his liking for schoolboy pranks.

SUNDAY, APRIL 3
Percy Thrillington trusts that all his friends were not offended by his April Fool's day little japes, to which he had no choice but to succumb on account of his liking for school-boy pranks.

MONDAY, APRIL 4
Percy Thrillington has announced that this week is Health And Happiness Week. The Thrillington personal routine will be vigorous and will commence each morning with twenty alternating single handed push-ups. Please read on tomorrow for further details.

TUESDAY, APRIL 5
Percy Thrillington implores all readers to adapt their daily bath routine, in the cause of Health and Happiness Week. Five minutes a day of "bath-bumping" works wonders. Your participation is invited.

WEDNESDAY, APRIL 6
It has come to the attention of Percy Thrillington that the general physical condition of the majority of London's residents is quite deplorable. He intends setting a personal example by taking a morning jog through Hyde Park. All other interested parties are asked to gather at the Bayswater fountain at 1.30.

THURSDAY, APRIL 7
Having travelled extensively Percy Thrillington wishes to comment that the early morning faces of commuting Londoners are amongst the most unhappy he has seen anywhere in the world. In the cause of Health and Happiness Week would all readers please smile warmly at their immediate neighbours. Thank you.

TUESDAY, APRIL 12
Percy Thrillington wishes to state that Health & Happiness Week has proven a big success & wishes to thank everyone for their kind participation. All readers are earnestly implored to continue their good efforts today by not wasting their free time.

Percy Thrillington will be in Paris today to advise his dear friend from the world of fashion on the design & musical presentation of her new collection.

WEDNESDAY, APRIL 13
Percy Thrillington is extremely flattered that rumours suggest that he is to be invited to ad-

WEDNESDAY, APRIL 13
Percy Thrillington is extremely flattered that r
that he is to be [illegible]
vise on Modern Mus[illegible]
Conservatoire, whi[illegible]
that city.

THURSDAY, APRIL 1[illegible]
Percy Thrillington [illegible]
thank Oliver & Richard for all their help & endeavours.

Percy Thrillington has been persuaded to prolong his stay in Paris as he finds the springtime atmosphere most conducive to musical creativity.

FRIDAY, APRIL 15
Percy Thrillington returns by air from Paris today, thoroughly invigorated and inspired, in full preparation for next week's announcement of his masterpiece

MONDAY, APRIL 18
Percy Thrillington regrets that he is forced to postpone this evening's planned soiree where his closest friends were to hear a preview of "Thrillington," his first long playing record.

TUESDAY, APRIL 19
Percy Thrillington with an armful of "Thrillington" LP records, has gone to Amsterdam to visit friends and to astonish the Dutch with his musical prowess.

WEDNESDAY, APRIL 20
Percy Thrillington was delighted that Mrs. Bedworthy was able to purchase a copy of his new album at her local music purveyor.

THURSDAY, APRIL 21
Percy Thrillington thoroughly recommends that his album "Thrillington" is used for therapeutic and relaxing purposes, particularly following arduous activities.

FRIDAY, APRIL 22
Percy Thrillington has returned to Newbury and is preparing to stay with friends for the Badminton Horse Trials. He feels that a copy of his new album "Thrillington" would make an ideal gift for his hostess.

SUNDAY, APRIL 24
Percy Thrillington thoroughly recommends that his album "Thrillington" is used for therapeutic and relaxing purposes, particularly following arduous activities.

MONDAY, APRIL 25
Percy Thr[illegible]

relaxing purposes, particularl[y] following arduous activities.

[illegible] will today b[e] [illegible]y Dress Sho[w] [illegible]hat "Admira[l] [illegible]ken from th[e] [illegible] be feature[d]

TUESDAY, APRIL 26
Percy Thrillington, delighted b[y] the ecstatic reception afforde[d] to his single 'Admiral Halsey' a[t] the Berkeley Dress Show, oblige[s] to young beauties by placing hi[s] moniker on the record sleeve[s] clutched to their breasts.

WEDNESDAY, APRIL 27
Percy Thrillington will be attending a few days at Newmarket fo[r] the racing, and has taken copie[s] of his single, Admiral Halsey, fo[r] the enjoyment of his many friend[s] within the racing fraternity.

Percy Thrillington wishes to inform all his friends that he will be taking an extended holiday in South America following the rigours of launching his first album Thrillington and the single Admiral Halsey. In his absence all enquiries should be directed to Miss Penelope Telfer-Smollett.

THURSDAY, APRIL 28
Percy Thrillington, pleased with his fortunes on the racecourse, was fortunate to meet an influential gentleman who assured him that Admiral Halsey could be included in the Trooping the Colour Ceremony in the near future.

FRIDAY, APRIL 29
Percy Thrillington wishes to inform all his friends that he will be taking an extended holiday in South America following the rigours of launching his first album 'Thrillington' and the single 'Admiral Halsey.' In his absence all enquiries should be directed to Miss Penelope Telfer-Smallett.

MONDAY, FEBRUARY 14
Percy Thrillington sends his warmest love and thanks to Miss Penelope Telfer-Smallett, Miss Debbie Dixon-Smythe, The Princess Francesca Visconte and Mrs. Ethel Bedworthy on this glorious St. Valentine's Day 1977.

WEDNESDAY, FEBRUARY 23
Percy Thrillington wishes to announce that today he has given up smoking, and craves support from

MONDAY, FEBRUARY 14
Percy Thrillington sends his warmest love and thanks to Miss Penelope Telfer-Smallett, Miss Debbie Dixon-Smythe, The Princess Francesca Visconte and Mrs. Ethel Bedworthy on this glorious St. Valentine's Day 1977.

WEDNESDAY, FEBRUARY 23
Percy Thrillington wishes to announce that today he has given up smoking, and craves support from all his friends.

THURSDAY, FEBRUARY 24
Percy Thrillington is basking in the sun in Mustique, and sends rays of sunshine to his friends in fog-bound London.

FRIDAY, FEBRUARY 25
Percy Thrillington wishes to advise his friends that he will be incommunicado for two days.

SUNDAY, FEBRUARY 27
Percy Thrillington wishes to announce that he has given up smoking, and craves support from all his friends.

MONDAY, FEBRUARY 28
Percy Thrillington wishes to advise all concerned that he will be represented at the Christie Sale of Chinese Ceramics by Miss Penelope Telfer-Smallett.

TUESDAY, MARCH 1
Percy Thrillington regrets that he will be unable to join Lady Metroland's party at the ROH performance of the Taming of the Shrew.

THURSDAY, MARCH 3
Percy Thrillington sends his congratulations to Mr. Sebastian McKindoe on the announcement of his engagement to Miss Sarah Wyatt.

FRIDAY, MARCH 4
Percy Thrillington will be attending the Torquay Relaxation Center for three days as from Saturday, March 5

MONDAY, MARCH 7
Percy Thrillington would like to send thanks to his friends for helping him acquire his latest Hispano Suiza.

TUESDAY, MARCH 8
Percy Thrillington wishes to thank Sir Jeremy Matthews-Ffitch and his party for a simply riveting evening at the opera.

WEDNESDAY, MARCH 9
Percy Thrillington looks forward

ning at the opera.

WEDNESDAY, MARCH 9
Percy Thrillington looks forward to meeting old school chums at the Canada Club Dinner.

THURSDAY, MARCH 10
Percy Thrillington wishes to advise that his gelding will not now be running at Sandown due to stable sickness.

FRIDAY, MARCH 11
Percy Thrillington regrets he will be unable to attend the Newbury Hunt this weekend due to prior commitments.

SUNDAY, MARCH 13
Percy Thrillington would like to send thanks to his friends for helping him acquire his latest Hispano Suiza.

TUESDAY, MARCH 15
Percy Thrillington has postponed all business engagements in order to spend time with a dear friend in Geneva.

WEDNESDAY, MARCH 16
Percy Thrillington wishes to advise friends that he is feeling thoroughly invigorated by the crisp & brisk skiing conditions in Gstaad.

THURSDAY, MARCH 17
Friends are mortified to hear Percy Thrillington has broken his arm skiing and wish him a speedy recovery.

FRIDAY, MARCH 18
Percy Thrillington is deeply irritated by the curtailment of his apres-ski enjoyment and is currently returning overland by private ambulance.

SUNDAY, MARCH 20
The princess Francesca Visconte is mortified to hear that Percy Thrillington has broken his arm skiing and wishes him a speedy recovery.

MONDAY, MARCH 21
Percy Thrillington is now en route to Paris despite the extreme inconvenience caused by a broken arm and suspected cracked rib.

TUESDAY, MARCH 22
Eccentricity is not one of my stronger attributes, dear ladies in Classified, but however, many thanks for your support, and to Mr. Stephen Clackson my sincere

TUESDAY, MARCH 22
Eccentricity is not one of my stronger attributes, dear ladies in Classified, but however, many thanks for your support, and to Mr. Stephen Clackson my sincere thanks for preserving my much valued privacy. Regard, Percy Thrillington.

WEDNESDAY, MARCH 23
Percy Thrillington is returning from Paris today with all haste to see his specialist in Harley St. to assess the damage incurred by the unfortunate incident in Gstaad.

THURSDAY, MARCH 24
Percy Thrillington wishes to announce that, comforted by his specialist's verdict regarding his condition he has departed, all smiles, for Yorkshire.

FRIDAY, MARCH 25
Percy Thrillington has been studying form & is confident that he has picked a winner for this weekend's activities at Doncaster.

SUNDAY, MARCH 27
Percy Thrillington will be enjoying a day of retreat at his Mayfair residence, following his recent frenetic and frustrating experiences.

MONDAY, MARCH 28
Percy Thrillington is delighte with the efforts of those con cerned at the YELLOWPLUSH GALLER to humour his aesthetic needs.

TUESDAY, MARCH 29
Percy Thrillington despite exces sive demands on both social an business time, hopes to lend hi support to today's DAFFODIL BALL

WEDNESDAY, MARCH 30
Percy Thrillington will be attend ing tonight's production of Do Giovanni and awaits with eager an ticipation a stimulating perfor mance from Miss Hayashi.

THURSDAY, MARCH 31
Percy Thrillington will be spend ing the morning with his tailo discussing plans for his sprin wardrobe, and taking luncheon a his club in Pall Mall.

FRIDAY, APRIL 1
Percy Thrillington trusts that a his friends will not be offende by today's little japes, to whi he had to succumb, on account his liking for schoolboy pranks.

SUNDAY, APRIL 3

THE McCARTNEY LEGACY

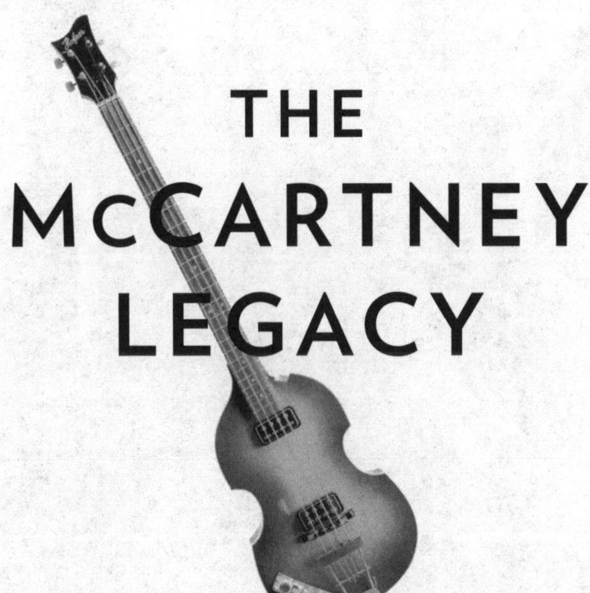

THE McCARTNEY LEGACY

VOLUME 2 | 1974–80

ALLAN KOZINN
ADRIAN SINCLAIR

DEYST.
An Imprint of WILLIAM MORROW

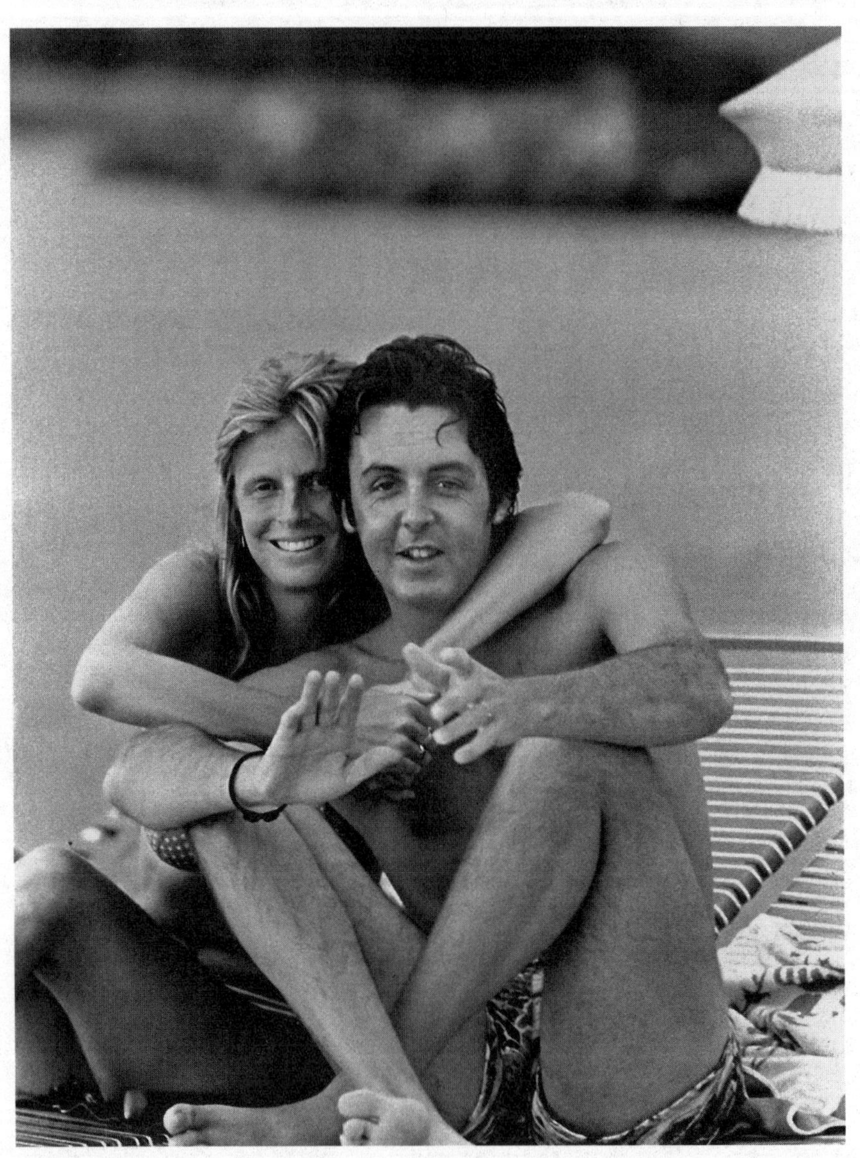

FOR LINDA, HENRY, JIMMY AND DENNY

CONTENTS

INTRODUCTION

When 'Now and Then' was issued as "the last Beatles single" on November 2, 2023, its release was covered in the press, globally, as a major event, as if the band had not broken up 53 years earlier. But then, the Beatles are always in the news, aren't they? Documentaries like *Eight Days a Week* and Peter Jackson's epic *Get Back*, or the remixes and archival issues of several of their albums, or Cirque du Soleil's *LOVE* show—the Fab Four are never far from a spotlight, even though only two of them still walk among us.

One interesting element of the 'Now and Then' story, from our perspective, is the degree to which it was a Paul McCartney project. The song was John Lennon's, composed and recorded on a cassette, as a demo, in 1977 or 1978—during the period covered in this volume—and McCartney, along with George Harrison and Ringo Starr, had tried to make something of it in the mid-1990s, when they transformed two other Lennon demos, 'Free as a Bird' and 'Real Love,' into updated Beatles tracks. But unlike the others, 'Now and Then' was a terrible recording, afflicted with a buzz that could not be eliminated using 1990s technology, so it was shelved.

The way McCartney tells it, the incomplete track had always nagged at him as unfinished business. When Peter Jackson developed a machine-assisted learning (MAL) program, during the making of *Get Back*, that allowed him to separate the components within mono recordings, McCartney saw a way to save 'Now and Then': Lennon's vocal could be lifted from the track, to replace the recording Paul, George and Ringo tried to expand upon in 1995. George Harrison's rhythm guitar from those sessions could be preserved, Paul and Ringo could add new parts, and harmony vocals from Beatles tracks could be lifted and repurposed.

That was not Paul's only use for Jackson's technology. He had the director make a remixed clip of 'I've Got a Feeling,' from the Beatles 1969 rooftop concert, with only John's vocal on the soundtrack, so that Paul could perform a virtual duet of the song with a celluloid Lennon on tour.

All this represents an approach to the Beatles—and an involvement in *being* a Beatle—that would have been unthinkable to the Paul McCartney we write about in this volume.

When the book begins, Paul's musical persona was wrapped up in Wings for a number of reasons ranging from a desire to establish the group as its own musical entity, to the psychic pain that the Beatles still represented for him, so he refused to perform songs he wrote that the Beatles recorded. That changed when he included a handful of Beatles tunes on the setlist for Wings' 1975–76 world tour. But he was still left to fend off the ghost of the Beatles at nearly every interview and press conference, and promoters seemed to mark the change of seasons by proposing increasingly lucrative offers for the Beatles to reunite.

Paul's responses to journalists' obsession with a Beatles reunion change over the period covered in this volume, often depending on the state of his disentanglement from Apple and his relationships with the others. But even when he is at his most open to the possibility of doing something—a show or a recording—it is hard to imagine him being the one pushing to complete "the last Beatles single." That was a luxury he had as an octogenarian who can legitimately claim to have enjoyed one of the most successful careers in pop music history, and was able to embrace—rather than be haunted by—the successes of his youth.

But the Paul McCartney of 1974 through 1980 was very different from the Paul McCartney of 2023. He was proud of his work with the Beatles, but he was in his mid-30s, with artistic ambitions and ideas that had not evaporated when the Beatles broke up. During this period, he was intent on pursuing those ideas, and having them not only embraced by record buyers and audiences but also respected by critics. The critical and popular success of *Band on the Run* assured him that such unalloyed success was possible for him, as it had been for the Beatles. The music he created in the period at hand pleased the public; critics proved more resistant.

When our first volume was published in 2022, our inboxes and social media feeds came alive with readers' overwhelmingly positive responses. The book also made ripples in Hollywood. Three months after it was published, Adrian was approached by the director Morgan Neville to work as a consultant on *Man on the Run* (working title as of July 2024)—a feature-length documentary about Paul's life beyond the Beatles.

One question readers asked after the publication of *Volume 1* is why we did not indulge our own critical opinions of McCartney's work, and given that Allan has spent 50 years writing criticism, it's a logical question. As in *Volume 1*, we have endeavored to tell the story as it unfolded, without foreknowledge of where the events we describe will lead. To that end, we have quoted the critical responses of the time, and though we have tried to include examples of both positive and negative responses to Paul's work, it was important to us to convey the tenor of the critical reaction in the 1970s. Those are the responses Paul was dealing with and that were influencing listeners. In that regard, our own feeling that, for example, *Back to the Egg* is woefully underrated is simply not germane.

Besides, our own opinions come through in the sections devoted to musical analysis: we would argue that showing how a particular chord progression, melodic twist or approach to harmony is fresh and innovative is an expression of opinion, just one that's stealthier than simply declaring likes or dislikes.

Some readers pointed out what they saw as a tension between the biographical narrative and the discussions of the sessions, and indeed, there are those who are fascinated by the session details but not the biography, and vice versa. We consider the two inextricable. When we began this project, we intended to write a sessionography, with short biographical synopses explaining what Paul was up to when he recorded each album. But we quickly discovered that while describing McCartney's sessions shows how he made the tracks we hear on disc, the inspiration for the songs themselves came from every aspect of his life—everything that happened between the sessions, even seemingly trivial things like reading a newspaper or a novel, or glancing at a spice rack in a rental home.

Going into this project, both of us were steeped in McCartney's work and familiar with the broad details of his life, yet we were constantly surprised by things we discovered in various archives—his fascination with science fiction, several tantalizing collaborations that failed to bear fruit, film projects that were left unrealized despite multiple attempts to get them off the ground, and the passion he brought to his side career as a music publisher.

We were surprised, too, by elements of Paul's personality that he normally shields from public view; in fact, one aspect of Paul that might surprise readers is the depth of his insecurities. As distant observers, we tend to take his thumb-up confidence at face value, and we might think, "*This guy was one of the Beatles and had a ton of hits—what does he have to be insecure about?*" Yet he was constantly second-guessing himself. The case of 'Mull of Kintyre' is a perfect example. Looking back, we know that it was a mammoth hit that sold more copies than every Beatles single. But those around Paul, in the months before its release, watched him vacillate between thinking that the song would be the biggest hit ever, and fretting that it was insane to release a Scottish waltz at a time when the charts were ruled by punk and hard rock. Almost invariably, he would go with his instinct, but only after an agonizing battle with self-doubt.

It may be that insecurity is the force that drives Paul's perfectionism—his need to fill reel after reel with takes before settling on one he can live with—and that his perfectionism is at the heart of his success. It must be uncomfortable and annoying to complete a piece of art and to then be plagued by doubts and fears, not just—or even principally—about what the critics will write, but about whether the completed work matches one's vision of what it ought to be. But that's the process, and if Paul didn't go through it, his work would not be what it is. As his friend and bandmate John Lennon once put it, "Genius is pain."

This second installment of *The McCartney Legacy* covers six years, from 1974 through the start of 1980. Thanks to the film *Rockshow* and the live album *Wings Over America*, most people are familiar with the huge tour Paul undertook with Wings during this period. But even among Paul's fans, the new music he created during this time is less known and appreciated than earlier albums, like *McCartney*, *Ram* and *Band on the Run* or later ones, like *Tug of War*, *Flowers in the Dirt*, *Flaming Pie* or *Chaos and Creation in the Backyard.*

Even fans who know the studio albums Wings recorded during this period—*Venus and Mars*, *Wings at the Speed of Sound*, *London Town* and *Back to the Egg*—are likely to have overlooked two other notable projects in Paul's creative life. We begin the book, in fact, with the sessions for a stealth Wings album that relatively few people know: *McGear*, the album Paul produced for his brother Michael, best known as Mike McGear. The album was not just a production job. Paul wrote or cowrote all but one of the album's songs, and Wings was Mike's studio band. Had the album been credited to the McCartney Brothers, it might have been a huge seller.

Similarly, Denny Laine's album of Buddy Holly covers, *Holly Days*, is often overlooked. But it was as much Paul's album as Denny's: with the exception of a few guitar lines Denny added late in the recording process, Paul played all the instruments and had prepared the backing tracks before Denny sang a note.

We also document a full album's worth of material Wings recorded for another of Paul's long-in-the-works projects—the songs he wrote for his prospective *Rupert Bear* film—during the *Back to the Egg* sessions, none of which has been released.

Paul's shelved projects have a way of turning up, eventually. The *Thrillington* album, recorded in 1971, was discussed at length in *Volume 1*, but it gathered dust until 1977, so its release is covered in the present book. *The Bruce McMouse Show*, produced in the wake of Wings' 1972 tour and discussed in *Volume 1*, was still in limbo during the period we cover in *Volume 2*, but was released in an archival box in 2018. The music for *One Hand Clapping*, a live-in-the-studio project recorded in 1974 and discussed herein, was released in 2024.

As was the case with *Volume 1*, McCartney did not make himself available as an interviewee for this volume. Allan had interviewed him several times for the *New York Times*, and used comments from those interviews where they were suitable, but for the most part our discussions focused on material relevant to later years. Paul has no problem speaking with journalists; newspaper and magazine interviews are part of the process of promoting whatever his current project is. But he regards biographies differently and prefers not to participate in them, having been burned in a couple of cases where he made himself available.

Being "burned" is, of course, subjective. "You're like the photographer showing photos to a guy and saying it looks great," Paul once told Allan, "and he says, 'Yeah, but my nose is too big.' To me, it's different than you looking at it."

We did not find this particularly problematic. Our print, audio and video archives include thousands of interviews with Paul from over the years, and our paper and digital archives of unseen documents, correspondence, session paperwork, and interviews is equally vast. Many previously unpublished comments from unedited interviews with Paul and Linda are presented here for the first time.

Often, details within Paul's own observations about his work have changed over time, and while this is sometimes because he later decided to reveal new information about a song or a recording, it also turns out that being a former Beatle does not shield one from the memory issues to which the rest of us are subject. A case in point is the song 'Let 'Em In.' At the time he wrote it, he told interviewers that he had written it for Ringo, who was at work on his *Rotogravure* album and wanted songs from each of the former Beatles. (He eventually gave Ringo a different song, 'Pure Gold,' and kept 'Let 'Em In' for Wings.) But in 2014, when he was interviewed for the archival edition of *Wings at the Speed of Sound*, he insisted that 'Let 'Em In' was *never* intended for Ringo (and cautioned the interviewer against believing what he read on the internet).

We have made it our practice, therefore, to regard interviews published close to the time of an event as likely to be the most accurate. That approach is not foolproof: sometimes interviews conducted close to an event are subject to particular agendas that can mean obscuring or obfuscating some aspects of a story and stressing others. We have therefore weighed contemporary and subsequent interviews against other evidence to determine where the truth most likely lies. But generally speaking, we have found that Paul's comments about his work near the time of creation have been straightforward and accurate, so for the most part, those are what we have quoted.

We have also spoken with a great many people who have worked with Paul, many of whom have not been interviewed frequently (or at all, in many cases), and the information they have imparted has been invaluable in filling out the picture. These include filmmakers like David Litchfield, Barry Chattington and Michael Lindsay-Hogg (who has spoken about his work with the Beatles, but rarely about the promotional films he directed for McCartney) and architectural designers like Steven Thomas, as well as musicians, recording engineers, photographers, tour managers, and painters.

Of the other members of Wings, we benefited from the memories and generosity of Geoff Britton, Joe English, Laurence Juber and Steve Holley. Denny Laine chose not to speak, possibly because his comments to a biographer in 1984 incurred Paul's displeasure, but his views are plentifully represented thanks to published (and unpublished) interviews.

Some readers may wonder about the ending of this volume. We tussled between two possible end points. During an interview for the *Things We Said Today* podcast, Allan mentioned our dilemma to Peter Jackson—a fan of *Volume 1*, it turned out—who gave us his two cents (and ultimately concurred with Adrian on where the narrative should end). And with that, the debate was over.

Let's face it—who among us is going to gainsay the plot advice of an Academy Award–winning director?

1

A FAMILY AFFAIR

"Looking back on it, we did used to say, it's like a divorce," Paul McCartney reflected on the Beatles' breakup, now a marathon heading into its fifth year. "It really was like that, but four fellas trying to divorce instead of a man and a woman. And then you get four sets of lawyers instead of just two. All of that kind of stuff was not making life easy at all."[1]

At the moment, the lawyers were not the problem.

As Paul, Linda and their three daughters—Heather (11), Mary (4), and Stella (2)—were enjoying some downtime at High Park in Campbeltown between recording sessions in Stockport, the attorneys representing each of the former Beatles convened in New York on Monday, February 11, 1974—the tenth anniversary of the Beatles' American debut concert in Washington, D.C.—to hammer out an agreement dissolving the Beatles' partnership.

This had been Paul's goal since early 1970, shortly after John Lennon announced to his bandmates that he was leaving the group. It was John, in fact, who first used the word *divorce*, likening his split from the Beatles—and the liberation he felt in declaring it—to his divorce from his first wife, Cynthia.

McCartney had not wanted to divorce the Beatles. He wanted to divorce Allen Klein, the brash New York manager whom John brought in to manage the Beatles and their company, Apple, which was losing money alarmingly by early 1969. Lennon's enthusiasm for Klein won over George Harrison and Ringo Starr, but Paul resisted, arguing that Klein's reputation in the music world was unsavory. The Rolling Stones, who had brought Klein to Lennon's attention, subsequently warned the Beatles that he was bad news: Klein had negotiated the Stones an improved contract with Decca Records while quietly buying their master tapes and publishing (through 1971) behind their backs. Paul feared that he could walk off with everything the Beatles had built, as well.

Nevertheless, when Paul refused to sign Klein's management agreement, the others overruled him, breaking the Beatles' longstanding rule that all major decisions be unanimous.

The idea of Klein being considered his manager, not to mention his taking a cut of the royalties on the Beatles catalog and his own albums, was galling to Paul, but the only way to get Klein out of his life was to extricate himself from Apple, and the only way to do that was to dissolve the partnership agreement that the Beatles signed in 1967. Unable to persuade the others to let him out of that agreement, Paul reluctantly followed the advice of his lawyers, Lee and John Eastman (who were also his in-laws, Linda's father and brother), and took them to court to force the dissolution of the partnership.

He took a publicity hit when he sued the other Beatles and Apple, but he prevailed. Yet, four years later, the battle still was not over. Because the Beatles did business as Apple, not as John, Paul, George and Ringo, their recording contract was between EMI Records and Apple, and according to that contract, all royalties for Beatles and solo recordings were paid to Apple. A receiver had been appointed to sort out Apple's byzantine finances, so that the money could be split. But finally splitting the company—and distributing those royalties—required a dissolution agreement signed by all four former Beatles.

The holdout was John, who had dangled the prospect of signing such an agreement before Paul several times since 1971 but always reneged. This was a significant inconvenience to Paul. In the summer of 1971, he had formed a new band, Wings, and he was paying his bandmates a weekly salary, underwriting touring and recording expenses, and running management offices (McCartney Productions Ltd., or MPL) in both London and New York to oversee it all. Yet his royalties for the last few Beatles releases, as well as his five post-Beatles albums (two solo, three with Wings), were frozen in Apple's bank accounts.

Now, at long last, the four sets of lawyers were meeting, and the end was in sight.

Much had changed over the past year. For one thing, Klein was no longer in the picture. When his contract expired in March 1973, the other Beatles opted not to renew it. "Let's say that possibly Paul's suspicions were right,"[2] John commented at the time.

More importantly, the personal relationships between the former Fabs were stronger than they had been since 1969. "Yeah, I miss Paul a lot," John told *NME* in mid-January 1974. "Course I'd like to see him again. He's an old friend, isn't he?"[3] Elsewhere in the same issue, John was quoted saying, "I think anything is possible now, and if it happens, I'm sure we'll all do something wonderful."[4]

All four were pursuing solo careers with notable success, if not quite at the level of (near) infallibility that they had enjoyed as the Beatles. Talk of potential collaborations, once angrily swatted away, were now offered as possibilities, however vague. In the February 16, 1974, edition of *Melody Maker*, Chris Charlesworth reported from New York that a joint statement from the former Beatles would be released in the near future, a tip that Charlesworth interpreted to mean the announcement of a new Beatles album.

Lee Eastman's first reports from New York were encouraging. The talks were productive, and the attorneys would press on, hoping to have an agreement by the end of the week. But there were complications. Klein was suing Apple for what he claimed were unpaid fees, and Paul's position was that since he had warned the others against signing with Klein, he should not be liable in the event that Klein prevailed. He therefore insisted that the other three indemnify him against that possibility.

Another issue was that the Beatles' individual homes were purchased through Apple and were technically among the company's assets—something that had to be considered when splitting those assets among the four musicians.

Yet another sticking point was that John had been charging his New York living expenses and the cost of his film projects with Yoko Ono to Apple, and by the end of 1973, those expenses totaled about $2 million (£860,000), money that Paul, George and Ringo wanted reimbursed to the company. And there was the not inconsiderable matter of how to deal with recording expenses that the individual Beatles, as well as Yoko, had charged to Apple.[5]

When Lee Eastman telephoned again on Friday, February 15, Paul was expecting to hear that after five days of negotiation, they had a contract that satisfied everyone, and that his freedom was at hand.

Instead, Eastman delivered the stunning news that with negotiations at an advanced stage, Lennon's attorney piped up with a last-minute demand from his client: Lennon would not sign unless he was guaranteed an extra £1 million ($2.3 million). It was a demand too outrageous to discuss, and the negotiations ended abruptly.

"I asked him why he'd actually wanted that million," Paul recalled, "and he said, 'I just wanted cards to play with.' It's absolutely standard business practice. He wanted a couple of jacks to up your pair of nines."[6]

In calmer moments, Paul recognized that the negotiations were a complex dance, and that all four former Beatles had priorities that were no longer in sync. Financially, there was a lot at stake for Paul, too. While the critics were often divided over his post-Beatles output, McCartney's record sales were healthy. In America alone he had sold over four million LPs, the royalties for which were currently sitting in Apple's bank accounts.

"I mean, there were many stumbling blocks. And just to keep the record straight, it wasn't always [John]. I mean, obviously they accused my side of doing plenty of stumbling too."[7]

But John's demand was more than legal poker play. In purely practical terms, Lennon forced the delay to be sure that neither he nor his lawyers had overlooked any details—whether, for example, the tax ramifications of the settlement would be more severe for him, as a British subject resident in the United States, than for the others.

On a purely emotional level, Lennon was also conflicted about the finality the dissolution agreement represented. Granted, he had occasioned the split and he had demonstrably moved on, musically and personally; but he was also the band's founder, and despite his public assertion that "it's only a rock group that split up, it's nothing important,"[8] he saw the Beatles as his own creation.

"Everybody changes," said May Pang, Lennon's companion at the time. "With John, things changed on a daily basis. Even though they had to break up to get to the next level in their musical careers, at the same time, he started this band that changed the world. It wasn't just a band that said, 'Oh, we made six albums.' It changed pop culture. It changed how we live and how we dress. And he knew that."[9]

To the other lawyers, Lennon's demand was little more than a stunt, something to be expected from the most mercurial of the Beatles. So in conveying the news to Paul, Eastman also offered his belief that Lennon's demand was just a hiccup in the proceedings and would soon be sorted.

But Paul was livid. Seemingly unconcerned about leaving Linda and the girls stranded at High Park without a car in the dead of winter, he stormed out of the farmhouse, hopped into "Helen Wheels," his Land Rover, and took the coastal road out of Scotland and toward Gayton, the Merseyside village where he had bought his father a house, called Rembrandt.

Linda contemplated the prospect of staying in Scotland and leaving space for Paul to cool off. But after a few hours, she decided to head for Rembrandt and ordered two cabs to accommodate a traveling party that included Linda and the girls, plus four dogs, each larger than the two youngest girls. Reggie McManus, the owner of the Campbeltown cab company, was taken aback when Linda requested two cars for the nearly 360-mile trip to Gayton but agreed, provided that Linda didn't mind making it an overnight journey.

McManus and another driver, Bob Gibson, collected Linda, the girls and their small menagerie at High Park at 12:20 A.M., and delivered them to Rembrandt on Saturday morning at around 10. The marathon journey racked up a fare of £70 ($170), which Linda paid from a roll of banknotes. To Linda's surprise, when she arrived in Gayton, Paul was having a cheerful breakfast with his father, his rage diffused by the head-clearing drive south.

Linda was used to Paul's temper, a characteristic that he had always carefully shielded from public view, projecting instead an enthusiastic Cute Beatle veneer. She and Paul quickly put his fit of pique behind them, and the next day, when Paul sat for a lengthy interview with the *New York Daily News*'s Sunday magazine section—a chat that began in early afternoon and continued that evening after a break for some horse riding—his paeans to marriage and family were laid on thick.

"Linda and I know that marriage is old-fashioned," Paul told his interviewer, Karin von Faber, "and we know the contract is just a piece of paper. It's up to the people what they make out of that piece of paper. I had my wild life. I really had a wild time, especially when we toured America in 1964. But I told Linda everything about that and all the rest. I have no secrets from Linda. I had my time, in my time. But I am much happier now. This new life means more to me.

"No matter how much money Linda and I may have, it means nothing to us without this kind of happiness. It's a great pleasure—and a tough job—to raise children. With female children, you want to try to teach them early to understand men as much as possible. Men and women are so totally different they spend a good part of their life trying to get closer to each other. Of course, they rarely get close enough. That's the problem. They should start early. I don't mean sex. I mean understanding, communicating, like the beautiful thing I have with this blond lady."

But Paul's anger about the inconclusive legal negotiations was not far from the surface, and he wanted to be sure his side was heard, and in perspective.

"All of us realized that this great thing we'd been part of was no longer to be," Paul told von Faber. "I think we've all accepted it as a fact since that day in the Apple office in London when John told us—'I'm leaving the group, I want a divorce.'

"Linda and I aren't rich people because so much of our money has gone into Apple. That's a disaster. Our former manager, Allen Klein, did some pretty strange things with the millions we made. Linda's dad is our attorney, and we've sued Apple, and we may get rid of the whole mess and get a settlement in the next few weeks. I sure hope I can clear it up. You know, the other Beatles didn't believe me when I said Klein wasn't the right man to handle our affairs. I took a lot of abuse from John, George and Ringo for my position. But it turned out I was right in the first place."[10]

Prior to Lennon's demand scuppering a possible divorce settlement in New York, the McCartneys could not have hoped for a more promising start to 1974. Wings' latest album, *Band on the Run*, in the stores since late November, was treated with a measure of nearly universal critical admiration and respect that McCartney had not experienced upon the release of his earlier albums. Record buyers loved it too: a week after its release, the Recording Industry Association of America (RIAA) certified the album Gold.

That was nearly enough to banish from Paul's mind the fraught circumstances under which the album was recorded.

Two weeks before the band was due to fly to Lagos, Nigeria, for the recording sessions—Paul was keen on abandoning London studios for an exotic locale—Henry McCullough, Wings' lead guitarist, resigned during a rehearsal in Scotland over Paul's refusal to let him construct his own guitar solo rather than play the solo Paul dictated. It was an explosion long in the making: Henry chafed against Paul's insistence that he play the parts Paul imagined, rather than those he crafted himself, nearly from the start.

Upon Henry's departure, Denny Seiwell, Wings' drummer—whom Paul met during the New York sessions for *Ram* and invited to help form the band—argued that the Lagos trip should be postponed until Paul was able to find and break in a new guitarist. But Paul wanted to forge ahead, and Seiwell, who had other (mostly financial) frustrations with Wings, quit the band by phone as a taxi waiting to take him to the airport idled outside his London flat. Paul went ahead anyway, recording the album with Linda and Denny Laine.

Driving McCartney, in his relentless push to finish *Band on the Run*—and to endow it with plenty of up-to-date stardust—was an undercurrent of "*I'll show you*," always an important motivation for him, but especially now, when he wanted to prove to McCullough and Seiwell that he could make a great Wings album without them.

He would need to replace those players if Wings were to continue as a band, of course, and McCartney gave no indication that the group was finished. But he was taking his time: six months had elapsed since McCullough and Seiwell quit, and they had not been replaced. It was almost as though he could not face starting again.

"It was a bit difficult for me to suddenly develop another band," Paul confessed. "Let's face it, the Beatles played Hamburg for a year solid, eight hours a day, before we ever were anything. Then we came back to Liverpool and still played for years in small places; so it took a long time. The idea was: we can't take quite as long with this band. . . . We did our university tour and a European tour, which had a bit of press, but we thought, 'We'll just have to swallow our pride and go right ahead.' You get any five people and it's pretty hard to get a band out of it, unless you've been going for about a year or so. It takes that long for five people to understand each other."[11]

Jimmy McCulloch, a 20-year-old guitarist who had played with Thunderclap Newman, Stone the Crows, and Blue, and whose path had already crossed McCartney's a couple of times, had the inside track on the lead guitar slot. In November, Paul had invited McCulloch to join them on a trip to Paris to record a couple of Linda's songs, and he made a strong impression. The drummer for those sessions, Davy Lutton, dropped out of the running quickly, joining Marc Bolan's T. Rex instead.

Now, as Big Ben rang in the start of 1974, Paul had the perfect side project to audition new musicians. He had promised his brother Michael*—officially Mike McGear, having changed his name when he began performing to distance himself from Paul's name and fame—that he would help him record a new LP. Paul would produce and would enlist the Eastmans to find his brother a new recording contract.

Mike was not a neophyte. In 1962, he formed the Scaffold, a Liverpool band that performed an unusual hybrid of rock, comedy and poetry. The Scaffold had enjoyed a few novelty hits, most notably 'Thank U Very Much' and 'Lily the Pink.' Although Mike played drums as a teenager, a broken arm at age 16 forced him to give them up. For a while, he abandoned any hope of becoming a

* Peter Michael McCartney, Paul's younger brother and only sibling, was born in Liverpool on January 7, 1944.

musician and took jobs as a Bible salesman and as a hairdresser. But the Scaffold gave him a shot at show business. Mike was the group's singer; the other members were the poet Roger McGough and a comedian, John Gorman.

Mike had released a couple of albums outside the Scaffold. He teamed up with Roger McGough for *McGough & McGear*, released by Parlophone in 1968, and featuring guest appearances by his brother, as well as Jimi Hendrix, Mitch Mitchell (the drummer in the Jimi Hendrix Experience) and the Yardbirds' Paul Samwell-Smith. His first purely solo effort, *Woman*, issued by Island Records in 1972, won enthusiastic reviews but failed to chart, leaving Island disinclined to underwrite a follow-up.

The Scaffold, meanwhile, had morphed into Grimms, an ensemble that included the three Scaffold members, as well as Andy Roberts, a guitarist who often backed the trio, and two members of the Bonzo Dog Doo-Dah Band, Neil Innes and Viv Stanshall. The new band's name was derived from the surnames of its original members; when other performers, including the poet Brian Patten, joined the troupe, the name remained unchanged.

After two years, personal differences were starting to surface in Grimms, and on October 24, 1973, Mike quit the collective, storming off the group's tour bus on the outskirts of Northampton, midway through a tour of Britain.

"[The tour] didn't seem to be going the way we wanted, and we weren't really making any money," Mike complained. "Then one night we were travelling back from one of our shows in our coach when one of the poets [Patten] in the show hit me over the head. It really hurt at the time, and I said to myself, 'That's it. What am I doing travelling around England earning no money and suddenly being hit over the head for no reason at all?'"[12]

By then, Mike had an ace up his sleeve. A few months before Wings left for Nigeria to record *Band on the Run*, Paul and Mike recorded a couple of tracks together. 'Leave It,' written by Paul, was tracked at EMI Studios during the sessions for Paul's 'Zoo Gang' theme, on April 26, 1973. A second song, 'Sweet Baby,' was written jointly by Paul and Mike and partly recorded at Mike's house in Heswall. They finished the recording in London, at Island Studios that June.

Paul—or as Mike habitually called him, "Our Kid," a homey Liverpool expression—sent the two songs to the Eastmans, who were encouraging.

"Linda's dad, Lee Eastman, and his son John, loved it," Mike recalled, "and they said, 'Why don't you do an album?' So Our Kid said, 'Have you got enough for an album?' I said, 'We've got lots of songs that I have been working on, we'll finish them.' And so that's what we did."[13]

By July 1973, Paul and Mike were sketching out a plan for the album, to be recorded the next time Paul was between projects. Paul would not only produce, but would also underwrite the sessions, making them an MPL endeavor.

With Paul picking up the studio tab, certain economies were necessary.

"Our Kid said, 'Right. Now we're not going to go to Abbey Road, it's too expensive. And too popular, too.'"[14]

Mike suggested using Strawberry Recording Studios in Stockport, a town just south of Manchester. He had worked there in 1971 with the Scaffold, recording 'Decimal 5,' a song for the soundtrack of a government film about decimalization, and he had recorded his *Woman* album there in 1971 and early 1972.

At the end of July 1973, Paul drove to Stockport to have a look at Strawberry, a roomy, well-equipped 16-track studio. At £25 ($55) an hour, roughly half the cost of comparable facilities at EMI, the price was right.

There were several agendas at play beyond Mike's need for a career reboot. The Beatles' contract with EMI and Capitol Records, which governed both group and solo recordings, ran through 1976, after which Paul would be a free agent. So the Eastmans knew that when they came calling at record labels with a Mike McGear album produced by Paul, executives would want to feel them out about Paul. Indeed, one label, Warner Bros. Records, was already sniffing around and had spent money on sessions for Denny Laine's *Ahh . . . Laine!* album as a way of inching closer to Paul.

Mike's sessions would also do double duty as an audition for Wings players. Since Mike had no band of his own, Paul, Linda and Denny Laine would be his session players and backup singers. Jimmy McCulloch, having impressed Paul during the Paris sessions, was invited along as the lead guitarist. After discussing potential drummers—Mike remembered Led Zeppelin's John Bonham being mentioned*—Paul asked his brother to invite Gerry Conway,† who played drums on *Woman*. If Conway worked out, Wings' personnel problems might be settled. In any case, Mike's album would be a stealth Wings disc, with Mike as the lead vocalist instead of Paul.

Just before Christmas, Mike put in a call to Strawberry Studios to arrange for session time starting on January 3, 1974. For Peter Tattersall, the studio's principal engineer and one of its founders, the rental was not purely a business arrangement. Tattersall was a Liverpool lad who not only played in local bands during the Beatles' early years but also worked briefly at a furniture store owned by Harry Epstein, whose son, Brian, was just starting to manage the Beatles. Tattersall ended up working with Brian as road manager for Billy J. Kramer and the Dakotas, a job that sometimes meant touring with the Beatles, Cilla Black and other Epstein artists.

* Bonham had jammed with Wings during the September 2, 1972, sessions for 'C Moon,' when Denny Seiwell was in New York.

† Gerry Conway (September 11, 1947–March 29, 2024) had recorded with Fotheringay, Al Stewart, Fairport Convention, Steeleye Span and Cat Stevens. He continued to work with Cat Stevens until 1978, and again starting in 2004. He was also briefly a member of Jethro Tull, rejoined Fairport Convention from 1996 to 2022, and worked with Pentangle, in which his wife, Jacqui McShee, was the singer.

Tattersall moved into the recording world in 1967, when he bought Inter-City Studios, a tiny room—roughly 20 feet square—above a record shop in Stockport for about £500 ($1,400). Tattersall's first clients were advertising firms, but soon Herman's Hermits, the Mindbenders and other groups began using Inter-City as a demo studio.

By the end of 1967, Eric Stewart, the Mindbenders' guitarist, invested £800 in the studio, becoming a partner and helping Tattersall upgrade the recording equipment. They changed the studio's unmemorable name to Strawberry Studios, after 'Strawberry Fields Forever,' Stewart's favorite Beatles tune at the time, and they moved to larger quarters at 3 Waterloo Road, in Stockport. The new studio was a 44-by-32-foot space with a 10-foot-high ceiling—room enough for an ensemble of 35 musicians.

Tattersall and Stewart soon took on more partners, including Graham Gouldman, who joined with a £2,000 stake. Gouldman, the Mindbenders' former bassist, was also a successful composer, with songs recorded by the Yardbirds ('For Your Love,' 'Evil Hearted You' and 'Heart Full of Soul'), the Hollies ('Look Through Any Window' and 'Bus Stop') and Herman's Hermits ('No Milk Today,' 'Listen People,' and 'East West'). Now he was writing songs for Kasenetz-Katz, a New York company that produced bubblegum hits, and he soon persuaded the firm to use Strawberry as the center of its British operation, with Stewart, Gouldman, Kevin Godley and Lol Creme as session players. The quartet, in turn, used their fees to further upgrade Strawberry.

In 1972, Stewart, Gouldman, Godley and Creme decided to make a go of it as a band and began recording under the name 10cc, starting with a single, 'Donna,' that climbed to No. 2 on the British charts. Strawberry Studios became 10cc's headquarters and laboratory, the place where the band made all its recordings.

By the time Paul visited Strawberry, in July 1973, it was the one of the best-equipped studios outside London, with a custom-built Helios 16-track mixing desk and tape deck, as well as a Studer stereo deck, Neumann and AKG microphones and EMT stereo echo plates, a Minimoog synthesizer, a Mellotron and a Bechstein grand piano. Paul was impressed: on July 25, he sent a postcard to the studio, addressed to "Eric, Pete, & Mob." The message was a drawing of three strawberries under which Paul had written "Nice one, Lads. Keep Rockin! Love From P+L Maccarooney."[15]

The studio was not quite available when Mike called: 10cc were at work on their second album, *Sheet Music*, and as Tattersall searched the studio calendar for the next free dates, Mike subtly reminded him of *the connection.*

"He said, 'Me brother wants to come as well—he's trying this new band out.' And it never bloody clicked who his brother was," remembered Tattersall. "I said, 'Ah, who's that?' '*Paul*.' Oh, shit! All right, fine!"[16]

A schedule was worked out that would keep the studio humming full time: 10cc would work during the day, wrapping up around 4 P.M., when Paul, Mike and company would arrive to work through the night, usually until about 3 A.M. This schedule was not entirely consistent, and it is possible that on some occasions the McCartneys and 10cc switched their studio hours.*

For Paul, who was still nursing a post–Wings Mark I hangover, collaborating with his little brother was a rousing prospect. This would be a Mike McGear album, not overtly a product of the Paul McCartney music factory; just as the Beatles had backed Tony Sheridan on record in 1961, Paul would simply be one of the gang, bass man rather than front man. For the first time in four years, the pressure was off. With that in mind, Paul solidified his plan to engage the services of a co-producer for the sessions.

In early January 1974, Paul telephoned Tony Visconti. Paul had known Visconti slightly from the Apple days, when the Brooklyn-born producer oversaw tracks for *Badfinger*. He was also married to Mary Hopkin, whose first Apple album, *Postcard*, Paul had produced, and Paul admired his production work for David Bowie and T. Rex. Those recordings made Visconti one of London's hottest producers, and in October 1973, during the final sessions for *Band on the Run*, Paul hired him to write arrangements for several songs and to conduct his arrangements at the overdubbing session, all on three days' notice. During that session, Paul invited Visconti to take a not-yet-defined role in the album Paul would be making with his brother in the new year.

Visconti, though, had a change of heart in the couple of months since the orchestral session. He had been put off by Paul's giving him so little time to create his scores, but chalked it up to Paul's being accustomed to the speed with which George Martin produced arrangements for the Beatles. But when *Band on the Run* was released, he was shocked to find that while his name was listed among the general acknowledgments, his role as arranger and conductor went unmentioned.

"When I looked at the credits for the Wings album," Visconti complained to *Record Mirror*, "I found it at the bottom of the sleeve, where it says 'Thanks to . . .' along with the roadies and the teaboy, etc. That's not exactly what I'd call fair credit."

Now McCartney added another last-minute invitation to Visconti's grievance list: as Visconti remembered it, Paul telephoned on January 2 to ask him to co-produce Mike's album, with the sessions starting the following day.

"I would never work with Paul McCartney again," he told *Record Mirror.* "He treated me the worst. . . . He phoned me the day before he wanted to begin [Mike's sessions] and said we were leaving the next day, expecting me to drop everything and go. When I explained that I just couldn't do that, he said not to worry and that he'd phone back, but never did."[17]

---

* Memories of who recorded when are strikingly muddled in non-contemporaneous interviews. In the earliest interview about the sessions, Peter Tattersall told the *Wings Fun Club* newsletter in June 1974 that Paul and Mike worked from about 4 P.M. to 3 A.M., information we have adopted because of the proximity of the interview to the events.

On January 3, Paul, Linda and the girls traded London for the Wirral, taking up residence with Jim and Paul's stepmother, Angie, at Rembrandt. The site of many a family get-together over the years, Jim's five-bedroom house was spacious enough to accommodate Paul's family and their dogs, Martha and Lucky. But living under the same roof for several months was an altogether different experience.

Jim and Angie lived a clockwork life—breakfast (two slices of toast and a cup of tea) at 8 A.M., lunch (Campbell's cream of chicken soup or Baxter's lentil soup) at 12 P.M., a cup of tea at 2 P.M., afternoon tea at 4:30 P.M., dinner at 6.30 P.M. and supper (tea and biscuits or a boiled onion) at 9 P.M. Suddenly, their spartan routine was turned on its head.

Unaccustomed to having full-time houseguests, Angie did not think to remove her diary from the kitchen drawer where she kept it and was put out when she discovered Linda casually leafing through it over breakfast one morning. And the fact that Paul funded his father's retirement by way of a monthly allowance was not lost on hosts or visitors.

"The kids [Heather, Mary and Stella] used the room that used to be Mike's bedroom, and by that time I'd refurnished it with white furniture, and a light carpet and everything," Angie recalled. "And I went in the bedroom one day and the three kids were playing with coloring pencils and crayons and drawing on the white furniture. And I said, 'Hey, girls, come on, you mustn't do this'—being mindful, as usual, not to be too stern with them because it wasn't my position. And I said, 'I'll get you some coloring books, I'll get you some paper to write on.' And Linda came in the door and said, 'Oh Ange, just let 'em be, I'll buy you more furniture if that's what you want. Don't inhibit them . . . just leave 'em be.'"[18]

But tensions aside, Angie's daughter Ruth, 13 at the time of Paul's extended visit, remembers that spending time with the McCartney girls also had its sweet moments.

"We were all in Woolworths [department store] on the high street one afternoon," said Ruth, "and Stella saw the chocolate counter. And she couldn't say chocolate and called it 'fokit.' And this two-year-old kid is yelling, 'Fokit! Fokit!' And everybody's looking at her. She was trying to say chocolate, but everybody's thinking Paul McCartney's kid is running up and down Woolworths shouting 'Fuck it!'"[19]

During Mike's sessions, the girls were left in Angie's and Ruth's care. Since Mike lived near Gayton, he would commute to Stockport, some 90 minutes away, with Paul and Linda. The rest of the band stayed at the Belfry Hotel in Handforth, another Manchester suburb.

Recording Sessions

Thursday, January 3–Thursday, January 10, 1974.

Strawberry Studios, 3 Waterloo Road, Stockport.

Recording and Overdubbing: 'Sea Breezes,' 'What Do We Really Know?' 'Norton' and 'Have You Got Problems.'*

With the sessions scheduled and the musicians lined up, there remained the question of what Mike would record. He had not made much progress on that stack of unfinished songs he told Paul he would finish. In fact, in some ways, Mike found the prospect of working with his brother a little terrifying.

"I was, like, shitting myself," he admitted, "because I've never really worked with Our Kid before, not serious; and to [make an album] with someone like Our Kid, who's been in the business for so many years and is such a good muso and singer, is a bit strange, even for a brother."[20]

One idea that Paul floated was making an album of covers. During the October sessions at AIR for *Band on the Run*, Paul had run into Bryan Ferry, the singer for Roxy Music, who was just about to release his own covers album, *These Foolish Things*, which included one of Paul's Beatles-era songs, 'You Won't See Me.' Two weeks earlier, David Bowie had released a covers LP, *Pin Ups*. So although the general expectation was that rock albums would comprise new, original material, albums of covers were suddenly in vogue.

With no new originals ready to go, Mike and Paul discussed various Buddy Holly and Fats Domino favorites. Paul's suggestions included 'Liverpool Lou,' a 1964 hit for its composer, Dominic Behan, as well as a tune from far into left field—'Sea Breezes,' a song Bryan Ferry wrote for Roxy Music's eponymous 1972 debut album. Mike resisted 'Liverpool Lou,' but he was intrigued by the Ferry tune.

"My brother chose that," Mike recalled. "I don't know why he chose it—it's not my type of song at all. But he could see it. He was convinced that it would be a good song, and it's always good to have another influence. I always loved Roxy Music anyway."[21]

Paul may have considered the gently melodic opening and closing sections of Ferry's song something Mike could easily master; its contours had elements in common with the title track of Mike's *Woman* album. And perhaps the contrast between Ferry's wiry falsetto and the driven, full-voice, rockier middle section reminded Paul of some of the Scaffold's style-mashing tracks, like 'Jelly Covered Cloud.'

* Because the session paperwork has been lost, the order in which the songs were recorded could not be definitively established. However, dates are known for specific occurrences during the sessions, including visits by other musicians, making a rough chronology possible.

In any case, he must have had the song in mind well before the sessions began: Peter Tattersall remembered him bringing the *Roxy Music* LP into the studio, cueing up 'Sea Breezes' and announcing that this was the song they were about to record.

"I liked the tune off [Roxy Music's] first LP which I've got, and I like Bryan Ferry—and being the producer of the LP I was just looking for stuff for Michael to do," Paul explained. "I just thought it was a catchy tune. . . . Bryan has good tracks, and it suits Mike . . . it suits him ducky."[22]

The arrangement Paul created was miles from Ferry's. Mike sings the outer verses in a light but full voice, and instead of the eerie backdrop Roxy Music provided for Ferry, Paul accompanied Mike on the piano, with solid guitar, bass and drum support on the repeated phrases at the end of each verse, and organ accompanying Paul's piano rendering of the melody in the instrumental break.

Mike was struck by the deftness with which Paul transformed the song into something closer to his own style, while also leaving room for Mike's own interpretive ideas.

"Our Kid merely picked the bones out of it," Mike said. "But then, the magic happened . . . 'Don't like that; like that; that's no good; let's try something better suited.' I'm not a musician and the problem I've always had is that the people you work with say, 'It's nice, but you can't do that because of the chord progression.' But with Our Kid, who had an ear for that, you'd hum what you wanted, and he'd work it out. He's always had a big head for music."[23]

By the end of the first day of the sessions, the track was virtually complete, although Paul thought it might benefit from light orchestration—a decision he would make toward the end of the project, depending how the rest of the album shaped up.

The speed with which Paul and Wings worked gave Mike the confidence to tell Paul that much as he enjoyed the Ferry tune, he would rather record originals. Together, they came up with a *modus operandi:* the drive from Gayton to Stockport was 90 minutes, meaning that Paul, Mike and Linda would be on the road for three hours every day. If they used the time to write—either completing unfinished songs they each had or starting anew—they could produce an album of material in no time. The plan was to write a song a day.

Before starting this exercise in carpool composition, though, Paul had a riffy idea he had been toying with. In truth, 'What Do We Really Know?' proved more a test for the band than a showcase for Mike, who had to make do with a constricted, talky vocal line, built mostly around repetitions of, and variations on, the title and a set of rhyming rejoinders ("*We know that birdies fly / We know that babies cry / We know that we'll get by*").

The track begins, though, with a burst of backward guitar that would have seemed at home on the Beatles' *Revolver*, leading into a steady drum figure that develops into a tight groove for Gerry on drums and Paul on bass, with Jimmy providing tense bursts of tightly focused guitar punctuation between verses. The vocal line, with its brisk tempo and the compressed hint of a melody, sails over the far more interesting band work, which includes brief drum, bass and guitar solos. When the vocal returns, it is supported with backing harmonies by Paul, Linda and Denny, whose vocal blend was by now an instantly recognizable element of the Wings sound.

A change of texture—the steady drumbeat vanishes, a piano underpins the start of each bar—gives Mike an opportunity to emulate an R&B singer before Conway's steady drumbeat returns, along with the backing vocals and Mike's chanted repetitions of the title, to bring the main part of the song to an end, Strawberry's plate echo repeating the final chords in the fade-out. As a coda, Paul took a minute of a guitar-heavy, between-takes jamming and attached it to the song after a five-second pause and a few seconds of delicate Minimoog sounds, played by Linda.

If the track provided scant illumination of Mike's abilities, it proved a fascinating look at Paul's chameleon-like approach to style and not incidentally, the strengths of this potential Wings lineup.

Other elements in McCulloch's arsenal showed themselves in 'Norton,' a track credited to Paul and Mike, but in which Mike's fingerprints are more clearly discernible. It is, for starters, spoken rather than sung, and pitched as a satire on the androgyny at the heart of the Glam movement personified by David Bowie, Marc Bolan and the New York Dolls—more in Scaffold's bailiwick than Paul's. A short sketch, depicting the effeminate title character in the army—enacted by Paul, Mike and Denny—is interposed before the final verse.

Paul's contribution was the musical backdrop against which Mike, approximating a posh London accent, intoned his lines. Central to this fabric was a steady beat provided by Gerry Conway, modeled on the drum accompaniment to Napoleon XIV's 'They're Coming to Take Me Away, Ha-Haaa!,' a 1966 American novelty record, the title of which is scribbled across the top of Mike's handwritten lyric sheet. The beat was reinforced by Paul and Mike stamping on Strawberry's hardwood floor.

Denny contributed a simple bass line, and Paul added a Jerry Lee Lewis–style piano part during the playout, under the second of McCulloch's two short, bluesy guitar solos. But the track's musical focus is the twin lead—a pair of tightly matched, tandem lines in harmony—that McCulloch plays between the verses.

The Beatles had used a similar effect in 'And Your Bird Can Sing,' but Paul's model here was more immediate: 10cc used parallel, harmonized guitar lines on several songs on their eponymous 1973 debut album, most notably 'Hot Rock Sun,' as well as 'Sand in My Face,' 'The Dean and I' and 'The Hospital Song.'

"Paul said, 'Give him some of that 10cc echo,'" Mike Tattersall recalled, "and he asked, 'How do you do that guitar sound?' And I said, 'Plug the guitar directly into the desk.' Basically, we overloaded the EQ modules. And that was all it was. We could experiment in our own studio."[24]

Indeed, the influences went both ways. "It definitely had a big influence on the music that we were recording at the time," 10cc's Graham Gouldman said of McCartney's presence at

Strawberry. "The control room was completely full of our gear, and Paul's gear as well. So we had, you know, the drum kit set up that [Conway] used, and we used that on some of the tracks on our *Sheet Music* album. And we borrowed Paul's Mellotron. We were listening to what he was recording, and he was listening to what we were recording, so it's kind of like a bit of cross-pollination."[25]

Although they were working at a brisk clip, it could not have been lost on either Paul or Mike that they were cobbling together a pretty diffuse collection, so far: a Bryan Ferry cover, the bare bones of a song decorated with a jam, and a comic novelty track. None of the new material approached Paul's 'Leave It,' the project's starting point.

The McCartney brothers remedied that with a more complex product of their composing-while-commuting project, 'Have You Got Problems.' A collaboration built on a lyric that was largely Mike's cynical look at government-promulgated lies, funneled through television news, with sets of repeated admonitions: *"Don't believe all you're told, all you read, all you're taught"* and *"Do what you want, do what you do, what do you want, do what you like."*

Paul made this into a hybrid Fifties-Sixties blowout, and a model of McCartneyesque texturing. Beginning with a simple piano introduction, then piano and voice, he gives Mike a simple but catchy vocal melody as he gradually adds bass, drums and guitars. Space was left for a solo, and given the song's Fifties DNA, both Paul and Mike agreed that a saxophone would be ideal, an embellishment that could wait until more tracks were completed.

The tempo picks up speed for the bridge—*"Don't believe, don't believe, don't believe all you're told, all you read, all you're taught, all you see"*—and upon the return to the verse, Linda, Paul, Denny and Mike add backing vocals, the men singing a low *"bah-bah-bah-bah-baaaah"* figure, seemingly lifted from the Beach Boys' 'Help Me, Rhonda.' And as the song winds to a chaotic ending, a bit past the six-minute mark, Paul again slips into Jerry Lee Lewis mode at the piano, steadily and energetically pounding out the chords. Add some reverb and slapback echo and, *voilà*, a lyrically feisty, musically retro track was in the can.

As soon as the session on January 10 ended, the McCartneys returned to London to catch a flight to New York. They were there for only 36 hours, principally to celebrate Lee Eastman's sixty-fourth birthday on January 12. Contrived though it may have seemed, who could resist having 'When I'm Sixty-Four' sung by its composer on the very day it became applicable?

Lee and John updated Paul on the Apple negotiations set to take place a month hence, and Paul updated the Eastmans on the quick progress of Mike's album. Lee Eastman also passed on to Paul a request from Al Coury, the marketing man at Capitol Records who had overseen the release of *Band on the Run* and was still working to shepherd it up the charts.

The album had sold 700,000 copies by then, significantly more than the half million sales required for Gold record certification. But sales were slowing, and the album had stalled at No. 13 on the *Billboard* 200. Coury's proposed solution was to release one of the album's catchiest tracks, 'Jet,' as a single.

Coury knew that the idea would be a tough sell to McCartney because they had discussed a similar notion only ten weeks earlier, just before *Band on the Run*'s November release, when Coury asked why the hit single 'Helen Wheels' was not on the album. Paul had explained that he preferred to keep albums and singles separate, as was common in Britain, but Coury cut through Paul's objections with a concrete example: after he persuaded Pink Floyd to release 'Money' as a single from *The Dark Side of the Moon*, sales of the album increased by 200,000 copies. Paul agreed to a compromise: 'Helen Wheels' was added to the American version of *Band on the Run*, but the British edition would be released without it.

Before approaching Paul about 'Jet,' Coury brought his pitch to Lee Eastman, and pointed out that radio stations across the United States had already identified 'Jet' as one of the album's strongest tracks and were giving it lots of airplay, creating a market for a single.

"I guaranteed him it would be number one," Coury related, adding that Eastman "kinda subtly threatened me. He said if it's not number one . . . we got demands . . . cut my balls off. I swallowed, took a deep breath, and said, 'Don't worry, it'll be number one!'"[26]

Paul made some pro forma objections, but Coury insisted that without singles drawn from albums, some potential buyers might be unaware that the album was available. Paul gave in, only to find that Coury had a second request. 'Jet' clocked in at just over four minutes, and although Paul had released longer singles—the Beatles' 'Hey Jude' was 7'10"—Coury felt that more stations would add it to their play lists if it were trimmed.

"I knew that," Coury later explained, "because in several different places in the country, radio stations started to edit the song down. My people in the field would say, 'Hey—you gotta listen to this, this guy in Seattle edited this track down, he's got it down to three minutes, or whatever, and he's getting a great reaction to it, he thinks it's gonna be a number one record.' So I realized that we had to do our own edit. . . . I proceeded to try to get Paul to authorize us to do an edit. But Paul would have no part of it. He didn't want any edits." [27]

After a vigorous back-and-forth, Coury prevailed. Paul left the editing to Capitol, where an engineer truncated the song's introduction by removing the repetitions of the opening "*Jet!*" and its pumping accompaniment. The first transitional guitar break, just before the synthesizer solo, was deleted, and when that transition returns, the song is faded out. The new version, at 2'58", was trimmed by just more than a minute. Capitol neglected to send Paul a copy of the edit, and uncharacteristically, he did not ask to hear it.

Capitol's handiwork was not to everyone's taste. "Must say, although my choice from Paul McCartney's great *Band on the Run* album for the follow-up single to 'Helen Wheels' was 'Jet'," a reviewer for *Cash Box* wrote, "the edited version of the track released is not a very neat one. No reason why the entire four minute plus track could not have been released. The song is strong enough and few jocks would have passed simply on the basis of its length. How about taking another close listen, Capitol, pulling back the edit and releasing the full album track?"[28]

At McCartney's insistence, the promotional single Capitol sent to radio stations included both versions of 'Jet'—the edit on one side, the full-length version on the other. On the commercial single, released in America on January 28, the full version of 'Jet' was backed with 'Mamunia,' but only on the first pressings; three weeks later 'Mamunia' was replaced with 'Let Me Roll It,' matching the British single, released on February 22.

Coury's hunch was quickly vindicated as *Band on the Run* resumed its climb up the charts. And the exchanges over 'Helen Wheels' and 'Jet' led Paul to realize that it was time to adjust his approach to marketing.

"With the Beatles," Paul said, "you had a collection of four very like-minded people, with very definite directions in things like marketing. The difference now is, I find it difficult to resist some sort of amazing marketing man really telling me how 'this is going to make the whole thing a sort of marvelous venture.' With the Beatles, it was very easy to resist those ideas: you'd just say, '*fuck off*,' because there were *four* of you saying fuck off. Now it's just me, and I've got to be absolutely sure that what I'm saying is the right thing."[29]

Recording Sessions

Monday, January 14–Thursday, February 14, 1974 (various dates).

Strawberry Studios, 3 Waterloo Road, Stockport.

Recording and Overdubbing: 'Rainbow Lady,' 'Simply Love You,' 'Givin' Grease a Ride' and 'The Casket.'

Having put in a solid week and set down half an album's worth of material, Paul and Mike began to work more intermittently, with Paul and Linda taking short trips to London and Scotland between sessions.

Nevertheless, Paul began his second week producing his brother's album as if he had not just spent the weekend on the other side of the Atlantic, the two sharing the drive from Gayton to Stockport, bouncing song ideas and lyrics off each other along the route.

'Rainbow Lady,' credited to both, brought a new element to the already varied project—an interesting hybrid that joined a melody redolent of early 1960s Mersey Beat, with a rich, thoroughly 1970s backing track, and a romantic lyric with just enough rainbow imagery to afford a hint of psychedelia. Here again, McCulloch's playing gives the track character, as do the backing vocals and a synthesizer solo, seemingly played by Paul, that points up the movement between major and minor keys that keeps the song harmonically unpredictable.

That Mike handled the song's tuneful verses with assurance may have emboldened him to ask Paul for something even more overtly melodic—perhaps something they could sing together, the way they did as young boys. They cobbled together 'Simply Love You,' an easygoing lyric that mainly danced around the title *("I simply love you, love you, love you, know that I love you")*, with a few easy rhymes *("Right from the start, straight to my heart")*, upon which Paul worked his melodic magic.

"In the McCartney family, doing harmonies, it's a big part of our history," Mike explained. "That's our lineage. The family parties, every one of them was a singsong, and the big thing was getting a good harmony. It's like the Beach Boys—they would have come from the same thing, from the family all singing 'round, and how can you get a better harmony than Uncle Joe.

"[Paul and I] used to sing Everly Brothers harmonies in Forthlin Road.* We used to love the Everly Brothers, and we were very good at singing [in their style]. So when it came to working together, I was fascinated to find that in the singing, we went back to being the Everly Brothers. You will hear so many checks on 'Simply Love You' and things like that, where it's just the two brothers singing like they used to sing."[30]

By the time the recording was finished, it was somewhat more complicated: Mike and Paul sang close harmonies, with Linda adding high parts, and the full vocal complement (Linda, Paul, Denny and Mike) singing answering phrases between lines. Paul suspected that 'Simply Love You,' like 'Sea Breezes,' might benefit from orchestral sweetening, so with the basic track and the lead and backing vocals complete, he set it aside.

For 'Givin' Grease a Ride,' the McCartney brothers took another sidelong glance at Glam, this time borrowing rather than parodying. Though their song is slower, and both its lyrics and its instrumental textures are more complex and varied, the influence of Marc Bolan's 1971 T. Rex hit 'Jeepster' is unmistakable, not least in the degree to which Mike channels Bolan's vocal style. Paul

* 20 Forthlin Road, Paul and Mike's childhood home in the Allerton district of Liverpool, from 1956.

disguises this brilliantly in the song's instrumental texture, with its multiple lead guitar lines (some presented as dialogues), steady drumbeat and phase-shifting effects.

Paul's practice of keeping tabs on 10cc's work during the session switchovers paid an unexpected dividend in the form of a new sound. Listening to the band's 'Baron Samedi' one afternoon while Conway, McCulloch and Laine set up for that evening's session, Paul wondered about the strange timbre at the end of the track. Was that a synthesizer, he wondered? No, Peter Tattersall told him, it was a Gizmo—a guitar attachment, designed by Kevin Godley and Lol Creme, and built with the help of Dr. Martin Jones at the University of Manchester Institute of Science and Technology.

Eric Stewart, who played the Gizmo on the track, brought out his modified guitar to show Paul how it worked. Attached to the bridge, the unit has six rotary plectrums that massage the strings, yielding notes that sound bowed rather than plucked. With experience, and the right tone modification boxes and pedals, a player could use the Gizmo to create what the ear perceives as an orchestra or a choir—or just strange, hard-to-identify tones.

Paul had heard a similar device during the Los Angeles sessions for *Ram*, when Greg Heet demonstrated his Energy Bow, which allowed a player to draw sustained notes from a guitar. Godley and Creme's Gizmo took the effect to another level.

"Wah-wah pedals, fuzz boxes and so on just gimmick the sound of the guitar," Creme explained. "The Gizmo changes the intrinsic nature of the instrument. It allows you to get any orchestration you like onto tape immediately. You don't have to work out parts for forty musicians. You just think the part and play it. It's the ultimate freedom for a musician.[31]

"When you press it down it sustains the string indefinitely. You can actually play the guitar normally, but as long as you hold the note with your finger it will sound. You can do a vibrato with your fingers with it. The first two strings sound like violins, the next two sound like violas and the bottom two like cellos."[32]

After a short acquaintance, Paul wanted a Gizmo of his own, so Creme got in touch with the University of Manchester to have another made. It would take a few weeks, so Creme loaned Paul a suitably kitted-out Telecaster. When Paul's Gizmo was ready, Godley and Creme made a gift of it. "You don't take money from Paul McCartney,"[33] Creme joked.

During the third week of the sessions, Mike and his mates from the Scaffold reconnected after Roger McGough and John Gorman phoned him, sang a verse of the Scaffold hit 'Lily the Pink,' and invited him to rejoin the group for a BBC television appearance. The group had been asked to perform, alongside the Liverpool actors Deryck Guyler and Rita Tushingham, on *Da Scouse Show*, to be filmed at the Shakespeare Theatre in Liverpool on January 27. Paul again suggested covering 'Liverpool Lou.'

"They wanted us to do our sketches, and poetry," Mike recalled, "and they asked, 'Can you do a song—a new one?' And so Our Kid said, 'I've always thought "Liverpool Lou" would be a great thing for Scaffold.' I said, 'No, it's too folky, it's a folk song.' And he said, 'Wait until you see what I do with it.'"

Mike looked into previous recordings, with some help from the BBC's library, and found Behan's 1964 original, as well as a BBC recording by the Spinners, a Liverpool folk group, and an uncharacteristically orchestrated, overproduced version by the American R&B duo Delaney and Bonnie.

"When I heard these, I understood what Our Kid was getting at," Mike confessed. "I'm just thinking about it as a little folk song, but he sees the bigger picture."[34]

Paul and the Scaffold met at Mike's house to rehearse his arrangement, which preserved the song's simplicity and folk character, and retained elements of Behan's version—most notably, the harmonica part featured in the Irish songwriter's introduction. Paul proposed having the harmonica run through the full song, and Mike invited Norm Yardley, a regular Scaffold guest, to play the expanded harmonica part. Paul also suggested replacing the quasi-classical fingerpicking on Behan's version with a strummed guitar part, as well as a simple bass line and a steady drumbeat. And he proposed that Scaffold sing the choruses in unison, with Mike singing the verses on his own.

The performance was a hit, and McGough and Gorman, eager to get Mike back into the fold, suggested recording the song as a new Scaffold single. Discussing the prospect, Mike and Paul agreed to bring Scaffold in to record 'Liverpool Lou' when Mike's album was closer to completion.

But the revived Scaffold already had a foothold at the sessions. Shortly after the 'Liverpool Lou' rehearsal, Roger McGough stopped in at Strawberry to watch the sessions in progress, and he brought with him a new poem, 'The Casket.' The title refers to a jewelry box, rather than a coffin, and describes the contents of such a box, washed up on a beach—love letters, a photograph of a World War I German sailor, and other mementos of a young girl, now mixed with seaweed and scuttled over by hermit crabs.

Paul was taken with the poem's imagery and set it to music, giving it a simple but attractive, folk-tinged melody not a world apart from that of 'Liverpool Lou.' The recording was equally straightforward, with Jimmy playing a fingerpicked acoustic guitar part and Paul at the piano, supporting Mike's vocal and sometimes doubling the guitar figures. The melody tested Mike's vocal range at times, but Paul joined him with a harmony vocal on the final lines.

"And there's Our Kid and I, going back to being young men, 15-, 16-, 17-year-old lads, after Mum died, singing harmonies. On 'The Casket,' at the end, where he and I sing together in harmony—it's very simple, and just the two brothers. There are some great feelings there."[35]

Paul and Mike agreed that bass and percussion were not necessary—but also that there was still something missing, to be dealt with at a future session.

Paul had other irons in the fire during these sessions. Paul and Linda, with Mike and the rest of the transitional Wings, attended Stevie Wonder's concert at the Rainbow Theatre in Finsbury Park on January 24.

"Linda and I really love Stevie," he enthused to a *Record Mirror* reporter. "We flew down from Manchester specially to see him when he appeared at the Rainbow. The dedication on the sleeve of *Red Rose Speedway* says it all,"[36] he added, referring to the Braille message, "we love you baby," on the cover of Wings' second album.

Bits of the past were cropping up, as well, in new guises that Paul wanted to keep tabs on. Having gained control of the Lennon-McCartney catalog in 1969, Sir Lew Grade's ATV was eager to exploit the material to ensure a steady stream of royalty income—that being one of the principal jobs of a publisher. The push was led by Sam Trust, the music publishing guru who declined Lee Eastman's invitation to manage Paul's own McCartney Music, Inc., in 1971, and who was now president and CEO of ATV/Northern Songs. When it came to inspiring others to tap into the Lennon-McCartney songbook, Trust argued, there were no losers.

"What's wrong with exploiting the catalog?" Trust asked. "The Beatles were out of business; if you exploit the catalog the money goes direct to them. So I did everything I could to exploit it."[37]

Paul had no problem with cover versions of individual songs; indeed, he and John presided over an hour-long television program with a diverse array of such covers, *The Music of Lennon and McCartney*, in December 1965.

But there were now some grandiose projects afoot, and he had mixed feelings about them. On January 19, *Melody Maker* reported that the producer Lou Reizner, who was best known for a 1972 symphonic recording of the Who's *Tommy* with an all-star cast (including Ringo Starr as the wicked Uncle Ernie), was planning a stage production and a recording of *Sgt. Pepper's Lonely Hearts Club Band.* Reizner had some experience with the Beatles' classic, having produced an instrumental version of the album by the Peter Knight Orchestra in 1967, shortly after the Beatles' version was released.

Four years after the Beatles split, the public's hunger for their music was as voracious as ever. Throughout the early 1970s, stage shows presenting moptop-wigged musicians performing Lennon and McCartney hits began popping up on stages across America. But these amateur productions were unregulated and unlicensed. Fearing this trickle of unauthorized shows would soon become a flood, and intent on protecting ATV's commercial interest, Trust attempted to form a united legal front with Apple to shut them down. But as Trust saw it, since Klein departed the company in March 1973, Apple was a rudderless organization.

"When the Beatles broke up, all these shows started swinging across America," explained Trust. "They were springing up in Texas, and Oklahoma, everywhere. So I had to hire a lawyer to go out and close the damn things, and that was at my expense. So I called Apple and said, 'Listen, can you join in on this? It's costing me a fortune.' And they said, 'No, we're not gonna do it. That's up to you.' I said, 'Wait a minute, I'm protecting the [Beatles'] copyright, but you own the image [rights] and everything else about the Beatles.' But they refused to do it."[38]

With the future of Apple uncertain amidst the former Beatles' ongoing efforts to dissolve their business ties, the only solution, in Trust's view, was to work closely with Broadway and West End producers to handpick projects for stage and screen and throw the full support of ATV/Northern Songs behind them.

What Paul undoubtedly found most irksome about the report of the proposed *Sgt. Pepper* show was that it would be presented by Robert Stigwood, the Australian-born entrepreneur. McCartney had formed a negative impression of Stigwood as far back as 1962, when the Beatles, shortly after the release of 'Love Me Do,' were keen to promote their debut single. The disc had climbed into the top 30 in *Pop Weekly*, a new magazine owned by Stigwood and Albert Hand. Brian Epstein bought an advertisement for the single in the magazine, in the hope of getting some editorial space, which bought the group an interview.

The visit was a disaster. Epstein had instructed the Beatles to introduce themselves to Stigwood, but the impresario refused to meet them. The interviewer he had assigned made it clear that he thought guitar-based pop groups were on their way out, and that they were wasting his time. After smiling their way through a handful of lightweight questions underpinned with scarcely veiled hostility, John turned to the others and said, "Let's fucking get out of here."[39]

Now, 11 years later, the encounter remained in Paul's memory. "I remember going to Robert Stigwood's office, and he wouldn't see us," Paul said. "Never been struck on him since."[40]

Not that Stigwood had to wait long to rue his refusal to meet with the young band. In 1967, when Brian Epstein was tiring of the music business—his fantasy, at the time, was to manage Spanish bullfighters—he merged his management business, NEMS, with Stigwood's firm, which by then represented Cream and the young Bee Gees. Stigwood's ambition was to manage the Beatles, and Epstein, whose contract with the group was due to expire that year, considered selling the Beatles to him outright.

"We dealt with it very quicky," McCartney recalled. "Brian said, 'Robert Stigwood wants to buy you.' And we said, 'Oh yes?' He said, 'And we're having a meeting with him and one of his businesspeople.' And we said, 'Oh yes, well, we're not very keen on this, Brian. You know that, don't you?' So we waited till the meeting, and they said, 'We were just talking about the conditions, you know.' And we said, 'Well, let's just get this straight. We're not going to be sold to anyone. If you can do it, you [Epstein] can continue to manage us. We love you. We're not going to be sold. In fact, if you do, if you somehow manage to pull this off, we can promise you one thing: we will record "God Save the Queen" for every single record we make from now on and we'll sing it out of tune. That's a promise. So if this guy buys us, that's what he's buying.'"[41]

But Paul also had reason to play nice with Stigwood. Following a brief stint in the Glasgow quartet Blue, guitarist Jimmy McCulloch—who was looking like a shoo-in for the vacant guitarist position in Wings Mark II—was managed by the Australian's company. Fearing a reprise of Denny Laine's contractual standoff with his former manager Tony Secunda between 1971 and 1973, Paul realized some accommodation with Stigwood might soon be in order.

Also in the mailbag around this time for the McCartneys were three Grammy nominations for 'Live and Let Die.' Paul and Wings were up for the Best Pop, Rock and Folk Vocal Performance by a Duo, Group or Chorus award; George Martin was nominated for Best Arrangement Accompanying Vocalists. And Paul, Linda and George Martin were in the running for Album of Best Original Score Written for a Motion Picture or Television Special.[42]

After taking a short break in London, the McCartneys and company returned to Stockport to continue work on Mike's album.

By the beginning of February, the fact that Paul had been working on Mike's album in Stockport was becoming broadly known, and publications from the local *Stockport Advertiser* to national music papers like *NME* were sending reporters and photographers to get what they could—in the case of the latter, a photo of Paul, Linda, Mike and Lol Creme at Strawberry Studios, and an interview in which Mike said that they were finishing a song a day and suggesting that the album might be released on Elektra in August.[43] His prediction proved incorrect, but it hinted at the discussions the Eastmans were having: they had set their sights on Warner early on, and Elektra had been a Warner subsidiary since 1970.

Paul was in the news on his own with the British release of 'Jet' set for February 22; it would be competing with Ringo Starr's 'You're Sixteen'—on which Paul sang a wordless line that was meant to evoke a saxophone but sounded more like a kazoo—due out eleven days earlier. Meanwhile, *Rolling Stone*, until now alternating between vaguely unsupportive and openly hostile to Paul, ran not only Jon Landau's favorable review of *Band on the Run* but also Paul Gambaccini's lengthy interview with Paul, conducted in London and New York between November 1973 and January 1974, in its January 31 issue.

The reviews of 'Jet' were a boost.

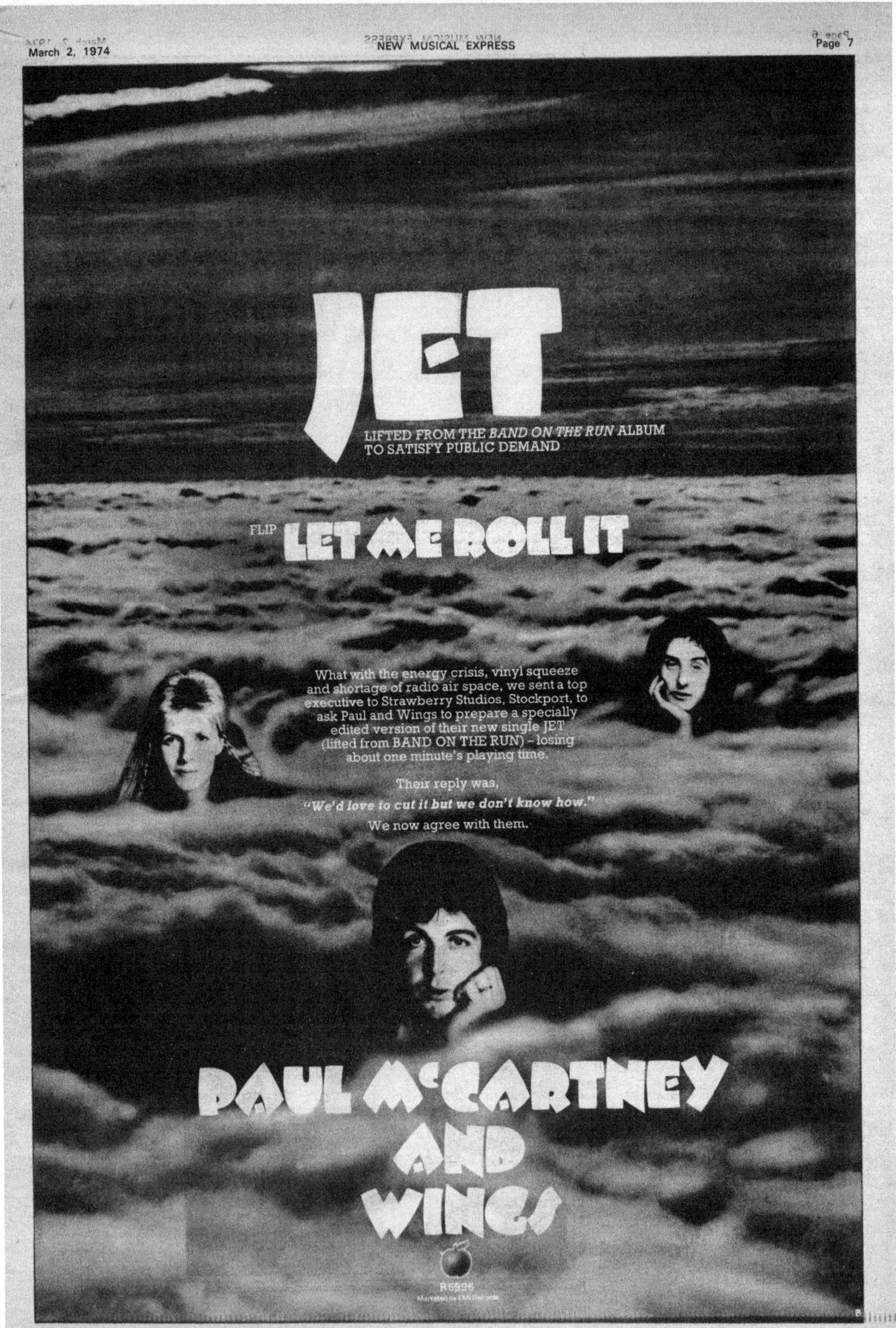

High in the clouds—Paul McCartney and Wings, 'Jet' single trade ad

Another from the exquisite Band on the Run *album, this tune is an overpowering smash both vocally and instrumentally.*[44]

Uncredited, Record World

'Jet' is representative of McCartney's talent—there's so much in it you don't know where to start. There are abrupt changes of melody and pace which make it a very unusual single. A hit, of course.[45]

Rosemary Horide, Disc

One of the outstanding tracks off the album, it's been played so many times, I thought it was a hit already. Original lyrics, fascinating instrumental ideas, exciting changes, what more can one ask in a single? Pure craftsmanship, and it should be a top ten triumph.[46]

Chris Welch, Melody Maker

'Jet' is the kind of quality pop that seems to have gotten totally out of fashion. Even if you've already bought the album, it'll sound so great on jukeboxes and radios that you'll feel a pathological urge to buy it anyway. The use of the synthesizer both to beef up the introductory chords, and to play the solo is nothing less than masterly. 'Let Me Roll It' is a brilliant but affectionate Lennon pastiche with the greatest chorus of the last twelve months.[47]

Charles Shaar Murray, NME

This is from the Band on the Run *album, a track recorded in Lagos, Nigeria.** *The first fact means that a lot of McCartney addicts will have it already. The second that it had a raw-edged, build-up excitement about it which is helped somewhat by the backing vocals. It's a whiplash sort of approach . . . the cracking biting staccato moments but varied by Paul's special style of phrasing. It'll be a big one, naturally, but with the proviso that it IS an album track.*[48]

Peter Jones, Record Mirror

* Actually, it was one of the few tracks on *Band on the Run* recorded in London, not in Lagos.

Recording Sessions

February 1974 (precise dates unknown).

Strawberry Studios, 3 Waterloo Road, Stockport.

Recording and Overdubbing: 'The Man Who Found God on the Moon' and 'Dance the Do.'

Back at work on Mike's album, the brothers spent several of their commutes between Gayton and Stockport working on an ambitious idea of Mike's that required tapping into one of Paul's specialties—the weaving together of unfinished songs to create a whole, a technique he used to help John Lennon finish off 'A Day in the Life' and to create the medleys on *Abbey Road*, as well as 'Another Day,' 'Uncle Albert/Admiral Halsey,' and 'Band on the Run,' among others.

"'The Man Who Found God on the Moon' was the best one," Mike said of the material he recorded at Strawberry Studios, "because it had all these different ideas. But I knew from [Paul]—from his *Sgt. Pepper* days, and his *Band on the Run* days—that he could segue in and out of tunes, and I thought he'd done those very cleverly. It's like a river bending, and different things you come across. All different songs. All different ideas. But if we could get them to all link together, that was the great joy of that one. It became a big jigsaw puzzle."[49]

Mike's stack of unfinished lyrics included a piece he wrote while driving from London to Liverpool on a summer evening and seeing a group of hot air balloons floating slowly across the sky. Later, on that same trip, he saw fireworks, duly noted in his lyric. Another scrap was about a young girl named Annette handing out Hare Krishna literature. Mainly, though, Mike was taken with a story he had heard about the astronaut Buzz Aldrin, who joined Neil Armstrong on the first moon landing on July 20, 1969, and who had reportedly found God during the experience.

Actually, the story as Mike heard it was incorrect. Aldrin did not find God on the moon—he brought God with him, in effect. Already a religious man, Aldrin was an elder at Webster Presbyterian Church in Houston, Texas, and had decided to take Communion while he and Armstrong were on the moon and Michael Collins was orbiting in the Command Module.

"I unstowed the elements in their flight packets," Aldrin later explained. "I put them and the scripture reading on the little table in front of the abort guidance system computer. Then I called back to Houston:

"'Houston, this is Eagle. This is the LM Pilot speaking. I would like to request a few moments of silence. I would like to invite each person listening in, wherever and whomever he may be, to contemplate for a moment the events of the past few hours and to give thanks in his own individual way.'

"In the radio blackout I opened the little plastic packages which contained bread and wine. I poured the wine into the chalice our church had given me. In the one-sixth gravity of the moon the wine curled slowly and gracefully up the side of the cup. It was interesting to think that the very first liquid ever poured on the moon, and the first food eaten there, were Communion elements."[50]

Mike, who listened avidly to the live broadcast of the landing—and recorded it on his Revox open-reel deck—would not have heard Aldrin's enactment of the sacrament. NASA, sensitive about public religious expression after fielding complaints (and a lawsuit) the previous year when astronauts on the *Apollo 8* mission read excerpts from Genesis, chose not to broadcast it, so only those at NASA's Mission Control knew about it at the time.

Still, the idea of Aldrin having a mystical experience was a great way to tie together balloonists, fireworks and a young Hare Krishna devotee, and Paul rose to the challenge.

One of the first things he did was jettison most of Mike's lyrics for the song's title section—lines like "*it was a total experience,*" "*it was a spiritual awakening,*" "*Dad's waiting on the moon, having breakfast out here in space,*" and "*Now I see you all down there in a new perspective.*" At one point, Mike got silly with rhymes—"*The man who felt God in a spacesuit / was the man who found God on the moon / And very soon / he'd be called a loon / now how's the tune!*" Paul retained only the first two lines, grafting on a rhymed section from elsewhere on Mike's working copy, after a small amendment. As originally written, the section reads, "*You should have seen him flip / It was a total trip / He should have got a grip on himself.*" As Paul and Mike reworked it, the finished version is, "*You should have seen him flip / He nearly lost his grip / It was a total trip.*"[51]

As in most of these songs, Paul gave Mike's song fragments melodies that are both graceful and easy to sing, and the basic track was simple but tightly focused: Paul played the piano (later overdubbing a bass line), Denny played acoustic guitar, with Jimmy on electric, and Conway played a carefully orchestrated drum part.

The song's complications were in the arrangement, which Paul built over several days. Paul, Mike, Linda and Denny, in various combinations, added a closely harmonized backing track that sometimes paralleled the lead vocal and sometimes responded to it. Paul suggested that Mike record his two oldest daughters, five-year-old Benna and three-year-old Theran, singing the 'Hare Krishna Mantra.' When he brought in the tape—along with his recording of the moon landing—Paul overlaid the girls on the "Annette" section and excerpted a fragment of a Neil Armstrong transmission to juxtapose with Mike's "*the man who found God in his spacesuit*" vocal. After a few days, it seemed clear to all that the track, clocking in at more than six and a half minutes, would benefit from orchestral strings, so it was set aside.

During the second week in February, Mike's sessions—and particularly labor-intensive tracks like 'The Man Who Found God on the Moon'—were an important distraction for Paul, who was keenly aware that 3,340 miles to the west, the lawyers for the four former Beatles were once again sitting in a conference room, hashing out the details of the agreement dissolving the Beatles' partnership.

Not that he was insulated from the proceedings entirely. He checked in with the Eastmans regularly, with one long debriefing on February 13 or 14, during which Mike and the musicians took off for the nearby Waterloo pub. Mike and company were celebrities at the Waterloo by then, having stopped by most days. On at least one occasion, Peter Tattersall remembered, Paul bought a round of drinks for the full house.

While they waited for Paul, the band began playing records on the jukebox and landed on Ike and Tina Turner's August 1973 single 'Nutbush City Limits.' As they bopped along to the pounding beat and sharp-edged guitar chords of Turner's autobiographical hit, one of the players suggested making a dance tune. Back in the studio, they began to set down a basic recording, in Paul's absence, with McCulloch and Laine (on bass) shaping the riff-based backing track, Conway putting together a nicely textured drum part, and McCulloch double-tracking an energetic solo.

Upon Paul's return, they finished off the track—first deciding what to call the dance, since repetition of its name makes up the lion's share of the lyric ("We've had the Twist, the Jive, the Shake, the Locomotive, the Funky Chicken, the Bump and all the rest," Mike said. "So what could I do except 'The Do'?"[52]), then adding a falsetto lead vocal and several layers of harmonies. In short order, 'Dance the Do' was complete, and the musicians headed off for a long weekend. McCulloch's and Laine's contributions notwithstanding, the finished song, 'Dance the Do,' was credited to Paul and Mike only.

Because Paul and Linda had been leaving their daughters in Gayton, rather than bringing them to the sessions, the long weekend was an opportunity to spend some quality time with them in Scotland on Friday and Saturday, before returning to Rembrandt in time for a Sunday afternoon interview with the *New York Daily News.* Lennon's demand for an extra million dollars and Paul's consequent explosion quickly put paid to that idea, although once Paul had time to think about it, he had to admit that it was typical of John to throw a spanner in the works at the last moment. As the new week dawned, he was ready to begin putting the final touches on Mike's album.

Recording Sessions

Monday, February 18–Friday, March 1, 1974 (various dates).

Strawberry Studios, 3 Waterloo Road, Stockport.

Recording and Mixing: 'Liverpool Lou' and 'Ten Years After on Strawberry Jam.'

Overdubbing: 'Givin' Grease a Ride,' 'Have You Got Problems,' 'The Man Who Found God on the Moon,' 'Liverpool Lou' and 'The Casket.'

Mixing: 'Sea Breezes,' 'What Do We Really Know?,' 'Norton,' 'Have You Got Problems,' 'Rainbow Lady,'

'Simply Love You,' 'Givin' Grease a Ride,' 'The Man Who Found God on the Moon,' 'Dance the Do,' 'Ten Years After on Strawberry Jam' and 'Liverpool Lou.'

Before settling in to finish overdubbing and mixing tasks for every song recorded during the sessions—with no thought yet to what would go on the album and what might be saved for later—there was some unfinished business involving Mike and the Scaffold. The BBC performance had gone over well enough that the group decided to record Paul's arrangement, with Paul producing.

The Scaffold reprised the arrangement they performed on the broadcast, with Norm Yardley on harmonica, Paul playing a simple bass line, Conway contributing a steady, uncluttered beat, and Jimmy's rich-textured acoustic guitar filling out the backing. The reconstituted Scaffold trio sang the choruses, leaving the verses for Mike alone. One chorus was left vocal-free for a solo, instrumentation to be determined.

The question of what to offer as a B side was settled when Paul decided to cobble together a novelty track, based on a jam between 10cc and the semi-Wings lineup, plus Peter Tattersall on piano, recorded one afternoon as 10cc handed over the studio to Paul and Mike. Winding through the reel, Paul took a nearly three-minute section of the guitar-heavy jamming and overlaid it with a conversation between the Scaffold players and possibly others. The Scouse-accented chat obscured the details and nuances of the music, though not enough to entirely hide the fact that the jam's jumping-off point was Jimi Hendrix's 'Third Stone from the Sun.'

Paul titled the track 'Ten Years After on Strawberry Jam,' with the composition credit given as Paul and Linda McCartney. Possibly because the nature of the track militated against its getting much play, no one appears to have noticed the use of Hendrix's melody—not even Warner Bros. Records, whose Reprise subsidiary had released the Hendrix recording in the United States, and which released the Scaffold single on May 3. But first pressings credited 'Liverpool Lou' as "Trad. Arr. Paul & Linda McCartney," and Dominic Behan immediately protested. He received an apology from McCartney, and subsequent pressings were credited Behan.

Tuesday, February 19, was a day of reviewing tapes and unspecified overdubbing, during which Paul had a pair of celebrity visitors, fresh from a performance of their own in Manchester.

"I got this phone call from Danny Betesh," Peter Tattersall said, referring to an artists' agent at Kennedy Street Enterprises, the Manchester-based management organization. "He said, 'Richard and Karen [Carpenter], um—can they come meet Paul?' So I said, 'Well, I'll just find out' . . . And Paul said, 'Yeah, I don't mind—so long as it's not a load of people.' So I went back to Danny, and said, 'Yes, okay, but I don't want a lot of people,' and he said, 'Hang on—Richard wants a word with you.' So he gives me Richard Carpenter [who] says, 'What I want to know—is it alright if my sister comes as well?'"

As a devoted student of Top 40 pop, Paul knew the Carpenters were a force to be reckoned with: their hits compilation, *The Singles 1969–1973* had just hit No. 1 in Britain and was preventing *Band on the Run* from sliding into that spot. When they walked into the studio, Paul sang the chorus of their 1973 hit 'Top of the World'—although he could equally have sung 'Ticket to Ride,' the Beatles cover for which their first album was titled—and Richard handed Paul a copy of *Band on the Run* that he had brought along, hoping to get it autographed. Paul signed it, "To Dickie, from a chum."[53]

"They were two timid little mice," is how Mike remembered the visit. "They just sat in the control room. That girl—one of the best singers, one of the best voices. Certain people, like k.d. lang and Dusty Springfield, Karen Carpenter, Stevie Wonder—they just have *voices,* God sent them these things. It's just such a joy to listen. And there she is, just quiet as a mouse."[54]

Upon discovering that his stepmother and stepsister were avid Carpenters fans—and wanting to thank them for looking after the girls—Paul also secured Angie and Ruth tickets to see the American duo in concert at the Liverpool Empire the following evening.

Slowly, Mike's recordings reached their final form. Mike invited Brian Jones, the saxophonist in the Undertakers—a Liverpool band whose best-known member was Jackie Lomax, one of the first Apple artists—to come in and play the vigorous, 1950's-style solo on 'Have You Got Problems' and to add some lighter touches to 'The Man Who Found God on the Moon.'

Listening to a rough mix of 'The Casket,' Paul decided that the track needed something a little unusual in a pop track, perhaps even defiantly so. He enlisted Paddy Maloney, a member of the renowned Irish folk ensemble the Chieftains, to add uilleann pipes (a variety of bagpipe), thereby giving the track a touch of antiquity to support the old photos in the broken jewel box.

Mike did some tweaking of his own. Pleased with the tape additions to 'The Man Who Found God on the Moon,' he compiled a tape of sound effects, including broken glass and automotive sounds. (Mike's eight-year-old Alvis "mic'd up through the bog [toilet] window of Strawberry Studios,"[55] he explained.) Some of these—a tire screech and crashing sounds—found their way to 'Givin' Grease a Ride.'

Mainly what was left to do, however, was orchestral sweetening. Paul asked Tattersall to see to the details, which principally meant engaging an arranger now that Tony Visconti was out of the picture. Tattersall hired Gerry Allison, who did a lot of work for Granada TV. Allison came to Strawberry for a meeting with Paul and Mike, and Paul ran down his ideas for the five tracks that he felt would benefit from orchestration. Allison did the arrangements, then contacted the Hallé Orchestra, a storied, Manchester-based ensemble, from which he engaged some 20 string, wind, and brass players for sessions on February 23.

On the day, Allison conducted, efficiently overseeing the addition of a brass section to 'Have

You Got Problems,' then adding a string bed and celeste to 'Simply Love You.' 'Sea Breezes' was adorned with strings, as was 'The Man Who Found God on the Moon.' And shapely solo oboe lines were added to 'Sea Breezes' and 'The Casket.'

Tattersall, monitoring the sessions from the control room, was taken with Paul's interaction with the classical players.

"He's marvelous, the way he deals with musicians," Tattersall said shortly after the sessions. "He's got this incredible oboe solo out of this middle-aged woman. He was sort of egging her on, saying, 'Yes, and bend a note here,' and stuff like that. She was pretty amazed at what she had been able to do. His whole approach, and friendliness, endeared him to the session musicians."[56]

The final week of sessions was devoted to mixing, and the atmosphere was loose, almost party-like. Linda, who had taken to bringing food to the studio to make lunch—Tattersall remembers being particularly impressed with a condiment she had brought back from New York, Hellman's mayonnaise—and on Shrove Tuesday, February 26, she made thin, fluffy pancakes on a Calor gas stove while Denny serenaded the others with Buddy Holly songs. Denny's mini concert turned into a two-hour sing-along, and as Tattersall remembers it, gallons of tea and wine were consumed.

Paul was in a bright enough mood during the final run of sessions that he even did some fraternizing with fans. One early evening he went outside the studio to wait for Mike to bring the car around and saw a couple waiting at a nearby bus stop.

"He had a guitar with him," Tattersall remembers, "and he starts singing to them. They must have thought, '*Is that Paul McCartney? It can't be Paul McCartney!*' Then he said, 'Cheers! Bye!' and got into the car. I remember seeing their faces, they just couldn't believe it."[57]

On March 1, Paul's Gizmo arrived—a receipt marked "Received on temporary loan, one 'Gizmo,'" signed by Paul, remains on file at the University of Manchester. Although the mixing was virtually complete, Paul added the Gizmo, playing it himself, to 'The Casket' and to 'Liverpool Lou.' And with the final mix of 'Liverpool Lou,' mixing was complete.

Only two tasks remained. One was sequencing the album. 'Liverpool Lou' and 'Ten Years After on Strawberry Jam' were set aside as a Scaffold single. But although Paul and Mike had thought 'Leave It' would be a strong single for Mike alone, with 'Sweet Baby' recorded the previous spring as the B side, they opted to put 'Leave It' in the sequence, saving 'Sweet Baby' and 'Dance the Do' for use on potential singles.

SIDE ONE	SIDE TWO
'Sea Breezes'	'The Casket'
'What Do We Really Know?'	'Rainbow Lady'
'Norton'	'Simply Love You'
'Leave It'	'Givin' Grease a Ride'
'Have You Got Problems'	'The Man Who Found God on the Moon'

Paul's final task was to honor a promise he had made to provide a musical greeting to Piccadilly Radio, a new Manchester radio station set to go on the air on April 2. He made short work of it, but given his talent for grabbing a fully formed melody out of thin air, it hardly sounds like a throwaway. Accompanying himself at the piano, he sings a single verse—"*Hello Piccadilly / Hello Albert Square / Hello Piccadilly / Keep doing it on the air*"—to a cheerful ballad-style melody.

Add this to 'Luxy,' the promotional track he made for Radio Luxembourg during the Paris sessions with Linda at the end of November, and 'All Together on the Wireless Machine,' a ditty he had recorded for the BBC deejays Kenny Everett and Chris Denning in November 1967, and he had the start of a sample reel, in the event that he wanted to embark on a sideline career as a jingle writer.

Not lost in all this was the sub-rosa reason for undertaking the McGear project—working out the future of Wings. When Paul spoke with the *New York Daily News* a couple of weeks earlier, it was clear that his anger at Henry McCullough and Denny Seiwell for quitting the band on the eve of the trip to Lagos had not abated; indeed, the story, as he told it now, was both inaccurate and mean-spirited, although for most readers, the takeaway was that he was readying a new version of the band.

"I hope that this spring we can try out the new group in Europe and be ready by fall to go on tour in America. But I want to be sure we're good enough. It's still very much on my mind that the Wings of 1972 were not good enough. Several reasons for that. One of the boys always came on stage drunk, and we couldn't cope with it—finally we had to get rid of him. The other boys unfortunately were not good enough musically. It was my fault. I didn't get the right people together. But I think the new boys will fit better with our personalities—Linda and me. I'll know for sure in a few weeks, after we get into serious rehearsals."[58]

But the personnel issue was not entirely settled. At the final session, on March 1, Paul invited Gerry Conway to become the band's drummer. But Conway had a previous commitment.

"I was offered the gig with Wings, and I was flattered beyond belief," Conway said. "However, I had been with Cat Stevens for about four years, and we were due to start a world tour shortly after Mike McGear's album. I said to Paul that I was committed to this tour but would love to join Wings when it finished, but I was not contacted again."[59]

Paul was not the only member of Wings disappointed that Conway was unavailable. "He would have got in the band," Denny Laine later observed, "because he was the right drummer and fitted in all the ways, you know."[60]

But Wings did have a new lead guitarist. Shortly before the sessions for Mike's album got underway, Jimmy McCulloch fielded an offer to tour with David Bowie. But he had enjoyed working with Paul in Paris, and the invitation to work with him again was too good to turn down, so he turned down the Bowie tour instead.

He may also have suspected that the Wings gig was his if he wanted it. And he did. McCulloch had played on a No. 1 hit single when he was 16—Thunderclap Newman's 1969 'Something in the Air'—and in the four years since, he had fronted his own Jimmy McCulloch band and played in Stone the Crows and Blue, as well as a few shorter-lived bands. He was also working on an album of his own with drummer Colin Allen. But at age 20, what he wanted most was the stability of a solid, long-term job, and playing in a band with Paul McCartney looked to be as solid as it gets.

Still, he was surprised at how Paul made the offer. During the final week of overdubbing, Paul asked him to play a slide guitar line, on a dobro, on 'The Man Who Found God on the Moon.' Between takes, Paul walked into the studio from the control room and said, "Yeah, sounds great, that. Do you want to join the band?"[61]

McCulloch remembered playing it cool, but explaining his feelings about joining Wings he revealed a hint of the volatility that he was already known for.

"I said, 'Yes. Why not?' I thought it was a great opportunity," said McCulloch, "because . . . I was sick and tired of being in and out of bands. I want to get something down on record that's going to be appreciated instead of always being in new bands, so few people hear. You know, I was really quite happy to leave Blue. It did nothing for me. They were a good group, and all professionals, but they didn't have any bollocks. They were good on record . . . but just never really got through to me playing live. The trouble was, there wasn't enough of that bluesy influence that was promised when the band was formed."[62]

Some interviewers asked him directly about his reputation for being pugnacious, the result, at least in part, of an incident during his time with Stone the Crows when he poured the entire contents of a soda bottle over the head of a journalist he considered obnoxious.

"Well, sometimes I am a bit weird," McCulloch admitted. "Immaturity I suppose. I've had a lot of experience in music, but experience of life—knowing how to treat people, when to say something and when not to, and when you've put your foot in it—I'm still green in that way . . . getting drunk and things like that. . . . Just sometimes, there's a Jekyll and Hyde within me. Sometimes I really blow it and get on people's nerves. I suppose it's partly growing up with older people. I mean, I left school as soon as I could and then I was an adult, you know?"[63]

Paul was certainly aware of this side of McCulloch's personality, but there were other sides of McCulloch that appealed to Paul, apart from the fluidity of his playing. The fact that he was fascinated with the Belgian jazz guitarist Django Reinhardt (also an idol of Denny Laine's), for example, suggested to Paul an eclectic taste that could be useful, given the stylistic breadth he liked to explore in his songwriting.

"I like a lot of brass," Jimmy told one interviewer. "It might sound corny, but I like dance bands, I really do. Jazz-style dance bands. That really turns me on. At one time I used to be a heavy rock fan, but now it doesn't appeal to me so much. I'm not putting anybody down, but it's just disappointing to me to hear a band just go bash-bash-bash 'til the end and then get off. I suppose, basically I like melody."[64]

In any case, there was an escape valve. McCulloch was under contract to the Robert Stigwood Organization (RSO), so there was no possibility, at that point, of Paul putting him under contract. For the moment, Paul adopted the same arrangement that had governed Wings Mark I: McCulloch would be paid a weekly retainer, whether or not Wings were working, topped up with super session fees for recordings, paid at a rate of £170 ($408) per session.

The day after the sessions in Stockport wrapped up, Paul was back in London to field some good news. At the Grammy Awards, in Los Angeles, 'Live and Let Die' won for Best Arrangement Accompanied by a Vocalist, and it was announced that the song was in contention for an Oscar as well, having been nominated for Best Song.

Within a few days, he learned that *Band on the Run* had reached the top of the charts in Spain, a country that had been shaping up as McCartney-mad ever since 'Give Ireland Back to the Irish' reached No. 1 there.

Soon it was time to throw himself back into the promotion of *Band on the Run*, the latest round led by an interview at MPL's offices with the American journalist Scott Osborne for the *Today* show, an NBC morning program. Not having been seen for a while on American television, Paul showed off a new look—a mustache not unlike the one he sported on the cover of *Sgt. Pepper*, and a soul patch sprouting under his lower lip. Osborne kept to familiar themes—Paul's interest in being a family man, how songwriting came easily to him ("It's not really hard for me to do music—it's like a footballer, he just kind of does it, you know") and whether, once the Beatles' business issues were settled, they might "get together and do something." Reluctant to say what that something might be, Paul added: "It would have been great had it carried on, but seeing as it didn't, well, what are you going to do?"[65]

Across the Atlantic, the Eastmans had persuaded Warner Bros. Records to consider Mike's album, now definitely titled *McGear*, with Paul's production and coauthorship of most of the songs as its principal selling point. And on March 8, while Paul was taping his *Today* show interview, MPL sent copies of Mike's masters to Ron Kass, the former head of Apple Records who was now running Warner's London office, and to Kass's boss, Mo Ostin, president of the label, in Burbank, California.

Paul agreed to offer further help if it were needed. But for the moment, his work on Mike's album was done.

2

"DADDY, ARE YOU SOME SORT OF POP STAR?"

In terms of what he hoped to achieve in the sessions with Mike, Paul was only partially successful. As a production, the project went well—not surprising, given that McCartney had long shown a heightened sensitivity to what will work well for another artist. Whether the Eastmans would be able to sell the album to a major label remained to be seen, but the McCartney name would go a long way.

But his goal of reconstituting Wings had not been achieved. He wanted a band at the ready when the time came to record his next batch of songs, but more importantly, he wanted a band so that he could tour on the strength of *Band on the Run*.

Young Jimmy McCulloch was a promising addition. His playing was focused and inventive, and at the sessions for Linda in Paris and Mike in Stockport he had no problem either coming up with fresh lines or taking direction from Paul. Wings was still short of a drummer, though, and Paul would not be able to address that immediately.

This was a source of considerable frustration because the experience of leading Wings Mark I showed Paul that finding the right players was only a first step: in matters of tightness and finesse, it was a long way from the 1972 university tour to the mid-1973 British tour. Perhaps that realization led him to take his time finding the last piece of the puzzle.

One strategy was to keep an eye on the music press for news of bands breaking up and drummers becoming free, much as he knew that Denny Laine was at loose ends in 1971 when he read about the breakup of Balls. Breakup news was not plentiful at the start of March 1974, as it turned out. But there was plenty of news about former bandmates.

Sounds, for example, reported that Henry McCullough was planning to move to New York, along with former Grease Band keyboardist Mick Weaver and bassist Chris Stewart, late of Spooky

Tooth, to form a band with Denny Seiwell. Their immediate plan was to record an album for Island Records and then tour.[1]

There was also plenty of news about his Beatle pals. Early in March, Apple confirmed that George Harrison was planning to tour the United States toward the end of the year, possibly with Ringo Starr drumming and Eric Clapton on guitar—although a couple of weeks later, Harrison insisted that he was merely exploring the idea.

Journalists wondered whether Paul was planning a tour as well, and Paul left it to Tony Brainsby to remind them of Wings' current state of disrepair. Brainsby also squelched rumors that Paul was planning to fly to Los Angeles to meet with John Lennon, who had been separated from Yoko since September 1973 and was living the California dream with May Pang. John had kept the relationship relatively discreet: although the press reported rumors that he and Yoko had split, it was not until a *Daily Mail* story on November 29, that the separation, and speculation about John's relationship with May, became widely known.

May met the Lennons while she was working for Allen Klein and became their assistant in 1970. In the summer of 1973, when the relationship between John and Yoko had grown tense, thanks in large part to John's barely disguised infidelities, Yoko decided that it would make sense to channel John's extramarital sexual energy into an affair that she could control. She settled on the attractive, 22-year-old May as a likely candidate, and suggested to May that she accommodate herself to this arrangement, a proposal that May initially resisted.

But resisting John was not easy, and once their romance began, Yoko found that controlling it was harder than she had anticipated. John's decision to move to Los Angeles with May was a significant challenge to Yoko's plan, and her first response was to cut off May's salary. Another was to suggest to John that they divorce, to which John's response, according to May, was, "Okay, fine, let's do it."[2]

But Yoko had distractions of her own. She was completing her *Feeling the Space* album and, shortly after the New Year, gossip columnists for the New York papers reported that she was spending a lot of time, both in and out of the studio, with a guitarist at the sessions, David Spinozza—the very same David Spinozza who had played on Paul's *Ram* LP.

With communication between Paul and John infrequent and tense, once the business of sorting the Beatles' post-Apple relationship was raised, as it inevitably was—it was hard for Paul to understand what was going on with John. What he knew was that John had been working on an album of rock oldies, provisionally called *Back to Mono*, since October 1973, as part of his settlement with Morris Levy, whose Big Seven Music Corporation was suing Maclen Music, Northern Songs and Apple over Lennon's pilfering from Chuck Berry's 'You Can't Catch Me' in the Beatles' 'Come Together.'

Phil Spector was producing, but when he fell ill in early 1974, the project was put on hold. By then, Lennon appeared to be running off the rails, judging from a couple of incidents that had made the papers. In the first, at a restaurant, Lost on Larabee, on January 12, John accidentally wandered into the ladies' room and emerged with a Kotex sanitary pad on his forehead. Later that night, John trashed the house he had borrowed from his lawyer, Harold Seider. Then, on March 12, he was ejected from the Troubadour after heckling the Smothers Brothers and brawling with the club's owner and bouncers, a misadventure he attributed to drinking too many Brandy Alexanders (a mixture of cognac, crème de cacao and fresh cream) and the encouragement of the equally inebriated Harry Nilsson.

"If you think about it," May explained, blaming the second incident on Nilsson, "if you go out with Harry, and you go out drinking, he'll start something. I've seen this happen many times, with and without John. And the next thing you know, they're screaming at whoever it is that [Harry's] with. Now, are they going to go to Harry, or are they going to go to John? They're going to go to John, even though Harry was the one who started it. And he wouldn't let up. I yelled at him, 'Please stop!,' and he said, 'Oh, everybody loves it!' And I said, 'No, they don't, please stop!' He kept going, 'Come on, John, let's go!' But they don't go to Harry, to shut him up, they go to John, because who makes better copy?"[3]

His issues with John over the dissolution agreement notwithstanding, Paul must have winced to read detailed reports about the second incident in the March 23 issues of *NME*, *Disc* and *Melody Maker*.

But there was more to the heckling story than the papers reported. By that point, John and Yoko were having at least superficial conversations about divorce, while John and May were growing closer. Still, Yoko called regularly—as often as 15 times a day, according to May—to check in, either directly with John, or by quizzing May about what he was up to. In these calls, she provided what May called "directives," the chief of which was that May and John should be discreet in public.

On the day of the Smothers Brothers show, Yoko played another high-risk card in her attempt to keep John under control. During her daily phone check-in, she told John that she had slept with someone else. She did not mention Spinozza by name, but May guessed it, pointing out that on the cover of Yoko's *Feeling the Space* album, released in November 1973, Yoko and Spinozza are side by side on horses, with John trailing in the background.[4]

Whether or not John considered the marriage over, he was still a Liverpool-born male who had only recently embraced feminism, so Yoko's news would likely have taken him aback. And while it might be that his introduction to Brandy Alexanders—and Nilsson's pushing them—had more to do with the degree of his inebriation than thoughts of Yoko's infidelity, Yoko's news undoubtedly led to another of the evening's less widely discussed events: during the wait for the start of the

Smothers Brothers' set, John pulled May close and publicly kissed her for the first time. A photographer for *Time*, on hand to cover the Smothers Brothers show, snapped a picture that was picked up by newspapers everywhere. May explained that John was "going through an emotional crisis."[5]

That crisis was taking a toll behind the scenes as well, in the form of trashed apartments and violent outbursts that did not make the papers. Ringo Starr was spending time in Los Angeles, too, as was the Who's drummer, Keith Moon, adding another couple of heavy-drinking musicians to John's posse.

John soon took matters in hand, telling Harry Nilsson that instead of spending so much time drinking and causing havoc, they should do something creative. Pending Spector's reappearance, he began producing an album for Harry.

"We always considered ourselves 'visitors' to L.A.," May said of that time. "We mostly stayed at other people's houses; the only time we ever had our own place was when Harry rented the beach house, and even that wasn't our own place really. We had Ringo, Keith Moon, Harry, and Klaus Voormann living there, and they fell into the 'boys back in England' behavior. John always had a problem with too much drink. . . . [former Beatles roadie] Mal Evans was even in L.A. basically reassuming the role of procuring anything for 'the boys.'"[6]

Paul was planning to visit Los Angeles at the end of the month, principally to attend the Academy Awards at the Dorothy Chandler Pavilion, on April 2, hoping to scoop up an Oscar for 'Live and Let Die.' For the time being, he and Linda were catching up with London's cultural life. On March 12, the night Lennon was lashing out at the Troubadour, Paul and Linda were watching more structured and professional fisticuffs. Sitting in ringside seats at the Empire Pool, Wembley, they saw the Liverpool-born boxer (and *Band on the Run* cover photo companion) John Conteh successfully defend his Light Heavyweight Champion title against Tom Bogs, of Denmark.

They were also photographed attending a fashion show by British designer Ossie Clark, and on March 22, they caught a solo show at the Rainbow Theatre by the virtuoso blues-rock guitarist Alvin Lee, whose band, Ten Years After, had just split up.

The McCartneys also had an unexpected visitor in late March. Yoko Ono turned up shortly before they left for America.

"Yoko came by, and we started talking," Paul remembered. "Obviously, the important subject for us is, 'What's happened? You've broken up then. You know, you're here, he's there. What's happening?' And she was very nice and confided in us that, yeah, it's kind of broken up, but she's been very strong about it, but very—not feminist, but being a strong woman rather than just submitting to it all.[7]

"So, being friendly and seeing her plight, Linda or I said to her, 'Do you still love him? Do you want to get back with him?' She said, 'Yes.' We said, 'Well, what would it take, then?' Because we were going out L.A. way. . . . And she gave me this whole thing, 'He would have to come back to New York. He can't live with me immediately. He'd have to court me. He'd have to ask me out. He'd have to send me flowers, he'll have to do it all again.'"[8]

Not having seen John since December 1971, Paul was unsure how a meeting with him in Los Angeles might go. But he tentatively agreed to have a word with his old friend in the hope of aiding a possible reconciliation. When the *Los Angeles Times* phoned Paul on March 26 for an interview about his Oscar hopes, and the discussion made its way to the inevitable Beatles question, Yoko was still on Paul's mind.

"There's a chance we might do something together," he said, dangling a carrot before inexplicably waxing historical, noting Yoko's presence during the *Let It Be* sessions, and explaining it with a sympathetic spin.

"John wanted her right there and then," he said. "Yoko was evident all the time. That was a sore point. It was John's first love; unreasonable things happen with a love like that. The fans wanted someone to knock. It was easy to knock Yoko. Japanese, older, an artist, leading John into ways that were considered freaky. The Beatles had gone full circle and what went down was no-one's fault."[9]

Two days later, on March 28, Paul and Linda flew to Los Angeles. They knew from Yoko where John was staying, and that he would be working on Harry's album at Record Plant West, at 1032 North Sycamore Avenue. It was, in fact, the first day of Harry's sessions; the day's work had been a cover of Dylan's 'Subterranean Homesick Blues.'

By the time Paul and Linda walked in, around midnight, the formal sessions were over and some of the musicians—including Ringo Starr and Jim Keltner, who had shared the drumming on the Dylan cover—had already left the studio. Those who remained were in the control room listening to takes, drinking whisky, and snorting lines of cocaine.

"I was a bit surprised, having heard all the stories of their rocky relationship, how quickly they resumed their warm friendship as if they saw each other the day before,"[10] May observed. "They couldn't be the two men who not only had been trading vicious attacks with each other in public, but also had squadrons of lawyers poised in battle against each other while they carved up their multimillion-dollar empire. They looked like any pair of old friends having a pleasant low-key reunion."[11]

Joining Paul and Linda among the late-night visitors to the studio were Stevie Wonder, who was working in an adjacent room, and producer Ed Freeman, who was working on an album with Don McLean elsewhere in the complex. Soon, the assembled players filed into the studio. Paul sat behind Ringo's abandoned drum kit. Stevie Wonder commandeered an electric piano, and Linda slid behind the organ. John and Jesse Ed Davis strapped on their guitars, Bobby Keys picked up his saxophone, and Ed Freeman grabbed a bass. Nilsson took his position at the microphone, although his voice was shredded after the day's session. May Pang and Mal Evans shook tambourines.

With vocal mics set up for John, Paul and Harry, and Roy Cicala engineering, this first musical encounter between John and Paul since August 1969 looked like it could be one of the greatest jam sessions of all time.

But it was a mess. The first thing you hear on the surviving tape, amid the sounds of guitars being tuned and drum patterns being tried out, is John offering Stevie Wonder a snort of cocaine. He then improvises an idiosyncratic stream-of-consciousness lyric over piano and organ flourishes, a steady, light drumbeat, and, after a while, distant guitar noodling. After a few more aimless minutes, John solicits suggestions about what they ought to play.

"If somebody knows a song that we all know, please take over, I've been screaming here for hours," Lennon begged. "It's got to be something done 'round about the Fifties, or no later than '63, or we aren't going to know it." Wonder obliged with a funky piano rendering of Barbara George's 1961 'I Know (You Don't Love Me No More)', with Paul gamely drumming along and Davis reaching with only intermittent success for a lead guitar line. Picking up on the similarities between the song's chord progression and that of 'Lucille,' Nilsson began a painfully hoarse rendering of the Little Richard tune, with Lennon and McCartney occasionally chiming in. John plays an aggressive chordal lead, of the type he played on 'The End,' on *Abbey Road*, but the only musician fully on his game is Wonder, who overrides the band's lackadaisical backing with a couple of fleet piano solos.

By now, John was dissatisfied with the mix he was getting in his headphones—he was unable to hear his vocals—and while Cicala was sorting that out, Lennon, Davis and McCartney offered a fumbling account of 'Sleep Walk,' the 1958 Santo and Johnny instrumental, punctuated with John's occasional attempts to fit a lyric to it. After taking a moment to tune ("Someone give me an E—or a snort," John says), they head into a song John was planning to include on his oldies album, the Ben E. King classic, 'Stand by Me.'

A couple of attempts falter, and when they finally go for it, John, Paul, Stevie and Harry all take turns at the mic. But the performance peters out, morphing into a medley of Sam Cooke's 'Cupid' and 'Chain Gang,' and Lead Belly's 'Take This Hammer.'

That ends the only available reel from the session, but the ad hoc band continued for a while. May remembered the session including a couple of takes of what she described as a "joyous" account of another Lead Belly classic, 'The Midnight Special'—during which, she said, John asked Linda to turn down the organ volume because she was drowning out Stevie Wonder—although this recording has never seen the light of day.

"We just jammed for about eight hours . . . playing and generally looning about,"[12] Paul told the

Daily Express a few days later, exaggerating wildly, but adding that he did not see much prospect of a Beatles reunion. Looking back on the evening later, Paul's assessment was franker: "It wasn't a very good session, and I don't think we recorded much of interest, but I ended up on drums for some reason."[13]

The next day, Paul and Linda turned up at the Malibu house John was renting for $5,000 (£2,100) a month in the hope that the musicians working on Harry's album would stay under the same roof. It was a house full of history. Built by the cinema mogul Louis B. Mayer and once owned by Peter Lawford, it was reportedly where both President John F. Kennedy and his brother Robert had assignations with Marilyn Monroe, a touch of historical gossip that tickled Lennon.

When Paul and Linda visited, Nilsson, Jesse Ed Davis and Keith Moon were staying there—"Three total nutters," as Paul described them, "three beautiful, total alcohol nutters plus John, forget it!"[14]

When the McCartneys arrived, it seemed like old times, to Paul: John was still asleep, as he had often been when Paul turned up for a songwriting session during the Beatle days. Here, at least, there was a pool, so Paul pulled up a deck chair and chatted with Harry and Keith, while Linda got to know the new woman in John's life.

"I remember Harry Nilsson offering me some angel dust," Paul recollected. "I said, 'What is it?' He said, 'It's elephant tranquilizer.' I said, 'Is it fun?' He thought for about half a minute. 'No,' he said. I said, 'Well, you know what, I won't have any.' He seemed to understand. But that's how it was there. Keith Moon was very sweet; we had a nice chat with Keith. He was very complimentary about *Band on the Run*. . . . He asked, 'Who drummed on that, man?' and it happened to be me."[15]

When John appeared and took a seat beside Paul, May snapped a handful of photographs of them together, John in a white long-sleeve shirt, jeans, and a black cap to shield him from the sun, and Paul sporting his porn mustache and soul patch, in white clamdiggers and a colorful jacket over a white shirt.

"I said to him, 'Ere, come on, come in, come in the back room, I wanna talk to you privately,'" Paul said of the conversation. "I said, 'Look, I feel a bit like a matchmaker here, with this girl of yours. She really still loves you, do you love her?' Because I felt like a judge or somebody in a divorce court. . . . And he said, 'Yeah, I do. But I don't know what to do.' And I said, 'Well, I've talked to her at home, and she does still love you. But you will have to work your little ass off, man. You have to get back to New York, you have to take a separate flat. You have to send her roses every fucking day. You have to work at it like a bitch and you just might get her back.'"[16]

Whatever John told Paul, May remembers him recounting the conversation with a somewhat different perspective.

"John didn't appreciate being told what to do," May said. "He wasn't interested in Yoko's terms and conditions. He simply said, 'I'm with May.'"[17]

Later that afternoon, the two couples, Nilsson and Moon moved to the living room, which was dominated by a piano—catnip to Paul, who could not resist slipping out of his jacket and into Liverpool Family Party Mode. He played through a selection of pre-rock Standards and show tunes, with Nilsson and Moon singing along. May snapped a photo showing Paul at the white piano. It was then that Mary, playing on the floor with Stella, began connecting the dots between her father's group of friends and her own experiences at home.

"Daddy, are you some sort of pop star or something?" she asked to the laughter of a room full of pop royalty.[18]

Strangely, given Linda's lifelong fear of flying, and the fact that they still intended to go to the Academy Awards ceremony on April 2, the McCartneys flew back to New York immediately after the visit. It is possible that Paul visited Yoko at the Dakota to brief her on his meeting with John, or that he had business with the Eastmans. They were photographed at Madison Square Garden on March 30, having taken the girls to see the Ringling Bros. and Barnum & Bailey Circus, the traveling tour de force of acrobats, clowns and performing animals that billed itself as *The Greatest Show on Earth*.

The girls were enthralled. Their mom was appalled.

Paul, Mary and Stella at the Ringling Bros. and Barnum & Bailey Circus, March 30, 1974

"Morgan stallions were lined up, chained," Linda complained. "They received no exercise. They were also given shots to calm them down. The elephants were also chained. . . . They did their act . . . then back to the chains. I found that horrific."[19]

Paul and Linda were back in Los Angeles on April 1, installed at the Beverly Hills Hotel, where one of the first items on his agenda was a poolside meeting with MPL managing director Brian Brolly and a pair of Capitol Records executives. Al Coury had prevailed upon Paul to release another single from *Band on the Run*—this time, the title track, backed with 'Nineteen Hundred and Eighty Five,' due out in exactly a week. Paul made no protest this time.

But he did have an issue with 'Jet.' Because Capitol had not sent Paul a copy of the radio edit, it was not until the previous week's visit to Los Angeles that he heard it while cruising down Sunset Boulevard. He found the slovenly edit so upsetting that he parked his car, found a telephone booth, and phoned Brolly in London. Coury knew how bad the edit was, but from his point of view, it was nothing more than a promotional tool to help sell the album. So when he heard that Paul would be in Los Angeles, he called the major stations and asked them not to play the edit while Paul was in town. When Coury heard from Brolly, he had to think fast.

"[Paul] called up his manager, who called me up," Coury said, "and was just crazy because Paul was crazy. So, I said, 'You tell Paul that record he heard was an edit the radio station did.' Which apparently Paul accepted, and which could very well have been true. I really don't know what edit he heard. And I got off the hook."[20]

Nevertheless, Brolly was summoned to the United States to act as Paul's tough alter ego during his meetings with Capitol, and the matter of Paul's displeasure with the 'Jet' radio edit was undoubtedly on the agenda.

For Paul, the definition of a first-class hotel involved having pianos available for guests—the kind of thing you would see in a Fred Astaire film from the 1940s—and having stayed at the Beverly Hills Hotel before (most notably at the start of his relationship with Linda, in 1968, when Paul was in town to make a presentation about Apple at a Capitol Records sales meeting), he knew that the hotel would provide him with a keyboard.

"There would be a Wurlitzer electric piano," he explained, "a simple Wurly, which is what Ray Charles used for the opening riff of 'What'd I Say.' It's a very distinctive sound and I always had one there."[21]

That sound, and its associations, pushed Paul toward a soulful bash, and it was during this visit that he wrote the chord progression and bluesy melody of 'Call Me Back Again,' a song with a soulful undercurrent that suggests a kinship with the Beatles' track 'Oh! Darling.' He had little in the way of lyrics—just the refrain, a single line that may have been a matter of Paul playing off a mutual promise that he and John made, now that he and Paul had broken through the permafrost, to meet again.

It is possible that they did spend more time together during Paul's Los Angeles visit. *Cash Box* published a pair of contradictory reports in consecutive issues, saying that John and Paul turned up at the Whisky-A-Go-Go, hoping to catch Captain Beefheart's sold-out tour-opener, on April 3. The first suggests that they got in;[22] the second (which incorrectly places the concert at the Troubadour) says they were turned away.[23]

Both John and Paul were known to be fans of Captain Beefheart's idiosyncratic blend of rock, jazz, avant-garde elements and a sepulchral blues growl, and although he had satirized their *Sgt. Pepper* phase in his 1968 song 'Beatles Bones N' Smokin' Stones,' there had been talk of signing him to Zapple Records, the experimental offshoot of Apple, before Allen Klein scuttled the label. The support act at his Whisky-A-Go-Go gig was Liverpool, a Canadian band that played only Beatles covers.

However, beyond the *Cash Box* reports, which were likely planted by Beefheart's publicist—having the famously estranged Lennon and McCartney attend a client's concert together would be a major credibility boost—there were no other reported sightings of the pair out and about.

The Academy Awards, held the night before the supposed Beefheart outing, provided little joy. 'Live and Let Die' was up for Best Song, the only nomination for the film, while 'The Sting' and 'The Exorcist' racked up 10 nominations each, and 'The Sting' won seven, including Best Picture. Absent a band, Paul did not perform his nominated song; instead, Connie Francis, dressed in a silver minidress and a silver feathered headdress, sang the number amid a company of dancers in transparent outfits with silver codpieces.

"The rock fans in the Oscar audience were more than a little disturbed by the tacky presentation of nominated song 'Live and Let Die,'" *Sounds* reported, adding that this "choreographer's nightmare" made Francis look "like a sack of potatoes being thrown around the stage in an alleged dance tribute to the McCartneys' song."[24]

In the end, 'Live and Let Die' lost to 'The Way We Were,' by Marvin Hamlisch and Alan and Marilyn Bergman. Still, Paul and Linda were on hand for an historic moment. During the ceremony, a streaker ran naked across the stage flashing a peace sign, prompting David Niven's off-the-cuff comment, "Isn't it fascinating to think that probably the only laugh that man will ever get in his life is by stripping off and showing his shortcomings?"[25]

"We didn't really expect to win," Paul told the *Los Angeles Times* a few days later. "A few people told us it was stupid to go to the Oscars. They said, 'Why go? This man's gonna say you lost and you're gonna have to sit there and . . .' But that's not the point to me. It's not just this thing of winning, winning, winning. There's also the matter of patience and long term and all that. I'm not too heavily into 'I've got to win everything.' I know I can't win everything, but I can win a lot. By attending the Oscars, we were just saying hello, glad to be here, we respect what you're doing."[26]

Paul and Linda paid another visit to John and May at their Malibu rental on April 6. The million-

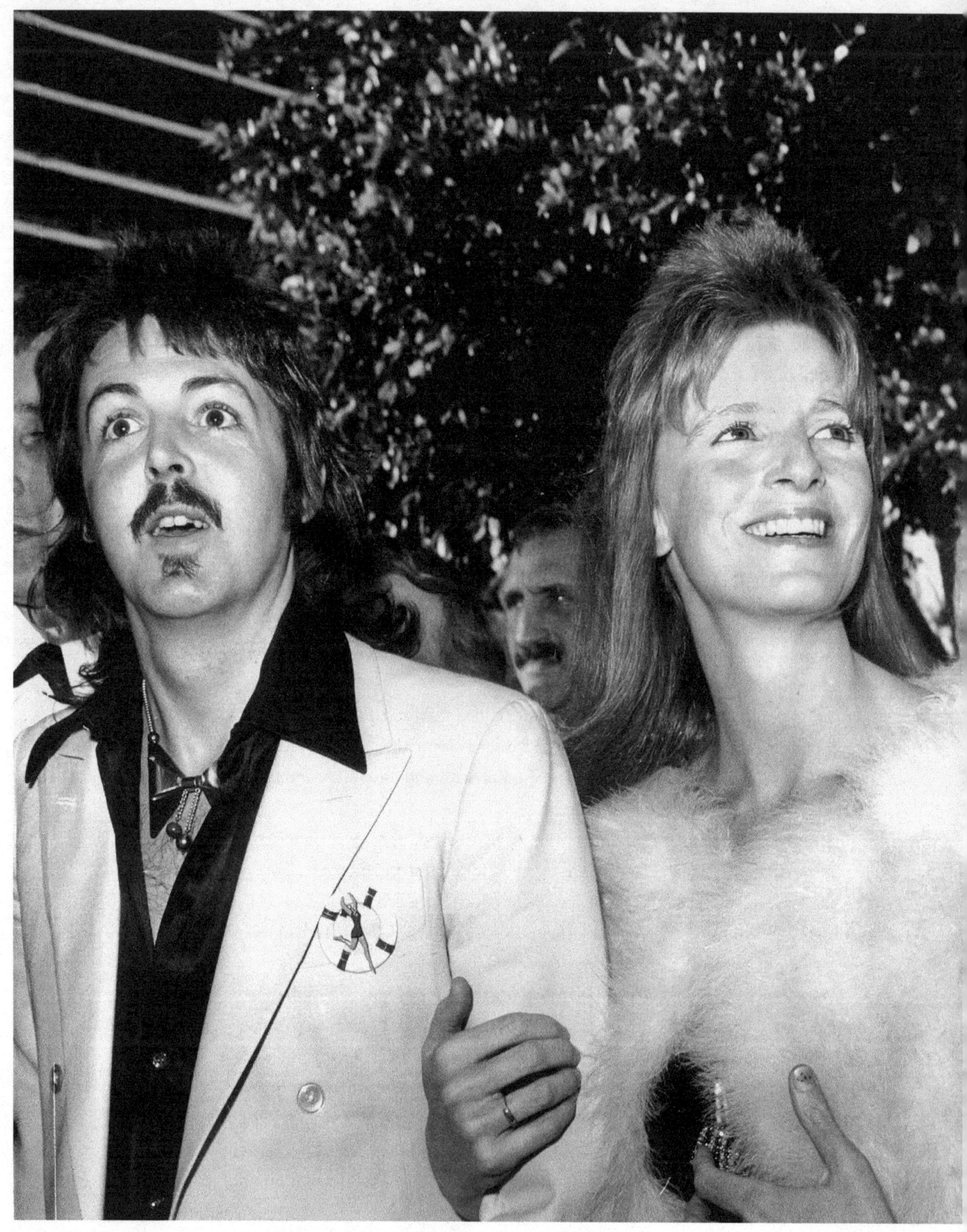

Paul and Linda McCartney at the Academy Awards, April 2, 1974

dollar demand that scuttled the last negotiation meeting among the former Beatles' lawyers still rankled, and although the time never seemed right to discuss it during their last meeting, Paul was intent on doing so now. This time he also sent word to Ringo that he and John would be meeting, and he tried to arrange for George to come as well, only to learn that visa problems were keeping George out of the United States.

When Ringo turned up, Paul sounded them both out on the Apple negotiations. Among the matters still unresolved were the individual Beatles' homes, John's now bicoastal living expenses, and Paul's desire to be indemnified against lawsuits by Klein.

Paul, John and Ringo discussed these concerns and fundamentally agreed in principle about what needed to be done to sort it all out.

"[We met] to settle all the money thing," John told *Melody Maker*. "We all agreed how to do it, now it's up to the lawyers to sort it out and tell us whether what we agreed is practical. That's all. We just want to make sure we all get paid. What a fucking mess."[27]

Also visiting John and May that day were Mal Evans, with his girlfriend Fran Hughes and her daughter Jody. Mal was there on a mission: still on the Apple payroll, he now resolved to leave the Beatles' employment and pursue a songwriting career. The first step was to inform the former Beatles, whom he hoped to approach separately, starting that day with John. Finding Ringo and Paul there as well was an unexpected bonus. He first spoke with John, who offered his enthusiastic blessings, then Ringo, whose response—silence—puzzled Mal, and finally Paul, who embraced the former roadie and said, "Good on you, lad. I know you'll be successful—you deserve to be."[28]

Given his long history with Mal, Paul's wishes were undoubtedly sincere. But for him, Mal's decision to leave Apple and forge a life of his own also had a symbolic importance: it was another element of the Beatles support structure falling away.

To mark the release of the 'Band on the Run' single, on April 8, Paul devoted the afternoon to interviews, holding court beside the pool at the Beverly Hills Hotel. The longest and most detailed of these was with Robert Hilburn, the chief pop critic for the *Los Angeles Times.* Hilburn had reviewed every one of Paul's albums, in most cases expressing disappointment that an artist of McCartney's caliber was not doing better work. As antagonists go, he was one who could perhaps be won over, if only he could be brought to see Paul's work as Paul saw it. When Hilburn asked how he regarded his post-Beatles albums, Paul was ready with an analysis that pitted the critical response against the fan reaction, and cast his approach to each LP as an attempt to address issues critics raised with its predecessor.

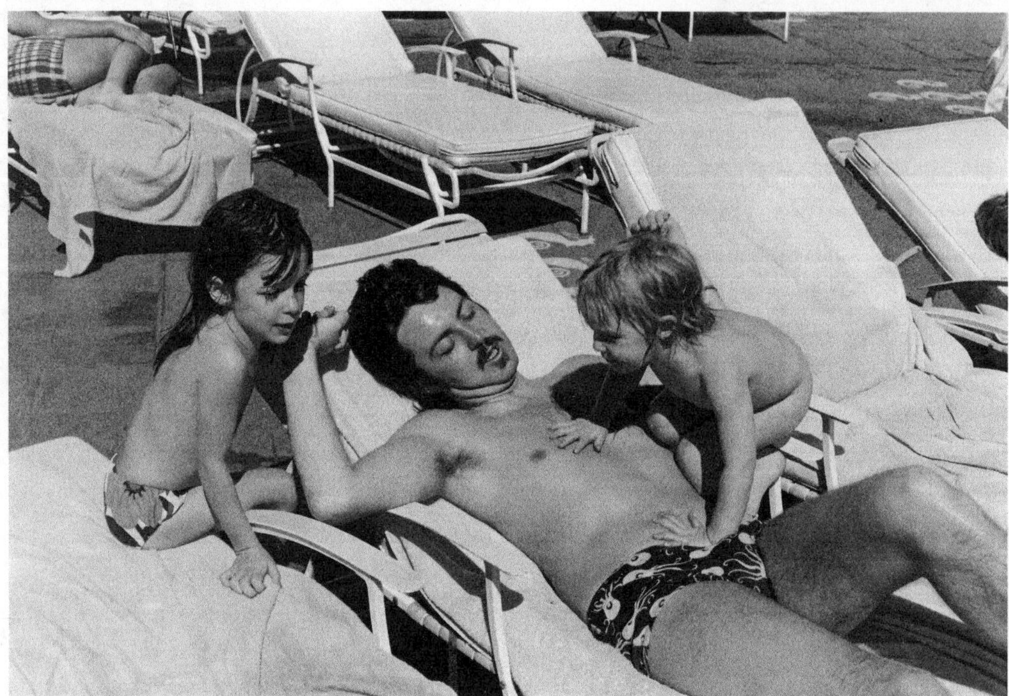

Paul, Mary and Stella McCartney, poolside at the Beverly Hills Hotel, April 1974

"I thought *McCartney* was quite good," he began. "Some people still think it was my best album. But then it didn't quite do it in every way. It did it sales-wise, but it didn't do it critically. It was very down home, funky, just me recording on my own, playing all the instruments. After it got knocked, I thought—it was very obvious in a way—I'll do just the opposite next time. So, *Ram* was with the top people in the top studio. I thought, 'This is what they want.' But, again, it was critically panned, though it did very well with the public.

"Then I thought, 'Oh, so they don't want the big production job.' So, I recorded *Wild Life* in two weeks. The whole thing was done around three days rehearsal. There's one track—'Mumbo'—where I just said to everybody, 'This one's in F, it goes like this.' I guess I was being inspired by Dylan, the way he just kind of comes in the studio and everyone falls in and makes the track. But that was kind of critically panned . . . so we thought we'd get it together a bit. We went in with the band for *Red Rose Speedway.* That was the first Wings thing really."

When Hilburn noted that *Band on the Run* had reached No. 1 on the American charts (specifically, in the April 13 edition of *Billboard,* which was already on the stands), and asked Paul why that album won a more positive critical response than its predecessors, Paul turned coy.

"Maybe it's just a good album," he said. "I'd say so. What happens to me is that I keep hearing it on the radio and, before it has registered that it's me, I think, 'That's good,' and I'm over at the radio trying to pinch a lick or something. In that respect I think the tracks come over great. But I feel the next one will be better."

Paul also discussed his hopes for Wings. He worked Jimmy McCulloch into the discussion as a full-fledged member, although his joining had not yet been formally announced. And he dangled the prospect of a tour, perhaps at the end of 1974. Tour plans were already being mooted in the British press; *Sounds* guessed that this was why Brian Brolly was in Los Angeles. And, of course, there was the perennial Beatles question.

"What might be possible," he told Hilburn, as if thinking aloud, "I mean, the easiest thing I could see is to record some tracks together and that would be a Beatles album. That I see as a possibility if we all fancied it, but please remember, this is purely guesswork."[29]

Four years after the split, Paul appeared to be gradually reclaiming his part of the Beatles' legacy. He had moved from refusing to perform Beatles' songs with Wings, to working up a Wings version of 'The Long and Winding Road' that was performed live three times in 1973,* and from dismissing talk of a Beatles reunion, sometimes angrily, to waffling about the possibilities, once Lennon, Harrison and Starr jettisoned Klein. Now he was hinting that he was open to the idea of the Beatles recording together again.

A few days later, Paul touched on a darker bit of Beatles-related trivia in a readers' questions column in *NME*. Responding to a question about the Höfner 500/1 violin-shaped bass guitar that had become his visual trademark during Beatlemania, Paul responded, "I've had three violin basses. One was stolen, and I was very upset indeed. I had a sentimental attachment to it. But I've still got the other two."[30]

The stolen bass was actually his first Höfner, the one he bought in Hamburg in 1961, a few months after taking over from Stuart Sutcliffe as the Beatles' bassist. It had been swiped from the Wings equipment van at Cambridge Gardens on October 10, 1972, while the band were nearby, recording 'Power Cut' at Island Studios. Ian Horne immediately reported the theft, and an appeal for its return went out on the LTW program *Police* 5, but Paul rarely acknowledged the incident.†

Paul and Linda were the guests of honor at a luncheon at the Capitol Tower on April 9. A group of Capitol executives—COO Brown Meggs, VP for Marketing Don Zimmermann and promotion guru Al Coury—presented the McCartneys with a platinum disc, signifying sales of one million copies of *Band on the Run*, and quizzed Paul about his plans for the immediate future.

That was complicated. Once Wings found a drummer, it would take time until the band sounded

---

* All three performances took place on March 18, 1973. The first two were taped before a live audience for the *James Paul McCartney* television special, but were not used in the broadcast. Later that evening, Wings repeated their set at the Hard Rock Cafe in London, in a benefit show for Release, an organization that provided legal advice and support to those charged with drug possession.

† The Höfner bass was found and returned to McCartney in early 2024, after a campaign seeking information about the instrument was launched in 2023.

as tight as it did in the summer of 1973, so there were no immediate tour plans. And Paul was only just starting to write material for a new album.

What Paul offered Capitol was a compilation that would bring together non-LP singles, perhaps odd tracks like 'Zoo Gang,' the instrumental theme for the British television series that just had its premiere (on April 5), plus outtakes from the *Ram* and *Red Rose Speedway* sessions.

There could be live recordings, as well; in fact, just the previous week, Ian Horne—one of Wings' roadies, who was also trained as a sound engineer—spent three days (April 2, 3 and 4) at EMI Studios remixing Wings' July 10, 1973, performance in Newcastle, with an eye toward including some live tracks in the collection.

Paul added what he considered a sweetener to his proposal. Since the session costs for the outtakes were already covered in the budgets for the original albums, why not release the set as a budget-priced disc?

The Capitol executives found Paul's idea perplexing.

"The project originally started out as *Hot Hitz and Kold Kutz*, with two k's and two z's," Paul explained, "but then someone at the record company said, 'Why have cold cuts on a hot hits album?' As a result of which it became simply *Cold Cuts*."[31] Paul's pricing idea did not go over well, either. "When I said I'd like to do a budget album, they said, 'You're so hot, what for?' I said, 'For the people.' 'Nah, man, fuck the people, they can afford it!' Those aren't *my* advisors, by the way. Mine are nicer."[32]

Still, noting Paul's enthusiasm for the project, Capitol assigned *Cold Cuts* a catalog number (3419),[33] and penciled it into the label's release schedule for November 1974, with the pricing to be determined.

By the weekend of April 12, the McCartneys were back in New York, spending Easter weekend with the Eastmans, who had made short work of selling Mike McGear's album to Warner Bros. Records. Actually, both Brian Brolly representing MPL in London, and the Eastmans, on hand to handle the contractual details in New York, began working on Warner in earnest as soon as the stereo master tapes were delivered to Ron Kass at Warner's London offices on March 8. Both were in a position to dangle the prospect of Paul signing with Warner when his EMI contract lapsed.

The day the tapes were delivered, Brolly wrote to Ostin, hedging his bets in case Ostin was not impressed, by noting that Paul might opt to make further changes. But he added, "Paul is very pleased, and we hope you will like it."[34]

Ostin decided quickly—possibly before even hearing the album—that being in the sweepstakes for Paul's next contract was worth taking a gamble on his younger brother's album. And there was a bonus of sorts: along with Mike's solo album, Warner would get the next Scaffold single, 'Liverpool Lou' backed with '10 Years After on Strawberry Jam,' both produced by Paul. Though by no means huge in America, the Scaffold were known to Beatles fans and British import fanciers, and that was enough to shift copies. A May 3 release date was scheduled.

In truth, there was no great enthusiasm for *McGear* at Warner. Mike sent a partly earnest, partly whimsical note to Mo Ostin on April 3, written with the clear presumption that the album had been accepted for release. But an internal memo from Bob Regehr, the label's senior vice president in charge of artists and repertoire, parodies and comments on Mike's handwritten missive.

Where Mike opened his letter with the hope that Ostin had "heard the album and agree with me that its [*sic*] by far the best of the year (and in fact any other year),"[35] Regehr drew a box containing the word JET, and quipped that "maybe he listened to Paul's album instead of his own." And responding to Mike's request that he be allowed a choice of the current Warner Bros. logo, or the version that appeared in classic films, Regehr suggested that another label's logo would be even better: "Hope he is not disappointed about the logo—how about EPIC,"[36] he wrote, referring to the subsidiary of Warner's East Coast rivals, Columbia Records.

Nevertheless, the Eastmans were able to confirm, during Paul's visit, that Warner would release the album in the fall. Ostin would have liked to convey that message to Paul in person while the McCartneys were in Los Angeles—as well as some concerns about what would be required to make the album a hit—but they did not connect. Instead Ostin sent a memo to Paul by way of Brolly, who telexed it to Paul in New York:

> *Since we never had an opportunity to talk to Paul directly relating to the Mike McGear album, I thought I might capsulize our thoughts in this memo for you to pass on to Paul.*
>
> *The album is a fine Paul McCartney album with one missing element . . . Paul. Mike has a pleasant voice but it has none of the power or personality of Paul. The songs range from very good, to good, to so-so (with most of the so-so's on the second side of the album). The production is consistently great.*
>
> *I think it will need a lot of help to sell in big numbers. This help can come from a hit single or from a well-planned tour (presuming he has stage presence). I don't think it will sell simply from the magic of Paul McCartney's touch or through the relationship. Nor is the album powerful enough to launch itself without aid.*
>
> *It might be worth trying a single before the album is released. If that is agreeable then I would submit that the track originally sent to us ['Leave It'] might be the strongest on the LP.*[37]

Paul could deal with the Ostin memo when he returned to London—or not. Having produced, played on, and paid for the recording, and having given it the power of his name, he regarded his role complete. Now it was time to move on to the next chapter of Wings.

But he could not resist an opportunity to spread some stardust when one presented itself. While they were in New York, Paul and Linda dropped in on James Taylor's sessions for his *Walking*

Man album at the Hit Factory, and enjoyed a brief reunion with Taylor and his wife, Carly Simon. The McCartneys sang backing vocals on two Taylor tracks, 'Let It All Fall Down' and 'Rock 'n' Roll Is Music Now,' with Simon joining them on the latter, before heading back to the Stanhope and out to dinner.

The press still routinely kept track of McCartney's travels, and a couple of stringers were on hand when the family arrived at Heathrow Airport on April 16, after three weeks in the United States. With time to fire only a couple of questions, Deborah Thomas, from the *Daily Mirror*, asked what his next project would be, and Paul mentioned the first thing on his mind, which was finding a new drummer. As a follow-up, Thomas wondered whether there was any chance Ringo Starr might join him.

"Ringo's a fine drummer," Paul responded, "but he's too busy." Paul had mentioned his need to find new Wings players in several interviews in the four and a half months since *Band on the Run* was released, but announcing that he was getting down to business had a stunning effect. The BBC had picked up on the *Daily Mirror* report, and within hours, MPL fielded more than 400 calls from drummers hoping to fill the position. Callers were told to apply by mail.

"We were getting letters from all over Britain," said Paul, "not just a few people applying for the job, but hundreds. And we felt that, to be fair to ourselves and to the applicants, we ought to see as many people as we possibly could."[38]

Paul rented the Albery Theatre* on St. Martin's Lane, a ten-minute walk from MPL's offices in Soho Square, and scheduled auditions on April 29 and 30. Paul enlisted Brian Brolly, Alan Crowder (Wings' manager) and David Minns, his personal assistant, along with Linda, Denny Laine and Jimmy McCulloch, to help him pick through the stacks of resumes, photos and letters, and identify players who seemed worth hearing.

All told, 52 drummers were invited to audition. Among them were Mitch Mitchell, the drummer for the Jimi Hendrix Experience; John "Twink" Adler, formerly of the In-Crowd, the Pretty Things and Pink Fairies, who had released an album of his own, *Think Pink*; Jim Russell, who had played with Curved Air and was currently in Stretch; Gilson Lavis, who had toured Britain backing Jerry Lee Lewis and Chuck Berry†; Damon Metrebian, a self-taught musician and entrepreneur‡;

* Known as the Noël Coward Theatre since 2006, this theater in London's West End opened in 1903 as the New Theatre. It was renamed the Albery Theatre in 1973.

† David Leslie Gilson Lavis went on to become the drummer for Squeeze, through 1992, and the Jools Holland's Rhythm and Blues Orchestra, from 1987 to the present.

‡ In 1978, Metrebian founded Super Bear Studios near Nice, France.

and Jack McCulloch, Jimmy's brother, who played with several bands, including Andwella and Andromeda.

"We look for someone who can play all styles, because the music is so varied," Paul explained. "The important thing is understanding, willingness, a personality that fits in. It was quite an experience.[39] I remember actually, Chris Jagger [Mick's brother] turned up on the day, not to audition as a drummer, but just 'cause I knew him as a mate. . . . And he was thinking of forming a band, so he sat up in the balcony while we listened to the drummers down in the stalls. I think he was looking for any leftovers! With 50 [*sic*] there, he must have had a bit of choice."[40]

For the first phase of the auditions, Paul hired a group of session players—a keyboardist, a guitarist and a bassist—and watched from the theater with the other members of Wings. Each drummer was asked to play five songs, including Duke Ellington's 'Caravan,' Booker T. and the M.G.s' instrumental, 'Green Onions,' Leiber and Stoller's 'Kansas City' and a couple of 1950's rock classics.

"I arrived at the stage door at 2:15 P.M., when I noticed Linda, Paul's wife, in a shop next door," recalled Steven Phillips, a 23-year-old Londoner who tried out for the position on April 29. "I waited 'til she came out of the shop and asked for an autograph, telling her I had come for an audition. We talked for a minute or so, then walked through the stage door and down some steps to the side of the stage."

Phillips had his turn at 3:30 P.M. "I sat down behind the kit making sure that all the drums were in the correct position," he remembered. "All the stage lights shone down on the drums so I could not see anyone out in the seats, however hard I tried. The keyboard player explained that we were first going to play 'Caravan' and after sixteen bars change to quickstep rhythm and after so many bars there would be stop breaks for the drums. I nodded in agreement as he counted us in.

"I played okay throughout, but would have been better if it hadn't been for nerves. Soon after the four numbers were finished and as I stood, I received a warm handclap and then I heard Paul's voice, 'That was great, Steve, really good. We'll be in touch next week.'"[41]

Phillips was not among the five drummers Paul invited to return for a second round. They were Geoff Britton, the drummer for the Wild Angels, a 1950's rock revival band; Rob Townsend, whose band Family had broken up in 1973, whereupon he joined Machine Head; Micky Waller, a member of the original Jeff Beck Group who followed that band's lead singer, Rod Stewart, into his solo career; Roger Pope, who drummed for Elton John; and David "Pick" Withers,* the drummer for the Primitives and Spring. Aynsley Dunbar, Frank Zappa's former stickman, was also recalled but had to pass due to a scheduling conflict.

---

* Two years later, David "Pick" Withers joined Mark Knopfler to form Dire Straits, and played on that band's first four albums, leaving in 1982.

Britton was stunned when he got the call. Once he saw Mitch Mitchell among the assembled players, he thought his prospects were nil. A Hendrix fan, Britton had seen Mitchell perform with the Experience at the Bag O' Nails, on November 25, 1966—a performance McCartney attended as well. He was nearly as intimidated once he heard who the other four contenders were.

"It terrified me," Britton remembered. "They were all guys who were in good bands that I used to go and see, so I thought, 'Game over.'"[42]

But it wasn't. The second auditions were held over two days, May 8 and 9, at the Carousel Ballroom* in Camden Town. This time the drummers played with Paul, Linda, Denny and Jimmy. "We were just like any band setting up in a garage," said Britton, who was heard on the first day. "I could probably have touched Paul with my drumstick. And that in itself was just the greatest thrill, because I'd seen the Beatles live."

McCartney asked Geoff whether he liked rock and roll—an odd question to ask a drummer who was not only auditioning for Wings, but whose current band, as Paul would have known, was a rock revival group. Britton must have suspected that he was being tested, and he answered accordingly.

"Paul," he said, "we're the same age, we grew up on rock and roll—you saw Buddy Holly the same time I saw Buddy Holly, back in the Fifties. Of course I do!"

As they got ready to play, Paul's probing continued.

"Do you know 'Lucille,'" he asked Geoff.

"Yes," Britton replied, "but there are two versions. There's the Everly Brothers, and Little Richard, and the drumming is different on both of them."

"Oh, you *know*," Paul said.

"*Of course* I know, Paul,"[43] the increasingly confident drummer replied. McCartney opted to play the Everly Brothers version, in which the drum pattern includes triplets on the cymbal.

Passing the 'Lucille' test helped Britton advance to the final round. So did a part of the audition in which Paul brought out a new mid-tempo rocker he was working on, as a way of testing how the drummers would respond to material for which there were no recordings they could use as reference points. The song was unfinished, with vague and slightly peculiar lyrics referring to a "poker man," an Eskimo, and a sea lion, but the music included several changeups and section breaks that would show how quickly each drummer reacted. Linda sat out those performances, instead recording them on a portable tape deck for Paul to review later.

The final round was just Britton and Rob Townsend. Each spent a full day with Wings, playing morning and afternoon sessions, with lunch in between. Britton's audition was on May 13, again at the Carousel. When the band went to lunch at an upscale restaurant barge in Camden Lock, Brian Brolly joined them, and spent part of the lunch quizzing Britton.

* In 1978, the Carousel Ballroom was renamed as the Electric Ballroom.

"He was trying to dig deeper," Geoff recalled. "Did I drink? Did I do drugs? [It had] the sort of undertones of an MI5 questioning."[44]

On the morning of May 16, Britton was out jogging in a field near his home in Kent, when his wife called out the window, "It's Paul McCartney on the phone." Paul did not come immediately to the point—he toyed with Britton a bit, saying that they had come to a decision, but waiting for Geoff to ask who they decided on before telling him, "You got the job."

Although he thought the auditions went well, he was surprised, and he said so. It turned out that the second audition—and particularly his work on the unfinished (and as yet untitled) new song—had largely clinched it.

"You were the only drummer who pulled the volume back when I went up to the mic to sing,"[45] McCartney explained. He added that when they listened to the recordings of the new song, the other four drummers played in a style that was virtually identical, but Britton took a different approach, which McCartney considered fresher and more original.

"We really liked the raw material that Geoff represented," Paul told an interviewer. "He's a great bloke who gets along with the others really well. He's a good personality to have in a band."[46] About Britton's drumming, he told *Melody Maker*: "It's very straightforward. I didn't want a drummer who plays a lot of fills. For the lack of a better word, I like 'spade' drumming. A real simple beat and they hold it like a metronome and occasionally put in some funky things. . . . That's the style I like. If you listen to a Black American record you won't find any drum breaks. . . . They just do it. Like Stevie Wonder's records. All the rhythm is in his voice and all the other instruments."[47]

Now the lineup of Wings Mark II was complete. And Paul had a plan: in June, they would fly to Nashville for a leisurely breaking-in period. They would work up some new material, rehearse the old Wings tracks that were likely to remain in the band's concert set, and not incidentally, soak up the sounds and atmosphere in the home of country music.

Britton had learned about the audition by way of his other passion, karate. Born in Lewisham, in southeast London, on August 1, 1943, Britton was drawn to drumming as a child, when he fashioned makeshift kits out of biscuit tins and begged his parents for a trap set. That was a request his parents were reluctant to meet: not musical themselves, they hoped to steer Geoff in a different direction, believing that his early interests in jazz and country music would lead him into a life of drugs and dissolution. Eventually winning that dispute and gravitating toward jazz, he took lessons briefly with Billy Jo Joes, a drummer from the be-bop era who had played with Miles Davis.

Britton's first band was a country outfit, the King Pins, which mostly performed in pubs around London. In June 1969, he joined East of Eden, a progressive band with jazz leanings that toured through Britain and Europe, sometimes sharing the bill with Yes and Free. Britton left East of Eden in February 1970, to join Gun, and a year later, he was offered jobs in both Uriah Heep and the Wild Angels. He chose the latter, he said, "because the music was fun, the guys were fun, and I liked the leather jacket idea."[48] The band took the cinematic 1950's rocker ethos beyond leather: they all rode motorcycles as well; in fact, Britton turned up for his Wings audition on his motorbike, in his leathers.

During his time with East of Eden, Britton got interested in karate. After a group of local toughs set upon the band during a tour of Germany, Britton decided it was time to learn self-defense. He trained seriously, becoming a black belt and competing in championship matches. He also taught, and when a friend with a martial arts school in West Wycombe decided to spend four years in Okinawa, Britton agreed to take over. One of his students was Clifford Davis, the manager of Fleetwood Mac and Curved Air. Davis had noticed an article in *Melody Maker* about McCartney's forthcoming auditions and mentioned it to Britton.

When Britton called MPL, he spoke with Alan Crowder, who told him that he was too late, the audition list had been finalized. But they continued chatting, and after a few minutes, Crowder said, "Do you know what—I'm going to put you on the list. Be at the Albery Theatre in St. Martin's Lane at 2 P.M. on April 29."

Having won the job with Wings, Geoff obtained a release from Decca, which had the Wild Angels under contract, but agreed to honor his commitments to the band through the end of May. There was also a spot of mischief to be sorted. During a tour of Scotland, the Wild Angels were booked into a hotel that they found so substandard that they left without paying. A few days later, the group's manager told the group that the hotelier had called the police and they were being prosecuted. They had a court appearance in Glasgow on May 29—something Britton kept to himself for fear of losing his spot in Wings—but much to Geoff's relief, the night manager's memory of the band was so vague that the judge ruled that the hotel had not proven its case and let the band off.

On May 24, Britton and the rest of Wings gathered at MPL for the first publicity photos of Wings Mark II. Afterward, he lingered to spend some quality time with Tony Brainsby, who needed to get to know Britton and McCulloch well enough to write their press bios.

Drummer auditions were hardly the only entries in the McCartneys' datebook for this period. On May 1, they attended the premiere of *Billy*, a musical by James Bond composer John Barry, with lyrics by Don Black and a book by Dick Clement and Ian La Frenais. Barry's music would have been the main draw for the McCartneys, although the subject—a Yorkshire lad's fantasies of moving to London at the dawn of the Swinging Sixties—would undoubtedly have struck a familiar chord.

The next afternoon, Paul, Linda and Denny attended a party to celebrate the release of the Scaffold's 'Liverpool Lou' single. The disc would reach No. 7 on the UK charts by the end of June and sell just over 133,400 copies. That was enough to persuade Warner to turn its vague acceptance of Mike's solo album into a more expansive contract. Negotiated by John Eastman, McGear was given a one-year deal, backdated to January 1974, with three one-year options, during which Mike was expected to make an album each year.[49]

The Scaffold party was held at The Den, the party space at the offices of Warner Bros. Records at 54 Greek Street, just across the road from the temporary headquarters MPL moved into that same week.

When MPL moved into the eighteenth-century townhouse in Soho Square in 1971, it had taken a pair of modest fourth-floor offices. Now Paul was in the process of purchasing the whole building,* and he was planning a top-to-bottom renovation. That meant that the businesses currently occupying the building, including MPL, had to clear out so that its interior could be gutted. Greek Street, a hub for film, television and music companies, runs off Soho Square, so the move kept them nearby—and they found temporary quarters with an artsy pedigree: 12–13 Greek Street had been the London showroom of the English potter Josiah Wedgewood from 1774 to 1795.

As if to compete with Mike for Paul's attention, EMI held a dinner for Wings at Julie's Restaurant, in Holland Park, on May 3, during which Paul, Linda and Denny were handed 14 gold, platinum and silver records for sales of *Band on the Run* and *Red Rose Speedway* in Britain, the United States and Australia. For the occasion, Paul shaved off the mustache and soul patch he had been sporting the last couple of months.

Paul also made a guest appearance between the drummer audition sessions. Visiting Faces guitarist Ronnie Wood at The Wick, Wood's home studio in Richmond, Paul played piano on a cover of the 1956 Jimmy Reed song 'Ain't That Loving You Baby,' and provided unspecified production assistance on 'Take a Look at the Guy,' a track Wood recorded with Keith Richards and Mick Taylor on guitars, Willie Weeks on bass, Andy Newmark on drums, and Rod Stewart singing backing vocals.†

There was a partly social, partly working dinner with Peggy Lee in early May. Paul was a longtime fan of Lee, whose 1960 recording of 'Till There Was You'—the lilting serenade from *The Music Man*, which Paul discovered in his cousin Bett Robbins's record collection[50]—was the model for the version he sang with the Beatles. Paul and Linda had seen Lee sing 'The Way We Were' at the Oscars during their Los Angeles visit, and when Lee was in London, she invited Paul to have dinner with her at the Dorchester Hotel.

---

* According to Land Registry documents, Paul became the owner of the entire building at 1 Soho Square on August 9, 1974.

† 'Take a Look at the Guy' appeared on Wood's debut solo disc, *I've Got My Own Album to Do*, in September 1974. The Jimmy Reed cover has not been released.

The way Paul told it, "I thought, 'I'm going to dinner—well, I'm either gonna take her champagne or a song.' So I took a song, and Peggy said, 'Great, let's do it.'"[51]

The song was 'Let's Love,' published as a collaboration by Paul and Linda. But charming as Paul's story is, the collaboration with Lee was in the works long before their dinner at the Dorchester. Lee had just signed with Atlantic Records, after nearly three decades (and 39 albums) with Capitol. When *Cash Box* reported on her new contract, in its May 4 issue, the details of Paul's involvement with her first Atlantic LP were already set. The album, *Cash Box* noted, would be co-produced by Dave Grusin and Lee, and 'Let's Love' would be its title track, to be produced by Paul.

"I am so thrilled about the whole thing," Lee enthused about her new project a few months later. "The material is strong, and I love the one Paul wrote. And to think that he would go to all that trouble. He said that it was his way of returning an inspiration . . . You know, I met him, and Linda in London and it was instant friendship. And somehow I feel that with all the great things Paul has done, his talent is just growing and growing . . . There's no generation gap at all. It's sort of a family feeling."[52]

Paul's "champagne or song" story also obscures who brought what to dinner. Lee had recorded a version of 'Let's Love' on April 23 in Los Angeles,[53] with Grusin playing piano, Chuck Rainey on bass, most likely David T. Walker on acoustic guitar, and unspecified players on electric guitar, drums, and celeste, and she brought Paul a rough mix. When the album was announced, Paul had not been certain that he would fly to Los Angeles to produce Lee's recording, but by the time the Dorchester dinner was concluded, Paul and Linda decided to add a detour to their Nashville itinerary, stopping in Los Angeles to work with Lee before meeting up with the rest of Wings in Music City.

Recording Session

Saturday, May 18, 1974.
EMI Studios, Abbey Road, London.
Recording: 'Let's Love.'

Paul was not knocked out by Lee's April 23 recording. The song was a classic McCartney love ballad with an interesting tension between the lyrics, which anticipate a night of romance ("*tonight is the flight of the butterfly*"), and the music, which is in a minor key and at a moderate tempo, giving it a wistful aura. The tempo Grusin took, however, was far too slow and crossed the line between wistful and mournful. Lovely as the light backing texture was, the track was almost a dirge.

Paul decided to remedy that by creating a backing track to which Lee would add her vocals, under Paul's direction, in Los Angeles. With Alan Parsons at the desk, Paul sat at the piano and recorded a part that was quite different from Grusin's. Where Grusin began with a fairly straightforward instrumental account of the verse, McCartney took a more nuanced, almost teasing tack, opting not to preview the melody, but to instead build a unique introduction around the song's chords.

He begins with a repeated, two-note falling figure, a D-sharp and a B—a major third, forestalling the song's minor key feeling until what sounds almost like a stray note is added. That note, a G-sharp, establishes the song's key, G-sharp minor. Two more falling figures follow, both minor thirds, before Paul reaches a stopping point—a G-sharp minor chord from which a bass line emerges, leading into the verse.

Paul added a second piano part to emphasize accented notes, as well as the bass line and, starting at the second verse, drums. Strings and winds join in the second verse as well, sometimes providing relatively unadorned support for the vocal line, sometimes providing such touches as flute flourishes between lines. Paul has never disclosed who did the arrangement or conducted the ensemble, but by the end of the session, he had a complete backing track, awaiting only Peggy Lee's vocal.

Linda pursued projects of her own during this period. One was piano study. She had taken to heart the criticism of her keyboard abilities, not only in the press, but from Wings' former lead guitarist, Henry McCullough, and when Paul engaged Tony Visconti to write the orchestral arrangements for *Band on the Run*, Linda asked if he knew anyone who could help her improve her technique. Visconti made a couple of recommendations; the problem was that Linda was rarely in London long enough to take them up. Now she had some time, so in the period between her return from America, in mid-April, and her next trip with Paul, to Nashville by way of Los Angeles, she took a few lessons, with improving her velocity and accuracy as her goal.

She also began work in earnest on a book of her photographs. Danny Fields, a friend from her days as a freelance rock photographer in New York, had suggested such a project when Linda reconnected with him in January 1971. It was an idea Paul fully supported: he wanted Linda to be taken seriously as an artist in her own right, not just as Wings' keyboardist-by-marriage. Fields had visited London to help Linda sort through her collection, but with Wings touring and recording, she had little time to look at old photographs. And even at the best of times, she blew hot and cold on the project.

"As you know, I've been taking a lot of photographs for years," she told *Hit Parader*. "I never had an agent—or really ever did anything with them. Then after I came to England, we were in Greece, and someone got into the house and took a lot of my stuff. . . . Anyway, even when we got married, I was taking a lot of pictures and not doing anything with them. I would just give them to people sometimes. I never really had a studio or wanted to be the next Richard Avedon.

"Then one day my friend Barney Wan, who used to be [the art director] at London *Vogue*, said that he was going to set them all up in a room with a projector, and then Danny Fields came over and we went through 10,000 of them. We cut them down to 5,000—I got sick of it, and then Barney took them and narrowed them down to 300 and that's the state of it now.

"You know," she added, "I only have about 8 pictures of the Beatles in there, and I have about 1,000. But also—like with Jimi Hendrix, he used to come around and go through my pictures and any that he liked he would put in his little brief case, so most of my color stuff of him is gone. Plus, I always felt a bit funny. . . . First of all, these people were friends and second of all a lot of them are dead now. And I thought well hell, I'm not going to cash in on that. That was one of the reasons I never wanted to do a book."[54]

If the book was meant to shine a spotlight on Linda's artistry in the field she had chosen, as opposed to her position as a draftee into Wings, there was also an effort to polish and project her image—to let the public see more of her warmth and humor. Doing so, Paul hoped, might undercut the criticism of her performances and perhaps blunt the continuing aggression of overly possessive McCartney fans.

It was clear, by now, that Linda was an excellent interviewee—frank, knowledgeable, often strikingly honest about both the joys and difficulties of living with someone as famous and accomplished as Paul. And though she could be guarded, if an interviewer caught her in the right mood, she could be surprisingly revealing. So a handful of interviews were set up for Linda on her own, in which she broadened the picture of life with the McCartneys.

"I've given him a home," she told *Woman's Own* of her principal contribution to Paul's life. "A lot of kids think I was lucky to marry Paul, but they don't realize the responsibility in marriage. Paul is a northern lad and family life's very important to northerners.

"I was a career woman before I met Paul, but I always had a base at home. I believe in equal pay and all that, but I wouldn't want my husband to do the ironing. You're right, though, it does get very busy. Let's face it, with Paul's money I needn't touch a pot, but I couldn't bear to have live-in staff. It's so impersonal. So I have the same problems everyone has. I'm trying to make order in my life, get my photography sorted out. There's my piano lessons for the band, the kids, planning holidays, packing suitcases . . . But I don't let worrying about things hold me up."

About her own image, she was alternately humble and militant, but seemed honestly puzzled why it should matter to anyone.

"I'm so surprised when people get me wrong. The things people say, 'The most hated but most envied girl in the world.' Rubbish. I'm not hated. Ordinary people don't hate me. People have put me in a category since I married Paul. They expect something more from me and then they find I'm an ordinary person. Why can't they just let me be Linda McCartney?

"I think some people are a bit afraid of me. I've never been a girlie girl. I'm very bad at small talk; I find it hard to chit chat. People who don't know me get me wrong. Too bad."[55]

Some interviewers took a look at Linda's pictures, the setup at Cavendish Avenue, and the way Linda ran her household, and then chronicled their visits in sharp detail.

"The McCartneys' big house in Regent's Park is neither a showpiece nor an Indian tent," Georgina Howell wrote in *Vogue*. "It is bright and comfortable, lived-in, has a Magritte and a set of Picasso etchings, a piano in the drawing/eating room and a lot of Linda's photographs stuck up with drawing pins. There are Tiffany lamps and a large sofa the children use for a trampoline.

"Linda [is] a lawyer's daughter who grew up in Scarsdale, New York. . . . She keeps the four dogs at bay in the garden, the children happy, makes lunch and changes the records. Paul, into imitations of Nigerians he met while recording *Band on the Run* in Lagos has four-year-old Mary on his lap and a glass of fresh orange juice in his hand. Music goes on all the time. . . . Conversation is punctuated by pauses for appreciation of a particular piece of phrasing or special effect: the presence of the outsider sails on oblivious. Lunch is a delicious vichyssoise, a cheese salad and a cup of tea. . . .

"What she is after with her photography, and Paul is after with his music now, is quality: for Linda, the grained, finished, deep quality or early photographs, the hand tinting she does herself; for Paul, technical perfection, quality of material and musicianship."[56]

Some more unusual invitations came Linda's way as word spread that she was assembling a photography book. David Bailey and David Litchfield invited her to showcase some of her photographs in their arts and graphics magazine, *the image*. And at a luncheon with the editor of the teen magazine *Mirabelle*, on a boat in Regent's Park, Linda agreed to write a monthly column, the first (of six) due to run in the July 27 issue.

As a kind of cosmic background noise, Beatles Universe was as active as ever. The latest offer, for a concert in Monticello, New York—a town in the Catskills with fewer than 6,000 people—was downright silly, but it was denied with only slightly more than the usual measure of pique. "It really is incredible where these reports come from," Apple's Tony King said. "This must make about 50 different comeback stories I've heard this year."[57] Paul issued his own denial, characterizing the reports as "a flagrant misrepresentation and a great disservice to the public."[58]

But a fictional Beatles reunion inspired by such reports came to the stage in Liverpool on

May 15, when Willy Russell's play, *John, Paul, George, Ringo . . . and Bert* opened at the Everyman Theatre. Russell was not simply mirroring the Beatles tributes that were sprouting up in American theaters. A 26-year-old Liverpudlian who was about to give up a job as a schoolteacher to become a playwright, Russell had grown up with the Beatles; at 14, he used to watch them at the Cavern, and like many Liverpudlians, he felt a sense of loss mingled with pride when the world wrested the Beatles from their home turf.

In *John, Paul, George, Ringo . . . and Bert*, Russell presents an idiosyncratic history of the Beatles, as seen through the eyes of Bert, whom Russell described as "that Liverpool figure who's always saying, '*Oh, I knew the Beatles—oh yeah, and I played with them for, like, two nights a week.*' That kind of local, you know, attaching oneself to the glory of the past, that was the inspiration for Bert."[59] In its Liverpool staging, the actors lip-synched to Beatles recordings, with further Beatles tunes, and some original music, performed live by Barbara Dickson, Terry Canning and Bob Ash.

"[Willy] decided that it would be wrong to have male singers impersonating Beatles songs," Dickson noted. "I had mentioned to him previously that if he needed a singer for any of his works to consider me because I really liked his writing."[60]

Russell was essentially a theater apprentice at the Everyman, his work until now consisting of adaptations of existing plays. The Everyman's artistic director, Alan Dossor, wanted him to adapt a Beatles play that was running in Manchester, but when Russell went to see it, he knew he could do better.

"What Alan Dossor didn't know was that I was steeped in Beatles lore," Russell explained, "having been watching them since I was 14, and anything about them, I devoured. So when I saw this [play in Manchester], I could see immediately that the dialogue was stilted because it had been culled from whatever biographies were knocking about, so it was not living and breathing in the way I knew Beatles dialogue could sparkle, and breathe, and be fully theatrical. So when [Dossor] asked me if I'd adapt it, I rather arrogantly said, '*No, I'll write my own play about them.*' And he took a chance—an enormous chance, really, with an unknown theater writer—and commissioned me to do it.

"I made an immediate decision that I would do no talking to the characters around Liverpool who laid claim to having a Beatles past. I didn't want to talk to Allan Williams, or Bob Wooler. I didn't try to get in touch with Cynthia Lennon. Even though I had tenuous connections, through the arts world, to people like Mike [McGear], I didn't want to be swayed by their vision of what happened. And I was very conscious, early on, that I didn't want to trade on the Beatles. I wanted to be my own man, and write a valid piece of theater, which happened to be *about* the Beatles."

What interested Russell was not the details of the Beatles' personal lives, but about how the Beatles had essentially been transformed into public property to become the phenomenon they were. As Russell put it at the time, "What I am saying in the show is not a criticism of the Beatles but what we did to them . . . This is a play about the effects of money, exploitation, growing up and it's as much about Brian Epstein and Allen Klein as about the Beatles. . . . I don't pretend to know them completely or to have attempted an analysis, so if they come to see the show and say they don't like it I'll be sorry, but I'll also say get lost, because it's not them I'm really showing."[61]

Indeed, Russell was under no illusion that the Beatles would like the play, and when it proved a success in Liverpool, attracting the attention of journalists, he came to understand how the former Beatles might perceive it.

"I knew how from seeing features and interviews with myself in newspapers how, no matter how sympathetic the journalist, the picture of yourself that comes back at you is such a false picture," Russell said. "It's like you've seen yourself in a hall of mirrors. It's you but it's palpably a distorted you. It's not a real you. So no matter how faithful we had been, and no matter how much we believe totally in the integrity and the truth and the strength of our musical play, I didn't for a second ever believe that the subjects of it would have the same benevolent attitude and welcoming attitude to it."[62]

The Liverpool premiere got onto Paul's radar, but he opted neither to comment on it, nor to throw any obstacles in its way. The other Beatles ignored the production as well. On the other hand, those in the business of promoting the Beatles' work—EMI and ATV, for example—thought the Beatles should be flattered that, five years after their breakup, they were the subjects of a new work of art. On the other hand, when the Ivor Novello Awards were presented on May 16—the day after the premiere of Russell's play—the composing members of the Beatles received no awards for the first time in a decade.

ATV, for its part, was not sitting around waiting to collect royalties on aging Beatles tracks. It was eager to exploit its newer holdings as well, and having commissioned Paul to compose a theme for *Zoo Gang*, a new ITV television series set in France during World War II, Lew Grade was chagrined that Paul had not released his April 1973 recording of the theme as a single, to coordinate with the show's premiere on April 5, 1974.

Paul, who thought carefully about what he released, particularly on singles, did not consider the short, Parisian-flavored instrumental suitable as an A side, and though he agreed to make it the B side of the British *Band on the Run*, he was not planning to release that single until June 28, by which time the series would have ended. So Grade sprang into action on his own, hiring an arranger, Colin Fletcher, and a producer, Tony Hiller, to assemble an ensemble of studio players and record a version that is nearly identical to Paul's. Grade released the recording on his own Bradley's Records, with the ensemble listed as Jungle Juice.

The performance is so similar to Paul's that some fans concluded that Jungle Juice was a pseudonym, and the B side, an instrumental called 'Monkey Music,' was an undocumented McCartney rarity. But the recording is simply a knockoff.[63]

At Apple, meanwhile, negotiation on the dissolution agreement continued to keep the company in limbo. But now Paul was not the only former Beatle eager for a resolution. On May 20, Herb Alpert and Jerry Moss, the founders of A&M Records, announced that they had signed George Harrison to a distribution deal for his boutique label, Dark Horse Records. George's own recordings would remain on Apple until the EMI contract expired in 1976, but nothing precluded him from producing other artists for Dark Horse, and when the label was announced, so was its first release, an album by Shankar Family and Friends, led by Ravi Shankar and produced by Harrison, due in September. George, Alpert and Moss lured Jonathan Clyde away from Elektra Records to run the new company.

Curiously, though Paul ignored a Liverpool play about the Beatles, he got involved in trying to preserve what would have been no more than a footnote in the Beatles story, a detail important only to the band, and at that, perhaps only to Paul. When he read that the Derby Arms, a derelict pub at the junction of Everton Valley and Walton Road, was about to be demolished, he remembered admiring the tiles that decorated the pub's exterior when the Beatles played some early gigs at nearby Blair Hall.

Paul hired an agent to look into getting the tiles preserved, and he started a minor groundswell: Geoffrey Lewis, director of the Museum of Liverpool, agreed that the tiles were fine examples of industrial ceramic art and was in favor of saving them, but lamented that the museum did not have the budget to do so. The Liverpool Housing Council Committee, and the city itself, were also unwilling to foot the bill—not, certainly, if there was a Beatle who might do it.

Having exhausted all official channels, Paul asked Angie and Ruth McCartney to visit the demolition site and make the foreman a cash offer for the tiles, plus the pub's ornate stained glass windows. But removing the tiles and windows without damaging them was a job for a specialist, and was likely to be time-consuming, so the foreman signaled the wrecking ball to move in.

"It *is* for Paul McCartney," Angie exclaimed.

"D'you know what, girl, I don't give a shit if it's for the Pope,"[64] the foreman replied.

Word of Wings' planned getaway to Nashville became public knowledge by way of a front-page article in *The Tennessean* on May 24. The Eastmans had seen to the details of the trip, engaging William Doyce "Buddy" Killen—executive vice president of Tree Publishing and co-owner of the Sound Shop Recording Studio in Nashville—as Paul's local fixer. Killen was still in the process of arranging a place for the McCartneys and Wings to stay—they wanted a ranch, ideally, with horses, and perhaps separate housing for the family and the band—and he had yet to speak with Paul directly. Nevertheless, Killen had plenty to say about Paul's plans for the visit, some of it more aspirational than factual.

"He's definitely not coming here to hide out," Killen said. "Paul's manager said he will be mingling with the musical community. He's going to be here six weeks so that he can get to know the people in the music industry and get the feel of Nashville and its music. If I can just get him into town and out of his house smoothly, I'll be greatly relieved. . . .

"He'll be doing some writing, and more than likely he'll do an album. Plans are at this point for me to work with him on the record. We can put together some phenomenal band. Paul is looking for something new and fresh. Although he's coming here for the influence of Nashville's music, I don't want to say anything that will indicate it will be country, because I don't know."[65]

In preparation for the trip, Paul and Linda traveled to High Park shortly after the drummer auditions. Paul had a handful of songs-in-progress that he wanted to finish, and ever since the fertile spring 1970 stay, when he recorded demos for more than 30 songs that would fill out much of *Ram* and *Red Rose Speedway*, High Park had been his go-to songwriting hideaway.

One song that needed work was the mid-tempo rocker Paul played with Wings and their five prospective drummers during the second stage of the auditions. With a band version at least partly worked up, it was time to finish the lyrics.

As he had done with 'Soily,' Paul let his imagination run wild, populating the lyric with strange characters, odd locutions and peculiar situations. Within the first few verses, he introduced a "poker man," an Eskimo, a sea lion, Ollie [Oliver] Hardy, and a "gee-gee" (British slang for a racehorse), and had everyone chipping in for a bag of cement at the Houses of Parliament—all leading to an easygoing chorus built around the invitation, "*Let's go, let's go, let's go, let's go—down to Junior's Farm where I want to lay low.*"

"I just get hold of a guitar and strum things and the words come out," Paul told *Disc*. "If you're feeling nice and loose, in a good mood, they just tumble out and you don't know what they mean. . . . 'Junior's Farm' was quite an easy one—there are only a couple of chords. The tune came first there, too. I wanted a bit of a bopper. . . . It has silly words, and, basically, all it means is let's get out of the city. Let's go down to Junior's Farm or Strawberry Fields or wherever. As for reading deep meanings into the words, people really shouldn't bother, there aren't any."[66]

Other demos recorded during the visit went straight into the archive, with no plan for immediate resurrection. They included 'Little Bass Man,' 'Rude Arab Nights,' 'You Look a Little Lonely,' and a song of Denny's called 'Children' (also called 'Children Children'), as well as a series of jams in the Oobu Joobu series he began at High Park with Wings in September 1971, toward the end of the sessions for *Wild Life*. (The title is a corruption of "mumbo jumbo," from which the *Wild Life* track 'Mumbo' got its name.) These included 'Latin Late Night (Oobu Joobu),' 'Oobu Joobu (Shaft Style),' and 'Moog Theme (Oobu Joobu).'

While the McCartneys were in Scotland, the tapes he recorded at the EMI Pathé Marconi Studios, in Paris, were pulled from EMI's archives, and the two songs Wings plus Jimmy McCulloch worked on—listed on the tape boxes as 'When I Was in Paris' (the working title for 'Wide Prairie') and 'Untitled' ('I Got Up')—were given rough mixes. 'Mood Music,' an instrumental worked up by Wings during the *Red Rose Speedway* sessions, was also pulled from the archives. It is possible that he was considering these for inclusion on *Cold Cuts*.

Work on Paul's recordings at EMI would continue without him even after he left for the States. On June 3, *Band on the Run* was given a Quadrophonic mix for new hi-fi systems that surrounded the listener with music, using four speakers rather than a stereo pair. It was a system with a tiny constituency—partly because only well-heeled music buffs were willing to invest in the decoding equipment and extra speakers, and partly because the music industry had not settled on a unified format, with labels individually committing to incompatible systems.

If all this activity was not enough for a musician about to travel halfway across the globe to break in a new version of his band, Paul had a couple of real estate deals in the works, too. Jim and Angie had decided to sell Rembrandt, the house Paul bought for Jim in the first flush of the Beatles' success. They listed the property for £38,500 ($92,160)—nearly £30,000 more than Paul paid for it in July 1964.

"We had to move, due to Jim's increasingly bad health," Angie explained, mentioning that his rheumatoid and osteoarthritis made managing the five-bedroom house too difficult. "We had a serious buyer, who eventually had to drop out for financial reasons, so Paul bought the house."[67] It would give him a comfortable place to stay when visiting family in Liverpool. Jim and Angie moved to a bungalow nearby.

The second transaction was a new country getaway for Paul and Linda. They had been scouting for properties since September 1969, and when their holidays did not take them to the Orkneys or other corners of Scotland—or to France, Jamaica or New York—they drove around the south of England, scouting for just the right property. Now they found Waterfall Cottage, in Peasmarsh, Sussex, three miles northwest of Rye—a two-bedroom cottage on 100 woodland acres, which they purchased from Mr. Jim Huggs for £40,000 ($95,750).

Everything about the place was idyllic. Although the cottage was built in the 1930s, its circular shape was characteristic of the area's oast houses, where hops were kiln-dried, and the forest land included a stream with a waterfall, from which the property's name was taken. There was plenty of history in the area, including a Norman-era church. Henry George Liddell had lived in the vicinity, in the second half of the nineteenth century. Besides being the vice-chancellor of Oxford University, the coauthor of an important Greek-English lexicon, and the author of a history of Rome, he was the father of Alice Liddell, the young girl who inspired Lewis Carroll to write *Alice's Adventures in Wonderland* and *Through the Looking-Glass*.

By the time the sale closed, in early June, the McCartneys were out of the country. Leaving from Heathrow Airport on June 2, they flew to New York, where they spent the night before heading to Los Angeles and checking into the Beverly Hills Hotel. Paul's instruments were shipped separately to Nashville, where he would arrive on June 6, followed the next day by Denny, Jimmy and Geoff.

Recording Sessions

Tuesday, June 4, or Wednesday, June 5, 1974.
Studio C, Record Plant, Los Angeles.
Recording & Mixing: 'Let's Love.'

The night they landed in Los Angeles, Paul and Linda had dinner with Peggy Lee at Les Restaurant, in Hollywood, picking up where they left off a month earlier in London. Socially, all was sweetness and light, a pair of stars comparing their experiences and discussing the music they loved. Professionally, though, there was an undercurrent of tension. A jazz singer whose recording career began in 1941—the year before Paul was born—Lee was used to making records in the time-honored way: singing to a backing ensemble that was playing in the studio with her.

She could deal with touch-ups, and with a producer deciding to add instrumental lines after the performance, of course; but the wholesale multitracking that was part of the technical toolbox of McCartney's generation was not her cup of tea, and she particularly disliked the idea of adding her vocal to a track that had already been recorded—a process that allowed for no interplay, however subtle, with the musicians backing her.

It may have bothered her as well that the 16-track master that Paul brought with him to the studio effectively countermanded the interpretive decisions that Lee and Grusin had made in their April 23 recording, most notably by quickening the tempo, but also by providing an orchestral backdrop quite different from the backing ensemble she and Grusin had used—elements that altered the character of the song.

But Lee maintained a professional veneer and was determined to perform the song as its composer thought it should be performed. Any irritation about the replacement of her original recording was tamped down—as was her well-known dislike of being told how to shape a phrase, something Paul did whenever a vocal take did not match his vision, just as he would at any other session.

Nevertheless, getting the right take—a brighter, more vibrant vocal than on the April 23 recording—took only a couple of hours, whereupon the track was mixed. Given that it was the album's title track, 'Let's Love' was meant also to be its opener. At the mixing session, a shorter edit was prepared as a "reprise," to be heard at the end of the album.

The ease and speed with which the recording was completed was apparently a surprise to no one: Atlantic had arranged for a press conference to be held in the studio that same afternoon, and Paul, Grusin and engineer Pat Stapley had a finished mix ready to play for reporters.

"This is something I've always wanted to do," Paul told the reporters gathered around the piano in Studio C. "Call it the Peg 'n' Paul show."[68] McCartney accompanied Lee in a couple of Standards, and took a few questions, with Lee asserting that she was a Beatles fan before Paul had heard of her, and Paul correcting her to say that he had some of her records in his formative years. Questions about a Beatles reunion were batted away—"We're not here to talk about that," said Paul—and the "champagne or a song" tale was told before reporters were shepherded into the control room to hear the finished track.

Before they decamped from Los Angeles and headed for Nashville, the McCartneys spent a few hours at Pip's, a private club on Robertson Avenue, having drinks and dinner with Elton John, Alice Cooper and Micky Dolenz. Other members of Pip's might have thought it was a peculiar assembly. But for Paul, an afternoon playing and singing Standards with Peggy Lee and an evening consorting with a sartorially spectacular queen of the keyboard, a shock-rocker who performed under a woman's name and in racoon-like eye makeup, and a former Monkee were all in a day's work.

3

NASHVILLE CATS

When the McCartney clan, accompanied by Brian Brolly, touched down at Metropolitan Airport in Nashville, on June 6, at 8:30 P.M., Brolly led the entourage out of the plane, carrying Mary, with Paul just behind him in a green, sleeveless jacket and a brightly colored shirt, his arm held aloft with a two-fingered peace sign. Linda followed, carrying Stella, with Heather behind.

Having a Beatle in Nashville was a Certified Big Deal, although by no means unprecedented: Ringo Starr recorded his *Beaucoups of Blues* album there in June 1970. A handful of reporters waited to ask Paul what he planned to do in the heart of country music. Paul was at his diplomatic and enthusiastic best. To a reporter who asked whether he was a country music fan, Paul said, "I was raised on it!"[1] He was here, he told the press, to rehearse the new incarnation of Wings and get in touring trim, adding that he and Linda also hoped to get some horse riding in and that he planned to meet, and hear performances by, some of Nashville's musical legends. Beyond that—who knew? "I may record here, I don't know," he told them. "It depends on how things go."[2]

Because Wings were in Nashville on tourist visas, they were legally prohibited from recording or performing, a point that may have slipped Paul's mind. But as it turned out, that didn't matter, because Buddy Killen, his Nashville fixer, was not only a co-owner of the Sound Shop, a highly regarded local recording studio, but was also well-connected in other ways. As the vice president of Tree International, one of the biggest publishers in country music, he would be able to finesse the legal and union complications that might arise if Paul decided to set down some tracks.

The connection between Paul and Killen was Eastman and Eastman, which counted Tree International among its clients. The Eastmans knew that there could be no more useful contact for Paul in Nashville, and Killen was thrilled to have a former Beatle in tow. He was on hand to meet Paul at the airport, and after allowing reporters to quiz him briefly, he led the McCartneys to a limousine, where Donna Hilley, his assistant; Bill Hudson, Tree's publicist; and MPL's Alan Crowder—in Nashville in his capacity as Wings' manager—awaited him.

Killen was a decade older than McCartney, but there was common ground beyond a relationship with Paul's in-laws. He had started his musical career as a bassist and worked at the Grand Ole Opry until 1953, when Tree's owner, Jack Stapp, hired him shortly after the publishing house opened for business. Killen had helped make Tree one of the biggest publishers in country music; it was he who discovered 'Heartbreak Hotel' and persuaded Elvis Presley to record it.[3] For a fledgling music publisher like Paul, Killen was a storehouse of knowledge and experience that he could tap during his stay in Nashville.

Paul planned to stay about six weeks, until the middle of July, and Killen, charged with finding them a farm with horses and swimming facilities, ideally within 50 miles of Nashville, had delegated the task to one of his star songwriters, Claude "Curly" Putman Jr.

When Putman, who was best known as the composer of 'Green, Green Grass of Home' and 'D-I-V-O-R-C-E,' reported that he was unable to find a place that met the McCartneys' wish list, Killen suggested that Putman rent the McCartneys his own 133-acre farm, located just off Highway I-40, between Lebanon and Gladeville. Putman agreed, letting Wings take over his property for $2,000 (£835) a week. With his own house now off-limits, Putman took his family on a Hawaiian vacation.

"I was kind of nervous," Putman admitted, having read wild tales of rock and roll misbehavior. "They paid me pretty good for leasing it for six weeks. And they didn't tear anything up. We had a reception in our home that first night. Paul was a very down-to-earth guy and friendly. We sat around, and then we went back and played the guitar a little bit together. Paul was very interested in country music. He was very nice. I thought he was just a regular guy."[4]

The house was a classic Southern two-story mansion, nestled into a hill overlooking a man-made six-acre lake stocked with fish, and with a stream running the eighth of a mile from the gatehouse—actually just a cottage near the gates to the property—to the main house. The mansion itself had large columns supporting a front porch and extending upward to a balcony, and windows framed with dark shutters. To Paul, it looked vaguely like Graceland, Elvis Presley's storied home in Memphis. Beside the house was a garage large enough for several cars, a perfect place for the band to rehearse.

The plan was that the McCartney clan would occupy the main house, and Laine, McCulloch, Britton, and roadie Trevor Jones would share the gatehouse cottage. The band's digs were hardly palatial, just mattresses on the floor, without air-conditioning, though temperatures were well above 80° Fahrenheit. Soon the musicians moved into the main house, leaving Trevor to share the cottage with Alan Crowder. The McCartneys and the band members individually rented cars.

The Putmans left their housekeeper at the McCartneys' disposal, although Linda did most of the cooking herself.

"They asked for certain things to be stocked in the house," Curly's wife, Bernice, noted. "Five gallons of Baskin-Robbins ice cream, cases of oranges and orange juice, Johnnie Walker Red and Ovaltine. Linda made all kinds of vegetable dishes."[5]

Not just vegetable dishes. Also on the provisions list the McCartneys asked Mrs. Putman to provide was smoked bacon. "I was a vegetarian for two and a half years," Linda told a local reporter, "but I have a husband who is the sort that craves his bacon."[6]

Nevertheless, Paul took another step toward a vegan lifestyle at the Putmans' farm.

"That was where I decided to give up fishing," Paul explained. "There was a lake Curly had put in and there were fish in it, and I was fishing, and I caught one, one time. And seeing him coming out and gasping for his life, I thought, 'You know what? I can give you your life back. I don't need you.' So I took him off and let him go. And I thought, 'I won't ever fish again,' so I never did . . . The only thing was if you swam in the lake you'd occasionally feel a nipping at you and the kids weren't too keen on that!"[7]

Besides swimming and horseback riding, Paul found a Honda XR75 motorcycle that belonged to the Putmans' 12-year old son, Troy, and took to riding it around the grounds; before the Nashville visit ended, he bought one of his own at Hunt Honda in Lebanon.

Dixie Gamble, whose job at Tree International was typing up lyrics, was enlisted to do the shopping for the McCartneys and to be generally available to them.

"Buddy said, 'Paul and Linda are going to be coming here for six weeks, how would you like to be their Girl Friday?'" Gamble recalls. "You know, my jaw dropped. I was a big Beatles fan, and of course, I was a Paul fan. But I had to keep my cool, I couldn't jump up and down and scream. I just said, 'Yeah, that sounds fun.' I didn't know how much direct contact that would give me with them. I had no preconceived notion about what it all meant, but it was just an honor to do it."[8]

Early in the trip, Paul and Linda stopped by the Sound Shop at 1307 Division Street, just off Music Row, to have a look around. The Sound Shop opened for business in 1970, when Killen, in partnership with three musician-songwriters—Bobby Goldsboro (best known for the 1968 hit 'Honey'), Bob Montgomery, and Kelso Herston—bought and renamed the recently closed Nashville Audio Recorders for $300,000 (£125,000). The studio was a spacious 30 by 40 feet, with a 20-foot ceiling, and offered the use of Baldwin and Yamaha grand pianos, a Hammond B3 organ with a rotating Leslie speaker, a Hohner clavinet, a vibraphone, and a Moog synthesizer. Chief engineer Ernie Winfrey presided over a 12-by-20-foot control room that included an MCI console and 16-track deck, as well as a Scully four-track and an Ampex twin-track, with an impressive selection of microphones—AKGs, Sonys, Beyers, and the Neumanns that were the go-to mics at Beatles sessions. Killen billed 16-track sessions at $110 (£46) an hour.

Paul and Linda arrived unannounced in the early evening, as Winfrey and Buddy Killen were in the middle of a session with rhythm and blues singer Paul Kelly.

Paul and Linda go for a ride at Junior's farm, Tennessee, July 1974

"I was working in the studio with Buddy," Winfrey remembered, "[and] Paul and Linda just walked in; he wasn't expecting them at all. So Buddy motioned them on in, and they sat down on the sofa in front of the console. And when we got through, they stood up and introduced themselves, and were just very pleasant. And Paul said, 'Man, I really like the sound in here.' I said, 'Good. I hope you like it good enough to record.' And as it turned out, he did."[9]

Exactly what Paul would record in Nashville was undecided, but he made it clear to both Winfrey and Killen that the prospect interested him.

Dixie Gamble also introduced herself to Paul and Linda that night. As the clock noisily ticked in the studio foyer, the red light illuminating everything in sight, she waited for a break in the session.

"Finally Alan Crowder came out. I introduced myself, and told Alan that Buddy had asked me to be Girl Friday to the McCartneys. Actually, Alan took care of most of that, but he was new in Nashville, he didn't know the ropes or where to go for things. So he said, 'Oh, that's brilliant. That's really brilliant. There's only one problem. Linda doesn't allow any women in the studio with Paul.' And he thought for a minute, and he said, 'Oh, I've got it, ask her to go shopping.'

"I was pretty scared about it, because Linda had a bit of a reputation for being pretty straight up—nice, you know, but a no BS kind of person. So, she came out and I kind of shakily walked up and said, 'I'm Dixie Gamble. Buddy asked me to be available for you guys for anything and everything that you need. But first of all, the most important thing we need to do is we need to go shopping, because there are incredible little boutiques in Nashville.' And she said, 'Brilliant! We'll go tomorrow.' And we did.

"I really liked her. I didn't know if I would or not, especially after that 'no women in the studio' thing. But she didn't seem possessive. We hit it off, and it became normal to hang out and chat with her."[10]

Often, Paul and Linda began their day with breakfast at the Loveless Motel, where the specialties were buttermilk biscuits, fried chicken, and country ham, and they would end their day unwinding after rehearsals by catching either a local gig or a film, or chilling out in front of the tube: on June 10, just a few days into their visit, they caught a TV appearance by Dolly Parton, their first glimpse of the singer who was then striking out on her own after seven years in Porter Wagoner's band.

"After hours," Britton explained, "it was sort of family orientated, because of the children. Poor Heather had to look after the two youngsters, and, until they got to bed, the guys couldn't sort of loosen up and get the booze out and the joints."[11]

Often, Denny, Jimmy, Geoff, Trevor and Alan Crowder opted out of the family atmosphere, instead eating—and soaking up another level of Americana—at a truck stop one of the band members discovered.

"They had a big sign that said Truckers Are Kings," Britton noted. "The truckers got served first, [but eventually] they got to know us, and we could be served with the truckers. The line of trucks in the car park—it was like the size of a small town. This place had movies, hairdressers, and hookers for the guys—I mean, truckers were kings in the motorways in America at that time."[12]

Paul had ample reason to start the Nashville sojourn in a good mood. On June 8, the day after his arrival, *Band on the Run* returned to the top spot on the *Billboard* 200. That same day, the British music press announced the imminent release (on June 28) of an otherwise unknown Paul and Linda McCartney song, '4th of July,' by the Australian singer John Christie.

Christie believed that Paul had composed the song specifically for him, but it actually dates to his long stay at High Park during the spring and summer of 1970, and it is included, under the title 'Why Am I Crying?,' on the 30-plus-song demo cassette that Paul carried with him to New York for the *Ram* sessions.

Paul never attempted to record the song formally himself, and though it has its charms musically, it is easy to see why he felt it was best left to someone else. On the surface, the song is quiet and downcast, the central conflict in its lyric—and the answer to the question in its original title being that the protagonist's lady has turned up with another man. Although jealousy songs were not out of the question for Paul, the ones he recorded tended to be quasi-cinematic fictions like 'Oh Woman, Oh Why,' with its shouted lyric, Ry Cooder–like slide guitar and gunshots, not introspective moans like this one. Celebrating thoroughly requited love and the joys of family was more to his taste.

But there was another, sub-rosa issue. Leaving aside the girlfriend-with-another-guy element, the song's central and most powerful image was in its refrain, "Why am I crying? It's the fourth of July." There was a clear autobiographical undercurrent in this diary-like scrap, composed on or around July 4, 1970—Independence Day in America—at a time when Paul faced the depressing prospect of suing the other Beatles to achieve his own artistic independence.

The song sat untouched for nearly four years, coming to life again early in 1974, when Dave Clark and Mike Smith (formerly of the Dave Clark Five) visited Paul and Linda, hoping to persuade him to write a song for Christie, whom Clark was managing and producing. At the end of an afternoon spent reminiscing, catching up and sharing a gourmet lunch whipped up by Linda, Paul ran off a cassette copy of the demo and handed it to Clark.

The rough guitar and vocal demo offered nothing in the way of production hints, and Paul did not attend the session at Lansdowne Studios, in Holland Park, London.[13] But Christie and Clark brightened it slightly, transposing it to B-flat major from A major, and playing it a bit faster than Paul's version.

"It was intended for the American market alone because the Fourth of July means something there," Christie said shortly after the single was released, "but it turned out so well that we decided to put it out here [in the UK] as well."[14] The single was released by Polydor in Britain and Capitol in the United States.

In Paul's absence, preparations were being made in London for Wings' next British single. An edited version of 'Band on the Run' was prepared at EMI Studios on June 11, reducing the song from its original 5'09" to 3'50." It was given the matrix number 7YCE.21746 and included only on promotional copies; commercial copies carried only the full-length version of the song, with 'Zoo Gang' on the flip side. The Quadraphonic mix of the *Band on the Run* album was mastered at EMI Studios on June 13.

Paul took a few days to settle in, get used to the Tennessee heat and to check out the Nashville social scene. On Saturday, June 8, the band was invited to a ritzy party—"All these people in sequins, and blokes with pompadour haircuts—yeah, very rich people, exclusive crowd," Britton recalled.[15] The next night, all of Wings went to the Nashville Speedway to hear Lynyrd Skynyrd, ZZ Top and the Marshall Tucker Band, and spent time backstage with the touring musicians, the cream of Southern rock.

Rehearsals began on Monday, June 10, with a freewheeling jam in the Putmans' garage. Paul, Denny and Jimmy started the day on acoustic guitars, plugging in as the afternoon progressed. It was not until the following day that they began to seriously tackle potential tour repertory, spending two days honing 'Jet' before taking up 'Band on the Run.'

At this point, Geoff had to admit to a problem he had been suppressing. On June 3, while Paul and Linda were in Los Angeles, Wings' new drummer was doing his karate training in his mother's garden, and a kick to his opponent's elbow resulted in a broken bone in his right foot. At Bromley Hospital in London he refused the recommendation that the foot be put in a cast, since it would affect his drumming. But nine days later Britton was in agony. He went to a local hospital for X-rays and was told that the bone was not healing. Still resisting a cast, he bought a pair of stiff shoes, on the theory that it would keep the bones lined up as they mended.

That evening, Paul, Denny and Geoff jammed for a while and then settled in front of the television; Jimmy went into town on his own, doing some advance scouting for the next night, when—after a day rehearsing 'Live and Let Die' and 'My Love'—McCulloch, Britton, Laine and the roadies would go barhopping in search of female companionship.

Jimmy and Denny got roaring drunk on that foray, leaving Geoff, who didn't drink, as the designated driver. At some point, the musicians got into a conversation with a Nashville policeman who, charmed by their British accents, starstruck at an encounter with Paul McCartney's sidemen, and aware that British police officers did not carry weapons, gifted Geoff a handgun.

"I nearly shot my fucking toe off with that gun," Britton said of an episode shortly before the afternoon rehearsal on June 14. "I had it in my hand, and it was like a .45, the bullets went in the handle. And I took the clip out, but there was one in the chamber. I was standing by the corral, and I was on my own, and I just pulled the trigger. It went off, and it just like went right beside my foot. Fucking hell, man! Talk about an idiot!"[16]

That afternoon, Wings added 'Let Me Roll It' and 'Hi, Hi, Hi' to the rehearsal list, but Paul soon heard about Geoff's souvenir.

"I just said, 'That's it, man. You're out unless you get rid of that fucking gun,'" Paul recalled of the encounter. Fleshing out his objections with worst-case scenarios, he admonished Britton, "'It'll go off in your pocket, shoot your balls off! Or mine!'"[17]

Some relatively innocent misbehavior in the wee hours of June 15 could easily have ended in tragedy. Late in the night, the McCartneys were disturbed by noise coming from the Putmans' garage and called the police to look in to it.

"I came out, and I said, 'What's going on?'" Britton remembered. "And they said, 'Someone's in the garage.' So I said, 'Well, aren't you going to look?' And the copper said, 'No! I'll get my head blown off.' They had the car doors open, the police, and they were tucked behind them. So I said, 'Well, I'll go and have a look.'"

It turned out to be Jimmy and Denny, sharing a joint. Geoff told the police it was just a couple of the guys in the band, and they drove off without further investigation. "They weren't the bravest of the brave," was the lasting impression Nashville's Finest left on Britton.

At rehearsals the next day, Britton, sleep-deprived and with an aching right foot, had trouble with the timing on 'Live and Let Die,' to the annoyance of his bandmates. Still, that night they attended a concert in town and partied until 5 A.M., Geoff once again driving everyone back to Curly's farm.

Britton had not been publicly announced as Wings' new drummer, but on June 15, *Melody Maker* carried the news (misspelling both Geoff's name—as Jeffrey Brittain—and his predecessor's, as Denny Serwell).

Absorbing the sound and spirit of Nashville's music scene quickly became an unstated priority for the band. On Sunday, June 16, they made their way to the Grand Ole Opry to hear the Third Annual Grand Masters Fiddling Contest: 20 violinists each had a six-minute slot, during which they had to play a waltz, a breakdown, and a tune of their choice, in the hope of winning a $1,000 (£418) prize. Not surprisingly, Paul became an unintended focus of attention.

"Instead of calling someone at Opryland and saying, 'I want to bring McCartney and his entourage out,'" Killen confessed, "I stupidly pulled up out there and bought tickets. We're walking toward the theater, and I look up and I see lips moving, forming the words, 'Paul McCartney.' Then the crowd started moving in on us. Suddenly it's, 'I want your autograph!' Paul was very nice. He said okay, and he'd sign them as we walked along. I don't know what I was thinking."[18]

Killen quickly arranged for Wings to sit in a cordoned-off area, where they were joined by the guitarist Chet Atkins. But Paul continued to draw attention, and he soon agreed to be taken to the stage and introduced to the crowd as a guest of the Opry. His brief appearance—just a wave, a hello and a thumbs-up—brought down the house.

Linda roamed the theater freely, photographing the competition, but Paul mostly kept to the cordoned-off area, listening to the performances and chatting with Atkins. George Harrison was a devoted Atkins fan during the Beatles' formative years, and the young Beatles tended to share each other's enthusiasms. And though Atkins inhabited a different musical world, he was by no means immune to the Beatles' melodic strengths: his twenty-eighth studio album, *Chet Atkins Picks on the Beatles* (1966), included a dozen Lennon-McCartney songs.

Between rounds of the violin contest, the Opry presented a performance by the singer-songwriter Porter Wagoner with Dolly Parton in what was billed as her last appearance in Wagoner's band. Parton had already made ten albums with Wagoner, and they were about to release their eleventh, *Porter 'n' Dolly*. But Parton had also been writing songs and recording on her own since 1959, and she recently had two huge hits on the country charts—'Jolene' (1973) and 'I Will Always Love You' (1974).

"We were just blown away with this singer," Britton said of Parton. "And Porter Wagoner was a real country character, with a big pompadour and a big suit with a sequin cactus all over it."

When Paul and Linda went backstage to meet Parton and Wagoner, taking the girls with them, the rest of the band followed—inadvertently disrupting the fiddling contest.

"It was really sad for one bloke, although he probably talked about it for the rest of his life," Britton remembered. "This poor geezer's onstage, and Opryland was really quite crowded. And it was like the sea dividing, [with Paul] as the front runner and everyone else following, like a V coming down the road. This bloke is onstage playing the violin, and he can see it coming, but the whole audience turned around. It was heartbreaking, but he's probably the only guy in the world who can say his fiddle tournament was ruined by Paul McCartney.

"So Paul brings it to a standstill, it's chaos, and then Porter Wagoner comes around the back of the stage with Dolly and meets us, and she's just as natural as apple pie. And we can't take our eyes off her cleavage for the ten minutes we talked to her. Yeah, she's larger than life, a lovely person."[19]

After their Opryland outing, Killen invited the McCartneys and Wings to his newly remodeled house to lounge around the pool and dig into a few buckets of deep-fried chicken. By the time they arrived, the Wings crew was famished, and they tucked into the dinner in Killen's den, preempting his plan to eat around the pool.

"The children finished first," Killen wrote in his memoir, "and without wiping the gravy and grease from their hands, immediately began to jump up and down on the white crushed-velvet couches as if they were trampolines, stomping mashed potatoes into the fabric. Each time one of them would touch the newly painted walls, a child-size oily handprint remained. Paul and Linda were very lenient parents and didn't seem to notice the children's antics."[20]

Appalled but intent on providing the best in Southern hospitality, Killen proposed taking his guests on a tour of Nashville, hoping to spare his freshly painted walls and new furniture further damage. As everyone headed for his Cadillac, Killen heard Stella yell that she had forgotten her shoes, followed swiftly by the sound of glass shattering as the two-year-old ran headlong into the den's glass door.

Linda bounded into the house, as did Britton, whose karate training gave him elementary first aid skills. Stella lay on the floor of the den amid shards of what had been the door to the pool, her arms and legs lacerated and bleeding profusely. Linda wrapped her shaking arms and legs in towels and carried her to Killen's car. The full troupe headed for the Donelson Clinic, where the gathering of doctors and nurses grew exponentially once word spread that there was a Beatle on the premises.

"Everywhere we looked, nurses and doctors were peeking around the corner, trying to get a glimpse of Paul," Killen remembered. "Since we were there for quite some time, I later jokingly told Paul that I wondered how many patients had died during our visit. The doctors and nurses had spent all their time sneaking peeks at him."[21]

A couple of hours later, with Stella's wounds cleaned, medicated and properly bandaged, the McCartneys and company returned to Curly's farm, and Killen went home to assess the damage. With Stella calmed down sufficiently, the adults in the Wings party unwound by catching a late show at a drive-in movie, where they devoured pizza and Cokes while watching *Culpepper Cattle Co.* and an oldie, *The Laughing Policeman*.*

When rehearsals resumed on Monday, June 17, Wings focused on 'Bluebird,' and finished early in the day, leaving Linda free to join Dixie Gamble and Donna Hilley on a shopping trip devoted mainly to finding a birthday gift for Paul's thirty-second birthday. She did not come up with much, apart from a cigarette lighter she thought Paul would like. She also bought a poster with photos of horses for Heather and broomstick horses for Mary and Stella.

But by then, Linda had arranged for Paul's main gift—the stand-up bass formerly owned by Bill Black, the legendary bassist who played (with guitarist Scotty Moore and drummer D. J. Fontana) on many of Elvis Presley's early recordings.

---

* Another incident involving Stella that Killen did not include in his memoir—but with which he regaled visitors for the rest of his life, and which was also reported in the July 21, 1974, issue of *The Tennessean*—occurred a couple of weeks later, when the McCartneys visited Killen at Tree International. Unencumbered by a diaper and not yet fully toilet trained, the child left a souvenir on the carpeted floor of Killen's office.

"We knew a guy in Nashville," McCartney said of Linda's acquisition of the instrument. "The bass was just in a barn, nobody bothered with it anymore, 'cause Bill Black himself, the player with Elvis, had died [in 1965]. So Linda actually got it for me for my birthday."[22]

Paul's birthday party was a low-key barbecue at the lake, back to the house for cake, and then a trip into Nashville for music and beers at Skull's Rainbow Room, a burlesque club.

Rehearsals continued, with 'Wild Life' added to the slowly growing setlist. But things were beginning to get strange. Jimmy and Denny were increasingly spending their free time getting stoned in the barn, and on June 20, Jimmy, Denny, Geoff and Trevor entertained a traveling stoner who claimed his name was Billy Shears. He and his girlfriend had driven through the night to see Paul and Wings in the belief that, because of his name, Billy was destined to replace Jimmy as Paul's lead guitarist.

The rehearsals took a dark turn the afternoon after the Billy Shears visit. When Linda had trouble with some harmony vocals, Jimmy rounded on her with little pretense of tact, leaving her in tears. "Various things were said, like they're said in any group—you can't deny that,"[23] Denny Laine later admitted. Indeed, in McCulloch's view, this was the way things should be. "We don't beat about the bush," the guitarist said, shortly after the event. "If there's a problem nobody holds back. You just have it out—there's no chance to bottle things up."[24]

For Paul, the fiery Scot's outburst echoed Henry McCullough's searing comments about Linda's playing during the 1972 European tour, leaving him with an unnerving sense of déjà vu. Here they were again: a lead guitarist with a taste for both drink and unmitigated criticism, and apparently little worry that his comments might draw the boss's wrath.

Calling a break, Paul went for a walk to shake off the tension; rehearsals resumed when he returned, 90 minutes later. "Heavy bad vibes," Britton noted in his diary. That heaviness lasted into the next day, when Jimmy and Denny were nowhere to be found by late morning, having stayed out late drinking. When they finally turned up for rehearsal in the early afternoon, Paul was unhappy with what struck him as a breakdown in band discipline. Cutting the rehearsal short, he went on another walk on his own. Linda confided to the others that Paul was depressed.

Linda was used to Paul's mood swings, but this was different: bringing together a second incarnation of Wings that gelled both creatively and personally, never mind following up an album as hot as *Band on the Run*, was weighing heavily on him.

"It's so easy to be negative, you get down and it's very easy to let yourself just go down,"[25] Paul reflected shortly afterward. "I'm just like anybody else. You wake up and it's a lousy day, and it's not going well and it all falls in on top of you. For me, it wasn't the job at the office that fell in. It was the idea that I'd pick up a newspaper and they'd say, 'Oh, you should have stayed with the Beatles, Paul.' So it got to me."[26]

"He's a complex person and very much a loner,"[27] Denny Laine observed of Paul. But at the moment, Denny was too caught up in carousing with Jimmy to notice the shift in Paul's mood. Buddy Killen noticed, however, and Paul was soon using him as a sounding board.

"Every day Paul discussed the problems he was having putting his new band together," recalled Killen. "They were a headstrong group, and he was having a difficult time getting them to rehearse and do things his way. Since this was Paul's first band after the Beatles, he was unaccustomed to administering discipline to a group of musicians and there were times when he was terribly upset. I told him that he was going to have to exercise control over them if he was ever going to accomplish anything."[28]

Almost as if Paul's frustrations were affecting the weather, a tornado warning on the afternoon of June 21 briefly kept the musicians close to home, but as soon as it was lifted, Britton decamped for a karate class, having found the local martial arts club, and Denny and Jimmy went barhopping.

Hoping that a break would help dissipate the heavy atmosphere of the last few rehearsals, Paul gave the band the weekend off and scheduled a late start on Monday, June 24. That morning, Britton drove to Gallatin to check out Randy's Record Shop, a venerable vinyl outlet that had supplied American records to collectors in England—and to the jukebox in Geoff's local café—since the 1940s. At 4 P.M., McCartney led the band through the brisk rhythmic changes of 'Soily' but was dispirited to find that the playing still did not gel.

After a short break, Britton returned to find Paul and the others deep in discussion and quickly realized that they were talking about *him*. In the band for barely more than a month, Geoff was already the odd man out—the rock and roller who did not smoke or drink, and who was devoted to karate, a discipline that was both physical and mental, and required a level of self-control that seemed rarified, perhaps even snobbish, to the more party-minded Jimmy and Denny. Geoff's tendency to sometimes wear his gi (the white outfit worn during matches and training) and black belt to band rehearsals was seen by the others more as an annoyance than an endearing eccentricity.

Nevertheless, when Geoff joined in the discussion, the subject changed abruptly to a dissection of the last few rehearsals and the problems that had arisen. Jimmy was particularly blunt, focusing not on any problems he was having with Geoff, but instead on Linda's shortcomings, a point he pressed until she was again in tears. When the meeting broke up, the band's mood was so low that Britton telephoned his wife, in England, and told her that he might be leaving soon. "This is not really going well," he said. "I'm not enjoying it."[29]

Paul and Linda forestalled that decision by meeting with Geoff the next morning, explaining to the drummer that it was crucial that Paul had "a happy band at all costs." Assured that his place in the band was solid, Britton called home again to say that all was well.

Paul found a way to placate Jimmy, too. While the band was setting up for rehearsals that afternoon, Jimmy spent a few minutes noodling around on the organ. "He happened to be singing this song, 'Medicine Jar,' that was a song that he'd written with former Stone the Crows drummer Colin Allen," Paul explained. "And I said to Jim, 'I like the tune. . . . Let's arrange it, let's do it.'"[30]

Allen was well known to the Wings musicians. When Stone the Crows disbanded, in 1973, he joined the Dutch band Focus, which had enjoyed a handful of international hits in the early 1970s. He also played drums on Denny Laine's solo album *Ahh . . . Laine!*

'Medicine Jar,' originally titled 'Itchy Fingers,' admonishes a friend who was abusing drugs—specifically, a girlfriend of Allen's, Jeanette Jacobs, a singer who had been in an American all-female band, the Cake, and joined Ginger Baker's Air Force after she moved to London. The song's immediate inspiration was an incident in which Allen found a pair of Jeanette's gloves, the fingers of which were filled with pills, mainly methaqualone, a form of quaalude popularly known as "mandies."

"Dead on your feet, you won't get far if you keep on sticking your hand in the medicine jar," the song warns.

"I had lots of lyrics lying around," Allen said of collaboration with McCulloch, "and when Jimmy joined Stone the Crows, he seemed very interested in songwriting, so I would often give him the odd page to motivate him. But we never worked together. That's the way it always was—I gave him the completed lyrics and he created a song."[31]

That evening, Wings made further incursions into Nashville's musical world, and Paul let the atmosphere become his muse. With Killen as their guide, the musicians went out for dinner and music in Printer's Alley, the historic district named for the vibrant newspaper business that was centered there in the late nineteenth century. After dinner at the Captain's Table, Killen took the band to the Hugh X. Lewis Country Club, a night spot opened in 1972 by its namesake, the singer-songwriter best known for 'What I Need the Most,' 'You're So Cold (I'm Turning Blue)' and 'Tonight We're Calling It a Day.'

In its newspaper advertisements, the phrase *"Where the Stars Meet"* was printed under the club's name, and indeed, the night Wings turned up, both Chet Atkins and the singer-songwriter Waylon Jennings were in house. On a curious stage set up behind the club's bar that night were the Nashville Cats (fronted by singer Brenda Clarke), duo Randy and Sandy Brunette, Bobby Borchers, and Josie Brown, a singer from upstate New York with country affinities who was then promoting her new singles, 'Satisfy Me and I'll Satisfy You' and 'Crackerbox Mansion.'

Paul may have had Clarke, Brown, Brunette—or even another female singer he had recently seen, one Dolly P—in mind as models for the heartbreaker in 'Sally G,' the song he started writing in the early hours of the next morning and completed by 11 A.M. Finding a bleary-eyed Britton lounging in Putman's den, Paul played him the new song.

The Tennessean, Hugh X. Lewis County Club ad for the night McCartney and Wings dropped by

'Sally G' is thoroughly in the country mold. Lyrically, it describes a trip to Printer's Alley that led to a romance with a guitar-playing singer first seen performing Hank Snow's 1957 hit, 'Tangled Mind.' In the spirit of the genre, she soon began cheating on him, and the relationship fizzled, inspiring some stereotypical country music wordplay: "*took the part that was the heart of me*," for example, and "*I never thought to ask her what the letter G stood for, but I know for sure it wasn't good.*"

Musically the song celebrates country simplicity, pivoting mostly around C major and G major chords, against which Paul lays a simple, strophic melody with the hint of a yodel on "*Sally*" in the refrain. It is a superb example of McCartney's ability to absorb the essentials of any musical style, although country music was by no means foreign to him: the early Beatles repertoire was rich in Carl Perkins, Elvis Presley, Jerry Lee Lewis and Hank Williams covers, and the embryonic Lennon-McCartney songbook included several country-style numbers that the band never recorded (except in passing run-throughs during the *Get Back/Let It Be* sessions), including 'Won't You Please Say Goodbye' and 'Because I Know You Love Me So.'

"When I'm in a place, it's not uncommon for me to want to write about where I am," Paul later

* The song became so beloved among Nashville musicians that origin stories took on a life of their own. Buddy Killen wrote in his memoir that Paul wrote the song in the car on the way home from Printer's Alley.

The club owner David "Skull" Schulman claimed that McCartney wrote the tune at *his* club, Skull's Rainbow Room, while watching a singer named Diane Gaffney. Other versions say that Sally is actually a barmaid of easy virtue, in that version, the G stands for gonorrhea. But an advertisement in *The Tennessean* listed the performers who played at Lewis's club the night Paul visited, and neither Gaffney nor Lee are mentioned. The singer is most likely to be an amalgam of female singers Paul saw in Nashville. There may also have been some input from Linda, who is credited as the song's cowriter. Geoff Britton noted in his diary that Paul told him he wrote the song between 3 A.M. and 11 A.M. on the morning of June 26.

said of the song's inspiration. "This bloke named Buddy took us out to Printer's Alley, which is a little club district. There were a few people just playing country music, and we imagined a bit more than we had seen for 'Sally G' . . . I didn't see anyone named 'Sally G' when I was in Printer's Alley, nor did I see anyone who ran her eyes over me when she was singing 'A Tangled Mind.' That was my imagination."[32]

Early that afternoon, Paul presided over a rehearsal, and though he did not add 'Sally G' to the song list, he played it for the band and challenged Denny to try his hand writing a country tune as well.

"Between me and Paul there was always that friendly competition," Laine said. "In Nashville, he wrote a country song and he said, 'Why don't you write one, and we'll see which one comes out the best.'"[33]

The rehearsals, however, continued to focus on songs from the Wings discography. Intent, as always, on having his concert performances hew closely to his recordings, Paul had brought with him a small stack of solo and Wings singles and albums, as well as acetates with unreleased tracks like 'Soily' that McCulloch and Britton could consult between rehearsals, to get the arrangements into their ears and under their fingers.

Paul scheduled a recording session at the Sound Shop for that evening, so when rehearsals ended, the band members went their separate ways, Paul and Linda heading to the studio at 1307 Division Street, in the heart of Nashville's Music Row, and Laine, McCulloch and Britton headed out to see the girlfriends each had cultivated.

Recording Session

Wednesday, June 26, 1974.
The Sound Shop Studio, 1307 Division Street, Nashville.
Overdubbing: 'Wide Prairie.'

Killen told Paul that the Sound Shop was at his disposal whenever he wanted to work there, and that as far as their visa restrictions went—well, just leave that to Buddy, who would smooth over any potential trouble with the local arm of the American Federation of Musicians. Shortly after gatecrashing Paul Kelly's session a few days earlier, Paul asked MPL to send over the 16-track masters for a handful of songs that he thought might benefit from some local color.

Included were the Paris recording of Linda's 'Wide Prairie' as well as a *Ram* outtake, 'Hey Diddle,' and the *Red Rose Speedway* instrumental leftover 'Mood Music.'

"Paul had tracks that they had recorded in Europe and in America," said Winfrey, "that he wanted to do overdubs on and finish up with the possibility of putting them on an album. They had those [tapes] sent over express, it didn't take them more than a day or two to get here. So we overdubbed on those tracks."[34]

For this first session, Paul had Winfrey thread up Linda's 'Wide Prairie,' a track meant for a potential Suzy and the Red Stripes album that Paul first mentioned publicly at the end of 1973, and that, so far, also included 'Seaside Woman,' a *Red Rose Speedway* outtake, 'Oriental Nightfish,' recorded during the *Band on the Run* sessions, and 'I Got Up,' the other Paris recording. Paul added two acoustic guitar tracks plus a track on which he played guitar and Linda played a simple electric piano line.

Much as she liked Linda, Dixie Gamble, who was present at the session, was not greatly impressed with her musicianship; she described Linda's keyboard line as "a part that probably a three-year-old could have played."[35]

Linda herself did not put a great deal of stock in the project. "I'm not career conscious," she said. "I'm not ambitious. I just do it 'cos it's such fun."[36]

As Winfrey recalled, at the sessions, Paul and Linda "were all over each other. They would come in to listen to a playback, and one would sit on the other's lap. I think Paul's attitude toward Linda showed a lot about him. He was willing to accept any criticism or derision that was handed out over him having her in the band."[37]

Beyond a few basic overdubs, Paul listened to the track with an ear to what Nashville musicians might bring to it. By the time he and Linda left the studio, Paul had sketched out ideas for string and brass additions.

For the rest of the week, the band pursued their routine of rehearsals by day, sometimes punctuated with talk of future plans for the band and chats about what Britton noted as "general togetherness." By night, it was either films (the group saw *Blazing Saddles* at the drive-in on June 27), barhopping, or in Paul and Linda's case, socializing in the country music firmament. The full band spent Friday night, June 28, at the Grand Ole Opry House, where they were the guests of honor at a pre-show cocktail party in the VIP Lounge, hosted by Killen's boss, Jack Stapp.

That night's show was broadcast live on local radio, with highlights televised on July 1. Paul was again introduced to the audience (this time by the "King of Country Music," singer Roy Acuff). But he took in the show from backstage, in the company of Acuff, Chet Atkins, Waylon Jennings and other Opry stars. He also did a bit of talent spotting that night.

"We performed on the Opry the night Paul McCartney came to visit," said Marcy Cates, who performed in a violin and vocal duo with her sister Margie, as the Cates Sisters. "I remember seeing him standing on the side of the stage. He gave us a thumbs up when we passed him on our way

By Overwhelming Demand!

**BAND ON THE RUN
IS
PAUL McCARTNEY
& WINGS'
NEW SINGLE
FROM THEIR
SMASH ALBUM**

BAND ON THE RUN

Single 1873 Album SO-3415

'Band on the Run' single trade ad

off stage. Buddy Killen called us the next day and said Paul wanted to book us for a session [on July 8]."[38]

Paul also grabbed headlines in the British music press on June 28, his absence notwithstanding. The single edit of 'Band on the Run' had its British release that day, as did John Christie's recording of '4th of July.'

By the time the British version of the single was released, the American single had not only reached No. 1 on the *Billboard* Hot 100 but helped Capitol Records sell another 500,000 copies of the LP, bringing its total sales in the United States alone to more than two million, and pushing it to the top of *Billboard*'s album chart for the third time. In Britain, the single garnered enthusiastic reviews, several critics making a point of praising the album as well.

> *The title track from the LP which restored the faith of a whole host of people, myself included, in young Paul's ability. It's an LP I still listen to—and when you have 40/50 new LPs to hear each week then you don't get to hear many for pleasure only. . . . You probably know the record well already but hearing it ten or twelve times on the trot brings it home to you just how good a song and performance 'Band on the Run' is.*[39]
>
> *John Peel*, Sounds

> *Suffice to say that the album is perhaps the first splinter product of the Fab Four that genuinely lives up to the legend, and the fact it's just topped the US chart for no less than the third time says enough for its sustaining power.*[40]
>
> *Ben Edmonds*, NME

The single entered the British Top 100 at No. 27 on July 6, and it peaked at No. 3 on August 3. But it did its job: for the week ending July 13, when the single was at No. 7 in the UK, *Band on the Run* reached the top of the album chart, giving Wings their first British No. 1 LP. The album held the top spot in the UK for seven weeks, remaining in the Top 100 for a total of 124 weeks.

John Christie's '4th of July' did not fare quite so well. The disc did not crack the Top 40 in Britain or the Hot 100 in the United States.

—

Although band rehearsals were the principal mission during the Nashville visit, Paul was also thinking about the follow-up to *Band on the Run*. Doing more recording in Nashville was a possibility; he was not convinced that the band was stage-worthy yet, but he had recorded Mike's album with essentially this group (except for Britton), and if that album had weaknesses, they had to do with the material and Mike's vocals, not with the band backing.

Paul did not have much new material ready to be recorded, but his antennae were always up and ready to transform anything he heard, read or saw into at least the basis of a song. 'Sally G' was a start, and he put the finishing touches on 'Junior's Farm,' noting the coincidence that although the lyrics had been mostly complete before the trip, Curly Putman, whose farm Paul was renting, was also known locally as "Junior."

Paul had a few other songs in the works, too. 'Baby, You Know It's True' was also in the country mold, at least melodically, and the lyrics, though still spotty, seemed headed that way too. 'Call Me Back Again,' a wide-ranging tune he started writing after reconnecting with John Lennon in Los Angeles, was promising but unfinished. And he had a gently wistful, ruminative piece, 'Treat Her Gently/Lonely Old People.' Though the title suggests that it was a medley, the song was actually a single, through-composed piece.

Mostly, though, Paul was in "soaking up" mode, taking every opportunity to hear new music and mining what he heard for any nuggets that might be useful. And it was not just country music that suggested ideas. On Saturday, June 29, Paul, Linda and Geoff drove into Nashville to catch David Bowie's concert at the Municipal Auditorium, followed by a backstage visit (where Linda easily slipped into pre-McCartney rock photographer mode and snapped dressing room shots) and an after-party at Bowie's hotel.

What struck Paul, though, was the difference in Bowie's band since the last time he had seen him. Gone were the Spiders from Mars; instead, Bowie had an expansive ensemble that included not only guitar, bass, drums and keyboards (Earl Slick, Herbie Flowers, Andy Newmark and Mike Garson, respectively), but also a pair of backing singers (Gui Andrisano and Warren Peace), a percussionist (Pablo Rosario), and a wind section, led by music director Michael Kamen (who played oboe as well as Moog and electric piano), with David Sanborn on alto sax and flute, and Richard Grando on baritone sax and flute.*

The idea of adding winds to the basic rock band model was nothing new. Common in the 1950s,

* The Bowie show that Paul heard on June 29 was recorded two weeks later, on July 11 and 12, at the Tower Theater in Philadelphia, and released as *David Live* on October 29, 1974 (with expanded versions issued in 1990 and 2005).

and an important component of the Motown sound that Paul had always loved, horns were now being embraced by bands that had been entirely guitar-driven in the 1960s. The Rolling Stones had a brass section when Paul saw them in New York in 1972, and George Harrison's band for his Bangladesh benefit used saxophones, trumpets and trombone.

But seeing Bowie, the consummate Glam-Rocker, now transformed into a quasi-R&B powerhouse, backed by winds and boasting a more soulful sound, impressed Paul. He was already thinking of adding brass to 'Wide Prairie.' Now he wondered about grafting horns onto Wings, for both concerts and recordings.

Raising the idea with Killen, Paul first proposed engaging the Memphis Horns. When they were unavailable, Killen suggested hiring Tony Dorsey, a trombonist and arranger who lived in Macon, Georgia, but was often in Nashville writing arrangements for the soul singer Joe Tex and others who recorded for Dial Records, another Killen-owned business. Killen arranged for McCartney and Dorsey to meet at the Sound Shop on July 8.

In the meantime, Wings continued to work out their kinks, personally and musically. They devoted two and a half hours to a photo session on July 1. They then retired to the garage for rehearsal, part of which was spent batting around ideas about the band's stage presentation. The subject was clearly important to Paul; it was part of the next day's post-rehearsal discussion as well. The band attended a local pool party, on an invitation secured by Crowder, on the night of July 2. And on July 3, they added the old Moody Blues hit 'Go Now'—a crowd-pleasing vocal spot for Laine during the 1973 British tour—to the rehearsal list.

Everyone but Geoff spent that evening at the home of Johnny and June Carter Cash, where singer-songwriter Roy Orbison was also a guest. Geoff had a date at the Speedway Stadium, where he and his girlfriend, Dottie, saw Freddy King, the Charlie Daniels Band, and Marshall Tucker. Heather spent much of the visit to the Cash home with four-year-old John Carter Cash and his nanny, a Mrs. Kelly, in the Cashes' barn, surrounded by goats, chickens and peacocks. Paul and Linda were amused that on the drive back, Heather "was talking Southern," as Paul joked soon afterward, adding an imitation in a mock Southern drawl, "'Oh, those chickens are so *beau*tiful.'"[41]

Paul and the band did not rehearse on July 4, instead attending a party on a guarded private estate. Rehearsals picked up on the fifth, with the band finally working up an arrangement of Paul's new country number, 'Sally G.' In the evening, the McCartneys threw another lakeside barbecue party, with a guest list that included Roy Orbison, Chet Atkins, Jimmy Reed, and Felice and Boudleaux Bryant, the husband-and-wife songwriting team that composed many of the Everly Brothers' hits. Unusually, the band's local girlfriends were invited as well.

"Linda was sometimes funny about other people hanging about," Britton remembered, "but [the girlfriends] were all accepted. They became friends with her, they were all okay."[42]

Dan Ealey, a 20-year-old bass player and McCartney obsessive who had befriended the band, and who turned up at the farm most days to chat with the players and listen (from a distance) to the rehearsals, was asked to man the gate. Ealey had arrived at Curly's farm several days earlier armed with press credentials that *Melody Maker*'s man in America, Chris Charlesworth, had sent him in the hope of getting on-the-scene reports. Ealey spent time with Laine, McCulloch and Britton in the gatehouse and hoped to scoop the rest of the music press by getting an interview with his idol, but Paul was not biting.

Ealey contributed to Britton's woes that evening. For reasons unknown, he had a powerful firework with him, and when Britton saw it, he thought it might be fun to blow up the Putmans' mailbox. That resulted in an upbraiding from Paul, Linda and Alan Crowder the next morning.

That was not the end of Britton's problems. His foot still bothering him, he paid another visit to the hospital, on July 8, where the foot was X-rayed and put in a plaster cast. Paul had scheduled another session at the Sound Shop that evening. Fortunately for Britton, who was told to remain immobile at the farm while his cast set, his drumming was not needed this time.

Recording Session

Monday, July 8, 1974.
The Sound Shop Studio, 1307 Division Street, Nashville.
Overdubbing: 'Hey Diddle' and 'Wide Prairie.'

Still focusing on material for *Cold Cuts* and Linda's Suzy and the Red Stripes projects, Paul's goal for the session was to add some Nashville fiddling to the unfinished tracks. The first part of the session was devoted to 'Hey Diddle,' an odd little concoction Paul wrote at High Park during the summer of 1970, affixing the opening phrase of a nursery rhyme to what is essentially a torch song. McCartney recorded the song's basic tracks with guitarist Hugh McCracken and drummer Denny Seiwell in New York on October 26, 1970—and then shelved it. But Nashville was clearly the right place to finish it: consciously or not, he may have got the idea for the finishing scoring from the part of the nursery rhyme's opening line that he did not quote: *"Hey diddle, diddle, the cat and the fiddle."*

It was to embellish this track and 'Wide Prairie' that Paul had Killen engage Margie and Marcy Cates, the violin-playing sister act he saw at the Grand Ole Opry on June 28. This proved a logistical challenge for the duo. On tour promoting their new single, a cover of Bill Monroe's 'Uncle Pen,' they had a show the night before in West Grove, Pennsylvania, some 600 miles northeast of

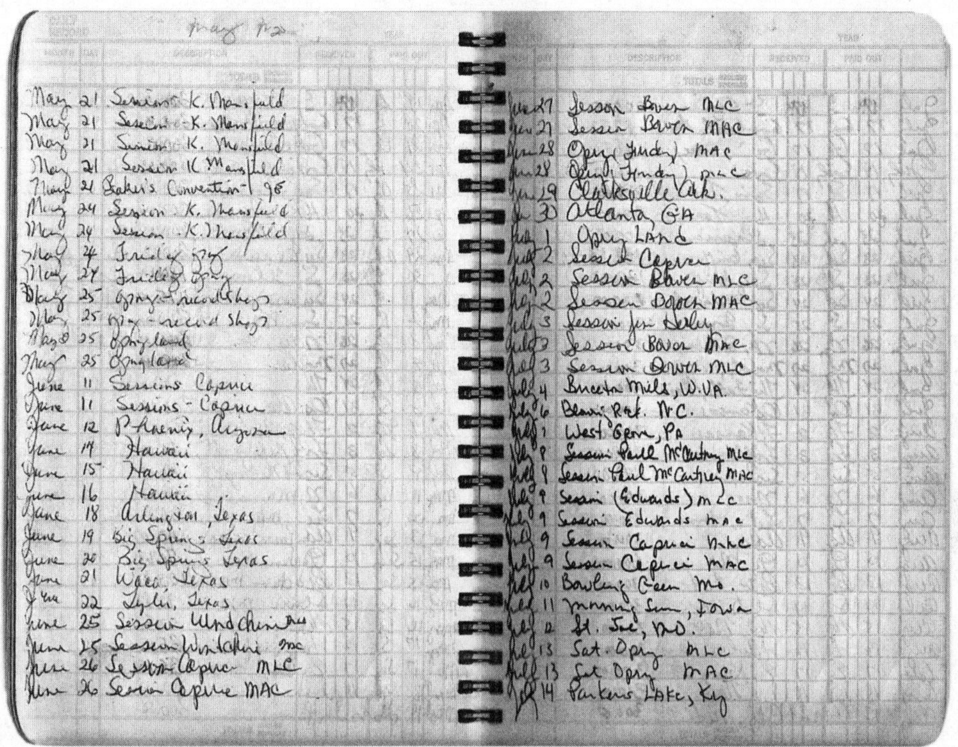
May 21 Session K. Mansfield
May 21 Session K. Mansfield
May 21 Session K. Mansfield
May 21 Session K. Mansfield
May 21 Baker's Convention
May 24 Session K. Mansfield
May 24 Session K. Mansfield
May 24 Friday Opry
May 24 Friday Opry
May 25 Opry–record shop
May 25 Opry–record shop
May 25 Opryland
May 25 Opryland
June 11 Sessions Capuci
June 11 Sessions – Capuci
June 12 Phoenix, Arizona
June 14 Hawaii
June 15 Hawaii
June 16 Hawaii
June 18 Arlington, Texas
June 19 Big Spring, Texas
June 20 Big Spring Texas
June 21 Waco, Texas
June 22 Tyler, Texas
June 25 Session Windchimes
June 25 Session Windchimes MAC
June 26 Session Capuci MLC
June 26 Session Capuci MAC
Jun 27 Session Baver MLC
Jun 27 Session Baver MAC
Jun 28 Opry (Friday) MAC
Jun 28 Opry (Friday) MLC
Jun 29 Clarksville
Jun 30 Atlanta, GA
July 1 Opry Land
July 2 Session Capuci
July 2 Session Baver MLC
July 2 Session Baver MAC
July 3 Session
July 3 Session Baver MAC
July 3 Session Baver MLC
July 4 Bruceton Mills, W.VA.
July 6 N.C.
July 7 West Grove, PA
July 8 Session Paul McCartney MLC
July 8 Session Paul McCartney MAC
July 9 Session (Edwards) MLC
July 9 Session Edwards MAC
July 9 Session Capuci MLC
July 9 Session Capuci MAC
July 10 Bowling Green Mo.
July 11 , Iowa
July 12 St. Joe, MO.
July 13 Sat. Opry MLC
July 13 Sat. Opry MAC
July 14 Parkers Lake, Ky

Marcy and Margie Cates' schedule for May–July 1974

Nashville. Up and on their tour bus well before dawn, they made the 12-hour drive back to Nashville in time for the 6 P.M. session.

"The session, for us as musicians, was typical—the Nashville way," Marcy Cates explained. "Listen to the song a couple of times, write a chord chart as you listen, start playing along, experimenting and getting ideas with the producer. When you find something he likes, start putting tracks down.

"On 'Hey Diddle,' the Cajun lick we played came naturally. Paul and everyone thought it was an obvious fit. The other lick we played towards the end of the song was an idea from Paul. He sang it to us and had us work it in. After we got the track recorded, we doubled it."[43]

For 'Wide Prairie,' the Cates Sisters were joined by two more violinists, Vassar Clements and Johnny Gimble. This was a more complicated overdub, a combination of what Marcy Cates described as "fiddle" and "string" parts—the fiddle parts played in a robust, folksy style, and the string parts in a more formal, orchestral way. As on 'Hey Diddle,' once the players and Paul settled on the parts, they recorded and then doubled them.

"Linda was there also and came in and chatted with us a little," Margie said. "We talked about

Southern cooking, and she said she would just as soon have a dinner of pinto beans and cornbread as a fancy gourmet meal. We said that if they came back to Nashville, we could fix them a real Southern meal. . . . Marcy and I were both so impressed with how humble and warm Paul and Linda both were. They both could not have been nicer."[44]

They were also struck by Paul's sense of humor.

"At one point during the session," Marcy remembered, "Paul came out in the studio and said they had a great idea for a title—'One Hand Clapping.'* At the time I didn't know if he meant it for a song title, album, or what. But we all had a big laugh about it."

During the session, Tony Dorsey stopped in to meet Paul and discuss the arrangements he was hired to make. The tracks in question were Paul's smoky quasi-jazz instrumental 'Mood Music' and Linda's 'Wide Prairie.' Paul gave Dorsey little to work with.

"When I got there," Dorsey said, "I didn't really get to interact with Paul or anything, because he was busy doing some other things with Buddy and some country and western studio players. So Paul just said to me, 'Look, I've got this cassette—I want you to make horn parts out of what I have here.' When I took the cassette home and played it, it was just a single line that he played on the guitar."[45]

—

Wings gathered in Curly Putman's garage on July 9 to run down all the songs they had rehearsed until now, a setlist that included 'Jet,' 'Band on the Run,' 'Live and Let Die,' 'Let Me Roll It,' 'Hi, Hi, Hi,' 'Soily,' 'Bluebird,' 'Wild Life,' 'Go Now,' 'Medicine Jar,' 'Junior's Farm' and 'Sally G.' That afternoon, the group began working up 'Send Me the Heart,' the song Denny wrote after Paul challenged him to write a country tune.

The band also met with Brian Brolly. Brolly had returned to London once Wings got settled in Nashville, and he was now back to dangle contracts before the band. Brolly proposed a two-year contract in which the musicians were guaranteed a percentage of the box office when Wings toured, plus royalties on recordings.

The band had mixed feelings about the offer: Britton and McCulloch—the latter optimistic that Robert Stigwood would soon release him from his contract with RSO—felt that a contract represented stability and were in favor. Laine, who had been through non-productive contract talks during the first iteration of Wings, objected that a contract would make him an MPL employee rather than a bandmate. It also bothered him that the contracts put him on the same plane as the

* The phrase comes from a Zen koan often attributed to the eighteenth-century monk Hakuin, who would ask his students, "Who can hear the sound of one hand clapping?" as a thought exercise to help them transcend logical reasoning in their pursuit of enlightenment.

newbies, McCulloch and Britton, when in his view, his longer tenure, and his work on *Band on the Run* should have entitled him to a more elevated status.

"The idea was really designed to make the other two guys feel more secure," Denny said of the contract proposal, "but first of all, I decided I didn't want to sign it because I'd never been on that kind of relationship with Paul anyway. Then it seemed like there was no point in having Wings on the basis of 'You're in the band—sign here.' We've got to have that fluid thing. Like, in the studio we might want to bring in other musicians, and maybe the other two guys won't be on every track.

"Also, with the three of us having been together for such a long time you can't expect the other two to be so established. They've got to grow into it just like we've had to."[46]

By the end of the meeting, the contracts in Brolly's briefcase remained unsigned, and three years after the two Dennys joined Wings on a "hippy handshake," Paul's new charges remained on the same bohemian deal while they argued the merits of freedom versus security.

Recording Sessions

Wednesday, July 10–Thursday, July 11, 1974.
The Sound Shop Studio, 1307 Division Street, Nashville.
Recording: 'Sally G' and 'Send Me the Heart.'
Overdubbing: 'Sally G,' 'Send Me the Heart,' 'Hey Diddle,' 'Bridge on the River Suite' (formerly 'Mood Music') and 'Wide Prairie.'

Having tinkered with old recordings at his Nashville sessions so far, Paul decided it was time to record something new, and to see how the current lineup of Wings worked in the studio. Having been charmed by the country players' contributions at the last session, he asked Killen to engage a couple of fiddlers and a pedal steel player for the session.

Paul had been mulling over pedal steel players in recent days, not only with Killen, but with band members and Alan Crowder, who had been asking locals who Paul should engage whenever he ran into someone who knew the local talent pool. Pete Drake, then one of Nashville's hottest and best-known players, was mentioned by several people, but Crowder said that Paul wanted someone else—not because he disliked Drake or his playing, but because both Ringo Starr and George Harrison had used him prominently, and Paul did not want to appear to be following their lead.

Killen's solution was to bring in Lloyd Green. Like Drake, Green was a member of the group of top-flight session players known as the Nashville A Team. Among the thousands of recordings he played on (he averaged 400 sessions a year), Green is heard on Tammy Wynette's 1968 recording of the Curly Putman song 'D-I-V-O-R-C-E.' Johnny Gimble returned on the fiddle.*

'Sally G' was committed to tape quickly, with Wings playing the basic track—Paul and Jimmy on acoustic guitars, Denny on bass, Geoff drumming with his foot in a plaster cast—followed by Green overdubbing a bright-edged, assertive pedal steel part and graceful dobro accenting, and Gimble adding atmospheric fiddling.† Before the end of the six-hour session, Green also added a pedal steel solo to 'Hey Diddle,' doubling the verse-long ocarina section that McCartney, Seiwell and McCracken recorded at the 1970 session. To give Green a live point of reference, Paul overdubbed another ocarina part alongside him in the studio.

"Paul was playing the ocarina," explains Winfrey, "but it's notorious for being out of tune. And it's unusual that Paul was able to play this thing and not be irritated by it. But he played the basic melody and Lloyd played a harmony part behind him. And Lloyd was really having to bend some notes in order to stay in tune with Paul's out-of-tune ocarina."[47]

When Green and Gimble left, Paul, Denny and Linda added lead and harmony vocals to 'Sally G.'

Paul booked a double session at the Sound Shop on July 11, working from 2 P.M. to 5:30 P.M. in the first, then from 6 P.M. to midnight after a short dinner break. Because the afternoon session was held when Wings typically rehearsed, the group took their places in the garage early that day, the main order of business being an arrangement of 'Send Me the Heart,' which had now morphed from a Denny Laine composition into a collaboration between Denny and Paul, and was set to be recorded at the evening session.

When Paul and company arrived at Killen's Division Street studio, Tony Dorsey was already there, as were the wind and brass players Killen had hired once he had a look at Dorsey's score: Thaddeus Richard, William Puett and Norman Ray, saxophones (with Richard listed as soloist in the American Federation of Musicians paperwork, and Ray specializing on baritone); George Tidwell and Barry McDonald, trumpets; and Dorsey and Dale Quillen, trombones.

Dorsey was still puzzled by Paul's having given him a tape with only the single musical line that he wanted orchestrated, rather than the full song, but he had no recourse but to do as Paul asked.

"All I did was transcribe what he had on the tape, and wrote it out for a horn section," Dorsey

* Many sources, including the *Venus and Mars Deluxe Edition* book, list Bob Wills among the players. However, Wills had stopped performing after a paralyzing stroke in 1969. He is not listed in the American Federation of Musicians paperwork for the session, which includes a single time card signed by Green and Gimble, and a contract for the two musicians. Also notable is that the musicians' union documents, which include contracts and time cards, list the session date as July 9. However, Geoff Britton's diary, which offers considerable detail about Wings' Nashville activities, lists only a rehearsal on the ninth, and places the session for 'Sally G' on the tenth. It is possible that whoever filled out the time card gave the incorrect date, which was transferred to the contract when it was prepared on July 25.

† Green opened his 1975 album *Steel Rides* with a cover of 'Sally G,' and released his version as a single. It was reported that McCartney wanted to engage him as a support act for Wings' 1976 American tour, but that Green, disinclined to give up studio work in Nashville, turned down the offer.

explained. "There was no conversation, no discussion of what kind of feel he wanted, and I had no musical input. It was just, 'Hey man, write me some horn parts.' When I returned for the session, the horns were there. We played it, and when we finished, he said, 'Good job,' and he wrote 'Good luck!' on one of the parts. And that was it."

'Mood Music,' as 'Bridge on the River Suite' was called when Paul last worked on it, on September 29, 1972, is an instrumental born of an easygoing studio jam on which McCartney and Seiwell laid down a solid, sometimes assertive rhythm track, against which Henry McCullough had a chance to stretch out with a solo line that moved between bluesy turns and harmonically more sophisticated jazz tracery, while Laine added light chording and occasional counterpoint to Henry's lead.

The line Paul wrote for Dorsey to score expanded upon a short figure Henry played near the end of the track. But where the guitar line is dreamy and exploratory, the horn figure is solid and driven, a melodic loop reminiscent of 'Ready for the River,' a 1928 foxtrot by Gus Kahn and Neil Morét. Paul asked for two more brief brass contributions toward the end of the instrumental—a laconic two-note (A-G) figure to fill out the texture behind Henry's lead, and sharp, textured chordal bursts, as punctuating figures. The brass additions completely transformed what had been a fairly bare track, magnifying its smoky lounge vibe.

Dorsey's memory of having no real musical input or interpretive freedom notwithstanding, the brass additions to Linda's 'Wide Prairie' were more freewheeling. Written during a February 1973 visit to Morocco, during the planning for the *James Paul McCartney* television special, and recorded in Paris nine months later, the song begins as a parody of a country tune that melts into an amorphous instrumental. In its Nashville incarnation, the track runs nearly 12 minutes, and while the brass contributions during the verses principally mirror the chords—played either solidly and syncopated against the vocal melody, or in arpeggiation—the seven-minute instrumental playout, to which the Cates Sisters, Vassar Clements and Johnny Gimble had already added a string bed, allowed for free-blowing saxophone and trumpet soloing.

The plan for the evening session was to record the new McCartney-Laine collaboration, 'Send Me the Heart'—a tune sung from the perspective of a man whose girlfriend has gone to Memphis to see her old lover and probably won't return, even though her old flame mistreats her. The protagonist's best offer, presented in the chorus: "*Send me the heart that's been broken in two / I'll mend it and send it back to you.*"

To supplement the Wings lineup and give the group the countrification the song needed, Killen brought in another of Nashville's star pedal steel players, Buddy Emmons, as well as pianist Shane Keister. Wings and company got a solid basic track—acoustic guitars, bass and piano—and the vocal harmonies, if not entirely polished, were well on the way. Emmons distinguished himself with a magnificent solo, as well as decorative figures throughout the song.

But there were problems along the way. Though the band had rehearsed potential parts for the song at the ranch, the addition of Emmons's lines left little space for McCulloch. After struggling to find a place in the song's texture, Jimmy lost his cool. Sensing the band's growing frustration, Alan Crowder asked Killen to play the heavy: walking into the studio and listening for a moment, Killen suggested that Jimmy sit out the rest of the session. McCulloch laid down his guitar and headed straight for the exit. A few hours later, angry and inebriated, he returned.

"Jimmy came into the studio, and it was obvious he'd been indulging in a few drinks," said Winfrey. "He sat down in front of the console, and he just kept mouthing off, he wasn't talking to anyone in particular. And next thing we knew, we see a Coke bottle fly at the glass, and clonk, hit it. So Buddy went down, and he got Jimmy by the arm and said, 'Jimmy, I think it's time to go.'"[48]

—

McCulloch's drunken tantrum cast a pall on the British encampment at Junior's farm the next day, and Paul was so unnerved and upset by it that he canceled the day's rehearsal. His frustration dissipated only at the end of the day, when he and Linda drove over to Chet Atkins's home at 1096 Lynnwood Boulevard, in Nashville, for dinner with Chet and his wife, Leona. In the course of the evening, Paul and Chet spoke about their work in progress, and Paul played several of his songs, old and new.

Somehow, the two musicians got to talking about their fathers, and Paul mentioned that his dad played in a dance band when he was young, and wrote a tune—apparently only one—in a lively jazz style.

"He used to have this one song," explained Paul, "which he'd play over and over on the piano. It was just a tune; there were no words to it. I actually remember him, when I was a real little kid, saying, 'Can anyone think of any words to this?' We all did try for a while; it was like a challenge."[49]

Vamping an off-the-cuff version of the song, called 'Eloise,' Paul mentioned that he had always fancied recording it—an idea Atkins encouraged.

"Paul played it for me and it's a pretty good little tune, kind of a [Hoagy Carmichael] 'Darktown Strutter's Ball' tune," said Atkins, "and I said, 'Why don't you record that sometime for your dad, it would be a great present.'[50] I knew it would be, because my dad wrote a song, and I recorded it and played it on guitar and published it. He made a few bucks off that thing, actually. He loved getting those $200 and $300 checks every quarter. He truly loved it, and it was one of the nicest things I could ever do for him, because I think he always wanted to be a songwriter."[51]

Atkins went beyond mere encouragement: he offered to round up some great players—Floyd

Cramer on piano, for starters—and record the song with McCartney at the Sound Shop. They penciled in the sixteenth—four days hence—for the session.

The evening yielded the seeds of a new McCartney song, as well.

"We were talking, and somehow we got on to him being very interested in ancient Egyptian history," Paul recalled. "And he said, 'Have you seen the book, *Secrets of the Great Pyramid*'?"

McCartney was not familiar with the 1971 book by Peter Tompkins, so as he and Linda were leaving, Atkins handed him a copy.

"I read it avidly, and it's a great little book because it goes into all the stuff, like the measurements of the circumference of the world being embodied in the measurements of [the Great Pyramid of] Giza; you know, the sacred measurements. . . . So I was now steeped in all these little legends and ideas that Chet had turned me on to."[52]

—

The evening on Chet Atkins's turf helped dispel Paul's irritation over McCulloch's breach of professionalism, and his growing alarm at the fact that the band was splitting into camps, with McCulloch openly critical of Linda and clearly not fond of Britton, and Laine trying to remain diplomatic but clearly becoming close with McCulloch and sharing his tendency to drink more than was prudent.

But the work had to go on, and Paul thought that perhaps a Wings-only recording session might reignite the band's enthusiasm and togetherness. The rehearsal session on Saturday, July 13, therefore, was devoted to getting 'Junior's Farm' into shape. The basics were already in place, since Paul had used a rough version of it during the drummer auditions, and he had completed the lyrics in Nashville. But it needed some arrangement touches to make it studio-ready.

Musically, 'Junior's Farm' is an unusually simple song with a purely visceral appeal. The first two lines of each verse are accompanied by a steadily pumping G major chord, then it's down to F major for the start of the verse-closing third line, which ends on an E minor chord. The chorus is even simpler, just an alternation of G major and F major.

Paul had written relatively few songs with a chord progression this simple since the early Beatles days. Melodically, too, the verses are pretty constricted, although he loosens up for the undeniably catchy chorus, "*Let's go, let's go, let's go, let's go, down to Junior's farm where I want to lay low.*" What catches the attention is the stream-of-consciousness lyric—a spliff in one hand, pen in the other exercise in lyric writing, with an idiosyncratic roster of characters filling no fewer than five verses (the sixth being a repeat of the first). But it also used an old trick that went back to the Beatles days and John Lennon's 'I Am the Walrus': present a colorful, other-world scenario, and listeners will feel challenged to figure it out, even if it's as opaque as "*Ollie*

Hardy should have had more sense / He bought a gee-gee and he jumped the fence / All for the sake of a couple of pence."*

The first order of business was to come up with an ear-catching intro. After trying several ideas, Paul settled on a fanfare-like figure with a harmonized twin lead guitar part and dramatic drum flourishes, repeated twice before settling into the steady rhythm of the verse.

With that sorted, it was time to take 'Junior's Farm' down to Buddy's studio.

Recording Session

Saturday, July 13, 1974.
The Sound Shop Studio, 1307 Division Street, Nashville.
Recording and Overdubbing: 'Junior's Farm.'

Wings arrived at the Sound Shop at 6 P.M. and played through 'Junior's Farm' with its new intro, but it struck Paul that something was still lacking. One obvious problem was that there was no bridge, just the verses, which were more talky than melodic, and the choruses. As the band continued rehearsing the song—with the Sound Shop's meter running at $110 (£46) an hour—Paul juggled the song's elements.

"Paul came in with the group and they had been rehearsing it," Winfrey recalled of the song's evolution in the studio. "But Paul in the course of running that song down, he would sometimes—if he wanted something in particular, from a particular instrument—he would go and play that instrument. Like, if there was a lick or two that he wanted Geoff Britton to play on the drums, he went and got behind the kit and showed Geoff what he wanted. Which was the case, actually, with Jimmy McCulloch too."[53]

After some experimentation, Wings arrived at a version that worked. After the intro, Paul would sing the first two verses, Jimmy providing short punctuating figures at the end of each, and then a single chorus. Jimmy would then take a verse-long guitar solo, which led to the third and fourth verses.

This time two choruses would follow, the second extended with a short line, *"everybody tag along,"* whereupon Jimmy and Denny would play the twin-guitar introduction again. Verses five and six would follow, along with two more choruses, the second including backing vocal repeti-

---

* A reference to American actor Oliver Norvell Hardy (1892–1957), one half of the famed comedy duo Laurel and Hardy. Paul was a big fan of their films, in particular *The Music Box* (1932).

tions of "*down to Junior's farm*," as well as *two* short extensions, "*everybody tag along*" and "*take me down to Junior's farm*."

To end the song, Paul introduced another new element. Instead of reinserting the twin-guitar intro, he had Jimmy play a short derivative of the figure, which he would double on bass before heading into an entirely new chord progression in E minor, played instrumentally first, then with a vocal vamp from Paul ("*take me back . . .*") before heading toward a G major finish.

"When he came into the studio to record a song, he had already formulated in his mind what he wanted it to sound like,"[54] Winfrey observed of McCartney's creative process. "He never missed a thing. If he heard something that was out of tune or out of pitch in the studio, he made sure that it was corrected."[55]

And with that, a song with a workaday chord progression, no bridge and peculiar lyrics was transformed into a prime contender for the band's next single—the first with the new lineup. At 10 P.M., Winfrey hit record, and Wings began tracking the song in earnest. For the basic track, Paul played bass, Denny and Jimmy played electric guitars—Jimmy's with a touch of fuzz—Linda played a simple (one chord per bar) Fender Rhodes electric piano part, and Geoff once again drummed through the pain with his plaster cast foot.

The overdubs included Paul's lead vocal, Paul, Linda and Denny singing harmony vocals, with Paul and Linda doubling their harmonies. Geoff added snare and high-hat touch-ups, and Linda added Moog synthesizer to the song's ending. With all 16 tracks used, Paul recorded a fresh bass line for the song's ending on the last few seconds of the track that had been used for Linda's harmony vocal doubling.

By 4 A.M., the song was finished to everyone's satisfaction. Paul and Linda headed home, while Jimmy, Denny and Geoff cruised off to meet their girlfriends.

Paul was hoping that the 'Junior's Farm' session would reset the band's collective spirit, and for a few hours, it appeared that it had: Geoff, perhaps with Denny and Jimmy, went to the Sunday afternoon show at the Speedway, where they heard Waylon Jennings, Poco and Leon Russell. After the show, they tagged along with Russell to a recording session at the Creative Workshop Studio.

But things began to unravel that evening. Dixie Gamble, who had been hearing from Killen about Paul's band-inspired woes, decided to see what she could do to help.

"I thought, 'Oh, I'll just throw a party for 'em, and maybe that will calm things down,'" Gamble explained. "I was living in a rental apartment, so I didn't have an appropriate space to do it, but a friend of mine had a beautiful home with a massive living room, and I was house-sitting for her. It was just Jimmy, Geoff, Denny and Alan Crowder, maybe a few others—it wasn't a lot of people.

"I felt pretty cool about it, everything was in control—until I looked up and Jimmy McCulloch was standing on my friend's antique glass coffee table. And I thought, 'Oh my God, I have made a serious mistake.' I was pretty naïve about drugs; I mean, in my world, the most anybody did was smoke a little pot and have a drink—it wasn't a heavy drug world, so I didn't have any concept of how things get out of control quickly. I just remember having this sinking feeling because my friend had white, shag carpet in her living room, and the house was all glass. And I'm thinking, 'Oh, my goodness, this is not good.'"[56]

Describing McCulloch as "batshit crazy," Gamble felt in peril of having her friend's house trashed, particularly since Laine's amusement at his colleague's misbehavior seemed only to fuel McCulloch. Gamble quickly enlisted Crowder to calm things down and get the musicians out of her friend's house without causing any damage.

Britton, Laine and McCulloch went their separate ways after the party, but when Britton walked out of the cottage on Monday, July 15, the first thing he saw was the Lincoln Continental that McCulloch had rented nose down in the stream that ran through the Putmans' property, its back end sitting on the bank. Once again, rehearsals were canceled.

Paul and Linda again dined with Chet Atkins, this time joined by Jerry Reed, at the Loveless Motel, where they ate country ham, buttermilk biscuits and okra, while running down the details for the recording of 'Eloise,' scheduled for the following evening. Paul also mentioned his desire to get out on the road with the latest incarnation of Wings. "Man, if I was Paul McCartney, I'd *buy* the road,"[57] Reed quipped.

Wings, meanwhile, continued to try Paul's patience. When he, Linda and Britton turned up at the garage for rehearsals the next day, Jimmy and Denny were missing in action once again. With the Nashville trip coming to an end, Paul was having second thoughts about whether this new Wings lineup was working. When McCulloch and Laine finally sauntered in, 45 minutes late, Paul read them the riot act—and they walked out.

"Jimmy and Denny buzzed off, and I sat around with Linda and Paul listening to them moan about the others and the future of the group," Britton noted.[58]

Laine was brooding on his own at the gatehouse when Dan Ealey arrived to collect some bootleg albums and a right-handed bass he had lent the guitarist a few days earlier.

"He was sitting on the sofa," Ealey recalled, "he never looked up, and he was glaring at a fly swatter. And I stepped in and said, 'Hey Denny, do you know where my McCartney stuff is?' and he said, 'Don't mention that fucking name to me.' And he never looked up."

The young fan quietly gathered his possessions and eased out the door. Outside he found a flustered Alan Crowder. "What's wrong with them?" asked Ealey, gesturing toward the gatehouse. "You have to understand, Dan, Paul is a superstar," Crowder said. "And he expects to be treated like one."[59]

That afternoon, Paul telephoned his father for a refresher on 'Eloise.' In particular, he could not remember the song's bridge. As he often did when Paul quizzed him about "that song you wrote," Jim McCartney denied having "written" it, taking the expression literally. "I don't really write songs," is how he put it. "I just think them up."[60] At 70, Jim was afflicted with arthritis, but at Paul's request, he played the tune to his son over the phone, whereupon Paul realized that the reason he could not remember the bridge was that there wasn't one.

Recording Session

Tuesday, July 16, 1974.
The Sound Shop Studio, 1307 Division Street, Nashville.
Recording and Overdubbing: 'Eloise' (working title of 'Walking in the Park with Eloise').

When Paul, Linda, Geoff and Denny arrived at the Sound Shop at 6 P.M., Atkins and his crew were setting up in the studio and chatting with Winfrey and Killen. The full ensemble included McCartney on bass, Laine on acoustic guitar, Britton on drums, Atkins on electric guitar, Floyd Cramer on piano, Bobby Thomson on banjo, Bill Puett on clarinet, Don Sheffield on trumpet and Dennis Good on trombone.

With the other musicians watching, Paul and Chet played through the song a few times, giving its minimal materials—an energetic melody, redolent of 1930's jazz, repeated several times—a sense of structure and variety by charting out scoring changes on each verse, throwing in a modulation to take the piece from G major to A-sharp major in the closing verses, and adding a stylistically apt chromatic figure to the ending.

Paul opted to record the tune with the full band playing live in the studio, the way it would have been recorded in the 78 rpm era, when his father wrote it for his Jim Mac's Jazz Band. The arrangement Paul worked out began with Puett, Sheffield and Good stating the melody on their own, and then with a bouncy accompaniment from the full ensemble. Atkins then took a fluid solo over Paul's walking bass line before ceding the spotlight to Cramer, who contributed a rippling piano solo. Cramer and Atkins then traded short variations on the melody, and the winds retook center stage to bring the song to a close.

It took only a few takes to get a performance that Paul found entirely satisfactory, but he decided to do one overdub after all—a percussive nod to his Liverpool roots, played on a Brass King brand washboard he found at a local flea market and brought to the session on a hunch that it might be useful.

"To them, a washboard was so comical," remembered McCartney, "but to us it meant skiffle groups. It was a steel one, too, which is much better than glass."[61]

As Winfrey was setting up to record that final touch, Paul had a couple of visitors, Gordon Stoker and his son Brent. Gordon was a friend of Killen's, whom the publisher knew Paul would be interested in meeting, since he had been a member of the Jordanaires, the vocal group that backed Elvis Presley.

"We got there around 7:30 P.M.," recalled Brent, who at the time was a serious enough Beatles fan to have scrapbooks full of articles about the group and its individual members. "We were in the control room when Paul recorded the washboard percussion. Linda was taking Polaroid pictures at that time, and I watched them develop as Paul continued to record. After he finished and came back into the control room, Buddy introduced him to my dad. He said, 'We listened to you guys singing harmony because that's what we wanted to do,' and they sat around talking about Elvis.

"Dad was always the soul of diplomacy and didn't want to overstay his welcome, so after a while he said, 'Paul, we should go—thank you very much for your time and hospitality.' And Paul said, 'Oh, no, no, please stay and listen to everything we've recorded in Nashville—we're going to listen to everything back.' So Dad said, 'Sure, okay,' and they played us everything. We were there for about 90 minutes. When we left the studio, Paul turned to us and said, 'See ya, chaps!'"[62]

Happy with 'Eloise' and the rest of the recordings, Paul asked Winfrey to do a mix.

When his part in the 'Eloise' session was finished, Britton met his girlfriend, Dottie, and went to another studio where Waylon Jennings was recording. They did not stay long, but when they left, they ended up in a car crash with a drunken Jimmy McCulloch, who plowed a borrowed Volkswagen into Dottie's car. Both cars were drivable so Britton had McCulloch follow him back to the Sound Shop, where Paul was still holding court, on the theory that he could stay there until he sobered up.

McCulloch soon thought otherwise, however, and left the studio, only to get himself into deeper trouble. In the early hours of July 17, McCulloch was arrested and thrown into jail for reckless driving. McCulloch called Crowder, who knew that if anyone could sort this out, Killen could.

"About three o'clock in the morning my bedroom telephone woke me from a deep sleep. It was Alan Crowder. 'I say, Buddy,' he said in his English accent. 'I hate to have to wake you this way, but it seems we have a slight problem.' 'What's the problem, Alan?' I asked.

"'Well,' he said, 'it seems that Jimmy has gone and gotten himself arrested and they have him in the clinker.' 'OK, I'll take care of it,' I said."[63]

Killen called his attorney, William F. Carpenter Jr., and the pair headed down to the police station in the early hours of the morning. Carpenter arranged for an emergency session at the local night court, and after agreeing to cover the cost of the damage to both cars, McCulloch was released. "You have some very powerful friends in Nashville,"[64] the judge commented.

Jimmy, Denny and Geoff were scheduled to leave Nashville on Thursday, July 18, with Geoff and Denny returning to London and Jimmy spending a few days in New York. That was not a moment too soon for Paul and Linda, who considered remaining a few more days so that they could enjoy Nashville without the aggravation of running a band.

Paul had little planned for July 17, other than an afternoon press conference and tying up loose ends with Killen and Putman. But he was angry and unsettled, and wondered whether continuing with Wings was worth the trouble. He was especially irritated with Jimmy, who had been a problem all through the trip and who appeared to exert a corrupting influence on Denny.

Geoff was more of a puzzle: Paul easily tolerated the eccentricity of Geoff's wearing his karate gi to rehearsals, and he respected Geoff's devotion to training, although his arrival at the band's first extended period of rehearsals with a broken foot, caused by a karate accident, was not a good sign. He also could have done without Geoff's firing a gun or blowing up the Putmans' mailbox, too, but those misdemeanors paled in comparison with throwing tantrums at the Sound Shop, running his car into Putman's stream or landing in jail, and at this point Paul found him to be not only a solid drummer, but the most reliable and easiest to work with of the current Wings.

"Paul and Linda had a talk with me about the group's future," was Britton's memory of the morning of July 17. "They came to see me about blowing out the other two guys and going back to England and re-forming the band. Paul said, 'It's my name out there, and they've done this, and they've done that.' And I didn't think that was a good idea.

"I defended them, saying that every band has people like that—we've just got to accommodate them, value them for the contribution they make, which is the music. And on that level, there were no problems. All right, Jimmy made Linda cry sometimes when he was a bit drunk and she was fluffing bits, but she held her end up, you know, it sounded great. And when it sounds great that's all you need to know. When we were in that garage, playing, there was magic, and you can't fabricate that. Musically, we gelled."[65]

But nerves were raw all around. "It was a trial for all of us," Denny Laine observed of Wings' time in Nashville. "It gave everybody a chance to say his piece, and for a while it was so pressurized that for the first time I really began to think seriously about leaving."[66]

Paul calmed down sufficiently to put off his decision to disband Wings, but the contracts drawn up by Brian Brolly were torn up, along with any chance of the group earning royalties on Wings records or percentages of box office receipts.

By the time of the press conference, Paul's optimism, or at least a persuasive facsimile, had returned. The press conference was a bit different—more homespun—than those Paul had typically given since early in the Beatles days, where he would sit at a table on a raised platform, the press lobbing questions from the floor. In keeping with the loose Nashville vibe, Paul held the conference on Curly Putman's front porch, Paul sitting on an old rocking chair, with Linda beside him, and reporters for the local papers, TV and radio stations loosely arrayed on the steps and lawn.

For nearly an hour, the McCartneys fielded questions about their experiences in Nashville, what they thought of the Sound Shop, which country stars they met or worked with, whether they were considering moving to America (Paul allowed that while the 90 percent income tax he paid in England was too high, he was happy not to deal with tornado or earthquake threats), and whether they might be touring soon. After Linda mentioned enjoying the country ham at the Loveless Motel, a reporter who had read reports of their interest in vegetarianism asked about that, to which Paul replied, "We were, for a while, vegetarians, but I like bacon too much."

Probably Paul's most revealing response of the afternoon—but one the gathered reporters, unaware of the tensions within Wings, would not make much of—came when Paul was asked to discuss Wings' current roster.

"Well, we've got Geoff here," he said, indicating Britton, who was standing behind him, at the corner of the porch. "Geoff Britton, who's drumming for us. And *at the moment* we've got Denny Laine and Jimmy McCulloch, who are two guitarists, and me and Linda. That's it, *it's not a strict format.*" [All emphases ours.] To which Linda added, "We might get other people in. We might change people." Whereupon Paul, emphasizing the fluidity that had never been part of his concept of Wings until now, added, "It's a kind of loose thing, you know."

"Did a member of your band get in trouble here the other night?" a reporter probed.

"Yeah, I think so, yes," Paul confirmed. "But I'd rather not talk about it."[67]

When the reporters left, and the photographers were satisfied that they had enough casual shots of Paul and Linda on the porch holding tea cups or riding Paul's new Honda XR75 together, Paul called another band meeting.

For four hours, Paul expressed his frustrations with the way the Nashville trip had gone and his feeling that while Jimmy was a great guitarist, he needed to get his personal life together if he was going to have a future in Wings. It was an intervention, of sorts.

"I think he realizes you can't be that untogether in this business," Paul said of Jimmy shortly after the Nashville trip. "You end up like a few of the people you can remember who died a few years back, just because they're not quite in control. I mean, it's a heavy trip. . . . It gets to you occasionally and that's when you've got to be able to think, 'I won't reach for the bottle' 'cos that's every film you've ever seen. I think you've just gotta learn to do it within yourself."[68]

At one point, both Jimmy and Denny said they wanted to quit the band, only to reverse course. Gradually, tempers were tamped down and everyone agreed to move forward. For Paul, though, the good vibes were provisional: the problems were settled for the moment but he knew that further eruptions were possible, perhaps even likely, and his patience was not infinite.

Recording Session

Wednesday, July 17, 1974.
The Sound Shop Studio, 1307 Division Street, Nashville.
Overdubbing and Mixing: 'Send Me the Heart.'

Wings' final session in Nashville was devoted to Denny's vocals on his country tune, the one element of the July 11 recording that both Denny and Paul thought needed improvement. After a handful of takes, they both declared themselves satisfied. Winfrey prepared a mix and appended it to the reel with his mixes of 'Wide Prairie,' 'Hey Diddle,' 'Bridge on the River Suite,' 'Sally G,' 'Junior's Farm' and 'Eloise.' Paul took that reel and his small stack of 16-track masters and was back at Putman's by midnight.

Denny, Jimmy and Geoff flew out of Nashville's Metropolitan Airport at 2:45 P.M. on July 18; limousines, arranged by MPL, were waiting for Geoff and Denny when they arrived in London the next morning.

Back at Junior's farm, Paul and Linda met with the Putmans, who quickly put an end to their hope of extending their stay. "The day they left," Bernice Putman said, "they really didn't want to leave. They asked if they could stay a couple of days longer and we had to tell them we were ready to get back to our house."[69]

Besides, there was damage to undo. Paul had already arranged to replace the Putmans' exploded mailbox, but Mary and Stella had drawn on the walls of the upstairs bedrooms. The Putmans were relieved that the children's artwork was the worst of the damage, and Paul wrote a check to cover the repair.

That afternoon, the McCartneys rented a car and a truck—the former for Paul, Linda and the girls, the latter for their 30 pieces of luggage and Paul's new motorbike—and headed east on Interstate 40 to begin their 1,025-mile trek to New York.

4

TEN HANDS CLAPPING

Paul told his Nashville friends that he planned to ride his Honda motorbike to New York, raising some skepticism from people who had seen him ride. As it turned out, even driving the car he rented for the trip proved to be a challenge. Having got a late start, they made it only to Knoxville, 180 miles to the east, before deciding to stop at a motel for the night. Upon checking in and checking out of their room, they returned to the car to hunt for a restaurant, only to find that it would not start. Paul left the keys with the motel clerk, asking him to get the vehicle repaired, and called a cab to take his clan to dinner. Upon his return he learned that there was nothing actually wrong with the car: it was equipped with an "interlock"—a device that prevented it from starting unless all the seat belts were fastened. The enterprising clerk told the story to a stringer for United Press International, and by the next morning, the embarrassing episode was in newspapers across the United States.

With that inauspicious start, the McCartneys made their way to New York, where they remained for two weeks, based at the Eastmans' summer house in East Hampton. Catching up with the music trades, Paul was pleased to learn that Wings and *Band on the Run* cleaned up at the *Record World* Awards, with the album taking the top prize in both the group and vocal combo categories and Wings also topping the Featured Vocalist from Group and Vocal Combo fields. Turning to *NME*, he found *Band on the Run* at the top of the paper's album chart, and the single at No. 5, coinciding with the appearance of full-page advertisements headed "We're Over the Moon" and thanking everyone who contributed to the album's success.

After a couple of days of family visiting, Paul and Linda went into Manhattan on their own. "We left [the girls] for the first time this summer when we were visiting my dad on Long Island," Linda reported. "We went into New York for two whole days without them. It was like a dirty weekend."[1]

In Manhattan, they visited John and May in their new apartment at 434 East 52nd Street, a penthouse overlooking the East River. It was a tumultuous time for John and May, who had moved into the apartment toward the end of June. Shortly after Paul visited them in Malibu, May began to feel that John was pulling away from her—behaving sullenly, spending hours reading beside the pool, and saying he wanted to be alone.

The sessions for Harry Nilsson's album kept John focused and out of trouble, but they had not been going well. Harry's excesses had taken a toll on his voice; indeed, when John finally responded to May's pleas to know what was on his mind, he told her that Nilsson had been coughing up blood—the consequence, he thought, of continuing to record vocals during a bout of the flu. In late April, John told May that he was taking Harry to New York to finish the album—and that he was going alone. May was hurt, puzzled, and unsure of her future, and reports that John was spending time with Yoko rattled her further.

Nevertheless, on May 27, a more cheerful Lennon asked May to come to New York. When she arrived, she found her mercurial lover intent on staying relatively sober—not giving up drink entirely but avoiding the drunken scenes that had brought him unwanted publicity in Los Angeles—and throwing himself into work. Moreover, he soon suggested they find an apartment—they had been staying at May's small studio apartment, and then at the Pierre Hotel, on 61st Street at Fifth Avenue—with a room for Julian, who was due to visit at the end of July. And with work on Nilsson's album virtually complete, John was writing songs for a new album of his own, although the return of 40 reels of multitrack masters for his rock oldies project, in Phil Spector's possession until now, temporarily delayed that plan.

If John seemed busy, his lawyers were busier. He was still fending off the United States government's attempt to deport him. There were two suits involving Allen Klein—*ABKCO Industries v. John Lennon*, and *ABKCO Industries v. Apple*. At the end of June, he settled a suit that ATV Music had brought against him in 1973, challenging his songwriting collaboration with Yoko, much as the company had challenged Paul's collaboration with Linda. John's settlement was similar to that ATV reached with Paul: John would remain an ATV composer until February 1980, in exchange for a cash payment and a co-publishing agreement with Ono Music, backdated to February 1973 (plus incidentals like space in ATV's New York offices).[2]

And, of course, negotiations continued on the Apple dissolution agreement. "I want to settle all this," John told May about the Apple talks, "but I still want to know what everyone wants from me and what I have to give away. And I don't want to give up *anything* that's mine."[3]

Before they drove into Manhattan, Paul telephoned Yoko to establish John's whereabouts, and was given the phone number at his new apartment. The McCartneys arranged to visit John and May at their new digs on July 26, and they returned for a second visit the next day. Julian, who landed in New York on July 25, had not seen Paul in several years, and told him he had memories of his dad and Paul playing music together at his house when he was growing up. And John and Paul reminisced about the Beatle years, finding that the passage of time had given them both some nuanced insights into those days.

"Paul was here, and we spent two or three nights together talking about the old days and it was cool, seeing what each other remembered from Hamburg and Liverpool," John told *Melody Maker*. "When we did a tour as the Beatles, we hated it and loved it. There were great nights and lousy nights. . . . I've got perspective now, that's a fact."[4]

May remembered the conversation as casual and friendly, though she thought both men were a bit wary. "They liked each other," she wrote in her memoir, "yet they seemed to feel fragile and uncertain, and they dealt with the feelings by pretending nothing at all had ever been wrong."[5]

Linda saw that simply as John having mellowed, but her view was also colored by the disillusioning experiences of the six weeks in Nashville, trying to mold the new version of Wings into a cohesive unit while getting their players to behave responsibly, rather than like newly minted rock and rollers. At the moment, however difficult the end of the Beatles was, there was still a lot to be said for a band that interacted as intuitively as they had.

"It was great," she said of John, "he's cooled down. We see all of [the other Beatles] now. Let's face it, they're all great, they are all immensely talented, and if they did get together, I don't think anybody would mind. Whether they will or not—who knows? They don't have Klein [as their manager] anymore. In fact, they're suing Klein now. John said to Paul, 'Yes, Paul, you were right, but, then, you always were.' I think that in a way they are all thankful."[6]

The visit happened, in fact, during an unusually Beatley moment, at least in the United States. February 1974 had been the tenth anniversary of the group's first visit to America, their epochal three-performance run on the *Ed Sullivan Show*, their American concert debut at the Washington Coliseum, and their first New York concerts at Carnegie Hall. The same evening that Paul and Linda visited John and May, Joe Pope, the editor of *Strawberry Fields Forever*, a Beatles fan magazine founded in 1972, presented the first Beatles Appreciation Convention, a weekend-long celebration of the Fab Four at the Hotel Bradford, in Boston. And in New York, Mark Lapidos, an assistant manager at a Sam Goody's record store in Manhattan, was planning Beatlefest, a similar gathering, scheduled for September 7 and 8 at the Commodore Hotel. At the end of April, Lapidos had approached John for his blessing, and got it. "I'm all for it! I'm a Beatles fan too," Lennon told him.[7]

On August 5, the McCartneys flew back to London, in time for Paul to sign the papers completing his freehold purchase of 1 Soho Square. Soon MPL would have a London headquarters worthy of its namesake.

—

It was time to write the next album, so Paul did what worked in the past: he took Linda and the girls up to High Park, where he could write and everyone could ride, their equine population now including three horses (Paul's Honor, Linda's Cinnamon and Jim McCartney's Drake's Drum) and two ponies (Coconut and Sugarfoot). Shortly after they arrived, in early August, they added a fourth horse, King, when its owner, a fan from Birkenhead who was unable to care for the animal properly, persuaded the McCartneys to adopt him.

For the McCartneys, part of the attraction of High Park was the routine of running the farm, something that appealed to their sense of having a place within the cycle of nature. In truth, they did not have to do farming's heavy lifting—that was handled by Duncan Cairns, the farmer they had hired as an overseer. But there were chores enough to impose structure on their days there.

"In the morning, there's the chickens' eggs to collect," Linda told *Mirabelle*, "and when that's done I set about preparing the breakfast. One good thing about being on the farm is that I've got time to do the cooking. After breakfast it's time to milk the cows and let the horses out. After all this has been done Paul often retires to his little studio and strums his guitar. By this time I'm probably preparing lunch.

"In the afternoon we might all go out riding, or sometimes I like to do some baking in the afternoons. By the time the evening comes everybody is pretty worn out. After the children are in bed, Paul and I often walk up a nearby hill and look out on the countryside. Everything's so peaceful, it's incredible."[8]

With a burst of confidence occasioned by the success of *Band on the Run*, Paul was toying with the notion of making the next Wings disc a concept album—a unified collection of songs that Wings could perform on tour. It was an idea that was in the air at the time. Asked by *Hit Parader* to single out albums he particularly admired, he pointed to Pink Floyd's *The Dark Side of the Moon* and, surprisingly, Mike Oldfield's *Tubular Bells*, a proto-Minimalist instrumental album on which each side plays without interruption, with repeating themes and instruments layered on gradually to create an expanding texture. The attraction, for Paul? "I just think they're very different," he said, quickly adding: "And I love Stevie (Wonder)'s stuff,"[9] a reference to albums like *Talking Book* and *Innervisions*, on which songs merged into each other.

"I play Stevie rather than Slade, and they probably do, too," he explained. "Yeah. I mean, there just is such a thing as Good Original Music. But I never closet myself off into a little corner and there's nothing else. Obviously, kids aged eight aren't going to be able to understand where *Dark Side of the Moon* is coming from. Me, I understand and associate with it totally."[10]

In Nashville, Paul had conveyed his observations about how popular music was changing to Laine, McCulloch and Britton, and gave them the sense that when it came time to record the next Wings album, he expected to keep pace with these developments.

"I think the next album will be more of a concept album than *Band on the Run*, a sort of *Dark Side of the Moon* in the sense of flowing things into one another," is how Denny Laine described the plan that summer, when Paul was in Scotland and the rest of the band were in London. "That's how the stage show is going to be as well. We're going to use more lights and effects and not so much of the 'the next number is . . .' Really, the whole album hasn't been wholly worked out yet, but it'll have some kind of lyrical theme, except I'm not going to say what it is. All I can say is Paul's been producing some sadder-type words than he's come up with for some time. Y'know, more like 'Eleanor Rigby,' that kind of feel."[11]

Laine may have based that last comment on having heard an early version of 'Treat Her Gently/ Lonely Old People,' but Paul's new crop of songs was hardly melancholy. One that he wrote fairly quickly was 'Spirits of Ancient Egypt,' a funky rocker with a chorus that suggested itself to Paul as he paged through *Secrets of the Great Pyramid,* the book Chet Atkins gave him.

The idea of a song about antiquity appealed to Paul, but beyond the first few lines of the chorus—"*Spirits of ancient Egypt / Shadows of ancient Rome*"—no story line came to him, so he vamped a verse, mostly around A major and E major chords, settling on a boilerplate lyric ("*You're my baby / and I love you*") and then toying with the succeeding lines until they were twisted into something from the world of 'Soily' or 'Junior's Farm.' "*You can take a pound of love / and cook it in the stew*" and "*You could sell an elevator / to Geronimo*" are not, after all, predictable rejoinders to the "*love ya baby!*" lines that open each verse, any more than "*hung on the tele' / hung on the tele' / hung on the telephone*" flows naturally from the evocations of antiquity that begin each chorus.

'Call Me Back Again,' the bluesy number he started in Los Angeles shortly before the Nashville trip, was more promising. He had only an opening verse and a refrain, but they were built around the kind of bluesy melody that typically drew inspired vocal embellishments from Paul.

Among the songs written fully at High Park, two—'You Gave Me the Answer' and 'I'll Give You a Ring'—suggested themselves to Paul on August 17, when he caught a Saturday morning broadcast of *Funny Face*, the 1957 film starring Fred Astaire and Audrey Hepburn, with songs by George and Ira Gershwin.

"Nearly always with me, it's something I've seen on telly, or film, or on radio," he said of his sources of inspiration. "I've seen something that gets me going, you know, a great act or something. And I can't help it, I sort of—you copy, or you adapt it to your own thing."[12]

Funny Face is an odd concoction. Though it uses the title of a 1927 Gershwin musical (which also starred Astaire), the film's plot and song list are quite different. But it sparked up Paul's inner music hall fan—the same side of him that was drawn to songs like 'Till There Was You' during the Beatles years, or that lapsed into the world of Jim Mac's Jazz Band to write pastiches like 'Honey Pie' or 'Gotta Sing, Gotta Dance' or, for that matter, what led him to record Jim's 'Eloise.'

'You Gave Me the Answer' channels both the spirit of the dance band era and Astaire's personality and vocal style, although as Paul imagined the song, it was by no means limited to an Astaire-like singer. On an early demo, he embellished the last line of the bridge—"*I can forget the airs and graces*"—first by repeating the final word in falsetto, with a piano flourish, and later by singing the same word in a mock operatic voice, with an almost Mozartian cadential decoration.

'I'll Give You a Ring,' which expands on an idea Paul played with earlier in the year, under the title 'You Look a Little Lonely,' is in the same spirit, with a wide-ranging melody inspired by the sophistication of 'Bonjour, Paris!' or 'On How to Be Lovely' (both included in *Funny Face*) and embracing the chromaticism that drives those songs.

"My dad never had [a record player], but he used to play on the piano, so that's how I heard them all," Paul said of the pop songs of the 1920s through 1940s. "I was a big fan of Fred Astaire. Still am. I just like that style: the wit in the old black and white movies, the little underdog who's really very sophisticated. The sophisticated underdog is a character I've always been very drawn to. I think in some ways it's because I've grown up in a working-class environment where there were some very clever people, but you wouldn't have known it to look at them. So this whole idea of the hidden talent in people I've always found very attractive.

"And I liked [Astaire's] voice. It was a funny little tenor, a soft little voice. And I liked a lot of the songs he did, so I was very attracted to that period through my dad, through Fred Astaire, through old movies, just through the general wit and sophistication of that era."[13]

Another notable song to emerge during this period was 'Now That She Is Mine,' a mid-tempo song with the potential to be a moderate rocker. Paul had only a few lines—"*Ah, she looks like snow / I want to put her in a Broadway show,*" and "*like a human being, so divine,*" plus the refrain, "*Oh—Now that she is mine.*" As he tinkered with the song through the summer, the refrain would be jettisoned and replaced with, "*Oh, I feel like letting go,*" and the title would change accordingly.

And finally, a paean to Scotland itself—and particularly, the area of Scotland where Paul's farm was located—was starting to take shape. Like the Astaire-inspired songs, this new one, called 'Mull of Kintyre,' was the product of Paul having assimilated a distinctive musical style and then synthesized a song with all the hallmarks of that style, mixed with Paul's own compositional thumbprints.

"I was just sitting around really, and I just thought about Scottish music," Paul said of the song's genesis. "And it occurred to me that all the Scottish stuff I'd ever heard, like, there was no real new stuff coming up. There were a few folk tunes here and then and a few comedy songs, but there wasn't the kind of things you think of as Scottish, you know, sort of 'Aye, by yon bonnie breeze.' There wasn't any modern stuff being written like that. So I decided to have a go at trying to do something that sounded like a kind of traditional type Scottish song."[14]

Like many Scottish ballads, 'Mull of Kintyre' has a slightly melancholy melody, but even more crucial, its tune can be sung easily over a sustained bass note—in effect, the drone of a bagpipe. And of course, the lyrics for this one could not be off-the-cuff; they had to embody the spirit of the place they are about. Paul had a start: "*Mull of Kintyre / Oh, fog rolling in off the sea / My desire is always to be here / Oh, Mull of Kintyre.*"

"Our place is on the Mull of Kintyre," Paul later explained. "But the Mull of Kintyre, there's about a hundred miles of it, I think. I was never sure actually—because I'd just always heard about it—and I had to ask them up there and said, 'Where exactly is the Mull of Kintyre?' Because I thought it might just be one little place.

"At first, I was just getting the melody [together]. I was just on the piano in Scotland, and you can't help seeing the mist rolling in from the sea because it does it quite often."[15]

By late August, Paul had a stack of new songs started, and a few completed, so he sat down at the more or less in-tune upright piano he and Linda kept in their bedroom, turned on a tape recorder, and played through the material he had amassed. What was captured was not a composing tape, as such: although he sometimes stops to experiment with a chord progression, or alters lyrics as he repeats verses, he generally has these songs under his fingers.

Mostly, this is just Paul having a lively bash with the songs he was considering for his follow-up to *Band on the Run*, occasionally throwing in unused tunes from his distant past. The running time is just over an hour, although there are starts and stops—places where Paul either wanted to listen to what he had just recorded, or where he took a break. It is unclear whether the full tape was recorded in a single sitting.

The tape begins with 'How Many Million Miles,' a gospel-like tune with scarcely any lyrics—just the title and *"Oh, Lord,"*—that runs for nearly six and a half minutes until its final chords morph into 'Mull of Kintyre.' Paul sings his verse a few times, changing *"fog"* to *"mist"* on one of the repeats. A second verse, *"Long have I travelled / And far have I been / Over the mountains"* trails off into placeholding nonsense syllables.

The cheerful 'I'll Give You a Ring' follows, and heads into 'You Know It's True,' a boogie number with vamped lyrics, played in a style that makes it sound like a parody in the spirit of the Bonzo Dog Doo Dah Band's 'Death Cab for Cutie.' Maintaining his satirical voice, Paul moves to 'Women Kind,' a song about harassment—*"From the age of 10 / they're chased by men"*—although his vocal style, to say nothing of the raspberries at the end of the performance, suggest that Paul was uncomfortable with the notion of exploring these issues in a serious song.

'Getting Closer,' a tune he was working on during the family's April 1973 visit to Jamaica, was revisited in an evolved state, with Paul switching between *"coming closer"* and *"getting closer"* in the refrain, and reversing the order of lines in the quirky opening couplet, which in 1973 were *"My salamander / Say you don't love me."*

'In My Dreams' sounds like the kernel of an idea that Paul opted not to continue exploring, although its grandiose melody and sliding effects suggest that it might have been an experimental piece with a comic underpinning. Its companion in this collection of piano demos, the 'Rockestra Theme,' takes keyboard grandiosity in a different, if more fully harnessed direction. Based on a short, melodically simple but attractive repeating figure, punctuated with chordal bursts, it seems intended as an instrumental, or an instrumental section of something larger—although Paul's following the melody with "*yeah, yeah*" vocalizations hints that he might have hoped to produce a lyric for it.

'Now That She Is Mine' follows and includes some chordal experimentation before moving on to 'Call Me Back Again,' sung in a comic voice. Another instrumental supporting a wordless vocal vamp, 'Lunch Box/Odd Sox,' follows. A complete performance of 'Treat Her Gently/Lonely Old People' moves seamlessly into 'You Gave Me the Answer,' complete with its operatic "*graces.*" 'Waiting for the Sun to Shine' is little more than a hint of one or two attractive melodic ideas, to which he sang the title, the song's only line.

That seems to have brought to mind 'She Got It Good,' another unfinished piece that had been kicking around since at least 1971, when Paul was filmed at High Park, singing and playing it on an acoustic guitar. With a gracefully winding, descending figure (to which he sang just one word, "*well . . . ,*" leading to the title line) as its main attraction, it had not changed much since the filmed version; it remained an idea in search of a broader context, but Paul seemed keen to document it alongside all the other works in progress.

Paul was, at this point, reaching deep into the unused song backlog, and he next produced 'Blackpool,' a jokey ditty inspired by the risqué seaside postcards produced by the West Yorkshire firm, Bamforth & Co. A couple of new fragments, another promising melody sung to the words 'Sunshine in Your Hair,' and 'Girlfriend,' a cutesy love song he had written during a secret skiing trip to Switzerland in 1973.* Sung in falsetto, with lyrics like "*Girlfriend / I'm gonna tell your boyfriend, yeah, . . . / I'll tell him what you do to me / Late at night when the wind is free.*" Paul was considering offering the song to American pop sensation Michael Jackson.

Another oldie follows: Paul's very first acknowledged composition, 'I Lost My Little Girl,' the final verse of which he sang in a style inspired by his recent Nashville visit.

As he winds down, Paul offers short glimpses of 'Upon a Hill,' another countryish tune; 'Sea,' with an arching melody set over block chords and shards of a lyric ("*Sea, Sea, the Sea / Go around the world with me*"); 'Love Is Your Road, Love Is My Road,' also a striking melody with lyrics that barely move beyond the title; the country-tinged 'Sweet Little Bird'; and a vaudeville parody, 'Partners in Crime.'

And with the cupboard apparently bare, he went back nearly as far as 'I Lost My Little Girl' for 'Suicide,' a song he wrote in 1956, with a voice and style like Frank Sinatra's in mind—and which he recorded during the living room sessions for his first post-Beatles album, *McCartney*, but mostly erased with his experimental 'Glasses,' leaving only a few seconds peeking through on the finished album.

All told, the tape had the makings of 25 songs.

---

* Paul has said that the song was written during a Swiss vacation, but the date and details of this trip cannot be clarified beyond the fact that it took place before the summer of 1974.

While Paul was in Scotland collecting eggs, milking cows and building the new Wings songbook, there was trouble afoot in London. Fresh from Nashville, Laine, McCulloch and Britton were not happy with the way things had gone in Tennessee—and they were not being discreet about it. By August 10, rumors that Wings were breaking up began appearing in the music press. *NME* reported that McCulloch and Britton were no longer in the band and quoted a spokesman for Laine citing "personal difficulties."

Paul held himself aloof from this discussion, and the response from an MPL spokesman seemed to confirm that Wings were in some disarray.

"Wings members are free to pursue their own musical careers," the unidentified spokesman told *NME*. "This will enable them to develop working relationships free of contractual ties. In future Wings will have a fluid concept, which will be adapted to suit current and future projects. It is wrong to say that Wings are no more, because Wings are Paul and Linda McCartney."[16]

McCulloch and Britton wasted no time finding other gigs. Britton's old band, the Wild Angels, had a cabaret gig near Newcastle, and the group's new drummer, Jim Russell, had other commitments, so Geoff headed north to play with them. Britton also sat in with the Baker Gurvitz Army at a rehearsal on August 10. McCulloch, meanwhile, was toying with an offer to join the James Gang. He had known the American band since 1970, when they toured Britain opening for the Who. Now they were in London auditioning guitarists to replace Tommy Bolin, who had left to join Deep Purple. Jimmy spent an evening visiting John Entwistle with the band, and as he drove them back to their hotel, he said he wanted to be considered for Bolin's position. He was offered the job and accepted it, but he backed out a few days later, telling the band that Linda had made a strong pitch for him to stay.

Denny Laine, for the most part, was busy with domestic duties: his girlfriend Jo Jo delivered their second child, Heidi, on August 13. But he found time for interviews with Capital Radio, *NME* and *Sounds*. Not surprisingly, the reports of Wings' personnel issues was among the topics Laine was quizzed about, and despite what one writer noted was a reluctance to say anything that might contradict Paul's as yet undelivered official line, he was fairly open.

"In Nashville it got to the point where we used to rehearse every day," Denny told *NME*, "which we've never done before except perhaps for a couple of weeks before a tour. We almost had to keep working to keep out of each other's hair, but that was the best thing we've done and from now on we're always gonna work that way. Nashville worked it out for us, because we were surrounded by all these musicians who were great—but who wouldn't have been in work if they'd turned up late for a session or something. It helped to bring it out in ourselves—or at least, we'd be an hour late instead of three. All of us needed that."

Addressing the breakup rumors, he offered a theory, with a personal twist.

"It was probably just people in Nashville, hanging around, hearing us talking and thinking it all sounded a bit heavy," he proposed. "All I can say is Paul and I have our arguments just like anybody else. But I couldn't stay in a band with a bloke I didn't basically like. There's always been plenty of criticism flying around since the early days—between us all. I couldn't respect a guy if I couldn't have a shout up with him occasionally. It's no good going around just saying, 'Yeah man,' to everything. An element of instability is no bad thing anyway. It makes you competitive. I just don't want people to get the wrong idea and think I'm actually leaving.

"After Nashville," he added, "I felt I had more say in the group, because it kind of turned out to be Paul and I telling the others what was wanted. We're too honest with each other to let [diplomacy] come into it now. For instance, if I don't like the way someone's singing I'll tell 'em. If Paul comes on strong with me I'll just tell him, 'Hold it, there's no need for that.' Neither of us have got that hang-up."[17]

The public talk of Wings splitting disturbed Paul, who had not definitively decided what to do about the band's future and resented being preempted by rumors—particularly when he was still basking in, and hoping to build on, the continuing glow of *Band on the Run*. And whether or not he saw Laine as his lieutenant in Wings to the degree Laine imagined he did, he was not happy to have him speaking publicly about the band's inner workings.

On August 15, the day Denny's *NME* interview hit the stands, Brian Brolly sent a manic memo to all MPL employees clarifying that nothing touching on MPL's business—which meant Wings, since the press rarely asked about the company's music publishing operation—could be discussed without being cleared first by Paul and Linda:

> DATE: 15th August 1974
> TO: ALL STAFF
> FROM: Brian Brolly
> SUBJECT: POLICY
>
> I would like to establish a very clear policy.
>
> Anything which directly relates to Paul and Linda McCartney of a personal nature which emanates from either of them or from them through their companies or the companies whose services they employ, must have Paul and Linda McCartney's own clear personal approval. Any statements attributed to them should be cleared by them; any pronouncements of any type whatsoever should be cleared by them. Any publicity release, advertisement, photograph, designs for T-Shirts or any other form of merchandize, promotional or for sale which does or

> implies their personal tastes likes and judgments must be approved by Paul and Linda McCartney.
>
> Please consult or show me materials prior to submission to Paul and Linda McCartney.
>
> In every other respect of the running of our professional companies, we will directly exercise the controls and approvals necessary to run our business affairs in the proper professional fashion.
>
> There obviously are distinctions between those matters on which Paul and Linda McCartney should be consulted for approval and those which are the direct concern of the companies' business, and clearly there are some areas which are grey, falling neither directly in one area or the other. IF IN DOUBT consult, but as an operating policy please be advised that personal or personally related or matters personally identifiable to Paul and Linda McCartney should have their approval in advance and certainly in advance of any incurrence of cost.
>
> [signed] Brian Brolly

Shortly before Brolly's memo landed on the desks of stunned MPL employees and in the musicians' mailboxes, Paul hatched a new idea. He booked time at EMI Studios from August 24 through September 1, and contacted Laine, McCulloch and Britton to tell them they would be needed during that period.

Paul was still uneasy about the band but accepted Britton's argument that all bands have their ups and downs. What he was not sure about was how the band would look onstage. So just as he had done in February 1972, when the stage-untested Wings Mark I began rehearsals at London's Institute of Contemporary Arts, he would hire a camera crew to film the band.

"As he said, when you're playing in a band, you don't see it from the punters point of view," explained David Litchfield, the man Paul hired to direct the film. "So what he wanted me to do was to set up in Abbey Road Studios and film the band playing, purely as a record of what it was then. Then he can look at it and see the band as the public saw it."[18]

Litchfield was an unusual choice of director for Paul, given that he had never made a film. His métier was photography, and his entrée to the McCartney circle was a chance meeting with the couple during Wings' concert at the Hard Rock Café, in March 1973. A year later, he met with Linda to discuss publishing some of her photographs in *the image*—a graphic arts and photography magazine he edited. The June/July 1974 issue carried a six-page spread with Linda's portraits of Frank Zappa, the Who, Brian Jones, Cream, Aretha Franklin, the Lennons, an unusually domesticated shot of Dylan, and artsy snaps of Paul, Heather, Mary and Stella.

"I met her, and I liked her," Litchfield said of Linda. "I mean, I found she was abrasive, and she was tricky and difficult and all that, but there was something about her that was not your normal sort of female photographer at the time. And her background stories on people apart from Paul were brilliant. So I did a piece about that. And that was what led to me staying in touch. Not with him, but with her."

But *the image* was not doing well: by August, its bank had foreclosed on a loan, and when Litchfield was no longer able to cover the magazine's office rent, he took up an offer from an employee who said he could put together the next issues at her flat, which was around the corner from the McCartneys' house on Cavendish Avenue.

"We were sitting there, and I said, '*What the fuck are we going to do?*'" Litchfield remembers. "Because we haven't got any money. '*Something will happen. Something will happen.*' And then the phone rang. I mean, it really was a movie scene. And it was Linda, saying, 'Paul wants to talk to you.' He said he wanted somebody to do some video for him, and that he'd seen *the image* and really liked it—and he thought maybe I could do something with that sort of feeling about it. Well, I didn't question. 'I'll be there!'"

Paul wanted to shoot the sessions on videotape, rather than film, probably because he intended it principally for his own use in assessing the band, and video, unlike film, allowed for immediate playback, with a full soundtrack.

Shortly after his conversation with Paul, Litchfield went to MPL's temporary offices on Greek Street to arrange the details with Brolly. As managing director of MPL, Brolly wanted the relationship formalized in a contract, but after Nashville, Paul was starting to think that contracts muddied the creative waters, and Litchfield was comfortable without one. He hired a crew that included Howard Sharp and John Druce, cameramen; Clive Matley, video engineer; John Page, to oversee the video sound; Brian Huberman, editor; and Keith Paisley, graphics designer.

"The first time I met Brian," Litchfield said of the encounter, "he'd just had his balls removed by Linda that morning, because Fortnum and Mason had delivered the wrong size of Hellmann's mayonnaise. This is rock and roll!"

EMI might have seemed an odd choice of venue for videotaping rehearsals, but Paul wanted more than that: while the cameras were running, engineer Geoff Emerick would record 16-track masters of the performances.

—

One thing that needed to be sorted out before Wings went into the studio was how the band would be paid. The contracts Brolly brought to Nashville were now off the table. An offer for Wings to appear at a fall festival alongside Stevie Wonder ("My cut would have bought me a house,"[19] Britton lamented) was also turned down. Brolly—whom the musicians had taken to calling "Mr. Crap" because they saw him as a corporate suit they did not entirely trust—summoned Britton to his office on August 23 to discuss a new proposal, and to put the drummer on the phone with John Eastman, who confirmed the details.

"Mr. Crap said, 'Well, it's now going to be like this,'" Britton recalled. "'You're going to be paid a sort of "super session fee" [of £170 ($405)].' Before that, we were going to have a retainer—so much a week, or month—and then we were going to get percentages when we toured, and points on the records. But after Jimmy and Denny fucked up, the whole deal went out the window."[20]

That suited Laine, who mentioned his suspicion of contracts and salaries in his *NME* interview and persuaded McCulloch to regard the situation in much the same way.

"We finally felt comfortable enough with each other to talk about the finances," McCulloch noted. "In the old Wings, you got your pay cheque weekly whether you were working or not, but I didn't want that. There's no use hanging about—if I'm in a band I expect to contribute a hell of a lot, and I also expect to get a hell of a lot as well. . . . I'm pretty happy with things as they stand now. I think we all trust each other, our agreements are more on trust now than legality, but next spring, when we go on tour, they'll be legal as well."[21]

Recording and Videotaping Session

Saturday, August 24, 1974.
EMI Studios, Studio Two, London.
Recording: 'Sally G,' 'Nineteen Hundred and Eighty Five,' 'Blackbird,' 'Blackpool,' 'Country Dreamer,' '20 Flight Rock,' 'Peggy Sue' and 'I'm Gonna Love You Too.'
Mixing: 'Junior's Farm' and 'Sally G' (Nashville recordings).

A freshly clean-shaven Paul, along with Linda, David Litchfield and some of the film crew, met at EMI Studios on the afternoon of August 24 so that Litchfield could get a sense of the space. "You could store a fucking [Boeing] 747 in there,"[22] was Litchfield's thumbnail description of Studio Two. Geoff Emerick, an engineer Paul knew from the Beatles days and who manned the console during the *Band on the Run* sessions, was in the control room again, overseeing the 16-track recordings and also running a second tape deck that captured a live stereo feed that was sent to the U-matic video machines.

By the time Paul and company arrived, Emerick had set up microphones for piano and vocals, as well as for acoustic guitar and vocals, while first-time visitor Litchfield was given a tour of the room that had become musical hallowed ground.

"He loved the studio," Litchfield explained. "And he said, 'Do you realize they've never painted the studio, because they were worried about the acoustics of it changing. So they'd never done anything to it.' And he said, 'Let me show you something.' He said, 'This is an echo chamber.'* He opened this little door, and we went in, and he flicked a switch and he said, 'Keep your head down. You can't really stand up in here.' I went in and there was this, it was like a cellar, full of bits of pipe. He said, 'Frank Sinatra loves this.' I said, 'Are you serious?' He said, 'Oh yeah.' I said, 'Even us talking sounds good.' He said, 'It's like singing in your bathroom.'"[23]

Litchfield's crew found spots for the three clumsy U-matic cameras on Studio Two's parquet floor, and Paul began to play an impromptu concert, first accompanying himself on guitar for 'Sally G,' then moving to the piano for 'Nineteen Hundred and Eighty Five.' Assured that Emerick was getting a good sound from both setups, he took up the guitar again for 'Blackbird,' 'Blackpool' and 'Country Dreamer,' followed by covers of Eddie Cochran's 'Twenty Flight Rock' and Buddy Holly's 'Peggy Sue' and 'I'm Gonna Love You Too.'

Once they were set for sound and vision, Litchfield and his crew left, and Paul turned to the next item on his agenda for the day—preparing Wings' next single, 'Junior's Farm' and 'Sally G,' for release. Paul decided that he could improve upon Winfrey's mixes. After seven stereo mixes of 'Junior's Farm' he marked the sixth (RS6) "Best," and turned to 'Sally G,' which required only three attempts before he settled on RS3 as the keeper.

Recording and Videotaping Session

Sunday, August 25, 1974.
EMI Studios, Studio Three, London.
Recorded rehearsals: 'Hi, Hi, Hi,' 'Jet,' 'Let Me Roll It,' 'Junior's Farm,' 'Blue Moon of Kentucky,' 'The Mess,' 'Nineteen Hundred and Eighty Five,' 'My Love,' 'Little Woman Love & C Moon (medley),' 'Maybe I'm Amazed,' 'Live and Let Die,' 'Band on the Run' and 'Wild Life.'

The rest of Wings turned up on August 25 for a day of preliminary rehearsals. Paul established a 10 A.M. starting time as a way to impose discipline, but as the week unfolded, that broke down, largely because of Paul's own sliding scale when it came to punctuality.

"Paul always used to say, 'We start at ten tomorrow morning,'" Litchfield explained, "so we all turned up at 10 and then he turned up at 2:30 in the afternoon. Well, by that time, Jimmy had had enough Special Brews. Plus, they used to get these groupies that arrived with drugs. So the

* The echo chamber in Studio Two was originally built as a bomb shelter.

amount of little white packages that were coming in the back door was enormous. With the influence of what was going down by the time Paul arrived, I found it quite staggering that there was any music made at all, of any kind."[24]

Yet, music was made with striking efficiency, and the band sounded better than Paul expected, not having played together at all in the five weeks since their last rehearsal in Curly Putman's garage.

As the videotape rolled, Wings powered through 'Hi, Hi, Hi,' 'Jet,' 'Let Me Roll It' and 'Junior's Farm' before Emerick asked for a break to change reels. The band resumed with 'Soily,' 'Blue Moon of Kentucky' and 'The Mess,' before Paul moved to the piano for 'Nineteen Hundred and Eighty Five,' 'My Love' and the medley of 'Little Woman Love' and 'C Moon.'

Paul remained at the keyboard for 'Maybe I'm Amazed' and 'Live and Let Die,' at the start of the third reel, then picked up his Rickenbacker bass to finish off the reel with 'Band on the Run.' On the fourth and final reel of the day, the band reprised 'Maybe I'm Amazed' and concluded their day's work with 'Wild Life.' Within a few hours, they had filled four reels of 16-track tape (each holding just over 25 minutes) with most—but not all—of the songs they had polished in Tennessee.

"Having done all that rehearsing and arguing," Linda observed, "we couldn't believe how good we were—we were so tight, and everybody knew their stuff."[25]

Recording and Videotaping Session

Tuesday, August 27, 1974.
EMI Studios, Studio Two, London.
Recording: 'Jet,' 'Let Me Roll It,' 'Junior's Farm,' 'My Love,' 'Maybe I'm Amazed,' 'Claps & Jam' (working title for 'One Hand Clapping'), 'Jet,' 'Junior's Farm,' 'Little Woman Love & C Moon (medley),' 'Band on the Run,' 'Live and Let Die,' 'Soily,' 'Go Now,' 'Bluebird,' 'Blue Moon of Kentucky,' 'Wild Life,' 'Hi, Hi, Hi' and 'Mama Don't Allow.'

The next day, Litchfield captured Wings recording most of the same songs—'Jet,' 'Let Me Roll It,' 'Junior's Farm,' 'My Love,' 'Maybe I'm Amazed' and the 'Little Woman Love'/'C Moon' medley. This time, Paul had Litchfield continue filming and Emerick continue recording when they stopped for discussions, since these moments could be useful in a documentary. Overdubbing became part of the proceedings as well, just as it would be if Wings were recording new material. Litchfield filmed this part of the process too, including some striking shots of Wings gathered around the microphones adding vocal harmonies and hand claps.

Watching the playbacks and seeing the new version of Wings in fighting trim, Paul's misgivings about the lineup were fast evaporating. Now he began reconsidering Litchfield's project. Instead of videotaping the band simply for the sake of seeing how it looked, why not make this a little documentary to promote Wings' new lineup? He even had a title: *One Hand Clapping*, the phrase he came up with during an overdubbing session in Nashville.

Fresh takes of 'Band on the Run,' 'Live and Let Die' and 'Soily' followed, before the group loosened up for a jam built around a synthesizer riff Paul and Linda devised in Nashville, called 'One Hand Clapping.' 'Go Now' and 'Bluebird' were now added to the setlist, and the band worked through 'Blue Moon of Kentucky' and 'Wild Life.' Wings saw out the day with the 1958 Frankie Lymon and the Teenagers' hit 'Mama Don't Allow It.'

All told, Emerick filled eight more reels on August 27.

Recording and Videotaping Sessions

Wednesday, August 28–Thursday, August 29, 1974.
EMI Studios, Studio Two, London.
Recording: (August 28) 'Power Cut,' 'Lazy Dynamite,' 'Hold Me Tight,' 'Tomorrow,' 'Love My Baby,' 'Lady Madonna,' 'Let It Be,' 'The Long and Winding Road,' 'Whole Lotta Shakin' Goin' On,' 'Ooh! My Soul,' 'Oo-Ee Baby,' 'Suicide,' 'Let's Love,' 'All of You,' 'I'll Give You a Ring' and 'Baby Face.'
Orchestral overdubs: (August 29) 'My Love,' 'Live and Let Die,' 'Band on the Run,' 'Bluebird' and 'Jet.'

Paul gave the band a day off on August 28, but went into the studio on his own to fill another four reels with solo keyboard performances.

Paul's repertory included some unusual choices, starting with 'Power Cut,' 'Lazy Dynamite' and 'Hold Me Tight,' from *Red Rose Speedway* and 'Tomorrow,' from *Wild Life*, as well as a new original, 'Love My Baby,' for which he accompanied himself on celeste. He revisited a few Beatles classics—'Lady Madonna,' 'Let It Be' and 'The Long and Winding Road'—as well as some pre-Beatles oldies, like Jerry Lee Lewis's 'Whole Lotta Shakin' Goin' On,' Little Richard's 'Ooh! My Soul' and Lloyd Price's 'Oo-Ee Baby.'

And like the all-around entertainer he had dreamed of becoming in the days before Bill Haley began rocking around the clock, he played a cabaret set, with his own 'Suicide,' 'Let's Love,' the otherwise unknown 'All of You' and 'I'll Give You a Ring,' plus Harry Akst and Benny Davis's 'Baby Face,' a 1926 song closely associated with Al Jolson, but which Paul probably also knew from the

1958 version by Little Richard. Interspersed between all these tunes were stretches of improvisation and noodling on piano, organ, celeste and jangle piano.

Now that he was thinking more expansively about *One Hand Clapping*, Paul arranged a last-minute orchestral session for August 29. He invited his old Liverpool friend Howie Casey to reprise the saxophone solos he had played during the *Band on the Run* sessions, and he hired the arranger and conductor Del Newman, who in turn contracted the necessary orchestral players to accompany 'My Love,' 'Live and Let Die,' 'Band on the Run,' 'Bluebird' and 'Jet.'

"Whenever Paul needed my services," Newman explained, "Alan Crowder from MPL, Paul's company, would call me and I would do whatever was required."[26]

Wings managed another take of 'Band on the Run' and 'Bluebird' before Newman and the orchestra—who were asked to wear full concert dress—turned up to overdub their contribution.

The orchestral session came off almost, but not entirely, without a hitch. Through several takes, the principal cellist seemed to be having difficulty phrasing the short cello obbligato in 'Live and Let Die.' The part was not that difficult, and Paul, noticing that it was 4:50 P.M., just ten minutes before overtime rates would kick in, walked down the long staircase from the Studio Two control room and took Newman aside.

"He wants to go into overtime, doesn't he?" Paul asked. "Do you mind if I take over?"[27]

Newman handed Paul the baton, and Paul told the cellist, "Right, I'll tell you what we'll do. I'll sing it, and you play it." He then sang the cello line, using the names of the chords as lyrics, leaving the player no recourse but to play the line as Paul sang it before doing a final take.

"It was so fucking brilliant," Litchfield marveled, "that when he finished, the entire orchestra stood up and gave [Paul] a standing ovation. The cellist got outgunned. It was wonderful; it was a private piece of musicianship the like of which I'd never seen before, and certainly never since."[28]

When the orchestral session ended, Emerick had filled another 11 reels, and Litchfield's U-matic tapes were stacking up.

Recording and Videotaping Session

Friday, August 30, 1974.

EMI Studios, Backyard and Studio Two, London.

Recording: 'Sweet Little Sixteen,' 'Loving You,' 'We're Gonna Move,' 'Look Over There,' 'Freight Train,' 'Cumberland Gap,' 'Rock Island Line,' 'When I'm Cleaning Windows,' 'Blue Moon of Kentucky,' 'Sally G,' 'Blackpool,' 'Blackbird,' 'Country Dreamer,' 'Peggy Sue,' '20 Flight Rock,' 'I'm Gonna Love You' and 'Nineteen Hundred and Eighty Five.'

McCartney and Litchfield returned to the studio the next day, apparently to gather some atmospheric shots that might be needed for the documentary. But Paul had an ulterior motive. With the rest of the band dismissed, he led Litchfield through a small door at the rear of Studio Two into the backyard of No. 3 Abbey Road—a spot where the Beatles used to go for "walks" during recording sessions and smoke "herbal jazz cigarettes"—and suggested that they film a few songs there. To contrast with the studio footage, they would film just Paul and his Martin D-28 acoustic guitar—a new, right-handed model on which he had reversed the strings but had not yet had the pickguard moved. Emerick brought out a chair for Paul, set up a pair of microphones, and ran the cables back to the Studio Two console.

"I think that some of this," Litchfield explained, "would have been like him showing me that musically he didn't need this backup band. There was no reason to do it. It was totally Paul's idea. In the next moment, he's got his guitar and he's singing 'Blackbird' and we're off."[29]

Litchfield brought out a cameraman and two cameras, one of which he operated himself. To Litchfield's chagrin, the other cameraman insisted on climbing a tree to shoot the session from above.

"No, you don't want to do that," Litchfield admonished him.

"Yeah, yeah, I do, I do," the cameraman insisted.

"Paul thought this was all quite funny," Litchfield said. "Anyway, he fell out of the tree while he was filming, and it served him right."

The performance was similar in spirit to Paul's wide-ranging keyboard performance two days earlier. He busked through Chuck Berry's 'Sweet Little Sixteen,' followed by a pair of Elvis favorites, 'Loving You' and 'We're Gonna Move.' He played a folk-blues-skiffle set that included 'Freight Train,' 'Cumberland Gap' and 'Rock Island Line,' and segued to a George Formby tune, 'When I'm Cleaning Windows,' and then a short country group, with 'Blue Moon of Kentucky' and 'Sally G.' To close this mini-concert, he repeated the material he played on the first day of the sessions—'Blackpool,' four takes of 'Blackbird,' 'Country Dreamer,' and his Buddy Holly/Eddie Cochran set, with 'Peggy Sue,' 'Twenty Flight Rock' and 'I'm Gonna Love You Too.'

The backyard performance filled three 16-track reels, and for good measure, McCartney and Litchfield returned to Studio Two and filled another two reels with solo piano performances of 'Nineteen Hundred and Eighty Five,' plus a third reel of live vocal performances, superimposed onto Emerick's original stereo mix of the song. And with that, the makings of *One Hand Clapping* were in the can.

But there was a fly in the ointment. Because of his inexperience, Litchfield did not realize that U-matic tape was the wrong medium for a proper documentary.

"You couldn't edit the stuff," he explained. "It was totally wild. You couldn't sync it. The only thing it had going for it was that you could put a soundtrack down, so the quality of the sound on all the stuff that I did with him is absolutely brilliant, but the quality of the vision is shit. I had to [transfer the material] from video to film to edit it, and once you've gone down one generation, the quality just disappears.

"But he was happy to experiment if I was, and I was. Neither of us knew what the fuck we were doing. We had a disagreement one day over the direction the video was taking, when we were editing it, and Paul said, 'You don't know what you're talking about.' I said, 'Neither do you,' and he said, 'No, I know—it's sort of our private film school, really, isn't it?'"[30]

The edit became a bohemian refuge for Paul, not only from the responsibilities of whipping a new band into shape but also from the day-to-day domestic demands on a dutiful husband and father. Famous faces would come and go from a makeshift edit suite in Litchfield's back bedroom (Neil Young, Litchfield recalled, once turned up with a cricket ball of cocaine in his coat pocket).

As McCartney and Litchfield reviewed the tapes, no topic was off-limits. When conversation turned to Beatlemania, and more specifically, notches on Paul's bedpost, Litchfield asked, "Ever had a threesome?" "Try a fivesome!" Paul joked. Yet Litchfield was struck by Paul's concern, if not insecurity, about his role as a partner within his marriage, and his awareness that one-night stands with groupies were one thing; maintaining a healthy, long-term sexual relationship was another.

Technical issues aside, Paul imagined *One Hand Clapping* as a television special that could help bring about a rethinking of how rock is presented on television.

"Television's never used rock music very well, that's where it's at," Paul told *Melody Maker* shortly after the sessions. "They never want to put you there," he said, using his hands to frame a head shot, "and another there on your guitar. I mean, if Keith Richards [is] on there, I wanna see his head and his guitar and his fingers. I wanna see what he's doing, y'know? [But] they don't think it's exciting enough! They don't! They never have! So I get the idea they always want to dress it.

"We've just done a thing at EMI where we just went in front of the cameras and played. It was originally just so that we could look at it and see if we're any good as a band. 'Cos we don't know really. You feel that it's okay and sometimes it goes great, but it's just nice to see if I look any good. There's no [set] dressing. It's straight, just us in the studio, and I think that could be really great."[31]

But though Paul was reassured by the sessions, tensions remained beneath the surface. Britton's devotion to karate continued to irk McCulloch, and when Britton wore his gi during filming, McCulloch needled him, and drew Laine into doing so as well.

The personality clash was not lost on Paul. He was fond of Britton, and he was okay with—even fascinated by—the drummer's devotion to martial arts. More importantly, Britton's intuition as a drummer made him a good fit for Wings. Similarly, if Jimmy's passion for alcohol and chemical stimulants led to trouble too easily and too often, he was a superb guitarist who could supply inventive fills and lead guitar lines. But he also did as he was told when McCartney had specific solos in mind, and if he was asked to reproduce the solo on a record—Henry McCullough's solo for 'My Love,' for example—he did it with precision.

Unwilling to choose between them, but also not wanting to be distracted by the friction, Paul opted to give Jimmy and Geoff time to settle into their roles, hoping that the experience of a week at EMI might help.

Paul kept up on the dysfunction in his former musical family as well. He would have heard scuttlebutt about marital problems in the Harrison family long before the August 24 issue of *Disc* reported that George and Pattie had split, and that Pattie had traveled to the United States on the arm of Eric Clapton, while George was spending time in the West Indies with Kathy Simmonds, an ex of Rod Stewart's. Ringo's marriage was on the rocks, too, after Ringo discovered that his wife, Maureen, had an affair with George Harrison.

Still, the latest news from Ringo and John was mostly musical: Ringo was at work in Los Angeles on the follow-up to his *Ringo* album, for which John supplied '(It's All Da-Da Down to) Goodnight Vienna.' When John and May returned to Los Angeles on August 6, John played piano on the song he supplied, which became the album's title track; on August 8—the night Richard Nixon announced his resignation as president of the United States—he played acoustic guitar on 'All By Myself.'

Two days later, John and May returned to New York, where John was still laboring over his *Walls and Bridges* album. But before they left, they spent an afternoon with Ringo and his girlfriend, Nancy Andrews, at the Hollywood apartment Ringo was renting.* Over in Britain, Paul's ears might have been ringing.

"In every family, there's a jealousy that goes on between siblings, you know?" Andrews observed. "We had a house up in the Hollywood Hills that overlooks the city, and I remember John coming up with a Wings LP. They played it, and then John took it off the record player and frisbeed it over the mountains, saying, *'That's just fucking bubble gum,'* like he was pissed off. And Richard† goes, *'Yeah, fucking bubble gum music!'* And you know, what I got from that was—it was sort of like,

* Ringo's marriage to Maureen was on the rocks, but they had not yet divorced.

† Andrews is referring to Ringo by his real name, Richard Starkey. She did not identify the album they played, but John is likely to have brought along Paul's latest, *Band on the Run*.

they were jealous. They were proud. And yet they were disappointed that the music was not up to what they felt was Paul's standard, or up to the Beatles' standard."[32]

Listeners not involved in the former Beatles' inner politics felt differently—including members of the New York Yankees,[33] who made *Band on the Run* part of their pre-game ritual in the summer of 1974. Bill Sudakis, a utility infielder and designated hitter during his single season on the team, had played the album in the clubhouse at top volume before a game. The Yankees won that day, and the album was played before games for the rest of the season.

Although the success of *Band on the Run* blunted comparisons between Paul's work with the Beatles and his post-Beatles output, it did not vanquish them entirely, and they continued to sting.

"Paul will get in a cab," Linda complained during an interview in mid-1974, "and the driver will say, 'Oh, it's not as good as it used to be, is it, Paul? It's not like the Beatles.' Well, sure, he gets hurt by that. If he's going through a bad period, give him a bit of positiveness and he might go out and write a great song. People are vulnerable. They're only so strong. It's like a great racehorse. If the owner whipped it and didn't treat it well, the horse would become a nervous wreck."[34]

Beatles connections remained part of the McCartneys' social life, as well. On Friday, September 6, Paul and Linda headed to the Ritz to attend the wedding reception of Mike Leander, who arranged the strings on 'She's Leaving Home' (George Martin was not available when Paul wanted the orchestration done, and patience was not among Paul's virtues), and Penny Carter.

And Paul participated, from a distance, in the first Beatlefest, in New York. Part of the event was a charity raffle on behalf of Phoenix House, the drug treatment program that had provided a statement in support of McCartney when he was trying to obtain an American visa after his drug convictions in Sweden (in 1972) and Scotland (in 1973). Paul had promised to play a fundraising concert on the center's behalf, but nearly a year later, Wings were not yet ready to tour, so Paul donated a guitar to the Beatlefest raffle, as did John. Ringo provided a pair of autographed drumsticks, and George donated a tabla that he had played on 'Within You Without You.' Phoenix House netted $3,000 from the event.

The opening of Beatlefest coincided with the release of Mike McGear's single 'Leave It.' Mike recorded a promo video for the song, and if the single was a success, he hoped to tour with a band that included keyboardists Zoot Money and John Megginson, guitarists Andy Roberts and Ollie Halsall, and drummer Gerry Conway.

Alas, Paul's involvement was not enough to push his brother's single into the chart's upper reaches: in Britain, it entered the Top 100 at No. 49 on October 5, and remained for only four weeks, peaking at No. 36. Mike's album was scheduled for release on September 27.

There was some drama surrounding the album's release. Through much of his correspondence with Warner Bros. Records since its completion, Mike pushed for a gatefold sleeve. Warner's policy militated against that, but Ron Kass, the managing director of Warner's British operation, decided to overrule that policy. This did not sit well with company president Mo Ostin, who had David Herscher, the label's general manager, send Kass a cable restating the policy. In his response, Kass reminded Herscher in veiled terms that this was not really about Mike, but about *the larger picture*—that is, the possibility of signing Paul to the label when his EMI contract expired.

> WARNERECS LDN
> 18.7.74
> DAVID HERSHER [*sic*].
> ---------
> REGARDING YOUR TELEX ABOUT MIKE MCGEAR'S GATEFOLD PACKAGE
> WE HAVE A PROBLEM HERE WHICH RELATES TO OUR ASSOCIATION WITH THE MCCARTNEY PEOPLE. WE HAVE HAD TO MAKE AN EXCEPTION
> IN OUR MARKET AND THE STAKES INVOLVED ARE MUCH BIGGER THAN THE MIKE MCGEAR ALBUM. I WOULD LIKE TO DISCUSS THIS MATTER WITH MO OSTIN AS I CANNOT CHANGE OUR PLANS AT THIS TIME WITHOUT POTENTIAL SERIOUS CONSEQUENCES.
> REGARDS,
> RON KASS
> WARNERS BUBK

McGear, complete with its hard-won gatefold cover, failed to crack the Top 40 album chart in Great Britain; its best American showing was on the *Record World* chart, where it reached No. 94 on December 12.

The McCartneys welcomed a few musical guests to Cavendish Avenue in late summer. When Crosby, Stills, Nash and Young played at Wembley Stadium on September 14, in what *NME* touted as the "Concert of the Year," Paul and Linda opted to skip the concert—missing the group's sweetly harmonized version of his 'Blackbird'—but they invited the group to visit them for a post-concert party. All but Crosby turned up, and McCartney jammed with Stills before the evening was out. At some point, Paul told Stills about his unfinished concert film, *The Bruce McMouse Show*, featuring Wings Mark I and a family of cartoon mice, and when Stills expressed interest in seeing it, Paul invited him back the next day for what was apparently a weed-fueled private screening that persuaded Paul to put the film back on his active projects list.

"Stephen Stills came 'round to see it," Paul told *Melody Maker*, "and he was 'Yeah, man, yeah!' Mind you, we were having a great evening. He probably would've enjoyed Mickey Mouse! So we'll do it as a kid's show, but do enough publicity so that adults can look in too."[35]

Recording Session

Sunday, September 22, 1974.

EMI Studios, Studio Two, London.

Recording, Overdubbing and Mixing: 'Proud Mother' and 'Tomorrow.'

Since 1970, Paul had fielded increasingly frequent requests from directors for songs to be used in films and other projects, and though he was selective about which of these he accepted, his agreement was not necessarily predicated on the purely artistic merit of the project. In the summer of 1974, for example, he turned down a commission from the American filmmaker Joseph Strick, who sought soundtrack music for a screen version of the James Joyce novel *Portrait of the Artist as a Young Man*. Yet having rejected that prestigious project, he accepted a commission to write a commercial jingle for Mother's Pride bread.

He was not asked to extol the virtues of the bread—the jingle was to be instrumental. And though he summoned Wings, plus a few brass players, to record the tune, they would be doing so incognito: the short jingle, running 30 seconds, as well as a two-minute version, for potential release as a novelty single, were recorded under the name the Whippets in a session that ran from 6 P.M. to 2:30 A.M., followed by nearly two hours of mixing.

"Recently, I have been doing a lot of commercial stuff," Paul later explained. "Not selling out, but stuff aimed at a special type of market. I've always been like that really. . . . I like writing frivolous things. All right, sometimes I do say to myself, 'What are you doing that for, Paul?' And maybe I should write one great song and not a hundred meaningless ones. But I'm not concerned with what people call my 'talent.' I've proved to myself, if no one else, that I'm capable of writing good songs. I've got no hang-up about going down in history as a great songwriter. I really don't care."[36]

The jingle, which Paul called 'Proud Mother,' is a bouncy, tuneful piece in the spirit of 'Zoo Gang' and the new 'Lunch Box/Odd Sox,' scored with a brass melody and a second theme played on Linda's Minimoog. With Geoff Emerick at the console, the musicians recorded six takes of the jingle, with Take 1 marked "Best," and 14 takes of the long version, the last of them noted as the keeper.

Taking the possibility of a Whippets single into account, Paul made an instrumental arrangement of the *Wild Life* track 'Tomorrow'—a favorite of Lee Eastman, who had told Paul that the song was essentially lost on the album and should be re-recorded. Eastman campaigned for a slow, sultry version, the kind of performance that might thrive in a jazz club,[37] but the version McCartney whipped up for the Whippets was more in keeping with Linda's tastes, supported as it was by a reggae beat.

Like 'Proud Mother,' it was an instrumental, but it had the same hallmarks as the jingle: the verse melody was played on synthesizer, the bridge handed over to the brass. Five takes were recorded; take 5 was reckoned "Best." A cassette was run off for Paul and Linda to take home. Two days later, at Paul's request, EMI sent over an open reel copy of the recordings and eight double-sided acetates, with both songs.

Recording Session

Wednesday, September 25—Tuesday, October 1, 1974.
EMI Studios, Studio Two, London.
Editing: 'Junior's Farm (Nashville recording).'
Overdubbing: 'Sally G (Nashville recording).'
4-Track and mono mixing (*One Hand Clapping*): 'Jet,' 'Let Me Roll It,' 'Junior's Farm,' 'My Love,' 'Little Woman Love' / 'C Moon,' 'Maybe I'm Amazed,' 'Band on the Run,' 'Hi, Hi, Hi,' 'Live and Let Die,' 'Soily,' 'Go Now,' 'Blue Moon of Kentucky,' 'Nineteen Hundred and Eighty Five,' 'Bluebird,' 'One Hand Clapping,' 'Piano tapes (August 28)' and 'Backyard tapes (August 30).'
Stereo mixing: 'Sally G' (Nashville recording), 'Blackbird,' 'Blackpool,' 'Country Dreamer,' 'Twenty Flight Rock,' 'Peggy Sue,' 'I'm Gonna Love You Too,' 'Sweet Little Sixteen,' 'Loving You' and 'There's a Leak.'

Exactly a month since the start of filming, David Litchfield had whittled down the playlist that would form the soundtrack of *One Hand Clapping*. Five days (September 25 through 29) were dedicated to mixing the 16-track recordings to 4-track and mono tapes for Litchfield and film editor Brian Huberman. Paul's piano and acoustic guitar performances, recorded on August 28 and 30, were given the same treatment, as the score for a vanity film Litchfield had put together, titled *Paul McCartney in 'The Backyard.'*

In preparation for the single release of 'Junior's Farm,' now penciled for October 25, a radio edit was prepared on September 26, when the track was trimmed from 4'30" to 3'02", most notably by lopping out the "Parliament" and "Ollie Hardy" verses. Two days later the edit was scrapped when Paul decided to discard Ernie Winfrey's mix. His next attempt to mix 'Junior's Farm' was at a session with Emerick on September 30, when mixes of both the full version and the radio edit were made. Those were scrapped as well, although at the same session, Paul replaced his lead vocal on 'Sally G' and oversaw the mix that would be released as the B side of 'Junior's Farm.'

Emerick and McCartney spent October 1 making stereo mixes of nine of Paul's August 30 acoustic guitar performances for *Paul McCartney in 'The Backyard.'*

—

The McCartneys did not have to look far for validation these days. When Linda turned 32, on September 24, the family celebrated privately, but in a sign that she was at long last winning acceptance among the British public, William Hickey included a warm birthday greeting in his *Daily Express* gossip column; Paul responded with a telegram, thanking Hickey for "the birthday greetings to the old lady."[38]

When *Melody Maker* published the results of its 1974 readers' poll, in its September 28 issue, *Band on the Run* was ranked the No. 2 album in both its British and international listings. The album's title track was No. 2 in the international singles section, while among the British results, Paul had two of the Top 10 hits—'Band on the Run' at No. 5 and 'Jet' at No. 10. Paul was also ranked No. 6 among composers, No. 9 among arrangers, and No. 10 among producers.

Nearly a year after *Band on the Run* was released, the McCartneys were still considered hot enough to be featured on both the cover and a poster in the October 5 edition of *Sounds*. The issue included a lengthy interview with Linda, in which she discussed Wings' plans for the immediate future.

"This band we have now will definitely do some big tour," she said. "England, America, Australia. . . '75 is going to be the big Wings year. We are just doing a TV show—the provisional title is *The One Hand Clapping Show*—and it is all down on video cassettes. . . . The quality won't be like a big TV studio, so we have to explain that somehow, but it's good."[39]

The focus now was on introducing the new incarnation of Wings. Britton and McCulloch were made available for interviews, and preparations for the release of 'Junior's Farm' continued apace. Clive Arrowsmith, whose cover shot for *Band on the Run* was by now an iconic image, was hired to shoot a photo for potential use on record sleeves and in trade advertisements. When Wings and Arrowsmith convened at the Park Tower Hotel/Casino in Knightsbridge, the band donned costumes representing some of the characters mentioned in the song, and assembled around a gaming table with cards and chips strewn across it.

Britton, seated at the table in a bow tie, vest and hat and holding a pair of playing cards, is the "poker man." Julie the seal* sits beside him. Denny is the song's Eskimo, clad in a fur-lined hood and

* Hiring a sea lion—as noted in Paul's lyrics—for the shoot proved impossible, so Paul had to settle for a seal.

holding a spear. Linda, standing at the table in a low-cut dress and holding a hand of cards against her hip, is the "honey"* mentioned in the song's second line, and Jimmy, hanging tenuously on the edge of the table, looks like he might be channeling Oliver Hardy. Paul, in a loose brown jacket, a straw hat and a patterned scarf, stands between Denny and the sea lion, holding his cards, seemingly representing the song's narrator.

"It looks very sedate in the picture," Paul explained, "but you should have seen it in reality. The table was all neatly arranged with stacks of cards until Julie, who was the seal, decided to rearrange things."[40]

"The table was laid out with all these chips stacked and everything," Britton picks up the narrative. "Now in order to keep the sea lion's [*sic*] attention her owner trainer was the other side of the table with fish, you see. And the first dollop of fish landed on the table and the sea lion [*sic*] just goes 'bosh' and knocks everything flying."[41]

"No seals next time: I think we'll put a bull in the next song or something easy like that," Paul concluded.[42]

The Arrowsmith photo would be used on the sleeve of the single in parts of Europe and South America, on the cover of the sheet music, and in advertisements. Alternative advertisements were prepared as well, one in the form of a comic strip showing the band on the farm and including the lyrics, and another with a black-and-white photo of Wings gathered on Curly Putman's front porch.

Paul was itching to get 'Junior's Farm' into the shops, and the October 4 release of John Lennon's *Walls and Bridges*, as well as the single from that album, 'Whatever Gets You Thru the Night,' got his competitive juices flowing. But he remained unsatisfied with the mix. Two engineers—Ernie Winfrey in Nashville and Geoff Emerick in London—had tried their hand, with Paul participating in both attempts, but it wasn't quite right.

Now, at Brian Brolly's behest, a third engineer—Alan O'Duffy—entered the picture. O'Duffy was only 26, but he had been hanging around recording studios since he was 17, working first at Pye Studios and then at Olympic. He had engineered recordings for the Kinks, the Nice, Procol Harum, Traffic, Blind Faith, the Rolling Stones, Deep Purple and Humble Pie. With producer Chas Chandler, O'Duffy had also overseen a string of No. 1 hits in Britain for Slade, including 'Cum On Feel the Noize' and 'Merry Christmas Everybody.'

O'Duffy had come to Brolly's attention through a project he had engineered for a couple of students, Andrew Lloyd Webber and Tim Rice, who came to Olympic in 1970 with an idea for a rock opera about the final week in the life of Jesus. Most labels had turned Lloyd Webber and Rice away, but their project, *Jesus Christ Superstar*, appealed to Brolly, who persuaded MCA to take

* In the line "*I had a honey and I bet a grand*," honey is a pun on "honey" (a girl) and "hunny," British slang for £100.

it on. It was an astute call: the recording was a multimillion-selling phenomenon, which quickly spawned stage productions around the world. Brolly's hand in its success was a factor in winning him the top job at MPL. And when Paul mentioned that he felt the mixes of 'Junior's Farm' were lacking something, Brolly suggested bringing in O'Duffy.

Paul was open to the idea, but as he had done when faced with a new engineer in the past—specifically, Eirik "The Norwegian" Wangberg, during the *Ram* sessions—he conditioned O'Duffy's engagement on the passing of an audition. If O'Duffy worked out, he could be a useful addition to Paul's go-to list. AIR Studios' managing director John Burgess, after all, was pushing to sign Geoff Emerick as an in-house engineer/producer, so while Geoff remained Paul's first choice, given their long history together, he might not always be available when Paul needed him.

Recording Session

Monday, October 7, 1974.
Olympic Studios, Studio Three, London.
Mixing: 'Junior's Farm.'

The 16-track master of 'Junior's Farm' was sent to O'Duffy at Olympic, and on October 7, O'Duffy prepared a mix that was both more full-bodied and more transparent than either Winfrey's or Emerick's mixes. Jimmy's lead guitar parts—not just the solo, but the between-verse commentary as well—were brought forward and centered, and O'Duffy applied a light phasing effect to strategic points in both the vocal and lead guitar lines. It was exactly the kind of production finesse that the song needed.

"There is nothing perfunctory about doing a mix at all," O'Duffy said, noting that the mix mirrored his own methodology as a recording engineer. "I'm only interested to know if I can do something that I think I like; can I make something beautiful out of what I've been given? And that's what I did with 'Junior's Farm.' I'm a fan of Paul, and I'm a fan of people who Paul loves, as well, like Brian Wilson. So, I just did what I could with what I heard."[43]

O'Duffy completed his mix the day he received the tape and delivered an acetate to Paul the next day. That was not quite the end of the mixing saga, however. Paul next sent the master to George Martin, at AIR Studios, and on October 11, Martin and his team filled two tapes of stereo mixes, three of which were complete. But these, too, were abandoned: listening to the Winfrey, Emerick, O'Duffy and Martin mixes, Paul chose O'Duffy's for release.

Recording Sessions

Tuesday, October 8 and Wednesday, October 9, 1974.
EMI Studios, Studio Two, London.
Recording: 'Junior's Farm' (Remake), 'Jet' (Remake) and 'Soily' (Remake).

While O'Duffy and Martin were preparing their contenders in the 'Junior's Farm' mixing sweepstakes, Paul, Wings and David Litchfield were back in Studio Two, rerecording some of the songs for the *One Hand Clapping* television special. At the first session, they filled three 16-track reels with performances of 'Junior's Farm,' one of which was earmarked as a potential promo video. A fourth reel was devoted to new performances of 'Jet.' The next day's session yielded five more reels, two devoted to 'Junior's Farm,' three to 'Soily.'

There was some tension in the studio this time. Geoff, whose foot was still not entirely healed, was having trouble with 'Soily,' trying the patience of both Jimmy and Denny, who took their complaints to Paul. Exacerbating the brittle atmosphere, Geoff wore his gi to the session, drawing sarcastic comments in McCulloch's Scottish brogue.

"Paul said, 'Why have you got it on?'" Litchfield remembers. "Geoff said, 'Cos tonight I've got [karate training]. It's a warm day, and I quite like wearing it, to get in the mood.' And Paul said, 'That's alright, I'm not complaining.'"

Geoff explained that he was training with the British team for a competition against Japan, at the Sobell Sports Center, on November 30. Paul turned to Litchfield and asked, "Do you want to film this competition?" Litchfield said he would love to—but he would want to shoot it on 16mm film, not on video.

"And that was all there was to it," Litchfield remembered. "There was no discussion about who was going to pay for it—Paul implied that yes, he would pick it up. It was very relaxed. Paul had taken me up an alley with this video thing, and—I'm surmising, but I think the karate film was a little bit of a 'guilt present,' to say, 'Look, would you like to go off and make a proper film, with other people and a proper camera?'"

Brolly again pushed the idea of a contract since the film was unrelated to Paul and his music. Paul again shrugged off Brolly's concerns, adding that he might write some music for the film.

"I remember MPL management going potty about it," Litchfield said, "and saying, 'But we haven't got a contract for this!' I said, 'Well, I don't need a contract, does Paul need a contract?' And Paul said, 'I don't need a contract.'" Brolly continued to push, so they repeated the exchange in reverse. "Paul said, 'Do you want a contract, David?' I said, 'No,' and he said, 'We're not going to have a contract, Brian, he's just going to do it. Let's move on to something else.'"[44]

The Country Hams, 'Walking in the Park with Eloise' single trade ad

'Junior's Farm' would not be ready for release in time to go head-to-head with John's 'Whatever Gets You Thru the Night,' but British retailers put in advance orders of 100,000 copies of the new Wings single as soon as its October 25 release was announced. Paul would, in fact, have releases on two consecutive weeks: on October 18, Jim McCartney's 'Eloise'—its title now expanded to 'Walking in the Park with Eloise'—was issued with 'Bridge on the River Suite' as its B side, not under the Wings moniker, but as the Country Hams.

The single failed to breach the Top 100 in either Britain or America, but it quickly became a collector's item for McCartney fans. The critics regarded it as an amusing indulgence.

> *While cutting Wings material down in Nashville, Paul McCartney found sufficient time to produce this pleasant piece of instrumental whimsy penned well over 20 years ago by Pappa McCartney. Ideal for theme tracking while rolling the credits for a P. G. Wodehouse teleplay, it highlights the droll finger pickin' of Chet Atkins, Floyd Cramer on piano, and a snappy trumpet section that sounds like a bunch of sozzled Bradford Mariachi players. Basically, the kind of jaunty ditty that Herb Alpert used to sell by the barrowload.*[45]
>
> *Roy Carr*, NME

> *Some family, the McCartney family, first Paul, then brother Mike, and now a number that Paul's dad, James, wrote some 20 years ago. And the talent doesn't stop there—Paul produced the single, Chet Atkins and Floyd Cramer play on it, as does Wings' drummer Geoff Britton. The tune is a la ragtime, nice and happy, and who knows—could be another McCartney heading for the charts.*[46]
>
> *Sue Byrom*, Record Mirror

But critical plaudits were, for once, the last thing on Paul's mind.

"He loved having a record out," Paul noted proudly in a *Disc* interview, "but he's very shy, me dad, and he didn't like all the publicity. I remember him being very emotional about it when I first played it to him—he said I really shouldn't have bothered, but I know he enjoyed it. And do you know what? My Uncle Joe has now written some words to go with it, so perhaps we'll do another version. How about that . . . brother, father, and now uncle! I'm told George Melly's written some words for it, too, I haven't heard them yet, though."[47]

5

LISTEN TO THIS BALLOON

It must have been difficult not to consider it simultaneously funny and irritating. When Paul suggested, at several points in 1969, that the Beatles return to live performance, John responded as if that was the most insane idea ever floated. And if there was anyone more implacably against returning to live performance than John, it was George.

Yet, in early October 1974, George announced that he would undertake a North American tour, starting in Vancouver on November 2 and ending in New York on December 20. And it looked like he was doing it right: Bill Graham, the founder of the Fillmore rock halls in San Francisco and New York, was the promoter, and Ravi Shankar, Billy Preston and Tom Scott were announced as support acts.

As the Beatle who wanted most to get back on the road, Paul could take some pride in having toured Britain and Europe with Wings, but George's tour announcement was a blow to his competitive side: he would not be the first former Fab to tour America, and given George's and Ringo's appearances at the Concert for Bangla Desh and John's handful of performances in the early 1970s, he remained the only one who had not performed in the United States.

If there was an upside, it was that George would now have an extended turn at answering the Beatles Reunion Question. He took a swing at it during a press conference at the Beverly Wilshire Hotel on October 23, ten days before the start of his tour, and gave his answer a nuanced spin that could not have pleased Paul.

"The Beatles was like being in a box, we got to that point," George responded, presenting his Beatles experience as both confining and psychologically damaging. "It's taken me years to be able to play with other musicians. Because we were so isolated it became very difficult, playing the same tunes day in, day out.

"Since I made *All Things Must Pass*, it's just so nice for me to be able to play with other musicians, and having played with other musicians, I don't think the Beatles were that good. I think they're fine, you know. Ringo's got the best backbeat I've ever heard. . . . Paul is a fine bass player, he's a bit over-powering at times. John's gone through all his scene, but he feels like me, he's come back around. We're all at that point. I mean, to tell you the truth, I'd join a band with John Lennon any day, but I couldn't join a band with Paul McCartney, but it's nothing personal. It's just from a musical point of view."[1]

The comment was widely quoted at Paul's expense, and George, insisting that he and Paul remained friendly, tried to do some diplomatic damage control.

"At this point now I've just got to meeting Paul again," Harrison explained, "because we drifted off away from each other through all the suing—*Sue Me, Sue You Blues* and that. But I've just met Paul, and I just know that whatever we've been through, there's always been something there that's tied us together. And it's like we've come through a big dark tunnel and we come back out the other end and, you know, we're ready to really pick up to be friends again."[2]

But George's sense of having been marginalized in the Beatles was something he could not suppress, and when asked to elaborate on his original comment, he delved into the dynamics of his relationship with Paul.

"Obviously if we did [play together], we'd compromise. But you know, I went to school with Paul. He was a year older than me; I met him when I was 13, and we were together for 17 years until we split. . . . When you're so close you tend to lock each other up in pigeonholes, and for me, it was difficult. Because musically with Ringo and John I had no problem, but with Paul, well, it reached a point where he wouldn't let me play on the sessions. It was a part of our splitting up. But at the same time, I have a tendency to defend Paul—John and Ringo too—if anyone else said anything without qualification about them. After going through all that together, there must be something good about it."[3]

Four years after they broke up, each of the former Beatles had his own way of exorcising the demons of Beatlemania. John's responses ranged from vehement lack of interest to hints that a reunion was possible, depending on his mood. Ringo tended to be dismissive: they were all busy and happy with their lives—why *should* they reunite? George, the relatively few times he was quizzed before now, sometimes held out hope that they would eventually settle down, get over their issues, and work together again. But time had not healed the wounds George felt he had sustained as a Beatle.

"Well, I can understand that," Paul told one journalist who quoted George's comments to him. "But basically you know, the real truth about any of this Beatles stuff is that we're just going to have to wait and see. I mean none of us know and none of you know, and that is what it is down to. Nobody knows what will happen on that scene. I wouldn't like the group to re-form and carry on as a group full time because it went full circle. Unlike George, I think it was a great band."[4]

It was not lost on John, George and Ringo, however, that had they listened to Paul in 1969, they would not currently be embroiled in a series of lawsuits with Allen Klein, one of which came before a judge at the end of October. When Klein sued Lennon, Harrison and Starr after they opted not to renew his contract, in March 1973, they countersued on the grounds that he had exerted undue influence in getting them to sign their original agreement with him, as well as a subsequent increase in his commission. Klein sought to have their suit dismissed, but on October 28, Sir Anthony Plowman, the vice chancellor of the High Court, denied Klein's motion.

Paul's way of conquering lingering demons from the Beatles days remained what it had been since he first switched on his borrowed Studer four-track deck to make the *McCartney* album, in December 1969: to press ahead. At the moment, that meant formally announcing the new lineup of Wings as part of the publicity for the release of 'Junior's Farm' and 'Sally G.' That involved some myth-weaving about the breakup of Wings' original lineup—but also, notably, a caveat about the new crew.

"It's taken a whole year and more to get the new band together. It's not easy you know," Paul told the music press, adding that Wings Mark I had been an eye-opener for him. "The personalities weren't right, we weren't interested in the same things. So when it came to the crunch, an argument, which it did, there just wasn't enough there to carry it through. Finally, it came to a good old argument and instead of saying, 'Let's patch it up,' I just said, 'Let's not bother.' Now this is another attempt, having looked around a bit more fully. We've still got some sorting out on a personality level to do—I really think that's the main and most important level."[5]

The release of the single on October 25 in Britain and America was meant to make talk of whether the new lineup's personalities might mesh seem beside the point: here, on this seven-inch piece of plastic was the new band in action, with 'Junior's Farm,' a punchy, guitar-driven rocker with idiosyncratic lyrics, and 'Sally G,' a country tune from inception to completion. Along with the release, Tony Brainsby let the press in on Paul's plan to record a new album, the release of which would be preceded by *Cold Cuts*, his album of unreleased material.

British critics were favorably disposed toward 'Junior's Farm.'

Julie the seal behaving for a brief moment

Having arrived at a satisfactory direction with Band on the Run, *the Mighty Macca continues to exude the utmost confidence as he hits his stride with this simple yet thoroughly effective full-tilt rocker. . . . 'Junior's Farm' reveals both McCartney and Wings to be among the coterie of musicians who really know what they're doing.*[6]

Roy Carr, NME

This has been described by Linda as a "real rocker." Seems a fairly accurate assessment to me. 'Junior's Farm' may lack the same kind of ruthless determination of, say, 'Jet,' which in some ways it recalls, but it drives along with a reasonable amount of power. . . . 'Sally G' on the B side, is an unmemorable piece of hokum, inspired by a night out in Nashville.[7]

Allan Jones, Melody Maker

Lots of instrumental in this one, with some guitar work that had a few memories of the Allman Brothers and some nifty drumming from new member Geoff Britton. Quick ending that should keep DJs awake if nothing else. Sticking my neck out, I don't put it up there with his best, but it's a change of direction.[8]

Sue Byrom, Record Mirror

Guitars are heard to whine, young Paul's bass is well to the fore, and a pretty good time seems to be had by all as the newly reconstructed Wings go a-struttin' and a-whoopin'. . . . Although this isn't as satisfying as 'Jet' or 'Band on the Run,' it's still a nifty single, slowing the tempo for a dramatic finale and ending on a startled yelp. Good on yer, Paul baby.[9]

John Peel, Sounds

Commercial success, however, proved more elusive. The single entered both the UK and American charts on November 9. In Britain, it enjoyed ten weeks in the Top 100, six of them in the Top 40, peaking at No. 16. In the United States, it cracked the *Billboard* Hot 100 at No. 59 and spent 17 weeks on the chart, peaking at No. 3, thanks to substantial airplay for both sides of the disc.

Hoping to foster the camaraderie he considered so crucial to a band's chemistry, Paul brought his bandmates to a live screening of one of the year's biggest sporting events, thanks to an invitation from John Conteh. The "Rumble in the Jungle," beamed from Kinshasa, Zaire, on October 30, pitted the unbeaten World Heavyweight Champion, George Foreman, against Muhammad Ali, the capricious challenger. Wings watched what turned out to be one of the most legendary bouts in the history of the sport, as Ali knocked out Foreman in eight rounds.

Shortly before the fight, Conteh introduced Paul to Michael Francis, a bodyguard. Paul engaged Francis to pick him up at Cavendish Avenue, ensure his safety throughout the evening—testosterone-driven boxing crowds could be unpredictable—and take him home.

"I could use a guy like you,"[10] Paul told Francis during the drive home. He did not need a full-time bodyguard at the moment, Paul explained, but he might call on Francis's services in the near future.

As the anniversary of the release of *Band on the Run* approached, Paul began planning the sessions for the next album. He wanted to record in the United States, which meant getting work visas. The recordings Wings made in Nashville were not, strictly speaking, legal; if their host, Buddy Killen, hadn't owned the studio and been willing to do some sleight of hand, Wings would have been confined to rehearsing and catching shows.

When he asked Brolly to work on getting Wings the proper visas, Brolly reminded him that he and Denny had drug convictions and now Jimmy had a police record in Nashville for reckless driving. Only Geoff and Linda, a United States citizen, were in the clear. To sort out these problems and help streamline the visa application process, the Eastmans hired an immigration lawyer, Austin Fragomen.

Until that could be settled, the idea of recording in America was shelved, and two blocks of time were booked at EMI Studios—November 1–15, and January 8–26, 1975.

Recording Sessions

Friday, November 1–Saturday, November 2, 1974.
EMI Studios, Studio Two, London.
Recording: 'Rock Show ("1st Version").'

In keeping with his idea that the new album would be the core of Wings' stage set, Paul had recently written 'Rock Show,' a song tailor-made to be performed in concert, its lyric namechecking some of the international venues he had played at over the years (and some he hadn't, like Madison Square Garden, in New York, and the Rainbow, in London).

"I start off with an idea," Paul explained. "'*Rock Show*,' boom. Concertgebouw came into my mind because that's one of the places you play in Amsterdam. We played there (during Wings' 1972 European tour), so I rhymed it with '*Rock Show*' in an English pronunciation of Gebauw. '*Long hair*' . . . well, where else? Madison Square. '*Rock and roll*' . . . well, that rhymes with Hollywood Bowl. Often these things that turn out to be great afterwards are just searches for a rhyme."[11]

Led Zeppelin's guitarist, Jimmy Page, was mentioned, too, as was a fictional character, Mademoiselle Kitty.

"In 'Rock Show' there's a line about, '*What's that man rolling across the stage / It looks like the one used by Jimmy Page / Like a relic from a different age.*' Personally, I was just thinking of a nice old amp and the people in the audience are saying, 'That's an AK300. Wow-eee, it looks just like the one used by Jimmy Page.' And he was the only guitarist who rhymed with 'stage.' John Cage? Not the same."[12]

Shortly before the session, Paul put in a call to Page, to be sure that his reference to the guitarist would not be taken amiss.

Regarding 'Rock Show' as the cornerstone of the new album, Paul chose it as the starting point for the sessions. What he wanted was a hard-edged rocker, but the band found it difficult to capture on tape the sound Paul had in his head.

"On one hand, I'm trying to put down the kind of things that are happening to me, in my life," he told Litchfield around the time he conceived the song. "And, on the other hand, I just write like a hack songwriter, some of them are just total imagination. Of course, Freud would say they're all connected with your life anyway."[13]

Indeed, beyond the references to concert venues, the song was full of veiled glimpses of Paul's recent past. "*The tension mounts / You score an ounce, ole!*" though certainly a line that seems natural enough in a song about rock shows, also referred to the band's fraught (if also comic, in retrospect) attempts to buy hash during their February 1973 trip to Morocco. Another line, "*Temperatures rise as you see the whites of their eyes,*" might strike a Freudian as a nod to being mugged in Lagos, Nigeria, the final phrase lifted from Terry Scott's line in the 1968 film *Carry On Up the Khyber*, "We don't fire until we see the whites of their eyes."*

With Geoff Emerick and Mark Vigars in the control room (they would oversee all of the November sessions), Wings recorded 34 takes, all but two of them complete. And because he wanted an electrifying performance that would seem as close as possible to the band's live sound, Paul played bass live on the basic takes—along with Jimmy and Denny on guitars, and Geoff drumming—rather than overdubbing it later, as was his usual preference.

* The origin of this phrase is much disputed, but many historians claim it was first uttered by American officer William Prescott at the Battle of Bunker Hill in the American Revolutionary War.

For Britton, the feeling among the band had warmed notably, thanks in large part to the *One Hand Clapping* sessions. Yet he still sensed a pecking order within the band, which gave old-timer Laine a slightly elevated status, as well as a cliquish friendship between Denny and Jimmy that left him feeling like an outsider. The switch from salaries to super session fees also contributed to making the studio feel like a pressure cooker.

"The social balance was so out of step from what I was used to," Britton confided. "And I found that particularly difficult. I had just come out of the Wild Angels, and we were mates. Every gig was just the greatest night out ever, we just had so much fun. I've gone from that to Wings with this incredible insecurity and imbalance of personalities, and it was just a big culture shock. I said to my wife at the time, 'Every day you've got to kind of re-establish yourself. You're not accepted for who you are and what you are.' And I said, 'It's ridiculous to say this, but I'm getting paid more than I'm happy to get. Because I'm miserable and it should be the best time of my life.'"[14]

But if Britton felt more insecure than the others, he was not the only one feeling the pressure of the studio. When the first 18 takes proved unsatisfactory, Paul had the band take a break while he reconsidered elements of the arrangement. They then started afresh with a new Take 1. After 16 takes, Take 16—which clocked in at 7'00"—was marked "Best," though Paul was still not completely satisfied.

When the band returned the next day, he opted to see whether some overdubbing might help the track blossom, so fresh guitar figures, as well as chimes and Minimoog lines, were added before Paul decided to abandon the track, which was archived as 'Rock Show 1st Version.'

Recording Sessions

Monday, November 4–Tuesday, November 5, 1974.
EMI Studios, Studio Two, London.
Mixing: *One Hand Clapping* soundtrack.
Recording: 'Letting Go.'

Monday's session was devoted to mixing the final soundtrack for Litchfield's production. In the hope of seeing his very first film shown on national television, Litchfield arranged to show a working cut to a BBC executive shortly after the session. Sadly, the documentary—not to mention the visual quality of the footage—left the unknown executive cold.

"I didn't do any of this with any expectation that it was going to get played [on television]," said Litchfield. "[But] somebody convinced me that I was out of my mind and that this was something that the BBC would love to get their hands on. So, I got somebody from the BBC to come around and look at what I'd shot. And they were horrified and told me that I had to be mad. Oh well, fuck you then! And that was the end of that."[15]

On Tuesday, Wings recorded the sultry rocker that only a month earlier had been called 'Now That She Is Mine,' and had now been transformed, with a new refrain, into 'Letting Go.' The fabric of the song, and the arrangement Paul devised as the track came together in the studio, owe something to his fondness for American soul records like Al Green's 1972 hit, 'Let's Stay Together.'

For the basic recording, Paul played electric piano and sang a pilot vocal, with Linda playing organ, Jimmy on electric guitar, Denny on bass, and Geoff drumming. Rehearsing the song before the first take, Paul was open to McCulloch's input—an approach notably different from the one he took during Wings Mark I, when his tendency to dictate guitar parts to Henry McCullough created an undercurrent of tension that led Henry to quit in frustration. McCulloch developed the song's bluesy guitar introduction through what he called "trial and error at rehearsals," adding that "apart from the chord structure of the songs, everything else is ad lib: you put in your own interpretation of a lead figure, according to how you feel that passage should go. There's plenty of freedom."[16]

Denny Laine noted this change in approach, but he ascribed it not to any change in attitude by Paul, but to differences between the two guitarists.

"Jimmy was more a team person [than Henry] as far as working out parts," said Laine. "You could jam with him a lot easier and that's where we took our ideas from. We'd jam an idea and then use it if we liked it. Again, Jimmy had a broader scope as far as the styles he was playing. He was a younger guy—he was into playing lots of different styles—but he was equally good at all of them."[17]

The band recorded 21 takes of 'Letting Go'—three false starts, 18 complete performances. Take 21, which ran 5'37", seemed to capture the feeling Paul was after, although he harbored some doubts.

"We finished playing back the track and there's that pregnant pause," Britton recalled, "and nobody wants to say what they think of it, and everybody's hedging their bets. So, Paul says to me, 'What do you think, Geoff?' And I said, 'We've got it. We've nailed it. But unfortunately, I don't think any of you lot realize it.'"[18]

As the standoff in the control room continued, Geoff decided to mimic a technique that the actor Robert Mitchum used as a way of persuading film directors to have faith in their actors.

"I said, 'I can't do it better than that.' So there was another pregnant pause. And [Paul] was like, 'Yeah, I think Geoff's right. I tell you what, send one of the roadies to my house to get an Al Green album.' So he went over to Paul's place and got an LP, came back, put it on, and then put on 'Letting Go.' And that was that. I knew I'd nailed it because I'd listened a lot to Al Green beforehand."[19]

Convinced at last that Wings had captured the spirit of Al Green, Paul overdubbed a new bass guitar part and a lead vocal. A rough stereo mix was made for Paul to take home.

Recording Sessions

Wednesday, November 6–Thursday, November 7, 1974.
EMI Studios, Studio Two, London.
Recording: *This Is Your Life* television insert, 'Love in Song' and 'Untitled Jam.'

Back in March, the television host Eamonn Andrews had invited Paul and Linda to participate in an episode of *This Is Your Life*, an ITV program that zoomed in on the lives of celebrities. Since the subject this time was a friend of Paul's, the McCartneys agreed to appear on the show. Each episode began with a sting, in which the celebrity guests would be surprised by Andrews before being whisked away to a television studio. After considerable back-and-forth during the planning, it was decided that the subject would be lured to EMI Studios on November 6, at 11:30 A.M., on the pretext of a photo shoot, in which he and Paul would be appearing together and Linda would be behind the camera.

"Tonight I'm with that world-famous man of music, Paul McCartney, and his wife Linda," Andrews said as the cameras rolled, "helping us to spring a surprise on a special friend of theirs. . . . And he's quite a guy, isn't he, Paul?"

"He sure is, Eamonn," Paul replied with a hammy smile.

Once the introduction was taped, Paul sat at the piano and led Wings through a rehearsal of 'Junior's Farm,' with the cameras rolling: when the guest of honor arrived, Wings were to look as though they were involved in a recording session. All this would be inserted into the program before it was aired a week later,* so playing 'Junior's Farm' made sense: it was Wings' new single, why not use their appearance on *This Is Your Life* to promote it?

At the appointed time, John Conteh, Paul's boxer friend, sauntered into the studio. If he noticed the television cameras, he probably thought they were for Wings' video shoot. Paul gestured that he should sit beside him on the piano bench, and Wings continued playing. When they finished, Andrews stepped out and announced, "Tonight, Light Heavyweight Champion of the World, John Conteh—this is your life!"

"Had he not been sitting at the piano with Paul, I swear I would have had the new world champion sagging at his knees," Andrews wrote in his memoir. "Was he surprised! The sharp left hand that had helped him to his hard-earned and well-deserved title was now raised in a gesture of bewilderment as he scratched the head that just 36 days before had been crowned in triumph."[20]

With the introduction complete, Conteh and the television crew raced across town to ITV's

* While *This Is Your Life* was recorded "as live" it did not air until November 13, 1974.

studios, where the rest of the show was to be taped, with guests that included eight other British boxing champions and the actor Kenneth Haigh. Paul and Linda added further comments about their friendship with Conteh by way of a live link between the TV studio and EMI.

Nothing more was accomplished on Wednesday, but on Thursday, it was back to business with a freshly written, moody ballad, 'Love in Song.' Like many of Paul's songs, from 'Eleanor Rigby' to 'Nineteen Hundred and Eighty Five,' the new tune was built around an opening line Paul had been toying with.

"I sat down—I had my 12-string—and started to write this thing," Paul said of the song's origin. "And I thought, '*My heart cries out for love and all that goes with loving*'—that's a nice opening, that'll do for the opening to a love song. And then one of the other lines was, '*My eyes cry out a tear still born misunderstanding*'—that's a nice little line. And it's just a tune that came forth.

"I don't feel like I have a lot of control over some songs. Some songs I do, and I really just sit down and work them out. But with that one I was just playing my guitar and I started singing those words. I wrote them down and said to Linda, 'How d'you like that?' And that was it."[21]

Paul asked Jimmy to bring a 12-string acoustic guitar to the session, but the guitarist did not own one, so he rented a Tony Zemaitis custom 12-string from Maurice Plaquet's music shop in Acton, West London. The model was similar to instruments McCulloch had heard Ronnie Lane, Ron Wood and Eric Clapton play on recent recordings, and Jimmy was charmed by its rich tone.

"I thought, 'I must have one,'" McCulloch explained. "So I phoned up Tony [Zemaitis], who had one left. It was exactly the same as the one I'd hired, but slightly better condition, so I zoomed down there, had a look at it, played it, and that was that."[22]

Though he wrote the song on a 12-string, Paul moved to the piano for the basic track, ceding the 12-string part to Jimmy, with Denny playing electric guitar and Geoff on drums. The band recorded 19 takes (including five false starts and two breakdowns), with Take 19, running 2'59", considered "Best." Before the session ended, Paul added bass guitar and a lead vocal; Linda added Minimoog; and Geoff laid down some extra percussion using glass objects he found lying around the studio.

"I was playing a drum part, and afterwards they had kept the tape running," said Britton. "I'd been fooling about on milk bottles. Paul thought it was great. But really it was a pure accident."[23]

Wings ended the session with a jam.

Recording Sessions

Monday, November 11–Wednesday, November 13, 1974.
EMI Studios, Studio Two, London.
Recording: 'Medicine Jar' and 'Medicine Jar (Remake).'

After a long weekend, Wings returned to EMI Studios on Monday morning to record 'Medicine Jar,' the anti-drug song composed by McCulloch and Colin Allen. Paul had committed to incorporating the song into their repertoire when the group rehearsed it in Nashville, but there was another reason for moving it up the priority list: with the band's work visas in question, it made sense to have a song that hinted that Paul and his band had moved beyond their herbal jazz cigarette days.

"It was used, when [Jimmy] got his visa revoked, to prove that he was making an effort," explained Britton, "because it was an anti-drug song. It helped his case when he got arrested."[24]

Beyond that, putting Jimmy in the spotlight reflected Paul's long quest to have Wings seen as a band, not just his backing ensemble.

"The idea was that we would have material for a stage show where everyone would get a go; each person would have their solo moment," Paul explained. "And that was really the policy. That was the strategy with Wings that it would be a group, worked from the bottom rather than plonked down as a super group. It would work its way up and write songs."[25]

But recording Jimmy's song proved tricky. With Paul on electric piano, Linda playing organ, Geoff drumming, and Denny and Jimmy playing electric guitar (with Jimmy singing a guide vocal), the band set down 28 takes (11 of them false starts). Take 28 (at 5'50") was marked "Best," but only temporarily: when Wings returned to the studio the next day and heard the recording afresh, Paul decided to rework the arrangement and try again.

Thirteen takes of this revised version were recorded, eight of which were complete, before Paul felt that the band had a good basic track. He sent one of the roadies to pick up some Chinese takeout, which the band ate while surveying the day's recordings. Take 13, running 3'45", was chosen as the new "Best," and Jimmy's lead vocal and a bass line from Paul were overdubbed before Paul had a copy made for home review, and called it a night.

On Wednesday, the band gathered at MPL's temporary offices on Greek Street to watch the finished Mother's Pride bread commercial, with Paul's 'Proud Mother' jingle as its soundtrack. For the occasion, Brian Brolly donned a whippet costume, something that struck David Litchfield as odd when he stopped at the office to file expenses for *One Hand Clapping.*

"He was sitting there at a large, beautiful office in Greek Street," Litchfield recalled, "and he was in a whippet suit. I said, 'What the. . . . ?' And he said, 'So, you've heard of the Wombles? Well, now it's the Whippets. They want to see what it looks like when they walk in.' I said, 'It's 10:30 in the morning, they're not gonna be here 'til 4:30 P.M.!' He said, 'I know, but I can't take it off, because then they'll walk in.' You know when people talk about tension? Often the tension was over quite ridiculous things like Brian in his fucking Whippet suit."[26]

Unfortunately, just over two weeks later, 33,000 workers at Britain's biggest bakeries—Sunblest, Homepride, Mother's Pride and Wonderloaf, which together supplied 70 percent of the nation's bread—went on strike, and though the strike lasted only six days, the advertising campaign was scrapped.

After watching the commercial and savoring the entire 30-second career of the Whippets at MPL, Wings cabbed from Soho to St. John's Wood to continue recording. Having listened to the previous day's work overnight, Paul concluded that 'Medicine Jar' still lacked bite. In Curly Putman's garage, the song had a raw sound that seemed perfect. But in the studio, more precision was necessary, and Wings took from 2:30 P.M. to 2 A.M. to try to capture a take that balanced those seemingly disparate qualities.

"I'm very aware of what I play in the studio," said McCulloch, who cited the 1950's and early-1960's precision pick masters like the Shadows and the Ventures among his earliest influences. "My approach is different. Everybody's afraid of making mistakes in the studio, so I think you play more carefully. But also in the studio I have a lighter touch because I don't have to worry so much about getting the sound across. In the studio if you've got a good engineer, he'll tell you if it's too loud or there's not enough bass, and you go and have a listen and experiment."[27]

Wings experimented with the remake of 'Medicine Jar' over the course of 15 takes (with

Wings and their roadies enjoy a Chinese takeaway at EMI Studios, November 11, 1974

seven false starts), with the same instrumentation as the first version, except that Paul played bass rather than electric piano on the basic track. Take 15 (which ran 3'46") was chosen for further work, whereupon Paul overdubbed an electric piano, Jimmy added more electric guitar, and Denny and Geoff added more percussion, with Denny playing congas and Geoff embellishing the cymbal and high-hat parts.

With the backing track complete, Jimmy recorded a new lead vocal, and Paul, Linda and Denny added harmonies.

Recording Sessions

Thursday, November 14–Friday, November 15, 1974.
EMI Studios, Studio Two, London.
Recording: 'Rock Show (Remake).'

After listening to the recording of 'Rock Show' at home and changing his mind several times about whether it was as tough and hard-rocking as he wanted it to be, Paul gave the recording a thumbs-down.

"I think it's easier for me to do melodies and ballads," Paul later reflected. "I think they come easier to me. I think they're actually easier songs to write than rockers. . . . Rock 'n' roll is deceptively hard to write. A lot of people will just think, 'Oh, it's three chords and all you've gotta have is a lot of soft lyrics and you've got a rock song.' And sometimes that does work.[28] Every time I attempt a heavy rock thing, I know it must be perfect. Otherwise I have people saying, 'That's a nice soft rock thing you've just done, Paul.' That's no compliment, believe me."[29]

So far, he had a soft rocker, 'Letting Go,' and a ballad, 'Love in Song.' 'Medicine Jar' qualified as a rocker, with a funky edge, but as Jimmy's song, with Jimmy singing, it didn't figure into Paul's own rocker/ballad scorecard. Also, to Paul's mind, 'Rock Show' was not just an item meant to increase the album's quotient of rockers; he saw it as the album's linchpin. There was no question about it—it had to be remade.

As it happened, Kenneth "Afro" Williams, a percussionist in the recently formed New Orleans funk band Chocolate Milk, was in London, and Paul invited him to the session, thinking that a second percussionist might give the track the spark it needed. With Williams on congas, Wings recorded six takes of the song, all but one complete. But at the end of the session, Paul had to confess that none of the new takes made the grade.

At home, Paul felt the need to clear his head and regroup. What he needed was the inspiration to make 'Rock Show' a worthy successor to the spirited and critically lauded 'Jet,' 'Let Me Roll It' and 'Helen Wheels.' It made sense to revisit those songs, in the hope of recapturing the feeling that drove them, so he slipped *Band on the Run* out of its sleeve and put it on his turntable.

"What I nearly always do is, I will listen to the album I did last, whilst I'm making the new one," Paul explained, "and kind of see where I'm up to. And I always did that with the Beatles [too]."[30]

Back at EMI the next day, he picked up Take 7 of 'Rock Show.' In the hope of ratcheting up the intensity of the basic track, Paul switched from bass to piano, picking up the tempo and providing a pounding Little Richard–style backing. Williams was still on hand to play congas, but the band struggled to find the right groove, and turned their frustrations on Britton.

"I had a problem with 'Rock Show,'" Geoff said, adding that he felt under extreme pressure to deliver. "We worked hard on 'Rock Show,' and it started getting worse. The band went all negative on me. I started wondering if I'd be okay. Went out to the toilet, started feeling dejected by it all. Ian [the roadie] suggested I try a joint, which, at that stage, I'd try anything. So I got stoned for the first time."[31]

Britton was likely mirroring Paul's own anxiety about recording the follow-up to *Band on the Run*, but the problem extended deeper than plain insecurity on Paul's part. There were issues with the song's arrangement—something a producer would normally remedy, but this time the producer was within the band's ranks. If Laine and McCulloch noted any problems with the arrangement, they weren't speaking out. Now, Britton, the only member of the group willing to voice an opinion, was under fire.

"The Beatles were all equals," said Britton. "[But in Wings] I felt Paul didn't have anybody around who would tell him when he was out of order, or to fuck off. You need that. It doesn't matter who you are. This was possibly my strength, and failing, within the band. It's alright if a band has come up together and they are all millionaires, they can talk to each other as equals. But with Wings there were these incredible imbalances."[32]

Paul addressed the weaknesses in the arrangement by trimming the playout and adding a short instrumental coda. And Geoff, having reduced his own stress thanks to a few tokes on some mellowing buds, found his rhythm. After Take 29, the band climbed the stairs to Studio Two's control room to hear what they had accomplished. They settled on Take 12, which ran 6'50", and returned to the studio to do overdubs. Paul added a bass line and lead vocals, and Jimmy added another layer of electric guitar.

Before the session ended, the best takes of 'Letting Go,' 'Love in Song,' 'Medicine Jar (remake),' 'Rock Show (remake)' and 'Rock Show (1st Version)' were compiled onto a master reel, and rough stereo mixes were made.

EMI Studios were unavailable beyond mid-November, so Paul discharged the band until January 8, when he had booked another three weeks in Studio Two.

Geoff slipped behind the kit again for a gig with the Wild Angels on November 16. That same evening, Paul and Linda gave Ringo's new album, *Goodnight Vienna*, a spin before settling in front of the box to watch the BBC's arts show *2nd House*, which was showing extracts from Willy Russell's Beatles musical, *John, Paul, George, Ringo . . . and Bert.* Paul had avoided the play ever since it opened at the Lyric Theatre in London's West End on August 15, although John Conteh told him that he found it so brilliant that he had seen it three times.

"I did think of going along one night and getting one of those little boxes near the stage," he told a reporter. "Then when he came on I was going to start heckling [the actor playing] Paul—shouting at him and perhaps jump on the stage yelling, 'You're not 'im.' I thought I'd get in on the play. A nice idea but I couldn't do it; I'd be too embarrassed."[33]

Watching the *2nd House* excerpts, Paul appreciated the humor in Russell's dialogue, and he was impressed with the prosthetics that made the actors look like the Beatles. But he worried that the loose, fictionalized narrative would be accepted as fact.

"Linda and I thought it was good fun," Paul told the *TV Times* shortly afterward. "The guy playing Paul looked pretty much like me. There was only one thing I didn't really like: as with anything else that's done from the press image, they never really got at the truth."[34]

Paul's specific objection was that he was portrayed, matter-of-factly, as the man who broke up the Beatles.

"They've got it all wrong, Paul was the last one to leave the Beatles," Linda complained, also taking exception to the way she was portrayed. "I saw part of it on TV . . . (mimicking the actress who plays her) 'Oh, Paulie!' I've got to go meet the guy who wrote it, just so he can see I'm not a stupid idiot. He should have done more research—at least met the people he was writing about."[35]

Artistic license on a West End stage was irritating, but soon Paul had another reason to find the play objectionable. The Robert Stigwood Organisation had been looking into acquiring the film rights to Russell's musical. EMI's film department, headed by John Hough, was interested as well, but Stigwood had the right of first refusal. He offered Russell £25,000 ($58,000) plus 2.5 percent of the profits.

"Stigwood—seizing the opportunity as always, thank you, Robert—wanted to make it into a film," Paul noted. "And then I really decided I just couldn't have *that.* All of us [former Beatles] agreed actually—it wasn't just me objecting to being cast as the villain. Everyone agreed that it wasn't anything like how it really was. It's the legend."[36]

"A lot of people like it," he told another interviewer, broadening his objections. "But now they want to make a film, and to me it seems that a film is going to be like *The Beatles Life Story*, inevitably. The plot of this little play is so weird and so wrong. Linda appears in a kind of crazy light. So do I. I appear as this total business-like character, which I only was towards the end of the thing. George is made to be a religious freak. It has nothing to do with how the Beatles were. My basic objection is that if they're going to do a thing, which in years to come is going to look like the official Beatles story, they must at least think about getting it right."[37]

Paul asked the Eastmans to explore ways of preventing the play from making its way to the silver screen. That, as it turned out, was not difficult, as Russell—who had dreamed of possibly collaborating with the Beatles on a film version—learned, to his chagrin.

"One thing I was unaware of was the great enmity between the Beatles and Robert Stigwood," explained Russell. "Obviously, the problems had been foreseen because Peter Brown* came on the scene to try to smooth the path. And there were debates about rights of image, which didn't exist in Britain, Europe and maybe Australasia at the time. But what eventually happened—this is my understanding of it, and I don't have chapter and verse because I was on the receiving end of this—is that Paul did not want this project to go ahead. I think Peter Brown reported this back. And what Paul had discovered [through the Eastmans] is that he did not have rights to his public image in Europe and Australasia, but in America he *did*."[38]

That was a crippling detail: without the right to use Paul's name and likeness in the United States, the film lost its biggest potential market.†

John, Paul, George, Ringo . . . and Bert was not, however, the only Beatles-related play on the boards at this time. Such was the continued demand for the Beatles as a band that another, very different music theater piece—the stage version of *Sgt. Pepper* dreamed up by Lou Reizner, and now called *Sgt. Pepper's Lonely Hearts Club Band on the Road*—was about to be unveiled in New York. And Stigwood's fingerprints were on this project, too.

Picking up on Reizner's idea, Stigwood had obtained the rights to use 28 Beatles songs, mostly from the *Sgt. Pepper* and *Abbey Road* albums. He hired Tom O'Horgan—the American director who made his Broadway debut with the musical *Hair* in 1968, and subsequently directed *Lenny* (Julian Barry's play about the comedian Lenny Bruce) and Andrew Lloyd Webber's *Jesus Christ Superstar*—to write and direct the show. O'Horgan collaborated with Robin Wagner on the script, about a young rocker named Billy Shears who wants to become a star.

"It will mark the beginning of a new kind of entertainment," O'Horgan commented, "combining elements of theater, opera and rock concerts in a novel way."[39]

---

* Peter Brown left Apple at the end of 1970 to run the Robert Stigwood Organisation's New York office as president and chief operating officer of the company.

† It took two years to establish whether Paul's image rights were indeed protected in America, and when it became clear that there was no way around this, the film project, then in pre-production, with John Hook directing, was shut down.

This was not to be a semi-biography, in other words, but a fantasy with fictional characters—which meant that American laws protecting name and likeness were irrelevant.

Apart from their collective dislike of Stigwood, however, there was little in the show for the former Beatles to find objectionable: they disliked being portrayed, but they had no problem with their songs being used in creative ways, as long as they were properly licensed; such efforts yielded extra income streams without trespassing on their images or reputations. Stigwood prevailed upon Peter Brown to get his former employers onside.

"I talked to both John and with Paul separately," Peter Brown remembered, "and they both thought it was a rather good idea."[40] He also sent photographs of the sets and costumes to John and Paul, to which Paul simply replied, "It looks fine."[41] And he lured John to a rehearsal at the Ukrainian National Home, in Greenwich Village. *NME*'s Lisa Robinson was on hand as well and reported that "Lennon laughed a lot and sang along with the songs, and called out occasional cues when the cast forgot their lines."[42]

The next day, John gave the show a public endorsement by turning up at the Beacon Theatre at Broadway and West 74th Street—just a few blocks from the Dakota—to hold up the street sign when the section of Broadway outside the theater was renamed "Sgt. Pepper Way" for the duration of the musical's run. After a seven-day tryout in Hartford, Connecticut, starting on November 4, the musical took up residence at the Beacon on November 17, and John and May attended the premiere—as did Yoko, for whom John arranged a seat on the other side of the theater.

"Peter Brown asked me to go, and he's been a friend for a long time, and he was involved with it, so I thought, 'I'm in town, so I might as well go,'" John told a reporter who was surprised to see him venture into a crowd. "It was pretty wild . . . At the *Pepper* thing, most of the audience were watching me! They were even popping off flash bulbs."[43]

Also occupying Paul's attention in mid-November were his plans for the future of his growing business empire, MPL. Having acquired 1 Soho Square, Paul was now about to bring the rundown building into the future.

In September 1973, Paul and Linda had visited Kensington High Street to have a look at Big Biba, a seven-story department store that had been given a chic Art Deco makeover that reminded them of scenes from Fred Astaire films and productions from the golden age of Hollywood. The flagship of the Biba fashion brand, Big Biba was designed by Chelsea School of Arts graduates Steve Thomas and Tim Whitmore. Its striking Art Deco interior exuded post-Depression New York glamor, and over several visits to the fifth-floor Rainbow Restaurant, Paul and Linda resolved to hire Whitmore and Thomas to design MPL's new offices in a similar style.

Paul telephoned the London offices of Whitmore-Thomas, but when Thomas's assistant handed him the receiver, he thought that perhaps his business partner was pranking him.

"I picked up the receiver to say, 'Hello, who is this?'" Thomas explained. "And this voice says, 'Hi, it's Paul McCartney.' And I went, 'Oh, don't fuck about, who is it?' He said, 'Paul McCartney.' So, I said, 'Alright, what's the second line to 'Yesterday'? And he sang it down the phone to me. So it got off to a weird start really, but he found it really funny."[44]

After working seven days a week for the 21 months to create Big Biba, Whitmore and Thomas were exhausted and not actively seeking another hefty project, but they agreed to meet with Paul and Linda at Soho Square the next day. Paul raved about the exquisite design and craftsmanship on display in Kensington before delivering his own vision for MPL's expanded London headquarters, which included offices, an apartment, and a basement rehearsal space.

He also wanted it to be durable, a quest prompted by events transpiring just across London at 3 Savile Row. The townhouse that had been the headquarters of Apple Corps had just been structurally condemned. Apple's operations, including the recording studio and the cutting room, were being wound down, and the small team running the company, headed by Neil Aspinall, was in the process of relocating Apple's offices to 54 St. James's Street, near Green Park.

Paul did not want MPL's offices to suffer a similar fate—1 Soho Square had to be built to last. Plastic laminates, wooden veneers or materials that would wear out would not do, Paul told Whitmore and Thomas: if something was to be oak, it would have to be solid oak. He requested that the designers seek out the best tradesmen in London and have them use the finest materials to create an office space that would be timeless in character and durable physically.

"Part of his brief," said Thomas, "and it was a very brief brief, considering it was Soho Square—was that he wanted it to be as British as possible. He wanted British-sourced materials, and British craftsmanship.

"He had emotional ties to 1 Soho Square because he took a room there when it was all going wrong at Apple, and it was his sort of hideaway. But it wasn't the finest of British architecture, it was a bit of an old rundown tip, to be honest. At the first meeting we zipped around the place, and he said, 'Oh, this is going to be the accounts floor, this is going to be our romping room, this is where we're going to have an apartment on top, and this is the basement where there was going to be rehearsal room.' So he went through it very fast, and we sort of took it all in.

"We had no idea what colors he liked, but we knew that he was going to use it like home, because he kept referring to how important this building was to him, and how he wanted to be as comfortable as possible, surrounded by really nice things for the rest of his life. So he wanted it to be a kind of office, obviously—it's got to work efficiently for the other people who work there day by day; but he wanted to feel that it had a domestic side to it as well, so he could feel comfortable and relaxed, and didn't feel like he had to play offices all the time.

"And then he said, 'Oh, by the way, we're off to America with Wings, so anything you want to show us, send it to Brian, Brian Brolly.'"[45]

Whitmore and Thomas agreed to work up some designs, and a rough timescale of two years was agreed on to complete the renovation work.

On November 18, Paul received encouraging news from the Eastmans. Immigration lawyer Austin Fragomen had worked his legal magic, and the band had been granted American work visas through March 1, 1975. Recording (legally) in the United States was now possible, and a world tour, including America, was in the cards.

That afternoon, Wings gathered in Soho to discuss finishing their album in the United States, as well as Paul's vision for their tour that would follow the album's completion. The entire building at Soho Square was now empty, and Wings had taken to using the basement as a rehearsal space, their workouts typically followed by drinks at a pub just around the corner. Paul had lots of ideas for that basement: at the moment, he thought of it as a place where the band could play impromptu concerts, in the same spirit as the Beatles' lunchtime gigs at the Cavern Club, in Liverpool.

Paul and Linda backstage at the Lewisham Odeon with Rod Stewart, November 18, 1974

A few hours later, the band made their way to the Lewisham Odeon to hear Rod Stewart in concert. Gathered backstage, and a bit worse for wear, having indulged in a fair number of celebratory pre-concert drinks, as well as the odd spliff, Paul and Linda were surprised to hear Stewart declare, midway through his set, that his "brother and sister" would join him for the next song—the one Paul wrote for him in the spring of 1973, 'Mine for Me.' Suddenly, the McCartneys found themselves onstage with Stewart, looking out at a packed house.

"We were sitting on an amp in the wings, having a good time, then Rod called us out and put us on the main mic,"[46] Linda told a reporter. Paul noted that "one journalist said I looked a little ungainly," Paul continued. "It was the alcohol. That wasn't ungainly, that was pissed!"[47]

Two days later, on November 20, it was Wings' turn to take center stage. The band trouped into Studio Two at Television Centre, in London, to record a lip-synced performance of 'Junior's Farm,' to be aired the following evening on *Top of the Pops*. The band also made a guest appearance alongside David Essex in a star-studded performance of Essex's new single, 'Gonna Make You a Star.'*

With a new single to promote, Paul kicked Wings into promotional mode, offering publicist Tony Brainsby a two-day window—November 20 and 21—during which the whole band would be available for interviews at MPL's offices on Greek Street.

"We enjoyed being on the road with Wings and this time it's going to be a global tour," Paul told one reporter about Wings' plans for the next year or two. "We're going east towards Australia, Hawaii and the States, finishing up in Britain. This is a new band and we'll not have had much chance to play together, so we're going to need an awful lot of practice. I reckon by the time we get back here we should be pretty good."[48]

He also offered a short preview of *Cold Cuts*—reverting to the original title that Capitol executives found so puzzling, *Hot Hitz and Kold Kutz*—which he said would be rush-released before Christmas.

"We've got a couple of little tunes from *Ram* which I did," Paul told Geoff Brown of *Melody Maker*. "It's like the [Who's] *Odds and Sods* idea, only it's a bit more 'studio' than that. We've done songs like the old Thomas Wayne song 'Tragedy' with the old Wings. We were hoping to do it, particularly in England, as a kind of budget album . . . what we're gonna end up doing is call it *Hot Hitz Kold Kutz* and instead of padding out the hits there'll be singles that didn't get on albums, certain, kind of, hit tracks, and all these others to fill it. And they're not bad."[49]

He couched the objections raised by Capitol when he first proposed the album as a transatlantic cultural issue.

---

* Essex's song lived up to its title, giving the Essex-born singer his first UK No. 1 single as 'Junior's Farm' labored to a peak position of No. 16.

"I would get record executives over in America saying, 'You're big, what do you want to do that for?' If I answered, 'For the people'—believe me, I would mean it—they would reply, 'Oh man, screw the people, they can afford it,' 'cos that's the way they look at business over there."[50]

Mostly, though, Paul, Linda and Denny stepped back to allow Jimmy and Geoff to introduce themselves properly as Wings' new members. McCulloch was intent on making it clear that times had changed since Denny Seiwell's and Henry McCullough's tenure.

"Wings wasn't a *band* before, it was Paul with session musicians," McCulloch explained somewhat paradoxically, given the band's new super session fee arrangement. "Now it feels like a band, and I'm able to say my own things and voice my opinion. I can say, 'Listen, why don't we do this?' If it works, we do it. It's everybody being able to speak up and contribute, even though Paul is so dominant."[51]

Britton took a humbler approach.

"Being in Wings is like stepping into a band that's in world terms," Britton enthused to Carroll Moore of *Beat Instrumental*. "There's your Led Zeppelins, your Stones, and Wings is in that class . . . [Being in the band is] a chance to see the world, to be a famous face, to make a lot of dough."[52]

Paul had some publicity photos taken with Geoff on November 25 to help promote his karate tournament. But Paul would not be on hand for the tournament itself: by Thanksgiving, on November 28, he was in Jamaica with Linda and the girls, sunning themselves on the golden sand and stocking up on the reggae records that had become an important source of spiritual refreshment for them. The Caribbean also offered the family an unexpected level of privacy.

"I remember reaching the point where I thought this is the point of no return—seeing our records sell in Greece, Turkey, Afghanistan. Thinking, now we're worldwide famous, it's not gonna be easy to find a country where they don't know us. Although, it's not true; there are plenty of places where they don't recognize me. If I go to Jamaica, they've heard of me, but they don't recognize me."[53]

On Paul's mind during this trip was the question of where to continue work on the new Wings album, now that the cleared-up visa problems made American studios a possibility. A chance encounter with Paul Simon in Jamaica, along with saturation airplay of the American vocal group Labelle's recently released single 'Lady Marmalade,' pointed McCartney in the direction of New Orleans.

Although Simon's last studio album, *There Goes Rhymin' Simon,* had been recorded in studios in New York and London, as well as Jackson, Mississippi, and Sheffield, Alabama, Simon had worked on the song 'Tenderness' with Allen Toussaint and spoke enthusiastically about the experience. Besides being a renowned songwriter and performer, Toussaint was the co-owner, with Marshall Sehorn, of Sea-Saint Recording Studio in New Orleans—where 'Lady Marmalade' was recorded. Wings' recent guest percussionist Kenneth "Afro" Williams also enthused about Sehorn's and Toussaint's two-year-old facility in his hometown, so the stars seemed to be in alignment. Paul telephoned Sea-Saint to scope out the possibilities.

"Paul first got in [touch] with the studio Thanksgiving of 1974," said Sehorn. "I gather that when he first called, he wanted to know if this was the studio where Allen Toussaint worked and was co-owner. We said yes, and his next questions was, 'Is this the studio where Labelle cut "Lady Marmalade"? 'Cos I loved the drum sound on that record.'"[54]

The EMI dates scheduled for January were canceled, and Sea-Saint Studio was booked for sessions starting on January 20.

Besides giving Wings a change of cultural and musical scenery, recording in America had a huge tax advantage for Paul. Production and copyright for songs recorded outside the UK could be credited to MPL Communications, Inc., the American arm of McCartney Productions, which meant that income from the recording would be taxed in the United States, not in England. In Britain, the super tax bracket for earnings exceeding £20,000 ($46,500) per year—a figure McCartney was in no danger of dipping below—was 83 percent, with a 15 percent surcharge for unearned income (for example, investments and dividends) that raised the tax rate to 98 percent. Paul's American income was taxed at 50 percent. Since the United States accounted for 50 percent of all records sold worldwide, Paul's savings would be significant.[55]

"We have to [record outside of the UK]," Paul explained to journalist Paul Gambaccini at the time. "I have to write all my songs outside the country, too, for tax reasons. Otherwise the government will say, 'Right, this is a British record, all the money has to come back to Britain.'"[56]

Jamaica also gave Paul an opportunity to clear his mind, and like most of the McCartneys' family vacations, the trip yielded creative ideas. One had roots in a peculiar story that John Lennon had told him during a recent discussion. Three months earlier, on August 23, John and May saw what they believed was an alien spacecraft both hovering and maneuvering over the East River in New York. They watched the object from their Sutton Place apartment for several minutes—long enough for May to run into the apartment to grab a camera, although she was unable to capture an image on film. John memorialized the event in the lyrics booklet of his *Walls and Bridges* album, noting at the bottom of page 2: "On the 23rd Aug. 1974 at 9 o'clock I saw a U.F.O."

Paul was, at the time, enjoying a science fiction phase in his leisure reading, and John's story fired his imagination. In Jamaica, he could be found beside the swimming pool, caught up in one of Isaac Asimov's Foundation novels or Frank Herbert's *Dune*, or with a small stack of Marvel comic books that Paul and the girls picked up at a supermarket in Kingston.[57] And soon enough, the influence of these otherworldly tales crept into Paul's songwriting.*

Asimov's and Herbert's novels inspired Paul to fantasize about intergalactic travel on a craft

* Coincidentally, at the end of 1974 an all-star ensemble recorded the sci-fi concept album *Flash Fearless Versus the Zorg Women Parts 5 & 6*. The album, issued in May 1975, was recorded between October and December of 1974. The LP, which was noted in the music press, features Alice Cooper, Elkie Brooks, John Entwistle, Keith Moon, Justin Hayward, Nicky Hopkins, Kenney Jones, and Bill Bruford, among others. The story was written by Rick Jones, Steve Hammond, Weston Gavin, and Dave Pierce, and produced by John Alcock.

like the one Lennon said he had seen. On his notepad, he jotted down a name for the spacecraft he imagined—"21ZNA9," designed to rhyme with another line from his work in progress, "*a good friend of mine.*" The song evolved from there.

"I was just sitting down and started singing *anything* and some words came out," Paul said of the gentle acoustic tune he was developing, which might otherwise have become a love song. "And I got this idea about a fellow sitting in a cathedral waiting for this transport from space that was going to pick him up and take him on a trip. The guy is a bit blotto, and he starts thinking about '*a good friend of mine studies the stars, Venus and Mars are alright tonight.*' And the next bit was [going to be] 'your ruling star is in ascendancy today,' but '*Venus and Mars are alright*' was better, it flipped off the tongue. I thought, well, I know Venus and Mars are planets so I can't go wrong there."[58]

Paul wrote two versions of 'Venus and Mars' in Jamaica—the first describing a singer in a sports arena "*wanting for the show to begin,*" and the second set in a cathedral where the narrator is "*waiting for the transport to come.*" These joined another new song with sci-fi roots, 'Magneto and Titanium Man,' a funky yet soulful rocker based entirely on characters from his freshly acquired trove of Marvel comics—specifically, *X-Men No. 91: "X-Men vs the Power of Magneto"* and *The Avengers No. 130 featuring Titanium Man, Radioactive Man, the Crimson Dynamo and the Slasher*.

"I'd been reading comics and science fiction and that does something to your head," Paul rationalized. "I used to agree with the general consensus, which I now think is daft, that comics are just for children or for American navvies who are stupid enough to buy them. But I think they're high art. It's really imaginative stuff."[59]

Written in what he later described as "a drunken moment,"[60] McCartney's comic book caper 'Magneto and Titanium Man' chronicles a conversation between an unidentified man and woman—possibly two of Jack Kirby's and Stan Lee's X-Men—about the aftermath of a foiled bank robbery. Marvel baddies Magneto, Titanium Man and the Crimson Dynamo are named as the central protagonists of the heist, which was ultimately foiled by "the law." Paul wrote the whole song in one sitting.

Much like one of Asimov's or Herbert's starships, McCartney's songwriting engine hit hyperdrive during the family's Jamaican break. By the end of their time in the Caribbean, Paul had sketched out a fully sequenced album, writing out 19 pages of lyrics for songs he had composed in Los Angeles, London, Scotland, Nashville and Jamaica throughout 1974, as well as Jimmy's 'Medicine Jar,' and taping the pages together to form a continuous roll of paper. The only other time he had done anything similar was during the recording of *Abbey Road*, when he planned out the medley on Side 2—but this was a full album organized before most of the songs were recorded.

"For the first time ever, I'd got all the songs together," Paul confirmed. "I wrote it all out and stuck it all together like a scroll."[61]

Paul's scroll reflected the running order of the album as he conceived it in Jamaica:

'Venus and Mars,' 'Rock Show,' 'Love in Song,' 'You Gave Me the Answer (You seem to like me),' 'Magneto and Titanium Man,' 'Letting Go,' 'Medicine Jar,' 'Venus and Mars (Reprise),' 'Spirits of Ancient Egypt,' 'Call Me Back Again,' 'Listen to What the Man Said,' and the conjoined 'Treat Her Gently' and 'Lonely Old People,' to be followed by an instrumental that he listed as 'Overture' and conceived as something akin to the "exit music" that played at the end of early Beatles shows as they walked offstage.*

An Overture, typically, is heard at the beginning of a work, rather than at the end, but Paul was probably using the term simply to indicate an instrumental piece that functions in a similar way: where an Overture would preview the musical themes in the work that follows, the Postlude he had in mind would reprise the themes listeners had just heard. He might have been put on to this by another recent disc that followed the "concept album" approach that he had been thinking about since Nashville—the Electric Light Orchestra's *Eldorado—A Symphony*, an album with both an Overture and an instrumental Finale, released in September.

Now that the follow-up to *Band on the Run* was ready to roll, at least on paper, Paul reconsidered his plan to release *Cold Cuts* as a between-albums stopgap. Though Capitol Records had given the project a catalog number, no master was assembled for the compilation, and the idea was quietly shelved.

Whether the former Beatles would enjoy a happy Hogmanay† depended entirely on the next leg of the McCartney family's winter travels. Paul was due to meet with John, George and Ringo on December 19 to sign the papers dissolving the Beatles partnership. After three years of negotiation, the attorneys for all four had reached the finish line; all that was needed were the four famous signatures.

With George touring the United States and performing in New York at the end of December—John had agreed to appear with him on stage—and with Paul in town for the holidays, the timing was right. Only Ringo would be absent: with Allen Klein trying to serve him with a subpoena in his latest suit against his former clients, he opted to stay in England.

"We're refusing to be sued by him, that's our answer," Ringo explained at the time. "Allen, well, I can't really talk about him because he'll sue me again. I mean, he's a nice guy . . . but naughty."[62]

Paul, Linda, and the girls flew to New York on December 18 and checked into the Stanhope

* Except for the placement of 'Medicine Jar,' that sequence remained unchanged through the recording and production process.

† Hogmanay is the Scottish New Year's Eve and has a number of associated traditions, the best known internationally being the singing of 'Auld Lang Syne.'

Hotel. The following day, Paul and Linda, along with Lee and John Eastman, cruised down Fifth Avenue to the Plaza Hotel—where the Beatles had stayed during their first visit to New York, a decade earlier—to sign the papers. George was there with his lawyer, David Braun, and his business manager, Denis O'Brien. Ringo's lawyer, Bruce Grakal, and his business manager, Hilary Gerrard, were present, and Ringo was on the other end of a telephone line. Neil Aspinall was on hand as well, with Apple's American and British lawyers. And John's lawyer, Harold Seider, patiently awaited John's arrival. Tensions and emotions ran high as the group cast their eyes over the documents in front of them.

"Neil had to read something out, deadly serious," Paul remembered, "[and] he just couldn't do it. He did a Nixon wobble. His voice went. And we were all suddenly aware of a sort of physical consequence of what had been going on . . . we really have broken the Beatles up."[63]

But there was no sign of John.

Since running into each other backstage at Elton John's Thanksgiving concert at Madison Square Garden—where John honored his promise to Elton that if 'Whatever Gets You Thru the Night' reached No. 1, he would perform there with him—John and Yoko had been on the brink of reuniting, although he continued to live across town from the Dakota, with May.

In truth, John was still panicking about the possible tax implications of the Beatles "divorce," and on the morning of the meeting, he locked himself in a room at his East 52nd Street apartment—a move that suggested to May that beyond the tax issue, there may have been an emotional component to his refusal to attend the signing.

It was, in fact, an unusually pressured time for John. Apart from the formal dissolution of the band he had formed as the Quarrymen in the mid-1950s, his older son, Julian, was visiting for the holidays, and although he had promised to appear on stage with George, the prospect terrified him.

May telephoned Yoko, in the hope that she could talk John into going. Yoko agreed to speak with him, but when she did, she told him that "the stars aren't right," and that he should not sign. John was generally amused by Yoko's mystical reliance on astrology and Tarot card reading, but he tended to go along with it—especially when, as in this case, it matched his own inclinations.

At the Plaza, meanwhile, the assembled lawyers, business managers, and former Fabs were getting antsy, and when Seider called John's apartment to ask when he would arrive, John refused to take the call, leaving May to tell Seider that John wouldn't be coming. Harrison and then the other lawyers soon turned on Seider, accusing him of telling John to stay away. George then picked up the phone, called John's apartment and, speaking to May, essentially canceled John's planned concert cameo. "Just tell him whatever his problem is, I started this tour on my own and I'll end it on my own!"[64]

Paul remembered the scene vividly. "We're all in New York at the Plaza for the big final settlement meeting," he said. "And John sent a balloon over, 'LISTEN TO THIS BALLOON.' I mean, you've gotta be pretty cool to handle that stuff. Oh, yeah. George blew his cool and rang him up. *'You fucking maniac! Take your fucking dark glasses off and come and look at us, man.'* He gave him a whole load of shit."[65]

"George and I are still good pals," John said soon afterward, "and we always will be, but I was supposed to sign this thing on the day of his concert. He was pretty weird because he was in the middle of that tour, and we hadn't communicated for a while because he doesn't live here. I've seen Paul a bit because he comes to New York a lot, and I'm always seeing Ringo in Los Angeles. Anyway, I was a bit nervous about going on stage, but I agreed to because it would have been mean of me not to go on with George after I'd gone on with Elton.

"I didn't sign the document on that day because my astrologer told me it wasn't the right day, tee-hee . . . George was furious at the time because I hadn't signed it when I was supposed to, and somehow or other I was informed that I needn't bother to go to George's show. I was quite relieved in the end."[66]

With the delivery of John's balloon, the meeting ended, and Paul, George, and a sizeable assembly of representatives filed out of the Plaza. But with three signatures on the legal papers, the end was near.

Back at the Stanhope, Paul could not have failed to note the apparent prescience of his lyrics for 'Venus and Mars.' The "*good friend of mine*" who "*follows the stars*" had been a genial tip of the hat to John that also dovetailed nicely with the album's science fiction undercurrent.

Paul generally avoided expressing skepticism about astrology, even when journalists noted—as they periodically did—that his being a Gemini could explain certain dualities in his personality. Linda, by contrast, had no problem joking about it. When a reporter asked what her sign was, she answered, "No Parking."[67]

The next day, Paul and Linda visited John and May at their apartment. "They said, 'Okay, what's going on, how do you feel?'—they were concerned," May recalled. "And John said, 'I felt awful not doing it yesterday, *but* . . .' And they said, 'Okay, let's see if things can be worked out.'"[68]

That afternoon, while Julian went to George's matinee at Madison Square Garden, John, May and Neil Aspinall met with Lee Eastman. George's anger, it turned out, did not last long: during John's meeting with Lee, Julian phoned to convey a message from George, saying that all was forgiven, and that he wanted John to come to his post-concert party that night.

Paul, Linda and John Eastman attended the evening show, and though they wore disguises—Paul donned an Afro wig, a false mustache and dark glasses, Linda a short, dark curly wig—the photographer Bob Gruen spotted them and snapped a few shots.

"We loved it," Paul said of the show. "I think there's a lot of people approaching the new shows like that. 'Oh, well, can they actually stand up there when they were once the Beatles?' You just

Paul, Linda and John Eastman watch George Harrison at Madison Square Garden, December 19, 1974

have to say, 'Well, this is me now, sorry, folks.' *Sgt. Pepper's* a big change from the record before it. That was us then. So I think George is just taking it very naturally and saying, 'This is me.'"

Yet Paul also approached George's show with the critical eye of a fellow performer.

"If I'd been producing him and if I'd been his impresario on that tour," he added, "I would have asked him to do a few more songs he was known for. And also, to stick to the arrangement a little bit. To which he'd probably say, 'Piss off,' and good luck to him."[69]

Paul's criticism in some ways reflected the reviews George had been receiving, in which he was excoriated not only for the state of his voice, which had become hoarse during the rehearsal period and remained so as the demands of almost-nightly performances punished it further, but also for the way he mixed his own music with an unusual Indian-pop amalgam performed by Ravi Shankar and Shankar Family and Friends.

"I thought it would give people another kind of experience other than just watching Led Zeppelin all their lives," Harrison said in defense of his show. "But the audience as a whole didn't want it. There was a great response from a lot of people, but on the whole it was negative. People really fear the unknown, they'd rather I just came out and sing 'She Loves You' or 'Here Comes the Sun.'"[70]

The evening show at Madison Square Garden was the finale of George's tour and was followed by a private party at the Hippopotamus Club, attended by Paul and Linda as well as John and May. John and George left together, in the wee hours, and repaired to George's suite at the Plaza, where they talked until shortly past noon the next day.

—

Alerted that the McCartneys were in town, Peter Brown invited them to see *Sgt. Pepper's Lonely Hearts Club Band on Tour*. They attended, with Heather and Mary, on December 22. Backstage after the show, they posed for photos with the cast, tried on costumes and signed autographs.

Behind the scenes, however, a legal battle was brewing between Lennon and McCartney and their music publisher, ATV—a disagreement that threatened to derail a planned national tour.

"There was a dispute between ATV and Lennon and McCartney regarding the split of royalties from the show," Peter Brown explained to *Billboard*. "ATV's Northern Songs offered to give us an indemnity against any action from John and Paul that might arise over the royalty deal, but I refused to go ahead until the dispute had been resolved because of my good personal relationship with the Beatles over the last 12 years. We, therefore, held up the show until Northern Songs had come to terms with Lennon and McCartney. That was the reason for the original holdup.

"John and Paul both loved the show," he added, "and I'm sure it will do well on tour."[71]

On the way back to the Stanhope after the show, the McCartneys ran into Sid Bernstein, the promoter who presented the Beatles at Carnegie Hall in 1964 and at Shea Stadium in 1965 and 1966, and who Paul had last encountered during the New York sessions for *Ram*.

"We were both with our kids, he was carrying his on his shoulders," said Bernstein. "We introduced the kids to one another, chatted. And I said, 'Paul every time I see you, or think of you, I remember that day at Shea.' He said, 'Sid, as long as I live, I'll never forget it.'"[72]

On a trip packed with blasts from the past, Paul and Linda also spent an evening with some of Linda's old friends, including Danny Fields, to whom they showed a galley of Linda's soon-to-be-published book of photographs. They visited John and May again as well. As a joke Christmas present, John gave Paul an advance copy he had been sent of *The Man Who Gave the Beatles Away* by Allan Williams, the early Beatles manager who had arranged the group's first Hamburg residency in 1960. The book was due to be published in January and was filled with tales of the young Beatles' antics and misbehavior—including one about John urinating from a window on a group of nuns walking past the Beatles' digs at the Bambi Kino. John thought the book was hilarious; Paul, ever concerned about the way he and the Beatles were portrayed, found it "terrible, a travesty," adding that "there are all the legends, but it's all exaggerated."[73]

After one too many drinks, John and Paul also paid a late-night visit to David Bowie at the Pierre Hotel.

"I got a knock at the door," Bowie recounted. "It was about three in the morning and John was there and he had Paul with him! The two of them had been out on the town for the evening. And John says, 'You won't believe who I've got here,' and I said, 'Wow I thought you two had . . .' and he said, 'Oh no, all that's going to change.' It was great! We just spent the evening talking. . . . They actually asked me if I'd join the two of them and become a trio with them, and we'd change the name to something like David Bowie and the Beatles because they liked the idea of it being DBB. But, you know, the next morning it just never came to anything."[74]

But perhaps Paul's most unusual encounter during his December 1974 visit to New York was a meeting with writer and professor Isaac Asimov. Besides inspiring some of his latest songs, Paul's fascination with science fiction carried him beyond his comfort zone as a pop musician. Toward the end of 1974, he wrote a treatment for a film musical that blended Lennon's UFO encounter with fictionalized elements from his own history, from the embryonic Beatles days to his post-Beatles world.

Provisionally titled *Five and Five and One*, the treatment was little more than a loose plot outline with a few fragments of dialogue. But Paul felt it had potential as a film vehicle for Wings; it even had plot turns that seem designed to incorporate some of his new songs, most notably 'Rock Show' and 'Magneto and Titanium Man.'

Having loved Asimov's Foundation books, Paul asked John Eastman to arrange a meeting with the Russian-born science fiction master in the hope that he might consider collaborating on the script. A meeting in London was out of the question: Asimov had a deathly fear of flying.

"He can imagine himself into far off galaxies," Paul noted with some amusement, "but he wouldn't get on a plane. It's funny, when I read Foundation, I remember it made me *more* confident about flying, because these huge distances, and I was able to see flying as we know it as merely an earth shuttle."[75]

A meeting was arranged during Paul's visit to New York, during which Paul outlined his film idea and Asimov made some off-the-cuff suggestions. Shortly after he returned to London, Paul sent Asimov a typed letter with his proposed plot:

> *A "flying saucer" lands. Out of it get five creatures. They transmute before your very eyes into "us" (i.e. Wings.) They are here to take over earth by taking America by storm and they proceed to do this Supergroup style.*
>
> *Meanwhile—back in the sticks of Britain—lives the original group whose personalities*

are being used by the aliens. They are a skiffle group, very down to earth and innocent in their own way. A friend of theirs (more a fan) is the type who collects comics, fan magazines and trade musicals from the U.S.

One day he is at a group practice and produces a magazine which contains a photo of "Supergroup." He says, "Look at this, it's just like you. And this photo too, just like you." "What do you mean—just like us," says the leader of the group. "That is us. There comes a time in the life of every . . ."

And with that they are off—by motorbike, and assorted vehicles—to the boat. Onboard the boat they are feeling depressed—huddling leather jacketed in the corner alcove of the dining room. "Another fine mess you got us into Stanley," says one of the group.

Picture dissolves to "Supergroup" where it is apparent that they too must be doing something depressed. They do a depressing blues—in a super way.

With the money gradually diminishing, the original five are taking odd jobs and trying to keep on the trail of the supergroup.

The "supers" hardly ever speak only to say "hi" and raise a hand but in the cool world of rock the only ones suspicious are the two sharp New York manager types who are forever trying to sign the group up. (By now they're BIG!!!) "How do you like that guy", all he ever says is "hi," "Really, man."

The originals are well into various adventures and are by now on a cattle drive heading northwest—still on the trail.

(Dawn scene with cattle drive. Sunrise, dust, smoke). The "supers" always keep one step ahead of the originals who are eventually tracked down by the naïve natives of Mother Earth. On confronting the aliens there is the opening; transmutation in reverse, and the "supers" change back to creatures and are off in their ship. Leaving the original group to work out . . . "What was all that about?"[76]

Asimov fleshed out McCartney's sketch into a five-page treatment, giving the aliens a backstory (they were wraith-like energy-beings from a dying planet—six of them, in Asimov's version), having them occupy the bodies of Paul and Wings rather than clone them (the sixth alien becomes Wings' manager), and injecting some emotional depth into the plot (the aliens did not understand human emotions such as love).

Ultimately, Asimov delivered a love-conquers-all tale, in which mankind escapes alien conquest and inherits the universe. But McCartney and Asimov failed to see eye-to-eye, and Paul rejected many of Asimov's amendments. By early 1975 the project was abandoned.

"Nothing ever came of this because McCartney couldn't recognize good stuff,"[77] was Asimov's succinct take on the pair's failed collaboration, scrawled across the first page of his 1,800-word treatment.

The McCartneys joined the Eastman family at their East Hampton getaway for Christmas and were back in London in time to hightail it up to Gayton to welcome in the New Year at Rembrandt with the extended McCartney clan.

John Lennon and May Pang, meanwhile, made their way to Florida, where the stars finally aligned: at the Polynesian Village Hotel at Walt Disney World in Orlando on December 29, John signed the papers dissolving the Beatles' partnership.

"He just sat down with the lawyer and went over the last clause, and made sure he understood everything correctly," said Pang. "And he knew, this was it. His was the last signature. As he started the Beatles, he was the one to end it."[78]

6

THE REUNION DIDN'T WORK OUT

At the start of 1975, the four former Beatles were enjoying a healthy competition that saw all four vying for creative bragging rights on the *Billboard* Hot 100. Paul led the way with 'Junior's Farm' at No. 4, trailed closely by Ringo's 'Only You' at No. 7. George's 'Dark Horse' was at No. 16, and John's '#9 Dream' had just broken into the top 50, at No. 47.

Riding above them all at No. 1 was a cover of a Beatles song—Elton John's recording of 'Lucy in the Sky with Diamonds.'

Staring at the *Billboard* 100 brought both their collective past and the present firmly into focus. McCartney often described the Beatles as being "like four sides of a square, without any side, the square collapses."[1] Now, four years and ten days after Paul filed his lawsuit to disentangle himself from the Beatles partnership and Apple, those four sides were about to be taken apart.

On January 9, representatives of Lennon, McCartney, Harrison, Starr and Apple met in London for a private hearing before a High Court master to formalize the agreement they had signed in December. As of November 1, 1974, Apple's holdings—which had been under the control of the court-appointed receiver, James Douglas Spooner, since 1971—were £8,915,912 ($20,770,000),[2] according to court papers. Of that total, £2,387,580.99 ($5,560,000) had been invested, at the former Beatles' request.

This figure, however, reflects only money collected on the Beatles' behalf since March 1971. As John Lennon once noted, the receiver controlled only a fraction of the money owed to the four of them; the rest was held in Apple's own bank accounts for which records are not available. It is also possible that EMI/Capitol was holding on to royalties for the four Beatles, as the label had been instructed to not pay out any money to the four of them while their business affairs were under the control of the receiver. In truth, we will never know how and when the money collected by the receiver was distributed to each of the Beatles, or how much each received.

But to anyone following the saga, from the filing of Paul's lawsuit through his many interviews in which he spoke about the need to dissolve Apple, there was a surprise: now that the four were friends again, Apple would continue to exist, in a radically altered form. The record label, shuttered years ago, would not be revived, although the individual Beatles could still use the Apple logo if they were so disposed. They would each receive royalties directly on their post-Beatles projects. But Apple would oversee their joint interests—mainly, the Beatles' recordings (original and reissued) and any historical projects that involved their collective work.

Immediately after the January 9 hearing, Apple issued a statement to that effect.

> John Lennon, Paul McCartney, George Harrison, and Ringo Starr are happy to announce that all legal and business disputes among them have been settled. All four have signed an agreement enabling each to pursue his own career. At the same time, the former Beatles become directors of Apple Corps Ltd. which will continue to operate from its St. James's Street offices in London.[3]

"In a nutshell," John Lennon told *Rolling Stone* later in the year, "what was arranged was that everybody get their own individual monies. Even up till this year—'til the settlement was signed—all the monies were going into one pot. All individual records, mine, Ringo's, Paul's [and George's]—all into one big pot. It had to go through this big machinery and then come out to us, eventually. So now, even on the old Beatle royalties, everything goes into four separate accounts instead of one big pot all the time.

"That's that. The rest of it was ground rules. Everybody said the Beatles have signed this paper, that means they're no longer tied in any way. That's bullshit. We still own this thing called Apple. Which, you can explain, is a *bank*. A bank the money goes into. But there's still the entity itself known as Beatles. The product, the name, the likeness, the Apple thing itself, which still exists, and we still have to communicate on it and make decisions on it and decide who's to run Apple and who's to do that. It's not as cut and dried as the paper said."[4]

John, George and Ringo were also still in litigation with Allen Klein on several fronts, and it was looking increasingly likely they would have to pay Klein outstanding fees to the tune of £3 million ($7 million).

The newly liberated Beatles remained tied to EMI through 1976, but the end of that contract was fast approaching, and now the four were free to negotiate solo deals with other labels. The Eastmans began talks with EMI and Capitol, likely leveraging interest from Warner plus the success of *Band on the Run*, to secure Paul a better deal.

On the same day as the hearing, word hit the American press that Paul and Wings had been granted temporary work visas, good through March 1, and that the band would be working at

Sea-Saint Recording Studio in New Orleans. Troy Adams, district director for the Immigration and Naturalization Service, told the Associated Press that McCartney and company were in a visa category for "highly qualified entertainers," but that while the visa covered recording work, the band would not be permitted to play concerts during their stay.[5]

The McCartneys flew to New York on January 10, planning to spend a few days in the Big Apple before heading down to the Big Easy on January 16. In Manhattan, Linda and Heather went to see the Royal Lipizzan Stallion Show at the Felt Forum, where they were treated to a program of exactingly choreographed production numbers involving 40 of the legendary horses—once regarded as treasures of the Austrian government but based in Florida since 1962—and a team of internationally renowned riders.

On January 15, Paul and Linda paid a visit to John and May. Although Paul now had a detailed roadmap for his new album, the amity between the newly appointed co-directors of Apple carried the moment, and he floated the idea of John joining him in New Orleans, where—if the stars were right—they might write and record some new music together.

John asked for time to think about it: he still had work to do on his album of rock oldies, and he had committed to play acoustic guitar on David Bowie's cover of 'Across the Universe,' on February 5. But if he left for New Orleans after the Bowie session, he could be there for Mardi Gras, on February 11—something, as he told May, he had always wanted to experience. On January 19, he mentioned the prospect in a letter to Derek Taylor:

> BOWIES CUTTIN "UNIVERSE" (LET IT BEATLE). AM A GONNA BE THERE (BY REQUEST OF COURSET). THEN POSSIBLEY DOWN TO NEW ORLEONS TO SEE THE McCARTKNEES.[6]

"I know that Paul was desperate to write with John again," Linda later recalled. "And I know John was desperate to write . . . *Desperate!*"[7]

But though they acknowledged that they would like to work together again, their relationship as songwriters was complex—as it had been even in the Beatles days. A healthy competition between the pair made them disinclined to pat each other on the back.

"I hardly ever remember it actually. There wasn't a lot of it flying about," Paul said of praise from his former writing partner. But he did remember one occasion when John let his guard down. "One time we were making *Help!* in Austria, we'd gone on location there. And I shared a room with John. More often than not, George would share a room with John, but on this particular occasion I was in with John. And we were taking our skiing boots off, and taking all the sweaty gear off, and getting ready for the evening and stuff, and we had one of our cassettes. . . . And there were like three of my songs, [and] three of John's songs on this one side that we were listening to. And for the first time ever, he just sort of said—he didn't say anything definite, but he hinted—he said, 'Oh, I probably like your songs better than mine.' And that was it. That was the height of the praise I ever got off him, I think."[8]

Still, judging by John's having only recently used *a Wings LP* as a frisbee—which, given John's mercurial personality, could have been either actual critical commentary or just clowning for Ringo—he may still have thought that Paul could do better. In any case, John and May planned a brief trip to Montauk, on Long Island, where they had rented a house that John was considering buying, after which they would join Paul and Linda in New Orleans.

"John was going to surprise the world by writing and recording with Paul," May explained, "but he needed a little time to regroup."[9]

—

When Paul, Linda and Denny traveled to Nigeria to record *Band on the Run*, EMI's Lagos studio was half-built and ill-equipped for multitrack recording. Yet thanks to the ingenuity of engineer Geoff Emerick, the sonic results were indistinguishable from the songs taped at AIR Studios in London. But when Paul contacted Geoff about engineering the new Wings album, Emerick told him that he would be on the West Coast, working with George Martin at the Record Plant in Sausalito, California, on *Hearts*, the fifth album by the folk-rock band America.

Luckily, Paul had a backup plan for exactly this situation. Having been impressed with Alan O'Duffy's 'Junior's Farm' mix, he decided to take a punt on the young engineer and invited O'Duffy for a chat at MPL.

"The first meeting was in their office," O'Duffy recalled, "Paul playing the piano and me sitting on the floor. And he just presented me with his concertina paperwork"—the Jamaican scroll—"and said, 'Well, we're going to do this song, and then we're going to do that song, and this is how this one goes.' There was an intensity and a clarity about what Paul was wanting to do, and that was a joy."[10]

O'Duffy then met with Brian Brolly to discuss the terms of his contract. "We would like you to join the McCartney family," was Brolly's opening gambit. O'Duffy would be paid £200 ($466) a week plus expenses, but family or not, Brolly took a hard line on the potential of post-recording income, adding "there's no royalties."[11]

O'Duffy traveled to New Orleans with Britton and Laine, arriving on January 13 along with Wings' roadies Trevor and Michael, a newcomer, the long-serving Ian Horne having recently left MPL for a job with the Frankie Miller Band. Two days later, Sea-Saint took delivery of several shipping crates with Wings' equipment as well as a 16-track master tape that included 'Baby Face' (Take 2, from the *One Hand Clapping* sessions), 'Letting Go' (Take 21), 'Love in Song' (Take 19),

'Medicine Jar' (remake, Take 15) and two versions of 'Rock Show' (remake, Take 12), marked "slow speed" and "normal speed." The studio's staff was given strict instructions not to discuss the sessions with anyone outside the studio, particularly the press.

The McCartneys landed at Moisant Field,* on the evening of January 16, the same day newspapers carried reports of the year's Grammy nominations, of which *Band on the Run* netted three: in addition to Album of the Year—the other contenders were Stevie Wonder's *Fulfillingness' First Finale*, Joni Mitchell's *Court and Spark*, Elton John's *Caribou* and John Denver's *Back Home Again*—the title track was nominated for the Best Pop Vocal Performance by a Duo, Group or Chorus Grammy, and the album was nominated for the Best Engineered Recording (Non-Classical) award.

Alan O'Duffy collected the McCartneys in a Ford Thunderbird convertible and ferried them to the French Quarter, where Wings would stay during the sessions. Sea-Saint Recording Studio co-owner Marshall Sehorn, himself a songwriter, publisher and entrepreneur who had been an important force in the New Orleans music scene since the 1950s, had arranged for Paul and Linda to stay at Le Richelieu Hotel, at 1234 Chartres Street. Suite 227† would be their headquarters while in town, and Sehorn saw to it that Paul had a spinet piano, a stereo system, and an assortment of cassettes and LPs that skewed heavily toward the New Orleans sound.

It was a sound Paul knew well, having been a fan of Antoine "Fats" Domino since his teenage years. He knew Allen Toussaint's work as well, and he had been interested in the Meters, a celebrated New Orleans funk quartet, at least since the release of their seminal 1969 single 'Cissy Strut.' Paul had even seen the foursome play in London. Now the Meters were, in effect, Sea-Saint Studio's house band.

But having been accused of musical carpetbagging by Fela Ransome-Kuti, during the *Band on the Run* sessions in Lagos, Paul was careful to deny having any thoughts of using elements of the Bayou Country's musical personality in his music.

"Mainly we're coming here to make our own album," Paul clarified. "I don't like to come to a place and use too much of the local talent, because you get people saying, 'Oh, they're taking our style.'"[12]

He added, though, that he was eager to get to know the city, having visited it only briefly with the Beatles in 1964. "I'd never been to New Orleans," he said, "except on tour, when we never saw anything except the inside of a trailer. The only thing I remember about New Orleans was the vibrating bed in the motel. And it was sweating hot."[13]

During the Beatles' visit on September 16, 1964, Paul asked to meet Fats Domino, and the local

* The airport, originally named for the aviator John Bevins Moisant, was renamed Louis Armstrong New Orleans International Airport in August 2001.

† To celebrate Paul's visit, Suite 227 at Le Richelieu was subsequently named "The McCartney Suite."

promoters made it happen, bringing Domino to the City Park, where he chatted with the Beatles in a trailer that doubled as their dressing room. Now, a decade later, Paul did not have to make any special requests: working at Sea-Saint, he would cross paths with the cream of New Orleans' musical life, starting with Sehorn's partner, Allen Toussaint, who was at the studio to greet the McCartneys when they stopped by to look at the facilities on January 17.

It's a striking picture—Toussaint, in a white tropical suit, walking through the studio's foyer alongside McCartney, who wore a black pinstripe vest, matching slacks, and brown and white wingtips, and carried a newly acquired walnut walking stick. In the control room, Toussaint played his guests cuts from *Southern Nights*, a rhythm and blues concept album that he was in the process of putting the finishing touches on.

Toussaint, the son of a railroad worker, was born and raised in New Orleans and had been a major figure in the Crescent City music scene since the 1950s. An exceptional pianist, he honed his skills further during a stint in the United States Army from 1963 to 1965, and when he returned to New Orleans, he soon made a name for himself as a session musician, arranger and songwriter for New Orleans musicians like Aaron Neville, Irma Thomas and Fats Domino.

By 1975 Toussaint had written more than 400 songs—some written under his mother's name, Naomi Neville—including hits like the Pointer Sisters' 'Yes We Can Can,' Lee Dorsey's 'Working in a Coal Mine,' the trumpeter Al Hirt's signature tune 'Java,' and 'Whipped Cream' for another star trumpeter, Herb Alpert. Several of his songs were championed by the Beatles' British colleagues, among them 'Fortune Teller,' recorded by the Rolling Stones, the Who and the Hollies, and 'I Like It Like That,' a hit for the Dave Clark Five. Only a few months earlier, Ringo Starr recorded Toussaint's 'Occapella' for his *Goodnight Vienna* album.

British pop musicians' fondness for Toussaint was not unrequited—certainly not so far as the Beatles' music was concerned.

"For melody and lyrics, the Beatles were unsurpassed," Toussaint told a journalist during Paul's visit, "and I always loved Paul McCartney's bass lines. Songs like 'Michelle,' 'Norwegian Wood,' and 'Yesterday' are so indisputably excellent. In my mind, I always thought they stretched on forever in both directions."[14]

Toussaint introduced Paul to Sea-Saint's two engineers, who would be assisting O'Duffy—Ken Laxton (who was also a busy trumpet player on the New Orleans scene) and Roberta Grace.

"You're an engineer here?" Paul asked Grace as he shook her hand. "I've never met a lady engineer before."[15] In fact, Grace was Toussaint's chief engineer and had been at Sea-Saint since the studio opened, in 1973. She presided over facilities that included a 24-track master recorder and a Harrison 24-track console, as well as several Studer tape machines. Paul's first impression was that the studio was plush, but not embarrassingly so: under the lights, everything was a serious red-brown, but on closer inspection, the shag carpet was already a bit frayed and the furniture, including the swivel chair Paul would use during playbacks, was Naugahyde rather than leather. Time in the studio was billed at $145 (£61) an hour.*

"We closed the studio down for business," Grace explained, "and Paul had the use of the studio any time. Whatever they wanted, we were there, it didn't matter if they wanted us to sit down and have ice cream with the kids. And Linda was such a charming person."

Grace had been warned that Linda was not keen on having women in the studio, but she was determined to head off any potential jealousy issues.

"I was told she was worried somebody would get next to Paul," Grace said. "But I'm gay. So she knew I was no threat to Paul, and we got along fabulously. And Paul was the same, he was just wonderful; he was an everyday dude."[16]

Paul and the band took the weekend to explore New Orleans and get a feeling for the city's rich music scene. They arranged for a visit to the outskirts of New Orleans to look in on the Superdome, with an eye toward an eventual tour. After Denny and Jo Jo arrived, on Saturday, Wings (minus Jimmy, whose work visa had been delayed) ventured out to Oak Street, a hot spot for college students, artists, musicians and writers. Because parts of New Orleans were known to be dangerous after hours, Paul and Linda were escorted by a security guard, arranged by Marshall Sehorn.

"He was an ex-Vietnam soldier," O'Duffy recalled. "You could see a plaster around his upper arm, and it was an injury that hadn't healed. But he was a lovely guy. And he had a gun. Paul and Linda weren't happy that there was somebody with a gun. But that was the way it was, and there was never any incident whatsoever."[17]

Late Saturday night, January 18, they settled in at Jed's University Inn, near Tulane University, to take in a performance by one of the city's jazz legends, Professor Longhair.

"That was great," Britton reminisced. "They let us sit right at the very front, we sat there, and we had our feet on the edge of the stage. And there was Professor Longhair. And it just shows you how out of touch they were [with the British music scene]—I was talking to the bass player, and he thought I was Ringo!"[18]

Shortly before Wings paid their first working visit to Sea-Saint Recording Studio, Paul told his entourage that John Lennon might be dropping by the studio to contribute to the album in some capacity. There was a combination of excitement and nervousness among the musicians, but MPL's

* Sea-Saint Recording Studio operated until 2005, when the facility was destroyed by Hurricane Katrina. Marshall Sehorn died on December 5, 2006. Allen Toussaint died on November 10, 2015.

top brass, Brian Brolly and Alan Crowder, regarded the prospect of Lennon's arrival as mildly alarming. Lennon, they worried, could only have a distracting and generally negative influence on McCartney.

"Alan Crowder and I were talking," O'Duffy explained, "and there was a conversation going on that maybe John would come down, and I was thinking that would be lovely. And I know we're making a record and we're getting on with it, but if John wants to come down, how much fun would that be? And Alan Crowder was saying, 'It would be a bloomin' pain in the neck! Because we wouldn't get on with our record. It would all go [wrong].' Alan was being an eyes-on-the-ball type of guy. But I thought it would have been a wonderful idea."[19]

Recording Sessions

Monday, January 20–Wednesday, January 22, 1975.
Sea-Saint Recording Studio, 3809 Clematis Street, New Orleans.
Recording: 'Lunch Box,' 'Odd Sox,' 'Spirits of Ancient Egypt' and 'Venus and Mars (Reprise).'

Jimmy, still without a work visa, had not yet arrived in New Orleans, but in addition to Denny and Geoff, Paul and Linda were joined in the studio by Tony Dorsey. Paul had been impressed with the arranging work Dorsey had done for them on the fly in Nashville, and with his performance as a trombonist and wind section leader during the overdubbing sessions for 'Walking in the Park with Eloise' and 'Bridge on the River Suite,' so in December, he had Brolly invite Dorsey to fly to New York to meet with Paul and discuss working on the new album.

"We spent most of the day together, going over the entire album," Dorsey said of his afternoon with Paul in New York. "He sat down at the piano—he played all of it and explained to me what he wanted to do. At certain spots, he would say, 'Well, I want to go from here to there,' and 'What do you think about this?' and I would give him my ideas about the easiest ways to do what he wanted. Because that's my concept—you know, do it the easiest way you can. And the next day, his manager called and said, 'Yeah, he definitely wants you in; we start work in January, in New Orleans.'"[20]

In Jimmy's absence, Wings took up 'Lunch Box' and 'Odd Sox,' a pair of jam-like instrumentals—intended to be heard together as 'Lunch Box/Odd Sox'—that both Paul and Linda had worked on in Scotland. When Paul recorded his piano demo, back in August, he shouted along, wordlessly, on the 'Lunch Box' section, while 'Odd Sox' was mostly instrumental, with a touch of scat singing. But he never wrote lyrics for either, so Wings recorded the two songs now as a pair of instrumentals, to be joined by an edit.

On both tunes,* Paul played piano with Linda on her Minimoog, Denny on guitar, Geoff drumming, and Tony Dorsey on bass. 'Lunch Box/Odd Sox' has a bit of everything—some jazz vamping, calypso rhythms, a touch of ska guitar—but most of all, it was something Linda had under her fingers, and would not feel nervous playing, even with some of New Orleans' finest musicians looking on.

Both Toussaint and Sehorn were present, although they were unsure what role they were meant to play in the sessions. Sehorn, the studio's A&R man, was keen on having Toussaint produce Paul's album. It was an idea that Paul did not have to push back on himself—he had Brolly and Crowder to do that, and they quickly made it clear that Paul produced his own recordings.

"You can be sure that Marshall would've tried to get Allen in there to produce," said Grace. "Allen was a masterful artist, and to have one produce another, they might bump each other's heads. Too much of a good thing—it would be like having two orchestra conductors."[21]

Sehorn was quick to observe that the studio environment had less of a bearing on Paul's music than the city itself.

"Paul had a very firm idea of what kind of thing *he* wanted to do," Sehorn noted, "the kind of instruments and the kind of sound he wanted. It wasn't, 'Let's go down to New Orleans to see what we can get together.' He knew from the beginning what sound he wanted to record, what he wanted it to sound like and, maybe in the midst of that, he could use Allen's ideas."[22]

Alan O'Duffy noted that the atmosphere that first day was loose, and that the session was fun. But watching the band at work also gave him an opportunity to put his role in the project in perspective.

"I'm the one with the experience in the studio," he realized, "but I couldn't pull rank on Paul McCartney. I couldn't say to Paul, 'Oh, no, we don't have a track for that.' Or, 'I don't really have a microphone that does that.' And I couldn't go, 'Paul, I think we should reconsider that because that's a bit of a stupid idea.' You couldn't say that to Paul McCartney, that's not on the agenda. You cannot outrank the guy. I wouldn't want to, and I didn't try."[23]

Tony Dorsey was also confused about his role. "When I got there, I didn't really know what my function was. And it never was really defined. Like, was I a producer, arranger, or whatever?"[24]

Wings returned to Sea-Saint on Tuesday, still minus a lead guitarist, and turned their attention to 'Spirits of Ancient Egypt,' which, Paul had decided, would be a vocal showcase for Denny. For the basic track, Paul picked up his bass, Linda played organ, Denny played electric guitar and sang a guide vocal, and Geoff struggled to come up with an interesting drum part.

But several takes yielded only frustration. Specifically, Paul felt that Geoff's drumming lacked

* The session documentation, reproduced in the *Venus and Mars Deluxe Edition*, does not give the number of takes required for each track.

the inventiveness that had enlivened his contribution to 'Love in Song,' when he added milk bottles and jugs to his drum kit to get the fresh effects Paul felt the song needed. 'Spirits' needed a fresh approach, but for Paul—and Geoff did not disagree—Geoff's contributions sounded oddly pedestrian.

Indeed, Britton's mind was not entirely on the task at hand, and his confidence, already suffering, was ebbing further. He still had doubts about his place in the band, both professionally and personally. Fitness and health were at the center of Geoff's daily regimen, but these concerns were at odds with the rock and roll lifestyle his bandmates pursued. And just before he left London for New Orleans, his already bruised ego took another hit: his wife filed for divorce.

The strain Britton was feeling was exacerbated by the fact that during the first two days of recording, it seemed as though just about every top-flight musician in Louisiana had decided to drop in—not least the Meters.

"The Meters were all hanging out at this studio," Britton remembered, "and the drummer with the Meters was a real hot potato, [Joseph "Ziggy"] Modeliste, great drummer. And 'Cissy Strut' was a groundbreaking piece of rhythmic playing. So, there's all these people just trying to get a piece of the action. I just felt it wasn't right, you know. I felt uneasy. And most artists are like that, we're all sort of insecure."[25]

On Wednesday, Paul turned to something simpler—'Venus and Mars (Reprise).' Paul played acoustic guitar and sang a pilot vocal on the basic recording, with Linda playing sparse piano fills, Denny on bass guitar (which Paul later replaced with an overdub), and Geoff providing cymbal flourishes. But Geoff's playing on the day's takes of 'Venus and Mars (Reprise)' was not enough to soothe the discontent Paul felt during the previous day's session, underpinning Geoff's own paranoia that other musicians hovering around the studio and playing in the city's clubs had turned Paul's head.

Britton's uncertainties, in fact, were now beginning to feed McCartney's own insecurities. With the sessions not moving as quickly as he had hoped, Paul was starting to feel the pressure of following an album as successful as *Band on the Run.* And because McCartney did not measure his work by a normal yardstick, that pressure was magnified. To his mind, just as the Beatles had followed *Revolver* with *Sgt. Pepper* and the *White Album* with *Abbey Road*, the follow-up to *Band on the Run* could not be second best.

Speaking about the challenge, though, he tamped down his insecurities.

"John always used to discuss the problems of following up records with others," he explained. "It never bothered me, but it worried John. I think [the next album] will be every bit as good as *Band* because the songs are better and we won't be doubling up on instrumentation, we will be recording the album with a full band, so there will be more continuity."[26]

Britton had been a member of Wings for only seven months, and the group had been in New Orleans for just more than a week. But midway through their third day of recording at Sea-Saint—

and having spent the last few days listening to the tougher and more varied drumming that is a standard element of music making in New Orleans—Paul decided that Geoff would not be able to provide the solid rhythmic backbone his new songs needed.

This was a realization Paul had been fending off since the EMI sessions in November, although in that case, when things started going awry, a few tokes on a joint helped Geoff find his equilibrium. Paul hoped that Geoff would settle in, with or without pot. But Geoff was disinclined to get marijuana into his life, and Paul now realized that the more uptight Geoff became, the greater the toll his insecurities would take on the sessions. And he wasn't alone. Alan O'Duffy had doubts about Geoff as well.

"McCartney's one of the best on the planet, end of story," O'Duffy observed, "so you would hope that the people in the room would be equally phenomenal. I just felt—as the man in the control room, as the man listening to what they were doing—I just thought that Geoff wasn't quite in the realm of that musical sphere that maybe was within Paul's mind."[27]

Midway through the session, Paul and Denny spoke alone in a quiet corner of the studio and Britton's fate was sealed. Paul decided that it was time to make a change, and having made the decision, he moved with a determination that bordered on ruthlessness. He took Tony Dorsey aside and asked him to find a session drummer as a temporary replacement—immediately. Sitting in Sehorn's office, Tony paged through his address book and began placing calls.

"All of the guys I thought about—drummers I had played with, and who I'd have liked to have given a break—couldn't be reached," Dorsey said. "And so, as a last, desperate thing, I remembered hearing Joe English play."

Dorsey did not know English personally, but he knew that he, like Dorsey, was based in Macon, Georgia. The band he had heard English perform with was the Tall Dogs Orchestra, which was rehearsing for a tour backing Bonnie Bramlett. Dorsey knew Earl Ford, who played electric trombone in the group.

"So I called Earl," he continued, "and I said, 'Hey man, I got an offer that Joe could come and play on an album with Paul McCartney, if he's interested.' Joe didn't know who I was, so he asked the drummer with the Allman Brothers, Jaimoe Johanson. And Jaimoe said, 'Man, if [McCartney] called me up, I'd leave the Allman Brothers.' So Jaimoe put him on an airplane to New Orleans."[28]

As Wings headed back to Le Richelieu after the session, Tony told Paul that Joe English would arrive in New Orleans at 10 P.M. that evening. Paul and Linda headed to Britton's room to deliver the bad news, as Britton noted in his diary:

> Paul and Linda turned up and gave me the sack, as yesterday's track hadn't gone right. I wasn't knocking them out. It was just based on that. [They thought I was a] Great guy,

> etc. At first, Paul wants me to move out the same day then realized that's mean and I can stay and sort things out. Alan [Crowder] and Marshall [Sehorn] hung around with me that afternoon.[29]

Paul's attempt to quickly hustle Geoff out of the hotel, before deciding that would be too callous, was based on a desire to prevent Britton and English from crossing paths. But as stunned and disappointed as Britton was, he felt like an outsider within the Wings ranks and defaulted to his martial arts training, which had taught him to be humble in defeat.

"I just didn't have any rapport with Jimmy and Denny," said Britton. "They were unapproachable—they just didn't like me. And to me, it was very apparent. Because I wasn't getting stoned and legless with them we had this barrier between us. I didn't erect a barrier. They did. You would think they would respect you and let you get on with your own lifestyle. It doesn't work that way. We would go to parties and the tables would be laid out with coke and anything you wanted was there. So everybody got absolutely legless, on the knowledge that I would drive them all home, and I would be straight. I would have thought it was a blessing to have someone like me around, but it didn't work out like that."[30]

Together, Geoff and Paul worked on an exit story. After the karate tournament that Litchfield filmed at the Sobell Center in November, Geoff had been approached about appearing in a martial arts movie, to be shot in Italy and Turkey. Now that project offered the perfect cover for his departure from Wings, as Tony Brainsby duly noted in a press release dictated by Paul:

> The parting is amicable. Geoff wants to work on his own project. It is a film about karate, and he hopes to start shooting it at the end of March. He is writing the musical score which will be percussion based. The film will be shot abroad, and Geoff's involvement will be extensive. It was an opportunity he didn't want to turn down, especially as it could open up a completely new career for him. Paul and Linda fully appreciated this, and the parting was completely amicable.[31]

Having worked on four tracks—'Letting Go,' 'Love in Song,' 'Medicine Jar,' and 'Venus and Mars (Reprise)'—that Paul was likely to include on Wings' next album, Britton was offered £1,000 ($2,385) on top of his session fees and travel expenses. Just 24 hours after his final session, Brian Brolly presented Britton with an exit contract. But after speaking with a music manager friend in England, Geoff refused to sign; he later agreed to an exit settlement much higher than Brolly's original offer.

Britton remained in New Orleans for the Mardi Gras National Karate Championships in early February, before flying back to England, where his streak of bad luck continued: arriving at Heathrow Airport, he found the spot where he had left his car was empty. He briefly considered an offer to join Lynyrd Skynyrd* but decided to withdraw from the music scene and focus on martial arts.

"My life had collapsed basically," Britton confessed. "My wife told me she wanted a divorce, I was out of Wings, and somebody had nicked my car. I'd lost the desire to play—it had all taken the wind out of my sails. But you know, life goes on."[32]

"He was a very good player," Paul later diplomatically declared of Britton, "but he still wasn't really what we wanted. I don't think auditions are much use. We won't do it again."[33]

Linda later confirmed what Britton suspected—chemical abstinence was not considered very rock and roll. "I know Jimmy wasn't that struck [by Geoff], and Denny, and we thought, well, let's keep trying."[34]

Recording Session

Thursday, January 23, 1975.

Sea-Saint Recording Studio, 3809 Clematis Street, New Orleans.

Recording: 'Spirits of Ancient Egypt.'

Jimmy McCulloch landed in New Orleans on Thursday morning, his work visa finally rubber-stamped, and he was called straight into action. But as he walked into Sea-Saint Recording Studio, he couldn't help noticing that there was a different drummer behind the kit, who was still stunned to have moved from a local Macon band to a gig with Paul McCartney and Wings.

"I was rehearsing with Bonnie Bramlett to go on the road," English said, "when I get a call from New Orleans to come and record. Got the call at three o'clock, landed at 10 o'clock that night, got up in the morning and started recording at 12. I had no idea what the music was like; they had no idea what I sounded like."[35]

Though lately a Southerner, English was born in Rochester, New York, on February 7, 1949, and like many young American kids, he decided he wanted to become a musician when, two days after his fifteenth birthday, he watched the Beatles' first appearance on the *Ed Sullivan Show.* He got his first drum kit soon after, and played with local bands until 1968, when he moved to Syracuse, New York, and joined a brass-heavy rhythm and blues band, Jam Factory.

---

* Missing out on the position of drummer in Lynyrd Skynyrd turned out to be a blessing in disguise. On October 20, 1977, the American group boarded a jet bound for Baton Rouge, Louisiana, where they were scheduled to play a concert the following night. After running out of fuel, the plane crash landed in Gillsburg, Mississippi. Singer Ronnie Van Zant, guitarist Steve Gaines, and backing singer Cassie Gaines died on impact. Other band members and their road crew were seriously injured.

Two years later, Jam Factory recorded an LP, *Sittin' in the Trap*, for Epic Records. After touring to support the album, some of the players returned to Syracuse while the rest, including English, settled in Macon and reconstituted themselves as the Tall Dogs Orchestra. English settled down on a farm owned by the Allman Brothers. And at the very moment Geoff Britton saw his life implode, Joe English could not believe his luck.

"I was flat broke," English said. "I was driving a 1964 Dodge Dart with bald tires. My drums were in it, and it had no backseat. . . . After I got the phone call, I took Jaimoe aside and said, 'Man, should I take this gig?' You should have seen the expression on Jaimoe's face. He made that funny face and said, 'Man, you'd *better get* on that plane.' I said, 'I don't have any money.' Jaimoe said, 'Don't worry about that.' He loaned me the money for the plane ticket to New Orleans."[36]

'Spirits of Ancient Egypt,' which had undone Britton, now became English's audition piece, and the position he was in—having to drum, in a recording session, on a song he had never heard, with musicians he had never worked with—was not lost on him. He looked for guidance from the man who brought him into this situation.

"I looked at Tony and said, 'Tony, I don't know *any* of this material,'" English explained. "He said, 'We're in the studio ready to go, just watch me, follow me, I'll direct you. It's gonna be okay.' So, I just took a deep breath."[37]

Paul led the session on bass, with Denny and Jimmy on electric guitars and Linda on organ. English, who was operating as a session musician rather than a member of the band, could see that the Louisiana scene had hit McCartney like a thunderbolt, and he adapted his style accordingly—alternating between sparse African rhythm and a funky rock pattern.

"I think Paul was looking for a more funky beat in the rhythm section, compared to that straight ahead, conventional sound,"[38] English said. McCartney apparently found English's musical instincts sound, because when the session ended, English was asked to stay for the rest of the album. "I was playing purely what I felt was needed at the moment, and McCartney must have been thinking that that was what the song needed, because I got the job. That's a good way to check out a musician. Put the person under pressure. They wanted to see if this horse could run."[39]

Once the basic track was finished to Paul's satisfaction, Denny attempted to record the lead vocal. But he struggled with it, particularly in the refrain, where the first syllable of the word "Egypt" was just beyond the top of his vocal range.

"You know what, Den, I think that's psychological, that," Paul told him after one failed attempt to hit the note. "I know you can get that," he added, singing the elusive top note and holding it, while Laine tried unsuccessfully to match him. Paul proposed that it might be easier to hit the note if Denny sang *"AY-gypt,"* which didn't work either, so perhaps to avoid further embarrassment, Paul changed the subject, addressing the song's opening.

“I think the first bit may be better down low—and kind of smoochy, to the mic,” he said, and offered a sultry reading of the line, *“you’re my baby . . .”* Denny made a few more attempts, at a couple of points singing *“I’m on the road again,”* to point up the similarity between the boogie-like playout and the 1968 single by the American band Canned Heat. After a few more tries, Paul and Denny agreed to tackle the vocal at a later session.

Laine was impressed with English’s contribution to the track, although he was suspicious of his reliance on Dorsey’s signals during the first takes. “He had to be himself,” Laine insisted, “he couldn’t be told what to do. What he could do was pretty well perfect anyway—there were just a couple of little things where we’d say, ‘Don’t fill that in so much,’ or something, but apart from that, every riff was more or less what everybody thought of.”[40]

Still, Denny thought a jam would be the best way to see what Joe could do, so as the session wound down, and Paul and Linda were in the control room with O’Duffy, he played a riff that Jimmy quickly picked up on, drawing Joe in as well. Tony, having played bass on ‘Lunch Box/Odd Socks’ a few days earlier, picked up the bass and joined in.

“But after a while,” Dorsey remembered, “somebody said, ‘What is it with this guy playing bass?’ And I kind of got the idea that maybe this is taboo. So I eased on away from the bass and left it alone.”[41]

Recording Session

Friday, January 24, 1975.

Sea-Saint Recording Studio, 3809 Clematis Street, New Orleans.

Recording: ‘You Gave Me the Answer.’

Although Paul had included ‘You Gave Me the Answer’ in the album layout he assembled in Jamaica, he had doubts about it as a potential Wings song. But after playing it for his aunt Millie in Liverpool on New Year’s Eve, he decided to go for it.

“Auntie Millie said to me, ‘You know, that’s just like Jack Buchanan!’* He was one of my favorites, old Jack, I used to like all those blokes. I thought, great, she doesn’t think it’s a con, it’s just a different style of singing, and she likes it. And I must admit, I do—it’s very romantic. A fruity approach, but I’m not against all that.”[42]

Denny and Linda sat out the recording of the basic track, on which Paul played the piano and,

---

* Walter John Buchanan (April 2, 1891–October 20, 1957) was a Scottish theater and film actor, singer, dancer, producer, and director.

channeling his inner Cole Porter, sang the finished vocal live, with Joe drumming and Jimmy playing electric guitar.

"When I started listening to music," McCartney explained, "I must just have been a kid, and the radio was on. In 1942, the kind of music that was on was Fred Astaire and the Billy Cotton Band Show, all that kind of old style of music. So I was brought up in a lot of that. And I like a lot of the old changes, the chords they use, and the certain types of lyrics; like Cole Porter, his type of lyrics, it's clever stuff. And it's lovely, it leaves you with a good feeling.

"So on this LP, I thought, 'Well, I'd like to get a bit of that in.' And it's just me imagining the tie and tails thing and really going back to my impression of the Fred Astaire era."[43]

During the first week of sessions, McCartney, Dorsey and O'Duffy could often be found at a piano, burning the midnight oil as Paul and Tony discussed arrangements. Though Dorsey had been hired as the album's arranger, he and Paul had slightly different interpretations of the task.

"He had already written the whole album," Dorsey noted. "He knew exactly what he wanted to do. He would say, 'Well, I want to go from this song to the next song. I'm gonna modulate from A to E—what's a good way to get there?' And I'd say, 'Well, we could use the harp, and use a glissando up to the next key, as if they're in the same key.' And he'd say, 'Okay.'

"If he asked me about an idea, I would try to adapt whatever musical ideas I could come up with to the style of the song that he's doing. Now, he's a clever guy. And I would say, 'Well, you could do this,' and I'd play a chord on the piano. And after a while, he'd say, 'Oh, I got it.' You know. *I* got it—it's *my* idea now, you know [laughs]."[44]

For 'You Gave Me the Answer,' Paul and Tony discussed a string and horn arrangement with muted trumpets that would capture the Cole Porter–Fred Astaire spirit Paul had in mind.

McCulloch, meanwhile, announced his arrival by quickly getting into a scrap. Leaving a club at 5 A.M., he approached what turned out to be a group of junkies to ask directions to the hotel. Sensing that the young Scot was drunk and ripe for robbing, the locals demanded his wallet, and when Jimmy responded by suggesting lewd acts they might perform on themselves, a fight broke out. Laine, fortunately, left the club at that moment and stepped in.

"They were going to beat him up," Denny recalled, "so I had to thump somebody and grab him and put him in a taxi and get the hell out. It was a very hairy situation."[45]

Alan O'Duffy had been warned about the guitarist's volatility. But having spent time in the studio with the Rolling Stones, the Small Faces, Slade and other bands known for their occasional rambunctiousness, he was unfazed.

"There was a little bit of sensitivity going on there," O'Duffy noted of Jimmy's more explosive tendencies. "I had been there and done that, to some extent, with some of the people I'd worked with. The man who ran the Small Faces (Don Arden), I'd seen him carried out of the studio. I'd seen people kick equipment and all that, so you would treat Jimmy with kid gloves, slightly."[46]

Recording Session

Saturday, January 25, 1975.
Sea-Saint Recording Studio, 3809 Clematis Street, New Orleans.
Recording: 'Treat Her Gently/Lonely Old People.'

Paul's plan for the session on January 25 was to set down 'Treat Her Gently/Lonely Old People,' for which he needed only his own piano and English's drums, so Denny and Jimmy were given the day to sleep off the previous night's brawl—an arrangement that also gave Paul and Linda time to get to know Joe.

The session was straightforward once Joe mastered the meter transitions between the song's distinct sections: 'Treat Her Gently' is in 4|4, 'Lonely Old People' is in 3|4, and the pairing is played twice (meaning three meter shifts). The basic performance was captured live.

"It was piano and drums, and that was it," O'Duffy remembered. "And Paul singing live. Paul was singing a love song to his beautiful wife, sitting beside her at the piano, live. I mean, at the time we were just doing a take, but when you look back that was special, and beautiful."[47]

Toward the end of the session Paul took his bass into the control room and recorded the bass line by direct injection—that is, with the bass plugged directly into the board. Paul and Dorsey then consulted about the orchestral arrangement that would complete the song.

"He breaks all the rules," Dorsey noted. "He invents such unusual chord changes that [the] first time you hear them you think, 'Did he really mean that?' His writing is so simple yet so meaningful, it's good, logical music. There's good and bad in all music, and the trick is to be able to sort it out, to take the good and throw out the bad. This is what Paul does so well.

"For the most part, it will never be complicated; he never writes anything that the average person couldn't play. But the end result is so simple and so effective and fitting that you wonder how on earth he came by it. He always ends up with something that was right there under your eyes all the time, and I'd wonder how he could have stopped at that, because if it had been me writing it, I'd probably have kept it right on, trying to reach something more dynamic, and maybe ruined it."[48]

After the session, Paul and Linda spent some time bonding with their new drummer. Where

Britton was larger than life, English was quiet, almost shy. But as they chatted, Joe—a part-time farmer in Georgia—and the McCartneys found common ground in their pursuit of bucolic bliss.

By now, Joe's initial reluctance to take the job had evaporated.

"I remember going into the studio with him and watching how he worked," said English. "It was like a quilt—he just wove things together. I'd sit back and go, 'You couldn't buy this. What an opportunity.'"[49]

Recording Sessions

Monday, January 27–Tuesday, January 28, 1975.
Sea-Saint Recording Studio, 3809 Clematis Street, New Orleans.
Recording: 'Magneto and Titanium Man' and 'Rock Show.'

By Monday—a week into the sessions—word of Paul's presence in town had spread, and between 20 and 30 fans began to gather at the studio daily, the size of the crowd growing as the sessions continued. At the *Ram* sessions, at the end of 1970 in New York, Paul established "rules" about fan gatherings—no photos in the morning, for example—and glowered at those who broke them. In New Orleans, he took a more laid-back approach. No fan who asked for an autograph was denied one, and many were handed Wings T-shirts, as well.

"The first week wasn't bad with the fans," Sehorn explained. "They hadn't yet caught on to the fact that he was actually here. But as soon as the TV started to pick up on it, it started to really snowball. By the time we were halfway through the album, every day at 2 o'clock the streets were filled, and it'd stay that way 'til 12 or 1 o'clock in the morning."[50]

Inside Sea-Saint, McCartney shifted gears. As broad as his own musical tastes were, he knew intuitively that just as 'Jet,' rather than 'Bluebird,' drove the sales of *Band on the Run*, the up-tempo entries among his new songs would be the key to the new album. So he set aside his music hall pastiches and love songs and upped the energy level.

As a warm-up, Monday's session began with Paul's Marvel Comics epic, 'Magneto and Titanium Man.' Hoping to inject some energy and heft into the rhythm section, Denny offered the new guy some advice. "The first thing we did," Laine said, "was give him a thicker pair of sticks and say, 'Right, get in there.'"[51]

Following a few introductory bars played by Linda on a Hohner clavinet, Paul's bass dominated the track, its rich tone owing as much to Paul's choice of instrument—a right-handed

Fender Precision Bass, played upside down—as to O'Duffy's recording method. In the hope of capturing a smooth-edged bass sound, O'Duffy tracked a direct feed from Paul's bass into the console, as well as the live feed from a microphone positioned near the bass speaker cabinet.

Along with Paul's bass and Linda's clavinet, Paul opted for a simple rhythmic backing, with Denny and Jimmy playing Fender Stratocasters, and Joe providing a compact, if uninspired, backbeat. With 24 tracks at their disposal, once a basic take was captured, other elements could be added at any time, so once the basis of 'Magneto' was in the can, it was set aside to be overdubbed another day.

"They were very professional," engineer Grace observed, something Killen and Winfrey would probably not have said six months earlier in Nashville. "They wanted to get it right. There wasn't any, 'Oh, we'll just let it slide, we'll catch it in the mix,' there was none of that. They wanted to get it right, there and then."[52]

Building on the morning's momentum, the band spent the afternoon working on a third version of 'Rock Show,' this time with a New Orleans accent: Allen Toussaint slid onto the piano bench, and Kenneth "Afro" Williams, back in New Orleans after his visit to London, again joined the band to play congas. Everyone but English and Toussaint knew the song from the EMI sessions, and as Paul blocked it out for the pianist, he tightened the arrangement, trimming the long instrumental break that had originally followed the bridge and inserting another chorus there, while also further shortening the playout—tweaks that trimmed a minute from the song's hefty running time.

Toussaint's brisk, bluesy piano figures sounded, at times, like Fats Domino's 'Ain't That a Shame' on steroids, but with considerably greater rhythmic variety and a bright edge, and he gave the coda a funkier feel than it had in the second EMI version. And with Paul on bass, Linda on Minimoog, Denny and Jimmy on electric guitars, Joe feeling increasingly more at home on drums, and Afro's congas filling out the percussion textures, the new version finally captured the intensity Paul hoped for.

"It was just like a party," English said of those early sessions. "As we didn't know each other, we were all able to capture a lot more energy. From the start it was good vibes, personally and musically."[53]

On Tuesday, the band added overdubs to the previous day's work: Paul doubling Linda's clavinet intro on 'Magneto and Titanium Man' on Moog, and the band stiffened the rhythm section of 'Rock Show,' with Joe adding extra bass drum and snare, Paul, Denny and Jimmy adding bells, and Paul supporting the basic beat on cowbell. Toussaint added more piano—this time on a Fender Rhodes, rather than the studio's acoustic grand—and Paul added Mellotron bursts.

Recording Sessions

Wednesday, January 29–Thursday, January 30, 1975.

Sea-Saint Recording Studio, 3809 Clematis Street, New Orleans.

Recording: 'Venus and Mars.'

The album did not yet have a title, but in the album layout Paul created in Jamaica, the planned opening track, 'Venus and Mars,' was to be reprised at the start of the album's second side, making it a strong contender to be the record's title song. It took on another life as well, when members of the band and studio personnel began referring to the McCartneys as "Venus" and "Mars."

"'*Venus and Mars are all right tonight*' was one of the lines that just came out as I was writing a tune," Paul innocently claimed of the song's origins. "And the funny thing is, Linda and I never thought of this idea of Venus being her and Mars being me, which is the classical idea—Venus as the female, Mars as the male. Throughout history they've been used as the classical figures. But this all occurred later; I mean I didn't realize any of this when I was writing."[54]

As they moved toward calling the album *Venus and Mars*, another idea struck the McCartneys as well. In its lounge, Sea-Saint Studio had a pool table with seven red and seven yellow balls, plus a black eight ball. During breaks, the band would drink whisky and Coke and knock a few balls around the table, and Linda liked the look of the red and yellow balls against the dark felt, and soon settled on using pool balls on the album cover, with a yellow ball representing Venus and a red ball representing Mars.

Having polished off the 'Venus and Mars (Reprise)' on January 22, Paul now turned to the main song, for which he used his Martin acoustic guitar, and Jimmy unpacked his new Zemaitis 12-string. "It's a very wide guitar and it's got a really big sound," McCulloch said of the Zemaitis. "When I took it over, I strapped it to the seat on the plane. No way was it going into the hold!"[55]

Paul had recorded the reprise with a clean guitar sound, but he wanted the album's opener to sound more "cosmic," in keeping with the song's theme. He and O'Duffy experimented with ways to capture that essence, eventually settling on sending the acoustic guitars through a rotating Leslie speaker.

"There was something really special about working with Paul," said O'Duffy, "something where you thought, this is different, this is on another planet from where I've been up to now. We were just having fun together exploring sounds, and we could be as mad as we liked, it didn't really matter. We were trying to make a beautiful record."[56]

McCartney and McCulloch joined forces for the song's delicate acoustic opening, with Paul picking an arpeggiated D major chord and Jimmy adding a simpler repeating pattern on his 12-string. To preserve the purity of the guitar sound, Paul decided not to sing a guide vocal, although in the introduction, Denny played the vocal melody on Linda's Minimoog. Linda on piano and Joe on drums were called into action for only the final few bars, which were designed to lead into 'Rock Show' by way of an edit.

With the basic track completed during the Wednesday and Thursday sessions, Paul added his bass guitar and Jimmy dubbed an electric guitar part. And to further boost the song's otherworldly aspect, Denny added a touch of sitar, Paul added finger cymbals, and Tony Dorsey contributed a clavinet line.

Recording Session

Friday, January 31, 1975.
Sea-Saint Recording Studio, 3809 Clematis Street, New Orleans.
Recording: 'Listen to What the Man Said,' 'Scottish Jingle,' 'Clematis,' 'New Orleans,' 'Goin' to New Orleans' (working title for 'My Carnival') and 'Crossroads.'

As Wings prepared to lay the groundwork for 'Listen to What the Man Said,' Paul told the band that he wanted the rhythm section, which supported the tune's simple rising and falling melody, to sound like a team of galloping horses—a pastoral aural image reminiscent of 'Maybe Tomorrow,' the Terry Bush and John Crossen tune used as the theme for the Canadian television series *The Littlest Hobo*. For English, who had barely had to lift a stick during the two days devoted to 'Venus and Mars,' it was an unusual approach.

"It was a completely different style [than] what I'd been used to," English explained. "I'd been used to jazz, soul, and progressive stuff, and I wasn't accustomed to working within the kind of limits that the Wings material presented. . . . The most difficult thing to accept was the discipline which that kind of music demands."[57]

Supplementing Joe's drums was a steady, repetitive rhythm that Denny Laine tapped out on the bongos with a pair of thin drumsticks. Paul led the session from the electric piano, while Jimmy, playing his Stratocaster, brought a measure of funkiness to the guitar chords. Satisfied that the backing captured the song's unassuming charm, Paul overdubbed his bass and set the track aside.

Wings finished their week of sessions by blowing off steam in a freewheeling jam, with Paul on bass, Linda on organ, Denny on acoustic guitar, Jimmy on his Strat, and Joe behind the kit. O'Duffy kept the tapes rolling while the band played a Scottish tune (listed as 'Scottish Jingle'); a Johnny

Cash–inspired Spanish number called 'Clematis'; a song Linda was working on, provisionally titled 'New Orleans'; and Paul's variation on a Louisiana workout, with a lovely rolling drum part, called 'Goin' to New Orleans.'

Paul's tune, which would soon morph into 'My Carnival,' saw McCartney in full magpie mode: its chord progression and its lyric—*"Well, I'm goin' to New Orleans, I'm going to see the Mardi Gras"*—borrow heavily from 'Kansas City,' the Jerry Leiber–Mike Stoller tune that had been a hit for Little Richard and was a staple of the Beatles' early setlists. But parts of its melody and its overall feel were pinched from 'Tell Me Pretty Baby,' a tune the McCartneys heard Professor Longhair play at Jed's University Inn shortly after they arrived in New Orleans.

"I just loved the style so much that I composed something called 'My Carnival,'" Paul said of the Professor Longhair song. "And it's got the same riff, basically, that he plays. I just couldn't play it as well! But it's the bass line definitely. It was very similar."[58]

Finally, after musical stops in Scotland, Spain and Louisiana, the jam morphed into a version of Tony Hatch's theme music for the British soap opera *Crossroads*.* Tony Dorsey, not having seen the show, set in a hotel in central England, thought the tune was a McCartney original. The song had not been intended for release, but Paul soon decided that it could serve as the instrumental closer to the album—the piece he had listed as 'Overture' on the scroll he made in Jamaica.

"It could just as easily have been *Coronation Street*," said Paul, referring to another well-known British soap opera, "but we knew the chords to *Crossroads*."[59] Paul wondered, briefly, whether including 'Crossroads' would be a British in-joke that the rest of the world would miss, but decided, "I'd still like to put it in. I don't care, it doesn't matter if no one gets it. I think if you don't get the joke, it still sounds like a closing theme." [60]

Since Dorsey liked the theme so much, Paul had him add it to the list of songs for which he was preparing orchestrations.

Recording Session

Monday, February 3, 1975.
Sea-Saint Recording Studio, 3809 Clematis Street, New Orleans.
Recording: 'Call Me Back Again.'
Overdubbing: 'Medicine Jar.'

On Monday, February 3, Paul took up a song he had not yet finished—'Call Me Back Again.' Although he vamped his way through it during his piano demo session at High Park over the

* *Crossroads* ran from 1964 to 1988 and from 2001 to 2003 on ITV.

summer, the song had not progressed much since he started it at the Beverly Hills Hotel in April 1974. Only a single verse had been completed—*"Well, when I / when I was just a little baby boy / Every night I would call / Your number brought me joy / I called your house / Every night since then"*—as well as a refrain, in which he begged the song's addressee to *"call me back again."*

But just as he had stretched a limited lyric to stunning effect on the *Abbey Road* cut 'Oh! Darling,' Paul embraced the challenge of transforming his limited start into a full-fledged song.

"I thought, I'll develop that and put a few more words to it," Paul said. "But I never did. In New Orleans, we just said, 'Well, let's just have a go with it anyway.' And I ended up sort of just ad-libbing a bit and stretching it out."[61]

There was some urgency about getting this song on tape: Dorsey had already written the horn arrangements for three of the album's songs, including 'Call Me Back Again,' and had booked the players for the next day.

Taking a seat behind the clavinet, flanked on either side by Denny and Jimmy, playing electric guitars, Paul had Joe count in the triple-meter song, whereupon the band provided a solid, energized backing. Paul's full-throated gospel-like guide vocal, which captured him channeling a hybrid of Little Richard and Aretha Franklin, was recorded live, with McCulloch filling in the blank spaces between the lyrics with inventive guitar fills, almost as if the song were a conversation between Paul's voice and Jimmy's guitar.

Once a solid take of the backing track was safely on tape, Linda overdubbed Mellotron chords on the refrains, using the same flute setting that Paul had used in the introduction to 'Strawberry Fields Forever,' and Paul added an active, bluesy bass line that quickly became a dominant element. McCartney, Laine and O'Duffy completed the session by adding three-part harmonies to the choruses.

Recording Session

Tuesday, February 4, 1975.
Sea-Saint Recording Studio, 3809 Clematis Street, New Orleans.
Overdubbing: 'You Gave Me the Answer,' 'Letting Go' and 'Call Me Back Again.'

"Paul McCartney doesn't really need an arranger," Dorsey humbly explained, "because he's a brilliant one himself. It's just that he can't put down on paper what he hears in his head, so he needs someone to do that for him. Doing the arrangements with Paul was really a collaboration."

"He would come in with a tune and sit down at the piano. He'd play bits and say, 'Here's this bit and there's that bit, and right now I want to get from here to there. Do you have any ideas how I can do it?' So I'd think of something and sometimes he'd say 'okay' and other times my suggestion would spark off an idea for him and he'd leap to the keyboard and say, 'I've got it, this is what we'll do.' So, although I was supposed to be the arranger, I ended up assisting him in all sorts of ways."[62]

Dorsey arranged 'You Gave Me the Answer' for clarinets (Michael J. Pierce and Vito Platomone), trumpet (Ronald B. Benko) and bassoon (Harold Joseph Ballam)—a sparse ensemble, but one that captured the romantic atmosphere of the 1930's and 1940's films that sparked Paul's imagination.

"He would listen to old records and try to copy the style," Dorsey noted. "Like 'Lady Madonna,' that's Fats Domino. He said he and John would sit down and listen to old records, and they'd get ideas from that for new songs."[63]

After the piano intro, Dorsey's winds join the texture subtly, voiced to mirror the chords, first in a rising progression and then following the contour of the melody. In the bridge, this chordal backing becomes rhythmically pulsing, staccato 16th notes until the instrumental solo, where Benko takes off with an embellished version of the melody, almost as a dialogue between unmuted and muted trumpet. Ballam's bassoon then picks up the tune, leading back to the final verse. During the wind overdub, Paul also added his final bass guitar part.

'Letting Go' and 'Call Me Back Again' shared the same instrumentation and personnel: three trumpets (Clyde Kerr, John Longo and Steve Howard) and three saxophones (Michael Pierce on alto sax, Alvin Thomas on tenor and Carl Blouin on baritone). Unlike 'You Gave Me the Answer,' these were not backward glances at an olden style, but fully contemporary, blues-based tracks that would benefit from straightforward R&B arrangements.

On 'Letting Go,' Dorsey left the guitar intro, first verse and most of the refrain unadorned, his horns entering in a two-chord blaze after the chorus's final *"oh, I feel like letting go."* With the next verse—*"oh, she looks like snow"*—Dorsey's horns become full participants in the track, adding decorative punctuation between lines, providing chordal support, and taking over the spotlight in instrumental connecting sections.

'Call Me Back Again' begins in true soul band fashion, the brass ensemble fully supporting the rising chords that open the song. Dorsey has his players step back for the rest of the introduction, but the brass returns to repeat the opening figure, leading into the vocal. Through the rest of the track, the ensemble supports and magnifies the song's chord progression, sometimes in a sustained underpinning, sometimes as a series of rhythmic brass stabs, and sometimes either tracing the vocal melody or winding around McCulloch's guitar lines.

Though he downplayed his input in the album's production, Dorsey's brass scores were transformative.

Recording Sessions

Wednesday. February 5–Friday, February 7, 1975.

Sea-Saint Recording Studio, 3809 Clematis Street, New Orleans.

Overdubbing: 'Rock Show,' Medicine Jar,' 'Venus and Mars (Reprise)' and 'Letting Go.'

Mixing: All album cuts.

The rest of the week was devoted to a miscellany of overdubs. On Wednesday, Jimmy played a dobro line and Denny doubled his electric guitar on 'Rock Show.' On Thursday, 'Medicine Jar' was touched up, with Jimmy adding an extra guitar part, using a Vox wah-wah pedal, while Joe fleshed out Geoff's drumming with additional cymbal crashes. That afternoon, Paul and Jimmy added more guitar lines to 'Letting Go,' followed by backing vocals from Paul, Linda and Denny. And 'Venus and Mars (Reprise)' gained Mellotron and Minimoog lines, played by Paul; an acoustic guitar, played by Jimmy; extra percussion from Joe; and backing vocals using an underwater effect from Paul, Denny, Joe and Jimmy.

Mardi Gras season was due to begin on Monday, February 10, with the main parade sweeping through town on "Fat Tuesday" itself—the date John and May had targeted for their visit to New Orleans. Sehorn and Toussaint warned Paul that the studio would be inaccessible during the peak of the festivities, and said they were considering closing Sea-Saint completely for the week starting February 10. Wings now had the perfect excuse to put the sessions on hold and throw themselves into the celebratory atmosphere.

But Paul's hope of sharing that celebration with John were dashed during the overdubbing sessions on February 6, when John phoned Sea-Saint and the receptionist patched his call through to the control room.

"The separation didn't work out,"[64] Lennon joked, telling Paul that he had moved back to the Dakota on February 3—just as Paul was recording 'Call Me Back Again,' the song he started just after reconnecting with John in Los Angeles—and that he and Yoko were hoping to work things out.

"I was just going over for a visit," Lennon told *Melody Maker* at the end of February, "and it fell into place again. It was like I never left, although I'd been there a few times. Suddenly, it fell back into place, and I realized that this was where I belonged. I think we both knew we'd get back together again sooner or later, even if it was five years, and that's why we never bothered with divorce."[65]

"I was supposed to be going down to join Paul in New Orleans," Lennon confessed a few months later, "but my personal life sort of interfered with that. I was too busy being happy. . . . I don't mind talking about that. [Yoko and I] are together and we're happier than ever before, it's like the old story. When you get someone back that you've lost it is better than ever. We were so wrapped up in each other that I just never made it to New Orleans. Sorry Paul."[66]

Tantalizing as the prospect was, the Lennon and McCartney reunion, like John and Yoko's separation, "didn't work out."

On Friday, McCartney and O'Duffy spent the afternoon making mixes of all the work-in-progress tracks, and cassettes were run off for the band before they were unleashed upon New Orleans for the carnival season.

7

MY CARNIVAL

"This time of the year in New Orleans," Paul observed, "there certainly is a great deal of lunacy in the air."[1]

From a balcony overlooking St. Charles Avenue, Paul and Linda watched the passing carnival floats and marching bands making their way through the upriver side of the French Quarter. Tens of thousands of partiers lined the streets—many of them enjoying King Cake, a blend of coffee cake and cinnamon roll—as revelers on the floats threw beads and other trinkets into the crowd.

To ensure that his guests enjoyed the full spectacle from a safe vantage point, Marshall Sehorn took over the upper floor of Kolb's restaurant at 125 St. Charles Avenue—just 12 blocks from the McCartneys' hotel—for the day.

"During the Mardi Gras we rented a place over a restaurant," said Sehorn, "where they could be away from the crowds, but they could see all the parades and all the people. Then, on Mardi Gras day itself, I think my secretary and I had the idea to have someone come over and dress them in clown suits so they could actually mingle in the crowd actively, feel what Mardi Gras was all about."[2]

The first American Mardi Gras ("Fat Tuesday"—typically the day before the start of Lent) took place on March 3, 1699, when French explorers of the Mississippi River landed about 60 miles downstream from present-day New Orleans at a spot they called Point du Mardi Gras. The first full-fledged parade took place a decade later. And now, in 1975, a touch of Beatleness was painted into the history of Mardi Gras, as the McCartneys and Wings, in clown costumes and face paint, rolled from Le Richelieu to Kolb's restaurant in their rented Ford convertible through a crowd so dense the car could barely move.

"Mardi Gras was extraordinary," said O'Duffy. "I was sitting up on the trunk of Paul's car, with Paul driving and the family in the car. We were just going through the town, and it was glorious fun, because the different floats would throw you trinkets, flowers and stuff and we were just surrounded by them."[3]

For once, Linda and her Nikon camera were separated for the day. Instead, 19-year-old rock photographer Sidney Smith was hired through the New York Pop Wire Service to document Wings over New Orleans. Smith arrived at Kolb's just as Paul and Linda made a brief appearance on St. Charles Avenue.

"I was invited to spend the day with them," Smith explained, "and when I arrived they were up there on the balcony; Paul was throwing beads down into the crowds below. He was under the assumption that no one knew who he was because they were all decked out in clown outfits. And so, at one point he and Linda thought they could go out into the crowds, but they came running back real fast. Somebody tipped off everyone, so they couldn't go down in the crowd without being recognized."[4]

That evening the party headed for the St. Bernard's Civic Auditorium, where another local legend, Mac Rebennack, better known as Dr. John, was playing a concert backed by the Meters. Paul and Linda arrived at the auditorium in their red and yellow clown costumes and white face paint, but the Meters, who had been seeing the McCartneys working at Sea-Saint, spotted them immediately and beckoned them to join Dr. John on stage. They were game, but the auditorium's bouncers did not recognize them.

"They were so well disguised that Dr. John's security people threw them off the stage," Smith said. "Literally, threw them off the stage."[5]

Having spent the day sipping scotch and Coke, the McCartneys were sufficiently well-oiled to see the humor in being tackled by the brawny security staff. They soon found seats near the stage with other musicians, including the singers Benny Spellman and Lee Dorsey, the singer and songwriter Earl King and the trumpeter (and Sea-Saint engineer) Ken Laxton. Linda was in her element.

"Their music was *my* music," Linda said. "After all, that jazz and blues stuff was what I was brought up on. Imagine what it was like for me, having seen it in the movies and then to meet all those people. I just can't tell you how it turned me on."[6]

Before the night was over, Paul invited some of his new friends to a session at Sea-Saint the next day.

Recording Session

Wednesday, February 12, 1975.
Sea-Saint Recording Studio, 3809 Clematis Street, New Orleans.
Recording: 'My Carnival.'

Sidney Smith had documented the McCartneys' Mardi Gras experience on film, but Paul was determined to capture the carnival spirit on tape as well. He assembled an all-star collective of New Orleans musicians at Sea-Saint for an impromptu recording session in which Wings and its guests revived one of their jams from January 31, the Professor Longhair–inspired 'Goin' to New Orleans.'

It was a mighty band Paul had at his disposal. He took his seat at the piano, Denny took up the bass, Linda played organ, Jimmy strapped on an electric guitar, and Joe got behind the kit, while Tony Dorsey unpacked his trombone, Ken Laxton moved from the control room to the studio, trumpet in hand, and George Porter Jr., played percussion. A starry vocal sextet filled out the lineup, with Benny Spellman, Earl King, Leo Nocentelli, Ziggy Modeliste, Art Neville and Cyril Neville gathered around a couple of microphones.

Over the next few hours, 'Goin' to New Orleans' morphed into a full-blooded celebration of Mardi Gras and was retitled 'My Carnival.' The song, built around an anthemic chorus—*"It's my carnival, it's a lovely day"*—was recorded and mixed in a single session. A crew from radio station WWOZ was on hand to document part of the session, and the song had its first hearing, alongside an interview with Paul, when the station aired its report.

"Any musician who comes to New Orleans, and hears the music and feels the culture of New Orleans, cannot leave without a little New Orleans in them," the Meters' guitarist Leo Nocentelli observed. "And I think Paul did that. I think he just fell in love with New Orleans, and he fell in love with New Orleans culture. I mean, he appreciated what Mardi Gras was, it was very inspirational to him."[7]

—

For most Americans, Mardi Gras is a single day on the calendar associated with some heavy partying down in Louisiana. But in New Orleans, the festival can last as long as four weeks. Jimmy McCulloch was in his element. "The clubs are open 24 hours a day," he beamed, "they just close for an hour to clean up. There were incredible bands playing all night. Trying to get from the hotel to Sea-Saint Studios was just impossible with all the street parades and stuff; it took about four hours to get across town. So we left it for a few days and joined in, and had a ball."[8]

But far from being mobbed for being Paul McCartney, when the McCartneys and Alan O'Duffy tried to find some place to eat on the second day of the carnival, they were turned away from multiple restaurants because they did not have a table reservation.

On Thursday, February 13, Paul hosted a river cruise and party on *Voyageur*, a 50-year-old riverboat. It was a two-part affair, the first leg for the press, the second for local musicians and some of the McCartneys' music business contacts. The cruise had been planned weeks earlier, possibly to coincide with Lennon's planned visit, but it became a part of Wings' continuing Mardi Gras celebration.

Paul and Linda were driven to the Canal Street docks in a white stretch limousine and made their entrance—30 minutes late—in good spirits, both sporting black top hats. Upon their arrival, the Tuxedo Jazz Band, which Paul had hired to provide suitably spirited party music during the cruise, struck up the longtime Macca favorite, 'When the Saints Go Marching In,' as a throng of fans and reporters from every underground newspaper and television station within 50 miles mobbed the couple and their bandmates. Dennis Fine, their American publicist, repeatedly yelled "Back up! Back up!" and as the crowd parted, Wings walked up the gangplank onto *Voyageur*, with the happily stoned Linda calling out the traditional Mardi Gras appeal, "Throw me something, mister!"[9]

For the press party leg of the trip through the Mississippi bayou, a menu of red beans and rice, sausages, mustard greens, ham hock and wine was laid on as Paul held court with the press. It was more of a crowd than they had planned for: about 20 reporters were invited, but at least

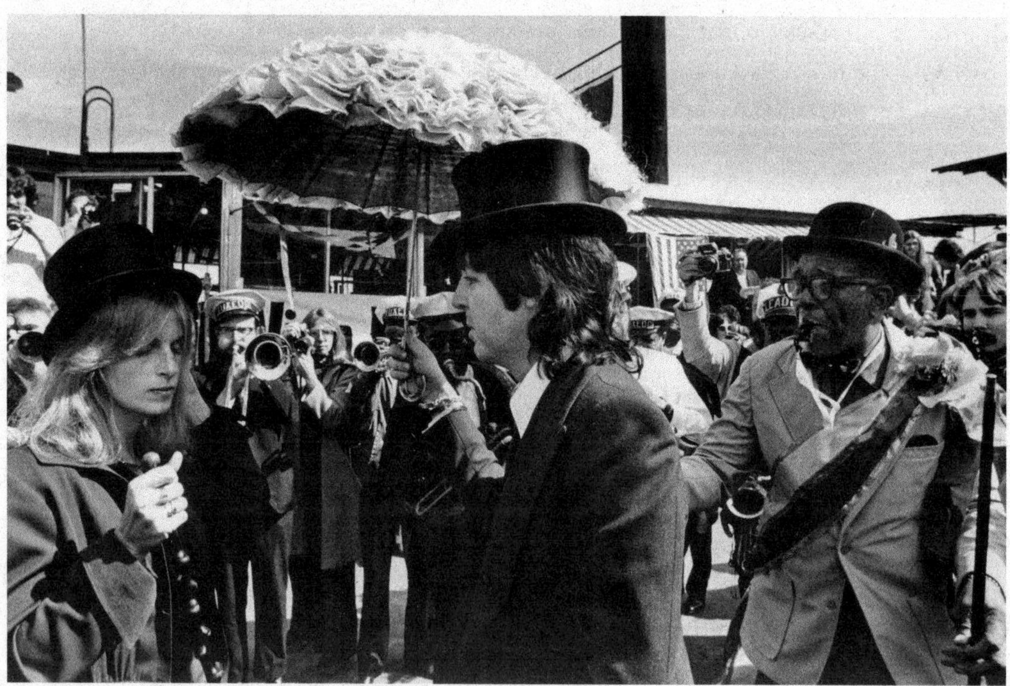

Paul and Linda board *Voyageur*, New Orleans, February 13, 1975

50 turned up, and the crashers were not turned away as long as they could show press credentials.

While the McCartneys turned on the charm, the rest of the band did their best to avoid attention. Joe English occupied a corner with his girlfriend, Dayle, who had flown in from Macon; Jo Jo, Denny's girlfriend, spent much of the trip being sick over the side of the boat; and a visibly hungover McCulloch was discovered by journalist Andy McConnell, "slouched into a chair, sour-faced, hiding behind a pair of sunglasses." McConnell documented what came next in his piece for *Sounds* less than two weeks later.

"After introductions, I said we had lived two miles away from each other at one time—him in North Weald, myself in Epping. 'Oh yeah,' he said, glancing the other way tight lipped, 'what musicians do you know in Epping, eh?' 'None,' I replied. 'So what do you know, then?' he snapped bitterly. A shout from Macca's roadie, Mike, for me to meet Allen Toussaint's horn section and the Meters averted any more embarrassment. But wondering what was up with the 21-year-old guitar player, I asked a fellow seafarer. 'Oh, he's been smoking pot in the lavatory.'"[10]

Rather than speaking to reporters individually, as he tended to do in party situations, Paul held a formal press conference, sitting at a table with Linda, a sea of microphones before them. Snippets of this fairly easygoing back-and-forth were carried by various newspapers, both in Britain and America:

Reporter: Why New Orleans?
Paul: Years ago, when we did the Beatles American tour people used to come over to us and say things like, "You never got to see the country, why don't you come back and have a look?" Well, I like traveling and sightseeing, as does Linda, so we thought of combining sightseeing with work. It's warm and it's a musical city and the studio's great. We are a little influenced by wherever we are.

Reporter: What did you do for Mardi Gras, Paul? Where did you see the parade?
Paul: We went on [St.] Charles Street.
Linda: And Canal Street. We were in the crowd man; we were right there!

Reporter: What about the music here in New Orleans? I understand you've paid a visit, incognito, to several places. What are some of the musicians you might have enjoyed here in New Orleans?
Paul: Well, we saw Professor play, Professor Longhair, and he's the greatest, he's a classic, I love him.[11]

Reporter: Will you play live soon yourself?

Paul: The band won't go out until we're musically ready.

Reporter: Did the disastrous reviews accompanying the Harrison tour discourage you?
Paul: No. We loved it. We had a ball [at George's concert]. In defense of the audience, though, I thought George should have played more of his hits, more of *his* music. George was not accustomed to a great deal of prolonged singing and perhaps the tour was too long.

Reporter: Do you have a name for the new album?
Paul: No, we haven't named the album yet . . . It'll be out in about two months . . . It'll be better than *Band on the Run*.[12]

Paul and Linda on *Voyageur*, New Orleans, February 13, 1975

Ninety minutes later, the riverboat docked again at Canal Street, where the press was offloaded and Paul and Linda welcomed Robert Parker, Earl King, Lee Dorsey, Ernie K-Doe, Mylon LeFevre, Clarence Henry, Allen Toussaint, Professor Longhair, several executives from Capitol Records, and two of Paul's American publicists, Lee Solters and Dennis Fine, among their guests for the cruise's second leg. For three hours, the boat navigated up and down the same stretch of water while guests ate, drank, and enjoyed live music played by the Meters and Chocolate Milk, with Ernie K-Doe joining the Meters to perform 'I Want to Hold Your Hand,' 'Get Back,' and 'Come Together.'

A splendid time was had by all, with one exception.

"I was shooting pictures *all day long*," explained photographer Sidney Smith, the only lensman allowed on the boat. "I had one camera around my neck, a couple of rolls of film in my pocket, and all the rest of my cameras and film rolls were in my camera bag. And toward the end of the day, I put my bag down next to me, just so I could watch Paul, and take the moment in, and think how lucky I was to get this job. And two seconds later, I go to grab my bag, and it's gone. And I flipped the fuck out. Somebody walked off the boat with all my cameras and all my film. Everything. It was a complete kick in the balls. As far as I'm concerned, I blew the biggest photography job I ever had."[13]

But all was not lost.* Between the beginning and the end of the boat trip, Smith did manage to salvage three rolls of film capturing Paul and Linda's arrival onboard the *Voyageur* and the closing

* 8mm film of the boat trip also exists, shot by filmmaker Joy Houck Jr. at Paul's request.

moments of the Meters' floating concert. "I had to go and tell them that I'd lost all my film," said Smith, "which wasn't exactly my finest moment."[14] For Paul and Linda, Smith's tale of woe must have brought back memories of Linda's camera bag being seized when they were mugged in Lagos, only 15 months earlier. But they quickly brushed off their disappointment and headed over to Sea-Saint for another spontaneous recording session.

Recording Sessions

Thursday, February 13–Friday, February 14, 1975.
Sea-Saint Recording Studio, 3809 Clematis Street, New Orleans.
Overdubbing: 'Baby Face' (for *One Hand Clapping*), 'Magneto and Titanium Man' and 'My Carnival.'

'Baby Face,' recorded in August for the *One Hand Clapping* television special, was an odd choice of song to dig out of the archives for Wings' New Orleans sessions, but Paul had a clear plan for the recording, virtually from the moment he decided to record in New Orleans. He wanted to enrich the song with the addition of a brass band, and listening to the Tuxedo Jazz Band during the riverboat cruise convinced him that he had found the right players—that, in fact, he had found the Louisiana equivalent of Jim Mac's Jazz Band. When the cruise ended, he offered each of the seven Tuxedo players $100 (£42) to come back to Sea-Saint that evening for an overdubbing session.

But the Tuxedo players—Gregg Stafford and Ted Reilly (trumpets), Walter Payton (saxophone), Frank Naundorf (trombone), Herman Sherman (alto sax), Joe Torregano (clarinet), Emile Knox (bass drum) and Laurence Trotter (snare drum)—were essentially street musicians, not session men, and it quickly became clear that translating the brass and wind lines that Paul hummed to them into a coherent ensemble recording was not going to be straightforward.

"I took the track and asked these fellows to overdub," Paul explained, "and like these guys don't know what earphones are; they're a trad band right? A genuine, New Orleans brass band. They couldn't get the tempo for a while, but then they started to get it. They're brilliant. The drummer plays bass drum with his . . . melon . . . and he has a coat hanger in his left hand, and the bottom half of a hi-hat, which he hits with his coat hanger. So it's boom, chick-a-boom, and his mate has got the snare drum. They have this ethnic talent—it's like a Morris dancing act."[15]

The next afternoon, Valentine's Day, Wings eased back into work on the new album with a short overdubbing session. 'Magneto and Titanium Man' was threaded up, and Jimmy and Denny added two new electric guitar parts to the master take, while Paul used a Fender Rhodes electric

We flipped over
Paul McCartney & Wings
latest single

SALLY G
is the flip side of 'Junior's Farm' – a Top 20 hit before Christmas. Now,
'Sally G' is breaking into both the national and country charts in the USA,
and we are re-promoting it, so that everyone has a chance to hear
another side of Paul, Linda and Wings.
Sally G c/w Junior's Farm – out now on Apple R 5999
EMI Records Limited. 20, Manchester Square, London W1A 1ES. Sales and Distribution Centre, 1-3 Uxbridge Road, Hayes, Middlesex. Tel: (01) 759 4532/5611 & 848 9811

Paul McCartney & Wings, 'Sally G' single trade ad (with Jimmy in the shadows)

piano to double the acoustic piano. Finally, Joe added drum crashes, designed to sound like monster footsteps after the first line of the fifth verse—"*So we went out.*" Backing vocals and clapping were then overdubbed onto 'My Carnival.' The session ended with Alan O'Duffy making new mixes of 'My Carnival,' 'Magneto and Titanium Man,' 'Call Me Back Again,' 'Letting Go' and 'You Gave Me the Answer.'

—

Three weeks into their stay, the Wings party was feeling at home in New Orleans, having sorted out the best places to eat, drink, score drugs, and stay out of trouble. With the weekend upon them, Denny, Jimmy, Joe and their lady friends hit the town, while Paul checked in with MPL in London and the Eastmans in New York.

A week earlier, Warner Bros. Records issued a second single from the *McGear* album in Britain. But the double A side, which coupled edited versions of 'Givin' Grease a Ride' and 'Sea Breezes (In Love),' failed to make the Top 40 singles.

EMI, meanwhile, made an unusual move in the hope of boosting the sales of 'Junior's Farm.' Noting that the flip side, 'Sally G,' with its Nashville connection and its country twang, was getting more airplay in certain parts of the United States than 'Junior's Farm,' Capitol Records' national promotion director Bruce Wendell decided to issue 'Sally G' as a promotional single, with both stereo and mono mixes.

"We've asked the trades and the stations to treat it like a separate record and drop 'Junior's Farm,'"[16] Wendell told *Billboard*. In its January 25 issue, *Billboard* flipped the chart title, listing the single as 'Sally G'/'Junior's Farm,' and a week later 'Sally G' alone was listed as a *New Entry* at No. 66. 'Sally G' peaked at No. 39 before slowly slipping out of the Hot 100. Capitol did not bother to produce a new retail version of the single for buyers who had ignored it when 'Junior's Farm' was the promoted A side.

In Britain, EMI regarded the move as a stroke of genius and followed suit, sending promotional copies of 'Sally G' to radio stations and reviewers. Paul had mixed feelings about this Capitol/EMI sales stunt, but he rationalized it when asked.

"We flipped that," Paul told *Melody Maker*, "and I thought it might seem we're trying to fool the public. But it isn't, it's only to get a bit of exposure on that song. Otherwise, it just dies a death, and only the people who bought 'Junior's Farm' get to hear 'Sally G.' I like to have hits, definitely, that's what I'm making records for. It's not for the bread, although I like that too, it's just that if you do something in my particular field, you want people to hear it."[17]

Reviewers who had already spun the song as the flipside of 'Junior's Farm' four months earlier were confused, though, and some aired their complaints.

Hats off for a hoedown! Genial young Paulie has gone all country on us, laying out a charming, carefree little piece with generous helpings of deep south fiddle, steel guitar, and round-the-campfire vocals. Wings don't somehow slot into the cowboy image, but it's pleasantly throwaway and Ringo will like it, even if it does sound a bit like an ad for Kentucky fried chicken. Apple are being a bit optimistic for this has already been out with 'Junior's Farm' (now relegated to the B side) on the top side and it didn't exactly change the world. Come on chaps, play the white man, and give us some new material. Miss.[18]

Colin Irwin, Melody Maker

No, of course he isn't running out of material. He just thought it would be a nice idea to flip the 'Junior's Farm' single over and release 'Sally G' instead, due to its success in the USA. A country style number featuring some really nice steel and violin, it was written in Nashville after a night out on the town. The lyrics are good and in Paul's impeccable style, every word can be heard! Should be in the charts soon.[19]

Lynne Thirkettle, Disc

Weeeee-ha let's go hoedown with Paul and the band to Tennessee, fiddle playing and all. Very pleasant and everything, but I wonder what the reaction would have been if it hadn't been sung by Paul McCartney and friends. Not really something to set the turntables on fire.[20]

Sue Byrom, Record Mirror

'Sally G' is just pleasant McCartney pick-and-strum country fluff with the pedal steel player getting a chance to wander up and down his axe. Nothing to get hung about.[21]

Charles Shaar Murray, NME

The British record-buying public was unmoved. While the single sold in substantial quantities in the country music–loving states in America, it failed to make an appearance in the British Top 100.

Checking in with the Eastmans, Paul learned that the acquisition of another addition to his growing portfolio of publishing interests—Wren Music Co., Inc., whose catalog included Gerald H. Nelson's and Fred B. Burch's 'Tragedy,' which Wings had covered during the *Red Rose Speedway* sessions but had not released—would be finalized in March.

One of the weekend's events tested Paul's patience. On Saturday night, Alan O'Duffy and Sidney Smith were invited to a party hosted by a local journalist. As the wine flowed, O'Duffy reached into his pocket and pulled out a cassette with mixes of the songs Wings had been recording, slipped it into his host's deck, and hit play.

"We palled around a lot together in New Orleans," Smith recalled. "I took him with me to a party, it was a party given by a writer at one of the local weekly papers. And, for whatever reason, Alan brought along Paul's unfinished tapes that he thought would be cool to play for people at the party. It was an innocent gesture on Alan's part, but the next thing we know, the fellow whose house it was wrote a review of the album based on the unfinished tapes. It got me in trouble with McCartney's management, and it got Alan in even more trouble."[22]

Paul was incensed when he read the review. It should have been obvious, he would have thought, that deciding whether and when to preview new material for the press was his prerogative. But these tracks were far from finished, and given the distance between their current state and Paul's vision for them, a leak could be damaging. When Smith and O'Duffy arrived at Sea-Saint on Monday, Paul took them into Sehorn's office and gave them a dressing-down: for Smith, it was strike two, after losing his camera bag; O'Duffy, who as a recording professional should have known better, was told that if he did anything like that again, he would be fired.

Recording Sessions

Monday, February 17–Thursday, February 20, 1975.
Sea-Saint Recording Studio, 3809 Clematis Street, New Orleans.
Overdubbing: 'Magneto and Titanium Man,' 'Spirits of Ancient Egypt' and 'Listen to What the Man Said.'

Wings began a new week with more overdubbing. 'Magneto and Titanium Man' was completed with the addition of Paul's lead vocal (plus a doubling) as well as a thick layer of backing vocals that brought a Beach Boys influence to the funky, comic book–inspired track. For a chastened O'Duffy, this was a chance to get back into Paul's good graces.

"I love harmony," said O'Duffy, whose father was an Irish tenor and who, as a teenager, played in a band that covered Beach Boys songs. "Brian Wilson was an amazing influence on my life, and also on Paul, and I used to analyze *Pet Sounds*, that remarkable record which Paul also loves. So when Paul wanted to put harmonies on, I was into it."

With O'Duffy encouraging him to make the harmonies more plush, Paul and company overlaid the backing vocals four times, rather than merely double-tracking them. "It's all the more glossy as a musical texture,"[23] O'Duffy explained.

The Tuesday and Wednesday sessions were spent fleshing out 'Spirits of Ancient Egypt.' Paul added Moog and Gizmo guitar, Linda recorded synthesized string swells, Joe added gong at the start of the track, and Alan O'Duffy recorded the sound of a telephone busy signal, to be used at the end of the song. Finally, the whole band, plus O'Duffy, gathered around a microphone to overdub the song's rich vocal harmonies.

Wings had visitors on Thursday—Dr. John and Meters guitarist Leo Nocentelli. Just before they arrived, Paul, Linda and Denny had recorded backing vocals, complete with a kiss from Linda, on 'Listen to What the Man Said.' Dr. John and Nocentelli were quickly drafted as a vocal trio with Paul (singing falsetto), for a second vocal harmony track. Paul finished the day's work by recording his lead vocal, introducing the song in a throaty imitation of his guests, "*Alright, okay, ha-ha. Very good to see you down in New Orleans, man. Yeah, hairy. Yeah, yeah.*"

"I put that on the beginning of the vocal track down in New Orleans," Paul acknowledged. "Leo No-Can-Telli, as the Faces called him, he talks like that. Dr. John talks like that too, sort of—very New Orleans voice. So that was me doing a little impression."[24]

After the session, the band went to see Dave Mason play a concert at the Warehouse. Mason was an old friend of both McCartney and Laine. Back in the *Sgt. Pepper* days, he used to spend time with Paul at Cavendish Avenue, and he filmed a clip with his old band, Traffic, that was intended for the Beatles' *Magical Mystery Tour* but did not make the final edit. He also sang backing vocals on a version of 'Across the Universe' that was never released.

Recording Session

Friday, February 21, 1975.

Sea-Saint Recording Studio, 3809 Clematis Street, New Orleans.

Overdubbing: 'Listen to What the Man Said' and 'Jam (with Dave Mason).'

Even after the previous day's vocal overdubs, Paul had mixed feelings about 'Listen to What the Man Said.' On one hand, it had clear commercial appeal, yet Paul felt that the backing lacked musical depth and variety, and he considered dropping it from the album.

"Whenever I would play it on the piano," Paul said, "people would say, 'Oh I like that one, you know.' So I thought, this will be a good one. But when we did the backing track, we thought we didn't really get that together at all."[25]

On what would be the final day of recording at Sea-Saint, Paul and the band undertook a series of overdubs, hoping to give the track the spark it was missing. Just as Paul and Denny began overdubbing electric guitar parts, Dave Mason walked into the control room.

Paul set his doubts to one side and told Mason that they were working on what might be Wings' next single and invited him to join in.

"I was playing a show at the Warehouse in New Orleans," Mason said, "and Jimmy McCulloch and a couple of the guys came over the night of the show. And I had a day off the next day, and they were like, 'Well, come down to the studio.' So I just went down there and they were working on this tune and Paul was like, 'Hey, grab a guitar—here, you see this lick—dum-dum-dum, dum-dum, dum-dum-dum,' he said. 'We're just gonna play that.' And I'm like, 'Okay, we're just gonna play the same lick?' And I just threw in this little harmony on the last few notes of the lick, and he was like, 'Oh . . . wait a minute . . . no, no, no. Okay, play it again.' And then he said, 'Oh, yeah, that's cool, I like that.' So that was my contribution."[26]

Even with the new guitar overdubs, the song still had plenty of breathing room for solo work, but Paul decided that further additions could wait. For the rest of the session, the band and Mason jammed, filling two reels in the process and working out the basis of a new song, entitled 'The Crawl of the Wild.'

—

Midway through the Sea-Saint sessions, it occurred to both McCartney and O'Duffy that for several reasons, a change of scene would soon be in order. Sea-Saint's studio was too small for the full orchestral sweetening that Paul wanted for some of the tracks. O'Duffy's suggestion was to move the sessions to Los Angeles at the end of the month, where they could work at Wally Heider's studio but would have the option to work in larger spaces as well. And thanks to the film industry, string players who could quickly and efficiently play anything you put in front of them were plentiful.

"We were loving New Orleans, and we had a great time," O'Duffy explained. "But, in my mind, there wasn't a possibility of doing string arrangement overdubs in New Orleans. Certainly you could do brass arrangement overdubs, which we did. And I had previously made records with guys where we'd record in one studio, and then went somewhere else to mix. My idea was that if we got to Los Angeles, there was a more accurate possibility of mixing."[27]

There was also the matter of the work visas held by the three British members of Wings, all due to expire on March 1. Since the permits had been arranged—and announced—by the local immigration office, Paul reasoned that the New Orleans officials would have an eye on whether they were overstaying their work visas, but that if they went elsewhere, they could fly under the radar.

Besides, Tony Dorsey would be conducting the orchestral sessions, using American musicians, so there would be nothing to alarm either the immigration authorities or the musicians' union. The only potential violations of Wings' visa status would be if Paul, Denny or Jimmy did any further overdubbing—and that, as they knew from their experience recording in Nashville, could be done on the down-low.

So, on Saturday, February 22, O'Duffy spent the afternoon making safety copies of all the 24-track masters the band had recorded in New Orleans—an effort that involved having a second 24-track deck shipped by Wally Heider from Los Angeles to New Orleans, since Sea-Saint had only one. And Wings prepared to fly to Los Angeles for the final push to complete the new album.

8

VENUS AND MARS ARE ALRIGHT

By Wednesday, February 26, Paul, Linda and the girls were sunning themselves by the swimming pool at a rented villa in Coldwater Canyon, Los Angeles. The rest of the band were put up at the Beverly Wilshire Hotel at 9500 Wilshire Boulevard. Paul brought over the players' significant others as well, and Joe English's daughter, Christy, spent time at the McCartneys' villa playing with Mary, Stella and Heather, and having the best in celebrity swimming lessons from Paul and Linda.

The villa Paul and Linda rented had a pool table, which reaffirmed their notion of using red and yellow pool balls on the album cover. Paul put in a call to Hipgnosis, the firm that assembled the cover for *Band on the Run*, and arranged for the principals—Aubrey "Po" Powell and Storm Thorgerson—to fly to Los Angeles to discuss the cover design.

O'Duffy had arranged for Wings to use Studio 3 at Wally Heider Recording, a studio founded in 1954 and located just off Hollywood Boulevard, near Grauman's Chinese Theatre. Studio 3 was a 15-by-40-foot room, with a 12-foot ceiling, and a spacious (19-by-20-foot) control room fitted out with a Medio 32-input console and an Ampex 24-track deck. Unlike New Orleans, where there was relatively little competition for business and recording time was charged at a premium, the studio scene in Los Angeles was thriving and competitive. Heider billed 24-track recording in Studio 3 at $90–$125 (£37–£52)* per hour, depending on the time of day.

The studio was just under half the size of EMI Studio Three—but since all that remained were instrumental and vocal overdubs it suited McCartney's needs perfectly. During the Los Angeles sessions, Alan O'Duffy was assisted by tape op Biff Dawes.

Unlike EMI Studios, which had a main entrance and reception area designed as a buffer for

---

* Unlike most studios, which charged a standard hourly rate, Wally Heider's rates increased throughout the course of the day. 8 A.M.–1 P.M. $90; 1–6 P.M. $105; after 6 P.M. $125.

visitors, hangers-on and groupies, Wally Heider had a quirky setup, which instantly made things interesting.

"The studio we had in Wally Heider's was opposite a car park," O'Duffy explained. "And it was street, pavement, door, control room—you could walk straight in off the street and you're in the control room. And we had all manner of guests, including Warren Beatty, Jim Webb, Micky Dolenz and Harry Nilsson. There was a little bit of a party atmosphere going on."[1]

Recording Sessions

Wednesday, February 26–Thursday, February 27, 1975.
Wally Heider Recording, Studio 3, 1604 N Cahuenga Blvd., Los Angeles.
Overdubbing: 'Venus and Mars,' 'Rock Show' and 'Love in Song.'

Recording in Los Angeles began on Wednesday, February 26, with Paul recording his lead vocals for 'Venus and Mars'—now acknowledged to be the album's title track. With a running time of just 1'24", of which the sung lyric accounts for only 30", it took little time for Paul to set down a vocal take he was happy with. He then added a second vocal track, harmonizing himself, starting with the line, "*red lights, green lights, strawberry wine.*"

His voice suitably warmed up, Paul also recorded his lead vocal for 'Rock Show,' and all five band members overdubbed backing vocals that evening.

Thursday's session was also dedicated to vocal work: Paul's lead vocal for 'Love in Song' was recorded in two passes, the master track a composite of the two takes. Paul, Denny and Linda then added backing vocals.

Paul and Linda took Friday off. Originally, they planned to fly to New York for the Grammy Awards ceremony at the Gershwin Theatre on March 1. But the National Academy of Recording Arts and Sciences had planned a second, low-key ceremony on March 4 at the Beverly Wilshire for those who were unable to attend the main event, so Paul and Linda decided against flying to the East Coast.

They may also have wanted to avoid an encounter with John and Yoko, who were guests of honor, with John tapped as a presenter. True, they had been getting along better than at any time since 1969. But John's U-turn on a reunion in New Orleans stung Paul, and though he wished the reunited Lennons well, the reconciliation created some awkwardness: less than a year earlier, Paul was flying across the country as a go-between, carrying Yoko's recipe for fixing their marriage, but Yoko may have regarded his more recent attempt to lure John and May to New Orleans as a dangerous distraction.

It was almost enough to make Paul regret getting involved. When he first brought Yoko's message to John, at the end of March, he did not know May and had not interacted with John and May as a couple. But having now spent several afternoons and evenings with them, he found that when John was with May, he was easygoing and open to working together. Now Paul remembered the degree to which he felt intimidated by John and Yoko when they were together.

"She's a very tough lady, and John and she made a very formidable couple. And often I would talk to them, and they would say, 'That's stupid,' which made me fearful. Often, I would get very nervous to talk to them. I couldn't do it."[2]

Paul's absence left the door open for Lennon's mischievous side. Presenting the award for Record of the Year, alongside Paul Simon, the pair, together with the ceremony's host, singer Andy Williams, delivered a wince-inducing scripted intro.

Lennon: Hello, I'm John, I used to play with my partner Paul.

Simon: I'm Paul, I used to play with my partner Art.

Williams: I'm Andy, I used to play with my partner Claudine.*

But the trio of musical legends reading lines on a teleprompter proved less awkward than the improvised banter that took place when they announced the winner, Olivia Newton-John (for 'I Honestly Love You'). Newton-John was not present, so Art Garfunkel, who had parted ways with Simon in 1970—around the same time as the Beatles' split, and with nearly as much acrimony—accepted the award.

Lennon: Which one of you is Ringo?

Simon: I thought I told you to wait in the car.

Lennon: Are you ever getting back together again?

Simon [pointing to John and Art]: Are *you guys* getting back together again?

Lennon: It's terrible isn't it?

Garfunkel: Still writing, Paul?

Simon: Trying my hand at a little acting, Art.

Lennon: Where's Linda? [No response.] Oh well, too subtle that one!

---

* Williams had married the French-born singer and actress Claudine Longet in 1961, but they had recently announced their divorce, which was finalized in 1975.

The evening was dominated by Stevie Wonder, who won four Grammys, including Album of the Year for *Fulfillingness' First Finale.* The McCartneys' admiration for Wonder might have lessened the sting of losing the Grammy for what had been his best post-Beatles album so far. But Paul could take consolation in winning the other two awards he was nominated for: 'Band on the Run' won for Best Pop Vocal Performance by a Duo, Group or Chorus, and Geoff Emerick claimed the Best Engineered Recording (Non-Classical) award.

Recording Session

Sunday, March 2, 1975.
Wally Heider Recording, Studio 3, 1604 N Cahuenga Blvd., Los Angeles.
Overdubbing: 'Medicine Jar.'

Wings spent Sunday working on 'Medicine Jar,' Jimmy's anti-drug tune, with all five musicians joining forces for backing vocals, and Paul adding an electric guitar. Paul, Denny and Jimmy were now in violation of their visa status, but it would take more than that to attract the eyes of the law.

As if on cue, Paul and Linda provided the necessary provocation. Leaving Wally Heider's at around 11:30 P.M., the McCartneys, including Heather, Mary and Stella, were driving back to Coldwater Canyon at just after midnight when they spotted the telltale flashing lights in their rearview mirror and pulled over. Rolling down the window of his rented silver 1974 Lincoln Continental, Paul faced a California State Highway patrolman who informed him that he had run a red light at the corner of Santa Monica Boulevard and Midvale Avenue. As the officer was writing up the citation, he couldn't help noticing the faint odor of burning marijuana, and when he ordered the McCartneys out of the vehicle, he found a half-smoked joint on the floor and a plastic bag with 16 grams of weed in Linda's purse.

Knowing the immigration, visa and touring implications of an American drug bust for Paul, Linda instantly took the rap, declaring, "It's my grass. Paul doesn't have anything to do with it."[3] Linda was arrested and taken to a cell in Division 91, where she was questioned for two hours. Because the girls were in the car, the district attorney was considering charging her not only with possession but with influencing minors as well. Her bail was set at $500 (£205).

Paying Linda's bail was surprisingly complicated for the multimillionaire pop star. Since their mugging in Lagos, Paul and Linda did not travel with much cash. After trying unsuccessfully to locate Alan Crowder, Paul drove across town, hoping to track down an old friend with whom he and Linda planned to meet later in the week.

"I was working for Stigwood," Peter Brown explained, "and Paul knew I was staying on business at the Beverly Hills Hotel. Paul came to the hotel and asked the night manager if he would ring my room. It was late but he wasn't going to say no to Paul McCartney, so he rang, and they came up to the room. 'Did I have any money?'

"He needed something like $500, and I didn't have that much cash. I rang down to the hotel desk and asked if I could cash a check and was told that they keep the safe locked at night. So the young man who was sleeping with me at the time, who lived in California, drove back to his apartment and got some cash, and came back to the hotel while Paul and I sat talking to each other in my hotel suite."[4]

Paul bailed Linda out, and she was ordered to appear in Division 91 Municipal Court on March 10. By Monday morning, news of Linda's arrest had already made the *Los Angeles Times*. "It's up to the district attorney," a police official told the paper. "If she is convicted she could go to jail for up to five years."[5]

Monday's recording session was canceled, as was the McCartneys' scheduled appearance at the Los Angeles Grammy Awards dinner on Tuesday evening. But if the bust was another demerit for the McCartneys, in the eyes of the law, Paul was as defiant now as he was in the wake of the Swedish bust in 1972, to which he responded by declaring, in his first post-bust interview, that marijuana should be legal. He now amplified that position.

"We don't really think it's a crime," said Paul, "and so we go about it as if it isn't. Unfortunately some people think it *is*, and go about it as if it is, so if you're hauled up by a highway patrolman in L.A. and he smells a bit in the car, he doesn't think that it's just an innocent little thing that's not going to harm anyone. He thinks of it as the whole dangerous what-is-this-depravity scene, y'know. I think it's as depraved as booze, which I think is . . . *slightly* depraved, but a lot of things are *slightly* depraved.

"The only really unfortunate thing about it, really, is that it starts to get you a reputation as a kind of druggie. It is really only a kind of minor offence. It isn't something we take too seriously, and of course the press image is really far worse. We're not serious drug addicts or anything. We just try to keep it quiet and not get into it a lot, because even talking about it in this interview is like adding to it."[6]

Recording Sessions

Tuesday, March 4–Wednesday, March 5, 1975.

Wally Heider Recording, Studio 3, 1604 N Cahuenga Blvd., Los Angeles.

Overdubbing: 'Listen to What the Man Said.'

When Paul and Linda returned from Europe in August 1972, their Swedish drug bust hanging over them, Paul's response was to issue 'Hi, Hi, Hi' as Wings' next single. Of the cuts Wings had been recording, 'Listen to What the Man Said' already stood out as the track most likely to be a hit, but now, thanks to the McCartneys' latest brush with the law, it was propelled upward on Paul's priority list. What better way to respond to a drug bust, after all, than to fill America's airwaves with lyrics like, "*Oh—yes indeed we know / that people will find a way to go / no matter what the man said.*"

Channeling his inner Stevie Wonder, Paul tinkered with the recording, doubling his electric piano part with a funky clavinet overdub on March 4, and adding Minimoog surges and additional rhythm guitar during the finale.

With nothing of her own to add, Linda decided during the Wednesday session that a shopping trip was in order. At around 1 P.M., she connected with Blair Sabol, an old friend from her salad days as a single mother/rock photographer in New York.

Sabol, like Linda, was from a well-to-do family, at home in Villanova, Pennsylvania, but with a Park Avenue pied-à-terre, which Sabol took over after graduating from Finch Junior College on Manhattan's Upper East Side. Waiting for a friend one day at the offices of the *Village Voice*, Sabol met Howard Smith, whose Scenes column was essential reading for anyone interested in the blossoming counterculture. She became Smith's assistant and soon had a column of her own, Outside Fashion. At the time, she was dating Joshua White, whose Joshua Light Show provided the psychedelic backdrop for concerts at the Fillmore East, which was where she met Linda.

Linda and Blair had not seen each other since Linda moved to London in 1968, and Linda would probably have known from their mutual friend Danny Fields—the only one in her New York circle who Linda kept up with after her departure—that Sabol had been furious not to have been kept in the loop. Another of Linda's friends from that time, the rock columnist and encyclopedist Lillian Roxon, had taken out her anger at Linda in a savage review of the *James Paul McCartney* television special in 1973, and Sabol had two years since then to observe Linda from a distance and keep her rhetorical knives sharpened.

Linda, though, thought the two might rekindle their friendship, so on March 5 they met for lunch and shopping on Rodeo Drive and traded stories of what they had been up to—including, in Linda's case, her recent drug arrest. "The bust didn't seem to affect her," Sabol later wrote, noting that Linda told her, "Well, you know, it happens to everybody and it's time consuming with the lawyers, but we'll get it taken care of."[7]

Linda insisted that Blair drop by Wally Heider's studio to watch Paul at work, and not incidentally, get a glimpse of Linda in her current role as both Paul's muse and an increasingly confident member of Wings. While Paul experimented with fresh sounds for 'Listen to What the Man Said,' and Denny, Jimmy and Joe chain-smoked and sipped bottles of Coors beer at the back of the control room, Linda showed Blair mock-ups of the album cover she had shot using the pool table at their Coldwater Canyon rental.

Perhaps thinking of Sabol as a fashion columnist and friend, rather than a general assignment reporter, Linda was blithely unaware that Sabol not only continued to harbor a grudge for those years of radio silence but intended to use their time together as fodder for what turned out to be the most vicious takedown ever written about Linda.

"The two hours I spent at Wally Heider's," she wrote in a *Village Voice* profile that ran six weeks later, "consisted of watching Linda order some of the roadies out for fresh strawberry juice at the Farmer's Market. She showed me her photos for the album cover at least four times and raved on about her work. I always admired her confidence and self-assertiveness. By the way, her album shot consisted of two billiard balls (one red and one yellow) on a black velvet background. Not exactly the hottest eye catcher of an idea for a cover photo, but, let's face it, can a cover really make or break a McCartney album?

"Linda then requested that I watch her as she played or dabbled at the celesta. She sat down, struck two notes, jumped up and was on to the Moog. She hit four Moog moans and went on to a guitar. She didn't complete one riff on one instrument nor did she complete one explanatory sentence. Meanwhile, Paul disappeared into total music meditation in the glass-enclosed booth. Earphones adjusted, he would sit there all night mainlining track after track and not paying too much attention to Linda's childish auditions."[8]

Sabol called it a day when Paul played what she described as "assorted types of catcalls and elephant roars with the volume turned up to Sensurround level," something she thought—or at least, wrote that she thought—he did principally in the hope that she would leave.

That night, the McCartneys and their bandmates were given VIP passes to see the Faces at the Forum in Inglenook, followed by a high-tone after-party thrown by Pacific Presentation and Warner Bros. Records. Linda devoted some effort to avoiding the few press photographers and reporters at the party—no need to discuss the other night's legal entanglement—and mingled with Paul in a crowd of 250 rock world A-listers.

Recording Sessions

Thursday, March 6–Friday, March 7, 1975.

Wally Heider Recording, Studio 3, 1604 N. Cahuenga Blvd., Los Angeles.

Overdubbing: 'Rock Show,' 'You Gave Me the Answer' and 'Listen to What the Man Said.'

Two new pop star visitors drifted through the revolving control room door at Studio 3 on March 6—the singer Tony Orlando and the singer-actor and former Monkee Davy Jones. After playing his guests a preview of the new album, Paul invited them to stay as long as they liked while he laid on a master class in record producing.

He first revisited 'Rock Show.' Listening to the track in Los Angeles, it occurred to him that Allen Toussaint's pulsating piano line had pushed the track decisively toward a New Orleans sound, which was not quite what he wanted. In the hope of toughening it up, Paul asked Jimmy to add a lightly distorted rhythm guitar track, to give the song a rough and raw rock-show feeling. McCulloch's new guitar part was transformative; Toussaint's spirited piano part was mixed out.

Next on Paul's to-do list was the lead vocal for 'You Gave Me the Answer,' for which he summoned his best impression of an urbane, 1930's cabaret style, complete with the slightly camp, upper-crust pronunciation favored by film stars and singers of the era, as well as whistling, scat singing along with the bassoon solo, and taking some of the top notes in a (not quite falsetto) head voice.

As Thursday night drifted into Friday morning, Paul asked O'Duffy to thread up the master tape for 'Listen to What the Man Said.' The song was still lacking something, and a debate broke out in the control about how to fill out the empty spaces in the rhythm track.

"We thought it would be great to have a very technical musician come in and do a great lyrical solo," said Paul. "Someone said, '[Saxophonist] Tom Scott lives very near here.' We said, 'Yeah, give him a ring, see if he turns up.' And he turned up within half an hour."[9]

Paul and Linda had seen the 26-year-old saxophonist at Madison Square Garden, in December, when his jazz-fusion ensemble, the L.A. Express, supported George Harrison. Music was in Scott's blood: his father, Nathan, had been composing, arranging and conducting music for film and television since the 1940s, his credits including music for *Dragnet*, *The Twilight Zone*, *Rawhide*, *The Untouchables*, *My Three Sons*, *Wagon Train* and *Lassie*.

Scott himself was enjoying considerable popularity at the time: having already released half a dozen albums, Scott and the L.A. Express toured as Joni Mitchell's backing band in early 1974; *Miles of Aisles*, a live album from the tour, was released that November, just before the Harrison tour. Scott also played the sax solo on Carole King's 'Jazzman' that year, and he had written the theme song for *The Streets of San Francisco*.

Paul and Linda made small talk with Scott when he arrived, discussing his work with George (besides the tour, he played on George's *Dark Horse* album) and asking after his father. He was soon ushered into the studio, where he barely had time to unpack his saxophone and warm up before O'Duffy played the song and hit the record button.

"I'd never heard the song before," Scott said. "I *thought* I was just learning it as I was warming up on my soprano sax with headphones on—I had no idea they were recording me. I had my eyes closed throughout, and when the fade of the song ended, I looked up at the recording booth. Everyone was applauding! I said, 'No, guys—I have no idea what I just played, let me do another take.'"[10]

"He went out and tried a few more," Paul continued the story, "but they weren't as good. He'd had all the feel on this early take, the first take in fact. So, we'd finished the session, we just sat around and chatted for a couple of hours."[11]

"Often the best performances occur when you react spontaneously, and this was one of those times,"[12] Scott concluded.

And that was that: 'Listen to What the Man Said' was still not complete, but it now had a solo that made it a highlight among Wings' new recordings.

At the Friday afternoon session, Paul met with Ken Caillat, an engineer from Sunset Sound, the Los Angeles studio O'Duffy had booked for orchestral overdubs on Monday, March 10. Paul played the half dozen tracks earmarked for Tony Dorsey's orchestral sweetening: 'Venus and Mars (Reprise),' 'Love in Song,' 'Listen to What the Man Said,' 'Treat Her Gently/Lonely Old People,' 'Crossroads,' and 'You Gave Me the Answer.'

Caillat stayed for the rest of the session, watching Wings tinker with 'Rock Show.' McCulloch's rhythm guitar overdub had brought the track closer to the sound in Paul's imagination, but it was not quite there. Now, in his quest to give the track more bite, Paul proposed doubling the rhythm guitar and drum tracks. So O'Duffy cued up the tape, Joe and Denny donned headphones, and as they recorded their additions, McCartney and Caillat watched from the control room.

But it still didn't quite click.

"Paul didn't like the part the drummer was playing," Caillat remembered, "so he went out and played it himself. Then after that he didn't like the part that Denny Laine, the guitarist, had played, so he went out and showed Denny how it should go. Then suddenly he was playing all of the instruments!"[13]

Frustration stifled progress, and Paul decided to let the band take a break. Walking out from the control room, a cigarette dangling from his lips, McCulloch hopped behind the drum kit and began casually thudding along as 'Rock Show' played through the studio speakers.

"That's what it needs!" McCartney exclaimed. Scanning the tape box, Paul could see there were multiple tracks available for overdubs, so he asked O'Duffy to roll the tape and capture McCulloch's performance on Tracks 7 and 8.

"I really wanted the backing [track] to be burning the balls off the whole thing," said Paul. "We came to do it and we had a lot of trouble, actually, with the drumming. We ended up with Jimmy overdubbing a track and he had much more of a dirty feel—he was out of his skull at the time—but he helped to give it a dirty feel."[14]

While McCulloch was making his recording debut as a drummer, Paul sat in the control room, his bass plugged into the console, and played along. By the end of the session, 'Rock Show' was complete.

Though Blair Sabol was unimpressed with the cover art mock-ups Linda showed her at Wally Heider, Paul and Linda were still committed to the idea of capturing yellow and red billiard balls against a dark background, as if they were Venus and Mars snapped through a powerful telescope. The Hipgnosis partners, Powell and Thorgerson, arrived in Los Angeles on March 9 to discuss the details.

Powell and Thorgerson had impressed Paul with their simple, eye-catching cover for *Band on the Run*, but that album's jailbreak concept, expertly photographed by Clive Arrowsmith, was Paul and Linda's idea, not their own. Although they had agreed to shoot the cover Paul and Linda had planned, Powell told them at the time that Hipgnosis' usual *modus operandi*—indeed, the point of the firm—was to conceive and execute their own cover designs.

Thorgerson and Powell were due to meet Paul and Linda at Wally Heider Recording on Monday morning, but before they left for the studio, they had a quiet word with Brian Brolly, who was staying at the Beverly Wilshire Hotel with the band.

"I said to Brian Brolly," Powell recalled, "'We'd like to come up with our own ideas.' And he said, 'No. Paul doesn't want that.' And he said, 'He wants you and Storm to go and see him and he has very specific views. It's called *Venus and Mars* and he's got the idea that he wants.'"[15]

Recording Session

Monday, March 10, 1975.

Wally Heider Recording, Studio 3, 1604 N Cahuenga Blvd., Los Angeles.

Overdubbing: 'Call Me Back Again.'

Hoping to persuade Paul to cut them some artistic slack, Storm and Po cabbed up Santa Monica Boulevard to Wally Heider's studio, where they found Paul, Denny and Alan O'Duffy, all slightly hungover after an evening spent partying with Elton John, in a vocal isolation booth adding backing harmonies to 'Call Me Back Again.' Once Paul was satisfied, Laine and O'Duffy left the studio, and Po and Storm made their case for a greater role in designing the album sleeve.

The meeting did not last long.

"Paul said, 'This is what I want to do,'" Powell recalled, "and Storm, I remember, turned around to him and said, 'Well, it doesn't need both of us to do this. Po can do this with you.' And Paul was slightly taken aback by that, I think, because Storm had very much been the leading guy with *Band on the Run*. He didn't take offense to it, but I think it's just one of those things where you don't say no."

Po took Storm aside to try to persuade him to stay involved in the project, but Thorgerson had no interest in it. "I don't want to do that idea," he told Powell. "I just don't. It doesn't work for me. I don't like it. I'm happy for you to do it with the [Hipgnosis] studio, but there's no point in both of us doing it."

Excusing himself from the meeting, Thorgerson pushed the control room door open onto the main street; 24 hours later he was back in London.

"After that he was not welcome in the Paul McCartney camp," said Powell. "'I'll work with you, man, but I don't want to work with him.' That was it."[16]

Powell agreed to remain in Los Angeles and make plans for the pool ball cover shoot. Paul had one more request. For the inner gatefold, he wanted a panoramic shot of the group—something that would make the band look like they were in an alien landscape, perhaps on a different planet—a vista, Paul told Po, something like the erosional mountain landscape in Michelangelo Antonioni's 1970 film *Zabriskie Point*, which had been shot in Death Valley. Powell hired a local fixer, Jeff Smith, to help him scout possible locations.

The McCartneys had two more items on their busy Monday agenda. One was the orchestral session at Sunset Sound, set to begin at 8 P.M. But before that, Linda was scheduled to answer charges of cannabis possession at a pretrial hearing at the West Los Angeles Municipal Court. Under California law, those charged with possession could avoid criminal prosecution by taking a voluntary rehabilitation course, an option taken by 3,000 pot smokers each month.

Linda, however, hoped to have her charges overturned. Loathe to allow a court date to interfere with her recording plans, she did not appear in court herself. Instead, she was represented by Richard Hirsch, a Beverly Hills attorney who argued that Linda's misdemeanor charge should be dropped because the evidence—the marijuana in Linda's handbag—had been illegally obtained.

"I expect the charges against my client to be dismissed,"[17] Hirsch told Municipal Judge Brian D. Crahan, who set a trial date of April 7.

Recording Session

Monday, March 10, 1975.

Sunset Sound Recorders, Studio 1, 6650 Sunset Blvd., Hollywood.

Orchestral overdubbing: 'Venus and Mars (Reprise),' 'Love in Song,' 'Listen to What the Man Said,' 'Treat Her Gently/Lonely Old People,' 'Crossroads' and 'You Gave Me the Answer.'

Six songs (seven if you counted the conjoined 'Treat Her Gently/Lonely Old People' as two) were dispatched on March 10 in just three hours by a handpicked company of Hollywood string players. The size of the ensemble is frequently said to have been between 30 and 60 players, but in fact only 21 (plus two copyists and Dorsey, as arranger and conductor) are listed in the American Federation of Musicians' contracts.* Studio 1 at Sunset, measuring 20-by-40 feet, could accommodate only 30 musicians.

The ensemble included 14 violinists (William Kurasch, Assa [Irene] Drori, Henry Ferber, Jay Rosen, Israel Baker, Sidney Sharp, Stanley [Ellison] Plummer, James Getzoff, Tibor Zelig, Arnold Belnick, Ronald Folsom, Murray Adler, Allan Marshman, and Yukiko Kamei), two cellists (Jesse Ehrlich and Raymond Kelley), two violists (Harry Hyams and Samuel Boghossian), a bassist (Peter Mercurio) and a harpist (Gayle Levant). The copyists who transformed Dorsey's scores into separate parts were Robert Ross and Ann Bartold. Ken Caillat supervised the recording.

"When I was asked to record the strings for *Venus and Mars*, I decided to get the best string sounds Paul McCartney had ever heard," said Caillat. "Before Paul arrived, I played back the instruments, and the session leader told me they sounded like he was hearing them from his seat as first chair."[18]

McCartney's music was in safe hands. Sidney Sharp, whose own orchestra cut records like 'Mashed Potatoes' in the early 1960s, was one of the first classically trained musicians to play on rock 'n' roll records, and together with Ehrlich, Kurasch, Getzoff, Zelig and Hyams, was part of the orchestral wall-of-sound that Brian Wilson used on the Beach Boys' 1966 album, *Pet Sounds*. Otherwise, these musicians had worked on everything from live albums by Nat King Cole and Frank Sinatra to recordings of Igor Stravinsky conducting his own music.

"Their day-to-day job was the film soundtracks," O'Duffy explained, "and we had the joy of having those fellows in front of us. And Paul stands up on the rostrum, he goes, 'Marvelous to be here, guys. We love your work.' Paul would maybe explain that 'this is a song about growing old, lonely

---

* The AFM bill of roughly $2,498.81 (£1,040), plus a percentage to cover health and welfare benefits, was settled on July 23, 1975. Delayed payment of the bill resulted in a late payment fee of 20 percent.

old people,' and he'd be funny about it. And these fellows were just bemused. But nonetheless, these guys had a heart and I think you can hear that in the passion—a spiritual passion—which they brought. It wasn't just another session. It was something special."[19]

As an arranger, Dorsey prized simplicity, and he had been guided, in any case, by Paul playing the songs to him on the piano and telling him what he envisioned, a remit from which Dorsey was reluctant to stray. For the most part, his arrangements either follow existing melodic elements—the strings in 'Love in Song,' for example, echo the Moog parts—or trace the underlying chord progressions.

"Every song, to me, has a certain flavor," Dorsey said of his arrangements, "and certain things that you can do musically that will fit into what the song is about. And so that's what I do, I basically do everything I can to put myself into the mood of whatever that song is, and to make it better—as opposed to trying to show how much I know, you know, how brilliant I am."

Still, he found conducting an ensemble of top-flight Hollywood string players intimidating.

"I said, 'Man, I'm in deep water here,'" Dorsey confessed. "It was nerve-wracking for me because I've got to [conduct these arrangements], and I've got all these big-time people here. So I was really sweating. But these guys were totally professional. The musicians had the charts, and they just played through them. And if there was anything that wasn't quite right, the concertmaster just straightened it out."[20]

Recording Sessions

Tuesday, March 11–Saturday, March 5, 1975.

Wally Heider Recording, Studio 3, 1604 N Cahuenga Blvd., Los Angeles.

Overdubbing: 'Treat Her Gently/Lonely Old People' and 'Venus and Mars (Reprise).'

Mixing: 'Listen to What the Man Said.'

McCartney and O'Duffy spent Tuesday afternoon reviewing Monday's orchestral work, during which Paul made a list of overdubs necessary to finish each track. 'Treat Her Gently/Lonely Old People' needed harmony vocals, and the next day—the McCartneys' sixth wedding anniversary—Paul and Linda huddled together in the vocal isolation booth to add them. As the happy couple donned their cans, Wally Heider's general manager, Terry Stark, rolled out a trolley filled with champagne and Mexican food to mark the occasion.

As Paul originally envisioned it, 'Treat Her Gently/Lonely Old People' was to have only a simple, two-part harmony, just Paul and Linda. But O'Duffy came up with another approach that meant inviting Denny to gatecrash the McCartneys' anniversary duet.

"During one of the playbacks," O'Duffy recalled, "Paul's on my right hand side, I'm doing a sort of working mix, and Paul starts to sing harmony with himself on '*here we sit, two lonely old people.*' Now I've been able to sing harmony since I was a kid, and I [started to] sing harmony with Paul. So we're listening to the lead vocal, Paul is singing harmony, and I'm adding the next part. And so he said, 'Can you teach your part to Denny?' So I taught my part to Denny."[21]

Finally content with the song's vocal blend, Paul returned to the track on Friday to add two celeste parts, although in the final mix he kept only one. Hearing the track with its orchestral backing also led him to reconsider the original piano part, so the Sea-Saint take was replaced with a fresh one. Paul then asked Jimmy to add guitar embellishments between the lines of vocal harmony toward the end of the track.

By the weekend, Alan O'Duffy was beginning to feel like a chef surrounded by a vast variety of ingredients with the task of turning them into a 13-course banquet. With the exception of 'Spirits of Ancient Egypt,' which still lacked Denny's finished vocal, the album was ready to mix. In the hope of coming to grips with it—and perhaps to score points to make up for having played the unfinished album to a New Orleans journalist—O'Duffy went into the studio to review each of the master tracks before mixing began.

He started with 'Listen to What the Man Said,' now virtually reborn thanks to Tom Scott's sparkling first-take saxophone solo and Dorsey's strings.

"Up to then we'd never actually mixed it," O'Duffy explained. "I had a few ideas of how I wanted to mix it. And there was a fashion at the time for: *How can we make a record that's the same volume as every other record, but sounds twice as loud?* Can you make a record that bounces whatever volume you play it at? Because I had done the Slade records, which the concept was volume, I had figured that one out.

"So I mixed 'Listen to What the Man Said' on the Saturday and had fun with it. Inspired by Brian Wilson and [producer] Andrew Oldham, who did the Stones stuff, I swelled the vocals."[22]

Pleased with his punchy mix, O'Duffy ran off a cassette dub, jumped in his convertible Volkswagen Beetle and drove up to Coldwater Canyon to deliver a copy—labeled as "Alan O'Duffy Saturday Mix"—to Paul and Linda. Paul popped the cassette into his portable deck and hit the play button, and he, Linda and O'Duffy listened to the track as they sat around the pool sipping lemonade.

Paul was knocked out, and any doubt that 'Listen to What the Man Said' would be Wings' next single vanished long before the final orchestral chord faded away.

Recording Sessions

Monday, March 17–Wednesday, March 19, 1975.

Wally Heider Recording, Studio 3, 1604 N Cahuenga Blvd., Los Angeles.

Overdubbing: 'Spirits of Ancient Egypt.'

Rough Mixing: All album cuts.

Mixing: 'Rock Show,' 'Love in Song,' 'You Gave Me the Answer,' 'Magneto and Titanium Man' and 'Letting Go.'

Joe English had been a provisional member of Wings until now, more a studio drummer and placeholder than part of the band. But Paul and Linda liked him, he got along well with Jimmy and Denny, and he clearly had both the chops and the necessary confidence for the job. So as they drove to Wally Heider's on March 17, Paul popped the question.

"Paul turned to me in the car and asked if I'd like to join," said English. "I said yes, and that was it."[23]

"Everything just clicked," said English. "Here I am with *Paul McCartney*. But it was never like putting him up on this big golden pedestal and I'm this low-life down here, it was never like that. It was an honor to work with him."[24]

When they arrived, O'Duffy was set up to record Denny's lead vocal on 'Spirits of Ancient Egypt,' the album's only missing element. He now had most of the song under control, and even brought some of the nuance to the opening lines that Paul demonstrated for him in New Orleans. But he was no closer to being able to hit the high G in the refrain. Paul was committed to Denny having a showcase on the album, though, so he found a way around Denny's vocal shortcomings: sharing a mic with Laine, Paul joined him in the chorus, taking the spotlight as Denny dropped back.

With 'Spirits of Ancient Egypt' now complete, Paul and O'Duffy set about making rough mixes of the album's 13 tracks—a process that stretched into Tuesday's session. At 4 P.M., Jeff Smith, Aubrey Powell's fixer, collected Linda at Wally Heider's and drove across town to a studio on West 3rd Street and Crescent Heights Boulevard that he had booked to shoot the album cover.

"I got the whole thing together—the pool table and the balls—and I wanted to shoot it on a five-by-four camera," said Powell, "which Linda was not familiar with because she normally shot on a 35mm Nikon, or something like that. I said, 'No, no, we have to have better quality than that.' I lit it all for her, she came in, she fired off some shots and that was it."[25]

Smith and Powell then went off to scout locations for the extraterrestrial inner gatefold. After about ten hours of visiting unusual sites in the Mojave Desert, Powell found the perfect place—an old talcum powder lake in the foothills of the Sierras, a four-hour drive northeast of Los Angeles, near Lone Pine, also known as the Alabama Hills.

But Paul had another idea: someone had told him about a place in Palm Springs that sounded perfect, and he instructed Powell to meet him there the next morning (March 19) at 6 A.M. Powell and Smith drove all night from Lone Pine to Palm Springs to meet with Paul at the appointed hour, only to learn that the shoot was canceled.

"We met at a Holiday Inn, I remember," said Powell, "and they were in this motor home. And as I got there, I opened the door to the motor home, and it was completely trashed inside. I thought, 'What the hell? There's been some murder!' Honestly, it was trashed that much. And then Paul and Linda came around the corner and he said, 'Listen, the guys are in the coffee shop. I want you to drive me straight back to L.A.'

"We'd already been up all night driving across there, plus the day before. I was like, 'Okay . . .' What had happened is Jimmy McCulloch had got completely out of it on the trip, and Jimmy could be highly volatile and temperamental, and he started to smash the Winnebago. And so, the moment was destroyed. I was relieved because I knew Palm Springs was not the right location."

On the way back to Los Angeles, Linda lit up a spliff, and Paul launched into what Smith described as "a monologue" about the demise of the Beatles, full of inside details, that lasted the entire drive. At 7 A.M., just as they entered Cathedral City, they were pulled over by a highway patrolman for the second time in as many weeks—this time because Smith had been clocked at 85 mph in a 55 mph zone.

Knowing that Linda was carrying a sizable bag of grass and was already facing possession charges, Smith jumped out of the car and walked toward the officer as he approached the smoke-filled car. Powell left the car a moment later and watched as Smith was handed his speeding ticket. The patrolman then glanced over at two passengers still in the car.

"There was blue smoke everywhere in the car," said Powell. "And [the policeman] said to me, '*Is that John Lennon?*' I said, 'No, it's Paul McCartney.' He said, 'Holy shit! Can you get me his autograph?' So I went to Paul, I said, 'Listen, the cop thinks you're John Lennon, but can you give an autograph? It's going to get us out of the shit.' He says, 'Anything, man.' He signed his autograph; I gave it to the cop and the cop waved us on. It was hysterical. Sometimes the word 'Beatle' works in your favor tremendously."[26]

Paul and Linda were rattled by the encounter, Smith said, but once they were back on the road, Linda lit up another joint. By early afternoon, Paul was back in the studio with Alan O'Duffy to begin formal mixing. Six stereo reels were filled with mixes of 'Rock Show,' 'Love in Song,' 'You Gave Me the Answer,' 'Magneto and Titanium Man' and 'Letting Go.' Only the mixes of 'Magneto and Titanium Man' and 'Letting Go' were marked as masters; the rest were rejected.

After Wednesday's mixing session, Paul and Linda attended the American premiere of Ken

Russell's film of the Who's rock opera *Tommy* at the Fox-Wilshire Theatre in Beverly Hills. The celebrity-filled evening was filmed by ABC-TV for a *Tommy* special, hosted by David Frost, who interviewed Paul and Linda as they left the theater.

After the screening, the McCartneys attended a reception at Studio One, a club managed and co-owned by the British actor and screenwriter Scott Forbes, who had it decked out for the occasion with pinball machines and transvestite dancers. Here, Linda fielded a question she had answered many times before, thanks to six years of lazy reporting in the press.

"Hey, are you Linda Eastman, of the Eastman Kodaks?" the man asked.

"No, no," Linda answered, explaining that her family had no connection to those Eastmans.

"I'm glad you said that," her interlocutor responded, "because I am!"*

And he said, "I've hated you for years because I thought you were going around saying you were Kodak, and I knew you weren't!"

Linda added, "And I just said, 'Hey, I'm glad, you know, don't hate me because of what [the press] say.'"[27]

Recording Sessions

Thursday, March 20–Saturday, March 22, 1975.
Wally Heider Recording, Studio 3, 1604 N Cahuenga Blvd., Los Angeles.
Mixing: 'Venus and Mars,' 'You Gave Me the Answer' and 'Medicine Jar.'

Light duties were the order of the day after a boozy night at Studio One, so Paul and Alan spent Thursday afternoon mixing the simple and short 'Venus and Mars,' a track rich in acoustic timbres. O'Duffy and McCartney spread the guitars across the stereo image, while Paul's lead vocals and Denny's Moog part were placed front and center. As the track reaches its conclusion, the instrumentation—including descending piano notes, bass, and electric guitar—build to a climax, orchestrated to crossfade with the opening chords of 'Rock Show.'

With 'You Gave Me the Answer,' mixed on March 21, the challenge was to evoke the spirit of *Funny Face*, the Fred Astaire and Audrey Hepburn film that inspired the song, without surrendering the benefits of modern sound techniques. They started with the piano introduction, using the fact that the keyboard had been recorded using three microphones, spread across three tracks

* The founder of the Eastman Kodak company, American entrepreneur George Eastman, took his own life in March 1932, leaving no heir. A philanthropist, he left his fortune to the University of Rochester. With no direct heir to his estate, Paul and Linda likely had an encounter with a grandchild of Eastman's only surviving sibling, Ellen Maria.

of the master (labeled 'left piano,' 'right piano,' and 'middle piano') to create an echo effect that suggested a pianist playing in a large, empty hall. The echo evaporated as Paul's piano intro kicked into the faster tempo that leads into the song.

From there, it was a matter of finding the right balance between the winds, strings, and basic track—plus making Paul's voice sound like that of a vaudeville crooner, something O'Duffy accomplished using a Pultec equalizer that thinned out the high and low frequencies.

"That was designed [to sound like it was] recorded through a vaudeville microphone," O'Duffy explained. "You're making a great singer's voice sound thinner and squeakier—removing the warmth of the man's humanity. You're screwing it up, essentially. But it's screwed up to give you an effect reminiscent of vaudeville."[28]

Denny, Jimmy and Joe were now backseat passengers, watching and listening as McCartney and O'Duffy mixed, but not taking a hand in it. The trio left the session early to drop in on a Mick Jagger session at the Record Plant, at 8456 W. Third Street; Rod Stewart and Ron Wood were also present.

Saturday was spent mixing Jimmy's 'Medicine Jar.' On playback, Paul decided the song could use a vocal injection, so new harmony vocals were overdubbed before the track was mixed. In the spirit of the *McGear* sessions, Paul decided that both the lead guitar and lead vocals should be treated with what he called "some of that 10cc tape echo."

Now in Los Angeles for a month, Paul and Linda were getting used to unwinding between sessions by partaking in a pastime enjoyed by Angelinos with similar connections and economic status—hobnobbing at parties packed with other A-listers. On Saturday evening, March 22, they rubbed shoulders with David Bowie, Barbra Streisand, Tatum O'Neal and Julie Christie at a bash that Stephen O'Rourke, Pink Floyd's manager, threw for the actress Charlotte Rampling in honor of her appearance in *Farewell My Lovely.* Besides appearing in the 1960's youth-culture classic *Georgy Girl* (1966), Rampling had made an uncredited appearance in the Beatles' first film, *A Hard Day's Night.*

The next morning they drove up to Lone Pine, having agreed to Aubrey Powell's choice of location for the gatefold photo. Powell and the band had driven up on Saturday and were staying at the Dow Villa Motel, and upon the McCartneys' arrival, Powell shot the band at three locations—near the big rocks by Movie Road, at a dusty shack off Highway 395, and in the white sands of Lake Owens. Paul and Linda wore striped serapes; Denny painted his face white at one of the locations. The red and yellow pool balls that would adorn the front cover were included in each of the band photos.

Between locations, Paul had their driver pick up a frying pan, a griddle, a spatula and groceries, and they cooked lunch over a campfire. After the shoot, the band slid into a red leather booth at Margie's Merry Go-Round for dinner and stayed the night at the Dow Villa Motel.

"It was one of the most memorable days of my life, actually," said Powell. "Having a barbecue with Paul McCartney in the middle of this desert and just drinking a few beers and just chewing the fat and just being very relaxed. And everybody was in the vibe. Everybody was in the mood. . . . And that really cemented my relationship with Paul and Linda."[29]

Recording Session

Monday, March 24, 1975.

Wally Heider Recording, Studio 3, 1604 N Cahuenga Blvd., Los Angeles.

Mixing: 'Venus and Mars (Reprise).'

On Monday, it was back to mixing. O'Duffy and McCartney devoted the afternoon to 'Venus and Mars (Reprise),' a notably more complex track than 'Venus and Mars,' with a running time nearly twice as long. They began by spreading the acoustic guitar texture across the stereo image, much as they had done on the album opener, but this time Paul's vocal was swathed in reverb, and the cymbal swells, synthesizer effects (ranging from tactile growls to strings of gurgles and bleeps produced by the Minimoog's sequencer), and backing vocals required balancing, all within a spacey, reverberant haze that evoked the cathedral mentioned in the lyrics.

That accomplished, Paul and Linda left the studio to don their glad rags and head off for another night of hobnobbing, this time as the hosts of a *Venus and Mars* wrap party aboard the *Queen Mary*—the famous British ocean liner that was now permanently docked in Long Beach Harbor—to which they had invited about 200 guests from the music and film worlds.

"We were going to have a launch party and I was looking around for something interesting, something exciting for us to do," said Paul. "And I heard that the *Queen Mary* was now in Long Beach, which is just outside L.A. And it was now some kind of a hotel thing and was available for functions. You could hire it; you could hire the big ballroom. So we think, 'Oh, well that's perfect! We should do that, and we should have a guestlist with all the L.A. celebs and people like this.' Which meant it was a pretty cool guestlist!"[30]

The party began at 8 P.M., when arriving guests were piped aboard by members of the United States Naval Sea Cadet Corps, and guided to the ship's Grand Salon, an enormous ballroom in which seven buffets decorated with ice sculptures and stacked with food chosen by Linda—and in

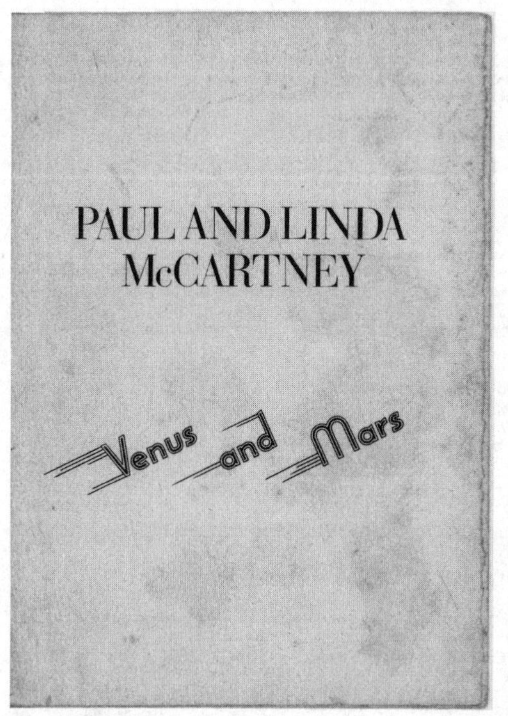

PAUL AND LINDA
McCARTNEY

Venus and Mars

Paul and Linda
cordially invite you and a guest
to join them and Wings
for a
Private Party
"on board The Queen Mary"
prior to their departure from America
and return to England

24th March 1975
8:00 PM to 1:00 AM
The Grand Salon
The Queen Mary at Long Beach

R.S.V.P. mandatory (non-transferable)
278-5692
Upon acceptance, parking and
deck passes will be forwarded to you

Invitation to the party on the *Queen Mary*, Long Beach

Paul and Linda hold court on the *Queen Mary*, March 24, 1975

some cases (the pea soup, for example) made from her own recipes—were set up along the walls, with bars interspersed. Mostly, the menu was built of gumbo pie, hurricane punch (drunk from authentic hurricane glasses) and other Southern specialties, in honor of Wings' recent sojourn in New Orleans.

The music was from New Orleans, too: Paul flew 57 musicians from the Big Easy to the party. Professor Longhair played the opening set, and the Meters performed later in the evening. Other New Orleans musicians at the party included Ernie K-Doe, Lee Dorsey, and Chocolate Milk.

"I still remember the great thing the Meters used to do," Paul later recalled, "was that they used to start their act in their dressing room. So they would start off . . . [Paul starts tapping a glass, air drumming and singing]. Somebody would have a drum. Somebody would have a tambourine. Somebody would have little claves. And they would just come into the hall from the dressing room playing. They just come walking in . . . [carries on singing]. Then they get up on the stage . . . [sings . . .]. Then they get their instruments on seamlessly . . . and suddenly it would be their opening number. It was such a great idea!"[31]

Meters guitarist Leo Nocentelli remembered being starstruck as he watched the audience during his band's set.

"The stars all came out," Nocentelli recalled. "I don't know if you can imagine, you're playing on the stage and you look out and you see Tony Curtis standing at the side of the bandstand, clapping, and people like that dancing to your music. The Jackson Five at the edge of the bandstand, watching us play. The guest list was phenomenal. It was an unbelievable experience."[32]

Between acts, Ev Segress and his Orchestra kept the crowd entertained. Some of the guests offered impromptu performances as well, including the 73-year-old Rudy Vallée, who sang 'Kansas City Kitty' and 'If You Were the Only Girl in the World.' Paul hired Wally Heider's mobile truck to record all the live music for his personal archive.

Candlelit tables with floral decorations were set up throughout the ballroom, with napkins and matchbooks bearing the message "Venus and Mars are alright tonight." And though no one had yet seen the album cover, the red and yellow of the billiard ball planets were central design elements at the party, which included yellow awnings and red carpeting.

The guest list of about 200 was a gossip columnist's dream, although Linda made a point of telling her pal Blair Sabol—still unaware that Sabol was preparing a slice-and-dice portrait—that there would be neither reporters nor gossip columnists present.

Among the guests were Bob and Sara Dylan, José Feliciano, Marvin Gaye, Mick Jagger, Dave Mason, Micky Dolenz, Davy Jones, Carole King, David Blue, Cher, David Cassidy, Phil Everly, Jim Messina, Joni Mitchell, Harry Nilsson, Helen Reddy, Linda Ronstadt, John Mayall, Nigel Olsson, Paul Williams, Jim Webb, Richard Perry, Klaus Voormann, and members of several bands, including the Hudson Brothers, the Faces, America, the Jackson Five, Chicago and Led Zeppelin. Tatum

O'Neal and her father Ryan, Dean Martin, Tony Curtis and Rudy Vallée represented the Hollywood elite.

George Harrison and his new girlfriend, Olivia Trinidad Arias, were there too, as were former Apple publicist Derek Taylor and onetime Beatles roadie Mal Evans. The only photographer invited to the party was Harry Benson, who had photographed the Beatles on several occasions, including during their 1964 stay in Paris, where he took an iconic photo of them in a staged pillow fight, just weeks before their first trip to America.

Elvis Presley, John Lennon and Ringo Starr had been invited but did not turn up. John and Yoko were otherwise engaged in New York, and Ringo, having just wrapped up an acting job in Ken Russell's eccentric *Lisztomania* (Ringo played the pope), was in London launching his new label, Ring O'Records, with *Startling Music*, an instrumental version of the 1973 album *Ringo* by former engineer David Hentschel.

The party, which reportedly cost Paul about $97,000 (£40,000), had its share of memorable moments. When an inebriated Peter Grant introduced himself to Dylan as Led Zeppelin's manager, Dylan was said to have responded, "I don't bother you with my problems." It was reported that Dylan later led a conga line.

Blair Sabol, in her fashion columnist guise, noted that Dylan wore "his trademark dirty denim jacket, baggy jeans and work shoes," and described "the usual array of Capitol Records salesmen who walked about in suits made of Ford Fairlane interiors." Nor was she much impressed by "George Harrison with his new artichoke haircut (now you really notice his lousy teeth) and wrinkled leisure suit."

Sabol stayed long enough to see Paul and Linda leave at about 2 A.M., Linda carrying a red and yellow carnation centerpiece from one of the tables. Sabol quipped waspishly: "You can take the girl out of the bar mitzvah, but you can't take the bar mitzvah out of the girl."[33]

Recording Sessions

Tuesday, March 25–Friday, March 28, 1975.
Wally Heider Recording, Studio 3, 1604 N Cahuenga Blvd., Los Angeles.
Mixing: 'Spirits of Ancient Egypt,' 'Call Me Back Again,' 'Rock Show,' 'Love in Song,' 'Listen to What the Man Said,' 'Treat Her Gently/Lonely Old People' and 'Crossroads.'
Compiling: *Venus and Mars* album masters.

A party as lavish as the one Paul and Linda threw on the *Queen Mary* had to have been planned weeks in advance, so it is striking how closely they predicted when the album would be finished. But there were still a few tracks to be mixed, and the masters had to be compiled before they were truly finished. On Tuesday, McCartney and O'Duffy mixed 'Spirits of Ancient Egypt,' before José Feliciano dropped in. Paul played Feliciano the mixes so far, and the band and the Puerto Rican guitarist ended the day with a friendly jam.

On Wednesday, 'Call Me Back Again' was given its final mix, and stereo mixes of 'Rock Show,' 'Love in Song,' 'Treat Her Gently/Lonely Old People' and 'Crossroads' were made on Thursday. O'Duffy also revisited 'Listen to What the Man Said,' in the hope of improving his earlier effort.

"Paul and I started to fiddle around with it, thinking about how this should sound," O'Duffy recalled. "Linda said, 'Can you find the "Alan O'Duffy Saturday Mix" thing you'd played us on the cassette?' So we put it on, played it, and Linda and Paul said, 'That's great. Next!' So that was the end of that."[34]

The album masters were compiled on Friday—not without challenges, thanks to the cross-fades between the two versions of 'Venus and Mars' and the tracks that follow them.

"For the segues," O'Duffy explained, "you needed to line up two machines, where you would play back one track, then press the button [on the second machine] so that the next track comes in on time. But when you press a button on a tape machine, it's not instantly up to speed. So you'd have to pre-judge the amount of time it takes to get the thing to come up to speed and be at the right time. So that was a conundrum."[35]

The album sequencing, which would normally require considerable thought, had been determined long before recording began in New Orleans. The compiled masters closely followed the scroll McCartney had assembled in Jamaica four months earlier:

SIDE ONE (EMI MATRIX NO. YEX.945)

'Venus and Mars'
'Rock Show'
'Love in Song'
'You Gave Me the Answer'
'Magneto and Titanium Man'
'Letting Go'

SIDE TWO (EMI MATRIX NO. YEX.946)

'Venus and Mars—Reprise'
'Spirits of Ancient Egypt'
'Medicine Jar'
'Call Me Back Again'
'Listen to What the Man Said'
'Treat Her Gently—Lonely Old People'
'Crossroads'

The McCartneys remained in Los Angeles until the end of the month, seeing to a few remaining obligations, including a photo shoot Paul had promised Harry Benson that he and Linda would sit for before they left town.

"I had a very good relationship with Linda," Benson later wrote. "She was helpful and would come up with suggestions about how to make the sessions more lively and natural. As a photographer, she knew what it took to make a good picture. Often the person closest to the subject can be a big pain for me and say things like, 'I hope this doesn't go on for much longer.' Linda was the opposite. Paul would say, 'Come tomorrow, 10 A.M. will be fine.' Linda would say, 'No, Harry, come at 8 and have breakfast.'"[36]

Benson photographed the whole family at their Coldwater Canyon rental. For most of the shots, Paul wore a green sweater commemorating 'Hi, Hi, Hi,' with a pattern containing the word "Hi" and a picture of an airplane repeated across it and down the sleeves. If 'Got to Get You Into My Life' was his musical way of preaching the virtues of herbal jazz cigarettes, the jumper he donned for Benson's photoshoot delivered a similar tongue-in-cheek message.

At the *Queen Mary* bash, Kenney Jones, the Faces' drummer, invited Paul, Linda and Denny to a recording session, at which he recorded two songs—'So High' and 'Baby Blue Eyes'—by Mentor Williams, the songwriter whose 'Drift Away' had been a hit for Dobie Gray in 1973. Though Jones had released a single, 'Ready or Not,' in 1974, he did not think of himself as a singer, particularly. But Williams persuaded him to give the songs a shot and booked a studio, as well as the guitarist Danny "Kootch" Kortchmar and the multi-instrumentalist Al Kooper.

"In the studio," Jones wrote in his memoir, "Paul enquired, while pointedly sitting at the piano, 'Kenney, what do you want me to play?' 'Bass.' His face dropped. We recorded 'So High' first. It's a slow song with a good, but strange feel. Mentor talked us through it and off we went, Paul on bass, Linda on keyboards, Denny and Kootch on guitar, and Al on everything else. I then added [the vocal], with Mentor assisting with the phrasing, while the others enthusiastically got stuck into the two-word backing vocals. 'So high!!!' In no time, we had the track nailed, quickly followed by Mentor's 'Baby Blue Eyes.'"[37]

Neither track was released, and Jones regarded the session as the end of his solo career.

Linda still had a court date on April 7, but she was uninterested; that's what lawyers were for. On April 2, the McCartneys landed at Heathrow Airport, where Paul was quizzed by journalists about Linda's drug bust and the new album, which he confirmed would be called *Venus and Mars* and would be released "in a couple of months."

9

CHASING WATERFALL

Much as Paul relished the glow of the Hollywood spotlight, the call of the countryside was equally strong. "We're desperate to split for Scotland," Linda told Blair Sabol in March, but with two children of school age, the practicalities of bolting to their Scottish refuge were less simple. During their US travels, a tutor kept the girls on track academically, but now that they were back in England, Linda wanted a return to normality, and for Heather and Mary that meant returning to school in London. Thanks to Paul's most recent property purchase, though, the best of both worlds was now within touching distance, just 75 miles south, in East Sussex.

Waterfall, the McCartneys' bijou rural cottage, three miles northwest of the historic harbor town of Rye, had been empty since Paul bought it in June 1974. The McCartneys acquired the eighteenth-century former industrial building surrounded by 100 acres of fields and ancient woodlands as a weekend retreat, as well as a spot to stable their horses and ponies during the winter months. But as the couple sought seclusion after ten weeks on the road, at the start of April, Waterfall became their somewhat unconventional family home.

When Paul and Linda first commissioned London estate agent Barry Mishon to find them a home in the south of England, in October 1969, their goal was radically different. Mishon was tasked with finding a large home set in 50 to 500 acres of land, in Sussex or Kent—a mansion that would be the McCartneys' equivalent of Harrison's Friar Park in Henley-on-Thames, or Lennon's Tittenhurst Park in Ascot. Mansions in rural England seldom come up for sale, though, and finding a property that matched Paul and Linda's wish list proved tricky.

When Waterfall cottage came up for sale in 1974, Paul shelved his plan to acquire a storied country house. The location was perfect, and the accommodation could be adapted at a later date to suit their needs.

But taking up residence at Waterfall was not as straightforward as just dropping anchor in Rye.

Travel arrangements would have to be made for Heather and Mary, whose private school was two hours away in central London. Promoting Wings' new album and working in some rehearsal time also had to be factored in to the McCartneys' plans. And then there was the question of what to do with Joe, their American drummer who would soon be moving to London.

Waterfall presented practical challenges for a family of five. The cottage only had two bedrooms, meaning the girls had to bunk together, and when the building was converted from a single-story industrial unit into a two-story dwelling, the upstairs walls were left open in places, allowing sound to travel around the building. This made privacy a problem for both the family and visiting guests.

But Paul and Linda were determined to get away from the city.

"I'm up at six in the morning at the moment to get the kids off to school," Linda told journalist Rosemary Horide of the family's new domestic routine, which began every day with the sound of a yodeling alarm clock. "You see, we've got this house down in Sussex with lots of trees and land and millions of birds around, and that's where we're staying while we rehearse. The kids moan about having to go to school—probably because they love traveling."[1]

With five O-Levels and an A-Level in English Literature, Paul was academically bright, but since the births of his children, he had developed a hippieish attitude toward education that was, at times, both inconsistent and contradictory.

"Heather goes to school, and so does Mary. Stella is still too young," Paul explained in late 1974. "I don't even like Mary going to school, I think she's too young. She likes going there and meeting the other kids, but she doesn't like everything about it all the time. Sometimes we keep her home, because I don't think five is all that brilliant an age to go to school. They are still very tiny at five, and school gets them growing up too quickly. I'm not fussy about education—Linda's not very well educated. She's educated, but I know a lot of people who aren't and they're still really great people. So I don't place very heavy emphasis on it; I know some people who are very well educated and are absolute bums. In a family I think you teach each other a lot simply by living together.

"I never enjoyed a lot of my lessons at school—looking back on it, I suppose it was okay, on the whole I quite enjoyed it. You get crazy teachers who think all there is in life is to pump information down you. I had a geography teacher like that, and I'm sure you've all had one. It was an all-boys school, and this bloke would come into class and say, 'Right, lads,' then he'd just read to you from a book, and we'd have to copy it down like secretaries. At best, it was just writing practice, because I never took any of it in. The only thing I ever learnt was maybe a bit of spelling. It was obvious the teacher hated his job, and he'd rather just thump you."[2]

But deep down, Paul recognized that fertile minds need a playground to escape to, and his dismissive comments seemed intended to deflect from his own insecurities at balancing life as a pop star and the responsibilities of fatherhood.

Throughout the spring, Linda ferried the girls to school in London, while Paul began making plans for the release of *Venus and Mars* and a world tour that would likely begin in late summer.

With EMI's help, he soon found a space in Rye where Wings could rehearse. Regent Cinema, a 700-seat theater at 42 Cinque Ports Street had been purchased by EMI in 1967, but closed its doors six years later, when the property was sold to Lawdon Ltd., a local property developer that planned to demolish the cinema and build houses. But Lawdon's plans were rejected by town planners, and the building had been empty for nearly two years.

Wings began rehearsals at the derelict cinema on April 28, and local press interest soon followed. Residents were told that the cinema had been booked by a band on the (fictional) MPL record label, but passersby soon realized it was Paul himself when they heard his unmistakable voice booming out through the cinema's walls. Band workouts noted by passing fans included 'Band on the Run,' 'Maybe I'm Amazed,' 'Live and Let Die,' 'Hey Jude' and 'Rock Show.'

During rehearsals Joe stayed at Cavendish Avenue with Paul's housekeeper, Rose Martin, and Linda shuttled the drummer to and from rehearsals as part of her daily school run. Joe had no connections in London and leaned heavily on the McCartneys during his bedding-in period.

"When I came to London he took me into his house, he didn't want me to stay in a motel,"[3] said English. "We used to ride around after rehearsals in their little car listening to tapes, and they'd show me different neighborhoods. They said, 'Listen, we'll buy you a house. You want a Porsche? Anything you want. We'll move your family here.'"[4]

Months earlier, English was scratching together a living as a jobbing musician. Now he was preparing to join a former Beatle on the road. The laid-back American could not believe his luck.

"I don't think I ever told Paul that when I stayed in that room, I opened the closet door and I hung some clothes up, and I looked and I went, 'Is that the *Sgt. Pepper* outfit that he wore on the album?' I never did ask him, but I think it was, and I was thinking, 'I'm really here! This is really it.'"[5]

When the band grew tired of dodging Kent and Sussex reporters, Paul and Linda could often be found enjoying lunch at the Mermaid Inn—a 600-year-old bar and hotel on Mermaid Street. The Liverpool-born jazz and blues singer George Melly was among the couple's lunchtime guests. The multitalented Melly, who also worked as a writer and critic, was hired to put together a press pack for *Venus and Mars*, which was scheduled for release worldwide on May 30. 'Listen to What the Man Said' would be released as a single on May 16.

Keeping London at arm's length also meant the McCartneys could dodge the backlash from the latest wave of anti-Macca headlines that followed the couple back across the Atlantic. The *Daily Mirror* set the tone for Paul and Linda's return to England with "Drugs and Me, by Beatle Paul," on April 3. The article, accompanied by snaps of the family at Heathrow Airport taken on April 2, centered on a fleeting comment Paul made to a reporter about Linda's Los Angeles drug arrest.

"It was hardly anything at all—only enough to make about four* cigarettes," Paul said of the marijuana police seized from their L.A. hire car. "Linda did a bit of quick thinking and said it was hers. They took us down to the police station and charged us with the offense. We said that we were sorry, and they let us go. That was that. In Los Angeles it's different from over here. Out there it is not such a big deal."[6]

When her case was eventually heard, in her absence, during hearings on April 7 and May 20, Linda was ordered to undergo a six-month drug rehabilitation program in London—six sessions in total. Judge Brian D. Crahan noted that Linda would face further action if she were busted again within six months.

But the *Daily Mirror* piece seemed like a slap on the wrist compared to the hand grenade that landed soon afterward courtesy of Blair Sabol, a two-page poison-pen assault on her old friend, published in the *Village Voice* on April 14.

Sabol's deeply unflattering portrait of Linda, "Who Does She Think She Is? Mrs. Paul McCartney?" accused her of everything from using her body to score photography jobs in the 1960s to being insincere and bereft of musical talent. Linda winced as her brother read the article to her over the phone from New York.

"I personally just deal with them," Linda said of hit jobs like Sabol's. "Paul gets upset because he always wants everybody to know the truth. He'll read and he'll get frustrated."[7]

In an effort to offset the damage done by the *Village Voice* piece, four days after Sabol's body-slam hit New York newsstands, Paul made what was for him an unusual PR move. The McCartneys supported many charitable organizations, but they typically kept their philanthropic endeavors private. One of their recent beneficiaries was the Elleray Park School, a center for the physically handicapped, in Wallasey, Merseyside. The McCartneys had bought the school a 12-seat minibus early in the year, and although the school normally did not reveal the names of its donors, on April 18, its head fundraiser was quoted in the *Liverpool Echo* saying that the McCartneys "are giving us about £4,000 ($9,500) for the purchase of a coach."[8]

Where Sabol painted the McCartneys as steely and disingenuous, the *Liverpool Echo* helped restore the balance by lauding one of their own as a local hero.

Paul was not alone in his pursuit of positive press. Having discovered during his "lost weekend" that even he was not exempt from his own edict that *"instant karma's gonna get you,"* John was

* In 2016, the *New York Times* reported that in a global drug survey conducted by academics, it was found that a joint typically contained about 0.33 grams of marijuana. The 16 grams in Linda's possession would therefore have yielded nearly 50 joints.

determined to wash away 18 months during which he was portrayed as being publicly out of control, and he had turned publicity for his *Rock 'n' Roll* LP into a form of self-therapy. Paul and Linda watched some of John's spiritual regeneration firsthand on April 18, when John appeared on the BBC's *Old Grey Whistle Test* in a pre-recorded interview with the show's host, Bob Harris, bookended by performances of 'Slippin' and Slidin'' and 'Stand by Me.'

Filmed soon after he rekindled his relationship with Yoko, John was in a chipper mood, and no topic was off-limits. After opening up on a broad range of subjects, from life and recording in New York, to depression, to missing Chocolate Olivers (his favorite English biscuits), John professed his remorse for targeting Paul with his 1971 broadside, 'How Do You Sleep?'

"It's not about Paul, it's about me," Lennon declared. "I'm really attacking myself. But I regret the association [with Paul] . . . The only thing that matters is how he and I feel about those things, not how the writer or the commentator thinks about it."

Harris asked whether this meant that the former Beatles might collaborate on future live or recorded projects.

"It's strange, because at one period when they were asking me, I was saying, 'Nah, never, go back? Not me,'" Lennon replied. "And then there came a period when I thought, 'Oh, why not?' if we felt like making a record or doing something. Everybody's always envisaged a stage show. To me, if we worked together [it would be in] the studio again."[9]

But as was often the case with John, this conversation with a journalist was not in sync with discussions he was having behind closed doors. After declaring on national television that there was nothing stopping the boys getting back together again, John told those closest to him that he and Yoko were trying to conceive and that he would be taking a break from public life.

Paul was disappointed not to reconnect with John in New Orleans but content that the war was finally over.

Six days after John's televised interview, singer-songwriter Pete Ham, the front man with former Apple act Badfinger, died by suicide at the age of 27. Ham's admission to the 27 Club* was a timely reminder that grudges were not worth taking to the grave.

The reality was, while the Beatles' four-year divorce battle ended amicably, the ghosts of the past were hard to exorcise. Paul accepted that the competitive streak between him and John never went away. "He was very jealous on the surface, and so was I, and it was all stupidness, on the

* The 27 Club is an unofficial list of celebrities who died at the age of 27. Others on the list include Jimi Hendrix, Janis Joplin, Jim Morrison and Brian Jones.

surface."[10] And he recognized that with music charts and sales figures pitting them against each other, jealousies were hard to conquer.

All four of the former Beatles had enjoyed commercial and critical success since parting ways. John's *Imagine* and *Walls and Bridges* LPs had topped the *Billboard* 200, as did George's *All Things Must Pass* and *Living in the Material World*. Ringo's 'Photograph' and 'You're Sixteen' were No. 1 hits on the *Billboard* Hot 100. But with three No. 1 albums and three No. 1 singles in America, Paul led the way commercially, and now the Eastmans were determined to cement his position as one of the biggest names in popular music.

Though the Beatles were still under contract with EMI through December 31, 1975, the Eastmans argued that once the Beatles dissolved their business ties, the group's existing contracts with EMI and Capitol should be annulled, and at the start of 1975 they began negotiating a new solo deal on Paul's behalf. With *Band on the Run* having gone platinum in both America and Canada, and preorders of *Venus and Mars* in the region of 1.3 million worldwide, the Eastmans had a strong hand to play.

Capitol's management was also under pressure from shareholders after a shaky start to the year. According to a report in the May 17 issue of *Cash Box*, in the first quarter of 1975 sales figures for Capitol Industries–EMI, Inc. declined by $10,842,000 (£4,510,000) compared with the first quarter of 1974.

In a statement designed to stop investors from jumping ship, Capitol president and chief executive officer Bhaskar Menon told stockholders: "Some improvement is foreseen for the fourth quarter, and indeed April sales were the highest for any month since last December. New albums for May reflect increased artist strength, and scheduled for release in June are albums from two of Capitol's most important stars: Paul McCartney and Helen Reddy."[11]

Now it was up to Menon to retain an artist he had just touted one of Capitol Records' biggest commercial assets. In past negotiations with Lee Eastman, Capitol blew hot and cold. Now Eastman wanted assurances that they meant business. Using McCartney's strong sales and interest from Warner as leverage, Eastman made an unpredictable opening gambit.

In July 1964, Capitol Records set up Morley Music, a joint publishing venture with the music publisher Edward H. Morris, bringing together Capitol's Ardmore Music and Morris's Morley Music. The joint publishing catalog boasted innumerable Standards, including 'After You've Gone' (by Henry Creamer and Turner Layton), 'I'll Walk Alone' (by Sammy Cahn and Jule Styne), 'Sentimental Journey' (by Bud Green, Ben Brown and Les Homer) and 'Autumn Leaves' (by Johnny Mercer and Joseph Kosma).

Much as Paul loved Standards—the songs his father played, the music of his youth—his real interest in the Morley catalog was that it would give him the publishing rights to a pair of songs published by EMI's Ardmore and Beechwood in 1962—'Love Me Do' and 'P.S. I Love You,' by a fledgling British composing duo, John Lennon and Paul McCartney.

Lee Eastman had been working on a deal to acquire Morris's portion of the Morley catalog, but when he began talks with Capitol, he proposed that the label should make a gift of its share of the company to Paul as a goodwill gesture for re-signing with them. It was a bold proposal, but Capitol agreed to it.

"He was a brilliant acquirer of catalogs," Sam Trust—who managed Morley Music for Capitol before he became CEO of ATV/Northern Songs in 1973—said of the elder Eastman. "[In] every deal he made, [including] the one he made with Bhaskar Menon, he would not even negotiate until he got catalogs for nothing. To me, Morley Music was the jewel in the crown of the publishing I had [when I worked for Capitol]. He would not go into negotiations until Bhaskar Menon had handed it over. Then he would start negotiating. So he got all those copyrights."[12]

Eastman also negotiated McCartney a weighty hike in his artist royalty rate. Over a four-year period—backdated to January 1, 1975—Paul would receive $1.20 (54p) for every album sold in Britain, and 15 cents (7p) per single. When the deal was announced, *Billboard* reported that McCartney would be paid an artist royalty of 24 percent.[13] Even if the amount was overstated—20 percent is likely a more accurate figure—this was still a significant uplift on the 17.5 percent the Beatles collectively received under the terms of the contract Allen Klein negotiated with Capitol in 1969.

Eastman also arranged for all of Paul's album masters to revert to him—a benefit neither Brian Epstein nor Allen Klein ever managed to negotiate on the Beatles' behalf.

Thanks to Eastman, McCartney joined Stevie Wonder and Elton John at the financial pinnacle of the pop pyramid. Paul's new "multimillion-dollar," four-year deal with EMI and Capitol, which would see all of his records issued under the Capitol umbrella, was announced in a press release on May 15:

> Capitol Records and Paul McCartney are delighted to announce that they have concluded an exclusive recording agreement for the USA, Canada and Japan. A separate agreement covering all other territories of the world has been concluded between Mr. McCartney and EMI Records. The first recording under the new agreement, the album Venus and Mars, will be released worldwide in May on the Capitol label.[14]

Looking to offset the advance he received (reported by *Billboard* as being in the region of $3,300,000 [£1,402,800], though this cannot be confirmed) upon renewing with Capitol/EMI, and more importantly, the substantial tax bill that came with it, Paul continued to hoover up music copyrights by adding Whale Music Corp. to his growing publishing portfolio. Formerly part of the T.B. Harms & Francis, Day & Hunter, Inc. group—one of Tin Pan Alley's "big seven" publishing companies—Whale Music held multiple copyrights by American songwriter Jack Lawrence, including 'If I Didn't Care,' 'Beyond the Sea' and 'All or Nothing at All'—all of them hits from Paul's childhood. But those songs represented only the practical lure of the catalog.

As in the case of the Morley catalog, Paul also had a purely personal reason to focus on Whale. Jack Lawrence was a client of Lee Eastman's, and in 1946, at Eastman's suggestion, he used the name of his lawyer's five-year-old daughter as a song title. 'Linda' was a hit for Buddy Clark and the Ray Noble Orchestra that year and was later covered by artists as diverse as Frank Sinatra, Willie Nelson, and the surf duo Jan and Dean.

When Paul first visited Linda's New York apartment, in 1968, the framed manuscript of the song, hanging on her living room wall, immediately caught his eye. Now he was married to the song's namesake, and he owned its publishing rights as well. The cost of the Whale catalog was not disclosed.

While the Eastmans negotiated on his behalf, Paul ramped up plans for the release of *Venus and Mars*. Thanks to George Melly, the album press release was good to go, but in a note to Brian Brolly, sent on April 22, Tony Brainsby complained that Aubrey Powell's photographs of Wings in the Mojave Desert were "disappointing for press use."[15] Denny Laine in white face paint, grasping a yellow billiard ball in his mouth, was deemed not fit for public consumption, and Brainsby didn't like the rest of the portfolio much better. In response, Brolly booked John Kelly for a photo session on May 6 but canceled when it was pointed out to him that 'Listen to What the Man Said' was due out only nine days later. Instead, Linda set the timer on her Nikon and snapped the band goofing off near the waterfall from which the McCartneys' cottage took its name, at the northeastern tip of their Sussex estate.

The cascading water also gave its name to a song Paul was noodling with. 'Waterfalls,' which he also called 'I Need Love,' was a fable set to music in which Paul called for his adventurous daughters to avoid "*jumping waterfalls*" and instead "*keep to the lake.*" 'Children Children,' a folksy tune Denny Laine was writing, drew on similar inspiration, but rather than calling for caution, Laine's composition painted a picture of the McCartney and Laine kids enjoying a magical adventure in Waterfall Woods.

"That came about as a result of being at Paul's house one day," said Laine, "where they've got a waterfall at the back. And it seemed a nice place for kids to play, you know. I sort of got the idea from that."[16]

Meanwhile, the design Paul and Aubrey Powell assembled for the *Venus and Mars* gatefold sleeve was causing headaches for Capitol Records. Having settled on Linda's photograph for the cover and one of Powell's shots of the band in the Mojave Desert for the inner gatefold, Paul decided to commission a modernist design for the inner sleeve, with yellow and red planets, white dotted lines showing their orbits (some standard, some strangely angular), set against a black background. Hipgnosis artist George Hardie drew this sleeve, but three complex elements were not enough for Paul. He also wanted to include two stickers and a double-sided poster featuring shots of Paul and Linda boarding the *Voyageur* in New Orleans, and the band in the Mojave Desert.

Production of a standard gatefold sleeve was normally a six-week process. But on April 27, a spokesman for Capitol told the *Los Angeles Times* that the sleeve had yet to be approved, meaning they were unlikely to meet the May 30 release date. Capitol blamed the album's elaborate design—or reading between the lines, Paul—for the holdup. In the end, production problems saw the single and album bumped by a week in Britain and other parts of the world.

Stretching the patience and resources of his record label did not trouble Paul, but after putting Tony Visconti's nose out of joint by not giving him a credit as the arranger on *Band on the Run*, Paul credited nearly every musician who played on *Venus and Mars*, including Geoff Britton, Allen Toussaint, Tom Scott, Dave Mason and Kenneth "Afro" Williams; only the string, brass and wind ensemble players are uncredited on the sleeve.

Tony Dorsey was given a co-arranger credit (with Paul). And Hipgnosis, unmentioned on *Band on the Run*, is credited for the centerfold (as "Po Hipgnosis"), with Aubrey Powell credited (as Po) for the "Balls Poster." Sea-Saint (without its hyphen) and Wally Heider are listed, as are photo locations in New Orleans and Northern California. The publishing credit reads, "McCartney Music, Inc." (as opposed to Ltd.)—confirming, for tax purposes, that the album was recorded in America (even though several tracks were started in London).

For the first time on one of Paul's post-Beatles albums, Paul was not required to include an Apple logo or any mention of the Beatles' boutique label—both the UK and US releases carry Capitol and MPL logos.

All songs on the LP—with the exception of 'Medicine Jar,' published by Jimmy McCulloch and Colin Allen's J.M. Music Ltd., and Tony Hatch's 'Crossroads Theme,' published by ATV Music—are credited to "McCartney" and published by McCartney Music Ltd./ATV Music Ltd.*

"Paul mentioned, on one occasion, that the royalties I should receive would keep me in ciggies for quite some time," Allen joked.[17]

* The credit "McCartney" was meant to embrace songs written by Paul alone as well as collaborations with Linda, but various releases muddy the waters. The British release credits the songs to McCartney. The labels on the American version say, "All Selections Composed by Paul McCartney" (with the exception of 'Medicine Jar' and 'Crossroads'). However, on the 2014 CD reissue, the credit reads "All tracks composed by Paul and Linda McCartney," with the same exceptions.

Recording Session

Late April 1975.

Apple Studios, 3 Savile Row, London.

Recording: 'Blowin' in the Bay' and 'Let's Turn the Radio On.'

By choosing to sign a new deal with EMI and Capitol, rather than entertaining a switch to one of their rivals, Paul inadvertently left his brother Mike's recording career vulnerable. Sales of *McGear* and its various singles were poor, and since Ron Kass was no longer chasing Paul's signature, Mike's future on the Warner label was uncertain. One thing was clear, though: if Mike wanted to prolong his solo career, he needed new material, so Paul offered to help his brother record a fresh batch of demos. If Warner did not take up the option to extend Mike's contract, the tracks could be taken to a different label. Paul even provided a studio for the session.

Apple Studios, the Beatles' underused recording facility, opened its doors on October 3, 1971, and since then Paul had only used the studio once to master 'Give Ireland Back to the Irish.' But now, as studio manager Malcolm Davies prepared to decommission the studio, Paul wanted to take it for a test drive.

"I had mentioned to my brother that I wanted to record a couple of demo songs," said Mike, "and he mentioned that we might be able to use Apple Studios. By that time, Apple was winding down. . . . As we were walking down the steps to the studio below the ground Our Kid said, 'Have you seen what's happened to the building above?' I remembered that it had some ornate fireplaces and when we walked through the main door, Paul said 'Look up.' Looking up, I saw that all the floors had been ripped out, with tarpaulin flapping at roof height, letting the rain in. I noticed the beautiful fireplaces were all against the wall getting soaked."[18]

Mike brought two songs to the session, 'Blowin' in the Bay'—a breezy funk melody with a moody middle eight, written in the spirit of Bryan Ferry—and 'Let's Turn the Radio On,' a cheerful pop tune with a ukulele accompaniment. Paul (drums) and Mike (vocals) were joined for the session by Viv Stanshall (vocals and ukulele), Johnny Gustafson (bass) and Zoot Money (piano and organ). According to Money, their precise roles during recording were interchangeable, as the studio became a sandbox for experimentation, much of which was not captured on tape.

"I was fascinated by the way Paul would just go for different sounds," Money explained. "He'd wander around the room and find something to hit to make a different sound. I played an improvised sound for a bass drum. Paul said, 'See what sound you can get out of this,' and it was a bass drum case, and I was hitting it with the bottom of a microphone stand to do a bass drum sound, while he plonked away on the piano."[19]

By the end of the session, Mike left with two master tapes—'Blowin' in the Bay' [2'31"] and 'Let's Turn the Radio On' [3'11]. The McCartney brothers' session was one of the last times Apple Studios was used before the building was closed for refurbishments.

"It's kaput," Paul said unsentimentally of Apple Studios in May. "There's no sense in having the shell of Savile Row if nothing's going to be in it. It's over, so we might as well close."[20]

Paul and Linda stayed in London for several days at the start of May to oversee the final stages of production and promotion for *Venus and Mars*. On May 2, Paul's restless pursuit of perfection took him to Master Room at 59–61 Riding House Street, where he oversaw the mastering of both *Venus and Mars* and the album's lead single, 'Listen to What the Man Said.' Record mastering—the process of transferring a master recording to vinyl—was viewed by many musicians as a technical dark art, but the practice of squeezing every ounce of life out of a tape and into the tiny grooves of a plastic disc fascinated McCartney. Like most recording artists, he believed that if his record was louder than anyone else's, it would sell more copies.

Established in 1974 by recording engineers Freddie Packham and George "Porky" Peckham, Master Room was the UK's first independent record-cutting facility. As an EMI artist, six in-house cutting rooms were at Paul's disposal, but going back to the Beatle days, he had considered EMI's cutting methods too cautious and clinical. He first questioned EMI's approach in 1966, when the Beatles issued the single 'Paperback Writer' and challenged cutting engineer Tony Clark to push the bass and overall volume levels.

"We were always pushing and asking, as younger engineers, as well as the artists, why American records were louder than ours," said Clark. "There was the fear, really, of records jumping. If you had a million-selling record and it jumped [the returns would be a problem], so English records were quite cautious. 'Paperback Writer' was the first high level cut. We did, I think, two cuts: one at the normal level and one at plus three. We actually played them back to George Martin and Paul in a test room, and they thought the loud one was fantastic, which pleased me because I took a lot of pains to make sure the grooves weren't touching."[21]

Nine years on, having pushed the limits at EMI, Paul wanted to explore what London's independent mastering facilities had to offer. McCartney had known Peckham for years: he had been a member of the Fourmost, a Liverpool band that was managed by Brian Epstein and recorded two embryonic Lennon-McCartney songs, 'Hello Little Girl' and 'I'm in Love' for EMI. He had also been the cutting engineer at Apple Studios. McCartney admired his penchant for pushing technical boundaries.

"Master Room had a bigger cutting room than Apple, and also a comfortable reception area for my clients," said Peckham. "I still had Paul McCartney's and George Harrison's cutting work to do which kept my link to Liverpool and my friends intact. All this assured I was able to keep the accountants happy."[22]

Peckham cut the *Venus and Mars* album masters on a brand-new Neumann UMS70 lathe, etching his trademark calling card—"A PORKY PRIME CUT"—into the dead wax beyond the run-off groove. Peckham's assistant, Melvyn Abrahams, oversaw the single, 'Listen to What the Man Said' (EMI matrix YEX.945), backed with 'Love in Song' (EMI matrix YEX.946).

In the United States, Capitol pressed promotional copies that included stereo and mono mixes of only 'Listen to What the Man Said' as a way of focusing radio program directors' attention on the A side.

The McCartneys split their time between the London districts of Kensington and St. James's, on May 5, when they ticked off two more promotional tasks. Paul believed that *Venus and Mars*, with its material ranging from straight-ahead rock to vaudeville pastiche, would have universal appeal, and what better way to showcase its variety than presenting a montage of tracks in a spiffy television commercial?

Having hired a non-filmmaker for his last foray into video, Paul made a complete U-turn and engaged the renowned Czech-born filmmaker Karel Reisz—whose CV included *Saturday Night and Sunday Morning* (1960), *Isadora* (1968) and *The Gambler* (1974)—to make this 60-second spot. For a reported daily rate of £1,000 ($2,340), the BAFTA award-winning Cambridge graduate directed the five musicians through a routine of hammy horseplay around a billiards table at a private house in Holland Park.

Back in Soho, the footage Reisz captured was edited to excerpts from 'Venus and Mars,' 'You Gave Me the Answer,' 'Listen to What the Man Said,' 'Treat Her Gently,' 'Medicine Jar' and 'Venus and Mars (Reprise).' It would have its first screening on ITV on June 25.

As soon as filming wrapped, Paul and Linda drove along the edge of Hyde Park to meet with Paul Gambaccini, a writer who wore several caps. A contributor to *Rolling Stone* and various British music publications, Gambaccini also hosted weekly radio shows for both the BBC and *Rolling Stone's* international News Service. On May 5, a sunny spring day, Gambaccini interviewed Paul and Linda at St. James's Park. But their conversation was quickly interrupted.

"Her Majesty's Guards were changing patrols with military precision in front of Buckingham Palace and Paul McCartney's Rolls-Royce was about to be towed," Gambaccini wrote. "A parking ticket planted on the windshield had failed to discourage the traffic warden who'd noticed the car on the sidewalk near the Palace, and it took a congenial conversation to convince the bobby that clemency was in order."[23]

After relocating to MPL's offices in Soho, the McCartneys and Gambaccini nattered for several hours, covering everything from the conception of Wings' new album ("I've been reading a little bit of science fiction"), to Geoff Britton's exit ("Henry left, and we get in Jimmy McCulloch, spelled differently but same kind of name. We got rid of a drummer called Geoff Britton who's English and got in a drummer called Joe English who's American"), to the couple's take on Blair Sabol's *Village Voice* article ("That was written by an ex-friend of Linda's. *Ex-friend* is the operative word"[24]). Paul also opened up on the recent death of Badfinger front man Pete Ham.

"Did you hear about Pete Ham? I was sad. He was good. It was one of those things where you hear about it and think, 'If only I had called him up a week earlier, I wonder if I could have helped and saved him?' It was like that with Jimi. The week before he died, we were talking about him and decided we had to invite him up to Scotland—but we didn't. A week later, he was dead."[25]

Gambaccini's conversation with the McCartneys was published in several music trades, and the audio aired as a BBC *Rock Week* special on May 24.

Recording Session

Monday, May 12, 1975.
EMI Studios, Studio Three, London.
Recording and mixing: 'Karate Chaos,' 'Sea Dance,' 'Backwards One' and 'Rudolph the Red-Nosed Reggae.'

Two MPL film projects* were in post-production—Karel Reisz's television commercial, and David Litchfield's karate feature, now titled *Empty Hand* (the English translation of the Japanese word *karate*). For several months Litchfield had been assembling a rough cut with editor Jonathan Lewis. Now his film needed a soundtrack.

The karate bouts between British and Japanese fighters at the Sobell Center on November 30, which formed the basis of Litchfield's short film, were brutal and at times disturbing.

"Theoretically, the Japanese team should have wiped the floor with the English team," Litchfield said. "What happened was they frightened the shit out of the English to the point where the

* Or three, technically, as *Bruce McMouse*—Paul's semi-animated, semi-live performance film from the 1972 European tour was still considered an active project. It was in the hands of a small team of animators in London at this time. Production was finally paused indefinitely in 1977.

English overreacted. And it became full contact karate. There were teeth going all over the place. I mean, it was very, very heavy indeed. One guy got a ruptured kidney."[26]

Yet somehow, in his 32-minute feature, Litchfield captured a beauty in the brutality, and portions of the film edited in slow motion lent themselves to abstract music, which Paul offered to provide.

Intent on reflecting karate's Japanese origins in his soundtrack, Paul called Maurice Placquet—an instrument hire company based in Shepherd's Bush—and arranged for a collection of Japanese percussion, a drum kit, and a harpsichord to be delivered to Abbey Road. Just before midnight, delivery drivers cum aspiring session players Bob Loveday* and friend Nigel dropped off the equipment together with a shameless sales pitch.

"By the way Paul, I play electric guitar," said Nigel as Paul checked over the drum kit.

"Oh, great man, I wish you the best of luck," Paul replied turning to Loveday. "I suppose you play an instrument as well?"

Expecting Paul to be underwhelmed, Loveday muttered under his breath, "Yeah, I play the violin," only to see his words have the opposite effect.

"Oh, great! Have you got it with you?" Paul beamed. Suddenly Loveday found himself booked for his first-ever professional recording session, paid at the union rate of £25 ($58).

With engineer Richard Lush at the console, Paul sat at the grand piano and tracked his first contribution to Litchfield's film soundtrack—a set of improvised chords, provisionally titled 'Sea Dance.' Loveday then found himself providing a one-man orchestral backing.

"He had this notion for a big string orchestra sweeping theme tune," said Loveday, "and he got me to record track after track of violins—I think it was about eight in all when he'd finished. It sounded absolutely mighty when it was done."[27]

Sound effects and percussion finished off the recording.

"It was a very nice piece of semi-abstract music, which I liked a lot," Litchfield explained. "He put bird sounds on it, and they were like those wader birds that have a cry rather than a song. And it was just beautiful, it was very haunting."[28]

Following playback, Loveday took a back seat while Paul and Linda recorded a pair of sparse Eastern-influenced percussion pieces, the first of which was titled 'Karate Chaos.' Lifting the lid on the studio piano, Paul first laid down a bed of abstract sound, created by plucking the piano's internal strings. Onto that basic track he and Linda then layered percussion, chimes and what sounds like metal objects being dropped inside the piano. Heavy use of echo, created using a new computerized echo system EMI was testing, obscured the piece's individual musical elements in the final mix.

---

* Loveday went on to work with a myriad of recording artists, including Van Morrison, Penguin Café Orchestra, Bob Geldof, Jeff Beck, Kirsty MacColl and Rachid Taha.

In a second film cue, 'Backwards One,' Paul used the same chimes and percussion, but the meat of the track was created by playing random sequences of piano chords in a Baroque style. During the mix, the tape was drenched in tape echo and played in reverse, creating a trippy effect.

By this time, the potent joints Paul, Linda and Bob had been passing around during session had taken hold, and tracking took an unseasonal turn.

"When I'd finished my other stuff," Paul explained, "he said, 'What are we going to do?' I said, '"Rudolph the Red-Nosed Reggae," of course!'"[29]

Paul hopped behind the harpsichord and played a couple of introductory bars of this reggae-tinged reworking of Johnny Marks's 1949 Christmas hit 'Rudolph the Red-Nosed Reindeer,' and Loveday took up the melody. Paul then overdubbed drums, and Lush made rough stereo mixes of all four cuts.

"We worked all night," said Loveday, "and at 8 A.M. they wandered off and I was left in the studio completely stoned out of my mind on popstar grade cannabis!"

No matter how many times he bared his artistic soul with a new collection of songs, the process—and that's exactly how he viewed it, as a mechanical exercise—of releasing a new record always stirred up mixed feelings for McCartney. Perhaps with the exception of *Red Rose Speedway*, which was released under a cloud of band infighting and discontent that liquefied his faith in the album, Paul rarely lacked confidence in his music. As a solo artist he had built a loyal fanbase, and his post-Beatles records were—on the whole—commercially successful. But one obstacle always blunted the pleasure of bringing out a new disc: the critics. And now it was time to run the critical gauntlet once again.

"We had a lot of ups and downs, and the critics and stuff made it very difficult," Paul admitted. "You know, it would be that insidious—it would get to you. It gets into there, wheedles its little way through the cracks—it's like water, criticism, it finds its way in."[30]

McCartney's appetite for writing and recording music was like that of a worker bee gathering nectar—innate and incessant, and never satisfied. Once the master tapes were delivered, though, he felt a cold detachment as the corporate wheels of EMI and Capitol took over.

"I let go of a record when I've finished it, and do the cover and everything, it's what the record company consider *product*. I let go of it, and it goes then, and I don't see it. I don't see someone going into the shop and buying it, I don't see them take it home lovingly and put it on and experience the joy, I don't see any of that. And what I do see then is when it arrives as a figure, on a sheet that tells you how many you've sold in Afghanistan."[31]

Paul wanted to see the whites of the critics' eyes as they listened to *Venus and Mars* for the

Wings, 'Listen to What the Man Said' single trade ad

first time, so together with EMI's director of repertoire and marketing, Bob Mercer, he hosted a private listening party at the company's Manchester Square offices on May 12.

One of Paul's American publicists, Dennis Fine, took charge of a similar event at Capitol's New York offices for a carefully selected group of American journalists on May 20.

The release of 'Listen to What the Man Said' offered a first glimpse of the critical response to the new material, and for the most part, the reviews made pleasant reading for McCartney.

> *Paul McCartney and his group take flight with this shuffle-paced single. Clarinets spice the song and give a distinct flavor while McCartney's supple vocal style will make this an automatic additional to almost anyone's playlist.*[32]
>
> Uncredited, *Cash Box*

> *Well, you know what Paul's records are like. "Charming, perfectly charming," you murmur to yourself on first hearing. "Not bad at all," you concede on the tenth. "That's a classic, what!" you allow on the 25th. I'm up to about 14 or 15 and moving towards a strong affection for the number. Anyway, it's a winner, with Paul singing romantically rather than aggressively, despite the tempo, and all the McCartney production agility and attention to detail on display.*[33]
>
> John Peel, *Sounds*

> *Typically precise production from master technician McCartney, applied to a bouncy little composition loaded with charm. Also loaded with an assortment of unidentifiable alterations to the sound of normal instruments and classy, character vocals. Jaunty, regular drumming in true Beatle-fashion allows Paul and Wings to expand on his sweet basic melody and hook, putting a tasty frosting on a great musical desert and containing nothing heavier than a sunny love message. Hope it's a killer.*[34]
>
> Lon Goddard, *Disc*

> *Ooh that Paulie (swoon swoon), he's a sly one. You play this single and in no time at all you're wondering how somebody so talented can produce something so inept and you're thinking it's safe to dismiss this as a loser. And then, involuntarily, the foot begins to tap, the head starts to nod, and by four or five spins, you're hooked. Paul sings in his creamy 'Yesterday' voice and there's a delightful arrangement that brings a distinctive clavinet to the fore. You can bop to it, you can sing along with it, or you can just listen to it, and it's equally successful on all levels. Hit.*[35]
>
> Colin Irwin, *Melody Maker*

Just what's needed in these troubled times, a happy, summery sound, fresh as a daisy with jaunty guitar parts, skittish brass, and a little mellow cello to end up with. McCartney's care-free vocal completes the mood. Lovely record, big hit and a tantalizing trailer for the new Wings album.[36]

Ray Fox-Cumming, Record Mirror

What a soppy song—this [is] McCartney on his "I'm no better than Peter Skellern or all those other guys" trip. Complacent backing and utterly trite lyrics—I can't tell you much about it because I don't remember much. After six hearings. Mercifully forgettable.[37]

Kate Philips, NME

For the record-buying public, 'Listen to What the Man Said' hit all the right notes and outperformed 'Junior's Farm' in both America and Britain. In the US the single enjoyed a 14-week ride on the *Billboard* 100, entering at No. 65 on May 31 and peaking at No. 1 on July 19. By September 4, it was certified Gold in America. In the UK, the song entered the singles chart at No. 33 on May 31, and peaked at No. 6 three weeks later. After eight weeks in the Top 100, it was gone.

Just before the album was issued, Tony Brainsby scheduled two days at MPL's offices, on May 26 and 27, with each band member speaking with a few reporters.

Buried among the fluff and self-promotion, each of the five musicians offered insights into the inner workings of Wings, and English, speaking with Eamonn Percival of *Record Mirror*, allowed readers (and former Wings members) a peek behind the MPL corporate curtain.

"The great thing is there's no contracts with Wings," English explained of the band's continued loose financial arrangement. "Paul's gone through the whole bit about being tied up with contracts and he doesn't want to get involved with that again."

Whether in denial, or just happy to be involved with McCartney in any capacity, English seemed intent on convincing Percival that not being tied down contractually was a good thing. In doing so, he inadvertently showed that he was no better off, financially, than Wings' first drummer, Denny Seiwell.

"We've got two weeks off," English noted of an upcoming break in the band's schedule, "so I'm going back to the States and making a few calls to see if there's anyone needing me for sessions or anything like that. The great thing about Wings is that if I want to go and record with Nilsson, Al Green, or anyone, then that's cool."[38]

If putting each musician in the spotlight was meant to perpetuate the idea that Wings was a band, not just Paul and sideman, it had the opposite effect. Though Denny and Linda referred to Wings as a collective, Joe and Jimmy seemed to imply that being a yes-man was the best approach to life in McCartney's group.

"I'm a very basic person," McCulloch explained. "I think that's why I'm so happy with this band. Paul *is* the writer—if I had a track record like his I wouldn't expect to be questioned about my ability or right to do [most of the songwriting]. I certainly don't question it—I'm quite happy just to be in the same band as a guy like that."[39]

Paul endured two starkly contrasting promotional encounters. The first was with Chris Welch of *Melody Maker*. Together the pair explored the difficulty of following the success of *Band on the Run* ("once or twice I thought, yeah, gotta follow that then. But y'know, it doesn't worry me") and touched on the sonic influence New Orleans had on *Venus and Mars* ("I think it always rubs off a bit, just in kind of arrangements and who's there. There's a couple of tunes we've got brass on and it's New Orleans brass"), before Paul confessed his frustration with his on-again, off-again *Rupert Bear* film project.

"I've got a big plan to do *Rupert*," he explained. "I've been saying this for years unfortunately, but I would like to get together a big *Bambi* if you like, a Disney style cartoon—which will be the first actual film score I've bothered to try and get into, and I'd really love to do that. The only disappointment to me is that it's such a big thing, I haven't got it together yet.* I'm going to have to clear some time.

"My idea is to make the [characters that appear in the] annuals move and have them talk. I can see it all in my head. But it's very expensive, and somebody has to get together the *Rupert* story and it's hard to write a very good plot. You could take one of the old stories, but they're all short, and you don't get all the characters in. If I manage to write the story and all the songs, it will be possible then."[40]

Paul's next encounter was with Charles Shaar Murray. The *NME* reporter had been sitting in MPL's reception area for some time, staring at a table of dried salmon sandwiches that were caught in a beam of sunlight, debating the question: "What can one say to an ex-Beatle who's made a crappy album?"

In his review of *Band on the Run*, Murray declared: "If anybody ever puts down McCartney in your presence, bust him in the snoot and play him this."[41] But he thought *Venus and Mars* was "a terrible album"—so bad, he quipped, that he "wouldn't use it to line a budgie cage."[42]

The underwhelmed reporter was sipping red wine ("warm and overly sweet," Murray complained) when Paul arrived late from a lunch appointment. Inviting Murray into a side room, McCartney, dressed in an ensemble of jeans, waistcoat, and white shirt, accepted a cigarette from his inquisitor, tore off the filter and held it over a flame, before settling into his chair.

At first, their conversation followed a familiar path—Klein, Apple, Paul's relationship with John, the usual post-Beatles questions—before Paul impatiently switched the subject to the promo-

---

* Barry Chattington, the director at the helm of *Bruce McMouse*, notes that Paul was actively working on *Rupert* in the mid-1970s. "I had storyboards of *Rupert Bear* for years when we were doing this," he told Adrian Sinclair in 2018.

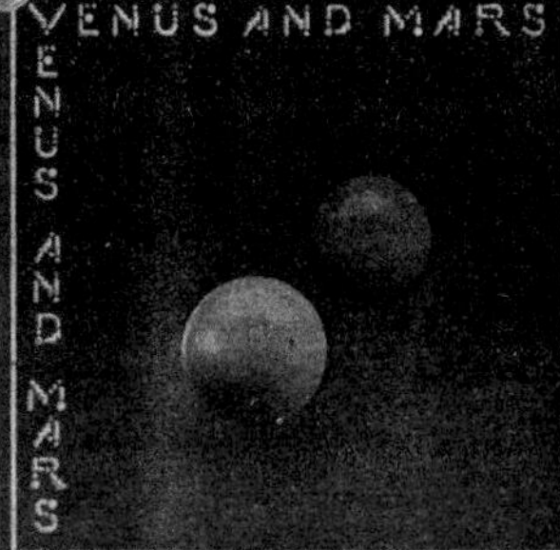

Wings, *Venus and Mars* album trade ad

tional business at hand, leading Murray into what quickly became a debate about the musical merits of *Venus and Mars*.

McCartney: New LP released soon. What do you want to know about it?

Murray: It's much lighter and simpler than its predecessor . . .

McCartney: It is?

Murray: It doesn't have as much attack as *Band on the Run*.

McCartney: Oh well, y'know, I mean the funny thing about that is, it's so much down to people's opinions, y'know. I'd take it up to Liverpool, y'know, to play it to a few people up in Liverpool, and they said just the opposite. They said, "Aww, man, I haven't heard you singing like that for years; it's got much more attack, much more bite." I don't myself think it's lighter. It might be, I dunno.

Murray: Yeah, but surely *Band on the Run* made gestures in the direction of being a rock album, whereas this is just an easy listening album.

McCartney: Yeah, some of it is, yeah. I mean, you've got a couple of tracks that aren't. You got 'Call Me Back Again' on the second side isn't easy listening. And you've got 'Letting Go.' And 'Rock Show' is kind of, hardish.

Murray: It sounds like David Essex.

McCartney: 'Rock Show'? Get out of it! Who has *NME* sent along, ladies and gentleman? He's been out all night, he's stoned out of his brain, he doesn't know what's going . . . No, it doesn't sound like David Essex to me. But thank you for the compliment.[43]

The young reporter's cross-examination was unrelenting. By the end of their sometimes heated back-and-forth, Murray had McCartney so fired up that he began rambling about politics; specifically, a referendum on Britain's status as a member of the European Economic Community (or Common Market) to be held on June 5. Paul was opposed to the Common Market* ("I just happen to think the Common Market's a stupid idea"[44]), as he feared it would dilute the United Kingdom's national identity. He also said he disliked Britain's switch from imperial to metric measurements, a change adopted in 1965.

Off-topic discussions were usually gossip column fodder for music papers like *NME*, but by the end of their conversation Murray was convinced that he had captured on tape a colorful portrait of a rambling, insecure pop star that should be published in full. Now he just needed to convince his editor to print every last word of it.

---

* The United Kingdom European Communities membership referendum, on June 5, 1975, was a public vote on whether the United Kingdom should remain a member of the European Economic Community. The UK joined the EEC two and a half years earlier, on January 1, 1973. On June 5, 67 percent of voters backed continued membership and the UK remained a part of the Common Market.

"When I was with the Beatles every new product was put down," Paul insisted, bringing a not entirely accurate historical spin to his experience with Wings. "Everyone kept buying it, but nonetheless it was put down. I think it's the same with Wings. But we're going to prove them all wrong again. We've got a tight little band here, and what's better than that is we've got nothing to prove. We make the music we like, and we hope the public likes it too. If they do, we're happy with our day's work."[45]

Paul often used self-deprecation as a tool to deflect criticism. But he was not fooling anybody. Even after 17 albums—from the Beatles' *Please Please Me* to Wings' *Venus and Mars*—he still cared deeply about how his music was received by both the press and the public. And having consumed Wings' sax-steeped entrée, the critics sank their teeth into the main course. Reviews of *Venus and Mars* were mixed, their tone perhaps best captured by Chris Welch in a largely positive review for *Melody Maker*.

"When an artist has just enjoyed a great success with a piece of creative work, there is often a problem in evaluating the next item on the agenda. Comparisons spring all readily to mind, anticipation is keen, and the tendency is to expect fresh miracles. Well, Paul McCartney's triumph with *Band on the Run*, which gave birth to hit singles as well as achieving its own artistic and commercial acclaim, crept up on us rather than making instant impact. And I think the same will be true of *Venus and Mars*. In repeated playing over the past week, new twists, different interpretations have become apparent, and this new collection of songs will eventually sink into the collective rock consciousness and become widely appreciated as another triumph for Wings and their songwriting bass player."[46]

Mike Flood, writing for *Sounds*, conveyed the same critical conundrum. "No way can you hear this album without making reference to *Band on the Run*, and that is where the trouble starts." Flood admired the production and performance, but unlike Welch, who noted 'Rock Show' and 'Listen to What the Man Said' among the album's highlights, and 'You Gave Me the Answer' and 'Crossroads'* as low points, he was unmoved by McCartney's new songs. "McCartney's in a class of his own given the right material," Flood concluded, "but something is lacking here. I suspect it's heart."[47]

Other critics were wholly positive in their analyses. Setting aside both preconceptions and

* The inclusion of a television theme on the album confused many reviewers. But ITV was so flattered that Wings chose to record a cover of Hatch's theme that the producers adopted the recording over the show's end credits from June 26. Not everyone was a fan, though. On August 10, one viewer wrote a letter to the *Sunday People*, remonstrating: "HELP! Please bring back the old version of the *Crossroads* theme tune. The one by Paul McCartney sounds like a chorus of old cats."

comparisons with other McCartney projects, *Record Mirror*'s Ray Fox-Cumming wrote that "of the 13 tracks only three are anything less than brilliant!,"[48] while *Disc*'s Rosemary Horide declared: "I love this album! A chart topper no doubt."[49]

At *Rolling Stone*, which had abandoned its longstanding Lennon-vs.-McCartney agenda to acknowledge the quality of *Band on the Run*, *Venus and Mars* reignited the pro-Lennon, anti-McCartney torch in spectacular fashion.

"None of the ex-Beatles has survived the first half of the Seventies heroically," Paul Nelson declared near the start of his two-page evisceration of McCartney's latest work. "George Harrison has become a musical Kahlil Gibran, Ringo Starr, a likably mediocre Everyman, Lennon, the consumed method actor unsure of what role to play, and McCartney, a latter-day Burt Bacharach trying to invent his Angie Dickinson—but, of the four, only Lennon's plight still reaches the rock & roll part of the heart."

Lennon, Nelson argued, could have saved McCartney from delivering an album of "computerized smoothness" and "insubstantial songs" with the "dumbest lyrics on record." Like Mike Flood, Nelson felt that the songs lacked depth and sincerity. "The McCartneys serve it all up with the offhand air of two uncaring jet-setters presenting us with the very latest in prefabricated TV dinners," Nelson opined, declaring the album a manifestation of "Paul and Linda's chic, unconvincing and blatant bid to be enshrined as pop music's Romeo and Juliet."[50]

Critical brickbats had little bearing on the record's commercial success, though. In May, *Billboard* reported that *Venus and Mars* had advance worldwide sales of 1.5 million (including 170,000 in Britain and 105,000 in Japan), and upon its release in America, on May 30, the album was already Gold certified. It entered the *Billboard* 200 on June 14 at No. 25, and hit the top spot on July 19; the same week, 'Listen to What the Man Said' topped *Billboard's* singles chart. In total, it spent 77 weeks in the *Billboard* 200, its run extended into 1977.

In Britain, where the record was issued on June 6, *Venus and Mars* enjoyed a healthy 29-week run in the Top 100, entering at No. 3 on June 21 and peaking at No. 1 twice—June 28 and July 19. By then, Paul's sixth post-Beatles LP was the No. 1 record in four countries: the United States, France, Japan and Britain.

The recording and promotion of Wings' fourth album left Paul drained, so just before his thirty-third birthday, he took Linda and the girls to the south of France for a head-clearing two-week vacation. Paul was unusually subdued, his songwriting engine powered down as he digested a book of press clippings and pondered his plans for Wings' world tour. *Venus and Mars* was selling well, but criticism always affected Paul's equilibrium. It was up to Linda to drag him out of a morass of self-doubt.

"He likes positive thinking," Linda explained. "He blossoms when he's around positive people. Negative people get a bit on his back. It's so easy, isn't it, with somebody who's written as many songs as him, to actually say, 'Oh, he's no good.' I mean, I just don't see how you can say it. But it's easy. It's easy to put down anybody. He's very self-critical. He is not like a person who thinks, 'I am great. No matter what they say, I am great. Look what I've done. I have it in me.' No, he doesn't have that much confidence in that way."[51]

There was validation from elsewhere, too. At a ceremony in New York on June 14, four of McCartney's songs—'Yesterday,' 'You Won't See Me,' 'Band on the Run,' and 'Jet'—were awarded Citations of Achievement by BMI. The Eastmans attended the awards dinner on Paul's behalf.

The holiday in France was also an opportunity to mitigate the effects of three months of State-side overindulgence that left Paul worrying that he was developing a dad-bod, a pudginess that was neither flattering nor healthy, particularly with an extended tour looming. So the vacation became a sort of pre-tour bootcamp, with ample exercise intended to sharpen his mind and trim his waistline.

"A grueling tour is a bit like being a boxer, you have another bout coming,"[52] he explained, using his favorite sporting analogy. "We went on holiday and got really fit."[53]

For almost a year Brian Brolly had been working with carefully selected promoters—Mel Bush (Britain), Paul Dainty (Australia), Andrew Miller (International Entertainment Ltd., Europe) and Concerts West alongside Jim Guercio's Caribou Management (USA)—to plan a world tour that would begin in small concert halls in Britain and end in 65,000-capacity sports arenas in America. But other than a proposed list of dates and venues, every other aspect of the tour was still up in the air, including staging, lighting and sound design.

When casual rehearsals began at the Regent Cinema in Rye, at the end of April, several English firms were invited to build custom PA systems and monitoring equipment for the band to try out. But while the PAs often made the grade, monitoring (the on-stage speakers that allow heavily amplified musicians to hear themselves) was always a problem. So Paul decided to play sonic sleuth. In late spring he and Linda attended concerts at a wide range of venues, from theaters to sports stadiums, making notes along the way about audio quality, staging and lighting design. The acts they saw included Frank Sinatra (London Palladium, May 30), Elton John (Wembley Stadium, June 21) and Bob Marley (July 18, Lyceum Theatre).

But one concert stood head and shoulders above the rest, sonically: Led Zeppelin at Earl's Court on May 25, the finale of a five-concert run, during which Zeppelin played a three-hour, 20-song set, including a three-song acoustic segment. Comparing Wings (a group unashamed to put out a nursery rhyme as a single) to Led Zeppelin was like comparing a comfy pullover with a studded leather suit, but just as the Bowie concert in Nashville had turned Paul on to the appeal of a live horn section, watching one of Britain's premier rock groups up close was eye-opening.

"The basis for our [1975–76] show was a Led Zeppelin concert we saw in London,"[54] Paul happily acknowledged. "We in Wings felt a little small-time, or 'Bush League' as the Americans would say, especially compared with other bands like Led Zeppelin who had been together for a long time. But I felt we had better get up there with them. We had to get a reputation, to show our faces, let people know who we were and dare to do it. And do it big. And commit everything."[55] *

The musical tautness of Zeppelin's 180-minute performance aside, Paul was particularly impressed with the band's sound and lighting production. Only a decade earlier, when Paul had performed at Shea Stadium with the Beatles, the band's performance was piped through the ballpark's tinny PA, which was no match for the incessantly screaming audience. Led Zeppelin's listeners had the benefit of a rich, full-bodied sound, as well as theatrical lighting, both thanks to systems built by Showco, a Dallas, Texas–based company founded in 1970 by musician and businessman Jack Calmes, mechanical engineer and part-time bass player Rusty Brutsche, and studio sound engineer Jack Maxson.

"What we were trying to do was not in the realm of the industry at the time," Brutsche said about why he and his partners founded Showco. "It was an industry where it was public address and their idea of a system was 10 watts, designed for a vocal at a basketball game or something like that. The idea of loud music, and loud amplifiers, there just wasn't any industry at all. So we decided that we would just wing it using Jack's experience as a recording engineer, and mine as a musician who built the stuff and played with it. And so we got the JBL catalog out—JBL at that time sold components, so you could buy individual speakers, you could buy cabinets—and we built a big system. It was a lot of trial and error, and we blew a lot of things up as we learned how to do things."[56]

Five years on, Showco was one of the biggest sound and lighting companies in America, with a client list that included the Rolling Stones, Led Zeppelin and David Bowie. Within weeks of the Zeppelin concert, MPL contracted the Texas-based firm to design and build a custom sound rig for Wings' upcoming tour. Jack Maxson offered to personally deliver the system to Elstree Studios, where Paul and Wings were set to begin formal rehearsals in the second week of July.

The McCartneys spent the July Fourth weekend with the Eastmans in East Hampton. Evenings, Paul and Linda slipped out to the local cinema to catch a handful of movies, including Robert Altman's musical drama *Nashville* and Steven Spielberg's killer shark thriller *Jaws*. During the day Paul

* Paul was not the only one inspired by the concert. After seeing Jimmy Page on stage that night with a twin-neck (6- and 12-string) guitar, Denny Laine invested in an Ibanez twin-neck guitar, which he used during Wings' 1975–76 world tour.

continued to hone his fitness levels off the coast of Long Island. "We saw *Jaws* on July 3," said Paul, "so the next day we were swimming cautiously."[57]

By mid-July the family was back in England, where they abandoned Rye for their home at Cavendish Avenue. A start date for Wings' tour—September 9 at the Gaumont Theatre in Southampton—had been confirmed but not announced, and on July 14, the five musicians traveled to EMI-Elstree Studios in north London to start arranging their live act. For nearly two months a soundstage at Hangar 6—a giant space surrounded by a wilderness of weeds—became Wings' temporary home. Rehearsals ran four hours a day, five days a week.

The first order of business was testing the custom 12,000-watt RMS, 30-input PA system—the most powerful and complex ever assembled for a touring act—that had been designed and manufactured at Showco's Dallas base and shipped to London. To satisfy the band's complex monitoring demands, Showco also prepared a 30-input, 11,000-watt RMS monitoring system. Sound engineers Jack Maxson, Craig Schertz, and Morris Lyda oversaw the delivery of the 12.5-ton Showco rig.

"Showco blessed me with a monitor system that was so powerful," monitoring engineer Lyda remembered. "Paul would tell you when he was happy, and if it changed much, he was unhappy. He wanted consistency. If something changed in the mix, he could hear it, because on the stage, they were amidst four big speakers [suspended] in the air, and then we had floor monitors scattered over the stage.

"The stage was so enormous that it was like a cloud of sound. And being in the midst of that must have been a pretty magical environment. I ventured into it only a few times because I dared not step away [from the mixing console], but it was always explosively right, and right on the edge. But anything that would change in that environment, Paul would notice and give me a look, or a hint that it needed to be readjusted. He didn't miss much when it came to audio."[58]

For Showco, the Wings tour promised to be a big payday. The US leg of the tour alone was a $453,500 (£214,820) contract, meaning the entire tour likely ran into the millions. With so much at stake, Calmes, Brutsche and Maxson did not leave anything to chance, assigning Maxson to oversee the tour from beginning to end. Lyda, too, became a permanent fixture, and having been around the block with some of the world's biggest acts, he found the inner workings of McCartney's group both fascinating and confusing.

"He was really the boss," Lyda observed. "There was really no question of who was in charge. And it wasn't a band in the same sense as the Band, or Genesis, or Pink Floyd—it was Paul McCartney and Wings.

"Linda, bless her cotton socks—I loved Linda to death, she had a heart of gold. She had some talent, she had really, really good coordination, and she was able to hit the right keys at the right times. Her rhythm was not bad. But she never was a musician.

"Joe the drummer mystically floated in and out of recognizing he had a job. Jimmy explained to me that he wanted to be a star, and he thought that was his launching platform, I guess. And he was a bit of a troublemaker. And Denny, I think in some respects, saw it as the only way he'd be on stage ever again. And all of them were very cooperative and participative, but when it came to suggesting what they were gonna do, it was all Paul running the show."[59]

Maxson's American sound crew was joined by four British technicians—Ted Sellen (drums), "Rocky" Morley (keyboards), John Hammel (guitars—all 37 of them) and Trevor Jones (chief roadie). On the lighting front, Showco's Kirby Wyatt and Alan Owen worked alongside Brits Ian "Iggy" Knight (show designer), Andy Collins, Ray Watouski, Derek Unwin and Ian Peacock.

Peacock, a 22-year-old Scotsman who grew up not far from Jimmy, was given a warm introduction to life in the Wings family. Standing at the side of the stage biting his nails on his first day, Peacock suddenly felt an arm reach over his shoulder as Linda plucked his hand out of his mouth. "Stop biting your nails," she said with warm motherly authority, "that's a terrible habit."

"I was responsible for putting up the stage set," Peacock explained. "And the stage set was beautiful, covered in black Plexiglas. The main floor was four-by-four squares of this hard, black shiny surface. Then there was a riser stage left upstage where the grand piano was, that was like three or four foot [high]. Linda had a riser stage left for keyboards. The drums were on a riser in the middle, and then the horn section had a riser stage right."[60]

Filmmakers Phil Mottram and Dick Spicer, who documented Wings' first rehearsals at the Institute of Contemporary Arts in February 1972, were hired to capture the latest chapter in McCartney's musical journey. As well as filming the five musicians shaping the live arrangements, Mottram and Spicer caught Paul in conversation with members of the technical crew, refining the lighting, sound and set design.

The first order of business at Elstree was to decide what songs should be polished further for the tour. *Venus and Mars*, an album written, sequenced and recorded with theatricality at its heart, provided a partial template for what became Wings' two-hour setlist. The opening lines of 'Venus and Mars': "*Sitting in the stand of the sports arena, waiting for the show to begin*," provided an obvious but fitting opening to the show, with the band—excepting Paul who stood in a spotlight—lost in a haze of dry ice. As on the album, it would lead into 'Rock Show,' another tune written with the stage in mind.

Filling out the rest of the setlist, and getting Joe and Jimmy up to speed on the numbers from before their tenure, took time. Rehearsals were further held up when Denny Laine was forced out of action for two weeks with a badly gashed finger.

"We did rehearse more than we've ever rehearsed for anything," said Paul, "because we just suddenly thought, well, we'd better know the numbers."[61]

By the end of July, the five musicians worked up live versions of 'Jet,' 'Let Me Roll It,' 'Little Woman Love/C Moon (Medley),' 'Maybe I'm Amazed,' 'Call Me Back Again,' 'Live and Let Die,' 'You Gave Me the Answer,' 'Magneto and Titanium Man,' 'My Love,' 'Listen to What the Man Said,' 'Letting Go,' 'Band on the Run,' 'Junior's Farm,' 'Hi, Hi, Hi,' and 'Soily' from Paul's post-Beatles songbook. Denny and Jimmy were each allowed time in the limelight with the inclusion of 'Spirits of Ancient Egypt,' 'Go Now' and 'Medicine Jar.'

"That was mainly at Paul's instigation," said Laine. "He didn't want the spotlight to be on him all the time. He was kind of sick of that. In Wings, he became the lead singer and that's it. And that was a lot on his shoulders, you know? So he wanted to bring us in to balance it out a little more."[62]

Paul's insistence that the group's live performances should perfectly match the LPs—the rigid attitude that contributed toward driving Henry McCullough out the door—remained firm.

"We took a lot of time taking the records apart and working out exactly what everyone should be singing," Paul explained. "When you're putting together the show, you think, 'Should we do the solos from the records? Or should we just ad-lib the solos and kind of just show how we can play?' But we decided that most of the people in the audience would like to hear the records exactly like the record, so Jimmy learned up a lot of the other solos."[63]

Replicating the records note-for-note also meant reproducing the horn and string sections, so Paul brought Tony Dorsey onboard to write the live arrangements, and hired a small horn section comprising saxophonist Howie Casey, multi-instrumentalist Thaddeus Richard (who had worked with such artists as Johnnie Taylor, Al Green and Paul Kelly), and trumpeter Steve Howard (who played on Labelle's *Nightbirds*, as well as on the New Orleans sessions for *Venus and Mars*), plus Dorsey on trombone. Paul's original plans, according to Dorsey, were even more ambitious.

"After we'd finished mixing in Los Angeles, Paul's manager talked to me about the idea of going on tour with Wings," said Dorsey. "He said hang loose for a while, don't make any commitments, so I relaxed for a few weeks and then he said they were putting a horn section together for the tour. At first it was going to be a big thing, 20 strings, plus a 12-piece horn section, but we got it down to six horns and four electric strings, which we had to drop as we couldn't get any string players. So it was just four horns in the end."[64]

Not having strings in the touring ensemble meant that Dorsey could take some liberties in his arrangements. In 'Yesterday,' the horn quartet hewed closely to George Martin's string quartet arrangement, although the change from string to wind and brass timbres gave the song a fresh edge. But in 'The Long and Winding Road,' Dorsey used elements of the Richard Hewson score heard on the *Let It Be* album but also included a solo turn for trumpeter Steve Howard. At first, Howard played a jazz-tinged solo, but by the end of the Elstree rehearsals, it evolved into an elegant, Baroque-influenced trumpet solo in the spirit of the one David Mason had played on 'Penny Lane.'

Paul did not drop strings from the live show completely, though. His Mellotron was preloaded with string samples, and if the sound was not that of a live string ensemble, it was a solid cost-saving alternative, so the Mellotron was added to Linda's keyboard rig, which already included a Hammond C3 organ, Hohner clavinet, ARP synthesizer, Minimoog synthesizer and Fender Rhodes electric piano.

All told, six songs—'Maybe I'm Amazed,' 'Live and Let Die,' 'You Gave Me the Answer,' 'Call Me Back Again,' 'My Love' and 'The Long and Winding Road'—required Mellotron samples. Paul and Linda agreed that she might benefit from some extra keyboard tuition to hone her speed and understanding of the instrument.

"Timing and syncopation I found very difficult. I just couldn't get it right," Linda said. "For the Mellotron arrangements I got a fellow named Fi, and Fi came around and showed me what the string arrangements would be on the keyboard. So I just practiced."[65]

Fi was the McCartneys' affectionate name for Fiachra Trench, an Irish musician and arranger who lived and worked in London. Trench, who also offered private piano tuition to supplement his income, was recommended to the McCartneys by David Katz, a violinist who EMI used as a contractor for orchestral sessions.

"Paul wrote to me in 1975 a request that I coach Linda on some keyboard stuff," said Trench. "He was writing parts to play on the Mellotron, which I suppose was string samples mostly. And actually, they had voice samples, Linda and Denny, and Paul's voices in blocks. So, I helped with that—not actually at a Mellotron, cos there wasn't one at the McCartney house in St. John's Wood, but on the piano; just you know, working with shapes and so forth. And she was an absolute delight to work with."[66]

Outside rehearsals, the band prepared for life on the road under one another's feet by hanging out after hours at Cavendish Avenue. Joe was still the McCartneys' houseguest, Jimmy lived close by in Maida Vale, and Denny spent the $100,000* (£41,590) bonus he received for his work on *Venus and Mars* and 'Listen to What the Man Said' on a house just around the corner from Paul and Linda, in St. John's Wood.

Laine's new status as a neighbor of the McCartneys had an unexpected effect on Wings' final setlist. Although George Harrison had been criticized for not playing "the hits" during his ill-fated 1974 Dark Horse tour, Paul remained unenthusiastic about performing Beatles tunes with Wings. It was Denny Laine, in the end, who persuaded him that he was making a mistake by not embracing his full songbook, past and present.

"One day I started playing 'I've Just Seen a Face' in Paul's back garden," Laine recalled, "and we decided to do it [on tour], simply based on that. We just could have done our songs alone, but

* Whether Jimmy and Joe received similar bonuses is unknown but (particularly in Joe's case) unlikely.

I wanted a selection. A lot of the time, and especially before this particular tour began, I've talked Paul into doing a lot of the Beatles stuff in the set. Things like 'Lady Madonna' and even 'Yesterday' were my ideas. He didn't particularly want to do it at first."[67]

Inspired by their backyard jams and Led Zeppelin's acoustic set at Earl's Court, the band developed an acoustic break made up of stripped-back versions of 'Picasso's Last Words (Drink to Me),' 'Bluebird' (played against a repeating beat pattern from a Roland Rhythm 77), 'I've Just Seen a Face,' 'Blackbird,' 'Yesterday' and Laine's rendering of the Simon and Garfunkel song 'Richard Cory.'

Denny's argument in favor of including some Beatles songs prevailed because the time was right: with *Band on the Run*, Paul had achieved the popular and critical success he craved as a solo artist, rather than as a former Beatle, and by refusing to play Beatles songs until now, he had made his point. Besides the Beatles tunes in the acoustic set, 'Lady Madonna' and 'The Long and Winding Road' were given the Macca thumbs-up. By late July, the show was starting to take shape.

—

Returning from Elstree on July 24, Paul unwrapped a package of newspapers waiting for him in the hallway at Cavendish Avenue. He had been warned by Tony Brainsby that Charles Shaar Murray, the journalist he had spoken with two months earlier at Greek Street, had written a lengthy, belated putdown of *Venus and Mars* for the latest edition of *NME*. But nothing could prepare Paul for the relentlessness of Murray's assault.

Murray's piece, titled "The Raps of Wacky Macca" with the subtitle, "What can a person such as myself say to an ex-Beatle who's made a crappy album?" spanned five pages and danced over the line of objective critique.

> *Venus and Mars* is . . . a terrible album.
>
> "McCARTNEY CAN make albums like *Band on the Run* anytime he wants to," claims a former associate of the Wings operation. "*Venus and Mars* is what he's actually into, though. He likes writing songs for his kids."
>
> *Venus and Mars* is not only one of the worst albums I've ever heard from a so-called "Major artist," but it's also the most decadent. Sure, it's got nothing to do with heroin or homosexuality or make-up or any of the other stuff that we used to think of as being "decadent" when we were young(er) and dumb(er) back in '72, but it goes much deeper than that.
>
> *Venus and Mars* is a symptom of decadence because it is the product of a considerable talent in an advanced stage of decay. It is totally lacking in either true beauty, true strength or true innocence; offering in the stead of these qualities—qualities which one could quite reasonably

demand from the work of an artist of Paul McCartney's eminence—a vapid, shallow prettiness which is ultimately more saddening than the work of even the dumbest no-hoper.

It's the whole lilies-that-fester syndrome: basically, nobody gives a shit if someone they've never heard of unloads a turkey because it's just another bad album. For someone of McCartney's level/status/importance to deliberately trivialize his talent is something of a blow.

The record review was not the worst of it. Murray went on to recount their entire conversation verbatim, including stumbles and superfluous words (like "umm," "y'know" and "really") that writers normally edit out. Very little of the piece touched on *Venus and Mars*, but rather captured journalist and superstar discussing drugs ("I don't take drugs at all. I categorically state—are you getting all this, tape?—that I do not take drugs"), British politics and bubblegum popstars like the Bay City Rollers and Donny Osmond ("The Bay City Rollers—I think that's all good, that stuff. I like those bands for the younger kids. . . . I even like the Osmonds for what they do"[68]).

Murray's low opinion of *Venus and Mars* came as no surprise to Paul; Murray had made that clear during their discussion. But by the time he finished reading, Paul was incensed.*

"One criticism started, 'How do you tell an ex-Beatle he has made a lousy album?'" Paul complained. "For weeks I didn't buy that paper. Let's face it, you have to do something to get back at them because they have got ultimate power. You can't write in the next week saying you don't agree, because you have then given them more copy and it makes it much worse. You know it's not true, but they say it and you end up wondering whether it is. Every time I make a record it takes me about three months before I can listen to it."[69]

Caught in the crossfire of Paul's fury was his 15-year-old stepsister, Ruth McCartney. Ruth—an aspiring dancer—was visiting London to make her television debut as a backing dancer for Mike McGear, who had just issued the quirky 'Dance the Do' as a single. Ruth was rehearsing with a dance troupe for Kid Jenson's ITV show *Rock on With 45* at a studio in Golders Green—just a few tube stops north of St. John's Wood—and decided to drop in on Paul and Linda to share her news.

Though the McCartney blood did not flow through Ruth's veins, Paul had generally treated her as an older brother would, with affection and protection. That all changed when he put down *NME* to answer the doorbell.

"When I called on Paul at Cavendish Avenue, I expect I blurted out all my good news in one gulp," Ruth recalled. "At any rate, my happiness must have been plain to see. My stepbrother didn't even smile. He launched into a long and stern lecture, painting the blackest possible picture of a show business career.

* Of all the bad press McCartney has received over the years, Murray's article got under his skin more than most. On May 26, 2016—some 41 years after the review was published—McCartney referred to Charles Shaar Murray specifically when discussing press criticism in an interview for the BBC series *Mastertapes*.

Trade ad for Wings' concerts in Britain and Australia

"There wasn't a word of encouragement for my efforts. Just a stream of destructive condemnation which brought a lump to my throat. I said, forcing back the first tears, 'Paul, I thought you would be happy for me. I thought you might give me some advice.' He said something like, 'You don't really think an important television producer would be bothering with you or your dancing if your name was not McCartney, do you?' I came away from Cavendish Avenue with the incredible impression that Paul did not want another McCartney to succeed in show business, at any level.

"I was firmly convinced by what he said that my own stepbrother, one of the most famous superstars the world of pop music has ever known, disliked the idea of another member of his family following in his footsteps, however far behind."[70]

The truth was more complex. Before reading Murray's article, the *Rolling Stone* review had already crept under Paul's skin and self-doubt had taken hold. Just five weeks before the tour was set to begin, the weight of expectation was playing on Paul's mind, and unlike the days of Beatlemania, when that weight was spread across eight shoulders, now it was on his alone.

"I've come home from rehearsals with Wings and just got the terrible feeling, it's not right," he confessed. "God, we could do so much more. We've got to get a producer. But I just have to say to myself, 'Get a grip on yourself, son—Don't think *that*. You're doing okay.'"[71]

10

BAND ON THE ROAD

Wings' British tour was scheduled to begin in Southampton on September 9, but on August 15—just three weeks until the opening chords would be struck—Tony Brainsby was still scrambling to get the publicity materials together. He planned to announce the tour on Monday, August 18, with local advertising set to run on August 20, followed by a wave of ads in the music press, starting on August 30. But he still lacked crucial materials, so on August 15 he sent an urgent plea directly to Paul: "We desperately need rehearsal photos to go with the release," he wrote, "as many different ones as possible."[1]

The next day Robert Ellis was dispatched to Elstree to spend the weekend photographing the band in action. He also took a series of profile photos to be used both as publicity handouts and in the program books.

Everything was printed and assembled with hardly a moment to spare. Brainsby distributed his press packets on Monday as scheduled, announcing a 13-date tour that would take Wings to venues in England, Wales and Scotland, including the Gaumont Theatre, Southampton (September 9); the Hippodrome, Bristol (September 10); Capitol Theatre, Cardiff (September 11); Free Trade Hall, Manchester (September 12); the Hippodrome, Birmingham (September 13); the Empire Theatre, Liverpool (September 15); City Hall, Newcastle (September 16); the Hammersmith Odeon, London (September 17 and 18); Usher Hall, Edinburgh (September 20); the Apollo, Glasgow (September 21); the Capitol Theatre, Aberdeen (September 22); and Caird Hall, Dundee (September 23).

At a time when the Rolling Stones and Elton John were entertaining crowds in excess of 100,000, some journalists were quick to question Paul's choice of modest halls and theaters. But he offered a simple explanation.

"In England," he said, "you can play certain special halls, but the normal venues in England are like 3,000. You just go to a town to play—unless you're playing in London—and play to about 3,000 people, and that's just about the right kind of thing. So very naturally we started off with the 3,000 people, and then we went to kind of 5,000 and 6,000. . . . For me, I like things like that. I like things step-by-step; you know. Maybe I'm square. Seems like the easiest way and I always go for the easiest way."[2]

Paul was also accused of hiding behind the name Wings. During their last British tour the group was billed as Paul McCartney and Wings, to the chagrin of his bandmates. For McCartney the promotional shift to just "Wings" had partly to do with his pushing the idea of Wings as a band. But there was also a current of deep-seated insecurity.

"It was a bit lonely [after the Beatles broke up]," he confessed. "You get very aware that the pressure's on you all the time, and it's nice to be able to spread it a bit.[3] The first stage appearance I ever made was at Butlins when I was 11 and I went up with my guitar and sang 'Long Tall Sally.' But I had to haul our Mike up on stage with me, although he had a broken arm in plaster and was just wailing along with me. Maybe I'm shy or something, but I work better with someone else on stage with me. To me I don't care what the band's called."[4]

The 30,000 tickets for Wings' British concerts were modestly priced, at £1.00–£2.80 ($2.10–$5.90), and they sold out quickly. And the crowds were not entirely local. One fan, Cindy Rosenthal, traveled 7,000 miles from her home in San Diego, California, to see Paul perform, and she was not alone: a delegation of nine fans from points all across America—Rosenthal, Marie Lacey, Ken Krinski, Barb Fenick, George Tebbens, Mary Ann Dolphin, Doylene Kindsvater, Lyndsey Vikios and Madeline Schatz—flew over to catch all 13 shows on the British tour.

Announcing the concerts, Brainsby also offered a look ahead. The shows would be the first leg of a planned world tour that would reach Australia and Japan by the end of 1975, and the United States in the spring of 1976.* He also noted that Wings planned to release a new single—'Letting Go,' coupled with 'You Gave Me the Answer'—on September 5, and that both songs would be included in the band's two-hour set.

For the single, a freshly remixed edit was created by Alan Parsons at EMI Studios on August 20. Nearly a minute of the song was trimmed, including 19 seconds of the intro. More strikingly, Paul's organ part, which had been recorded during the original London session but dropped when the song was mixed in Los Angeles, was restored during the shortened intro. Parsons also reduced the bass, using only the direct-injection feed Paul recorded straight into the console, and he reduced the reverb on the vocals and lead guitar. 'Letting Go' and 'You Gave Me the Answer' were sent for mastering and assigned the matrix numbers 7YCE.21771 and 7YCE.21772.

If dropping a second single from *Venus and Mars*—an LP released four months earlier—was meant to keep Wings flying high in the charts and dominating the airwaves as they took off on tour, it did

* A report in the Random Notes column in *Rolling Stone*, on September 11, claimed that McCartney had originally planned to tour the United States in the fall of 1975, but that the tour was postponed because the band had not applied for work visas in time. A Capitol Records spokesperson is quoted saying, implausibly, that the band "were so busy rehearsing" that they forgot to apply.

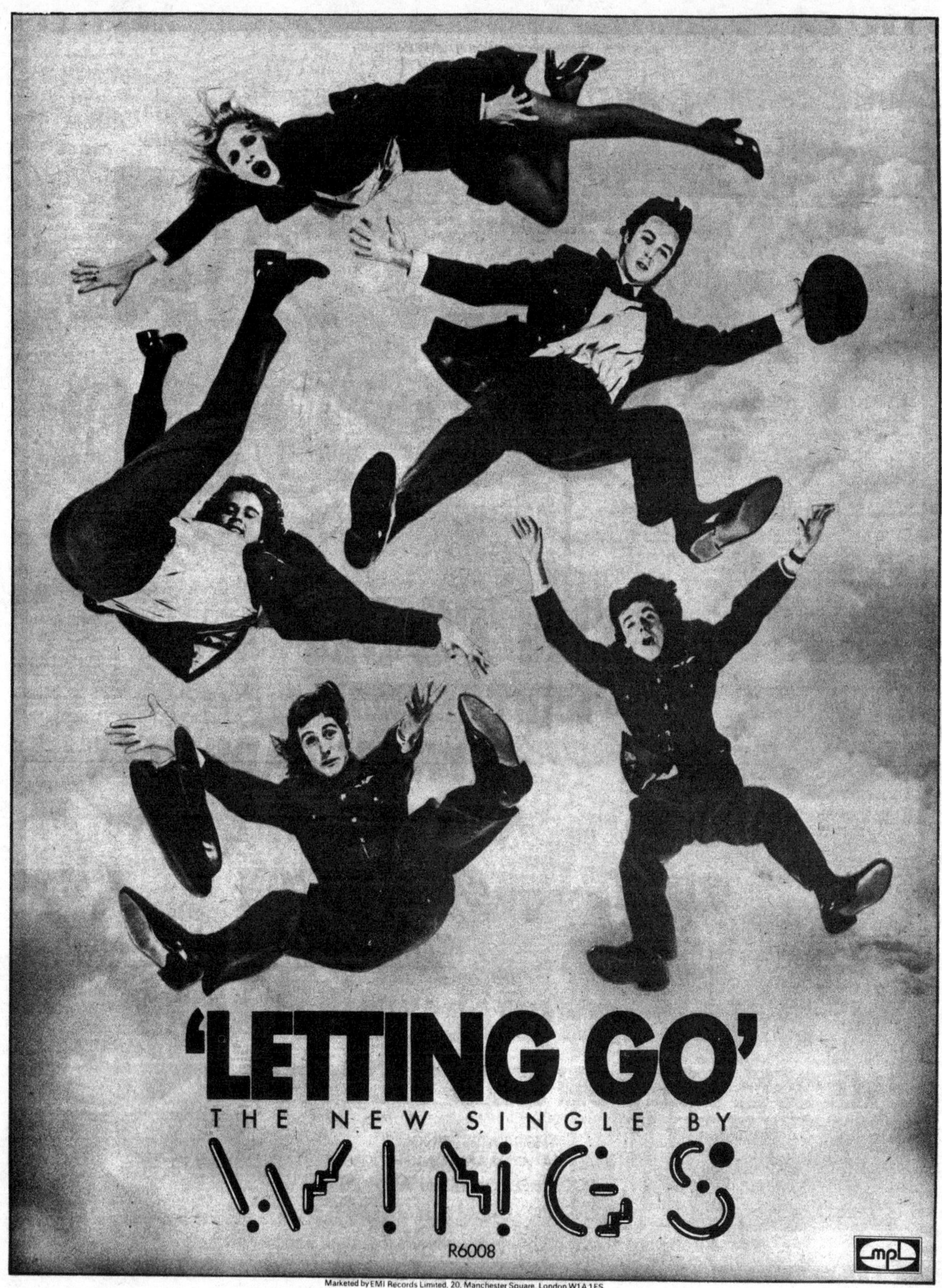

'LETTING GO'
THE NEW SINGLE BY
WINGS
R6008
mpl
Marketed by EMI Records Limited, 20, Manchester Square, London W1A 1ES

Defying gravity—Wings, 'Letting Go' single trade ad

not quite work out that way. First, the single's release was postponed a week, but when MPL realized that George Harrison's new single, 'You,' was due in the UK on September 19, 'Letting Go' was delayed until September 19 in the United States and October 3—after the tour wound up—in Britain.

'Letting Go' managed just three weeks in the British Top 100, peaking at No. 41 on October 25, becoming Paul's worst-performing post-Beatles single. The single also bombed in America, where McCartney's solo work usually enjoyed greater commercial success. After entering the *Billboard* Hot 100 at No. 74, on October 4, it peaked at No. 39 four weeks later, and dropped off the chart after six weeks.

Reviewing the single for *Record Mirror & Disc** in an issue where Bob Marley and the Wailer's 'No Woman, No Cry' was the single of the week, Sue Byrom was quick to note the problem.

> *Taken from* Venus and Mars, *this single is being released to coincide with the start of Wings' second UK tour, the first in two years. Driving bass line, and those familiar rising chorus lines, it's a firm favorite for those who already have the album. And speaking of which, so many people have the album, will there be enough people to buy the single and make it the hit it should be?*[5]
>
> *Sue Byrom,* Record Mirror & Disc

> *Wings themselves are on sale again—this time with 'Letting Go,' from the justly-castigated* Venus and Mars *ticket. Everything you've read about it is true and it will thus be a minor hit.*[6]
>
> *Ian MacDonald,* NME

> *Not one of the most memorable tracks from* Venus and Mars *released hastily to coincide with Macca's tour which opens this week. A low, lurching ballad in strict tempo with bluesy overtones but pretty monotonous after a few hearings. The superhuman success of* Band on the Run *and the three singles that were pulled from that album has obviously given EMI the idea to try their luck again, but I can't see it happening with this weaker material. A minor hit.*[7]
>
> *Chris Charlesworth,* Melody Maker

The next item on the pre-tour checklist was dealing with the press. Terry Pritchard, EMI's regional promotion manager, sent memos to promoters around the country on August 21, noting that "Wings Over Britain" was "the most important tour this year, and it is imperative that ev-

* *Record Mirror* and *Disc* merged in September 1975 becoming *Record Mirror & Disc.*

erything from the Regional Promotion aspect runs like clockwork." Pritchard promised window displays and radio promos, to be recorded by Paul, and he offered a total of eight press tickets at each stop—one ticket, not pairs, for every reviewer—as well as four tickets for contest giveaways.

Paul would be happy to do interviews, Pritchard continued, but the schedule was tight, so he suggested a daily one-hour interview slot (between 1 and 2 P.M.) for all requests, with the possibility of post-concert interviews backstage. And with a stunning lack of insight into how journalists work, he suggested that promoters "devise, along with your most original disc jockey and journalist, some unique approach to an interview with Paul." He also offered some insultingly tone-deaf advice to be passed along to reporters unwilling to ask questions handed to them by promoters:

> Let's try to avoid the "how did you start in the business" routine; and "will you and the Beatles get back together again?" Apart from the fact that it's dead boring, it's all been said a hundred times before![8]

For most journalists, the suggestion was the kind of effrontery that all but guaranteed that Beatles questions would be asked—or, in some cases, that the restriction itself would be ridiculed. "Publicity men warn prospective interviewers that mentioning his former group 'makes him cross,'" Wendy Hughes wrote in the *Sunday Times*, later noting that "despite his publicity men's strictures the subject somehow crept in"[9] when Paul brought it up himself.

Still, enterprising journalists like Chris Welch from *Melody Maker* were able to negotiate special access. Welch, whose coverage of Wings had been generally (but not exclusively) supportive, arranged for a three-day berth on Wings' bus—a proper modern touring coach, with a kitchen, toilets, a television and a bar—starting after the second show, in Bristol, in order to write a two-part feature chronicling the band's time on the road.

Local presenters also received a two-page directive from Alan Crowder covering security issues (everything from how telephone calls to the band were to be handled and how backstage passes were to be distributed to the importance of preventing "theater staff or hangers-on" from attending the soundchecks), and detailing the band's backstage requirements:

> **FOOD:**
>
> - Paul and Linda don't really like meat.
> - Heavy emphasis on salads. Also like cheeses, fruit, fried chicken, potato chips. Tomato ketchup and pickles.

- Coca cola, spring water, fresh orange juice, one bottle Johnny Walker Red Label whisky. Lots of ICE.
- Kettle, teapot, etc. for orange pekoe tea.
- Denny, Jimmy and Joe like cold meats, salads, fruit, cheese, potato chips.
- Beers, Coca cola and one bottle of whisky. Lots of ice.
- The horn section (4) like seafoods especially shellfish. Three of them do not like meat, one does. They all like cheeses, salads, fruit.
- One bottle of whisky, Coca cola, beer and Ice.

ENTERTAINMENT:

- Dartboard (and darts), playing cards, magazines.

GENERAL:

- It is essential that all dressing rooms should be heated when necessary.
- Most important that the dressing rooms are covered by security at all times, especially when the band are on stage.[10]

MPL made its own contribution to keeping the band and crew entertained. A collection of recent films and projection equipment was rented for post-concert screenings.

For Paul and Linda, the children were another consideration. From Wings' earliest touring days, Paul and Linda had made a point of bringing Heather, Mary and Stella with them, and they intended to continue doing so. But during the 1972 and 1973 tours, Mary and Stella were preschoolers, and because Wings touring was limited to Britain and Europe—the latter taking place during the summer—it was not difficult to ensure that Heather kept up with her school work.

But now Heather was nearly 13, Mary was 6 and Stella was 4—nursery school age—and Wings would be away for extended periods in places as distant as Australia and America.

"We had decided our policy in the early days," Paul said. "We had children, we wanted to tour, what to do? We had long talks with teachers and other people about it, and the consensus seemed to be that we shouldn't remove them from school, that it would make life too unstable for them. Our reaction was, 'Yes, but what happens if we're in Australia and somebody rings up to say that one of the kids has a fever of 103 degrees?' Get back quick from Australia? So we just said, 'No, we're a close family, we've got to take them with us. Whether it's a good thing or not, we want to be with them.' We just felt that it was right."

Several people around Paul and Linda recommended sending the girls to a boarding school, but that was a nonstarter: besides wanting the children with them, the idea of boarding school went against Paul's working-class grain. Instead, he explained, "we hired tutors and encouraged them to find out what the children were learning at school and to continue the same work. Obviously it

Paul and Stella talk news, Linda relaxes; taken during the British tour, September 17, 1975

wasn't as good as them actually staying in school, but they all went on to do better academically than Linda and me."[11]

Recording Session

Thursday, August 28, 1975.
Olympic Studios, London.
Recording: 'Beware My Love.'

The adrenaline of preparing to go out on tour again got Paul's creative juices flowing, and in late August he came up with an idea for a song—'Beware My Love,' a dark-hued rocker tailor-made for an emotive growl. Its lyrics were not quite finished, but he had several verses that address a woman who is attracted to someone the singer believes will do her harm. He would have time to beat the lyrics into shape, but for the moment, he wanted to get a draft on tape.

One problem: Joe English had returned to the States for a long weekend to visit family before the start of the tour. But Paul and Linda ran into their pal Bonzo from Led Zeppelin and invited him to the session.

"John Bonham was a good friend of mine, and I was a great admirer of his," Paul said of the drummer. "So I hooked up with him that one time and said, 'Fancy recording something? I've got this song.' So we just went into the studio. . . . I got on the piano and did 'Beware My Love' and he thrashed his drums."[12]

With Phil Chapman engineering and Nigel Brooke-Harte assisting, Bonham settled in behind the kit as Paul took his seat at the piano. Jimmy McCulloch played bass, Denny Laine played electric guitar, and Linda played both Moog and ARP synthesizers set for an organ-like sound. As Linda put it, "I'd play ARP on my left hand and Moog on my right hand, but Paul showed me what he wanted."[13]

Using a version of the verse chords as an introduction, the band kicked right into the song, which at this point started with the verse "*Beware, my love / he'll bowl you over / Beware, my love / Before you're much older.*" After an instrumental verse, dominated by Paul's piano, Paul sang a verse he would soon delete because it broke away from the format he had established: "*Take my regards / And don't forget it / Beware, my love / And never regret it.*"

Throughout, Bonham's drum part was less to do with power than fine detail: a tightly focused cymbal figure accompanies the intro section (which returns on Paul's shouted cue, "*Intro!*" after the second verse), and when he deploys the rest of the kit, he follows the rhythmic accents of the vocal line.

Paul's rough vocal hints at the variety he might bring to the song when the time came for the finished performance, some verses nuanced with a touch of vibrato, others with a brusque, bluesy sound. Linda essentially traced the chord progression, while Paul's piano performance channeled Jerry Lee Lewis, with repeated chords and ascending and descending glissandos. Denny contributed a tentative lead guitar line, sometimes with a wah-wah pedal, that must have had Jimmy wondering why he was stuck playing a simple but solid bass part.

Three days later, Paul brought the tape to EMI Studios and made a rough mix.

Joe returned for a final week of rehearsals leading up to a dress rehearsal on September 6, during which the band played the full 29-song set for an invited audience of 900, among them EMI brass, friends, family, 100 members of the Wings Fun Club and a handful of celebrities, including Ringo Starr, Elton John, Dave Mason and Twiggy.

Some of the setlist had been determined from the start: the show was always going to open with 'Venus and Mars' and 'Rock Show,' and the acoustic set would take place around the halfway point. The positions of other songs were juggled during the weeks of rehearsals, but now McCartney had a running order he felt worked.

The energy and drive of 'Rock Show' would be maintained with 'Jet,' which would follow without a break, and 'Let Me Roll It.' The quirky 'Spirits of Ancient Egypt,' Denny's first vocal showcase, lightened the mood somewhat; then it was time for a glance backward, by way of the 'Little Woman Love/C Moon medley,' 'Maybe I'm Amazed' and the set's first two Beatles tunes, 'Lady Madonna' and 'The Long and Winding Road.' Jimmy would take the spotlight for 'Medicine Jar' before the first part of the show ended with the punchy, hard-rocking 'Soily.'

At that point, wicker chairs would be brought to center stage and Paul, Denny and Jimmy would switch to acoustic guitars, with Linda and Joe on hand for light percussion and vocal harmonies. They would play six songs in this configuration: the stripped-down 'Picasso's Last Words (Drink to Me),' with Denny singing the opening lines and Paul taking over later, then over to Denny for 'Richard Cory,' back to Paul for 'Bluebird' and three more Beatles classics: 'I've Just Seen a Face,' 'Blackbird,' which Paul would play alone, and 'Yesterday,' in which he was accompanied only by the horns.

The full band would return to their electric instruments for 'You Gave Me the Answer,' 'Magneto and Titanium Man,' and Denny's final vocal spot, 'Go Now,' after which the band would raise the temperature with 'Junior's Farm,' 'Letting Go' and 'Live and Let Die,' complete with a pyrotechnic display—and then dial it back with the bluesy 'Call Me Back Again,' and the smoochy balladry of 'My Love.' 'Listen to What the Man Said' and 'Band on the Run' closed the show, with Wings' celebration of sex, drugs and rock and roll, 'Hi, Hi, Hi,' as an encore.

Opinions of the Elstree dress rehearsal show vary. "[Paul] actually brought in an audience," lighting technician Ian Peacock said, "and it seemed like everybody was having fun."[14] Morris Lyda remembered the rehearsals and concert at Elstree as being "inspiring."[15]

Paul disagreed. "I thought we were terrible," he said of the Elstree preview. "Everyone was nervous. I swear, our trombone player, Tony Dorsey, who is black, went white. Nothing could be as bad again as that night."[16]

Denny offered a more forgiving analysis. "I thought we were a bit over-rehearsed. We had to be well rehearsed because we are going to be taking this band everywhere, so we wanted to make sure everybody knew exactly what each other was playing. We don't want the band to be that rigid, but it had to be like that to start with."[17]

After the concert, Elton John threw a birthday party for his manager, John Reid, on another of Elstree's soundstages. Paul and Linda stopped in, but left early. The next night, they caught Dave Mason's show at the Hammersmith Odeon.

On Tuesday, September 9, the band left London at noon and arrived at Southampton in the early afternoon, giving them time to check into the Polygon Hotel and relax for a few hours before the 5 P.M. soundcheck. Not that it was a restful afternoon for everyone. Watching the band's equipment being unloaded, Howie Casey looked on in horror as one of the roadies adopted a perilous approach to moving the wind and brass instruments.

"He's carrying them all in, stacked on top of one another," Casey recalled, "and my sax is on the top. Of course, it fell off. It went wallop, hit the ground. It was in its case, but it didn't matter: when I opened it, it was damaged. Paul got annoyed, but he said, 'We'll sort this out.' Brian Brolly called an instrument shop in London, and they sent down a Selmer Mark VI, which I used, and the other was sent off for repair."[18]

If Paul had any last-minute misgivings, it was about the acoustic set, and he openly confessed to some insecurity about the prospect of singing 'Yesterday' on his own.

"At first I thought, 'Oh, God. I've never done it before. Never sat in front of all these people and just played on my own, I'm going to be so nervous.'" But he was quick to remind himself that this was not his first rodeo. "I suddenly realized I'd played it in front of forty million people on the *Ed Sullivan Show* once, so I thought well it's mad, you know, why don't I just get up there and do it again."[19]

Nerves aside, the concert proceeded without hitches, the songs given tight, solid performances, with Paul ad-libbing introductions and adding odd snippets of music here and there. At the start of the acoustic set, for example, he sang the opening line of the Frank Ifield hit 'I Remember You,' complete with its characteristic yodel, before diving into 'Picasso's Last Words (Drink to Me).' And a burst of feedback after the first chords of 'Yesterday' forced him to start again, after a moment of banter with the audience, and to strum for a few more seconds until he felt it was safe to begin again.

The reviews of the tour-opener were generally positive, if restrained. Ray Fox-Cumming, in *Record Mirror & Disc*, wrote that the show "isn't the last word in presentation—doesn't even attempt to be," but immediately clarified that this was not an issue. "Most of us emerged from the opening night of the Wings tour elated. We'd heard 29 songs, loved 'em all, and seen two hours fly by as if they were but 40 minutes."[20]

One dose of snark got under Paul's skin, though. "For all his latter-day success," Bart Mills wrote in the *Daily Mail*, "McCartney remains a throwback. He has written a lot of good songs since 'Yesterday,' but none better, and his fans know it. Onstage, despite his advancing years, McCartney is gawky and boyish. He has no chat, and his repertoire of gestures hardly extends beyond pointing an index finger." Mills also, strangely, criticized Paul for trying to front a band rather than going out as a solo act. "McCartney obviously feels better working with his wife and three guys named Joe. The rock scene he knows is about bands, not solo shows." [21]

Speaking with *Melody Maker*'s Chris Welch on the drive to Manchester the day after the review appeared, Paul addressed some of Mills's barbs. "What do they mean?" he asked with what Welch described as real bewilderment about the assertion that he should be a solo act. "Don't they think

I'm at the center of the show already?" He then turned diplomatic. "But I think I can see what this guy means when he says I'm a throwback. Yes—I suppose I am from another age."[22]

But the "throwback" comment still irked him, and he revisited it during another chat with Welch a few days later.

"In our profession what pisses you off is when you get someone saying, 'He's a throwback,'" Paul snarled. "And it could be that the critic who said it was [expletive], or his wife stamped on him and he's in a right state."[23]

On Wednesday, September 10, the Wings' tour bus headed north to Bristol, where the band and crew checked into the Post House, in Alveston, where they would remain for two nights—the first enlivened by a post-concert screening of Woody Allen's *Play It Again, Sam*—given the proximity of the third concert, in Cardiff, the next night.

Reviewing the Bristol show for *Melody Maker*, Chris Welch admitted that he had not seen McCartney on stage since catching one of the Beatles' 30-minute sets in London in 1963, and that he had not been expecting much in the way of showmanship. "I suddenly became aware," he wrote, "that I'd always thought of the man, subconsciously or otherwise, as simply a face with a bass. A clever songwriter, but not exactly a musician, and certainly not a performer, outside the hot house of the recording studio."

But as Welch watched Paul lead his band, wearing his outfit for the tour—a wide-sleeved black kimono jacket with a wide white collar and cuffs, over a red shirt—and either wielding his Rickenbacker bass, sitting beside Jimmy and Denny playing an acoustic guitar, or perched behind the piano, he reconsidered his long-held notion of what McCartney was all about.

"The bass with the face suddenly swam into focus," he wrote, "demonstrating an unobtrusive authority. . . . Paul applied that same authority over acoustic guitar, piano or whatever instrument he chose to accompany a voice that rang with simplicity and power, on songs that are nearly all minor—and in some cases major—gems of the imagination. . . . McCartney's all-round ability puts him into a special category reserved for very few. I became more impressed, not merely by the originality of so much of Wings' material, and Paul's emergence as an instrumentalist, but by the ability of this master record producer to reproduce those records on the bare boards of a stage, where so many reputations can teeter and crash. This may seem like unstinting praise. I see no reason to stint."[24]

Neil Spencer, writing for *NME*, had less problem stinting. Though he praised Paul's "almost contemptuously brilliant bass runs" and Jimmy's "scorching solos," and tipped his hat to Joe, he lit into Linda, noting that she "floats amiably but fairly purposelessly 'round the stage, adding one-handed keyboards here, tambourine there, and lamentably flat harmonies just about everywhere." He then batted around the format and spirit of the show—"It's just that sometimes Macca and Wings' one-big-happy-family-singing-yer-fave-songs approach gets a little too cozy and cloying for comfort"—and casts Paul's versatility as a songwriter as a *bad* thing.

"If you like 'You Give Me the Answer' [*sic*], good luck to you . . . And that McCartney should sing 'Yesterday' and 'Blackbird' side-by-side is obvious enough, but that he should be unable (apparently) to discriminate between the chocolate box emotionalism of the former and the powerful symbolism of the latter is, I think, a real problem."[25]

Before the Cardiff show, Wings sat for interviews with Harlech TV and BBC Wales in the afternoon, and with the radio station Swansea Sound after the sound check. Apart from a few bland questions about what keeps him going ("Drugs," Paul quipped), Beatles questions dominated the discussion, and Paul gave the 1975 version of his standard answer: "We run into each other—we're just good friends."

Chris Welch sat on the sidelines during the television interviews, then drove to the Cardiff show with Paul and Linda. After noting their annoyance with the Beatles questions ("I think they'll go on asking those questions forever," Linda ventured, with Paul wondering, "Why can't they let us get on with something new?"), he asked Paul how he thought the first couple of shows had gone.

"It's better than I thought it would be," Paul responded without elaborating. "We had worried that it'll be over-rehearsed. I didn't mind the silences during the songs at all, and nobody seemed to mind the tuning up when Jimmy broke a string last night [during 'Junior's Farm' in Bristol]. We saw Dave Mason's concert in London, and he tuned up between every number, and I used to think that was death.

"We rehearsed the band down in Rye in Sussex in an old cinema last summer, learning all the numbers. We could have rehearsed the chat between numbers too, but we thought that might make it seem too formal. Originally, we weren't going to allow that—chatting ad-lib. But audiences don't seem to mind, and in any case, they seem to be Wings fans, calling out requests for old Wings B sides."[26]

The idea that there were *Wings fans*—as opposed to Beatles fans who followed Wings because Paul had been a Beatle—was a revelation for Paul. "After the Beatles—well, I didn't think anyone could be a Wings fan. The TV man asked me why I kept going, and I wish I'd told him about Wings fans. That's what's left for me to do!"[27]

At Cardiff's Capitol Theatre, Wendy Hughes of the *Sunday Times* noted that ticket holders, who had queued for hours before the doors opened, included teenagers as well as "pinstripe-suited gents and matronly-looking ladies," and that the screams and applause for 'Yesterday' were only marginally more enthusiastic than the response to songs from *Band on the Run* and *Venus and Mars*.

For father of three McCartney, more comfortable with dropping dad-jokes than off-the-cuff, Beatle-sharp quips ("I'm exactly 33 1/3 years old and I look forward to speeding up to 45 and eventually 78,"[28] he joked with Hughes), Wings provided a bridge between two generations of music fans.

In Manchester, Wings and their support crew—which at this point included not only Showco technicians, MPL and EMI staff, but also a tutor to keep Heather's, Mary's and Stella's schooling on track, and Rose Martin, McCartney's housekeeper and the children's nanny—took over 41 rooms at the Midland Hotel. Wings had stayed at the Midland during their notably less elaborate university tour in 1972.

Chris Welch had seen three shows by now, and he had developed an appreciation for the straightforwardness of the presentation.

"There is barely any stage gimmickry throughout the concert," he wrote, implicitly comparing the Wings show to those of more spectacle-oriented bands. "No dry ice, laser beams or pantomime horses, just an occasional slide projection. And yet it holds the attention and provides more continuous enjoyment than any concert I can recall this year."[29]

The tour's next two stops, Birmingham on September 13 and Liverpool two nights later, were homecomings for Denny and Paul, respectively. Not that Randall Northam, the critic for the *Birmingham Post*, offered much in the way of a welcome. Finding Wings to be "only an ordinary band" coasting on McCartney's charisma and Laine's enthusiasm, he was unimpressed with McCulloch and English and hostile to Linda. Mostly, though, he was fighting a war that had ended elsewhere in 1973: "I suppose in the end it boils down to the fact that if you like John Lennon you tend to dislike Paul McCartney," he wrote in an unusually transparent declaration of his prejudices. "Let's hope Lennon gets his [US immigration] problems sorted out soon so that he can come to Britain and perform."[30]

Barbara Charone offered an alternative view in *Sounds.* Having attended both the Manchester and Birmingham shows, Charone observed that in the two years since their last British tour, Wings had evolved from a *pop band* to a *band*—a distinction that implied a step up in seriousness and credibility. Noting that the set drew heavily on the last two albums, Charone reported that "the complicated arrangements lose nothing in their onstage transition with a four-piece horn section that captures every vinyl nuance," and that while the group's performances closely mirrored those on the discs, "the reproduction is far from sterile. In fact, most songs sound a good bit rockier onstage."[31]

By Birmingham, Paul was getting an idea of what the audiences liked and reconfigured the set order slightly.* 'Call Me Back Again' was moved up three slots to follow 'Go Now,' switching places with 'Junior's Farm,' which now took its place between 'Letting Go' and 'Live and Let Die.' 'Soily'—an oddly popular number, given that it had never appeared on record—was moved from just before the acoustic set to the encore position, and Paul made the Birmingham audience wait

---

* Audience recordings of all but the Manchester, Liverpool, Edinburgh, Aberdeen and Dundee shows circulate, so while the earliest extant recording on which the set reconfiguration is first heard is the Birmingham show, it is possible that they went into effect the night before, in Manchester. Recordings of nearly all the concerts in the Australian, European and American legs of the tour circulate as well, and descriptions of the performances in these pages are based on those recordings.

for it, rhythmically chanting, stomping and clapping for nearly three minutes before Wings returned to the stage and Paul announced, "We've got one more for you!"

Backstage at the Hippodrome after the show, the full band spoke with a German television crew and Denny had a solo interview with a local radio station before the musicians made their way back to the Holiday Inn for a late supper and a screening of *Blazing Saddles*.

Sunday was a rest day, and as the band settled in at the Adelphi Hotel in Liverpool, Paul retrieved his Rolls-Royce to buy himself and Linda some freedom of movement in the city. The McCartneys stayed at Rembrandt, which he now maintained as a Liverpool-area pied-à-terre, and they visited Jim at his new bungalow on Beverley Drive. Jim's poor health made it impossible for him to attend the show, but Angie and Ruth were there.

"We love to come back up here and see the folks and meet friends," Paul told Peter Trollope of the *Liverpool Echo*. "It's nice because people never bother us and we can all have a great time."

"I don't like what they've done to the city with all their concrete buildings, though," he added. "It's a bit like New York, but I suppose that's what people would call progress. Still the people haven't changed."[32]

Having the Rolls available also allowed Paul a symbolic moment that, even after all the Beatles' success, he could not resist: a young scruff only 15 years earlier, he now arrived at the Empire in a Rolls, the star of the show.

But an immediately recognizable Rolls-Royce was a double-edged sword. At the end of the evening, a crowd estimated at being somewhere between 400 (in the *Liverpool Daily Post*) and 1,000 (in *Record Mirror*) fans gathered at the backstage exit. The theater's security crew cleared a path for Paul and Linda to get to the Rolls, but it had to inch its way forward as the crowd pressed in on the car, causing £2,000 ($4,205) in damage.

Paul got a good reading of the Liverpool fans' enthusiasm two hours earlier, during the transition from 'Venus and Mars' to 'Rock Show,' when the audience rushed the stage. It was a moment when Paul's duality was at its strongest: to the man who liked being in control, the crowd surge was alarming; but to his inner rocker, who missed the messy, quasi-outlaw heyday of Jerry Lee Lewis, Chuck Berry, Gene Vincent and the young Elvis—and who had personally winked his share of crowds into going wild—it was definitely a kick.

When the Empire's manager, Charles O'Neill, announced after 'Rock Show' that if concertgoers did not return to their seats, the show would be stopped, Linda took a rebellious stance, telling the crowd, "Ah, don't listen to him!"[33] But Paul had it both ways, telling the audience, "Take it easy, it's not a football match,"[34] but claiming to a reporter that, "We don't really believe in [crowd control]. We think, 'It's rock 'n' roll,' and people should be able to get up and enjoy themselves. I feel safe with a rock 'n' roll crowd. I don't feel there are loonies—maybe one or two—but you get them everywhere."[35]

As it turned out, "one or two" specific loonies had come to represent the dark side of fandom in Paul's mind.

"There was a guy and a girl who completely freaked Paul out when he was performing," said the director Barry Chattington, who had joined the tour to film some shows,* "and they always seemed to get bloody tickets. Anyway, we were all staying in the Adelphi—me, John [Hammel] and Alan [Crowder]—and Paul had gone off to his dad's after one of his triumphs. And it's my turn to buy drinks. So I get the drinks, and this rather attractive lady goes, 'Hello, how are you?' And suddenly out of nowhere, Trevor arrives and says, 'Alan needs to speak with you, very quickly, Barry, I'll get the drinks.' And Alan says, 'That's the fucking woman—if Paul sees her he stops completely in his tracks, he's completely freaked by her.' But this woman, she would always sit in the middle, nine rows back, and they could never work out how she got the tickets."[36]

Although Jim McCartney could not attend the concert, 68 members of the McCartney clan turned up to cheer Paul on, with brother Mike declaring that he had never heard Wings play so well, and that the show was "a gas."[37]

The critics were swept up in the excitement as well, with Peter Trollope describing the show in the *Liverpool Echo* as "a night of sheer magic," and noting that 'Yesterday' received "the biggest ovation of the night," apart from the ten minutes of roaring demand for more between 'Band on the Run' and the two encores.[38]

Not that the show was without mishaps. At one point toward the middle of the performance, the onstage monitoring system began feeding back, and soundman Morris Lyda was at a loss to stop it.

"I hit every button and shut everything down and muted everything and slammed every knob, and the thing continued to feed back," an exasperated Lyda explained. "The horn players are lying on the [stage] with their hands over their ears. We're talking about a PA going mad, screaming—it must have been between 110 and 120 decibels onstage, at 3,000Hz, which would have been the most painful experience artists could endure, other than electrocution. The show came to a complete stop, and Paul introduced me—'Ladies and gentlemen, Morris Lyda!'"[39]

After the concert, Paul and the band did brief interviews with *Rolling Stone*, Paul Drew from the American RKO Radio chain, and Radio Merseyside, and then headed to the Adelphi Hotel for a post-concert party for friends and family. One family member who was not invited was Paul's stepmother, Angie. But Alan Crowder, running into Angie McCartney in the Empire's foyer, assumed that she was on the guest list and told her to bring her party directly to the Adelphi after the show. Angie turned up with her daughter, Ruth, her sister and brother-in-law, and the couple

* Besides helping to create the still-in-progress *Bruce McMouse Show*, Barry Chattington had been enlisted to film several shows on Wings' 1972 European tour. His work with Wings to this point is detailed in *The McCartney Legacy: Volume 1, 1969–1973*. From the 1975 British tour, clips of 'Letting Go' and 'Venus and Mars—Rock Show,' edited from performances likely filmed in Liverpool, Newcastle and Glasgow, were released as promotional videos.

that lived next door to her and Jim. Like everyone else in the room—she estimated that there were about 80 people present—Angie waited for Paul and Linda to turn up and congratulated them on the show.

"The following morning, Paul phoned his father at Beverley Drive, and he was obviously going on at great length about something," she remembered. "I frequently used to just get out of the way so Jim wouldn't feel embarrassed when he was having an up-and-downer with Paul on the phone. . . . But I could still hear what was going on. And I could hear Jim say, '*No* son, no I'm *not* going to get rid of her. She's a good woman and I love her, and she takes good care—No. *No.* I am *not* going to get rid of her, you can't tell me to do that. You know, I'm ill, I'm old, and I need her, she takes care of me. I mean—because she went to a party after the show? I mean, what is it? Be *reasonable* son. No, I'm sorry, I'm not going to.' And I heard the phone slam, and I waited a few minutes discreetly and went through, and Jim was sitting, crying, in the chair."[40]

There may have been more to Paul's insistence that Jim jettison Angie than pique over her appearance at the party. Jim's health was failing quickly, and there was a feeling among the Liverpool McCartney relatives that Paul should put him in a nursing home. This was an idea that Angie would not entertain because it directly contravened Jim's wishes, so from the family's point of view, she was an obstruction to the care they believed Jim needed.

"Jim had always said to me," Angie later confided, "'I'm a creaking gate. You'll know when the end is coming and I want you to promise me something—I want you to promise me that you'll never let me finish up in a hospital bed. If I ever wake up and see a sea of faces around the bed looking at me, I'll hate it. So, promise me that when you know the end is near you'll just let me die peacefully in my own bed.' And I said, 'Oh, of course I will, love.'"[41]

The next day, September 16, Wings were in Newcastle-Upon-Tyne, performing for an audience of 2,250 at City Hall. Just over three and a half years earlier, Wings had turned up unannounced at Newcastle University and played one of their first concerts. Philip Crawley, a student then, scored a ticket to Wings' North East debut; now he was the reviewer for the *Newcastle Journal* and noted that the demand for tickets in 1975 was such that "this time there were more people locked out than saw the February 1972 concert."

Crawley described the show as "one of the finest rock concerts" the Newcastle audience was likely to see and reported that the Beatles numbers—particularly 'Blackbird' and 'Yesterday'—won the loudest applause. "It was a moment to savor," he wrote, "the greatest pop composer of the last decade, singing one of its most beautiful ballads and stirring thousands of memories (even if half of the audience were still in short pants and gymslips when it was first written)."[42]

No interviews were scheduled for Newcastle, but one intrepid reporter, Ian Penman, of Radio Newcastle—whose request for an interview had been turned down by MPL—made the rounds of hotels until he found Wings at the Gosforth Park Hotel and knocked on the McCartneys' door. Paul spoke with Penman, but back at the station, the reporter discovered that the tape was blank. "McCartney had been playfully fiddling around with the tape recorder and must have accidentally pressed the rewind button," Radio Newcastle DJ Dick Godfrey theorized at the time.[43]

The show itself, however, was professionally recorded, one of several for which MPL had arranged for a 24-track mobile recording unit.

Now London beckoned. The entourage began the long drive from Newcastle at 9 A.M., to make it to London by mid-afternoon. The McCartneys and the band spent the next few days in their own homes, while the crew was put up at the Holiday Inn in Swiss Cottage, a short walk from EMI Studios. Tickets for the Hammersmith Odeon shows on September 17 and 18 were scarce, and scalpers were selling them for as much as £45 ($95), 15 times the original top price.[44]

Reviews were plentiful, and generally enthusiastic. "The atmosphere in the hall was both happier, more exciting, more emotional and more celebratory than at any other London concert this year," Robin Denselow wrote, setting the scene in the *Guardian.*

Having covered Wings in concert and on disc several times since 1972 (when he reviewed the band in Châteauvallon, France), Denselow offered some historical perspective, suggesting that in the glow of the first Hammersmith show, "those semi-disastrous early [Wings] concerts and the string of mildly depressing albums that ended with the magnificent *Band on the Run,* are now forgotten," and noting that "though she looks worried as ever," Linda had improved as both a singer and keyboardist since he had last heard her.

Chris Charlesworth, who had also covered Wings since their early days, took a historical view too, writing in his *Melody Maker* review that "the current Wings band is a vast improvement on the previous rather scraggly lineups,"[45] and praising Paul for coming to terms, at long last, with the music he wrote during the Beatles years.

For Paul, the reactions of these seasoned Wings-watchers confirmed that he was right to rehearse Wings long and hard before going on the road, rather than working out the setlist in a short rehearsal period and allowing the spirit of the moment to take over on stage.

"We tried it the other way, when we first came to Europe with the very first line up of Wings," he told an interviewer, referring to the more freewheeling approach Wings took in 1972. "This is where the stories about drinking came. But the truth is, I mean, we were pretty out of it on the stage; there was no discipline just in case that was a better way.

"When you think of discipline, you almost think of it as a bad thing—like you think of people slapping your hand *[makes a slapping noise and continues in a German accent]*, 'You vill be playing good.' But that's not the kind of discipline we have; we have discipline where we know the songs."[46]

Nevertheless, the first show had a few quirks. At the start of 'Let Me Roll It,' Linda hit the synthesizer effect that begins 'Spirits of Ancient Egypt,' apparently jumping the gun on the next song in the set. And Paul moved 'Maybe I'm Amazed' to between 'Lady Madonna' and 'The Long and Winding Road,' only to reconsider the next evening when he restored the song to its original place.

At the second Hammersmith Odeon show, on Thursday evening, a fan called out, "*What about John Lennon?*" Paul responded, "What about him," and then launched into a song before the dialogue could go further. The exchange became a jumping-off point for Ray Coleman, whose *Melody Maker* review suggested that although he may have just seen a Wings show, for him—and, he believed, the audience—it was really all about the Beatles.

"It wasn't that Wings were a bad rock band; their performance was professional and fairly tight throughout, even if the songs were as unmemorable as Paul's solo spot was memorable," Coleman opined. "It's just that old Beatle problem rearing its head again. The pure fact is that McCartney will have to live forever as an ex-Beatle, and yet here he was, on the Hammersmith stage, acting out a role that sought to kill off his past. By that yardstick, the show was just another rock band racing through some hot licks; yet we all knew things were different and nobody should judge it as just another rock band—if it was that, the theatre would not have been full. . . .

"In fairness," Coleman continued, "it must be recorded that the audience was ecstatic, and the band received the mandatory encore; but nothing will shake my conviction that they were applauding an ex-Beatle's appearance rather than the Wings concert."[47]

After the show, Paul threw a post-concert party backstage, attended by a hefty roster of show business royalty. Ringo Starr attended, as did Pete Townshend (who told his old Thunderclap Newman protégé, Jimmy McCulloch, that Wings' performance "should remove whatever stigma the band had in this country"[48]), Alice Cooper, Harry Nilsson, John Baldry, Jon Anderson of Yes, Marc Bolan, Olivia Newton-John and David Frost.

At one point during the party, Paul joined Ringo and Nilsson for a loose rendition of Harry M. Wood's standard 'Side by Side.' And Paul, chatting with a reporter from *Rolling Stone*, admitted that the oldest of his girls, Heather, was among his tougher critics.

"She doesn't like my solo bit," he confessed. "She likes Jimmy's song better. She's 12, and there are a lot of people aged 12 these days."[49]

The London shows, played to crowds of 4,000 each, were the climax of the tour, but there was a coda—three shows in Scotland that, conveniently, would leave Paul, Linda and their daughters within striking distance of High Park, where they planned to take a post-tour break.

Paul made one staging change for the three concerts in Scotland: when Wings left the stage after 'Band on the Run,' they slipped on kilts and slipped off their pants, returning for the encores in traditional local dress.

The Edinburgh concert came just after the publication of the annual *Melody Maker* readers' poll, in which McCartney and Wings were plentifully represented, but did not hit the top spot in any category. Paul was listed as No. 10 on the Top 10 male singers list and Wings were the No. 9 band. 'Listen to What the Man Said' was No. 8 among British singles and No. 10 among international singles, and *Venus and Mars* was No. 6 on both the British and international albums lists. Paul scored in four other categories as well—as composer (No. 4), bass player (No. 2), producer (No. 7) and arranger (No. 3).[50]

In Scotland, Paul continued to fiddle with the set order, moving 'Medicine Jar' down the list to the second half of the show, between 'Letting Go' and 'Junior's Farm,' and moving 'Live and Let Die' up to provide a spectacular finale to the show's first half, before the acoustic set. He also tweaked his arrangement of 'Lady Madonna' to include a short instrumental reprise, although he played it only at select shows, seemingly deciding whether to add it on the spur of the moment. The Glasgow show was another for which MPL had a 24-track recording made.

After the show, Wings and the crew repaired to their digs at the Albany Hotel and unwound by watching another film from their traveling library, *American Graffiti.*

The band was joined in Glasgow by Norman Dunn, a reporter for the *Aberdeen Evening Express* who, like Chris Welch, talked MPL into letting him not only catch a couple of the shows (Glasgow and Aberdeen) but also travel on the tour bus, interviewing Paul and Linda along the way.

"I remember coming up here with the Beatles," Paul said as the bus made its way through the Scottish countryside, Paul again countermanding his publicist's attempt to suppress Beatles questions. "We did Elgin, Dingwall—I don't recall all the gigs." Dunn noted that it had been two years since Wings last visited Scotland. Was it likely, he wondered, that they would return? "I want to go on tour as often as I can," Paul told him, immediately rendering his comment a non-answer by adding "until I get bored with it, that is."

Barry Humphrey, a freelance publicist hired for the tour, told Dunn that the British tour was, in effect, preparation for touring Australia; Australia, in turn, would be preparation for Japan, and "when we hit America, we'll be in overdrive." As Paul explained, there was a reason these tours were preparation for the American leg: they were the investment, and the American tour was the cash-out.

"Sure, [touring Britain] doesn't make money," Paul told Dunn, "but we've got a world tour coming off in four months—Australia, then Japan and finally America. I reckon America will pay for the present tour." But lest he seem too mercenary, he added, "The tour also means we're playing together all the time. The current LP [*Venus and Mars*] is going well, but we'll be working for another one in about four months' time."[51]

When the bus pulled up to the Sheraton Inn Hotel in Bucksburn, on the outskirts of Aberdeen,

Dunn went on his way as the band checked in and got ready for the afternoon soundcheck and the evening concert.

"One outstanding feature of Wings is their energy," the reviewer for the *Aberdeen Evening Express* told readers the following day. "They worked their way non-stop through a two-hour programme which would have left lesser musicians gasping. But they still came back on stage to answer an encore. Then quietly filed out. There hadn't been a single incident to mar the evening."[52]

From the band's point of view, that was not entirely correct. Apart from a delay at the start of the show because of sound problems, there was a pyro mishap during 'Live and Let Die,' occasioned by one of the crew throwing a temper tantrum during the load-out in Dundee and kicking the control box for the flash pots from the stage into the sixth row of the theater.

"Needless to say, the little controller was broken," Ian Peacock explained. "One of the other guys on the lighting crew knew how to rewire it, so he did, and he showed me what was happening. Usually, I preset the first lot of bangs and then hit the button [when the explosions were due to occur], but either I misunderstood what the guy who rewired it was saying, or he hadn't explained it properly. So I set the switches and turned the key, and right in the middle of the slow part of the song—about four or five bars in—*Boom!* Everybody is looking over at me, on the corner of the stage, because they knew where that was being controlled. I was just totally mortified, and Trevor came running over and gave me an earful. It was an embarrassing moment."[53]

After the show, Norman Dunn turned up backstage to get the final touches for his feature, which was mainly a matter of watching a French television crew interview Wings. Most of the questions were directed to Paul, including an unusual Beatles query. Having been asked over the last couple of years why he did not perform any Beatles songs with Wings, he was now asked why he *was* playing them.

"Why?" Paul asked, a little startled. "Why not. I haven't gone away from the songs because they're my songs. If I didn't sing them, they would just vanish. People like them, they make them happy, and that's what they are there to do."[54]

Back at the Sheraton Inn Hotel, Paul had trouble unwinding. What was playing on his mind—his father's deteriorating health, perhaps, or concerns about the tour—is unknown, but he reached for a guitar and began work on a new tune with a refrain meant to keep him focused on the bright side.

"We were on tour in Scotland, and we're having quite a time of it," he later said. "We were up in Aberdeen, and I was sitting in a hotel bedroom just before we were gonna turn in for the night, and I had my 12-string guitar with me. And I just started plonking out a little tune, and it became 'Don't Let It Bring You Down.'"[55]

From Aberdeen, the coach and two equipment trucks drove south along Scotland's east coast to Dundee, where the band checked in at the Angus Hotel. The concert was filmed by a crew making a documentary about Wings' Scottish shows.

The one departure from the standard setlist came at the end of 'Soily,' when a birthday cake for Linda (a day early) was wheeled onto the stage, and the four brass players serenaded her with a New Orleans-tinged rendering of 'Happy Birthday.'

The critic for the *Dundee Evening Telegraph* judged the concert to have been "one of the best shows on Tayside for some time." The paper's coverage also included an interview with Paul, in which he was still trying to formulate a succinct comment about why he was playing Beatles songs.

"Well, this was the first time we started playing the Beatles songs again," he said. "Previously all of the efforts had been to establish Wings and to make something that wasn't like a Beatles tribute band. But once we had a few hits with Wings—and *Band on the Run* was a really big hit album—we had some of these hits in our repertoire, and it did feel like, 'Oh, it's okay, now we can do Beatles stuff!' And it was quite a relief in a way because I'm always sort of conscious of what the audience wants, because my audience isn't a narrow audience, it's quite a wide group of people."

And then it got a bit stranger with Paul, who only four weeks earlier had his publicists warn journalists not to ask Beatles questions, telling his interlocutor that he dreamed—*literally*—about the Beatles reuniting.

"It would have been great to get the Beatles back together again," he mused. "People always say what if? But we can't, so sadly, that's not going to happen. If by some strange fluke it was to happen, it would be beautiful. But do you know where it does happen? In my dreams. As a musician, you often have dreams about being in the studio or on stage so I'm often with the guys. Just the other morning I woke up and I was with George. And that was very nice. That's how I run into John and George these days. So the Beatles have re-formed. In my head."[56]

After the show, the McCartneys were asked to sign the guest book at Caird Hall and noticed that the Queen Mother had signed it a few weeks earlier. Paul drew a smiling face with a crown, eyes pointed to the top of the facing page where the Queen Mother signed, and an arrow running from his inscription—"And love from another subject"—to her signature. Linda's message was, "Keep it up Dundee, you take the cake!"

11

WINGS FLY SOUTH

It was a nearly 200-mile, four-and-a-half-hour trek from Dundee, on the east coast of Scotland, to High Park, clear across the country and down the Kintyre peninsula, and Paul was ready for some relaxation on his Scottish farm—relaxation, for Paul, meaning writing songs for the album he had already told the press Wings was about to record.

Technically, of course, the sessions for this prospective album had already started, with the recording of 'Beware My Love.' Now, in the cool autumn at High Park, he sat at the piano exploring and fleshing out ideas that had been germinating during the tour.

One of the new songs, 'She's My Baby,' was a new addition to his catalog of songs inspired by Linda. Rather than singing straightforwardly about what she means to him, as he did in 'Maybe I'm Amazed' and 'My Love,' Paul toys here with metaphorical imagery: in the morning she's a baby "*when the sleep is in her eyes*," but by the time the rest of the world is awake, "*she has arisen.*" But she also "*comes out at night*" and is "*the lady of the evening tide / when the stars are in the sky*," which is when "*she changes back into a kitten.*" For good measure, and with Linda's passion for cooking as a backdrop, there's a food metaphor, which some listeners hear as sexual innuendo, as well: "*Like gravy / down to the last drop / I keep mopping her up / she's my baby.*"

At this stage, the song's musical heart was a rising and falling chordal piano figure that sounds like a stylistic remnant from Wings' visit to New Orleans, as does the playful melody that enlivens both the verses and the bridge. The bridge, rather than offering a contrast, is an expansion on the verse, but with an interesting quirk: it is always played twice, first with the *morning/baby/sleep in her eyes* lyric, then with the *evening/kitten* imagery.

"The interesting thing about this period," Paul later confirmed, "is there is a kind of New Orleansy feel, a sort of bluesy feel to a lot of the songs. Some of them were completely the opposite, but this one's got a slightly sort of funky little feel to it. And it's very simple, that's my ode to Linda."[1]

Linda was also the inspiration for 'Warm and Beautiful,' a piano ballad with a lyric that reads as effortlessly poetic and direct, and an ingenious chord progression that unfolds by Paul's shifting a single note (or in one case, two notes) within a chord up or down a half-step. Understanding how this gradually morphing progression works tells us a lot about how Paul's piano technique and his approach to the keyboard often led him to fresh ideas.

He begins with a simple C major chord (C-E-G), and then raises the G to G-sharp to transform it into a C augmented. From there, he moves to an F major chord (F-A-C), which is just a matter of retaining the C and shifting the other two notes up a half step—the G-sharp to A and the E to F. Paul next moves from F major to F minor by lowering the A to an A-flat, and then back to C major by holding the C from the F minor chord, moving the A-flat down to G and the F down to E. Dropping from C to B changes the C major chord into an E minor—whereupon Paul abandons this procedure for the final two chords of the verse, F major and G major, which do not share any notes.

The introduction to one of Paul's favorites among his Beatles-era songs, 'Here, There and Everywhere,' works similarly, and the connection was not lost on him. "I wrote 'Warm and Beautiful' just the same way as I did 'Here, There and Everywhere' on the Beatles' *Revolver* album," he explained a few months later. "It's the same kind of effort. But I'm not a great analyzer of my own stuff."[2]

Paul was sufficiently taken with the chord progression to record an instrumental demo on an electric piano. Typically, Paul's demos include vocals, the lyrics often a work in progress, hammered out during the demo process. Here, it's just the chord progression in the left hand and the gracefully flowing melody in the right, and though the completeness of the melody suggests that he had lyrics in mind, he clearly wanted to focus on the harmonic mechanism that drives the song.

Also among Paul's new creations was 'The Note You Never Wrote,' a minor-key narrative in 3|4 time about a message in a bottle. The song's nautical inspiration likely came from a story in the British press earlier in the year about a German sailor, Rolf Decker, who found himself marooned after a shipwreck. A manhunt to locate Decker began in late August when a message he wrote was found bobbing in a bottle in the Mediterranean Sea off the coast of France. "I am on an unknown island, the position of which I do not know, but presumably south of Corsica," Decker wrote in a desperate rescue plea. "I have been shipwrecked and am the last survivor of five people. Help!"[3]

Paul begins with a graceful image, in *media res*: "*Later on, the story goes / a bottle floated out to sea.*" When the bottle is found, the narrator tells us, "*I read the note you never wrote to me*"—an unusual twist, because in song lyrics, "*you*" is typically someone the singer knows, and "*me*" is usually the singer. Here, "*you*" is the unknown author of the note, who wrote it for whomever finds it (that is, it was not written "*to me*").

From there, the song grows more surreal, and seems partly motivated by a search for rhymes, and partly by a yen for *sub-rosa* political commentary, much in the same way his reference to being tarred and feathered in '1882' touched on recent news stories about the Irish Republican Army meting out that punishment to collaborators with the British Army. In 'The Note You Never Wrote,' Paul leaves the floating bottle aside to tell us that the Mayor of Baltimore is on the scene, but that "*he never is gonna get my vote / 'Cause he never is gonna get a quote / From the little note you never wrote to me.*"

The 1975 Baltimore mayoral race was widely covered, and Paul is likely to have read about it during his Stateside visits. The reference may have been simply a contrarian response to the popularity of Baltimore's Democratic mayor, William Schaefer, who was reelected in 1975 with more than 85 percent of the vote.

Obscure as the lyric is, it fits a category of McCartney song that dates back to 'Monkberry Moon Delight,' in which Paul adopted John Lennon's 'I Am the Walrus' strategy of toying with listeners by giving them lyrics that appear to convey a meaning that is just out of reach but may actually be just a combination of wordplay and in-jokes.

"I never usually write a song and think, 'Right, now this is going to be about something specific,'" Paul told an interviewer a few weeks later. "It's just that the words happen. I never try to make any serious social point. Just words to go with the music—and you can read anything you like into it."[4]

By the time he left Scotland, Paul had decided that the song should be sung by Denny, who had been airing complaints about the shape of Wings' current agenda, both in private discussions with Paul and now in a whingeing interview with Peter Harvey.

"I don't want to go in the studios for another year," Denny told Harvey. "I just want to stay on the road. It gets so boring being in the studio for a long time. In America, we were in the studio for three months doing nothing but recording. That's not my idea of fun."

Paul had been encouraging Denny to write for Wings albums since 1972, hoping that he might enjoy recording more if he were singing his own songs. Denny had complied, haltingly: Wings recorded his 'I Would Only Smile' for *Red Rose Speedway*, but the song was left unreleased when EMI demanded that the album be trimmed from a double to a single disc. His 'No Words,' which ended up as a collaboration with Paul, made it onto *Band on the Run*, but his Nashville effort, 'Send Me the Heart,' remained in limbo. So Paul put him before the mic for 'Spirits of Ancient Egypt' on *Venus and Mars*, and now, even if he wrote nothing for the next LP, he would have 'The Note You Never Wrote.'

"To tell you the truth, I don't write much anymore," Laine told Peter Harvey. "I'm the sort of bloke who has to be away from it all before I can write songs. It's not impossible to write on the road but you only get about one hour a day [to yourself], and that's not much of an opportunity."[5]

Another song Paul brought near to completion during his High Park visit was 'San Ferry Anne,' a title based on a corruption of the French phrase "Ça ne fait rien" (it doesn't matter, or don't worry). Paul and Linda first heard the phrase during their November 1973 recording trip to Paris. Wings' instruments had been held up at Calais and were unavailable for their first session at EMI's Pathé Marconi Studios, leaving Paul to borrow guitars, drums and keyboards from Les Variations, a French band that were also working at the studio. When Paul mentioned the missing instruments to Duncan Richards, the studio's press officer, his response, "Ça ne fait rien," quickly became a band in-joke in its Anglicized form.

As Paul began toying with a bouncy, French-sounding melody to match the phrase's rhythm, 'San Ferry Anne' became his new 'Michelle,' a song that began as a party piece in a French *boulevardier* style.

Revisiting the song, Paul made it into a word game. Each of its six verses has three lines. The first two lines rhyme; the third is a short phrase that, in the first four verses, end with "*dear.*" The third lines of the final two verses end with a rhyme, "*after*" and "*laughter.*" In the four verses that end with "*dear,*" the words preceding *dear* rhyme—"*I'd say you're doing well, dear*" and "*You're looking swell, dear.*"

"I like doing that, playing with words," Paul explained, countering earlier comments in which he defensively responded to critical dismissals of his lyrics by saying that he was more interested in a song's *feel* than whether its lyrics said much. "My dad was always very into words and he was a crossword man, so my love of words probably comes from there. And I had a very good English literature teacher, who encouraged that love of words. . . . And so 'San Ferry Anne,' it's a little atmospheric thing—it's very Parisian."[6]

As always, Paul kept an eye on the other Beatles. After crossed signals in an effort to prevent Paul's and George's releases from competing directly, George's new album, *Extra Texture*, was released on October 3 in Britain. Four days later, the US Appeals Court in New York City overruled the Immigration and Naturalization Service in its attempt to have John deported, granting him permanent resident status. And on John's thirty-fifth birthday, October 9, Yoko gave birth to Sean Taro Ono Lennon, John's second son.

John's victory in his four-year fight with the United States immigration authorities returned to him the ability to leave the country without fear of being barred from entry upon his return. Consequently, there was immediate press speculation that he might visit Britain. He even had a reason to go: the playwright, actress and director Denise Coffey had adapted his books, *In His Own Write* and *A Spaniard in the Works*, for the stage, and had invited him to see the show. But he remained in New York.

After two weeks at High Park, Paul felt sufficiently refreshed. And now that he had a handful of new songs, he arranged for studio time at EMI, and summoned Wings.

Recording Sessions

Tuesday, October 14 and Thursday, October 16–Friday, October 17, 1975.

EMI Studios, Studio Two, London.

Recording: 'The Note You Never Wrote' and 'Beware My Love (Remake).'

Mixing: 'The Note You Never Wrote' and 'Beware My Love (John Bonham version).'

Hoping to get Denny more enthusiastic about recording at the very start of the project, Paul handed over 'The Note You Never Wrote.' The official story would now be that Paul wrote the song specifically for him. "I'd written a song for Denny because I always felt that the tunes he was producing weren't big enough for him, so I wanted to write something that was a bit more epic,"[7] was how he put it.

"'The Note You Never Wrote,' it was in a waltz tempo, 3|4 time, which is the same tempo as 'Go Now,'" Laine added, "and I'm sure Paul was influenced by 'Go Now' very much when he wrote that song specifically for me to sing. I love the song because it's a kind of a folk song to me, and it's almost a political thing. It's not too heavy, but it's like a statement, like a, I won't say a protest song, but it's just the sort of song that I like to sing."[8]

EMI assigned Tony Clark to engineer the sessions. Clark's and McCartney's professional paths had not crossed since the stormy 'Give Ireland Back to the Irish' session in February 1972. The McCartneys' fondness for Thai Sticks* did not sit well with Clark, and he was surprised when he was assigned to the sessions.

"I can honestly say," said Clark, "my experiences of that whole drug-taking world, it was completely alien to me. I was there first hand and I didn't like what happened. I didn't like what happened to the Beatles—you could see it unfolding and it became a psychological battle."[9]

The band set to work on what was, at this point, a sparse, atmospheric arrangement. For the first verse, Denny's rough vocal is accompanied only by Paul's electric piano and a light organ part, played by Linda. Denny joins in on acoustic guitar at the second (Mayor of Baltimore) verse, with Joe soon following with a drum pattern that fills the spaces between the lyrics. In a short instrumental section, Joe and other members of the band added light percussion, and Jimmy provided a blistering solo that instantly raised the track's temperature and intensity. Paul had ideas for other additions—strings, for starters, and vocal harmonies—and Denny would have to replace his lead vocal. But for now, the basic track was complete, Take 2 marked as the keeper.

---

* Thai Sticks were a particularly potent cannabis "cigar" that originated in Thailand. According to Litchfield, Paul and Linda "exclusively devoted" a huge fridge to maintaining a fresh supply of them.

Paul did not plan another session with the band until Friday, so on Thursday, Clark prepared mixes of 'The Note You Never Wrote' and 'Beware My Love,' and had copies delivered to Cavendish Avenue. Reviewing both tracks, Paul decided that 'The Note You Never Wrote' was fine for the moment, and the Bonham take of 'Beware My Love' had the vigor and rawness it needed. But though he was selling Wings now as a "fluid concept" that was open to guest appearances and collaborations, in this case heart overruled head, and he decided to give the song another try with the full Wings lineup.

Joe, now living alone in a flat near Paul's house, was in the habit of stopping by Cavendish Avenue most days, so Paul was able to play the recording and show the drummer what he had in mind, ideas Joe drank in as if he were an apprentice.

"I used to go over to his house almost every morning and have eggs, tea and toast and sit at the piano with him, right next to him as he was writing songs," Joe reminisced. "I told him, 'I'm going to sit here and maybe some of it will rub off on me.'"[10]

On October 17, Wings returned to EMI to record a new version of 'Beware My Love.' They filled two 24-track tapes before settling, with misgivings, on a temporary master take for possible use if further recording did not yield something better.

—

While Paul and Wings were getting a start on their next LP, fans in Australia were getting ready for Paul's first performances Down Under since the Beatles toured there in June 1964. Wings' compact, two-week tour would include nine concerts in five cities, starting at the Perth Entertainment Centre on November 1 and then powering through pairs of concerts at the Apollo Stadium, Adelaide, November 4 and 5; the Hordern Pavilion, Sydney, November 7 and 8; Brisbane Festival Hall, Brisbane, November 10 and 11; and finally, the Sydney Meyer Music Bowl, in Melbourne, November 13 and 14. All told, there were 62,400 tickets, selling at A$6.80 ($8.56, £4.20) to A$9.80 ($12.40, £6).

Less than a month before the first show, there was pandemonium at the ticket windows. In Sydney, where tickets went on sale on Saturday, October 18, fans had lined up outside the Hordern Pavilion by 3 P.M. on Friday; by midnight, the line was more than a mile long. The ticket windows opened Saturday morning at 8:30 A.M., and by 9:30, the 11,000 tickets were gone. People who had joined the queue as early as 5 P.M. on Friday were shut out—unless they happened to win tickets in contests announced the next morning by the *Sydney Morning Herald*, the *Mirror* and the *Sun*.

Similar situations prevailed in all five cities on the tour, and by the end of the weekend, tickets were scarce everywhere.

Paul and Linda gave a few interviews to Australian news outlets before they left England, but for the most part Paul was able to duck the promotional chores thanks to Chris Welch, who repurposed his *Melody Maker* tour bus interviews as a two-part feature—one devoted to Paul, one to

Linda—for the Sydney *Sun*. These proved to be unusually frank portraits that pointed up deep wells of insecurity that McCartney more typically kept hidden.

"I've gotta remind myself that the main thing is to enjoy myself," Paul told Welch. "You can get easily wound up in the super-hip world of 'that's wrong' or 'that's out of tune, man. I can't stand it.' Sometimes you feel as if you have a ten-ton weight on your shoulders. And you can't entertain so well, unless the weight is off your shoulders.

"When I go out there on stage, if I saw anyone walk out, or light a cigarette, I'd think, 'Oh, God. I've lost 'em.' You see, I must misread so badly, all the time. If I do see someone leaving the theater while I'm singing I've got to remind myself they might be going to the lavatory. It really could be that. But instinctively, I just go, 'Oh, no, they hate me. I'm no good.' I'm just a born worrier. It's like the old Indian saying, 'I walk down the street and I'm crying because I have no shoes, and then I see a man with no feet.' I must try and remind myself that I've got feet."[11]

And in an unusual moment of public self-criticism, he admitted to finding the 1973 *James Paul McCartney* television special unwatchable ("It wasn't a hip show at all. In fact, I couldn't watch it.") and fretted about recent rehearsals with Wings—possibly referring to the Elstree preview show.

Linda leaned into some of her insecurities, too, but quickly shrugged them off.

"I married Paul and all of a sudden I was this ogre," she told Welch, before turning to the critical reaction to her playing in Wings. "I think I became a perfect, what is it, foil? I was just a perfect person to knock in every way. They think I'm getting on the bandwagon and stuff . . . but I'm not and never intended to. I just like to sit down at the piano and have a play, whereas I couldn't do that a few years ago."

But surely, Welch wondered, having a brilliant musician like Paul to teach her must have been helpful?

"No, really—no," was Linda's emphatic answer. "He has no patience. I had to learn myself. The few things he'd show me, if I didn't get it right off, he'd get really angry. So I said, like, 'Forget it.' I just practiced by myself. No, Paul hasn't taught me anything, actually."[12]

Meanwhile, following the disappointing chart performance of 'Letting Go,' Capitol determined that it was time to peel another single from *Venus and Mars*. The selection this time was Paul's show opener, 'Venus and Mars' and 'Rock Show,' with 'Magneto and Titanium Man' on the B side. An edit was necessary to encourage radio play, so the songs on the A side were trimmed from 6'49" to 3'42". The American release was on October 20; in Britain, the single hit the shops on November 28.

If anything, the release proved that Al Coury's take-the-singles-from-the-album gambit was not infallible—although a different way to look at it was that *Venus and Mars* was no *Band on the Run*, or at least, there was not a limitless appetite for singles from it. In America, the disc spent only nine weeks on the *Billboard* Hot 100, and climbed only to No. 12.

The modest success of the American single was not enough to scuttle plans for its British counterpart. A separate edit was made on November 11, while Wings were in Australia, this version taking the combined 'Venus and Mars' and 'Rock Show' (EMI matrix 7YCE.21777) down to 3'43". As on the American version, the B side would be 'Magneto and Titanium Man' (EMI matrix 7YCE.21778). In Britain, the single did not crack the Top 50.

The American trade press mustered polite approval; their British colleagues treated the single as what it was—a couple of tracks from an album that had been in the shops for six months.

> *Already on the charts at a starred 82, the latest single from one of our few super-groups may be acting as a bit of a preview for their upcoming spring tour. Same kind of goodtime feel as 'Band on the Run.'*[13]
>
> *Unsigned,* Billboard

> *'Venus and Mars' grows from a slow beginning, as we wait for the 'concert' to begin, into another extremely strong show of shows from the most prolific of the ex-Beatles. McCartney again demonstrates a remarkable aptitude as not only a writer and performer, but as a producer, and he's showing no signs yet of slowing down.*[14]
>
> *Unsigned,* Cash Box

> *Equally adept with a soothing ballad or a moving rocker, McCartney gets the chance to flex his vocal muscles after a brief prelude on this ode to the road. Visiting places like the Hollywood Bowl and the Garden on the way, Wings takes off once again.*[15]
>
> *Unsigned,* Record World

> *First half has a certain teasingly romantic quality, second half drags till you're glad it's a single.*[16]
>
> *Vivien Goldman,* Sounds

> *It must still be a bit of a mystery as to why 'Letting Go' never really made the charts, but here's Wings' follow-up, taken, like the B side, from the album of the same name. As so many thousands of people already have the album, this probably doesn't need too much introduction, except to say it's a lot raunchier than 'Letting Go,' and should do a lot better.*[17]
>
> *Sue Byrom,* Record Mirror & Disc

Recording Sessions

Tuesday, October 21–Thursday, October 23, 1975.
EMI Studios, Studio Two, London.
Recording: 'Silver,' 'Same Mistakes,' 'Candy Man (Jam)' and Concert Set.
Mixing: 'Silver,' 'Same Mistakes' and 'Candy Man (Jam).'

Paul's bet that Denny would drop complaining about spending time in the studio if he had a share of the spotlight seemed to be paying off: when Wings returned to EMI Studios on October 21, he had two new songs, which Paul gamely slotted into the recording schedule. On Tuesday, the band filled one reel with attempts to record Laine's 'Silver,' a punchy tune that called out for additions from Wings' touring horn section. They did not return to the track on Wednesday, opting instead to take on Denny's other new song, 'Same Mistakes,' a more easygoing ballad with attractive melodic ideas but not quite finished. After several attempts, the band lapsed into a jam based on the Anthony Newley–Leslie Bricusse tune 'Candy Man.'

The Thursday session was essentially a studio rehearsal for the Australian tour, a run-through of all but the acoustic section of the set, plus a couple of jams, all captured on five reels of 24-track tape:

Reel 1: 'Venus and Mars' / 'Rock Show' / 'Jet' / 'Let Me Roll It' / 'Spirits of Ancient Egypt' / 'Little Woman Love / C Moon (Medley)' / 'Maybe I'm Amazed'
Reel 2: 'Jam' / 'Lady Madonna' / 'The Long and Winding Road' / 'Live and Let Die' / 'You Gave Me the Answer' / 'Magneto and Titanium Man'
Reel 3: 'Jam' / 'Go Now' / 'Call Me Back Again' / 'My Love' / 'Listen to What the Man Said' / 'Letting Go'
Reel 4: 'Medicine Jar' / 'Band on the Run' / 'Hi, Hi, Hi'
Reel 5: 'Soily'

After the session, Paul and Linda caught the Who's concert at Wembley Arena and a post-show party at the venue.

—

The plan was to arrive in Australia a few days ahead of the tour's November 1 start date so that the players and crew could acclimatize, but there was a touch of rock star drama at the start of the trip. McCulloch, Laine and English were on board Quantas flight QF8, along with the two dozen technicians on the Showco crew, and about 225 other passengers. Nowhere to be seen on the A747 Jumbo jet were Paul, Linda and their three girls. As it came time to seal the cabin, Crowder bounded toward the cockpit and begged the crew to hold up the flight—*we're not waiting for just* anyone, *you know*—and calls went back and forth between the cockpit, the gate, the control tower and Quantas's offices.

When the McCartneys turned up, another 15 minutes was needed to load their 20 pieces of luggage. All told, Paul and Linda delayed the flight by 45 minutes.[18] "We slept in," was Paul's explanation. Quantas billed him $3,000 (£1,450) for the delay.

Landing at Perth Airport on October 28, after a 17-hour flight, Paul could not have helped noticing the difference between the Beatles' arrival in Melbourne in 1964, and Wings' arrival now. On that first visit, some 5,000 fans greeted them at the airport, with many more (the police estimate was 250,000)[19] lining the route into town and awaiting them at their hotel. But as ego-gratifying as that reception was, it had its downside: the Beatles were driven twice around the airfield in an open, flatbed truck so that their fans could see them. But it was windy and raining, and the Beatles could do little to shield themselves from the elements. They regarded the episode as a symbol of the indignities Beatlemania visited upon them.

Fandom had changed immensely in 11 years. Now, as Wings stepped onto the tarmac, they were greeted by only a handful of fans who barely outnumbered the reporters on hand—a circumstance that allowed reporters to refer to Paul as "the man who once enjoyed superstar rating and was part of a group that affected millions of teenagers,"[20] while also acknowledging that there had been a rush on tickets for his Australian shows.

Tickets had become a headache for Paul Dainty, the promoter. When the shows sold out within hours, some of the fan ire was directed toward Dainty's office. "The public is pretty hard to satisfy," a spokesman told the *Sydney Morning Herald*. "If we stage an outdoor concert, someone complains. If we have mail bookings, someone complains. We decided that one booking office was the fairest way of selling the tickets. Those at the head of the queue who waited all through the night naturally got the best seats."[21]

Now Dainty faced a new ticket problem: forged tickets sold at premium prices. Dainty had foreseen this, so he had the tickets printed on matte stock, with reproductions of the band's signatures and several anti-counterfeiting features.

"The tickets cost me about three times as much as normal concert tickets because the printing was so intricate," Dainty explained. "We included a secret marking that only a handful of people will know about. It will take a real professional to reproduce the tickets—but even if he does we will still be able to pick the fakes. . . . I've no doubt that most of the tickets went to genuine fans but I wouldn't be surprised if scalpers are at work outside the Pavilion before the concert."[22]

Dainty also arranged, at Paul's behest, for a film crew, led by Gordon Bennett, to shadow Wings during the tour. Bennett,* a cameraman who had covered Beatles press conferences in Sydney, Adelaide and Melbourne for Australia's Seven Network, was at Perth Airport with his 16mm camera when Wings landed and was astonished to find, when he was introduced to the McCartneys, that Paul remembered him.

"He said to me, 'Have we met before?'" Bennett recalled. "It was probably because at the press conferences, the cameramen went in close—you did braver things than the reporters would have to do."[23]

Bennett was given an Access All Areas pass for the duration of Paul's visit. All told, he filled 24 rolls of 400-foot 16mm film and 16 900-foot Nagra audio reels—roughly four hours of mostly offstage, backstage and between-concerts footage—at a cost of A$10,000 ($12,670, £6,110).

"The pitch was," Bennett added, "would I cover, in documentary style, the tour of Australia. I shot a lot of stuff showing the group preparing to go out onto the stage, a lot of crowd material, and then a lot of material onstage [although] my stuff was never meant to be complete songs. We went out to where they were staying and did a lot of material with the kids, and with Paul and Linda playing bongo drums. And there was a lot of them meeting people at concerts, and that sort of thing, that never saw the light of day."[24]

The band and crew made the Sheraton Hotel in Perth their headquarters for the next six days, with the McCartneys occupying the fourteenth-floor penthouse Presidential Suite. Never far from the McCartneys was Billy Manne, a 23-year-old karate instructor from Melbourne who was hired as their bodyguard.

"I'm an ordinary guy," Manne told a reporter. "I don't want to frighten people. But if trouble breaks out I can handle it. . . . The last thing they want me to do—the last thing I want to do—is hit anybody. Mostly I just ask the fans to leave him alone. Most are happy to respect his wishes."[25]

Soon after their arrival, Paul and Linda began tinkering with a new song, inspired not by their new surroundings but by a quirky vision of London.

"Linda and I were sitting in the hotel in Perth, which was a Sheraton, you know, top floor, 'Elton John Suite,'" Paul said with a laugh, adding, "I don't mean that how it sounds, actually! We started doing this thing, and we came up with these lyrics: '*Walking down the sidewalk on a purple afternoon.*'"[26]

During their stay, they came up with the rest of the first verse: "*I was accosted by a barker playing a simple tune upon his flute / Silver rain was falling down upon the dirty ground of London Town.*"

---

* Bennett's name was the source of much amusement for the British visitors. For decades, the phrase "Gordon Bennett!" had been used by Brits to express surprise, or even outrage. Though the precise roots of this idiomatic phrase are unknown, it is thought to derive from the controversial reputation of James Gordon Bennett Jr. (1841–1918), son of the founder of the *New York Herald*.

Although Showco's stage, sound and lighting rigs would not be loaded into the Perth Entertainment Centre's main hall until 7 A.M. on October 31, the center made its rehearsal room available to Wings during their stay, and the band practiced there most afternoons. On October 29, their second day in Perth, Paul, Linda and the girls spent the early afternoon sightseeing around Perth and Rottnest Island, just off the coast, before returning to the rehearsal space late in the day to run through part of the set and celebrate Denny's thirty-first birthday.

And then, finally, the curtain rose on the Australian tour. A crowd of 8,000 responded with a gratifying roar as a single spotlight and a cascade of glitter illuminated Paul in his kimono, standing at the microphone with his Rickenbacker bass, shin-deep in a cloud of dry ice wafting over the platform—a newly added staging touch—singing about a good friend of his who follows the stars. When 'Venus and Mars' segued into 'Rock Show,' the full stage panorama was gradually illuminated. Denny with his double-neck Ibanez guitar, Jimmy with his red Gibson SG Special, Joe on his drum riser and Linda behind a bank of keyboards, all came into view, pink bubbles slowly rising behind them.

Paul in his kimono at the Perth Entertainment Centre, November 1, 1975

The setlist, unchanged since Dundee, unfolded smoothly, with sharp-edged, fluid guitar contributions from Jimmy, solid drumming from Joe beneath a subtly shifting rhythmic backdrop by Paul, Denny and Linda, and tightly matched backing vocals. For an audience that had not seen Wings live—and for fans from the Beatles days who remembered their concerts as 30 minutes in which only hints of the hits could be heard between waves of audience shrieking—it was an ear-opening evening. And though the Perth crowd was usually subdued, according to local journalists, Paul's exhortations to get up and dance, toward the end of the set, brought the crowd into the aisles, where they overwhelmed a security force that had been able to keep order until then.

"The audience responded with unfettered enthusiasm," Zoltan Kovacs wrote in the *Western Australian*. "Many people said it was the greatest concert staged in Perth and the deafening, almost frightening roars and whistles of applause that filled the Center after each number testified to this." Greg Kelton, reviewing for the *Australian Advertiser*, described the show as "the most exciting rock concert I have ever witnessed,"[27] and Brandon Stewart, in *Hamersley News*, noted that "the entire performance was quite an emotional experience for many, bringing some almost to tears."[28]

After his decade-long absence, every Australian media outlet from Perth to Canberra was set on securing some face-to-face time with Paul, so Dainty's office scheduled a press conference for early Sunday afternoon at the Cottesloe Civic Centre. Some 200 reporters were on hand, including writers from the United States and Japan, eager to file reports previewing McCartney's planned visits to their countries.

Dainty's scheduling was not optimal for Paul, but that hardly mattered: musicians, producers, record executives and jet planes had had to wait upon his pleasure, so a bunch of reporters could, too. He and Linda turned up about 90 minutes after the scheduled start time. The Australian actor Garry McDonald, on hand to host the news conference, settled into his popular Norman Gunston character—a clueless television interviewer with greased hair combed straight forward, around whom the recently launched *Norman Gunston Show* was built—and kept the gathered writers entertained while they waited.

"We had a show last night," Paul offered as a reason for their tardiness. "Anyway, who wants to get up on a Sunday morning to come to something like this?"[29] He fielded questions for about an hour, eating prawns and sipping wine (which he exchanged for a beer once he noticed that there was a choice).

McDonald/Gunston's presence as host allowed Paul to reconfigure annoyance as humor at a couple of points. "I don't like giving press conferences," he noted. "We used to have to give a lot when I was with the Beatles. I don't have to now. Usually they're too formal, but Norman Gunston helped us loosen up in front of the cameras." When he was asked whether the Beatles would reunite, he said, "No chance, no—we're getting back together with Norm; we're forming a group with Norm here."[30]

Taking the opportunity to introduce each band member, including the four-man horn section, Paul redirected the discussion from the Beatles to Wings. Acknowledging that "trying to follow the Beatles" was the band's toughest challenge, he added that there were compensations.

"This is new, this is exciting," he said. "However, the feeling of being on stage is not much different from the feelings when I was working with the Beatles. There are a series of thoughts going through my head—it terrifies me. I am always thinking of whether I am doing the song justice or what is going to happen when I get back to the hotel after the show."

He insisted, too, that Wings would come to be seen as a real band, not just his backing group.

"It will get to a stage later on where I will be taking a lesser role," he predicted. "We are trying to work it out so that everybody gets a bit of a go on stage and on record."[31]

After the press conference, Paul and Linda lingered in the Civic Center's garden, sitting under a striped umbrella and continuing the discussion with individual writers from several Australian publications before hopping into a rented Jeep and driving off.

The next morning Wings flew east to Adelaide, where about 400 fans were on hand to greet them when they arrived at 5 P.M. The band and crew headed to the Parkroyal Motor Inn; the McCartneys opted this time to rent a house from an Adelaide physician—a place outside town with a kidney-shaped swimming pool, cactuses that reminded Linda of her time in Arizona and, to the family's delight, a corral with four horses (and a hefty stock of carrots to feed them).

In Adelaide, soundchecks were at 5 P.M. both days, with the concerts starting at 8:15, for audiences of 4,000 at each show. While both Adelaide concerts went down well, there were several technical problems at the November 4 show: tuning issues affected 'Jet,' and 'Live and Let Die,' and 'Junior's Farm' was sufficiently out of tune for Paul to stop the performance a few bars into the introduction and have the band tune up before starting again. 'Maybe I'm Amazed' was marred by howling feedback.

Unwinding after the show, Paul discovered that his decision to rent a house paid an unexpected musical dividend. As Linda prepared a late-night supper, Paul strummed an acoustic guitar and took in the scene. In no time at all, the pair captured an idiosyncratic musical snapshot of their Down Under digs.

"Around the kitchen," Paul recollected, "there was all these little pots, there's seco, macaroni, marijuana, and various other things. And I just kind of read them all off—rice, seco, macaroni—and I put them down into the song. And then I was looking around for the second verse, because I wanted to do it exactly with the stuff that was in the house and not make up anything of my own—I just felt like taking it down, like taking dictation almost—just whatever was in the room. Then I noticed a little plaque on the wall, you know these little plaques that you see in kitchens that say, 'Welcome to Cornwall,' or something, and this one said, 'No matter where I serve my guests, they seem to like my kitchen best.' So, I had the second verse.

"And then, for the middle of that, I was just watching what Linda was doing. And she had rice cooking and she had some beans going and salad and stuff. So I just wrote it all into the tune. And then afterward I said, 'Well, that'd be a good song for you [to sing], you know.'"[32] *

Within days, Paul was mentioning the song in interviews. "I'm calling it 'Cook of the House,'" he told John Hamilton of *The Herald*. "You've got to be in the right mood to write a song—if it ever became a formula, you'd be finished."[33]

Paul was not playing his new songs to the band yet, but some of the musicians knew he was working on new material.

"There's no doubt about it," Howie Casey remembered. "Of course, we didn't stay with him, because he, Linda and the kids would stay at some ranch or whatever, and do their thing. But he'd pick up ideas—you could see him. He was almost like a sponge. Something—a lick, something that he said—he *had* it, and it would come out somewhere else, as a song or whatever. He had that ability. His ears were always there, listening, listening."[34]

About 50 fans and 15 reporters were at the airport in Sydney when Wings landed at 5:15 P.M. on November 6. Accommodations were split, with the crew heading toward the Commodore Chateau and Town House Motel, and the band, including the McCartneys, staying at the Sebel Town House. The soundchecks were at 5 P.M. at the Hordern Pavilion, with the concerts on November 7 and 8 starting at 8:15, each for a crowd of 5,200.

Judging from the review in the *Sydney Morning Herald*, the audience was torn between listening quietly and going crazy—the latter response reserved mostly for the handful of Beatles classics. When the concert ended, the audience refused to stop stamping and shouting until Paul and the band returned to the stage, each with a bouquet from which they threw individual flowers into the crowd, as Paul apologized that the band had "run out of songs" and waved good night.

That night saw a brief scuffle between McCartney and a drunken McCulloch. Paul spoke about the incident through the veil of diplomacy, telling Paul Du Noyer that "you'd want your kip, and [Jimmy]'d be in the next hotel room to you, blasting music after coming in off the piss at four in the morning. I'd have to go to him, 'Hey, Jim, do us a favor, man.' 'Oh, sorry man, were ya asleep? Oh, okay, aye.'"[35]

But one of the road crew remembered the encounter ending differently, telling a friend: "When Paul approached him, [Jimmy] told Paul to 'fuck off.' Paul's response was to knock him out cold."[36]

Wings and company headed to Brisbane on November 9, for shows at the 4,000-seat Festival

* In an interview with Barry Miles for the *Wings at the Speed of Sound* archive edition (2014), Paul said, "'Cook of the House' was something that Linda wrote, as I recall, in Australia." He also included the track in Linda's posthumous *Wide Prairie* album, although writing about the song's origin in the liner notes for that disc, he discussed the inspiration for the song in terms of "we," rather than either taking credit or attributing it to Linda. Here we have opted to quote what he said about the song shortly after it was written.

WELCOME TO JAPAN

WINGS

THE GREATEST CONCERTS

AT BUDOKAN ●EVER IN THIS COUNTRY● TOKYO

NOVEMBER 19.20.21

Sold Out!

LETTING GO

●EPR-10863 ¥500

McCartney
●EPS-80231

RAM
●EPS-80232

Wings Wild Life
●EPS-80233

Red Rose Speedway
●EPS-80234

Band On The Run
●EPS-80235

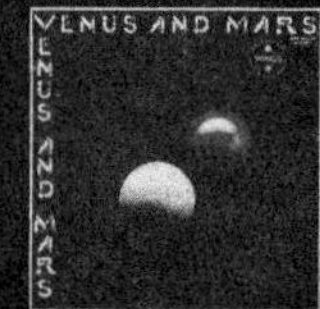

Venus And Mars
●EPS-80236

TOSHIBA-EMI LIMITED

UDO ARTISTS, INC.

Wings, 1975 Japanese tour trade ad

Hall on November 10 and 11. A crowd of 500 at the airport awaited them, with more at the Parkroyal Motor Inn, where the band and crew stayed. Paul and Linda again rented a private house.

Knowing the McCartneys' fondness for animals, EMI Australia arranged for a visit to the Lone Pine Koala Bear Sanctuary in Brisbane, where Gordon Bennett filmed Paul and Linda holding the bears and speaking to one of the wardens about unique aspects of koala bear behavior.

"I felt a bit privileged because I was getting into areas of shooting material of the McCartneys that no other press photographer, or cameraman could get close to," said Bennett. "Because I was employed by McCartney to do whatever the McCartneys wanted, and they never requested anything. It was always left up to me as to what we wanted to do."[37]

They were back in time for the 5 P.M. soundcheck, to which a dozen winners of a local radio contest were invited to watch the band rehearse and collect autographs. Two of the fans, Enrica Molinaro and Agatha Rametta, both schoolgirls, told the McCartneys that they had been unable to get tickets to the show. "I'll see what I can do," Linda told them, and moments later, Alan Crowder appeared with tickets for the girls.

That night Paul's most notable ad lib during the set was a fake-out introduction to 'Yesterday,' in which he strummed the opening chords but sang *"Once a jolly swagman . . ."* the opening line of 'Waltzing Matilda,' the turn-of-the-century Australian favorite by Andrew Barton "Banjo" Paterson and Christina Macpherson. The single line was enough to draw laughs from the Brisbane audience, and if the introduction prematurely signaled that 'Yesterday' was next on the setlist, the joke did nothing to lessen the roar of delight once he began the song. He kept the fragment of 'Waltzing Matilda' in the show for the three remaining Australian concerts, and fake-out introductions to 'Yesterday' became a running gag.

One destination Wings would not be waltzing to, however, was Japan. Before the second Brisbane show, MPL received word that Japan's minister of justice, Osamu Inaba, had revoked Paul's visa because of his 1972 and 1973 drug convictions. Laine had a marijuana arrest as well, and although the charges in Linda's Los Angeles drug bust would be dropped by the end of November, her arrest did not sit well with the Japanese authorities. Wings concerts scheduled for November 19–21 at the Budokan Hall in Tokyo were therefore canceled.

"It was the minister of justice's fault," Paul told a reporter, shortly after he returned to London. "I suppose he'd say it was my fault for having smoked some of the deadly weed. But we had our visas signed by the London Japanese Embassy. Everything had been cleared, David Bailey was coming over to do a film and we were in Australia, just about a week out from going to Japan when a little note arrived saying sorry, the Japanese minister of justice says 'No.'

"They're still old-fashioned out there. There's a generation gap and the wrong end of the gap is in the ministry of justice, as it is here. The older folks see a great danger in allowing in an alien who has admitted smoking marijuana, and supposedly they're trying to stamp it out, using all the wrong methods as usual. . . . It was just one of those things, but we felt a bit sick about it. It's so short-sighted."[38]

With the cancellation of the Tokyo shows, Paul proposed using the dates for concerts in New Zealand, but promoters were unable to find suitable venues on such short notice.

Wings left Brisbane at 3:50 P.M. on November 12 and flew to Melbourne. When they arrived at Tullamarine Airport at 7:15, only three fans and eight reporters awaited them, the reporters eager to hear his response to the Japanese cancellation.

"The annoying thing really," he told them, "is the whole affair is two years old, and in America, we made a lot of representations and stuff, and said to the American government, 'Will you let us in?' And they said, 'Yeah, okay, you know, you're a good boy now, so that's okay.' So we're allowed in America. And Australia!"[39]

Wings were whisked away in a motorcade that included five Rolls-Royces and a Mercedes, the musicians and crew ferried to the Southern Cross Hotel, and the McCartneys to a house they were renting in nearby Kilmore. Once the family settled in, Paul began mulling over the Japanese cancellation. Japan was a significant market for the Beatles, collectively and individually, and it made sense to make a gesture of some kind to the Japanese fans, so Paul summoned the band and Gordon Bennett to his rental house to film a short message.

"Hello, people of Japan," he began. "It's Paul McCartney, of Wings, saying that we're very sorry we can't come to Japan to play our music to you this time. But if the minister of justice says we can't come in, then we can't come in. So, we'll see you next time, don't worry, we'll see you when we come back to your beautiful country. Sayonara. And, uh . . . rock on."[40]

The band—with Paul, Linda and Jimmy sharing a love seat, Denny perched on its left back edge, smoking a cigarette, and Joe standing behind them—then launched into a laid-back performance of 'Bluebird,' with Paul and Jimmy playing acoustic guitars, Joe keeping time by striking the back of the love seat, and the full band joining in for the vocal harmonies.

The two Melbourne shows were special, not only because they were the final stops on the tour and were performed to the largest audiences—at each show there were 3,000 reserved seats and 11,000 lawn seats—but also because both shows were filmed for a television special (although only the November 13 show was used), to be broadcast by ATV-0 on November 24. There was a radio broadcast of the show as well.

Now the film would have a secondary purpose: a version of it was sent to Japanese television as another offering to disappointed fans, and to counter the negative publicity from Wings' visas being rescinded. As it turned out, the Japanese television producers had ideas of their own.

"We did the TV show for all the people who couldn't get in to see us in Australia because some of the tickets were going for Sinatra prices," Paul explained. "And we immediately got a print of it up to Japan, so that the weekend we were supposed to have arrived, they had a big TV show and they turned it round into a big current affairs programme, too, with an hour and a half of people discussing the merits of marijuana. In a way we had become martyrs for the cause, which is a drag."[41]

For the Melbourne shows, the soundchecks were moved up to 2:30 P.M., but although the sound and lighting equipment may have been tested with special care because of the filming, they followed a ritual that Paul put in place during the British tour. While the band was setting up and tuning, Paul would head out into the hall to Morris Lyda's mixing board. Sitting next to Lyda with a microphone, he would ask each band member to play, and whether they were comfortable with the sound from their stage monitors.

"Everyone wanted a different mix, of course," Lyda explained. "At the time, coming up with discrete mixes wasn't sophisticated, but we were able to patch together a number of different sub-mixers so that we could come up with individual mixes for the horns, for the guitars, and the drums, and then multiple mixes for Paul and Linda, depending where they were sitting."[42]

Reviewing the first show for *The Age*, Bryan Patterson was struck by the sheer volume of the show and by the band's musicianship. "McCartney has been hailed as one of the greats of contemporary music. His performance confirmed the description. Shifting effortlessly from bass to piano, 12-string guitar and organ, he had the audience dancing in the aisles with a spirited set of songs from his latest albums and old Beatle favorites like 'Lady Madonna' and 'Yesterday.'"[43]

For the second show—the tour's finale—Heather, Mary and Stella were in the front row; one reporter took note of four-year-old Stella standing on her seat, blowing kisses at the stage and calling out, "Hello Daddy!"

"We let them go to selected concerts," Paul told John Hamilton, of *The Herald*, after the show. "I think it's right that they should know what their mum and dad do and why we do all this travelling. Why? It's the enjoyment. It's like one long holiday, staying at the best hotels. But instead of going to the bar for a drink in the evening, you do a gig. You get your kicks by seeing the people out there, people with candles waving . . . people bopping . . . people just going crackers."[44]

At the end of the set, Paul and Wings let the audience demand an encore for a full five minutes before coming out to play 'Hi, Hi, Hi' and 'Soily,' the latter accompanied by fireworks and the release of 400 helium balloons.

Paul never lost the affection of his friends Down Under after the Beatles parted ways. *Red Rose Speedway* and *Band on the Run* both topped the Australian hit parade, and as the helium balloons ascended in Melbourne's Myer Music Bowl, *Venus and Mars* was heading for the No. 2 spot. "Paul was very happy with the Australian tour," Brian Brolly told a reporter as the group signed off in Melbourne, "and wants to tell people that he will be back. He was delighted with every aspect of the tour—it was one of the best."[45]

With Japan off the schedule and New Zealand not a possibility, the McCartneys decided to spend the rest of the time they had allotted to their Pacific tour on an impromptu vacation. When the band flew back to London on November 15, the McCartneys and Brian Brolly flew to Honolulu, Hawaii, where they were met by the photographer David Bailey and his new wife, the Hawaii-born fashion model Marie Helvin. Bailey had been in Tokyo to shoot a documentary about Wings in Japan for ABC-TV, the American network, but like the McCartneys, he and Helvin now had time on their hands. One Hawaiian paper noted that Bailey was considering making a film about sumo wrestling with backing from MPL.[46]

The trip was not entirely idyllic. On November 24, violent thunderstorms lashed Honolulu, bringing two inches of rain, 25-foot waves and winds in excess of 40 miles an hour. The storms continued on and off for several days, but during a respite on November 26, Paul felt the ocean was calm enough for some swimming and body surfing near Koko Head. Locals told him *never* to swim in that area the day after a storm, but he ignored their advice. It was a miscalculation that nearly cost him his life.

"In Hawaii, I used to swim off a rock about ten feet above the water level," Paul later explained. "The huge Hawaiian waves would roll in without breaking. You'd wait for one and get in the water on the crest of a wave, then you'd wait for another wave to lift you up the ten feet onto this little rock platform. It was a thing all the local kids did. So me, I like to see if I can do those things local kids do, I like to go native a bit. So I do it and get it off to perfection.

"But I forgot that if there's been a storm the waves are going to behave differently. And one day I went in after a storm. It looked alright, but when I tried to catch a wave to lift me out, it dumped me. I was about 30 feet out, struggling to get back. I felt myself getting weak and beginning to perhaps accept that this was it. But eventually, I pulled myself together and said to God, 'Please put me out.' And He did."[47]

He was not unscathed: as the waves swept him back toward the shore, he was dragged across rocks that caused cuts and abrasions, some deep enough to leave scars. He spent a quiet Thanksgiving recuperating, on November 27, and the following day, he and Linda joined Bailey and Helvin for an unusual photo shoot Bailey had been commissioned to do for Alpha Cubic, a clothing line. Bailey and McCartney set up a pair of poles and hung a lime-green clothesline between them, from which a pair of pink rubber gloves were hung, their fingers dripping water. Bailey photographed the line and gloves against the stormy sky, Bailey commenting, "I found this stuff in a hardware shop in Tokyo. You can't think of two nastier colors. It's an image you can't forget. It's a very chic picture."[48]

That afternoon, Paul was leafing through the *Honolulu Star Bulletin*, and after scanning the news, features, sports and gossip columns, he found, on page F8, listings for adult films that were playing at cinemas on the island of Oahu. He jotted down the names of some of the films—*Kid Sister, Spanish Doll, Oriental Princess, The School for Girls*, and *Sleepy Head*, as well as references he found elsewhere on the page, to "Hawaii's original outcall massage" and Rosanna, a dancer at Club Hubba Hubba.

He began tweaking some of these—Rosanna became Roxanne, *The School for Girls* became *Girls' School*, and the "18 years or older" warning on one of the ads was changed to "18 years or younger"—and soon he was stringing them together with narrative phrases to create four verses for an up-tempo number he called 'Girls' School.'

"I picked up one of these American newspapers," Paul explained, "and at the back, in the entertainment section, they've got a big page where it's all the porn movies. And they're all called great titles. So, I just took all the titles, and if you read through the lyrics of the thing, it's nearly all just porn titles. *Sleepy Head, School Mistress, Woman Trainer,* and *Spanish Doll*. I must see them sometime, 'cos I don't go to that kind of thing, you see."[49]

Another song Paul wrote in Hawaii was a response to critics who insisted that he wrote nothing but fluff. In his lyrics, Paul characterized "fluff" more pointedly as "silly love songs," which became the song's title. Some of the ideas were still being worked out at this stage: near the line "*what's wrong with that?*" he scrawled, (*"OR I'm ONE of THEM!!"*), a less subtle alternative that he soon dropped.

From the start, he envisioned a complicated piece with several strands of vocal counterpoint, as if to make the point that whether or not one considers love songs silly, they can have more than their fair share of musical complexity. On his manuscript from Hawaii, the lines sung contrapuntally are listed as "first line" (the rising "*I love you*"), "second line" (the rising, then falling "*Ah, I can't explain, the feeling's plain to me / say can't you see?*") and "third line" (the descending "*How can I tell you about my loved one?*"), indicating their order of appearance in the thickening texture he had in mind. When he recorded a piano demo of the song, Linda sat beside him and sang some of the counterpoint against his own vocal.

"'Silly Love Songs' is basically just saying, 'What's wrong with that? What's wrong with being romantic?' I think the majority of people do feel like that. But I think critics, and harder people who have to listen to 300 records a week, haven't got, really, much romance in their souls after a couple of years of doing that. I think it's really just me saying, 'Look, I'm likely to write a lot of other love songs, 'cause I like doing it, and it seems to go down well, and most people I meet like that kind of thing anyway. So . . . Sod you, I'm gonna do it, whether you like it or not.' And yet in a little way, by saying '*What's wrong with that?*' I'm anticipating their criticism."[50]

A third song Paul started in Hawaii was 'Must Do Something About It,' a darker vision of life without anyone to sing silly love songs to. The song's protagonist watches a sunset, plays solitaire, tries (unsuccessfully) to reach a friend by telephone—all couched in attractively wistful music in which major chords melt into minor key rejoinders. The line *"All day long I've been alone"* is repeated in a couple of verses, leading to the refrain, *"Must do something about it,"* although the underlying sense is that the loneliness captured in the song continues unchanged.

The McCartneys spent much of their time in Honolulu with Bailey and Helvin, and Helvin's local roots came in handy—not least when it came time to find recreational smokables. Helvin showed them an especially strong local strain, called pakalolo, the Hawaiian word for cannabis (a literal translation would be "crazy weed"). She also took Heather on a shopping trip for vintage clothing, during which Helvin set aside 50 outfits for Linda to try.

The McCartneys were useful to Helvin, too, if only to counter what Helvin described as Bailey's more curmudgeonly impulses. Helvin and the McCartneys made common cause in refusing to credit Bailey's claim that he disliked all music except the Rolling Stones, and they dragged him to a concert by Loggins and Messina, who were touring to promote their *So Fine* album. The McCartneys' only request was that the outing be kept quiet so that they could spend their time in Honolulu unbothered by the press or fans.

Unfortunately, a friend of the Helvins—a local television personality, Robert M. "Lucky" Luck—arranged for Bailey, Helvin and the McCartneys to have . . . *stage seats.* Paul quickly arranged to watch the show from backstage, but they were spotted by at least one reporter, and by the time they left the concert, a crowd of fans awaited them. "Hey Paul!" one young man called out. "Have you read *Helter Skelter*?" Helvin, who *had* read Vincent Bugliosi's book about the Manson murders, was horrified; Paul just shouted back, "I wrote it, man!"[51]

The day after the Loggins and Messina concert, the McCartneys attended a party thrown by Linda Helvin (Marie's mother) to celebrate her daughter's marriage. Helvin was having a rough time: her parents had recently split, and she had just been introduced to her mother's new boyfriend. Helvin, then 23, confided in Paul that thinking of her mother as sexually active was difficult for her.

"Paul picked up on my discomfort," Helvin wrote in her memoir, "and was really supportive about it. 'I've been there, and you just have to deal with it in this way, y'know, Marie . . .' It was a huge relief to me to talk about it with him; it was a delicate situation and he responded with great sensitivity."[52]

The McCartneys' immediate plans were governed by the holiday season. Following the pattern they established early in their relationship, they planned to spend time with the Eastmans in New York around Christmas, then back to London and up to Liverpool for New Year's Eve.

“It’s a ritual,” McCartney told a reporter in Melbourne about the Liverpool visit. “It’s something I’ve done ever since I was five . . . and Uncle Joe, who can play the bagpipes, always comes along to pipe in the New Year.”[53]

They decided on a gradual progress from Honolulu to Liverpool, flying first to Los Angeles and spending a couple of days there. The Los Angeles correspondent from *Melody Maker* reported that they were spotted having a hamburger at the Rainbow Bar and Grill on Sunset Strip on December 5, and they caught the Canadian band Hammersmith at the Starwood Club on December 6.

They also checked in on Mal Evans. Evans was writing a memoir of his years as a Beatles roadie and assistant, to be called *Living the Beatles Legend*, and had engaged a ghostwriter, John Hoernie, to put his ideas into shape. Earlier in the year, Mal had asked Paul’s permission to proceed, and Paul sent his blessing:

> Dear Mal,
> Sure you can do your book, as long as you tell ’em how lovely I am. I agree to you writing the story—and wish you luck with it, you great big POOFTAH!
>
> Love,
>
> Paul McCartney[54]

Mal and Hoernie sold their project to Grosset & Dunlap, which gave them a January 12, 1976, deadline. When he completed his first draft, Mal sent copies of the manuscript to all four Beatles, who signed off on it, although he continued to tweak it as the deadline approached. At the moment, however, he was having financial difficulties, and he spoke to Paul about some possible remedies, including looking into whether he was due any back pay from Apple, and whether he might have further payments for some songs—mostly notably ‘Fixing a Hole’—to which he contributed lyrics. Paul suggested that Mal discuss these issues with John as well, and hinted that they could come to some accommodation.

Paul, Linda and the girls flew to New York around December 10, and on December 13 they dropped in on John and Yoko at the Dakota. The Lennons were entertaining the photographer Bob Gruen that evening, and as Gruen remembers it, they were watching TV and smoking a joint when the doorbell rang. It was not a welcome sound: part of the point of living in a building like the Dakota was that security was tight, so anyone visiting the building had to get past doormen on the sidewalk and in the reception area, where visitors waited behind a locked door as the attendant called up to announce them. Paul and Linda wanted the visit to be a surprise, and the Dakota security guard was not immune to Beatle magic, so the McCartneys were let through.

"Understandably, John was a bit paranoid when he heard his doorbell," Gruen recalled. "Only John, Yoko, Sean, and myself were in the apartment, so John asked if I would answer the door and try to keep the visitor from coming inside. The Lennons' apartment had a small foyer between two doors. When I opened the inner door, I heard what sounded like Christmas carols. 'Don't worry,' I yelled back to John and Yoko. 'It's just some kids caroling.' When I opened the outer door, I saw it was actually Paul and Linda. They'd been singing 'We Wish You a Merry Christmas.' I was really surprised and said, 'I think you're looking for the guys in the bedroom.'

"As they came in, everyone was really happy to see each other. John and Yoko jumped up when Paul and Linda walked into the bedroom. They were obviously excited to see each other again. There was a lot of hugging and catching up, and we had a round of tea."[55]

Paul telephoned Mal Evans on December 14 with an offer that would alleviate Mal's financial distress. In a last-minute addition to his memoir, Mal wrote that McCartney "phoned me at home asking me to consider going on the road with him for his upcoming American tour in the spring of 1976." He added, "I do feel our friendship is as strong as ever."[56] They may also have discussed the back-pay issue further; within days, Mal was telling friends that he had been in touch with both John and Paul, and that he had reason to expect a "five-figure cheque"[57] from Apple.

The Lennons and the McCartneys met again for dinner on December 20, this time at Elaine's, a restaurant and bar on Second Avenue at 88th Street that was a favorite haunt of actors, writers and musicians. Elliott Mintz, a television journalist who had befriended the Lennons in 1972, was at the dinner as well, and he remembered it taking an unusual turn that could have unfolded in a number of ways, given that Elaine Kaufman, who opened the restaurant in 1963, was known to eject, berate or even get into physical altercations with patrons when she had issues with them.

"The [Lennons and McCartneys] didn't see anything they liked on the menu," Mintz recalled, "so Linda said that there was a great pizza place not far away. 'Do you think Elaine would mind if we sent out for pizza?' I had the feeling that would be a social faux pas, but I also sensed that Elaine wouldn't ask the group to leave. The pizza was delivered, and we had our Christmas meal."[58]

Part of the dinner chat was a nostalgic look at the ways John and Paul celebrated Christmas growing up, and the very different family dynamics they each experienced.

"We were very close, with aunties and uncles always coming in, sing-songs and parties," Paul said of his family a few months later. "I saw John and Yoko the last time I was in New York, and I happened to mention, for some reason, our family sing-songs. He said he never had them. He didn't have the sort of family life I had, being brought up by his aunt, having his mother killed [by] a car outside his house. Yoko didn't either. She had to make appointments to see her dad. I realize now how lucky I am to have a close, loving family."[59]

Paul and Linda spent Christmas in East Hampton with the Eastmans and flew back to London on December 29.

Back in England, the McCartneys traveled directly to High Park, where they would spend a couple of days before heading to Merseyside to ring in the New Year with Paul's family. One reason for their trip to Campbeltown was so that Paul could use the four-track Studer in Rude Studios to make demos of the songs he composed in Australia and Hawaii, as well as updated versions of the songs he wrote before the Australian tour.

He had some new ideas, too. Ringo was gathering material for a new album and was hoping to reprise one of the attractions of his successful 1973 *Ringo* album—songs from John, Paul and George. Paul volunteered to compose a new song for the project, and during his brief stay at High Park, he polished off two that would suit the drummer, the rough lyrics (and some production ideas) for both scribbled on the back of the same envelope.

One was 'Pure Gold,' which ponders a new relationship—"*Tell me, is she everything I see / Or is she really not the one for me / We know and though some may disagree / But do they know the way we want to be?*"—in a 1950's-tinged ballad style. That was a strong contender: the lyrics about the unknowns of a fresh romance reflected Ringo's relatively new relationship with Nancy Andrews, and if parts of the attractive, arching melody might test the limits of Ringo's vocal ability, the tune was similar in character to some of the songs on *Ringo*.

The other was 'Let 'Em In,' a song built on a nursery rhyme–like metrical scheme, with a melody etched from short, simple, mirroring phrases, exactly the kind of thing that suited the character of Ringo's voice. Much of the song had been written over the summer, and Paul rehearsed it with Wings during the Elstree sessions before the British tour. But it remained unfinished until now. It describes a party in progress—a touch of 'Yellow Submarine' for the mid-1970s—and its straightforward, non-rhyming opening verse sets the scene: "*Someone's knocking at the door / Somebody's ringing the bell / Do me a favor / Open the door / And let 'em in.*" That led to a list of friends attending the party, with Ringo at the door inviting everyone in.

"It was half-written with Ringo in mind, actually,"* Paul said of 'Let 'Em In.' "There was that and another one ['Pure Gold']. In the end I told him I was nicking it and he could have the other one. I just got this idea for a song about someone knocking at the door, someone ringing the bell, and then in the middle I got into the idea of naming people, just sort of symbolic of a crowd coming around."[60]

---

* Paul has offered contradictory remarks about whether he intended the song for Ringo. The present quote is from April 1976, roughly five months after he composed the song. However, when asked whether he wrote the song for Ringo in an interview published in the archival edition of *Wings at the Speed of Sound* (2014), he said, "No, don't trust the [inter]net. . . . I wrote a couple of songs for Ringo, but not that one."

Once he decided that the song was for Wings, rather than for Ringo, he produced a fanciful, personalized guest list, the kind of crowd he would love to see at the family's New Year's Eve party a few days later. Naturally, there were relatives, including Brother Michael (Mike McGear), Auntie Gin (his paternal aunt, Jane McCartney Harris) and Uncle Ian (Jane Harris's son, and therefore actually *cousin* Ian), and, of course, Linda (as Sister Suzy, using her Red Stripes pseudonym). Also included are a historical figure (Martin Luther—a reference to the American civil rights leader Martin Luther King, according to Paul,[61] not the sixteenth-century theologian), a pair of his musical heroes (Phil and Don, the Everly Brothers), one of his Beatles colleagues (Brother John, although Paul has said that this is also a reference to John Eastman), and a fictional character (Uncle Ernie, from the Who's *Tommy*).

"The whole meaning behind it starts to occur to you after you've written it," Paul mused. "I suppose it's like going to a psychiatrist; you have a dream and you take it to the psychiatrist, and I suppose it's filled with meaning, but it's down to the psych to get it out. You just tell him you dreamed about walking around in your knickers, and he says, 'Well, this means . . .' It's the same with a song; you write a song in order to put some words to your tune, stuff just comes out. . . . Like Sister Suzy will come out, and then you think, 'Sister Suzy, Brother . . . John, great, Martin Luther, that just came out . . . Phil and Don, rhymes with John, great.' And then you just go on—Uncle Ernie, Brother Michael, Auntie Gin, Uncle Stephen if you like."[62]

As he worked on the song, Paul also imagined the kind of production he wanted. On the other side of a page with the guest-list verse, he wrote a schematic for the production he envisioned, including several interludes of military-style drumming:

Intro—Racket, elec. Bells / wooden knocking
Gives way to RIFF
1. Instrumental RIFF
2. With vocal
3. Repeat with distant voices
4. Verse with 40 drums
5. Flutes join in riff—middle / vocal end on harmony thing (brass too)
6. Vocal verse, distant voices
7. Instrumental 40 drums RE-ENTER (sax)
8. Flutes / repeat their riff twice with break in the middle
9. Middle again
10. Vocal verse
11. Drums and EVERYTHING—FADE UP![63]

With the year coming to an end, some of the music papers published their year-end chart rankings and critics' picks, and as he did every year, Paul leafed through them for an overview of where he and Wings stood, from the press's perspective.

In the December 27 issue of *Record Mirror & Disc*, Ray Fox-Cumming included *Venus and Mars* among his Top 10 albums and 'Letting Go' on his Top 10 singles list. In the same publication, Dave Wright included the two-year-old *Band on the Run* among his Top 10 albums.

Cash Box, in the same week's edition, listed *Venus and Mars* as No. 30 on its 1975 albums chart. On the singles chart, 'Listen to What the Man Said' came in at No. 45, and 'Junior's Farm' was listed at No. 92.

Sounds, which based its survey on information supplied by the British Market Research Bureau and *Music Week*, published a sales chart for the year that put *Venus and Mars* at No. 9 and *Band on the Run* at No. 24. A similar listing in *NME* ranked albums and singles using "chart points" (based on a disc's number or weeks on the chart, as well its chart position), and also placed *Venus and Mars* at No. 9, with *Band on the Run* at No. 37. *Melody Maker* published a list showing the number of weeks albums had been on the British albums chart—66 weeks for *Band on the Run*, 22 weeks for *Venus and Mars*.

After a few productive days at High Park, the McCartneys headed to Liverpool. The partying was somewhat muted because of Jim's poor health. But Uncle Joe, as always, piped in the New Year, which for Paul would see tours of Europe and, at long last, America.

12

RECORDING AT THE SPEED OF SOUND

Much of 1976 would be devoted to touring, which suited Denny and Jimmy, who preferred live performance to recording. But with a stack of new songs ready to go, Paul was eager to return to the studio. With a focused push, a new album could be completed and released by the time the tour resumed in March. That would give Paul an opportunity to spruce up Wings' setlist with new material.

Studio time was booked by the time Paul and Linda returned to London, and Wings were summoned for the first sessions of the year.

Paul had by now established a pattern in which each album was a departure from its predecessor, and after the fanciful *Venus and Mars*, with its competing sci-fi, comic book, Fred Astaire and pop-rock influences, it was time for something more stripped-down and direct.

"I think the conscious thing was to get back to basics and sort of make some simple music," Paul said. "The songs that we came in with were a bit simpler and there didn't seem to be any reason to complicate them."[1]

Recording Sessions

Monday, January 5–Tuesday, January 6, 1976.

Abbey Road Studios,* Studio Two, London.

Recording: 'Must Do Something About It' and 'She's My Baby.'

Overdubbing: 'Must Do Something About It.'

---

* Ken Townsend, who joined EMI as a recording engineer in 1954—and was responsible for such innovations as ADT (Artificial Double Tracking)—proposed changing the name of EMI Studios to Abbey Road Studios when he was promoted to general manager of the facility in 1974. The name change became official in 1976.

As Wings set up in Studio Two, Paul ran through 'Must Do Something About It' for the rest of the band, while upstairs in the control room, Peter Henderson set preliminary levels on Paul's acoustic guitar, then walked down the long staircase to set up microphones around Joe's kit. Once again, Paul's go-to engineer, Geoff Emerick, was otherwise engaged, this time recording albums with Gallagher and Lyle and America. Henderson, who had turned 21 on New Year's Day, had been working as Emerick's assistant at AIR Studios for just over two years, but he had already engineered Jeff Beck's *Wired* and had been the remixing engineer on *History: America's Greatest Hits*, both George Martin productions.

"I always laugh," Henderson said of work on the America compilation, "because I never got the credit on it, it was just: *Mixed by George Martin*, even though, basically, he never was even around. He'd pop in at the end of the day, have a listen and say, 'Yeah, that's fine.'"[2]

Henderson came to McCartney with a strong recommendation from Emerick. "It was kind of a little bit of a baptism of fire," Henderson remembered. "I'd been an engineer at that point about six months, so I kind of knew what I was doing. But certainly, you know, this was my first real break, as it were."[3]

That break was not without challenges, even apart from the pressure of working with a demanding former Beatle. As an AIR employee, he was given a chilly reception at Abbey Road at first. But EMI's engineers were not short of work. Elsewhere Queen dropped in occasionally to work on their upcoming album *A Day at the Races*, and Pink Floyd compiled sound effects for their next LP, *Animals*.

"Pink Floyd was in the studio," said English. "I made my way to where they were and all the lights were out, and all I heard was animals; like barking dogs. And I said, 'Yeah, that's Pink Floyd!'"[4]

For the basic take of 'Must Do Something About It,' Paul played acoustic guitar and laid down a guide vocal, with Denny on bass and Joe drumming. Paul also set up an electronic rhythm box to provide a steady beat for the backing track, the first of several experiments with new percussion timbres during these sessions.

"We started getting into different tunings," English explained. "For certain sounds, I'd use one size plastic-tipped stick in my cymbal hand and a heavier stick in my right hand, or vice versa. And I'd use different cymbals. I started realizing what my gear was all about. I guess you can do that in a live playing situation, too, but in the studio, it's like putting the drums under a microscope. You really start to hear what stuff is like. You start to hear textures and other things."[5]

'Must Do Something About It' is not a complicated song, and Paul, Denny and Joe produced a suitable basic track fairly quickly. Paul then moved to the electric piano for the backing track for 'She's My Baby,' again with Denny playing bass and Joe on drums. Jimmy sat in the control room with Linda, patiently waiting to be called into action.

But 'She's My Baby' did not go as easily or as quickly as 'Must Do Something About It,' and the session was derailed entirely when Paul received word that Mal Evans had been shot dead the previous evening at the Los Angeles house where he lived with Fran Hughes and her four-year-old daughter, Jody.

Just days before his book deadline, and with the prospect of his financial problems being sorted both through a payment from Apple and a gig with Paul, Mal was nevertheless battling severe depression. When Fran Hughes phoned the police and told them that Mal had a gun and had taken Valium, and was upstairs with her four-year-old daughter, four officers came by to try to talk him down. But when he pointed the rifle at them, they fired six shots, killing him instantly.[6]

Paul was stunned—it was just three weeks since he and Mal had spoken. Before the day was out, he asked Tony Brainsby to issue a statement to the press, saying simply that he was "very disturbed at the loss of a close friend."[7]

He reminisced about Mal with Linda and Denny, who had both known him since the '60s, and tried to get back to work, adding a second acoustic guitar part to 'Must Do Something About It' before calling it a day.

Wings returned to 'Must Do Something About It' on Tuesday, spending from 2:30 P.M. to midnight adding overdubs. Jimmy added single-line guitar phrases throughout the track, alternating between a bluesy tone that reflected the downhearted lyric and sun-kissed figures that reflected the tune's Hawaiian origins. Joe replaced the rhythm box with a cowbell and added other light percussion sounds. And Paul made a pass at a finished vocal, but it was, by his own admission, lackluster. "I put a main vocal down," he said, "but it was never too good."[8] After a few tries, he decided to revisit it another day.

Recording Sessions

Wednesday, January 7–Thursday, January 8,1976.
Abbey Road Studios, Studio Two, London.
Recording and Overdubbing: 'She's My Baby.'

Paul described 'She's My Baby' as "essentially a series of little enigmatic statements, snatches from a diary that seemed to sum up our relationship at that time."[9] Having failed to get a basic take on Monday, he took up the song again at the January 7 session, with the same configuration as the original attempt: Paul played the electric piano—which was recorded both directly into the console, and from a mic'd amplifier—and sang a guide vocal; Denny played bass, and Joe manned the kit.

It took 35 takes (18 of them false starts or breakdowns), on four reels of 24-track tape, to get a basic track that Paul found satisfactory. Take 35 was marked "Best" and Paul overdubbed his lead vocal. Listening to the track again on Thursday, however, he felt he could improve on the vocal, so he did several more takes, using a varispeed effect—slowing the tape deck during recording so that when it played back at normal speed, the vocal sounded slightly sped-up and higher in pitch.

"His idea of doing a vocal," Henderson said, "would be, he'd go out into the studio and do two takes, and he would say, 'Which one was the better one?' And I'd say, 'Well, I think take two was slightly better.' Then he would listen to it, and if there was anything he didn't like he would just say, 'Okay, just knock across that line from take one.' And that would be it."[10]

Paul had a clear idea of how he wanted the lead guitar part to sound, and instead of demonstrating it for Jimmy, he strapped on an electric guitar and recorded the part himself while the wee Scot looked on from the control room. That, at least, was the diplomatic explanation.

"He was a boozer *par excellence*, and a stayer-upper-later," Paul said of the Wings' lead guitarist. "He'd be out of it [during] sessions, so I'd have to play the stuff."[11]

McCulloch may have been getting restless, as well. Shortly after these sessions, *Sounds* reported that the guitarist, along with Boz Burrell, Bad Company's bassist, were spotted sitting in on sessions with the band Snafu. And the fact that in four days of recording, he played nothing but the between-the-lines fills in 'Must Do Something About It' may help to explain Jimmy's generally negative attitude toward the recording process.

"Actually, I find being in the studio bloody boring," McCulloch confessed, "and I'm relieved when it's over. My forte is being on the road. I get much more of a buzz out of that."[12]

Even so, he preferred the relatively business-like atmosphere at Abbey Road to the open-door policy in New Orleans, where groupies, visitors and hangers-on became a distraction.

"It got a bit ridiculous," he said of the *Venus and Mars* sessions. "The recording sessions were made during the Mardi Gras carnival and people kept milling around and dropping into the studio.[13] [For the new album], we didn't have nobody about—just the band. It was a question of total concentration on this one, whereas the last was a bit more of a loon."[14]

Paul wound up the Thursday session by making a rough mix of 'She's My Baby,' and then turned his attention to old material that he requisitioned from the archives, tracks that he had thought about for *Cold Cuts* before the Nashville trip.

The tapes that were sent over include two of the tracks he had set aside for his *Rupert* film (now heading into its sixth year on Paul's project list), 'When the Wind Is Blowing' and 'Sunshine Sometimes.' There were three leftovers from the *Ram* sessions, 'Rode All Night,' 'The Great Cock and Seagull Race' and 'A Love for You'; a *Red Rose Speedway* outtake, 'Jazz Street'; and Linda's songs, 'When I Was in Paris' (the pre-Nashville version of 'Wide Prairie') and 'Oriental Nightfish' from the *Band on the Run* sessions.

Paul left the studio with rough stereo mixes of the eight older tracks, as well as the October 1975 recordings of 'The Note You Never Wrote' and 'Beware My Love.'

Recording Sessions

Friday, January 9 and Monday, January 12, 1976.
Abbey Road Studios, Studio Two, London.
Recording: 'Wino Junko' and 'Wino Junko (Remake).'

Sensing that he needed to engage Jimmy's interest and attention, Paul proposed on Thursday evening that they devote Friday to 'Wino Junko,' another of Jimmy's songwriting collaborations with drummer Colin Allen.

Like 'Medicine Jar,' 'Wino Junko' is about a drug abuser—this time with a touch of alcohol abuse thrown in—but where 'Medicine Jar' is sung from the perspective of a friend warning where drug abuse will lead, 'Wino Junko' is sung mainly from the perspective of the drug abuser: *"My soul is spent and so's the rent / But I'll go down again,"* with an observer taking over at the refrain: *"Wino Junko can't say no / Wino Junko eyes aglow / Pill freak spring a leak / You can't say no 'til you go down again."*

"I got into a situation with [the former Cream bassist] Jack Bruce for a short period," Allen explained, "and spent a few days running through some material at his house, much of which was odd-time-signature stuff. It was pretty intimidating playing with a guy who had been in a band for quite some time with the genius drummer Tony Williams. Jack was intending to make an album but from what I heard, it was put on hold until he did something about his dependency on alcohol and heroin. It was out of my short association with Jack that the lyrics for 'Wino Junko' were born. I had pondered the dichotomy of Jack, battling I believe with heroin addiction—and from his comments at the time—also sounding like a connoisseur of fine wines."[15]

Paul could not help but see a trace of McCulloch in Allen's lyrics, and worried that the young guitarist could lose himself to drink and drugs.

"He was . . . a little bit over the top, young Jim," Paul observed. "He was a lovely fella but he'd been raised in Glasgow and had a pretty tough upbringing, he'd hit fame young and he didn't find it too easy. I remember saying to him, 'What are you going to be doing when you're 30?' It kind of stopped him in his tracks.[16]

"I was very much thinking that with Jimmy's tracks that we heard—'Medicine Jar' and 'Wino Junko'—those are about someone who knows he can't resist extremes. And this was very much

Jimmy! It was the story of his life. A great player, but could easily be knocked off the straight and narrow by drink, drugs, whatever, and that period of course was particularly rife in it all. We did have talks in the band, because he was a young guy compared to us. We were sort of saying, 'Hey Jim, come on now, look at your life as a long story.' We'd try and have pep talks and things with him, which he would listen to, and for a short period he'd be cool. But then he may run into someone, and they'd have a crazy night."[17]

Peter Henderson's assessment was similar to Paul's, but he saw a different kind of vulnerability in Jimmy's personality.

"I could sense that he was very shy, incredibly shy," Henderson said. "And then he would drink quite a lot, I think. And then at some points he could be a little bit sharp, I would say. But generally [he was] just a really, really sweet person, very laid back. I mean, it's hard to be a member of Paul's band. . . . and it's all about him, really, so you kind of have to subjugate your own personality when you play in a band with Paul, I would have thought. So that's tough, too. But Jimmy, he was really good. I mean, he always had a lot of fire about him."[18]

The band worked on 'Wino Junko' from 2:30 P.M. until 10 P.M. in search of a basic track, with Jimmy playing acoustic guitar, Paul on bass and Joe drumming. But it failed to click. They made a stereo mix (RS3) of Take 8, the best of the day's efforts, but the players knew they would start afresh after the weekend.

On Monday, Jimmy, Paul and Joe continued chasing a basic take of 'Wino Junko.' But then a new problem arose. After two takes, the band climbed the stairs to the control room and listened to what they had. But before they could begin another take, Joe put down his sticks and walked out of the studio.

Joe joined Wings when the opportunity was offered to him, as most ambitious musicians would. It was only later that he considered the ramifications for his personal life. He and Dayle barely had time to discuss, let alone work out, how they would manage a long-distance relationship. But that was only part of the problem. Though he was not unfamiliar with city life, having grown up in Rochester and Syracuse, New York, he had settled into a simpler life in Juliette, Georgia, a rural village surrounded by 500 acres of pine trees, some 20 miles northwest of Macon. Now in London, he was homesick and lonely and had turned to drugs in search of psychic and emotional relief.

Joe had spoken with Paul and Linda about missing home, but he kept his extracurricular drug-taking (apart from smoking with the band) to himself until now. But 'Wino Junko' made Joe uneasy. It had bothered him on Friday; on Monday it seemed even more oppressive.

There was something beyond homesickness that led Joe toward drugs, though. Even with the *Venus and Mars* recording sessions and tours of Britain and Australia behind him, he did not feel entirely prepared for the bright spotlight he was thrust into, playing drums behind one of those guys who made him resolve to become a musician when he 15.

Joe was motivated, and he had paid his dues. As a child, he had ankle surgeries that left him wearing a brace, and his response to classmates who taunted him as "crippled" was a determination to do something outstanding. When an aptitude test pointed up his strength in music, he begged his parents for a drum kit, and they took out a loan to buy him one. But the budget did not cover lessons. As Joe put it, "I just played what I wanted, so I developed my own style—which is backwards, very unorthodox."[19]

More involved with bands than with schoolwork, Joe did not graduate from high school; instead he moved to Syracuse to play drums in Jam Factory. "It was a really good experience," Joe said of that time, "six of us together for five years solid, live, playing."[20] And when part of Jam Factory morphed into the Tall Dogs Orchestra, Joe resettled in Georgia, driving his 1964 Dodge rust bucket and playing what gigs he could. He was, until now, always in the support band, never at the top of the bill.

Now he was halfway around the world, in the headlining act, and making lots of cash. Paul was acutely aware of the degree to which financial worries helped scuttle Wings Mark I, but circumstances had changed since then. In the wake of the Apple settlement, he now had access to his earnings, and MPL had evolved into an efficient management machine that could negotiate with promoters and make sure expenses (including band fees) were paid expeditiously. Joe, Denny and Jimmy stood to make $122,222 (£67,000) each for the world tour, and in addition to their supersession fees, they would each pocket a $50,000 (£27,400) bonus for the new album.

Joe's Wings paycheck allowed him to buy 200 acres of land in Georgia, and a few cars, but he still felt out of his element in London. Staying at Cavendish Avenue and stopping by for all those breakfasts after he moved out brought him close to Paul and Linda, but he had not become especially friendly with Denny or Jimmy.

"Generally we never really socialized," Denny Laine said of his troubled colleague. "The only people that socialized were me, Paul and Linda. And that was sort of in a songwriting aspect. That was me going over to their house, or vice versa, just to get some songs together, or we'd go on vacation and write some songs. But other than that, it was just down to the work, and outside of work we just wanted to get away from it all and have some peace."[21]

It was the "getting away from it all" that left Joe feeling at loose ends.

"I would spend time in my flat in London," English said. "I had a Porsche, I had a Jeep, all the things that you would think would make somebody very, very happy. On the outside, you look happy. But on the inside, I spent many days in England, just lonely. And it got to a point where every two weeks, I'd fly home, I'd fly home to Atlanta because I just wanted to go home to see Dayle."[22]

Joe's departure on January 12 put the session on pause while Paul decided how to proceed, not only at the session, but generally. It was not clear whether Joe intended to return to the band or head home to Georgia—and there was the question of how Paul should handle this breach of band decorum if Joe intended to stay. Jimmy offered a logical proposal for the session at hand: why not bring in the song's cowriter, Colin Allen?

"During the recording sessions, Joe English was getting restless," Allen recalled, "and it seemed he was longing for his wife and was seriously considering leaving the band. So I was asked to go and play a little with the band, as a possible replacement for Joe should he leave."[23]

Colin turned up at the session a couple of hours after Joe left, and Paul and Jimmy rehearsed 'Wino Junko' with him. They recorded a single take, marked 'Wino Junko Remake,' Take 1. But Paul knew that the better course was to determine Joe's status before proceeding further, and the band soon called it a day.

"I had no serious discussion about joining Wings," said Allen. "Running through 'Wino' a couple of times was hardly an audition."[24]

After the session, Paul and Linda went to Joe's flat, prepared either to read him the riot act or find out how to fix what was broken in him. Joe kept the focus on being homesick and lonely, soft-pedaling the drug aspect, and Paul and Linda proposed a solution: they would arrange for Dayle and her daughter Christy to come to London. Perhaps if they spent some time with Joe in his new environs, they might want to stay, and all would be well.

Joe was willing to give it a try, as were Dayle and Christy. But their visit to London proved that a transcontinental move for the family was not a long-term solution.

"I could not handle London," Dayle said. "I couldn't handle being in an apartment. I didn't have anything to do. Christy was there, she didn't have anything to do, we were bored to tears. So I kept going back home."[25]

Recording Sessions

Tuesday, January 13–Wednesday, January 14, 1976.
Abbey Road Studios, Studio Two, London.
Recording: 'Wino Junko.'
Overdubbing: 'Wino Junko.'

At 2:30 P.M. on Tuesday, Wings were back at Abbey Road with Joe behind his kit, ready to continue work on Jimmy's song. This time Paul switched to electric piano, with Denny playing bass. Jimmy continued to play acoustic guitar. Beginning with Remake Take 2, the band recorded another 20 takes (only 12 were complete), and marked the 5'33" Take 21 as "Best." During the playout, Jimmy tipped his hat to Pete Townshend, his mentor from the Thunderclap

Newman days, playing a chord figure using a suspended fourth, a move borrowed from the opening of 'Pinball Wizard,' played with a rhythm borrowed from Elton John's 'Saturday Night's Alright for Fighting.'

The Wednesday session, which ran from 1 P.M. to 10 P.M., was devoted entirely to Jimmy's additions of a lead guitar part and his lead vocal.

Recording Session

Thursday, January 15, 1976.
Abbey Road Studios, Studio Two, London.
Recording: 'If I Have to Run' (Demo) (working title for 'Time to Hide').
Overdubbing: 'Wino Junko.'

The degree to which Paul tried to coax material from Denny has not been widely noted because except for some public encouragement in interviews, it took place behind the scenes. But it was an important part of Paul's hope that Wings would be seen as a band. But his efforts engendered pushback from EMI, which was happy to promote a former Beatle on its roster but less interested in Wings, as such.

Paul may have felt unable to challenge EMI in 1973, when it urged him to drop the other band members' showcases from *Red Rose Speedway*. But the success of *Band on the Run* and, to a lesser degree, *Venus and Mars*, emboldened him to make an album that would demonstrate that Wings were not just his backing band. With Denny singing 'The Note You Never Wrote,' and Jimmy as composer and singer of 'Wino Junko,' he had a start.

There was also a more practical reason Paul wanted more music from Denny. Wings were playing a two-hour show, and on the first two legs of the current world tour, he sang lead on everything but Denny's three spotlight moments and Jimmy's 'Medicine Jar.'

"I don't like the idea of me doing all the lead vocals and Denny just harmonizing," Paul complained at the time, "because it seems a waste of him."[26]

"Paul was always on my case to try and write more and to do more," Denny admitted, "which I took as a friendly compliment really, because I always felt that Wings was more his vehicle, and I was just one of the band, and he was trying to push me to the fore."[27]

Laine turned up at Abbey Road on January 15 with a new tune, provisionally named for its opening line, "*If I have to run.*" An outlaw song in the spirit of Bob Marley's 'I Shot the Sheriff,' it is sung from the perspective of a man running from the law but trying to assure his paramour that he is not running out on her.

The song was new to the band, so almost the entire session, which ran from noon to 10 P.M., was devoted to learning and arranging it.

"The fact that Paul wanted to record it," Laine said of the song, "was a compliment again, so his contribution was the arrangement, helping with the arrangement, putting it together as a Wings song."[28]

Before packing it in for the day, the band recorded a demo of Denny's song, and Joe overdubbed congas on 'Wino Junko.'

Recording Session

Friday, January 16, 1976.
Abbey Road Studios, Studio Two, London.
Recording: 'Silly Love Songs.'

Paul ended the week by getting a start on the most complex of his new compositions, 'Silly Love Songs.' He brought in his piano demo, with his and Linda's approximations of the vocal counterpoint, but he had worked on it further since then: the demo lacked the bridge—"*Love doesn't come in a minute / Sometimes it doesn't come at all / I only know that when I'm in it / Love isn't silly (repeated three times) at all.*"

He had a surprising model in mind, according to Peter Henderson, who remembered Paul suggesting a reference point. "He said, 'Think along the lines of "Bohemian Rhapsody,"'" Henderson recalled. "He was very aware of other stuff going on at the time."[29]

The Queen song, from *A Night at the Opera*, had been released ten weeks earlier, and began 1976 at the top of the British singles chart; it soon became the first million-selling single in Britain since Gary Glitter's 'I Love You Love Me Love,' two years earlier. Coincidentally, along with eight cuts sung by front man Freddie Mercury, Queen's fourth studio album also featured lead vocals from both drummer Roger Taylor and guitarist Brian May, giving Paul extra ammunition should EMI argue against him democratizing Wings' next record.

'Silly Love Songs' and 'Bohemian Rhapsody' are very different songs, but they share certain features, beyond vocal counterpoint—namely, an episodic structure. The recording would have to be carefully planned if all the song's elements were to fall into place.

"Most of the songs we do," explained McCulloch, "we only hear them in the studio. Paul will come in and say, 'I've got this tune that I want to do,' and that's it. So you sort of fall in and you listen to it and say, 'Well, I can hear something I'd like to put on it.'"[30]

But on this day, there was nothing for Jimmy to do. At around 1:30 P.M., Paul began work on the sparest possible backing track—just his piano and scratch vocal, and Joe's drums. Given the song's irregular structure and its many changes of texture, the drum part was complicated—and the fact that Joe would be playing against only the piano and a single vocal line meant that he was dependent on Paul's direction and what he could glean from the bridgeless demo.

For the verse, Joe played a standard 4|4 pattern, accents on the second and fourth beats—but at the end of the instrumental intro, there are two hits on the first beat of the fourth bar, then a pause before the verse begins. The verse then proceeds with the standard beat, but when Paul reaches its closing lines—*"What's wrong with that? / I'd like to know / 'cos here I go again"*—Joe switches to a pattern similar to that of Phil Spector's Ronettes hit 'Be My Baby.'

With the rising *"I love you"* section, Joe returns to the standard pattern, with a quick fill at the point where the second voice was to enter with *"Ah, I can't explain / The feeling's plain to me."* Another changeup occurs when Paul reaches his newly written bridge—*"Love doesn't come in a minute"*—where Joe is silent during the vocal lines, but fills in the short instrumental sections between them, alternating between two patterns: one in which all four beats are emphasized, and another emphasizing only the second and fourth beats.

But that was just the start of the track's drumming complications. Moving beyond his demo and arranging on the spot, Paul left long sections for instrumental workouts that would be arranged later, and though Paul had a vision for those sections, Joe had to proceed on faith, coming in or laying back as Paul directed. There were also sections where Paul pulls back the texture entirely, leaving only vocals, lightly accompanied by piano chords—for example, the third *"I love you"* section, which comes in after one of those phantom instrumental breaks, about 4'20" into the song.

Linda, Jimmy and Denny watched from the control room, along with a guest, Barbara Charone, who was invited to write up the session for *Sounds*. Charone watched as Paul, clad in a loose Hawaiian shirt, played his demo for the band, with Linda swaying in her seat and adding harmonies. As recording got underway, Charone described Linda and Denny listening in the control room, trying out harmonies as they listened to Paul's vocal through the monitor speakers, while Jimmy sank into the couch across from the console, reading a newspaper.

After several takes, Charone and Linda adjourned to an adjacent room for an interview. Apart from some promotional enthusing about 'Silly Love Songs' ("This one's gonna be great"), Linda offered an overview of the current edition of Wings, with a focus on Joe. "Onstage," she said,

"Joe added the thing that was lacking with all the other drummers. That's why Wings never stayed together. It's not Beatle Paul, it's a band." By the time Linda and her interlocutor returned to the control room, Paul had a basic track he liked. "Shit hot rocking," Charone quoted Paul mumbling as he listened to the playback.[31]

Paul began the overdubbing process with a hyperactive bass part that transformed the song from a ballad into something closer to a funk/disco track. Although the style was something new for Paul, the line's inventiveness and drive were not: during the Beatles' years, his bass lines were often full-fledged strands of counterpoint that bounced off the vocal melody and fit between the rhythm and lead guitar figures. In his solo work, though, his bass playing had been simpler and more direct, and on Wings recordings, the bass was often played by Denny, who was not the virtuoso bassist that Paul was.

From Paul's perspective, 'Silly Love Songs' was not a return to form for him as a bassist, but simply a matter of what the song needed. It accomplished two things: it gave the song yet another rich line of melodic counterpoint, and it locked tightly into the changing patterns of Joe's drumming.

"I wanted to have a melody on bass," is how he explained it. "We really pushed the bass and drums right out front. But it drove the song along nicely. Pushed it hard. We wanted to make something you could dance to."[32]

As Henderson recalled it, no one—even Paul—knew how the bass line would sound before he hit the record button. "I remember with that particular song, Paul walking out there and getting his bass sound set up," Henderson said. "And literally within half a run-through, he had that bass part. He didn't have that when he started playing, so it was amazing to see him come up with that, which is the signature riff of the whole song, out of thin air."[33]

Laine, as a part-time Wings bassist, was also struck by Paul's ability to consistently create bass lines that perfectly suited the song at hand, whatever the style.

"I would just watch him making up parts in the studio," Denny observed. "Sometimes he'd be there for hours working on the part and just getting it right. I mean, he's a very tuneful bass player, and able to play a very simple bass part that fitted, and then be able to sing on top of it. So, that's an art in itself."[34]

With the basic track plus the bass line sorted, the band gathered around the console and made rough mixes of 'Wino Junko,' 'Silly Love Songs' and the demo of Denny's 'If I Have to Run' to listen to over the weekend.

Recording Sessions

Monday, January 19–Tuesday, January 20, 1976.

Abbey Road Studios, Studio Two, London.
Overdubbing: 'Silly Love Songs.'

Work on 'Silly Love Songs' continued on January 19, with the band spending an entire session overdubbing extra percussion. After considerable experimentation, Paul settled on adding congas to the short, almost a cappella, third "*I love you*" section, and tambourine plus a hollow tube played with drum sticks for the final part of the song. Occasional sizzle cymbal hits, treated with heavy echo, were added throughout.

On Tuesday, Wings spent from 1 P.M. to 8:30 P.M. creating a mechanical-sounding percussion intro for 'Silly Love Songs,' similar in texture to the chorus of mechanical devices that kicked off 'Money' on Pink Floyd's *The Dark Side of the Moon*. As with the previous day's percussion overdubs, this involved plenty of trial and error, but in the end, Paul, Denny and Joe combined four elements to create the effect Paul had in mind: a conga hit, sandpaper, metal being struck and metal being scraped. Paul referred to that short intro, according to Henderson, as "the robot on the front."[35]

Several tracks of vocal harmony were added, sung by Paul, Linda, Denny and Joe, including a falsetto part, suggested and sung by Joe.

"Paul was impressed when Joe came up with that high line on the end of 'Silly Love Songs,'" said Henderson, "and I think that was the first time he thought, 'Wow, Joe's got a really interesting voice.' It was like a real revelation to him that Joe came up with that harmony, and I think that might have been what led to him suggesting that he might sing 'Must Do Something About It.'"[36]

While Wings were hard at work on 'Silly Love Songs,' a telegram from the American promoter Bill Sargent landed on the desks of each of the former Beatles' representatives. Sargent offered a mammoth fee—a $30 million (£14.8 million) advance against a percentage of the gross—for a single, televised concert. Sargent wasn't taking any chances on creative interpretations of his offer: he specified that the four former Beatles would have to perform simultaneously, under the group name, on the same stage.

Sargent estimated that a global telecast of a Beatles reunion concert would bring in nearly $150 million (£74 million), with three million people paying $50 (£24.70) for tickets to a closed-circuit screening. Album and film sales would double that take. If his estimates were accurate, the Beatles stood to make about $200 million (£98.6 million). A date and location for the concert were mooted: July 5 at Olympic Stadium in Montreal, effectively inaugurating the new stadium for the 1976 Olympic Games, set to begin on July 17.

"There is nothing to it at all," John Eastman said on Paul's behalf. "We received a telegram. We have not even considered it." Ringo's lawyer Bruce Grakal was equally dismissive. "I have the telegram," he said, "but I don't think they have had any discussion about it. It's not the first offer, and the numbers for all of them have been staggering."

Sargent dismissed the dismissals, and when it was pointed out that Paul's planned tours of Europe and the United States made rehearsals with the Beatles unlikely, the promoter said, "I'll buy out McCartney's tour. I'm known in the business as a professional winner."[37]

Paul noted that Sargent never contacted him directly—not that it would have made any difference. Like all calls for a Beatles reunion, Sargent's was dead on arrival.

"People have said to me, 'Well you'll have to do it, won't you? You can't go turning down that sort of money,'" Paul said shortly after the offer. "But to me there's more to it than that. It's a group that's broken up, for Christ's sake; what do they want us to do? Re-form just for money? I think that's a bit sordid, for what the Beatles were. It's a bit like puppets, isn't it? I'd like to think that the Beatles came back together, if they ever did, because they really wanted to—musically. That's the only reason I'd ever do it.

"Like I'm always saying, I'm not against it. But not being against it and going and doing it are two different things. He sent a telegram, this bloke: *You are hereby offered . . .* I framed it, put it on the wall."[38]

Deep down, though, Paul knew that the group's unified refusal to consider such offers masked the hope that, at some point, all four might feel otherwise.

"I know, without knowing, because there's no proof," Paul later told an interviewer, "but I know in my mind that [John] must have missed—as I did, and as I think the other two did—actually sitting down with that unit. That was a cozy glove, a very cozy glove, well-worn glove that any time you just pulled it on, you didn't even think, 'Have I got a glove on?' You just were in this glove. . . . And then beyond that, there was our songwriting ability, which meant that we could throw things at this glove, to stretch it and to get it working, to give it a bit of something to do. . . . It's very rare that you do that—and that was the big, special thing."[39]

Recording Sessions

Wednesday, January 21–Friday, January 23, 1976.
Abbey Road Studios, Studio Two, London.
Overdubbing: 'Wino Junko' and 'The Note You Never Wrote.'
Recording: 'Beware My Love.'

Joe missed the Wednesday session because of illness, but the others carried on, creating an introduction to 'Wino Junko' using bells, chimes and "sparkly" electric piano to capture a mysterious, otherworldly sound. Paul also had an idea for a mind-bending effect to be used on the line "*'til you go down again*" when it is repeated toward the end of the song, heading into the long coda.

To produce the effect as he imagined it, Paul made a Mellotron tape loop of the sung line, with the idea of using the instrument's pitch-shifting capability to make the vocal slide downward when it was played against Jimmy's lead vocal.

But the effect proved less interesting than Paul had hoped, so he decided to try something else: a vocoder. Invented at Bell Labs in 1938, and originally used as a method of encryption that shielded voice transmissions from interception, the vocoder had more recently come into its own for musical use, thanks to experiments by Siemens, the German electronics company, as well as Robert Moog and the electronic music composer Wendy Carlos. Its attraction was its ability to blend the human voice with input from an electronic keyboard instrument, so that speech could be "played," the result sounding like a robot choir.

To test the vocoder, Paul recorded a message to the absent Joe, saying that he hoped the drummer felt better and explaining (briefly—the full message runs 24 seconds) about the effect he was trying to create. "It's very rough," Paul said/sang, "but it will have to do for now."[40] Paul then added vocal overdubs to 'Wino Junko' through the device.

Two sets of backing vocals were then added to the song, the first with just Jimmy and Denny, the second with Paul, Linda, Jimmy and Denny. And with the band's energy levels still high as the session headed into the wee hours, Denny replaced his lead vocal on 'The Note You Never Wrote.' Mixes were made of 'Silly Love Songs,' 'Wino Junko,' 'The Note You Never Wrote' and the remake of 'Beware My Love' before Wings left the studio at 2 A.M., after nearly 12 hours' work.

Heading to Abbey Road on Thursday morning, Paul picked up a copy of the *Daily Mirror* with an early photo of the Beatles on the cover, beside the headline "Will the Beatles Be Back in 1976?" Bill Sargent's offer had hit the news, and as the paper reported it, there seemed to be a chance it might happen. Tony Brainsby, speaking for Paul, and Jonathan Clyde, the managing director of George's new Dark Horse Records label, both said that their employers had no comment, but these were seen as non-denials, as was a comment from a spokesman for Ringo's Ring O'Records label to the effect that "offers are usually channeled through advisors and just occasionally they may then approach the boys."

John, however, was quoted as speaking for himself—although the attribution is questionable, since after the birth of Sean he had retreated from public life. "I'd like it more than anything," he supposedly told the paper. "I've always felt that splitting up was a mistake in many ways. Coming back together again would undoubtedly produce some great music." That was enough to justify Sargent's assertion that "My offer is getting serious consideration. We have agreed there is no insurmountable problem."[41]

Paul was actually less interested in the Beatles reunion story than another front-page headline trumpeting the maiden commercial voyage of the Concorde. The supersonic jet had completed its first commercial flight between London and Bahrain, with roundtrip tickets on what the *Daily Mail* called "The World Shrinker" costing £676 ($1,370). The paper noted that the jet made its journey at the speed of sound—and Paul, having scanned the ether in search of an album title in recent weeks, suddenly had one—*Wings at the Speed of Sound*.*

Before he left Cavendish Avenue that morning, Paul had given the previous night's mixes a spin, with particular attention to 'Beware My Love.' When that version was recorded, in October, the band had reluctantly settled on a master take, but they were not thrilled with it. Hearing it again, Paul knew it was not what he wanted: it lacked the sizzle of the version with John Bonham.

Thursday's session was therefore devoted to taking the song apart, reassembling it and rehearsing it with the tapes running. Between 1:30 P.M. and 7 P.M., 14 rehearsal takes were recorded, with Paul and Jimmy on acoustic guitars, Denny on bass and Joe drumming.

When Wings turned up at Abbey Road at 2:30 P.M. on Friday, they set about recording 'Beware My Love' in earnest. But it remained elusive: when they gave up at 3 A.M., they had recorded 20 new takes (called Takes 15 through 35) on four reels. Only nine of the new takes were complete, and although several of these were close—Take 19 was marked "not far off," and Take 22 was marked "pretty good, best yet"—the band did not consider any of them a keeper. Reconsidering the October 17 recordings, the best take was appended to the end of the first reel and marked "Take 20."

"We weren't in an aggressive mood when we made the record," said English in an attempt to analyze the problem. "I mean, aggressive to the point when you say, 'Well, we gotta knock 'em dead, show 'em how heavy we are.'"[42]

Recording Sessions

Monday, January 26–Tuesday, January 27, 1976.
Abbey Road Studios, Studio Two, London.
Recording: 'Beware My Love' and 'Time to Hide.'

* Joe English has claimed that the band flew on the second commercial flight of Concorde, which would have been on Saturday, January 24, to Bahrain. This cannot be confirmed, and it is more likely that Wings flew on Concorde later in the year when flights began between London and Washington, D.C.

Work on 'Beware My Love' continued on Monday. Another 17 takes were recorded, taking the total, including those recorded in October, to 53. Paul marked Take 53 "good," but asked to revisit Take 19 from Friday's session. On reflection, the beginning and end of that take were fine, so Paul edited those sections onto Take 20 from October 17.

Edited backing tracks were rare for Paul, though: he preferred complete takes, played live in the studio, and he knew it would take some work to make it hang together.

"We aimed to get all the excitement in the backing track so it's human: you can hear we're all in there," said Paul. "Build on a great take and there's no problem. If it's a ropey take, which you're hoping to save further down the line—which I've also done—then it is a problem because it's like a rickety building that's going to fall down any minute. No foundations."[43]

Before Paul called an end to the session at 11:30 P.M., lead and backing vocals were added to the composite master take.

"The other thing that I always remember with him that is very, very different to most other people," Peter Henderson said, "is that when he's playing anything, or singing, or anything he did, it was a performance, and he would lay into it in a way that people generally didn't really do in overdubs. It was a performance and he's obviously good enough to pull it off."[44]

When the musicians turned up on Tuesday, they took up Denny's new song, now retitled 'Time to Hide.' But in ten hours of work, no master take was captured.

—

Wings took a two-day hiatus from recording, during which the *Daily Mirror* followed up its story on the Sargent offer with a piece in which George offered a sliver of hope for a reunion. Tracked down in Cannes, George told the paper, "I've been quoted as the only one to say no. But now I'm saying yeah. I'd do it if the others would. I'm not going to say no to my share of £15 million ($30,430,000). It would be fun just to see what happens at such a get-together."

But George also spelled out the practical hurdles they would have to overcome on the way to Sargent's proposed concert—and given George's dry sense of humor, it was unclear whether his claimed enthusiasm, his analysis of the pitfalls, or both, were said tongue-in-cheek.

"It would take months and months to get it organized," he said. "Messages going between lawyers trying to get us all to meet up somewhere, decisions over what to play—which and whose music to use. It'd probably all end up in lawsuits over the music alone. Then we'd most likely want to use mainly new material not the old stuff. That new material would almost certainly get the lawyers going again."[45]

Recording Sessions

Friday–Saturday, January 30–31, 1976.
Abbey Road Studios, Studio Two, London.
Recording: 'Time to Hide.'
Overdubbing: 'She's My Baby,' 'The Note You Never Wrote' and 'Time to Hide.'
Mixing: All songs.

Between 2:30 P.M. Friday and 1:30 A.M. Saturday morning, two more reels were filled with 'Time to Hide,' this time resulting in a master take with Paul on organ, Denny on bass and Joe on drums. Initial overdubbing included tom-toms, bass guitar, organ and an electric guitar played through a rotating Leslie speaker.

On Saturday, Paul, Denny and Linda added vocal harmonies to 'She's My Baby.' But most of the session was devoted to overdubbing the two songs that featured Denny's lead vocals.

Paul and Linda created a mysterious "from out of the depths" introduction to 'The Note You Never Wrote,' using faded-in Mellotron sounds and the bass grumble of the Moog, as well as other Moog overdubs—six tracks' worth—scattered throughout the song. Turning their attention to 'Time to Hide,' Denny added harmonica, and Paul and Jimmy split a lead guitar solo, with Paul playing his section on a Stratocaster fitted with 10cc's Gizmo, and Jimmy picking up the end of the solo on an unmodified Strat.

Immediately following the session, Paul met with Fiachra Trench, the arranger (and Linda's occasional piano mentor), at Cavendish Avenue to discuss orchestral additions for 'The Note You Never Wrote' and the as yet unrecorded 'Warm and Beautiful.' Sitting at the piano in his music room Paul played 'Warm and Beautiful' for Trench, who suggested a delicate arrangement for string quartet plus a pair of euphoniums (tenor horns similar to tubas), the latter to be used sparingly for textural variety.

Paul then switched on his open-reel deck and played Trench the latest mix of 'The Note You Never Wrote.' The theatrical ebb and flow of the Wings recording left ample space for strings, and McCartney proposed an arrangement that would first expand and then taper down.

"There's a nice feature in 'The Note You Never Wrote,' when it starts off with solo strings—a string quartet—and it finishes with solo strings," Trench pointed out. "That may well have been Paul's idea, you know, that it should ease in from quartet to the big band and go back to [quartet]. It suited the song very well.

"It was a privilege to be working with them in a home environment," Trench added, "because they would be at their most unguarded, you know, just like good mates. It made it very pleasant.

He was the Beatle who had the most sense of what arrangement was about, and what it could bring to a track—an orchestral sweetening and so forth. So from that point of view it was easy for me because he had such a feeling for that, an understanding for it. He pretty much gave me a free hand, which was nice."[46]

Paul sent Trench off with cassette copies of 'The Note You Never Wrote' and his electric piano instrumental demo of 'Warm and Beautiful,' with Trench promising that the scores would be ready, and the ensemble booked, for a February 13 session. Trench completed the arrangements quickly and had the violinist David Katz round up the necessary players.

Peter Henderson devoted Sunday to making rough mixes of all the songs Wings had recorded so far.

Recording Session

Monday, February 2, 1976.
Abbey Road Studios, Studio Two, London.
Recording: 'Warm and Beautiful' and 'San Ferry Anne.'

Only Joe was present when Paul and Linda arrived at Abbey Road at midday on February 2, so Paul ran through 'Warm and Beautiful' at the piano and decided to record the song alone. Half an hour later, a master take—Paul on piano with a live vocal—was in the can.

For all the ingenuity of its slowly morphing chord progression, the song is surprisingly spare, with only a single verse and a bridge, each sung twice. The verse opens and closes the song (there is a single lyric difference between the two performances of the verse—"*Stands when time itself is falling*" the first time, with "*falling*" changed to "*calling*" on the repeat); the two bridge stanzas appear between the verses, separated by space for an instrumental break, using the verse chords. When Jimmy and Denny turned up, Paul had them record tandem slide guitar parts in the section reserved for the solo.

"I find it a very emotional melody," Paul said of the song, "and in the middle there's a sort of slide guitar in the instrumental thing where it suddenly goes into harmonies. And it's funny I always think of that song in close harmony, but the rest of the song isn't—it's pretty much just a solo—me and a piano."[47]

Lyrically, the directness and poetic imagery in 'Warm and Beautiful' make it a close second to 'Maybe I'm Amazed' among Paul's songs inspired by Linda. And it was almost enough to make him reconsider his insecurity about writing lyrics.

"I've never thought I had a relationship with words that's very strong. I feel as though it's more music. But that's my particular hang up. I think what I'm saying is, there are some people who string words together that I admire to the degree that I don't think I'm that good. I mean, that's my natural response—'No, I'm not very good with words.' But when I think about it I know I have some moments when suddenly a little flash has come to me and I've thought, 'Okay, that's good, those are good words.'"[48]

In Paul's own estimation, 'Warm and Beautiful' was one of those sudden flashes.

"That one really does get to me," he later admitted. "It captures some of my innermost feelings for her."[49]

With 'Warm and Beautiful' finished but for Trench's orchestration, Paul picked up an acoustic guitar to record the backing track for 'San Ferry Anne.' Denny played a second acoustic guitar, with Joe drumming and Jimmy on bass. With the addition of a bass drum and cymbal overdub by Joe, Jimmy's lead guitar line, Paul's lead vocal, and harmonies by Paul and Linda, the track was virtually complete when the session ended at 11 P.M.

"Linda and Paul were given a hard time about Linda being in the band and all the rest of it," Henderson observed, "but her vocals are fantastically good, and what people never realize is she has a voice that's just got such a fantastic tone to it. It blends really well with Paul's voice, and it's got this airy quality that is just fantastic for backing vocals."[50]

Recording Session

Tuesday, February 3, 1976.
Abbey Road Studios, Studio Three, London.
Recording: '1st Day in No. 3' and 'Let 'Em In.'
Overdubbing: 'Time to Hide.'

Wings moved to the smaller Studio Three for their February 3 session and after a quick jam—which they called '1st Day in No. 3'—to get used to the space, they worked on the basic track for Paul's party song, 'Let 'Em In.' Paul played piano and sang a guide vocal, Joe drumming and Jimmy playing bass.

The full group then filled four tracks with snare drums, using layering to create their own marching band. "They overdubbed the military kits," Henderson said. "What I've got written down in my diary is, 'three kits plus 40 snares.' The five of them each tracked it a few times, and then we bounced it down."[51]

The three kits Henderson mentioned each had their bass toms detuned to create a dynamic "on the street" effect. Before the session ended, at 1 A.M., Joe recorded a new bass drum track on 'Time to Hide,' replacing the one he originally recorded, and Henderson made a quick stereo mix of '1st Day in Studio Three.'

Recording Session

Wednesday, February 4, 1976.
Abbey Road Studios, Studio Three, London.
Recording: 'Cook of the House' and 'Whirling Derbisher's Dance.'

When Jimmy, Denny and Joe filed into Studio Three at 1 P.M. on Wednesday, Paul was already there, plunking out resonant riffs on the double bass that Linda bought for him in 1974, an instrument heard on many early Elvis Presley discs. Paul brought it to Abbey Road because he thought it would help give 'Cook of the House,' the next song on his to-do list, the 1950's feel he felt it required.

Sitting at the piano, with Joe drumming and Denny playing electric guitar, Paul quickly dispatched the backing track, and then overdubbed the double bass part.

"I think it's the original bass that he played 'Heartbreak Hotel' on," Paul said of the instrument. "I've been mucking around on it, trying to learn stand-up bass. It's very hard, you know. A whole other set of muscles from what you normally use. So, I took that in the studio, I was just banging away—I play it terribly—but it gave the record this very interesting old '50's gymnasium sound."[52]

From the time he wrote it, Paul imagined Linda singing it, but now that it was time to actually record the lead vocal, Linda was reluctant, and it took some persuasion to get her in front of the microphone. As part of his argument, Paul appealed to Linda's inner 1950's rocker, setting up an era-appropriate slap-back echo for her vocal.

"So, we decided to just try it, and if it didn't come off, maybe I would have done it, or somebody else would have done it," Paul said. But the contingencies were not necessary. "Linda sang it great, and we just got off on it that evening, we had a nice time."[53]

Another jam, listed as 'Whirling Derbisher's Dance,' was recorded as well. Before everyone left, Henderson made rough mixes of the jam as well as 'The Note You Never Wrote,' 'Warm and Beautiful,' 'San Ferry Anne,' 'Let 'Em In,' 'Time to Hide,' and 'Cook of the House.'

Recording Sessions

Tuesday. February 10–Thursday, February 12, 1976
Abbey Road Studios, Studio Three, London.
Overdubbing: 'Beware My Love' and 'Let 'Em In.'

After a brief hiatus, Wings returned to Studio Three on February 10 for a short session devoted to 'Beware My Love.' The editing of several takes to get a solid backing track meant that certain elements of the joined recordings would have to be reworked. Chief among them was Jimmy's lead guitar part, which he rerecorded at a session that ran from 2:30 to 8 P.M.

Work on the track continued the following day, with Jimmy adding another electric guitar line, and Joe adding two more passes at the complete drum track, giving the band the option of using the original or either of the new versions in the final mix. Double-tracked clapping was added as well, and Linda overdubbed Moog and ARP sounds at various points in the song.

On Thursday, Paul's lead vocal and harmony vocals by Paul, Linda and Denny were overdubbed onto 'Let 'Em In.'

"Wings was a great harmony band," said Laine. "That became established fairly early because we all liked harmonies. You know, everybody sang, and that song epitomized that."[54]

Recording Session

Friday, February 13, 1976.
Abbey Road Studios, Studio Two, London.
Overdubbing: 'Warm and Beautiful' and 'The Note You Never Wrote.'

The orchestral session on February 13, starting at 7:30 P.M., went easily, with Paul conducting the ensemble for both songs. For 'Warm and Beautiful,' Fiachra Trench engaged the Maggini Quartet and two euphoniums, all of which join the texture at the second bridge. The Maggini players remained as part of a larger string ensemble, which also included members of another London quartet, the Gabrieli, whose first violinist, Kenneth Sillito, was the concertmaster for the session.

Paul made one change to Trench's score for 'The Note You Never Wrote.'

"The first he heard [the score] was when we were there in the studio with a fairly sizable string orchestra," said Trench, "and he wanted it slightly less fussy in the double bases—he just took some of that out. Some of the kick notes [after the line *"but he never is gonna get my vote"* and also preceding the guitar solo], he said, 'No, no, just keep them fairly straight.' Otherwise, it went down exactly as I had written and presented to him. It's nice when somebody puts that much trust in you."[55]

For dramatic impact, the double bass part was doubled by an electric bass guitar, which Denny played live with the orchestra, plugging directly into the console (and monitoring the string ensemble and the original track through headphones) in order to avoid spillover from the bass amp.

The session lasted five hours, at the end of which Henderson made rough mixes of both songs, as well as a stereo mix of some of the between-takes chatter from orchestral players.

Recording Sessions

Monday, February 16–Wednesday, February 18, 1976.
Abbey Road Studios, Studio Three, London.
Overdubbing: 'Cook of the House' and 'Must Do Something About It.'

Ever since the Beatle days, Paul's relationship with Abbey Road was such that he could *usually* turn up with relatively little advance notice and get some recording time. At the moment, though, Abbey Road was tightly booked—hence the move from Paul's preferred Studio Two to Studio Three. Now there was pressure on Studio Three as well, so with the new album close to completion, Paul booked three short sessions—Monday through Wednesday from 7:30 to 11 P.M.—for overdubbing.

The first matter of business was backing vocals for 'Cook of the House,' and once that was complete, Paul saw an opportunity to further democratize Wings. Denny now had two vocals, and Jimmy and Linda had one each. That left Joe, and it was not lost on Paul that the lonely protagonist in 'Must Do Something About It' had a lot in common with the drummer.

"I suggested to Joe that he try it to see if he could," said Paul. "I'd heard him sing before and he's got a very good voice, but it's just not a normal thing to ask your drummer to do a track, it's more an old-fashioned thing really. Get everyone to have a sing.[56] And when he'd done it we were all surprised. He can sing well."[57]

Indeed, Joe brought a strong voice to his deeply felt reading to the song.

"When I read the lyrics, it was kind of obvious that was about me," said English. "*I've just seen another sunset on my own*—Paul knew that I'm over there alone, the person I loved was over there [in America], and he understood that part of it."[58]

Now every member of Wings had a vocal on the album, something Paul had not managed even on the double-album version of *Red Rose Speedway*. The only one with any doubts was Peter Henderson, and he kept his opinion to himself.

"He's got a great voice," Henderson said of Joe. "But I have to be honest, I would prefer to hear Paul sing it. You know, having heard Paul sing it originally, I always thought that was a slightly odd decision."[59]

Recording Session

Thursday, February 19, 1976.
EMI Mobile Unit, 7 Cavendish Avenue, London.
Recording: Harmonium links and sound effects.

Some of Paul's ideas for the album were best recorded not at Abbey Road, but in the comfort of his home on Cavendish Avenue. For example, he wanted to record a couple of short pieces on a harmonium, to be used as links between 'She's My Baby' and 'Beware My Love,' and 'Time to Hide' and 'Must Do Something About It.' He had a harmonium at home, and he liked it better than those in EMI's instrument closet, so he hired EMI Mobile Unit 7, and had Henderson record him playing his own harmonium.

While planning for the harmonium recording, it occurred to Paul that two of the album's songs needed sound effects that could also be recorded at his house. For 'Let 'Em In,' he wanted to record the doorbell, with its Big Ben chimes—a gift from Joe, when he was staying with the McCartneys. 'Let 'Em In' seemed a natural opening track for the album, and starting the track with the doorbell seemed perfect.

'Cook of the House' also cried out for sound effects that would root the song in Linda's kitchen. And what could do that better than the sound of bacon and chips, sizzling in a deep fat fryer?

"Paul and Linda decided to cook a meal and get cooking sounds recorded, and then fed the meal to us and the engineers," said Peter. "We all had a laugh and a drink. The mobile was outside the house, and we just ran wires into the kitchen. 'Take one. Bacon frying.' The first British cooking on record. There are chips [frying] at the end which is great because it sounds like applause."[60]

All told, Henderson filled three reels of tape—two with harmonium links and a third marked 'One Wild Piece'/'Cook of the House,' with the doorbell and cooking sound effects.

Recording Sessions

Friday, February 20 and Monday, February 23, 1976.
Abbey Road Studios, Studio Three, London.
Overdubbing: 'Silly Love Songs' and 'Time to Hide.'

Wings were able to get time for short sessions (2:30 to 7 P.M.) on Friday, February 20 and Monday, February 23. On Friday, Paul recorded his lead vocal for 'Silly Love Songs,' using EMI's proprietary ADT to create the impression that the vocal was double-tracked, without Paul's having to actually sing it twice. Wings' horn section, back in London to rehearse for the next leg of the tour, enlivened 'Silly Love Songs' with bright wind and brass work in the style made famous by Philadelphia soul bands.

This was tricky, though. The Musicians Union frowned upon non-union players recording in British studios, particularly when some of them were not even British. That rule worked both ways, of course: Capitol Records had intended to record the Beatles' two performances at Carnegie Hall in 1964, but was prevented from doing so by the American Federation of Musicians for the same reason. Paul tiptoed around the rules, recording his horn players in a couple of stealth sessions, conducting the ensemble.

Paul had distinct ideas for the brass and wind parts on 'Silly Love Songs,' and he gathered the players around the piano to show them what he wanted.

"Paul had already prepared the brass parts," Howie Casey said. "There were no charts as such, it was all his. He did all the harmonies and everything for us. I put a little lick on out of the blue at the end when they're doing '*I love you*,' just a little daft lick. He said, 'Oh yeah, keep that.' So you *were* allowed to contribute, there was no doubt about that."[61]

By now, Paul saw 'Silly Love Songs' as a possible single, and he spared no detail making it sound dazzling. "When I came in," Tony Dorsey recalled, "he just told me, 'Well, it's a disco song, so it needs some string parts. Just write something.' So I went and did some string parts."[62]

Further horn and string overdubs were scheduled for later the following week. On Monday,

Wings spent some quality time with Denny's 'Time to Hide,' adding two tracks of harmony vocals—the first by Denny alone, the second with the entire band.

Recording Sessions

Tuesday, February 24–Wednesday, February 25, 1976.
Abbey Road Studios, Studio Two, London.
Overdubbing: 'Silly Love Songs,' 'San Ferry Anne,' 'Cook of the House,' 'Time to Hide' and 'Let 'Em In.'

Coming into the home stretch, Wings reclaimed Studio Two for a pair of nighttime sessions, on Tuesday from 7 to 10 P.M., and Wednesday from 7 P.M. to 1 A.M., devoted entirely to orchestral overdubs. On Tuesday, Dorsey arrived with his fresh new charts, and soon a complement of freelance string and brass players contracted by David Katz filed into the studio. With Paul conducting, 'Silly Love Songs' was given a coat of bright orchestral color.

Because of the Musicians Union restrictions, the American players had to lay low on Tuesday, but on Wednesday, only the Wings horns were required, so the session took place under the union's radar. Paul had not asked Dorsey to create parts for the songs to be sweetened that day—rather, the day's additions were improvised, with some guidance from Paul about what he needed for each.

"He said, 'Okay, gather around the piano,'" Casey recalled. "There were no charts, so he said, 'This is what I want,' and he showed us the various licks that he wanted. He said, 'Okay—trumpet, you do that, alto that, tenor, trombone you play that line,' and so on. So that was cool, and we did. We went through them one by one, and we built it up like that."[63]

Trumpeter Steve Howard added that after Paul demonstrated some of the riffs he thought would work, "we would work them out with the section and decide who was going to play what. And then there were a couple of spots where he wanted us to come up with some little parts, and I was actually able to contribute a couple of lines. . . . We just pretty much did what [are known] in the business as 'head arrangements.'"[64]

On 'San Ferry Anne,' flute, saxophone and flugelhorn flourishes alternated with full ensemble figures throughout the song, becoming an elaborate dialogue during the song's long playout.

"That was probably my favorite because it had a pretty little melody and I got to play a flugelhorn solo in there," said Howard. "It kind of featured the horn section more, and in rock and pop music, there's not a lot of space for horn solos unless you're a saxophone player. So it was nice to get a little spot there on the recording."[65]

Thaddeus Richard and Howie Casey added improvised clarinet and saxophone lines, in a 1950's sock hop style, to 'Cook of the House.' The full horn section mirrored the structural guitar riffs in 'Time to Hide.' And on 'Let 'Em In,' the horns bolstered the party atmosphere with bursts of improvisation—as well as a double-tracked, reggae-inspired trombone solo by Dorsey.

"When I was in Jamaica, I heard a reggae record which featured a trombone all on its own," said Paul. "It sounded daft, and fruity, and I filed it away at the back of my mind that I'd love to use a trombone. And, of course, we have Tony Dorsey, who plays trombone for us, so we could use it as a solo instrument on the album."[66]

Paul had another instruction for 'Let 'Em In' that fell under Henderson's purview.

"Paul said he wanted the brass arrangement to be really nasal," Henderson explained. "So he made me EQ them in a way that they sound really middly, so that's why they sound like they do."[67]

With those additions, *Wings at the Speed of Sound* was complete but for mixing and sequencing.

As the sessions wound to a close, Paul had a visit from Hunter Davies, a journalist he had known since the 1960s, and the author of *The Beatles*, the group's 1968 authorized biography. Davies was preparing a profile for *The Times*, to appear in May, just before the start of the American tour. The interview began at Cavendish Avenue, where Linda made breakfast—fried bread, fried eggs, bacon and freshly squeezed orange juice—and then headed to Abbey Road, where Paul played Davies tracks from the new album.

The McCartneys felt comfortable with Davies and Linda, especially, explored feelings that she usually kept under wraps. She confessed, for example, that she would be happy to do less touring, even as she faced 31 shows over nearly two months in the United States and Canada, as well as concerts in Europe.

"What worries me most about America," Linda said, "is that we'll have to start again. *Rolling Stone* will be waiting for me. I'll obviously be criticized, and I'll hate it. I'd love to put the critics up on stage and see them do better. You lose a few years of your life on stage. You live on your adrenaline. When it's over I want to crash out and go and live in Scotland for a while. We've got to do America to prove we can do it, but after that, I hope we'll just stick to occasional concerts, playing a big festival, or a little club. I don't want to spend my life touring."

"America will be okay," Paul countered. "I've told you, there's nothing to worry about."

"There will be all those questions, the same old stupid questions," Linda responded.

"It doesn't matter," replied Paul. "John was always best with the smart answers, but any jokes go down well. They ask what brings you here and you say you 'came on a Jumbo' and they all go ho-ho. You don't have to be Oscar Wilde." Eventually, Paul guided the conversation back to the party line, but with an unusual nonchalance about where it all might lead.

"They now seem to like us, at least in Britain," he told Davies. "I know in America the press will be sitting in the first three rows, their pencils ready. But it really doesn't matter what they say. I'm not as precious about Wings as I used to be. If it folds, hard luck. I'll be very upset, but we'll survive.

"I'm pleased with Wings. I'm as happy as when I was playing with the Beatles. Not happier. As happy. No more, no less. But what I have got now is an extra—the family. I had chicks in the Beatles days and now I have kids. I don't miss the old way of life at all."[68]

Recording Sessions

Thursday, February 26–Sunday, February 29, 1976.
Abbey Road Studios, Studio Two, London.
Mixing: 'Let 'Em In,' 'The Note You Never Wrote,' 'She's My Baby,' 'Beware My Love,' 'Wino Junko,' 'Silly Love Songs,' 'Cook of the House,' 'Time to Hide,' 'Must Do Something About It,' 'San Ferry Anne' and 'Warm and Beautiful.'

Mixing the new album took four sessions in Studio Three, each beginning in the early-to-mid afternoon and stretching into the early hours, the final mixing session ending at 3 A.M. 'Let 'Em In,' 'The Note You Never Wrote,' and 'She's My Baby' were mixed first, on Thursday, with 'Beware My Love' and 'Wino Junko' following on Friday. Saturday was devoted to 'Cook of the House' and 'Time to Hide.' And the ballads—'Must Do Something About It,' 'San Ferry Anne' and 'Warm and Beautiful'—were all mixed on Sunday.

"Paul was very involved in all that," said Henderson. "He always knew what he wanted and would direct you, 'Can you make it sound more glamorous? Can you put something on the voice to make it sound a bit different,' or whatever else."[69]

The rest of the band was on hand for the mixing sessions as well. "We all made suggestions in the mixing," English said, "but Paul made the final decisions, and it was all done very simply."[70]

By the time mixing was complete, Paul had a good idea how he wanted the album sequenced. 'Let 'Em In,' with its newly affixed doorbell, was a logical opener, and his fondness for 'Warm and Beautiful' dictated that it close the album. The rest fell into place, with an ear toward spreading the varied vocals through the album without strictly alternating with Paul's vocals.

SIDE ONE (EMI MATRIX NO. YEX.953)

'Let 'Em In'
'The Note You Never Wrote'
'She's My Baby'
'Beware My Love'
'Wino Junko'

SIDE TWO (EMI MATRIX NO. YEX.954)

'Silly Love Songs'
'Cook of the House'
'Time to Hide'
'Must Do Something About It'
'San Ferry Anne'
'Warm and Beautiful'

And then, without time to unwind, it was on to rehearsals for the European leg of Wings' world tour, which would begin in Copenhagen on March 20.

13

LE DOIGT OF BLAME

Each of McCartney's albums to this point, whether solo or with Wings, had a distinct sonic personality. But whether the production was rough-hewn, like *McCartney* or *Wild Life*, or finely polished, like *Venus and Mars*, Wing's essential sound was that of a late-1960s/early-1970s rock band, sometimes with orchestration, often without. Even the group's most updated sounds, from Linda's Minimoog and ARP synthesizers, were part of the accepted rock palette by the time Wings used them.

Wings at the Speed of Sound was something different—an acknowledgment, by Paul, that pop music was changing, that new timbres and song styles were being embraced. The album was a declaration that he intended to stay current.

In a way, this was another aspect of Paul's duality. He had developed a distinctive musical personality, built on wide-ranging tastes and a remarkably facile command of styles, and he could have followed his instincts and deeply rooted tastes indefinitely. But he was also the guy who, ever since the Beatle days, studied the Top 10 singles every week, poring over them to be sure that no fashion, fad, or trend escaped his notice.

But until now, when he took note of a trend, he did so subtly, often as a reference rather than as wholesale adoption of the style—for example, his nod to Glam Rock in the line from 'Rock Show,' *"And the ring at the end of my nose makes me look rather pretty."*

On *Wings at the Speed of Sound* the influence of new styles and sounds is bolder and more direct. An example is his prominent use of the electric piano. For decades, electric pianos mostly approximated standard piano timbre, but now they were using synthesizer technology to expand the instrument's palette.

Paul was hearing these sounds everywhere—in progressive rock and jazz fusion, for example, but also on recent albums by one of his heroes, Stevie Wonder. On *Wings at the Speed of Sound*,

Paul drew on some of the bright, sparkly timbres offered by newer pianos, giving them a prominence that ties the album thoroughly to its time.

The new album also took account of disco. When the Beatles wanted to get their audience dancing, they would crank up a fast rocker, like 'Hippy Hippy Shake' or 'I Saw Her Standing There.' With Wings, Paul presented the rockier tracks as an opportunity to get up and dance, but the aesthetics of danceability had not fundamentally changed for him. Now, nearly two years after Gloria Gaynor's 'Never Can Say Goodbye' topped the very first *Billboard* American Disco chart, the mainstream emergence of a new dance music style, with a steady, pounding beat and heavy bass lines, got Paul's attention and fired up his competitive juices.

'Silly Love Songs' was Paul's move in that direction. It must have been strange for a musician who was used to establishing trends and watching others follow, to now be picking up on what younger musicians were doing. But in 'Silly Love Songs,' Paul put his own spin on disco. The bass line was active and prominent, but the beat was by no means mechanical—it included changeups and turnarounds, even stopping points. McCartneyesque melody was plentiful—so plentiful that competing melodies were overlaid against each other. And Tony Dorsey's horn and string score kept the ear engaged between verses and stretches of vocal counterpoint.

It was clear, in any case, that Paul was keenly aware of the changes in the pop audience's tastes, and he was determined to remain current—but on his own terms.

Shortly after he settled on *Wings at the Speed of Sound* as the new album's title, Paul summoned Aubrey Powell of Hipgnosis to Cavendish Avenue to discuss cover ideas.

"I went to see him," Powell said. "I remember him sitting at the piano—he was always playing the piano—and I remember he put his cup of tea on the piano, and I happened to glance at it, and it was [sitting on] a Magritte painting. I said, 'Paul, you've just put your cup of tea on a Magritte painting.' He said, 'Magritte won't mind.' I'll never forget that; Magritte was one of my heroes."

As was the case when he commissioned Hipgnosis to assemble the cover art for *Band on the Run* and *Venus and Mars*, Paul brushed past the firm's preference for pursuing its own concepts and presented his idea, which was not negotiable. This time what he had in mind was a theater marquee—specifically, the large marquee of the Leicester Square Theatre—with lettering reading *Wings at the Speed of Sound*.

"So I organized it," said Powell. "I went to them, and I said, 'This is what we want to do. It's for Paul McCartney.' Everybody falls over themselves to help." There was a proviso, however: the theater's lettering would have to be changed after the West End theaters let out, and when foot traffic in the area was relatively sparse. That, as Powell remembers it, was at about 1 A.M. "I brought a cherry picker," he continued, "and went up in it with Linda and shot it," while Paul watched from the street.

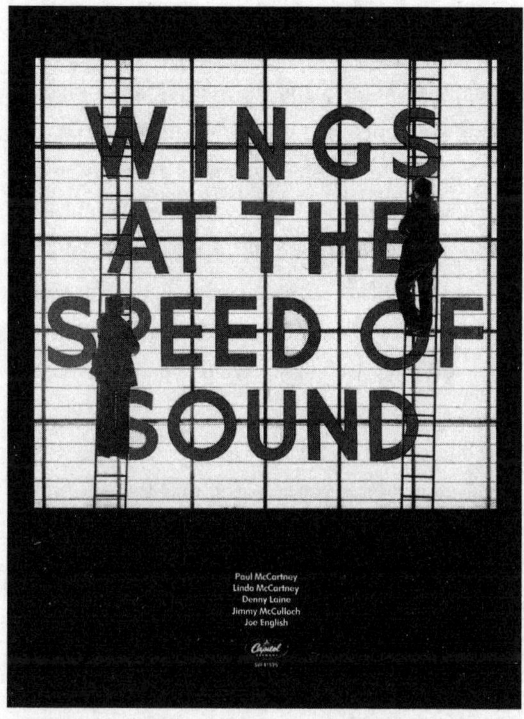

Early morning in Leicester Square, Wings trade ad

"It was a fun evening out," Powell added. "I got the pictures back the next day and they loved them. And I liked it too, because I thought it was a different approach—it was an interesting way of doing things, without having [the band's] pictures on the front."[1]

Through Powell, Paul commissioned a painting for the inner sleeve from Humphrey Ocean. The 25-year-old Ocean—born Humphrey Anthony Erdeswick Butler-Bowdon in 1951—had been a student of Ian Dury's* at Canterbury Art College and had played bass in Kilburn and the High Roads, a band in which Dury was the singer. Powell had told Ocean about the marquee front cover, and Ocean maintained the theatrical connection in his painting, which shows the exterior of a theater, the doors open to show a Robert Ellis photograph of Wings onstage, beneath a banner reading *Speed of Sound*. The commission, Ocean maintains, was an audition for a new position on the MPL roster, and the McCartneys had done their homework.

"They had an idea that they wanted to take an artist on their Wings USA tour," Ocean explained. "Linda McCartney, who was from a background of high art in America—you know, her dad was best friends with de Kooning, they knew Rothko and Franz Kline—she'd grown up with art, very good art. Paul married up when he married her, he married into what he was already interested in, you only have to look at the Beatles covers. And, you know, they knew about art. They'd done a bit of research. Paul knew Kilburn and the Highroads, he also knew that I'd worked on a film with the BBC where I played the part of Captain Cook's artist, Sidney Parkinson, on the *Endeavour* voyage."[2]

Ocean's inner sleeve/audition piece shows the theater's brick exterior, as well as the side-

---

* This is the same Ian Dury, born May 12, 1942, who became a new wave icon with the release of the single 'Sex & Drugs & Rock & Roll' in August 1977, and the album *New Boots and Panties!!* a month later, followed by a string of era-defining recordings with the Blockheads. Dury later became an actor, with many film appearances to his credit, and he wrote a musical, *Apples*, with his Blockheads colleague Mick Gallagher, which ran at the Royal Court Theatre in 1989. He died at 57 of metastatic colorectal cancer, on March 27, 2000. McCartney recorded one of his songs, 'I'm Partial to Your Abracadabra,' with the Blockheads for the tribute album *Brand New Boots and Panties*, released in April 2001.

walk and street. The front end of a 1950's vintage automobile is pulled up to the entrance, and a handful of people—among them, Dury and Eddie Speight of Kilburn and the High Roads—linger outside. Most of the picture is monochrome, with some elements—the theater doors, part of the *Speed of Sound* banner, some of bystanders' clothing—colored in. When he submitted his artwork, Ocean was formally engaged as artist in residence for the upcoming Wings Over America tour.

Ocean had to share creative bragging rights, though, as the other side of the inner sleeve includes recording session photos taken mostly by Linda. And for the back cover, Paul engaged Clive Arrowsmith to take multiple-exposure photos of each band member, which were arranged in five rows—from top to bottom, Paul, Linda, Denny, Jimmy, Joe—like a Wings version of the Beatles' *A Hard Day's Night* album cover.

For all but Joe, only faces are seen; Joe's picture continues down through several inches of his shirt, which is the backdrop for five short rows of album credits, in red ink—the first two are the song titles (with lead singers noted); the third and fourth list the members of Wings and the horn section, plus McCartney's production credit, Henderson's engineering credit and the album's catalog number; and the fifth noting that "Special Speed of Sound Badges Go To Tony Clark, Mark Vigars, John Hammel, Trevor Jones, Fi, Hipgnosis & Hardie," followed by the label and MPL logos, MPL's address, and photo credits for Linda, Arrowsmith and Ellis.

Even the dull administrative part of the record's production received a few obligatory demiurgic brushstrokes. The disc labels had information on the top half—song titles, composing credits (the McCartney songs, whether by Paul and Linda or just Paul, are credited McCartney) and publishing information. For the McCartney songs, this was "MPL Communications Inc. (By Arrangement with ATV Music Corp)," with "Naimad Laine Songs Ltd" for 'Time to Hide,' and "J.M. Music Ltd." for 'Wino Junko,' both administered by MPL Communications, Inc., in the US and McCartney Music Ltd. in the UK. The American LP included Capitol and MPL logos; the British edition did not include logos as such but listed "M.P.L" (without the final period) in the same typeface as the Parlophone catalog number.

The album's release was scheduled for March 25 in America and April 2 in Britain.

With the next leg of Wings' world tour about to begin, the band gathered at Elstree Studios on March 1 for two weeks of rehearsals. This was a short tour—two concerts at the Falkoner Theatre in Copenhagen, on March 20 and 21; and single shows at Berlin's Deutschlandhalle on March 23, Rotterdam's Ahoy Sportpaleis on Mach 25, and the Pavillon de Paris on March 26.

Instead of merely polishing the British-Australian set, Paul took the opportunity to promote Wings' new long player and to tweak the running order. He moved 'Call Me Back Again' up from the second half of the show to a slot between 'Maybe I'm Amazed' and 'Lady Madonna.' He dropped the 'Little Woman Love' and 'C Moon' medley, as well as 'Junior's Farm,' to make room for three *Wings at the Speed of Sound* tunes—'Let 'Em In' (with Denny playing a strapped-on marching band drum), 'Silly Love Songs' and 'Beware My Love,' all slotted in as a block just after 'My Love.' And he reversed the order of the songs that had previously followed 'My Love,' putting 'Letting Go' first, followed by 'Listen to What the Man Said.'

Wings worked up a version of 'Time to Hide' at Elstree as well, as a replacement for 'Go Now,' but Paul ultimately opted to leave both songs off the European setlist, with the possibility of adding 'Time to Hide' and restoring 'Go Now' for the North American leg.

Paul's goal for the live versions of the new songs was the same as it was for the rest of the set—to sound as close as possible to the recorded versions. When players deviated, Paul would keep drilling the song until it was exactly as he wanted it.

"Paul had a way of getting you to do what he wants you to do, without telling you," Tony Dorsey recalled. "One day we were rehearsing 'Silly Love Songs,' and he kept doing it over and over and over."

From what Dorsey could tell, the problem was that Joe was trying different drum patterns in parts of the song where the beat changed. "He was a very creative drummer," Dorsey said, but given Paul's preference for live performances that precisely mirrored the recordings, creative drumming was not the order of the day.

"So he kept us going," Dorsey said. "Finally, we took a tea break, and Joe came over to me, and he said, 'Man, what the hell does he *want*?' And I said, 'Well, you know that section where [there's a tempo shift], he wants you to play that exactly as we recorded it.' So he went back and played it, and we got out of there! But it was, like, 11 o'clock at night. That was his way of chastising you when you're not doing what he wants you to do."[3]

At Abbey Road, meanwhile, Henderson made a set of test pressings on March 4, and mastered the disc on March 7. The mastering proved unsatisfactory, so Henderson mastered the album again on March 9.

The same day, Henderson also made rough mixes of Wings' live recordings from Melbourne, assembling two reels of live material for use in a *Wings Over Australia* television special that would draw on Gordon Bennett's footage as well as film from the television broadcast of the Melbourne show. Eight days later, on March 17, MPL contacted Bennett in Australia and engaged him to make the film, and to shadow Paul and Linda during the North American tour, as he had done in Australia.

"I received a letter from Brian Brolly after the event saying, 'Now that the tour is over, how would you see *Wings Over Australia*? Concerts or documentary? How would you see it happening?' So, I sent back the ideas that I had with the footage that I'd shot, and they set me up in an editing room there [in Soho] for four weeks. I synced everything up and then edited a one-hour programme for them out of the Australian material."[4]

There was Beatles activity, too, which served to boost the profile of Paul's upcoming tour as well as his bank balance. EMI reissued the Beatles' 22 British singles, both individually and in a boxed set, each disc packaged in a newly designed picture sleeve with a period-appropriate photo of the Beatles. An extra disc included 'Yesterday,' backed with 'I Should Have Known Better.' 'Yesterday' had been released as a single in the United States (with the more contemporaneous 'Act Naturally') in September 1965, to capitalize on the Beatles' performance of the song on the *Ed Sullivan Show*. Now that Paul was playing Beatles songs again, 'Yesterday' had been cited by critics in Britain and Australia as the highlight of his concert set, and EMI did not want to miss a trick.

The Bill Sargent offer was still clinging to life, too. The March 8 edition of the *Daily Mirror* carried a piece in which Harold Harrison, George's father, is quoted saying that "George has relented after some hesitation, and the boys have all agreed to do the show in the United States and possibly stay together for other shows."[5]

Around this time, Paul telephoned John Lennon for a chat about the singles reissues and other plans EMI had for Beatles compilations, plans that Paul was not against in principle, although he found some details that emerged during the conversation concerning.

"We were talking about re-packages," Paul told an interviewer a few days after the call, "and he was saying that in the States they want to repackage all the old Beatles stuff, but they want to use [the] American mixes"—mixes that in some cases were re-channeled stereo, and in others were drenched in excessive reverb. "He was saying that I should get it together, because I'm over here, to see that they get the official versions that we as Beatles sat 'round and mixed in London. All the little spin-offs and Capitol re-mixes and stuff is just what we don't want because they distort what we actually did. For historical reasons, we want to get it down as right as possible. It's never going to tell the whole story. There's only four of us know the whole story, and we're beginning to forget it.

"Anything that was genuine, anything that we did, I stand by. It's all the spin-offs, all the things that got it a little bit wrong, that start to get up your nose."[6]

It was not until later that evening that Paul realized that he and John had just chatted about the Beatles for over an hour, but it had not occurred to either of them to mention, let alone discuss, Bill Sargent's multimillion-pound offer.

An item in the news that caught Paul's attention (and that of most Britons) in early March was the Sterling Crisis. A large-scale sell-off of sterling currency, the crisis was occasioned by inflation (which had been close to 25 percent in Britain in 1975) as well as balance of payments and public funding deficits, and the continued fallout from the 1973 oil crisis. The British pound rapidly lost value against the American dollar, and its value continued to drop, making imported goods and overseas loans more expensive and exacerbating inflation.

Paul was shielded from these fluctuations to some degree, thanks to his investments in music copyrights. But as a songwriter able to find inspiration virtually anywhere, stories like "Holiday Haze Over Sinking Pound," which ran in the *Sunday Telegraph* on March 14, and detailed the volatility of the pound, the Spanish peseta and the Italian lira, had him scribbling notes for a potential tune. Dire as the situation was, he was able to set *"The pound is sinking . . ."* to a simple, attractive melody.

Jim McCartney's failing health was high on the list of concerns occupying Paul in March 1976. Now 73, Jim's health had started to deteriorate five years earlier, and Paul was in the habit of checking in on him by phone almost daily, speaking either to Jim directly or to Angie if Jim was not up to speaking. In recent years Angie began paying a National Health Service doctor an additional £300 ($650) a year to look in on Jim every Tuesday, and to run various tests to be sure that the drugs he was taking to alleviate his arthritis pain were not causing other problems.

But there were family rifts shaping up behind the scenes. At one point, Jim's sister-in-law, Joan McCartney, offered to stay with Jim and Angie to help out, but it turned out that Joan and Angie had different views about how to run the house, and Angie soon decided that she did not need Joan's help. Angie began to sense animosity from parts of the McCartney family, including aunts who believed that Jim would be best served in a nursing home, despite Angie's promise to Jim (with Paul's assent) that she would avoid that route. Rumors circulated within the family that Angie was romantically involved with a neighbor who visited the bungalow frequently to help care for Jim.

In the few weeks before the European tour, Jim's health declined more dramatically, and on March 13, Paul, Linda and the girls drove north to spend the weekend with him. When they arrived at the bungalow, Cynthia Lennon and Billy Hatton, formerly of the Fourmost, were visiting Jim. Paul and Linda brought a framed portrait of themselves and the girls, which they placed on Jim's bedside table.

"Paul spent a lot of time with his father that night," Angie remembered. "I just left the two of them alone. And Linda went in for a little while, and the kids went in one by one, and Linda said, 'Grandpa Jim's sleeping, and he's not very well, so don't disturb him, but you can go in and see him.' There was a very severe air of doom at that stage because it was obvious that Jim was deteriorating rapidly."[7]

According to Angie, Jim's decline was so steep that he began hallucinating, and bedside visitors adopted disturbing unearthly forms. Opening his eyes one afternoon, Jim mistook Ruth for his long-deceased mother, and when a dark figure passed by the window, he muttered, 'He's there, tell him I'm not ready yet,' convinced that the Grim Reaper had come for him. Then he would lapse into unconsciousness again.

After spending the evening at Rembrandt, Paul, Linda and the girls returned on Sunday morning, and again on their way to the airport. The visit left Paul shaken.

"Paul was very choked emotionally as they left," Angie said. "As we stood in the hallway, he hugged me. Normally we didn't have physical contact, he and I—he wasn't a kissy-kissy kind of person; none of the McCartney men were. But he hugged me and said, 'Ange, I'll never forget what you've done for my dad. Honest, you'll never want for anything.'"[8]

Back in London, Paul phoned Angie on Wednesday with a request. "I want you to promise me, Ange, that I'm gonna be the first one to know," he told her. "You tell me before you tell anybody, okay?"

But unless the European tour was going to be rescheduled at the last minute for the sake of a Jim McCartney death watch—an idea that was not seriously considered—preparations had to proceed.

Moreover, *Wings at the Speed of Sound* was due out in America on March 25, and in Britain a week later—by which time the band was scheduled to be in the United States rehearsing for the *Wings Over America* tour that was to open in Fort Worth, Texas, on April 8.

If you're Paul McCartney, you don't just slip an album into the shops without some kind of press event. Tony Brainsby, therefore, rented a suite at the Palace Hotel with tables full of sandwiches and bottled beer, and a waitstaff to serve mixed drinks, for a launch party and free-form interview session on March 18. Journalists from distant cities had the option of phoning in for interviews with band members.

Even at the event, as it turned out, access to Paul was not guaranteed. Brainsby deftly shepherded journalists toward individual Wings players, making sure to press the point Paul made in his press kit interview (lifted from Steve Peacock's recent *Street Life* column): *"This is much more of a group album."* Paul spoke mainly with Peacock and Chris Welch, who was on duty for *Melody Maker*, but he occasionally disappeared from the room entirely.

Jimmy and Joe were slightly the worse for wear, having been at a release party for the Sensational Alex Harvey Band's new album *The Penthouse Tapes* until the early hours the night before. Jimmy did his part, talking up the album in a phone interview with a writer in Bristol—but also showing his independent streak.

"We can plan a year ahead with Wings," McCulloch said, "and if I find the right people during my time off from Wings, I can go out and gig with them. I do it quite a bit."[9]

Talking up the new album with Gary Herman, from *Circus*, Jimmy spoke about the disc's "laid-back sound," but also undercut Paul's push to get journalists thinking of Wings as a democracy.

"Paul will come in and say, 'I've got a tune I want to do,'" Jimmy said, "and that's it. So you just sort of fall in, and you listen to it, and say, 'Well, I hear something that I'd like to put on it.'"

Joe, in his interview with Herman, tried a bit harder to toe the democracy line, but with mixed success. "We'd all go into the studio, hear a number, play it through and when we were hot, we'd cut it. We all made suggestions in the mixing, but Paul made the final decisions, and it was done very simply."[10]

Since he had already spoken with Steve Peacock about the making of the album, a conversation quoted at length in the press kit, Paul went slightly deeper in their discussion at the press launch, anticipating the critical response to the album—and confiding some of the insecurity he invariably felt when sending a new album out into the world.

"I have had a feeling over the past five years or so that people are getting a bit too psychiatric about it all, analyzing it like you analyze dreams," Paul observed. "Whereas the whole fun about music is just to dream it. Like dreams, the whole fun is just to dig 'em. Once you start taking them to the psychiatrist to find out what they meant, you're in the problem area.

"I nearly always think I could have done it better," he confided. "But then again, you're faced with the thing of, why should I go telling you when I'm dissatisfied? I should really—for all the people—be saying 'I'm awfully satisfied and it's really lovely, Steve, and I hope you're all going to buy it.' I'm always torn between telling you the truth . . . giving you a totally polished answer or trying to tell you what's actually going on."[11]

Asked how he felt about EMI releasing 'Yesterday' as a single, 11 years after it was recorded, Paul told Peacock, "I'm very proud. I think it's a lovely song. . . . I'm always pleased to hear any of my tunes on the radio. Just the other day I heard 'Tomorrow' by David Cassidy, 'Here, There and Everywhere' by Emmylou Harris, and Stackridge's 'Hold Me Tight.' That was just [on my way] to the studio. I love that."[12]

Paul had made a similar comment to Barry Chattington, when they were working on *The Bruce McMouse Show*, in 1972. Chattington asked Paul, "What's the nicest thing about being Paul McCartney?" To Chattington's surprise, Paul's response was, "Sitting in the bath, hearing yourself earn money"[13] as his music played on the radio.

It was a response that made his sideline business of investing in music publishing seem all the more tailor-made for him: though it remained a matter of frustration for Paul that he and John failed to acquire the publishing rights to their catalog when they lost Northern Songs to ATV Music, he nevertheless felt a thrill—and could almost hear the coins drop into the coffers—when he heard a new cover of a song he had written, or one that he owned, whether it was by Buddy Holly, Sammy Cahn or Jack Lawrence.

Paul was mid-conversation when Brainsby whispered in his ear that Angie McCartney was calling from Liverpool with urgent news.

"Paul came to the phone, and I said, 'Paul, I'm sorry to tell you son, it's just happened,'" Angie remembered. "And he shouted, 'Are you sure?!' His reaction was such shock, you know. I said, 'Yeah, I'm sorry son, it was very peaceful, but he's gone.' And he said, 'Okay, I'll call you later, I'm in the middle of this big thing. I'll call you later.' Poor bastard—going back to a room full of press."[14]

Jim's death notice, with details of the funeral, appeared in the *Liverpool Echo* the following morning. He was given a dignified send-off—no "Beatle Paul's Father Dies" front-page splash, just a simple listing in the obituaries column:

> McCARTNEY—March 18, 1976, peacefully at home, 20 Beverley Drive, Gayton, Wirral. JAMES McCARTNEY, beloved husband of Angela, and dear father of Paul, Michael and Ruth. Private service in his residence, Monday, March 22, followed by cremation at Landican, at 10.30 a.m. No flowers please, but donations may be sent for Arthritis Research, c/o Doctor T.R. Littler, Leasowe Hospital, Wirral.

The funeral was a between-concerts travel day for Wings, but Paul did not attend, and was not expected to. Mike helped Angie make plans for the funeral, and during a telephone conversation with his brother, Paul stated his case for his absence. His argument was simple: should he turn up, so would the press. But as Mike put down the receiver, he could sense that Paul's reasons for skipping his own father's funeral ran deeper than celebrity paranoia.

"It was no coincidence that Paul was on the continent at the time of the funeral. . . . Paul would never face that sort of thing," Mike later wrote. "As Dad would say, 'It's just the way you're made, son.'"[15]

By his own admission, the death of his mother at age fourteen left deep scars.

"When my mum died, I said, 'What are we going to do for money?'" Paul once noted. "And I've never forgiven myself for that . . . But that's all I could say then. It's like a lot of kids; when you tell them someone's died, they laugh. My mum died when I was 14. That is a kind of strange age to lose a mother . . .'cause you know, you're dealing with puberty. . . . And for a boy to lose a mother, it's not easy. You're starting to be a man, to be macho."[16]

George and Ringo sent Angie flowers, as well as donations to Leasowe Hospital. Paul asked her to arrange for flowers as well. "On the run up to the funeral," Angie said, "Paul said to me, 'Will you do some nice flowers from me, do little posies from the children—just to go on the coffin. I know we're not supposed to do flowers, but we have to have some flowers.' I said, 'Oh yes, of course.' It was never a question that he could come. So when people say, 'Oh, Paul was a no-show,' that is not true."[17]

"I'm a private kind of person," Paul later reflected. "You know, crying is not done. And it was definitely not done when I was a boy, and you were definitely considered a sissy if you cried. We tried to change a lot of that—our generation tried to change a lot of things and did. Some would say we shouldn't, but I figure if we've got tear ducts, there's got to be something there. I cried as a kid [when] anything hurt, but I slowly learned to repress that. From what people generally say, repressing stuff like that isn't too clever."[18]

Paul was not exaggerating when he said he described himself as a private person, at least as far as personal and family issues went. For fear of killing the buzz on the next leg of their world tour, he did not mention Jim's death to Denny, Jimmy or Joe. It was not until the end of the European tour, when a French interviewer asked Paul whether his parents were still alive, that the rest of the band heard that Jim had recently died.

"I was fond of Jim McCartney and knew him well, but Paul didn't even tell me he was dead," Denny said. "I was stunned. I knew his mother had died when he was 14 but he had never mentioned a word to me about his father. . . . When Paul dropped that bombshell, I felt utterly deflated. Paul loved his dad—there's no doubt about that. But death scares him, and he didn't go to the funeral because he couldn't handle it. It wasn't lack of love that kept him away—he didn't want to cry in public. He wants to appear like he's got his act together whenever anyone is around. That's the kind of person he is."[19]

Wings flew out of Heathrow at 6:30 P.M. on March 19, and checked into the Palace Hotel at 9:15. During his arrival in Copenhagen, Paul's spooky ability to split his persona into the two manifestations he has called *Him* (the public Paul) and *Me* (the real person) came into full effect. *Me* was mourning his father, but *Him* was thumbs aloft for the waiting television cameras and reporters, primed to entertain.

The next morning, Paul and Linda took the girls sightseeing in the Danish capital, with stops to see *Den lille Havfrue* (the Little Mermaid), a bronze statue by Edvard Eriksen of the Hans Christian Andersen fairy-tale character, as well as the Amalienborg Palace, the official residence of the Danish royal family. The girls wanted to stop in for tea with Queen Margrethe II,* but if an impromptu visit was more than even Paul's celebrity could leverage, Paul and Linda turned the episode into a comedy routine later that evening, in a post-concert interview.

Interviewer: I've been told you went to visit the Danish queen today. What happened?

Paul: Well, you see, we were touring around, and we went to see the mermaid first, and then we went to see the queen.

---

* Margrethe Alexandrine Þórhildur Ingrid, born April 16, 1940, became the longest-reigning female monarch in Danish history when she abdicated the throne after a 52-year rule on January 14, 2024.

Denny: She had a hangover. *[band laughs]*

Paul: We saw a car go in, so we rang the bell, you know. And we heard she's only 34, so we thought . . .

Linda: . . . She might like to have us in for tea.

Paul: . . . She might like a cup of tea or something, a bit of Danish bacon, you know. So, we rang on the door and there was a man there and he said, "No, no, no, no." And we said, "But we'd like to see the queen," and he said, "No, no, no," and he was closing the door. I said, "Well, tell her the McCartneys called."

Linda: And he went *[makes noise of door slamming closed].*

Paul: "No, no, no." And closed the door! So, we're hoping to see her tomorrow.

Linda: Let 'em in![20]

At the Falkoner Theatre opener, Wings picked up where they left off in Melbourne, except that now the band were playing three songs from the not-yet-released *Wings at the Speed of Sound* that few in the audience of 2,000 would have had a chance to hear. The live premiere of 'Let 'Em In,' complete with its opening doorbell and its vibrant horn arrangement, won appreciative applause. The band negotiated the vocal complexities and rhythmic changes of 'Silly Love Songs' without a hitch, and drew a marginally more enthusiastic response. The driven 'Beware My Love' seemed to strike a sympathetic chord as well.

But as had been the case in Britain and Australia, the most vehement and sustained applause came at the start of 'Yesterday'—which Knud Orsted, reviewing the show for *Billboard*, jokingly called "his new old single." Orsted added that "the concert brought together in one hall both the Beatles generation and the Wings generation," and that "the audience responded with vociferous acclaim and towards the end was dancing around the hall."

After the second Copenhagen show, on March 21, the band did backstage interviews for Swedish television, a handful of Danish newspapers and radio stations, and two magazines—*Musik Express* and *Pop*—from Germany. Among the interviewers, the new album was a topic of particular interest, especially 'Silly Love Songs.' Asked whether the song was written in response to criticism, Paul first denied it, saying, "You don't think about all that, you're just writing something," but then added a comment that made it clear that the song was defensive. "The line that sums it up is, 'What's wrong with that?' There's nothing wrong with love songs, you know, a lot of people like 'em."[21]

Paul was vague when asked whether the song would be Wings' next single, saying that he wanted to see how audiences reacted to it. But the thinking at EMI and Capitol was that it would be a superb single, and as they awaited final word from Paul, EMI's mastering engineer Chris Blair prepared cuts of 'Silly Love Songs' (EMI matrix 7YCE 21785) backed with 'Cook of the House' (EMI matrix 7YCE 21786)—Paul's and Linda's choice of B side, not EMI's.

Wings had another full day in Copenhagen, but MPL in London and New York were in overdrive, announcing the schedule for *Wings Over America*, the largest and only truly lucrative part of the band's world tour. Wings would spend nearly two months in North America playing 31 concerts in 20 cities:

April 8–9, Fort Worth, TX, Tarrant County Coliseum
April 11–12, Houston, TX, The Summit
April 14, Tempe, AZ, Tempe Stadium
April 15, Tucson, AZ, Community Center
April 17, San Diego, CA, Sport Arena
April 19–20, Los Angeles (Inglewood), CA, The Forum
April 22–23, San Francisco (Daly City), CA, Cow Palace
April 25–26, Vancouver, Canada, P.N.E. Coliseum
April 29, Denver, CO, McNichols Arena
May 2, St. Paul, MN, St. Paul's Civic Center Arena
May 4–5, Chicago, IL, Chicago Stadium
May 7–8, Detroit, MI, Olympia Stadium
May 9, Toronto, Ontario, Canada, Maple Leaf Gardens
May 10, Cleveland (Richfield), OH, The Coliseum
May 12–13, Philadelphia, PA, The Spectrum
May 15–16, Landover, MD, Capital Center
May 18–19, Atlanta, GA, OMNI Center
May 21, Long Island (Uniondale), NY, Nassau Coliseum
May 22, Boston, MA, Boston Garden
May 24–25, New York, NY, Madison Square Garden[22]

Such was McCartney's stature that he could have booked and sold out every major sports stadium in America, playing—as the Beatles did in the mid-1960s—for crowds in excess of 50,000. But the booked venues were mainly hockey and basketball arenas with far lower capacities. Showco advance man Allen Branton, a lighting designer in his mid-20s, was responsible for scouting each arena, together with a rigging expert, to make sure that the venues could sustain Wings' bulky sound and lighting rigs.

For Branton, it was clear that McCartney was haunted as much as he was energized by his memories of Beatlemania.

"The venues that they chose were very consistent," said Branton. "They never tried to go to any stadiums, just the stadium in Seattle, the Kingdome. . . . I think that he was so worried about the quality of the performances that he just wasn't willing to go to these places where the sound would get away from him, so to speak. I think that experience with the Beatles really scarred him."[23]

At 6:50 P.M., the band and crew were on a plane to Hamburg, where they had just enough time to change gates and grab a beer and a bite before the 40-minute flight to West Berlin departed at 8:55 P.M. The band made their way to the Schlosshotel Gehrhus; the crew lodged at the Hotel Schweizerhof. They would perform the following evening, March 23, for a crowd of just over 5,000—about twice the audience Wings drew when they performed in Berlin in 1972,[24] but well under the hall's capacity of 8,770.

On the afternoon of the show, in a move reminiscent of John and Yoko's peace vigils in 1969, Paul painted 'Silly Love Songs' in large letters on a bedsheet, and he led Wings through West Berlin with the makeshift banner unfurled. Gordon Bennett filmed Wings' march as it reached its end point at the Berlin Wall, and Aubrey Powell snapped photos of the band holding up the banner near Checkpoint Charlie, the crossing point between East and West Berlin. It may be that the procession was prompted more by vanity and a promotional instinct (should Paul approve 'Silly Love Songs' for release as a single, Powell's photos would prove useful for trade advertisements and possibly picture sleeves) than any real hope of bringing down the East-West divide, but Paul made an event of it.

That evening Paul presided over an electrifying performance, with the band sounding particularly polished, even in cases where the tempos were a bit brisker than usual. Jimmy added showy lead guitar flourishes throughout the set—most notably in 'Let Me Roll It,' 'My Love' and 'Soily'—and Paul revived the German he learned during the Beatles' Hamburg residencies, introducing songs in a combination of German and English, with Linda throwing in the occasional word or phrase *("Wunderbar!")* as well.

Wings' next stop gave Paul an opportunity to try out his more limited Dutch. Having flown from West Berlin to Hamburg and then Amsterdam, on March 24, arriving just after 5 P.M., Paul and Linda were met at the arrivals lounge at Schiphol Airport by executives from EMI Holland, and a film crew gathering footage for a Wings special for Veronica TV.

"Hello, goedenavond, good morning, how are you?" Paul cheerfully called to the Dutch television crew. Puzzlingly, his Dutch greeting was correct for the time of day—it was his English "good morning" that was wrong. "Goedenavond," Linda chimed in, quickly adding the names of Dutch painters—the contemporary artist (and Lee Eastman client) Willem de Kooning, and the seventeenth-century portraitist Frans Hals. A moment later, she added Rembrandt and van der Meer, and Paul introduced Heather, Mary and Stella to the crew as Rembrandt, de Kooning and Picasso ("non-Flemish!" Linda quickly pointed out).[25]

By the time they reached the Amstel Hotel (the crew went ahead to Rotterdam, where they stayed at the Hilton), Paul had acquired a spray of tulips from a small group of fans that had gathered outside holding a sign that read, "We Love Paul McCartney and Wings."

But just as it had been when Wings toured Europe in 1972, trouble was never far from Wings' rank and file.

"He drank a lot, fell down a lot, got up again and drank more," a *Daily Mirror* reporter who was shadowing the band wrote of Jimmy's night in Amsterdam. "He fought a lot, too. . . . He was musically more than ready for such big-time rock music, but he was far from emotionally ready to shed his wildness. In Amsterdam, his mid-morning lager wasn't to his satisfaction, so he hurled it across the plush hotel lounge, just missing the head of a waiter."[26]

The band traveled to Rotterdam the next day for the show at the 5,000-seat Ahoy Sportpaleis that had the same energy and drive as the Berlin show. The Veronica team continued to film, capturing excerpts from the show and from a handful of post-concert interviews with print, radio and television journalists. The Veronica interviewer broached the subject of the Bill Sargent proposal.

"Well, that's a very big offer," Paul said, lightly scratching the side of his nose—a movement that was quickly becoming one of his tells, indicating that he was about to give an answer that was more diplomatic than candid. "Nobody has yet spoken about it. We've talked to each other, and we've talked about ordinary things—you know, what's happening—but no one has actually said, 'do you wanna do it?' yet. None of the other three have asked me. But we might do it, and if we did do it, we'd try to make it good. But then again, we might not do it! But then again, we might!"

"It's a yes-no," Linda offered.

"It's a positive maybe," Paul added. "No one's against it, but for a thing to happen you have to have people *for* it. Not everyone *not against* it. Everyone has to be positive, and that's what we're waiting for."[27]

The day of the Rotterdam show, *Wings at the Speed of Sound* was issued in the United States, without a single to herald it, although Capitol continued to push for 'Silly Love Songs.' Paul thought the song would make a strong single, too—so what was he waiting for?

"We've released the album before any singles," he told one journalist, "mainly because the radio stations haven't been told what our preference is, and they can decide for themselves. And they'll play various cuts and see which rises to the surface."[28]

Reviewing the album in the *New York Times*, John Rockwell noted that "*Wings at the Speed of Sound* has been greeted in some quarters as a disappointing throwaway after the more ambitious *Venus and Mars*. As far as this listener is concerned, the new disc is a more refreshing testimony to Mr. McCartney's current skills and ambitions than the earlier, more pretentious effort was." But Rockwell left some question about what those skills and ambitions were. "Mr. McCartney seems to have had his fill of significance during his Beatle days and settled into his solo career for the straightforward production of 'disposable' pop"[29]—an observation he supported by quoting the refrain of 'Silly Love Songs.'

Jon Tiven, in *Audio*, gave *Wings at the Speed of Sound* an A+ grade for the performance, and an A for sound quality. He began by calling out the dogmatic McCartney vs. anti-McCartney divisions, arguing that "if you weren't going to like this album, you made up your mind that you didn't like McCartney long ago." To Tiven's ears, "Macca has truly exceeded himself without overpowering the rest of the band." That said, though he singled out 'Warm and Beautiful' as "a Standard in the making," and described 'Let 'Em In' as "thrilling," he found 'Cook of the House' only "mildly amusing" and didn't much like 'Time to Hide' (which he attributed to McCulloch rather than Laine). [30]

At *Rolling Stone*, Stephen Holden damned McCartney's post-Beatles career with faint praise, asserting that he "has proven himself a clever miniaturist whose records resemble collages built around simple musical fragments, each of which is painstakingly produced. While some have discussed McCartney's music as insufferably cute, uninspired trivia, all of his albums contain at least some good music."

But he was hard-pressed to find that good music on *Wings at the Speed of Sound*. He described 'Silly Love Songs' as "a tract in defense of moon, June and spoon," but also as "a clever retort whose point is well-taken." And he found 'Warm and Beautiful' to be "one of the worst songs Paul McCartney has written," packed with "the stalest pop ballad clichés ever to emerge from an English music hall."

But the *coup de grace* was a comparison of the new album to McCartney's own best work. "Ultimately," Holden concluded, "this album lacks the melodic sparkle of *Venus and Mars*, which in turn lacked the energy, passion and structural breadth and unity of *Band on the Run*. . . . As a whole, *At the Speed of Sound* seems like a mysterious, somewhat defensive oddity by a great pop producer who used to be a great pop writer."[31]

More brickbats awaited the British release, eight days later. Barbara Charone, in *Sounds*, began her review by declaring *Wings at the Speed of Sound* "a major disappointment," adding that "all the magic and excitement evident in concert is mysteriously absent from this soporific piece of vinyl." Disagreeing with the notion that Wings should be—or could be—a democracy, Charone objected to the fact that Paul sang only 6 of the 11 songs. Still, she found 'Silly Love Songs' to be the "one genuine chunk of inspiration" on the disc, a "well thought-out production and arrangement, a musical tease wrapped around an infectious melody."[32]

"This is not an album that hits you with the sustained power of *Band on the Run* or *Venus and Mars*," Chris Welch wrote in his *Melody Maker* review, "but, as Linda says: 'It grows on yer!' And indeed, it does. After five or six hearings, many of the subtleties of the arrangements, the choice of instruments for a particular passage (like an unexpected burst of trombone during 'Let 'Em In'), the feeling Paul puts into a particular phrase, or simply the effectiveness of a melody, begin to swim into focus." All told, Welch felt the album would "undoubtedly increase the growing worldwide appeal of Wings."[33]

Like vinegar in a paper cut, criticism never failed to sting. But after a ten-year absence from the American touring scene, 31 life-affirming concerts were now tantalizingly close, so McCartney remained tunnel-vision focused on the only balm he needed to lift the critical blues: the love of the masses.

One more concert remained on Wings' European tour itinerary, and then it was off to America. The entourage was driven from Rotterdam to Amsterdam for a 12:30 P.M. flight for Paris, landing at Charles de Gaulle airport an hour later. Wings checked into the George V, with the McCartneys taking over three suites (118 through 120); the crew stayed at the Novotel Bagnolet.

Before the show that evening, Paul spent half an hour with Nicky Horne, recording an interview for Horne's Capital Radio show, *Your Mother Wouldn't Like It*. They discussed *Wings at the Speed of Sound*—Paul's stories about the writing of 'Cook of the House' and the solo turns by Denny, Joe and Jimmy were fast becoming interview set pieces—as were his thoughts about the Sargent offer.

But there were also a few less guarded moments, like when Horne reminded him that he once said he "half expected Wings not to work."

"Yes," Paul admitted, "like everyone else, you know? But I couldn't join in with everyone else and say, 'yes, I agree with you, it's never going to work,' 'cause no one in the band would have believed in it then, you know? Everyone would have just said, 'Oh, it's not going to work, right, let's jack it in now,' which—there was enough of that *anyway*. But you know, yes, I did half suspect it mightn't happen, just because it's very difficult to get a thing together after something like the Beatles."

Talk soon turned to reviews, and his vulnerability to them.

"I think anything people say influences me a bit," he admitted. "I'm sort of plugging ahead trying to keep positive and get on to the next one. It can drag you down a bit. It doesn't help when you've got to kind of wake up and read a few newspapers and say, 'Oh what? Rubbish!' And you've got to go through the day with that on your head, then."[34]

The concert, like the previous four, showed that Wings had hit their stride on the eve of the American tour. Paul seemed fully at ease, and Denny sounded comfortable in his vocal showcases. Linda played and sang with a new level of confidence. Joe's drumming was solid, flexible, and heavy when it needed to be, particularly in the two foot-stomping encores, 'Hi, Hi, Hi' and 'Soily.' And Jimmy was on fire in 'Beware My Love' and 'Letting Go.'

After a post-concert television interview for *Les rendez-vous du Dimanche*, with a reporter for the newspaper *Bon Soir* also in attendance, during which Paul mentioned for the first time that his father Jim had died, the band was set loose on Paris.

Jimmy went out drinking with David Cassidy, who was in Paris to see Wings at Paul's invitation. It was a free pass Paul quickly came to regret. Having played beer glass shotput in Amsterdam, McCulloch was itching to take misadventure to the next level. After a night sampling Parisian bars, McCulloch and Cassidy ended up at Cassidy's hotel, where, as Cassidy wrote in his memoir, "Jimmy was just out of control, and because of his alcoholism, he went nuts."[35]

Going nuts, in this case, involved smashing the television in Cassidy's room, during which he sustained a fall and broke the pinky of his left hand. Cassidy got Jimmy to a hospital, where his finger was placed in a cast. He was told it would take about three weeks to heal. McCulloch left it to Cassidy to phone Paul in the middle of the night to tell him what happened. "I think Paul somehow blamed me," Cassidy wrote.

With a finger on Jimmy's fretting hand in a cast, the American tour would have to be postponed. When Brolly informed the Eastmans the next morning, they pointed out a further potential ramification, if not for this tour, then for subsequent ones. Since in this case, MPL was eager to reschedule the concerts that were canceled because of Jimmy's accident, presenters were unlikely to sue for breach of contract; but in a case where the circumstances were dire enough to require outright cancellation, MPL could be liable. The Eastmans, therefore, took out an insurance policy—with an annual premium of $40,000 (£77,000)—to protect Paul against such events.[36]

Jimmy had, by now, an impressive list of demerits—a tirade at the Sound Shop Studio in Nashville, as well as an arrest, smashing up a Winnebago while scouting photo locations with Aubrey Powell and the rest of Wings, a growing list of incidents involving drunkenness or brawling, and now this.

Paul made his displeasure clear to the diminutive Scot, but there was also some public relations to be done. Tales of drunkenness and television destruction were fine for the likes of Led Zeppelin or the Who, but Wings projected a more wholesome image, so a fib was concocted for Jimmy to tell in interviews: he had returned to the George V after the show, had a bath, and slipped on the bathroom's polished marble floor.

Tony Brainsby sent the British and American press the bathroom story, along with statements from Jimmy and Paul, and a photo of a smiling Jimmy, showing his finger in a thick cast.

"What can I say?" Brainsby wrote, for attribution to Jimmy. "It's one of those things that happens and I'm sorry that the accident should cause such carefully prepared plans to be rearranged. I hope our fans will remain patient until I get the cast off."

Brainsby's magic typewriter also converted Paul's anger to something closer to compassion.

"We're all disappointed about the delay. As soon as Jimmy's playing again, we'll be there. Jimmy is the one who is suffering the physical pain of the fractured hand, and we just want him to get well quickly."[37]

By now, McCulloch's slurred brogue and dilated pupils were enough to send his bandmates scurrying out of hotel bars to avoid getting swept up in his chaotic whirlwind.

"We were always putting Jimmy in his place," said Laine. "I would shout at him to grow up, literally. Once he'd sobered up, though, he was quiet as a mouse. I guided Jimmy through lots of things, you know. I even got him out of jail for drinking and driving. We were with Frank Zappa once and he fell over the table, face down on the floor. I mean we've all done it, don't get me wrong. We've all had our moments, but Jimmy seemed to have more moments than anyone else."[38]

Jimmy was not the only one to leave his mark on Paris. While Wings were playing at the Pavilion, six-year-old Mary and four-year-old Stella undertook an art project in their suite at the George V. Using the hotel's handmade Japanese wallpaper as their canvas, they liberally contributed drawings using felt-tipped pens, which the hotel staff quickly discovered could not be washed away.

"Kids will be kids," the hotel's manager, André Sonier, told the *Daily Mirror*. "We made no fuss about it."[39]

14

WINGSMANIA

I was trying very hard to play it all down, keep casual," Paul confessed of his mixed feelings about returning to the American stage. "We're just taking a band to America, and we'll have a good time, lads. But then you start getting the journalists saying, 'It's ten years since former Beatle Paul McCartney has been back to the Beatle stage,' and, 'Is it going to be as good as the Beatles? And will they play Beatle songs?' Suddenly, that kinda thing starts piling in on you and you start to have these horrible thoughts—well it just might not be as good like . . . but we'll have a good go like."[1]

But McCartney's American second coming was on hold. Paul and his Wings returned to London with time suddenly on their hands, and Jimmy's injury sent MPL into overdrive. Reconfiguring the North American tour meant not only shuffling the tour dates but also revising the complex logistics of moving a huge tour around the continent.

But the revisions to the tour schedule came together with surprising rapidity. Allowing nearly a month for Jimmy's finger to heal, it was determined all the shows between May 7 (Detroit) and May 25 (New York City) could go ahead unchanged. The Fort Worth tour opener was moved to May 3, with Houston the following evening. The other pre-Detroit dates were moved to after what had originally been planned as the tour's finale at Madison Square Garden.

All told, five concerts were scrapped—the second shows in Fort Worth and Houston were dropped, as were concerts in Tempe, Arizona, and two in Vancouver, British Columbia, because the venues were not available for proposed new dates. However, three cities—Cincinnati, Ohio; Kansas City, Missouri; and Seattle, Washington—were added to the itinerary, and shortly after the new schedule was announced, on April 7, extra shows were added in Chicago and Los Angeles to fulfill high demand. The final itinerary:

May 3, Fort Worth, TX, Tarrant County Convention Center
May 4, Houston, TX, The Summit
May 7–8, Detroit, MI, Olympia Stadium
May 9, Toronto, Ontario, Canada, Maple Leaf Gardens
May 10, Cleveland (Richfield), OH, The Coliseum
May 12–13, Philadelphia, PA, The Spectrum
May 15–16, Landover, MD, Capital Center
May 18–19, Atlanta, GA, OMNI Center
May 21, Long Island (Uniondale), NY, Nassau Coliseum
May 22, Boston, MA, Boston Garden
May 24–25, New York, NY, Madison Square Garden
May 27, Cincinnati, OH, Riverfront Coliseum
May 29, Kansas City, MO, Kemper Arena
May 31, June 1–2, Chicago, IL, Chicago Stadium
June 4, Saint Paul, MN, St. Paul Civic Center
June 7, Denver, CO, McNichols Sports Arena
June 10, Seattle, WA, Kingdome
June 13–14, San Francisco (Daly City), CA, Cow Palace
June 16, San Diego, CA, Sport Arena
June 18, Tucson, AZ, Community Center
June 21–23, Los Angeles (Inglewood), CA, The Forum

The 21-city tour was expected to gross in the neighborhood of $5 million (£2.8 million), but it also involved significant technical and logistical upgrades. Showco built a larger stage, to reflect the bigger American venues, and new projection equipment was added. The set, lighting and audio equipment would be carted around the continent in five large semi-trucks. At Gordon Bennett's suggestion, three of the trucks had the words "Wings," "Over" and "America" painted on their roofs. Bennett and Powell captured aerial shots of those trucks from a Cessna light aircraft, as they tooled along the highway just outside Tucson.

"Technically speaking," sound designer and Showco co-owner Jack Maxson boasted, "this is probably the best concert tour that has ever been put on. It's all so well thought out. . . . All of our help comes straight from Dallas. The nucleus of the crew is 27 people. And we also work with the stagehands union at the local hall[s]."

As a co-owner of Showco, which built equipment for dozens of tours every year, Maxson had his hands full, but he had decided to travel with the Wings tour. "This is the only tour I'll do myself this year," he told *People*. "It's important to me to do at least one tour a year to keep my feet wet and also not to lose touch with what the crews are going through."[2]

The band and staff—23 people—would travel in a private 24-seat BAC 111 jet, leased from Braniff International Airways and customized with a blue-and-white Wings logo and the words *Wings Over America* to the right of the passenger door.

"When you're touring like this, and it's a very big tour, you either hire a plane or you take scheduled flights," Paul explained. "And by the time you've taken a lot of little scheduled flights it's the cost of a private plane anyway—when you've got this many people to cart around. And it just means you're not rushing through airports late and stuff, so it's a thing that a lot of people do. It just becomes part of the way you live."[3]

Having a private plane at the band's disposal made another unusual element of Paul's tour planning possible. Instead of booking hotels in every city where there was a show, MPL arranged the tour almost like a military operation, establishing a handful of bases around the United States, to which the band could return on their private plane after each concert.

This was not just a matter of efficiency. An unstated benefit was that getting the band onto the jet and back to base after each show would limit the musicians' post-show barhopping and tail chasing (and, consequently, turning up late or drunk the next day). As on earlier legs, MPL rented a handful of recent films, including *Moses*, *Dog Day Afternoon* and *Next Stop* and *Greenwich Village*, to keep the band entertained during their downtime.

From April 24 through May 5, that base was the La Baron Hotel, in Dallas, where the band and crew stayed (the McCartneys rented a private house in Dallas) during the pre-tour rehearsal period and for the Fort Worth and Houston shows. From May 6, the night before the first Detroit show, through the second Madison Square Garden concert, on May 25, Wings' moveable headquarters was New York—the Gramercy Park Hotel, for the band, the Stanhope for the McCartneys. For the dates in the Midwest, from Cincinnati through Saint Paul, the band were based at the Whitehall Hotel in Chicago, while the McCartneys rented a farmhouse outside the city. And for the last batch of shows, in the Southwest and on the West Coast, Paul and Linda rented a house in Los Angeles, and the band's home base was the Beverly Wilshire Hotel.

Paul and Linda remained committed to the idea that where they went, their children went, too. But as Heather, Mary and Stella got older, it made sense to consider the logistics of that policy. Renting houses rather than staying in hotel rooms provided a sense of normalcy and "hominess," and also put some distance between the children and any manifestations of raucous band life that might be playing out among the band and crew.

"Some people said, 'Oh, you can't drag these children 'round the world!'" Paul explained. "We didn't think of it like that, we just thought, 'You know what? What's the sense of us being in America and them being in England?' We were always a close family, it just seemed like the thing to do.[4]

"I thought that either the kids were going to be with me and influenced by me, or with some babysitter or nanny. So, they came to all our bases. They only came to four shows as treats—special nights—so they would not be camp followers. We treated it as if we were on holiday and us parents would go out during the evening."[5] The McCartneys' preference for keeping families together did not apply just to them.

"Linda would say, 'Where's the missus?'" Tony Dorsey remembered, "And I'd say, 'She's at home, she knows I'm here to work.' So Linda said to Alan [Crowder], 'Get his wife out here!' You know, my daughter would be out there, playing with his kids, and the dog—it was a real relaxed thing. I thought of it as a big vacation."[6]

For at least part of the tour Joe's girlfriend Dayle and her daughter Christy traveled with the band. Like the McCartneys, Joe and Dayle engaged a tutor to travel with them and keep Christy on course with her studies.

Paul arranged to add a 24-track recorder to the band's hefty equipment list so that all the shows on the tour would be recorded for a potential live album. This was not the first time he had harbored such hopes: the last five shows of the 1972 European tour were recorded, principally for use on the soundtrack *The Bruce McMouse Show*, although several live cuts were considered for inclusion on *Red Rose Speedway*, and one, 'The Mess,' was issued as the B side of 'My Love.' Wings' 1973 show in Newcastle was considered for release as a live album as well but was ultimately shelved.*

Paul had Brainsby extend invitations to three photographers he knew and trusted, to travel on the band's plane and have backstage access, for at least part of the tour. They were Aubrey Powell, of Hipgnosis; Robert Ellis, who traveled with Wings during their 1972 European tour; and Harry Benson, the Glasgow-born photographer Paul had known since the early days of the Beatles.

"He was quite comfortable being photographed by me," said Benson, "although we never became close friends. It was a professional relationship—I never tried to become friends with any of my subjects. I wanted to photograph what I see."[7]

Gordon Bennett, the Australian cameraman who trailed the McCartneys around Australia and Europe, had been engaged to do the same in America. Like the band, he was cooling his heels in London. Since MPL now had both Bennett's Australian footage and the Melbourne concert film, Bennett was installed at Roger Cherill's editing facility in Soho (where *The Bruce McMouse Show* was edited) to start work on *Wings Over Australia*.†

And it was time to pull the trigger on a single from *Wings at the Speed of Sound*, on the theory that having a hit in the charts would help sell concert tickets. Not that McCartney needed

---

* Nineteen tracks from the 1972 tour, and one from the 1973 Newcastle show, were released as *Wings Over Europe* in the *Wings 1971–73* Limited Edition Super Deluxe set in 2018.

† Bennett's documentary, *Wings Over Australia*, only ever reached rough-cut stage and has never been issued commercially or otherwise.

WINGS SINGLE

R6014

SILLY LOVE SONGS

From the album
Wings At The Speed Of Sound

Wings, 'Silly Love Songs' single trade ad as captured in Berlin

to worry about that: on March 25, shortly before the ticket sale dates for the original tour schedule was announced, the box office manager at the Los Angeles Forum jumped the gun and put tickets on sale; the first two Forum shows were sold out before ticket sales were formally announced.

Still, it made sense to keep Wings in airplay rotation, so Paul finally agreed to release 'Silly Love Songs' and 'Cook of the House' as a single. The disc was in the shops on April 2 in America, and on April 30 in Britain.

For reviewers, 'Silly Love Songs' had an element beyond the normal questions of whether it was well written, well performed and well produced: with Paul's response to criticism of post-Beatles work as the song's lyrics, the reviews were a measure of the value critics placed on those love songs of Paul's.

> *What's wrong with silly love songs, McCartney asks? There's certainly nothing wrong with this one; the production is slick, and the arrangement filled with drive. The ex-Beatle's voice is as good as ever, and this is headed straight for the top.*[8]
>
> *Uncredited,* Cash Box

> *I don't think very much about it at all. They've done better. The song's not very nice. It IS a silly love song. It's all OK until he starts singing. But it'll probably get in the chart.*[9]
>
> *Carolyn Coon,* Melody Maker

> *It would seem that even the Beatles themselves are currently having a bit of trouble producing really great singles. Wings' 'Who Wants to Fill the World With Silly Love Songs,' has a wonderful drum sound and immaculate brass but is also silly.*[10]
>
> *Mick Farren,* NME

> *What could have been a brilliant song remains half formulated. There are some fantastic moments in this, and the production is uniformly magnificent, but the thing doesn't grab the way it should. I haven't yet heard* Wings at the Speed of Sound, *and this doesn't increase my desire to.*[11]
>
> *Jonh Ingham,* Sounds

Obvious choice for a single really and has had a lot of plays as an album track. Wings haven't had too much success with singles lately (lots with albums though) but this is a lot more commercial than some of the previous selections. Bright and bouncy and just right if you're feeling a bit daft.[12]

Sue Byrom, Record Mirror & Disc

There was nothing silly about the record's chart performance. Defying its critics, 'Silly Love Songs' spent 19 weeks on the *Billboard* Hot 100, entering at No. 58 on April 10, and peaking at No. 1 twice—for a single week, on May 22, and for four weeks starting June 12. In Britain, the single spent 11 weeks in the Top 100, entering at No. 29 on May 15, and peaking at No. 2 on June 12.

As the source of the hit single, *Wings at the Speed of Sound* proved the perfect backdrop for the band's first American tour. The album entered the American charts at No. 32, on the same day 'Silly Love Songs' first charted. It reached No. 1 three times—on April 24 and May 29, for a week each, and for five weeks starting on June 19. By May 1, it was certified Gold, and it remained in the Top 200 for 51 weeks. It entered the UK album chart at No. 2 on April 17, and though it did not reach No. 1, it spent 35 weeks in the Top 100.

Paul was also on the British singles charts as a Beatle: all 22 reissued singles, plus 'Yesterday,' charted in early April, with 'Yesterday' climbing the highest—to No. 8—during its nine-week stay.

Tickets for *Wings Over America* went on sale—again—on Friday, April 23. At Madison Square Garden, where lines of ticket buyers spilled out onto Eighth Avenue, two shows, accounting for about 40,000 tickets, sold out within hours, with the other shows in the new itinerary following quickly. The stage was set for Beatlemania Mark II, or as sections of the American press dubbed it: "Wingsmania."

But as Paul was heard singing 'Silly Love Songs' through radios everywhere, the rumblings of a cultural shift were being heard in London and New York, as a new style was emerging that Paul would have to consider. In London, Malcolm McLaren was presenting concerts at the old Paradise Club on Brewer Street, in Soho. On Sundays, between 2 and 7 P.M., the Sex Pistols were McLaren's resident band. Across the Atlantic, bands like the Ramones, Television, the Patti Smith Group, Talking Heads and Blondie were entertaining America's impressionable (but also influential) youth at the CBGB & OMFUG club in Manhattan's East Village.

These nascent punk scenes were regarded (and regarded themselves) as "underground," but they were on the verge of a commercial breakthrough. Patti Smith made her first London appearances on May 16 and 17 at the Roundhouse; the Ramones would make their British debut at the Roundhouse on July 4.[13]

Making the most of the respite caused by Jimmy's accident, Paul, Linda and the girls flew to Martinique before the start of the American tour. It was not long before the surroundings—specifically, the island-tinged French and Creole that were Martinique's dominant languages—revived memories for Paul of his visits to Paris in the early 1960s, with John and later with the Beatles.

It was one such a trip, in October 1961, that John and Paul persuaded their Hamburg art student friend, Jürgen Vollmer, who was then living at the Hôtel de Beaune on the Left Bank, to give them the haircuts that would thereafter be associated with the Beatles. And it was in Paris, in January 1964, that the Beatles learned that 'I Want to Hold Your Hand' had gone to No. 1 in America, where they were headed a few weeks later.

Now images were coming back to him—sitting at a café, watching the girls, overhearing tourists speaking English too loudly. He jotted down these impressions, juggled them until they fit a minor-key chord progression, and *voilà*, the lyrics for 'Café on the Left Bank' were soon scrawled in pencil on the back of a sheet of Hotel Bakoua stationery. The line *"Café on the left bank"* is circled, twice, capturing the moment when Paul knew he had a title for his new song.

He made a few minor amendments, mainly to reduce the number of syllables per bar—changing *"Discotheque after midnight"* to *"Dancing after midnight,"* and *"Sprawling to the streetcar"* to *"Sprawling to a car."* And he reconsidered the order of the verses, with arrows and circled numbers showing the process. When he was satisfied, he turned the sheet over and rewrote the lyrics with a red felt-tipped pen.[14]

"I used to go to Paris occasionally, and this is my memoir of it," Paul said. "I'd sit by the cafés and watch all the girls walking past, and I'd just drink a glass of wine or something. It's just a fond recollection of when I went there. I just strung together the things I remember.[15] You just, sort of, go walking 'round the streets and you see all sorts of things. And it's the kind of thing I used to do in Paris, you know, so it's just a sort of reminiscence of the old 'Ooh-la-la' days."[16]

From Martinique the McCartneys stopped in New York on their way to Dallas, where the band and crew arrived on April 24, nine days before the tour's opening show, leaving a week for rehearsals—necessary, in Paul's view, not only because the band's lead guitarist was recovering from a broken finger, but also so that the band and crew could get used to the larger stage set and expanded visual elements.

Since they were in New York for a couple of days, Paul and Linda dropped in to see John and Yoko at the Dakota just as Wings were getting settled in Dallas. John and Paul spoke, at long last, about the Bill Sargent offer and agreed that the time was not right, however much money was involved. The conversation turned to whether John would attend one of Wings' Madison Square Garden shows in May.

"Everyone's kind of asking me, am I going? Should I go?" Paul quoted John as asking. What worried John was that if he attended the show, he would feel pressure to get up on stage and perform.

"If any [of the former Beatles] comes, they feel like they've got to get up," Paul explained to an interviewer a couple of weeks later. "Then they get up, we've got to be good. Can't just get up and be *crummy*, 'cause then they say, 'The Beatles really blew it on the Wings tour,' or something."[17]

They left the question open; John could attend if he wanted to, if it felt right in the moment.

Since the birth of Sean, John and Paul found common ground in parenthood, and that became another element in the healing of their post-Beatles rift. Responding to a questionnaire mailed to him by a fan, John made his feelings toward his former bandmates and a range of other subjects clear:

Today, how do you associate the following, described in one word?

> New York: *great*
> Elvis: *fat*
> Ringo: *friend*
> Yoko: *love*
> Howard Cosell: *hum*
> George: *lost*
> Bootlegs: *good*
> Elton: *nice*
> Paul: *extraordinary*
> Bowie: *thin*
> M.B.E.: *shit*
> John: *great*[18]

John was keen on introducing Paul to *NBC's Saturday Night,** a live satire-plus-music show that began airing in October 1975. Only 17 episodes into its first season, the show was still finding its legs, but it had a strong cast that included several actors who had appeared in *National Lampoon: Lemmings*, a show that opened at the Village Gate nightclub in 1973 and ran 350 performances, a skewering of the Woodstock festival and the top tier of rock stars (including several who were not at Woodstock). Highlights included a Dylan parody, performed by Christopher Guest,† who slipped into Dylan's *Nashville Skyline* style to sing, "*Knee deep in cow shit / Shovel my blues away,*" as

* The show's original name was meant to distinguish it from *Saturday Night Live with Howard Cosell,* a variety show on the competing ABC network that ran from September 1975 to January 1976. The cancellation of Cosell's show enabled NBC to drop the network moniker and rename the show *Saturday Night Live* in 1977.

† The British American actor and musician—formally Christopher Haden-Guest, the Fifth Baron Haden-Guest—went on to a prolific career that included the role of Nigel Tufnel in the rock mockumentary *This Is Spinal Tap.*

well as Chevy Chase's impersonation of John Denver and the Joe Cocker impression that became a signature piece for John Belushi.

Chase and Belushi were now part of the *Saturday Night* cast, and on April 24, the evening John and Paul watched the show, Belushi slipped into his Cocker imitation for a performance of 'Superstar,' the 1971 Carpenters hit, in a duet with the show's guest host, Raquel Welch. But for John and Paul, the episode's centerpiece was an appearance by Lorne Michaels, the show's producer and co-creator, about halfway into the 90-minute program.

Playing off Bill Sargent's reunion offer, Michaels sat at his desk and calmly invited the Beatles to appear on his show.

"Now, we've heard and read a lot about personality and legal conflicts that might prevent you guys from reuniting," he added. "That's something which is none of my business. You guys will have to handle that. But it's also been said that no one has yet to come up with enough money to satisfy you. Well, if it's money you want, there's no problem here. The National Broadcasting Company has authorized me to offer you a certified check for $3,000."

Holding up the check, Michaels added, "As you can see, verifiably, it is a check made out to you, THE BEATLES, for $3,000. All you have to do is sing three Beatle tunes. 'She Loves You,' yeah, yeah, yeah—that's $1,000 right there. You know the words, and it'll be easy. Like I said, this check is made out to The Beatles—you divide it any way you want, if you want to give Ringo less that's up to you. I'd rather not get involved."[19]

"Paul and I were together watching that show," John remembered. "He was visiting us at our place in the Dakota. We were watching it and almost went down to the studio, just as a gag. We nearly got into a cab, but we were actually too tired."[20]

The show did, however, give Paul the idea that it might be fun to have some of the show's actors—especially Belushi, with his Cocker impression—among the performers at the large after-party he was planning to throw at the end of the tour.*

Paul and Linda flew to Dallas the next day. On Monday, April 26, they visited Showco's headquarters before attending the band's first rehearsal at the 3,000-seat Will Rogers Auditorium, in Fort Worth, which they would use as a rehearsal space until May 1, when the equipment would be moved to the 14,500-seat Tarrant County Civic Center for a full dress rehearsal on May 2, and the opening show the next night.

Joining Wings and their production crew was a beefed-up security contingent, headed by Orrin

---

* Paul has said, in interviews in 2011 and 2020, that he and John did *not* watch the show together, but that he visited John a week later (May 1). It was then, Paul said, that John introduced him to the show and told him about Michaels's offer, whereupon they discussed turning up at the studio. However, on May 1, Paul was rehearsing with Wings in Dallas, and in any case, *NBC Saturday Night* was not broadcast that week. The following four Saturdays, Paul was performing (in Detroit, Landover, Boston and Kansas City), after which *Saturday Night* was off the air until late July (by which time Paul was in Scotland). So the only time he could have seen the show with John in New York—and got the idea of hiring *Saturday Night* actors for Wings' end-of-tour party—was on April 24.

Bartlett,[21] a former FBI agent, who would scout out each venue in advance, take note of bomb threats and other menacing phone messages, and scan for snipers—a worry of Paul's, not only because of America's peculiar romance with firearms, but because of a specific memory of the Beatles' last American tour, in 1966. When the band played in Memphis, Tennessee—with white-hooded Ku Klux Klan members outside protesting Lennon's comment about the Beatles being bigger than Jesus—a firecracker exploded during the performance, causing the four Beatles to glance around the stage to make sure none of the others had been shot.

Sitting in her perch behind her keyboards, Linda found that while Jimmy, Denny, Paul and Joe were anxious to get back on stage, the band's enforced downtime meant that she had to psych herself back into performing nightly. "It would have been better if we had gone straight from Europe, right into it without a break," she told a reporter. "But when Jimmy broke his finger then things got put back. We went off to Martinique for a holiday. It was lovely but it meant that when we got here, we had to start building ourselves back up to facing it."[22]

But there were compensations for Paul's horse-loving wife. On the 32-mile drive between their rental house in Dallas and rehearsals in Fort Worth, Paul and Linda spotted some American Appaloosas out grazing as they drove through the town of Hurst. Linda was instantly besotted. On April 29, they took a detour to find the horses' owner.

"I'd decided I wanted more than anything an Appaloosa," Linda explained. "Appaloosas are the original American Indian pony. I asked the promoter of the tour, 'Do you know of any Appaloosas? I want the Indian type though.' They usually cross them with thoroughbred Quarter horses for the color. But they don't have the temperament—you know, that Indian frame of mind. So, they showed me all these fancy horses. No way. They weren't what I was talking about.

"We used to drive from Dallas to Fort Worth, and one day I saw this Appaloosa exactly the way I dreamed it. He was in a field like a paddock, with a palomino. I thought, 'That's it. . . .' So, we pulled off the freeway and we finally found this little farmhouse that said: Lucky Spot Appaloosas.

"I told the old farmhand about the one I'd just seen, and he said, 'I've put him away.' I'd just missed him. But he took us to see this little stallion. The farmer didn't want to sell him as his kids loved the horse. So, I said I understood, and we were happy to have seen him. Anyway, to cut a long story short, they . . . very kindly sold him to us. Afterwards we became very friendly with the family and the kids came to the concerts. But the horse was wonderful. A lovely, lovely temperament, so beautiful, and I realized my dream."[23]

During their week of rehearsals, Paul made a few small but telling setlist changes. 'Time to Hide' was added between 'Let 'Em In' and 'Silly Love Songs,' expanding the block of *Wings at the Speed of*

Sound songs to four. And because Jimmy was champing at the bit for some solo time, Paul gave him a moment in the spotlight all to himself: when Wings returned to the stage for its second encore, Jimmy improvised for 60 to 90 seconds, typically starting on a sustained low note and exploring a stream of controlled feedback and melodic, note-bending blues phrases before settling into a chunky, rhythmic figure that was the cue for the rest of the band to come blasting in with 'Soily.'

The show's visual component was upgraded, too. 'Live and Let Die,' which at the start of the tour involved just flashpots and strobe lights, now gained lasers, bigger flashes and more smoke bombs. 'Magneto and Titanium Man' gained projections of its major characters, which Marvel Comics artist Jack Kirby provided for the single's picture sleeve. Film of the *Band on the Run* cover shoot was used as the backdrop for that album's title song. And for 'Soily,' the lighting crew found a way to project a thin "sheet" of light over the heads of the audience, with smoke effects and a pulsating laser creating the impression of a marbleized, ethereal ceiling suspended in midair.

It was not lost on Paul how much had changed in the decade since he last toured North America, as a Beatle. There were no light shows or visual elements back then, just four young men in suits and ties, their instruments plugged into small, 100-watt amps, piped through public address systems built for ball game announcements.

His return to America was a bona fide occasion, and he wanted to be sure it was thoroughly documented, not only by the small army of photographers, artists and filmmakers traveling with the band on MPL's dime but also by major publications from around the world. Alongside local media, MPL invited writers from the *New York Times*, the *Los Angeles Times*, *Newsweek*, *Rolling Stone*, *Time* and the Associated Press, as well as several British music publications, including *Melody Maker* and *Record Mirror & Disc*, to the Fort Worth opener. Contingents from MPL, EMI and Capitol were also on hand, as were Lee and John Eastman.

What no one but Linda knew, however, was that Paul's Gemini dualism lurked just beneath the surface—that alongside the glitz and hoopla lurked a current of insecurity. No matter how many miles Wings had logged in Britain, Europe and Australia, how well his post-Beatles recordings had been selling in America, and how quickly tickets had sold out, Paul knew that concertgoers could still leave the concerts unimpressed, as some had done when George toured.

"To be honest, he was scared to death," Linda admitted. "After all, it's been a long time since those fantastic days and nights as a Beatle. He didn't know if the kids today would like him or not. Everything changes so fast. Kids can be screaming their heads off for you today and next week, you're a member of The Father Time Club."[24]

At 8:15 P.M. on Monday, May 3, the band sauntered onto the stage amid clouds of dry ice and bubbles—and an audience greeting that momentarily edged toward Beatles-era shrieks—and quickly settled into 'Venus and Mars.' "Howdy, Texas!" were Paul's first words to the crowd, after

Wings performing at the speed of sound during the Wings Over America tour, May 4, 1976

Paul and Linda on stage during the Wings Over America tour, May 4, 1976

'Jet.' (Denny tried to go local as well, but momentarily forgot where he was. "Dallas! How are ya?" he asked the Fort Worth crowd.)

The performance was hard-driven and solid, the audience's enthusiasm turning several songs into clap-alongs and feeding into the band's opening-night energy. Paul's pre-show insecurities quickly evaporated, and six years of post-Beatles ghosts were exorcised. Backstage afterward, in a rare moment of emotional weakness, Paul burst into tears.

"It would be impossible to describe how I feel about it all," McCartney told an interviewer after the show. "It was like it was way back in the beginning. I saw kids crying in the audience—the love that was pouring out to us was unbelievable. It inspired me to even do better work."[25]

Paul braced for the prospect that the press would not share his elation. But the reviewers were impressed with the show's energy.

"Fort Worth crowds are reportedly reserved about most pop acts," John Rockwell observed in his *New York Times* review, "and indeed before the concert the clean-cut, denim-clad crowd seemed subdued. But when the lights went out the audience came suddenly alive, standing and cheering, and it remained enthusiastic for the whole two hour, fifteen-minute set. People liked the five Beatles songs McCartney included, needless to say. But they also responded warmly to his post-Beatles efforts, and that is of course the real key to his continued health in the music business."[26] Rockwell described the concert as "a spiffy show, nicely paced with a clear, solid sound system and some pleasing special effects," of which the smoke and light illusion during 'Soily' rated special mention.

The reviewer for *Sounds*, Tony Maimis, concluded a long, detailed review with the startling observation that "Wings . . . just may be the new Beatles."

"Musically," Maimis wrote, "there were few surprises. In fact, for the first ninety minutes you might have thought you were listening to the records. Well not quite. Joe English's drumming turns out to be superb, extraordinarily forceful and dynamic, a far cry from his recorded sound. And the stinging attack of the guitars played by both Jimmy McCulloch and Denny Laine was something to behold—also a pleasant surprise after listening to the record. But the arrangements were just like the records, with little or no extended solos or jamming in the tunes."[27]

Several reviewers cited the extra-explosive 'Live and Let Die' as the highlight of the show, the first time a Wings song eclipsed 'Yesterday' as the reported showstopper. And virtually all the critics were taken with the lighting effect accompanying 'Soily.'

After the show, the band entertained friends and spoke with journalists backstage. Linda showed off photos of her new Appaloosa stallion, which she told reporters was 18 months old and named Lucky Star. And Paul, chatting with Maureen Orth of *Newsweek*, offered an unusually flexible response to the Beatles reunion question.

"We're all good enough friends still," Paul told her. "We all know that possibly something may happen. Two weeks ago, I was talking to John about this exact point, and I was pleased to hear his feelings were exactly mine—which is, if anything really happens, we won't close the door on it, but until it does, we'll all go on opening doors."[28]

Denny, for his part, had mixed feelings about performing in halls as large as those in America. "The very first night was an amazing experience," he admitted before citing a downside. "Even though it was an enjoyable thing, I never enjoyed it onstage with an audience that you really can't have a rapport with. That's kind of a contradiction in a way. I enjoyed it for what it was, but I kind of missed the smaller thing, because to me that's what I was used to."[29]

The band flew (and the crew drove) on to Houston on Tuesday for the sold-out show at the 16,000-seat Summit that evening. There was a touch of mayhem: when the crew was rigging the stage and lighting arrays, just before the soundcheck, a scaffolding pole fell, hitting Trevor Jones on the head. The roadie was rushed to the hospital, where it took 13 stitches to close a nasty gash.

Paul could almost have written the reviews himself.

Dale Adamson's *Houston Chronicle* review declared that "McCartney proved quickly that he hardly needed the rest of the Fab Four to dazzle an audience his own way. . . . The keynote of the show was its variety—a full two-and-a-quarter hours of invigorating and refreshing music."[30]

On May 5, Wings flew to Teterboro Airport, in New Jersey, from which they were driven to their second home base, in Manhattan. Paul and Linda spent the evening with Linda's friend, Danny Fields.

Danny had stepped away from his editing and publicity careers and become co-manager, with Linda Stein, of the Ramones, one of the bright lights of the new punk movement. Fields told Paul that the Ramones had taken their name from a bit of Beatles lore—specifically, the stage name Paul used, Paul Ramon, when the Beatles toured Scotland in May 1960 backing the singer Johnny Gentle.

"He was, like, '*You're kidding!*'" Fields recalled. "And I said, 'No, they really did.' I don't think he really believed me."[31] A few weeks later, when Fields visited Paul and Linda backstage at Madison Square Garden, he brought them early issues of *Punk* magazine. Humphrey Ocean snapped a photo of them reading the issues with raised eyebrows, pretending to be shocked.

The McCartneys and Fields picked up a pizza for dinner, and while slicing it, Paul cut into a finger on his left hand. That could have proved disastrous during Wings' acoustic set, which required Paul's semi-classical fingerpicking on 'Blackbird.'

"For a few days, I was worried about hooking a string under the nail when I played," Paul told a reporter once the injury had healed. "I had to wear a thimble on it." But the remedy might not have been that extreme: Linda was photographed backstage cutting a bandage for Paul's finger.

"I was in New York yesterday—this is true—and I got myself a pizza," he told the Detroit audience before 'Blackbird.' "And I was slicing it, and I was just starting to slice a piece of my finger. So, I got a thing on it tonight, so I can't play that well—but you don't mind, do you?"[32] He then launched into 'Blackbird' with little concession to his injury—the fingerpicked introduction to the song largely drowned out by the audience's applause.

The Detroit Olympia, where Wings performed on May 7 and 8, was the home of the Detroit Red Wings, the ice hockey team; Humphrey Ocean described the arena's sound as "a bit echoey"[33] in his tour diary. The band arrived late to the soundcheck, which Paul later complained was "rushed." The rush had ramifications: a moment into 'The Long and Winding Road,' feedback howled through the hall. "Watch it, Morris," Paul said to Morris Lyda under his breath between verses, his microphone picking up the warning. But sitting at the monitoring soundboard, Lyda found that there was little he could do, and feedback marred 'My Love' and 'Silly Love Songs,' too.

"That system got away from me," Lyda recalled, "and it was just a battle all night long trying to control feedback. It sounded bad to me, it sounded bad to the people on the stage, and I don't know why it was. But I was called backstage by the band—which was, effectively, Paul—and it was '*what the fuck?!*' And I just apologized, and swore that I would come in early, which I did—I got in at three o'clock the next day and started working through the system, trying to get it back in shape. And the second night was fine."[34]

Before the second show, Wings took greater care with their soundcheck, playing a half hour of jams and oldies, including the early Elvis hit 'Just Because,' Sam Cooke's 'Bring It On Home to Me,' Carl Perkins's 'Matchbox' and a rocked-up version of the vaudeville tune 'If I Were Not Upon the Stage,' as well as Paul's own 'C Moon.'

Now they had a couple of visitors: the writer Ben Fong-Torres and the photographer Annie Leibovitz, from *Rolling Stone*, would be trailing the band for a few shows. During the soundcheck, Linda gave them a tour of her keyboard setup, with particular attention to the Mellotron, on which the standard instrumental tape loops were augmented by loops of Paul singing the line "*'Til you go down*," from McCulloch's 'Medicine Jar,' animal sounds (a pig, a hyena and a bull), the mechanical opening of 'Silly Love Songs' and the frying bacon-and-chips from 'Cook of the House.'

Fong-Torres wondered what Linda thought of the harsh reviews of her singing on 'Cook of the House.'

"My answer is always, 'Fuck off!' Look, we had a great loon in the studios that night. All the hung-up people don't have to buy it, don't have to listen to it. It's like having parents on your back, this criticizing. I've grown up. I had a great night last night, this is a great band, and this is great fun. And that's all we care about."

Walking back to the dressing room with Fong-Torres, Linda thought better of her remarks and asked him to forget them. But when they ran into Denny, the conversation about criticism resumed, this time about 'Silly Love Songs.'

"You have criticism in school," Linda continued. "When you get out of school, you want to be free."

Denny, always in his element when there was complaining to be done, added: "We're pretty good critics ourselves. We don't need all the bums coming along and telling us, 'Hey man . . .'"

Fong-Torres suggested that criticism offers an outside perspective, a sense of how the band's work sounds to people who don't have a personal stake in it. Linda wasn't buying it.

"We always know what's wrong," she told him. "We know with every album what's done wrong." When Linda turned aside to speak with Paul, Fong-Torres and Laine spoke about working with Wings while Beatlemania continued to bubble beneath the surface.

"The main thing about us is we want to be able to work on the stage without too much adoration, if you know what I mean," said Denny. "They're a bit in awe, you know, of Paul. And that's a bit of a drag."

Paul offered a different view when Fong-Torres ran Denny's comment past him.

"There is this feeling that I should mind if they come to see me as a Beatle," Paul told him. "But I really don't mind. They're coming to see me; I don't knock it. It doesn't matter why they came, it's what they think when they go home. I don't know for sure, but I've got a feeling that they go away thinking, 'Oh, well, it's a band.' It lets them catch up. I think the press, the media, is a bit behind the times, thinking about the Beatles a lot. And I think the kids go away from the show a lot hipper than even the review they're going to read the next day."[35]

The performance was stronger than the first night's, and free of technical glitches. He told the pizza story again before 'Blackbird,' and he tipped his hand, for the first time, about the inspiration for 'You Gave Me the Answer,' dedicating the song to Fred Astaire.

After the show, Paul spoke with *Daily Mirror* reporter Pauline McLeod. Floating on post-show adrenaline, he told McLeod that "the kids gave us such a feed-back that we did not want to finish the show." He then took up a theme from his talk with Fong-Torres earlier in the day. "I think a lot of people came to see Paul the Beatle, even though he's dead and gone. But I feel sure they left the place tonight with Wings on their brains."[36]

Wings headed back to the New York base that night, and from there to Toronto on the afternoon of Sunday, May 9. Paul was meant to start the afternoon by meeting with Capitol/EMI of Canada executives, who brought a stack of Gold and Platinum Discs to the arena, followed by interviews with Canadian TV, radio and newspapers. Running late, he asked Brolly to reschedule the interviews for after the show, and to tell the EMI representatives that he would be with them shortly. He then corralled the band for an early, extended soundcheck.

Although the second Detroit show had been fine, McCartney worried that setting up again in a new arena might create new problems, so during the first part of the 60-minute soundcheck, he sat at Lyda's desk while the soundman tested every instrument and monitor.

With the concert's 8 P.M. start time fast approaching, Paul told Brolly that Wings would go on at 8:30. As the hour approached, Paul and the band headed to the makeshift wardrobe room, where costume designer Pamela Keats oversaw the full collection of stage clothes, and suited up. But instead of heading to the stage, the band climbed the stairs to a backstage room where the Capitol/EMI of Canada executives were waiting to bestow six Gold and Platinum discs upon them—Platinum for *McCartney*, *Ram*, *Band on the Run* and *Venus and Mars*, and Gold for *Wild Life* and *Red Rose Speedway*. Paul accepted the awards, did a quick round of glad-handing, apologized for having to run, and headed off to the stage. Elapsed time: less than five minutes.

A moment later he was singing the opening lines of *Venus and Mars* for a crowd of 18,000, cloaked in what had become his nightly sci-fi moment, standing on a planet with an atmosphere of bubbles and dry ice smoke.

Some of the audience—including those who had paid scalpers as much as $365 (£200) per ticket—had been inhaling whiffs of Beatles reunion rumors for several weeks and were hoping that the Wings Toronto show would be the magical night. In the days leading to the show, newspapers were reporting this might be the case, partly on the flimsy theory that Canada was neutral ground—neither England, where Paul and George lived, nor the United States, where John and Ringo were based. The *Toronto Star* mentioned in its gossip column that John, George, and Ringo had all taken hotel rooms in town.

The press outside Toronto took it from there. A piece in the *Daily Mail* quoted Stan Obodiac, speaking for Maple Leaf Gardens, saying, "We have been notified the three other Beatles are coming to watch the show." When the *Daily Mail* reporter wondered aloud whether this could be a ploy to sell tickets, Obodiac said that the show had sold out weeks earlier.[37] *Rolling Stone*, however, reported that George was in the Bahamas, John was in New York, and they were unable to locate Ringo.

Why, after years of denials, would fans have regarded such a report as credible? Partly because a spokesman for Paul from Solters & Roskin, his American publicity firm, hinted that a reunion could, just possibly, take place.

"If the former Beatles do meet up with one another, it would be no surprise," the spokesman told a reporter days before the tour began in Fort Worth. "They tend to turn up at one another's concerts. Paul would be delighted to see them. They are all friends despite their old disputes." To which he added, "Paul McCartney's answer to the question 'Will there be a Beatles reunion on stage?' is a definite maybe." Even Lee Eastman's attempts to dampen such hopes left some wiggle room. "At this point," Eastman said, "there is absolutely no plan of any kind to get together. That may vary tomorrow, but at this moment there is no decision by any of the four to get together."[38]

Beatles obsessions found their way into the reviews as well, the headline of the *Edmonton Journal* declaring, "Beatles Reunion Untrue but McCartney Wins Praise." The paper's critic, Michael Lawson, noted fans' disappointment that the reunion didn't happen, but added that "few, if any, were disappointed by the concert given by ex-Beatle Paul McCartney with his group Wings."[39]

By now, McCartney's pizza injury was essentially healed, but he preceded 'Blackbird' with the finger-slicing story one last time. He preceded 'Yesterday' with the 'Waltzing Matilda' fake-out from Australia, but the "jolly swagman" drew relatively few laughs from the Canadians. Backstage after the show, he caught up with the interviews he had postponed earlier, including a chat with Peter Goddard of the *Toronto Star*.

"I recognize this place," said Paul of the Maple Leaf Gardens dressing room, a space he last visited with the Beatles in 1966. "I remember its shape." Asked whether he had heard that the other Beatles were in the audience, McCartney simply shrugged. And when Goddard wondered whether he worried about Wings' ticket sales, he pretty much shrugged that off too. "We knew that our record sales had been good," he reasoned, "and we knew that if your records sold well that there were several million people who bought them, and they'd be there to see us."[40]

The band flew back to New York for the night, and the next afternoon, May 10, it was on to Cleveland, Ohio—the hometown of the Lindners, Linda's maternal relatives—for a performance at the sold-out, 21,000-seat Richfield Coliseum, a relatively new venue, opened in 1974. Paul alluded to the connection when he introduced Linda onstage: "I'd like hand over for a minute to a girl whose mother was born in Shaker Heights—Linda!"[41]

The trip did not begin well: the plan was for Wings' private BAC 111 jet to land at Cleveland Hopkins International Airport—where their limos awaited them—but the plane was directed instead to the smaller, more distant Burke Lakefront Airport, used principally by private business travelers.

"We all hopped off the plane," Gordon Bennett recalled, "and the pilot was all very apologetic. That was a case of Paul overriding Brolly. Brian wanted to take the plane, but because they had cars waiting there, Paul said, 'No, no, forget that—we'll just get a couple of taxis and drive in; we're so close.' And that's what we did."[42]

As Brolly arranged for the cabs to take the entourage to the Richfield Coliseum, Denny unpacked an Ovation acoustic guitar and busked, while Paul played with Stella and Mary, all captured on film by Bennett.[43]

For some in the traveling party, the mishap had an upside.

"It was a really wonderful day," the group's artist in residence, Humphrey Ocean, recalled. "We were miles away, and we had to get cabs to the stadium. And I actually saw a bit of the American countryside for the first time. Because we were living this hermetically sealed existence of being in a hotel or on an airplane or in a stadium. So, it was a lovely moment."[44]

Ocean noted in his tour diary that his cabdriver got lost, and that he arrived at the venue about

90 minutes later than the band, which shared another cab. But the show, he wrote, was "the best concert so far."[45] Reviewers were impressed as well. One, Bob Von Sternberg of the *Akron Beacon-Journal*, couched his review within an essay on Paul's battle against his fans' memories of the Beatles.

"When Paul McCartney bounded onstage at the Coliseum Monday night," Von Sternberg wrote, "he was trailing a lot of ghosts—whether he wanted them or not. Even before he rapped his bass into the opening notes of 'Venus and Mars,' the capacity crowd was on its feet, screaming and howling." Von Sternberg then offered a sober comparison between Wings, as he heard them that night, and the Beatles toward the end of their touring years. "With each song, the five members of Wings and their four-man horn section gather strength, momentum, and polish. This is a well-rehearsed, hard-edged rock and roll band—something the Beatles never claimed to be in their later years."[46]

During the post-concert interviews, backstage, Paul and Linda were in a jokey mood, with Paul asking the press what Fonzie, a character on the popular American sitcom *Happy Days*, feeds his horse. When reporters shrugged, Paul and Linda together struck a characteristic Fonzie pose and delivered, in unison, his introductory catchphrase, "*Hey!*"

By now, Paul had prepared a rhyming response to the inevitable Beatles reunion question, and when it was asked, he adopted the accent and cadence of the boxer Muhammad Ali, and recited it:

The Beatles split in '69,
And since then, they've been doin' fine.
But if that question doesn't cease,
Ain't no-one gonna get no peace![47]

As he and the band walked out of the dressing room, he added, "And my next fight will be against Joe Bugner."*

Because there was a free day between the Cleveland and Philadelphia shows, Paul, Linda and the girls were able to spend the night and the next day with Linda's family in Cleveland. The rest of the band flew back to New York. As was often the case, the band spent at least part of the night unwinding at the Gramercy Park Hotel's bar, keeping a wary eye on Jimmy.

---

* József Kreul Bugner, a Hungarian-born boxer and actor who held Hungarian, Australian and British citizenship, fought Muhammad Ali twice—on February 14, 1973, and on July 1, 1975. Ali was the winner of both matches, the second of which took place in Kuala Lumpur, Malaysia, for the undisputed heavyweight title.

"Jimmy had a kind of attitude," Tony Dorsey observed. "I don't know if he really liked Americans, or maybe he didn't like horn players. So, I would just kind of stay out of the way, because I knew what the situation was: Jimmy was more important to the band than I was, that was how I saw it, so if we couldn't get along, I figured that I'd be the one who had to go. So, when Jimmy came down to the bar, and I'd see him getting loaded, I would just say, 'Hey, I'll be right back, I've got to go to the restroom.' And I'd go up to my room and wouldn't come back, and the next day I'd get the story about what happened."[48]

Fellow horn player Howie Casey put McCulloch's volatility down to biology rather than malice.

"The thing is, Jimmy, bless him, he was a very small, slight guy," said Casey, "and of course, most of us in the band were bigger than him. And all right, we did stupid things as well. I mean, I used to drink quite a bit. I didn't do dope or any drugs—I'm a nice clean boy and all that—but a lot of the other guys did, and Jimmy would try to keep up with that. And of course, it would affect him, physically. There were times when they couldn't wake him up in the morning, they'd be banging on the door—he's unconscious, totally gone. But that was Jimmy."[49]

Thankfully, a fifth of the way through the America tour, Jimmy was toeing the line, and was in superb form onstage.

On May 12, the entourage flew to Philadelphia for the first of two shows at the Spectrum, for audiences of 18,500 at each. Paul continued micro-tweaking the set. At the first show, he restored the 'Lady Madonna' reprise, which he had played in Fort Worth and Houston but omitted at the shows since then. He also tried a new pre-'Yesterday' fake-out—the opening line of 'The Star-Spangled Banner.' Neither of those additions was retained at the second show, on May 14. But that night, someone in the audience set off firecrackers two lines into 'The Long and Winding Road.' Without stopping the song, Paul admonished the culprits, singing the next line as *"Don't leave me burning here."*[50]

In the audience the first night was the Beatles' early manager Allan Williams. Since 1973, Williams had been trying to interest the former Beatles in a tape of the band, recorded in December 1962 by another Liverpool musician, Ted "Kingsize" Taylor, at the Star Club, in Hamburg. Williams had visited George and Ringo at Apple and left them with a copy, which they had transferred to multitrack tape at Apple Studios in 1974. But they had no interest in having the recordings released.

Now Williams wanted to try his luck with Paul, but he was having no luck getting a backstage pass. Williams could not help noticing, however, that another old friend from early 1960's Liverpool, Howie Casey, was in the horn section. He persuaded a security guard to get a note to Casey backstage, saying that he wanted to say hello. Casey obliged, but when Williams turned up backstage after the show, he made a beeline for Paul, who greeted him cheerfully, if warily. Williams handed him a copy of his recent autobiography, *The Man Who Gave the Beatles Away* (which Paul had already read and disliked), while hyping him on the Star Club tapes, and promising to send a copy.

Among the reviews, Jack Lloyd's coverage in the *Philadelphia Inquirer* predicted, "The Wings tour, marking McCartney's first performance in this country since he toured here ten years ago with the Beatles, just might end up by being regarded as his greatest personal triumph, removing any lingering doubts about the validity of his solo stardom," and compared McCartney's show favorably to Harrison's. "Unlike the rather aloof, somewhat self-indulgent concert appearance more than a year ago at the Spectrum by George Harrison, McCartney knew exactly what his fans were shelling out their money to experience. And McCartney was more than willing to oblige."[51]

—

During one of Wings' New York layovers—perhaps between the two Philadelphia shows—Paul and Linda were walking along Fifth Avenue when they spotted Ringo and Nancy Andrews. Ringo had started work on his new album—his first under a new contract with Atlantic in the North America and Polydor elsewhere—in April at Sunset Sound Recorders, in Los Angeles, with Atlantic's Arif Mardin producing. The couple were enjoying a layover in the Big Apple.

"We happened to be in New York," Andrews recalled. "[Ringo] was wrapping up some vocals with Arif Mardin for his album, and we were walking down Fifth Avenue, close to Tiffany's, and I hear someone yell, *'Ringo! Ringo!'* I said, 'Someone's yelling your name,' and Richie [Ringo] said, 'Don't look, don't pay attention, it's probably just a crazy fan.'"

Turning to look anyway, Andrews saw Paul and Linda on the other side of Fifth Avenue, running toward them.

"It's Paul and Linda!" exclaimed Andrews, who had not yet met the McCartneys.

"What?" Ringo exclaimed, turning to look. "Oh my god."

"So here we are, in the middle of Fifth Avenue, saying hello, and we took them back to our hotel and ordered up some tea and sandwiches."[52]

Ringo told Paul the sessions for his album were going well, and that he was enjoying working with Mardin.

"I always have producers, because I don't know an E-flat from an F demented," he later explained. "Also, I'm a lazy kind of person. And Richard Perry would kick my ass. And Arif is a strong producer too, although he's a bit more subtle than Richard. I really need to have a producer to take care of the musical situation. I can't tell if a guitar is a little bit flat, I can only tell when I sing."[53]

Having retained the Ringo-suitable 'Let 'Em In' for his own record, Paul had sent Ringo 'Pure Gold' for the album. As Ringo had hoped, the project was shaping up as a Beatles reunion, at least compositionally.

"Paul *asked* to write a song," Ringo said of the lineup he had arranged for the new disc. "I asked

John, and he worked on it and worked on it and came up with 'You Got Me Cooking' [*sic*]*, you know, he's really into that now—cooking. I also asked George to write one, but there was an old one of his that was never released by anybody that I always loved—I was on the session when it was recorded—so in the end I asked him if instead of writing one, could I have that old one? He said, 'Fine,' it saved him a job. It's called 'I'll Still Love You'—big ballady thing."[54]

Paul promised to attend the sessions for 'Pure Gold' when the tour brought him to Los Angeles.

Wings flew to Baltimore on the afternoon of May 15 for the first of two shows at the 22,000-seat Capital Center, in Landover, Maryland. At the first show, the crowd's enthusiasm proved a challenge for the police: as soon as the lights went down, the crowd surged forward toward a thin wooden fence that served as a barrier to the stage. Several attendees were plucked from the crowd amid the crush, and by the time the show was in full swing, there were 11 arrests, mostly for alcohol possession, and two girls had to be revived after they fainted.

The performance left positive impressions with Tom Basham of the *Baltimore Sun* and Larry Rohter of the *Washington Post.* Basham was particularly impressed with Denny, dazzled not only by his double-neck guitar, but by the ease with which he (like McCartney) moved between guitar, bass and keyboards. Jimmy, Basham wrote, "played like a monster," and Joe "abused his drums to maximum advantage."[55] Rohter acknowledged "a sugary streak" in Paul's music, but found that "in live performance he showed a toughness that's missing in much of his recorded work,"[56] an observation a growing number of critics shared.

Speaking with a *Washington Post* feature writer after the show, Paul was still struck by the pandemonium at the start of the concert. "They don't scream like they used to," he said, "but then I looked out at the audience tonight, they were going pretty potty out there, weren't they? This was a crazy audience, one of the craziest we've had on this tour."[57]

The tour's next stop was Atlanta, for two shows at the Omni Coliseum, each for 16,500 fans, on May 18 and 19. Instead of returning to New York between shows, Paul, Linda and some of the entourage stayed over at the Westin Peachtree Plaza Hotel, partly because of the distance between Atlanta and New York, but also because this was Joe's (and also Tony Dorsey's) home turf, and Joe planned an excursion to his home, an hour south of Atlanta. Humphrey Ocean, Aubrey Powell and Gordon Bennett tagged along, and Ocean, for one, was grateful for the break in routine.

"I think if you spent 24 hours around a rock band," he said, "you'd be in awe. But after two months, it becomes a bit of a process and quite procedural."[58] As Ocean elaborated in his tour diary:

---

* The song John Lennon supplied was 'Cookin' (In the Kitchen of Love).'

> Staying over makes a change from the up at midday, have breakfast, drive to airport, onto plane, off plane, drive to concert, from concert, on and off plane again, back to hotel and collapse routine to which we are now conditioned.[59]

Upon their arrival in Atlanta, Wings were meant to add their names, handprints and footprints to the walk of fame outside Peaches Records and Tapes on Peachtree Road. The store was only a year old, but with 16,500 square feet of sales space, it was already enough of a force in the record market to warrant visits from touring superstars. Because the Atlanta police worried that an on-the-street appearance by Paul would attract a mob, the store's manager arranged to have wet cement poured onto the back of an 18-foot truck, which was driven to the Omni after the show so that Wings could immortalize their prints and signatures.

On May 19, Joe drove off with Ocean, Powell and Bennett for an afternoon at his house, with Ocean sketching and Bennett filming along the way.

"I remember the house that Joe English had was very, very American," Ocean said. "Those timber frame houses, with clapboard or what have you—you get them in Sussex and Kent, but they're particularly American, and I was quite intrigued by the quaintness, the down-home ruralness of it."[60]

Joe, however, still had mixed feelings about his place in the band, and about the sheer magnitude of the tour. As Ocean put it, Joe "was a little more bewildered by it all than some of the inner circle."[61]

"I had a gig that most musicians dream about," Joe mused. "I had people opening limousine doors for me. We flew on chartered jets—first class. People were always wanting to do things for me. I had no other worries. All I thought about was playing my gig at night. I didn't worry about where my clothes were or what I was going to wear. We had people with trunks of clothing that were pressed and ironed, all sewn and custom-made for the tour. You'd walk into a room, and they'd ask, 'What do you want to wear?'

"I was a kid who'd seen the Beatles on the *Ed Sullivan Show.* All that was going through my mind. I was thinking, 'Hey, I've got a chance. This is Paul *McCartney.* This guy is no *slouch.*' I'm not talking about working with some mediocre guy in the rock 'n' roll business. There are a few people in the business on the top, and he's *one* of them. I got a chance to work with him, and he turned out to be a great guy. A lot of people in that situation don't *have* to be great guys. But Paul made it as nice as possible, and it paid off. All we had to concentrate on was what we were doing."[62]

Yet there was something missing, for Joe.

"I always wanted to be a rock star," he explained. "Okay, I became a rock star, played in the biggest band in the world and had everything I always wanted. But it wasn't right. I was unhappy. I'd go back to hotel rooms after shows and just read the Bible. I felt a terrible void."[63]

Living a detached existence in rented homes rather than sharing hotels with the rest of the touring party, Paul was not witness to Joe's post-concert blues. But the American's fragility was not lost on his bandmates.

"Joe was into all sorts of chemical things," said Casey. "He used to go into chemists and buy things; medicines, he'd drink like whole bottles of it. Then he'd be off his face, you know."[64]

Onstage, Paul was loosening up with his ad-libs, dedicating 'You Gave Me the Answer,' at the first Atlanta show, to Gene Autry, the Depression-era country and western singer, actor and rodeo performer best known for his 1939 hit, 'Back in the Saddle Again,' reverting to Astaire at the second show. He sang 'Yesterday' without a fake-out at the first show, and reprised 'The Star-Spangled Banner' at the second.

"I wouldn't want to speak for anyone else," Denny Laine told a reporter after the second show, "but, tonight was one of the better nights we've had. The audience allowed us to set a pace, the way we like to. You know, start slowly and build as we go. It keeps us from getting tired but, from a show point of view it seems to work best. Personally, I prefer the raving bit, completely, from beginning to end, but I don't think we'd be able to carry it off for an entire performance. It would be too much of an energy drain. The audience tonight, and last night, seemed to relax a bit before getting up and letting loose. An audience like that always makes it easier for us."[65]

The critical take was not vastly different.

"The concert is a study in controlled flash, spectacular but not gaudy," James Willwerth wrote of the first show in *Time*. "Even the trappings of the typical rock super-production—smoke bombs, laser beams, meticulous lighting and shifting backdrops—are used sparingly, for maximum effect. McCartney, wide-eyed, boyish, bounces along eagerly on the warm good will of the crowd. . . . His group, Wings, provides him with full force backing, surprisingly stronger in performance than on records."[66]

Joe Roman, of the *Atlanta Gazette*, admitted to keeping McCartney's post-Beatles work "at arm's length" because of what he perceived as "a disturbing tendency toward the insipid." But the show led him to revise his opinion: it was, he wrote, "perhaps the most outstanding concert I've seen in 16 years of close involvement with music."[67]

Paul's interviews in Atlanta were more direct than those at many other stops. When Jim Jerome of *People* asked whether taking his children on tour is good for them, Paul responded that the girls are at their best under their parents' influence.

"Our kids go with relatives for a few days," he said, referring perhaps to their recent family visit in Cleveland, "and come back with sweets comin' out of their ears, Coke on their teeth, and talkin' back: *'I don't WANNA do it.'* [Soon] they get back to the old working class way of *'You bloody WILL do it.'* This is the way I grew up and it still works—acting on that tribal instinct. Now Dr. Spock has come out years later and said he was afraid he was wrong—the kids are running away with it. Well, that's what I could have told him right at the beginning. If the kid doesn't respect the parent as the boss of the house, you're in for trouble."[68]

Jerome also contacted John Eastman for his piece and got another nugget not typically among the McCartney talking points. "Paul's very worried about losing his fans because of being too Establishment," Eastman confessed. "He didn't want to be a businessman, but he really didn't have any choice." [69]

—

A few days earlier, Paul gave an interview to John Rockwell of the *New York Times* for a piece that would run on May 21 as a preview for the three New York–area shows—that night's concert at the Nassau Veterans Memorial Coliseum, in Uniondale, New York, and the Madison Square Garden performances on May 24 and 25—in which he spoke openly about his hopes and fears for the tour.

Sitting on a sofa in his suite at the Stanhope, McCartney said that he was pleased with the way the tour had gone so far. But his responses to Rockwell's questions revealed his own internal struggle between establishing Wings as credible band, and accepting that many fans come to see a former Beatle play rather than Wings as a collective.

"When I went to George Harrison's concert at the Garden in late 1974, in an Afro wig," he said, "there was a guy standing behind me who kept shouting, 'Ringo, Ringo,' and I thought, 'Oh Lord, that's the last thing I want.' We haven't had much of that. There's always some idiot who shouts out, 'Where's John?' And you shout back, 'He's at home.'

"I definitely thought it was going to be a strain," he said of the tour more generally. "But it's like someone who has a big part in an opera—you develop more stamina if you have more to sing. I must sing thousands of notes in an evening. I know which ones I miss. But if I let the couple I do miss hang me up, I'll have a bad time the rest of the show. . . . I'm not a great analyzer of my own stuff. I just look and see if the tickets are selling. You see, you can get too precious about what you are. You can start to try to live up to it all. I like to think of myself as just some songwriter who has some songs."[70]

Paul was not always so forthcoming in his interviews. The post-concert chats, in particular, could be downright peculiar if he was feeling drained. After the Nassau Coliseum concert, where Wings played for an audience of 16,000, Paul gave an interview to Stan Mieses of the *New York Daily News*. It quickly became clear that Paul had little interest in another installment of the nightly interrogation.

"A few minutes into the interview," Mieses wrote, after first describing how excited he had been at the prospect of speaking with Paul, "I felt as trapped as the Beatles did in the press conference scene in *A Hard Day's Night*. Talking to McCartney is like playing tennis with a badminton racket, or being sent upriver without a paddle, if you like. He's quite skilled at the game of non-interview, which consists of glib one- or two-word responses that drop like stones into deep silences."

Sipping a scotch and Coke while Linda took Polaroid photos and Ocean sat on the arm of a chair holding his sketchbook, Paul told Mieses that he was "quite taken with America," adding that his wife was American and that "I know about America; I know about pizzas." From there, the conversation degenerated into farce, with Mieses avoiding asking Paul questions about the Beatles, having read his responses elsewhere on the tour, and Paul prodding him to ask the perennial Beatles question.

"You're not going to ask me the same question, are you?" Paul prompted.

"Do you mean about the rumored $50 million offer to reunite the Beatles?" Mieses asked.

"I'd like to end it as far as people asking about the x-million dollars, but I'd like to keep the door open if the other Beatles thought there was something worthwhile in doing it," Paul said, with Mieses noting in his report that this was an answer Paul had also given elsewhere.

When Mieses asked whether Paul still had to defend Linda against angry fans and the barbs of critics, Paul replied, "Used to. We just keep smiling through." To a question about where the McCartneys' children were, Linda answered, "They're at home dreaming of White Christmases."

As the interview continued, Paul, Linda and Ocean showed all the characteristics of three teenagers who had just scored some killer weed, which may have been the case. At one point, Ocean stood up and announced, "What we need here is some balance," whereupon he put a plastic cup half-filled with Coke on the back of his hand and walked around the room until it fell off, to the amusement of Paul and Linda.

Paul again encouraged Mieses to ask questions about the Beatles, as if his old band were a straw man that he wanted Mieses to set up so that he could knock it down.

"You don't want to know about the Beatles?" Paul asked. "It's all right. All that stuff, Beatle cartoons, Beatle handbags—the most important angle for most people is the living angle, yes, the now angle. It's all very well, these tokens of the Beatles, but it all fades out when you come to play."[71]

Mieses asked why Paul was keeping Beatles rumors alive if part of the point of touring with Wings was to dispel those memories. Ocean declared that to be a good question, but Linda sensed that it was too close to home and changed the subject before Paul could answer, asking Mieses to tell them something about himself. And from there, the interview hobbled to an end.

Paul was probably not happy to read Mieses' write-up of their interview, but he would have had little complaint about the evening's reviews. Wayne Robins, of *Newsday*, admitted between the lines that he had not cared much for most of McCartney's post-Beatles albums, but was won over by the live performance. He noted, moreover, that "the younger members of the audience seemed to truly like Wings' music and with good reason. McCartney has overcome the tendency toward mawkishness that marred his early post-Beatles solo albums like *Wild Life* and *Ram*, and he obviously knows it: None of the more than 20 songs Wings performed were from those albums."[72]

As the band headed to Boston on Saturday, May 22, it was with the news that 'Silly Love Songs' had reached the summit of the *Billboard* Hot 100. In Boston, they would perform for 15,500 fans at the Boston Garden. In the days before Wings' arrival, radio stations saturated their airwaves with Wings and Beatles music, and on Friday one of them, WRKO, ran an interview with Ringo. Not surprisingly, the drummer was asked about the prospect of reunion. His response was similar to what had become Paul's standard answer, but with the door cracked open a bit more widely.

"We've all said, 'Maybe,'" Ringo commented. "None of us has said, 'No.' I'd like to try it . . . It would be nice to see if it worked in some studio somewhere. I think it's the best band I've ever played in."[73]

The interplay between McCulloch, Laine and English was particularly energized at Boston Garden, and one critic, Nick Fountas, of the *Lowell Sun*, was especially taken with the two guitarists, writing that their "individual performances often overshadow the efforts of the leader Paul." He was less taken with Linda, suggesting that Wings would do well to replace her, but that "this move seems doubtful for obvious reasons." Still, Fountas declared that "Wings were the tightest, most polished band to play Boston for some time."[74]

What the reviewers did not see was a moment of offstage drama. After 'Band on the Run,' the band did what it had done at every show since the tour began the previous September—the players walked off stage, where they lingered for a few moments while the audience lit matches and called for more. When Paul deemed that they had soaked in enough stomping and shouting, the group would return to the stage to play 'Hi, Hi, Hi' and 'Soily.'

But in Boston, Jimmy said he was not going back on stage.

"He refused to come on for the encore. So, of course, I ran into the dressing room and hit him—'*Get on!*'"[75] was Paul's succinct memory of the incident.

"He was pissed off about something, I don't know exactly what," Tony Dorsey recalled. "But he said he wasn't going to go back out. So, he and Paul got into tussling a little bit, and Paul picked him up and slammed him down on the floor, on the concrete floor."[76]

As Howie Casey remembered it, the tall, muscular trombonist had to physically intervene. "Tony grabbed hold of him, and he grabbed hold of Paul, held him off. He's a big guy, Tony. Of course, Paul was livid, and Jimmy—he was off his head, and being a brat, really."[77]

The entire interaction lasted less than five minutes, whereupon the band went out and gave a charged performance of 'Hi, Hi, Hi,' but omitted 'Soily' and the introductory guitar improvisation that was Jimmy's moment to shine.

Afterward, Jimmy complained to Dorsey, whom he saw as an ally for coming between him and his irate boss. "Jimmy said, 'Look what he did to me!' And I said, 'Don't make him mad—it's an easy solution.' I think, on that tour, both Joe English and Jimmy McCulloch were fighting drug and alcohol addictions—they were pretty heavy users of everything."[78]

Aubrey Powell put the altercation in perspective, noting that Jimmy was "the kind of guy that, if he really didn't like something, he would just walk off. Paul couldn't afford for that to happen. But Jimmy only misbehaved a couple of times. He was a sweet boy. But he was basically a bit lost, I think."[79]

"Jimmy McCulloch was a great player, but he had an attitude," Paul later said of his guitarist and his demons. "This is rock and roll—people do have attitudes. You can't expect everyone to be choirboys."[80]

—

On the original tour schedule, Wings' concerts at Madison Square Garden on May 24 and 25 were to have been the tour's closing performances. That made sense: with Eastman and Eastman and MPL's American headquarters in Manhattan, New York was essentially Paul's home base in the United States.

He had seen concerts at the Garden—the Rolling Stones in 1972, George Harrison in 1974—but although he was the only former Beatle to mention the venue in a song ('Rock Show'), he was also the only one of the four never to have performed there. The fact that New York was John Lennon's home, which naturally led both fans and journalists to hope he might show up and join Paul onstage, as he had done with Elton John in November 1974, added to the sense of occasion.

Newspaper reports described a crowd of 20,000—the entire capacity of the Garden—milling around on Eighth Avenue and both West 33rd and 34th Streets in the hours before the first show, with a contingent of 110 police (a dozen on horseback) managing the crowd, and scalpers commanding $60–$100 (£34–£56) for $10.50 (£5.90) tickets. Reports from inside the Garden noted a number of A-listers in the crowd, including Jacqueline Kennedy Onassis, her two children (John Jr. and Caroline Kennedy), and her sister, Lee Radziwill, who were shepherded backstage by John Eastman after the show. Lou Reed, Warren Beatty and Allan Williams were reportedly spotted as well. And there were 250 British fans, winners of a contest to see Paul in New York.

Denny Laine's parents, Herbert and Eva Hines, had flown to New York for the concert as well, and they were backstage before the show to see Denny and his bandmates receive a Platinum Disc for one million sales of *Wings at the Speed of Sound* from a contingent of Capitol Records brass. After the presentation, Paul spoke with reporters from the *Daily Mail* and *Jackie*, to whom he admitted that he regarded these shows as special.

"This is what we were really doing it for," he told the *Daily Mail*, "always aiming toward playing

Madison Square. In the beginning it was just a crazy thing and I guess I didn't even really think we'd get there. . . . I wanted it to be a biggie. And I guess I was a bit scared."[81]

At both shows, the crowd roared predictably at the line *"long hair at Madison Square,"* and radiated a level of excitement that the band played off throughout the show. On May 24, Paul used his 'Star-Spangled Banner' introduction to 'Yesterday,' but on May 25 he played it straight. 'Lady Madonna' had its reprise both nights, and at both shows Paul sought to inject a local element into his dedication of 'You Gave Me the Answer' to Fred Astaire and Gene Kelly, mentioning that both were in town the previous week. And the full double encore, with Jimmy's improvisation, was restored.

Looking back some months later, Paul used the Madison Square Garden shows as his yardstick when discussing how to overcome performance jitters. "The funny thing about being famous," he pointed out, "is that people don't think you get nervous. But I am nervous every time I go out, sometimes more than others. On the night of Madison Square Garden, New York, people were saying how relaxed I was, and I should have been nervous. But what they did not realize is that a few months before I had been in a taxi driving past Madison Square Garden, and I thought, 'We're not going to play that, are we?' I had got my nerves over in that taxi because I was actually shaking at the thought of coming to this huge city and being the only attraction on the night. My God. It worried me stiff. So, I imagined when I actually got there, I would be terrified. Thinking that made me quite relaxed.

"I have a joke which I do when I'm nervous by saying, 'I'm not going on.' And I walk around panicking people by saying it. I know that I am going on, but it is just something to relieve the nerves. But of course, you go through the nerves and cross the barrier and you feel ten times better for doing it. You have beaten yourself. Afterwards, when it's working and it's been a great show, there's no feeling like it. It takes me at least half an hour to come down."[82]

Backstage after the first show, McCartney phoned his old songwriting partner at the Dakota. Paul had expected John not to attend, but hoped that he might. He would miss the second show, too, because he and Yoko were flying to Los Angeles that day. "They said they were glad the show went well. And we left it at that,"[83] Paul reported. John did, however, request a pair of tickets to the second show for Sean's babysitter.

With the show on May 25, Paul quietly kept a promise he had made to Phoenix House in December 1973, when the drug rehabilitation center wrote a letter supporting his request for a visa. Thinking, at the time, that he would tour America with a new version of Wings in 1974, he said he would play a benefit concert for the center. Now, without publicity, he donated the proceeds from the May 25 show to Phoenix House.

As if to justify McCartney's professed fear of playing in New York, some of the reviews had a harsh edge. "The Wings show isn't just rock," Robert Palmer wrote in the *New York Times*. "It's also

Paul and Linda backstage during the Wings Over America tour, May 1976

Paul and Linda pose for photographers during the Wings Over America tour, May 1976

music-hall vaudeville, middle-of-the-road pop, and sheer schmaltz—all the ingredients that made the Beatles the most popular group in the '60s. The trouble with the show from a rock standpoint—and it is as a rock group that Wings asks to be judged—is that Mr. McCartney's hardest-hitting music is also his most ordinary."

Palmer went on to offer a broad and not especially flattering assessment of McCartney as a songwriter. "When heard one after the other, Mr. McCartney's songs do not indicate the presence of genius. A handful are enduring pop standards, and they deserve to be. Quite a few more are memorable. The rest are well-crafted but forgettable, like Loggins and Messina songs. One enjoys them while they are going on and forgets them as soon as they are over. . . . His rock fails to generate the sort of communal ecstasy the Rolling Stones and a handful of other bands create, and his ballads, which would be affecting in a more intimate environment, sound frail and disembodied in a hall as cavernous as Madison Square Garden."[84]

Backstage after the Garden shows was more tumultuous than usual, with print and television journalists angling for stories and teams from the two biggest rock FM stations, WNEW and WPLJ, collecting sound—music and interviews, both nights—for McCartney specials they were assembling. Not surprisingly, given the number of times Paul had addressed it over the past three weeks, the Beatles reunion question was beginning to fade. But as he had done a couple of nights earlier in Uniondale, Paul pulled it back into the spotlight himself.

When Mary Campbell interviewed him for the Associated Press, Paul launched into the subject, both posing and answering the reunion question ("Probably not, let's leave it at that") before Campbell had a chance to ask. But with the subject in the air, Campbell pursued it, wondering whether he missed the adulation that was part of the Beatles days.

"I don't know if I miss that," he said. "I'm not really in it for the adulation. That is sort of a side issue. You can't help feeling good if people like you. It's not the adulation you like but the fact you're going down well in anything. I mean, you know, we just play our music and if it gets us to the top, great. If it gets us to the middle, that's all right as long as we're enjoying it. We're at the top of the hit parade at the moment with our song, 'Silly Love Songs,' you can't get much higher than that."[85]

Alison Steele, WNEW-FM's sultry-voiced "Nightbird," took the discussion a step further, asking whether Paul found it dismaying that people were so obsessed with a Beatles reunion. "I think the Beatles reunion was a very hot issue before we came to America and played," he told her. "I've got a feeling it's sort of dying as an issue. I think people are kind of saying, 'Well, maybe they shouldn't come together,' or 'Maybe Wings is kind of the new thing.' I think it's going that way."[86] When Steele ventured that she found the question "a terrible bore," Paul slipped into his Muhammad Ali impression and regaled her with his rhyming response.

Having reached the halfway point in the tour, Wings spent the night in New York. On May 26, the entourage flew to Chicago, where the band set up a new home base at the Whitehall Hotel, and the McCartneys drove to their rented farmhouse outside town.

But while Paul was talking up the band's recent performances and chart success with the American press, Jimmy McCulloch was ready to quit. Since day one, when the two Dennys toasted the formation of the group with mismatched cups of scotch and Coke at High Park, there had always been an undercurrent of dissatisfaction within Wings' ranks, grumblings that normally centered around two issues: money and artistic input. Much as it had been for his Guinness-sipping almost-namesake, Henry McCullough, Jimmy's drinking had become a way of silencing the disaffected voices inside his head. Now those voices were shouting a question: *"Are you in a band, or just a sideman for McCartney, hired to play his music his way?"* And Jimmy was not comfortable with the answer.

As the musicians were settling into their rooms in Chicago, Jimmy knocked on Howie Casey's door. Casey invited him in, and the guitarist flopped down on Howie's bed and said, "I'm fed up with this."

"What are you talking about?" the saxophonist asked.

"I can't be arsed with it," said Jimmy. "They always want me to play the same thing."

"Yeah," Howie replied, "but it's *his band.*"

As Casey remembers it, "You could see that Jimmy was getting really dissatisfied, and wanted to pack it in. I said, 'Jimmy, you're mad—you're on a 100-grand-a-year retainer, you can do what you like as long as you turn up for the gigs.' He was totally disgusted with that. I couldn't understand him. None of us could."[87]

15

WINGING HIS WAY BACK TO THE TOP

As Wings continued to make their way around the United States, Apple boss Neil Aspinall and lawyers for all four Beatles met at the Capitol Tower in Hollywood during the week of May 24. What they discussed was never revealed, but it is likely that both Capitol's executives and the Beatles' representatives wanted to discuss the label's plans for exploiting the Beatles' catalog.

The Beatles' contract with EMI and Capitol had ended in January 1976, and now only McCartney had signed a new agreement with the company. But of course, EMI owned the Beatles' recordings, including the session masters, including outtakes and unissued tracks. And EMI had made it clear that they were not content to merely administer royalties for the canonical albums, *Please Please Me* through *Let It Be.*

Now that the contract had lapsed, EMI wanted to establish an active reissue and compilation program. With Hollywood, the West End, and Broadway also mining the group's catalog of 213 songs, just six years after their split, the Beatles were an industry. And though the former Beatles were now more concerned with their individual careers than their collective one, they understood that it was in their interest to be involved (even if only through their representatives) in decisions made in their name.

EMI had tested the waters with its two double-LP compilations, *1962–1966* and *1966–1970* (the "Red" and "Blue" albums). There was no real pushback from any of the Beatles, and the sets sold well. Nor had the Beatles objected to this year's reissue of their British singles, in March, all 22 of them.

Now EMI was considering revisiting the concert recordings the Beatles had made at the Hollywood Bowl in 1964 and 1965, even though the performances were overlaid with a layer of shrill screaming. EMI had reason to believe that the Beatles might challenge the release. When the recordings were made, the company sent acetates to the Beatles, who refused to consider issuing them.

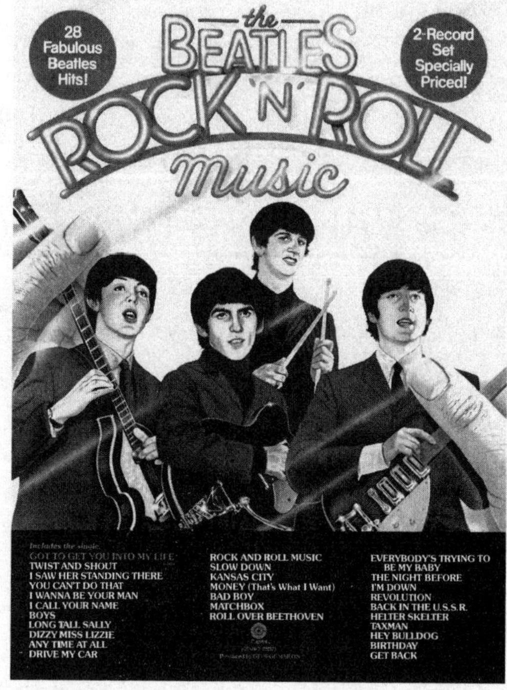

The much debated *Rock 'N' Roll Music* artwork

The label also considered raiding the January 1969 *Get Back/Let It Be* session masters, hoping to assemble an album of the rock oldies the group jammed on between takes, but abandoned the idea when a preliminary listen, early in 1976, yielded few complete, release-worthy performances.

Instead, EMI cobbled together an album of 28 hard-rocking tracks from the standard catalog, with both covers (like 'Twist and Shout' and 'Roll Over Beethoven') and originals (from 'I Saw Her Standing There' to 'Get Back'). The set, *Rock 'N' Roll Music*, was assembled with no input from the former Beatles, and was set for release in the United States on June 7 (along with a single, 'Got to Get You Into My Life' and 'Helter Skelter'), and June 11 in Britain.

Each Beatle was sent an advance pressing, and for starters, they were unanimously unimpressed with the cover art. Printed on silver, the cover sported a drawing of the Beatles holding their instruments, beneath neon treatments of "The Beatles" in red and *Rock 'N' Roll Music* in blue. The labels were straight out of *American Graffiti*—fountain glasses filled with cola and ice, a straw sticking out—as was the inner gatefold filled with '50's iconography.

Paul shrugged off the project. "I don't mind the *Rock 'N' Roll Music* album," he said. "When it's over, you really don't care what they do with it. If someone comes up to us and says, 'That's a terrible rip-off!' we say, 'It has nothing to do with us.'"[1]

But John and Ringo saw the album as the record industry at its worst, a reaction that would likely have been on their representatives' agendas for the Capitol Tower meeting.

Not normally one to challenge the status quo, publicly or otherwise, Ringo was unusually outspoken.

"I'd like some power over whoever it is at EMI who's putting out these lousy Beatles compilation albums," he complained to *Melody Maker*. "They can do what they like with our old stuff, we know that. It's theirs. But Christ, man, I was *there*. So, listen, EMI, if you're reading this—*Please let us know what you're doing with the records we made. We'd like it done, how do I say, nicely.*"[2]

Starr unloaded further in an interview with *Rolling Stone*. "When Capitol put out *Rock 'N' Roll*

Music, John and I tried to have it stopped," he said. "The cover was disgusting. When we worked, we spent as much time on the cover as on the tracks. We didn't put some crap-house cover on something we'd done. John even said he'd do them a new cover. . . . At least he went to art school. It made us look cheap and we were never cheap. We were *the Sixties*. All that Coca-Cola and cars with big fins was *the Fifties*. I was also annoyed that they didn't call us and ask what we thought of the running order. Just because we're not on the label, you don't treat us like dogs."[3]

A more serious issue that was undoubtedly raised at the meeting was that the Beatles' contract with EMI allowed the company, under certain conditions, to refuse a raise in royalties due to them in 1972, so their royalties for *Rock 'N' Roll* were going to be paid at the old rate. "In those days it was alright," Ringo said of the old royalty, "but now it's a silly royalty rate. No one would sign for that if they were blind, deaf and dumb." [4]

Capitol, for its part, argued that the release would be so heavily promoted—the label had reportedly committed $1 million (£570,000) to the task—that whatever the Beatles thought of the cover, the track listing and the royalty rate, Capitol projected that the group would take in as much as $150 million (£85 million). Moreover, the entire back catalog—all the albums in their original form—would be repromoted as well.

"It will be the single greatest promotional effort in the history of the recording industry," Don Grierson, Capitol's merchandising director, insisted. Capitol spokesman Bruce Garfield added, "There is every likelihood that the Beatles will sell more records and make more out of this than they did the first time."[5]

John and Ringo were in Los Angeles during the Capitol meetings, but did not make an appearance, leaving it to their lawyers to represent them. During the two weeks John was in Los Angeles, he played keyboard on 'Cookin' (In the Kitchen of Love),' the song he wrote for Ringo's new album-in-progress.

"Truth is, I never knew what it actually meant to be a Beatle until we split from each other," Paul confessed in mid-1976. "The impact on fans—people everywhere—was fantastic. I guess I sort of died for a while when it was all over. There was a numbness inside that's inexplainable. There were times when I couldn't sleep—when I would try to compose or think of another musical idea; nothing would happen. If you want to talk about nightmares, I could fill volumes."

Now McCartney's nights were sleepless out of choice. Hopping between concert venues and the family's various rented homes in the band's private BAC 111 jet, he had time to reflect on half a decade spent clawing his way back to the top. Midway through the North American leg of Wings' world tour, the adoration of tens of thousands of fans was intoxicating.

"When the American audience like you, they let you know in every way possible. They cry, throw their clothes at you and even throw money onto the stage. Americans love with a certain passion which is unequaled any place else in the world. I love performing in this country—it's a very special place."[6]

As the five 40-foot 18-wheelers carrying the *Wings Over America* stage, sound and light rigs pulled into Riverfront Coliseum, Cincinnati, on May 27, the venue's crew wondered what was about to hit them. Cal Levy, the director of the venue's concert division, noted that Wings traveled with two trucks more than was typical, in his experience, and estimated that the group's equipment load was about 40 percent bigger than anything he had seen previously.

Wings' technical fleet also included two Continental Silver Eagle buses, with facilities that included bunk beds, televisions, stereo systems and refrigerators, inhabited by the Showco road crew; a van packed with merchandise (program books, posters, T-shirts) for sale at the shows, as well as ping-pong and foosball tables for backstage entertainment, and a camper for the band's roadies, who were joined for a few days by Ocean and Powell, intent on capturing the technical side of the show in drawings and photographs.

MPL had requested that a security staff of 25 be present while the stage was assembled, five more than were required when the Who performed at Riverfront five months earlier. Riverfront also supplied a crew of 25 to help Showco's crew of 35 unload the equipment.

Riverfront was normally the home of the Cincinnati Stingers ice hockey team, and Cal Levy took it upon himself to make the backstage area—usually locker rooms for the home and away teams—as homey as possible, unrolling a large Turkish rug and fitting out the dressing room with sofas, a glass coffee table and end tables, lamps and comfortable chairs, and both hanging and potted plants. And he saw to the McCartneys' specific requests for backstage refreshments, including whole wheat bread, tea and lemon, pastries and homemade soup.

One delivery, integral to the show's theatrical opening, was missing, though.

"In Cincinnati the dry ice was not delivered," advance man Allen Branton explained, "and we weren't able to do the effect that night. And that was sort of embarrassing for everybody. But the audience never knows about the things that you wanted to do but didn't do. They're not missing it."[7]

An unruly crowd of 18,500 continually pushed toward the front during the show, and the discomfort of listeners close to the stage was so noticeable that Denny, Jimmy and Paul each encouraged the crowd to move back a bit. Musically, there were few surprises: 'Lady Madonna' was played with its reprise, and 'Yesterday' elicited the mighty roar that Paul expected by now. 'You Gave Me the Answer' was dedicated to "a couple of fellas called Fred Astaire and Ginger Rogers."[8] And 'Blackbird' had an unusual music hall ending, a chromatic guitar line leading to the final chord—a departure accompanied by a string of what one reviewer interpreted as vaudeville gestures.

"At the last sung note," Cliff Radel reported in the *Cincinnati Enquirer*, "his left hand shot out in a wave. He stomped his right leg, grinned, turned his head in rhythm, turned it back, made several quick salutes and then strummed the last chord."[9]

Wings had a free Friday in Chicago, the day *Time* magazine's issue with McCartney on the cover (dated May 31) appeared on newsstands. On Saturday, they boarded their private jet at O'Hare Airport, flew to Kansas City Municipal Airport, and were driven, in a small fleet of limousines, to the Kemper Arena, a sports complex built in 1974.

"Pre-show tension had peaked in the 30-minute wait since the show was supposed to begin, and 18,000 fans were getting antsy," Bil Tatum wrote in the *Springfield Leader and Press*. "Suddenly, the Kemper Auditorium lights blacked out and an overwhelming roar went up as Paul McCartney and Wings rushed to the stage amid a blitzkrieg of flashbulbs. All was forgiven. The half-hour wait, the hazards of dodging errant frisbees, and ticket prices scalped as high as $100 (£43) were in the past. . . . Smoke machines engulfed the band and front rows of the audience in a multicolor fog as the group began 'Venus and Mars.' Only the applause, screams, whistling and stomping were louder than the amplifiers. . . . The smoke billowing from the floor of the stage was met halfway by snow falling from above and the entire scene was strafed by colored lights pulsing with the rhythm."

After his painterly description of the show's opening, Tatum offered an assessment that matched what was quickly becoming the critical consensus on the tour—specifically, that "insipid and 'silly love songs' that fail to impress on disc were transformed into gutsy, smashing music," and that the audience response saw a generational split among McCartney fans, where "old people (over 20s)" were dazzled by the Beatles tunes while "the teens boogied to 'Let 'Em In' and 'Time to Hide,'" and pretty much everyone loved 'Yesterday' and 'Live and Let Die.'[10]

After the show, reporters from radio stations KBEQ, KWKI and KADI stationed themselves in the green room and caught Wings members as they turned up—Jimmy first, then Denny, then Paul and Linda; only Joe avoided the microphones. Paul mostly fended off Beatles reunion questions ("I'd like to give a scoop to Kansas City, but I can't") and Denny was asked mostly about the experience of recording *Band on the Run*, which he suggested might not have turned out as well had Henry McCullough and Denny Seiwell remained in the group, his theory being that the pressure of recording as a trio helped make the album what it was.

Jimmy was quizzed about his background, going all the way back to Thunderclap Newman, and was asked whether he was getting tired of playing the same set night after night. "Maybe after this tour, yeah," he responded diplomatically. He then fended off questions about staying up late and partying, suggesting that he was going to go straight to bed after the show, adding, "I mean, there's too much responsibility."[11]

The next stop was Chicago, where they played three shows at Chicago Stadium, on May 31, June 1 and 2—each for an audience of 20,000. Paul's most notable ad-lib, in the third show, was a new 'Yesterday' fake-out—the first word (and a third) of Fred Fisher's 1922 hit 'Chicago,' a song Paul regularly cited as a favorite of his father's.

Chicago had its own Beatles rumor: shortly before the first show, the *Chicago Tribune* published an item saying that John Lennon was expected to join Wings onstage. Lennon, however, was still in Los Angeles. In an interview after the third concert, Paul brushed the rumor aside, noting that he had visited John before the tour ("Shared a cup of tea with him in his kitchen," he said to which Linda added, "Japanese tea"[12]).

One reunion reported in the *Chicago Tribune*, however, did take place.

"In 1976 I was producing an album for RCA in Chicago," former Wings drummer Denny Seiwell explained. "When they passed through, Paul invited us over to the show; they were staying on a farm somewhere."[13] Nevertheless, conversation between the Seiwells and the McCartneys was brief and frosty: Paul had seen Denny as a kindred spirit during Wings Mark I, but his exit on the eve of the *Band on the Run* sessions angered Paul, and neither party was willing to accept responsibility for the breakdown in communications.

As in other cities, the critics worked hard to place Wings in some sort of context—either as a Beatle's post-Fabs endeavor, or as an avatar of contemporary stagecraft. *Chicago Tribune* reviewer Lynn Van Matre joined the list of critics around the country whose view of McCartney was altered by the show.

"The Beatles are done," she wrote, "and for my money, McCartney has emerged as the best of the bunch. While many of his pleasant-enough recorded songs have been criticized for their unfortunate tendency to go vapidly in one ear and out the other, his live performance of them is something else again. On stage, the tunes took on a real rock 'n' roll edge." Van Matre also noted that having endured considerable criticism over the years, Linda "fit in well enough," but seemed "ill at ease when she's not behind the keyboards."[14]

Two nights later, Van Matre saw Wings again, and stopped backstage for an interview. Although he rarely commented to critics about their reviews, Paul responded to Van Matre's comments about his recordings and Linda.

"Yeah, I know a lot of critics haven't liked our records," he admitted. "Lightweight music, that's what they've called it. I can tell the difference in our playing live and our playing on records, though. It's true. The thing is, when you make a record you're putting the music down on vinyl forever, making a statue, as it were, encasing it in cement. On stage, we're just throwing the music into the air, letting it happen. The pressure's off, a little."

About Linda, he said, "Some reviewer from *Rolling Stone* wrote that when Linda stands downstage for the song 'My Love,' she looked funny standing there with her hands on her hips for the whole number. So, for Monday night's show, she took her hands off her hips for a while, and you wrote that she looked fidgety."

"I *like* to fidget," Linda interjected.

"We're just having some fun with you,"[15] Paul told Van Matre.

For some of the crew, the criticism Linda was still drawing was excessive, even if they conceded that she was not a seasoned player.

"I was the keyboard tech on the *Wings Over America* and *Wings Over the World* tours," Peter "Rocky" Morley later recalled. "I looked after Linda's keyboards. Linda did a lot more playing than people think she did. I would change the settings on the Minimoog as she was playing in certain songs. As for some people saying that the keys were numbered and had letters on them, that was only on the Mellotron, so she knew where certain sound effects were, from doorbell sounds to violins and other instrument sounds. Having previously worked for Keith Emerson for six years, I wouldn't say she was a great keyboard player, but she helped make the Wings sound, and would have been noticeably missed had she not been there."[16]

That said, it was not only the press that was critical of Linda. "Linda is a nice chick and I really like her," Joe English said in a dyspeptic moment, "but let's face it, she can't play, and she can't sing. And Denny Laine can sing, but he tends to sing off-key."[17]

Jimmy took a more nuanced view. "She had no musical background, and it was very hard work for her to walk straight into a grade A band," he observed. "She's a tough nut, but she's got a big heart. She can only get better and better. I find her innocent approach refreshing. All the stick was to be expected. But if the keyboards player had been a real professional like Billy Preston, it wouldn't be Wings. Linda has the innocence."[18]

One of Paul's backstage interviews in Chicago was with Roy Leonard, the host of the popular *Roy Leonard Show* on WLS. Leonard joked with Paul about a muddled lyric in 'The Long and Winding Road'—a performance also marred by feedback—noting that Linda shot him a glance, and wondering whether Linda knows the lyrics to Beatles songs better than Paul does.

"I don't know about that, but she just notices my goofs. I think she gets off on that. She likes to see me goofing, just occasionally." He then seemed to take slight (if good-natured) umbrage at the question. "I've got two hours of songs there, so I don't know how many words that is, I've never counted, but to miss about three or four in an evening, I don't mind too much."[19]

Leonard also had a chat with Jimmy, from whom he hoped to hear the *real* story of the accident that led to the delay in the North American tour. But McCulloch was not going for it: he repeated the story about the slippery marble floors at the hotel in Paris. Leonard tried again: "That's the story we read, but I figured that after the concert, backstage, we'd get the *real* story from Jimmy McCulloch!" But Jimmy just repeated the official story once more.

After the soundcheck before the second show, Bruce Meyer spoke with Paul for United Press International, and after the expected Beatles reunion question—this time Paul shrugged off Sargent's multimillion-dollar offer by likening it to be offered a lot of money to jump off the Empire

State Building—they discussed Paul's long-held but not widely discussed desire to host a radio show.

"Radio is the thing I like," Paul told Meyer. "It's very imaginative. You can say, 'Now here we are in the country' (a few bird whistles), and here we are. I was brought up on radio. So maybe once a week, we'd just introduce recordings that are favorites of ours—not necessarily new ones—and we'd play a bit of Wings, and maybe have some guests, some high-powered guests, friends of ours. We have lots of little plans."[20]

Minnesota was next on the midwestern itinerary, and Wings landed there on Friday, June 4, for a concert at the St. Paul Civic Center in Saint Paul for an audience of 17,500. It was Jimmy McCulloch's twenty-third birthday, which earned him a song dedication from Paul. "This is a tune we normally dedicate to Fred Astaire, 'cause he's groovy," Paul told the crowd. "But today we're gonna dedicate it to a friend of ours whose birthday it is—Jimmy McCulloch."[21]

In a backstage interview after the show, Jon Bream, of the *Minneapolis Star*, wondered whether Wingsmania might be for the 1970s what Beatlemania was for the 1960s—a prospect that Paul seemed to find uninteresting, even objectionable.

"I'm sure it won't, and I hope it doesn't, and it really shouldn't," he told Bream. "Because I think we've moved ahead. It's a new time. The symptoms of these years are different, and the audiences are different. I wouldn't want to re-create the old audiences and get it back to the '60s. That's been and gone. It was great! You don't really want to be back there. I don't. I don't think most people do."

But if McCartney had moved past being a teen idol, Bream wondered, what about the Beatles' later role as political and social models—culture heroes for the '60s generation? He read McCartney a quote from a review that suggested that his post-Beatles ballads and love songs indicated "an ambivalence toward the culture that he helped deliver." It had been some time since Paul had made a point of the distinction between his public persona (*Him*), and his real self (*Me*), but Bream's question pushed him to revisit it.

"I don't agree," Paul said of the review quote, tartly adding that "people spout off and think they've got the gist of it. And I don't pretend anyone's got the gist of it. I like what happened and believe in what went on in the '60s, and still want to see wars come to an end. I want to see the kind of wrong things in life changed, but I don't necessarily want to see it change the way some other people do. So we differ.

"There is the hero side," he added. "It exists in the papers—at arm's length. It's nothing I really get into. I don't want to have to behave like a hero all the time. 'Cause I also know myself as a person. That's the real thing."[22]

With the Midwest leg of the tour complete, the band flew back to Chicago for a final night before moving their base of operations to the Beverly Wilshire Hotel in Beverly Hills (with Paul and Linda again renting a private house nearby) on Saturday. Although the McCartneys were not staying at the Beverly Wilshire, Paul regarded it as his favorite Hollywood hotel. But in the aftermath of some egregious behavior by traveling rock stars—most notably Keith Moon, who was now banned from the hotel—the Beverly Wilshire had been refusing rooms to musicians, or charging "breakage deposits." Given the size of Paul's entourage, and talk in the press that the McCartney girls had taken to redecorating hotel rooms with crayons and colored pens, the manager asked him to pay a $15,000 (£8,443) deposit before the band and crew were allowed to check in. The amount was reportedly handed over in cash, without objection.[23]

After a free weekend in Los Angeles, Wings flew two hours east to Denver on Monday, June 7, for a single concert at the McNichols Sports Arena, a new venue that opened in August 1975. Although the local press reported that a capacity audience of 19,000 was on hand, reports in the music trades suggest that it was not sold out, apparently because of a predatory move by the Denver-based concert promoter Barry Fey.

"When Concerts West took Paul McCartney around the country, they sold out every city except for one—Denver," observed Chet Hanson, of the Los Angeles–based Athena Artists. "And that was because Barry Fey was not going to let them sell out in Denver. He surrounded [the Wings concert] with seven shows and the day before [Wings] tickets went on sale, seven of Barry's shows went on sale. He took so much money out of the marketplace that there was no way to get in there. So the next time Concerts West came into that market, they split [the production credit and fees] with Barry Fey."[24]

The *Los Angeles Times* critic Robert Hilburn flew to Denver to interview Paul and Linda for a preview to be published before Wings' three Los Angeles shows. Hilburn was acutely aware of Paul's eagerness to escape the specter of the Beatles: at their last encounter, in 1974, Paul answered a few Beatles questions before snapping, *"That's enough about the Beatles, okay?"*

But now, in the midst of an undeniably successful tour, with *Wings at the Speed of Sound* at No. 2 on the *Billboard* albums chart (just under the Rolling Stones' *Black and Blue*) and 'Silly Love Songs' topping the singles chart, the Beatles were in hot pursuit: the newly released single, 'Got to Get You Into My Life,' had just entered the Hot 100 at No. 64. When Hilburn pointed that out, McCartney's comments about the Beatles were more nuanced.

"It's funny," he told Hilburn, "because we have had some people come up to me on this tour and say how great it must be now with Wings because people can hear the music. They say it must be more satisfying because there isn't all that screaming from the Beatles concerts. Well, that is satisfying about the shows now, but it isn't more satisfying than the Beatles' shows. Those shows were great. But it's great, now, too. This is as satisfying, but in a different way. As long as the audience digs it, it doesn't really matter to me what form the digging takes. The truth is I don't really feel that much different on stage than I did ten years ago. The circumstances are different, but I'm not that much different. It's still a buzz.

"We realize we have a lot of people coming to the show with a certain viewpoint," he added. "It's like, 'We'll let him be a Wing for a little while. He's not doing too bad. But we know, really, he's still a Beatle.' This tour has convinced us that we're a group and I think it has convinced audiences, too. This wasn't just a one-time trip. This is going to be a working band. We'll be back."

For perspective on how the tour was affecting Paul, Hilburn sought a behind-the-scenes report from Linda.

"This tour has been a beauty for Paul," she responded. "It has been the most positive thing that has happened to him for years, and he works very much on positive vibes. When it's positive, he flowers. So, he's very much his old self again. He's got his thinking cap on again. He has got a team together in Wings and the audiences have accepted it. Seeing him on this tour, I can realize now what he had before the Beatles broke up. He had friendship and a creative community to work with. He could turn to John and say, 'Let's try this' or, 'What about that?' It was all very positive. That's what hit him so hard when the Beatles broke up. He had lost his world. And there was so much negativity in the air. That was definitely the low point for him. Now, it's a high point again."

Hilburn also offered a brief evaluation of the show, which included a few of Paul's on-the-spot variations—'Lady Madonna' with its reprise, the 'Star-Spangled Banner' fake-out before 'Yesterday' and the dedication of 'You Gave Me the Answer' to both the corpulent British character actor Fred Emney ("You may not have heard of Fred, but he's a fab comedian from England"[25]) and Fred Astaire.

"His new band, Wings, may not carry either the full musical range and/or social impact of the Beatles," Hilburn wrote, "but it is a solid, convincing unit. And the concerts, concentrating on post-Beatles material, were rousing, celebrative events."[26]

After the show, Paul had a brief backstage reunion with Jim Guercio, the producer who had scuttled his own honeymoon to help Paul put the finishing touches on *Ram*, only to part ways with McCartney and company after a few days.

After two free days in Los Angeles, Wings flew to Seattle, Washington, for the biggest concert of the tour, a performance for 67,000 people at the newly opened King County Multipurpose Domed Stadium, popularly known as the Kingdome. Wings' performance, which took in about $600,000 at the box office (from which the arena took 13 percent), was the first rock show at the Kingdome, and it went directly into the record books as the largest attendance for an indoor concert. It also demolished the attendance record the Beatles established when they played for an audience of 55,600 at Shea Stadium on August 15, 1965.

Keen to capture on film the cavernous size of the venue, Linda had a request for Showco lighting engineer Warren Cunningham.

"Linda was out in the arena," Cunningham remembered, "looking up at the massive ceiling, and she noticed a structure hanging from the center of the dome. She asked me if it would be possible to go up there so that she could take some pictures."

Staring up at the rig, several hundred feet above the auditorium floor, Brian Brolly immediately tried to dash the idea on health and safety grounds. But Linda persisted.

"I checked with the local building managers and with the tour management," Cunningham continued, "and they said there was a way up there that was safe. With her security detail in attendance, we climbed the ladder to the center of the dome to a trap door where we then climbed inside, and down another ladder to the gondola. Linda took several pictures from there."[27]

As Humphrey Ocean noted in his tour diary—and captured in drawings in his sketchbook—such was the enormity of Kingdome that an Airstream trailer had been driven into the huge dressing room, offering privacy for those who were changing into or out of their stage costumes while others were conducting interviews or were otherwise engaged in the backstage area, which was kitted out with artificial grass, fake boulders and tables of food.

The size of the venue had ramifications for the Showco crew, as well.

"Seattle is the only really big show we're doing on this tour," Jack Maxson explained to *People* magazine. "The rest are standard coliseum-type shows. The others are not on this scale at all. We've had to build a huge scaffold here for the show and the equipment that we didn't have to do anywhere else." In terms of electricity, he added, "We'll use about 3000 amps at 120 volts. That's about enough to run a small town. This is the largest PA system used for anything, anywhere, as far as I know. This is much bigger than Woodstock or California Jam or anything you ever heard of."[28]

That shift in scale created technical difficulties that had not occurred elsewhere.

"At the Kingdome in Seattle, the riggers had to do huge, long cable runs from the roof," lighting man Ian Peacock recalled. "There were two or three motors that took up the [projection] screen, and two or three motors upstage of that, that took up the front truss. And the cable runs were so long that it was hard to tell which motor was which."

When Peacock needed to move something in the stage set by operating those motors—which could not be seen from his position—he had to hope he engaged the correct one, something he determined by watching which cables either went slack or remained taut, quickly correcting if necessary. "There was two or three times, possibly, that I got the wrong motor," he added. "I remember that day as being quite technically challenging."[29]

Because only 15,000 of the seats were reserved—the rest were first-come-first-choice festival seating—tens of thousands of fans hoping to get close to the stage gathered outside the Kingdome hours before the show. "I remember Paul, Denny and I going to a place where we watched people line up forever,"[30] English remembered. Once the doors opened, it took more than 90 minutes for the crowd to file in. Inside, the crowd—average age 21 or 22, according to one reporter—floated frisbees across the venue, with groups of fans bouncing balloons, and a few setting off firecrackers and cherry bombs. The concert was delayed, in fact, when someone lit a firework jammed into the stage rigging, sending a piece of it sailing over the crowd, fortunately without causing injuries.

"I was hanging around backstage after the soundcheck," Ian Peacock remembers of the hour before showtime, "and I found myself in a tented area where they had a dartboard and a television. And the next thing I know, I'm playing darts with Paul, Denny and Jimmy—we were playing doubles. I was waiting for somebody to come in, at any minute, and tell me, 'Ian, what are you doing here? Get out,' but it didn't happen.

"At some point," Peacock continued, "the television was on, and Ray Charles appears on the TV.* And Paul goes over to watch, and lo and behold, Ray Charles starts playing 'Eleanor Rigby.' I remember Paul was just glued to the TV, and I'm standing there thinking, 'Ray friggin' Charles is singing a song on TV by the guy in front of me, and we're watching it.' That was a special moment."[31]

When Charles finished performing and the dart game broke up, Paul turned his attention to an interview with journalists from newspapers in Washington and Oregon. As Heather, Mary and Stella darted behind the fake boulders and under the tables, wardrobe mistress Pam Keats ironed costumes, and Linda sat in a corner being sketched by Humphrey Ocean, Paul lit up a Senior Service cigarette and held forth about—of all things—bad decisions made on behalf of the Beatles. After criticizing EMI's recent release of all the British singles—"I thought they should concentrate on one or two of the biggest hits at a time, like 'Hey Jude,' instead of releasing them in a bunch"—he launched into a discussion of Beatles royalties, asserting that the group "lost millions" over the years.

"I'm not complaining, we came out all right," he said. "But the Beatles sold, what?, 300 million records, they say. Now, we were supposed to get five cents a record or about that, and we certainly didn't. We made a lot, but not what we should have."[32]

Ten minutes later, Wings were onstage amid the dry ice fog and bubbles, soaking up the roar of 67,000 fans. To Jimmy, it was "just like playing Wembley Stadium with a roof on it."[33] Tony Dorsey found it a somewhat stranger experience.

"That's a huge place," Dorsey said of the Kingdome. "When you're playing [an arena] like that, it's more like a dress rehearsal than a performance. Before [touring with Wings] I had worked with soul bands, and the audience would be right up at the stage. But [at the Kingdome] we were so high up, away from the people, we didn't really see them until they turned on the lights. We could hear them applauding at the end of a song, but other than that, it was just like they weren't there."[34]

* The show may have been a repeat of Charles's appearance on NBC's *A Touch of Gold*, first aired in January. The night of Wings' Kingdome show, Charles was performing at the Great American Music Hall in San Francisco.

For Linda, that detachment from the colossal crowd was a plus.

"We played to 67,000 in Seattle and it didn't worry me one bit," she later confessed. "I was much more nervous when we did our first stage shows in Europe and Britain. That was the worst part of all. Nothing has been as bad since."[35]

Paul may have heard unverified reports that Little Richard was in the audience. "Let's have a big cheer for Little Richard!" he exhorted the crowd before 'You Gave Me the Answer,' adding "Yeah! Alright. We love you Richard," and then, imitating Little Richard's accent, "*My, my, my!* This next tune we usually dedicate to Fred Astaire, but we're going to dedicate it to Little Richard tonight. Why not?"[36]

For the critics on hand, both Wings and the Kingdome were under review, and both fared well. Patrick MacDonald declared in the *Seattle Times* that "if there was any doubt that the Kingdome was suitable for rock shows, Paul McCartney and Wings wiped it out." Calling the show a "spectacular extravaganza," MacDonald wrote that Paul was "full of boundless energy throughout the two-hour show, mugging, prancing and joking. He said he was having a good time and he looked it."[37]

Roaming through the hall that night was a camera crew from ABC-TV, filming the show for use in a *Good Night America* Wings special that would also include an interview with Paul by Geraldo Rivera. When the special was aired, 18 days later, it ended with Paul's Seattle performance of 'Yesterday.' But overlaid faintly on the concert clip as a ghostly backdrop, silent and haunting, was footage of the Beatles performing in the concert scene from *A Hard Day's Night*.

—

After another two-day break, Wings flew from Los Angeles to San Francisco for two sold-out shows at the 17,000-seat Cow Palace on June 13 and 14. San Francisco looms large in Beatles history: the group opened their first full-length American tour at the Cow Palace on August 19, 1964, and closed their second North American tour at the same venue on August 31, 1965. Their performance at Candlestick Park on August 29, 1966, was their final public concert.

Before the show, Denny Laine's girlfriend, Jo Jo, ran into a cocaine dealer she knew from years past, who promised to get her, for $2,000 (£1,130), enough coke to last through the rest of the tour. Jo Jo knew she couldn't ask Denny for the cash; although he enjoyed the odd snort when it was available, he would rebel at the price tag, not to mention the danger carrying that much cocaine could mean for his employer and bandmates. Rooting around backstage, she found a suitcase with a small stack of front-row seats for the McCartneys' invited guests. She pocketed the tickets, disguised herself in an old raincoat and headscarf—"As a rock 'n' roll bag lady," she said—and scalped the tickets outside the Cow Palace.

"I had more than enough for the coke," Jo Jo explained, "which I used to put in smaller packages so that no one actually sussed how much I had. Old Jimmy and I, especially, used to like having some blow around, as did Denny. . . . I wouldn't say that the band was strung out, but everyone certainly enjoyed a good buzz."[38]

At the end of the second show, after singing 'Hi, Hi, Hi' Paul stepped up to the microphone and said, "I'll tell you what, just before we go here, just want to bring out some fella, an old friend of ours for years. . . ."[39] Adrenaline flowed and anticipation filled the hall during those few seconds—*could it be John?*—but it was a tease: the old friend Paul brought out was the promoter Bill Graham, who nevertheless won fervent applause in his capacity as a legendary force on the San Francisco (and national) rock scene. Paul and the band then filed off the stage without performing 'Soily.'

Two days later, Wings landed in San Diego to play a concert for 15,000 at the San Diego Sports Arena. "It was significant that the group was stressed in the billing," wrote Jim Guthrie of the *Times Advocate*, "that indicated a certain symbolism, an understanding by one of pop music's most eminent superstars about the idiom's integral relationship between the individual and those around him. McCartney's name alone would have been enough to guarantee the tour's success, but by itself, it wouldn't have reflected what, in purely musical terms, the tour was all about—where the man was now musically."

Guthrie rhapsodized briefly about the importance of 'Yesterday' in the pop canon, but argued that the song was not the highlight of the concert. "Hearing it was nice enough, but somehow only in a nostalgic way. What made the concert memorable was the 'new' McCartney sound, the sound of five musicians playing together as Wings. Wings is still developing as a group, and it may never reach the Beatles' status or preeminence. Probably no group ever will. But I can't wait for its next tour."[40]

On their flight back, Wings welcomed a guest onboard their private jet, and with the McCartney girls safely in their beds in Los Angeles, the journey was more colorful than usual.

"We flew from San Diego back to L.A. after a concert," Aubrey Powell reminisced, "and gave John Bonham a lift, who was a wild man. And on the BAC 111, there was a kind of disco, and I remember John doing coke in there. But, you know, drugs and rock 'n' roll, what's new?"[41]

With another free day in Los Angeles before Wings' next show, Paul and Linda dropped into Cherokee Studios, where Ringo was working on his new album, having moved from Sunset Sound Recorders on June 12. While still at Sunset, on June 3, Ringo set down the backing track for Paul's 'Pure Gold,' with Klaus Voormann on bass, former Apple artist Lon Van Eaton on guitar, Jen Getz and John Jarvis on keyboards, George Devens on congas, and Jim Keltner and Ringo sharing the drumming. At the June 17 session, Paul and Linda contributed backing vocals.

"Paul said, 'I wrote this song for you, Nancy,'" Andrews remembered him telling her during a playback. "And I said, 'Really?' He said, 'Yes.' It's a lovely, lovely song, and I thought, 'Oh my God, that was so sweet!'"[42]

Shortly after his sessions with John and Paul, Ringo reflected on his former colleagues' recent work. "Y'know, it's difficult to stand back and judge them as ordinary records," Ringo explained. "I listen to Paul's things and sometimes I've thought, 'No, not this time.' Then I've been in the hotel lift and his song comes out of my mouth as a whistle, and I think, 'Sod him! He writes bloody catchy tunes.' Paul's always been like that. John's records take more time to get into, but he's lovely. George seems to have come back from the East now. What'd you want me to say? They're my brothers."[43]

The collaborations also got him to think about the virtually constant reunion talk and how such a thing might work.

"What we really should do," Ringo suggested, "is get into the studio and be with each other for a while if we were to do anything. Even when we were the closest band in the world, it would take us a week or so when we'd get back to record to relax again with each other. Despite what anyone's said, we have talked about doing something. But it's not for the money. If we did it, it would be because I wanted to. I'd probably do it for free."[44]

Paul, meanwhile, had a new single on deck: 'Let 'Em In' and 'Beware My Love,' originally scheduled for release on July 23, was instead rushed out on June 18—Paul's thirty-fourth birthday—in order to hit the market during the final stretch of the tour. (In Britain, the release plan remained unchanged, and it was issued on July 23.) Both the American and British releases used an edit, the 4'18" song trimmed to 3'34". (The British single was mastered at Abbey Road on June 29, in Paul's absence, and assigned the matrix numbers 7YCE 21789-DJ and 7YCE 21790.)

> *We thought this should have been the first single from* At the Speed of Sound, *but 'Silly Love Songs' went straight to number one. It's hard, therefore, to predict that this will do better, but it is a better, more substantial tune. McCartney's voice is at its best, and the rhythm of this one is dangerously addictive. Headed straight for the top.*[45]
>
> *Uncredited,* Cash Box

> *One of the group's more dazzling stage numbers on its recent tour, this* At the Speed of Sound *track makes an impressive follow-up to 'Silly Love Songs.' With a loping beat and a brisk, military drum sound, this should be another chapter in McCartney's success story.*[46]
>
> *Uncredited,* Record World

July 31, 1976 NEW MUSICAL EXPRESS Page 7

LET 'EM IN

WINGS

NEW SINGLE RELEASED 23 JULY

R6015

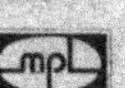

Marketed by EMI Records Limited, 20, Manchester Square, London W1A 1ES

Wings, 'Let 'Em In' single trade ad

Ultimate hummable whistleable or whatever you like pop song that's even better than 'Silly Love Songs.' Staring with an 'Avon calling' bell and mentioning Martin Luther King, it can't fail. Anybody for No. 1?[47]

David Hancock, Record Mirror & Disc

Taken from the relentlessly boring At the Speed of Sound *LP. Actually this has the pace of a sloth with hangnail. Leave me out Paulie.*[48]

Giovanni Dadomo, Sounds

Tour exposure notwithstanding, 'Let 'Em In' failed to dislodge the Elton John and Kiki Dee duet, 'Don't Go Breaking My Heart,' and the Bee Gees' 'You Should Be Dancing' from the summit of the *Billboard* Hot 100. In total, 'Let 'Em In' spent 16 weeks on the chart, peaking at No. 3 (where it remained for four weeks) on August 14. In Britain, where the record enjoyed a 10-week run in the Top 100, the single climbed one rung higher (but was again held off the top spot by Elton and Kiki), peaking at No. 2 on August 28.

Just as the new Wings single was hitting the shops, EMI announced that it would release another single from *Rock 'N' Roll Music*, 'Back in the U.S.S.R.' backed with 'Twist and Shout,' on June 25.

—

Paul spent his birthday onstage in Tucson, Arizona, playing for a crowd of 11,000 at the Tucson Community Center Arena. Upon their arrival in late afternoon, the temperature was 100° Fahrenheit—"Like warm oil," was how Humphrey Ocean described the feeling in his tour diary.

Tucson was one of the few cities on the itinerary that Paul had never visited, although he and Linda had connections with it, Paul having namechecked the city in the Beatles' song 'Get Back,' and Linda having lived there in the early 1960s. Paul and Linda had a local jeweler make Paul a gold pendant for $300 (£169) while they were in town, but a planned reunion with some of Linda's friends was canceled for lack of time.

Still, the visit rekindled in Linda a love for the area, and she and Paul began discussing the idea of buying a ranch there. "Arizona is the most beautiful state in all of America," Linda told an interviewer shortly after the tour. "After growing up in the East, it opened my eyes up to the wonders of light and color."[49]

It was not lost on the audience at the Tucson Community Center Arena that it was Paul's birthday, and the band made several references to the occasion in their song introductions, and Paul himself sang a line from 'Happy Birthday,' with a piano flourish, just before 'You Gave Me the Answer' (which was dedicated to Gene Autry).

"[The audience] held up banners and gave him presents and sang 'Happy Birthday' to him," Larry Fleischman wrote in a rhapsodic review in the *Tucson Daily Citizen*. "In response, Wings performed 2½ hours of some of the best rock 'n' roll ever to come to town. . . . It was truly a celebration, this rock concert. It was a time filled with nothing but good things, nothing but joy."[50]

After the show, the road crew laid on a birthday party for Paul, in the best southwestern tradition, with Mexican food (tortillas and enchiladas), and a mariachi band. There was even a piñata, which Paul, blindfolded, had to smash apart with a pole, liberating the candy and toys inside.

The revelry continued back in Los Angeles. Richard Perry, whose birthday was the same day as Paul's, threw a joint party for Paul and himself at Studio 55 on June 19; Ringo, Ronee Blakely, Leo Sayer and Al Coury were among the guests. And the next day, Paul and Linda attended Brian Wilson's birthday party.

Paul celebrates his 34th birthday in Arizona, June 18, 1976

All that remained on the Wings Over America itinerary were three concerts at the Forum, in Inglewood, a suburb of Los Angeles, each for an audience of 18,700. These shows, on June 21, 22 and 23, were presented in the finest Hollywood fashion, complete with a red carpet for arriving celebrity guests—who were legion—plus a marching band circling the stadium, and a hot air balloon flying above the Forum, sporting the Wings logo. MPL had even helped arrange for a planeload of Japanese fans—members of Japan's Wings Fan Club—to attend the show, yet another make-good for the canceled Tokyo concerts.

At curtain time, the Forum was packed with musicians, including Brian Wilson and members of the Beach Boys, Elton John, Diana Ross, Robbie Robertson, Leo Sayer, Adam Faith, members of Chicago, Jesse Ed Davis, John Bonham, Helen Reddy, Natalie Cole, Harry Nilsson and Ringo Starr, as well as quite a few actors, including Dustin Hoffman, Jack Nicholson and Yul Brynner. Most waited until the lights went down to slide into their seats, although Ringo made his entry ten minutes earlier, to the sound of girls in nearby seats screaming. When George Martin, who was seated nearby, asked Ringo what the hubbub was about, the drummer shrugged and said, "I don't know, I'm just the guy they cheer for before the real act comes on."[51]

One pair of celebrities that was not spotted by many, and not mentioned in the press reports, was Gene Roddenberry, the creator of *Star Trek*, and his wife, Majel Barrett, who played Nurse Christine Chapel on the show. As busy as the tour was, Paul found time to revive a project that had been tugging at his imagination the last few years—the science fiction film starring Wings, which had lain dormant since his hoped-for collaboration with Isaac Asimov fizzled.

Paul does not give up ideas easily, and it would not have been lost on him that David Bowie's science fiction film, *The Man Who Fell to Earth*, hit the theaters in April, confirming for Paul that he had tapped into the Zeitgeist. A significant difference was that the Bowie film was based on an existing story, Walter Tevis's 1963 novel; Paul wanted his film to be new and fresh, something just for him and Wings.

In any case, the Wings sci-fi epic had not been abandoned so much as placed on Paul's "to be revisited" shelf, alongside *Rupert Bear*, *Thrillington*, *The Bruce McMouse Show* and *One Hand Clapping*. Early in the tour, he arranged to meet with Roddenberry when he reached Los Angeles.

"Gene received a phone call from an agent representing Paul McCartney," Susan Sackett, Roddenberry's personal assistant, wrote in her memoir. "He was a huge *Star Trek* fan and he wanted to hire Gene to write a screenplay that would star his rock band, Wings. Gene was impressed, and also grateful for the opportunity to do some writing, since Paramount hadn't approved his script for the *Star Trek* movie."[52]

Sackett attended the show with Roddenberry and Barrett and accompanied them backstage after the show, where they sat at a table with Paul and Linda chatting over drinks about the show and the prospect of working together, and arranging for further discussions. To kick-start the creative process, Paul handed Roddenberry a short written treatment that had evolved from his short-lived collaboration with Asimov.

"What I recall of the outline from Paul," Sackett explained, "is that it was about some sort of contest between his band, which he called *The Stix*, and a band from some alien planet. I think the proposal was about two pages long."[53]

For the Forum shows, Paul restored Denny's Moody Blues hit 'Go Now,' but otherwise did not tinker with the set (apart from playing the 'Star-Spangled Banner' fake-out before 'Yesterday,' at the first show only).

The big moment in the first show, though, came at the very end, after 'Soily,' when, as Robert Hilburn reported in his *Los Angeles Times* review, "a familiar, bearded figure joined them on stage, carrying a bouquet of flowers."[54] Ringo handed the bouquet to Denny, kissed Linda's hand, and picked up McCartney's Rickenbacker bass, waving it over his head the way Paul used to do (with his Höfner) at the end of Beatles shows.

"For a few seconds," Hilburn wrote, "the two ex-Beatles—who hadn't been on stage together in the United States since 1966—seemed uncertain about their next move." But being seen together, and an embrace, was all they offered before Paul told the audience, "See you next time!" and everyone walked off the stage.

"He's my friend," Ringo told Hilburn after the show. "I thought I ought to do something to welcome him on his first night in town. It was great. I loved it. Always been a ham, you know!"[55]

Before the second show, Paul had a visit—and a bespoke drawing—from Jack Kirby, the artist who created Magneto in Marvel Comics' *X-Men* series, as well as the painted flat of the character unrolled as a backdrop to the performance of 'Magneto and Titanium Man.' Kirby had not planned to see Paul in Los Angeles, but Gary Sherman, the brother of Kirby's assistant, Steve Sherman, hatched a plot to get Kirby and McCartney together. Sherman contacted MPL to say that Kirby had created a drawing for Paul and Linda.

Paul and Ringo reunite on stage at the Los Angeles Forum, June 21, 1976

That was not true, but once MPL agreed to

send a backstage pass, Sherman persuaded Kirby to create the artwork, "Wings Over Magneto"—a pencil drawing of Magneto looking upward as Paul and Linda, in top hats, followed by the rest of Wings, flew over him. He signed it, "To Paul and Linda, Best Wishes, Jack Kirby."[56] In return, Paul asked Denny, who introduced 'Magneto and Titanium Man' at each show, to add a dedication to Kirby in his introduction.

Backstage after the June 22 concert, the entourage celebrated Humphrey Ocean's birthday. "There are festivities in the road crew room," Ocean wrote in his tour diary. "I am swathed in champagne and custard pies like a tribal sacrifice." Photos from the party show Ocean and McCartney laughing together, Paul's face also covered with the remnants of a custard pie.

At the final show, Paul made one last change to his 'You Gave Me the Answer' dedication. "As you probably know, this is the last night of our American tour. And I want to tell you from all of us, we've had a fantastic time, really. No doubt about it. We want to thank all you people for coming. The next tune we're gonna do, we normally dedicate it to Fred Astaire and Ginger Baker [*sic*]—but then again, *sometimes* it's Ginger Baker. And then again, sometimes it's Carl Worthington. Anyway, listen, for a change tonight I'd like to dedicate this to the whole of the road crew who helped us put this show on the road. *Best road crew!*"[57]

And with another extended farewell before 'Band on the Run,' and "Good night, America! See you next time!" after 'Soily,' Wings Over America—much to the relief of an exhausted Showco crew—was a wrap.

"It was kind of sweet in its way," Allen Branton reflected. "This wasn't the Rolling Stones, or someone who was likely to misbehave, or create problems, or be controversial, or bite the head off a bat, or any of that shit. This was a beloved figure, and everybody wanted to do a good job. And it was pretty bloody smooth, frankly."[58]

After the show, the McCartneys and company repaired to the estate of the silent film comedy genius Harold Lloyd for a party that made the McCartneys' other celebrity bashes—even the party on the *Queen Mary* after the *Venus and Mars* sessions—seem restrained. Their plan for the party was so extensive that they had to rent the Lloyd house for four days to prepare the rooms, tents and outdoor spaces. A catering staff of 200 was engaged, and a telephone station, with a dozen phones, was set up so that guests could make and receive calls. (During the party, a loudspeaker periodically boomed out "there is a call for . . ." announcements.)

Guests were asked to wear all-white—Paul wore a white shirt and trousers, Linda wore a short white dress with aqua feather epaulettes—and Linda engaged a Hawaiian artist she had met during their November 1975 visit to spray paint designs onto the outfits of guests who were interested in taking home a piece of art on their clothing. (For those unwilling to ruin their outfits, white T-shirts were provided.)

A bandstand was erected near the pool, from which Nelson Riddle and his Orchestra provided dance music, as well as accompanying a set of ballet excerpts with dancers from the Los Angeles Ballet. Partygoers were free to swim, although a few hours into the event, the pool was covered with a disco dance floor.

Also among the entertainers: the cast from *The Wiz* performed 'Ease on Down the Road' from the show; actor and martial arts expert Chuck Norris gave a karate demonstration; the Los Angeles Mime Troupe performed; and John Belushi reprised the Joe Cocker imitation that Paul watched at the Dakota in April, also performing a sketch with his *Saturday Night Live* colleague Dan Aykroyd.

The evening was anything but staid. "Boxer's percussionist and wild man of rhythm, Tony Newman, went to Wings' party in Los Angeles," *Melody Maker* reported in its next issue, "where Nelson Riddle was playing with the Los Angeles Ballet, and got up onstage with the dancers. To the fearful amazement of the honored guests, who were too stunned to do anything about him, he began prancing about in his white jumpsuit. Then, rumor has it, he performed his celebrated party trick whereby he's said unleash his (oh, how to put this delicately?) . . . his testicles and apply a lighter to them—briefly, one hopes and presumes."[59]

In a moment of family nostalgia, some three months after his father's death, Paul had phoned his brother Mike and offered to fly him over, with his family, for the closing concert and the party.

"The Scaffold were due to play a particularly difficult club in London (Dingwalls, Camden, in late June 1976)," Mike explained. "I say difficult, because the audience is always drunk, and our humor doesn't go down very well there. I was feeling pretty depressed about the whole thing when out of the blue I got this phone call from Our Kid in Los Angeles. He invited me and the wife and the kids to L.A. for, of all things, a party. 'Come first class,' he said, 'bring the lot, everybody.' That's typical of him, the spontaneous off-the-cuff gesture—and just at the right time."[60]

And then there was the guest list. Among the 400 invitees were the actors Dustin Hoffman, Jack Nicholson, James Caan, Tony Curtis, and Warren Beatty (with supermodel and actress Maud Adams). Naturally, a broad swath of the pop music world was there too, including Ringo, Keith Moon, Harry Nilsson, Bob Dylan, Roger McGuinn, Linda Ronstadt, Peter Asher, Joni Mitchell, Rod Stewart, John Denver, David Cassidy, Jesse Ed Davis, Barry White, Carole King, Kenny Loggins and Jim Messina, Dolly Parton, Dave Mason, Ricky Nelson, Mickey Dolenz, Alice Cooper, Keith Emerson, Yvonne Elliman, John Mayall, Olivia Newton-John, Helen Reddy, Diana Ross and members of Chicago, America, the Beach Boys and the Jackson Five.

Traffic outside the estate was so congested that the McCartneys were fined $50 (£28) by the Beverly Hills Chamber of Commerce—barely a rounding error on the full bill for the party, which reportedly surpassed $80,000 (£45,100).[61]

Wings backstage during the Wings Over America tour, May 1976

Paul told guests that he planned to spend some time in Scotland, and that he wanted to work on his *Rupert Bear* film. But he was also still buzzing about the prospect of a science fiction film vehicle for Wings, and he and Linda were seen huddled in deep conversation with Gene Roddenberry.

The party came to an unplanned end at 3 A.M., when the property's power generator went down, plunging the estate into darkness.

Before they left Los Angeles, the McCartneys attended one more party, this one not at their expense. They, and Wings, were invited to a swanky do at the Bel Air Sands Hotel. The dress code noted on the invitation called for white suits for men and evening dresses for women. Wings turned up in jeans and T-shirts.

But a jeans-clad McCartney was back on top.

"We worked our way up," Paul later reflected, "we then clawed our way back, just little bit by little bit. And it hurt, and it wasn't nice. But we had to get up—we couldn't go back to bed—and had to slap ourselves about our face, and have that shave, and do all the cliché things anyone had ever said about clawing your way back. And that was how we did it in the end."[62]

16

HOLLY DAYS IN SCOTLAND

Driving up the rough road to High Park, Paul looked forward to a stretch of relieving post-tour downtime. But wear and tear notwithstanding, he had found the last ten months thoroughly energizing. He had ticked off a reasonable number of items on his wish list: he was in a working band, but he was also unquestionably its front man and its creative engine. More crucially, in the past 16 months he had led this band on tours of Britain, Australia, Europe and North America, and cut an album between jaunts.

The band was sounding good, tight and polished, and was seen to be so by critics across the globe. So downtime—*great*, but then it's time to build on the work of the last few years, and to consider where to point the ship next.

Linda had a different perspective. She had worked hard to bring her keyboard and vocal performance to a level that would not be skewered in the press at every performance. And she gamely played both band member and vehemently supportive wife in interviews, while also mothering three young girls. But unlike her husband, Linda had not spent her adolescence and early adulthood mastering an instrument (or four), learning the ins and outs of songwriting, and hankering to stand up in a crowded room and sing. If it were up to her, she would stay at High Park indefinitely, throwing herself into raising plants and animals, cooking, bringing up the girls and having more children.

"You lose a few years of your life on stage," Linda observed shortly after returning from America. "I could feel I was living on my adrenaline the whole time. When it was over, all I wanted to do was come back to Scotland. I've already decided that I'm not spending my life on the road. With its incredible beauty, old rocks, moss, ever changing sky and weather, Scotland is good. Very good. And that's all I'll ever want.

"Even though my home had been New York," she continued, "I'm a country girl at heart. I love the isolation and I could sit in a field all day to watch what's going on. We have a very peaceful existence in Scotland. No frills. Whenever we're away from home, we yearn to be back. Sometimes we ride our horses bareback over the hills, and we often go down to the sea to swim. I'm constantly thrilled by simple things, like dew on the grass every morning. It's wonderful living so close to nature. And we don't only like it when the sun shines. There's a special feeling in Scotland even on a rainy day—and the mists make me feel good, too."[1]

For Paul, the return to High Park meant quality time in Rude Studio. He had a new toy—a Rhythm Ace drum machine, similar to the Roland rhythm box Wings had used on stage. Capitol Records had sent Paul the Rhythm Ace as a gift—small compensation for the millions of dollars his records had made the company. Made to play a variety of styles and beats, it had settings for Basic Rock, Slow Rock, Waltz, Tango, Swing, Fox Trot, Rhumba, Samba, Mambo, Cha-Cha and Shuffle, and had a dial that allowed for mid-song tempo shifting. Paul nicknamed the unit "Robert the Robot," and quickly put it to use recording demos.

"I've always liked drum machines," Paul admitted, referring to the device as "he," as if it were a live drummer. "A lot of drummers couldn't get on with them, at least in the early days, but I found that if I believed that he did know what the real tempo was, I'd be alright. It was believing that maybe he'd got it wrong that caused trouble. . . . Once you acknowledge he's got the right tempo then it's like a crutch, you just can't make a mistake."[2]

Working on his own, Paul filled two reels, mainly with experimental solo jams. He gave them provisional titles:

> ***Reel 1:*** 'Dervish Crazy Moog' / 'Fishy Matters (Underwater)' (with tremolo guitar) / 'Second' (soul song) / 'Hey Man' (R&B riff-driven guitar song with reggae-style vocal) / 'Cards Up on the Table' (mumbled rocker) / 'Norfolk Broads' (blues rock) / 'All It Needs Is a Darn Good Song' (short guitar piece)
> ***Reel 2:*** 'Don't You Wanna Dance' / 'E Moog Melody' / 'Super Big Heatwave'* / 'How D'you Like the Lyrics?'

While beavering away at his own projects, Paul kept tabs on the music world, where there was plenty of activity that involved him, directly or indirectly. The Beatles' *Rock 'N' Roll* compilation that Capitol released in May had gone platinum by early July.

The first book-length collection of McCartney interviews was published on June 25. *Paul McCartney in His Own Words*, a large-format paperback, drew on interviews Paul had conducted since 1973 with the London-based American journalist Paul Gambaccini, an interviewer Paul particularly trusted, not least for having helped him crack through the Lennon-centric attitude at *Rolling Stone*.

---

* This jam was the basis of what became 'Old Siam Sir.'

Gambaccini was not the only journalist to hit on the idea of repurposing old interviews. David Wigg, an enterprising columnist for the *Evening News and Post*, whose work also appeared in the *Daily Express* and on the BBC, compiled *The Beatles Tapes* from interviews he had conducted with each of the Beatles between December 1968 and December 1973. Wigg had written to each of the Beatles about his plan to release the recordings, and Ringo sent word that he had no objection. But just as Polydor was about to release the two-LP set, at the end of July, Ringo and George sought an injunction, claiming that the interviews did not represent their current views. But their application was denied, and the album was released worldwide. Paul never commented publicly about the set.

There was news from a precinct normally beyond Paul's reach, as well. Since the 1930s, EMI had been distributing classical recordings made by the Soviet Union's state record label, Мелодия (Melodiya), through HMV in Britain and Angel in the United States. The company was now in the process of expanding its agreement to allow the Soviet label to release recordings from EMI's pop catalog. Until now, rock music had been frowned upon by Soviet officialdom, who characterized it as a symptom of the West's decadence, although bootleg copies of albums by the Beatles and other bands circulated underground, the ultimate *samizdat*.

"We loved the idea of that, that we were getting smuggled along with Levi's jeans," McCartney later confessed. "This was like true cultural arrival."[3]

An album of Paul's music was selected as the first rock album to be released officially by Melodiya. Technically, the album chosen for release was *Band on the Run*, but because the title track was replaced with 'Silly Love Songs,' the album was renamed ПОЛ МАККАРТНИ+Ансамбль *(Wings)—Paul McCartney + Ensemble (Wings)*. The release, EMI cautioned Paul, would not make him appreciably more wealthy: as classical musicians who toured in Russia already knew, fees and royalties were paid in rubles, which were not freely exchangeable for Western currency. Classical players found that they were best off spending their fees in Russia and returning to the West with fur coats, vodka or other Russian goods.

"We get less royalties from an album sold in the Eastern bloc than from a single in Britain," explained David Finch, EMI's controller of licensing services and business affairs. "The Communist way of thinking is that they would prefer to barter their locally produced goods for our records. Other companies have agreed to these terms, and I can remember one who, in exchange for a record license, received a consignment of 50 tons of potatoes. For all I know, they've still got them in a warehouse somewhere. That's not our way of doing business."

But EMI's "way of doing business" was not much different. Typically, the company would license a recording to its affiliate in India, which would pay EMI in cash, and would then press the discs and trade them to the Soviets for industrial equipment. Finch implied, in interviews with the British music press, that EMI was working out a more direct licensing deal for *Paul Mc-*

Cartney + Ensemble (Wings). But for Paul, the symbolism of the deal was more important than the money.

"[The Soviets] have allowed *Band on the Run* to be released," he said when the deal was announced, "so we're very proud of that, breaking down the barriers, cultural barriers, East and West, maybe the twain shall meet." He added that "there's some talk about maybe going there next year. So we might end up—Moscow, watch out!"[4]

Paul and Linda were also honored by BMI during the post-tour summer, as the organization celebrated the composers of the 101 most performed BMI-affiliated songs on the radio in 1975. The McCartneys won BMI Awards for 'Junior's Farm,' 'Sally G' and 'Listen to What the Man Said'; Paul won a fourth, with John Lennon, for 'Lucy in the Sky with Diamonds.'

Lennon, meanwhile, having won his four-year battle with the United States government, was granted a green card on July 27. He now had the right to remain in the United States indefinitely, as well as the ability to leave the country and return at will.

"It's great to be legal again," Lennon enthused. "It's been a long and slow road, but I am not bitter. On the contrary, now I can go and see my relations in Japan and elsewhere. The main thing is that I can travel now. Until today my attorney wouldn't even let me go to Hawaii for a vacation in case I couldn't get back. Whenever I flew to Los Angeles I was paranoid in case the plane was diverted to Toronto on the way."[5]

Bill Sargent's reunion offer continued to ricochet through the columns of the music press, and Sir Bernard Delfont, the theater impresario, joined the queue, inviting the Beatles to perform together as part of Queen Elizabeth II's Silver Jubilee festivities, planned for June 6 and 13, 1977, at Earl's Court and Wembley Arena. "I have spoken to Paul McCartney, and he hasn't said 'no,'" Delfont told the *Liverpool Echo* on July 2. "I think there is a chance."[6]

But despite Paul's soft spot for Her Majesty, Delfont was less sanguine when he spoke to the *Daily Mail* the next day. "It's just possible they may be tempted to re-form because of the honor and importance of the occasion, although it must be said I don't know whether it is very likely. These boys are perfectionists. It is impossible to say whether they would want to work and rehearse together for months for just one show."[7]

Far more interesting to Paul, at the moment, was the Eastmans' latest acquisition on behalf of MPL, Edwin H. Morris Music. Morris Music was a big company with thousands of copyrights, including songs by Harold Arlen, Sammy Cahn, Jule Styne, Jimmy Van Heusen, Jack Lawrence and Johnny Mercer, and acquiring it was a crucial part of transforming MPL from a company that owned a handful of catalogs to a music publishing empire. And it wouldn't come cheap: Edwin H. "Buddy" Morris, who founded the company in 1941, told *Billboard* that including interest (MPL would pay for the company over several years), the cost was expected to be between $9 million and $10 million (£5.15 million and £5.73 million).

Morris was born in Pittsburgh in 1906, and was working for Warner Bros. when, at age 21, he was asked to establish a music publishing division for the company. In the process, he acquired several existing publishers for Warner, including T. B. Harms, which published several Rodgers and Hart scores and much of George Gershwin's theater music.

When Morris left Warner in 1940, he enlisted Lee Eastman, then a young attorney who already had some experience in music publishing, to help him set up Edwin H. Morris & Co., Inc. Over the next 35 years, Morris published roughly 12,000 titles.

But in 1976, Morris turned 70, and told Eastman—still his attorney—that he wanted to sell the company. Eastman had the perfect buyer—his son-in-law. When Paul paged through the list of Edwin H. Morris's copyrights, he was immediately sold: with this acquisition, he would become the owner of countless Standards, including 'Autumn Leaves,' 'Ac-cent-tchu-ate the Positive,' 'Tenderly,' 'Sentimental Journey,' 'Ghost Riders in the Sky,' 'Witchcraft,' 'The Christmas Song,' 'Basin Street Blues,' 'Mister Sandman' and 'One for My Baby (And One More for the Road).'

And there was more! Morris also owned dozens of successful Broadway musicals, including *Guys and Dolls; Mame; How to Succeed in Business Without Really Trying; Hello, Dolly!; Peter Pan; Applause; Promises, Promises; Grease; and Bye Bye Birdie.*

Wearing his Budding Publishing Magnate hat, Paul found the prospect of acquiring E. H. Morris irresistible—but also a little scary.

"This particular company was *the* company, really, in New York," Paul later explained. "My father-in-law knew a lot about [it] and advised me to buy it. And so I had to take everything I'd ever earned off the Beatles to buy it. . . . [It cost] a huge amount of money, as I say, which was like, all my savings plus. So it was a big, big move.

"I really just looked through the catalog," Paul said. "There's a song, 'Tenderly,' and I love that melody so much that I just thought, 'Right, I'm gonna do this,' even though I'm taking all my savings and spending it all in one go. 'Stormy Weather' was a big convincer. The songs that I've grown up with all my life, and I've always been in awe of them. I loved them. And my dad loved them. And all my Liverpool family loved them. So there's a huge heritage."[8]

As he had done when he bought Buddy Holly's publisher, Nor-Va-Jak Music, in 1973, Paul decided to leave the company's administrative structure intact, at least for a while. Chappell Music, which had won the rights to administer the catalog in 1975, would continue in that role, with sub-publishing rights to the catalog in Europe. Morris and his general manager, Agnes Kelleher, would stay on with five-year contracts, with Morris devoting himself principally to developing theater works.

"I had been approached over the years by many individuals and corporations and had resisted their offers for one reason," Morris told *Record World.* "I felt the situation would mean the loss of the relationship between the purchaser and the original owner. I am very pleased with the

McCartney deal because I know that the present catalog will be actively promoted, and new writers will be brought in."[9]

Lee Eastman later bragged that the deal only took him 90 minutes to secure. "We made the deal with a 1½-page contract," Eastman said, "while other companies seeking the catalog spent six months on the deal, all contained in a six-inch-thick contract."[10] Since Eastman could not represent both sides of the transaction, he negotiated for MPL; Alvin Deutsch, of Linden and Deutsch, represented Morris.

Paul immediately had an opportunity to show that he was in the publishing business for the love of music, not as a corporate raider. Shortly after he agreed to buy Morris Music, Paul received a call from the company about a show by Charles Strouse, an estimable composer who had studied with Aaron Copland and Nadia Boulanger, and had written several hit shows, including *Bye Bye Birdie, Golden Boy, Applause* and *It's a Bird, It's a Plane, It's Superman,* as well as a handful of film scores (among them, *Bonnie and Clyde* and *The Night They Raided Minsky's)* and the old-timey theme song to the popular sitcom *All in the Family.* Strouse and his lyricist, Lee Adams, had another show that was then in development.

"Someone from the company rang up," Paul recalled, "and said, 'Look, seeing as you're going to become the new owners, we've got a little show here, which is now in Boston. And we're hoping to bring it to New York. Will you continue to fund it? Or, do you want us to sort of lay them off and say, there's a new owner?' And I said, 'Well, no way am I going to lay them all off! You kidding?' An artist comes in, lays everyone off? That's not my kind of game. I said, 'No, no, *encourage* them, you know, and yeah, of course we will continue to fund it.' That turned out to be *Annie.*"[11]

As much as Paul believed that publishing was the right investment choice for him—and though he was willing to nearly go into hock for the sake of the Morris Music purchase—he also maintained a healthy respect for the value of land, both as an investment and, almost more importantly, as a buffer between himself and anyone inclined to intrude on his privacy. On June 2, through his solicitors, Paul began negotiating with Ingram Alistair Thomson Legge to buy Low Park Farm (formerly known as Skeroblinraid), Legge's 16-acre property bordering High Park. On August 16, Paul filed the paperwork to purchase Low Park for £24,000 ($42,800)*; the sale would be finalized on December 2.

With Wings on hiatus, Joe was spending time in Georgia. Jimmy swanned around London, working on solo material and becoming a fixture at post-concert parties and, as a consequence, a bold-

* Confirmation of the sale price can be found in Registers of Scotland document 89–222, Search Sheet, Country of Argyll, 15555.

face name in gossip columns. Among his solo projects was a single with White Line, a band that included his brother, Jack McCulloch, on drums and Dave Clarke, a bassist and keyboardist who had worked with the Noel Redding Band, fronted by the bassist for the Jimi Hendrix Experience. The disc—'Call My Name,' written and sung by Clarke, backed with 'Too Many Miles,' written by McCulloch and Colin Allen and sung by Jimmy—was set for release by EMI in November.

Only Denny was at loose ends. He had been hoping to use some of his downtime to record a new album—a tribute to Buddy Holly, provisionally titled *Denny Laine Sings Buddy Holly*.

"Originally Linda's father, Lee Eastman, suggested it," Denny said, quickly adding, "it was my idea, a long time ago, to do something like that. I wanted a package album—a set album of a certain thing, not just separate songs away from the group. It was Lee's original idea, but as I say, it's always been at the back of my mind anyway, he just sparked it off."[12]

Eastman was undoubtedly less concerned with coming up with a project for Denny than with showing Paul, by example, the kind of thing a publisher does to increase his catalogs' value while also creating royalty income. It had been three years since Paul bought Holly's publishing, and although Norman Petty had been kept on to promote the music—and Holly's songs continued to be covered—a high-profile release that would focus record buyers' and other performers' attention was always a good idea.

Paul had an idea of his own, along those lines. September 7, 1976, would have been Holly's fortieth birthday, and Paul thought the milestone should be celebrated, so he made plans to kick off "Buddy Holly Week" to honor the occasion. There would be concerts, parties and other events, and if it was the success Paul hoped it would be, it could be an annual celebration.

"I think it's important to remember him," Paul told a reporter, "because not only was he a major influence on rock 'n' roll, but there must be a lot of kids who never heard of him. You have all these weeks, like Litter Week, so we thought we'd have a Buddy Holly Week, so people won't forget about him."[13]

Denny's project could be part of the celebration if it were done in time. His idea was to return to Nashville, where he would work

Artful trade ad for the first Buddy Holly Week

with Ray Stevens and a group of session players. Discussing the prospect with Paul, Denny mentioned a visit to Rod Stewart's 1975 sessions for *Atlantic Crossing*, which took place on a boat.

"I've always loved boats," Denny said, "and thought it would be an interesting way to record an album."[14] The idea appealed to Paul, who had Brian Brolly contact Stevens to present a plan in which Paul, Denny and Stevens would charter and outfit a boat and record Denny's album of Buddy Holly covers. Stevens was not entirely sold on the idea.

"I was very busy at that time in my life," Stevens recalled, "and the offer was to produce the project on a boat that had a recording studio on it. The idea of working with or for Paul McCartney was and still is very flattering since I admire his talent greatly, and if the offer is still open I'd love to get in the studio with him. At the same time, the prospect of working on a boat and not being able to come and go as I saw fit was a little unattractive, and so given that and my busy schedule I reluctantly passed."[15]

Paul, not surprisingly, had a Plan B, and put it into effect as soon as MPL heard back from Stevens.

"Paul put it together on his farm in Scotland," Denny said. "He put these very, kind of, basic tracks together. So I went up there, and he had it virtually done except for a bit of guitar and the voices. So, it was really his album in a way.

"I liked it, I didn't mind it," Laine continued. "It was a little like his *McCartney* album, very similar in feel to that. If you wanna know the truth, I would've liked to have done it with Ray Stevens with all of these other guys, for sure. But these are the way these things go. What are you gonna do?"[16]

Actually, the backing tracks Paul made were more sophisticated than the home recordings he made for *McCartney*, although they retained a distinct do-it-yourself quality. He recorded both albums on a Studer four-track deck. But now he also had a four-track mixer, which allowed him to do what the Beatles did when they found four tracks insufficient: he could make "reduction mixes" to free up tracks for extra instruments and vocals.

For Laine's medley of 'It's So Easy' and 'Listen to Me,' for example, Paul laid down the drums on track one, guitar on track two, piano on track three and bass on track four. All four parts were mixed to mono on track one, freeing up tracks for Denny's vocal on track two, a guitar solo on track three and harmony vocals by Paul, Linda and Denny on track four.

Denny arrived at High Park by the end of July and took three weeks to record his contributions to the album.

Between Holly sessions, Denny and Paul worked on songs for the next Wings album. "There's no pressure there," Denny said of the songwriting sessions at Paul's Scottish hideaway, "just peace and quiet. Sometimes, he'd write a verse, then I'll write a verse. Or I might play him just a fragment of a song idea I've had, he'll react well to it, so we build an entire number from it.

"We are very critical of each other. One had to be, of course, neither of us is inspired all the time. If things don't work out, Paul will say, 'Shall we call it a day?' and we'll have a walk around the farm."[17]

One collaboration was a song Paul had started in Perth, at the start of the Australian tour. Provisionally called 'Purple Afternoon,' after an image in its opening line, "*Walking down the sidewalk on a purple afternoon*," Paul and Denny "just sat down and finished it all and arranged it up a bit,"[18] as Paul put it. By the time they finished the gentle tune, a different title suggested itself, by way of the refrain—"*Silver rain was falling down / Upon the dirty ground / of London Town.*"

They also finished a song Paul had started during the British tour, 'Don't Let It Bring You Down,' a folksy piece in 3|4 time, with a D minor melody that has the simplicity and attractiveness of a Renaissance ballad, and an arresting melodic twist in the refrain—a leap of a major sixth between "*bring*" and "*you*," and a little turn (F-G-F) on "*you*" before dropping a minor third on "*down*."

Both songs were credited McCartney-Laine, but others that they worked on together were credited to Paul alone, including the cheerful 'With a Little Luck' and the folksong-like 'Famous Groupies.'

"I was just sitting around," Paul explained, "and this idea came to me about doing a song about groupies. I thought it would be a nice idea to send it up instead of getting all serious about them, and so, it's a joke track really."[19]

Some of the inspiration was historical. "There's a famous pair of groupies from years ago called the Plaster Casters.* It's not really modelled on them, but it's that kind of idea, you know—a couple of groupies who go around together and are notorious."[20]

Though mostly a fictional tale, a reference in 'Famous Groupies' to a musician who kept a "*Dunlopillo mattress in his van*" was rooted in fact. Often found parked outside Abbey Road Studios during this period, Wings' roadies maintained a portable hotel room that was used by both the road crew and members of the band.

Other songs Paul worked on either on his own or with Denny during this visit included 'Yes Sir, I Will,' 'Twelve of the Clock,' 'How Do You Like the Lyrics,' 'The Pound Is Sinking,' 'Love Awake,' 'Mull of Kintyre,' 'Dress Me Up as a Robber,' 'Down San Francisco Bay,' 'Winter Rose,' 'Find a Way,' 'After the Ball,' and a song Denny started in 1974 and had demoed with Paul around then, 'Children Children.' Using the four-track Studer in Rude Studio, he tracked demos for these, and polished off demos for songs that had been written earlier, including 'Girlfriend,' 'Girls' School,' and 'Café on the Left Bank.'

The McCartneys made a quick trip to the Netherlands on August 19, principally to visit the Van Leer/DeLange printing plant in Deventer, where *Linda's Pictures*—the collection of Linda's pho-

* The Plaster Casters—Cynthia Albritton (known as Cynthia Plaster-Caster) and a friend (known originally as Pest, later as Dianne Plaster-Caster)—were famous for creating plaster casts of rock stars' erect penises. Among their first conquests was Jimi Hendrix, on February 25, 1968. Albritton, who later made casts of women's breasts, as well, donated her Hendrix cast to the Icelandic Phallological Museum shortly before her death in 2022.

tography that they began discussing with Danny Fields back in 1971—was being printed. Landing at Schiphol Airport in Amsterdam, they were met by Jan Slagt, a driver and bodyguard who had worked for the McCartneys when Wings performed in Rotterdam in March.

The visit was kept secret, but even so, when Slagt's black town car arrived at the publishing house at 4:45 P.M., eight fans and a photographer were on hand. Paul and Linda met with Jan Boreel, the director of Van Leer/De Lange, who gave them copies of Rembrandt and Van Gogh books printed there before showing them proofs of Linda's book. The visit lasted only an hour, after which Slagt drove them back to Amsterdam, where they spent the night before returning to Scotland.

On Saturday, August 21, Paul and Linda flew to Knebworth to see the Rolling Stones with their new guitarist, Ron Wood. Wood had played with the Stones on their 1975 American tour, but did not officially join the band until April 1976. Watching backstage, Paul and Linda were photographed speaking with David Gilmour of Pink Floyd. The Stones' audience of 200,000 eclipsed the crowd of 67,000 who had come to see Wings in Seattle.

Upon Paul's return to High Park on Sunday, he and Denny reviewed the tapes of the Buddy Holly album—the title was now changed to *Holly Days*—and declared themselves satisfied, while leaving open the possibility of sweetening some tracks orchestrally in London.

They mixed the tracks in mono as a tribute to the sound world Holly worked in, but the performances were by no means tethered to Holly's sound or the songs' original arrangements. In truth, what Paul and Denny had on tape was a motley bunch of tracks, some clear-textured and straightforward, some with lovely vocal harmonies that magnified Holly's melodies, some woven around the mechanical beat of Paul's Rhythm Ace (which left those tracks sounding like demos) and some with zany touches involving guitar effects pedals or unusual vocal filtering.

"He doesn't really know the technical side of getting a sound," Denny said of Paul as a producer. "He knows what he wants. Paul's got that 'reach out and grab it' sort of attitude. And a pioneer, you know. He's like a pioneer to work with. And that's what I like. I don't like to sort of be working with anybody who says, 'That'll do, man. That's good enough.' I like somebody who says, 'Could be better.' He goes for things that aren't there. He finds them. That's why I like it. And that's a producer. He's hypersensitive to what he wants out of the artist."[21]

By the end of the day, they had established a track sequence:

SIDE ONE (EMI MATRIX NO. YAX.5215)

'Heartbeat'
'Moondreams'
'Rave On'
'I'm Gonna Love You Too'
'Fool's Paradise'
'Lonesome Tears'

SIDE TWO (EMI MATRIX NO. YAX.5216)

'It's So Easy/Listen to Me'
'Look at Me'
'Take Your Time'
'I'm Looking for Someone to Love (Instrumental)'

The next day, Paul and Denny filled five reels with copies of all the *Holly Days* material, plus non-Holly experiments that were recorded during the sessions but not used ('12 of the Clock,' 'Little Mice' and an instrumental, 'Wah-Wah').

Although he was invited, Paul chose not to attend the first British Beatles Convention, at St. Andrew's Hall in Norwich on August 28. According to Dave Chisnell, the self-employed stockbroker who organized the convention, however, Paul had given his seal of approval. "I got the idea for it when I met Paul McCartney in New York on the Wings tour," Chisnell said. "I mentioned it to him, and he thought it was great."[22]

By then, Paul and Linda were in New York, possibly for meetings to do with the acquisition of Edwin H. Morris Music. Their return to London on September 1 brought Wings' summer vacation to an end: now Buddy Holly Week beckoned, as did a second hop over to Europe for another four concerts.

Paul had no plans to take Wings on the road again in 1976, but he could not resist a plea from UNESCO (The United Nations Educational, Scientific and Cultural Organization) to play a concert in aid of Venice. Paul's appearance with Wings would be the highlight of the UNESCO "World Week for Venice" festival, staged to raise money to help revive a city that was in an alarming state of decay, and was beginning to sink into the lagoon in which it was built—a dire situation that began with the Great Venetian Flood of 1966, which raised the water level of the lagoon by six and a half feet.

Paul agreed to bring Wings to Venice for the festival, which would also feature appearances by the sitar virtuoso Ravi Shankar, the Brazilian musician Jorge Ben, the American singer-songwriter Mort Shuman, the actor Peter Ustinov, and Le Chunga Flamenco Ballet. Besides raising money, the festival would bring the world's attention to the city and its unique problems.

Since the eyes of the world would be on the UNESCO concert, Paul asked Brian Brolly to schedule a handful of concerts—public woodshedding—prior to the Venice date. A couple of days after Paul's involvement in the Venice festival was revealed, MPL announced the schedule for the rest of the mini-tour. Wings would perform at the Stadthalle in Vienna, Austria, on September

Buddy Holly left us many memorable songs...
and on the 40th anniversary of his birth
DENNY LAINE
has recorded a couple of his best...
IT'S SO EASY/LISTEN TO ME

Denny Laine, 'It's So Easy' single trade ad

19; Dom Sportova Hall in Zagreb, Yugoslavia, on September 21; on the Piazza San Marco, in Venice, Italy, on September 25; and at the Olympiahalle, in Munich, West Germany, on September 27.

Denny's album would not be out in time for Buddy Holly Week, but Paul persuaded EMI to release a single on September 3 in Britain (the American release was delayed until October), with the 'It's So Easy'/'Listen to Me' medley as the A side, backed with the funky instrumental, 'I'm Looking for Someone to Love.' In the meantime, MPL lobbied successfully for Linda Ronstadt's cover of Holly's 'That'll Be the Day' to be released in August as the first single from her *Hasten Down the Wind* LP.

It was not lost on reviewers that although Laine was the front man, the single was in every other way McCartney's work, as both player and producer, and that as Holly's publisher, he had an interest in the single's success. The reviews were generally brutal:

> *What a terrible waste of time and talent. . . . It may well be in Paul McCartney's vested interests to gain mileage out of Buddy's publishing, but if he was so intent on recording this material then why not with Wings? Indeed, though McCartney is credited as producer, the same kind of care and attention that one expects from Wings product isn't apparent on this. OK, so it's a quick one-off, but I'd much prefer to hear Denny Laine singing something that will enhance his career. He can't go on singing 'Go Now' for eternity.*[23]
>
> *Roy Carr*, NME

> *Yuck! Even backed with Wings' genius this single is redundant when you can buy four original Buddy Holly tracks for 70p.*[24]
>
> *Carolyn Coon*, Melody Maker

A remake of the old Buddy Holly tune by Denny Laine (lead guitarist of Wings). Clean production is provided by Paul McCartney, with Paul and Linda on backup vocals. How can it go wrong? Expect instant adds on both FM & AM playlists.[25]

Uncredited, Cash Box

The upbeat prognostication in *Cash Box* notwithstanding, the disc got little airplay, and although it found a place on the *Record World* chart for four weeks, peaking at No. 121, it did not make the *Billboard* Hot 100, nor did it breach the Top 100 singles chart in Britain.

Still, at the champagne launch for Buddy Holly Week on September 7 at the Orangery, in Holland Park, London, Denny's 'It's So Easy'/'Listen to Me' was among the sunbeams emanating from the Holly legend being celebrated.

Paul, sporting a wax-sculpted version of his *Sgt. Pepper* mustache, presided, and Norman Petty, Buddy's former manager and publisher, was the guest of honor. Petty, who attended with his wife, Vi, presented Paul with a pair of Buddy Holly's cuff links—a gift that left McCartney speechless until some in the press asserted that the cuff links were those Holly was wearing when he died, and that the gift was therefore in questionable taste.

"For bad taste," Paul offered in defense of Petty, "you look to how the person meant it. . . . He meant it with a lot of heart, and that's how I took it."[26]

Paul spoke at the event, telling a crowd dominated by rock royalty that "Buddy was one of the first singer/songwriters I ever noticed. His style was so simple you could easily copy it. Yet no one has ever come close to him. To me, he is a special man. I was just starting when he was popular, and he brings back a whole era. Oh boy, he's terrific."[27] Other speakers extolling Holly's influence were Graham Gouldman, Dave Cousins and Phil Lynott.

One invitee who did not turn up was George Harrison, who said at the time that he was getting over a bout of hepatitis, but whose comments a few weeks later revealed the still touchy, on-again/off-again nature of his relationship with Paul.

"I haven't seen Paul since his party on the Queen Elizabeth [*sic*] a few years back," he said, referring to the *Venus and Mars* wrap party on the *Queen Mary*. "That's the only time you see him, anyway, when he's having a big party. Who wants to be invited to a party of Paul's, and you walk in and find yourself another statistic in a pop paper? They have all these camera people to show who came to his party . . . I don't want to meet an old friend like that."[28]

Paul, on the other hand, was entirely supportive when, on the same day as the Buddy Holly bash at the Orangery, Judge Richard Owen, a musically trained opera-composing jurist in New York, found Harrison guilty of plagiarizing the refrain of the Chiffons' hit 'He's So Fine' in 'My Sweet Lord.'

“We pinched ideas from records all the time,” Paul asserted. “There’s nothing immoral or dishonest about it because the imitation’s only a way of getting started. In my mind ‘Hey Jude’ is a nick from the Drifters. It doesn’t sound like them or anything, but I know the verse, with those two chords repeating over and over, came when I was fooling around playing ‘Save the Last Dance for Me’ on the guitar. There’s no mystery involved. Plenty of people who don’t know anything about music can do it.”[29]

Other events during Buddy Holly Week included a launch party on September 9 for Denny’s single at the Zanzibar Club, which Paul attended in Teddy boy dress, and a concert that same evening at the Lyceum Ballroom, sponsored by MPL, in which three bands—Flying Saucers, Flight 56, and Mike Berry and the Outlaws—played live sets, and the Wild Wax Roadshow spun records.

Even as Paul pointed the spotlight at Holly, he and his former bandmates continued to commandeer headlines. Ringo’s engagement to Nancy Andrews was announced in the middle of September, followed by a *New York Times* interview in which Ringo brushed away talk of the Sargent offer, but raised a rhetorical question that suggested he was thinking about what the Beatles would do if they did reunite.

“The four of us aren’t talking,” he said about the Sargent plan. “Others are talking, but we’re not. *Maybe* in a couple of years. And *maybe* we’ll get into the studio. The question is, which way we’d play—like then or like now. If we went out with new stuff, I think it would be better.”[30]

Inspired, perhaps, by Ringo’s comments, Sid Bernstein took out a series of full-page advertisements in the *New York Times*, the *International Herald Tribune* and other papers, couched as an open letter to the four former Beatles, presenting a plan he had been mulling over for the last few months. Ignoring comments by each of the Beatles about huge amounts of money not being sufficient reason to re-form, Bernstein out-Sargented Sargent, dangling a potential $230 million (£130 million) before the four musicians.

Sunday
September 19, 1976

Dear George, John, Paul and Ringo,

You have made the world a happier place to live in. Your music has found its way into the hearts of millions of people in every corner of the world. For almost ten years now, your dedicated old friends, and countless new friends—have hoped, have waited, and patiently watched for a signal from you—that you might play from one stage, just one more time, individually, or together.

In a world that seems so hopelessly divided, engaged in civil war, scarred by earthquakes, and too often living in fear of tomorrow's encore of tragic headlines—more than ever, we need a symbol of hope for the future. Simply by showing the world that people can get it together.

Let the world smile for one day. Let us change the headlines from gloom and hopelessness to music and life and a worldwide message of peace. You four are among the very few who are in a position to make the dream of a better world come together in the hearts of millions in just one day.

The burden of the world is not on your shoulders—we all share that responsibility. This proposal is made for your consideration—only if you can find the time—and the strength to put it together.

We out there would welcome your return.

1. The Plan: Your appearance on one stage; whether you play individually or collectively, or both, would be seen by an audience of millions. Moderately priced tickets would be sold in advance, at every theater, auditorium, concert hall, and arena—where closed circuit television cable could be placed.
2. On the day of the event, ticket holders would be required to bring, in addition to their ticket of admission—a can of food, or an article of new or useful clothing, to be deposited in boxes at each facility. These gifts could feed and clothe an impoverished nation for years.
3. A 'volunteer' foundation or worldwide organization such as CARE or UNICEF could lend their resources to pick up these life-giving gifts, the day after your concert, and distribute them five days later to an area, changing overnight into a nation of hope and life.
4. The Possible Revenues: $100 million from the sale of an album recorded 'live' of this event . . . $40 million from the sale of seats at a moderate ticket price to every closed circuit venue around the world . . . $15 million for TV rights around the world; to be shown the next day, or the next week, free, to all who couldn't buy tickets, the night of the concert . . . $60 million from a movie of the event itself, and an equal amount of footage devoted to each of you—to talk, play, or share in your own way, your lives as individuals—with your friends who want to see you . . . $15 million from the sale of program books and souvenirs.
5. THE TIME: New Year's Day or Easter 1977.
6. The Place: Bethlehem! Liverpool! Or wherever it is right.

Respectfully,
Sid Bernstein [signed]

*Twenty percent of these figures could be directed toward the feeding and educating of the orphaned children of the needy nations.

505 Park Avenue, New York, New York 10017[31]

Paul did not comment on the Bernstein plan until September 27, and when he did, he offered a potted history of offers the Beatles had received and ignored. Asked whether this greatly inflated offer was likely to lead to a reunion, Paul looked into the camera and said, "No, it isn't. I've been saying this for about four years, you know—looking earnest and saying, 'I don't think so.'"[32]

Wings flew from Heathrow to Vienna on September 18, the band split between the Hotel Bristol and the Hotel Kummer, and the road crew staying at the Hotel de France. The setlist had not changed, and the performance the band gave for the 16,000 fans at the Stadthalle was as polished as any of the North American shows. For the Austrian date Paul brought in a new ad-lib: before 'Lady Madonna,' he asked, tentatively, whether there were any British fans in the audience, followed by Americans and Austrians, receiving cheers for each nationality. After the show, the full band gave backstage interviews to Austrian television and radio, the German Press Agency, and a handful of German and Austrian newspapers and magazines.

The smoothness with which the show now ran may have led some of the crew to be slightly too comfortable. Wings made their way to Zagreb, Yugoslavia,* on Monday afternoon, the band checking into the Intercontinental Hotel and the road crew heading on to the Belgrade Hotel. It was the first concert for Paul and the band in a Soviet bloc country, and common sense suggested some wariness. But during the soundcheck, not everyone was as careful as the situation dictated.

"The projectionist ran some material that was somewhat risqué," sound engineer Morris Lyda recalled of the X-rated pre-show entertainment, "and he was arrested. During the course of the tour, I had at least three understudies that were there to relieve me if I should ever fall ill or become incapacitated to the point that I couldn't mix. But we didn't have an understudy for the projectionist. Fortunately, they were able to get him out of jail in Zagreb just before the show took off, and he was able to run the projector."[33]

EMI had an affiliate in Yugoslavia, and Paul's recordings were available there, but Eastern Europe was still largely *terra incognita* for touring bands. Although the Rolling Stones had performed

* Croatia, where Zagreb sits, declared independence from Yugoslavia in 1991.

in Warsaw in 1967 and Procol Harum had played in Eastern Europe more recently, the Zagreb audience would have had few opportunities to hear an artist at McCartney's level.

But the crowd's anticipation, mixed with Paul's eagerness to please—particularly in a part of the world so politically and culturally different from Britain or America—yielded an electrifying performance, and months later, Paul was still calling the concert at the 5,000-seat Dom Sportova Hall on September 21 "our greatest triumph." The audience knew Paul's Beatles, solo, and Wings material as well as any audience anywhere, and responded to even the newest songs with whistling, foot-stomping, shouting and applause.

The highlight, as at most stops on the tour, was 'Yesterday,' but even Paul was taken aback by the response. The crowd had barely reacted to Paul's introductory "See if you know this one," and the song's opening guitar chords. But when he sang, "*Yesterday . . .*" a roar arose that gave way to whistling and did not subside until the end of the first verse, whereupon the audience began clapping in a steady rhythm and sang along for the rest of the song.[34]

"They're just singing at the top of their voices, in English," Ian Peacock remembered. "Paul is playing away, and he's looking over towards where we were all sitting with this *what the fuck?* look on his face. So he gets to the end, stands up, and he does his usual thing—you know, he holds up the guitar. And the next thing we know, he goes back over to his seat, sits down and he starts playing 'Yesterday' again."[35]

The audience joined in again, too, singing and clapping rhythmically.

"It's the first time we played in an Iron Curtain country, and the reaction was fantastic," Paul said when he returned to London. "Any ideas one might have had of Communists standing sternly in grey coats was completely wrong. They were a marvelous audience—they all went loony![36] I did an encore for 'Yesterday' and they knew every word. It was a blinder of a show."[37]

After the show, Velco Despot, the head of EMI's local affiliate, presented Paul and Wings with a Gold Disc for sales of *McCartney* through *Venus and Mars*, and Paul entertained a parade of journalists from Yugoslavian television, radio, and magazines. But the success of the concert lingered in Paul's mind and became a symbol of something larger than a rock show.

"We played in Zagreb," Paul said on the BBC's *Tonight* less than a week later, "and we thought it was gonna be very grey and Communist, and it was the best show we've ever had. They were singing along with 'Yesterday.' So, you know, maybe there could be some kind of breakthrough like that, where young people kind of decide, through getting to know each other through something like music, that the old politics of always fighting each other and killing off the young, and all this stuff—there may be something like that to come out of it, you know? I've got that sort of thing at the back of my mind."[38]

The Wings entourage flew from Zagreb to Venice on September 22, arriving at 4:50 P.M., and traveling by speedboat to the Helvetia Hotel on the Lido di Venezia, while some of the crew stayed at the Centauro Hotel in Venice itself. Building the stage for the concert on the Piazza San Marco, which had never before hosted a rock concert, was a daunting task; in the meantime, the band had three days' liberty in Venice.

"The enormity of this operation has been incredible," Brian Brolly told Pauline McLeod, reporting for the *Daily Mirror.* "There were problems we have never had to surmount before—chiefly the water."[39]

That "enormity" involved 40 tons of sound, lighting and stage equipment, worth about $2 million (£1.16 million), including seven lasers. This equipment was brought to Venice on a convoy of barges. UNESCO agreed to cover the cost of the stage and seating, as well as the hotel bills for Wings and a technical crew of about 70 (up from the usual 45 because of the site's complexity). But the cost of transporting and setting up the equipment was covered by McCartney, who kicked in about £30,000 ($51,600) of his own money to cover the show's expenses and donated Wings' fee, as well as the band's box office cut of about £25,000 ($43,000). Some 350 journalists and six television crews were on hand to cover the performance.

On Friday, the night before the show, Wings did several photo sessions, including one in a gondola on the Grand Canal, during which they were mobbed by about a dozen motorboats full of reporters and photographers. The band splashed water at the reporters and mugged for the cam-

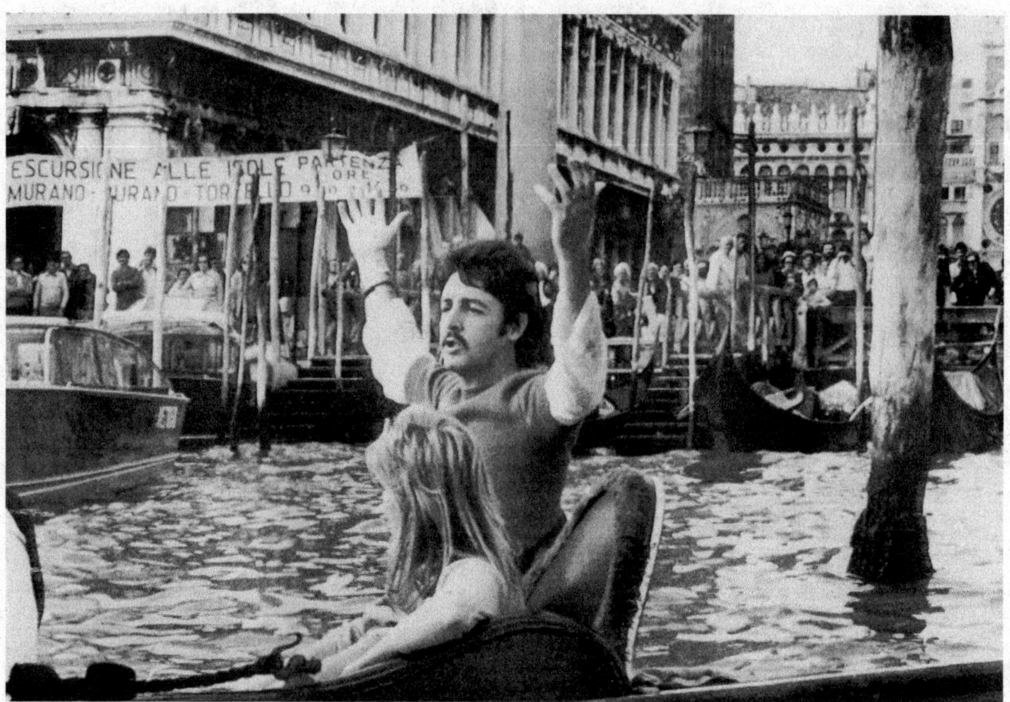

Paul and Linda take a gondola ride, Venice, Italy, September 24, 1976

eras, making what had become their customary "W" for Wings sign with their hands. That evening Paul and Linda were joined by Mike McGear, his wife, Angela, and their children, who had flown in to celebrate Linda's thirty-fifth birthday at a local restaurant.

Because of the extraordinary weight already on the twelfth-century piazza, which is built on wooden pilings driven into the floor of the lagoon, the city limited the audience for the concert to 15,000—3,000 in reserved seats, at £10 ($17.20), and 12,000 in standing room, at £2 ($3.40) a ticket. The police cleared the Piazza at 6 P.M., but by 9 o'clock, when Paul stepped out from the billowing smoke and bubbles to sing the opening lines of 'Venus and Mars,' the barriers had been toppled and some 30,000 people filled the plaza, half of them without tickets.

To suit the occasion, Paul loosened up his stage patter. Before 'Maybe I'm Amazed,' he reprised the nationality survey he had conducted in Vienna, with the audience responding with equal volume when he asked if there were English, American and Italian fans in the crowd. He acknowledged that the audience was more tightly packed than expected by preceding 'Lady Madonna' with the suggestion, "If you've got any room, we'd like you to clap your hands, or stamp your feet, or crack your knuckles." And he dedicated 'You Gave Me the Answer' to Fred Astaire, Gene Kelly and Tony Curtis.[40]

At the climax of the performance, Wings' technical crew deployed its lasers, lighting up the Renaissance Clock Tower in green and St. Mark's Basilica in red.

Geoff Brown reported in *Melody Maker* that the crowd was oddly subdued early in the set. But that changed. "By the time 'Band on the Run' closed the show at 11 P.M.," Brown wrote, "there was enough of a sustained shout to bring Wings back for an encore ('Hi, Hi, Hi'), and it carried over for a second encore, the excellent rocker 'Soily.' As the grand finale, the laser burned out from the back of the stage toward the tall red brick clock tower at the opposite end of the piazza and played games on it, ultimately forming the embroidered 'W' Wings emblem, a spectacular sight and climax which left most of the crowd satisfied at last."[41]

After the concert, Wings repaired to the Danieli Hotel for dinner, while Paul and Linda fielded questions at a news conference. The evening's event, naturally, topped the list of questions, Paul extolling the festival as "a good cause" and adding that "the chance to play in a setting like that was a wonderful experience. We were all very conscious that nothing like this had ever been done before. The whole band was determined to respond to that."[42]

He acknowledged that "the audience were a bit quiet,"[43] and then turned the subject to his recent experience in Zagreb, where he "expected it to be very grey and stuff," but found the audience as appreciative as their British and American counterparts—they were, in his words, "rockin' Commies."

"We've been saying for quite a long time," he added, "we'd like to go to Russia and China, just because they're places behind the Iron Curtain and we in the West don't really—well, *I* don't—know too much about them. But I've got a feeling that they're very like the West, and it's just sort of politics that makes it seem grey and drab. So after Zagreb, we'd like to go and play in Russia next year."[44]

At midday on Sunday, the band and crew packed into a coach for the five-hour journey to Milan, then boarded a flight to Munich, where they arrived at 7:55 P.M. and were taken directly to the Hilton Hotel. A handful of reporters seeking interviews were invited to the soundcheck on Monday afternoon, where band members were deployed to field questions. Denny spoke with the German music paper *Sounds*, Jimmy spoke with *Pop* magazine, Linda was interviewed by *Neue Revue*, while Paul had his photo taken with 14-year-old Regina Israel, the winner of a competition held by *Freizeit* magazine, and signed a copy of *Wings at the Speed of Sound* for her before gliding into some obligatory smiling and hand-shaking with executives from EMI Germany.

If the audience in Venice was restrained, the Munich audience of 9,100 (the 15,500-seat house did not sell out)[45] was energetic and demonstrative, rhythmically clapping and stamping along with virtually every song from 'Lady Madonna' to the end, even if that meant laying back momentarily for tempo shifts in 'Richard Cory' and 'Silly Love Songs.' The band, seemingly inspired by the audience's enthusiasm, responded in kind, with Paul pulling out his best blues growl for 'Call Me Back Again' and 'Beware My Love,' and Jimmy soloing aggressively in 'Medicine Jar,' 'Magneto and Titanium Man' and 'Letting Go,' and covering considerable ground in his 40-second improvised intro to 'Soily.' Denny also had an unusually good night, with 'Go Now' again restored to the setlist. And the horns were at their edgiest. Intermittent feedback problems marred 'Call Me Back Again' and 'Let 'Em In,' but the band powered through them.

After the show, some of the journalists who had been at the soundcheck—including the writers for the German *Sounds*, *Neue Revue* and *Pop*—were joined by representatives from Radio SWF, Bavarian Radio, and the American military newspaper *Stars and Stripes* for a post-concert debriefing, although the questions were unusually inane: "Will your next album be a concept album?" "How do you get an idea?" And of course, "Will the Beatles get back together?"

"We love that question!" Linda said. "It's a new one!"

"I'll tell you the real reason," Paul said, sipping Johnnie Walker and Coke. "It is that I'm in a group called Wings. And that's it—that's the answer."[46]

Back in London, Paul caught up with the music papers, noting the delayed release of Ringo's *Rotogravure* album on September 27 (a single, 'A Dose of Rock 'n' Roll,' would follow on October 15) and more legal problems for George—this time, a lawsuit against him by A&M Records, the distributor of his Dark Horse label, which claimed that he had reneged on an agreement to provide four albums and failed to return a £558,000 ($941,000) advance.

There was McCartney news in the annual *Melody Maker* readers' poll, in which Paul, Wings and their recent releases appeared on eleven Top 10 lists. In the British section, Paul was No. 10 on the Male Singer list; Wings were No. 8 among British Bands; 'Silly Love Songs' was the No. 6 Best British Single; and *Wings at the Speed of Sound* was the No. 10 British Album. On the International list, 'Silly Love Songs' was the No. 7 single; *Wings at the Speed of Sound* was the No. 10 album; and Paul charted in the Male Singer (No. 8), Composer (No. 8), Arranger (No. 7), Producer (No. 6), and Bassist (No. 2) categories.

Paul would have taken note of punk rock's inroads as well: the first Punk Rock Festival was set to be staged at the 100 Club in London on October 2. And within a week, one of Britain's signature punk bands, the Sex Pistols, became Paul's label-mates when EMI signed the band to a two-year deal with a one-year option, handing them an advance reported to be £40,000 ($66,600). But in announcing the signing, EMI's A&R manager, Nick Mobbs, made comments that could be taken as a thinly veiled swipe at Paul, Wings and the brand of family-friendly music they championed.

"Here at last is a group with a bit of guts for younger people to identify with," Mobbs said, "a group their parents actually won't tolerate. And it's not just parents that need a little shaking up, it's the music business itself. . . . For me, the Sex Pistols are a backlash against the 'nice little band' syndrome and the general stagnation of the music industry. They've got to happen for all our sakes."[47]

Recording Sessions

Monday, October 4–Friday, October 15, 1976.

Abbey Road Studios, Studios Two and Three, London; De Lane Lea Studios, Wembley, London.

Playback and overdubbing: Various live recordings.

Paul had recorded a number of his concerts since 1972 in the hope of releasing a live album, or at least individual live tracks. But though these recordings were mixed and remixed over an extended period, only a single live track—the 1972 Hague recording of 'The Mess'—had been released (as the B side of 'My Love').

Now he was determined to release a live album from the North American tour, and he had 24-track masters from all 31 concerts to choose from—a total of 90 hours of material (which must also have included soundchecks, since the concerts ran just over two hours). Jack Maxson and Tom Walsh had overseen the recordings, and Maxson compiled a listing—dubbed "The Bible"—in which each performance of every song was graded on a scale of 1 to 10 to help whittle down the potential selection.

There was also the question of how much music to include. In 1972 and 1973, Wings played sets that ran slightly more than an hour, and when he considered releasing the 1973 Newcastle concert, he trimmed a few songs to yield a single LP. But Paul wanted to release the full 1976 set. That meant the live album would require three discs and would carry a proportionally elevated price tag.

Paul tussled over that, briefly. He did not want to lose potential sales because the set was too expensive. But he soon realized that this might not be a problem. The tour had been one of the year's major musical events, and if he could get the live album out quickly, he could take advantage of the afterglow—not to mention that here was not only a live album by a former Beatle playing most of his biggest hits of the last six years, plus concert performances of five Beatle tunes. It was a comparatively safe bet, particularly if he could have the album in the shops by Christmas.

"Our sound engineer has listened to 800 hours of tapes," Paul told Paul Gambaccini, greatly exaggerating the amount of material that needed to be reviewed, "and selected the top five takes of each tune. We're now going through those five takes. That's five takes of 30 tunes. We'll remix them and make a three-record set. . . . If the two million people who saw the show all over the world buy the record each, we'll be okay."[48]

Because Abbey Road Studios were not consistently available at this time, Paul and Wings, along with engineers Phil McDonald, Mark Vigars and Tom Walsh, shuttled between Abbey Road and De Lane Lea Studios to review the tapes and do some repair work—that is, overdubbing fixes to vocal and instrumental lines where there were flaws, or where band members thought they could improve their contribution. Nearly everyone found something to touch up: Linda was reportedly disturbed by the sound of some of her vocals.[49] For Denny, it was less a matter of fixing his parts as beefing them up.

"You've gotta remember, the main thing about any live album is the feel," Denny said of his overdubs. "Everybody's parts were more or less spot-on, musically—maybe not the harmonies, maybe not every note was exactly right—but the general feel was pretty good. But I had the feeling that it could have been a better feel, a fuller sound, so I said, 'We're gonna go in and I'm gonna put my electric guitar on again.' In other words, to fill it out and to sort of join some of the gaps.

"Because this is what happens: the drum fill might not fit exactly with the bass line, the vocal might come in a bit late, so the one thing that could tie all that stuff together, really, would be a real driving rhythm guitar. I don't know if I did it for the whole album, but I definitely did it to some of the tracks that weren't quite what they could've been, and it definitely helped. I think I did it on most of them. Having a rhythm guitar that's driving all the way really makes a hell of a difference."

Jimmy, Denny added, "might have had to replace a couple of notes, but we kept most of the solos, and we kept most of the bass parts as it was. That's why I did that, otherwise they would've had to have gone in and done a lot of stuff. That's my point. By doing that, it saved them a hell of a lot of [work]. Just to make things flow more. It's not like there were bum notes, but sometimes the feel wasn't right."[50]

At the first overdubbing session, Paul revisited 'Venus and Mars,' 'Richard Cory,' 'Bluebird,' and 'I've Just Seen a Face,' and in the 11 days that followed, the band made their way through the full set.

"It took us forever to get those *Wings Over America* tapes ready for the live album," Joe English revealed. "The keyboard had the most [overdubs], Denny the second most, and then most of the vocal harmonies. Paul had to do a few lead vocals because of a bad mic or something, but most of the harmonies were out of tune. It was an abnormal amount of overdubs."[51]

While Wings were hunkered down at Abbey Road, MPL announced the final dates of the world tour—three concerts at the Empire Pool, Wembley, on October 19, 20 and 21 would bring the tour to an end in Britain, where it began in March 1975. All three shows would be filmed by Barry Chattington.

To promote these final dates, Paul invited Annie Nightingale to Abbey Road to interview Wings for the BBC program *London Scene*. Paul settled into his comfortable talking points—mentioning the "800 hours" of live tape the band was sorting through, and the plan to have a live album out by Christmas. He spoke about the Zagreb concert and compared the venues—and profit potential—in America and Britain, and suggested that performing the full set Wings had played in North America during the upcoming Wembley shows was a bargain for British fans (even though Wings had played nearly the same set in Britain the previous year).

"It's the size of the halls, isn't it?" he asked rhetorically. "There just aren't the venues here that hold 20,000, so you can't make money from concerts in Britain like you can in America. We did think of putting on some small shows in England, scale the whole thing down. But eventually we decided to do the same shows as we did in America. We'll do the full one, even though the country is in a depressive state."

When Nightingale noted that Jimmy's broken finger seemed to have healed, the guitarist said, "I'm playing better than ever with it now."

"Yeah," Paul agreed. "We're going to break his arm next week."[52]

Late on the afternoon of October 19, Wings gathered at the Empire Pool for the soundcheck for the first of their three shows. Shortly after 4 P.M., the Showco team and the Wings roadies were all over the stage and at various outposts in the venue, making sure Denny's, Jimmy's and Paul's guitars were tuned and on their stands, and that Linda's bank of keyboards and Joe's drums were set up the way they liked them. Microphones were tested, cables taped down, and a handful of camera crews—Chattington's team, as well as cameramen from the BBC and ITV, the latter there to record Eamonn Andrews interviewing Paul for *Tonight*—saw to their lighting setups. Robert

Ellis, in his capacity as Wings' official photographer, moved freely around the stage, shooting players, instruments and technicians from all angles.

Out in the arena, Jack Maxson, wearing a red Wings Live sweatshirt and a tan cowboy hat, was at his mixing board, adjusting balances as the horn section ran through 'Silly Love Songs.' Then it was the band's turn—individually, starting with Joe, then Linda, then Jimmy, and Denny, with Paul sitting beside Maxson listening to their warm-ups before walking back to the stage. With an eye on Morris Lyda, overseeing the stage monitor levels, Paul slid onto the piano bench and played the rollicking keyboard part to 'Lady Madonna,' then picked up his Rickenbacker bass so that Lyda could set its levels. With the levels set to everyone's satisfaction, he led Wings through 'Letting Go' and 'Band on the Run.'

The lighting crew had a complaint that would be echoed in some reviews and fans' letters to music publications. Because of Greater London Council safety regulations, the house lights would have to be left on through the performance, diminishing the variety and drama that was an important part of Showco's lighting design. Moreover, the large speaker stacks blocked the views of some fans. (McCartney offered to refund the £3.50 [$5.80] ticket cost to those in affected seats.)

When the band and Showco's team completed the soundcheck, Eamonn Andrews walked out onto the stage, checking the positions of ITV's two cameras and finding a place between the drum and keyboard risers. Paul and Linda walked over to greet him. Andrews asked Linda whether being in Wings interfered with her duties as a housewife, which she denied. Paul added, "She's a good cook, Eamonn, you should come around for a nosh." They talked about the recent American and European shows—Paul enthused about Zagreb again, and wrestled for the camera with one of his bodyguards.

After a news break, Paul noted that *Band on the Run* was about to be released in Russia, adding that he hoped to perform there. Representatives from Tass and Soviet radio, he added, would be at the second Wembley concert to check him out. When Andrews asked the expected Beatles reunion question, Paul was ready: he reprised the Muhammad Ali–style poem he first used backstage in Cleveland, this time adding a new couplet: *"An' if you ask it jus' once more, I think I'll have to break your jaw."*

Wings repaired to a dressing room for their BBC interview, Paul stopping along the way to exchange his light blue dress shirt for a colorful T-shirt, but retaining his sport coat. He was in a playful mood: asked whether the world tour had had any effect on the group, he said, "We're a lot tighter," adding, "it's all the drink." When the interviewer wondered whether they were nervous about playing for a London audience, Joe responded, "After 62 concerts, you're not *too* nervous."[53]

Three hours later, Wings were onstage before a crowd of 8,000, clouds of dry ice and bubbles billowing from behind and around the sides of the band. All three Wembley shows were sold out, and each night Wings glided easily through their thoroughly practiced set, with Paul, comfortable before his home audience, giving his song introductions an easygoing ad-libbed quality.

But the patter, by now, was nearly scripted. 'You Gave Me the Answer' remained dedicated to Astaire and Kelly, but on the first night the actor Victor Spinetti (who appeared in *A Hard Day's Night*, *Help!* and *Magical Mystery Tour* and was in the audience) was added to the dedication list; on the second he added the British footballer and television personality Jimmy Hill, reverting to just Astaire and Kelly on the third night. At the October 21 show, Paul asked the crowd to supply bird sounds before 'Blackbird,' unleashing the sound of 8,000 whistles and warbles. And because Brian Brolly was celebrating his birthday that evening, birthday wishes were conveyed before 'Go Now' and later in the form of a cream pie in the face during a post-concert party backstage.

The reviews of the three Wembley shows were rapturous, overall, the occasional barbs mostly putting Wings' elevated performance level in high relief. But they also pointed up elements that made Wings less of a band than a superstar-plus-sidemen, and they sometimes skewered the wholesomeness of the McCartneys, Wings and even their audiences, a quality considered outside the self-defining ethos of the rock world.

"The sound is excellent," Jonh Ingham wrote in *Sounds* about the October 19 show. "Paul's playing is a dream, ably matched by Joe, who is consistently the most exciting person on stage. Denny is a competent rhythm support, and Jimmy makes all the right noises without actually challenging Paul. This is the most annoying feature of the evening: no one challenges Paul's supremacy, no one pushes him (and the band) into taking risks, taking that step beyond excellent playing and recreation into innovation. . . . The audience is a mixture of young and middling, nearly all representatives of clean living."[54]

Covering the Wembley opener for the *Guardian*, Robin Denselow recalled catching Wings' first European concert, in 1972, and finding it "one of the most depressing almost embarrassing concerts I can remember." But the Wembley show was different. "[Wings] played non-stop for more than two hours and gave one of the happiest, most exhilarating, and most brilliant rock concerts London has seen in recent years.

"It was a show so well executed, so well performed, so well lit, and with such excellent sound, that one came out with all the old enthusiasms for McCartney as one of rock music's few true geniuses rekindled. Above all, he was to be admired for his courage in sticking with Wings (and in keeping a now musically improved Linda in the band) while they slowly built up to this peak. To be an ex-Beatle can be a massive disadvantage, as well as advantage, and this concert was remarkable because almost all the material was post-Beatles and all of it compared well with the few inevitable Beatles classics that he threw in."[55]

Reviewing the second of the three Wembley shows in *Melody Maker*, Chris Welch lamented the difference between hearing the band in an intimate space, as he had done during the tour's first leg, and hearing them in a large arena.

"I recalled seeing the band in a relatively small cinema in Wales last year," Welch mused, "when they played a tight, trim show, and the atmosphere was *absolute magic*, as Billy Connolly might say. The songs were the same and the band were the same, but then the audience was raving, and the band were cooking. The Empire Pool induced the feeling we were watching some distant event, an ice spectacular, glamorous but cold."[56]

For the final night at Wembley, a dozen of McCartney's relatives were bused down from Merseyside. Other friends of the McCartneys who turned up for the final show, as well as the world tour wrap party laid on by EMI, included Elton John and his lyricist, Bernie Taupin, Kiki Dee, Lynsey de Paul, Victor Spinetti, John Conteh, Cliff Richard, Mike McGear, Steven Tyler of Aerosmith, Andy Mackay and Phil Manzanera of Roxy Music, Lorna Luft, and Jake Hooker of Arrow, as well as all of Pink Floyd and 10cc.

On the morning of October 21, the family contingent gathered at Cavendish Avenue, where Linda cooked a lavish breakfast. She later reflected on that morning in an interview with a Liverpool reporter, contrasting Paul's northern roots with her own background, and again declaring her desire to put some distance between herself and the modern world.

"There we were eating breakfast together," Linda told Derrick Hill of the *Liverpool Echo*, "and there was lots of chatter and noise and that marvelous family warmth that Paul's people generate, and it suddenly struck me how different it was to my own background—happy though that was. I get on really well with Paul's family. I love them.

"I suppose I grew up in a false value world. All my friends still live in posh New York suburbs, married to rich men who go off on the train every morning to make money, lots of diamonds, they're members of country clubs, and so on . . . well, I didn't want that sort of thing.

"To me, the whole thing with people is 'niceness,' just to sit around and talk and be warm. Like Paul's family. But although Paul and I have been together pretty long, I still don't really know how it happened. I tend to think it was a gamble. Paul sort of gambled on me.

"You see, Paul has remained very much the boy from Liverpool. He's kept his own personality and he's someone who enjoys the warmth of his family background. Now, in the middle 1960s he'd been living a 'cold' sort of life in London, on his own, going to parties, dating a different girl every night . . . a sort of superficial world. And I think that finally he began to want a family, and warmth, and I just happened to come along at the right time. He probably thought I was a 'nice' girl."[57]

Having traveled around 100,000 miles to visit 66 cities in 10 countries, and having performed for around two million fans and brought in a reported gross of £6 million ($9.9 million), Wings had landed safely back in London, strengthened by the experience. But though Linda seemed finally to have sharpened her musical chops and found her place within the band, she was making it clear that life on the road was not for her.

During one of their final tour press conferences, a more unusual exchange, occasioned by Linda's mentioning her desire to tour in China, brought out a slight tension between Paul's love of work, both on tour and in the studio, and Linda's desire for a simpler lifestyle. Asked why she wanted to visit China, Linda said, "I like their peasant way of life and their farming. They're not as materialistic as we are. I'm interested in going as a photographer, really. This was all before Mao died. Now that he's gone I don't know what's going on there. What worries me is that all the good work that Mao did with the people—that's what interests me, the way he got—I think, anyway—all those people working together.

"It's funny," Linda added, "but I'm not that interested in money. And everyone can say, 'Oh, you can say that, you've got it,' but I know—because I've done it—I could go up to our house in Scotland and grow vegetables and never long for the big cities, no newspapers, and be happier, I think. Really. . . . Okay, it's crazy—you're really going to laugh when I say this—but I think we should go back to dirt roads, walking to work or riding a horse or a bike. We're covering the world with concrete and not getting anywhere. Where are we going to go when there's no more earth?"[58]

Privately, Linda confessed that she would be happy if the band never toured again. Within the Wings ranks, alarm bells began to ring.

17

SILVER RAIN WAS FALLING DOWN

The post–world tour revelry continued at Denny Laine's home in Chertsey on October 30, when Denny threw himself a birthday party (a day after the occasion). Paul and Linda attended—Paul now shorn of the mustache he had been sporting in recent months—and the McCartneys joined Eric Stewart, Graham Gouldman and Jimmy McCulloch on guitars, Linda Lewis on vocals, Denny on harmonica and backing vocals and Kenney Jones on drums, to provide entertainment.

Soon after the tour ended, Paul received an invitation to perform at a Peace Concert for Northern Ireland, scheduled for November 20. Elton John and the Bay City Rollers were also approached to support the cause. Inviting Paul made sense, given the sympathy he expressed, as an Englishman with Irish roots around the time Wings' first single was released as a plea to the British government to 'Give Ireland Back to the Irish.'

But it did not take into account the degree to which the response to the single scarred Paul, psychologically. Radio and television stations had banned it, and EMI barely supported it. And there was confusion among the student audiences for Wings' February 1972 university tour about whether Paul was supporting the Irish Republican Army. There was also a sense of physical peril, after the brother of Wings' guitarist Henry McCullough had a bottle smashed in his face when he admitted that his brother played on the disc.

He sent his regrets, citing "current work commitments."[1] It was not just an excuse; those commitments began in early November.

Recording Sessions

Monday, November 1–Saturday, November 20, 1976.
Abbey Road Studios, London.
Mixing: Live recordings.

After several weeks of listening, note-taking, accepting or rejecting the suggestions in Maxson's "Bible," and a heavy dose of overdubbing, Paul and the band selected what they considered the best performance of every song on their setlist to create an idealized representation of the North American tour. Paul opted to include Denny's performance of 'Go Now,' although it was performed at only a few American shows, but not to include the 'Lady Madonna' reprise or any of the pre-'Yesterday' gags. Ultimately, recordings from only 9 of the 31 North American shows were used.

Paul named the album for the leg of the tour it represents, *Wings Over America.* The tracks were mixed in the order they would appear on the album (also the order in which they were performed):

SIDE ONE (EMI MATRIX NO. YEX.963)

'Venus and Mars' (Cincinnati, May 27, mixed on November 1, 2, 3)
'Rock Show' (Cincinnati, May 27, mixed on November 2)
'Jet' (Cincinnati, May 27, mixed on November 3)
'Let Me Roll It' (Cincinnati, May 27, mixed on November 4)
'Spirits of Ancient Egypt' (Seattle, June 10, mixed on November 4)
'Medicine Jar' (Cincinnati, May 27, mixed on November 7)
'Maybe I'm Amazed' (Kansas City, May 29, mixed on November 7)

SIDE TWO (EMI MATRIX NO. YEX.964)

'Call Me Back Again' (Cincinnati, May 27, mixed on November 8)
'Lady Madonna' (Detroit, May 7, mixed on November 8)
'The Long and Winding Road' (Kansas City, May 29, mixed on November 8)
'Live and Let Die' (Boston, May 22, mixed on November 8)

SIDE THREE (EMI MATRIX NO. YEX.965)

'Picasso's Last Words (Drink to Me)' (Boston, May 22, mixed on November 10)
'Richard Cory' (Los Angeles, June 23, mixed on November 10)
'Bluebird' (Cincinnati, May 27, mixed on November 10)
'I've Just Seen a Face' (Los Angeles, June 23, mixed on November 10)
'Blackbird' (Boston, May 22, mixed on November 10)
'Yesterday' (Unknown venue, mixed on November 10)

SIDE FOUR (EMI MATRIX NO. YEX.966)

'You Gave Me the Answer' (Los Angeles, June 23, mixed on November 12)
'Magneto and Titanium Man' (Boston, May 22, mixed on November 12)
'Go Now' (Los Angeles, June 23, mixed on November 12)
'My Love' (Uniondale, May 21, mixed on November 13)
'Listen to What the Man Said' (Kansas, May 29, mixed on November 15)

SIDE FIVE (EMI MATRIX NO. YEX.967)

'Let 'Em In' (Los Angeles, June 23, mixed on November 15)
'Time to Hide' (New York, May 25, mixed on November 15)
'Silly Love Songs' (New York, May 25, mixed on November 16)
'Beware My Love' (Denver, June 7, mixed on November 16)

SIDE SIX (EMI MATRIX NO. YEX.968)

'Letting Go' (Kansas City, May 29, mixed on November 16)
'Band on the Run' (Denver, June 7, mixed on November 17)
'Hi, Hi, Hi' (Denver, June 7, mixed on November 17)
'Soily' (Denver, June 7, mixed on November 20)

At the final mixing session, on November 20, stereo mixes were also made of tracks listed as 'Denny's Laugh' and 'Various Stages of Madness,' but these were not used. With the mixing complete, the tracks for the triple LP were compiled for mastering, which took place on November 23. To take advantage of the holiday season, EMI would issue the album in Britain and America on December 3.

—

After the mixing session on November 4, all of Wings attended the British premiere of Led Zeppelin's concert film *The Song Remains the Same*—a production that was filmed at shows in 1973 and had been in the works nearly as long as *The Bruce McMouse Show.* At the after-party at the Floral Hall in Covent Garden, guests consumed fish and chips, with ale from Wolverhampton, while being entertained by clowns, acrobats, men on stilts, and drag queens, not to mention Peter Grant, Led Zeppelin's manager, punching out a photographer.

Save for a patchwork ten-minute prologue—which features everything from a reading of *Jack and the Beanstalk* to a *Godfather* pastiche—*The Song Remains the Same* is essentially a concert film, Led Zeppelin's near two-hour 1973 set, uninterrupted. For Paul, who was still forming a plan for the footage that Gordon Bennett and a string of American film crews had captured, the evening was as much business as pleasure.

Twenty-four hours later, with the creative cogs still turning, the McCartneys arrived in Liverpool for bonfire night—Paul's first visit to Merseyside since Jim's passing.

Luckily, distractions were plentiful. 'Let 'Em In' had just been certified for a Gold Record, and the music press was reporting on the November 5 release of the soundtrack album for *All This and World War II*, Susan Winslow's film built of World War II newsreel footage with a soundtrack devoted entirely to covers of Beatles tunes. Two of them—Rod Stewart's version of 'Get Back' and Frankie Laine singing 'Maxwell's Silver Hammer' (both written by Paul)—were issued as a single a week later.

Also on Bonfire Night, EMI released 'Call My Name,' the single Jimmy McCulloch and White Line recorded during the summer. The band had no management and given that its lead guitarist was a member of Wings, it was unlikely to undertake an extensive tour. But White Line played casual gigs in London pubs, and there was always the possibility, if the disc was a hit, that Jimmy might reconsider his priorities.

"I played Paul a copy of the single to see what he thought," McCulloch said when the single was released, "and he said, 'You might well have a hit there.' There is a lot of freedom within Wings itself. Everyone is working on their own projects as well as the band's. It's more fun that way.

"Wings are pretty close; I've been with them now for three years and they've gone by so fast, it proves how good it is. We sit down and tackle things. Wings is a very open band. Likewise White Line have a lot of good ideas—not all of which will surface, but you have to pick the right songs to release. You have to be proud of it rather than just knock something out. When we took the two songs to EMI they thought they were good enough for two singles and have something else done for the B sides, but we wanted the two strong numbers together."[2]

Despite the Wings connection, the single failed to make the Radio 1 playlist and did not chart in Britain or America. EMI scrapped the planned second single. McCulloch may have downplayed the White Line project in the press, but it was clear to those around him that his lack of solo recognition stung.

"He explained to me, he wanted to be a star," said Morris Lyda. "And he thought that [Wings] was his launching platform. I guess in the end, he was very disappointed that it wasn't."[3]

George Harrison also sprang back into the news after being off the radar for some time. The same weekend McCulloch's single was released, the British music press reported that Harrison had settled his disputes with A&M Records out of court, and that his new album, *Thirty-Three & 1/3*, would be released by Warner Bros. Records on November 19. At the same time, EMI was readying *The Best of George Harrison*—a shameless bit of catalog exploitation, bringing together seven of his Beatles songs and six early solo recordings for release on November 26.

And in late November, *Record Mirror & Disc* picked up on one of Paul's occasional comments about Linda recording her own album, suggesting that it would be released in the coming year. No sessions for such an album were planned, however; it remained an entry on Paul's list of projects he hoped to complete . . . sometime.

But another element in Paul's ongoing battle to win respect for Linda was finally coming to fruition: *Linda's Pictures*, published on December 2 by Jonathan Cape in the UK and Alfred Knopf in the US. Included among the 112 monochrome and 67 color photos were shots from the Rolling Stones 1966 floating press conference that started her photography career, as well as Buffalo Springfield; the Beach Boys; Ray Charles; Crosby, Stills and Nash; the Jefferson Airplane; B. B. King; Simon and Garfunkel; Cream; the Who; the Yardbirds (Jimmy Page era); the Mamas & the Papas; Jimi Hendrix; Janis Joplin; Jim Morrison; Bob Dylan; and, of course, the Beatles and Wings, plus non-rockers like Dustin Hoffman, Steve McQueen, and Willem de Kooning, and artsy shots from Scotland and London.

That most of the rock portraits predated her time with Paul, and quite a few had been published in *Rolling Stone* and other rock magazines, underscored her bona fides for anyone who hadn't paid attention to photo credits back then. Linda gamely promoted the book, giving interviews to the *New York Times* and other publications on both sides of the Atlantic, and appearing on the BBC's *Tonight*.

Press copies dealt with another old myth: along with the promotional materials, each copy was packaged with a note pointing out that Linda had no connection to the Kodak Eastmans. She was still asked about that occasionally; the note was intended to head off the error in reviews.

"I don't even use Kodak film, if you want to know the truth,"[4] Linda later confided to an interviewer.

Terry O'Neill, the fashion and celebrity photographer, was unequivocally enthusiastic in his review for *Melody Maker*. "I had heard many varying opinions about Linda McCartney's book," he wrote. "(a) 'It is amateurish'; (b) 'Being Paul McCartney's wife gives her easy access to the subjects'; (c) 'Who'd pay £7.50 for that!'; (d) 'If she wasn't who she was it would never have seen the light of day,' and so on. . . . However, I was very pleasantly surprised and can only take my hat off as one professional to another. Well done!"[5]

The press was now also getting wind of Paul's nascent collaboration with Gene Roddenberry. The possibility of a Wings film directed by Roddenberry was mentioned in both *Record Mirror & Disc* and *Melody Maker* as something that might materialize in 1977. Roddenberry visited London in November, while the live album was being mixed, and held further discussions with Paul. Jimmy McCulloch went so far as to tell *Melody Maker* that the film was about an invasion by space aliens, adding that "everyone's very excited about it, and it's the band's number one project at the moment."[6]

Intent as always that his album covers be more than just a bit of cardboard to hold the records, Paul began discussing ideas for *Wings Over America* with Aubrey Powell during the tour, and kicked the discussions into high gear during the production of the album. With Robert Ellis and Powell snapping rolls of film at every show, and Humphrey Ocean sketching every aspect of the tour, there was no shortage of visual material.

But Paul was open to the possibility of random events pushing him in different directions. One such event was the appearance, during the summer, of a young freelance artist, Jeff Cummins, who called MPL looking for work. Fresh out of school in 1974, he worked for advertising agencies in Surrey and Hartford for two years before going freelance, and in recent months he had done illustrations for *Kung Fu Monthly* and for the poet and publisher Felix Dennis. What he really wanted, though, was to make paintings that would be used as album covers. Filled with both confidence and gumption, he called MPL and asked to speak with Paul McCartney's manager. When Brian Brolly took the call, Cummins said, "Look, I want to do album covers—can I come in with a portfolio?"[7]

Brolly agreed to see Cummins, and after paging through his work, he offered the young artist a trial—a cover for *Thrillington*, the orchestral version of the *Ram* album that had been sitting on a shelf ever since it was recorded in 1971. Paul had conceived the project shortly after *Ram* was completed and had engaged Richard Hewson to write the arrangements and conduct the sessions (with Paul as producer),* although the plan was to release the album not under Hewson's name, but as the work of Percy "Thrills" Thrillington, a fictional persona dreamed up by Paul and Linda.

Now Paul wanted to revive the long-dormant project, and although Aubrey Powell of Hipgnosis would be the art director, there had been only the vaguest discussions of its jacket art, so Cummins's appearance was timely.

As his audition, Cummins created a set of sketches that impressed Brolly sufficiently that he sent the artist to Hipgnosis to meet with Powell. As a connoisseur of album art, Cummins knew and admired Hipgnosis's work, and he and Powell hit it off instantly. Seeing promise in Cummins's portfolio and *Thrillington* sketches, Powell contracted Cummins to create the *Thrillington* cover, and offered him freelance work on other projects. MPL would retain ownership not only of the original *Thrillington* artwork, but of Cummins's sketches as well.

As he beavered away at *Thrillington* and other Hipgnosis assignments, Cummins heard from Brolly that there might be some work for him on *Wings Over America*. What Paul wanted was a

* The arrangements and recording sessions are discussed in detail in *The McCartney Legacy: Volume 1, 1969–1973.*

painting of the band onstage, based on Ellis's photographs. Powell went to Cavendish Avenue to select the shots with Paul, from dozens that Paul had spread across the floor of his music room.

"In the end, he had to choose one of each [musician]," Cummins recalled, "and when I was briefed by Po on these photos, he just said, 'try to make it look like the show, with all the lasers and explosions, and all the gear.'" Cummins was given ten days to complete the artwork. "It was just mad," he said, "and I literally just worked through. I used to work quite long hours anyway, but I had to cut a lot of corners. But it all worked out."[8]

Cummins's painting, based on Ellis's stage shots of each player, had an almost photographic precision, but the composite portrait of the band was a fantasy—Wings are in a configuration that never occurred onstage: Paul is seated with his 12-string Ovation acoustic guitar, singing into a microphone, his left arm raised; Linda, to his left (the viewer's right), stands behind her bank of keyboards, her hands in the air exhorting audience to clap along; Joe, to Paul's right, bashes away at his kit; Denny sings harmony while playing his double-neck guitar; and Jimmy strikes a power chord. The horn section is seen in shadow over Jimmy's right shoulder.

"Po took the painting to Paul," Cummins said, "and the next time I saw him, I asked, 'What was his reaction?' Paul apparently said, 'Fab gear trip.' I asked, 'Is that good?' and Po said, 'Yeah, I think so.' So that was it—'Fab gear trip.' I've been calling [the painting] that ever since."

Paul was sufficiently taken with the painting to consider using it as the album's front cover.

"I said to Paul, 'Honestly, I don't think it's good enough for the outside cover, I really don't,'" Powell remembered. "We had a long conversation about it and he kind of agreed that perhaps it would be better to do something else. And I said, 'But I have an idea which is based on something that struck me, flying around on a private jet.'"[9]

Powell had already made drawings and taken photographs to further this idea, which was to use a section of the BAC 111 fuselage, with its door cracked open and a blaze of light emerging from it. Paul was immediately won over when Powell showed him his drawings. "I love it," Paul told him. "Let's do it."

"I took lots of images of the [jet], and we put together a collage," Powell said. The collage gave him a composite close-up of the fuselage long enough to wrap around both sides of the album cover. Powell sent this to Richard Manning, who worked for Hipgnosis as a photo retoucher, and had him, as Powell puts it, "paint it in what I call a highly stylized, realistic way. And then we hand tinted it all."

In the end the fuselage on the album jacket had a more striking color palette than the actual jet, which was white. On the album jacket, the jet body is metallic gray, captured from close enough to see the jet's rivets, with sharply delineated red, black and blue stripes, as well as ripples and blemishes that suggest the miles the tour covered.

Powell's original idea for the inner gatefold was to use a selection of Ellis's photos that captured Wings in the context of the large arenas and stadiums they played in, showing both the band at work and the vastness of the settings. But one afternoon, while Cummins was working at Hipgnosis's Denmark Street studio, Linda called Powell to deliver Paul's veto and his desire to use the Cummins painting in the gatefold instead.

"Po came over to me and said, 'Jeffery, good news,' and I punched the sky in my head," was how Cummins remembers getting the news.

But the outer and inner gatefold art was only part of Hipgnosis's album design. There was also a poster—one side showed the faces of Wings' five musicians, arranged as if they were on a clock face, with *Wings Over America* at the center, also in a circular design; the other side included ten stage shots by Robert Ellis.

The text additions to the cover were deliberately unobtrusive: *Wings Over America*, printed across the top edge, is the only text on the front cover. On the back, six lines of song titles—a line for each LP side, in small type—are printed in the upper left. The lower left lists the five members of Wings and the instruments they play, with the horns listed under them (Dorsey is not credited for his arrangements, or as the section leader). Paul's production credit follows, with Phil McDonald, Jack Maxson, Mark Vigars and Tom Walsh listed as recording engineers. MPL and Hipgnosis share the design credit, with Manning and Cummins credited for the outer and inner painting; graphics and lettering attributed to Richard Evans and Geoff Halpin, respectively; and the poster credited to Bob Ellis. A catch-all (". . . and a special thanks to everyone involved") follows, just above the MPL logo.

The inner sleeves were gray, each bearing a different size version of the cover's arc of light seen shining out of the jet door from the cover, plus color registration markings. Each of the six disc labels carried a different stylized meter, dial, or in the case of side 6, a thermal map of North America.

"Paul loved the labels, which were all about flying and navigation," Powell said. "That was all Hipgnosis studio work—for once he let us get away with [our own ideas]."[10]

With the release imminent,* Paul directed a 30-second television spot, shot at Elstree Studios. As the camera pans across the exterior of an apartment building, we look in on an architect at a drafting table, a hippie couple dancing, and a young, racially mixed group sipping wine, one of them playing a guitar, all listening to cuts from *Wings Over America.* Finally, the camera pans to a window through which we see a couple asleep in separate beds. "Well," the voiceover tells us, "not *everybody* is into *Wings Over America.* Wings' new live album. 30 songs, three records, recorded on stage in America."

Triple albums, though rare in pop music, were becoming more plentiful. George Harrison had already released two (*All Things Must Pass* in 1970, and *The Concert for Bangla Desh* in 1971). *Wood-*

---

* Originally scheduled for December 3, the American release was delayed a week to avoid clashing with *The Best of George Harrison.* In the UK, manufacturing issues delayed the release until December 24.

stock: Music from the Original Soundtrack and More was a must-have triple album in 1970, and the Nitty Gritty Dirt Band's 1972 *Will the Circle Be Unbroken* achieved classic status among folk-country fans. Record shop bins were bulging with triple live albums by the Grateful Dead (*Europe '72* in 1972), Yes (*Yessongs* in 1973), Emerson, Lake and Palmer (*Welcome Back, My Friends, to the Show That Never Ends* in 1973) and Leon Russell (*Leon Live* in 1973).

But Paul was not entirely comfortable with releasing an album with a triple price tag, and he was defensive when interviewers raised price as a discussion point.

"[*Wings Over America*] had to be a triple in the end," Paul told more than one interviewer, "because what we were doing was the two-hour show that we did, so there was no other way to get two hours on record . . . If we could have got it onto a double album it would have been a double album.

"[I] don't really like releasing high-priced items. I don't. Because I know what I was like when tickets were high and when I was part of the audience. I'd prefer for everything to cost 50p, because, after all, I'm not really in it for the profit, despite what some people might think."[11]

Nevertheless, several reviewers, particularly in Britain, either took issue with the decision to make the album a triple-disc set, or mentioned that they would *usually* object, but liked this one.

Harry Doherty, in *Melody Maker*, argued that the album's length undercut its energy. "Paul McCartney is still the most gifted vocalist in rock," Doherty wrote. "His band is tight and extremely flexible. And Linda is by no means the incompetent she's portrayed as being. *Wings Over America* succeeds in establishing those points.

"Unfortunately, it also proves that six sides is two too many for this 'live' album. While I sympathize with McCartney's logic in releasing the entire undiluted stage set, this collection would have been much more striking and exciting if it had been trimmed to four sides. Instead, then, of tautness from beginning to end, as we could so easily have had, we're presented with an album that, like the stage act, sags in the middle." Specifically, Doherty could have done without sides four and five. "Otherwise," he concedes, "it's a superb album, the best live recording I have ever heard."[12]

In *Sounds*, Hugh Fielder noted that he was "not usually in favor of three-album sets," but that this was an exception—one that arrived just as "my faith in Wings was in need of being restored" after his disappointment with the last two studio albums. "Nearly two hours long," he wrote, "the set makes up virtually an entire Wings concert and those who have seen them live will not need reminding of the quality of their stage show. The material was whittled down from some 90 hours of tapes and the final result is one of the best live albums I've heard."[13]

Size was an issue for Tony Stewart too. "Three albums is going over the top, because by the fifth side no amount of instrumental virtuosity can justify the inclusion of songs like Denny Laine's 'Time to Hide' and Macca's own 'Beware My Love.'" He objected, as well, to the audience reactions being suppressed (something *Melody Maker*'s Doherty admired) and the spoken introductions being trimmed. But he praised most of the performances, as well as McCartney's

Wings, *Wings Over America* album trade ad

ability to "give credibility to what is essentially pop music in much the same way that he did with the Beatles and inject it with such refreshing energy that yet another generation can find it acceptable."[14]

Rolling Stone ran a short, mixed review by Ken Tucker, who praised most of the set as "a legitimate alternative" to the studio albums, noting that most of the performances are "rawer and more driven than the original recordings and, in many cases, much the better for it." But he found the acoustic performances to be "unremittingly maudlin," and noted that Wings songs he had always considered mediocre—'My Love,' 'Listen to What the Man Said' and 'Silly Love Songs'—"successfully resist transcending mediocrity."[15]

In Britain, *Wings Over America* entered the chart at No. 13 on January 15, 1977, and spent 23 weeks in the Top 100, peaking at No. 8 on February 12. In the United States, the album was clearly on many holiday gift lists: it leaped onto the *Billboard* 200 at No. 7 on Christmas Day and spent 65 weeks on the chart, peaking at No. 1 on January 22. Long before it reached the top of the chart—within ten days of its release—*Wings Over America* qualified for Platinum status, for sales of a million copies. It was, *Cash Box* reported in its January 1 issue, the biggest-selling album of the holiday season.

The non-McCartney members of Wings did not get royalties for record sales, but they were paid "artists services fees" through MPL, including three big payments in 1976—£50,000 ($101,300) for *Wings at the Speed of Sound*, $122,000 (£71,850) for the world tour, and $100,000 (£58,900)* for *Wings Over America*.[16] Compared with Wings Mark I's weekly retainer of £70 ($118), a bonus of £500 ($1,250) for *Red Rose Speedway*, and an end-of-year loyalty bonus of £1,000 ($2,500), each member of Wings Mark II earned (in sterling) 35 times more, in 1976, than the Wings Mark I lineup took home three years earlier.

The McCartneys threw a Christmas party for MPL's staff and other guests at the company's Soho Square offices on Thursday, December 16, despite the continuing renovation work at the building. Ten MPL staff and the McCartneys' nearest and dearest—50 guests in total—filled a large room on the second floor, where catering was provided from a small kitchen designed for tea and coffee making. "How the caterers crammed themselves into that tiny little kitchen to cook for 50 people I will never know," Suzy Melville, MPL's 22-year-old switchboard operator, marveled. "The number of times the fire alarm went off was beyond belief. And the fire brigade was very upset that they kept getting called out; by the third time they didn't care if it was Paul McCartney or not, they'd

* The payment denominations were governed by whether the fees were paid by MPL's London or New York offices.

had enough of it. And then, of course, somebody decided to light the Christmas pudding! And off it went again."[17]

Typically, the McCartneys spent Christmas in New York, visiting Linda's family, and New Year's in Liverpool. But Jim's death made the Liverpool tradition less of a priority, and having spent considerable time in New York during the spring, they opted to skip the holiday visits this time. Paul and Linda caught Rod Stewart's show at the London Olympia on December 23, and the next day, girls in tow, they hopped on a plane to Puerto Vallarta, Mexico, where they remained through New Year's Day.

Their obscure choice of location was meant to guarantee the family privacy, and for the most part it did, but it is virtually impossible for Paul to spend time anywhere unnoticed. Strolling through town, Paul and Linda discovered Alberto's, a family-owned jewelry-making business started by Roberto Ballesteros Rico and run by his son, the store's namesake. Enchanted with Alberto's silver work and original designs, Paul bought several pieces of jewelry and spent some time at the shop creating his own designs and making jewelry for Linda, who photographed him at work, Alberto hovering over him offering guidance. Linda signed the photo, and Alberto displayed it proudly in his shop.

The family flew to Los Angeles on January 2, and stayed at the Beverly Hills Hotel. For the moment, the spotlight was on Linda, who had agreed to a few interviews to promote her photography book.

In New York, meanwhile, the Eastmans had been discussing the prospect of Paul leaving Capitol at the end of his current contract, with Warner and Columbia courting him most aggressively. Warner had been playing a long game, supporting Mike McGear and Denny Laine projects, but when the Eastmans dangled Linda's 1972 recording of 'Seaside Woman' before Columbia, the label grabbed it, agreeing to release it as a Suzy and the Red Stripes single on its subsidiary Epic label. Paul had MPL ship a copy of the 16-track master to CBS Studios in New York. Neither Paul nor Linda was present when a new mix—labeled the "Eastman Special Mix"—was created on January 5.

Three days later, and half a mile north of CBS Studios, lawyers for Allen Klein's ABKCO Industries and for each of the Beatles worked late into the night at the Plaza Hotel, hammering out an agreement that would bring an end to four years of lawsuits, in which Klein claimed £20 million[18] ($34,100,000) in unpaid fees and commissions, as well as unrecouped expenses incurred on behalf of Apple. Curiously, the relationship between Klein and Apple ended much the same way it began—with John, Yoko and Klein having dinner together.

"Shall I tell you how it all ended after all these days, years and weeks?" Klein asked rhetorically. "Yoko Ono came up to me and said, 'I have two questions. One: if we settle now, is that an end to it all?' 'Yes.' Then she asked, 'And secondly, will you come and have dinner with John and myself tonight?' Well as you can imagine, we went off and got very merry. That was how we boiled it all down. But it would never, never have happened if Yoko had not been there to calm us down and be a total diplomat when the going got tough and rough. That woman is extraordinary." When the settlement was announced, Klein released a statement praising Yoko's "tireless efforts and Kissinger-like negotiation brilliance."[19]

After the Lennons and Klein negotiated the broad terms of the settlement, the lawyers saw to the contractual formalities, which involved Apple paying Klein £2,912,644 ($4,966,470), after Klein paid Apple £1.5 million ($2.6 million) in costs, with each side paying its own legal fees, estimated at about £10 million ($17 million) together: in the end, neither side did as well as the lawyers.

Paul and Linda returned to Britain in time for the *Daily Mirror* Rock and Pop Awards at Bingley Hall in Stafford, on January 9, where the rest of Wings joined them. The band picked up awards, presented by Sir Richard Attenborough, for Best Pop Group and Best Rock Group, and Paul took home the Best Group Singer prize. Paul was also named the No. 2 Instrumentalist (guitarist Eric Faulkner, of the Bay City Rollers, took the top prize), and *Wings at the Speed of Sound* was named the No. 2 album (after the Bay City Rollers' *Dedication*). The ceremony was broadcast on ITV on January 27.

Wings did reasonably well in the turn-of-the-year awards season. *Sounds* offered a year-end

Wings attend the *Daily Mirror* Pop Club awards, January 9, 1977

rundown of the albums issued that year, and though *Wings at the Speed of Sound* was called "a major disappointment: a fast seller," the notation for *Wings Over America* was, "Now that's more like it—*triple* live album."[20] Both *Sounds* and *Record Mirror* listed *Wings at the Speed of Sound* as the year's No. 4 album (No. 1 was Abba's *Greatest Hits*), and 'Silly Love Songs' was No. 23 on the singles chart.

Before January was out, the Grammy nominations were announced. Wings were frustratingly underrepresented, given that they had released two albums and several singles in 1976: only 'Let 'Em In' was nominated, for Best Arrangement Accompanying Vocalists. Paul also turned up in the *Sunday Mirror*'s list of Britain's best-earning pop musicians, on January 30: he placed third, after Elton John and Led Zeppelin.

When *Record Mirror* published its Readers' Poll results in its February 12 issue, Paul was No. 2 among songwriters and No. 7 among male singers, while Wings were No. 3 among group and No. 2 among live groups. *Wings at the Speed of Sound* was voted the No. 8 album of the year, and 'Silly Love Songs' was the No. 2 single. *Sounds* published its Readers' Poll a week later, with Paul listed as No. 7 among musicians and No. 5 among bassists. Wings were voted the No. 9 group.

Few of these prizes involved ceremonies and personal appearances, but Paul and Linda stopped in at the Grosvenor House Hotel on February 4 for the Capital Radio Awards, listeners having voted to give the Best London Concert Award to Wings for their Wembley shows. An unfortunate interviewer who caught up with Paul at the ceremony asked him where he got the energy to keep performing, to which he responded, "It's the drugs, love," adding, "Where do you get the energy to ask such stupid questions?"[21]

Four days after the *Daily Mirror* awards, on January 13, Joe English was back home in Georgia, where he married Dayle Betts in a ceremony at City Hall in Forsyth, Georgia, 60 miles south of Atlanta. The newlyweds had a small reception at their house, and then took off on a road trip in Joe's latest purchase, a Jeep CJ5. The wedding was an item in the premiere issue (February/March 1977) of *Club Sandwich*, a new magazine created for the members of Paul's fan club.

And then it was time once again for a high-stakes Beatles reunion offer, this time from boxing champion Muhammad Ali, who appeared not to have heard about Paul channeling his style and accent in his reunion denials. Ali had joined forces with two businessmen, Joel Sacher and Alan Amron, to create the "International Committee to Reunite the Beatles," which was predicated on the notion that if the Beatles could not be lured with money, perhaps getting them involved in a cause might work. The plan was to present a concert that would raise an estimated $200 million (£120 million), which would be used to create a fund to help clothe and feed the poor, particularly children, around the world.

"I don't need the money and neither do the Beatles," Ali told the *New York Daily News* for a story that appeared on January 15. "The idea is to create this fund and to help people develop a quality of the heart." He added, "It would be a personal joy to see them together again. The man who helps unite the Beatles makes a better contribution to human happiness than an astronomer who discovers a new star."[22]

Five days later, Ali and Sacher attended an inaugural gala for Jimmy Carter, the newly elected president, an event also attended by the Lennons. Ali mentioned his plan to John, who would not commit but asked Ali to get in touch. But Paul made it clear, through the Eastmans, that the plan was a nonstarter—*"If that question doesn't cease, Ain't no-one gonna get no peace!"*

It must have been some relief to Paul that when a reporter for the *Daily Mail* called, just as word of the Ali project was hitting the papers, it was not to discuss the unlikely prospect of the Beatles re-forming. Instead, the reporter, Garth Gibbs, wanted to talk about drugs. Although his marijuana busts in Scotland and Sweden had meant turning legal cartwheels to get an American visa, Paul maintained what had been his policy ever since the tussle in Sweden—or, for that matter, ever since the press asked him, in 1966, whether he had taken LSD: answering the question honestly.

"I don't think grass is dangerous," he told Gibbs. "I find whisky is more dangerous. But I do think it is vitally important that someone sat down somewhere and produced a list of the dangers of drugs and the dangerous drugs. Drugs are a reality. We owe it to the children to say, 'If you take this, this is going to happen to you, and if you take so much of this, this is going to happen to you.'" Gibbs spoke with Denny Laine as well, who added, "There are a lot of pressures in any creative business and people do tend to take stimulants."[23]

By late January, sales of Paul's latest record also needed a shot in the arm. With *Wings Over America* selling well, both EMI and MPL were determined to keep it that way as long as possible. It was decided early on that this was a chance to rectify what many of Paul's fans, as well as some Capitol executives, regarded as a historical error—not releasing 'Maybe I'm Amazed' as a single from the *McCartney* album in 1970. Now they had a live version calling out to be issued as a single—and there was 'Soily,' the second encore, which had never been released in any form until the live album.

"It was one of the only songs we hadn't recorded," Paul explained, "and we always used to end our show with it. And people would say, 'What's that song?' So we thought we'd put it on the single because we're trying to keep as much unreleased stuff as possible."[24]

Thus the new Wings single, 'Maybe I'm Amazed (Live)' (EMI matrix 7YCE 21791) backed with 'Soily (Live)' (EMI matrix 7YCE 21792), was released in the United States on January 28, and in Britain on February 4. Both EMI and Capitol issued promo discs for radio on which 'Maybe I'm Amazed' was trimmed from 5'11" to 3'43".

Wings, 'Maybe I'm Amazed' live single trade ad

It seems extraordinary that one of Paul McCartney's best songs since he left the Beatles, 'Maybe I'm Amazed,' has never been a single before. It originated on one of his early solo albums. Later Rod Stewart recorded it, and the song cropped up again on Wings' current hit album Wings Over America. *A superb live recording, released this week.*[25]

Anne Nightingale, Daily Express

Macca lets his voice rip and he brings the roof down on an alive "live" recording which is sound-perfect enough to have all those out there in mobile recording units heading back to the studio for good. A hit.[26]

Caroline Coon, Melody Maker

Quite emotional stuff, although the production seems a bit flat. Fab gear guitar solo though.[27]

Pete Makowski, Sounds

One of Fab Paulie's finest hours and a truly majestic cut from Wings' Bird Droppings Over Baltimore triple-decker layer-cake. Almost as good as Rod Stewart and the Faces' unsurpassable in-concert rendition. The hitherto unrecorded 'Soily' depicts Wings toying most effectively with The Feelgoods familiar 'Roxette' ridhem. A true hit. What else?![28]

Roy Carr, NME

This onstage version of one of McCartney's first major solo career ballads is grittier and shows more rock roots than the original tender-and-romantic studio cut. A rough-edged McCartney single would seem to be coming along at the most appropriate time to contrast with preceding releases.[29]

Uncredited, Billboard

With live-recorded singles more in fashion than ever, this version of McCartney's terrific song, just as it was heard on the Wings Over America tour, is right on target. FM stations have been programming this cut for a while, and top 40 should follow in short order with the singles chart not far behind.[30]

Uncredited, Cash Box

Yeah, well maybe we're not amazed. We expected it to be brilliant and it is. Has to be a number one, or I'll eat it. 5 stars.[31]

Rosalind Russell, Record Mirror

It is unknown whether or how Russell munched on her copy of the 45, but 'Maybe I'm Amazed' barely got within shouting distance of No. 1, either in Britain or America. In the UK, it entered the Top 100 at No. 42 on February 19 and peaked at No. 28, a spot it held for two of the five weeks it lingered on the chart. In the US, where it faced stiff competition from Stevie Wonder's 'Sir Duke' and the Eagles' 'Hotel California,' it entered the *Billboard* Hot 100 at No. 59 on February 12, and peaked at No. 10 two months later, spending a total of 13 weeks on the chart.

—

Throughout January, Paul was intent on getting back into the studio to make Wings' next album, but he also wanted the sessions to involve a change of scenery. He considered returning to Strawberry Studios in Stockport, but the studio was booked when Paul wanted to start work. Instead, he planned for a week of recording at Abbey Road Studios in mid-February, leading up to a holiday he and Linda planned to take in Jamaica.

There were other projects to oversee, too, among them the belated release of *Thrillington.* In 1971, Paul and Linda placed a series of fanciful personal ads mentioning Percy Thrillington in London newspapers to create a buzz about their fictional conductor, and they went as far as to persuade a random Irish farmer to don white tie and tails to pose for publicity photos as the supposedly legendary musician (although in the end, they decided he did not look sufficiently musicianly, and filed the shots away).

Now they decided to revive the whispering campaign. Paul and Tony Brainsby engaged Cream Creative Marketing Ltd., a Kensington firm, to create and place a more formal series of personal ads, more than 50 of them, in the Classified sections of the *Times,* the *Evening Standard*, and the *Observer.* The ads ran almost daily between February 14 and April 29.

Monday, February 14, 1977

PERCY THRILLINGTON sends his warmest love and thanks to Miss Penelope Telfer-Smallett, Miss Debbie Dixon-Smythe, The Princess Francesca Visconte and Mrs. Ethel Bedworthy on this glorious St. Valentine's Day 1977.

Tuesday, March 29, 1977

PERCY THRILLINGTON despite excessive demands of both social and business time, hopes to support today's DAFFODIL BALL.

Tuesday, April 5, 1977

PERCY THRILLINGTON implores all listeners and readers to adapt their daily bath routine in the cause of health and happiness week. Five minutes a day of bath bumping works wonders for slack posteriors. Your participation is invited.

Friday, April 29, 1977

PERCY THRILLINGTON wishes to inform all his friends that he will be taking an extended holiday in South America following the rigours of launching his first album *Thrillington* and the single 'Admiral Halsey.' In his absence all enquiries should be directed to Miss Penelope Telfer-Smallett.

A fictional conductor needed a fictional staff, so one was created: Penelope Telfer-Smallett sprang into existence as Maestro Thrillington's personal secretary, to deal with his correspondence from her fictional office, Flat 4, Curzon Mews, London, W1. A country pile was invented for Thrillington as well, the address given as Endsleigh Manor, Nr. Newbury, Berkshire. And there was a backstory, which involved young Percy traveling to the United States, where he studied music in Baton Rouge, Louisiana, before moving to Los Angeles to learn marketing, conducting and arranging, and then to London, where he formed his own orchestra and, as if by wizardry, was befriended by Paul McCartney.

They took this as far as having Telfer-Smallett undertake correspondence, on Thrillington's behalf, with EMI Records; an actress posing as her was also interviewed on Capital Radio. And on February 14—Valentine's Day—female staffers at several music papers received a single red rose with an elegant card bearing Thrillington's name in gold lettering.

Cummins had by now completed his *Thrillington* art to everyone's satisfaction. The front cover was a ram with long, curled horns, dressed in a tuxedo with white gloves and seated on a folding chair, playing the violin. Before him is a music stand bearing an open score; the title, *Ram*, can be seen through the stand's black metal elements. To the ram's side is a potted palm, hinting at the Palm Court Orchestra flavor of Hewson's jazzy arrangements. The album's title appears in an Art Deco font in the upper left, with Deco border elements in the three other corners.

For the back cover, Cummins adapted a photo Linda took at A&R Studios during the orchestral sessions for *Ram* to present a view through the glass window of a studio control room, with orchestral musicians seated around the standing ram, who is holding score pages in his left hand and gesturing with his right. On the other side of the window, we see a line of VU meters (the top of a recording console), and a shadowy view of Paul—whose reflection can be seen in the glass. Beneath this tableau is Thrillington's ostensible biography, as well as the track list and a production credit for Percy "Thrills" Thrillington. In the small print beneath that are credits for Richard Hewson (arranging and conducting), Cummins and Hipgnosis (cover art), and Tony Clark (engineering the recording at Abbey Road Studios). The sleeve note—Thrillington's bio—is attributed to Clint Harrigan—the pseudonym Paul used for the *Wild Life* jacket notes.

On March 18, following a reader tip-off, the *Evening Standard* published a half-page editorial on the enigmatic Percy Thrillington, putting to an end any illusion that Mr. Thrillington was anybody other than one James Paul McCartney.

A week before Maestro Thrillington sent his Valentine's Day roses, Paul and Linda invited journalist Judith Simons to Cavendish Avenue for a chat. Simons, who had been one of the most supportive voices in the press from the start of Paul's post-Beatles life, discovered upon arrival that the news the McCartneys had for her was personal rather than musical: Linda was pregnant with her fourth child, their third together.

"The idea of having a big family," Paul joked, "is to have a band. We're providing for our old age—when we're 64!" Then, turning more serious, he outlined the professional ramifications for themselves and Wings.

"It's just going to be a slightly lighter year than it might have been," he told Simons. "We were not planning a tour anyway. We will be writing and recording instead. I suppose the biggest difference the baby will make is that we won't be traveling so much. We do take our children along when we go on tour, but we make it as much like a holiday for them as possible, so that they don't get too much show business.

"We don't push careers on to our children, although they are all good singers. So far we play the records for them—except for Heather who is now a rocking teenager."[32]

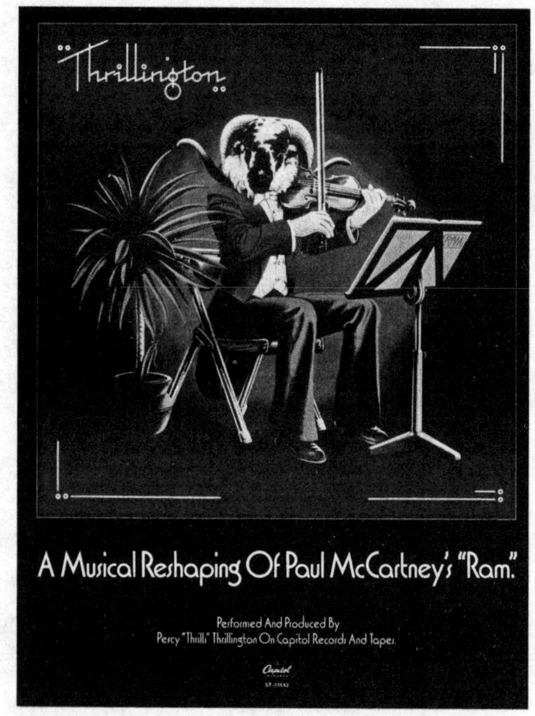

Percy Thrillington, *Thrillington* album trade ad

Linda's pregnancy also meant slowing down the social whirl. The night after the

Simons interview, they attended Bryan Ferry's concert at the Royal Albert Hall but opted not to attend the after-party. But the McCartneys did find time to catch a performance of *A Chorus Line*—a musical now in Paul's copyright portfolio, by way of the E. H. Morris catalog—at the Theatre Royal on Drury Lane.

Around the time the McCartneys spoke with Simons, Paul gave a lengthy interview to Garth Pearce of the *Daily Express*. With Wings having toured the world to considerable acclaim, and with a successful triple-LP souvenir of that tour still on the charts, Paul was eager to seize the narrative and discuss his post-Beatles work on his own terms. So with Pearce as his scribe, he presented "The McCartney Memoirs," a first-person manifesto that ran in three parts, on February 9, 10 and 11, under Paul's byline.

"I would never have left the Beatles if everyone else hadn't," was his stark opening line, and after a brief elaboration, he took on Willy Russell's play, *John, Paul, George, Ringo . . . and Bert*. "In the play," he complained, "John is saying to me, 'For the sake of the group, Paulie, let's stick together.' For one thing, he never called me 'Paulie' and for another it's totally bananas to the way it really happened. . . . It sets me down in history as the one that broke the group up. The opposite is true."

He revisited the various temporary exits from the Beatles by Ringo and George, and John's divorce announcement, and his own post-Beatles tussling over how to proceed. From there, it was on to Wings, which, he argued, had to make their mistakes in public, unlike the Beatles, who had the luxury of developing as a band of unknowns. No fewer than 11 paragraphs were devoted to how hurtful (and angering) negative reviews had been, referring in particular to Charles Shaar Murray's scathing *NME* assessment of *Venus and Mars* (though without mentioning the author's name or the publication).

But he was not without criticism for his own work. "After I heard *Wild Life,* which was Wings' first album, I thought, 'Hell, we have really blown it here.' And the next one after that, *Red Rose Speedway,* I couldn't stand."[33] A brief defense of Linda's place in Wings followed, with the first installment ending on the eve of the trip to Lagos to record *Band on the Run*, under the shadow of lead guitarist Henry McCullough's and drummer Denny Seiwell's departures.

He began Part 2 with the more harrowing details of the Lagos trip—getting mugged and collapsing in the studio—but skipped over the music he recorded there. Edging into Wings Mark II, he reminisced about various aspects of the world tour—getting nervous before performing, taking his children on tour, and excessive partying.

Some of this was propaganda and self-justification, and some was broadly inaccurate—for example, his assertion that Northern Songs was sold to Lew Grade during the Beatles 1968 trip to India; the sale happened a year later. But there are also sections that offer readers insight into things Paul found irksome. His comments about partying, for example, may at a glance seem to counter his consistent argument that marijuana is harmless, but a closer reading suggests that he may be referring less to his own penchant for unwinding with a joint than with Jimmy's and Joe's more serious problems with substance abuse.

"The trouble with the whole scene of pop and booze and drugs," he observed, "is that if you have got any weaknesses they will find you out. You don't realize when you are being one of the lads that it is a hectic pace. You just go out and have a good time. But when you find yourself still doing it at 30 you have got to hang on and say, 'Wait a minute. Do I really enjoy this? Or has it just become a habit?'"[34]

And in the final installment, he aired some financial frustrations.

"In the last two years I have earned more money than I have ever earned in all the other so-called boom years put together," he said, before torching Allen Klein, both during his time running Apple and as the instigator of the recently settled lawsuit. "He's been stopped now, if you can call getting £4 million ($6.8 million) [*sic*] being stopped. And part of that money was mine, which hasn't been reported. . . .

"What was happening with Apple was crazy," he complained. "Anything I earned right up to the LP *Band on the Run* three years ago, went to Apple. All the Beatles ever earned was our living expenses—which admittedly were high compared with ordinary people—and the money which is left in Apple now. We were supposed to have sold 300 million records. If you compute that and say the group should have had 10p (17 cents) a go, then where did that money go? I don't think anyone really knows.

"All the merchandising—the Beatle bags, Beatle talc, Beatle badges, Beatle this and that—Brian Epstein was ripped off so badly. He gave it to a bunch of people who did him silly and we never saw any of that money for promotional material. . . . All of this business made me think: 'There has just got to be an easier way.' So, with the help of Linda's dad I got it all together and formed my own company."

After offering a simplified accounting of the formation and growth of MPL, he launched into a complaint about music publishers' owning the copyrights to the songs they publish—an unusual choice of subject for this mini-jeremiad, given MPL's ownership of a quickly expanding portfolio of copyrights. Specifically, his target was Dick James, the publisher of the Lennon-McCartney catalog until he sold the company to Lew Grade.

"We never did badly," he admits, "and it's a bit much to grumble because we have had a lot of money off him. But compared with what we *could* have had, it's peanuts."

The rest of the third installment is a tapestry of random memories of the Beatle days that were becoming set pieces—how he dreamed 'Yesterday'; the origins of 'Michelle' as a party gag; early compositions like 'I Lost My Little Girl,' 'When I'm Sixty-Four' and 'Suicide'; that he has a notebook with "more than 100 songs written around the age of 15 or 16," which he hoped to dig out one day;

how he and Lennon had tried to write a play about Jesus when they were in their mid-teens; and about how only the four of them knew "what it was really like."

In the final few paragraphs, though, Paul looked ahead, saying that he and Denny Laine had written about 30 songs together, and that he expected to make his *Rupert Bear* film in the near future, his ambition being "to make a better film than Walt Disney" and to supply his own musical score, "a totally new step for me."

"There are so many things left to do in life," he concluded. "And for me, really the success with Wings is only just beginning."[35]

Recording Sessions

Monday, February 14–Friday, February 18, 1977.
Abbey Road Studios, Studio Three, London.
Recording: 'Name and Address,' 'Girls' School,' 'London Town,' 'Girlfriend,' 'Children Children,' 'B Side to the Seaside,' 'Moog & Drums,' 'Evening Jam' and 'Auto Harp & Denny.'
Overdubbing: 'Girl's School,' 'London Town' and *Holly Days* cuts.

Geoff Emerick was again unavailable—this time he was in New York with George Martin, recording a Neil Sedaka album*—so freelancer Peter Henderson was enlisted to oversee a preparatory session on February 10, as well as the first week of sessions for Wings' new album. EMI's Mark Vigars assisted.

The sessions began on February 14, with both Henderson and Vigars curious to hear the start of Paul's next musical chapter—although both knew that with Paul, it was impossible to know whether the first tracks he recorded represented the album's musical direction, or whether that would change over the course of the sessions.

The song Paul began with was 'Name and Address,' a straightforward rockabilly track about an unsuccessful and uncommonly brief romance ("*Our love affair was over on the second day*") built on a simple, three-chord progression, with most of each verse vamped on an A major chord, pivoting to E major only on the final line—"*If you want my love, leave your name and address.*"

"It was a sort an affectionate tribute to Elvis,"[36] Paul said of the song, also noting that it was

* The album was Neil Sedaka's *A Song*, released in 1977 on Elektra in the United States, Polydor elsewhere.

written in London. "It's like a throwback to the old days of just kind of straight three-chord rock 'n' roll; tape echo on the voice and very Elvisy sounding."[37]

Paul felt that it was so well suited to Elvis's voice and style, in fact, that he thought the King might cover it. "I thought I'd try and write one that Elvis could sing. I was just thinking, well, I'll send it to him and enclose a little joking note: 'What do you think of this, El?'"[38]

With Jimmy and Denny playing electric rhythm guitar, Linda on electric piano using an organ-like setting, and Joe at his kit, Paul played bass and sang a live vocal. After filling two reels of 24-track tape, the band agreed that they had a master take. The one they liked best was actually a breakdown, with Paul laughing at the end, but they agreed that "feel" was the most important quality in a parody track like this one.

The track was set aside for later overdubbing, and Wings moved immediately onto another basic rocker, 'Girls' School,' the song Paul wrote in Hawaii using the titles of pornographic movies. Following the same live-in-the-studio approach, Paul delivered a good approximation of Jerry Lee Lewis's chord-pummeling piano style as well as a rough guide vocal, with Jimmy and Denny on electric guitars, Linda on Moog synthesizer and Joe drumming. Two more reels were filled, and a hard-driven master was selected.

Aside from Paul's rollicking piano, these raw early takes of 'Girls' School' were characterized by Jimmy's free-flowing guitar lines. "All the guitar stuff has really come out of my head, except for maybe some part that's really a line in the song," Jimmy said. "I like to sit down and listen to a song, and what comes out depends on how I'm feeling."[39]

Already having an unusually productive first day of sessions, Paul moved on to 'London Town,' a gentler and more subtle tune that he finished with Denny amid the post-tour glow. Two more reels were filled, with Paul at the piano, Joe providing a steady drumbeat with occasional punctuating turns, Denny on acoustic guitar, and Jimmy doing relatively little on electric guitar until the coda, when his solid chording suggested momentarily that the band might launch into a jam before Paul returns to the song's tuneful refrain and brings it to an end. Again, Paul was sufficiently pleased with the results to select a master.

With time left and the band's energy not flagging, Paul pressed ahead with a fourth song, 'Girlfriend.' Paul had written the song in 1973 and had given it a run-through when he recorded a set of piano demos in August 1974. But its Motown-inspired vibe had not suited anything else he was recording at the time, and he had considered sending it out for someone else to cover before it slipped his mind entirely. Having recently run into his lyric sheet again, he decided it might be worth seeing what he could make of it with Wings.

"I had the song from a couple of years ago," Paul said of its origins. "I write quite a bit of stuff when I'm on holiday, because I just feel very relaxed. And Linda and I had gone to a place in Switzerland where we were doing a bit of skiing. Well, I was trying to do a bit of skiing, and

Linda was doing a bit of 'pullder' getting pulled around on a rope. She's just learning stuff, you know. But one evening in the hotel I just started doing that song. And I always thought of it as something that one day I might give to the Jackson Five or something because it's a souly type track."[40]

Paul returned to bass and sang a guide vocal, supported by Joe's light drumming, with plenty of brush and cymbal. Denny played acoustic rhythm guitar, and Jimmy's electric rhythm guitar part was built around funky figures in the style of the backing on a Chic record. The band filled a single reel with takes of 'Girlfriend' before agreeing on a master backing track.

When Wings returned to Abbey Road on February 15, they devoted most of the day to rehearsing 'Children Children,' a McCartney-Laine addition to Wings' catalog of children's songs. But unlike 'Bip Bop,' in which Paul simply expanded on a tune Mary sang as a toddler, and 'Mary Had a Little Lamb,' for which he wrote a new melody to a nursery rhyme, 'Children Children' is a full-fledged ballad in the spirit of Donovan's occasional children's tunes, etched with a sense of fantasy—"*I know a tiny waterfall / A magic little place / Where we can play together / And watch the fishes race.*"

The basic arrangement included an autoharp, played by Denny. Paul played bass, Jimmy played acoustic guitar, and Joe found a non-intrusive beat. Linda sat this one out, as she had done on the basic tracks for 'London Town' and 'Girlfriend,' but it became clear during the rehearsals that it would benefit from an intricate vocal arrangement, in which she would have a role.

The song was not ready to record at this stage, so the band (including Linda) settled into jamming for the rest of the session, with the tapes rolling. Before they left for the day, they made stereo mixes of three jams, which they called 'Moog & Drums,' 'Evening Jam' and 'Auto Harp & Denny.' The Wednesday and Thursday sessions were devoted to overdubbing, although it is unclear from the available documents what songs were worked on; it is possible that at least one of the sessions was devoted to adding orchestration to *Holly Days* tracks.

But on Friday, February 18, Wings worked on four songs, starting two afresh and adding to two others. The basic track for 'Children Children' was recorded, largely in the arrangement Wings had rehearsed on Tuesday, but with the addition of Joe playing harmonica. And an attempt was made the record 'B side to Seaside,' a funky, lighthearted ditty that Paul and Linda cooked up for use, as the title suggests, on the Epic release of 'Seaside Woman.' This version was not used, however. Unspecified overdubbing was also done on 'London Town' and 'Girls' School.'

Toward the end of the Friday session, Geoff Emerick dropped in, having completed his work on the Sedaka album and eager to hear some of the material he would be working on when the Wings sessions resumed after a short break. After some chitchat about the Sedaka sessions, Emerick told Paul about sessions he and Martin had overseen in Hawaii with the folk-rock band America, for the group's just-released *Harbor* LP.

"We were sitting in the studio in London," Paul recalled, "and it was raining and doing its usual thing at the beginning of the year—February in London . . . and the engineer we were working with, Geoff Emerick, came back and he'd done an album in Hawaii with America . . . and he said, 'We hired a house in Hawaii, and we had the whole studio there, it was fantastic.'"[41]

Emerick's report actually understated the preparations for the sessions.

"We did absolutely everything that could be done without an orchestra [in Hawaii]," Martin explained, "because it was a pretty expensive process just recording out there. We found an old, large house on the seashore that had a good room in it and we made that our recording studio. I did a kind of reconnaissance with Geoff. We gave the realtor the specifications as to what we were looking for, and then had carpenters build what we needed, batten screens and things. We hired a Yamaha piano from Japan and brought in Record Plant's mobile truck."[42]

Listening to tales of Hawaii and the beach as the silver rain fell on London town, McCartney's Wings were feeling shortchanged. But for Paul and Linda, Jamaica was calling.

—

With a week of productive studio work behind them, Paul, Linda and the girls headed to Heathrow Airport on the morning of February 19, and flew to Montego Bay, Jamaica, for a two-week holiday. There was some discussion of canceling the trip: a spate of shootings in recent months had claimed some 300 victims, and though not all the shootings were fatal (Bob Marley had been shot and wounded in December, when seven armed men broke into his home in Kingston), outside Jamaica the island was thought to be in the grip of chaos. But the McCartneys felt safe in Jamaica; more to the point, they considered it a spiritual second home, and would not hear of missing the trip.

This time, however, the visit was devoted partly to business. Shortly after they arrived in Montego Bay, the Eastmans landed there as well, as did Brian Brolly. They had a full agenda: plans for the releases of *Holly Days*, *Thrillington*, and 'Seaside Woman' had to be discussed. And there was some Beatles business. Capitol had firmed up its plan to release an album of the Beatles' 1964 and 1965 Hollywood Bowl concerts. To keep the former Beatles onside, George Martin was hired to produce the record and the foursome were assured that they would hear the album before its release, although whether they would have the right to veto the project is uncertain. At the same time, Allan Williams was pressing forward with his plan to issue the 1962 Hamburg recordings, a prospect that George and Ringo opposed, but that John and Paul seemed unconcerned about.

Through all this, Paul was hatching a plan to move the sessions for the new album to a more exotic location: the Virgin Islands.

His recent discussion with Emerick got him thinking about putting together a studio where you would not expect to find one—a train of thought that led back to the original idea of recording Denny's *Holly Days* album on a boat.

"We decided to see if we could get a studio on a boat," Paul explained. "So, we rang up some people in L.A. who do that kind of thing, Record Plant, and they got it together. They just said, 'Yeah, we can do it, if you're mad enough to want to try it.'"[43]

Also on the business agenda in Jamaica was a potential legal tussle. Michael Grossman, an American theatrical producer, was planning to bring over Willy Russell's *John, Paul, George, Ringo . . . and Bert* for a tour of the States, starting at the Ahmanson Theatre, in Los Angeles, and expected to run nine months. Paul wanted that stopped, if possible, and since the Beatles had control of their name and likeness in the United States, Eastman told him that stopping it would not be difficult.

"[We've] heard nothing, except that [Eastman will] sue if we go ahead," Grossman told the *Liverpool Echo*. "We've offered to discuss things with Eastman, even to adjust the text, but he won't communicate with us."[44]

Toward the end of the trip, Paul and Linda booked time at Black Ark Studios, in Kingston, for work on Linda's prospective album.

"We were really into reggae," Paul said, "and we asked the producer Lee Scratch Perry—who is one of the famous producers from Jamaica—if he'd make some backing tracks for us of certain songs."[45]

They asked Perry to create backing tracks for three songs that Linda thought she might want to sing: 'Sugartime,' by Charlie Philips and Odis Echols, which dates to 1957; 'Mr. Sandman,' by Pat Ballard, which was a hit for the Chordettes in 1954; and 'Dear Hearts and Gentle People,' a 1949 Sammy Fain and Bob Hilliard song that was a chart hit that year in versions by Bing Crosby, Dinah Shore and Gordon MacRae. Both 'Sugartime' and 'Mr. Sandman' were published by MPL. Among the musicians Perry used were Billy Gardner on guitar, the bassist Boris Gardiner, the drummer Mikey "Boo" Richards, and the organist Winston Wright, all respected Jamaican players.

Paul and Linda made no additions to these tracks in Jamaica. Instead, they took Perry's 24-track recordings back to London with the idea of working on them further at their leisure. By the end of February they were back home, ensconced at Cavendish Avenue and ready to get back to work on Wings' next album.

Before the Wings sessions could begin again in earnest, there was some housekeeping to be done, which Paul left to Emerick. On March 1, the engineer assembled a 24-track master reel with the basic tracks for 'Name and Address,' 'London Town,' 'Children Children' and 'Girlfriend,' and a second reel with the provisional "Best" take of 'Girls' School,' a song Paul had decided to remake.

Two days later, on March 3, Emerick returned to Studio Three at Abbey Road with a stack of four-track reels full of demos Paul had recorded in Scotland. Proper recordings of a few of the songs were already underway, but Paul wanted to consider the full selection of these Rude Studio demos and asked Emerick to make a set of stereo mixes. The songs Emerick worked on, which filled three reels, were: 'Yes Sir, I Will,' 'Purple Afternoon' ['London Town'], 'Twelve of the Clock,' 'With a Little Luck,' 'How Do You Like the Lyrics,' 'The Pound Is Sinking,' 'Girls' School,' 'Café on the Left Bank,' 'Famous Groupies,' 'Love Awake,' 'Mull of Kintyre,' 'Dress Me Up as a Robber,' 'Down San Francisco Bay,' 'Winter Rose,' 'Find a Way,' 'After the Ball,' 'Girlfriend' and 'Children' ['Children Children'].

Paul was hoping to find the missing pieces that would shape his next record among these amorphous ideas and rough demos.

18

THE *FAIR CAROL*

At the end of February, Frank Sinatra began an eight-night run at the Royal Albert Hall, a charity gig in aid of the National Society for the Prevention of Cruelty to Children. Paul and Linda attended the seventh concert, on March 4, as did George Harrison, whose 'Something' Sinatra had covered in 1970 (and which he periodically introduced as "my favorite Lennon and McCartney song"). George had mixed feelings about Sinatra—he was more interested in hearing his song done by Ray Charles or James Brown; Sinatra, he noted, was more interesting to his parents' generation.

Paul, though, was a fan, partly because his father had been one, and Paul always imagined that one of his earliest tunes, 'Suicide'—a song that comes up again and again in his reels of home demos—was perfect for Ol' Blue Eyes.

Generally, though, liking the music your parents enjoyed was frowned upon in the edgier corners of the pop world, and some of the younger generation were thinking of Paul's music in just that way. At the very moment he and Linda were soaking up Sinatra at the Royal Albert Hall, the Sex Pistols—the band that best represented the punk vanguard in Britain—was having a dustup that resulted in their bassist, Glen Matlock, being fired. One and only one reason was given for Matlock's dismissal: *he admired Paul McCartney.*

In its March 12 "Mailbag," *Melody Maker*—which had been gleefully following the group's headline-grabbing antics—reproduced a memo from Malcolm McLaren, the Pistols' manager, to one of its writers, Harry Doherty, confirming this:

YES HARRY, GLEN MATLOCK WAS THROWN OUT OF THE PISTOLS SO I'M TOLD BECAUSE HE WENT ON TOO LONG ABOUT PAUL MCCARTNEY. EMI WAS ENOUGH.* THE BEATLES WAS TOO MUCH. SID VICIOUS THEIR BEST FRIEND AND ALWAYS A MEMBER OF THE GROUP BUT UNHEARD AS YET WAS ENLISTED. HIS BEST CREDENTIAL WAS HE GAVE NICK KENT WHAT HE DESERVED MANY MONTHS AGO AT THE HUNDRED CLUB. LOVE AND PEACE, MALCOLM MCLAREN.[1]

McLaren went on to describe what a problem Matlock's taste was for the band. "We always knew Glen was into the Beatles and at first we lived with it," he told *NME.* "It was alright Johnny Rotten having a go at him because of it, but when it became three of the band against one the pressure was too much and I had to deal with it. . . . They thought Glen had become a pain in the back 'cos they hate the Beatles."[2]

It must have come as a source of amusement to Paul that the man behind the Sex Pistols' sound on disc was Chris Thomas, a classically trained former EMI engineer turned producer, who had worked on the *White Album* and *Abbey Road* LPs.

The day after the Sinatra show, Paul and Linda flew to Liverpool, where they had ringside seats at Liverpool Stadium to watch their friend John Conteh fight Len Hutchins to retain his World Light Heavyweight title. Conteh won the bout with a technical knockout in the third round.

Joe English, meanwhile, had his moment in the sun, courtesy of *Record Mirror.* Regarded as Wings' quiet one, English was rarely the focus of attention in articles about Wings. But in a discussion with Sheila Prophet, he had a chance to speak at length about his interests and his experience in the group.

"I enjoy working with this band," English said, "because it's—well, on the last album, the one before the live one, it was the first time we'd started experimenting, with everyone having a go at arranging, writing and producing. Everyone was playing together as a unit. I'm looking forward to this next album because everyone's playing exactly what they want. That comes through people playing together for a certain length of time, and understanding each other's gives and takes and wants, and knowing how many sugars everyone takes in their tea—that sort of thing."

He said that Wings planned to take their time completing the next album. "We don't have a deadline or anything, which is how we choose to do it. It means we can all go a bit lunatic—play them fast, play them slow, play them backwards, shuffle, country, everything. And it's real good because everyone gets a chance to have their say. We had a few problems with that at the start, but that was just part of the growing process. We're over that hump now.

---

* EMI Records signed the Sex Pistols in October 1976, and released their debut LP, *Never Mind the Bollocks, Here's the Sex Pistols*, as well as a single, 'Anarchy in the U.K.,' a month later. In January 1977, EMI dropped the band.

"We'll meet each other somewhere in the sun," he said of the band's immediate plans, without tipping his hand about the still-in-formation plans to record in the Virgin Islands. "With our families, and music, and alone. This is a good time of year—springtime, I'm happy, the band is going good. . . . Linda's going to have her baby in September. . . . We're really not in any hurry."

But for all that, he hinted at a need for a broader musical palette than he was finding in Wings. "I was listening to jazz bands when I was 15," he said. "I still dabble in jazz these days, but not the serious heavy stuff—more the Billy Cobham sort of thing. James Brown, Bootsy's Rubber Band and Billy Cobham—that's who I listen to. You've heard of Bootsy's Rubber Band? Well, everything you've heard is true. They're the lowest-down, funkiest funk band you've ever heard. I get into all kinds of music when I have a break from Wings. If somebody wants me to do something, I'll do it."[3]

Recording Sessions

Tuesday, March 8–Wednesday, March 30, 1977.
Abbey Road Studios, Studio Three, London.
Recording: 'Suicide (Demo),' 'Girls' School (Remake),' 'London Town (Remake)' and 'B Side to Seaside.'
Mixing: 'Australian TV Interview,' Various cuts.
Overdubbing: 'London Town,' 'B Side to Seaside,' 'Children Children' and 'Name and Address.'

Upon his return from Liverpool, Paul visited Abbey Road to work on a variety of projects, of which Wings' new album was only one. The first order of business was to record a demo of 'Suicide.'

It might seem surprising, given Paul's habit of earmarking songs for specific performers and sending them tapes in the hope that they might cover them, that he had never sent 'Suicide' to Sinatra, whom he envisioned singing the song ever since he wrote it in 1956. But there was a reason: with its single verse, the song worked nicely as a party piece, or as a way to loosen up in lightly jazzy style during a demo session. But it was not really a finished song.

Shortly after the Royal Albert Hall concert, Paul remedied that, adding a 45-second intro in the style common among 1940's-era Standards—a slow, gentle, almost spoken melody leading easily into the body of the song by way of a thematic link (in this case, the couplet, "*Taking her for a ride / I call it suicide*"). He also added a second verse, as well as a bridge built around the word *suicide*. And he shuffled these elements into the form a Standard would take: intro, verse 1, verse 2, bridge, repeat of verse 1, bridge and ending. Having rumbled around in Paul's head (and fingers) for 21 years as a song fragment, 'Suicide' was now a full-fledged composition.

Paul spent the first part of the March 8 session recording a version with piano, bass and light percussion, the piano part filled with jazzy turns and tripping figures between the lines.

When he was satisfied that he had a take that would sell the song to Sinatra, he turned his attention to the material Wings had recorded in February, adding an organ part to 'London Town.' As the session ended, he oversaw stereo mixes of 'Suicide (Demo)' and 'London Town,' as well as the February recordings of 'Girls' School' and one of the band's jams.

Details of the sessions on March 9, 10 and 11 are unavailable, but on March 14, Wings filled three reels of tape with a remake of 'Girls' School,' producing a version that replaced the provisional February 14 master.

Emerick was now back behind the mixing desk. Though Paul had been happy with Henderson's work in Emerick's absence, he had known Geoff for more than a decade—he had engineered most of the Beatles recordings from *Revolver* on, and he had shared the Lagos experience, recording *Band on the Run*. And Emerick felt that he and Paul were generally in sync.

"You know, I really get on well with Paul," Emerick once said. "He knew the way I was thinking, and he knew musically that I was thinking the way he was thinking."[4]

The key to their relationship was patience. Emerick didn't get frustrated when Paul recorded take after take in search of perfection, or in some cases, when they had different ideas about what perfection was. But having reviewed the work Wings did with Peter Henderson, Geoff found the slightly faster original recording of 'Girls' School' rawer and more dynamic than the remake and was puzzled by Paul's preference for the latter.

"That first [version] of 'Girls' School' was awesome," he insisted. "It was more than awesome. It was exciting."[5] Paul listened to Emerick's arguments on behalf of the original version but maintained his preference for the remake. But either the debate put a damper on progress, or Paul was unsure what he wanted to do next, because the session on March 15 was devoted entirely to jamming, with Wings filling three reels—close to 90 minutes—with untitled jams.

Paul gave the band the rest of the week off, time he spent working on Linda's 'B side to Seaside.' Scrapping the February 18 take, he spent the March 16 session building a backing track on which he played Mellotron, electric guitars, Moog, congas and banjo. Linda then added the lead vocal, and they recorded backing vocals together. Paul spent the next two days overdubbing bass and extra percussion.

Paul and Linda held on to the track until they were sure nothing more could be usefully added, then shipped the multitrack master to New York, where engineer Steve Popovich was preparing the masters for the Suzy and the Red Stripes single. 'B side to Seaside' was given a rough mix at Columbia Studios.

The rest of Wings returned to Abbey Road on March 21 and spent some of the day working on a remake of 'London Town.' By the end of the session they agreed that they couldn't better the performance they had already recorded, so the February 14 version remained the master take.

On March 22, Wings set aside serious work on the new album to entertain an Australian film crew. ABC's weekly music show *Countdown* was celebrating its one hundredth episode, and Paul and Linda agreed to an interview with presenter Ian "Molly" Meldrum. Sitting against a backdrop of amplifiers and guitar cases, Paul explained to Australian viewers how Wings translated his ideas into finished recordings.

"Well, the way I do it is," he explained, "I think of it in my mind, and think of the way I'd like it to be and then tell everyone that. And then we do this thing of kicking it around a bit, and some little things will start to suggest themselves because of a style someone else is playing that I wouldn't have thought of. And that gets included—all the good ideas we keep. We'll change a [song] in the course of recording it from my original idea, but hopefully for the better."[6]

Footage of the band recording overdubs that was intercut with the interview, however, tells a different story. Sitting at the grand piano in Studio Three, Paul can be seen coaching Jimmy through the guitar solo that will fill the closing moments of 'London Town.' In the same way as he would communicate ideas with arrangers, Paul taps out chords on the piano and invites Jimmy to replicate the sequence of notes on guitar. McCartney winces to the camera as McCulloch hits the odd bum note, before the Scot finally replicates Paul's piano line, note for note. To the viewer—and to Jimmy—it looked a lot more like musical dictation than "kicking it about."

The band spent the next three days adding overdubs—vocals and harmony vocals principally—to the tracks they had already recorded. 'Name and Address' and 'Children Children' were now deemed complete, and the March 30 session was devoted to mixing them. They had visitors, that day, as well: Tony Visconti having made peace with his arranging and conducting going uncredited on *Band on the Run*, dropped by with his wife, Mary Hopkin. And Brian Shepherd, the executive manager of Capitol Records' European operations, arrived with Gold and Platinum discs for sales of *Wings at the Speed of Sound*, *Wings Over America* and the group's recent American singles.

Emerick compiled the 24-track masters of the basic takes recorded so far onto a pair of compilation reels. Master Reel 1 included 'Name and Address,' 'London Town,' 'Children Children' and 'Girlfriend.' Master Reel 2 included only the remake of 'Girls' School.'

—

By this time the band was eager to get on with Paul's plan to move the sessions to the United States Virgin Islands. As Emerick observed, "A third of the way through recording the album, it was, like, 'Why are we working in the studio? Why don't we go somewhere more exotic?'"[7]

With arrangements for the sessions well underway and recording in sunny climes set to begin in May, Paul gave the band a month off. Joe flew to Florida for a vacation with Dayle. Jimmy and Denny remained in London. The McCartneys headed up to High Park, followed by a taxi, hired at the cost of £100 ($172) to ferry a group of hens that the family had been keeping at Cavendish Avenue.

Heavy snow fell throughout the nearly two weeks they were in Scotland, reinforcing their desire to transfer Wings' recording sessions to the Virgin Islands. Nevertheless, they took an opportunity to demonstrate that they were solid citizens of the peninsula, responding to a local fundraising effort to buy a kidney dialysis machine for Vivian Dewar, a resident of Campbeltown, by writing a check for £1,700 ($2,925), nearly half the effort's £4,000 ($6,880) target.

While Paul was in Scotland, EMI announced the May 6 release of the Beatles' *Live at the Hollywood Bowl*, a single LP produced by George Martin that combined songs from the band's 1964 and 1965 performances. The objections the Beatles raised upon hearing the recordings shortly after they were made had apparently vanished now that the band was no longer a going concern.

"John heard it last week and was delighted with it," Martin told *Rolling Stone* in late March, although one could argue that the reaction Martin quoted was not entirely delight. "After hearing it, John said, 'We did all that rubbish? That's all we did in those days.'" Martin added, "I don't know if Paul's heard it; if he doesn't like it, then it probably won't be issued."[8]

Disinclined to involve himself in Beatles business that the others (and Martin) had signed off on—and when he was consumed with projects of his own—Paul did not object.

"If I were still in the Beatles, I'd be worried about all of that," Paul explained. "I'd care how they repackaged it and how they did it all, but I'm not in [the Beatles] anymore. I mean, the group split up and the record company has all the tapes and stuff and they're allowed to do [whatever they want]."[9]

But the fact that he shrugged the set off did not mean he had no opinion about it. "*Hollywood Bowl* is an old thing," Paul told Paul Gambaccini. "It's something we as the Beatles never wanted to put out. That's the truth about it. We listened to it and said, 'It's not good, lads' . . . They were very early days, it was an American tour with lots of screaming, and nobody had done many live rock and roll records. We had the chance for years to put it out as the Beatles, and we always said no to it, but what's happened is like vultures picking over a corpse."[10]

He also kept his distance in cases where his former colleagues objected—for example, the 1962 Hamburg Star Club recordings that Allan Williams and Paul Murphy (with whom Williams formed a label, Lingasong) were about to bring to market.

Apple hoped to thwart that plan by bringing a lawsuit instigated principally by George and Ringo, and on April 5, their suit was heard in the High Court, before Vice Chancellor Sir Robert Megarry. Apple argued that the recordings were "informal and unrehearsed," and could "damage [the Beatles'] reputations." Kingsize Taylor asserted that he had asked the Beatles whether he could record them, and they gave permission, which Vice Chancellor Sir Robert Megarry construed as a binding oral agreement in his refusal to grant the injunction Apple sought.

"I wasn't even in on trying to stop the Hamburg album, to tell you the truth," Paul noted. "I know some of the other fellas were trying to have it stopped but I just don't get into all that these days. When the Beatles stopped in 1969, that was it for me. A vacuum was created, and the business side of things filled the vacuum."[11]

The disinclination of the High Court to block the release of *Live! at the Star-Club in Hamburg, Germany; 1962* only added new urgency to EMI's decision to release its Hollywood Bowl recordings. If there were going to be live Beatles recordings on the market, EMI wanted its share. Besides, they pointed out, bootleg recordings of the Hollywood Bowl shows—sourced from the acetates EMI struck in the 1960s—had been trading hands since the early 1970s.

Paul's desire to put the Beatle years behind him notwithstanding, he must have indulged in some schadenfreude upon hearing the news in mid-April of Allen Klein's latest legal travails, particularly as they involved an attempt to profit from his involvement with the Beatles. To the United States government, this was a tax case: Klein was charged with federal tax evasion for failing to report $216,000 (£125,650) in 1970 through 1972. For Paul the salient point was that this undeclared income came from a scheme in which Klein obtained large numbers of promotional copies of *Let It Be, The Concert for Bangla Desh* and other Beatles and solo albums and sold them to wholesalers and distributors.[12]

Across the Atlantic, Joe's Florida vacation with Dayle and her daughter Christy was coming to an end, and on Easter Sunday, April 10, Joe drove Christy back to Macon while Dayle remained in Fort Myers. That night Dayle went to a bar, and on her way home, at about midnight, she got into a serious car crash.

There are two versions of what happened. "Somebody in a bar had slipped her a mickey, as they call it, and she had completely passed out in the car while driving 50–60 miles per hour,"[13] Joe explained. As Dayle told it, she was awake at the time of the crash. "A guy was following me, and I think I got scared and gunned the car, and it was a Porsche, so you know how it took off. But I didn't see the s-curve, and I hit the pole."[14]

Either way, she plowed into a concrete utility pole on Estero Boulevard, and when the police arrived they had to use the jaws of life to extract Dayle from the mangled Porsche. She was ambulanced to Lee Memorial Hospital, where she underwent surgery to reconstruct her broken left leg—15 pins were required—and was treated for internal injuries and a significant number of cuts and abrasions.

Paul and Linda sent flowers and telephoned Dayle during her monthlong stay in the hospital. "A lot of people ask me what Paul and Linda are like," she told an interviewer a few weeks later. "I guess the best way to describe them is to say they're just regular people. They're nice; they love children—Paul has three with another on the way—and they love their farm and their pets. Wings is a real family-ish group. Wives and kids always go on tour, and we all get along pretty well. It's a pretty straight and together group."[15]

When she was released, Dayle was wheelchair-bound and faced the possibility, at age 30, of never being able to walk again. She had also become addicted to painkillers while hospitalized.

"She was literally strung out," Joe remembered. "We were staying in this basement apartment; she was lying in bed, and it was weird. I mean, the devil had a hold of her. She was swearing, hollering, moaning, and screaming in pain. It freaked me out."[16]

Joe was left with a difficult decision: should he stay in Georgia and oversee Dayle's recovery, or join the rest of Wings in the Virgin Islands? He had three weeks to decide.

Joe let Paul know what the situation was, but Jimmy, still on break, was oblivious. On April 16, Jimmy McCulloch entertained a writer from *Record World* at his flat in Maida Vale, ostensibly to promote his other band, White Line. But much of the discussion centered around Wings, Jimmy's place in it, and his relationship with Paul.

"We're off to the Virgin Islands to record the new album," Jimmy said with some measure of eagerness, while also noting that he preferred touring to studio work. He then expanded on his short-term plans. "Touring with Wings is out of the question this year because of Linda's pregnancy. Just now I'm working with a couple of bands with a view to producing. We're preparing demos, but I don't want to say any more at present. I might knock a band together and get on the road. . . . Wings are very together, but we've also got time and room to do our own things."

Asked what working with Paul was like, Jimmy offered a nuanced response in which his principal complaint—one he shared with his predecessor, Henry McCullough—was presented more as his own problem than Paul's.

"I'd heard people say he was difficult to work with," Jimmy said. "Paul knows what he wants. Ninety-nine percent of the time he's great. Sometimes I go to the studio and all I want to do is blow, play away, but nine times out of ten he'll have something [i.e., a specific guitar part] lined up for me. That's why in my spare time I like doing my own thing—blowing. I've always been in blowing bands, and Wings isn't one.

"It's very much Paul McCartney's Wings," he added. "He's got a definite policy and he's in complete control. Don't get me wrong, I'm not moaning. Wings has priority over anything else I do, and I like it that way."[17]

At MPL, the commercial wheels continued to turn. 'Moondreams,' recorded by Paul and Denny in the summer of 1976, was released as the second single from the still-unissued *Holly Days* album on April 15, with 'Heartbeat' as its B side. It did not fare well with the critics, and it failed to chart in either Britain or America.

Buddy butchered, can't see the point. 2 stars.[18]

David Brown, Record Mirror

Despite the adverse critical consensus towards Laine's Holly covers, both cuts here are tastefully done, with the B side 'Heartbeat' having the edge. McCartney produces with the care of a man protecting his investments. 'Moondreams' is typically Holly, veering slightly towards the schmaltzy, but Macca rescues it with a subtle, crisp arrangement. The album Holly Days *from which this comes should be a small treat.*[19]

Bob Edmands, NME

Exquisitely crafted version of the Buddy Holly song. Very nice in a ho-hum sort of way.[20]

Al Lewis, Sounds

Back in London after his Scottish break, Paul spent April 26 at Apple Studios producing another demo for brother Michael, whose career once again needed to be kick-started. Backing Mike on 'Knocking Down the Walls of Ignorance,' a song he planned to bring to EMI in the hope of signing a new recording deal, were Denny Laine on guitar, Zoot Money on keyboards, Paul on drums and Viv Stanshall filling out the texture on various instruments in his arsenal. EMI's staff producers were unimpressed and made a point of noting that the "drummer leaves a lot to be desired."[21]

The next morning Paul and Linda flew to New York on their way to the Virgin Islands. They had a full schedule that included meeting with Ira Beal, the newly hired executive vice president of MPL Communications. When Beal was hired in early April, Lee Eastman told *Record World* that "I believe we are the fastest growing independent—privately owned—publishing company today. Since we started I don't think there's been a week that we haven't been on the charts."[22]

Paul had an opportunity to see some of MPL's holdings in the wild—and to have a brief reunion with a former bandmate. On the morning of April 28, Paul and Linda brought the girls to Madison Square Garden to see Ringling Brothers and Barnum & Bailey Circus. As they were walking back to the Stanhope, they ran into Ringo and Nancy Andrews, who were staying at the Plaza, and whom they hadn't seen since the end of the Wings' American tour the previous June.

At 8 P.M. Paul and Linda slipped into the Alvin Theatre to see the Charles Strouse–Martin Charnin musical *Annie*—the show that was in out-of-town tryouts when Paul bought Edwin H. Morris Music. They were photographed backstage with Andrea McArdle, the 13-year-old actress playing Annie.

The next evening, Paul and Linda had a look at *Grease*, another show owned by MPL, at the Royale Theatre. Robert Stigwood was in discussions around this time to make the show into a film, and Paul's longstanding dislike of Stigwood notwithstanding, he did not stand in the way of such a potentially lucrative proposal. Stigwood was planning a blockbuster production with the singer Olivia Newton-John and the actor John Travolta in the lead roles of Sandy Olsson and Danny Zuko. The Bee Gees' Barry Gibb was drafted to flesh out Jim Jacobs's, Warren Casey's and John Farrar's original score.

During their trip the McCartneys were also hoping for a springtime reunion with John and Yoko and paid a surprise visit to the Dakota. But their timing was terrible: John and Yoko were busily preparing for an upcoming trip to Japan while also dealing with Sean as he approached the Terrible Twos. The McCartneys did not make it past the front door of Apartment 72.

"That was a period when Paul just kept turning up at our door with a guitar," John said. "I would let him in, but finally I said to him, 'Please call before you come over. It's not 1956, and turning up at the door isn't the same anymore. You know, just give me a ring.' He was upset by that, but I didn't mean it badly. I just meant that I was taking care of a baby all day, and some guy turns up at the door."[23]

Paul's alter ego, *Thrillington,* was also given a cold reception. The album had its British release—along with a single, 'Uncle Albert/Admiral Halsey'—on April 29, with the American edition following on May 17. With Paul out of the country, Tony Brainsby fielded press inquiries, maintaining Paul's denial of any involvement with the album, other than to acknowledge that he had signed Maestro Thrillington to MPL. When asked to come clean about Thrillington's identity, Brainsby would simply ask, "But darling, doesn't everyone know who Percy Thrillington is?"

Reviewers saw the project as a musical piñata waiting to be smashed open. "More money for the destitute McCartney family,"[24] David Brown wrote of the single in *Record Mirror*, giving it two stars.

"Holy Practical Japes, Batman, you don't think that Percy Thrillington is Paul McCartney?" Patrick Humphries asked rhetorically in *Record Mirror.* "'Fraid so, and it's what we've always feared—McCartney's gone irrevocably MOR! He has of course displayed these tendencies in the past, as far back as *The Family Way*, but he's managed to keep it under control—until now. Not that it's a bad album, just rather bland, sort of 'Bland on the Run.' It's as if Dylan's *Self Portrait* had been 'All the Tired Horses' carried through four sides."[25]

Pete Silverton, in *Sounds*, marveled at the press materials, which included reproductions of the personal advertisements and an *Evening Standard* article purporting to look into the mystery of Percy Thrillington—and which Silverton summarized as a master class in "creating an aura of mystique around an otherwise solidly drab piece of product." Silverton described the recording itself as "a collection of 'band' arrangements of Macca tunes of such crushing vapidity that James Last probably wouldn't listen to it."[26]

The McCartneys' final chore before leaving New York was an April 30 visit to CBS Studios to pick up acetates of Steve Popovich's mixes of Linda's single. Upon hearing the mixes, Paul and Linda noted their suggestions in a memo they left for Popovich, who remixed the two songs in the McCartneys' absence on May 10. The McCartneys signed off on Popovich's amended mixes.

—

While the McCartneys were taking in hot Broadway musicals that they happened to own, Geoff Emerick and Mark Vigars, along with Mark Eschliman from Record Plant, plus Trevor Jones, John Hammel and Mike Walley from Paul's road crew, were in St. Thomas preparing for the sessions.

Their principal task was to reconfigure the *Fair Carol*, a 105-foot yacht, under the watchful and somewhat apprehensive gaze of its owner, whom the band knew only as Captain Carlo, his partner, Vashti, and the ship's mascot, a white poodle named Cupid (renamed Q-Tip by the band). Things nearly went awry when it became clear that although Carlo had agreed to allow the *Fair Carol* to be used for recording, he did not fully understand how much equipment a professional recording environment required.

"The Record Plant people chartered this boat, and the owner didn't know what the hell was going on," Jimmy McCulloch related. "He thought the group was coming to record with one of these little cassette things. He had no idea. Then all this stuff goes on the boat, and it was, 'No, no. I want to cancel the charter! No way, you can't come on with all that stuff—the boat'll sink.'"[27]

Carlo's mind was quickly put at ease by Emerick and Vigars, who also assured him that the boat could sustain the equipment, and that although they would be building a wooden enclosure on his aft deck, for use as a control room—something else he had not counted on—they would not be doing any damage to the boat. Carlo calmed down when the recording crew agreed to pay a bonus to cover any damage.

But though the *Fair Carol* was securely moored in the US Virgin Islands, Emerick and his crew were slowly drifting into unchartered waters. Recording studios are precision-engineered, soundproofed spaces, with control booths for playback and monitoring, isolation booths for audio separation, and crucially, a steady source of AC electrical current. A boat offered none of those things, and from a safety perspective, a studio on a boat was a floating liability.

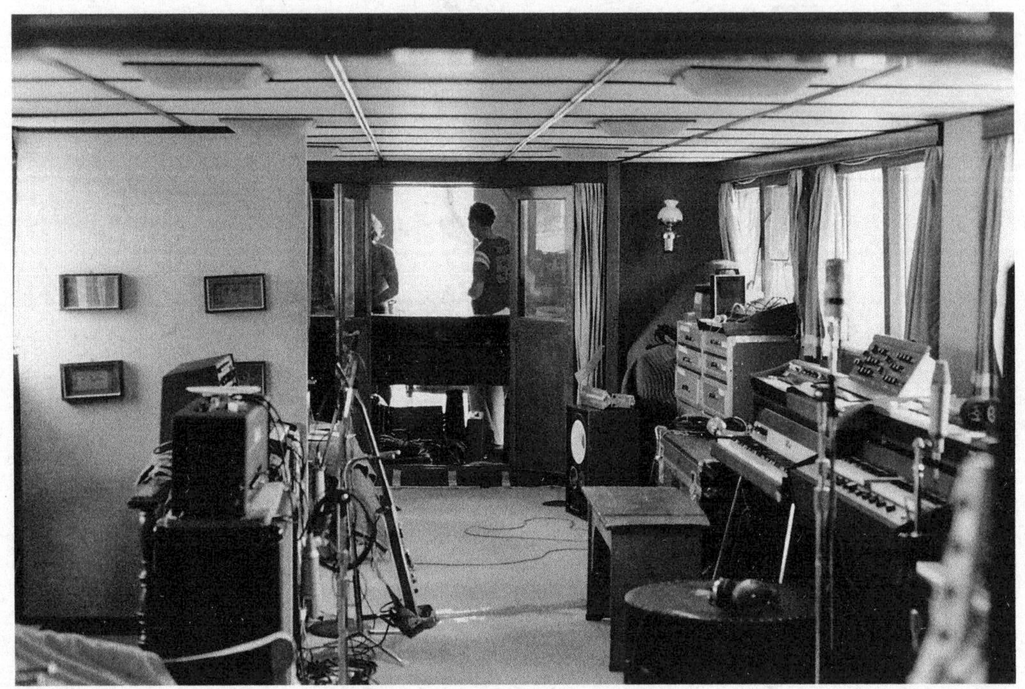

Wings' recording equipment on the *Fair Carol*, May 1977

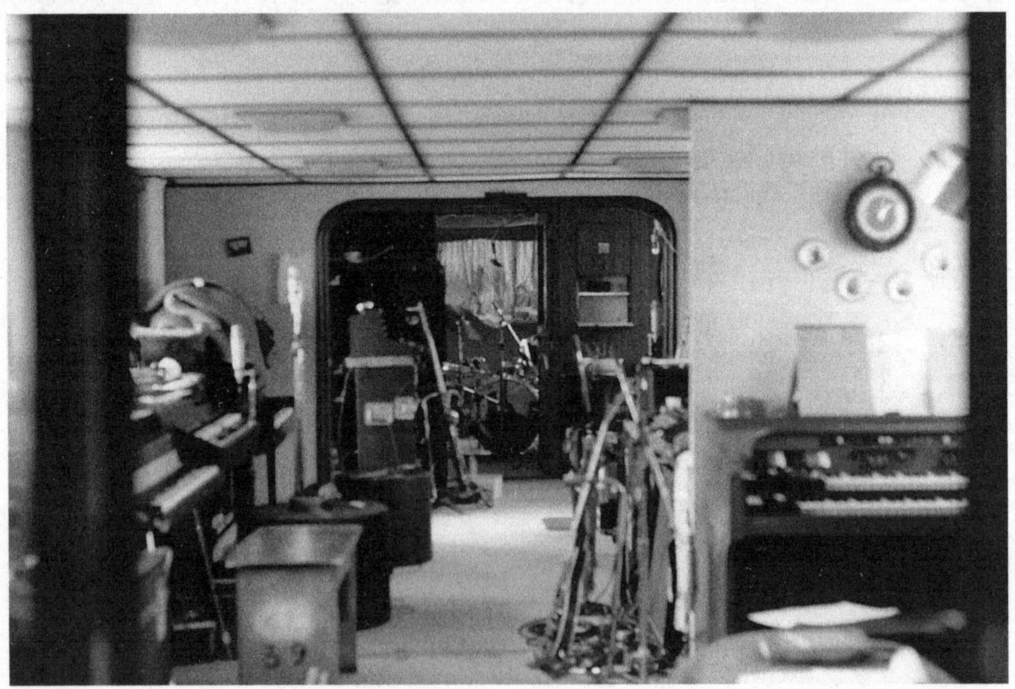

Reverse view of Wings' recording equipment on the *Fair Carol*, May 1977

Emerick and Vigars thought carefully about how the spaces on the *Fair Carol* should be allocated for maximum separation between the instruments during recording. Just behind the control room, they put up three plywood panels to make an open-sided isolation booth for recording acoustic guitars and vocals, with the opening looking out on the water.

Amplified instruments—guitars and keyboards—would be recorded in the carpeted main salon, with Paul's bass rig—an 18-inch speaker on the bottom, two 12-inch speakers in the middle, and one or two high-end drivers at the top—placed in an alcove. There was also a direct injection box, for when Paul wanted to record the output of his bass directly into the board.

The boat's forward salon, which was separated from the main salon by a set of folding doors, was the drum room. All interior walls were covered with thick blankets.

The equipment they installed included an Auditronics 24-input console and a 3M 79 24-track deck, as well as a 3M 64 two-track deck, a Yamaha cassette deck, four compressors (a Fairchild 360 and three UREI 1176s), AKG spring reverb and several Neumann U-87 microphones.[28] After several days of strategic thinking and creative construction, the team had built Paul a floating Abbey Road Studio Three.

Besides the *Fair Carol*, Wings' miniature fleet included two more boats, to be used as floating quarters—*El Toro* for the McCartney family and the *Samala*, a converted British minesweeper, for the rest of the band, Emerick and Crowder. The rest of the recording crew and the roadies had berths on the *Fair Carol*.

"Communication was often simplified between the three boats," Vigars observed. "Everyone just swam from one to the other for planning meetings and sessions. On the first day Brian Brolly did not want to wet his clothes so dived into the sea clad in nothing but a towel, revealing all as the towel took off! Denny learned to sail but most [of us] swam around in clear, blue seas studying starfish, sea urchins, brightly hued coral and small, harmless barracuda, with snorkels."[29]

On April 30, the three boats sailed from St. Thomas to the island of St. John and docked in Francis Bay, on the island's north side, where they were to rendezvous with Wings, Crowder and Brolly. Wings—including Joe, who had engaged a nurse to oversee Dayle's recuperation in Georgia—flew into St. Thomas the following day and engaged the trimaran *Wanderlust* for the eastbound trip to Francis Bay. Along the way, Jimmy tripped and injured his leg, which had him limping through the first few days of the sessions.

Though technically not part of the Wings armada, *Wanderlust* remained in the vicinity. Trevor Jones noted in his diary that Brolly, Walley, Terry Stark—the liaison between the Record Plant and MPL—and some of the crew stayed on *Wanderlust* the first couple of days before transferring to the *Fair Carol*. Paul, Linda and the girls stayed on *Wanderlust* one night toward the end of the sessions.

By now the technical crew was rounded out by two members of the Record Plant staff besides

Eschliman and Stark—recording engineer Tom Anderson and technical engineer Jack Crymes. Emerick knew Crymes from the America sessions he recorded in Hawaii, and insisted that he be part of the team.

"We used the Record Plant Mobile," Emerick said, "basically because of the guy who comes with the equipment, Jack Crymes. He's superb. I wouldn't have done the project without Jack because he knows that equipment inside and out."[30]

A modus operandi was quickly established. "Recording took place most days in the morning and evening," Crowder wrote in his diary for *Club Sandwich*. "The mornings were really beautiful in the bay, with jumping fish called Jumping Jacks, laughing seagulls, pelicans, and very large birds called Frigates."[31]

"Alan Crowder of McCartney Productions is our task master," Joe English joked. "Every morning it's '15 minutes lads! 10 minutes lads!'"[32]

The evening session would often be followed by a late-evening dinner and a swim—or on lazier evenings, sitting on deck watching bats trying to catch flying fish and drinking tropical cocktails. The musicians became enthusiastic about local rum.

There was a very clear sense that although Paul expected to complete all or most of the recording necessary to finish the album, the trip was also a vacation. Between the morning and evening sessions, the musicians were at liberty to swim, soak up the sun or take a dinghy to the island. The only holdouts during the first days of recording were Emerick, a non-swimmer, Crowder, who begged off because of an ear infection, and Jimmy, who was nursing his sore leg. Joe and Denny soon tired of splashing about and joined Jimmy on deck for a relaxed jam.

"We created an ideal situation to take the sweat out of work," Paul explained. "I hate the grind of trying to make myself be inspired. This was an experiment to see if we could produce good songs in a holiday setting. The change of scene was exhilarating. It restored our enthusiasm. The acoustics were amazing. There was total peace and stillness.[33]

"We didn't work much in the mornings. We'd just get up and have a swim, and do all the nice holiday things. Then we'd have something to eat, bop across to the boat and record a little bit, and then leave for the afternoon, go back in the evening. On holiday I always find there's a little boring part to the day where you've got to find something to do, and I normally end up just going to dinner . . . But instead of going to dinner, we went to the studio. It's a very different buzz from being in a normal studio."[34]

The first day was devoted to settling in, so after a group breakfast aboard the *Samala*—the captain, Tony Garton, formerly of the British navy, was a superb chef who would lay on several feasts for the Wings party during the sessions—much of the crew dove off the side of the boat for a first swim. As Crowder noted, "The *Samala* became the 'in' place to be."[35]

Paul and Linda turned up on the *Samala* after lunch and relaxed on the rear deck, staying for a pot of Earl Grey tea at 4 P.M., after which the band and crew went snorkeling. With all that relaxation out of the way, Trevor returned to the *Fair Carol* to help with some final studio setup tasks. Paul and Linda stopped by in the early evening with the recordings from Abbey Road, which they played to hear how they sounded in the newly constructed control room.

When the McCartneys returned to *El Toro*, the rest of the crew swam over to the *Samala* for drinks, games of backgammon and a Clint Eastwood film (Paul continued the practice, started during the world tour, of renting films for the entertainment of the band and crew).[36]

Recording Sessions

Monday, May 2–Thursday, May 5, 1977.
Fair Carol, Mobile Studio, St. John, US Virgin Islands [Offshore].
Recording: 'Café on the Left Bank,' 'I'm Carrying,' 'I've Had Enough,' 'Find a Way Somehow' and Jams.
Overdubbing: 'I'm Carrying.'

Wings climbed aboard the *Fair Carol* for their first day of work on Monday, fully aware that they were unlikely to commit much to tape. There was still the matter of testing how the instruments recorded and doing whatever they could to tailor the acoustics of the space. Much of the first session, in fact, was devoted to setting up and tuning the drums, experimenting until they got a drum sound that pleased Joe and Paul.

"We'd just finished the studio," Paul said, "and we just kind of leapt in there and we were just trying it out. And with the kind of holiday feeling."[37] Paul was hoping to end the first day of recording with a basic take of 'Café on the Left Bank,' but after a few attempts, it was clear that the drum sound was not yet quite right. After a few experiments, they called it a day.*

On Tuesday, Wings took up 'Café on the Left Bank,' and though they again left the studio without having nailed the basic track, the arrangement—which included sharp-edged, flowing guitar lines from Jimmy through nearly the entire song, with Paul and Joe playing steady, interlocking bass and drum parts that pull back for a solo from Jimmy midway through—was falling into place.

When they returned on Wednesday, they continued playing through take after take, filling two reels of 24-track tape, before settling on a master. Besides Jimmy's lead guitar, Paul's bass and Joe's drums, the basic take included an electric rhythm guitar part from Denny; Linda played the

---

* Paul quickly put the travails of testing the studio out of mind: when the album was released, he gave several interviews in which he said that despite his fears that the untested studio would take time to break in, Wings were able to record 'Café on the Left Bank' on the first day. That was not the case.

electric piano. To that, they overdubbed more percussion in a Caribbean style to bring some variety to Joe's simply accented drumming. Paul went up on deck to sing (and then double-track) the lead vocals. Backing vocals were added as well.

"All vocals were recorded topside," Anderson noted, "which allowed the vocals to sound as open and natural-sounding as possible."[38]

A final touch—at least for the moment—was a Moog synthesizer line, played by Paul. With their first truly productive day behind them, Wings settled into a jam, letting the tapes roll as they recorded jam takes of 'Girls' School' and 'Girlfriend.'

"On the morning of the fifth," Mark Vigars noted in his *Club Sandwich* diary, "Paul recorded a track playing acoustic guitar on the stern deck looking out over a sun splashed sea. A dolphin surfaced to enjoy the super sound and splashed around the boat for some time."[39]

The track was 'I'm Carrying,' a gently melancholy song with an opaque lyric, sung from the perspective of a neglectful lover returning after an absence—a circumstance that has led some commentators to surmise that the addressee is not Linda (who, given her heavily pregnant state at the time of writing, may have inspired the composition's title), but a former girlfriend.

The title is the most strongly accented part of the refrain, *"I'm carrying something for you,"* with the listener left to guess what that something is. In the first verse, that something is clear enough: *"By dawn's first light I'll come back to your room again / With my carnation hidden by the packages / I'm carrying."* And the rest of the song—just one more verse and varied repetitions of the refrain—doesn't depart much from the notion that he is carrying gifts. But in context, he could equally be carrying a torch. He did rule out two interpretations based on other common uses of the phrase—carrying a gun and carrying drugs. But otherwise, he enjoyed the ambiguity.

"Some songs you can't really say what they're about," Paul teased. "In this song I know what it's about. Some people I've played it to know what *they* think it's about. It could be lots of things. It could be about a girl carrying a baby, or it could be about someone carrying something much more romantic than just packages. You almost can't talk about it—if you pin it down to just being parcels, or just carrying love or a baby, you're only taking one of the meanings. You know, for me, what I like about it is it's four or five meanings in there all at once."[40]

Musically, the song appears both simple and sophisticated at first glance, its graceful melody flowing naturally, with the refrain climbing high in Paul's range, supported by a progression of only four chords, played as fingerpicked arpeggios. But the progression is unusual—E major, E diminished, F-sharp minor 7, B major sus 4. And though an analysis may make it sound complicated, Paul seems to have hit upon this progression by simply moving a two-finger pattern down the fretboard, an ingenious, chord-morphing technique similar to the one that yielded 'Warm and Beautiful.'

As Paul plays it, the song begins with the third string played on the 13th fret (G-sharp),

Paul records vocals for 'I'm Carrying' on the top deck of the *Fair Carol*, May 5, 1977

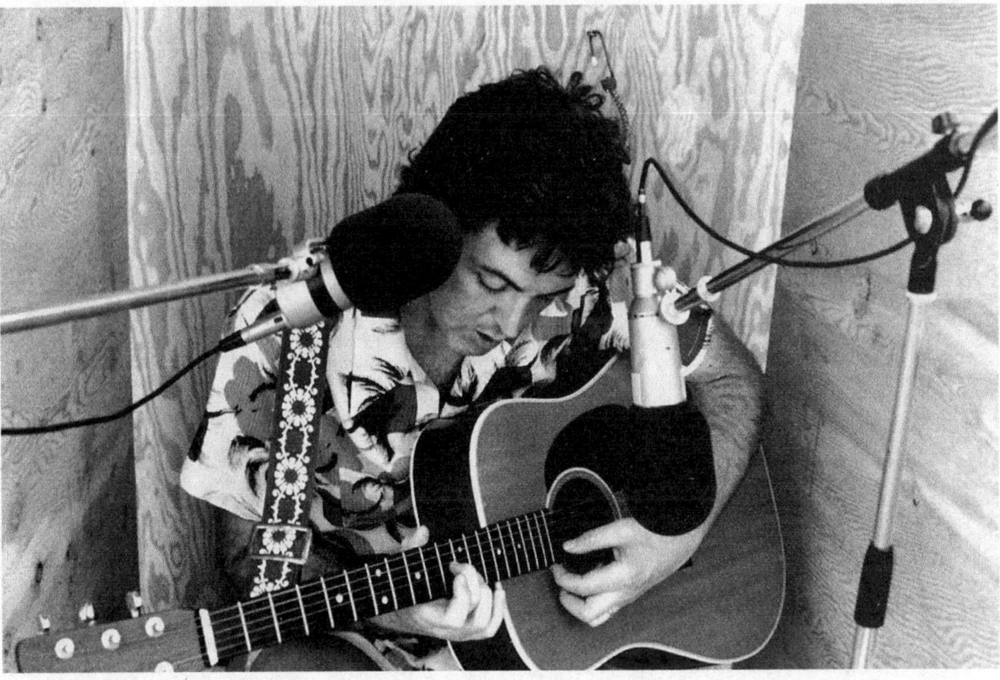

Paul tracks 'I'm Carrying' on the top deck of the *Fair Carol*, May 5, 1977

the second string stopped on the 12th fret (B), and the top string open (E). Sliding the two fingered notes down one fret each, while maintaining the open top string, creates the E diminished chord, and moving the two fingers down one more fret (again, with the open E) yields the F-sharp minor 7. Only the final chord requires a change of hand position, with the top two strings open (the open E is the suspended 4th), the third string stopped on the 11th fret and the fourth on the ninth fret.

"The delicate acoustic guitar sound was captured in the plywood isolation booth on the aft deck," Tom Anderson remembered. "We used one Neumann U-87 with a doubled-up Neumann-supplied pop filter."[41] A master, with guitar and guide vocal, was captured fairly quickly, whereupon Paul added a second acoustic guitar with the chords voiced differently. This posed a challenge—diplomatic rather than technical—for Emerick and Anderson.

"[Paul] was doing an acoustic guitar overdub," Anderson noted, "and I think he put new strings on. New strings squeak until they get finger oil on them, so I said, 'Geoff, should we tell him? Paul's very particular.'" Although Paul would certainly have heard the string squeaks as he was playing, Emerick opted to raise the point. But Paul was untroubled. He stopped and said, "It's just music, lads. Imperfections are part of the hunt."[42]

At the evening session with the full band on hand, Paul introduced a song based on a simple chordal riff that had come to him at an earlier session and that he thought had the makings of a new rocker. "I was sitting in the studio one day and I was just working on some chords, and just clunking along," he explained. "I didn't have any words to it. I just had the chorus, just *'I've had enough / I can't put up with any more,'* that was the only bit I had."[43]

Besides lacking lyrics, the song had no bridge, but that was something that could be finessed with a solo or a change of focus. Paul created a simple schematic for the recording: an eight-bar introduction that presented the D major chordal riff, then a verse built around a straightforward A major rock progression. An A major chord with a suspended fourth creates the tension needed to push the verse into the chorus, which uses the intro chords and Paul's single line of lyrics, sung twice, each time followed by a taunting *"No, no, no, no, no, no."* After three verses and choruses, a fourth verse progression would serve as the backing for a guitar break, and an extended version of the chorus would bring the song to a hard ending on *"I've had enough."*

A basic track was completed quickly, with Paul playing bass and singing a nonsense vocal during the verses. Denny played rhythm guitar with a phase shifter pedal, and Joe provided solid, steady drumming with some inventive punctuation to signal section breaks. Jimmy added a lead guitar line, including the basis of his solo break, and Linda contributed a Moog line, with one of the technicians playing tambourine.

Though the basic track was promising, Paul harbored some insecurity about it, occasioned largely by criticism of another track he thought made a great rocker, 'Rock Show.' Seven years after the Beatles, with seven studio albums, a handful of tours, and a triple live album behind him, he could still be rattled by criticism, or the possibility of it.

"When someone comes along and says, 'Wimpish, middle of the road,' it's like school," he said, adopting a trope about music critics that Linda used in interviews during the American tour. "You get an essay and you try to do something for the buggers, and they turn around and [*slaps his own hand and adopts school master voice*], 'You were late for school today, don't do it again.' Fucking hell, man, tell me it's alright, better luck next time, give me some kind of encouragement, but don't do that to me 'cause it makes me go worse. Next time you come to do a rocker you think last time didn't come off and they're gonna hate me for it again and they're building your paranoia. I suppose it's [the critics'] job, and they've got to do it, but I don't think it helps."[44]

The day ended with another jam session, largely led by Denny. Paul wanted these documented along with the finished tracks, so two reels were filled before Wings turned their attention to 'Find a Way Somehow,' a track from Denny's *Ahh . . . Laine!* album. The instrumentation was the same as for 'I've Had Enough,' except that Linda moved from synthesizer to electric piano. But the song's bluesy character brought out the best in Jimmy, who filled it with hard-edged but fluid solos and between-the-lines bursts—the kind of playing he rarely had the opportunity to do in formal Wings recordings.

Wings filled three reels with performances of Denny's song, and identified a 5'36" take as the master. Denny's guide vocal needed to be replaced, but instrumentally, this version ran circles around Denny's original recording. Whether it would be considered for the album, however, was an open question, given that Denny had already released a version.

"It felt really good on the boat," Paul beamed. "I mean it can't feel bad that; you get a take and then you just leap over the side to celebrate, you know, into the blue water and that, and the sharks."[45]

Wings took a long weekend off to recharge by cavorting in Francis Bay and exploring the island. "The majority of St. John is National Park land with lots of peacocks and donkeys," Crowder mused in his diary. "One day Denny saw this fin gliding through the water and shouted 'SHARK!' but it turned out to be a dolphin."[46]

Given that studios often take a week or two to break in, Paul was lucky to have completed four masters in his first four days of recording. "We didn't have any problems with saltwater in the machines or sharks attacking us," Paul later said. "At night there was much merriment, leaping from top decks into uncharted waters and stuff. I had a couple too many one night and nearly broke something jumping from one boat to another. But then you always break yourself on holiday."[47]

Recording Sessions

Monday, May 9–Friday, May 13, 1977.
Fair Carol, Mobile Studio, St. John, US Virgin Islands [Offshore].
Recording: 'With a Little Luck,' '*El Toro* Passing,' 'Untitled Jam' and 'Jam (On Arrival) at Watermelon [*sic*] Bay' and 'Famous Groupies.'
Overdubbing: 'I've Had Enough' and 'With a Little Luck.'

When the band gathered on the *Fair Carol* on May 9, the first order of business was to add overdubs to 'I've Had Enough.' Jimmy was pleased with his short solo, but had an idea that would give it a more current spin: a tandem harmony line that gave the solo the fat chorus effect that was the signature sound of Boston's 'More Than a Feeling,' a hit in the autumn of 1976 (and before that, UFO's 1974 song 'Doctor Doctor'). The addition was accomplished quickly, with Paul adding a piano part at the same time.

The full band session planned for the evening was canceled when Denny suffered a case of sunburn sufficiently nasty to require being looked at by a doctor at the hospital in nearby Caneel Bay. "I went out on a Sunfish," he explained, "and got lost for five hours and had sunburn for five days."[48] He was not alone: earlier in the day, Crowder slipped on a wet flight of stairs and broke his heel, landing in the same hospital.

This was not going to stop Paul, however. He and Linda went to the *Fair Carol* alone, where they filled two reels recording the basic tracks for 'With a Little Luck,' producing a master, by the end of the session. Paul then laid down a drum machine track, played electric piano and sang a guide vocal, and Linda contributed whooshing sounds on her synthesizer.

But the day's bad luck continued: shortly before the session, Jimmy reported that he had lost hearing in one ear, and during the session itself, Geoff somehow sustained an electric shock to his foot. The Record Plant's Jack Crymes came down with a throat infection. At a stroke, the creative gains of recording on a yacht were offset by the realities of mixing business with pleasure.

With Denny and Jimmy convalescing, the Tuesday morning session was scrapped. In the evening, Joe made an extended but unsuccessful effort to add drums to 'With a Little Luck,' working until midnight before giving up.

"Overdubbing drums can take a little work," said English. "You can either do it or you can't. It's one of those that if you can't [get it right], it shows up and you don't use it."[49]

Wednesday was similarly disappointing: Paul hoped to add a bass line to 'With a Little Luck,' but like Joe the night before, he was unable to produce a part that satisfied him.

Paul returned on Thursday morning to try again, this time completing the finished bass line within a couple of hours. But as he was listening to the playback, he noticed a white National Park Service skiff cruising toward the *Fair Carol.* Mainly, the park police lectured Paul about noise—amplified music was prohibited after 10 P.M.—and warned him about other potential infractions like, say, drug use. They did not conduct a search but implied that they might at any time. And they handed Paul a citation, carrying a $15 (£8.72) fine for playing amplified music the previous evening, Paul's attempted bass line for 'With a Little Luck' apparently being the offending noise.

Paul may have found a humorous side to being fined $15 for his bass playing, but Captain Carlo was decidedly unamused. No captain wants the authorities visiting his ship, and Carlo was aware—and not entirely happy—that the occasional reefer had been fired up during the sessions. Emboldened by the Park Service visit, he chose that moment to lay down some rules for Paul.

"The captain was threatening us that he was gonna keep turning the generators off, so I had to take him into a corner and talk to him very discretely, 'Now, come on, Cap,'"[50] was how Paul later remembered the lecture. But at the time he was incensed. "The captain of the boat that we were on was a little, sort of, heavier than the other captains—you know, he sort of took it a little more seriously—and at some stage we had an argument with him, and I sort of said, 'You know, we don't need all this aggro and stuff,' and we wanted to get off onto this other boat that happened to be in the harbor."[51]

The other boat was *Wanderlust*, and Paul cooled off by spending a few hours there with his guitar. Unwinding after his altercation with Captain Carlo, Paul wrote a song, taking the name of the boat as its title and alluding to the argument in the opening verse: "*Light out wanderlust / Head us out to sea / Captain says there'll be a bust / This one's not for me.*"

"It became like a symbol of freedom to me, this catamaran, as it was, called *Wanderlust*. . . . After this hassling that this other fellow had given us, to get on this boat was like freedom, you know? So the song for me is actually just carrying on the idea. You know, just head us out to sea and take us away from all these headaches, and just wanderlust kind of free."[52]

But while writing a new song was a productive response to the "aggro," it did not address the immediate problem of not being able to record after 10 P.M.—something that was increasingly necessary because the Caribbean heat made the morning sessions unbearable.

"It was so hot," Jimmy explained, "we ended up just doing night sessions. We would get up about 8 o'clock in the morning, start working about 10, and by the time midday came, it was so hot we just jumped into the water."[53] The evening sessions, Jimmy noted, went on until as late as 3 A.M.

After consulting with the three captains, Paul decided to move the three boats eastward, around Mary Point, past Anna Point, to Waterlemon Bay,* where they were less likely to be hassled.

* Paul and members of the crew who have written or spoken about the sessions typically, and incorrectly, refer to the location as Watermelon Bay (as do several bootlegs of material from the sessions).

Leaving Francis Bay at 6 P.M., when amplified music was still legal, Wings jammed as they sailed, with the tapes rolling. All told, three jams were committed to tape—'*El Toro* Passing,' 'Untitled Jam' and 'Jam (On Arrival) at Watermelon [*sic*] Bay.' Crowder, on the *Samala*, waved his crutch at the jamming musicians on the *Fair Carol* as they sailed, looking like Long John Silver moonlighting as Percy Thrillington.

Paul had feared that engine noise would ruin the jam recordings, but that proved not to be the case. There were other problems, though. "We couldn't really record under sail," Emerick said, "although we did once, and found it a bit impractical: people had to hold on to speakers and things to stop them falling over."[54]

Upon arrival, they headed for the beach and had a barbecue to celebrate Jack Crymes's birthday, a celebration that continued with champagne three days later.

Wings spent the final session of the week, on Friday evening, drinking piña coladas and recording the basic tracks for 'Famous Groupies,' the not-quite-but-sort-of paean to the Plaster Casters Paul had cobbled together with Denny (uncredited) in Scotland. The song was not, Paul was quick to point out, a personal memoir. Although he famously bedded female fans by the dozens back when, as Lennon put it, "the Beatles' tours were like Fellini's *Satyricon*,"[55] that was all behind him. "I don't do that kind of thing anymore," he said, "'cause I'm a married man now with kids. I don't go in for all that kind of stuff. I'm not celibate, but extremely un-rude."[56]

Paul played acoustic guitar and sang a guide vocal, with Joe playing a stripped-down kit, Denny playing bass, Jimmy on electric guitar and Linda playing Moog. A master take was completed quickly, the takes filling only a single reel. Still, there were attempts to vary the arrangement during the course of the session.

"There was one point where we were thinking, it really could be a kind of real serious shouted rocker, you know—'FAMOUS GROUPIES!!!'—and really holler it and really get mean on it," Paul related. "But every time we tried that, basically it's in the wrong key to do that with, because it's neither here nor there for singing it, so it came in a sort of medium key. So, I ended up just goofing it and just being silly on the session and just trying to have a laugh."[57]

That meant letting the character of the song—almost a folk melody, with each verse presenting a comic scene involving groupies and their would-be paramours—dictate the arrangement.

Recording Sessions

Monday, May 16–Friday, May 20, 1977.

Fair Carol, Mobile Studio, St. John, US Virgin Islands [Offshore].

Recording: 'Deliver Your Children' and 'Morse Moose.'

Overdubbing and mixing: 'Deliver Your Children' and 'Morse Moose.'

After a weekend at liberty, Wings convened on the *Fair Carol* on Monday without a definite plan, and for two days they listened to demos Paul had made in Scotland or at Cavendish Avenue and worked out arrangements for a few of the songs while Paul decided which worked best. By Wednesday evening, he settled on 'Deliver Your Children,' a song Denny started in April 1975, and that Paul helped him finish.

"I wrote that in L.A.," Denny said. "I'd got so far with it and Paul came along with a couple of ideas for the arrangement. So—I do this all the time—I write the song and it'll probably be the words and a tune, but it'll need something and I'm not happy with it. And he'll come and help me with it."[58]

Its lyrics are wildly eclectic. The opening verse evokes a flood—perhaps even the biblical flood—from the perspective of a non-religious man praying for safety. The second is the complaint of a man whose woman is a fastidious housekeeper but spreads her love around town. The linked third and fourth verses are the tale of a man who forces an auto dealer, at gunpoint, to repair his truck, and the fifth verse is a throwaway—"*If you want good eggs / You gotta feed that hen / And if you wanna hear some more / Well, I'll sing it again.*" Between verses, the chorus offers down-home parenting advice—"*Deliver your children to the good, good life / Give 'em peace and shelter and a fork and knife*" (the utensils being, presumably, metaphorical).

Musically, the song is a stylistic hybrid. The verses have the character of an old English strophic folk song in the Fairport Convention/Steeleye Span mode, but the choruses shift into more of a Laurel Canyon pop groove that calls to mind Jackson Browne.

A notable element is the Spanish guitar filigree that threads through it—a touch Denny brought to the track, drawing on his study of flamenco during an extended trip to the Spanish Canary Islands in 1968. Denny played that part on the basic track and sang a scratch vocal, with Jimmy playing a second acoustic guitar, Paul on bass and Joe on drums.

Wings spent the evening creating an improvised piece that evolved from Paul experimenting with putting the electric piano through various sound-processing units. As the cocktails began to flow, the session descended into what sounds more like a Laurel and Hardy slapstick routine than a recording session.

"The electric piano was set up through a couple of gadgets and you had this weird sound on it," Paul explained. "I just started hitting it one evening and I was doing a sort of Morse code beat on it. Denny was just leaping over to the piano and sort of hitting it occasionally with his head. And we had this thing that just sounded like Morse code for about six minutes. And we quite liked it, you know, it sounded like a germ of an idea."[59]

From what the public could tell, Paul's experimental side had been subdued since 'Loup

(1st Indian on the Moon)' on *Red Rose Speedway* and 'Picasso's Last Words (Drink to Me)' on *Band on the Run.* But he never stopped; experimentation was an ingrained element of his musical personality. He continued to record experimental material privately, periodically having the masters logged into either EMI's or MPL's archives. And occasionally, he would pursue a seemingly bizarre idea that occurred to him during a recording session, as was the case this evening.

Once he had his electronically processed Morse code piano track, the next step was to add to it, the first overdub being a second piano line that provided a sense of harmonic movement.

"We started just making up bits to go on it, and overdubbing stuff," Paul said. "We just made that up as we went along, so it's a kind of crazy track, that one."[60]

Before the Wednesday night session ended, Emerick mixed both 'Deliver Your Children' and the new keyboard instrumental, which Paul was calling 'Morse Moose.' When the band returned on Thursday, Denny replaced his guide track on 'Deliver Your Children' with a proper lead vocal, and then doubled it. Denny and Paul then added harmony vocals throughout the track.

And then it was back to 'Morse Moose,' which they spent the rest of Thursday night and all of Friday embellishing.

Paul added a funky, sometimes hyperactive bass line with Joe following closely on drums, providing fills that either signaled section breaks or offset the monotony of the repeating bass figures and the Morse code underlay. Denny and Jimmy added guitar parts, with Jimmy's improvisations taking off about halfway into the track. Not much thought was given to lyrics at this point. After three days of tinkering, 'Morse Moose' was a 6'40" instrumental that listeners in a blindfold test would be hard pressed to identify as a Wings track.

It could have been stranger. "There was a request made involving doing vocal overdubs underwater,"[61] Tom Anderson recalled. But with one electrocution already logged in the accident book, Paul's impractical request was politely denied.

With three weeks of recording behind them, Wings and the technical crew were developing cabin fever.

"There were some trying times," recording engineer Tom Anderson observed. "You've got some serious egos working on a 100 [*sic*] foot yacht, and that's as far as you can go. You got nowhere else to go. Go back to your home yacht, Paul could go back to his. I won't say tempers flared, but it wasn't *all* beautiful."[62]

On Saturday morning, the *Fair Carol* and the *Samala* headed west to St. Thomas with everyone but John Hammel, Mark Vigars and Joe English, who remained on *El Toro*. After a few hours shopping for supplies on St. Thomas, everyone reconvened in Waterlemon Bay, whereupon all three boats headed east to Hurricane Hole, a group of bays and creeks surrounded on three sides by land.

The British contingent—everyone but Linda, Joe and the Record Plant crew—lamented not being able to see the FA Cup Final between Liverpool and Manchester United on Saturday, but Paul had anticipated that and arranged with his travel agent to have a videocassette of the game flown to them on Sunday, everyone agreeing to avoid news of the game for 24 hours.

"We waited impatiently as the FA Cup Final, the big match of the season, was being played in Britain," Paul wrote in *Club Sandwich*. "No one was to tell each other if they found out the result by radio or newspaper, so that everyone could watch the video that had arrived hot from London with frantic travel agent."[63] (The final score: Manchester United 2, Liverpool 1.)

Recording Sessions

Sunday, May 22–Friday, May 27, 1977.
Fair Carol, Mobile Studio, St. John, US Virgin Islands [Offshore].
Recording: 'Hurricane Hole Jams' and 'Don't Let It Bring You Down.'
Mixing: 'Café on the Left Bank,' 'I'm Carrying,' 'Find a Way Somehow,' 'I've Had Enough,' 'With a Little Luck,' 'Famous Groupies,' 'Morse Moose,' 'Deliver Your Children' and '*El Toro* Passing (Jam).'

After watching the FA Cup Final on *El Toro*, the band and crew had dinner and repaired to the *Fair Carol* to listen to the work they had completed over the last three weeks, Geoff having made stereo mixes of their Virgin Islands cuts on Sunday.

For their final week in the Virgin Islands, Wings had a pair of visitors. The photographer Henry Diltz arrived on Monday and got a good start on his shooting assignment while Wings worked out in an extended jam session. As was now the practice, the 3M 24-track deck was running during the jamming, and in this case, the music—four reels; worth (close to two hours)—was driven and perhaps even inspired by external stimuli.

"'Hurricane Hole' was recorded while we were having a race between the three yachts as we were changing anchorages," Tom Anderson pointed out. "The number of reels of tape it consumed would indicate a lengthy 'composition.'

"Paul was playing a Rhodes electric piano while watching the other boats pull ahead of us and then fall back while the race ensued. His playing speeds up and slows down periodically. I would say that this was an emotional response from the piano player linked to the unfolding of the race as it progressed. As in, his response to winning and then falling into second or third place while the race was run! I wouldn't be able to tell you which yacht won. It was fun, though!"[64]

Paul Gambaccini arrived on Tuesday to cover the sessions for *Sounds* and *Rolling Stone*. Gambaccini would be staying for the duration, and Paul wanted him to understand what he regarded as the sessions' atmosphere and philosophy.

"I like to record and not have to feel like too much work," Paul told him. "I hate to think, 'I'm going to work now, I'm going to grind out some music.'"[65] He added that there was no deadline for the album. "We're not even worried about having it out by the end of the year. We may be just having summer, like people, you know how people take the summer off? They go on little boats and jump in the water. They lie back. We might be doing that. With Linda being preggers, she's gonna need a bit of that, she's been working hard."[66]

Jimmy, though fighting off the boredom he felt after three weeks in the islands with not much to do on the boats beyond the sessions, and even less to do when they headed for land, painted the band's self-imposed isolation as a *benefit*.

"You don't have the gas man coming in or mail you have to act on," the guitarist told Gambaccini. "It's more peaceful and relaxed this way. There are no telephones and nobody interrupting with messages."[67]

With Gambaccini and Diltz looking on, Paul played his cassette demo of 'Don't Let It Bring You Down,' another collaboration with Denny. This one, in 3|4 time, begins with a slowly descending melody and a faux Renaissance accent. Picking up an acoustic guitar, he gave a performance that was somewhat more fluid than the one on the tape, with Denny vamping along on an acoustic guitar.

Paul then switched to bass, and he, Denny and Jimmy rehearsed the song, with Paul singing and Joe taking his place at his kit in the forward salon-turned-drum-room, connected to the others through headphones. They spent the rest of the session rehearsing, with Paul making suggestions about phrasing and asking Joe to take a relaxed approach and to use brushes at certain points.

They took up the song again on Wednesday, filling three reels with takes that did not satisfy Paul at the moment—all were marked as outtakes—although by the end of the week, Paul changed his mind and identified one take as a master for later overdubbing.

As the day's takes were being played back, Paul chatted with Gambaccini about his plan for the still untitled album—Denny proposed that it be called *Water Wings*—and about how the record market had changed since the Beatle days.

"We've got 26 songs to do," Paul said. "We've done 5 in London, 10 here, and we've got the rest to do. We'll pick the best for a single album. We're not planning a double because we've just had a triple album, and it's a drag when someone can't have your record because it's too expensive.

"It would be nice," he added, "to use the best songs as a series of singles. That's the way it used to be in the Beatles days. You'd have a single every three months; you'd release the next one when the record was just beginning to go down. You'd try to be number one at Christmas and the other festive times of the year. That was easy to do when others were doing it with you. The Stones had a new single, somebody else had a new single, so it was alright for you to put out a new single and make it an event.

"Now nobody does that. The emphasis is on albums. The Beatles may have been responsible for part of this with *Sgt. Pepper.* Now you make albums, and if a song sounds like a single, fine, it's a single. The business is bigger now. Sales have grown. Albums make more money. Sometimes I think it would be a bit more exciting if it happened like it used to, but the fact is that it has changed."[68]

Gambaccini also let Paul unload on critics, a conversation that flowed out of Gambaccini's reference to 'Silly Love Songs' being listed by *Billboard* as the No. 1 song in America in 1976.

"I *liked* the song," Paul said, "but I listen to people and I just get crackers. All someone has to say is, 'A bit poppy,' or 'That was a bit sickly, that one,' and I expect the song to flop. Well, I *know* that. What do you think goes through my mind when I'm writing a song about *silly* love songs? I'm flashing on all of this: 10cc have done a song called 'Silly Love,' so I'm in danger there. The hard nuts of the music business, the critics, are gonna hate me because I'm not writing about *acne.*

"You weigh all those problems up and you still write it. You know all those problems; you don't need somebody to tell you that it doesn't cook or whatever the critics are going to tell you. Unfortunately, it still tends to get to me. I still hear them saying it's no good. I wonder if they're right. I wonder if I'm right. And it's great when something wins a poll and you can say, 'Nyahh, nuts to you! I thought I was right.' It's vindication."[69]

The band ended the Wednesday session with a jam that filled two more reels of tape, the material including a reprise of some of the 'Hurricane Hole' themes, as well as loose accounts of oldies, standards, made-up tunes, and Linda's 'Wide Prairie.' Gambaccini noted that Irving Berlin's 'Easter Parade' was among the songs played; also played were 'Rock Away the Blues,' 'Till There Was You,' 'You Are My Sunshine,' 'Monkey Song,' 'Train Song' and 'The Lady Is a Tramp.'

On Thursday, the three boats moved from Hurricane Hole north and west to Leinster Bay, adjacent to Waterlemon Bay. Along the way, the band jammed on the deck of the *Fair Carol* with Henry Diltz shooting rolls of film. After a while, Diltz put down his camera, took a harmonica out of his pocket, and joined in a jam listed as 'Mellotron Jam.' Paul also oversaw the recording of sound-effects tracks for possible use on the album. These were listed as 'Dinghy Starting (SFX),' 'Dinghy Moving Away (SFX),' and 'Dinghy Up & Past (Several Times) (SFX).'

With the Virgin Islands sessions winding down, Emerick saw to some important clerical chores: cutting the master takes out of the 24-track reels and compiling them on a series of master reels to add to the two he had assembled in London. On Tuesday, he compiled Master Reel 3, which included 'Café on the Left Bank,' 'I'm Carrying,' and 'Find a Way Somehow,' and Master Reel 4,

DENNY LAINE

Holly Days

DENNY LAINE'S TRIBUTE TO THE LATE, GREAT BUDDY HOLLY

PRODUCED BY PAUL McCARTNEY

ST-11588

Capitol

Denny Laine, *Holly Days* album trade ad

with 'Deliver Your Children,' 'I've Had Enough,' and 'With a Little Luck.' He finished the job on Thursday, assembling 'Famous Groupies,' 'Morse Moose' and 'Don't Let It Bring You Down' on Master Reel 5.*

On Friday, the band gathered around Emerick and Paul as they made new stereo mixes, replacing those Emerick made earlier in the week. And then they had a farewell party, during which Paul played the captain's mini-piano while Mary and Stella acted out a play, *The Two Little Fairies*. Paul also played one of his own party tunes, 'Running 'Round the Room/Standing Very Still,' as Denny led a procession around the captain's table. The evening ended with an adaptation of the game "man overboard," in which everyone ended up splashing around in the bay.

Wings flew out of St. Thomas on May 28, and stopped in New York on the way back to London. The McCartneys arrived at Heathrow Airport on June 2, where a photographer for the *Daily Mirror* snapped a shot of a heavily pregnant Linda.

"Yes, another on the way!" Linda told a reporter, to which Paul added, "I don't mind which it is [a boy or a girl]—but we're expecting another girl."[70]

* That accounts for nine songs recorded on the *Fair Carol*. When Paul told Gambaccini there were ten, he might have thought one of the jams might have some further use and included it.

19

MY DESIRE IS ALWAYS TO BE HERE

While Wings were recording in the Virgin Islands, several recordings involving Paul or other band members were released. Most notably, Denny's *Holly Days* was finally issued on May 13, having been put back a week to avoid a direct conflict with the Beatles' *At the Hollywood Bowl*. Roger Daltrey's *One of the Boys* was released the same day, with Paul's 'Giddy'—a reworking, with lyrics, of the *Ram* sessions jam 'Rode All Night.' Paul did not play on Daltrey's album—but Jimmy McCulloch did.

Holly Days, a passion project for Paul, did not get the reception he would have hoped for it, either as the album's producer, arranger and principal instrumentalist, or as Buddy Holly's publisher.

Although Jim Evans of *Record Mirror* found the album "enjoyable" and "worthwhile" (and gave it three out of five stars)[1] and *Cash Box's* unnamed reviewer deemed it "a good team project that should find a place on album-oriented rock and top 40 playlists,"[2] others treated the project with outright contempt.

"This record is not only nasty," Mick Farren wrote in *NME*, "it's plain offensive. It tramples over Buddy's best work to the point where it's reduced to a cutesy pulp, awash with piping organs and syrupy singing that I guess is supposed to pay tribute to the master, but only serves to muddy up the legend so that anyone who grew up loving Holly simply gets disgusted."[3]

Dave Marsh, in his *Rolling Stone* review, mentioned the importance of Holly's music to McCartney as a backdrop for his surprise that the album was "a misconceived failure." For Marsh, everything is wrong: Holly is credited as the composer of only 5 of the 11 songs, many of which come from the more obscure end of his catalog; Denny "seems strangely distant from the music," bringing none of the commitment he brought to his own 'Time to Hide' on the last Wings album; and some of the arrangements "erode much of the power that Holly's versions have."

But what would have sparked Paul's ire was Marsh's kicker. Comparing the album negatively to Mike Berry's recent *Tribute to Buddy Holly*—which he calls "a trivial one-shot"—he concludes that

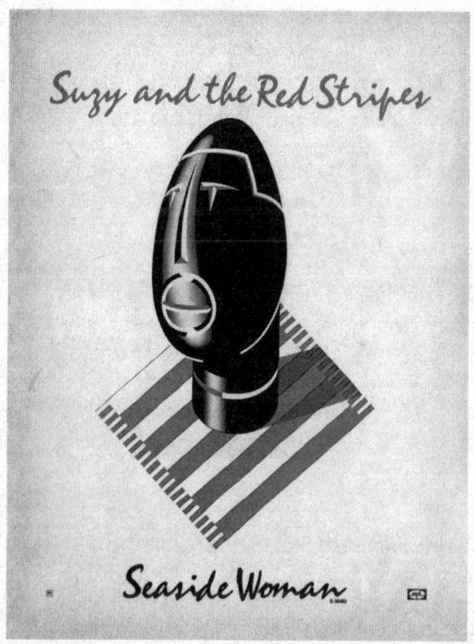

Linda's 'Seaside Woman' single trade ad

"*Holly Days* may do swell things for Holly's publishing catalog, but it does nothing but damage to Paul McCartney's already sagging reputation as a rock artist."[4]

Between them, Farren and Marsh touched on all the epithets that Paul had told Gambaccini he found particularly irksome, and Marsh's final sentence had to sting. Suddenly it was as if *Rolling Stone*, his old nemesis, had decided that the rock 'n' roll street cred he had established as a Beatle, lost with his first few solo and Wings albums, and clawed back with *Band on the Run* and the world tour, had been swept away again, just like that—and in a matter-of-fact swipe in a review of an LP that wasn't even nominally his own.

The American release* of Linda's single, 'Seaside Woman' and 'B side to Seaside,' by Epic Records on May 31, received generally supportive reviews from the trade press, although *Billboard* regarded it as a novelty record. But *NME* took a dim view of Paul's mock Caribbean accent vocals, and once again, delivered a blistering attack.

> *Lynda [sic] McCartney nauseates on white man's reggae with hubby joining in for the background vocals. Sounds like 'Oob-Blah-dee, dah-dee-dah' played at 16 RPM. Fake Uncle Tom voices are insulting, Paul. Almost as insulting as the perennial MOR wallpaper Muzak churned by the Macca clan.*[5]
>
> *Tony Parsons*, NME

> *With a lighthearted reggae beat, 'Seaside Woman' is the most novelty-oriented single from the McCartneys since 'Uncle Albert/Admiral Halsey,' Paul and Linda's 1971 hit that was his first post-Beatles No. 1 million-seller. The flip is an equally off-beat 'B side to Seaside.'*[6]
>
> *Uncredited*, Billboard

* 'Seaside Woman' was not released as a single in Britain until 1979.

A record for pure fun only, combining a reggae-influenced rhythm with Caribbean pidgin-lyrics. Since Red Stripe is the favorite beer in Jamaica, it all makes sense. We hear the lead vocalist here is Linda McCartney, though the entire Wings crew has obviously joined in. Aimed right at top 40.[7]

Uncredited, Cash Box

Yes, that is Linda McCartney backed by Paul and Wings, on a lighthearted reggae song with any number of unusual instrumental touches. It recalls McCartney circa Ram, and the beat and the family name should make it a hit.[8]

Uncredited, Record World

Nevertheless, solid radio play pushed the single onto the *Billboard* Hot 100 on June 18 at No. 83. It remained on the chart for five weeks, peaking at No. 59.

Amid these critical swipes, Paul could take some solace in Billy Paul's R&B cover of 'Let 'Em In.' Released in America in 1976, it had a UK release in March. The cover charted at the end of April and spent five weeks on the UK hit parade, peaking at No. 26. But more crucially, for Paul, it was getting British press attention just as *Holly Days* was taking its lumps.

"I was in Miami when I first heard Wings' version of that song," the R&B singer told *Record Mirror.* "I couldn't get it out of my mind. . . . When I got back to my hotel that night, there was a telegram waiting for me from Kenny Gamble, asking me to go back and record on Monday. That was strange, because Kenny never, ever bothers me when I'm on holiday. But I went back, and he said, 'I called you back because I've got a great song for you to record'—and the song was 'Let 'Em In.' I freaked out; it was so weird."

What Billy Paul heard in the track was not just a party song; for him, it had a political underlay: waving all those people into the party was an expression of equality and inclusivity. For his version, he altered the guest list (Louis Armstrong rather than Phil and Don, for example), interpreted Brother John as Kennedy rather than Lennon (or Eastman), and wove in snippets from speeches by Malcolm X, Martin Luther King and others.

"I don't think we changed the song, because Paul laid the groundwork," he added. "I knew what he was meaning—I could see his train of thought, especially in the chorus where he mentioned people like John Kennedy and Martin Luther King. We just brought the meaning out. We took one aspect of the message and emphasized it."[9]

MPL and the Eastmans also had plenty on their plates while Paul was in the Caribbean. Having been unable to stop the stage version of *John, Paul, George, Ringo . . . and Bert,* Paul was determined to stop *Beatlemania*, a show conceived and produced by Steve Leber and David Krebs that told the Beatles' story through the band's music and contemporaneous photographs. Four musician-actors—including the guitarist Les Fradkin, whose album Paul and Linda contributed to during the *Ram* sessions in New York—played the Beatles, with changes of costumes, wigs and facial hair to help them move through the eras.

The show had opened in Boston in April and moved to the Winter Garden Theatre in New York for its Broadway opening on May 19. Paul asked the Eastmans to get the show stopped, but that was not going to be easy because Leber and Krebs had negotiated with ATV, the owner of Northern Songs, to license what they thought was all of the Beatles' music. George Harrison's songs, however, were not published by Northern, and since he also objected to the show, he forced the producers to remove 'Here Comes the Sun' from the setlist.

John Eastman took an aggressive approach on Paul's behalf, despite the fact that the songs were duly licensed and royalties were being paid. He told *Rolling Stone* that "Leber is doing a pirate production, because it is opposed by the Beatles. We were thinking of seeking a preliminary injunction, but we didn't want to give them any free publicity."[10]

Lee Eastman took a different approach. He took his old friend Sam Trust, who was then running ATV Music, to lunch at the Drake Hotel in New York and asked him to withdraw the right to use Lennon-McCartney songs. To Trust, this was madness: the show was paying $32,000 (£18,620) a week to license the Beatles' music.

"Look, I hate to do this," Eastman said to Trust, "but Paul is very upset—he doesn't like the idea of *Beatlemania*, he wants to close the show.'"

"Are you out of your mind?" Trust asked.

"It would be a personal favor if you closed the show," Eastman continued.

"I noticed that he hasn't sent back any of the checks," Trust observed, pointing out what Eastman, as the owner of several publishing catalogs, already knew—that *Beatlemania* was the kind of opportunity songwriters and publishers dreamed of. Not only was it pure income, requiring neither effort nor involvement, but it was also likely to spur fresh sales of the Beatles' own recordings.

"So he says to me, in confidence," Trust later explained, "'Sam, I hope the damn show runs for ten years. But he's my son-in-law, and I'm speaking on his behalf, and he'd like you to close it.'"

"Well, I can tell you this right now," Trust replied, "I'm not going to close it. And he said, 'Okay, well he's going to call you.'"

When Trust was in London a few weeks later, Paul telephoned to pursue the discussion further.

"I guess you talked to my father-in-law, and he wanted you to close the show," Paul began, "and you refused. I'm asking you to close it now."

"I'm not going to close it, Paul," Trust said. "And what the hell is wrong with you? You're making a fortune out of it. What's the real reason?"

"I had the idea myself," Paul ventured. "I simply had never spoken to anybody about it."

"Well, someone else had the idea, too," Trust pushed back. "They negotiated with us, and we went ahead, and it was a success. So, I'm sorry we scooped you, Paul."[11]

Nevertheless, Paul exploited the show's Beatle-look-alike cast for its comic potential, telling no fewer than three versions of a mistaken identity story in interviews. In one, he was walking past the Winter Garden box office when a ticket buyer asked whether he was Mitch Weissman, the actor who played Paul in the show. In that version, Paul responded, "Sorry, mate, but show business ain't my cup of tea."[12] In an alternate telling, Paul said his answer was, "That's right, I'm him."[13] In the third version, he ran into Mitch Weissman's mother, who told him that her son plays him in *Beatlemania*, an encounter that, he said, "almost made me sick,"[14] because, as he saw it, people who are portrayed by actors on stage or in film are usually old or dead.

In the aftermath of the Beatles losing their bid to buy the Northern Songs catalog, and ATV's taking control of it in late 1969—a loss that, Paul now saw, allowed productions like *Beatlemania* to be staged—Paul had built a corporate brick wall around his work to safeguard his control of it. With the exception of *McCartney* and half of *Ram* (which ATV held) Paul owned his solo music, and by hiring photographers and artists to work directly with Wings, the copyright of most still and moving images of Paul on the road and in the studio was retained by MPL. By 1977 it was near impossible for outsiders to exploit Paul's post-Beatles work.

By June 1977, MPL was back in its newly refurbished offices at 1 Soho Square. Part of the company's workforce continued to be occupied with the 1975–76 world tour, and that would be the case for some time to come, for although the tour was receding quickly into the past, as was the triple album it yielded, other by-products had not yet seen the light of day—Aubrey Powell's and Robert Ellis's photographs, Humphrey Ocean's sketches, and canister after canister of material from Gordon Bennett's film crew, plus concert footage and material from television stations.

One project was an audiovisual overview of the tour. Two variations were currently in the works: a documentary about the tour, mixing concert footage, offstage elements and interviews, to be called *Wings Over the World*; and a straight concert film, essentially a visual counterpart to the *Wings Over America* album, to be called *Rockshow*.

Before the film project was bifurcated, Paul reconnected with Michael Lindsay-Hogg, whom he had not worked with since *Let It Be*, and engaged him to direct. Working at the Music Centre in Wembley, Lindsay-Hogg sorted through the materials with a team of editors that included Robin Clarke and Paul Stein. A few months into the project, they were joined by Thelma Schoonmaker, a young but widely respected editor who had been nominated for an Academy Award for her work on *Woodstock*.

Paul also engaged Chris Thomas, the former EMI engineer who had worked with the Beatles and was now producing the Sex Pistols.

"I saw [Paul] a few times here and there," Thomas recalled, "and then when they did the *Wings Over America* triple album, he sent it to me to have a listen to, and I made some comments on it; he wanted an extra pair of ears to hear it. And then they were gonna make a film, *Rockshow*, from that tour, and I was invited then to work on *Rockshow*.[15] I was doing the Pistols album at the same time, which is a weird one. We did 'God Save the Queen,' and that was banned. And then at that time, Paul asked me to work on what became the film. So, you know, I needed a job, I needed the money, basically, nobody was getting paid for the Pistols."[16]

Thomas's job was to oversee the music that would be used in the film, but as he quickly learned, it was not a straightforward production job. He had been brought in, in fact, to solve a thorny problem that the film crew ran into—or, from Thomas's point of view, created. The concert footage was edited with a focus on what *looked* best, meaning that an edit of a particular song might include shots from two or more performances, on different nights and in different cities.

"They put this film together," Thomas said, "and whoever had organized this, they'd cut the film from five different performances. So, it was visually cut. But the music didn't make sense, because you went from a gig in Seattle to a gig at Madison Square Garden, and the guitars suddenly had a different sound, different level, different this, different that.[17]

"The sound went all over the place. So, the producer of the film said, 'We need someone to come in and fix the sound' . . . And I said, 'Well, you can't [fix the sound], you've got to do sound edits that work correctly, and then you fit pictures to the sound.'"[18]

Thomas explained the problem to Brian Brolly, whose response was "that's why we've employed you—to sort it out." It was around then that Schoonmaker was brought in as well. In the end, the only solution was to rerecord some of the music—"A hell of a lot,"[19] according to Thomas—including virtually all the backing vocals, much of Denny Laine's work, and even some of Paul's bass lines, all for the sake of sonic consistency.

"Jimmy, believe it or not, had a consistent sound and consistent performance throughout all those edits," Thomas said. "So there was hardly anything for him to do. So we're in the studio for months, and he's probably in about two days. He grumbled about his situation in the band. He was very unhappy."[20]

Thomas began to prepare the recordings for the film soundtrack while Wings were in the Virgin Islands. With Phil McDonald engineering, Thomas oversaw five sessions at AIR Studios, between May 23 and 30, making stereo mixes (as well as 24-track safety copies) of recordings from Los Angeles, Seattle and New York, representing virtually Wings' entire set, so that the band could begin overdubbing when they were back in England.

Between June 6 and July 1, Wings made frequent appearances at the Music Centre to overdub parts that needed to be adjusted. It was not a simple task.

"We would sit in a giant recording studio," Joe English said, "and you'd watch yourself singing or playing on the screen and have to make the same inflections with your voice, just like in the movie. It was funny, a real trip."[21]

During the process, Thomas shuttled between Wembley for McCartney sessions and Wessex Studios in Highbury, North London, for Sex Pistols sessions. As production jobs went, Thomas's work with the Sex Pistols was unusually perilous, particularly once the band's single 'God Save the Queen' climbed up the UK charts, irritating "patriots" who found the Pistols' message—"*God save the Queen / She ain't no human being / And there's no future / And England's dreaming*"—deeply offensive.

On June 17, with the single at No. 2, Paul Cook, the Pistols' drummer, was set upon by a gang at the Shepherd's Bush tube station and required 18 stitches to the back of his head. The next night, as Thomas, his girlfriend Mika, engineer Bill Price, and Sex Pistols' lead singer John Lydon (aka Johnny Rotten) were leaving the Pegasus Hotel after a post-session pint, they were attacked by 11 people, some with knives.

"We were probably marked down for attacks when Johnny Rotten was recognized in the pub," Price theorized. "The gang cut his face and his arm but didn't manage to do any serious damage. Chris also had his face cut, and I got a deep cut in my arm. It was obvious Johnny was not too popular because of the record about the Queen."[22]

Thomas returned to the McCartney sessions on Monday and didn't mention the attack. The next day, the *Daily Mirror* had a story about the altercation on its front page.

"I walked into McCartney's studio and they went, 'Oh, you're alive! Oh my god!'" said Thomas. "And I went, 'What?' He said, 'We've been phoning all the hospitals in London to find out where you are.' I said, 'What are you talking about?' They said, 'Look at this!' They showed me a copy of the front page of the *Daily Mirror*. I said, 'That happened on Saturday. I was with you yesterday!'"[23]

The overdubbing sessions ended with Paul touching up 'Blackbird,' but he remained in the studio late into the night to work on 'Waterspout,' a song he had written during the family's last visit to Jamaica. It is not known why the image of a waterspout—the funnel of water that forms at the bottom of a whirlwind over the ocean—occurred to him. But he had made a four-track demo, which he now transferred to 24-track tape. Before leaving the Music Centre, he added unspecified overdubs.

Wings' new album was still very much unfinished, but work was largely on hold for the moment. Paul and Linda caught the last of Bob Marley's shows promoting his *Exodus* album at the Rainbow

Theatre on June 4.* They also likely caught up with the big film of the moment, George Lucas's *Star Wars*, which had opened in America on May 25—they may have actually seen it during their few days in New York. Given Paul's love of science fiction, it would have been a must; and like everyone else who saw it, Paul would have been struck by the sophistication of its visual effects—and the vast difference between those effects and what was available to his erstwhile collaborator Gene Roddenberry just a decade earlier, when *Star Trek* was made.

The McCartneys would also have noted that George and Pattie Harrison's divorce was finalized on June 9. Divorces often have the collateral effect of shaking up friends of the divorcing couple, and the attention given to celebrity divorces only increases the pressure—not least when tabloids and magazines had been using the Harrisons' marital troubles as jumping-off points for examinations of all the Beatles' marriages. But just a couple of months earlier, Linda gave an interview to *Woman* in which she painted her marriage to Paul as secure, if not without the occasional turbulence that all couples experience.

"My life is not perfect," she told reporter Bonnie Estridge. "But whose is?" Estridge asked whether Linda was ever sorry she married Paul. "No, I'm not," Linda responded. "I can honestly say that. But if we ever broke up, I wouldn't kill myself. Just because the other Beatle marriages went wrong doesn't mean to say we have to follow suit. Everyone tries to make you think the Beatles were one big person—or four sides of a square. But each one is an individual within his own right. Paul's completely different to John, George and Ringo—and anyone I've ever known before.

"We row, naturally. And every couple gets to a point when they feel trapped and think, 'What the hell's this about, anyway? I could be free.' But then, the next day life seems better. The good outweighs the bad for me . . . I don't pretend that I can't ever see things going wrong. I've never been on the point of leaving him, but I've been able to see how it could happen."

She also offered some insight into Paul's offstage personality.

"I've always been a romantic person. I like to dream. But Paul's less romantic than you may think from his pretty songs. He can be a softie but don't be fooled by his silly love songs. He's got his head screwed on the right way. He's an astute businessman as well as a pop singer."

Linda also addressed their relationship with their daughters—and some ingrained aspects of Paul's Liverpool upbringing.

"Our kids must like us. We're fun people as well as loving parents. I was hard on my parents, a real rock 'n' roll kid. I wish I could have had the same rapport with them as our kids have with us. But that doesn't mean we spoil them. At least, not with gifts and things. We spoil them with love, especially Paul. And he says what he thinks; he doesn't stand for any nonsense. When we're at

* Such was Paul's affection for Bob Marley's music that he hired a film crew, fronted by David Litchfield, to film Marley's final UK show at the Rainbow Theatre. The film recorded that night remains unreleased.

home, the young ones have to be in bed after dinner and an hour of TV. There's no staying up all night around our place.

"Paul's taught them good manners and they're very polite. I don't think the kids feel our way of life is different from the norm. We're not showbizzy. We're not flash. We're cozy. We only go to parties that we want to go to. If we think a party is going to be cold and impersonal, we don't accept. We'd rather stay in.

"I hate clearing up, though. Heather helps me out there. She's 14 now and quite domesticated. You won't find Paul near a sink, he's a typical Northerner; believes a woman should do the housework and the man bring the money home—even though I bring the money home, too. But he's not [a] chauvinist as you probably think after hearing that. He's just old-fashioned in his ideas. That's nice, I like it."[24]

One of Paul's old-fashioned ideas due for reconsideration, however, was his approach to Wings. It was not lost on him that Joe was still having trouble settling into life in London, and that Dayle's accident gave his homesickness a fresh urgency. And Jimmy had made no secret that he found the recording process tiresome and preferred to be on the road—although, his finger-breaking wild night in Paris and his encore rebellion in Boston suggested that roadwork was not an entirely reliable cure for what ailed him.

Moreover, work on the new album exacerbated Jimmy's and Joe's sense that they would always be "the new guys," even after a couple of albums and a world tour. Although Jimmy had songs on both *Venus and Mars* and *Wings at the Speed of Sound*, he had nothing for the new album, while several of the songs Wings recorded were McCartney-Laine collaborations. There had been talk of Jimmy, Joe and Denny receiving a 2 percent royalty on record sales, but there was never any follow-through.

"McCartney said I would get two points on the royalties," Joe complained, "but I never did. Once I asked [Lee] Eastman if I could have it down on paper, and he told me that I was an unknown boy from Georgia who's lucky to be playing with McCartney. He told me to 'just forget it' and that he wasn't going to give in. That kind of thing doesn't make you feel very secure, does it?"[25]

Around the end of June 1977, Paul decided to address any financial discontentedness in the band by reconfiguring the way his bandmates were paid. Denny, Jimmy and Joe were offered service contracts that clarified that the musicians were sidemen, employees of McCartney Music, Inc. Each would now earn an annual salary of $100,000 (£58,100), with bonuses for tours and recordings.

McCulloch was happy for the freedom this arrangement allowed. "I know I've got the freedom to do anything [outside of Wings], as well as being involved in Wings," he told an interviewer around the time the contracts were signed. "We have quite a bit of time off, so I can start getting back into what I would do if I was on my own. I haven't done anything myself in commercial terms, just getting back down to writing, and producing a band called Glasgow."

But Jimmy's interview also revealed an undercurrent of frustration with his musical role in Wings. "An extension of your personality, that's what your guitar is," he said. "Instead of putting it into words you just say it through your instrument. Now maybe sometimes that may not work in a certain song. [Paul's] got his ideas about how he wants to hear it, because it's his song, right?"[26]

—

The McCartneys planned to spend the summer at High Park, once school let out in mid-July. Britain was celebrating the Queen's Silver Jubilee, and for residents of Campbeltown, that meant street parties, a yacht race and parades led by the local pipe band.

Linda was in her element at High Park. Her own diet now was entirely vegetarian, and at High Park, she adopted a back-to-the-earth approach. Although their groundskeeper and resident farmer Duncan Cairns, saw to the gardens when the McCartneys were away, when they were at High Park, Linda planted and harvested her own vegetables, including tomatoes, sprouts, cabbages and beets. She did her own canning and pickling, and made jam. And she tended to the flock of chickens that the McCartneys brought back to Scotland after spending the rest of the year in a hut in the back garden at Cavendish Avenue so that the family could have a continuous supply of fresh eggs.

Paul spent long stretches in Rude Studio recording four-track demos of songs he had written recently and improvisations that might be refined as songs. Paul's latest batch of demos ranged from synthesizer workouts in various styles, to a punk parody, 'Boil Crisis,' motivated by a late-night television report about the British *oil* crisis. The news piece Paul saw looked at four years of disruption to oil supplies, as well as inflated fuel and petroleum prices, caused by the 1973 oil embargo imposed by members of OAPEC (Organization of Arab Petroleum Exporting Countries).

"Linda and I used to watch the *News at Ten* each night, religiously," said Paul, "but it got so bad and everything was so terrifying, from the oil crisis to the threat of nuclear war. You know, you're in the middle of all this and you just have to slog through it."[27]

By summer's end he had compiled five reels of new and recent demos, including some (like 'Waterspout') that he had recorded during previous visits to High Park, or in London:

> ***Tape 1:*** 'Firebird Drama' (jam) / 'Back in Time'* / 'Drum Tests (Back in Time)' / 'After You've Gone' (recording of the Henry Creamer and Turner Layton song) / 'Boil Crisis' (a punk parody) / 'Instrumental Piece' (jam)

* 'Back in Time' and 'Drum Tests (Back in Time)' would soon become 'Backwards Traveller.'

Tape 2: 'Yamaha Link (aka Off the Cuff Link)' (keyboard jam)*
Tape 3: 'Jamaican Hilite' (Jamaica-inspired synthesizer demo) / 'Scottish Air' (demo) / 'Mull of Kintyre' (with lyrics and synthesized pipe band part) / 'Waterspout'
Tape 4: 'That Strange Old Fashioned' / 'Agoo Mr. Didi' / 'Jail Break' / 'Sleepy Time Rag' / 'I Love You Madly' / 'Sweaty Mouth Piece' / 'Feeling'
Tape 5: 'Late Night' / 'One Woman' / 'Keep Under Cover' / 'Average Person'

Among these, there was one song in particular that had been tugging on Paul's imagination for at least three years, and that he now had an urge to complete. That song, 'Mull of Kintyre,' was already in the works by August 1974, when he included it among an hour's worth of piano demos. Its melody, in 3|4 time, boasts a distinctive Scottish accent and its simple chords seem to imply the drone of a bagpipe.

On the 1974 piano recording, the melody for both the verses and the chorus is complete, as are the chorus lyrics—*"Mull of Kintyre / Oh, mist rolling in from the sea / My desire is always to be here / Oh, Mull of Kintyre."* But for the verses, Paul had only a single line: *"Far have I traveled and much have I seen."*

"It was a love song really," he later explained. "About how I enjoyed being there and wanting to get back."[28]

Early in July, Denny and his family were on the estate as well, their caravan parked in Low Ranachan. One night at dinner, Paul told Denny, "I have an idea to do a Scottish song" and played him the unfinished 'Mull of Kintyre.' Denny's immediate response—"That's got to be a hit song!"[29]—reinforced Paul's own feeling that there was something worth mining. The music already tapped into the spirit of traditional Scottish folk song and seemed to be begging for a bagpipe accompaniment, a sound not typically heard on rock discs.

Granted, some listeners were bound to find the lilting tune and the nostalgic chorus a bit mawkish. But for Paul, that was a risk worth taking, because he sensed that if it were done right, 'Mull of Kintyre' could become the kind of Standard that 'Auld Lang Syne' and 'Amazing Grace' were—and mawkish or not, 'Amazing Grace' had topped the British charts for five weeks in a bagpipe-heavy recording by the Royal Scots Dragoon Guard. Nor would it have been lost on Paul, in his capacity as a publisher, that a song with that kind of heartstring-tugging appeal could be a gold mine.

But there was still the problem of the unfinished verses. Sitting on the steps of one of the cottages sharing a bottle of Famous Grouse whisky, Paul and Denny set about completing the song.

"The place has spectacular views out over the Mull and the inspiration for the [lyrics] came to us as we got more and more drunk,"[30] Denny remembered. "We just kind of got in the mood and

* 'Yamaha Link' would soon become 'Cuff Link.'

sat there and looked out to sea and got the whole vibe of the Scottish countryside and that was it."[31]

Like Wordsworth describing the wonders of Grasmere in his 1804 poem 'Daffodils,' Paul and Denny needed only to open their eyes and write down what they saw. Wild deer bounding through the glen, lush green valleys, and distant mountains like the nearby Beinn an Tuirc (the Hill of the Wild Boar), all joined low sea mist on a lyrical checklist of sights the McCartneys were blessed with every time they stepped out of their house at High Park.

When the song was finished, Paul contacted Tony Wilson, the pipe major of the Campbeltown Pipe Band, and invited him to High Park. Paul had never written for bagpipes, but he knew from working with George Martin on the string arrangement for 'Yesterday' and the orchestral scores for other songs, that instruments had specific ranges and limitations. So he had two questions for Wilson: would the band be available to record one of his new songs, and what did he need to know about writing for bagpipes?

"You're a bit limited if you're thinking of using bagpipes because they've got a limited range," Paul noted. "They only can play certain notes. So it had to be in a particular key for the bagpipes. So I wrote it all around that idea. And I was quite happy with the tune of it, 'cause I thought it was like reminiscent of Scottish songs, which is what I'd wanted. But it sounded fresh."[32]

It turned out that the song would need some rearranging. The version Paul and Denny worked out was in the key of A major, but that was awkward for the bagpipes. Paul wanted them to have a solo section that was essentially the melody of the chorus, but they were unable to play all the necessary notes in the key of A. Paul transposed the song to D major and recorded a demo with Denny, overlaying a synthesizer version of the proposed bagpipe part.

When they met with Wilson in mid-July, they learned that there was actually some flexibility: the pipes could not play the melody in A major, but they could play a counterpoint to it. Paul had a brainstorm: the song could begin in A major, with him and Denny on acoustic guitars, strumming a simple pattern—bass note, chord, chord—and then modulate to D major for the pipe band's solo section. The second verse ("*Sweep through the heather like deer in the glen*") would be sung in D major as would the chorus that followed.

Key changes can have an interesting effect, in that even if the listener has no idea (or interest in) what key a song is in, repeating an already-heard melody in a new key can make it sound fresh, even surprising. So for good measure—once Wilson assured him that the pipers could play the harmony line he had in mind—Paul threw in a few more key changes. The third verse ("*Smiles in the sunshine and tears in the rain*") returns to A major, but the final chorus moves back to the bagpipe-friendlier key of D.

Paul and Denny made another quick demo, this time with vocal harmonies and lyrics, as well as a synthesized bagpipe part.

"We just worked it up," Paul said. "I gave [Wilson] a tape, he went back, he rehearsed it with his lads, and they came up a couple of weeks later and I said, 'Have any problems with it?' He said 'No, nae problem.'"[33]

Paul had another idea as well, one that occurred to him as soon as he revived 'Mull of Kintyre.' Rude Studio, he decided, was nice for making demos, but he thought it was time for something larger, for proper recording—somewhere he could record 'Mull of Kintyre' so that his paean to Scotland could be recorded locally.

With his money disentangled from Apple, and with the proceeds from the world tour and *Wings Over America* pouring in, Paul was feeling flush, and having a better studio on his Scottish estate made sense. In fact, he was already imagining a grander move: why not install a proper studio in every location where he owned a home and spent a significant amount of time?

Paul contacted Steve Thomas and Tim Whitmore, the designers who had just finished revamping MPL's Soho Square offices, and summoned them to Campbeltown.

"Having got there," Thomas said, "he dumped us in his Land Rover, took us over to Ranachan, and went into the cow barn, which is about five foot deep in cow shit from, I suppose, 100 years ago, with no roof at all, no windows, no doors, no anything."

When they walked in, Paul clapped his hands, which Thomas understood was to test the acoustics—an odd thing to do in a building with no roof, but it was Paul's way of introducing the assignment.

"Not the perfect place for a studio," he told Thomas, noting that it was under the flight path to Machrihanish airport. "But that's what you're going to do."

"What, a studio *here*?"

"Yeah," Paul responded, "this is the studio. I want a mezzanine with a solid wall in front of the mezzanine so that if you're down here, you can just see the tips of the violin bows when they play a top C."

"How high is that?" Thomas asked.

"I don't know, work it out," Paul told Thomas, and then led him to the next room—the milking area—and said, "This is going to be the control room. You don't have to worry about [the equipment], because that's all going to be coming up from London in a lorry. But the windows have to be double or triple glazed, and each glass panel has to be at a different angle so that the sound doesn't go through, and I want soundproofed double doors. And the farmhouse has to be completely redone for human habitation, because that's where the band is going to stay, and the technicians."

Thomas looked over at the farmhouse and began organizing his thoughts about what would be necessary, and how to approach it, when Paul added one more requirement.

"Oh, by the way," he said, "you've got a month."

"*What?*" Thomas and Whitmore asked in unison.

"Yeah, yeah, you're fine," Paul said. "People are very willing to work quite hard up here. Use everybody local you can, because there's so much unemployment up in Campbeltown."

But why, Thomas wondered, must the studio be ready in a month?

"Because this record I've got in mind is going to be the biggest seller of all time, and we all know that's down to Christmas," Paul told him. He then explained the timeline, working backward from the release. "EMI need a month to press and distribute it, and I need a week to record it, so therefore you've got this bit, which is a month."[34]

Whitmore returned to London, leaving Thomas in Scotland to oversee the studio project. "We flew in a structural engineer from Glasgow," Thomas said, "who did the structural calculations for the mezzanine on the bonnet of his car, handed them to us, and said, 'I'll phone the steel works and tell them what it is.' We had the steel work helicoptered in, and the guys turned up from Glasgow to install it."

Thomas contracted a local building firm, Weir, Ferguson, Martin Ltd., who supplied enough workers to fill two eight-hour shifts daily. By the last weekend in July, the studio was built (but for the recording equipment) and the farmhouse was renovated. Weir, Ferguson, Martin celebrated by throwing a full-fledged cèilidh, complete with traditional Scottish dances like Strip the Willow and the Gay Gordons, for the entire building crew.

Paul and Linda, meanwhile, popped down to London on Saturday, July 30, for the final day of the weeklong CBS Convention at the Grosvenor Hotel. The Beach Boys, who had left Capitol in 1970 for their own Brother imprint, distributed by Warner, were about to move their business to Caribou, a CBS imprint, and were on hand to perform. Other guests at the closing-day bash were Mick Jagger and Ron Wood from the Rolling Stones, Jeff Beck, Stephen Stills, Neil Diamond, Ray Davies, Patti Labelle, Heart, and the Clash.

But Paul had not left Scotland on the eve of his new studio's completion just to rub shoulders with his starry peers or to hear the Beach Boys. With his EMI and Capitol contract up for renewal, several labels had been courting him through the Eastmans, and recently CBS had pulled ahead of Warner as the label most likely to lure him away from his longtime affiliation. Walter Yetnikoff, the CEO of CBS Records, insisted that releasing Linda's Suzy and the Red Stripes single had "no bearing"[35] on a deal with McCartney, but most observers thought otherwise.

Paul had the rest of Wings attend the convention as well, and the rumor that Paul's new agreement with CBS was a done deal was so prevalent that at the convention, someone congratulated Denny Laine on Wings' new contract. Jimmy McCulloch shared a table with Chris Thomas, who didn't find him much happier than when they spoke during the *Rockshow* overdubbing sessions.

Publicly, Paul was cagey, if not disingenuous, while negotiations were in progress. "It was just a rumor," he told Roger Scott in a Capital Radio interview. "Our record deal with Capitol is up for renewal soon and the talk was that if we were going to go with anyone [else], it was going to be CBS. It wasn't talk from us, it was talk from the executives and people. . . . And then CBS people started to hear about it and put it around a bit."[36]

On Sunday, Wings were back at High Park. Paul brought with him the backing tracks Lee Scratch Perry made for Linda in Jamaica, reduced from the 24-track master to a four-track reel. That afternoon, with Paul manning the Studer deck, Linda added her lead vocal to 'Mr. Sandman' and 'Sugartime.' Wings also recorded 'One Woman,' a jam that ran nearly 12 minutes, and by the end of the day, Paul made stereo mixes of the jam, 'Mr. Sandman' and 'Sugartime.' It is possible that Paul and Linda were considering these for a follow-up to 'Seaside Woman,' but if so, the project never went further.

Now Paul's new studio was complete and even had a name—Spirit of Ranachan Studio. It was time to break it in. As crazy as his idea of getting the space built in a month was, Thomas accomplished it. But Paul recognized that installing the electronics and working out the bugs before it was time to record 'Mull of Kintyre' would not be possible. Instead, he hired the RAK Mobile Recording Unit from producer Mickie Most, who had it built in 1974, before his RAK Records label had its own studio. The mobile was run by Doug Hopkins, RAK's chief engineer, and Tim Summerhayes, his assistant.

In its full glory, the RAK mobile was an air-conditioned truck that worked as a moveable control room, equipped with an API 2488 mixing desk, two 3M multitrack decks (including an M79 24-track) and a full complement of limiters, compressors, an echo plate and a closed-circuit TV system that gave the engineers a view of the ensemble they were recording.

"But all the equipment could be easily de-rigged from the truck and into a location control room,"[37] Tim Summerhayes explained. "It would take about a day. This is what we did in Scotland." Summerhayes and Hopkins, along with Geoff Emerick and Mark Vigars, assembled the Spirit of Ranachan control room. Hopkins returned to London, leaving Summerhayes to assist Emerick and Vigars and oversee RAK's equipment.

Trevor Jones and John Hammel shared the newly renovated farmhouse near the studio with Jimmy and Joe. Three caravans were parked near the farmhouse: Laine and Emerick each had their own; Tim Summerhayes and Mark Vigars shared one. "We would normally eat together, dinner and breakfast, in the cottage," Summerhayes said.

Recording Sessions

Tuesday, August 2–Friday, August 5, 1977.

Spirit of Ranachan Studio, Low Ranachan Farm, Campbeltown, Scotland.

Recording: Untitled Jams.
Overdubbing: 'Girls' School' and 'Famous Groupies.'

Wings inaugurated the new studio with an afternoon of jamming on August 2, while the engineering team tested the equipment and ensured that everything was working properly. The following day, the band added unspecified overdubs to the March 14 remake of 'Girls' School' and added Jimmy's lead and slide guitar parts, Joe's bongos and Denny's acoustic guitar (on the choruses only) to 'Famous Groupies.' Paul then double-tracked his lead vocal, and added backing vocals by the full band.

It did not go entirely smoothly. "Paul and I were discussing the guitar solo," Emerick recalled, "and there was an issue with the guitar solo that Jimmy had started. And I said, 'Well, he should do this, or he should do that.' Paul said, 'Go out and tell him.' I made a remark to Jimmy [and] he was very obnoxious. He swore at me, because he'd been drinking and I asked him to do something. . . . I didn't take it personally because these musicians are under so much pressure, they need an outlet, whether it's drinking or drugs. You've seen it happen to so many artists."[38]

Recording Session

Monday, August 8, 1977.
Spirit of Ranachan Studio, Low Ranachan Farm, Campbeltown, Scotland.
Recording: 'Mull of Kintyre.'
Editing and Mixing: 'Mull of Kintyre' and 'Girls' School.'

The basic track for 'Mull of Kintyre' required only Paul on acoustic guitar and Denny on bass, with Paul singing a guide vocal. It is likely that Joe kept time for the duo by playing a steady beat on his bass drum that was never intended to be heard in the finished mix. Although Paul had Spirit of Ranachan Studio built specifically for this recording, it was a glorious summer's day, so he opted to record the track outdoors, surrounded by the landscape that inspired it. That meant that his vocal mic needed a wind guard, something that was not part of the RAK Studio's kit. Trevor Jones was dispatched to find something, and returned with a Union Jack sock, adding a Silver Jubilee touch to the session.

‘Mull of Kintyre’ is not an especially tricky song, even with its multiple key changes, but he and Denny filled six reels of tape before they were satisfied that they had a master take. They spent the rest of the session making trial edits of the song, as well as rough stereo mixes of both ‘Mull of Kintyre’ and ‘Girls’ School.’

During the mixing, a crisis in the control room threatened to scuttle the day’s work. The 3M M79 deck used a bright light and a photo sensor between the capstan and pinch rollers to detect when a reel of tape ran out and shut down the machine. But the light had the unfortunate side effect of attracting moths. The engineering staff had batted away several of the insects during the evening session.

“However, one of these creatures became attracted by the bright light, got caught in the mechanism and exploded across the tape,” Summerhayes recalled. “We had a problem.

“Geoff, Mark and myself spent time thoroughly and carefully cleaning the affected tape. We did have another recorder there and were planning to make a copy as soon as we were convinced that we could still even play the original. After another thorough clean of the M79, we carefully rethreaded the tape and pressed the play button. All was good. I think we also tried recording a test tone across some free but contaminated tracks. Again, all was good.”

They made a safety copy of the master take but never used it. The next day, Trevor was dispatched to buy wire mesh to moth-proof the control room.

Exploding moths, it turned out, were only the start of the evening’s problems. Jimmy, perhaps miffed at having nothing to play on a song Paul was touting as Wings’ next single—a new frustration added to those he was already bearing—went into town and got roaring drunk. When he returned to Low Ranachan farmhouse, he went on a rampage in the new kitchen, smashing crockery, breaking the dishwasher and hurling food at the walls, including a dozen of Linda’s hand-collected eggs, as well as ketchup and whatever sauces he could find.

In the morning, Denny walked from his caravan to the farmhouse to grab some breakfast, saw the wreckage Jimmy had left, and hoofed it up to High Park to warn Paul about the mess, adding “it’s nothing to do with me.” The other caravan dwellers slowly discovered the scene. No one had any doubts about who caused it.

“Damage had been done to the cottage, and this became apparent to me when we went up for breakfast,” Tim Summerhayes related. “I know that Paul had become involved and he was coming down to the cottage.” Summerhayes returned to his caravan. “It seemed fitting that I should not be there. I don’t know what was said, but I never saw Jimmy again.”[39]

One witness who remained, however, reported that Paul went into Jimmy’s room, pulled him out of bed and ordered him to pack up and get off his property, adding that if he came near Paul again, Paul would kill him.[40]

"Jimmy was just Jimmy," Denny Laine observed. "He was just a young kid who was bit stroppy, he was a little Scotsman who used to drink too much sometimes and go over the top. But apart from that, he was a nice kid, y'know? Nobody took [his behavior] that seriously. We just dealt with it."[41]

"Yes, he had some problems with drinking," English acknowledged. "But I know the other side of Jimmy where you could just sit down and talk and have a good time—it wasn't all rock 'n' roll all the time. But he did have these situations with drinking, and it saddened me. Because when you take away all the bad stuff there was a Jimmy who did have a tender heart."[42]

In a more reflective moment, Paul acknowledged that Jimmy's departure was inevitable.

"Jimmy's story is a long one," he told a reporter. "You see, I have these weird little influences that I can't do much about. So it ended up that he wanted to do things differently. So naturally we weren't fitting and were having a few bad vibes.[43]

"What's the use of having a brilliant guitarist in the band when he's such an unpleasant pain in the ass who makes the whole thing so uncomfortable for you? With Jimmy he felt I was directing him too much. He'd never say, 'No, I want to do it this way.' I could just feel the tension rise. If he'd stayed, recording the next LP would have had problems."[44]

Recording Sessions

Tuesday, August 9–Thursday, August 11, 1977.
Spirit of Ranachan Studio, Low Ranachan Farm, Campbeltown, Scotland.
Recording: 'Jam (Day After Pipers)' and 'Jam (Good One).'
Overdubbing: 'Mull of Kintyre.'
Editing and Mixing: 'Mull of Kintyre.'

With the morning's drama sorted, the farmhouse cleaned up, and Wings now a quartet, the technical crew prepared to record the Campbeltown Pipe Band's contribution to 'Mull of Kintyre' in the late afternoon on August 9. The band, 14 strong, turned up in full traditional dress. Paul liked the fact that the players were amateurs in the original sense of the word—people who played music for the love of it rather than professionally.

"They all live there," he told Capital Radio's Roger Scott. "They're farmers and farmers' sons, and an ex-copper from Glasgow, a few nutters, and they're a nice bunch."[45]

All told, there were seven bagpipers (Pipe Major Tony Wilson, Pipe Sergeant Dougie Lang, John McGeachy, Ian McKerral, Archie Coffield, John Lang Brown and David McIvor) and seven drummers (Drum Sergeant Campbell Maloney, Ian McKenzie, David Hastie, Jimmy McGeachy, bass drummer Tommy Blue, and tenor drummers Ian Campbell and John McCallum).

"It was a beautiful summer's night," piper John Lang Brown remembered. "We turned up with the full regalia on—we had our kilts, uniforms, everything on—and Paul was totally surprised. He was delighted that we went to the effort to actually get dressed up for the occasion, you know, because he was expecting us to turn up in our civvies and just play on the track. But the Pipe Major, big Tony, he said, 'No, we'll do it properly.'"[46]

After Tony Wilson's visit, Paul bought a set of bagpipes, possibly in the hope of joining the band during the session. But that was not to be. "It was hard getting a note out of them, and for weeks I would turn red as a London bus—practically blowing my head off. But one day a moaning noise came from the pipe and I knew I'd made a start. But Denny just fell about laughing."[47]

There was some discussion of how to record the pipe band. When Tony Wilson visited High Park to go over the arrangement with Paul and Denny, it quickly became clear that a bagpipe was too loud to be played indoors, so seven of them, plus seven drummers, would create quite a racket. Nevertheless, Emerick decided that the pipers could be recorded in the new studio, and he set up ten Neumann KM84 microphones. The only problem was that the volume of sound the bagpipes produced militated against the close miking that was one of Emerick's signature techniques.

"So we used a few room mics and a couple closer to get the drones rather than the chanter part,"[48] Emerick said. It was decided, too, that the pipers would be recorded first, inside the studio. "The pipers were arranged in a straight line inside the barn," Summerhayes recalled of the session. As Lang Brown remembers the session, "two or three takes, at the most" were required to capture their performance. The microphones were then set up outside the studio to record the drums.

"We did the drums at about 10 P.M.," said drummer Jimmy McGeachy, who at 15 was the youngest member of the band. "I remember that because we did them outside to get [the] sound, and Paul stood amongst us. We laid it down, and then we did it again—we double-tracked it."[49]

Once the drums were successfully captured, Trevor Jones pushed a wheelbarrow full of McEwan's Export beer, Famous Grouse whisky, Coca-Cola and lemonade over to the studio, and the pipe band joined Wings for a post-session party, with Mary and Stella playing waitress. As the musicians drank and bantered, Paul was having second thoughts about whether it made sense to release 'Mull of Kintyre' as a single at a time when punk ruled the charts.

"When I first heard it," he said, "I thought, 'Oh well, it's a nice track and everything, but it can't be a single really 'cause everybody's doing really rocking stuff . . . How can you come out with a Scottish waltz?' But the pipers, when we did it, they said, 'Aye, gotta be a single, aw, grand, aye. The exiles will love that,' and all of this. And I was saying, 'Oh yeah, well, we'll see.'"[50]

While the older musicians were drinking, young Jimmy McGeachy peeled off from the group and headed back into the studio.

"I was in my first band at the time—like a school punk band," he explained, "so, I was obviously keen about the recording side. There was a mezzanine floor, and when we finished recording, I buggered off upstairs, and all the guitars that Paul's got, they were all up on this mezzanine floor, and I'm like, *'Man!'* Joe was using this Pearl Concept kit at the time, and it was all set up. And I'm just mucking about, tapping away on the kit, and Linda comes up. I had a great time there with Linda—we were both jamming away on the kit, and she had the shakers and tambourines. And then Joe English comes up, and we had a great wee moment up there."

Linda and Paul, it turned out, had heard McGeachy's band rehearsing when they were in town. So before the pipers and drummers filed into their minibus to return to Campbeltown, at about 1 A.M., Linda signed a cigarette packet for McGeachy. "Good luck with your group Jimmy,"[51] she wrote above her signature.

"I do remember," Summerhayes added, "that some of the musicians were found, still unconscious, on the farm the following day."

On Wednesday afternoon, Paul and Denny edited the master take of 'Mull of Kintyre.' As it was recorded, the song ended with the drums trailing off beneath a sustained bagpipe chord. That now struck Paul as flat, so he edited on an earlier section of the pipe band playing the chorus, trimming the track's running time by ten seconds in the process.

The recording was by no means complete at this point—Paul's original guide vocal had not yet been replaced, and there were other touches he wanted to add. But for the moment, 'Mull of Kintyre' was filed away, a fresh reel of tape was threaded onto the 3M deck, and Wings unwound with a loose improvisation titled 'Jam (Day After Pipers).' On Thursday, too, Wings put serious work aside and recorded another jam, called 'Jam (Good One).'

Before leaving Scotland, Paul summoned Steve Thomas to Spirit of Ranachan once more.

"I have a fantastically high regard for Paul," Thomas said. "I admire the man a lot. But I don't like his music. I never have. I was a Rolling Stones fan, not a Beatles fan, and if I'd been a Beatles fan, I would have favored John, not him. And Paul knows that. But he used the fact that I didn't like his music, because it meant that he'd found someone who would be honest, would tell him the truth.

"When I got there and found no one at Ranachan, I went to High Park, where he lived. He always liked a bit of theatrics, Paul. There was just a tape player, standing on this table that fell to bits if you leaned on it, with a cassette tape leaning up against it. I made myself a cup of tea, sat down and waited for him.

"Paul turns up and he says, 'Ah, great. You obviously want to hear the results of your labor.' And he played 'Mull of Kintyre,' which I thought was awful. Just fucking dreadful. So he played it again.

And again. And again—he must have played it about 14 times. I said, 'No, I give in, I like it!' And he said, 'I know you don't. But I'll tell you, this is going to be the biggest hit record of all time.'

"Then he pulled out of the back pocket of his Levi's another cassette tape and slammed it in. It was 'Girls' School,' which is a rock and roll number. And he said, 'That's for you—that's my way of saying thank you for doing the job.' I thought it was a really sweet gesture."

—

Two days after the final session at Spirit of Ranachan, Joe English was back in Georgia, attending Capricorn Records' annual barbecue and summer games at Walden Lakeside Park, near Macon. He was having a difficult time. Dayle's accident exacerbated the homesickness he had been feeling ever since he joined Wings and moved to London, and he was increasingly discontented in other ways, too.

It bothered him—as it had bothered Jimmy—that as high as Paul was on 'Mull of Kintyre,' he had no part in it, other than to be a human metronome during the recording of the basic track. Jimmy's dismissal left a bad taste in his mouth as well. And there was more. Dayle, after her accident, had become a born-again Christian, and Joe was not only amenable to her new religious fervor but had a superstitious side that began to unnerve him during his stay at Low Ranachan.

"He had an experience up on the farm in Scotland with Paul," Dayle related. "He said one night he woke up and he looked out the window, and he said he saw the standing stones on the property. And you know, Paul liked odd things, but it scared [Joe] really bad. He said all he could feel was this presence of evil."[52]

Joe attended the Capricorn party as the guest of Bonnie Bramlett, with whom he was about to tour when he was invited to record with Wings in Nashville. Bramlett was aware of Dayle's accident and Joe's discontent, and most likely alerted Irwin Steinberg, Capricorn's president, that Joe would be at the barbecue. Although it is unlikely that Steinberg hoped to lure Joe away from Wings, he gave him a possible exit ramp in the form of an open offer to work with Bramlett and other Capricorn artists at the label's studio in Macon.

Paul and Linda remained in Scotland for several more days, and they were still there on August 16, when they were shocked to learn about Elvis Presley's death, at age 42, in Memphis.

By August 22, they and the girls were back in London for the start of the school term. There were also discussions to be had at MPL about parting ways with Jimmy, who was under contract. Jimmy and Paul agreed on an official story—that Jimmy felt that his talents were not best suited to Wings, and that he left of his own volition. When he began touring with the re-formed Small Faces, in early September, the official line became Jimmy left Wings to join Small Faces (although he was enlisted for tours, not as a full-fledged band member).

While the details of Jimmy's severance were being negotiated, the guitarist gave a couple of interviews in which he made no reference to his departure from Wings; in one, he even spoke about the Campbeltown Pipe Band session and its hard-drinking aftermath as if he were there, which both Summerhayes and McGeachy insist was not the case.*

Sipping a pint while fielding questions outside the Beacon Hotel in Glasgow, McCulloch was oddly detached; referring to the Wings as "they," and offering some interesting observations about Paul and the band.

"I don't see Wings staying together much longer," he predicted. "Maybe another three years; Linda will soon have her fourth kid, and she's got all that to contend with. They'll keep working in the studio, but there may be another world tour and that will be the end of touring. I don't think Paul could tour without her; he could have in the past and he chose not to.

"Wings is as democratic as it could possibly be," he added, "because of [Paul's] influence and know-how, and having that much experience. He's not that easy to work with, he sets a very high standard and he's a perfectionist."[53]

It was not until the second week in September that Jimmy announced his departure.

"I learned a lot from Paul," he said of his time with Wings, "but I felt it was time for a change and the ideal change for me was the Small Faces. They are old friends of mine whose music I have always enjoyed."[54]

For his part, Paul issued a prepared statement that diplomatically avoided saying that Jimmy had been canned, but also expressed relief that he was gone.

"Jim had been playing some great guitar recently, and it is a pity he is leaving. But problems have been building up for quite a while now, so the rest of us are happy to carry on without him."[55]

Another bit of aggravation for Paul turned up in the form of a September 4 *Sunday Times* interview with Willy Russell, under the headline "Beatles Veto Kills a Film," about Russell's supposed anger at Paul for preventing a film version of *John, Paul, George, Ringo . . . and Bert.* It was old news—Paul's objections had put an end to the film project three years earlier, and Russell had written three plays since then. The *Sunday Times* interview was meant to be about his latest show, *Breezeblock Park*, which was about to open, with Norman Rossington, who played one of the Beatles' road managers in *A Hard Day's Night*, in its cast.

"At the end of the interview about my current play," Russell said, "the interviewer asked me,

* A group photograph taken on the day of the pipe band session and published in *Club Sandwich* did not include McCulloch, further confirming that he left Wings before the session. Any details he relayed to reporters about the overdub session were secondhand.

'Whatever happened to the film of *John, Paul, George, Ringo . . . and Bert,*' and I just told him it was stopped, but that it was no great concern of mine, and I certainly bore no ill will to Paul or anyone who stopped it. Well, two weeks later, I open the *Sunday Times* thinking I'm going to read a story about my play *Breezeblock Park*, and it's a story about how Paul stopped the film. Which, for the *Sunday Times* is a more enticing headline than, 'New Play Opens at the Mermaid Theatre.'"[56]

Irritated, Paul fired off an angry letter to the editor of the *Sunday Times:*

> Dear Sir,
>
> In last week's *Sunday Times* there was a story in which Willy Russell told how I had stopped his play and film "John, Paul, George, Ringo . . . and Bert" from being produced.
>
> Well, sorry Willy, but the main problem for me about the film being made is that it lays out a story which in many details is true to life, but in certain ways, distorts the truth.
>
> In the play, I leave the group and John Lennon begs me to stay "for the good of the group," whereas, in real life the opposite was true. He left, and the others and myself waited a few months before deciding to do likewise.
>
> It may seem unimportant to most people what the truth actually was, but the play might, in time, have come to be accepted as fact . . . something that has happened to many a story through the ages . . . And I myself would have had to live with the consequences of something that never actually happened!
>
> Paul McCartney[57]

"Because of that [story], Paul tracked me down and invited me over to Cavendish," Russell said. When Paul called Russell, he told him that the specific objection that he mentioned in his letter to the *Sunday Times* was based on having seen an excerpt from the play on television. Russell then understood that Paul's issue was not with the play as it was written, but with an edit the BBC had made for the sake of concision.

"They included a scene in which Paul is in a massive argument with John about the breakup," Russell explained. "In my play, the scene ends showing that, as history is now well aware, it was John Lennon who broke up the Beatles, not Paul McCartney. But the edit didn't [show that], and that was what Paul had seen. So when I said I'd be happy to go around and meet with him, I asked, 'Have you read the script?' No, but he saw it on Melvyn Bragg's show. 'Look,' I said, 'that was a travesty, I couldn't watch it myself. I'll bring you the script.' And I did. I went around to the house and took the script with me and said, 'Read it, you'll see—there's no way this was meant to be any

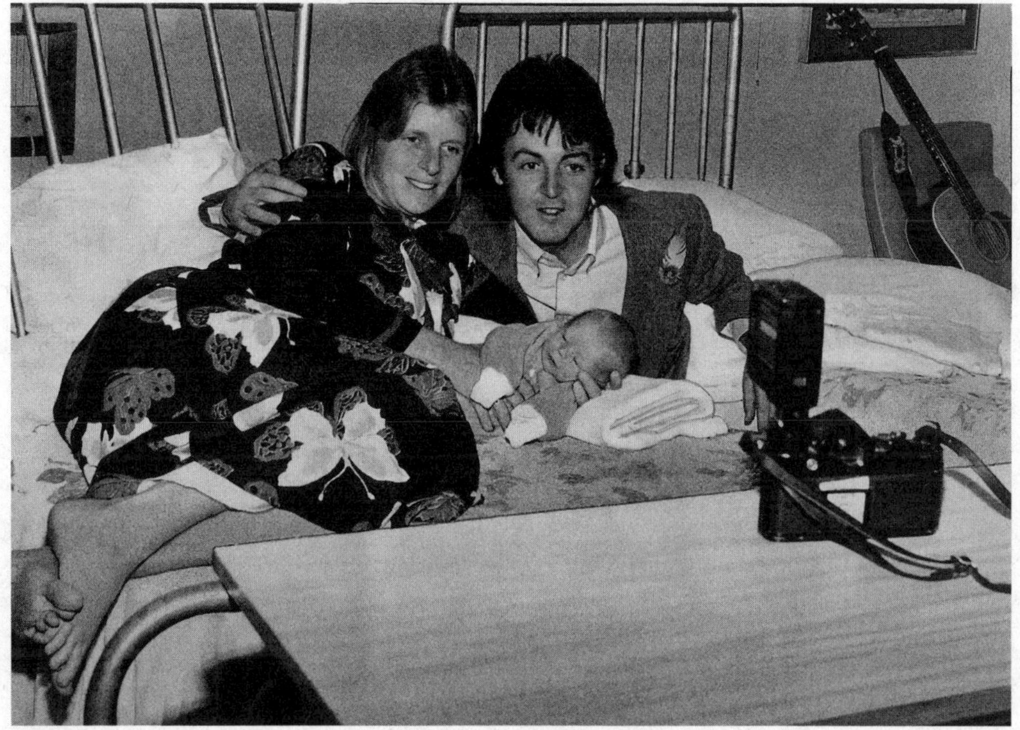

Paul and Linda welcome James McCartney into the world, September 12, 1977

kind of a hatchet job. . . . I wouldn't want to falsely depict something as crucial as the breakup of the Beatles.'"

They ended up having a friendly chat that lasted a couple of hours, Russell said, during which Paul offered him a tour that included a look at the Bill Black bass Linda had bought for him.

Paul oversaw the second Buddy Holly Week in London, September 7 to 14, and though it was a lower-key celebration than the previous year's bash, he was able to point to several record releases he had campaigned for. Among them were a Buddy Holly maxi-single with 'Maybe Baby,' 'Think It Over,' 'That'll Be the Day' and 'It's So Easy,' as well as *Western and Bop*, an album of Holly's collaborations with Bob Montgomery, plus a cover of 'Think It Over' by one of Paul's Liverpool friends, Freddie Starr.*

The main event of this year's celebration was a free concert by the Crickets, Buddy Holly's backing band, at the Gaumont State Theatre on September 14. It was the first time the band's original lineup—Jerry Allison on drums, Joe Maudlin on bass and Sonny Curtis on guitar and vocals—had performed together in 17 years. Paul attended the show with Mick Jagger, Ronnie Wood, Eric Clapton, Lol Creme and Kevin Godley.

* In return, Paul sang backing vocals on 'You've Lost That Lovin Feelin,' which appeared on Freddie Starr's 1978 eponymous album.

And in the aftermath of Jimmy's disruptive departure, there was a welcome arrival. On Monday, September 12, Linda checked into the Avenue Clinic in St. John's Wood, where James Louis McCartney was born by Caesarian section.

"I'm over the moon," Paul told reporters outside the hospital the next day. "When I knew the baby was a boy I really flipped. I was waiting outside the door when he was born. The baby weighs 6lb 1oz, has fair hair and looks like Linda. Linda is still a bit tired, but otherwise she's smashing, I don't know how she does it.

"Though my first name is James too," he added, "we are really calling him after my late father. The 'Louis,' as in Armstrong, is after Linda's late grandfather. We have called all our children after people we loved who have died. We don't go in for crazy names."[58]

Recalling the time around James's birth sometime later, Paul hinted that it was a bit more stressful than he let on.

"I remember many times [during Beatlemania] just sitting outside concert halls waiting for the police to escort us inside and thinking, 'Jesus Christ, I really don't want to go through this. We've done enough, let's take the money and run! Let's go down to Brighton, or something.' Linda and I felt like that when she was having our last baby. We were driving to the hospital and there was this terrible desire to say, 'Let's go to Brighton instead.' If we could have gotten away with it, we would have."[59]

20

SADDELL UP

With a new addition to the family, Paul spent the rest of September as a homebody, ensconced at Cavendish Avenue with Linda and their four children.

When BMI hosted a luncheon in London to honor British composers and publishers whose BMI-licensed works had racked up a million performances in America, he had Brian Brolly pick up his award. He and his former songwriting partner were well-represented: of the 34 songs honored, 11 were McCartney compositions, 10 were by Lennon.

Toward the end of the month, the McCartneys had a visit from Ringo and Nancy. Ringo had released his *Ringo the 4th* album on September 20, but any joy he felt about the release was tempered by the news that T. Rex front man Marc Bolan had been killed in a car crash four days earlier. Paul and Linda knew Bolan well, but Ringo was closer to him and had produced, directed and appeared in *Born to Boogie*, the 1972 film about Bolan and his band.

The friendly visit began to founder, however, when Paul raised the issue of a *still* unsettled bit of detritus from the Apple settlement, the matter of untangling and dividing up the Beatles individual and collective pre-1975 royalties.

"The Apple thing is very complicated," Paul said a few weeks later, "as it has been for many years. Ringo came to see us when we had the baby and we were chatting and polishing off a bottle of wine. We were having a great time until we started talking about Apple and the minute we did it was like *urgh*. So we thought, 'Christ, we'd best start talking about the light things again.'

"So this is the situation and as soon as anyone brings up the word 'Apple' there are these incredible rows. It's like a divorce—'Well, I'm not letting you have that unless you give me this,' and it gets so daft you end up thinking, 'Who needs it?' Really, it's nothing to do with what it was ever to do with."[1]

Apple had once again become a flashpoint with John too. Since his unsuccessful visit to the Dakota earlier in the year, Paul had seen another door slammed in his face when trying to persuade John to accept an agreement to untangle this last unsettled detail in the Apple divorce.

"If you knew the truth of what goes on in the business thing," Paul related two months later, "it gets a bit bitchy in there, and so we don't really have a chance to have a talk about anything normal . . . it tends to be business. I do not get on too well with John at the moment, because he's playing funny; he's being a bit weird, you know. He's doing funny things, and he's sort of holding everyone up actually. George and Ringo, I can see them, but John has got certain objections at the moment, and Lord knows what they are, but he is being a bit funny at the moment."[2]

If getting four parties to come to an agreement on how to divide the pot was not hard enough, John was no longer making business decisions for himself. Since playing peacemaker between the former Beatles and Allen Klein, Yoko had been overseeing John's financial interests, including Apple, causing friction in an already stalling legal process. Yoko's glacial bedside manner soon earned her a new private nickname: Madame Defarge, a moniker Paul and Linda plucked from the pages of Charles Dickens's *A Tale of Two Cities*.

With the rest of Wings at liberty, Denny appeared as a guest on David Essex's eponymous BBC television show on September 27, performing with the house band, which included Ronnie Leahy on keyboards, Alan Wakeman on saxophone, Barry De Souza on drums, and Mark Griffiths, Phil Palmer and Laurence Juber on guitar. Between segments, Denny chatted with Juber, a busy young session musician.

"David [Essex] was an old friend and admirer of mine," Denny noted. "Anyway, Laurence's brother* [*sic*] happened to be the conductor of the studio band and Laurence was the guitar player. So he came up to me and said, 'The guitar solo on "Go Now," do you want me to do this or that? Who played it on the record anyway?' And I said, 'I did.' So he copied my guitar solo and played it on the show."[3]

With his hands full at home, Paul seemed uninterested in bringing new musicians into the fold. But Denny, who—like Jimmy—often felt like a caged animal in the studio, saw things differently. If the band wanted to take their next album on the road, they would need a new guitarist, so Denny added Juber to a list of guitarists he was planning to bring to Paul's attention.

Juber had actually met Paul, sort of. Earlier in the summer, the guitarist was recording a jingle session at CTS Studios, where Wings were doing overdubs for *Rockshow* and *Wings Over the World*. Walking into the men's room during a break, he encountered Paul.

"We had our musicians' union 15-minute break," Juber said with a smile, "and went to the toilet. And there's Paul McCartney, zipping up his fly!"[4]

By the end of September, Paul was ready to get back into the studio to finish the next Wings album. It had been more than a year and a half since he had released a new studio album, and his absence from the rough-and-tumble resounded in the 1977 *Melody Maker* Readers Poll, published in the

* The music director for the *David Essex* show was Richard Niles, Juber's brother-in-law.

September 24 edition: Wings did not make it onto any of the best-of lists, and Paul's only appearance was in the International section, at No. 5 among bassists—after Chris Squire of Yes, John Paul Jones of Led Zeppelin, Mike Rutherford of Genesis, and Greg Lake of Emerson, Lake and Palmer.

A three-sided test pressing of the material Wings had recorded over the past seven months was made at IBC Studios on September 29; sessions would resume the following Monday.

Recording Sessions

Monday, October 3–Wednesday, October 5, 1977.
Abbey Road Studios, Studio Two, London.
Overdubbing: 'Mull of Kintyre.'
Mixing: 'Mull of Kintyre' and 'Girls' School.'

Paul was going back and forth on the idea of releasing 'Mull of Kintyre' as a single, sometimes convinced it would be a huge hit, as he insisted to Steven Thomas even before it was recorded, and sometimes worried that with raucous punk as the sound of the moment, his Scottish waltz might be seen as the 'Mary Had a Little Lamb' of 1977. The sentimentalist in him was eager to create a little anthem for a part of Scotland that had been his sanctuary; but the guy who felt sucker-punched when a *Rolling Stone* reviewer questioned his credibility as a rocker hated providing another target.

Nevertheless, Paul liked the song and the recording, and he knew that as varied as the material for the new album was, it would be hard to find a place for it alongside any of the new tracks. Its distinctiveness demanded the attention it would get as a single. So whatever doubts he harbored, he continued to prepare the recording for release.

At the October 3 session there was the added pressure of a film crew from London Weekend Television, there to film Paul at work, for use in the inaugural episode of Melvyn Bragg's new omnibus ITV program, *The South Bank Show*.

Bragg had met Paul socially but had never interviewed him. He knew that Paul was well disposed toward him: his previous show, *Read All About It*, was a book program for which he had used 'Paperback Writer' as his theme, and the first time he was introduced to Paul, Paul told him, "I was dead chuffed you picked that as your signature tune."[5] (*The South Bank Show* would use Andrew Lloyd Webber's ebullient rescoring of Paganini's Etude No. 24.)

As the television crew rolled film, Paul added an additional bass line to 'Mull of Kintyre,' as well as a new vocal to replace the scratch vocal he recorded in Scotland. He also overdubbed a new acoustic guitar part—this time with a capo on the seventh fret to add more high-lying harmonies to the guitar sound—as well as vocal harmonies, both on his own (singing a falsetto line) and with Linda, Denny, and a couple of musicians he drafted from Alan Parsons Project sessions in Studio Three,* guitarist Ian Bairnson and drummer David Payton.

"While at Abbey Road recording, some guy in the studio next door enlisted me and David to provide some authentic Scottish backing vocals to a song he was working on," [6] joked Shetland-born Bairnson, whose baritone voice can be heard during the song's first chorus.

The filmed part of the session was rounded off with a jam on Little Richard's 'Lucille,' with Paul singing and playing drums and Denny playing his double-neck guitar. Before the session ended, Paul made a stereo mix of 'Mull of Kintyre' and had EMI cut several dozen acetates, to be sent to members of the Campbeltown Pipe Band.

On Tuesday, Bragg and his crew returned to film an interview with Paul. Sitting at the piano in Studio Two discussing his music—going all the way back to 'I Lost My Little Girl,' his first song—Paul decided to offer Bragg and his viewers a quick songwriting class.

"It *is* a kind of magic," he told Bragg. "You're just plunking along on a chord, and you decide—for some reason, you decided to reach out and see what's there. See what you can pull down. And you can do it any time. You just do this," he said, turning to the keyboard, hitting a chord and singing *"Melvyn Bragg was in the parlor / And he said he was going to have some tea."* Turning again to the camera, he continued: "I mean, that's not very good, but we could work on that." He sang it again, adding a third, somewhat more melodic line, *"Will you have some tea with me / Melvyn Bragg"* joking that "it's not a very good name, that's the only problem. Now, Melvyn Rigby . . ."[7]

Bragg was stunned to see Paul produce the kernel of a song on the spot—let alone one in which he was the protagonist. "I was so taken aback when he finished the first verse," Bragg later lamented, "I omitted to ask him to go on with it. What a mistake!"[8]

After Bragg and his crew left, Paul made a fresh stereo mix of 'Mull of Kintyre' and filled two reels with mixes of 'Girls' School,' without settling on a master for either. He had better luck on October 5, when he remixed 'Mull of Kintyre' and 'Girls' School' once more, this time signing off on the masters for both sides of the single.

After the Bragg visit, Paul and Linda found themselves sitting in Paul's MPL office listening to Joe English telling them that the clear solution to his existential pain was to leave Wings and return to Georgia. When he phoned them to say he wanted to leave, he couched his resignation in humor. "I joked a little and told him that he had a bright future in this business and didn't need me,"[9] he said. But he agreed to come to MPL to discuss his decision.

"We were at Soho Square and I told them that I'd made the decision to go back home and leave

* The Alan Parsons Project were recording their *Pyramid* album.

Paul, Melvyn Bragg and Joe English during *South Bank* show filming, October 3, 1977

the band,"[10] said Joe. "McCartney once wrote this song [with the line] 'happiness is a homeland'* and I reminded him of that. I told him, 'The US is *my* homeland. I miss the US. I miss *my* family. I'd had enough of the hype and big glamour.' I mean, you can sit there and fool yourself all you want. But when you work with McCartney, the people are there for one reason. And it wasn't to hear me. I told Paul that. I said, 'They're here for you and I've got to get on my own feet before I stay too many years.' He saw this wild and crazy look in my eyes and told me to go home, mellow out for a month and think about it. But I never went back."[11]

Paul and Linda were aware of Joe's homesickness, and they knew that he was getting through it by self-medicating. What they did not know was how far his drug habit had taken him—or that in the days after Jimmy's dismissal, when he stopped at his London flat on his way back to America, he overdosed on heroin.

"At an early age, I started smoking marijuana," Joe later said of his drug journey. "Then I took LSD. And then as the years progressed the drugs got worse. And when I was with Wings, I was living in England and I was introduced to heroin, and there were a few times that I overdosed. I was by myself in my apartment."[12]

---

* The lyric, from 'Love in Song,' is actually "*happiness* in the *homeland*."

And though he was less outspoken about it than Jimmy, he felt a measure of musical frustration, as well.

"The music was sort of getting on my nerves," the former jazz-funk drummer complained. "It was pure commercial stuff and nothing else. . . . In Wings, I could never interfere with McCartney's thing. You've got to be happy with your job, otherwise it all catches up with you and you wind up miserable."[13]

Within a couple of days, Joe was back in Georgia. Hoping he might reconsider, Paul held off announcing Joe's departure until November.

"We'd been in that situation before, when we were about to record *Band on the Run*," Paul told an interviewer when news of Joe's exit went public. "We panicked then because there was just three of us, but as we recorded Denny and I found we could do most of the things ourselves. So the three of us are the nucleus. There's no sweat; we can add people when we go out on the road. I've tried to keep the lineup stable because when I was a kid it used to really annoy me to see the band that I was into chop and change, but that's the way it is."[14]

Paul could handle any drumming or lead guitar playing that might prove necessary to complete the new album. Nevertheless, the loss of two key players was going to have an effect.

"It got broken down when they both left," is how Denny put it. "And then we went into the studio to continue it. It lost us continuity, basically, and it became one of those albums. 'Well, what are we gonna do to put this right?'"[15]

"Making music in a band is all about chemistry,"[16] Paul once observed of the Beatles' enduring success. In the end, though chemicals propped up Wings Mark II, the lineup failed to spark a lasting chemical reaction.

By now, Paul had overcome his qualms about the chart prospects for 'Mull of Kintyre,' and decided that his best option was to have it both ways: 'Mull of Kintyre' and 'Girls' School' would be a double A side release. If radio stations and listeners thought a Scottish waltz-ballad was too unfashionable, they could flip the disc and hear a hard-rocking track with a lyric built from X-rated film titles.

"I've got past the stage when I really worried too much if I am in fashion or not," Paul argued. "I mean, there were times when I thought I should get a bigger, higher pair of platform heels and that [Glam Rock] came and went. So, after you have been through a few of these phases and seen all the dyed hair and stuff, you just end up thinking, 'Well, if I make good music that people like, then that's alright.'"[17]

EMI fought against the double A side plan; in fact, to the company's ears, the obvious choice for single release, among Paul's newest tracks, was 'Famous Groupies.'

“Record companies are always telling you things like, ‘You’ll be splitting your plays.’ And that means that you’ll get half the plays,” Paul told a radio interviewer. “So, we just didn’t listen to them anyway. We said, ‘Well, we’ll split the plays, but we wanted to get the other one noticed a bit.’ And it means that anyone who prefers that side now can buy the record. Because they know there’s something else other than just a ballad on it.”[18]

Having finally decided that ‘Mull of Kintyre’ would be Wings’ next single, Paul borrowed Michael Lindsay-Hogg from the *Wings Over the World* team for a few days to shoot a promo film for the song. They discussed the shoot over drinks at Cavendish Avenue.

“As we were talking, the phone rings, and it’s obviously a business call for him,” Lindsay-Hogg related. “And he said, ‘Listen, would you mind going outside in the garden while I take the call, and I’ll come and get you as soon as I’m finished. You can play with Stella and Mary.’ So I went out in the garden, and I say, ‘Hi girls, do you want to play?’ And they said, ‘Yeah, we have a good game for you,’ and whichever of them was the ringleader said, ‘It’s called tie you to the tree.’ Okay, how does that work? They said, ‘Here’s what happens. You come and stand by the tree, and then put your arms on the back of the tree.’ And one of them found a ribbon or something and tied my hands behind the tree.

“So then I said, ‘This is fun, but girls, listen—I’ve gotta go back and talk to your mother and father in a minute, so untie me.’ And they said, ‘Yeah, we will,’ and then they ran off inside. I’m there, still tied to the tree, and in a minute or so, Paul comes out into the garden and says, ‘Where are you?’ And I said, ‘Oh, your daughters tied me to the tree.’ He said, ‘Oh, that’s a game they like,’ and he untied me and we went back in.”[19]

Lindsay-Hogg, Brian Brolly, and Tony Richmond, who was to be the director of photography (as he was for *Let It Be*), took an overnight train to Scotland to scout out locations, and were entranced by Saddell Bay, a long, isolated stony beach set in the shadow of Saddell Castle, not far from Campbeltown.

Lindsay-Hogg and Geoffrey Forster, who produced the film, employed a crew of 13, including two assistant directors, electricians, and staff for lighting, focus, makeup and sound, from James Garrett and Partners, Ltd., a London film company, augmented by four members of the MPL staff. Jim Miller, a reporter for the *Campbeltown Courier*, was given exclusive access to the October 13 film shoot under strict terms.

“We approached the management company—a man called Alan Crowder—about getting access to the story,” said Miller, “and they agreed on the condition that it was for the *Campbeltown Courier* only, and it wouldn’t be sold to any other outlet. And we agreed to that. And I kept that promise throughout the entire time.”[20]

Filming began at around 10 A.M., focusing on the Campbeltown Pipe Band marching up the stony beach, with close-up shots of some of the players. After a dozen takes in full Highland dress, the pipers were exhausted. Following a lunch break, Paul, Linda and Denny were filmed walking along the embankment, with the surrounding hills and Saddell Castle in the background. The crew took another short break before filming crowd shots, for which two busloads of Campbeltown residents were invited to the shore and given a quick lesson in singing the chorus in preparation for the final sing-along shot.

"Fortunately, given the month, it was pretty good weather," Lindsay-Hogg said. "And it may not have been what the drum major was used to, doing it on the beach, but there's a wonderful moment when Paul and Denny walk away from the house, and they look down at the beach and the bagpipes come in. There's a shot of two little girls playing down by the rocks at the water's edge—that's Mary and Stella.

"The design of the video was not to seem what I'd call sophisticated in any way—it was really to celebrate that part of Scotland, the people who are from there, and the eternal seasonal idea of the place—you know, the waves rolling in. There were a couple of shots we couldn't get because it was October and the dark came on early. So we went to night a bit sooner than I'd like, but it was very good."[21]

Filming at Saddell Bay with the Campbeltown Pipe Band, October 13, 1977

Paul and Denny during the filming at Saddell Bay, October 13, 1977

As the afternoon light ebbed, floodlights lit up the castle walls, wood was chopped and a bonfire was lit. The filming ended with Paul, Denny and Linda playing and singing near the blazing fire, surrounded by a crowd of locals who joined in on the final verse and chorus.[22]

During a break, Linda explored the white cottage that is seen at the start of the film and discovered that the song had an unexpected nautical connection. Inside Linda found a navy hat marked H.M.S. *Mull of Kintyre*—a repair ship built in Canada for the Royal Navy and launched in 1945.

Paul and Linda spent the weekend at High Park, returning to London on Sunday. By the end of October, the *Campbeltown Courier* reported that the Campbeltown Pipe Band had signed a deal to record an album of bagpipe music at AIR Studios in London. The record, to be distributed by Chrysalis Records, was funded by Paul.

On October 24, 'Mull of Kintyre' (EMI matrix 7YCE 21793) and 'Girls' School' (EMI matrix 7YCE 21794) were mastered by Nick Webb at Abbey Road. Airplay versions with an edit of 'Mull of Kintyre,' trimmed from 4'42" to 3'37," were prepared as well. The American version of the single had been mastered by John Golden at Kendun Recorders on October 17, with mono DJ mixes prepared on October 21.

As Paul readied 'Mull of Kintyre' for release and prepared to resume work on the tracks Wings had recorded since February at Abbey Road and in the Virgin Islands, he took in another rush of Beatles news, the band still filling columns nearly eight years after the four musicians parted ways. John Lennon, largely absent from the news since Sean's birth in October 1975, held a news conference in Tokyo on October 12. John, Yoko and Sean had been in Japan since May and were about to head back to New York, but they wanted to announce that John's absence from the music scene would continue.

"We've basically decided, without great decision, to be with our baby as much as we can until we feel we can take the time off to indulge ourselves in creating things outside the family," John announced, taking Paul's focus on family life to another level. "Maybe when he's three, four or five, then we'll think about creating something else other than the child." He also offered his belated feelings about Elvis's death—"Elvis died when he went into the army"—and noted that he might visit England "at some point." Asked whether the Beatles might get together, he replied, "I doubt it very much."[23]

John's declaration that he was not interested in creating anything "other than a child" was a bit of a fib.

"There's this impression that my dad stopped doing music for a while to raise me," his son Sean later said. "But he was always playing music around the house, he was always making demos, and I can remember him recording into these tape cassette recorders."[24]

Demos to roll off the Lennon production line during this period included 'Real Love,' 'Now and Then,' 'Free as a Bird,' 'What Ever Happened To?' and 'She Is a Friend of Dorothy's.' Creatively, John was as prolific as ever, but he was not yet ready to begin publicly sparring for creative bragging rights with his old songwriting partner.*

In Liverpool, there was a contretemps about a proposed £18,000 ($31,800) life-size statue of the Beatles. Liverpool's General Purposes Committee voted down the plan, its chairman, Roy Stoddart, saying that "the Beatles have made no real contribution to this city," and "aren't worthy of a place in our history." Other council members chimed in to criticize the Beatles for leaving Liverpool, and Lennon for returning his MBE. Supporters of the statue proposal, including John Chambers, the 29-year-old joiner's mate who started the campaign, as well as Allan Williams and Harry Harrison, George's father, demanded an apology from Stoddart.

The intensity of the response forced the Liverpool Council to reconsider its stance, and on November 9, three weeks after the initial vote, the council reversed the General Purposes Committee's decision. When Paul finally weighed in, the day the council voted to approve the statue, his response was that having a statue erected while the band members were still alive was a bit macabre.

---

* With a little help from the former Fabs, three of John's unfinished 1977–78 home demos—'Free as a Bird' (1995), 'Real Love' (1996) and 'Now and Then' (2023)—were completed and issued as Beatles singles.

"I would rather be remembered by the council using money to set up a center for underprivileged children,"[25] he told the *Liverpool Echo*.

EMI, certainly, was not finished cashing in on its Beatles masters. The label released another double LP of previously issued material, *Love Songs*—the gently melodic mirror image of *Rock 'N' Roll Music*—on October 24 in the United States, with a November 4 release for the rest of the world. Nor was the label alone in wanting to celebrate the Beatles' music. ITV assembled *The Beatles Forever*, with Ray Charles, Diahann Carroll, Anthony Newley and others performing their interpretations of Beatles tunes, for airing on November 19.

Recording Sessions

Tuesday, October 25–Saturday, October 30, 1977.
Abbey Road Studios, Studio Two, London.
Overdubbing: 'Café on the Left Bank,' 'I'm Carrying,' 'Name and Address,' 'Morse Moose and the Grey Goose' and 'Children Children.'*
Mixing: 'Sweetest Show in Town.'

Sessions for Wings' sixth studio album were now into their ninth month, and recording fatigue had set in, exacerbated by post-pregnancy sleep deprivation. Returning to Abbey Road on October 25, together with engineers Geoff Emerick and Mark Vigars, Paul, Denny and Linda decided to enliven the proceeding by giving Studio Two a makeover. Their choice of décor was inspired by the song the trio chose to overdub that afternoon, 'Café on the Left Bank.'

"To get the atmosphere down at Abbey Road Studios, we had the whole place done out with like potted plants, and little café umbrellas, and little stripes," Paul explained, "to make it look like a café on the Left Bank. And there was some visiting bloke from an American record company, and he kind of walked in all serious—it was half a joke to us really, having a big café in the studio, but it was nice, the atmosphere and everything—anyway, this fella came in and he said, 'This is very interesting, Paul. What, er . . . ? What temperature do you keep it at?' So I said, 'Oh a constant 68, constant, absolute constant 68.' So I think he must have gone away and done a string of them up and down the West Coast."[26]

Drawing the line at donning a beret, Paul added his lead vocal—double-tracked—and joined

---

* It is impossible to precisely date all the overdubs done during this period. Those that could be determined appear in the week of sessions when they are known to have been done. The songs listed at the start of the current entry were known to have been overdubbed this week.

Denny and Linda for the backing vocals. As a finishing touch, Paul added cowbell. Besides the unnamed record executive, visitors to the studio during this block of sessions included the actor Victor Spinetti, Rolf Harris, Andy and Jay Mackay, Steve Harley, and Tony Garton (the captain of the *Samala*).

Moving on to 'I'm Carrying,' the acoustic track Paul recorded on the deck of the *Fair Carol*, he replaced his pilot vocal. It needed strings—nothing fancy, just a velvety string bed to add heft to the arpeggiated guitar chords. For the moment, Paul used the Mellotron and the Gizmo to create a light orchestration, pending a decision about whether this was adequate.

'Name and Address' was polished off with a double-tracked guitar solo by Paul, and backing vocals by Paul, Linda and Denny. The track was then given a dollop of tape echo to underscore its rockabilly elements. Paul had a touch of competitive inspiration here: while they were recording his guitar solos, Hank Marvin, the Shadows' lead guitarist, watched from the control room.

Also likely worked on during this week was 'With a Little Luck,' to which Paul added three keyboard parts (including a polyphonic synthesizer) and a double-tracked lead vocal, with Paul, Linda and Denny joining forces for two, possibly three tracks of backing vocals.

One song that needed considerable work was 'Morse Moose,' which at the end of the Virgin Island sessions was an experimental instrumental. Back in London, Paul and Denny wrote lyrics for the song's outer sections—actually only three lines, "*Right on down at the bottom of the sea / Tell me are you receiving me? / My name is Morse Moose and I'm calling you,*" repeated several times. The idea, as Paul explained it, played off the Morse code–like keyboard figure that is the basis of the track.

"We didn't have a song to go with it, but we decided to make one up as we went along. So, we thought of the words, 'Morse Moose' and decided we'd have this big sort of sea drama with this fella saying, 'I'm Morse Moose and I'm calling you'—he is like someone trying to rescue anyone in distress who is on the sea."[27]

But even with the repeating verse overlaid at several points in the track, there remained a section of about 1'20" duration where something different was needed. They considered trimming the track, which ran a hefty 6'35". But they opted instead to write a four-verse song in the form of a sea shanty, about a boat called the *Grey Goose*—"Which," Paul added, "is another bit of sea drama. We just strung it all together and it's like a mad sea epic."[28]

Creating this "mad sea epic" required a lot of overdubbing. Playing up the sea shanty idea, Paul and Denny adorned the 'Grey Goose' section with acoustic guitars, and Denny also added bongos. Paul added his lead vocal, heavily processed to give it a constricted, almost electronic timbre. Paul and Denny also recorded multiple tracks of backing vocals. The finished track became 'Morse Moose and the Grey Goose.'

Paul added Mellotron strings to the track, but he ultimately decided he also wanted real strings, brass and an accordion. He commissioned an arrangement from Wil Malone, who had scored the 1972 orchestral version of Pete Townshend's rock opera *Tommy*. Paul was tempted to commission orchestrations for other songs as well, but Emerick argued against it.

"We did rough mixes when we got back into port," Emerick explained, "[then] we got back to England and Paul wanted to dub some orchestra stuff. I did these rough mixes in seven hours—they sound amazing, they really do. The album should have been left as it was."[29]

After considering Emerick's point of view, Paul overrode his opinion. But instead of engaging a single arranger, as on earlier albums, he enlisted three, including Malone. Mike Vickers, the former multi-instrumentalist for Manfred Mann and the conductor of the orchestra during the Beatles' global telecast of 'All You Need Is Love,' was hired to orchestrate 'Girlfriend.' And Bobby Richards, who Paul knew from film work and arrangements for the Seekers, was asked to write a string score for 'I'm Carrying.'

'Children Children' needed sweetening too. Paul and Denny played recorders, and Paul tried his hand at the violin, which joined Denny's autoharp and Jimmy's harmonica, on the original recording, to amplify the song's childlike magic.

"We thought we should do it like a kind of fairytale kind of thing,"[30] Paul said of his aim for the track. "It is supposed to be the kind of thing you imagine—it's like an animated film going on with lots of little dwarfs and fairies and elves, all down in Dingly Dell, with little violins, and little flutes and stuff, all singing. It's just a children's song, this one."[31]

For the most part, though, Paul saw the sense in Emerick's preference for simplicity and directness.

"Most of it is just the straight backing tracks where we decided to not really put too many strings on stuff," Paul said of his new material. "We have ended up doing it with guitars, and doing it with synthesizers, rather than big string sections. And some of the tunes are a bit simpler than we've been doing. It just comes in phases—at one moment you've been listening to some records that are really produced, and you think, 'Ooh, yeah, I want to do that kind of thing.' Another moment you're listening to something that is very simple, and you think, 'Yeah, I really like very simple music.' So, we sort of come in the middle of that, probably. It's not dead simple, 'cause [there's] a lot of stuff there in the mixes. After a few times when you listen, if you listen on headphones or good equipment, there's all sorts of stuff appears."[32]

Paul is known to have worked on one other track during this week. On October 26, he brought in one of the four-track demos he recorded in Scotland, a slow ballad called 'Sweetest Little Show in Town,' that could go in any of several directions—as a bluesy acoustic guitar ballad, for example, or fitted out with brass and winds as a 1930's-style tune. The demo suggested that the former was what Paul had in mind. For the moment, he was content just to make a stereo mix of the demo.

In early November, work on the film versions of the world tour continued apace, with Chris

Thomas completing his mixes for *Wings Over the World* at the Music Centre on November 1. He filled four reels with mono mixes, labeled as *Wings Over America '76 (Concert Film)*, and handed them over to the film production crew.

—

Recording Sessions

Friday, November 4–Thursday, November 10, 1977.
Abbey Road Studios, Studio Two, London.
Recording: 'Guitar and Drums Jam (Paul & Denny),' 'Join the Army (Jam),' 'Yamaha Links (Off the Cuff Links),' 'Backwards Traveller' and 'Boil Crisis.'
Overdubbing: 'Yamaha Links (Off the Cuff Links),' 'Backwards Traveller' and 'Boil Crisis.'
Mixing: 'Guitar and Drums Jam (Paul & Denny)' and 'Join the Army (Jam).'

Paul had no specific agenda when he returned to Abbey Road with Denny on November 4, but he had Emerick keep the tape rolling as he and Denny unwound with a couple of jams, one with Paul on drums and Denny playing guitar, listed as 'Guitar and Drums (Paul & Denny).' The instrumentation for their second jam, 'Join the Army (Jam),' is unknown, but Paul found both jams worthy of mixing to stereo, either to be worked on further or plundered for chord changes and melodic flashes.

Nothing was documented from the Monday and Tuesday sessions, long stretches of which were devoted to interviews. With 'Mull of Kintyre' about to be released, Tony Brainsby invited Ray Bonici of *Record Mirror* and Chris Welch of *Melody Maker* to Abbey Road. Both were given the official story of 'Mull of Kintyre'—that the idea was sparked by Paul's desire to write a new Scottish tune once he realized that most of the Scottish music you heard was either traditional or comedy—and they were told about the off-color Hawaiian origins of 'Girls' School.' Both interviews also covered Wings' two recent departures, with Joe's attributed to his homesickness and Jimmy's to his need to do something else.

"He wanted to make a move," Paul told Welch about Jimmy. "A bit like football, really. I don't know how long he was with us. . . . He's a good lad, Jimmy, a good guitar player, but sometimes he's a bit hard to live with. It's pretty well known in the biz and we just decided it would be better if we didn't bother anymore. It got a bit fraught up in Scotland. He's with the Small Faces now, but he's done a lot of nice guitar on the new album, and on the boat he was incredibly together."[33]

Oddly, while Paul usually argued that Wings should be seen as a band rather than as a star and his sidemen, his discussion of Jimmy's and Joe's departures made them both sound expendable. Both, he said, had completed the work required of them for the new album, and since the band was not going to tour soon, there was no hurry to replace them. In fact, he told Welch, they were barely even needed for studio work.

"Me and Denny both play guitar, and if it's not live we can work out the guitar things. And if we need to overdub, I can play drums too. . . . So here we are . . . back to a trio. No sweat. We'll just continue like this. It's easier now there are less people to deal with. We can make decisions quicker among ourselves."[34]

Paul also spoke with both writers about the musical backdrop for the release of his Scottish ballad—the British punk scene. "I think it's healthy," he told Bonici. "We're getting a younger wave of people coming up and that's good. I like punk and I like their attitude and the looks and fashion, though I'm not really into it myself. We learn more about what's happening from our daughter Heather. She's into punk and plays all the stuff all the time. For me it's just another style."[35]

His thoughts had crystalized more fully by the time he spoke with Welch the next day. "It's a different audience altogether. To me, punk is more important than glitter, and a lot of the stuff that's been going down in the past few years, just because it's got a bit more balls to it. . . . I can hear a lot of Who in it, Bryan Ferry and Dylan too, and Lou Reed. It's Velvet Underground, New York type stuff, but the British kids do it best at the moment. But I'm not into it. I wouldn't pretend to be. It's just a different kind of music. Instead of sitting down, they're jumping up and down. Great. Nice one."[36]

Anticipating that 'Mull of Kintyre' would likely receive a critical mauling, Bonici was also treated to one of Paul's disquisitions on how the music press pressure cooker affects him—and how the public's response helps him defeat the insecurity that criticism creates for him.

"Critics didn't like *Wild Life* when it came out, so I started thinking like them, that it was rubbish," he said. "Then when I heard it a couple of years later I really liked it and found it interesting. . . . But what made *Wild Life* okay for me was when I saw this fella heading for the hills in California holding a copy of *Wild Life*. So someone liked it. The same with *Wings Over America*. This bloke who works with handicapped children wrote to us saying—the children wrote to us saying—the album was the one that really lifted the children and he wanted to thank us for that.

"I never really liked *Venus and Mars* until I heard it at a party one night and saw everybody leaping around. That's the funny position you're in and there's no way you can tell who's into what. So I ignore all the bloody critics, get on with my stuff and think in the terms that someone somewhere liked it. Let's face it, critics never liked the big stuff in history. They never liked Van Gogh's pictures and has he got a name?"[37]

Welch also got an earful about critics, but his lecture was both more personal and more whimsical. Welch, who knew Paul from the Beatles days, and who had accompanied Wings on part of their 1975 British tour, had developed a good rapport with Paul. But he had also reviewed one of Wings' 1976 Wembley shows, and in the course of saying that he found the band more electrifying in 1975, he asked, tongue-in-cheek, "Who can fail to be moved on hearing 'Yesterday' at least once a year?"[38]

"I thought your review was shit," Paul told Welch as the writer walked into the Studio Two control room. Welch denied having written anything particularly damning, but Paul, pretending to be offended, refused to let up. "Oh yes you did. Prat. I remember everything. All that stuff about 'Yesterday'—it's engraved on my forehead. I'll never play it again!" When Denny joined them, well into the conversation, Paul introduced Welch by saying, "This is that cunt who gave us that bad review. Fucking 'it 'im!" To which Denny replied, "No hard feelings."

"My daughter went to see the Stranglers," Paul continued, still on the subject of criticism. "She's very into punk . . . well, she's the right age. She came back a changed person, over the moon, just loved it. And the next week a review appeared in one of the papers, and it was like a terrible review. 'The bass player was inefficient . . .' same old technical crap, you know. But come on, let's get off critics."

Paul gave Welch an overview of Wings' current recording sessions but declined to play any of the tracks, saying that the still-untitled album was unfinished, and anything he played Welch might be reworked before it was released. "But there is an up feel to the music from being on a boat," he said before teasing a tour.

"Next year, we won't do anything live until the album is out," he added, "because we wanna go out with some new stuff. I mean *you* didn't like us playing all the old stuff. Yes, I could quote your bloody review to you, Welch."

And he added a new twist.

"We actually fancy playing in some small, steamy clubs and get back to the people right there and playing to them for a laugh," he said, revisiting the university tour idea, except this time with clubs. He then expanded on it. "We keep wanting to do a residency. We'd like to get a little club somewhere and build an audience. We'd like to get a little scene going for a couple of weeks.

"There's a scene in the film we're doing," he added, referring to Gene Roddenberry's latest script proposal, "where a fellow is offering a girl £3 tickets for £20. We'd like to get away from that situation of, 'You are now coming to see this extremely expensive group!' I'd much rather have people come in at lunchtime, or after work, have a little dance and a cheese roll. We might have a couple of lunchtime sessions next year."[39] (Shortly after Paul's remarks were published, the Hope and Anchor, an Islington pub, invited Wings to perform there, but even if Paul was entirely in earnest about playing small venues, Wings were in no position to accept the invitation without a drummer and lead guitarist.)

Paul invited another journalist into the studio on Wednesday, this time Alasdair Buchan of the *Daily Mirror*, who conducted his interview in the early afternoon as Paul tucked into shepherd's pie and chips. At the same time, Linda was in another of Abbey Road's rooms for an interview with Maggie Norden of *Hullabaloo* to promote *Linda's Pictures.*

Buchan pressed McCartney on John Lennon's recent assertion that he had made his contribution to society and did not plan to work again. "He's full of wind, isn't he?" McCartney scoffed. "Maybe he isn't going to work anymore, but it's no skin off my nose. It's really up to John. I've heard him talk like that before. . . . I think he must be very bored now."

Like Bonici and Welch, Buchan quizzed Paul about punk, but got a strikingly different kind of answer—possibly because Buchan couched his question in terms of Glen Matlock's dismissal from the Sex Pistols for liking the Beatles and McCartney.

"I haven't heard them saying they hate Paul McCartney, but I expect them to," he said. "I like the music but I wouldn't buy it. It's youth music. But it's not new. When we came along, Cliff Richard was the establishment figure. We did interviews knocking him and the Shadows, saying they'd had it. We were the big new wave. . . . But I don't think many have really suffered on dole queues. Most I've met have been slightly upper class if anything."

Returning to work after Buchan and Norden left, Paul, Denny and Linda considered material from the collection of demos Paul recorded in Scotland during the summer. With his dismissive comments about punk still fresh, he and Denny made a quick and dirty recording of Paul's punk pastiche 'Boil Crisis' but agreed that it did not really fit with the material they had already recorded.

They worked more seriously on 'Back in Time,' which Paul quickly renamed 'Backwards Traveller' (both names are drawn from the lyrics). In its demo form, the song 'Back in Time' ran about 3'50", much of it a drum and guitar backing that seemed to be waiting for either further verses or solos.

Paul had written only one verse, in which the song's narrator mentions, matter-of-factly, that he was "*always going back in time*," a science fiction notion, hinting that the song may have been written with Roddenberry's film in mind. But this verse has an ear-catching rhythmic twist. The song is mostly in 4|4, but the third line—"*Rhyming slang 'Auld lang syne' my dears*"—begins with a displaced beat in "*Rhyming slang*," then switches to 3|4 for "*Auld lang*," also with a displaced beat, then back to 4|4 as the rest of the line comes spilling out.

The demo also includes the chorus—"*I am the backwards traveller / Ancient wool unraveller / Sailing songs wailing on the moon*"—which was all he needed for the song's intended purpose, to lead into the new album's existing bit of time travel, the 1950s throwback 'Name and Address.' But though 'Backwards Traveller' offers little in the way of narrative detail, it boasted a characteristically fetching McCartney melody.

Wings, 'Mull of Kintyre' single trade ad

"I was trying to get this song 'Backwards Traveller' to explain on the album why the album suddenly went to a '50s-type sound," Paul explained.[40]

Paul and Denny filled two 24-track reels with attempts at a backing track, with Paul on acoustic guitar and Denny on electric guitar. A basic take eluded them, however, and they abandoned the song for the moment, turning their attention instead to another curio from Paul's Rude Studio demo collection, 'Yamaha Links (Off the Cuff Links).' An expansive instrumental funk vamp, mostly on an unchanging D minor chord, it struck Paul as something he, Denny and Linda could turn into a short piece to link two of the tracks they had already recorded.

Paul, on a polyphonic Yamaha synthesizer, and Denny, on bass, recorded the basic track, with Linda playing a second synthesizer line. They filled two reels before completing a master take, then turned their attention to overdubbing. Between Wednesday evening and Friday afternoon, Paul added drums and two more synthesizer parts, treated with a combination of phase-shifting and wah-wah.

Recording Session

Friday, November 11, 1977.
Abbey Road Studios, Studio Two, London.
Recording: 'Backwards Traveller (Remake).'
Overdubbing: 'Backwards Traveller.'
Mixing: 'Children Children,' 'I've Had Enough,' 'Backwards Traveller,' 'Off the Cuff Link,' 'Deliver Your Children,' 'London Town,' 'Don't Let It Bring You Down' and 'Famous Groupies.'

The Wings trio returned to 'Backwards Traveller' on Friday and nailed a master take in short order. This time, Paul played drums on the basic track, with Denny playing acoustic guitar and Linda on keyboards. Paul then overdubbed another acoustic guitar as well as bass and synthesizer (playing underwater sounds) before adding a lead vocal and, with Denny and Linda, backing vocals.

They finished out the week by making rough stereo mixes, for review at home, of 'Children Children,' 'I've Had Enough,' 'Backwards Traveller,' 'Off the Cuff Link,' 'Deliver Your Children,' 'London Town,' 'Don't Let It Bring You Down,' and 'Famous Groupies.'

The journalist visits to Abbey Road were part of an MPL press blitz meant to put Paul back into the newspapers just as 'Mull of Kintyre' was being released, but not all the coverage was prompted by Tony Brainsby. The first weekend in November, *Record World* picked up on the buzz from Columbia Records' London convention and reported that Paul was considering signing with Columbia for the United States and EMI for the rest of the world when his current EMI deal expired in January 1979.

That same weekend, *News of the World* ran a large feature about Paul by Stuart White that drew mostly from interviews with others, including his brother and stepmother, and various friends and business associates (former Beatles manager Allan Williams and Apple Records head Ron Kass, for example).

Among the more illuminating sections of White's piece was a glimpse of an interest of Paul's that had not been much in the public eye—painting. Describing Paul sitting in his kitchen at High Park painting the Scottish landscape and stacking up completed canvases, the paper sought an assessment of Paul's talents from Dane Dixon, a California painter who had been an assistant to Willem de Kooning and had become friendly with Paul.

"Paul's oil paintings are mostly of views of the farm and the Scottish scenery around it," Dixon said. "From what he tells me, he just sits there with the wife and kids around and paints. Make no mistake, music is first with him, and he paints for relaxation. But like a lot of talented people, everything he does he does well. I've no doubt he could make a living out of art if he had to. Paul could even have a one-man show some day, he is that good. I don't think he's too anxious for anyone to know about his painting. I can't think why. A guy with talent like that shouldn't hide it."

Mike McCartney offered some unbuttoned observations about Paul's personality, including his vulnerability to criticism. "People may think he's cute, cuddly old Paul," Mike said, "and in a way he is. But there's a sharp side to him which comes out if people are trying it on with him. He can still come up with the killer retort. He's no pushover. . . . I wouldn't say he's cynical, but he has got a good memory. He remembers who his friends are.

"When he first went solo and then started his present group, Wings, and particularly when his wife Linda joined the band, a lot of the music papers got their knives out. Imagine how you would feel if half the papers were slating your missus. Well, they came through despite that and they made it. But Paul hasn't forgotten the people who were happy to knock him then. . . . Paul feels criticism very strongly. He's human and capable of being hurt. What he hates particularly is criticism if he thinks it is uninformed or done with the intention of getting at him."[41]

Indeed, Paul's ribbing of Chris Welch was one thing—he knew that Welch admired his work and was teasing him about a single snarky phrase in a concert review. But pointedly not invited to participate in the current round of interviews was *NME*, against which he nursed a grudge that went back to Charles Shaar Murray's confrontational interview at the time of *Venus and Mars*, an animus more recently topped off by the paper's slice-and-dice reviews of *Holly Days* and 'Seaside Woman.' *NME*, for its part, noted the boycott when Don Van Vliet (Captain Beefheart) joined what it called "the elite list of people who categorically refuse to talk to *NME*," a list that also included Paul, Lou Reed, Ian Anderson (of Jethro Tull) and Margaret Thatcher.[42]

To celebrate the release of 'Mull of Kintyre' on November 11, Paul threw a launch party at the new Dial 9 Club in Soho, for which guests were served traditional Scottish fare: a choice of avocado or smoked salmon to start, haggis or poached salmon as the main course, and Scottish cheeses, fruit salad and coffee for dessert. At the party, EMI presented Paul, Linda and Denny with Gold discs for *Wings at the Speed of Sound* and *Wings Over America*, and Silver discs for *Venus and Mars, Wings at the Speed of Sound* and *Wings Over America*, as well as for two singles—'Silly Love Songs' and 'Let 'Em In.'

Recognizing that the airplay necessary to make 'Mull of Kintyre' a hit might be difficult to come by, EMI hired Johnny Beerling, a BBC Radio 1 producer, to drum up interest—or, as Beerling put it, "so they had someone to blame if it didn't take off."[43] Among Beerling's colleagues at Radio 1, Paul Williams and Dave Price outright hated the single. Tim Blackmore at Capital Radio, Beerling reported, was not mad about the song either but persuaded Roger Scott, at Capital Radio, to play the single on his *People's Choice* program, in which listeners voted for the station's record of the week. The week Scott included the song, it was voted in fifth place among five discs.

Blackmore shortly called Beerling to say that 'Mull of Kintyre' was growing on him, so he added it to the playlist, and Radio 1 soon reconsidered as well. And over at Capital, Roger Scott had Paul and Denny in the studio to plug their new single on November 12. The same day, Paul spoke with Phil Griffin of Piccadilly Radio.

After a week of promotion, most of the reviews of 'Mull of Kintyre' and 'Girls' School' were in, and except for the ever-supportive American trade press, the critics either disliked the single outright or were at a loss to know what to make of it, other than that it reminded them of Rod Stewart's cover of 'Sailing.' Charles Shaar Murray, writing for the exiled *NME*, did not hold back.

> *Nice cover pic of the Isle of Davaar on the West Coast of Scotland. This is a tribute-in-song to the area in Argyllshire where Friendly Macca has his twee little hideaway. The Campbeltown Pipe Band, with whom Wings posed for the cover of* The Campbeltown Courier, *all sound good, especially Johnny Sinclair, but the song sucks on ice.*[44]
>
> *Charles Shaar Murray*, NME

Singalong-a-macca on the first track. Ol' flat voice just saved by the chorus and none other than the Campbeltown Pipe Band. Somehow it reminds you of the everlasting 'Sailing.' 'Girls' School' changes the atmosphere completely, rock and roll from Abbey Road Studios.[45]

Sheila Prophet, Record Mirror

'Mull' lies somewhere between a traditional folk song (the pipes and drums of the Campbeltown Pipe Band are enlisted for full malt flavor), a scarf-waving chant (in the Rod Stewart vein) and a late night at the boozer.[46]

Ian Birch, Melody Maker

Double A side. What couldn't be done with a song called 'Girls' School'?! What couldn't be done in a girls school?! A damned sight more than McCartney and spouse do. 'Mull' threatens to be this year's 'Sailing' . . . dancing on the terraces. Aaaaarrgh . . . [47]

Jane Suck, Sounds

First product from Wings in nine months is a double A sided single. 'Girls' School' is a powerful rock 'n' roll tune that describes that kind of female institution. McCartney's vocals are pitted against a driving guitar and bass. 'Mull of Kintyre' is a mellow acoustic ballad about a favorite Wings retreat in Scotland. The tune features bagpipes where the acoustic guitars leave off.[48]

Uncredited, Billboard

The British public, however, responded more enthusiastically. 'Mull of Kintyre' entered the charts at No. 48 on November 19, and it sold 250,000 copies within two weeks of its release—enough to send it to the top of the charts, making it McCartney's first post-Beatles No. 1 single in the UK. By its fourth week, it had sold 500,000 copies in Britain. It remained in the Top 100 for 17 weeks.

"I remember joking with our fella in the office who looks after the charts and plugs the records for us," Paul told a BBC interviewer. "And he'd come to me, and he'd said, 'We had 11,000 sales the other day.' I said, 'No, that's no good.' I mean, actually it was good, but I was just kidding him. . . . I said, 'Don't come to me until you've done 30,000.' Anyway, he came back about three days later, and he said, 'Well, will 100,000 do?'"[49]

Americans, unsure what a Mull was, where to find Kintyre, or why they were hearing bagpipes on a McCartney disc, found the record puzzling, but its double A side status made it easy enough for DJs and listeners to shrug it off and focus on the flipside. 'Girls' School' was more in keeping with what DJs thought their audience wanted to hear, so that was the side they favored. 'Girls' School' entered the *Billboard* Hot 100 at No. 83 on November 19 and remained on the chart for 11 weeks, peaking at No. 11 on January 14, 1978.

It was around this time that Gene Roddenberry delivered the first draft of his script for the Wings science fiction film. Roddenberry had explored several directions, trying to find a concept that would please Paul, but the treatment Paul had prepared for Isaac Asimov still seemed to be at its heart. "Paul's story was about two bands (one from Earth, one from another planet) entering into a competition,"[50] Roddenberry's personal assistant Susan Sackett noted.

Recording Sessions

Thursday, November 14–Saturday, November 26, 1977.
Abbey Road Studios, Studio Two, London.
Overdubbing: 'Don't Let It Bring You Down.'
Mixing: 'Famous Groupies,' 'Don't Let It Bring You Down,' 'Backwards Traveller' and 'Blues (Longest Song Title in the World)' [also known as 'The Great Cock and Seagull Race'].

Paul, Denny and Linda had another guest when they returned to Abbey Road for a Thanksgiving Day session on November 24, but this time it was an in-house visit by Dave Gelly, who was writing a piece about the session for *Club Sandwich.* Parts of the interview would later be used in the press kit for the still nameless album.

"Because they spend so much time there," Gelly reported, "[Paul and Linda] have added a few touches to the barn-like Studio Two to make it a bit more homey. There are some enormous plants in pots, chairs grouped round a café table surmounted by a beach umbrella and even a few Christmas decorations."[51]

By the time Gelly arrived, Paul, Linda and Denny were working on the backing vocals for 'Don't Let It Bring You Down,' to which they devoted at least three tracks. By then, Paul had overdubbed an electric lead guitar part, and he and Denny had added flageolets—"A posh word for an Irish tin whistle,"[52] Paul explained.

"We tried a lot of stuff in the studio," said Laine. "We tried [recording] glasses with water in to get sounds. We'd both play piccolos or flutes; we'd try instruments we couldn't play. We were experimental."[53]

The overdubs continued to flow as Paul added another acoustic guitar, and he and Denny recorded, and then double-tracked, acoustic lead guitar lines using the same phase-shifting effect that Paul used prominently in 'Yamaha Links (Off the Cuff Links).'

The backing vocals, particularly in the second half of the song, are tightly harmonized, and at times—particularly on the lines *"Up and down your carousel will go"* and *"When the price you have to pay is high"*—both the phrasing and harmony call to mind the work of Crosby, Stills, Nash and Young. But the balance and phrasing were tricky, and Gelly witnessed the frustration of multiple attempts stopped by Emerick when one of the voices veered slightly off pitch, or when an entrance was late—as well as the exhilaration when the part was finally nailed.

"Everything goes like clockwork," Gelly wrote, "and Geoff gives the thumbs-up sign through the glass. Suddenly a crazy rustic hullabaloo emerges through the loudspeakers. 'Arrh! When the proice yew 'ave to pay is 'oigh' (Paul).' 'Aha, Jim lad! Shiver me turnips' (Denny and Linda). They are all addicted to funny voices and can keep up a barrage of assorted accents for ages when the mood takes them."[54]

When the session ended at 7:30 P.M., Paul and Linda repaired to Cavendish Avenue for a Thanksgiving dinner that Linda prepared that morning.

The Friday session was spent making rough stereo mixes of 'Famous Groupies,' 'Don't Let It Bring You Down' and 'Backwards Traveller,' and on Saturday, for reasons unknown, Paul revisited a *Ram*-era outtake, 'The Great Cock and Seagull Race,' listed this time by its original title, 'Blues,' and a new subtitle, 'Longest Song Title in the World.'

Recording Session

Wednesday, November 30, 1977.
Abbey Road Studios, Studio Two, London.
Overdubbing: 'I've Had Enough.'
Mixing: 'I've Had Enough.'

Most of the songs Wings had recorded since February were now complete, but one holdout, 'I've Had Enough,' needed work. Completing it was the principal task of the November 30 session, which Dave Gelly was again on hand to chronicle for *Club Sandwich*.

Paul began with instrumental touch-ups. He and Denny added electric guitar parts, and Paul added a Mellotron line, using the instrument's pipe organ setting and deciding in the process to drop the piano line he recorded on the *Fair Carol*. Handclaps were added as well. But all this was buying time: what the song most needed was a lead vocal. But Paul had not completed the lyrics.

"He's been singing it with sort of mumbles up to now," Linda told Gelly, who watched from the control room as Paul sat at one of the umbrella-enhanced tables scribbling lines. When he was done, he had Emerick cue up the tape so that he could rehearse the vocal a few times, and then went for a take. Listening to the playback, he asked Emerick to send some reverb through the headphones, and tried the vocal with Elvis Presley and Jerry Lee Lewis vocal moves before settling into another take.

"This time," Gelly wrote, "he sings quite differently, almost conversational. There are a few false starts and another, completely new style emerges, a kind of blues-cum-gospel treatment. He attempts a high falsetto phrase. It doesn't work and he stops. The next take is a mixture of the first (straight) version and the last. It sounds good, but Paul is still searching for exactly the right feeling for the song. Between takes he is constantly singing little phrases, trying out different tones of voice."[55]

Paul sang a few more takes, sometimes stopping to second-guess the lyrics—wondering, for example, whether the end of the line *"And then you wonder why I stand at the bar day and night"* should be *"overnight,"* and singing it both ways before deciding the original was best. After a few more takes, Paul asks for the reverb to be dialed back slightly because it is now distracting him. On the next take, he tries a spoken section with a touch of Otis Redding influence—*"Baby, you know, sometimes you get a little we-e-ea-ry."*

"You see, I'm after singing it like a real old rock 'n' roll song," he explained to Gelly. "It's a bit difficult when you've only just made it up. Tricky, this old trad stuff!" After a few more takes, he felt satisfied that one of the performances captured the song, and went into the control room to decide which one to use.

Before leaving for the day, Paul and Geoff made a rough mix. Emerick thought the track was still missing something. Paul disagreed—he wanted a simple, straightforward rocker, and it fit the bill. But for good measure, he took home a cassette copy for further review.

Recording Session

Friday, December 2, 1977.
Abbey Road Studios, Studio Two, London.
Filming: 'Mull of Kintyre' Promotional Video #2.
Mixing: 'Name and Address,' 'With a Little Luck,' 'I'm Carrying,' 'Café on the Left Bank,' 'Morse Moose' and 'Girlfriend.'

With the completion of 'I've Had Enough,' the new album was essentially finished but for the mixing and sequencing. And at this point, in addition to the multitrack recordings, there were several reels of mixes to sort through. Paul, Denny and Linda began their Friday session listening to their November 11 mixes of 'Children Children,' the unfinished version of 'I've Had Enough,' 'Backwards Traveller,' 'Off the Cuff Link' (Yamaha now dropped from the title), 'Deliver Your Children,' 'London Town,' 'Don't Let It Bring You Down,' and 'Famous Groupies.' Fresh mixes were made of 'Name and Address,' 'With a Little Luck,' 'I'm Carrying,' 'Café on the Left Bank,' 'Morse Moose and the Grey Goose' and 'Girlfriend.'

Besides working to complete the new album, Paul was keeping an eye on the promotion for 'Mull of Kintyre.' Sales of the single in Britain were rocketing skyward, and as a result Michael Lindsay-Hogg's promo film was in line for significant airplay. But Paul was annoyed when *Top of the Pops* faded the video nearly halfway into the song on its November 24 show. The DJ edit, running 3'30", was ideal for television airplay, but editing Lindsay-Hogg's video to the short version would have been tricky, since the promo moves from day into night. Paul decided, therefore, to direct a second promo himself, specifically to be cut to the DJ edit. He hired a film crew to shoot him, Linda and Denny at Abbey Road on the afternoon of December 2.

It was a peculiar shoot, with all the markings of one of the McCartneys' herbal jazz cigarette–inspired ideas. For the occasion, Paul and Linda guided their new pony, Jet, across the Abbey Road zebra crossing to the studio, which was still fitted out with the umbrella tables and Christmas decorations that they had brought in to liven up the last few sessions.

With no clear idea of how the promo film might come together, the camera operator filmed Paul, Denny and Linda lip-syncing with sections of the single, as well as overdubbing instruments and vocals onto other random album tracks. Shots of Geoff Emerick, Jet the pony (now inside Studio Two), and a mannequin of Santa Claus were thrown in for good measure, together with a scrap of the unseen *Bruce McMouse Show* film, with one of the cartoon mice proclaiming, "Wings is here!"

On review—once the spliff haze had cleared—Paul realized the promo had no connection with the song's subject and scrapped it, arranging instead to bring the Campbeltown Pipe Band to London to shoot a third promo—a proper one. The pipers, coincidentally, recorded their own first single, a cover of 'Mull of Kintyre,' at Craighall Studios, in Edinburgh, on December 3.

Recording Sessions

Monday, December 5–Friday, December 9, 1977.
AIR Studios, London.
Overdubbing: 'Oriental Nightfish.'
Mixing: 'Oriental Nightfish,' 'Mull of Kintyre' and 'Girlfriend.'

Wings moved to AIR Studios to complete the mixing of the album, as well as a few other tasks, with Geoff Emerick engineering and Steve Churchyard assisting. Much of December 5 was devoted to reviewing the masters and mixes. They worked until around midnight, when Nicholas Ferguson, whom Paul had engaged to direct the third promotional film for 'Mull of Kintyre,' came to the studio to discuss the details of the shoot, to be done at Elstree Studios.

"It was very last minute," recalls Ferguson, who had not worked with Paul since he directed the four promotional films for 'Mary Had a Little Lamb.' "I got the job on Monday morning, and I went to see Paul [that same day] at midnight, at AIR Studios in Oxford Circus. They were giggling, and there was birthday cake,* and that's when we discussed 'Mull of Kintyre.'

"It sounds impossible now," Ferguson said of the tight schedule. "I had to call Paul the following morning and tell him that I couldn't find a studio. And Paul said, 'Ring the managing director [Sir Lew Grade] and tell him, "Paul says you owe him a favor—you'll have to empty a studio." And a studio was made available. I got a designer, John Clark, and I said I wanted to build the Mull of Kintyre in the studio—the mountains, everything else. And he managed to get it all designed and built by the Friday morning."[56]

While Ferguson was getting the shoot together, Paul and Linda turned their attention on Tuesday to Linda's 'Oriental Nightfish,' a track recorded during the *Band on the Run* sessions and set aside for the Suzy and the Red Stripes album. Now the artist and director Ian Emes was planning to use the song as the soundtrack for an animated film, so Paul needed to prepare a mix. After transferring the 16-track master to a 24-track reel, he overdubbed sound effects suggested by the Emes's visuals, and made a stereo mix.

On Wednesday, Paul made two new mixes of 'Mull of Kintyre'—one labeled 'Master Backing Track—full length,' the other 'Edit backing track.' The latter was to be used for the Ferguson shoot, the former for Wings' appearance on the *Mike Yarwood Christmas Special.*

As Paul was preparing the mixes, the Campbeltown Pipe Band were on a coach headed for London. They arrived mid-afternoon, checked into the Swiss Cottage Hotel and unwound with a few pints at the hotel bar with Alan Crowder. On Thursday, some of the pipers visited Wings at AIR Studios. "Well congratulations—we're number one!"[57] Paul told the pipers as they entered the control room.

Also in the control room were two representatives from the Musicians Union.

"So they're there to check that we're going to record the song again [to comply with union

* It was Geoff Emerick's thirty-second birthday.

Wings and the Campbeltown Pipe Band at AIR Studios, December 8, 1977

rules]," said McGeachy. "And we're like, 'Fuck! We've got to record it again, how are we going to do that? That's a lot of work.'"

Paul had no intention of recording the track again, but he and Emerick encouraged the pipers to play along. Soon they were dutifully tuning their instruments and readying for a take. Two hours later, before a single note was taped, one of Paul's roadies shepherded the union reps to the studio exit.

"And as soon as they left the studio, 'Right lads, in you come, don't worry, we'll use the original soundtrack!' Then they opened the beer again,"[58] McGeachy joked.

On December 9, Wings and the Campbeltown Pipe Band reconvened at Elstree Studios, where John Clark's set looked plausibly woodsy, with lots of greenery and what appeared to be boulders and rock outcroppings. The ground is never quite seen, thanks to *"the mist rolling in,"* supplied by a dry ice machine. Paul, Linda and Denny perform the chorus much as they had done in the Abbey Road shoot, with Paul and Denny using the same guitars, Linda seated between them, but now surrounded by foliage instead of Christmas decorations. Paul is seen singing the verses as he walks a path through the faux woods, Denny joining him. And when the bagpipe music begins, the pipers appear in full regalia, walking along another path, the mist at their feet.

After the shoot, Wings returned to AIR, where they mixed 'Girlfriend,' and Ferguson took a couple of days to edit the film. The new promo had its premiere on *Top of the Pops* on December 15.

When the music papers hit the stands the day after the shoot, they reported that 'Mull of Kintyre' had sold 500,000 copies in Britain, qualifying it for a Gold Record. All the papers carried an advertisement placed by MPL with a message from Paul:

> 'Mull of Kintyre' is number one.
> Thanks a lot, folks!
> Paul McC . . . Thanx a half-million.
> Up your kilt!

The Campbeltown Pipe Band remained in London for the taping of the *Mike Yarwood Christmas Special* on December 10, arriving at the BBC Television Centre in Shepherd's Bush to a greeting from the Scottish comedian Billy Connolly, who shouted from a balcony, arms outstretched, "*We*

Paul filming the third promo for 'Mull of Kintyre,' Elstree Studios, December 9, 1977

arra people! It's the start of a revolution boy! You take them on the west bank and I'll take them on the east!" as a stunned and somewhat embarrassed Michael Parkinson stood beside him.[59]

There was an afternoon dress rehearsal, and taping began after the audience was let in at 8 P.M. The 'Mull of Kintyre' segment was taped at 10 P.M., with Wings wearing matching faux-military tunics and seated on chairs before a backdrop of Christmas trees, with dry ice wafting around them. Paul also gamely appeared in a comedy sketch with Yarwood, in which the comedian played a punk version of Denis Healey, the much-maligned chancellor of the exchequer. The show was broadcast on Christmas Day at 8:20 P.M. and was seen by an audience of 21.4 million, making it the most-watched program in Christmas television history.[60]

Sales of the single were already healthy before December 25, but the performance on national television before such a huge audience guaranteed that 'Mull of Kintyre' would remain the toppermost of the poppermost.

"[When] we did the *Mike Yarwood* show at Christmas time with it, that made it huge,"[61] said Laine.

Recording Sessions

Monday, December 12–Wednesday, December 14, 1977.
AIR Studios, London.
Mixing: 'Off the Cuff Link' and 'Yamaha Jam.'

Work on the new album continued on December 12 with stereo mixing of 'Off the Cuff Link,' but the following day, Paul turned his attention to a variation on that track recorded at the same session and called 'Yamaha Jam.' It is possible that he was considering this either in addition to 'Off the Cuff Link,' or instead of it. In any case, he made a stereo mix of the jam on December 13. But when he compiled a pair of reels with all the work in progress mixes, on December 14, he did not include it. Acetates of the two reels were cut for review over Christmas.

The first acetate included the most recent mixes of 'Café on the Left Bank,' 'I'm Carrying,' 'Backwards Traveller,' 'Cuff Link'—its title now whittled down by two more words—'I've Had Enough,' 'London Town,' 'Don't Let It Bring You Down' and 'Children Children.' The second acetate included 'Morse Moose and the Grey Goose,' 'Deliver Your Children,' 'Girlfriend,' 'Name and Address,' 'Famous Groupies' and 'With a Little Luck.'

There may also have been an orchestral session scheduled this week. According to a report in the *Campbeltown Courier*, Malone's, Richards's and Vickers's arrangements were to have been recorded in mid-December, but Paul sacked a 27-piece ensemble of freelancers when they arrived late for the session.

—

Maintaining their tradition of spending the start of the holiday season in America, Paul, Linda and their brood flew to the United States before the end of the week to spend Christmas with the Eastmans in East Hampton.

Paul, naturally, kept tabs on the British music press over the holiday. *NME* reported in its December 17 issue that sales of 'Mull of Kintyre' had reached 800,000[62] in the UK, and that the millionth copy of the disc had been pressed. The paper also published its annual Readers' Poll. Wings, absent from the concert stage and without a new LP on the market, did not win in any category, but Paul was voted No. 14 among male singers, No. 9 among songwriters and No. 8 among bassists.

He had reason to be happier about the *Daily Mail* Rock and Pop Awards, published two weeks later: he was voted Best Male Group Singer, and was given a special award for Outstanding Contributions to British Music, the first year that award was bestowed.

While Paul and Linda were visiting the Eastmans in New York, they slipped into Manhattan to see the latest Steven Spielberg film, *Close Encounters of the Third Kind.* Paul loved the film—"He's making films like rock shows," he said of Spielberg. "He's grabbing you at the beginning with a big special effect. He's very plugged in with the average head, Mr. Spielberg, isn't he? You know, television, corn flakes, the mother who lives on her own with the children . . . My family is like the families that happen in Spielberg movies. . . . The kids come home from school with new words and the boys want to be rougher than the girls. It's all the same as it ever was. I don't know how it is in the States. I know how it is around me."[63]

But seeing the film soured Paul on the Gene Roddenberry project. He had already harbored doubts, ever since seeing *Star Wars* at the end of May and noting the degree to which George Lucas's grandly scaled yet gritty vision of life in space made the *Star Trek* shows of a decade earlier look quaint. Now Spielberg took more of the wind from his sails.

"I did something with Gene Roddenberry of *Star Trek* fame," he said. "But the big thing in that was gonna be this flying saucer, this incredible flying saucer. Now like two weeks after [Roddenberry's script arrived] Spielberg brought out *Close Encounters*, so that sort of knocked that one on the head—there was no topping that saucer."[64]

By the end of December, the McCartneys were back in England for some close encounters of the Scouse kind. The family drove up to Liverpool to ring in the New Year along with Twiggy and her new husband, the American actor Michael Witney. Twiggy's presence was requested by

Linda to inject some life into a gathering that could otherwise have been overshadowed by death; though it had been 17 months since Jim's passing, this was Paul's first New Year's Eve with his family since then.

"Not as often," was Paul's response to Capital Radio's Phil Griffin when asked in November how often he visited Liverpool since Jim's death. "I used to mainly go up to see him. I really haven't been up quite as often. I have got to go up and show them the baby."[65]

They stayed at Rembrandt, but the family celebration was at the home of Paul's uncle Joe, where they were expected at 9 P.M. Arriving in time for a light supper before heading out, Paul went upstairs after dinner, and soon summoned Linda and their guests to join him for a bit of show-and-tell, starting with a box of exercise books he had kept since his school days.

"And this is my first guitar," he said, pulling down a beat-up but carefully preserved Zenith Model 17 steel-string acoustic, for which he had traded in his previous instrument, a trumpet, in July 1957. After a while, Linda reminded Paul that they were expected at his uncle's house, and they packed into the Land Rover, taking a scenic route that allowed Paul to show Twiggy and Michael the Liverpool Institute ("this is my old school") as well as Strawberry Field and Penny Lane.[66]

"I just go to all my old haunts," Paul said of his routine when in Liverpool. "It's like a sort of nostalgia thing when I go up there. I always go out late at night, drive round with Linda and say, 'And there's where I went to school. And there's the little part of the playground where we used to smoke, and I remember hearing about Buddy Holly dying there.' And I just kind of go through all that and say, 'There's where I used to live, and there was my room.' Some people don't like to do that, but it's irresistible for me. I mean, it's not even nostalgia actually, it's mainly to clue Linda in on how I used to live, because she met me after all of that."[67]

Paul had reason, beyond the turn of the year, to be in a celebratory mood, and to want to look back to see how far he had come. Shortly before he left for Liverpool, he got word that 'Mull of Kintyre,' still No. 1, had sold its millionth copy.

21

CHOCKS AWAY! (AGAIN)

As 1978 got underway, the competition among labels to lure Paul away from EMI came more fully into public focus. Until now, Warner's moves toward that goal were executed in the background and indirectly, by being amenable to projects by Denny Laine and Mike McGear, while CBS's interest had lately moved into the public domain. Now there was another suitor—Phonogram, the British arm of the German-Dutch Polygram family of labels. And its managing director, Ken Maliphant, seemed confident of his company's chances.

"Everyone is after McCartney," Maliphant said. "No one draws a bigger check than us. . . . Because we are part of Polygram, we will not lose any act because we can't pay."[1] CBS, however, knew that while cash was a draw, there were other paths to getting Paul's signature on a contract. In his discussions with the label, Lee Eastman let it be known that Paul was opposed in principle to *Beatlemania*, and though the label's executives found that puzzling—the show was basically a cash machine funneling royalties into the Beatles' bank accounts nightly—they took his opposition to heart and cashed in the company's investment in the production.

Paul found himself in the midst of a small tempest in early January, when Melvyn Bragg was skewered for making *him*, rather than a "serious" artist, the focus of the inaugural episode of *The South Bank Show*. Bragg was having none of it. "That's the trouble with 'art' programmes," he told the *Daily Express* a week before the show's January 14 premiere. "They exist in a private little world of their own. I just take it for granted that rock music is as good as contemporary classical music. To be able to write songs like McCartney does is a remarkable talent. As great as writing lyric poetry. That is the intention of our new programme; to present the art of our generation. Nothing exclusive, nothing prissy. We're in the popularizing game."[2]

Bragg had been unusually lucky. When he taped the show, his cameras captured McCartney working on 'Mull of Kintyre,' and how the single would fare was anybody's guess. When the show aired, the song had been No. 1 on the British singles chart for seven weeks and had been declared, with sales of 2 million, the bestselling British single of all time—eclipsing 'She Loves You.' To celebrate, Paul sent each member of the Campbeltown Pipe Band a £200 ($383) bonus check,[3] topping up the fees of £365* ($670) and £30 ($55) they received for the recording session and appearance on the promotional film.

During the first weeks of 1978, music press polls brought further reminders that Wings had slipped out of the spotlight. In *Melody Maker*, *Wings Over America* was down at No. 41 on the list of 1977's bestselling LPs (Abba's *Arrival* held the No. 1 spot, followed by Fleetwood Mac's *Rumours* and the Eagles' *Hotel California*). But *Record Mirror* listed Wings in the Top 10 groups (at No. 7) and 'Mull of Kintyre' at No. 3 in the Best Singles category.

Paul began the year working to rectify the absence of new Wings material in the shops.

Recording Sessions

Wednesday, January 4–Wednesday, January 25, 1978.
AIR Studios, London.
Recording: Jamming with Kenney Jones.
Overdubbing: 'Girlfriend,' 'Morse Moose and the Grey Goose' and 'I'm Carrying.'
Mixing: 'London Town,' 'Café on the Left Bank,' 'Name and Address,' 'Famous Groupies,' 'I'm Carrying,' 'Backwards Traveller,' 'Off the Cuff Link,' 'Children Children,' 'Girlfriend,' 'With a Little Luck,' 'Deliver Your Children,' 'Don't Let It Bring You Down,' 'I've Had Enough' and 'Morse Moose and the Grey Goose.'

Paul had spent the holidays listening to rough mixes of all the material for the album, and when he arrived at AIR, he was still tussling over what worked and what could be improved. On January 4, he completed the mixes for 'London Town' and 'Café on the Left Bank.' Thinking he could better the mix of 'Café,' he began the January 5 session with that track, but after a few attempts he marked the previous day's mix as the master and turned his attention to 'Name and Address' and 'Famous Groupies,' creating the master of the former and setting the latter aside. The January 6 session was largely devoted to recording Wil Malone's orchestration for 'Morse Moose and the Grey Goose,' Bobby Richards's strings for 'I'm Carrying,' and Mike Vickers's woodwind score for 'Girlfriend'—to which Paul also added bursts of electric guitar, including a solo, an element McCulloch failed to complete before he vanished in a blaze of ketchup and eggs.

---

* Because of the unexpected success of the single, years later the fees paid to the pipe band would become the source of music press consternation. But at the time they were paid above the normal Musicians Union rate. None of the pipers complained about their rate of pay in 1977. (For perspective, £1 in 1977 is worth £7.37 [$9.38] in 2024 money.) The single also had the add-on effect of boosting tourism in the Campbeltown area considerably.

After the orchestral session, Paul quickly made the final mixes of 'I'm Carrying,' 'Backwards Traveller' and 'Cuff Link,' the last two now edited together as a single track. Taking a long weekend, Paul returned to Abbey Road on Tuesday, January 10, and completed the stereo master of 'Children Children.' The final mix of 'Girlfriend' was completed on January 12, and the master mix of 'With a Little Luck' was finished on January 13. A final mix of 'Famous Groupies' remained elusive: on January 16, Paul filled two reels with mixes before settling on a master. A mix of 'Morse Moose and the Grey Goose' was attempted toward the end of the session but abandoned.

Now into the final week of mixing sessions, Paul finished mixing 'Deliver Your Children'—the only song in the current batch recorded entirely in the Virgin Islands—on January 17, with stereo masters of 'Don't Let It Bring You Down' following on January 18, 'I've Had Enough' on January 19, and 'Morse Moose and the Grey Goose' on January 20.

For part of the session on January 19, Paul and Denny jammed with Kenney Jones, the drummer for the Faces until 1975 (and before that, the band's pre–Rod Stewart, Steve Marriott–fronted incarnation, the Small Faces). Paul and Denny were courting drummers, and Jones was an experienced prospect. Paul felt good enough about the session to mix it to stereo for close listening at home.

By now Paul, Denny and Linda had agreed that 'London Town' would open the album and would be its title track. A reel of sound effects (labeled 'Bow Bells Chimes SFX,' 'Whittington Chimes' and 'Queens Chimes') was logged into the archives, suggesting that Paul was considering garnishing the LP with sounds of London. But like the reel of prison sound effects prepared for inclusion on *Band on the Run*, this new effects collection went unused. And with a cross-fade between 'Famous Groupies' and 'Deliver Your Children,' completed on January 23, the mixing and editing of the album was complete but for sorting out the track sequence.

After trying different track layouts, on January 24 and 25, the production masters were assembled and handed over to EMI for mastering.

Glancing down the final track list, the profound effect that fatherhood has on the music Paul commits to vinyl is as clear as it was when he released *McCartney*, a record written and recorded just after Mary's birth, with "home, family, love" as its stated themes. *London Town*, delivered soon after James's arrival, does not stray far from that path. 'Café on the Left Bank,' 'Backwards Traveller,' 'Name and Address' and 'Don't Let It Bring You Down' see Paul reflecting on and sometimes mourning the past, while in 'I'm Carrying,' 'Children Children,' 'Deliver Your Children' and 'With a Little Luck' he looks to the future with optimism and hope.

SIDE ONE (EMI MATRIX NO. YEX.975)

'London Town'
'Café on the Left Bank'
'I'm Carrying'
'Backwards Traveller'
'Off the Cuff Link'
'Children Children'
'Girlfriend'
'I've Had Enough'

SIDE TWO (EMI MATRIX NO. YEX.976)

'With a Little Luck'
'Famous Groupies'
'Deliver Your Children'
'Name and Address'
'Don't Let It Bring You Down'
'Morse Moose and the Grey Goose'

Acetates of the two sides were pressed and sent to Paul's promotional teams in London, Los Angeles and New York, prompting a mixed response.

"Well, it'll be all right when it's finished," was promoter Tony Bramwell's reply when asked for his thoughts on the album.

"What the fuck do you know? I fucking brought you down from Liverpool!"[4] was McCartney's touchy response to the former NEMS and Apple man.

Recording Sessions

Thursday, January 26–Friday, January 27, 1978.
Abbey Road Studios, London.
Mixing: Various jams and demos.

With the album in EMI's hands, Paul settled in behind an Abbey Road mixing board to mix material that had been recorded during the past year but would not be used. These included 'El Toro Passing,' 'Hurricane Hole,' 'Spirit of Ranachan Jam' and the demo for 'Sweetest Little Show in Town,' all mixed on January 26, as well as 'March 1977 Jam 1, 2, 3, 4,' 'Jam/March 1977' (a separate recording, or possibly an edit of the other four jams), a demo for 'Dress Me Up as a Robber,' and the previous week's jam with Kenney Jones.

London Town, meanwhile, was mastered by Nick Webb at Abbey Road on January 27, and a provisional date of March 17 penciled for worldwide release. Hoping to avoid a repeat of the mastering problems that saw buyers return poorly pressed copies of *Band on the Run* (the last record he and Paul made together), Emerick flew to Los Angeles to oversee the mastering of the American version by John Golden at Kendun Recorders.

Aubrey Powell discovered that Paul's allowing him to take the reins on the cover of *Wings Over America* was a onetime fluke. For *London Town*, Paul had a simple idea: Denny, Linda and Paul would be seen on both the front and back, with London's Tower Bridge in the background. On the front, Wings are photographed in black and white, wearing winter coats; on the back, the trio are shot in color, Denny wearing a denim jacket and the McCartneys in tropical attire.

"[The album] was started in London town, and it was finished in London town," Paul said. "And the opening track on the album is called 'London Town.' I suppose you could have called it any of the other titles, actually, but that was the one that seemed to fit the most. Then we had the idea on the cover to show London town as if it's in the Virgin Islands. On the back cover of the album, it's all London town looking like it's been moved to the Virgins."[5]

Powell was not taken with Paul's idea. The Hipgnosis aesthetic tended toward not having portraits of the artists on the cover. Wings appeared on *Band on the Run*, of course, but they were in a crowd of other celebrities, and the photo was built around the jailbreak concept. The covers since then were more in the portrait-averse Hipgnosis style.

"It was a conscious decision to have the basis of Wings back on the front cover," Powell noted, "and it was Paul's idea to have the Tower Bridge. He gave me the photographs and said, 'Collage these together and put this in front of Tower Bridge.' Which I did. It was the one album cover that I really felt didn't work for me, I didn't like it at all. I said to Paul, 'I don't think this is good enough,' and he said, 'I don't care what you think, that's what I'm doing.'"[6]

On the album jacket itself, information is sparse: the title on the front and Wings on the back, both in colored, shadowed lettering, with the song titles and timings on the back cover. (The disc labels mirror the front and back covers, but without Paul, Linda and Denny.) The inner jacket, however, presents the lyrics against a cream backdrop with diagonal rows of Tower Bridge images, in pink (on side one) and green (on side two). Black boat-shaped symbols appear next to the titles recorded in the Virgin Islands. Side one of the inner sleeve includes the MPL and label logos and the publishing information (mostly split between MPL Communications Ltd. for songs written in Britain and MPL Communications Inc. for songs written elsewhere, with the McCartney-Laine songs also claimed by Denny Laine Ltd.).

After the lyrics on side two of the inner sleeve, the musicians (including Jimmy and Joe) are listed, with the instruments they played—or most of them: Denny's autoharp was lost in the shuffle. Paul is listed as producer, Emerick as engineer, with Henderson, Vigars and Churchyard as assistants. The recording venues and dates are given, and the cover design and photography are attributed to "Paul, Linda and Denny," with Powell and George Hardie credited with "cover coordination," and Henry Diltz and Graham Hughes acknowledged for "additional photography."

Finally, there is the cattle call of thank-yous. The three arrangers are thanked, although as usual for arrangers, there is no reference to the nature of their contribution, just their names (with Wil Malone's first name given an extra *L*). The technical staffs from MPL and Record Plant, and the captains and crews of the boats Wings frequented in the Virgin Islands, are thanked as well.

A poster was included, too (hence the expansive photography credits), with a group portrait of Linda, Paul and Denny on one side, and a collage on the other, built around a portal with a shot of the *Fair Carol*. The collage is full of casual shots taken mostly in the Virgin Islands, with Wings both recording and clowning around. One shot includes a package of Bambú rolling papers, set upon a letter to Crowder emphasizing that marijuana is illegal in the Virgin Islands. Jimmy and Joe are nowhere to be seen.

Recording Session

Monday, February 6, 1978.
Abbey Road Studios, London.
Recording: 'Goodnight Tonight (Demo).'
Mixing: 'Goodnight Tonight (Demo).'

Apart from jamming with Kenney Jones, and no doubt hearing out Denny on his encounter with Laurence Juber, Paul had barely considered the future of Wings. But ideas from the McCartney songwriting factory, sometimes fragmentary, sometimes complete, sometimes experimental and quirky, continued to pour forth. And as a musician who prided himself on understanding his audience, he listened to the hit parade with an analytical ear. Disco was now ascendant: *Saturday Night Fever* hit the movie theaters in December 1977 and was on its way to breaking records, and it was not lost on Paul that the film's musical driving force was music by the Bee Gees, who began their career in the stylistic shadow of the Beatles (and were represented by someone near the top of Paul's swerve-to-hit list, Robert Stigwood). So as the aftershocks of the punk earthquake gave way to the rhythm-heavy rumble of disco, Paul's musical imagination kicked into gear, finding ways to incorporate elements of the style into his own.

Just ten days after *London Town* was mastered, Paul returned to Abbey Road to record 'Goodnight Tonight,' a disco experiment with a bass line so animated and attention-grabbing as to be almost a character within the song, as well as layers of percussion, an element central to the style as he perceived it.

"That was one of those that, after a visit to a disco, the next day you can't help it—when all those tunes are thumping round in your head you can't help writing a disco one the next day,"[7] was Paul's take on the song's genesis.

Not quite certain whether he was making a demo or the basis of a formal recording, Paul explored the idea at length: although he filled two reels before he had a take that satisfied him, the keeper was 7'18", so it is unlikely that there were no more than four takes on each reel. He began by laying down a drum machine track, but where he had previously used the instrument mainly to put down a repeating, steady beat, here he assembled a complex beat pattern that made the most of the drum machine's electronic timbres.

He then added real drums and a keyboard bed using a chord sequence full of sevenths and ninths to create a mildly dissonant feel. Then came the assertive, syncopated bass line.

"Paul is a better bass player than a lot of people think," said Denny, an odd comment given Paul's stature as one of rock's greatest bassists. But with a few exceptions—'Silly Love Songs,' for example—Paul's bass lines for Wings were decidedly less showy than his Beatle bass lines had been, something Paul himself attributed to the simpler style of the time. With the advent of disco, bass lines were changing again. "'Goodnight Tonight' was quite a good song for that," Denny continued, "where he started to change style—which he always does, you know—to stay [current] with everything. And he played quite a complicated part on that."[8]

Continuing to overdub on his own, Paul added an acoustic guitar part, more high hat, two electric guitar parts and a guide vocal for a first verse *("Don't get too tired for love / Don't let it end")* and the repeating chorus that made up most of the song *("Don't say it! Don't say it! Say anything, don't say goodnight tonight!")*.

"It's like a disco version of 'Let's Spend the Night Together,'" Paul joked, "only put more genteelly."[9] Two more reels were filled with rough mixes before Paul called it a day.

Paul, Linda and the children flew off for a family break in Jamaica in the early weeks of February, leaving it to Denny to pick up a pair of awards for 'Mull of Kintyre' at the *Music Week* Awards at the Savoy Hotel. Paul sent a telegram, read by Denny at the ceremony, in which he took the opportunity to promote the forthcoming album, mentioning for the first time publicly that it would be called *London Town*.

The McCartneys were back in London by February 24, when they popped into AIR Studios, along with Denny, to remix 'Oriental Nightfish' once again for Ian Emes's animated film, now scheduled to have its premiere at the Cannes Film Festival in May. As they were finishing up, Denny ran into Laurence Juber in the hallway and brought him into the control room.

"I was early for my session, and they were running late," Juber recalled, "and Denny invited me in. That's when I got to meet them all."[10]

With *London Town*—tne last remnant of Wings Mark II—finally in the rearview mirror, Paul was beginning to consider the future of Wings. Denny, eager to get Wings back up to touring strength, had kept tabs on Juber since their appearance together on the *David Essex* show.

"Apparently," Juber explained, "Denny called Richard Niles a couple of days later to find out if I was versatile."

Versatility, as it turns out, was a quality Juber could claim without fear of contradiction. He was born in Stepney, East London, on November 12, 1952, and began playing the guitar when he was 11, under the influence of bands like the Shadows and the Beatles. But he was soon learning jazz chords as well, and when he was 15, he started studying the classical guitar—his principal instrument when he enrolled at Goldsmith's College as a music student (where he also took up the lute).

During his student years, Juber was also a member of the National Youth Jazz Orchestra, which he has described as "something of a farm team for studio musicians."[11] By the time Denny met him, Juber had played in West End pit orchestras and on recordings by Rosemary Clooney, Charles Aznavour, Shirley Bassey and Cleo Laine, as well as on Al Stewart's *Year of the Cat*, the Alan Parsons Project's *Tales of Mystery and Imagination* and the soundtrack for *The Spy Who Loved Me*. Paul was instantly struck by Juber's professionalism and easygoing manner. But Denny's push to expand Wings notwithstanding, Paul was noncommittal on engaging the services of another guitarist just yet.

One decision Paul did settle on was what to release as Wings' next single. His choice was 'With a Little Luck,' backed with 'Backwards Traveller/Cuff Link,' and on March 1, a DJ edit of the A side was made for radio play, trimming the track from 5'46" to 3'12." The tracks were mastered for release on March 6 (their matrix numbers were 7YCE.21795 and 7YCE.21796).

Around this time, Paul took a phone call at Cavendish Avenue from Warren Beatty, who asked him to write a song for his new film *Heaven Can Wait*.

"Fine, Warren," Paul told him. "Send me a video of the film."

"Well, I'd like to come over and talk about it," Beatty responded.

"No, it's all the way from L.A. Don't bother."[12]

Beatty insisted, however, and visited Paul at Cavendish Avenue. He brought a rough cut of the film about a football player (and amateur soprano saxophonist) who was mistakenly transported to the afterlife by an overzealous guardian angel and is allowed to return to life, albeit in another body because his own had already been cremated. Paul agreed to send Beatty a song.

Now that Denny and Jo Jo had two children, the guitarist at long last decided to trade in caravan living for home ownership, and bought Yew Corner* in Laleham, Middlesex. Shortly after he moved in, he was introduced by a local guitarist, Nick Pearson, to another Laleham musician, Steve Holley.

Stephen Jeffrey Holley, born in London on August 24, 1953, was the son of a jazz band musician; his mother was the singer in his father's band. He was drawn to music early: he was given his first drum kit when he was five years old, and he began learning his instrument from Keith Brown, the drummer in his father's band. He also studied the piano and the guitar, and played his first paid gig, as a drummer, at age 11.

As a teenager, Holley spent his free time in London watching John Mayall's Bluesbreakers, with Eric Clapton and other six-string warriors who passed through Mayall's group. He played in several bands, including G. T. Moore and the Reggae Guitars. Now 24, he had his own band Vapour Trails, which had backed Kiki Dee on tour between 1974 and 1976. At the time he met Denny, he was playing drums on the sessions for Elton John's forthcoming *A Single Man* album.

Denny knew none of this—he thought of Steve as just an interesting young neighbor, who Pearson had introduced as a drummer without giving details.

"We had a couple of beers and started chatting," Holley recalled of their first encounter, "but I really didn't talk about my background. He was having a housewarming party, and he invited me. And he told me to come early, because he knew that Paul and Linda would not stay once a lot of people arrived."[13]

Walking in, Holley heard music coming from one of the rooms. When he looked in, he saw Linda at the piano, Paul playing bass and Denny playing guitar. A drum kit, set up in the corner, was unmanned. Catching Denny's eye, Holley pointed to the drum kit, then to himself, then walked over to it, sat down and picked up the sticks.

"I just couldn't believe it," Steve said with a laugh. "This guy moves into the village and a couple of months later I'm sitting there playing with Wings. It was very lighthearted. I remember Paul saying, 'Hey, can you play some rock and roll?' I can't remember what we played. Then he said, 'You can't play any reggae, can you?' and my years with G. T. Moore and the Reggae Guitars—and my devotion to Bob Marley—paid off."[14]

After the jam, Denny approached Steve and said, "I knew you played drums, but I didn't know you were *a drummer*. Do you think you could hold a professional gig?"

---

* Denny later noted that children's author A. A. Milne once owned Yew Corner, and that the house provided the inspiration for his Winnie-the-Pooh books, but this is not the case. Milne lived at Cotchford Farm in the village of Hartfield.

"Well, depends on what you're talking about," Steve responded. "But I'm working on Elton John's album, and I've been with Kiki Dee for a couple of years."

"*What?*" Denny said, his eyes widening. They also had a chat about Denny's kit. "It was a decent kit," Steve recalled, "but there was one cymbal that was just exceptional—perfectly tuned, beautiful sound."[15]

The next morning, when Steve opened his front door, the cymbal was on his porch. "I didn't know Denny even knew my address, but he found it and left the cymbal. It was a lovely thing to do." Later that morning, Holley's mother was visiting, and when the telephone rang, she picked up. "She turned a very strange color and looked at me and said, '*It's-it's-it's P-P-Paul Mc—P-P-Paul McCartney on the phone!*'"[16]

When Holley took the receiver, Paul said, "That was fun last night. I enjoyed the way you played. I'm looking for a drummer, and it's a strange way for this to happen, but could you come up to London for a more formal audition?"[17] The audition was a second jam session with Paul, Linda and Denny, with Paul calling out the titles of rock oldies and Wings tunes, and taking the measure of Holley's spontaneous responses.

Hiring new band members was not at the top of Paul's priority list, though. More pressing was promoting 'With a Little Luck,' which was released on March 17 in the US and March 24 in Britain. He realized that Holley could be of some use there.

Just before the single's British release, Paul again commandeered Michael Lindsay-Hogg from the *Wings Over the World* team to direct promotional clips for 'With a Little Luck' and 'London Town' (a likely choice for a future single). Lindsay-Hogg booked Twickenham Studios for a shoot that was to have taken place the week of March 13, but Lindsay-Hogg, then Paul, and then Linda came down with the flu, forcing a postponement until March 20 and 21.

Twickenham was a haunted place for McCartney: he and Lindsay-Hogg last worked there together during the *Get Back/Let It Be* sessions in January 1969. But these were different times: Paul was now returning as an artist whose last single had outsold all 22 of the Beatles' singles.

For 'With a Little Luck,' the band mimed a performance of the DJ edit, with Denny and Linda playing keyboards on either side of Paul, who had his Rickenbacker bass. Behind them was a potted tree and a cyclorama, lighted in yellow and orange. And off to the left, to the side of the tree, Steve Holley undertook his first Wings gig, amiably miming to Joe English's drum part.

"'With a Little Luck' is a simple video, and is meant to be an optimistic one," Lindsay-Hogg noted. "We have them playing with a tree behind them, and there are some kids dancing. And then there are some little kids who were on the shoot as well. We had them just to make it seem a joyous occasion, and also because Paul likes kids a lot. He understands them."[18]

'London Town' was a similarly minimalist shoot that took its cues from the song's lyrics. Lindsay-

Hogg had Denny, Linda and Paul link arms and slowly walk down a mocked-up street, a purple spotlight on the cyclorama behind them *("walking down the sidewalk on a purple afternoon")*. They are dressed in raincoats (*"silver rain is pouring down"*), Paul wearing a fedora and Linda a cap. During the guitar solo, Paul plays his Epiphone Casino, Denny plays slide on a National Steel Guitar, and Linda bops along.

Extras plucked from the streets outside MPL's Soho offices walk past Wings during the song *("People pass me by on my imaginary street")*. And Paul engaged Victor Spinetti to don white makeup and mime the travails of the song's out-of-work actor.

"We were using ingredients of, you might call it, semi-real life, and exposing that it was in a studio," said Lindsay-Hogg, who found 'London Town' the more interesting of the two films. "So we had built a little street, and then when certain things are mentioned, like 'people walking by,' they just walk up the side of this little fake street, and step off at the end and gather in the background, just chatting away. And then there's the actor who's talking to his mate, played by the wonderful Victor Spinetti. I hadn't worked with him before, but I knew him to be a very special actor, someone who would do whatever he could to make it work. He's basically inventing jokes for his wife at the breakfast table, and that all came from Victor—it wasn't like I said, 'Hold your tea cup like that' or do whatever." [19]

THIS WEEK'S #1 SINGLE
WINGS
WITH A LITTLE LUCK
FROM THE PLATINUM-PLUS ALBUM
LONDON TOWN
LONDON TOWN
ON CAPITOL RECORDS AND TAPES

Wings, 'With a Little Luck' single trade ad

Following the still billowing success of 'Mull of Kintyre,' the new single had some critics wondering why bother reviewing a disc that was guaranteed to be a hit; others were so disdainful that they couldn't get the titles right—*Record Mirror*'s critic calling it 'With a Little Love' and *Sounds*' reviewer calling the second half of the B side 'Cufflinks.'

> *Yes, the one you've all been waiting for, and why isn't it Single of the Week you might ask. Well, quite simply because it's just an ordinary, slight pop tune with a catchy hook and little more. Bound to be a hit, but then Wings could release a Scottish bagpipe anthem and it would sell!*[20]
>
> *Philip Hall*, Record Mirror

Paul and Linda in front of Tower Bridge, London, March 22, 1978

Regardless of the fact that at this point a 45 of Paul McCartney cutting his toenails in mono would top the charts, this 45 would sound specially sweet, lyrical and tender, without being an all-time classic either. The flip's a poignant ditty called 'Backwards Traveller' and a medium-paced instrumental called 'Cufflinks.'[21]

Vivien Goldman, Sounds

Oh gawd! Count to ten. They are the easiest targets in the world. Critics abuse while the public lap up in ever-increasing-quantities. Look at the phenomenal success of 'Mull of Kintyre.' This will clearly be a massive hit, but when you remember that so much good stuff can't even get on the anachronistic BBC playlist, does it deserve the inevitable exposure? Smooth, self-congratulatory optimism burbles against pure MOR electric piano patterns. With a bit of luck, some elbow grease and, of course, lots o' love there is no end to what we can do together. The instrumental break is little more than an elongated filler with a noise that sounds like the clucking of a synthesized chicken.[22]

Ian Birch, Melody Maker

Here's another puzzler: How does this 35-year-old man keep on putting out singles for which chart success is a forgone conclusion? What's his secret? The elixir of eternal schmaltz perhaps . . . ?[23]

Paul Rambali, NME

This is a strong mid-tempo pop tune that picks up momentum. As with previous McCartney songs, the lyrics, as are the mood and music, are optimistic and celebrative. Should be one of the most commercial songs McCartney has penned in some time.[24]

Uncredited, Billboard

The single made its debut in the UK Top 100 on April 1 at No. 42, and peaked at No. 5 on April 22. Its chart life in Britain was brief: after nine weeks, it dropped out of the Top 100. It fared better in America, entering the *Billboard* Hot 100 at No. 70 on March 25. Following a nine-week tussle with the Bee Gees' 'Night Fever,' 'With a Little Luck' reached No. 1 on May 20. McCartney's twenty-sixth No. 1 single in the US, it held the top place for only two weeks, and spent 18 weeks in the Top 100.

London Town—the album—had been scheduled for release on the same day as 'With a Little Luck,' but was pushed back, reportedly because Paul wanted to tweak the cover art; it was now set to be issued on March 31.

In the first burst of promotion for the album, Paul invited a few reporters to the filming sessions for the two promotional clips, setting aside his *NME* boycott for a chat with Roy Carr. One telling exchange enlivened Paul's interview with Carr. Referring to 'Boil Crisis,' he told Carr that he'd written a punk song "but I daren't do it" because "people will only slag me off and say 'Oh look, McCartney's going punk! He's just trying to keep up with the trends.'" That led to a discussion of his own broad tastes, and his desire to do something unexpected, musically.

"I don't feel like any one age group myself," he said. "I see all age groups. . . . I've always had very wide musical tastes. I mean, I love all those old songs in that *Pennies From Heaven* TV series on BBC*. . . . For me, on his own terms, Fred Astaire can be just as heavy as Robert Plant—see, it doesn't matter what era they come from. I'd like to do an adventurous album and we're discussing the possibilities of doing just that for the hell of it. No formula style . . . I'd welcome the change . . . love having fun with the music instead of getting my head down and thinking along the lines of, 'I am Led Zeppelin and I've got to come out with something heavy because that's what they expect from me.' And that probably is the biggest problem . . . getting pigeonholed."[25]

He spoke with Peter Trollope of the *Liverpool Echo*, as well, but seemed to be on autopilot, responding blithely to questions about the success of 'Mull of Kintyre,' the new album, Beatles reissues and criticism. He also revisited—and defended—what he now recognized was an archaic attitude about releasing singles from LPs.

"Singles and albums are completely different as far as I'm concerned," he insisted to Trollope, even as he was filming a promo for an album track about to be released on a single. "I like it when you can buy an album without any singles on it. A lot of people these days are dictated to by record companies who put out about three tracks from one album. We're just not into that."[26]

Also in the mix of reporters was *Record Mirror*'s Barry Cain, who had been refused an interview with Paul ("He has already said all he wanted to say," Brainsby told him) but was invited to speak with Linda instead. Armed with a list of snarky questions, he ended up so charmed by Linda ("Hey, wait a minute. This girl is shy. I mean, really shy. . . . It makes her cute as well as nice and that's a pretty lethal combination"[27]) that he discarded his questions—and resented it when Paul turned up to end the interview.

He published his article at the end of the week, and it charted both his shift from antagonism to sympathy for Linda and his parallel journey from admiration to hostility toward Paul.

"I wouldn't mind," Paul said after reading Cain's feature. "It was obviously bottling up inside

---

* *Pennies From Heaven* is a six-episode series written by Dennis Potter and directed by Piers Haggard that ran from March 7 to April 11, 1978. Set in the 1930s, it stars Bob Hoskins as a traveling sheet music salesman. Paul's reference is to the scenes in which the songs Hoskins is selling—among them, 'Roll Along, Prairie Moon,' 'Did You Ever See a Dream Walking?' and the title song—come to life as fantasy scenes, using vintage recordings on the soundtrack.

him, and I wouldn't mind if he'd come out with it, but he was so meek. Why didn't he come out with it then? I would have hit him, and he would have got his story."[28] (Cain fired back a couple of weeks later, writing in the April 8 *Record Mirror*: "Maybe you should have hit me. Then I could have beaten you up."[29])

Press-courting on behalf of *London Town* continued on Wednesday, March 22, with a boat trip up the Thames. The boat was scheduled to leave from Charing Cross Pier (the exact spot from which the album cover shot was taken) at 1 P.M., but at the appointed hour there was no sign of Paul and Linda. It was a tough call for Brainsby: he didn't want to multiply the cost of the event by having the boat rental go into overtime, but proceeding without Paul and Linda made little sense. At 1:35, Brainsby decided to go ahead with the cruise—only to be summoned back when Paul and Linda turned up ten minutes later.

"Of course, he does turn up," Colin Irwin wrote in *Melody Maker*, "arm-in-arm with Linda, and of course, all malice towards him is instantly forgotten and everyone fawns around him. And off we go on our little boat trip. *The Mail*, *Express* and *Mirror* cling to McCartney, while the *Evening Standard* and the *Sun* content themselves with Linda. We sail towards Tower Bridge and Paul, Linda and Denny Laine are ushered to the front of the boat to have their photo taken, eating fish and chips out of newspaper with the bridge in the background."[30]

After the boat trip, Paul invited Irwin to join the Wings party as they repaired to Trillion Video Post-Production, in Soho, where Lindsay-Hogg was editing the promotional films. As Lindsay-Hogg responded to Paul's and Linda's on-the-spot editing notes, Irwin couldn't help notice Steve Holley drumming in the 'With a Little Love' clip, an observation heightened by Linda's suggestion that Holley should have a close-up. Irwin's curiosity was further piqued by Denny's agreement with Linda's request—"It might make people stop phoning me up asking for the job." Irwin, naturally, asked about Holley's status in the band.

"The answer is no, he's not our new drummer," McCartney told him, shattering Irwin's hope for a scoop, "though we've been playing with him. We're not in any hurry. Last time we were trying to get people in quickly and . . . well . . . last time we did auditions they were all too hard-headed and professional and weird. We're not really bothered. We've got an album out, so we can coast for a while.

"We have the luxury of not having to decide what we're gonna do next, so we're gonna take it. That's what it's supposed to be all about, coming up in groups, being able to indulge yourself and be able to do music the way you want to do it, so that's exactly what we're gonna do next. We wanna go on the road, we fancy it and stuff, but you never know. It may be an amazing summer and the idea of going for a row in a boat may be more appealing."[31]

Having started the day's press rounds on the Thames and continuing it during an editing session, Paul and Denny had one more stop, a visit to Nicky Horne's Capital Radio show, *Your Mother Wouldn't Like It*. Besides talking up the new album, Paul took up one of his recent and still evolving hobby horses—the notion of playing small venues, as if he could somehow return to lunchtime shows at the Cavern.

"Because the last thing we did was so big time—tons of equipment and everything," he told Horne, "lately, we've been talking, if we go back to doing some live stuff, we'd really like to try and get it down to little funky places, and the idea is to do something like a residency. Because, in the old days, when you were a really young struggling group, you'd get to have a lot of fun, actually, just by playing down little places, lunchtimes, where it's just kids from the office turn up and it's not a big serious crowd. And you'd get to know 'em after about a week, and they'd send up requests, and you could have a real nice easy time. It's good for your music, it's good for your whole thing, really."

Expanding on the idea, he slipped into Utopian Dreamer mode.

"Imagine if you had like a great gig in London with a house band something like Area Code . . . where it was a really red-hot band who just played for three hours. The things that would happen off something like that would be great, because there would be a lot of people who would want to jam with the band, a lot of people who'd want to sing with them, a lot of vocalists knocking around. And you'd find a lot of bands who'd want to come and just be noticed, and play. So that idea of creating some kind of scene—even if we take an already existing place, and just play there for a week or two, so that you build up a scene."[32]

Recording Session

Thursday, March 23, 1978.
RAK Studios, London.
Recording: 'Did We Meet Somewhere Before.'
Mixing: 'Did We Meet Somewhere Before.'

Paul wasted little time meeting his Warren Beatty commission. On March 23, he, Linda and Denny headed to Mickie Most's 24-track RAK Studios to record the song, 'Did We Meet Somewhere Before,' a ballad that brings together several McCartney compositional hallmarks—arching melodic hooks, the fluid juxtaposition of major and minor (a trait that dates back to the Beatle days), and a more recent touch, a plentiful sprinkling of seventh and ninth chords to give the song a jazzy tinge.

The song's structure is an alternating verse (*"Did we meet somewhere before / Far behind that half-closed door?"*) with an unvarying chorus (*"Happening time and time again / Happening over and* *over / Will the king's horses and all the king's men* / Ever find out / What it's about?"*). At the third verse, Paul introduces a slight variation—repeating the last line of the final couplet (*"Or is this just one more thing / That's happening to both of us? / It's happening to both of us"*).

Paul played electric piano on the basic track, with Denny playing electric guitar and Linda on synthesizer; they filled two reels before capturing a nearly five-minute master take. Paul overdubbed drums and percussion, bass and electric guitar, Mellotron strings, plus a lead vocal, with all three adding backing vocals.

The track's most striking element, though, is a clarinet solo that runs through it—a reference, perhaps, to the fact that Beatty's character is seen playing a soprano saxophone (which looks similar to a clarinet) in several scenes. The soloist on Paul's recording was not documented. Before leaving the studio, Paul filled two more reels with stereo mixes and ran off a copy of the keeper to send to Beatty.

"I like doing it," he said of film composing in an interview with Paul Gambaccini a week later, "and if good stuff comes up, I'll try it again. It's quite interesting, because it's a different way of working. You've got to do something that's like *them* and not like *you*. Normally, I made records sort of based on me. But when they've got a film that's all finished and it's two other people, say, acting throughout the whole film, then I've got to tailor it. . . . But the big danger is that they're going to end up saying, 'It's a very nice song, but it doesn't fit the film,' you know, and then you've done all that work for nothing. So I went away, wrote [and recorded] it, sent it to him, and he was back in L.A. at that time. And he said, 'Fine, I really like it. It's fine.'"[33]

One of Paul's New Orleans heroes, Professor Longhair, came to London for a performance at Ronnie Scott's Club on March 26, a performance Paul helped arrange. Professor Longhair had played at the *Venus and Mars* wrap party on the *Queen Mary*, and Paul had his set—and all the other music performed that night—professionally recorded. So when the gig approached, Paul arranged to have Fess's wrap party recording released by Harvest, an EMI subsidiary.

From Paul's point of view, the album, *Live on the Queen Mary*, was a gift to Professor Longhair, a collection that his concert at Ronnie Scott's would help sell. But Fess and his manager had mixed feelings about it.

"I got an invitation to play at [Paul's] party on board the *Queen Mary*," the pianist said of the set McCartney recorded. "I went with four guys out of New Orleans and we played a set for the party.

---

* James McCartney junior's tiny fingerprints quickly made a delicate impression on his father's lyrics. *"All the king's horses, and all the king's men"* was extracted from the nursery rhyme *Humpty Dumpty*, no doubt part of Paul's bedtime reading to his son.

I didn't really enjoy it. . . . We had no monitors or nothing, the sound was bad, and the people were all lit up, partying. I didn't think they was paying much attention to me, so we didn't try very hard for them, it was one of those kind of situations. Next thing I hear, they're putting an album out."

His manager, Allison Kaslow, added, "We were mad when we heard about the album. In fact, we were going to sue, but in the end they gave us enough money that we've gone along with it. In all honesty, though, I have to say that it's not truly representative of Fess."[34]

All you knead is love: Paul baking bread, Scotland, April 1978

When school holidays arrived at the end of March, the McCartneys headed for High Park, where in addition to overseeing the end of lambing season and attending the annual Cattle Show, Paul spent time pursuing a new activity: baking bread, which he was shown doing in a picture spread, under the headline "All you knead is love!" in the *Daily Mirror* on April 10.

He also had another film assignment. The American producer Walter Mirisch had contacted the Eastmans to enlist Paul to write a theme for *Same Time, Next Year*, a film starring Alan Alda and Ellen Burstyn that had gone into production in February. Based on a 1975 play by Bernard Slade, the film is the story of two people, each happily married with children, who meet for an annual tryst.

Paul accepted the commission and wrote a slow ballad with verses built around a dotted rhythm (alternating long and short notes, *"Must we wait another year for the celebration dear / If we do we'll hold it here"*) leading to a refrain on steady quarter notes (*"Same time next year"*). The bridge was simply a single line—*"Ah, nothing changes"*—repeated twice. He completed two four-track demos of 'Same Time Next Year' (losing the comma in the film's title) in Rude Studio.

Paul and Linda were still in Scotland when *London Town* was released on March 31, but they had reason to believe that album's fate was in good hands: in America, it shipped Platinum (one million copies, a category established in 1976), and Capitol mounted a campaign that included extensive consumer and print advertising, posters and a Spectacolor animated billboard in Times Square.

The reviews ranged from supportive to brutal, with even the generally positive reviews carrying a few barbs. "Genial effortlessness" was Janet Maslin's double-edge description of McCartney's work in *Rolling Stone*. "*London Town* is so lighthearted," she wrote, "that the album's feeling of familiar strength and affection is virtually the only thing that binds it to earth. . . . Even the best songs here—and a couple of them, like 'Deliver Your Children' and 'Children Children' are wonderful—sound as if Wings were only half trying."[35]

John Rockwell, in the *New York Times*, found the material "prime McCartney . . . which means very listenable indeed," adding that "by this time, everyone knows that it's not necessary to look to Mr. McCartney's lyrics for philosophical profundity, and even his music rarely probes beneath a sweetly sentimental surface. But his ear for tunes and for classically simple yet clever arrangements remains acute, and the result here is often delightful."[36]

In his *Los Angeles Times* review, Robert Hilburn noted that eight years after the Beatles' breakup, McCartney was "the most consistent and successful of the old foursome," and that *London Town*, McCartney's first album of new material since Wings' world tour, "is his most confident and comfortable work." Hilburn found that the album's "melodic fibers and arrangements are as solidly crafted as anything he has done in the '70s," yet he missed the "hard, adventurous edges of *Band on the Run* and *Venus and Mars*."[37]

A common thread in many of the reviews was that McCartney's music is safe rather than adventurous, tailor-made for either children or aging suburbanites. *London Town*, Bob Edmands's *NME* review tells us, is "the familiar Wings mixture of medium to soft rock and MOR mawkishness," filled with lyrics in which "McCartney has nothing in particular to say, and says it at some length." He singled out 'I'm Carrying' as "a useful reminder of McCartney's remarkable gift for potent, emotional pop songs," adding, "It's a gift that is deployed all too rarely here."[38]

Donna McAllister's *Sounds* review was an unrestrained slugfest. "Paul McCartney has entered senility," she wrote before characterizing the album as "an acetate collection of Nursery Rhymes." She seemed, in fact, to take it personally that Paul made an album that she disliked. "I'm humiliated that he has put me in a position where I have to slag him," she wrote. "What did we ever do but make him rich?"[39]

London Town entered the British album chart at No. 6 on April 15 and peaked at No. 4, a spot it held for three weeks starting on April 22. It remained in the Top 100 for 23 weeks. In America, it entered the *Billboard* 200 at No. 20 on April 15, and reached No. 2 on May 6, the *Saturday Night Fever* soundtrack blocking its ascent to the top. It remained at No. 2 for six weeks and spent a total of 28 weeks on the chart.

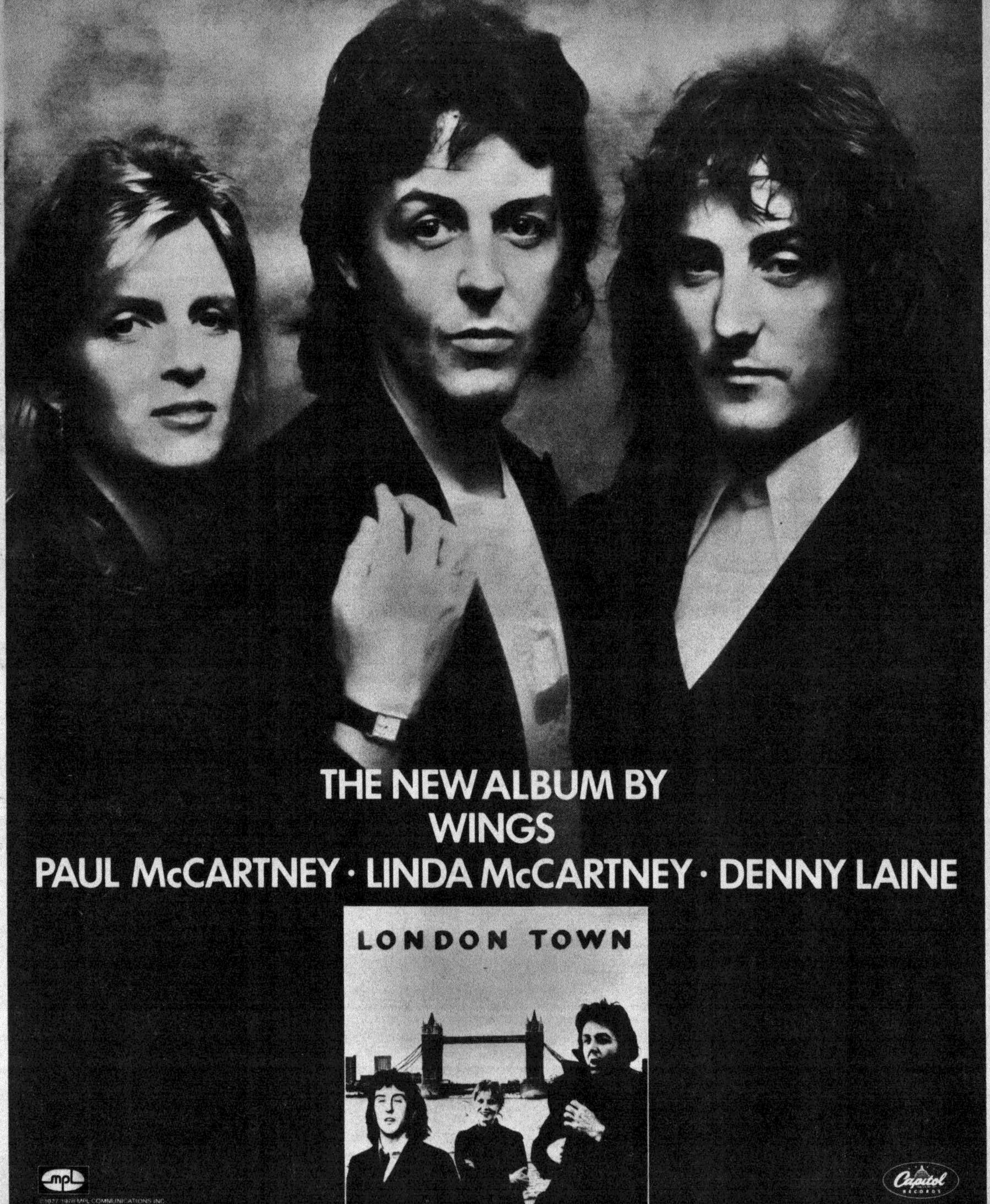

Wings, *London Town* album trade ad

Paul distracted himself from the mixed critical response to *London Town* by throwing a first anniversary party for his in-house fan magazine, *Club Sandwich.* It was, basically, an MPL staff party, but Paul invited a single journalist, the sympathetic and supportive Judith Simons of the *Daily Express*. "I run the fan club paper myself," Paul told Simons, exaggerating his involvement and adding a hefty dollop of wide-eyed spin. "I personally select all contributions and do some writing. I do it for the same reason I keep on writing songs; simply because I love this whole pop business." For good measure, he also told Simons his small-venues plan. "We want to get close to our audiences again, not have them stuck away behind barriers. We'd like to find some old warehouses to play in, or small theaters."[40]

A Freudian, noting the critical mauling his most recent work had suffered, might interpret Paul's desire to return to his Cavern days as a form of *Regressus Ad Uterum*—the wish to return to the start of one's life (or in Paul's case, the start of his career).

But in truth, the grandeur of the large-venue American tour was something he was not ready to consign to the past. *Hands Across the Water—Wings Tour USA*, a book of Aubrey Powell's photographs from the tour, was due for publication on April 14. And work continued on the two tour films, *Wings Over the World* and *Rockshow*, although it was around this point that Michael Lindsay-Hogg left the project.

"Thelma [Schoonmaker] and I were in the cutting room," Lindsay-Hogg recalled, "and we ran some footage of Paul up in Scotland after [the Beatles] had broken up, which Linda had taken. He looked like he was trying to collect himself and figure out where to go next. And I thought, we've got to put this in the film early on, to show that Paul had been in quite a deep hole, emotionally. He looked like he was going through a kind of grieving. So I told Thelma, 'Let's put this early in the movie, so the audience can see Paul's sense of resolve, and his kind of guts that made him go from this low point in his life to what became the great tour *of Wings Over America.*' So we opened with that—the sequence ran two minutes, maybe, and then immediately we go to one of the venues with 50,000 people cheering."[41]

The sequence rubbed Paul the wrong way, though, and when Lindsay-Hogg went to New York to make promotional clips for the Rolling Stones' *Some Girls* album, he got a call from Brian Brolly, who was also in New York.

"Look, Michael," Brolly told him. "I'm not sure you and Paul are seeing things exactly the same way at the moment. Paul doesn't want to have any reference to the Beatles. He wants that to be put in a box and forgotten about. He wants this to be totally about Wings."

Lindsay-Hogg offered his rationale—that the documentary sequence helps audiences understand Paul better. "Paul doesn't want to go that way anymore," Brolly told him, before handing him a check and thanking him for his work on the project. "There were no hard feelings," Lindsay-Hogg said.

In London, the music press had been taking note of Steve Holley's work on the 'With a Little

Luck' promo, but Paul remained noncommittal. When *NME* reported that Holley had been working with Wings, an MPL spokesman told the paper, "It doesn't necessarily follow that Holley will join them permanently. But you could say it's an indication that Paul is taking the first steps toward augmenting Wings in readiness for live work."[42]

Not that there were any concrete plans for live work, beyond the empty warehouse fantasies Paul mentioned to journalists with increasing frequency. Linda was not inclined to tour with James so soon, or to leave him behind. And Paul himself was doing little to reconstitute Wings: so far, all the moves in that direction were driven by Denny. Having brought Steve Holley into the Wings orbit, Denny now pushed to bring Laurence Juber in as the band's new guitarist.

"I got the call when I was doing a session at Abbey Road Studio Two," Juber said of Alan Crowder's summons to audition. "Alan said, 'Denny wants to know if you can come and jam—and oh, by the way, Paul and Linda will be there.'" Juber went to MPL on April 28 and was sent to the basement, where Paul, Linda, and Denny were waiting, with Steve Holley sitting behind the kit. Juber was under the impression that Holley was also auditioning, but since Holley had already done his audition, it was more likely a matter of testing the chemistry between Juber and the rest of the band, including Holley.

"I didn't know any Wings tunes really," Juber admitted. "I borrowed some LPs from my brother over the weekend, but I wouldn't know what to really learn out of it. I figured I would wing it, as it were."[43]

The band played through Chuck Berry tunes and other rock oldies, as well as some reggae—a workout that Paul had been using to break in new musicians since the very first Wings jams at Rude Studio on July 22, 1971. But Paul quickly saw that Juber, with his classical training and experience in jazz and pop, brought a breadth that was new for Wings. So he popped the question: "What are you doing for the next few years?"

"At that point I really had to make a decision," Juber remembered, "because I'd spent many years getting myself to the point where I had a successful studio career. And then, for a nanosecond, I had to think about it, but I wasn't going to turn down the opportunity to work with Paul. So I said, 'Well, I guess I'm working with you.'

"I think what Wings were looking for was versatility," he added. "And Steve is a versatile drummer, but still basically kind of an English heavy backbeat rock player, which actually kind of set a direction for the band that became apparent when we started recording."[44]

Paul was not yet ready to make a formal announcement, but after nearly nine months as a trio, it was "Chocks away!" for Wings Mark III.

22

DOWN TO MACCA'S FARM

Having passed his audition, Laurence Juber was soon sitting across a desk from Brian Brolly at MPL's Soho Square offices for what the guitarist described as "a very kind of general conversation" about his future in Wings.

"He respected the fact that I was approaching this from a professional perspective," Laurence said, "not 'Oh, boy, I'm in a band!' kind of thing. My approach to it from the business angle was very much, 'This is a job, and this is something that needs to be dealt with on that level.'

"I was pretty much sober," he added. "I was meditating—I did transcendental meditation. In fact, my first real McCartney encounter was with Mike McCartney on a meditation retreat in August of '77; I remember being in the room when Mike walked in with a newspaper declaring that Elvis had died. I mean, the fact is that I came into it with a reputation for professionalism. They clearly didn't want another Jimmy McCulloch on their hands."[1]

Recording Sessions

Friday, May 5, Saturday, May 6, and Monday, May 8, 1978.
RAK Studios, London and Abbey Road Studios, Studio One, London.
Recording, Overdubbing and Mixing: 'Same Time Next Year.'

For the new version of Wings there would be no playing-in period in Nashville or anywhere else—it was straight to the studio, even before Laurence and Steve signed their new contracts. "The very first session we did," Laurence remembered, "was 'Same Time Next Year,' for the movie of the same name. And that was a big, orchestrated McCartney 'My Love' type of ballad. It was a very cool tune."[2]

The bare bones of McCartney's proposed title track for director Robert Mulligan's movie was recorded at RAK Studios, with Paul at the piano, Denny on bass, Laurence on electric guitar, Steve behind the kit and Linda on tambourine. They filled three 24-track reels before settling on a master, to which Paul added his lead vocal, as well as an acoustic guitar part, for which he was joined by Denny. Backing vocals, by Paul, Linda and Denny, completed Wings' work on the track; only the orchestration remained, and on Saturday, Paul brought the tape to Abbey Road Studio One to oversee the orchestral session. He had enlisted Fiachra Trench to do the scoring, but as Trench discovered, Paul had a very specific sense of what he wanted.

"Paul had written out the arrangement—every note that he thought the individual string lines should be," Trench said. "And he'd written them out as 'G, G octave, F-sharp' or whatever—the names of the notes, because he didn't write or read music notation. I had no problem with that, but it was enormous—I think it was on sheets of A2 paper [16.5 by 23.4 inches]. He handed it to me and said, 'Now you go and make it better,' which meant 'Now you transcribe it into musical notation and amend it as you see fit.' He was quite easy about that, but the arrangement is very much his concept."[3]

Trench enlisted 68 string players, four clarinetists, four recorders (members of the Dolmetsch family, who had played on the *Wild Life* and *Thrillington* sessions), and John Leach, who played the cymbalom (the Hungarian hammered dulcimer most famously heard in the film *The Third Man*). Paul spent the early hours of Sunday morning making rough mixes of the completed track at Abbey Road and returned to RAK Studios on Monday for the final mixing. The finished recording was quickly dispatched to California where the film was being shot.

Paul did not have to wait long to learn the fate of his contribution: the production company sent word back that they could not use it because it telegraphed the plot too clearly.

The next project for the new Wings lineup was one that would announce the new players—albeit miming to a *London Town* track on which Holley and Juber did not perform. Perhaps as a response to critics who found 'With a Little Luck' too lightweight, and *London Town* as a whole too inclined toward balladry, Paul chose the album's toughest rocker, 'I've Had Enough,' as the band's next single, with Denny's 'Deliver Your Children' as the B side.

"You assume that anyone who puts out singles has got a huge marketing division behind them saying, 'This is the single,'" Paul told the BBC, "but really, in most cases, it's just up to what you fancy at the time. I was driving back from Scotland down the M6, and I . . . had the radio on, and the DJ came on and he was playing 'I've Had Enough' and it really sounded good on the radio. And I thought, 'Wow!' You know, I hadn't even noticed that one too much on the album. And the [DJ] came on late after it, he said, 'Oh magic! Yeah, great track!' And these are the kinds of things that sway you. I thought well, 'Yeah, it's great. He's right. Definitely ought to be a single.'"[4]

At the suggestion of EMI, Paul used a new video production company run by Keith "Keef" Mc-

Wings, 'I've Had Enough' single trade ad

Millan and John Weaver. The company—Keef & Co. in the UK, Keefco in the US—had produced one of the two music videos for Kate Bush's debut single 'Wuthering Heights' and were known for their pioneering use of lighting and visual effects. "[Bush] turned the corner for us with EMI," Weaver told *Billboard*, "and helped get us to Paul McCartney."[5] The 'I've Had Enough' promo was a $55,000 (£30,280) shoot, staged in Paul's barn-turned-studio at Low Ranachan Farm.*

The video is strikingly simple, but matches the song's dark, energetic mood. Paul and Linda are seen mostly in facial close-ups; their instruments are never shown. By contrast, Denny, Laurence and Steve are seen in full shots, Laurence bouncing around in a leather coat playing a black Gibson Les Paul, Steve bashing away at his kit, and Denny with a sunburst Les Paul. The bodies of Denny's and Laurence's guitars get close-ups too, and the two guitarists are shown miming Jimmy's double-tracked solo. McMillan made two edits of the video, one showing the straight performance, the second beginning with freeze-frames of each player—a signal to fans that Wings were back to full strength.

When the day's miming was complete, the band cranked up their amps to do some actual playing. "We spent some time just kind of jamming and kicking ideas around,"[6] Laurence recalled of that first visit to Scotland.

On May 16, Paul and Linda flew to Cannes for the premiere of Ian Emes's 'Oriental Nightfish' video. Like some of the McCartneys' more left-field creative projects, Emes's trippy short film—which pits a naked woman against supernatural forces—was rooted in chemical influence.

"I got pissed on whisky and put the music on as loud as it would go," Emes explained of the film's origin, "and lay on my back in the living room and let it wash over me. The whisky did indeed

* The exact date of the shoot is unclear. The McCartneys' only known trip to High Park during this period was in late March/early April, but Juber did not audition for Wings until April 28, and he has said that his first job for Wings was the session for 'Same Time Next Year' on May 5. One source lists the production date as June 17, but the McCartneys were in New York then, and the single had already been released. So the video was most likely shot in mid-May, before the McCartneys flew to Cannes for the premiere of Linda's 'Oriental Nightfish' video.

help, and I came up with this weird idea where alien forces enter this building where someone who looks like Linda McCartney is playing a Gothic Expressionistic Wurlitzer. This blonde female is penetrated and inhabited by the alien force, then she's replicated, before becoming a comet that explodes. The film was a bit weird and scary and a little bit sexual."[7]

Emes's racy film failed to win any awards at the Cannes Film Festival, but in Paul and Linda's absence, 'Mull of Kintyre' won an Ivor Novello award for Best-Selling A side at a ceremony in London. (It was also nominated for the Best Pop Song award but lost to the Bee Gees' 'How Deep Is Your Love.')

The single 'I've Had Enough' coupled with 'Deliver Your Children' (assigned EMI matrix numbers 7YCE.21797 and 7YCE.21799) was released in America on June 2 and in Britain on June 16. But any hope that delivering a single with a rocky edge would win critical applause was soon dashed; in fact, the reviewers for *Record Mirror* and *Melody Maker* began their eviscerations with the same wisecrack, playing off the single's title. Denny's lyrics for 'Deliver Your Children' also came in for some criticism.

So have I. Another band who are capable of producing excellent material, but who are palming us off with sub-standard wares. A weak rocker, which like the B side originated from their London Town *album. Another non-event.*[8]

Kelly Pike, Record Mirror

So have I. Paul McCartney's artistic poverty has been as crippling as his material wealth has been excessive in recent years. . . . EMI call this thoroughly mediocre record a "raunchy rocker"—sorry, but I find his attempts to rip-rock it up these days as offensive as the astonishing lyrical banality in evidence on the flip: a musically attractive strum-along which treats the Last Deluge with such insights as 'I had me a woman / She was good and clean / She'd spend all the day with the washing machine / When it came to loving she was never around / She was out getting dirty all over town.' You forgot to mention that you cleaned your teeth that day, Paul.[9]

Chris Brazier, Melody Maker

You've already heard this stomper on the radio by now: one of the few tracks with any spunk on the current album, most of which sounds like it was written for (or even by) his daughters. In fact, this one comes dangerously close to rock and, own up, ain't at all bad. Think what a great album he could make if he wanted to, and if he left you-know-who at home.[10]

Alan Lewis, Sounds

The single performed poorly on both sides of the Atlantic, entering the British Top 100 at No. 65 on July 1, and made it only as high as No. 42 during its seven-week run. In the United States, it entered the *Billboard* Hot 100 at No. 81 on June 17, and peaked at No. 25 on August 5, a spot it held for two weeks before beginning its descent. It dropped off the Hot 100 after only 11 weeks.

"When it came out it was—I don't know really, just some of them just don't make it," was Paul's stoic take. "You can't spend your life sweating about the ones that don't make it."[11]

The assertion in the *Sounds* review that Paul could make a great album "if he left you-know-who at home" came as a reminder of the lingering anti-Linda sentiment in certain corners of the press just as Linda was beginning to feel that this was behind her—at least as far as the fans were concerned. In an interview conducted around this time that would soon appear in both the *Daily Mirror* and *Women's World*, she said, "I think the kids like me these days. Well, they're fans of Wings and I'm established there. They respect me now, I hope."

The interview otherwise offered a quick overview of Linda's ambivalence toward show busi-

The McCartneys at Heathrow Airport, June 16, 1978

ness, a feeling that had only grown stronger since James's birth. "I certainly wouldn't go mad if I had to give it up," she said. "I'm more likely to go mad if I don't!" Nevertheless, she admitted that Paul sometimes calls her to account for not pulling her weight in Wings. "When he says it, I know he's right. But he understands that I love our home; and our family is more important than work."[12]

—

Paul, Linda and the kids, along with Laurence and Steve, made a quick trip to New York on June 16—although the travel itself was not as quick as they had hoped, having booked seats on the Concorde only to arrive at Heathrow too late for the supersonic flight. At Heathrow, Paul was cornered by David Wigg, of the *Daily Express*. Confirming what McMillan's promo film had already hinted at—that Juber and Holley were now part of Wings' lineup—Paul added, "This means all the men in the group are English, so you can say that Wings are flying the flag."[13]

But having seen five players come and go since 1973, Paul remained cautious. When an *NME* reporter questioned Tony Brainsby about the new lineup a few days later, the publicist said, "I can confirm that Holley and Juber are now playing with Wings. But please note that I didn't say they have necessarily joined Wings."[14]

That "necessarily" was a dodge, because the principal order of business in New York was meeting with Lee and John Eastman in East Hampton to discuss their contracts. "It was a one-page contract—just what the financial terms were, and a reference to music publishing [saying] that anything we wrote would be recorded and released by the band, and that MPL would have the publishing." Laurence related. "It was a pretty basic one-year contract that then got renewed the following year."[15]

Steve saw the contract as a sort of extended probation. "I was paid an annual salary under a contract that was renewable at one-year intervals," he said, "so in other words, they could let me go, or I could walk away, at a yearly review."[16]

Paul and the Eastmans had more business to discuss during that June visit, namely, the still unresolved matter of dividing up the millions of dollars in record royalties that had accumulated in Apple's coffers since March 1971. Dissolution papers, signed by the four Beatles in December 1974, severed their business ties, but the Beatles recording royalties continued to flow into Apple, with each Beatle receiving 5 percent, while 80 percent went into Apple's bank account.[17*]

According to Paul, the main sticking point in reaching a financial settlement was John's insis-

* This division of royalties was noted in 1980 by John Eastman. Whether this financial division applied to solo recordings made by the four former Beatles before they agreed to a legal split in December 1974 is unclear.

tence that the others indemnify him against both US and UK tax claims. Until now, the Eastmans had resisted any such agreement, but keen to break the deadlock, Paul sought their blessing to accept Lennon's terms; after all, what good was a divorce without a settlement?

Paul reached for the telephone and dialed John at the Dakota. After some small talk, he cut to the chase.

"Look, as I understand it, you need this indemnity," Paul explained, getting ready to offer his former bandmate a legal olive branch.

"Fucking indemnity!" John cut in. "You don't need to give me a fucking indemnity, you fucking . . ."

Their conversation quickly descended into a swearing match.

"Fuck you, ya big cunt!" Paul shouted, slamming down the receiver. Keen to relay the news to John Eastman, Paul picked up the phone once more, hastily dialing his brother-in-law's number. Or so he thought.

"Of course, I got the phone numbers wrong," said Paul, "I rang John Lennon back instead . . . But it was Yoko this time, and then I said, 'Look, I didn't mean for it to get like that—but, shit, you know, it seems to have got . . .' The funny thing was, they knew I was trying to ring John Eastman immediately after, so that would have reinforced their little feeling about me—double-dealing."[18]

Paul's rage turned to embarrassment. Desperate to set the record straight and not leave New York under a storm cloud, Paul took a taxi ride to the Dakota building. The Lennons' interior gardener, Mike Meideros, was watering plants when Paul pulled up outside.

"It was maybe like five o'clock in the evening," Meideros recalled, "and the concierge called up. I don't know the exact conversation because I didn't hear it, I just heard Yoko saying, 'No, he can't come up now.' And I thought that was pretty cold."[19]

Luckily, distractions during their Stateside visit were also plentiful. Besides visiting the Eastmans, Paul and company attended a Rolling Stones show at the Palladium, a semi-secret gig (announced only two days earlier) to promote their new *Some Girls* LP. But what particularly interested Paul was that the Stones were playing in a venue that seated only 3,000. Fifteen months earlier, on March 4 and 5, 1977, the Stones had played at the El Mocambo, in Toronto, a club that seats only 650, and released recordings from the shows as *Love You Live* six months later. Here was one of the biggest rock and roll bands on the planet, demonstrating that Paul's idea of occasionally playing in small and medium-size venues was plausible.

The Stones concert also prompted a subconscious creative outburst.

"I woke up," Paul recalled, "and I could remember dreaming that the Rolling Stones were onstage doing this amazing number called 'No Values.' It was a song I pictured them doing and it suited them down to the ground.[20] And then I woke up and thought, 'What's that one?' and they had never recorded it."[21]

After discovering that 'No Values' was not a Jagger-Richards original, but rather something he had dreamt up, Paul noted the chord progression for a later date.

Immediately upon their return to London, Paul and his family headed back up to High Park, eager to get to work not only on Wings' next album but also on other projects that had been hanging fire. Denny, Laurence, Steve and producer Chris Thomas, whom Paul had drafted to produce Wings' next album, soon joined them, but before they turned up, Paul saw to some housekeeping—specifically, compiling four-track demos.

On June 23—perhaps with a view to developing the radio show he first discussed with Bruce Meyer during the *Wings Over America* tour—he compiled two reels, the first of which included remakes of the 'Oobu Joobu' jingles he first recorded in 1971:

> ***Tape 1:*** 'Seattle Build Up' (five mixes) / 'Oobu Joobu' (seven jingles)
> ***Tape 2:*** 'Nearly Rebel Music' (two mixes) / 'Slow Claves' / 'Give Us a Chord Roy' (three mixes) / 'Seattle Build Up' (three mixes)

Over the next few weeks, he compiled three more reels of demos, including multiple versions of 'Cage,' a song that took its name from its chord progression (C, A minor and G with an E in the bass), and a Denny Laine tune, provisionally called 'Little Woman,' as well as a version of 'I'm Getting Closer,' a song that dated back to at least 1973.

> ***Tape 1:*** 'Little Woman' (working title for Denny Laine's 'Again and Again and Again') / 'Emotional Moments' [aka 'Cage'] (three mixes) / 'Praying Mantis Heart' (ten takes) / 'Reggae Moon' (two takes) / 'Old Fashioned'
> ***Tape 2:*** 'I Can't Write Another Song' (three takes) / 'Tremolo' (five takes) / 'I'm Getting Closer' (two takes)
> ***Tape 3:*** 'Take Me to Your Garden' (four takes) / 'Love Awake' (one take) / 'Busy, Busy Bo (Whole Wide World)' (one take) / 'S.M.A.' (punk song, two takes) / 'Butterflies' (with Stella and Mary, one take) / 'Dee-Dee' (with James, one take) / 'Denny's Little Woman' (one take) / 'Cage'

Recording Sessions

Thursday, June 29–Saturday, July 1, 1978.
Spirit of Ranachan Studio, Low Ranachan Farm, Campbeltown, Scotland.
Recording: 'To You.'

Laurence and Steve had been at Low Ranachan Farm only briefly for the 'I've Had Enough' shoot, but now they would be making it their home while Wings recorded a new album and whatever else Paul had in mind. For starters, Paul had the space above the studio set up as a kind of dormitory for the band, with dividers creating separate accommodations; soon they moved into the cottage at Low Park. But for a couple of musicians used to studio work in London, Paul's studio was surprisingly quaint, not least because it had no actual equipment of its own, relying instead on hiring the RAK mobile setup.

"The studio part of the building [at Low Ranachan] doubled as a grain reserve," Steve observed. "But it had been fitted with an equipment room, so it could be turned into a recording studio very quickly. The barn and the control room just suddenly became a studio: the trucks rolled up, the equipment was installed, and there we are. It was magnificent. It was really lovely, just to be sitting in the countryside on a farm with the windows open. I'd never had that experience before. I've been to some great studios in idyllic places, but nothing quite as private and personal as that."

Once they moved into the cottage, each of the players had several rooms, Holley recalls. "It was a very large farmhouse, very clean, very bare bones. I remember having a room with a window and a wooden desk. I also remember doing some finishing work on it, in my downtime: I stained the floors, and did some painting. I think I did the hallways upstairs as well. I thought, if I'm going to be here for a long time, I'll make it as comfortable as possible. That's just the kind of person I am. But yeah, it was very clean, very pleasant, just a work environment, a fun environment. Plenty of room to open up boxes and boxes of new toys and play with drums and mess around with tunings and stuff.

"I had some pretty crazy ideas, at that time, about sound, with drums and tuning—and extreme tuning sometimes. And everybody was game, you know—like, Paul would love that. And I was just trying to consider what he'd done, and the sounds that he liked, and then what I liked and what I could bring to the plate. So it was a great working environment. And the songs would come in, and we'd play for quite a while, just to get a sense of how we would fit together. I found that whole entry process very, very enjoyable."[22]

The band spent much of June 29 jamming and playing through 'To You,' the song Paul wanted to record once the studio was set up and tested. If having two new band members wasn't enough of a wild card for Paul, there was also his decision to bring Chris Thomas in to co-produce. Paul had mixed feelings about producers, George Martin excepted.

It was handy having another pair of trusted and experienced ears in the studio, and *in theory* having someone who would challenge you could yield a better album. But Paul was secure enough in his ideas that challenges were often batted away. "*I don't care what you think, this is what we're going to do.*" The few times Paul tried working with a producer, post-Beatles, had ended in grief. Jim Guercio, brought in to help get *Ram* over the line, lasted only a few days. Glyn Johns left the sessions for *Red Rose Speedway* early, complaining that Wings were unfocused.

Thomas, Paul told Roger Scott in a Capital Radio interview, "had done some work on the film we'd done," referring to the as yet unseen *Wings Over the World* and *Rockshow*. "We just said, 'Would you fancy coming on this next record?' And he did. But it wasn't out of, like, a *need* or anything." He added that having a producer "is a help, really. . . . It just takes a bit of work off me."[23]

Steve saw the value of Chris's presence immediately.

"You gotta have somebody in control," he said, "and I think he was very good at doing that without being oppressive. If he thought something was nonsense, he'd tell you, and if he thought it was good, he'd encourage you. So he was the epitome of a producer for me."[24]

Working with Thomas were engineers Phil McDonald and Mark Vigars from EMI and Tim Summerhayes from RAK. Once the equipment was set up and tested, Paul transferred the masters for 'Sunshine Sometimes' and 'When the Wind Is Blowing,' *Ram* session recordings he had set aside for the *Rupert* animated film project he had been hoping to make since the late 1960s. *Rupert* had again moved up his to-do list: he had written more music for it, and wanted to get it on tape.

But first, there was 'To You,' a track for the next album and an early clue to the new direction. Its chord progression is a parade of simple major and minor chords—none of the jazz voicings heard in Paul's two recent film songs—played with a chunky guitar sound against a pounding backbeat, at a brisk pace. Paul adopted a punk style for his shouted guide vocal, an approach he maintained for the finished vocal take, later in the day.

"It was just what I was into at the time," Paul claimed, sweeping aside his previous ambivalence about punk. "The New Wave thing was happening, and I realized that a lot of New Wave was just taking things at a faster tempo than we do. 'We' being what I like to call the Permanent Wave—little joke there."[25]

Paul played a Zemaitis acoustic bass, Denny and Laurence played electric guitars, Steve drummed and Linda traced the chord progression on the organ, although she is nearly inaudible except on the refrain, "*What if it happened to you*," where she accented the final word. The band filled two reels before Paul settled on takes 6 and 7 as "Best," editing together the strongest parts of each.

"Paul was trying to do stuff that was kind of simple and rocking again," Denny later recalled. "Not too much of a big production. And he wanted to get the band into shape, as a live band, to tour the world, starting with that album. So, I think he stuck down to basic, simple, rocky type songs for that reason."[26]

On Saturday, Paul overdubbed an acoustic guitar part, recording his Martin D28 through the soundhole pickup to get a dirty part-acoustic, part-electric sound that suited the spirit of the track. He also added slide guitar, a lead vocal and, with Denny and Linda, backing vocals supporting the refrain. Laurence then overdubbed a guitar solo, with an experimental contribution from Paul. As Laurence played the solo on his Fender Stratocaster, Paul sat in the control room altering the notes Laurence played.

"The guitar solo on that went almost atonal," Laurence said. "It was just me playing, and Paul manipulating an Eventide Harmonizer in real time. I would play a note, and what I'd hear in the headphones was something completely different. So it was like a joint thing, where I was responding to what he was doing, and he was responding to what I was doing. It was kind of cool.[27] Once I got a sense of where it was going, I would play some random things, and it all worked. I like that kind of outside-the-box thinking and playing."[28]

The raw take ends with a moment of feedback and crashing, distortion-drenched chords from Laurence, altered surreally by the Eventide Harmonizer.

The two new recruits, who were used to studio work at a session man's pace, were taken with the laid-back atmosphere.

"Just coming into the business, you go to a recording session, and it was just in and out as quickly as possible," Steve observed. "And everything was about costs and watching the clock. But here, we were in a world where it didn't seem like the pressures were there, timewise or financially, and it was the first time I'd really experienced that. So there was time to experiment. There was a lot of jamming and just what you do normally to feel out players."[29]

Recording Session

Wednesday, July 5, 1978.
Spirit of Ranachan Studio, Low Ranachan Farm, Campbeltown, Scotland.
Recording: 'Rupert Song (1st Version),' 'Parents Theme (Tippi Tippi Toes),' 'Flying Horses,' 'Sea Melody,' 'Rupert Song (2nd Version),' 'Storm,' 'Nutwood Scene (French Waltz),' 'Whistling in the Meadow,' 'The Palace of the King of the Birds' and 'Sea—Cornish Wafer.'
Overdubbing: 'When the Wind Is Blowing' and 'Sunshine Sometimes.'
Mixing: 'Tones,' 'Rupert Song (1st Version),' 'Tippi Tippi Toes (Parents Theme),' 'Flying Horses,' 'When the Wind Is Blowing,' 'The Palace of the King of the Birds,' 'Sunshine Sometimes,' 'Sea—Cornish Wafer,' 'Storm—Sea,' 'Nutwood,' 'Whistling in the Meadow,' 'Sea Melody' and 'Rupert Song (2nd Version).'

With one track recorded for the new album, Paul shifted gears, turning his attention to *Rupert*. All told, he had 11 new songs for the project, plus the two 1970 tracks, which needed only textural elements and a light lead vocal and backing vocals on 'Sunshine Sometimes.'

"If you're English, Rupert the Bear is this really iconic character in your childhood," Steve explained. "All I actually remember was Paul saying, 'Yeah, tomorrow we're gonna do something different. I've got all these bits and pieces sitting around.' So, a big aside to what we'd been doing, and it just took one day. [We] took a deep breath and piled in, and just sort of approached the stuff not as a band, but just as a relaxed day of doing 'something completely different,' to quote Monty Python—which is normal for a session musician!"[30]

Paul had created a story for his planned film, and on his own, he recorded a plot synopsis, reading from his script. When the songs were mixed, at the end of the session, the relevant sections of Paul's narration were affixed to the top of each piece of music.

In the story, Rupert and his family home in Nutwood are introduced before a black-winged stallion and a herd of white flying horses whisk him off to meet the King of the Birds. The King tells him that the North Wind has gone out of control and plans to freeze the planet, whereupon Rupert is taken away by a giant bird, who drops him on a tropical island. There, Rupert meets Sailor Sam. After a celebration, Rupert and Sam sail off in a small boat, but a storm washes their boat onto the shore, where friends find the traveling party and return them to Nutwood. Rupert is looked after by Dr. Lion and goes for a walk in the meadow before deciding to resume his mission. Setting off in a flying bubble in search of the Wise Goat of the Mountains, he meets Jack Frost, with whom he is buried in an avalanche until the South Wind thaws them, and then defeats the North Wind's nefarious plans.

Paul had written songs to illustrate most of these events and characters but appears to have left the ending incomplete: there is no music representing the flying bubble, Jack Frost, the avalanche or the South Wind's saving victory, only 'Sea Melody'* is an attractive piece etched in short descending figures, with the character of a thanksgiving hymn. The fact that the song is in the key of C major, and there is no role for the sea in this part of the tale, suggests that the title of the piece should actually be (or was originally) 'C Melody.'

On the new songs, Paul alternated between piano, acoustic guitar or 12-string acoustic guitar; Denny handled most of the bass lines, occasionally playing acoustic guitar instead; Linda played Mellotron, principally string lines, and a synthesizer programmed with sound effects; Laurence played electric guitar with effects pedals, and Steve played drums and percussion.

"It was a day of donning different hats," Steve explained, adding that for the new songs, Paul "would just play them once, and we'd rehearse them a couple of times, commit them to tape and move on."[31] Laurence recalled, "We just basically did one or two takes of each song."[32]

These included a cheerful 'Rupert' theme built around a repeating five-note Mellotron figure,

---

* Paul revisited this music in the mid-1990s, giving it new life as 'Celebration,' the finale of his second large-scale classical work, *Standing Stone* (1997).

and piano- and guitar-based 'Parents Theme' (also called 'Tippi Tippi Toes') with alternating jaunty and slow sections. A second version of 'Rupert' was recorded as well, to be used in the closing sequence.

Rupert's adventures begin with 'Flying Horses,' which features a prominent, seemingly improvised electric guitar part over static bass and piano tones, overlaid with the sound of galloping horses. 'When the Wind Is Blowing' serves as gentle traveling music that brings Rupert to 'The Palace of the King of the Birds'—an instrumental that dates back to 1968; Paul played it as an expansive solo piano piece with a plangent melody during the January 1969 *Get Back/Let It Be* sessions. Now revived after a decade in Paul's "For *Rupert*" stack, it had changed considerably. Quicker, with the piano sharing the limelight with guitar, bass, drums and wordless harmony vocals, it has shed the melancholy character of the 1969 version; here it is a full-fledged pop song with a rock-steady beat and punctuating flourishes, its melody fitting snugly on the beat.

'Sea—Cornish Wafer' alternates easygoing sea music and a hornpipe-like dance piece, both with placeholder lyrics. 'Storm' uses a slower version of that track's 'Sea' section, overlaid with noise effects, electric guitar and cymbal crashes, leading to a reprise of 'Sea' in which Laurence's guitar line winds around Paul's vocal. Chirping birds run through 'Nutwood,' a delightfully antique-sounding waltz for bass, electric piano, guitar and Mellotron. 'Whistling in the Meadow' is also a waltz, slower and heavier, with Laurence contributing jazz-tinged guitar figures over Paul's whistled and scat-sung melody. The cathartic conclusion, 'Sea Melody,' has Paul playing the main melody on the piano, with a steady bass and drum accompaniment, bursts of guitar counterpoint, and a choral element toward the end.

At the end of the day, Paul settled into the control room and compiled three reels of mixes from the session, one labeled 'James and chat, etc,' the second '*Rupert* Rehearsal,' and finally a reel with rough mixes of the finished tracks in the order of their appearance in the film, complete with Paul's narration.

Steve remembers later discussing plans for the *Rupert* film with Paul and Linda, and hearing Linda's ideas about animation. Both were taken with a TV ad campaign that British Telecom had run the previous winter. "I found the cartoon imagery of a melting snowman was just beyond belief," Steve said of the advertisement. "And I mentioned it to Linda in a discussion." The animation Steve was so taken with was by Sergio Simonetti, but when Linda looked into it, she was told that the animator was Oscar Grillo.

"Oscar Grillo actually ended up doing the first video [for *Rupert*]," Steve added. "What made his work so good was that he did everything himself. There was no reallocating to a team or the staff, so it took forever to complete a few minutes. And it became painfully obvious that to do a full-length feature movie was gonna cost a fortune. So, it never came to fruition with Oscar Grillo."[33]

The *Rupert* session left Laurence amazed at Paul's creative range, and lucky to be observing it so closely. It was, after all, only his third session with Paul, but the three—for 'Same Time Next Year,' 'To You' and the *Rupert* songs—could not have been more different.

"I had three or four years of solid studio work under my belt," Laurence noted, "but I had never had the luxury of being able to watch somebody on that level developing material, and having the kind of interaction that I was getting with Paul. . . . It was just how broad his palette was, and how easy it was for him to switch gears from one style to another. Because there was this kind of *Über*-consciousness—this artistic consciousness that wasn't just driven by being in one genre, but by being an artist, and a musician, and a multi-instrumentalist, and a producer, and being able to wear many hats, some of them at the same time. One would assume that there's a very strong ego at work there, which there is, but a very collaborative ego too."[34]

Recording Sessions

Friday, July 7–Monday, July 17, 1978.
Spirit of Ranachan Studio, Low Ranachan Farm, Campbeltown, Scotland.
Recording: 'You Don't Wanna Be My Little Woman' [working title of 'Again and Again and Again'], 'Arrow Through Me,' 'Winter Rose' and 'Love Awake.'
Overdubbing: 'You Don't Wanna Be My Little Woman' [working title of 'Again and Again and Again'], 'Arrow Through Me,' 'Winter Rose' and 'Love Awake.'

Paul's ideas about whether Wings were a band or his steady backing group had evolved since the early days, when he promised his bandmates joint ownership of Wings, with everyone sharing equally in the spoils. Now his conception of the band was more nuanced.

When it came to contracts and payment, it was clear—and he *wanted* it clear—that Wings members were employees of MPL, contracted to be on hand when Paul needed them, but with plenty of freedom in between. They would be well-paid for their work in the studio, but would not share in the royalties generated by record sales.

It is striking that after starting sessions for a new album, Paul veered off to work on *Rupert* material. He had done exactly this during the *Ram* sessions, when he was working with a pair of New York session players. It was almost as if he saw Laurence, Steve and Denny as this year's Hugh McCracken and Denny Seiwell—sidemen hired to do whatever Paul wanted, or as Denny described his role in the recording of *Band on the Run*, utility men. But the other side of the coin was that Paul encouraged his players to contribute songs to Wings albums—not because he was low on material of his own (as his continuous demo-making shows), but because it furthered the notion of Wings as a band in the traditional sense. In theory, players who composed could have their time in the spotlight, and as songwriters, they would receive composing royalties (as would MPL, as their publisher).

So when the sessions for the next Wings album resumed on July 7, Paul put the spotlight on Denny, who had two incomplete songs—'You Don't Wanna Be My Little Woman,' a simple burst of teenage romantic angst ("*You don't want to stay in my school / You don't want to be the one that's cool / You don't want to be the little woman / I love*") set to a simple C major chord progression, and 'Again and Again and Again,' a catchier tune in a more varied harmonic frame, with lyrics about a relationship going sour over time.

Paul suggested one of his own strategies for dealing with unfinished songs: combine them, making 'You Don't Wanna Be My Little Woman' into the verses and 'Again and Again and Again' into an extended bridge and refrain.

"I think that Denny was part of the rock 'n' roll-folk-R&B axis of the band," Laurence suggested, "and you get it right from the get-go, even with 'Go Now,' which is an R&B song that Denny brought into a kind of an English consciousness. And then you add Denny's folkiness to it; he's like a soul-folk musician. So I think that Denny was a part of the balance of the band, you know, as much as Linda was bringing her New York rock 'n' roll sensibility to things. And Paul could be influenced by that. Even Denny's voice modulates Paul's voice in a way that John Lennon would modulate Paul's voice. You need that extra dimension sometimes just for variety, and in the context of the band. And I think that was an important factor. It wasn't like we were just hired to be Paul's backup musicians; we were encouraged to have a band consciousness. And I think that Denny was our kind of anchor within that."[35]

Working in what was essentially Wings' stage configuration—Paul on bass, Denny on rhythm electric guitar, Laurence using his Strat to get what he described as a "Steve Cropper meets George Harrison"[36] soul-pop lead guitar sound, Linda on a Hammond B3 organ and Steve on drums—the band recorded a reel of backing tracks before settling on a master take. The addition of lead and backing vocals completed the song.

On Monday evening, July 10, Paul held an impromptu session with only Steve, to record 'Arrow Through Me,' a soft-rock number with an R&B tinge. The arrow imagery evokes Cupid's arrow, but with a darker turn: "*Ooh baby, you couldn't have done a worse thing to me / If you'd have taken an arrow and run it right through me.*"

Its most striking aspect is that it sounds as though it was built around a bass guitar riff, but that full, rounded bass tone is actually a Fender Rhodes electric piano. Paul recorded the piano track and a rough vocal with Steve drumming, and then, at Chris Thomas's suggestion, Steve added a second snare part, recorded at half speed—a trick from the Beatle days—so that when played back at normal speed the drum is pitched an octave higher and has an unusual timbre.

In keeping with the song's R&B character, Paul envisioned overlaying a brass section, and on the basic track he can be heard singing the melodies he intended for the horns.

"The sun was coming up by the time I staggered out of the barn with Paul," Holley recalled, noting that the pair had been drinking neat whisky all evening. "I'm standing there, and I'm exhausted, and we were both really hammered to be honest, and then Paul said, 'Do you hear that?' I said, 'What?' He said, 'The horse. That's Linda coming to get me, she's gonna be really mad.' The sun is coming up and we're standing there hammered. And the horse came along, and [Linda] says, 'Look at the state of you two, you disgust me!' And we're there holding each other up. And I remember looking up at her and saying, 'Err, would you let this man marry your daughter?' and she said, 'Yes, but that's a whole other point, Paul get on the horse!'"[37]

The full band returned to the studio on July 12 to work on another pairing of two incomplete songs—Paul's, this time—'Winter Rose' and 'Love Awake.' The latter appears always to have been intended as the second half of a pair: in 1977, Paul recorded a demo in which 'Love Awake' was attached to 'I Can't Write Another Song' (aka 'Keep on Believing'). Paul subsequently jettisoned 'I Can't Write Another Song' in favor of the more colorful 'Winter Rose,' but because their instrumentation and basic feel were so different—minor-key, wintry bleakness for 'Winter Rose,' a bright, folkish sound for 'Love Awake'—the two were recorded separately.

'Winter Rose' draws on a musical current that Paul had not previously tapped: the neo-Renaissance spirit explored in certain corners of progressive rock (Gryphon, for example), and also in a piece that was among Paul's classical favorites, Benjamin Britten's "'The Courtly Dances from *Gloriana*," which Paul knew from a 1964 recording by the Julian Bream Consort. Paul presided over the basic track from the piano, with Denny and Laurence playing acoustic guitars and Steve on drums.

Laurence used an Ovation nylon-string classical model equipped with a pickup that contributed an interesting stereo effect by sending the notes played on the sixth, fourth and second strings to the left channel and the fifth, third and first strings to the right channel. Since his part involved fingerpicked arpeggios, the sound of his guitar danced back and forth across the stereo image.

Over the next few days, Paul added bass and harpsichord, Denny added an acoustic 12-string, and Steve layered on more percussion. The lead and harmony vocals were saved for another time, not least because Linda, splitting her time between Wings and mothering four children, was often engaged with James during the sessions, either in the studio or at High Park.

"I don't think Wings would have been Wings without Linda," Laurence observed, "whether that was because of her modulating Paul's tendency to go toward the pop end of the spectrum, or just her contribution to the backing vocal sound."[38]

Concurrent with the overdubbing on 'Winter Rose,' the band began work on 'Love Awake,' the second part of the joined pair. Paul and Denny strummed acoustic guitars, Laurence played bass and Steve provided a light beat that became more varied as Paul sang the guide vocal. Linda added

Mellotron flute flourishes during the song's second half. In three reels of takes, the band tried several approaches including a calypso version, before settling provisionally on a version with a gentle folk spirit that suited the characteristically rich McCartney melody.

During the week, Steve and Laurence gave their first interviews as members of Wings. Speaking to journalist Pauline McLeod, both credited Denny with their introductions to Paul, Laurence noting that he had done lots of session work with big stars, but that "the call came just at the right time because I wanted to express myself more," and Steve saying that Wings "will be going out on the road as soon as possible."[39]

In their downtime, Steve, Laurence and Denny, and sometimes Paul and Linda, toured the countryside and spent time in Campbeltown. One evening, the full band attended a preview screening of *The Buddy Holly Story*, the biopic directed by Steve Rash and starring Gary Busey, which had been released in the United States in May, and was due for its British premiere during Buddy Holly Week, in September.

Besides taking the defibrillator pads to his long-dormant *Rupert* project, Paul wanted to give the kiss of life to the film project he had been developing as a vehicle for Wings. After the blockbuster success of both *Star Wars* and *Close Encounters of the Third Kind* saw his film project with Gene Roddenberry fizzle out, he decided to bring his narrative back down to earth and—at the suggestion of Brian Brolly—hired a writer with an appreciation of both his past and present: Willy Russell.

"I got a call from Brian saying that Paul was interested in making a movie," Russell explained, "and the invitation was for me to go up to the farm and to hang with them for a week or so. I have to say that I was at once flattered enormously, excited, and extremely wary, because I had enough background knowledge, and enough experience of stars [to know that] if you're working *for* them, you will arrive at a day where you will have to give up something of your fiercely held writerly independence. Not because of any intention or malevolence, but if you're working with one of *the* greatest stars on the planet then you're gonna rub up against that. It's inevitable."[40]

Setting aside his reservations, Russell spent a week with Wings in Scotland, getting to know the players who would be characters in his film script.

"I got up there and I realized how remote it was," Russell joked. "And the brief [from Paul] was, 'Come up and see me, and come up with an idea. And it has to be a film that would include me [Paul], and all of the members of Wings,' who were very new members. The time that I was there was a playing-in session for them, and I remember Steve being cautious and tentative—everybody was feeling their way a little, I think, when I was there. Not so much Laurence, I think, who was much more centered anyway."

Recording sessions, Russell observed, began late in the afternoon, and were typically followed by nightly workouts during which the band would jam old rock 'n' roll and R&B Standards.

"It was phenomenal for me, it was like I was back in the Cavern!" Russell rhapsodized. Besides playing fly on the wall at the Spirit of Ranachan, Russell was handed rough mixes of Wings' work in progress, and an idea for a script soon began to form, provisionally titled *Band on the Run*.

The film's principal characters were Jet, a singer; Lilly, a keyboard player from New York; Benny, a guitarist and singer from Birmingham; Snav, a drummer from London; and Lorry, a guitarist (whose listing among the dramatis personae notes "no regional accent")—as well as three businessmen, four groupies, another band and a slate of incidental characters, including unnamed "well-known musicians."[41]

Back in Liverpool, Russell would flesh out the script with stage director Mike Ockrent.

Recording Sessions

Tuesday, July 18–Friday, July 28, 1978.

Spirit of Ranachan Studio, Low Ranachan Farm, Campbeltown, Scotland.

Recording: 'Old Siam, Sir,' 'Maisie,' 'Spin It On,' 'Simon Game,' and jams including 'Denny's Silly Announcement,' 'Country Verbal,' 'Jam (Conga jam),' 'Steve Outside,' 'Jam (Harmonica blues),' 'Crazy Jam,' 'Sunday Jam,' 'Wonderbar' and 'Jam.'

Overdubbing: 'Old Siam, Sir,' 'Spin It On' and miscellaneous vocal overdubs.

After tinkering with the Renaissance-folk combination of 'Winter Rose' and 'Love Awake' for a few days, on July 18 Paul again shifted gears, bringing 'Old Siam, Sir,' a song with musical roots in a mostly instrumental demo Paul recorded in 1976 as 'Super Big Heatwave.' Its ear-catching element is a riff based on octave leaps. Otherwise, it boasts a melody that wanders freely against the simplest of backdrops—just an E minor chord, with a drop to D major at the end of each line. Toward the end of the demo, Paul sings a largely incomprehensible lyric, although the phrase "*Old Siam, Sir*" comes through a couple of times.

Now he had completed lyrics for the song, taking that single intelligible phrase as a starting point and winding it into an unusual narrative about the travails of a lady from Siam (the Southeast Asian country that had been known as Thailand since 1939). Between verses furthering the story, the protagonist "*waited 'round in Walthamstow*" and "*scouted 'round in Scarborough.*"

---

* Russell may have been alluding to the degree to which Juber had suppressed the Cockney accent of his youth.

"'Old Siam' is . . . silly lyrics, as usual," he admitted. "It's just about some chick coming over from the Orient.

"When you see them written out they make quite a bit of sense. Because in the second verse she meets like a film director, and he takes her home to see his mam, and then she gets a letter from Siam. Some tragedy happens there, and she needs some money. And she wanders around in Walthamstow and Scarborough again, and then the director finds out that she's been getting money from unsolicited—so, this is totally crazy. But all my stuff is mad. Most of it is, anyway. And then he directed her not to stay. The film director *directed* her not to stay.

"All clever stuff. It's just there, it's just something to sing, really. And I really worried about those lyrics, I didn't like them. And then this guy Willy Russell has been doing some scriptwriting for us, he really loved it, you know, and he's a writer. He writes plays, so I was all chuffed. So, I loved it."[42]

Paul had by now developed a strategy for commenting on songs, or even full albums (*Wild Life*, most notably) that have either been strongly criticized, or that he had doubts about. The format is: "The press disliked [the song or album] so I began to think it wasn't very good—but then I ran into [someone respected in popular culture] who said he really liked it [or even that it was his favorite], so there you go."

What the song lacked when the sessions began was a bridge. That problem was remedied during a jam.

"Steve Holley came up with the chord progression for the second section of 'Old Siam, Sir,'" Laurence confirmed. "That came out of a jam where I think Linda was playing drums and Steve was playing piano, and I think Paul was playing guitar."[43]

Holley's uncredited addition—a descending chord progression starting on A minor and working its way down to C major—became an instrumental break, heard after the third and sixth verses.

For the basic take, Paul played the Fender Rhodes electric piano, doubling the melody of the vocal line, Denny and Laurence played electric guitars and Steve returned to his kit. The master was created quickly; the band filled only a single reel of tape before Paul was satisfied. Figuring out what to do with Steve's bridge was more complicated. Paul decided it was the place for a solo, but a composed rather than improvised one. Picking up his Epiphone Casino, he was joined by Laurence, playing a Gibson Les Paul Custom, in a series of short, harmonized phrases, Paul playing the lower line and Laurence taking the high part.

The track was finished off with Paul's lead vocal, delivered in his best rock-shouter style.

"'Old Siam' was definitely punk influenced," Chris Thomas observed. "I never bought the whole ethos of punk particularly, [but] the good thing that came out of it was that fact that even if you couldn't play, you could join a band. It returned music to ordinary kids, which was just great. But the most important thing that happened was that it really went back to rock 'n' roll roots. If you

Wings, 'London Town' single trade ad

listen to the Sex Pistols, it's all Chuck Berry style stuff, and I think the same thing happened with 'Old Siam, Sir'—it's Paul rocking out."[44]

In the spirit of keeping Wings on their collective toes by exploring a different musical style at virtually every session, Paul asked Laurence whether he had any tunes to contribute. Despite holding a degree in music, Laurence had not done much composing. But working with Paul, and watching him at close range, inspired him to try.

"I was learning that the process of inventing licks and riffs, the connective tissue of guitar parts, was not that far removed from composing," he wrote in his memoir. "Witnessing Paul put together the elements of songs was something of a revelation, that it did not require a bolt of lightning from above to bring inspiration."[45]

Laurence turned up at the July 21 session with an instrumental, 'Maisie,' a country-tinged tune in the spirit of Chet Atkins that he had written between sessions. The band sat in a semicircle and worked up a lively arrangement, Juber playing his Gibson Super 400, McCartney with his Rickenbacker bass, Laine on harmonica and Holley playing a light drum part. "[Steve and I] had both been listening to the retro-blues picking of Ry Cooder, so Steve immediately clued in to the feel I was looking for,"[46] Laurence recalled. As was the case with the rockier 'Old Siam, Sir,' the band quickly completed a master.

Although Sundays were generally set aside for family time, Paul summoned the band to the studio on July 23 to record 'Spin It On,' a song he had written that morning. Reprising the punk spirit that enlivened 'Old Siam, Sir,' Paul built his new song around only two chords, A minor and E7, both chords punctuated with a G in the bass on alternate beats. Its lyrics, like those of 'Old Siam, Sir,' are an almost stream-of-consciousness fantasy, with internal rhymes that, at the speed Paul was proposing the song be played, were guaranteed tongue-twisters: "*Off to the flicks with the piddle* [urine] *in her nicks* [underwear] */ To the fair with her hair in curlers*," in the first verse, "*Off to the fields with a missionary zeal for the life / Of the wife of the farmer*" in the second. The verses alternate with a repeating chorus—"*Spin it on, don't stop, take it back to the top / 'Cause I've got another lot of love for you*"—and a pair of short guitar breaks take the place of a bridge.

"'Spin It On' I wrote one morning in Scotland and brought it in to everyone," Paul explained, "and they said, 'Ha, ha, ha—you're kidding,' because it sounds really daft on one guitar. But you know, I was kinda like, 'I haven't done a fast one for a long time.'"[47]

He was also reacting to the reviews of *London Town* that criticized his focus on mid-tempo ballads—and to punk rockers' habit of trashing their predecessors in interviews, something he believed the press put them up to.

"The only pressure [I feel]," he told Paul Gambaccini, interviewing him for the BBC, "is the one that the media creates, which is—I mean, I don't know if the media creates it or if it's just there anyway, which that kind of pressure of, 'Well, the older rock 'n' rollers can't rock and the younger ones can,' which gets you a bit annoyed . . .'Cause if you talk to [young musicians], I mean, there's not that much of that going on anywhere. It's created a lot by people who want to write about it. A lot of the young kids I see are just really into [the music] just exactly as I was. They just like guitars, they like electric stuff, and they want to bang away at it. The singing styles may be a little bit different from how it was—but that we were always changing anyway, so they're only doing what we did."[48]

For proof that younger musicians did not necessarily regard their elders as useless geezers, Paul had to look no further than Steve Holley. As a member of G. T. Moore and the Reggae Guitars, Steve had played on bills with the Clash, Rat Scabies, the Damned and Dr. Feelgood. Paul's memory of Wings' initial response to 'Spin It On' notwithstanding, Steve recalls being entirely enthusiastic.

"I was just totally there," he said, "'cos I was ten years younger, at least, than everybody. So that was an interesting time period, because it was already a part of my energy and my makeup. I was bringing that full-on punk aspect to my rock playing. . . . I just think it was a reflection of the times, really, and some of it was just pure fun. It's really an attitude more than a style, because you're still playing within the same fundamental structures. 'Spin It On' is a prime example of that.

"Very often, Paul would come into the studio and play a song, it was pretty obvious what needed to be done. And then he would have something like 'Spin It On,' where it was just a blank pattern: you can do *anything* with that. So, I just heard bombastic double-speed, sixteen-stroke fills, just flat out."[49]

Wings again used their stage configuration for the basic track—Paul on bass, Denny and Laurence playing guitars with a touch of distortion to give them the right amount of spark-creating crunchiness, and Steve driving them with his rapid-fire fills. The band filled three reels with basic takes before choosing the master, to which Paul added his lead vocal, then double-tracked it before Denny and Linda joined him for backing vocals. The only other notable overdubs were Laurence's guitar solos, heard in the choruses and in the space left for the break.

"I was just sitting with my Stratocaster in the control room with Paul right next to me, and just kind of eyeballing each other," Laurence recalled, emphasizing the collaborative nature of the process. "There was space for a solo, which I filled with what I felt was appropriate. Paul liked it and brought stuff out of me in that process."[50]

The band spent Tuesday, July 25, playing with a new toy, Milton Bradley's Simon, a round disc with four pads, each a different color, which flashed as different tones were played. It was, in effect, a primitive sequencer, which would add new notes with each round.

"You have to copy the sequence that it plays each time," Steve explained, "and it gets more complicated as you go."[51] The band found its testing of their musical memories both fascinating and challenging, and Paul ran tape while they played, the resulting recording entitled 'Simon Game.'

Otherwise, Wings spent their final week at Spirit of Ranachan touching up vocal overdubs and jamming. Among the jams were 'Crazy Jam,' with Steve playing piano, and an untitled jam on which Alan Crowder's son, Paul, played drums. By the end of the week, Thomas, McDonald and Vigars compiled two reels of 24-track masters from the sessions, as well as a reel of jams. Paul gave the band a six-week break.

—

At the end of July, Paul and Linda had their Scottish hideaway all to themselves. Press reports mentioned that Ringo visited the McCartneys around this time, but that cannot be verified; in any case, Ringo was busy at the time promoting his latest single, 'Tonight,' which was issued on July 21.

George Harrison had his hands full as well: he and his girlfriend, Olivia Arias, celebrated the birth of their son Dhani on August 1; a month later, on September 2, George and Olivia were married at the registry office in Henley-on-Thames. It was announced, too, that George was working on a book, *I Me Mine*—part memoir, part collection of lyric manuscript reproductions—for Genesis Publications, a publisher of high-quality limited editions, based in Guildford, Surrey. George's book, due out in 1980, would be limited to 1,000 copies and priced at £116 ($224).

John Lennon was quietly spending his second consecutive summer in Japan with Yoko and Sean. Like the others, he kept tabs on the ever-churning Beatles industry from a distance. Paul took note of the opening of the *Sgt. Pepper's Lonely Hearts Club Band* film on July 21, and though he expressed little interest in seeing it, he heard the soundtrack album, and told Paul Gambaccini that he particularly admired Earth, Wind & Fire's cover of 'Got to Get You Into My Life.' The album sold well and brought renewed interest in the Beatles' own recordings, sufficient to push the original *Sgt. Pepper* album up 20 places to No. 32 on *Billboard's* Top LP & Tape chart, bringing with it the two 1973 compilations—*1962–66*, which popped back onto the chart at 142, and *1967–70*, which climbed ten places to No. 92.

The McCartneys spent much of their August downtime traveling in the south of France, and as was often the case, their vacation yielded musical by-products. In Nice, Paul and Linda attended a concert by the Mills Brothers, an American vocal group that flourished in the 1930s and '40s and were a childhood favorite of Paul's.

"There they were, singing away, singing up a storm, doing all their old hits," Paul recalled, "and I really loved them. . . . [I] went backstage to say hello to them 'cause I'm a fan of theirs, and one of them just pulled me to the side—Herbie [Mills], I think it was—and he said, 'Hey, Paul, why don't you write a song for us?' So I said, 'Oh, okay, great, I'd love to.'[52] It'd be quite an honor, really, that they would do my stuff. I've still got quite a feeling for all that, so I went back to the hotel and wrote a song in the next couple of days, which was 'Baby's Request.'"[53]

While the McCartneys were away, *Record Mirror* published an introductory interview with Juber and Holley. They covered all the expected ground—what they like about recording, what they like even more about touring—but the interviewer, Robin Smith, also took the opportunity to ask about reports that Paul paid subpar wages.

"That just isn't true," said Juber. "Put it this way, we're being paid enough to be in a situation where we can concentrate on the music and not have to worry about finances."

Smith also quizzed the pair about life with the Macs.

"The Paul McCartney and Linda McCartney you see on television or in the papers is how they really are," Juber reported. "The closeness of his family ties has meant that he can survive anything people hurl against him and come up smiling. I don't see how anybody can call him complacent though, the man is a genius. There's that indefinable quality in his songs which makes each one a masterpiece. It's difficult to describe it any other way."[54]

Though they were members of Wings, Juber and Holley could take some solace in the fact that the next round of insulting reviews had nothing to do with their work. In the hope of extending the shelf life of *London Town*, EMI released the title track (EMI Matrix 7YCE.21799), paired with 'I'm Carrying' (EMI Matrix 7YCE.21800) as a single on August 21 in America and four days later in Britain. Having read the press's dismissals of the album and earlier singles, Paul was under no illusion that reviewers would be kind.

Yet another cut excised from the album of the same name, and doubtless you're expecting the usual McCartney putdown. Really, it's not worth it. Wings are a self-professed, upmarket family unit and play cozy tunes to match. Of course there's nothing new or provocative: to expect that at the moment is pure delusion.[55]

Ian Birch, Melody Maker

Typical faceless Wings album track. No substance for a single and certainly shouldn't shift much vinyl, reads like a dyslexic Jane Austen.[56]

Bev Briggs, Record Mirror

Wings' single needs no review. It's not even hip easy listening, it just sort of lies there. . . . My sister climbed Buckingham Palace gates for this???[57]

Danny Baker, NME

This is the third single and title track from the group's Platinum LP and it's a melodic, atmospheric ballad about the city of London. As usual Paul McCartney's voice is a standout.[58]

Uncredited, Billboard

'London Town' entered the British singles chart on September 9 at No. 72, and climbed only as far as No. 60, which it reached on September 23. Its run in the Top 100 lasted only four weeks. In the United States, the single entered the *Billboard* Hot 100 at No. 75 on September 9, and remained on the chart for eight weeks, peaking at No. 39 for two weeks starting on October 14.

By late August, the McCartneys were back at High Park, where they remained until the end of school holidays. It was a farewell, of sorts: Paul and Linda had decided to make their property in Peasmarsh, East Sussex, their principal residence, and the process of transforming the property into their home inevitably meant spending less time in Scotland, particularly since many of the attractions of High Park—farmland for horse riding, for example—were part of the package in Peasmarsh too.

Cavendish Avenue would remain his London pied-à-terre, to be used mainly when he was recording in London. And it was there that he discovered, on September 3, that Warren Beatty's *Heaven Can Wait* was in the theaters.

"I opened the paper," he said, "and there was a big ad for the film—and no mention of my song, at all." Miffed, he asked the Eastmans to look into what had become of 'Did We Meet Somewhere Before.' When they reported back, he was astonished to learn that not only was it not used, but that he was not the only songwriter Beatty had approached.

"He asked five separate people to write songs," Paul explained, "and like me, they all apparently sent him a song. I don't know who the other four were, probably John, Ringo, Bert, and Harold. And eventually, he got all the five songs, turned them all down, didn't use the songs and didn't ring anyone up to tell them!"[59]

23

THE ELECTRICIANS

When she was last seen publicly, Heather McCartney was a lively six-year-old, scampering through a scene of *Let It Be* while the Beatles jammed. Now she was an attractive 16-year-old whose musical tastes skewed toward punk and were an influence on Paul's own sense of what was popular with teenagers. But Paul and Heather did not always see eye-to-eye.

Paul had been a central figure in Heather's life for more than a decade—five years longer than her biological father, Joseph Melville See Jr., with whom she had minimal contact. During that time Paul and Linda had sculpted Heather in their own image—she adored animals, craved fresh air and open space, and lived and breathed popular culture. But like any teenager, she maintained a delicate balance between her willingness to appease her parents and her desire to fit in with her peers. At the start of the summer, the scales began to tip toward the latter.

It was the aftermath of an argument between Paul and Heather at Cavendish Avenue earlier in the year that led Paul and Linda to make the drastic decision to uproot the whole family from London to East Sussex.

"We'd been talking about the kind of things that fathers and daughters talk about, and we'd had a row," Paul explained. "I suppose I was becoming the hard father figure to her. She left the house, and sometime later, when she came back, we were talking about this row, after we'd made up, and she'd told me what her friends [at the private school she attended in London] had said.

"They were all the sons and daughters of famous and influential people and they'd said to her, 'You've no need to worry about your dad,' and she'd asked, 'Why?' and they'd said, 'Because if he gives you any more trouble you can tell the newspapers.' Just realizing that she was mixing with children who had this mentality was very worrying. It was the thing that sparked off this whole change for me.

"I know it's not easy for them. I remember once in Scotland when we were on holiday, my kids rode past me on their horses and one of the little ones said, 'Oh look, there's Paul McCartney,' I said, 'Oh, don't do that to me.' The schools there [in London] were always trying to make them believe they were superior. I asked them, 'What is it like at school having a famous daddy? Is it weird?' and they tell me little things that people have said about me. So, I say to them, 'Well, I can't become unfamous for you!'"[1]

Just as he had experienced a modest, working-class upbringing in Liverpool, Paul wanted his children to spend their formative years surrounded by down-to-earth folk whose problems could not easily be remedied by daddy's checkbook. But while the earthy, rural community of Peasmarsh offered the perfect antidote to central London life, the move meant giving up some comforts, initially: Waterfall, the three-room, two-bedroom cottage on their East Sussex estate, would be inadequate for the long term.

For Heather, the upheaval was unsettling.

"I never actually fitted in," Heather later confessed. "When I was at school, I was always the one who was standing back. I remember thinking, 'Those people over there are doing that, and I am

Wings at Lympne Castle, 1979

over here—and I don't know quite why.' We were moving around so much that I never settled in any school. There are a lot of gaps in my education. But I didn't feel isolated—I actually felt lucky. I was never told to behave in a certain way; I was just encouraged to be who I am."[2]

To help oversee the land and buildings Paul hired two full-time stockmen and a part-time bookkeeper. Schools were found for the girls in nearby Rye. Linda drove them to school daily, often stopping at Jempsons, the local bakery, for fresh bread and pastries on her way home. Paul also began making inquiries into purchasing a bigger home for the family nearby; building a larger house on the plot where Waterfall sat was another option.

Recording, formally or otherwise, was also tricky. Abbey Road Studios was a two-and-a-half-hour drive north, and nothing on the property was suitable for use as a studio. But Paul hit on the idea of renting Lympne (pronounced Lim) Castle, a medieval pile roughly 40 minutes to the east of Peasmarsh, from its owners, Harold and Deirdre Margary. Set on 139 acres, on an escarpment overlooking the English Channel—on clear day, the coast of France can be seen from its east-facing towers—the castle was built between the eleventh and thirteenth centuries on the ruins of a Roman settlement. If you're a band looking for an atmospheric place to work, you couldn't do better.

Using the castle as a recording venue, however, required careful planning. The RAK Mobile Studio was brought in through the castle gates, which are operated using an ancient wheel system, and the console and tape decks had to be carried up a steep, narrow spiral staircase to a room called the Vaulted Chamber, the walls of which had to be covered in felt to deaden the acoustics. Cables were run back down the stairs to the rooms where the band would record.

Mostly, that was in the castle's Great Hall, a large wood-paneled room with stunning views of the Kent coast. Steve's drums (and an acoustic enclosure) were set up there, in front of the large fireplace. But experimentation turned up other useful locations. Laurence, for example, found that acoustic guitars sounded especially rich both in the kitchen, where Linda's keyboards were set up, and in the winding stone staircases.

"We like to record in unusual places because it gives the recordings a healthier and brighter approach,"[3] Paul said of the move to Lympne. "We secretly hired the castle and moved everything in. The locals were told that the electricians were doing wiring work. Nobody was supposed to know. They did, but never let on. They just called us 'The Electricians.'"[4]

The first day of recording at Lympne Castle, September 5, was mainly an equipment-testing day, so the band filled two reels with jams. It would be nearly a week before work began in earnest; meanwhile, Paul went to London to oversee the third annual Buddy Holly Week.

The celebration began with a party at Peppermint Park, a hamburger restaurant in Covent Garden, with Eric Clapton, Keith Moon, all of Led Zeppelin, Gallagher and Lyle, Mary Hopkin, Elvis Costello, Tom Robinson, George Melly, John Cleese, and John Hurt among the guests. From there, Paul and his guests headed to the Odeon, in Leicester Square, for the British premiere of *The Buddy Holly Story*.

The festive spirit ended abruptly the next day when Keith Moon, the Who's drummer, and one of Paul's guests at Peppermint Park and the film screening, was found dead in his flat in Curzon Square, Mayfair, having overdosed on Heminevrin (also known as clomethiazole), a sedative.

The music world reacted with shock, if not necessarily surprise, given Moon's status, at age 32, as one of rock's wild men, known for trashing many a hotel room, driving a Lincoln Continental into the swimming pool of a Holiday Inn, and blowing up toilets with cherry bombs—not to mention consuming copious amounts (and dangerous mixtures) of alcohol and drugs.

But at Paul's party, Moon told other guests that he was planning to marry his Swedish girlfriend, Annette Walter-Lax, and Walter-Lax believed that he was, at long last, beginning to temper his behavior.

"Keith was not drunk at the party," Walter-Lax said. "As far as I saw, he had only a few glasses of wine because he was cutting down on his drinking a great deal."[5] According to Walter-Lax, Moon had taken some sleeping pills, woke up around 7:30 A.M. and ate a steak, then went back to sleep. When Walter-Lax checked on him again, at around 3:40 P.M., he was not breathing and she could detect no pulse.

For tea-leaf readers, there were decidedly spooky coincidences surrounding Moon's death. One was that just over four years earlier, the American singer Ellen Naomi Cohen, better known as Mama Cass Elliott, had died in the very same Mayfair apartment (which was owned by Harry Nilsson). And on the cover of *Who Are You*, the album the Who released only three weeks earlier, while the rest of the band is dressed casually, Moon is dressed as a country squire, in a tweed coat, tan pants, a jockey's cap and knee-high boots, holding a riding crop in his gloved hand, and straddling a folding chair bearing the legend "Not to Be Taken Away."

Although Moon had been friendly with the McCartneys, and had died just hours after attending an event Paul was hosting, Paul made no public statement on the drummer's untimely passing, his silence rooted in the same aversion to death that kept him away from his own father's funeral. Flowers were dispatched to Moon's widow, and on September 13, when the rock world bid farewell to "Moon the Loon," Paul and Linda were back with the rest of Wings at Lympne Castle.

Recording Sessions

Monday, September 11–Friday, September 29.*

RAK Mobile Recording Unit, Lympne Castle, Kent.

Recording and Overdubbing: 'Radio' (aka 'Radio Bit' and 'Reception'), 'After the Ball' (First Version), 'No Details' (further elements for 'Radio Bit') and 'Love Awake' (Remake).

* The master takes of the songs recorded during this period were compiled over a period of two days (September 22 and 23), and although the compilation reels most likely present the songs in the order they were recorded, paperwork showing the actual recording dates has not been located.

Bad luck followed Paul and Linda back to Kent. Sessions resumed on September 11, but were almost immediately put on hold when Chris Thomas discovered that a batch of defective tape rendered the recordings made during the first few days unusable.* While Thomas and the RAK engineers dealt with the problem, Paul pondered the direction of the album in progress. At some point after the Spirit of Ranachan sessions, he began thinking about a concept, or at least a thematic frame, for the record. As he explained it, it was "a rough idea of someone in a car, goes to a gig, then gets out of it, and then [there's] a song about the morning after . . . and then it rocks off again."[6]

What was required, therefore, was a starting point—the person driving. Paul's vision for this was an instrumental track that was part funk jam and part electronic experiment involving the sound of random radio broadcasts.

"It was supposed to be like when you're in a car, and you're trying to get a station, and you get four other stations as well," Paul said of the track, which at that point was called 'Radio Bit,' but was soon renamed 'Reception.' "You're trying to listen to a rock and roll record, or something, and you get the Berlin Symphony, and the BBC World Service and other stations, and you get four of them at once. We were trying to make up [that kind of] sound. And then you suddenly hit the right station—and then the album starts."[7]

The basis of the track was what Laurence described as "a Meters-like groove," in which he and Denny played tightly interlocking figures over a punchy, repeating bass figure from Paul. Coming out of the bass-heavy funk groove, Laurence overdubbed a higher melody line, using an ARP Avatar guitar synthesizer. The band then collected effects—the high-pitched sound of a reel of tape rewinding, for example, which was overlaid at the start of the track—and radio recordings, both real and newly manufactured by Wings, to overlay throughout the track.

While building this sound collage, Paul hit on the idea of getting the Margarys involved—it was their castle, after all—by having them read selections from their library as if they were on a BBC Radio 4 show, like *The Afternoon Play* or *The World at One*—programs Paul and Linda frequently tuned in to.

"The fellow who owns the castle here has got a very BBC voice," Paul explained. "He and his wife have very similar home counties accents, very sort of proper. They're great people. So, we were sitting and having a drink with them one evening, and I said, 'Look would you . . . just as a laugh . . .' He said, 'Oh yes,' he'd be pleased to. So, we got him in the old kitchen there. There was a big fire crackling, and he got his headphones on, and he sat down, and we started doing this."[8]

* Exactly what was recorded and lost during this period is undocumented.

Harold Margary gave emotional (within the bounds of British propriety) readings of passages from Ian Hay's *The Sport of Kings* and John Galsworthy's *The Little Man*. Deirdre Margary read Vivian Ellis's lyrics for 'The Poodle and the Pug,' a number from A. P. Herbert's 1946 opera *Big Ben*. Since the idea was to weave these readings through the tapestry of music, effects and radio recordings, Paul decided that orchestral music best suited the Margarys. So Laurence again took up his ARP Avatar, Linda took her place at the Mellotron, and Paul strapped on his Gizmo-equipped Telecaster and produced an orchestral track.

"We did that 'Reception' piece, which was like an overture," Laurence recalled, "and I distinctly remember recording that with a guitar synthesizer, and then Paul overdubbing the Gizmo. I mean, he and I kind of built up this orchestra with the guitar synth and the Gizmo, which then also played into the play reading, with the orchestra behind it."[9]

It soon became clear that the group was amassing far more than was necessary for a short introductory track. But deciding what would be used, and how much, was a decision to be made later; for the moment, the plan was to assemble as much, and as varied, material as possible.

"We started off at the castle here, working on the thing, and we did the basic riff that was gonna be the rock 'n' roll thing you were trying to tune in," Paul told an interviewer, referring to the funk groove the band recorded. "We just played that live, we just carried that on for a while. [Then] we started working on little bits and pieces, and started recording radios. All for atmosphere. And then we wanted the classical thing, you know, we wanted the big classical orchestra. So, we made up a classical orchestra of our own, with Mellotrons and Gizmos and everything, and had this big theme going."[10]

During the several days Wings assembled 'Radio Bit/Reception,' they also worked on 'After the Ball,' a bluesy ballad in 6/8, with a wistful, old-timey character that may reflect the fact that Paul borrowed the title (as well as the waltz meter and overall spirit) from an 1892 song by Charles K. Harris that was popular in both public vaudeville houses and private salons.

It was a song Paul probably knew: Nat King Cole included a version on his 1963 LP *Those Lazy-Hazy-Crazy Days of Summer*, and it was the title track of a popular 1974 collection of such period pieces by Joan Morris and William Bolcom. And given his fascination with music publishing, he probably knew about the song's place in publishing history: offended by the pittance publishers had paid for his earlier songs, Harris published 'After the Ball' himself. It became the first song to sell a million sheet music copies, and ultimately sold five million.[11]

But where Harris's song is a tale of betrayal and lost love, Paul's is almost an antidote. His protagonist, lost among strangers at a ball, finds his sweetheart waiting for him out in the hall (easy rhymes being something Paul rarely resisted).

The first version Wings recorded began with a light texture. Paul sings the opening words (*"after the"*) alone, in a slightly raspy voice, with the third (*"ball"*) supported by piano and Linda's organ, which soon supplants the piano as the main accompanying instrument. Paul's overdubbed bass joins the texture, adding a slow but prominent line of counterpoint that is tightly interlocked with Steve's simple but sharp-edged drum punctuation. Denny's and Laurence's electric guitars gradually thicken the backdrop, from which a slowly climbing, fluid solo by Laurence brings the track to the point where Paul planned to join it to a second antique-sounding character piece, 'How Many Million Miles' (the first two words of its title soon to be dropped).

For the moment, this version of 'After the Ball' was marked "Best," though Paul suspected he could better it.

In the meantime, he turned his attention to 'Love Awake.' Unsatisfied with the Spirit of Ranachan recording, he presided over a remake with the same mostly acoustic instrumentation and the same expansive spirit—Juber called it "anthemic"[12]—but this time in a tighter, more focused performance. Paul, Denny and Laurence played acoustic guitars, with Laurence using an unusual tuning in which the guitar's bottom four strings were tuned an octave higher than usual. Laurence overdubbed the bass line, as he had done in Scotland. The other overdubs completed at Lympne were a light organ part, played by Linda, and an electric piano, played by Paul.

Recording Sessions

Monday, September 11–Friday, September 29, 1978 (continued).
RAK Mobile Recording Unit, Lympne Castle, Kent.
Recording and Overdubbing: 'We're Open Tonight,' 'Cage & He Didn't Mean It' (Lympne Version), 'Getting Closer' (first version), 'After the Ball' (Remake), 'How Many Million Miles,' 'Rockestra' (Band Demo) and various jams.

To the extent that he was toying with the idea of a concept for the album, the song Paul had in mind to follow 'Reception' was 'We're Open Tonight.' Its lyrics—"*We're open tonight for fun / So bring all your friends, come on*"—would set up the concert that the protagonist was driving to, much as 'Venus and Mars' set up 'Rock Show.' Like 'Venus and Mars,' 'We're Open Tonight' is slow and contemplative, and would lead naturally into a more rambunctious track, with one of Wings' recent punk-inspired songs most logically fitting the bill.

It is a deceptively simple song, pivoting around only two chords, but slightly unusual ones: G6 (a G major chord with an added E) and G minor 6, both played in gentle arpeggiations against the rising and chromatically falling melody. Sitting in one of the castle's spiral staircases, Paul and

Laurence recorded the guitar parts, Paul playing his Martin D-28 and Laurence accompanying him on a 12-string acoustic with the third pair of strings tuned "a step or two" flat.[13]

"That was great, sitting in a spiral staircase playing 12-string guitar," Laurence recalled. "There was some cool stuff about [recording in a castle]; we took advantage of the circumstances as much as we could."[14]

The acoustic guitar parts were run through a wah-wah pedal, used subtly to create a slight phase-shifting effect rather than full-fledged wah-wah. Paul overdubbed a sparse bass line—a single note, faded in with a volume pedal at strategic points—and Steve added percussion to punctuate the short spaces between verses. Laurence added an electric guitar with a tremolo effect, and either Linda, Steve or Paul added a glockenspiel. The track was finished off with Paul's lead vocal and backing oohs and aahs by Paul, Denny and Linda.

The next song Paul brought in was a peculiar but musically fascinating medley. The first part, which he had demoed during the summer, was a lively track built over an energetically bouncing bass line, alternatively called 'Emotional Moments' (after the opening lines, "*Emotional moments / You left in a rage*") and 'Cage' (after the refrain, which immediately follows, "*And if you could love me now / I wouldn't be in a cage*"). In the demos, the bass figure, shadowed by a synthesizer, continued in various permutations through the full track, and included a brisk, ear-catching chordal interlude dominated by the synthesizer.

Now Paul added a second verse, which more or less explained the "cage" reference: "*Provisional license** */ I'm under arrest / But if you could get me out / I'd like to take another test.*" The chordal interlude was moved to the end of the song, where it precedes a final verse.

In the medley, Paul has interposed an entirely different song between the opening and closing verses of 'Emotional Moments.' Called 'He Didn't Mean It,' this second song is slower and more melodic. In its lyrics, Paul revives a trick the Beatles had used in 'She Loves You'—presenting a narrative in which the singer is a third party, interceding with the two people in a romance. "*I've been sent to tell you / That the man you were with last night / Is feeling sorry*" for lying to his paramour. A second verse moves along similar lines, replacing *sorry* with *lonely* and *lying* with *crying*. Between the two verses is a chorus, "*He didn't mean it, no / Said he didn't mean it, no,*" the rhythmic emphasis on each line coming on the final "no."

Getting this strange concoction on tape proved a challenge. On the basic track, Paul played bass, Denny and Laurence played electric guitars with light distortion and a chorus effect, Linda layered-in idiosyncratic synthesizer lines, and Steve contributed a solid drum part with punctuating flourishes that help set off the song's distinct sections. The overdubs included Paul's lead

---

* British citizens can apply for a provisional license—the American equivalent is a learner's permit—at the age of 17 but cannot drive unaccompanied until they have passed their driving test.

vocal and rich, tight harmonies by Paul, Denny and Linda on the chorus. An attempt was made to record the horn on Paul's Rolls-Royce for the track as well; eventually that idea was abandoned, the needed sounds provided by Linda's synthesizer instead.

"'Cage,' in particular, was one that a fair amount of time was spent on," Laurence recalled. "I think that was our version of 'Not Guilty'*—a lot of time was spent on it, but it never coalesced into something that would make the album. I think that if the ballad—that mid-tempo *'I've been sent to tell you'* section was the [whole] song, it would have fit very much into that traditional, commercial side of previous versions of Wings. But there was also this riff-driven bit—and of course, the title, 'Cage' was [also] C-A-G-E,† the notes of the riff."[15]

Paul too had doubts about whether the song fit with the rest of the material for the album, but it remained a prospect and was set aside for further work.

Paul next turned the band's attention to 'Getting Closer,' a catchy rocker that he had been sitting on since 1973, although in both his 1973 acoustic guitar demo and his 1974 piano recording, he had the music and lyrics for only the chorus. Now the song had verses, the first of which describes driving through the rain, looking for something good on the radio—basically, an explanation of 'Radio Bit/Reception,' even if the chorus—*"I'm getting closer to your heart"*—turns it into another McCartney love song. It also had a quirky touch, the apparent endearment *"my salamander"* mentioned in several verses.

"Sometimes you just like a word, so you try and find an excuse to put it in," was Paul's explanation. "I remember Linda telling me a story about how when she was a kid, she was a fan of nature, just like I was, and she would look under stones to find a lizard or a newt, which she would call a 'salamander.' I loved the idea that in her world it was 'salamander'—much more exotic. Salamanders have a mythical aspect, born in fire, so that's how the salamander made its way in."[16]

Looking for a driven, texturally crunchy sound, Paul played an insistent bass line on the basic track, with Denny and Laurence playing electric guitars, Linda playing organ and Steve again provided the strong backbeat and rolling punctuation that was becoming one of his thumbprints on Wings recordings. Paul thought the song might be a good vehicle for Denny, so Laine sang the lead vocal.

The recording of 'Getting Closer' that the band made at Lympne Castle crackles with energy, but something about it seemed off to Paul, so it was set aside without overdubs.

While considering what to do about 'Getting Closer,' Paul returned to a recording from earlier in the Lympne sessions that had left him unsatisfied, his salon ballad, 'After the Ball.' The new recording used the same arrangement as the attempt from a few days earlier. But the band now

* 'Not Guilty' was a George Harrison song recorded during the *White Album* sessions but abandoned after dozens of takes. Different mixes of Take 102 were released on *The Beatles Anthology Vol. 3* and *The Beatles (Super Deluxe Edition)* in 2018.

† It is actually more complicated, as Juber acknowledged in a comment on X (formerly Twitter) on June 13, 2022: "The title was from part of the opening riff: C-E-A - C-E-A - C-A-G-E - G-A-C."

played it with greater confidence. Laurence's solo was slightly less showy this time, and Paul played an extended bass line at the point where the song was meant to join the hymn-like 'How Many Million Miles.'

Paul recorded 'How Many Million Miles' alone, accompanying himself on the accordion-like concertina, outdoors on the castle grounds, beginning the take with steady tones that would ease the crossfade from 'After the Ball.'

In a way, 'After the Ball' and 'How Many Million Miles' are two sides of a turn-of-the-century coin, the former evoking a thoroughly secular type of popular entertainment, the latter, with its squeeze-box accompaniment and its simple, gospel-style lyric (*"How Many Million Miles, day-oh / When I get up, up, up in the morning, whoa! Lord I know"*), sounding as if it were made for a revival meeting. Although the song dates back to 1974, Paul's decision to perform it on the concertina was almost certainly inspired by a character in *Pennies from Heaven*, a BBC series Paul had mentioned in interviews, in which a nameless character (he is referred to only as "The Looney," played by Kenneth Colley) turns up repeatedly, playing hymns on an accordion.

Wings made one more formal recording at Lympne Castle, but it was actually a demo for a larger project Paul was pulling together. Its roots were a concert film idea Paul had as early as 1968, called *The Death of Variety*. It was a cross-genre battle of the bands—Paul also likened it to a boxing match—with a classical orchestra and an expanded band of rock and rollers sharing the Royal Albert Hall stage. Pieces of music would be written for the event, and the two ensembles would duke it out in performance. "And like, we were going to leave it open as to who would win," Paul explained. "We'd just give them an equal balance, and let's see who won."[17]

By the mid-1970s, this idea had grown into a kind of musical soap opera, which Paul pitched unsuccessfully to Lew Grade at ATV. "I wanted to have someone like [Peter] Frampton up front as a kind of leader of the band," Paul said. "But also, it was gonna be like, you go backstage, and you see that the trumpet player has a problem with drink. It was like *Crossroads*—the day-to-day life of a rock band. . . . It was gonna be all these sordid stories of all the backstage things, which I think still could be good."[18]

Although he was unable to interest Grade in the project, Paul wrote a pulsing, sharply accented instrumental theme for the show and recorded a piano demo of this 'Rockestra Theme' in 1974. Now he was reviving a fragment of the idea—the huge, star-studded rock band, playing his song. By early September, Paul had arranged for session time at Abbey Road and spoken with a few dozen of his peers about participating in the project. He had also summoned to England the horn section he had used for his world tour. And he enlisted Barry Chattington to document the proceedings on film.

Now what he needed was a full-band demo, so toward the end of their stay at Lympne Castle, Wings filed into the Great Hall, listened to Paul run through the tune at the piano, with breakouts of what he wanted each instrument to play—a pounding bass line and churning rhythm guitar, in the spirit of 'Hi, Hi, Hi,' a lead guitar melody, and a steady, rolling drumbeat.

"We did a demo of 'Rockestra,'" Steve Holly remembers, "where we recorded the piece on eight tracks of a 24-track tape, then double-tracked it, and then triple-tracked it, just to get some idea of what it sounds like." [19]

Although the track was an instrumental, Paul sang a single lyric—*"Why haven't I had any dinner?"*—a third of the way through the recording. Strange as it was, he not only repeated the line, but sang it with Denny and possibly Laurence on both full-band overdubs. The only other vocal is an R&B-style, *"No, no, no, no, no, no, no, no, no, no"* at a stopping point before the long, crashing final chord.

"I thought that [*'why haven't I had any dinner'*] was going to be the horn section," Steve said. "He just sang that randomly. . . . As far as I know, it just came out, and it stuck. And it might just have been a reflection on not having had anything to eat—it might be that simple. I mean, I have no idea what that was or where it came from."[20]

Recording Session

Friday, September 29, 1978.
RAK Mobile Recording Unit, Lympne Castle, Kent.
Mixing: 'We're Open Tonight,' 'Cage & He Didn't Mean It,' 'Cage' (two versions), 'He Didn't Mean It,' 'Rockestra' (Band Demo), 'After the Ball,' 'How Many Million Miles,' 'Love Awake' and various jams.

As Wings' time at the castle wound down, Paul and Chris Thomas reviewed the work the band had done and compiled the master takes onto two reels of 24-track tape. The first, assembled on September 22, included 'Radio Bit,' 'After the Ball' (first version), 'No Details' (further recordings for 'Radio Bit') and 'Love Awake.' The reel compiled on September 23 included 'We're Open Tonight,' 'Cage & He Didn't Mean It' (Lympne Version), 'Getting Closer,' 'After the Ball' (second version), 'How Many Million Miles' and the band demo of 'Rockestra.'

On September 29, Paul oversaw mixes of most of this material, leaving himself some options. 'We're Open Tonight,' for example, was mixed both with its full instrumentation and absent one acoustic guitar. 'Cage' and 'He Didn't Mean It' were mixed both together and as separate tracks, with two versions of 'Cage' mixed separately. The 'Rockestra Theme' demo, 'After the Ball,' 'How Many Million Miles' and 'Love Awake' were all mixed to stereo as well.

Paul also took away a reel of jams, including 'A/C (He's Cracking Up),' 'Freight Train,' Paul and Laurence in an acoustic guitar duet, 'Messing About on the River,' 'Control Room Blow & Chat,' 'Control

Room Lunacy,' 'Fun and Frolic with Paul and Denny,' 'Phil Changed the Mic,' and a 'Rockestra' reggae jam. A recording labeled 'End of Sessions Party (September 29)' was affixed to the reel as well.

While Paul was working with Wings, his music publishing sideline was having an especially successful run. *The Buddy Holly Story* and an associated six-LP set of Holly's recording issued by MCA Records would produce a healthy stream of royalties, as would the release of the film version of *Grease* and its soundtrack album. By the end of 1978, the Holly soundtrack album had qualified for multiplatinum sales in several countries, as had multiple singles from it; *Grease* would eventually sell 30 million copies worldwide.

Much as Paul disliked Robert Stigwood, the *Sgt. Pepper's Lonely Hearts Club Band* film, as well as the *Beatlemania* stage show, were keeping the Beatles' royalties flowing, and they enjoyed further boosts at the end of September when EMI followed Capitol's lead in releasing colored vinyl editions of the *Red* and *Blue* compilations, and in November, when the company issued *The Beatles Collection,* a boxed set with all the Beatles' British LPs plus a *Rarities* disc.

The downside of this success was increased activity by record pirates, as well as producers presenting Beatles stage shows without the proper licensing. "A large amount of our profits is being set aside for pursuit and prosecution of these producers,"[21] ATV's Sam Trust told *Billboard,* estimating that they had defrauded Maclen Music out of $1 million in royalties over the previous decade.

Recording Sessions

Monday, October 2–Wednesday, October 4, 1978.
Abbey Road Studios, Studio Two, London.
Recording and Overdubbing: 'Rockestra Theme,' 'So Glad to See You Here,' 'Day After Rockestra' Jam, and 'Arrow Through Me.'
Mixing: 'Rockestra' (Band Demo), 'Radio Bit,' 'Radio Bit (Mix No. 1, starring Mrs. Margary)' and 'Radio Bit (Mix No. 2, starring Mrs. Margary).'

In preparation for the 'Rockestra' session, scheduled for October 3, Wings spent October 2 in Studio Two, first making a new mix of the 'Rockestra Theme' demo and then tinkering with 'Radio Bit.' The track was significantly longer than a noise experiment intended to open an album ought to be, but Paul liked so many things in it that he decided to split it into multiple parts. With that in mind, he made a stereo mix of the full track and two mixes of Deirdre Margary's reading.

Amid all this, Barry Chattington spent the day setting up his filming position—which Paul wanted to keep secret.

"See, with all the paranoia of even inviting all these people," Paul reasoned, "I just thought, well, if it works, we've got to film it, because it's going to be some big kind of deal. But I thought, the only thing is, you've got that many rock musicians, and they're gonna hate the cameras and lights, and being dabbed down with makeup—we won't be able to do the session, we'll all be too involved [with those details] . . ."

There was also the matter of getting a large assembly of rock stars to sign releases granting Paul permission to use the film. That was a detail too fraught to deal with. Paul figured that if the production was a success, it could be dealt with retrospectively.

For the moment, Paul's solution was to have Chattington film the session the way nature photographers film wildlife—hidden, so as not to disturb the subjects of the filming.

"Paul didn't want lots of camera men bouncing around," said Chattington. "So we actually moved the walls in about a meter on two sides, so the studio just looked exactly the same, but now it's got little holes where the cameras could poke through."[22]

"I said, 'We don't even want to see you all day,'" Paul explained. "'We don't even want anyone to know it's being filmed, 'cause then you get all the real reactions.'"[23]

Nearly everyone Paul invited to the session agreed to participate, and on October 3, the players gradually filed into Studio Two before the session's 10:30 A.M. start time. Augmenting Wings and its horn quartet were Pete Townshend, David Gilmour and Hank Marvin on guitars; Ronnie Lane, John Paul Jones and Bruce Thomas on bass; Gary Brooker and Tony Ashton on keyboards; and John Bonham and Kenney Jones on drums, with additional percussion by Morris Pert, Speedy Acquaye, Tony Carr and Ray Cooper. Paul would play bass on the basic take and keyboard on the overdubs; John Paul Jones would do the same.

It could have been grander still: Keith Moon had agreed to participate, just before his death. Ringo Starr had been invited, but was out of the country, and Elton John begged off because he had a television rehearsal that day. Jeff Beck was interested but wanted veto power on the guitar part he would play, and on the completed track, a nonstarter for Paul. Eric Clapton bowed out with a case of the flu; Jimmy Page had agreed to play but failed to turn up. Paul had also considered a celebrity vocal section with Mick Jagger and Rod Stewart, among others, but that proved impossible to arrange.

To guarantee as much control of the recording and mix as possible, Chris Thomas arranged to have a second 24-track tape machine sync-locked to the 24-track deck in Studio Two, giving himself 48 tracks to work with.

Once everyone was assembled, Paul played the band demo. The piece was not complicated, but Pete Townshend volunteered to lead the guitar section, seeing to it that the sharp cut-off bursts were tightly executed.

"I was worried that what I was giving them to do was too simple," Paul said. "I kept going around to everyone saying, 'Look, you know, all you got to do is play those few notes. Not too simple for you, is it?' They'd say, 'No, keep it simple, mate.' You know, everyone was keen to keep it real kind of easy. So that was the only thing I was worried about. And also, in case it was just going to be a shambles."[24]

As Chris Thomas saw it, the simplicity of the 'Rockestra Theme' largely guaranteed that the session would be a success. "It is very simple," he said of the tune, "and it was important to keep it very simple. Because you've got a doubling-up of drums—you can't have one guy doing one fill and another doing another, it would be like kicking a drum kit down the stairs.[25] It had to be structured, that's the point—it had to be done like an orchestra."[26]

When it seemed to Thomas—during one of the overdubs when Paul and John Paul Jones switched from bass to keyboards—that complications were creeping in, he stepped in.

"John Paul Jones was playing piano," he explained, "as was Gary Brooker, and John Paul Jones was playing lots of extra stuff. I went down there, and I said—and I meant it tongue-in-cheek—'No jazz.' And then later in the evening, once it was all finished, I bumped into him and I said, 'Did you enjoy it?' And he said, 'Yeah, until you said, "No jazz,"' and walked off!"[27]

The simplicity of the tune did not, however, prevent the two newest Wings from being starstruck.

"I was kind of in awe," Laurence recalled, "because I'm looking down the guitar section and it's Pete Townshend, and Dave Gilmour, and Hank Marvin and Denny Laine. And it's like, you know, 'What am I doing here?' Oh, and Jimmy Page's amp. His amplifier showed up, but he didn't."[28]

Steve's reaction was similar. "That session was just amazing because of the cast of characters," he said. "I just thought, 'What in God's name am I gonna do?' Drummer-wise, it was originally intended to be John Bonham, Keith Moon and myself, but of course, we lost Keith. I'd never met John Bonham, and that was terrifying, really. I knew they were gonna come in with monster kits, so I stripped mine down to about four or five drums, sat in the middle and hoped for the best."

Curiously, the vocal that Holley thought was just a placeholder for the horn parts was retained for the finished version, the expanded band dutifully intoning "*Why didn't I have any dinner?*"

"That's what it says, yeah," Paul responded when queried about the odd lyric. "You should be able to hear it, but you can't—they get drowned, I think. It was just gonna be like . . . all those jazz records, where everyone in the band stands up, and they all go, '*Pennsylvania, oh, oh, oh!*' Everybody was supposed to jump and shout."[29]

When Paul and Thomas were satisfied that 'Rockestra Theme' was in the can, Paul enlisted the mammoth band for another song, 'So Glad to See You Here,' walking the players through it at the piano before going for a take. Again, simplicity was the byword: the track was a churning rocker, the verses and choruses each built around only a couple of chords plus a short between-verses chordal transition. Before the session ended at 6:30 P.M., Paul dubbed on his lead vocal.

"The session was bordering on chaotic, but a lot of fun," Hank Marvin concluded. "I wasn't aware that the session was being filmed, just as well I behaved myself!"[30]

With the recording in the can, Paul turned his attention to the film, which he wanted to make into a documentary about recording the track. But his candid-camera approach torpedoed the plan in several ways. One cropped up the next day, when he proposed shooting control room scenes as if they were taking place during the session. Chris Thomas wasn't having it.

"I refused to turn up," he said. "I thought, I can't go in there and *act*. So I didn't turn up when they filmed the control room scenes. I'm on in bits downstairs, in the studio, wandering around and talking to the musicians, but the control room footage was filmed after the event, and I thought, what's the point of doing a documentary if it's bogus?"[31]

But that wasn't the main problem.

"Nobody was really aware of the filming," Laurence noted. "The cameras were not visible—that was the idea. And of course, what it did was it kind of screwed up the potential of actually making anything of it, because nobody signed releases saying that they were okay with being filmed. It was a little presumptuous to imagine that you could do that."

After the doomed attempt to film control room sequences, the band spent Wednesday jamming and poring over the recordings of the Rockestra session, in some cases soloing the individual contributions of their celebrated colleagues.

"All I kept thinking is, '*What is David Gilmour going to do?*'" Steve related. "So the next day we went in, and I said, 'I just want to hear what David played.' And all he did was, you see him look around a bit, and he hits—I think it's a low D—and sustains it for the entire performance. And that's all he does. He just plays one note from beginning to end. One of the greatest guitarists in the world had the sense to just play one note and hold it. That was priceless!"[32]

Later in the week, Wings' horn quartet returned to Abbey Road to add horn parts to 'Arrow Through Me.'

Recording Session

Tuesday, October 10, 1978.

Abbey Road Studios, Studio Three, London.

Mixing: 'Rockestra Theme' (with and without horns).

Overdubbing and mixing: 'Arrow Through Me.'

Mastering: *Wings Greatest.*

Paul oversaw mixes of 'Rockestra Theme' on October 10, keeping two mixes featuring the full ensemble, plus a rough mix without the horns. He also made an addition to 'Arrow Through Me' after a visit from Pete Townshend.

"He popped in to say hello to Paul," Chris Thomas remembered, "and as usual, we played some songs, and we played him 'Arrow Through Me.' And Pete went, 'That is fantastic. Absolutely bloody brilliant!' He loved it. And he said, 'It's a stroke of genius not to have a bass on it.' And the basic track was great; there wasn't anything to do to it. Pete went home, and Paul put a bass on it!"

EMI was clamoring for a Christmas release, and though Wings had enough new material in the can for an LP, Paul was not going to be rushed. The label's marketing department, which had by now heard the increasingly likely reports that Paul would be signing with Columbia for the United States (but remaining on Parlophone for the rest of the world), proposed a hits compilation, which would not only satisfy the company's desire to have a McCartney album out for Christmas but would also bring together several of Wings' non-LP singles.

Paul compiled the set and spent the rest of the session overseeing the mastering with cutting engineer Nick Webb (the US release was mastered by Capitol's Kenneth R. Perry).

SIDE ONE (EMI MATRIX NO. YEX.983)

'Another Day'
'Silly Love Songs'
'Live and Let Die'
'Junior's Farm'
'With a Little Luck'
'Band on the Run'

SIDE TWO (EMI MATRIX NO. YEX.984)

'Uncle Albert/Admiral Halsey'
'Hi, Hi, Hi'
'Let 'Em In'
'My Love'
'Jet'
'Mull of Kintyre'

Paul contacted Aubrey Powell to do the cover art—and Powell once again set aside Hipgnosis's insistence on formulating its own design concepts. Paul's idea this time was extravagant to the point of wastefulness.

Paul and Linda acquired *Semiramis*, an Art Deco sculpture by the Romanian artist Demétre Chiparus, at a Sotheby's auction, and decided to make their new acquisition the focus of their album cover. At first, they had the piece photographed against a black background, but Paul felt that the picture was not sufficiently striking for an album cover (although he used the shot in trade ads). Instead, he proposed that Powell fly *Semiramis* to Mount Everest and photograph the sculpture there. Both in terms of location and subject, he was one-upping Supertramp, who used a photo of a piano on a mountaintop at the Eldora Mountain Resort in Colorado as the cover of their 1977 album *Even in the Quietest Moments.*

Powell discovered that transporting *Semiramis* to Mount Everest was impossible, and proposed shooting the sculpture on the Matterhorn, in the Swiss Alps. That, too, proved unfeasible.

"It just so happened that a helicopter couldn't fly to the top of the Matterhorn," Powell explained, "but there was a mountain next to it called the Rothorn, which a helicopter couldn't land on, but it could go at a 45 degree [angle], which would allow us to open the door and put the statue on top of the mountain. And Paul said, 'Yeah, okay, great. You know what I want—I want the mountains behind, and snow, and stuff like that.'"

On October 14, Powell and a team that included the photographer Angus Forbes flew to the Rothorn for the shoot.

"It was a lot of fun," Powell said, "and very dangerous, and absolutely terrifying. I think it's one of the most frightening shoots I've ever done, because the top of the Rothorn is about the size of four sitting rooms, with a 10,000-foot drop below you, on all sides. And the funniest thing was, if you look at the cover, you can't see the Matterhorn behind, although the Matterhorn was there. I did shoot pictures that showed it, but Paul didn't want them. He wanted it very much to be about the statue.

"When we finished the cover he was really happy. And I'll always remember, it was just before I walked out of the door of his house, he said to me, 'You know, we could've shot this in a studio with an effect drop.' And I said, 'Yeah, I know, but we didn't—we did it for real, and it's all in *Club Sandwich*, and there are photographs everywhere, and it's great PR.' And he said, 'I know, man, it's terrific.' So again, this shows Paul's sense of humor and understanding about how to do things."[33]

The back cover used a shot from the Rothorn showing the nearby mountains in the distance with a black-and-white portrait, by Clive Arrowsmith, of Denny, Linda and Paul at the center. Running down each side are the names and years of the included tracks, each accompanied by the relevant single or album art. The inner sleeve is black, with an alternate of the album cover shot on one side, and *Semiramis* from behind, plus the track listing, production and publishing information on the other. *Semiramis* adorns the disc labels as well.

The album would not be a gatefold, but it would include a poster with Arrowsmith's portrait of Wings on one side, and on the other, a color shot of *Semiramis* atop a woodgrain Bechstein piano, upon which a pair of parrots are perched. On the right side of the piano lid is a framed version of Arrowsmith's group portrait, and a window looks out over an Alpine scene taken from the cover shoot.

Getting the parrot shot also presented difficulties: the first attempt had to be abandoned when the parrots went berserk and defecated all over the photography studio. The photo ended up being shot at Cavendish Avenue, where the birds soiled Paul's piano.

Recording Sessions

Monday, October 16–Thursday, October 19, 1978.

Abbey Road Studios, Studio Two, London.

Recording and Overdubbing: 'Emotional Moments,' 'He Didn't Mean It,' 'Getting Closer' (Second version), 'Baby's Request,' Jams, including 'Looney Version' (Emotional Moments, etc.), 'Radio Intro for Ref,' 'Reggae Denny' and 'Space Jam.'

Mixing: 'Loony Version' (Emotional Moments, etc.), 'Jam,' 'Radio Intro for Ref,' 'Reggae Denny,' 'Cage,' 'Getting Closer,' 'Baby's Request' and 'Harmonizer Ramblings.'

Several tracks were left incomplete or were deemed unsatisfactory when the Lympne Castle sessions ended, and this week Wings revisited them, along with the new tune that Paul wrote during his French holiday. The October 16 session began with that song, 'Baby's Request,' and the band filled a reel with performances, although it is unclear whether those were rehearsals or earnest attempts to capture the song. The recording was intended not for Wings' own use, but as a demo for the Mills Brothers. But the band failed to produce a satisfactory take.

Two more reels were taken up with recordings of the two parts of 'Cage'—'Emotional Moments' and 'He Didn't Mean It,' recorded separately—and 'Getting Closer.'

To Paul's ears, none of the day's recordings were keepers. There was, however, plenty of jamming during the session, and before leaving the studio, Paul and Chris Thomas made stereo mixes of a few of the session's more free-blowing moments, including 'Loony Version' (Emotional Moments, etc.), two simply marked 'Jam,' 'Radio Intro for Ref' (apparently a reference mix of 'Radio Bit'), and 'Reggae Denny.'

They began a new version of 'Baby's Request' the next day. The song has been likened to 'Honey Pie,' a pastiche in a 1930's pop style, but there is a difference. While 'Honey Pie' was a sly parody of the style, 'Baby's Request' is a straightforward adaptation of the style's hallmarks, commissioned by a vocal group that specialized in it. It also suited one side of Paul's compositional sensibility at the moment: except for the overt punk-influenced tracks, a growing number of his recent compositions used a harmonic language more germane to jazz than rock. In 'Baby's Request,' augmented chords, and chords with added sevenths and ninths are plentiful and support a gentle, eminently croonable melody.

The lyrics suited the style as well and offer a consistently focused, carefully crafted narrative. A man's request to a cocktail pianist to play his lady's favorite song—a tune from long ago when they first met, before their children grew up and fled the nest—is couched in the imagery of a 1940's ballad: *"When the moon lays his head on a pillow / And the stars settle down for a rest / Just do me one small favor, I beg you / Please play me my baby's request."*

"It was a cool song," Laurence noted, "but quite radically different from where we started with 'To You' and 'Spin It On.' But, I mean, the Beatles could quite happily put 'Maxwell's Silver Hammer' and 'She's So Heavy' on the same album."[34]

Steve also recalled being struck by how different the song was from everything else the band had recorded in recent months.

"I thought, 'Wow, this is so diverse. How does that work on an album?'" Steve said. "It just seemed like almost a huge swath of random pieces. I couldn't see how the whole thing fit together, to be honest."[35]

To capture the mood and spirit of 'Baby's Request,' Paul brought in his Bill Black standup bass and Steve played the drum part with brushes. Denny played the piano and Laurence used his Gibson ES 335, producing a mellow tone in the chordal accompaniment, as well as a warm, slinky tone in the opening solo flourishes, for which he drew on his experience playing jazz as a student, as well as things he had picked up more recently in lessons with the jazz guitarist Ike Isaacs.

Once a live master take was captured, Wings picked up where they left off on Monday, with the component elements of 'Cage,' for which masters were also completed before they made another pass at 'Getting Closer.'

For the basic track, Paul played electric guitar while Laurence and Denny played acoustics, Linda played organ, and Steve supplied the tight drum patterns he had played on the original version. Laurence and Denny then added electric guitars, Paul recorded his driving bass line, and then a Mellotron on the playout. Denny again sang the lead vocal.

Here Laurence and Paul had different visions of what would make the track sparkle. "I think the most frustrating aspect of it," Laurence related, "was the coda. I must have played a couple of dozen really cool and interesting guitar solos, and Paul's just not into guitar solos. So that evolved, eventually, into more of an orchestrated melody."[36]

With 'Getting Closer' in the can, the band recorded another freewheeling workout, 'Space Jam.' Rough mixes were made of the 'Cage' elements, 'Getting Closer' and several jams.

The band returned to Abbey Road on October 19 for a day of overdubbing. 'Baby's Request' was completed with Paul's lead vocal and harmony vocals by Paul, Linda and Denny on the bridge sections and the last couple of refrains. Paul had left half a verse between two bridges for a horn solo.

"It needed a trombone sound," said Laurence. "Don Lusher, who is the greatest trombone player ever, was [recording] next door, and I said, 'This is the best man you could possibly have for a trombone solo.' Paul said, 'I've got this new synthesizer and I'd rather do it myself.' He preferred the challenge."[37]

Paul's solo was achieved by approximating the sound of a trombone on Minimoog.

Two visitors dropped by while Wings were working on 'Baby's Request' overdubs—first George

Martin, followed shortly by George Harrison. Laurence, who was not needed for the vocal or Minimoog overdubs, was sitting in the control room reading Swami Hariharananda Aranya's *Yoga Philosophy of Patañjali*, a book about meditation, which Laurence practiced. Harrison spotted the book, and as Laurence later wrote, "He recognized my spiritual inclination, and the universe gave us a bonding moment."[38]

The song got a thumbs-up from Harrison as well. "We were playing him some stuff and we happened to be working on 'Baby's Request,'" Paul recalled, "And he was saying, 'Oh, that's nice, I like that.' Because he likes mellow stuff."[39]

Dubbing was done on the 'Emotional Moments' section of 'Cage,' as well. During an extended, prog-influenced chordal passage meant to link the end of 'He Didn't Mean It' to the return of 'Emotional Moments,' Paul wanted a calliope sound.

"We all gathered around a microphone and were handed bottles of Scotch whisky," Laurence explained. "Blowing across the top of a bottle produces a quite pure tone, but the only way to change the pitch was to drink some of the amber contents. Needless to say we were quite tipsy at the end of the session."[40]

They were not too tipsy to make a stereo mix of 'Baby's Request,' which was dispatched to the Mills Brothers, and 'Harmonizer Ramblings,' mostly likely a section of 'Space Jam' in which Paul continued the Eventide Harmonizer experiments he had started during the 'To You' session.

Recording Sessions

Friday, October 20–Saturday, October 27, 1978.

Abbey Road Studios, Studio Two, London.

Mixing: 'Radio,' 'Emotional Moments,' 'He Didn't Mean It,' 'Getting Closer,' 'We're Open Tonight,' 'Spin It On,' 'Again and Again and Again,' 'Old Siam, Sir,' 'To You,' 'Arrow Through Me,' 'After the Ball,' 'Million Miles,' 'Winter Rose,' 'Love Awake,' 'Radio Bit,' 'Rockestra' and 'So Glad to See You Here.'

On October 20, Wings took stock of everything committed to tape since June. Stereo mixes were created from the 24-track masters of each song, and they were compiled onto two reels, each representing one side of the prospective LP, sequenced to reflect Paul's current thinking about the album's running order:

Master Reel 1: 'Radio' / 'Emotional Moments' / 'He Didn't Mean It' / 'Getting Closer' / 'We're Open Tonight' / 'Spin It On' / 'Again and Again and Again' / 'Old Siam, Sir'

Master Reel 2: 'To You' / 'Arrow Through Me' / 'After the Ball' / 'Million Miles' / 'Winter Rose' / 'Love Awake' / 'Radio Bit' / 'Rockestra' / 'So Glad to See You Here'

'Baby's Request,' as a demo for another group, was not regarded as part of the project, and Laurence's 'Maisie' appears to have dropped out of sight. After listening to these mixes for a few days, Paul returned to the studio on October 25 to make new rough mixes of 'Rockestra Theme' and 'So Glad to See You Here.' He also spent time at Abbey Road on October 27, and though it is unclear what work was done to further the completion of the album, a stereo tape was logged, its contents listed as 'Control Room Ramblings' and 'Paul Echo Guitar.'

Paul now ran into the problem he faced during the final stages of mixing *Band on the Run*. He needed more time at Abbey Road, but other artists—principally, Cliff Richard—had booked the studio, and Wings had to clear out. Paul mooted various remedies, including booking Studio Two for a year and canceling when he didn't need it, but that would have been impractical, and EMI is unlikely to have agreed to it.

What Paul needed at this stage of the project—mixing, mostly—was Studio Two's control room, a room he knew intimately both in terms of acoustics and layout. There was an obvious solution a decade in his past: the Beatles had built a studio in the basement of Apple; why not build, if not a complete studio, at least a replica of the Abbey Road Studio Two control room in the basement of MPL?

He approached Steven Thomas with the plan, but although Thomas had already transformed the basement of the Soho Square building into a rehearsal space and turned a Scottish barn into the Spirit of Ranachan Studio, this replication job did not appeal to him.

"It's not the sort of thing we do, to be quite honest, or have any experience in," he told Paul. "Why don't you get a film crew in, because they do that every day?"[41]

Paul next approached Alan Brown, who had designed the Studio Two control room in its present form and asked if creating a replica was possible. Brown told Paul that it was, and that it would not be that expensive once you contrast owning a functional replica of the control room against hiring Studio Two for extended periods at EMI's hourly rate.

With Brown advising on the technical side, Paul took Thomas's advice and hired a film crew to make the reproduction exact, his only proviso being that they use real wood and other materials, rather than the inexpensive facsimiles they might use for a film set. But the reproduction was to be exact, down to the cigarette burns on the engineering console. One of Linda's photographs, showing the view of the studio as the producers and engineers would see it, would be blown up to the size of the control room window.

There were limitations. Studio Two's control room could be replicated, but certain crucial effects—the echo chamber beneath Abbey Road Studios, for example—could not be. So a way was found to get actual Abbey Road echo: a high-resolution phone line would connect the Replica Studio to Abbey Road, and tracks requiring reverb would be sent there and back.

Building what McCartney would call Replica Studio would take until early December, so Wings were given some time off while Paul switched focus to another project—the final sound mix for the *Wings Over the World* documentary.

Between October 30 and November 14, Paul and Chris Thomas mixed 17 songs at AIR Studios: 'The Long and Winding Road,' 'You Gave Me the Answer,' 'Live and Let Die,' and 'Letting Go,' on October 30; 'Yesterday,' 'Venus and Mars,' 'Rock Show,' 'Jet,' 'Maybe I'm Amazed,' and 'Magneto and Titanium Man,' on November 1; 'Go Now,' 'Let 'Em In,' 'Silly Love Songs,' 'Beware My Love,' and 'Band on the Run,' on November 6; and 'Hi, Hi, Hi' and 'Soily' on November 9. A second mix of 'Venus and Mars' was also done on November 9, and 'Letting Go' and 'Go Now' were remixed on November 14.

Denny Laine and Jo Jo LaPatrie, his companion since 1972 and the mother of his two youngest children, used the pause to fly to Boston, where they were married on November 5.

"We've been together on and off for seven years," Denny told the *Daily Mirror*, "and decided to get married a few weeks ago. It was a smashing wedding. We got hitched on a boat in the harbor in Boston—Jo Jo's hometown—and our kids were our attendants. They had a great time."[42]

Five days later, Brian Brolly stepped down as managing director of MPL, a position he had held for five years, to head up Andrew Lloyd Webber's Really Useful Group. Paul left the business of finding his replacement in the hands of the Eastmans.

Recording Sessions

Monday, November 13–Monday, December 4, 1978.
Abbey Road Studios, Studio Two, London.
Recording: 'Space Tune.'
Mixing: 'Emotional Moments,' 'He Didn't Mean It,' 'Getting Closer,' 'Again and Again and Again,' 'Love Awake' and various jams.

Time opened up at Abbey Road for mixing sessions on four Mondays in November and early December, as well as Friday, December 1. Mostly, Paul used this time to mix some of Wings' copious jams. The November 13 session yielded stereo mixes labeled 'Jam (Parts Good)' and 'Jam (Continued).' The following Monday, Paul mixed 'Jam' and 'Jam (Using Radio Transmitter on Guitar),' each taking a full reel. November 27 was spent mixing 'Jam (Whole Reel).'

On December 1, Wing recorded something new, although it may well have been another jam, called 'Space Tune.' It is unknown how (or whether) this is related to the earlier 'Space Jam,' but the same session also yielded fresh mixes of 'Emotional Moments,' 'He Didn't Mean It,' 'Getting Closer,' and 'Space Jam.'

While Paul was mixing, Linda became friendly with a band making its third album in Studio Three, Eddie and the Hot Rods, and sang backing vocals on one of their tracks, 'Power and the Glory.' "Wings were recording in the next studio and Linda McCartney seemed to spend more time with us than she did with them,"[43] joked Barrie Masters, the band's singer, to the *Daily Mirror* several weeks later.

Paul made new mixes of 'Space Jam,' 'Again and Again and Again,' and 'Love Awake' on December 4.

For McCartney-phobes in the press, the release of *Wings Greatest* on December 1 was an early Christmas gift. Monty Smith took the opportunity to note, in *NME*, that 'Mull of Kintyre' "is only tolerable if the listener is half hammered and thus susceptible to its dirge-like qualities," and that the album as a whole is a "clump of those irritating songs with which Ringo used to interrupt proper Beatles albums." For good measure, he added that "a horrible poster comes inside the horrible sleeve."[44] Barry Lazell, in *Sounds*, was only slightly more civil: "Better than most Wings albums," he wrote. "Fewer of those annoying shallow jingles on it."[45]

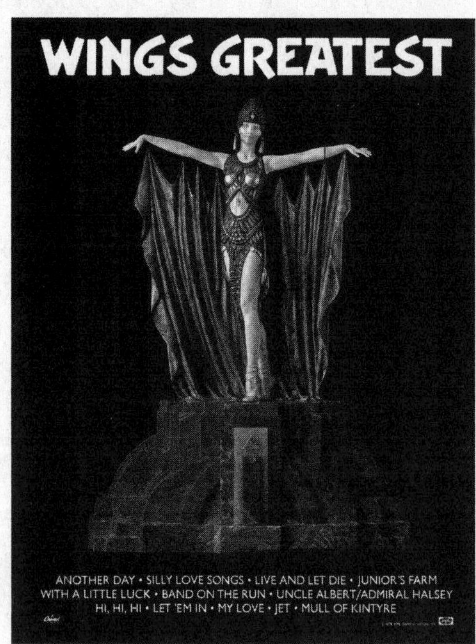

WINGS GREATEST
ANOTHER DAY • SILLY LOVE SONGS • LIVE AND LET DIE • JUNIOR'S FARM
WITH A LITTLE LUCK • BAND ON THE RUN • UNCLE ALBERT/ADMIRAL HALSEY
HI, HI, HI • LET 'EM IN • MY LOVE • JET • MULL OF KINTYRE

Wings, *Wings Greatest* album trade ad

One publication that offered an informed perspective—positive but not without criticism—was *Beatlefan*, a new fanzine that reviewed the album in its first issue.

"Well, finally Capitol (which is not sure it will have McCartney and Wings on its label much longer) has gotten around to releasing a McCartney greatest hits package," wrote William P. King, the magazine's publisher (and also a pop music writer for the *Atlanta Constitution*). Though he considered the disc a "must," he was disappointed at the number of non-LP singles that were not included. "What we need," he continued, "is for McCartney to revive his *Cold Cuts* idea so we can have some of those singles which weren't smash hits and haven't been on an album, and all those marvelous B sides, such as 'Country Dreamer' and 'I Lie Around.'"

Commercially, Paul's first solo hits compilation fared well in Britain but became his worst-performing long-player in America since *Wild Life*. The album entered the British Top 100 at No. 50 on December 6, and reached No. 5, its highest position, on February 5, lingering on the chart for a total of 32 weeks. In the United States, it entered the *Billboard* Top 200 on December 16 at No. 85, and climbed only as high as No. 29 on January 20. It spent only 18 weeks on the chart.

Recording Sessions

Wednesday, December 6–Monday, December 18, 1978.
Replica Studio, MPL, 1 Soho Square—Basement, London.
Recording: 'So Glad to See You Here' (coda).
Mixing: 'So Glad to See You Here,' 'Winter Rose' and 'Jam.'

Replica Studio was ready the first week in December, and Wings spent some time becoming familiar with it and working out how it could be used for recording as well as mixing. There were possibilities: direct-injection recording, where instruments were plugged into the console, was one. And the rehearsal space in the basement, while not a proper recording room, would be suitable for overdubbing, with Steve's drums set up in the kitchen and screens isolating the band's amplifiers.

The band's first task in the studio—apart from entertaining visiting members of the Swedish pop group Abba—was to add a 50-second coda to 'So Glad to See You Here' on December 11.

By then, Paul was thinking of calling the album *We're Open Tonight*, given that song's centrality as the "destination" song in the "going-to-a-gig" concept. And following that plan, 'So Glad to See You Here' would close the album. So in the added coda to 'So Glad to See You Here,' Paul sang the lyrics and melody of 'We're Open Tonight,' a reprise meant to create the impression of thematic unity.

Wings spent December 14 making stereo mixes of another untitled jam. 'So Glad to See You Here' was mixed, with the new coda edited on, on December 18. The opening of 'Winter Rose' was also given an overdub this week, a brief Mellotron addition, using a pitch-shifted loop of Linda's voice. The track was mixed on December 18 as well.

And with that, it was time for a holiday break. Paul and family flew to New York for their annual Christmas visit with the Eastmans and discussions about Paul's impending new deal with Columbia Records, probably the industry's most poorly kept secret. *Billboard* reported in early December that it was a done deal, but the Eastmans continued to insist that Paul was still in negotiation and had not signed with any label.

The annual polls carried in the British music press carried little weight in contract negotiations—and the Eastmans were negotiating for a US rather than a UK deal—but this year's batch did not paint a flattering picture of Paul's place in the pop firmament or his relevance to young listeners.

For the first time since the start of his solo career, Paul did not make the Top 10 in any category in the *NME*, *Sounds* or *Record Mirror* readers' polls, and *Melody Maker*'s readers ranked him in only one category, as No. 7 among bassists. In *Melody Maker*'s list of top-selling discs, *London Town* came in at No. 33 on the album chart (*Saturday Night Fever* was No. 1), 'Mull of Kintyre' was listed at No. 36 among singles, and Wings were No. 15 among the Top 50 singles artists.

Brightening the publicity picture was never heavy lifting for Paul, though. Back in London at the end of the year, the McCartneys made the New Year's Eve papers with a donation of 1,000 teddy bears—£5,000 ($10,150) worth—to be distributed to needy children throughout Britain, with 100 of them earmarked for the Royal Hospital for Sick Children in Glasgow.[46] The article noted that Paul and Linda's "favorite home is in Scotland." But just a year after the release of 'Mull of Kintyre,' that was no longer the case.

24

EGGS OVER EASY

During Wings' sessions in Scotland, Lympne Castle and Abbey Road Studios, the press reported virtually no information about what the band was up to, apart from taking on two new players whose names the public barely knew. When the press finally checked in on Wings, Denny agreed to field questions, telling the *Daily Mirror* that he expected the new album to be out in February—but also throwing down the gauntlet about touring.

"I'm desperate to be out on tour," he said. "I get very twitchy sitting around in a studio. When I was with the Moody Blues, recording was something you did between tours. I am sure that Paul enjoys touring, but I am also sure that when he was in the Beatles he got used to being off the road for long periods. I am quite sure we will be touring soon, though—otherwise, I honestly feel that I wouldn't be able to stay in Wings."[1]

On Friday, January 12, Wings met in MPL's boardroom to map out their immediate future. It was an unlikely scene, for a rock band. "We all sat around one of those big boardroom tables with notepads and glasses of water," Laurence recalls, "and we talked about what the next step was going to be."[2] The next step, Paul told them, was to release a single.

"What did the Beatles do when they needed a single?" someone asked.

"We'd write one over the weekend," Paul replied.

Steve remembered Paul proposing a full-band contest.

"I remember him saying, 'I challenge you all to go home and write your best effort, and we'll review them all on Monday. And whoever's written the best song is the one we record.' I honestly don't remember what I did, but I know I put something together and Denny put something together, and Laurence, and we all came in and one by one played what we had. And then I remember Paul saying, 'Well, I wrote this,' and that was 'Daytime Nighttime Suffering.' And we all collectively went, 'Ahh, okay. Well, let's record that one then!'"[3]

Linda offered a closer look at Paul's side of the competition. "He's actually incredible," she enthused to Ray Connolly four months later. "On Friday he decided he needed a new single, on Saturday and Sunday he messed around the house writing it, on Monday he explained to the group how it should go, on Tuesday we recorded it. He just never stops. Ideas seem to come to him all the time."[4]

Recording Sessions

Monday–Tuesday, January 15–16, 1979.
Replica Studio, MPL, 1 Soho Square—Basement, London.
Recording, Overdubbing and Mixing: 'Daytime Nighttime Suffering.'

'Daytime Nighttime Suffering' was a shift back from the jazz voicings of 'Baby's Request' to the pop music lingua franca of (mostly) major and minor chords, but deployed with a sophistication that allowed for fluid movement between vibrancy and melancholy. The music thoroughly suited the lyric, which asks, through a handful of metaphors, why all women get in return for their love, support and effort is 'Daytime Nighttime Suffering.'

"What does it pay to play the leading lady," the verse lyric asks, *"When like the damsel in distress / Daytime Nighttime Suffering / Is all she gets."* The bridge, by contrast, draws on the classical association between water and femininity in a paean to women's power: *"Come on river, flow through me / Don't be stopped by insanity"* and *"You are the river, I am the stream / Flow mighty river through me."* Paul characterized the song as being about "the plight of women."[5] Laurence likened it, in that regard, to 'Another Day.'[6]

The song's musical appeal is its inventive and continuously changing arrangement, which moves smoothly between unaccompanied vocal harmonies and bright ensemble pop powered by Paul's bass, Laurence's compressed, crunchy chordal punctuation and subtle arpeggiation, and Steve's sharp, precise beat.

The band spent Monday working on the backing track. "Paul was playing an RMI [electric] piano," Laurence recalled, adding, "I remember Paul having a very specific guitar part that he wanted me to play, so I did that." Denny played electric guitar on the basic track, and Steve drummed, his part often providing the cues for shifts in the arrangement.

Recording the basic track "couldn't have taken very long," Laurence recalled. "It typically didn't take that long to get a track down once you had all the parts." Actually, Wings filled six reels of tape before settling on a master, but the session was apparently relaxed: on three of those reels, formal takes end in extended jams.

Much of the song's magic was added on Tuesday, when Paul recorded an autoharp part as well as his lead vocal, plus triple-tracked harmonies with Denny and Linda, in one of Paul's most varied vocal arrangements since the *Ram* sessions. The song's introduction is a modified, slow-tempo version of the opening verse. The first line is harmonized and sung a cappella; Paul's bass joins to underpin the second and third lines. Throughout the song, the third line is usually the refrain (the song title). But in the intro, that refrain is replaced with a preview of the water imagery (*"Mighty river give her all she gets"*). Paul sings the "mighty river" lyric solo as the backing vocals peel off into a wordless counterpoint.

Four brisk drumbeats kick the song into a faster tempo and introduce the full instrumental backing, with Paul singing the verse on his own until the refrain, where he is joined by the triple-tracked Paul-Denny-Linda trio. The second and third verses follow the same layout, with the bridge between them sung by Paul, his double-tracked voice occasionally splitting into a tight harmony. A new element is introduced after the third verse—a four-line call-and-response interlude in which Paul's first three solo lines are repeated by the harmony trio, the final line sung together.

A repetition of the bridge follows, heading into another verse—except that this time, all but the refrain are sung in a triple-tracked wordless counterpoint, with Linda's soprano and Denny's tenor taking the melody, while Denny and Paul sing multiple strands of a bass line, starting their notes with hard consonants to suggest the plucking of bass strings.

All this was done in the tightest of spaces. "It was like a home studio—it was really basic," Laurence said of Replica. "There was a kind of kitchenette and then the lobby area before you got to where the control room was."[7]

That setup yielded an accident that Paul decided to leave in the track. "At one point," Steve recalled, "the elevator opened, and Linda came out with baby James in her arms, and he actually went, 'aaaah.' And that's on the recording—you can hear it if you listen carefully, it's right over one of the stops where there's a little drum break,"[8] about two minutes in.

Once the overdubbing was complete, Paul made a rough stereo mix to take home and consider.

Recording Sessions

Monday, January 22–Wednesday, January 24, 1979.

Replica Studio, MPL, 1 Soho Square—Basement, London.

Overdubbing: 'Goodnight Tonight.'

Mixing: 'Daytime Nighttime Suffering.'

'Daytime Nighttime Suffering' was the clear winner of the Wings single-writing competition, but after listening to it at home for a few days, Paul had second thoughts. The band was summoned to Replica Studio once again, and when they settled into the control room, Paul played the recording of the disco-tinged 'Goodnight Tonight' he had made on his own nearly a year earlier. The track was not new to the band: McCartney had played it for them in Scotland over the summer, but it was never a contender for the album, so it went back on the shelf.

"It's one of those that I played all the instruments, originally," he said. "I had it hanging around for a little while and I always liked the beat of it, the backing track. . . . Everyone liked it, so we put a couple of overdubs and things on it and just freshened it up."[9]

Those overdubs, recorded on January 22, included electric guitar parts by Denny and Laurence, and percussion from Steve. "That's not my drum track," Steve pointed out, "it's Paul. But I played some Moroccan drums, and bits and pieces."[10] Paul made some vocal additions, riffing on the phrase "I gotta go home," sung through a vocoder to give his voice a robotic quality. Paul asked Laurence to add some flamenco-style guitar flourishes at the start of the song and at nearly five minutes in.

"I did a warm-up pass," Laurence later wrote, "and asked, 'Something like that?' Apparently it was exactly 'like that,' and the first-take flourish is what's on the record."[11]

Rough mixes of both 'Goodnight Tonight' and 'Daytime Nighttime Suffering' were made on January 23, and after listening to them overnight, Paul decided he could sing 'Goodnight Tonight' better, so on January 24, he rerecorded the lead vocal.

Now Paul began tussling, internally, with whether *either* of the new songs should be the single. "We sat around for years—well, it seemed like years—discussing it," he told Paul Gambaccini a few months later. "You know, the normal soul-searching you go through. And we decided, 'No, it isn't right, we won't put it out.' So we scrapped the whole thing. And about a week later, I played the record again. I thought, 'That's crazy, we've made it—it's stupid, why not put it out? Just because people are going to pan it?' I liked it, and other people had taken it home and played it to people at parties. So we decided to do it."[12]

Although Paul's move from Capitol Records to Columbia in the United States had cycled through the industry rumor mill for months, it was only in recent weeks that the final details had been settled and the contracts signed. The deal would be announced at a CBS Records Sales and Promotion meeting in Dallas on February 1. Around the same time, EMI would announce that Paul's recordings would remain on the Parlophone label for the rest of the world.

For record-industry watchers, the Columbia deal was astonishing. In what was described as the most lucrative recording deal in history,[13] Paul would receive $20 million (£10 million) over the next three years, with an annual $2 million (£1 million) advance plus a royalty of 22 percent—roughly $1.55 (£0.78) per album, compared with $1.20 (£0.60) under his 1975 EMI contract. The industry standard royalty at the time was 3 percent, or about $0.275 (£0.14) per album.[14]

The deal also demonstrated the upside of Paul's having licensed his albums to Capitol, retaining ownership of the masters. Capitol had the right to distribute McCartney's albums for five years, but once that period ended, the albums would be released by Columbia for distribution in the United States and Canada at the new royalty rate. His most recent LP, *London Town*, would therefore make its way to Columbia in 1983. The arrangement with Columbia would be the same: Paul's masters would continue to be owned by MPL, and leased to Columbia.

But the most important blandishment was Columbia's transfer to MPL ownership of the Frank Music Corporation—the publishing company started by the composer Frank Loesser in 1950. Besides boasting Loesser's Broadway musicals (including *Guys and Dolls*, *How to Succeed in Business Without Really Trying* and *The Most Happy Fella*) and songs (including 'Baby, It's Cold Outside,' 'Heart and Soul' and 'Let's Get Lost'), Frank Music controlled the rights to music by other composers as well, most notably Richard Adler and Jerry Ross (*Damn Yankees*) and Meredith Willson (*The Music Man*—the source of one of Paul's star turns from the early Beatle days, 'Till There Was You').

At the time, both MPL and CBS downplayed any connection between Paul's new recording contract and MPL's acquisition from CBS of Frank Music. But Walter Yetnikoff, the president and CEO of CBS Records at the time, had acknowledged that it was this element that gave CBS an edge over its nearest rival in the negotiations.

"I knew about [Paul's] interest in publishing," Yetnikoff said. "I figured it was going to be either us or Warner Bros. I just remained persistent, and I hoped the publishing would close the deal. People on the CBS board criticized the deal, saying it was too much—to which I reminded them that there were not a lot of Beatles around to be signed. They finally came around. It was a unique arrangement—an unusual deal [because of our] adding Frank Music."[15]

To retain the distribution rights for Paul's music worldwide and in the United Kingdom, EMI agreed to increase the royalties McCartney received on the Beatles' back catalog. Lennon, Harrison and Starr were kept in the dark about McCartney's royalty uplift.

Recording Sessions

Friday, January 26–Tuesday, February 13, 1979.

Replica Studio, MPL, 1 Soho Square—Basement, London.

Recording: 'Violin Concerto,' 'Intro to Violin Concerto,' 'Spin It On Busker' and 'Three Cool Cats.'

Mixing: 'Goodnight Tonight,' 'Daytime Nighttime Suffering,' 'Violin Concerto,' 'Intro to Violin Concerto' and 'Spin It On.'

Paul McCartney And Wings

Linda McCartney · Denny Laine · Paul McCartney

NOW AVAILABLE AT COLUMBIA RECORDS

Now available at Columbia Records trade ad

By now EMI and Columbia were pleading with Paul to let them hear his work in progress, so on January 26, the band and Chris Thomas spent the day compiling the best mixes so far—none considered final—of the new tracks, in a provisional running order:

SIDE ONE

'Reception'
'Getting Closer'
'We're Open Tonight'
'Spin It On'
'Again and Again and Again'
'Old Siam, Sir'

SIDE TWO

'To You'
' Arrow Through Me'
'After the Ball—How Many Million Miles'
'Winter Rose—Love Awake'
'The Broadcast'
'Rockestra Theme'
'So Glad to See You Here'

Acetate discs were made for each band member and both record labels. The album also had a new title—*Back to the Egg*, a name Paul alternately claimed credit for or attributed to Linda.

But Paul found himself in a situation similar to what he experienced during the *Ram* sessions at the end of 1970 and the start of 1971. He had recorded plenty of material, more than enough to fill an album, but he was having trouble drawing the double bar and letting go. It was as if the enormity of the Columbia deal triggered and magnified his insecurities.

He now drifted into an unhealthy routine of mixing songs again and again, without settling on a final version. For the moment, the single was a welcome distraction. He acknowledged that the full 7'16" recording of 'Goodnight Tonight' needed to be trimmed, and on January 29, he made a 4'19" edit. He spent the rest of the session mixing both the long and short versions, plus 'Daytime Nighttime Suffering,' but left the studio unsatisfied with any of the mixes. Final mixes of both songs eluded him on January 30 and February 1, as well.

The other Wings players were present for these mixing sessions but generally deferred to Paul. "Were we hands-on [in the mixing]? Not really," Steve admitted. "But if you had an opinion about something, it would definitely be entertained."[16]

Chris Thomas, however, was becoming irritated with the constant mixing and remixing. "*Back to the Egg* did become very long and it did become laborious," Thomas said. "It was very difficult because, to be frank about Paul—I mean, Paul is very determined about what he wants, and he's right. He is a genius. It's extraordinary: he doesn't work very quickly but he works at this high level all the time. So, I would [make suggestions] sometimes and normally it was pretty collaborative, but towards the end it wasn't. And it got to the point where he started wanting to introduce new songs—different things that he'd done on his own—and try to bring them into the record, which was pretty dispiriting, to be quite honest, because it meant that he had sort of lost faith, a little bit, in what we were doing."[17]

Paul gave himself a few days' space before returning to Replica, and when he did, on February 5, he left the single alone and turned his attention to another experimental piece along the lines of 'Radio Bit.' It was listed on the tape box as 'Violin Concerto' and included a number of new radio recordings, its most notable elements drawn from a performance by mezzo-soprano Carole Rosen and pianist Paul Hamburger of four songs by the Finnish composer Jan Sibelius, broadcast on BBC Radio 3 on January 31. At the end of the session, he made stereo mixes of 'Intro to Violin Concerto' and 'Violin Concerto.' For good measure, he mixed 'Goodnight Tonight' again, without success.

Fruitless attempts to mix 'Goodnight Tonight' took up the February 8 and 9 sessions, before Paul set the song aside to mix 'To You' on February 12, also with no joy. The logjam was finally broken on February 13: Paul completed the master mix of 'Spin It On,' and was so elated that he brought his guitar and a microphone out into Soho Square for a short busking session, playing 'Spin It On Busker' and 'Three Cool Cats,' both preserved on a 24-track reel. For Chris Thomas, monitoring the performance in Replica Studio, the sound of one couple passing by as Paul busked on a freezing cold London street provided some light relief.

"You could hear them approaching, and this guy said, 'That's Paul McCartney.' And his girlfriend goes, 'What?' And he says, 'It's Paul McCartney.' 'Don't be stupid.' He said, 'Seriously, it's Paul McCartney.' She says, 'If you're gonna carry on like this, I'm leaving you.' And we were just absolutely howling, it was fantastic."[18]

Meanwhile, Paul continued the process of expanding the East Sussex property that was now the family's main abode. In early January, the neighboring property, Lower Gate Farm, came up for sale, and Paul immediately snapped it up, completing the purchase on February 14, just six weeks after the property was listed for sale. Lower Gate included a farmhouse, a gatehouse, and 60 acres of land, bringing Paul's total East Sussex acreage to 160. He and Linda renamed the property Blossom Wood Farm.

Recording Sessions

Friday, February 16–Friday, March 2, 1979.

Replica Studio, MPL, 1 Soho Square—Basement, London.

Mixing: 'Static Changes' and 'Radio Bit' ('Reception'), 'Radio Bit—Mr. Margary' ('The Broadcast'), 'Rockestra Theme,' 'Baby's Request,' 'After the Ball—How Many Million Miles,' 'Again and Again and Again,' 'Old Siam, Sir,' 'Goodnight Tonight,' 'Daytime Nighttime Suffering' and 'A Minor Chord.'

A couple of Paul's radio experiments, 'Static Changes' and 'Radio Bit' were mixed to stereo on February 16. 'Radio Bit' now incorporated a snippet of Carole Rosen's Sibelius performance from the 'Violin Concerto' recording. With this new addition, Paul completed a master mix of 'Reception.'

Paul hoped to polish off the mix of the 'Rockestra Theme' on Monday, but after filling a reel with attempts, he gave up and mixed an unspecified jam from the band's now sizable archive. After two more reels of mixes on Tuesday, the 'Rockestra Theme' master mix was added to the slowly growing compilation reel of completed tracks. On Monday, February 19, Paul returned to the radio recordings, this time extracting Harold Margary's Galsworthy and Hay readings, which would be renamed 'The Broadcast.'

By now, Paul had received a puzzling response from the Mills Brothers to his 'Baby's Request' demo. The group's manager informed Paul that the group would be happy to record the song for a $1,000 (£500) fee. That was not quite the arrangement he envisioned, so Paul decided to use the track on *Back to the Egg* instead. He made a new stereo mix on February 26, filling less than a reel with attempts before deciding on the master. And on February 27, he added a fresh stereo master of the conjoined 'After the Ball—How Many Million Miles' to his compilation reel.

The streak continued with 'Again and Again and Again,' mixed on March 1, and on March 2, the master mixes of 'Old Siam, Sir,' 'Goodnight Tonight' (both the long version and the edit) and 'Daytime Nighttime Suffering' were completed, along with an unknown song listed as 'A Minor Chord.'

'Goodnight Tonight' and 'Daytime Nighttime Suffering' now had a prospective release date—March 23—so for good measure, Paul sent five mixes to be mastered by EMI, three of which would be released. These were 'Goodnight Tonight' (Master, A side, EMI Matrix No. 7YCE.21803); 'Daytime Nighttime Suffering' (Master, B side, EMI Matrix No. 7YCE.21804); and 'Goodnight Tonight' (long version for the 12-inch single, EMI Matrix No. 12YCE.21803). The remaining two mixes were 'Goodnight Tonight' (old edited version, using the January 29 mix) and 'Goodnight Tonight' (instrumental version).

A Paul McCartney disco single was not something anyone in the music business expected, and since record labels prefer the predictable, much as they claim otherwise, executives at both EMI and Columbia were taken aback when 'Goodnight Tonight' landed on their desks. But whatever insecurity Paul was feeling at the start of the year was tamped down once he settled on a course of action.

"The record company said, 'It won't be a good single, [you] probably shouldn't release it,'" Paul told an interviewer. "So we did."[19]

At the end of the March 2 session, Paul made a new compilation reel with a combination of finished and rough mixes and had a cassette dubbed for review at home.

Whatever calm Paul expected to enjoy while listening to his rough assembly of *Back to the Egg* over the weekend was shattered when he learned about a *People on Sunday* interview with his stepmother, Angie, entitled "My Bust-Up with Paul McCartney." The root of their dispute was Angie's decision in September 1977 to start a talent agency with a partner, Michael John Mingard, called Cloth Cap Management, to sign and promote young Merseyside acts.

Paul made it clear that he was not happy about her career choice, which he considered to be trading on his name. Not so, Angie insisted, arguing that the McCartney name was actually a hindrance: "We found that we invariably had to play Twenty Questions whenever we phoned anyone," she insisted in the *People on Sunday* piece. "The person at the other end, whether we were phoning the States, Australia, or Timbuktoo, would say, 'Are you the McCartney who's related to Paul?' Then they'd go on to ask how Paul and Linda were getting on and how was the baby."[20]

Paul and Angie had sparred in the press on and off through 1977, and things appeared to have calmed down. It is not clear what occasioned Angie's interview with *People on Sunday*, but she detailed their last conversation, at the end of 1977, as a screaming row in which she told him that she had given up 12 years of her life to take care of his father, and that as a widow she had to make a living, which he had no right to begrudge her.

"But there we are," she concluded, "what's done is done. I don't suppose I'll be seeing Paul again, or his wife, Linda. That's a pity because I like Linda a great deal and she works so very hard for Paul. But I'm determined to get somewhere in this life—with or without Paul's blessing."

What was perhaps most frustrating for Angie and daughter Ruth, whom Paul had also accused of trading on the McCartney name, was his backing of his second cousin, Kate Robbins. Bett and Mike Robbins's daughter, Kate, a talented pianist and vocalist, had moved to London several months earlier and had been working with the arranger Del Newman as a backing singer on sessions for artists as diverse as Rosemary Clooney, Howard Keel and José Feliciano. When she decided to go it alone, Paul arranged for Robbins to record 'Tomorrow'—one of his *Annie* copyrights—together with her own 'Crowds of You.' The songs were later issued in Britain as a double A sided single on Anchor Records.

"I came down to London and my second cousin, Paul McCartney, helped me a little bit," Robbins confirmed, "in that he paid for me to have some demo tapes done. And so people kind of heard me, because he had a bit of faith in me."[21]

Paul was disinclined to respond to Angie's accusations through the press, and when he eventually did, he noted that "I've smoothed it all over now, so I don't wanna go digging it all up." But he acknowledged that "sometimes there'd be mistakes"—his way of admitting that he might have handled the dispute poorly. Not that he was accepting the full blame: "Sometimes it would be that she wasn't mentioning the other side of the coin. She'd just say, 'He was mean about that,' and forget to mention the bit where I was generous, which would have balanced it out."[22]

George Harrison was commenting about Paul in the papers as well, during a round of interviews meant to promote the release of his *George Harrison* album. When asked about Paul, he noted that Paul was giving audiences who wanted the Beatles at least a taste of what they craved. "Paul was always the one with a smile, a wave and an autograph. We'd always be sitting in the car waiting for him—'*Come on, Paul!*'—and he'd be signing away. Paul is a workaholic; he likes to be out there. That's not to say that's wrong."[23]

About Paul's music, George declared it "inoffensive," but added, "I've always preferred Paul's good melodies to his screaming rock and roll tunes. The tune that I thought was sensational on the *London Town* album was 'I'm Carrying,' but all the noisy, beaty things I'm not into at all." He said that he and Paul were on friendly terms, but within limits. "We don't have any problems whatsoever as far as being people is concerned, and it's quite nice to see him," he said. "But I don't know about being in a band with him, how that would work out. It's like, we all have our own tunes to do. And my problem was that it would always be very difficult to get in on the act because Paul was very pushy in that respect."[24]

What George wanted to make clear was that he was, at this point, the polar opposite of Paul, uninterested in pleasing or answering to anyone but himself. Although readers would not yet have known it, he couched this distinction in terms that reflected directly on the music Paul had been recording in recent months.

"I don't go out of my way to sell records," he said. "When I've made a record, I'd like the people to know it's there, and then if they like it they can buy it. I'll do what I can do as honest as I can, but I'm not gonna turn into a punk or do disco. I don't *like* disco, so what's the point of my tryin' to do something like that?"[25]

Recording Sessions

Monday, March 5–Friday, March 30, 1979

Replica Studio, MPL, 1 Soho Square—Basement, London.

Recording: 'Champagne Corks Popping.'

Overdubbing: 'Getting Closer.'

Mixing: 'Winter Rose,' 'Arrow Through Me,' 'Getting Closer' and 'So Glad to See You Here.'

Mixing continued on March 5, when the final mix of 'Winter Rose' was accomplished quickly. The master stereo mix of 'Arrow Through Me' was completed on March 9. Paul and Linda celebrated their tenth wedding anniversary at Replica with the rest of Wings on March 12, and recorded the popping of the champagne corks as the party got underway. No mixing was completed that day, although several jams were recorded, and on March 15, three full reels of jams were mixed and logged. The same day, an attempt was made to mix 'Getting Closer,' but no mix was deemed a keeper.

The unsuccessful attempt to mix 'Getting Closer' led Paul to reconsider aspects of the performance—specifically, Denny's lead vocal. On March 19, he replaced it with his own, and then spent two more days (March 20 and 22) attempting to mix it, without success. On March 23 everything fell into place, and 'Getting Closer' was added to the compilation reel. 'So Glad to See You Here' took three days to mix, with failed attempts on March 26 and 27 and success on March 30.

One day in late March, David Bowie paid a visit to Replica, and Paul played him most of the album, as well as a few other tracks, including 'Cage,' which Chris Thomas had persuaded Paul to drop from consideration.

"Bowie came down and we played him the album in random order and not all of it," Thomas recalled. "And then all of a sudden, Paul put this track on, and I'm like, '*Why is he playing this? That's not on the fucking album? What's going on?*' And it was amazing because, I think the first three tracks that we played to Bowie, Bowie went, 'This is fantastic. This is fantastic. This is fantastic.' Then Paul slipped one in, and Bowie went like, 'I don't like that one so much.' Bowie got it 100 percent right. He chose all the ones that we'd done for the album, and rejected all those that Paul slipped in."[26]

Bowie also told Paul that 'Broadcast' was his favorite of the tracks he heard, and that Paul should release it as a single—a suggestion that might seem cynical but for the fact that Bowie's two most recent releases, *Low* and *"Heroes,"* skewed toward experimentalism.

Wings, 'Goodnight Tonight' single trade ad

—

'Goodnight Tonight' and 'Daytime Nighttime Suffering,' Paul's first single in seven months, and his first release to be split between Parlophone and Columbia, was released worldwide on March 23. In a typically canny move, Paul had arranged for some free promotion—not so much for the single itself, but as a way of ensuring that Paul and his accomplishments were front and center in listeners' minds as the new disc was hitting the airwaves. The first of the two Wings concert films, *Wings Over the World*, had its American premiere on CBS-TV on March 16 and its first British screening on BBC Two on April 8.

It was no coincidence that Paul's long-in-the-making, outdated documentary found a home on CBS-TV, the broadcasting arm of the Columbia media conglomerate. While the version of Wings in the documentary was strikingly different than the current band, the show offered context for anyone interested in Paul's (and Wings') next move, as well as providing a promotional vehicle for Paul's back catalog—*coming soon on Columbia Records.*

It might have occurred to Paul, too, that having his audience see him singing his biggest hits, along with some Beatles oldies, might offer a counterweight to the critics' tart takes on his latest effort.

> *I really don't want to slag off yet another Wings offering, but they haven't given me any option. A year or so ago, everyone who was anyone did their token reggae cut. Nowadays it's switched to the token disco track, so that's what Wings have done. . . . The song is a non-existent throwaway while the 'disco effects' have zero robustness or sensuality. Paul may never have claimed to provoke, but even if you only want to entertain, it's got to be more substantial than this.*[27]
>
> *Ian Birch,* Melody Maker

> *Young whippersnappers don't believe me when I tell them that the bloke who wrote this dismal frippery used to be in a rather good band. Can't say I'm surprised.*[28]
>
> *David Hepworth,* Sounds

> *McCartney's gone disco. He and his band Wings have turned their latest record into a slowish smooched disco number, most of which is taken up with Paul repeating the words 'don't say it.'*[29]
>
> *Anne Nightingale,* Daily Express

Disco must now be doomed. Yes, down on the farm, old Paulie had wakened up to the fact that popular music has undergone a transformation since the days of Abbey Road. *Naturally, a one-time innovator must keep up with current trends, at least for the sake of appearances, so in addition to a disco rhythm track (all fussy Latin percussion), there's a touch of dub (multiple moaning) and a Vocoder (hitherto intended as an aid for duff singers). The only thing absent is a bit of a tune. Still, you're bound to admit it's the best thing he's done since his* London Town *album.*[30]

Bob Edmands, NME

Slight reggae tendencies creeping into the bass line on this new song—which, for some reason brings back fond memories of their Band on the Run *LP, which can't be bad. Better, and less blatantly commercial than their recent releases. It does drag on a bit though, and I'm not so sure that I'll be so enamored when I've heard it 87 times on the radio. Still, we shall see.*[31]

Kelly Pike, Record Mirror

The single's chart performance was respectable, but not stunning, and certainly not the kind of commercial return Columbia was expecting from its sizeable investment. In Britain, it entered the Top 100 at No. 43 on April 7, and spent ten weeks on the chart, peaking at No. 5 on May 5. In America, it entered the *Billboard* Hot 100 at No. 38 on March 31. It peaked at No. 5 on May 26, and held the spot for two weeks. It remained on the Hot 100 for 16 weeks.

Both EMI and Columbia wanted Paul to put both sides of the single on *Back to the Egg*, but having been hammered in the press for releasing too many singles from *London Town*, he resisted the suggestion.

"Yes, the companies here and in America, worldwide, would like a single on the album, and it makes more sense merchandising-wise," Paul conceded. "But sometimes, I just have to remember that this isn't a record retail store I'm running; this is supposed to be some kind of art. And if it doesn't fit in, it doesn't fit in. . . . We've got a lot of artistic control, thank goodness."[32]

Recording Sessions

Monday–Friday, April 1–5, 1979.

Abbey Road Studios, Studio Two, London.

Overdubbing: 'Love Awake.'

Mixing: 'Love Awake.'

By now the working relationship between Paul and Chris Thomas was fraying, and Paul's plan for an overdubbing session at Abbey Road on April 1 was the perfect example, for Thomas, of where Paul was going wrong. Three days earlier, Paul had engaged the conductor and arranger Martyn Ford to write a brass accompaniment for 'Love Awake.' The Black Dyke Mills Band—an ensemble that was founded in West Yorkshire in the mid-nineteenth century and had recorded Paul's 'Thingumybob,' an instrumental (credited Lennon-McCartney) for Apple Records in 1968—was enlisted to record this addition, with Ford conducting.

Thomas did his best to persuade Paul that 'Love Awake' was perfect in its gentleness and delicacy, and that the acoustic guitar textures were all the song needed.

"We screwed it into the ground," Thomas said of the track, "and it just got worse. The more we did to it, the worse it got and it just got overblown. Once there was an amazing song on there, which we messed up with the Black Dyke Mills Band—I mean, an amazing, beautiful song. It could have been much more simple. I just found it very frustrating."[33]

Paul had the option, of course, of scuttling the Black Dyke Mills Band overdub if, after hearing it, he agreed with Thomas. But he liked it, and the rest of Wings lined up with Paul, arguing that the brass additions gave some bite to the chord changes and beefed up the texture in the later verses. Laurence, for one, thought the brass "added a bittersweet dimension to the song."[34]

An attempt to mix the newly augmented 'Love Awake' on April 2 came to nothing, but the session was late in the day, after rehearsals for a video shoot for 'Goodnight Tonight' and an interview with Ray Connolly, so it seems likely that Paul's focus and energy were flagging.

The 'Goodnight Tonight' video, directed by Keef, was shot at the Hammersmith Palais on April 3. A few weeks earlier, the band had done a photo shoot for the single's picture sleeve, in which they appeared as a 1930's lounge band, the group's men dressed in tuxedos, with slicked-back hair, and Linda in a purple dress with a fan, her hair and makeup in the style of the time. They recreated that look for the video. Paul sings into an antique radio microphone borrowed from EMI, and other vintage mics are seen as well. The only anachronisms are Paul's, Denny's and Laurence's more recent model guitars.

The master mix of 'Love Awake' was completed on April 4, and on April 5—the final day of mixing—the master for 'To You' was quickly finished. The mixes for *Back to the Egg* were now complete. On Friday, April 6, the album was sequenced as per Paul's original loose concept, and sent to EMI's Nick Webb for mastering:

'Love Awake' overdub session, Abbey Road Studios, April 1, 1979

SIDE ONE (EMI MATRIX NO. YEX.987)

'Reception'
'Getting Closer'
'We're Open Tonight'
'Spin It On'
'Again and Again and Again'
'Old Siam, Sir'
'Arrow Through Me'

SIDE TWO (EMI MATRIX NO. YEX.988)

'Rockestra Theme'
'To You'
'After the Ball'/'Million Miles'
'Winter Rose'/'Love Awake'
'The Broadcast'
'So Glad to See You Here'
'Baby's Request'

Toward the end of the mixing marathon, Aubrey Powell met with Paul to discuss the cover. Paul was back in a sci-fi mood: the plan was to have Wings in a spaceship that looked like a cozy living room, peering through a portal in the floor at Earth, floating among the stars in the black of space. Powell hired John Shaw to shoot the cover in a photography studio above the Belsize Park tube station, between Regent's Park and Hampstead Heath, a few minutes north of Cavendish Avenue.

The studio was done up as a living room, without furniture, but with a fireplace and mantel behind the group. Paul's *Semiramis* sculpture sat atop the mantel, with lit wall sconces in the shape of the Wings logo to either side. The room's wooden floor was actually a platform with a rectangular hole cut out of it, and the band members are seen sitting, kneeling or lying prone on the floor, peering into the hole, onto which the portal and its view of Earth would be composited. During the shoot, as a way of establishing an intergalactic mood (albeit a comic one), Shaw played recordings of Douglas Adams's *The Hitchhiker's Guide to the Galaxy*, the first season of which had been broadcast by BBC Radio 4 a year earlier.

The album's back cover was kept simple: against a cloth backdrop, portraits of the five Wings players (photos credited to Paul and Linda) stretch across the cover. Above the portraits, the track titles are listed, with side one parenthetically labeled "sunny side up" and side two called "over easy." Below the pictures is the production credit, shared by Paul and Chris Thomas, and a list of the recording locations.

One side of the inner sleeve is what looks like the inside of an ornate church tower shot from below, a dove within a sunburst at its center. The other side is black with a cut-out hole showing the disc label, which has the track listing and copyright information printed on a sunny-side-up egg on side one and an over-easy egg on side two. On the sleeve itself, the track titles are listed above the label cut-out, with the same egg-related side designations; below it is the roster of Rockestra and credits for the Black Dyke Mills Band, RAK Mobile, and other contributors to the project. In keeping with Paul's practice of not properly crediting arrangers, Martyn Ford, listed only as Martyn, is included in a list of miscellaneous thank-yous.

Steve Holley's name is misspelled (as Holly), but that was deliberate: because journalists had frequently referred to him as "Holly," and because of his boss's reverence for Buddy Holly, the drummer changed the spelling of his surname during his time with Wings.

Paul was already thinking about a video production to accompany the album, so he hired Keith McMillan—Keef—to come to the cover shoot to capture what would become the intro and outro to the video, based on the shots John Shaw was taking.

Like the album cover, the video includes nods to Paul's onetime science fiction film collaborator Gene Roddenberry. Wings fade into picture, before the fireplace, as if they had beamed-in, *Star Trek*-style. They roll up a large rug, revealing the portal, which opens to show the view of Earth. In the outro, Paul closes the portal and the band rolls back the rug, walks back to the fireplace, and fades away.

While the shoot was being set up, Paul did an interview with Paul Gambaccini for *Rolling Stone* (they had also spoken a few weeks earlier at Abbey Road), which offered one especially revealing moment—Paul's almost fatalistic look at his own musical personality, in response to a question about whether his new album will break new ground.

"Slightly, yeah," he responded, tentatively. "You start off really wanting to do something very new, but eventually you come back to what is *you*. So it always gets an imprint of what is *you*, and

12 ROLLING STONE, JULY 26, 1979

WINGS
BACK TO THE EGG

Wings, *Back to the Egg* album and 'Getting Closer' single trade ad

you always do what you do. You know what I mean. The sort of magnetic forces, or whatever it is around you, make a certain mold, I think you must listen to the music because I can't really talk about it. I think so many different things about it. So if anyone asks me what it is, I can't tell you."[35]

EMI and Columbia jointly agreed to a provisional release date, June 6.

With that, the McCartneys flew to Barbados for a two-week holiday. Upon their return, Paul saw to some musical housekeeping: between April 24 and May 9, he made stereo mixes of no fewer than eight reels' worth of band jams, with titles like 'Heavy Metal Waltz,' 'Harmonic Groove,' 'Stomp,' 'Ba-Da-Da Jam' and 'Lympne 24-Track Jam 1 & 2,' as well as unused oddities like 'Simon Game' and various versions of 'Space Jam.'

Since the birth of James, in September 1977, touring had not been a priority for Paul, even as Denny, in particular, stressed his eagerness to get out on the road. But now that *Back to the Egg* was finished, a tour to promote it was the next logical step—and most likely expected by Paul's new label Columbia. Paul had hinted that a tour was in the offing early in the year, when the 1,200-seat Royal Court Theatre, in Liverpool, was under threat of closure. Making a £5,000 ($10,000) donation to help keep the theater open, Paul also promised to perform there with Wings before the year was out—a promise in keeping with his recent fascination with the idea of playing in small venues, something he continued to push in interviews.

"We'll probably do something in a couple of months' time," he told *Record Mirror*, "but we want to do something different this time, like playing smaller halls and clubs. We want to turn up somewhere and offer them a gig for that evening. We want to have that kind of freedom, instead of being tagged in the superstar mold. We will of course play a few big halls because it is expected of a band of our size anyway, but we will do the smaller clubs as well." There was talk, he added, of Wings performing an Iron Curtain–defying show in Red Square, in Moscow, "but as yet, nothing is definite."[36]

What this version of Wings did not yet have was a stage show. In the hope of putting one together at a leisurely pace and well away from the public glare, Paul again rented Lympne Castle, where the band would rehearse for four weeks starting on May 7. The musical diet included oldies like 'Shake Rattle and Roll,' "Whole Lotta Shakin'," 'Johnny B. Goode' and the early Wings staple, 'Blue Moon of Kentucky,' along with songs from the pre-Juber and Holley Wings songbook and a few Beatles tunes.

Mostly, though, the sessions turned out to be more about the band getting to know each other and testing each other's limits in ways that recording and overdubbing don't really provide. Jamming was plentiful, and early in the visit Paul had the RAK Mobile return to document it, as well as a handful of new songs that emerged from the rehearsals.

Not that Paul shielded himself from distractions from the outside world. On May 19, he and

Linda, along with Denny and Jo Jo, attended Eric Clapton's wedding to Pattie Boyd at Clapton's mansion in Ewhurst, Surrey. The guest list also included Pattie's ex, George Harrison, as well as Ringo Starr, Mick Jagger and Bill Wyman of the Rolling Stones, Clapton's former Cream band-mates Jack Bruce and Ginger Baker, Elton John, David Bowie and others. After a few crateloads of champagne were imbibed, some of the guests moved onto the bandstand for a jam, and although it has been reported that Paul, George and Ringo were onstage together at one point, no one seems to remember who actually played with whom.

"Everyone was sitting around in a big marquee having drinks," Paul explained, "and they had some microphones and a bit of a stage thing down the end, and all the kids get on, screaming away. So the grown-ups turfed off, and we had a little play. It was just crazy, you know, but then the newspapers noticed that the next day. There was Ringo, George, me—is it a reunion folks? Nay. Denny? Eric Clapton, Ginger Baker . . ."

How did Paul describe this jam?

"Terrible, oh, it was shocking—all out of tune and that, but no one noticed. It's pretty good. Denny's recorded it* and he's got it out as a bootleg."[37]

Around the time of Clapton's wedding, John Eastman closed on another land purchase on Paul and Linda's behalf, this time a 151-acre spread on the eastern edge of Tucson, Arizona. Linda had been fond of Tucson when she lived there in the early 1960s, and her memories of learning the art of photography, and riding horses, were rekindled during Wings' American tour. The property included a house and a guesthouse, and although the purchase price was not disclosed, the owners had listed a portion of it (107 acres) for $1 million (£500,000) earlier in the year.

For Paul and Linda, the Arizona property was a potential hideout, and though the sale was reported publicly (it was front-page news in Tucson), they hoped it would drop off the public's radar. To that end, John Eastman shrugged off any talk about their plans for it. "It's just going to be [left] as is," he told the *Arizona Daily Star*. "It will probably become a preserve."[38]

Mid-May also brought the news that Apple Records Inc. and Apple Corps Ltd. had filed suit against Capitol Records and EMI in New York Superior Court, seeking damages of $16,050,000 (£7.8 million) for underpayment of royalties on Beatles and solo Beatles recordings under the September 1969 contract negotiated by Allen Klein. Apple's lawyers had been quietly working on the suit for several years, and while the timing, so soon after Paul severed his ties with Capitol Records in America, is likely coincidental, it is impossible to rule out a direct connection between Paul's exit from Capitol and the start of legal action against his former label. The suit, however, would test his working relationship with EMI in Britain.

Among other things, the suit claimed that Capitol had inappropriately debited the cost of pro-

---

* As Paul's tone suggests, he was joking; no audio recordings of the wedding jams were ever bootlegged, though photographs exist.

motional records and scrapped overstock, which the Beatles contract required the label to pay for, and that Capitol had sold Beatles recordings through record clubs, which the contract prohibited. Royalties were also said to have been underpaid on tapes, and in a part of the suit that must have been embarrassing to John Lennon, Apple argued that by encouraging Lennon to release *Some Time in New York City*, his album of political broadsides, Capitol deliberately subverted a contractual clause calling for a higher royalty rate after August 1972, so long as all discs released before then sold at least 500,000 copies, a threshold the Lennon album failed to meet. Capitol's failure to adopt the increased royalty rate, Apple said, cost the Beatles $10 million.[39]

Neither the land purchase nor the lawsuit required Paul's presence; the Eastmans did the heavy lifting on his behalf. They would also have forwarded on the advertisement John and Yoko took in the 'Week in Review' section of the *New York Times* on May 27—a full page, at a cost of $18,240 (£8,900), titled "A Love Letter from John and Yoko to People Who Ask Us What, When and Why," in which they couched a plea to be left alone in quasi-mystical terms: "Remember, our silence is the silence of love and not of indifference."

Nor would Paul's presence have been required at Abbey Road on May 24, when 'Old Siam, Sir' and 'Spin It On' were mastered for release as a single (and assigned matrix numbers 7YCE.21809 and 7YCE.21810), to be issued on June 1. 'Old Siam, Sir' was Paul's choice: besides liking its quirkiness, he thought British listeners would be amused by the location references in the lyrics. Columbia Records, on the other hand, felt that 'Getting Closer' was a more commercial choice, so that was the A side of the American single, scheduled for June 4. It was the first time since 1971—when 'Uncle Albert/Admiral Halsey' was released as a single in America and 'The Back Seat of My Car' was the single in Britain—that Paul released different singles on each side of the Atlantic.

The single would give Paul an inkling of how the press would receive the new album, although the response to 'Goodnight Tonight' did not leave him much hope that reviewers were ready to declare his new material a *Band on the Run*-level return to form.

> *All we get is some spineless pretend-rock from the clapped-out old phony. John Lennon, I raise my chalice to ya. Get well soon me old son, please . . .* [40]
>
> *Garry Bushell*, Sounds

> *What a big, ringing sound. Congrats, Chris Thomas . . . the song is so stripped down to the hook that you can't miss it. Enter the headbanger—I don't begrudge this one its obvious success.*[41]
>
> *Vivien Goldman*, Melody Maker

> *So when the world discovers that without a McCartney there wouldn't be a Gerry Rafferty, Andrew Gold, Steven Bishop, Squeeze, Badfinger, Jeffrey Lynne and all their hybrid cousins, we'll all start being a bit nicer to Paul. When the man the word 'photogenic' was created for, finally stops making these awful records and starts realizing that only he can take over from Sinatra I'll stop taking these handfuls of vitamins. Paul created 'pop,' without him where is it?*[42]
>
> *James Parade and Monique*, Record Mirror

> [Listed with other singles] *None of these singles have picture covers. None of these singles have any soul.*[43]
>
> *Paul Morley*, NME

The public was not much more enthusiastic. 'Old Siam, Sir' made its debut on the British Top 100 at No. 73 on June 16, and limped to its peak, No. 35, on June 30. It remained in the Top 100 for only six weeks. Sunny side up or over easy, the single did not appeal to the tastes of British music fans.

In America, 'Getting Closer' did slightly better. The anonymous reviewer for *Billboard* found the song to be "an uplifting rocker" and praised McCartney's vocals, as well as lyrics and instrumental hooks that were "subtle but effective."[44] The single entered the *Billboard* Hot 100 at No. 64 on June 16 and remained ten weeks. It took until July 28 to hit its peak, No. 20, a spot it held for a fortnight.

At Lympne Castle, meanwhile, Wings were filling reels of tape with jamming, and Paul was bringing in new material. One of his new tunes was 'Ebony and Ivory,' a song he had started after a row with Linda at High Park in the summer of 1978, but that looked at relationships more globally, using the keyboard as a metaphor for racial harmony: "*Ebony and ivory live together in perfect harmony, side by side on my piano, keyboard, oh Lord, why don't we?*"

"One good time to write songs," Paul revealed of the tune's overcast genesis, "is when you're not in a very good mood. It's like a kind of psychiatrist's couch in a way, and often what you do is take your guitar or piano, your musical crutch, and go off in a room and sort of sulk almost; you sulk to the song. It makes you feel better because you're getting it out. And as I recall, I wasn't feeling brilliant."

Though the melody was fresh, the song's title—extracted from a Spike Milligan sketch—had been up Paul's sleeve for several years. "I heard Spike Milligan make this analogy with black and white notes on the piano; he'd say, 'You know, it's a funny kind of thing—black notes, white notes, and you need to play the two to make harmony folks!' I thought, 'Yes, this is a good analogy for harmony between people' because if you've just got the black notes you're limited, and if you've just got the white, you're limited; eventually you've got to go into them both."[45]

Another, 'How Come You're Never Home,' was rehearsed and abandoned.

Toward the end of Wings' rehearsal period at the castle, the activity shifted from rehearsing and jamming to formal recording.

Rehearsals/Recording Sessions

Wednesday, May 23–Tuesday, June 5, 1979.

RAK Mobile Recording Unit, Lympne Castle, Kent.

Recording: 'Weep for Love,' 'New Orleans,' 'Robber's Ball' and 'Cruisin' Ahead.'

Denny had introduced 'Weep for Love,' an acoustic ballad with a bluesy acoustic guitar figure supporting a plea for the betterment of mankind on May 22, and after working up an arrangement, the band recorded the track the next day. "Interestingly, Paul plays bass on that with a drumstick," Steve noted. "He's actually banging the strings as he plays the part, it's a really cool sound. And I played it with mallets on the toms. I loved that tune actually, that had a lot of potential."[46]

The band filled a patience-testing seven reels with takes before settling on a master, to which Denny added his lead vocal, and Paul, Linda, Denny and Steve added widely spaced harmonies.

Since the band was recording new material during what was meant to be a rehearsal period, Paul had the master of Linda's 'New Orleans' retrieved from MPL's archives and sent down to Kent. Linda had recorded the basic track at Sea-Saint Studios in February 1975.

Sung with a sassy, 1950's girl-group timbre, the lyrics are steeped in local references, most of them culinary—*"Gumbo and Po' Boys are all that I've seen in New Orleans / Creole Dish and Crawfish are all that I've seen in New Orleans / Oysters on a half shell, Bourbon Street got its own smell, yeah."* On the basic track, Linda played a rudimentary but energetic piano part, Denny played electric guitar and Joe English played drums. At the May 24 session, Linda double-tracked her vocal, Denny added an acoustic guitar and Paul overdubbed a rollicking New Orleans–flavored piano solo.

'Robber's Ball,' the strangest of the new tracks, was the product of a jam between Laurence and Paul. "I should get some writing credit on that because the basic track of that was just me and Paul," Laurence said, half-joking. "It was just Paul jamming and rolling tape, and then we built the other stuff on top of it. But as it never got a commercial release, it's hardly worth [chasing a credit].” When they were finished, they had a cheerful parody of an operatic chorus, with a group of robbers tweaking the noble men of Padua (in Italy) and Halifax (in West Yorkshire—the verse is sung in a Yorkshire accent), whose towns they rob at will. But for its heavy disco beat, sequenced synthesizer tones, and varispeeded vocals, it could almost be mistaken for Gilbert and Sullivan.

The band also spent part of May 31 touring around Kent, visiting places like the Eagle Parachute Club, at an airfield near Lympne Castle, looking at locations for an upcoming video shoot and posing for publicity photos, shot by David Thorpe. Officially, Paul was still considering a choice of directors for the shoot, but Keith McMillan had the inside track, having shot footage of the band during the *Back to the Egg* cover shoot. Another new song that emerged from the band’s jamming on June 4, ‘Cruisin’ Ahead,’ saw Paul channeling his inner Elvis and Carl Perkins. When the band recorded the song the next day, it took only nine takes to perfect it, the last marked as the master. June 5 was the final day of rehearsals and recording at Lympne Castle.

But Wings would be back at the start of the next week, when they switched fully into promotional mode.

25

PLAYING WITH HIMSELF (AGAIN)

Back in East Sussex, Paul decided at last that Keith McMillan was the right director for the *Back to the Egg* special he was planning, and on June 7, he called McMillan to offer him the job—the catch being, as so many of Paul's collaborators have discovered, that Paul wanted to start immediately, which in this case was the following Monday, June 11. For McMillan, that meant that any planning—hiring staff, obtaining equipment and materials, preparing rough storyboards and getting permissions from filming locations—had to be done instantly. As was usually the case, Paul's collaborators turned cartwheels to meet his schedule. McMillan and his staff—Phil Davey and Hugh Scott-Symonds—saw to all the preparation in time for the shoot.

"If a record gets in the Top 30," McMillan explained soon after filming, "record companies will phone me up and say, 'Can we have a finished clip by six o'clock tomorrow afternoon,' and we're set up to do that. It is a problem because a lot of the time we have to come up with the ideas very fast, get a crew, build a set. I would much prefer it if we were given as much notice as possible, obviously, because we could do a more careful job. When we have to tape very fast, we're working mainly on instinct."[1]

Paul had given Keef a cassette of *Back to the Egg* and asked him to select seven songs that he felt would lend themselves to video treatment. It turned out that the songs Keef chose—'Baby's Request,' 'Spin It On,' 'Winter Rose/Love Awake,' 'Again and Again and Again,' 'Old Siam, Sir,' 'Arrow Through Me,' and 'Getting Closer'—matched Paul's own choices, boosting his confidence that Keef was his man.

Wings and McMillan, with a crew of about 40, a Titan crane, two generators (for lighting), five cameras and sound equipment (for playback during the shoots), all converged on Lympne Castle on the rainy morning of June 11. The first order of the day was . . . a change of plans: 'Again and Again and Again' was meant to be shot outdoors that day, but since the rain showed no sign of

Paul and Linda launch *Back to the Egg* at Abbey Road Studios, June 11, 1979

letting up, the crew set up in the castle's Great Hall to shoot 'Old Siam, Sir,' capturing an energetic mimed performance with lots of close-ups.

That was it for the first day; Wings were due at Abbey Road Studio Two for the *Back to the Egg* launch that afternoon. Paul, Linda and EMI arranged for an over-the-top thematic party, with tablecloths sporting a fried-egg design and parasols printed to look like eggs sunny side up. On the tables were rubber hard-boiled eggs, and boiled egg jigsaw puzzles. The one idea dreamt up by Supotco—the agency hired to coordinate the event—that Paul and Linda vetoed, now that they were both almost entirely vegetarian, was having the sofas done up as bacon and sausage sandwiches. Guests—about 150 writers and EMI personnel—were fed Chinese food, with a heavy emphasis on seaweed, while video from the Rockestra session was screened.

Back to the Egg had been released the previous Friday, June 8, and Paul did not have to wait long for the critical verdict, with the first reviews appearing in music papers published that weekend. The press was overwhelmingly negative, with even writers who had been supportive in the past falling back on a trope that was common in criticism of Paul's early albums—"He is capable of so much more than this." Otherwise, reviewers lambasted the album as much for what it was not as for what it was.

"There are no messages in these songs, no evidence of urgent need to put the world to rights through the power of rock 'n' roll," Tony Mitchell opined in *Sounds.* "They're just songs that you can remember easily if you care to, or just as easily forget." The music, Mitchell wrote, "is complacent and formula-ridden," and shows no evidence that McCartney is "interested in pushing forward the barriers of his art."[2]

Ray Coleman noted in his *Melody Maker* review that McCartney is the most commercially successful of the former Beatles, but that he "seems to be on a treadmill of banality." Not that he found the album entirely without merit. He singled out the two Rockestra tracks as "creditable, rolling, raunchy and at least efficient." 'After the Ball' struck him as "a good ballad with a light country tinge," and 'Getting Closer,' he wrote, was "a natural single in the 'Jet' league." But he closed his review with a plea for Paul to drop Wings and go solo, writing that the band was "created as an edifice marking The Beatle Who Carried On, rather than as an artistic attempt at something brave and invigorating (which is what Paul is *capable* of attempting)."[3]

One problem critics had with the album was the variety of styles it embraced. This kind of versatility was considered an asset during the Beatles years—consider the vast range of styles addressed on the *White Album*. But in June 1979, when the top albums on the chart—discs like Donna Summer's *Bad Girls*, Supertramp's *Breakfast in America,* Electric Light Orchestra's *Discovery,* Blondie's *Parallel Lines*, Dire Straits' *Communique* and Cheap Trick's *At Budokan*—each had a consistent style and sound, critics found an album that embraced punk, folk, turn-of-the-century salon music, 1930's pop, Renaissance pastiche and a bit of gospel to be diffuse rather than varied.

In *Record Mirror*, for example, Ronnie Gurr judged the album "a tremendously muddled lucky bag of half-baked concepts," and "a competent rock album with no strong direction and no instant classics."[4] And Timothy White, in a disdainful review in *Rolling Stone,* called the album "just about the sorriest grab bag of dreck in recent memory," complaining that "McCartney's gross indulgence is matched only by his shameless indolence, and *Back to the Egg* represents the public disintegration of a consistently disappointing talent."[5]

John Rockwell, in his review for the *New York Times*, focused on only one of the styles represented on the album, calling *Back to the Egg* "Mr. McCartney's own coming to terms with punk." The upside, Rockwell wrote, was that "Mr. McCartney sounds looser and freer than he's sometimes done." But he did not find Wings-style punk particularly persuasive. "Punk is also about passion," he wrote, "and passion has generally been an intermittent quality in Mr. McCartney's pop confections. Here the pop is less shiny and smooth, but there isn't much real emotion to compensate."[6]

Wings, *Back to the Egg* album trade ad

Even the generally positive review by Paul Du Noyer in *NME* was awash in backhanded compliments. "Finally, McCartney gets on with it," he wrote. "*Back to the Egg* might not be enough of a departure to delight the cynical or, by that token, to disappoint the faithful. But it is the sturdiest, the least twee and the most rigorous offering we've had from Wings in much too many years." But is this, he wonders, "The Sound of the Suburbs? Yes, I suppose it is—although given the guy's apparent contentment and his honesty I doubt if there's any other kind of music, we could reasonably demand of him."[7]

In Britain, Paul insisted that the album be priced below £4.50 ($9), at a time when LP prices had just crossed the £5 barrier, engendering a debate about whether this reflected his lack of confidence in the album, or his wanting to give his fans a break (and himself a price advantage) at a time of high inflation and high unemployment numbers. EMI complied, but those same economic pressures made it a rough time for them to do so.

Record company executives across the industry had become besotted, over the past year, with the fantasy that mega-sellers like *Saturday Night Fever* and *Grease* would turn up annually. But when a global economic downturn put a squeeze on discretionary spending and mega-sellers failed to materialize, those same executives started to panic, some hyperventilating in the press that the industry was facing the worst time since the Great Depression. Things were particularly dire at EMI, which sought to right its financial problems—caused mainly by development costs in its medical technology division—by selling 50 percent of its worldwide music business to Paramount/Gulf & Western for £70 million ($147.5 million).*

Back to the Egg made its first appearance on the UK album chart on June 23 at No. 27, and hit its peak, No. 6, a week later. It remained in the Top 100 UK albums for 15 weeks. In America, the album entered the *Billboard* 200 at No. 45 on June 30 and peaked at No. 8, a spot it held for two weeks starting on July 21. It remained on the *Billboard* chart for 24 weeks. Like the singles that preceded it, *Back to the Egg* offered Columbia a poor initial return on their much-publicized multimillion-pound investment in the former Beatle.

On the morning of Tuesday, June 12, the day after the launch party at Abbey Road, Wings were back in Kent for another day of filming—three of them this time. Embryonic video concepts were concocted and storyboarded in advance by McCartney and McMillan, then adapted on the fly to incorporate wardrobe and props found on location.

* The Paramount/Gulf & Western sale fell through in September, but toward the end of the year Thorn Electrical Industries made a bid worth £169 million ($356 million), leading to a merger and a name change to Thorn EMI.

"Paul McCartney is certainly the most aware artist I work with," McMillan explained several months after the shoot. "There's nothing that I can do that I can fool him with. With Paul it's a matter of working very closely with him. He's a very intelligent man, he knows the business inside out, so that makes it very easy for me to work with him because I can go down and discuss what we're going to do, and I don't need to tell him the technical problems because he understands them."[8]

Two of the day's videos were shot in a hangar at the Eagle Parachute Club. Phil Davey struck a deal with the hangar's owner to allow McMillan's art director to paint a ten-foot-high Wings logo on the top part of the hangar, and repaint that part of the hangar when the shoot was finished. But the logo had only a few seconds of screen time: except for the opening scene, when a biplane is seen wheeling out of the hangar, the clip was shot indoors on a 50-foot-by-25-foot stage built for the shoot, along with six 40-foot trusses with lighting towers. Wings were filmed miming 'Spin It On,' dressed in leather bomber jackets, with parachute suspension lines falling around them from above.

When the shoot was complete, the crew prepared to paint over the Wings logo, but the hangar's owner liked the look of it and decided to keep it.

Wings mimed 'Again and Again and Again' that afternoon in a nearby field of waist-high yellow oilseed rape. That evening the band returned to the hangar for a performance of 'Getting Closer' similar to the one they filmed for 'Spin It On,' but without the bomber jackets and parachute

Wings filming a promo for 'Again and Again and Again,' June 12, 1979

Paul gets hammy while filming a promo for 'Again and Again and Again,' June 12, 1979

lines. Inserts showing the five band members crowded into the front seat of a tour bus, barreling through the rain with Paul at the wheel, were filmed later in the week.

Mark Williams of *Melody Maker* was invited to spend the day with the band, interviewing the players between filming. Ray Coleman's review for the paper was in the current issue, but if that created any awkwardness, Paul kept it under wraps. Laurence, on the other hand, took the opportunity to comment on criticism of his boss.

"I think he comes in for a lot of criticism because of who he is," Laurence theorized. "But you can choose any group or any artist—they're bound to come up with some stuff that you don't particularly like and maybe the critics don't like . . . maybe even the artist doesn't like! But you can't turn your nose up at the best people—and he's one of the best. I'm not saying everything he's done is perfect, but I think he's got his own style, which has got nothing to do with the Beatles."[9]

Williams spent a good deal of his time with Steve and Laurence, getting a sense of "the new guys," and asking Paul to assess the new lineup, now that they had an album behind them.

"The truth of the matter is," Paul said, "I find this new lineup very easy to work with. Steve's very good, no messing about and he can play anything. He's a good stable kind of a character, too, you can lean on him a bit. And Laurence, too, is super-professional. It's just very much easier."

Williams noted that whenever the cameras were not rolling, Wings started jamming. "There was a reggae version of one of the album's more, er, poignant ballads, 'Love Awake,'" he wrote, "and a Chuck Berry riff with McCartney on drums (not bad) and Holly on keyboards (hammy). And despite all the ghastly stories about Linda miming onstage, I heard her playing a pretty nifty 12-bar at one point." [10]

Wednesday's shoot for 'Winter Rose' was at Lympne Castle. In the opening shot, the castle is seen undergoing a gradual transformation from springtime to winter, a trick accomplished by shooting the castle on Tuesday and leaving the camera tripod in place while thick layers of soap, posing as snow, were applied to the castle's walls, turrets, lawn and trees. That view was filmed on Wednesday, and Tuesday's and Wednesday's footage was crossfaded so that the snow gradually appears in the picture.

For 'Winter Rose,' Paul and Linda are seen alone, Linda riding a horse up the snowy path to the castle, Paul coming out to meet her. 'Love Awake' was supposed to have been filmed on Wednesday as well, but 'Winter Rose' was completed late in the day, so 'Love Awake' was put off until Thursday. Another mimed performance clip, it was filmed in the castle's kitchen before an open fire.

The 1940's-ish 'Baby's Request' was shot on Friday, June 15, at Camber Sands, 40 miles from

Wings film a promo for 'Baby's Request,' June 14, 1979

Wings taking a break during filming of 'Baby's Request' promo, June 14, 1979

the castle—an oddly surreal beach set in the shadow of the Dungeness Nuclear Power Station, where scenes from *Dunkirk* (1958) and *The Longest Day* (1962) had been filmed. McMillan's team built a small army encampment with jeeps and trucks, tents and a stage. Wings donned World War II army uniforms (without insignia) and mimed the song for a uniformed group of extras, like Humphrey Bogart or Vera Lynn performing for a crowd of wartime soldiers in the early '40s. Fanciers of Paul's instrument collection would have been amused to see Linda plucking on the Bill Black bass.

'Arrow Through Me,' shot on Wednesday, June 20, is an unusual clip: reflecting the song's deceptive instrumentation, Paul, Linda, Laurence and Denny all play keyboards, with Steve drumming. The clip also uses split imagery, with multiple images (often a dozen or more) of a player in a tight sequence, the video equivalent of tape echo, created with a device called a digital frame store, which splits the image electronically.

With the promo clips and the video bookends that were shot at the cover art session, all the elements for a *Back to the Egg* special were in hand. But Paul was not in a hurry to get the completed special on the air: its first screenings were scheduled for November on American television.

In the opulent executive suite at Black Rock, the 38-story CBS headquarters at 52nd Street and the Avenue of the Americas in New York, a handful of extremely irritated men walked through a corridor lined with Gold Record awards and artist photos to Walter Yetnikoff's office, ostensibly to discuss promotional plans for Paul McCartney's *Back to the Egg*, but really to express their exasperation with their new ultra-high-ticket roster acquisition.

For starters, Paul flat out rejected Columbia's request that 'Goodnight Tonight' be included on the album, and the label did not have anyone as persuasive as Al Coury on staff to talk him into it.* And now, after the label committed itself to a $20-million contract, stripped its own portfolio of a venerable publishing company, and earmarked $200,000[11] (£95,000) to advertise and promote *Back to the Egg*, it turned out that McCartney was not lifting a finger to help sell the album. He was not touring, and with the exception of a radio interview with the RKO Network, he was doing no press.

Instead, he sent Steve and Laurence to New York to handle the promotional chores.

"Oh, Columbia weren't happy," Laurence admitted. "They weren't happy because the album would have sold at least another million if Paul had included the single. It was an odd time. You're coming out of this period where there was an expectation, with Fleetwood Mac's *Rumours* and *Saturday Night Fever* selling 10 million copies. And *Back to the Egg* comes out and sells well over a million without the hit single being on it, simply because of Paul's fan base. But there's no tour, the promo special comes out in November—almost six months after the album's released—so it was not necessarily launched in a fully commercial way.

"I think that Columbia didn't necessarily know how to market Paul," Laurence added. "Capitol had learned how to market Paul, but for Columbia, it was a new thing. And it just didn't have the traction. Plus, the American economy radically slowed down in that period, so, the market had kind of shrunk anyway. There were a number of factors that conspired to not give it the launch it needed."[12]

But Paul did press in Britain. He had boiled down the experience of writing and recording the album to a selection of colorful tales, and he had told them all, with only minor variations, to Mark Williams, Paul Gambaccini, Roger Scott and a few other journalists in England. Rather than repeating them again in Europe and America, he reasoned, why not send Steve and Laurence, who would have stories of their own.

* Capitol no longer had Coury either: he left the label 1976 to become the first president of RSO Records, which he formed with Robert Stigwood. It was under Coury's watch that RSO released the *Saturday Night Fever* and *Grease* soundtrack albums.

"It was suggested," Steve recalls, "that Laurence and I do the early promotion of *Back to the Egg* through Europe and then in the US, since nobody really knew who we were. I think we did 110 or 115 interviews in a week. So that was used as a way to introduce us to people who otherwise wouldn't have a clue who we were, and it gave Paul a chance to rest."[13]

The newest Wings made the most of their time in New York, going to shows—a photo of them meeting Ian Hunter backstage after his show at the Palladium ran in *Billboard*—and jamming with the soul duo Sam and Dave. Laurence decided to remain in New York for another week after Steve returned "because I was having a good time, and getting my feet wet with New York"[14]—and besides, Wings were on a between-projects hiatus.

Not that there wasn't plenty afoot in various corners of Paul's fiefdom. Barry Chattington was at work on the *Rockestra* film, and from July 9 to 13 its soundtrack was compiled, edited and mixed to mono at Abbey Road.

Willy Russell's *Band on the Run* film was still a prospect, too, with EMI's new chief executive, Lord Delfont, speaking enthusiastically about it to the *Daily Mail*, saying that the film was expected to go into production in 1980 with the company's backing.[15]

It was also decided, possibly by Paul but more likely by the Eastmans, that it was time to bring some attention to MPL's publishing business. On June 18, Paul's thirty-sixth birthday, the *Washington Post* published an article that detailed some of his more lucrative and better-known holdings, noting, "McCartney makes a little money every time somebody buys a copy of Linda Ronstadt singing 'You're No Good' or Judy Garland mourning 'The Man That Got Away,'"[16] and that MPL owns popular shows like *A Chorus Line, Annie, Mame, Grease, Hello, Dolly!* and *Bye Bye, Birdie*, plus the Buddy Holly catalog, Scott Joplin's rags, Standards like 'Autumn Leaves,' 'Sentimental Journey,' 'Stormy Weather,' and 'Dinah' (which was played daily as the theme for Dinah Shore's talk show), and even some college sports teams' fight songs like 'Rambling Wreck from Georgia Tech' and 'On Wisconsin.'

John Eastman told the *Post* that MPL was the world's largest independent publisher, and though he declined to comment on reports estimating Paul's net worth at \$80 million–\$120 million (£38 million–£57 million), the *Post* put the value of his publishing holdings in perspective by estimating that if *Back to the Egg* sold two million copies, Paul's cut as the publisher—without factoring in his earnings as a performer and songwriter—would be \$660,000 (£313,000).

Within days, the *New York Times* and United Press International ran similar explorations of Paul's publishing empire, and on July 7, *Billboard* carried an interview with Lee Eastman, who told the magazine that MPL had recently acquired two more companies, Cherio Music and Warock Corporation, as well as a 20 percent stake in the Mills Music Trust.

For Paul, a between-projects hiatus—"a chance to rest," as Steve put it—was generally a time to dream up new projects. He and Linda repaired to East Sussex, where Paul decided that the farmhouse on the newly acquired Lower Gate Farm would make a decent home studio. He enlisted his technical guru, Eddie Klein, to rent a Studer A-80 16-track deck with a varispeed control and drive it down to East Sussex, along with everything else Paul would need—microphones, stands, cables, a 16-track mixer Klein built himself, and ten rolls of Ampex 456 two-inch tape.[17] After Klein set up and tested everything, Paul was ready to get to work.

What Paul had in mind was a collection of recordings he would make on his own, multitracking all the parts, as he did on *McCartney*, in 1970. The point, at the outset, was not to record songs from his backlog of compositions, but to experiment.

He had a new sound, or range of sounds, in mind. Just as he had been keen to experiment with punk moves, Paul was fascinated with the broad timbral palette and motoric rhythms of the nascent synthpop style. In May, Gary Numan and Tubeway Army released 'Are "Friends" Electric?,' which topped the UK singles chart for four weeks. Paul most likely saw Numan and his band play their hit on the May 22 edition of *Old Grey Whistle Test.*

Over the years, Paul had acquired an arsenal of electronic instruments for Wings' tours and recordings, among them a Yamaha CS-80, a Roland Jupiter 4, an ARP and the Minimoog, as well as the Mellotron, a Univox rhythm box and the vocoder. Now he wanted to explore their potential.

The plan was to turn on the tape deck and see what happened, without having to explain or justify what he was doing. And just as he had no preconceptions about the music he would be recording, he had no idea whether these private sessions would yield an album, demos or just wild experiments. That was largely the case when he started work on *McCartney*, as well. But this time he had much more sophisticated equipment.

"Actually, I was trying *not* to do an album," he insisted. "It was just after *Back to the Egg,* and I wanted to do something totally different. So, I just plugged a single microphone into the back of a Studer 16-track tape machine; didn't use a recording console at all. The idea was that at the end of it I'd just have a zany little cassette that I'd play in my car and never release."[18]

But there was something else behind this do-it-yourself project. Paul's attitude toward Wings was starting to change. It was not something he had come to terms with fully, or even consciously: in interviews, he still discussed Wings as his principal creative outlet, and he planned to take the band on tour. And as he had acknowledged in his interview with Mark Williams, Wings now had an exceptional lineup, with a powerful young drummer and a guitarist who could move easily between rock, jazz and classical styles. Holley and Juber both understood whose band it was, and they did what they were asked without drama or argument. No surliness, no homesickness, no one complaining of feeling undervalued. This was the Wings he had been aiming for all these years.

Yet, something was bothering him. The Lympne Castle rehearsal period, when the band should have been creating and polishing its live show, turned out to be days of jamming and, at the end, recording. But that was as much his fault as anyone's. It's possible that the early reviews of *Back to the Egg* had gotten into his head. Of Wings' albums, only *Band on the Run* was received as a masterpiece, and he had made that album nearly on his own. The other Wings albums had been trashed, with the complaint that *"It's not a real band, it's Paul and sidemen"* coming through either overtly or between the lines.

Or maybe it was just restlessness, a seven-year itch. Whatever the reason, what he needed now was to work alone—to go where his instruments and imagination led him, and to make music that was unlike the focused pop he had been recording with Wings.

As he did on *McCartney*, Paul kept carefully annotated track sheets showing what he played (or sang) on each track of the 16-track tape. He did not, however, make note of the recording dates, or where each recording was started and finished.* All that is known about these recordings is that Paul began work on them in East Sussex in July, and that in August, Eddie Klein dismantled the recording setup, drove it to Campbeltown, and installed it in the Spirit of Ranachan Studio, where Paul continued to work. Also unclear is whether the five reels of master tapes include the songs in the order they were created—as was the case with the *McCartney* masters—or whether the reels are compilations. The former seems likely, given that Paul has said that the first two compositions he recorded were 'Front Parlour' and 'Frozen Jap'—the first two songs on Tape 1.

The five reels, which were each labeled "WINGS (Paul McCartney)," included:

> ***Reel 1:*** 'Front Parlour' / 'Frozen Jap' / 'Summer's Day' (listed on the spine as 'Summer Down') / 'You Know I'll Get You Baby' / 'All You Horse Riders' / 'Blue Sway'
>
> ***Reel 2:*** 'Temporary Secretary' / 'Slow Down' (working title of 'On the Way') / 'Mr. H Atom' / 'The Bogey Wobble' / 'Wonderful Christmastime' / 'Darkroom' (30 IPS†—listed as "30 mph!!" on the spine)
>
> ***Reel 3:*** 'One of These Days (Breathe Fresh Air)' / 'Secret Friend' / 'Bogey Music'
>
> ***Reel 4:*** 'Hi George—Morning Terry' / 'Check My Machine' / 'I Need Love' (working title of 'Waterfalls') / 'Nobody Knows' / 'Coming Up'
>
> ***Reel 5:*** 'Steve' / 'Let There Be Pillows'

---

* In the *McCartney II* Deluxe Edition book, all the tracks are listed as having been recorded "at Lower Gate Farm, Sussex, Summer of 1979," except for 'Blue Sway' and 'Wonderful Christmastime,' which are both listed as having been recorded on August 30, 1979. However, interviews Paul gave closer to the time suggest that this information is not reliable. Besides stating that the music was recorded at both Lower Gate Farm and Spirit of Ranachan, Paul has said that 'Wonderful Christmastime' was written and recorded in July (and, in one interview, in June). The erroneous dating in the Deluxe Edition is most likely drawn from MPL's tape log, in which the five reels of Summer 1979 recordings are listed with August 30 as their recording date.

† A reference to the tape speed, 30 inches per second. The other recordings were made at 15 i.p.s.

Paul's studio at Low Ranachan during the making of *McCartney II*, August 1979

At some point during the summer, he decided that the recordings were fit for release, a decision that, in the telling, sounds oddly passive—and one that actually downgraded the experience for him.

"In the end I had a few tracks," he said, "played them for a couple of people, and they said, 'I see, that's your next album.' And I thought, 'Right, it probably is.' So then I got a bit serious about it and tried to make it into an 'album.' That was the worst part of it—I was having fun till then."[19]

Recording Sessions

July–August 1979.
Lower Gate Farm, Sussex and Spirit of Ranachan Studio, Low Ranachan Farm, Campbeltown.
Recording and Overdubbing: 'Check My Machine,' 'Front Parlour,' 'Frozen Jap,' 'Summer's Day' (listed on the spine as 'Summer Down'), 'You Know I'll Get You Baby,' 'All You Horse Riders' and 'Blue Sway.'

Even before he recorded 'Front Parlour,' Paul tested the Studer by filling 10 of the 16 tracks with a wild test piece, 'Check My Machine.' Its appearance on Reel 4 (preceded by 'Hi

George—Morning Terry,' a snippet from a Sylvester the Cat cartoon, which Paul attached to one of his edits of 'Check My Machine'), rather than at the start of Reel 1, is a slight mystery. A likely explanation is that Paul recorded the test piece on one reel, then set it aside, starting the project proper with 'Front Parlour' on a fresh reel. But he liked the groove he built on 'Check My Machine,' so later in the process—probably after he decided to release these recording as an album—he added a vocal track and began to consider 'Check My Machine' as a full-fledged composition and a contender for release. Once he filled Reel 3, he recorded new material after 'Check My Machine,' converting the test reel into Reel 4.

To record these experiments, Paul returned to a process that served him well when he recorded *McCartney*: he recorded the drums first, giving himself a beat to work against. In the case of 'Check My Machine,' he used two tracks for drums—track 4 for the snare, track 5 for the bass drum. A repetitive, slowly evolving bass line on track 6 begins by outlining chord changes, but eventually becomes simpler (in some cases, single notes per bar). Paul fills in the space around the bass line with fluty synthesizer figures, on track 3, two banjos—one mirroring the synthesizer melodies, the other strumming chords—on tracks 1 and 7. He added a synth, run through a Harmonizer, on track 9, and an electric guitar on track 11. With that, he set the nine-minute track aside, later adding a vocal on track 2.

The vocal track begins with a cacophony of shouting (Paul), plus other voices (sampled on Mellotron keys, as 'Hi George—Morning Terry' mostly likely was), but soon gives way to falsetto repetitions of the track's title, for which Paul used varispeed to give his voice a cartoonish, helium-inhaling effect, as well as so much reverb that the consonants in the lyric bounce around to become a secondary percussion figure.

Even in the late 1960s, Paul was completely comfortable behind a console, but in interviews, he downplayed his knowledge of the technical side of recording, as if that was something an artist shouldn't know.

"I liken it to when people buy records," he said of his approach to engineering this project. "People who've got a nice stereo or a hi-fi at home, when they get home, they kinda mess with the treble and bass and they sort of fix it the way they like it. . . . I got a very simple recording thing fixed up for me by an engineer. Instead of having the whole mixing console, which I couldn't handle, 'cause I'm not technically minded enough to do that, I had something a bit similar to a sort of home stereo. You know, I could just tweak this and just do that and make it sound like I wanted it. . . . This was really me fiddling around as if I was just on my own home hi-fi."[20]

'Front Parlour,' named for the room in the old farmhouse that was now Paul's studio, has a more overtly pop sound and is built on a melody that hints at John Denver's 1971 hit, 'Take Me

Home, Country Roads.' Paul began by laying down a snare and bass drum on track 3, later replacing them with separate bass drum and snare parts on tracks 1 and 5. The rest of the tracks are synthesizer, labeled as "Synth main" on track 2, "Synth chug" on track 4, "Flute synth" and "Flute" on tracks 6 and 8, and "Moog chug" on track 7. The synthesized flutes carry most of the track's melodic weight, with the other synths providing texture and rhythmic counterpoint. Some of the synthesized backing sounds vocalized, suggesting that Paul ran a vocoder through one of the instruments.

Paul records drums during the making of *McCartney II*, August 1979

"[I] used the kitchen as an echo chamber. It was a big echoey kitchen," Paul remembered. "If I wanted any kind of echo, I'd just have to stand in this big kitchen with a snare drum and belt it! That's how I got an echo snare."[21]

The echo snare he referred to first appears in the project's next installment, 'Frozen Jap,' an instrumental with the heavy, steady beat of a dance track, produced by a rhythm box on track 1. Paul added a bass drum and snare part on track 6, but later marked it "don't use," preferring instead a new bass drum part on track 7, tom-toms on track 5 and the "echo snare" on track 12. Woven through the insistent dance beat are two synthesizer melodies—a high-pitched tune with a pentatonic ending that gives it an Asian accent (Paul marked it "Synth—oriental") on track 11, mid-range, entirely Western-sounding tune on track 8; another synthesizer track marked "Synth sustain," on track 9 may simply have been an effect on one of the two melody tracks. Three tracks of handclapping—tracks 2, 3 and 4—completed the 5'45" instrumental.

"What happened, originally," Paul said, "was that I was working around on synths, again, experimenting and I suddenly got something which sounded very Oriental. When the track was finished, I tried to think of a suitable title and things came to mind like 'The Ice-Capped Mount Fuji,' or 'A Snow Scene in the Orient.' But all the titles sounded clumsy. Then I thought of 'Frozen Jap'* as a working title—frozen being the ice bit for the snow scene idea, Jap meaning Oriental and somewhere over in that part of the world. And the title stuck."[22]

* When the track was released on *McCartney II* in May 1980, the title was changed on the Japanese release to 'Frozen Japanese' because, Paul said in an interview at the time, "we didn't want to offend anyone."

An important part of the project was being open to random influences and running with them, and one morning Paul heard a classical piece on the radio and decided to take that influence into the farmhouse studio and record 'Summer's Day Song,' a short (3'26"), slow track in a classical style.*

He began with a rhythm box on track 1, used as a click track rather than as a musical element; once the other elements were added, it was eliminated from the mix, except for a faint beat in a short section beginning two minutes in. An electric piano on track 2 is also buried in the mix, suggesting that, like the click track, its use was preparatory: Paul probably played the skeleton of the piece on the piano and then replaced it with two tracks of Mellotron strings (tracks 3 and 4), synthesizer cellos and basses (track 7), a French horn timbre, using an ARP synthesizer (track 6), two tracks of Mellotron flutes (tracks 8 and 9) and another synthesizer track reinforcing the low tones (track 11).

"Synthesizers are amazing things," Paul observed. "Instead of spending hours scoring string sections, you can just sit down at this machine and get a very similar sound immediately. It's a bit more spacey than a real string section, but you can do your own writing as you go and experiment more easily."[23]

To finish the recording, Paul wrote a single verse, about waking from a bad dream to a summer's day. He sings the verse twice, using the melody of the flute line; the first time, he merely double-tracks his voice (tracks 14 and 15), but when the verse is repeated, he adds harmonies (tracks 10, 12 and 13).

Paul's detailed track sheets for the rest of Reel 1 are unavailable. With 'You Know I'll Get You Baby,' Paul returned to dance mode, with a heavy, repetitive beat, and the title (with variations) chanted by a chorus of varispeeded voices. Paul expands his command of his instrumental arsenal here: the pounding beat is provided by a sequencer—a synthesizer module that allows you to program a series of notes and rhythms, which it repeats—and he brings in spacier synth timbres as well, including sliding tones paired with whooshes that evoke cinematic sci-fi weaponry. There is plenty of acoustic percussion, including a cymbal at the start of the track and tactile porcelain and metal sounds. And the vocals have an almost ritualistic quality: the ensemble vocals are not tightly matched, and there is plenty of free vocalizing woven around them, suggesting that Paul may have been recalling the powerful sound he heard when he attended a Fela Kuti concert in Lagos during the *Band on the Run* sessions.

'All You Horse Riders' is an amusing, 3'52" overtly painterly celebration of equestrianism. Over

---

* Though he has never said what the influential classical piece was, aspects of his recording provide some clues. His use of an occasional trill suggests a Baroque influence, and elements of the piece, including his slow tempo and alternation of flutes and strings, call to mind Bach's 'Schafe können sicher weiden' ('Sheep May Safely Graze') from Cantata 208, although harmonically, structurally and melodically, Paul's piece is more freewheeling and modern. His lyric, on the other hand, hints at another Bach work, 'Wachet auf, ruft uns die Stimme,' commonly known in English as 'Sleepers Awake,' from Cantata 140 (although that work lacks flutes).

a steady bass and snare beat, Paul plays a basic blues progression on a synthesizer, using light, transparent, organ-like timbres. But the chord progression is just a backdrop here. Paul overlaid a voice-over (not really a vocal, in the musical sense) in a varispeeded, vaguely American accent, calling out the moves that a group of riders are about to undertake. The synthesizer texture expands, with low tones and whistles, and the percussion becomes a gallop as the riders begin their journey. When the riders jump a stream, Paul uses a rising and falling synthesizer glissando to follow the action.

For the ambitious 'Blue Sway,' Paul laid down a drum track and an attractive but frequently morphing chord progression on the synthesizer, using a hybrid wind and string timbre as the track's skeleton. He added bass, plenty of hand percussion—most notably maracas and cowbell—more synthesizer, using timbres that never imitated acoustic instruments, and bluesy guitar figures that play off the synthesizer lines. There are vocal lines as well, including some that sound like they could be Linda but were actually Paul, varispeeded into the soprano range. But the vocals are processed, recessed, and largely unintelligible; Paul uses them almost as another instrumental timbre.

"I felt like the nutty professor in his laboratory," Paul said, adding that as much as he was enjoying creating these pieces, there was a downside to the longer ones. "That's all very well when you're doing your first take. But then you've got to put a cowbell on it, and I would sit there in real time and put a cowbell on for ten minutes, occasionally glancing at my watch, and I've got five more to go: dink-dink, dinka din-dink. . . . Your thoughts come swimming in: 'Are you kidding me? Are you really gonna stand here and do this? Right! Now we'll do maracas!' Ch-ch-ch-ch, looking at the watch again."[24]

Recording Sessions

July–August 1979.

Lower Gate Farm, Sussex and Spirit of Ranachan Studio, Low Ranachan Farm, Campbeltown.

Recording and Overdubbing: 'Temporary Secretary,' 'Slow Down' (working title of 'On the Way,' 'Mr. H Atom,' 'The Bogey Wobble,' 'Bogey Music,' 'Wonderful Christmastime' and 'Darkroom.'

With the exception of 'All You Horse Riders,' the recordings Paul had made so far had an overly earnest quality—an occupational hazard of experimentalism. So his next track, 'Temporary Secretary,' was meant as a joke—or at least, the lyrics were: an employer calls the Alfred Marks Staff Bureau (an employment agency that advertised in the *London Evening Standard*) in search of a temporary secretary—"*Someone strong and sweet fitting on my knee.*"

"The story behind it was sex, I suppose," Paul said with a laugh, "but that's always the story."[25]

Musically, though, the track is as sophisticated as the overtly serious selections. Its basis is a brisk pattern Paul programmed into a sequencer and recorded on track 1. It is heard through the length of the track, although at its bridge—spoken lines, rising a step between each couplet (*"She can be a belly dancer / I don't need a true romancer / She can be a diplomat / But I don't need a girl like that"*)—it is faded slightly. Paul has admitted that the middle section was influenced by Ian Dury, and that he meant to tinker with it to make the influence less obvious but ended up leaving it as is.

With the sequencer providing the basic rhythm, Paul added drums—bass drum on track 2, snare on track 3, a second snare with kitchen echo on track 4 and tom-toms on track 13—and two synthesizer parts, on tracks 5 and 7. An acoustic guitar part and an Ovation guitar (acoustic with an electric output) on tracks 11 and 12 fill out the instrumental texture, except for a banjo on track 16 that Paul opted not to use.

The song's lead vocals were double-tracked on tracks 14 and 15, with chorus vocals on tracks 8, 9 and 10. In what was becoming a signature sound in the collection, he used varispeed on some of the vocals to make them sound not quite human.

At this point Paul appears nearly to have exhausted his desire to pursue pure experimentalism. As a palette cleanser, he recorded 'Slow Down,' a blues tune with few McCartneyesque melodic twists, using classic Beatles instrumentation: two electric guitars, on tracks 5 and 6, bass guitar on track 3, and drums split between tracks 1 (bass drum) and 2 (the top of the kit). The reverb-drenched vocal is on track 4, and there are several guitar solos; if Paul had brought this track to a Wings session in 1973, Henry McCullough would have been in his element.

The one puzzle is the song's title, which may have been more an annotation of the song's function within this batch of experiments than a real title: the words "slow down" do not appear in the lyric, and Paul soon changed the title to 'On the Way,' from the end of the refrain, "*So I hope you don't mind / The things I say / On the way.*"

Paul returned to his synthesizers and eccentric structures, but from here on, the compositions would meld experimentalism with more recognizable song forms.

Not that he was against a bit of whimsy when the opportunity presented itself. During a visit by Twiggy and her husband, Michael Witney, a discussion about the differences between men and women over dinner, and perhaps a spliff or two, brought everyone into Paul's studio to record 'Mr. H Atom,' a satirical rock track.

The track begins with Paul's announcement, in a Jamaican accent (with varispeed raising the pitch), "Shangri-Las versus the Village People"—a hint that the track would feature Linda and Twiggy doing a Shangri-Las impression while Paul played a Village People–style dance beat. To that steadily pounding drumbeat Paul added a tightly matching bass line, electric guitar flourishes, and a restrained synthesizer using a light organ timbre.

Set against this, Twiggy, Linda, Paul and Michael sing the song's single lyric, "*Mr. H Atom lives in a flat on the male side of town*" as a double-tracked, varispeeded chorus through the full track, interrupted by two short breaks. In the first, Paul, drenched in echo, presents the song's rationale: "*It has been suggested that the only difference between a male and a female / Is one atom of hydrogen.*" The second is a short instrumental section.

Paul's recent experiences fruitlessly writing songs for films did not sour him on further requests, and earlier in the summer Paul was asked to write music for a film adaptation of Raymond Briggs's 1977 quirky picture book *Fungus the Bogeyman.**

"The story is a bit bizarre," Paul said about what attracted him to the project. "The basic idea is that the bogey men are the people who make bumps in the night. They live beneath the ground and come out at night and frighten people, and they like everything that's opposite to what we like. If we like warm dry clothes, they like wet slimy ones. If we like pictures of live animals, they like pictures of dead sheep, and if we like music, they hate it. And they've got all sorts of crazy books in their library, like *Lady Chatterley's Bogey.* It's a great book, you know, but it's crazy and it just tickled my fancy when I got it."[26]

Paul's first piece earmarked for the prospective film was 'Bogey Wobble,' a three-minute instrumental that begins with a sequencer quickly repeating a single tone with an almost vocal timbre; it calls to mind a moment in *The Beatles Sixth Christmas Record*, sent to members of the Beatles Fan Club in 1968, where the opening sound of the word "once" is repeated similarly. The sequence fades and returns several times in 'Bogey Wobble,' sometimes in altered timbres, but at the start, it gives way to bashing on the echo snare, a few sepulchral bass tones and bright, expansive keyboard chord progression.

That pattern—sequencer, snare, chord progression—is repeated, although the chord progression is altered each time. Bursts of synthesizer sound (drips, slides, spacey timbres) and percussive rumbling are overlaid along the way, with the track ending on a sunny C major chord.

Paul's second Fungus piece, 'Bogey Music,' is quite different—a rocker in an updated 1950's style, with lyrics that play on the similarity between "bogey" and "boogie" and celebrate the rebellious joys of bogey music.

"I had that book in the studio one day," Paul explained, "and opened it to a page where the young people in Bogeyland rebel against the old people who hate music. They all start to get dressed in warm clean clothes—kind of Teds' outfits! Then they start to actually take baths, which

* Paul has never identified the director who approached him, but the film was never made, and subsequent adaptations—Stuart Orme's series for the BBC (2004) and Catherine Morshead's for Sky One (2015)—did not use Paul's music.

is unheard of, and get into rock and roll. So I just took that page, looked at it a bit and just thought: 'Well, it looks like a bit of rock and roll.' So, I made up the track and called it 'Bogey Music.' It's a crazy fantasy, really, but that's what I was thinking of when I did it."[27]

Work began with a simple rhythm box, set to produce a clapping sound on track 1 with real drums—snare, toms, and bass drum—on tracks 2, 3 and 6. Paul underscored the 1950's sound by playing a bass pattern typical of the time on track 10. To this he added two electric guitars on tracks 4 (rhythm) and 5 (quirky solos), Mellotron saxes on tracks 7 and 13, and a synthesizer on track 12.

Three vocal tracks completed the song: Paul's lead vocal on track 9, an echo vocal (a delayed repetition of track 9) on track 8, which gives the song an amusingly chaotic quality, and Paul singing sections of the song in a lower-pitched voice on track 11.

At this point it occurred to Paul that he should record, of all things, a Christmas song.

"It was a boiling hot day in July," he remembered. "And this boiling hot day was so ridiculous that, for some reason, I thought of Christmas. It'd be just ridiculous to write a Christmas song while it's this hot. So, I sat in the room and made up a Christmassy backing track and wrote the song all around it. And it was just ironic, sitting there going, 'Hee, hee, hee! This isn't Christmas, it's a boiling hot July day!' And that's how I did that one. . . . I immediately got out the sleigh bells and went 'ching-ching-ching' on them, and I worked it all up from there and just got things that suggested Christmassy sounds to me."[28]

It was a canny move, if not quite in keeping with the "I'm just experimenting" idea. In Britain, there had been a growing appetite for Christmas singles in recent years: Johnny Mathis scored his first No. 1 hit with 'When a Child Is Born' (1976); the unlikely duo of David Bowie and Bing Crosby reached No. 3 with 'Peace on Earth/Little Drummer Boy' (1977); and 'Mary's Boy Child—Oh My Lord' (1978) was a No. 1 single for Boney M. This was a club Paul wanted to join, so the summer heat notwithstanding, he set about crafting what he hoped would be a contender.

"To me, Christmas is mainly all the parties, and the good humor everyone gets into suddenly for those few days a year. So, the song's just basically about '*The mood is right, the spirit's up, we're here tonight, and that's enough.*' It's very simple."[29]

Paul used all 16 tracks to create the song, starting with bass drum and snare on tracks 1 and 3, and using the Yamaha CS-80 on track 7 to create the basis of a bouncy, festive backing. That track includes the ear-catching opening gesture—a series of bass tones and chords, each followed by ricocheting echoes—that establishes a pattern underlying much of the song. Synthesizer strings were added on tracks 4 and 5, with an echo track for the string synthesizers on track 16. With the addition of sleigh bells on track 2 and an electric guitar solo on track 15, the backing was complete, leaving Paul eight tracks (6 and 8 through 14) for his lead and backing vocals, including several in falsetto, heard particularly during the sections in which *"the choir of children sing their song."* The unedited song came in 4'15."

At some point—possibly in Scotland, but more likely in London in September—Paul had second thoughts about his drumming and asked Steve if he could improve upon it. "I remember trying to overdub the drums," Steve recalled, "but I couldn't really beat his drum track."[30]

Paul did, at some point, invite Steve to visit him at High Park. "He actually wanted some cymbals or something," Steve explained, "and I spent a night or two up there." Paul played him the tracks he was working on, which left Steve feeling uncertain about the future of Wings. "I just felt like it was over at that point."[31]

'Darkroom' was another hybrid, a fairly conventional song form mixed with some sonic zaniness. It is almost an update of the early Lennon-McCartney tune 'There's a Place,' with *"There's a place / Where I can go / When I feel low"* replaced by *"Got a place we can go / Lights are low."* But where the Beatles track was about solitary introspection, the new McCartney version is more social, even a bit salacious, its bridge being a seductive invitation: *"Come a come along with me to my darkroom,"* the lyric punning on a photographer's darkroom (although he has said he did not have Linda's darkroom in mind) and a dark room.

Paul set the lyric to a slight but catchy melody, but everything else about the track pushes it toward the experimentalism of the summer's earlier recordings—starting with the drums, which are heard at double speed, a choice Paul made for the sake of the altered timbre rather than the increased tempo. To get the effect, Paul played the drum part slowly, recording it at 15 i.p.s. (inches per second), the Studer's slowest speed. Playing the track back at 30 i.p.s. gave the drums the sound he was looking for—but it meant that the other instruments and vocals would have to be recorded at 30, making this the only song in the set recorded at that speed.

Alongside his double-speed drums on track 1, Paul recorded a snare on track 2, tom-toms (and a teacup) on track 7, and two tracks of maracas—one at double speed on track 4 and one at normal speed on track 5. He played a repeating bass pattern in a loping rhythm on track 6, and electric guitar improvisations on track 10. Synthesizers, however, provided the song's peculiar overall texture, and here Paul went for a varied palette: besides a synthesizer producing an organ-like sound on track 9, he used synthesizer strings on track 12, and what he called "atmosphere synth"—high-pitched, transparent tones that create an otherworldly texture, on track 13. (A fourth synthesizer part, on track 3, was marked "Don't use.") Playing off the "atmosphere synth," Paul added a freewheeling slide whistle line on track 8.

Paul recorded his vocals on tracks 11, 14, 15 and 16, sometimes double-tracking, sometimes with a falsetto counterpoint winding around the main vocals, and often with expostulations of various kinds, in both falsetto and full voice. Most of the vocal tracks—or sections of them—are varispeeded to sound faster and stranger.

Recording Sessions

July–August 1979.

Lower Gate Farm, Sussex and Spirit of Ranachan Studio, Low Ranachan Farm, Campbeltown.

Recording and Overdubbing: 'One of These Days (Breathe Fresh Air),' 'Secret Friend,' 'Hi George—Morning Terry,' 'I Need Love' (working title of 'Waterfalls'), 'Nobody Knows,' 'Coming Up,' 'Steve' and 'Let There Be Pillows.'

'One of These Days' is almost an antidote to the tracks like 'Dark Room' and 'Mr. H Atom'—a graceful, uncomplicated three-and-a-half-minute ballad in G major with a McCartneyesque melody and a lyric about striving for simplicity. As with 'Summer's Day Song,' though, it is the product of simply being open to the influences of the moment.

"'One of These Days' all happened when a Hare Krishna bloke came round to see me," Paul explained. "He was a nice fellow, very sort of gentle. After he left, I went to the studio and the vibe carried through a bit—I started writing something a bit more gentle that particular day. The song seemed right as a very simple thing, and it basically just says: 'One of these days I'll do what I've been meaning to do the rest of my life.' I think it's something a lot of people can identify with."[32]

The recording is built of just acoustic guitar and vocals, with nary a drum or a synthesizer to be heard. That said, he uses a *lot* of his guitar and voice: the main acoustic guitar is on track 1, with a doubling on track 3, another guitar part on track 9, and echo of the track 9 guitar on track 10. Paul's lead vocal is on track 2, with a doubling on track 4 and harmony vocals on tracks 6 and 7. Track 5 is devoted to echo for the vocal parts.

As straightforward as 'One of These Days' is, in 'Secret Friend' Paul bolts back toward experimentation, with a synthesizer and percussion extravaganza that runs just over 10'30" and seems almost a sequel to 'Temporary Secretary'—this one seemingly an invitation to a clandestine affair: *"Here we are where are we / Cast adrift on some uncharted sea / I know we'll find our way / If you will say you'll be my secret friend."* The lyrics are set to a free-ranging melody that moves slowly against a tumultuous instrumental backdrop and an almost static harmonic background that slides between F and F-sharp (the backing is too busy to settle on major or minor), sometimes by way of varispeed manipulation.

A sequencer on track 5 immediately establishes a sci-fi "computer-gone-mad" feeling, which Paul made even stranger by fiddling with the varispeed, sometimes mid-sequence. A second sequencer, on track 7, adds an alternative sequence, but apart from the brisk, repeating sequencer figure and the heavily echo-laden vocal (doubled on tracks 15 and 16), an especially ear-catching element of the song is its dense, multi-layered percussion. Here, Paul counters the synthetic sound of the sequencer by bringing in his drum kit—bass drum on track 1, snare on track 3, toms on track 6, floor tom on track 8 and high hat on track 9—as well as additional noisemakers, including claves (which he notes on his track sheet as "little knockers!") on track 2, maracas on track 4, and cowbell sharing the high-hat track. Some of the percussion takes advantage of the echoic kitchen at Lower Gate Farm.

The sequencers and percussion create a thick, busy texture, but Paul did not leave it at that; he added bass and rhythm guitar on tracks 13 and 14, a Mellotron sax on track 10, and synthesizer strings on track 12.

In 'Secret Friend,' Paul came close to his ideal for these recordings. "I wanted something that sounded nothing like me," he explained, "but inevitably, you start to creep through even that, your sense of tune or whatever it is."[33]

By his own account, Paul was becoming bored with the *creatio ex nihilo* aspect of the project. And since he was making the rules, he could break them, including the one that precluded working on existing songs. In recent days, an item from his stack of unfinished tunes had been nagging at him—a 1975 song, provisionally called 'I Need Love.'

Rather than a verse and bridge structure, 'I Need Love' is an alternation of two distinct verse forms, with distinct melodies. The first, in A major, is simple and plaintive. The second, in E minor (with a sudden shift to E major at the end) is more wide ranging and cathartic. The title was taken from the second verse—*"And I need love, yeah I need love / Like a second needs an hour / Like a raindrop needs a shower"*—but Paul soon changed the title to 'Waterfalls,' drawing instead on the opening verse, written as advice to his daughters about playing near the waterfall on his Peasmarsh property: *"Don't go jumping waterfalls / Please keep to the lake / People who jump waterfalls / Sometimes can make mistakes."*

This was going to be a comparatively soft-edged song—no drums, no sharp-edged sequencer figures, not even electric guitar or bass. Paul began the recording with an electric piano part on track 1 and added a second electric piano on track 2. Six tracks of synthesizer—string lines on tracks 6, 7, 10, 11 and 12, and a "melody synth" that mirrors the vocal line on track 5—fill out the instrumental texture, but for one detail: an acoustic guitar solo was added to a verse without lyrics. Paul finished the song with two vocal tracks, deployed flexibly: sometimes his voice is heard solo, sometimes double-tracked, and sometimes closely harmonized.

Paul has described 'Nobody Knows' as "craziness,"[34] and it has its freewheeling aspects, both musically and lyrically. But at heart it is a rockabilly blues track with a heavy beat and an edge of wackiness. Among the highlights of the lyric: *"Samson and Delilah would have made a crazy pair / If that silly woman hadn't shaven off his hair."*

The song was inspired by a documentary, *The Devil's Music*, Alexis Korner's four-episode BBC series about the blues.* Having already recorded a straightforward blues track during the sessions ('On the Way') what Paul decided to explore this time was an anomaly he had noticed among bluesmen.

"One of the funny things for me," Paul explained, "is that in blues you'll get what is supposed to be a 12-bar blues, then you get odd timings coming in. For instance, sometimes they just hold over on one chord—like one bar longer than you should or than most people would do. On many blues records they're never very exact so, on this track, I do the same thing. That was the basic inspiration behind it."[35]

Paul did not switch on the synthesizers for this one, relying instead on the basic rock band configuration. Setting down the drums first—bass drum on track 5, snare on track 6, high hat on track 4, with a composite drum track mixed to track 7, and some foot stomping later added for good measure on track 2—he added rhythm guitar on track 1 and bass guitar on track 9. Two more electric guitar parts were needed, one to play the lead solos, on track 10, and another on track 8 to execute the rhythmic "chord stabs" heard at various points. Echo for the guitar parts was sent to track 3. Paul recorded three vocal performances on tracks 11, 12 and 15 (the last shared with handclapping), and devoted track 14 to vocal echo.

'Coming Up' was another track inspired by something Paul heard and decided to try his hand at, although he was vague about the exact source of his inspiration. "I believe I heard something on the radio by Sly Stone or Sister Sledge," he said. "The song I heard might even have been [Sister Sledge's] 'We Are Family.' But I went into the [studio] with that vibe and began to make something up around my own groove."[36]

That groove was a repeating, funky guitar figure—a single, four-beat vamp built on an E-flat major chord, each repetition ending with a pivot in which a passing C and then a dissonant D-flat are added. This hypnotic figure lies beneath the verses—*"You want a love / to last forever / one that will never / fade away"*—as well as most of the instrumental sections, and is abandoned only at the choruses—*"Coming up / Coming up, yeah / Coming up / like a flower / Coming up."* As simple as the chorus lyric is, McCartney illustrates it in the music: the chorus, though melodically minimal, is sung over an inexorably rising chord progression—A-flat major 7, B-flat minor 7, C minor 7, D-flat major, E-flat major, F-sharp diminished, then back down to E-flat major.

Building that edifice began with a rhythm box on track 1, used as a click track to which Paul set the drum line, bass drum on track 2, snare on track 3. The rhythm guitar figure is on track 4 and doubled on track 5. He added three synthesizer tracks—a piano timbre on track 6, fluty sounds on track 12, and a variety of sounds sharing track 14 with tambourine. Mellotron saxophones, on

* The first part of Korner's American blues chronicle—which featured the musicians Booker White, Houston Stackhouse, Sonny Blake and Sam Chatman—played on BBC One on July 9, 1979.

which Paul used varispeed to make them sound "like tight little munchkins,"[37] were recorded on tracks 15 and 16. And Paul's consistently inventive bass line is on track 11.

Paul used varispeed when he recorded the vocals, creating the impression that it included both men's and women's voices, although all the voices are Paul's. Four tracks (7 through 10) were devoted to the vocals, three of them with handclaps as well.

Little is known about the two songs on Reel 5, 'Steve' (possibly an experiment recorded during Steve's visit to High Park) and 'Let There Be Pillows,' or about 'Twelve of the Clock,' a 16-track recording listed as having been recorded at Abbey Road on September 18, but which may actually date from these sessions as well. (Paul had recorded two demos of 'Twelve of the Clock' since 1976.)

"Originally, I was just going to go in and do two weeks of kicking around, and just do the craziest stuff I could think of just for my own fun," Paul said of his solo project. "Hence things like Christmas songs in July! Anyway, I ended up doing about twenty tracks, but that set of recordings was all very off-the-cuff. I'd do a drum track, and I'd stick a bit of bass on it, and then try and think of a song to go with it. So, that was all very different from how I normally do it, but probably next time I'd do it differently again so as not to just repeat myself."[38]

Back in London, in September, Paul played a few of the tracks for Chris Thomas. He had, by then, determined to release his new recordings as a solo project rather than as a Wings set, and given the amount of material he had, he was thinking in terms of a double LP.

"He played me about three backing tracks that were going to go on to this double album," Thomas recalled, "and he was singing the lyrics over them. These backing tracks were amazing, because they're all basically done in the bloody kitchen, like bashing things. And he sang these incredible [improvised vocals]—because there were no lyrics—he was just making up the lyrics to these backing tracks. And that was just the best stuff I'd ever heard in my life. I wish we'd actually recorded that, you know, just him doing that."[39]

While Paul was in Scotland, Wings—both under its own name and as Suzy and the Red Stripes—had singles released on either side of the Atlantic. The belated British release of Linda's 'Seaside Woman' was issued by A&M on August 10. It did not chart, and was barely noticed by critics, although Kelly Pike in *Record Mirror* used it as a cudgel to batter Paul with, noting that "it's certainly better than her old man's 'Mull of Kintyre.'"[40]

On the same day, Columbia released 'Arrow Through Me,' coupled with 'Old Siam, Sir' in America. *Billboard* praised it as a "light and bouncy midtempo tune,"[41] but in its ten-week stay on the *Billboard* Hot 100 it barely dented the Top 30, entering at No. 83 on August 25 and peaking at No. 29 on October 13.

EMI, disappointed with the sales of 'Old Siam, Sir,' wondered whether Columbia was right to release 'Getting Closer' (EMI matrix 7YCE 21811) instead. Coupling the song with 'Baby's Request' (EMI matrix 7YCE 21812), the label released it as the second British single from *Back to the Egg* on August 17. Some reviewers covered 'Getting Closer,' some covered 'Baby's Request,' and *NME* just lashed out in general.

> *A self-consciously forties, smoochy lullaby. I think Linda's singing in the background, which might explain things. Still, I love Paul's warm voice and there's a vaguely bluesy feel to the song.*[42]
>
> *Simon Tebbutt,* Record Mirror

> *If 'Closer' had been given to Cliff Richard and produced by Bruce Welch, it could easily have been a minor-league nugget. To compensate for Paul's sloppy vocals and those hideous harmonies by Linda and Denny (won't they ever learn?) there's an unexpected sizzling fade. 'Baby's Request' is another of those doe-eyed McCartney pastiches, a nightclub soft-shoe shuffle with staggeringly inane lyrics.*[43]
>
> *Ian Birch,* Melody Maker

> *Y'know humility is a wonderful thing. Only the other day I was bowling along the Hertfordshire lanes in my Rolls when I spotted a rustic chappie whistling to himself and chewing on a sweet blade of fresh mown hay, not a care in the world. Hey ho, just as I was musing on the vagaries of wealth vis a vis true happiness, I chanced to catch the ancient's refrain. Blow me down, if it wasn't the coda to Macca's latest waxing. Naturally enough, I ignored the fellow's request for paper money and fetched him a swift clout across the temple. I think we can all benefit from that simple lesson.*[44]
>
> *Max Bell,* NME

The single bombed, entering the Top 100 at No. 70 on September 1 and peaking at No. 60 on September 15, managing only three weeks in the Top 100. EMI did not make use of the 'Getting Closer' promo film Wings made in June at the Eagle Parachute Club, but Columbia did: when Paul was invited to appear on Jerry Lewis's annual Labor Day telethon for the Muscular Dystrophy Association on September 3, the label persuaded him to send a copy of the video, which was given its first airing. Coincidentally, Ringo Starr appeared on the show as well, answering telephones and taking mailing addresses from callers making pledges.

Buddy Holly Week rolled around again, and this year, Paul brought Maria Elena Holly, Buddy's widow, as well as his backing band, the Crickets, to London for the festivities. Paul had been spending an average of £50,000 ($105,300) a year celebrating Buddy, but as MPL's accountants could attest, Paul's efforts to keep Buddy's music in the public eye, two decades after the singer's death, were paying off handsomely. Paul performed with the Crickets at Hammersmith Odeon on September 14—as did Denny, Laurence and Steve. Other musical guests included the Moody Blues, Boomtown Rats, Squeeze and Jack Bruce, all of whom donned 1950's attire for the occasion.

"His popularity is growing," Maria Elena said of her late husband, "and I'm so thrilled that Paul McCartney is keeping Buddy's music alive."[45] As well she might have been: making the case to *Billboard* that MPL was a benign redistributor of publishing income, Lee Eastman noted that "Buddy Holly's widow was making $2,000 a year when we acquired the catalog, four years ago, and now it's up to $200,000."[46]

September also brought Sid Bernstein's virtually annual bid to bring the Beatles together for concerts. Finally realizing that even the most extravagant financial offers could not sway the group, Bernstein wondered whether the Beatles, like their cartoon representations in *Yellow Submarine*, might be persuaded to play together if it meant saving the world. In a full-page advertisement in the *New York Times*, Bernstein implored the Beatles to "appear on one stage, individually, collectively or both" in Cairo, Jerusalem and New York, to demonstrate that mankind can overcome any obstacles, and to raise more than $500 million (£225.7 million) for Southeast Asian "Boat People"—refugees from Laos, Vietnam and Cambodia.

Bernstein's plea soon morphed into a story, carried by the *Washington Post*, in which the Los Angeles–based filmmaker Dirk Summers, together with Kurt Waldheim, the secretary general of the United Nations, had persuaded George Harrison to reconvene the Beatles. Picked up by newspapers around the world, the story continued to blossom: soon it was reported that the Beatles had agreed to play a series of shows at the 4,000-seat Grand Opera Theatre in Geneva, Switzerland, to benefit Southeast Asian refugees.

Denials, including one from MPL's New York office, were quickly issued. But the hoax nearly gained some traction.

"A lot of people got letters from some fella who was supposed to represent Kurt Waldheim," McCartney said to *Rolling Stone*. "He wrote on Mayfair Hotel stationery saying that he was staying at the hotel and that Waldheim had asked if we would do something for charity. I took it to mean a Wings thing and said okay. I talked to George [Harrison], who had been asked by the same fellow.

He said, 'If I get something together, will you do it?' I said yes. But we just left it there and it got a bit lukewarm."[47]

There were signs that the Beatles could work together, if only as plaintiffs in lawsuits. Having agreed in May to let Apple's lawyers loose on Capitol and EMI, they now adopted Paul's obsession with the *Beatlemania* stage show. Apple sued the producers to stop the show, which had done well on Broadway and was due to open in London on October 11. Apple's position, summed up by the company's Los Angeles–based lawyer, Bert Fields, was that "[The Beatles'] appeal is unique and distinctive, and they generated enormous good will which others are now trying to exploit."

Steve Leber, the impresario behind the show, was taken aback by the suit. "I'm amazed," Leber said. "They haven't sent us back any of the hundreds of thousands of dollars that we have paid in royalties for the Beatles songs that we use in the show."[48]

Just over a month later, in mid-November, Apple sued to stop Dick Clark Productions and the American Broadcasting Company (ABC TV) from producing *Birth of the Beatles*, a biopic for which Pete Best, the Beatles' drummer from August 1960 to August 1962, was a technical advisor. The TV film had gone into production in Liverpool on June 11, with a budget of £1.25 million ($2.64 million); Apple argued that the Beatles would be damaged both by actors playing them and by any potential spinoff recordings, and sought $40 million (£19 million) in exemplary damages.[49]

At the United Nations, meanwhile, Secretary General Waldheim wondered whether the idea of getting the former Fabs involved raising money to address humanitarian catastrophes—as George had done on behalf of Bangladeshi refugees in 1971—was really such a crazy stretch. Once the rumor disappeared from news columns, Waldheim wrote to McCartney, who was in the process of sketching out—but had not yet announced—a tour with Wings.

"A letter came from Kurt Waldheim," Paul reported, "saying, 'I have never authorized anyone to ask on my behalf if you'd do anything. There seems to be someone going around, but it is a hoax. Seeing as you're now involved, would you do something?' We sent back a telegram saying yes, we'd do a show." [50]

Paul referred the matter to Harvey Goldsmith, the promoter assembling the Wings tour. And he convened Wings to discuss the setlist and to rehearse, although the kind of focused rehearsals that were necessary would not begin until late October.

"There was definitely a question of whether or not we should use the horn section or something different, that was put to the table," Steve remembers. "And my feeling was, I actually loved having the horn section behind me. My father was a sax player, for God's sake, and I couldn't imagine it without it, so I was all for that.

"And then there were a few ideas that came up about playing in the round, and I couldn't understand the concept of having to turn and look behind me to see somebody else in the group. I didn't see how that was gonna work."[51]

At the moment, though, Paul's head was still in his new set of 16-track solo recordings.

Recording Sessions

Tuesday, September 25–Thursday, September 27, 1979.
Studio Three, Abbey Road Studios, London.
Mixing: 'Front Parlour,' 'Frozen Jap (Full length),' 'Summer's Day Song' (Without Vocals), 'You Know I'll Get You Baby,' 'All You Horse Riders,' 'Blue Sway,' 'Temporary Secretary,' 'On the Way,' 'Mr. H Atom,' 'Link,' and 'Bogey Wobble.'

Paul booked several days at Abbey Road to mix his new recordings, with Eddie Klein engineering. The plan was to make rough mixes, to be revisited later. But the mixes Paul marked as keepers proved to be the final mixes of these tracks. 'Front Parlour,' 'You Know I'll Get You Baby' and 'All You Horse Riders' were mixed, and marked as keepers, on September 25; the day's mixes of 'Frozen Jap,' 'Blue Sway' and an instrumental version of 'Summer's Day Song' were set aside for reconsideration. Paul and Eddie also completed final mixes of 'Temporary Secretary,' 'On the Way,' 'Mr. H Atom,' 'Bogey Wobble' and a section of an unidentified recording that Paul thought might make a useful link track.

While Paul was mixing at Abbey Road on September 27, less than two miles to the south, the Metropolitan Police were searching the Maida Vale flat of Jimmy McCulloch, trying to piece together why the 26-year-old guitarist had been found dead that morning. McCulloch had last been seen on September 24, and things had been looking up for him: less than a week earlier, his newly formed band the Dukes had released their eponymous debut album on Warner, and they were about to play at Dingwalls, in London, on September 28. When Jimmy failed to turn up for rehearsals on September 25 and 26, his brother Jack went to his flat, gaining entry by climbing through the bathroom window. He found Jimmy sitting motionless on the floor.

The circumstances were strange: the police found no money or alcohol in the flat, and no signs of drug addiction. The flat itself was tidy—there was no sign of a struggle—but although the door had been bolted, the security chain was broken, and there was sawdust on the floor near his door.

After an autopsy, the cause of death was given as morphine poisoning, but the coroner ruled, a few weeks later, that given the circumstances, the true cause of McCulloch's death would never be known. An open verdict was recorded.[52]

"He was a great guitar player," Paul told reporters. "I am very, very sad."[53] Paul and Linda sent flowers and a tribute to be read at Jimmy's funeral at the City of London Crematorium on October 4.

"He was from a hard-drinking, poor Glasgow family," Paul later reflected on his former bandmate's life of excess, "where to be a man you just had to drink hard. To Jimmy, you just had to be out of it. And preferably with a lot of whisky so that you were absolutely incapable and then you couldn't play the solo, but you felt great. Or something like that. I felt very sorry for Jim in that respect, really. I saw his folks once, his uncle and dad showed up. And it was a binge. It wasn't just meeting his uncle and dad—it was, 'Get the bottle out!' I guess he just grew up in that kind of thing. It isn't easy for some people to cope with that."[54]

Recording Sessions

Thursday, October 4–Tuesday, October 16, 1979.
Studio Three, Abbey Road Studios, London.
Recording: 'Pipes for Mellotron,' 'Tape Loop for Drones,' and 'Bagpipes for Mellotron No. 1–27.'
Mixing: 'Raining in My Heart,' 'It's So Easy,' 'Bo Diddley,' 'Wonderful Christmastime (Full Version),' 'Darkroom,' 'One of These Days,' 'Secret Friend,' 'Bogey Music,' 'Check My Machine,' 'I Need Love' (working title of 'Waterfalls'), 'Nobody Knows,' 'Coming Up,' 'Front Parlour (Rye Mix),' 'Frozen Jap (Rye Mix),' 'Frozen Jap,' 'Summer's Day Song' and 'British Johnnies (Edit Piece),'
Editing: 'Wonderful Christmastime.'

Paul and Eddie returned to Abbey Road to continue mixing Paul's experimental recordings but took part of the October 4 session to make stereo mixes of Wings' performances from the September 14 Buddy Holly Week concert at the Hammersmith Odeon. The show had been videotaped, and there was talk of using some of the Wings segment—which included Paul singing 'It's So Easy' and 'Bo Diddley,' and Denny duetting with Don Everly on 'Raining in My Heart'—in a documentary.*

* The documentary, *The Music Lives On*, was not seen until September 8, 1984, when it was aired in the United States on MTV. All three songs were included.

Once the Buddy Holly material was sorted, Paul shifted his focus back to the summer recordings, mixing the full-length version of 'Wonderful Christmastime,' as well as 'Darkroom,' 'One of These Days,' 'Secret Friend' and 'Bogey Music.' They returned on October 11 to mix 'Check My Machine,' 'I Need Love (Waterfalls),' 'Nobody Knows' and 'Coming Up,' although only 'I Need Love' and 'Nobody Knows' were marked as masters.

On October 14 Paul edited the full 4'18" version of 'Wonderful Christmastime' to 3'49" for release as a single. The next day, he met with Judd Lander, a multi-instrumentalist Paul had engaged to record loops for Linda's Mellotron, to be used on Wings' upcoming tour. Lander recorded "Pipes," "Drones" and "Bagpipes," and Paul arranged for Lander to return in November to record other sounds and spruce up some of the existing Mellotron loops.

Paul and Eddie returned to Paul's solo project on October 16, revisiting mixes of 'Front Parlour' and 'Frozen Jap' that Paul had made at Lower Gate Farm, deciding that the 'Front Parlour' mix from September 25 was superior and making a new mix of 'Frozen Jap' that was marked as the master. Another edit piece, called 'British Johnnies,' was mixed but set aside, and master mixes of 'Summer's Day Song' and 'Check My Machine' were completed.

With the mixing complete, McCartney and Klein assembled four reels of masters:

Master Reel 1: 'Front Parlour' / 'Frozen Jap' / 'All You Horse Riders' / 'Blue Sway'
Master Reel 2: 'Temporary Secretary' / 'On My Way' / 'Mr. H Atom' / 'Summer's Day Song' / 'You Know I'll Get You Baby' / 'Bogey Wobble'
Master Reel 3: 'Darkroom' / 'One of These Days' / 'Secret Friend' / 'Bogey Music'
Master Reel 4: 'Check My Machine' / 'I Need Love' / 'Nobody Knows' / 'Coming Up'

Acetates of each reel were cut, and Paul distributed them to friends and family. He had decided to release this material as a double album, but he sent the acetates under the guise of soliciting opinions about the music and what to do with it. For the most part, he got the answer he was looking for: "*You've got to release this!*" In some cases, he knew the recipients well enough to know what they would say, and so circumscribed their responses.

"He phoned me up and said, 'Oh, I finished that record,'" Chris Thomas recalled. "And he said, 'I'm gonna send it over to you, have a listen and tell me what you think.' And he said, 'And don't bother to tell me it should be a single [rather than a double] album.' So I listened to it. And of course, it wasn't a double album at all. He's already told me I can't tell him otherwise, so obviously, this is what everybody had told him. So I was actually able to turn that around slightly because I had spotted something. I said, '"Coming Up" is a smash hit. You've got to release it.'"[55]

Recording Sessions

Thursday, October 18, 1979.
Studio Three, Abbey Road Studios, London.
Mixing: 'Emotional Moments (aka. Cage),' 'He Didn't Mean It,' 'Cage,' 'Waterspout,' 'Lunch Box—Odd Sox,' 'Rock and Roll Rodeo' (with Mike McGear), 'Jazz Street,' 'Hey Diddle,' 'Oriental Nightfish,' 'Same Time Next Year,' 'Did We Meet Somewhere Before,' 'Going to New Orleans' (Working title for 'My Carnival'), 'Suicide,' 'Wide Prairie,' 'Twelve of the Clock,' 'Best Friend (Live),' 'Mama's Little Girl,' 'I Would Only Smile,' 'Tragedy,' 'Night Out,' 'When the Wind Is Blowing,' 'Sunshine Sometime,' 'Great Cock and Seagull Race,' 'A Love For You' and 'So Glad to See You Here.'

Decisions about marketing the new material could wait, however. Rehearsing for the upcoming tour was more pressing—but not so pressing as to keep Paul from beginning to sort out *another* prospective album—one that had been on his mind for the last five years: *Cold Cuts*, the collection of outtakes he first mentioned to Capitol Records executives in 1974. Capitol had looked askance when he proposed issuing the disc at a budget price; perhaps Columbia would see the album as quick, near-cost-free compensation for the poor sales of Wings' most recent album and singles.

With that prospect in mind, Paul and Eddie devoted a day to sorting out the likely candidates and mixing them. Much of the material was left over from *Ram* and *Red Rose Speedway*, and had been the basis of *Cold Cuts* from the start. But the outtake list had grown since then, with songs written for films, leftovers from more recent albums, *Rupert* tracks and even some demos.

Paul and Eddie assembled three reels of stereo masters for consideration (titles with asterisks were marked as master stereo mixes):

Reel 1: 'Emotional Moments (aka Cage)'* / 'He Didn't Mean It' / 'Cage' / 'Waterspout'* / 'Lunch Box—Odd Sox' / 'Rock and Roll Rodeo' / 'Jazz Street'*
Reel 2: 'Hey Diddle' / 'Oriental Nightfish'* / 'Same Time Next Year'* / 'Did We Meet Somewhere Before'* / 'Going to New Orleans' / 'Suicide'* / 'Hey Diddle'* / 'Wide Prairie' / 'Twelve of the Clock'
Reel 3: 'Best Friend (Live)'* / 'Mama's Little Girl'* / 'I Would Only Smile' / 'Tragedy' / 'Night Out,'* / 'When the Wind Is Blowing'* / 'Sunshine Sometime'* / 'Great Cock and Seagull Race' / 'A Love for You'*

Paul took home cassettes of these sequences, and after living with them for a week, he and Eddie returned on October 24 to assemble *Cold Cuts Sampler 1,* adding the recent outtake 'Robber's Ball' in the process. The running order of this version of the album is unavailable, but was likely:

SIDE ONE

'Night Out'
'A Love for You'
'Mama's Little Girl'
'Hey Diddle'
'Best Friend (Live)'
'Tragedy'

SIDE TWO

'Cage'
'Waterspout'
'Same Time Next Year'
'My Carnival'
'Did We Meet Somewhere Before?'
'Robber's Ball'

Having sorted two new albums long before they were needed, Paul turned his attention to his next single. 'Wonderful Christmastime' was the obvious choice, given the proximity of Christmas and his deep-seated desire, going back to the Beatle days, to hold the top spot on the charts on Christmas Day. But he could not dismiss Chris Thomas's enthusiasm for 'Coming Up,' and Thomas was not alone in being knocked out by the track.

So on October 18, he assembled a master reel with 'Wonderful Christmastime (Edited Version)' and 'Coming Up.' Paul also made a new mix of 'So Glad to See You Here,' apparently with the idea of making it the B side of whichever song was chosen to be the single. Soon he had a better idea: when EMI agreed that 'Wonderful Christmastime' was the obvious choice, Paul exhumed from the archives his May 1975 reggae-tinged recording of the Johnny Marks Christmas classic, 'Rudolph the Red-Nosed Reindeer,' which he had renamed 'Rudolph the Red-Nosed Reggae.' On October 29, 'Wonderful Christmastime' (EMI matrix R6029A-1U) and 'Rudolph the Red-Nosed Reggae' (EMI matrix R6029B-1U) were mastered at Abbey Road.

But at a time when Pink Floyd's 'Another Brick in the Wall (Part 2)' and Abba's 'I Have a Dream' dominated the airwaves, 'Wonderful Christmastime,' even with its festive spirit, was not guaranteed a clear run at the top spot.

26

IN A CAGE

When Wings toured Britain, Europe, Australia and North America between 1972 and 1976, Paul made a point of setting aside hefty rehearsal periods and working until the arrangements were tight and the performances were polished. But in October 1979, with a British tour set to begin at the end of November, Wings had barely rehearsed. And the British tour was just the start of what promised to be an extended touring period, with a visit to Japan planned for January pending the approval of the band's visas—still a matter of concern, given the Japanese government's refusal to allow Wings into the country in 1975 because of Paul's earlier pot busts.

Now, barely a month before their British tour was set to open, Wings did not even have a setlist.

Paul had been able to suppress his feeling of discontent with Wings—not its current incarnation, particularly, but the idea of fronting a permanent band—while he was working on his solo project, and through all the activity in the weeks that followed. The question now was whether he could rekindle his love for the concept.

The fact is, leading a band had been more of a slog than he bargained for, and the natural chemistry he had with the Beatles—developed as they grew from adolescent amateurs into stage-tested adults—had been impossible to replicate with a group of experienced players. He had been so desperate to have a band, after the Beatles broke up, that he approached it naively, believing it could be a band of equals.

It took the departure of Henry McCullough and Denny Seiwell—the implosion of Wings Mark I—for him to realize that this was implausible. As the only marketable star in the band, it would never be equal, and more crucially, equality was not something he was suited for: he always had a clear idea of what he wanted to do and how he wanted to do it, and he was unwilling to brook any opposition.

When Jimmy McCulloch, Geoff Britton and then Joe English joined the band, they were

Paul receives an honor from the *Guinness Book of Records*, October 18, 1979

younger and the power relationships were clearer. But in Wings Mark II, Paul found himself having to sort out his young charges' personal problems, and while he was generally there for them, the combined role of musician and guidance counselor grew tiresome. Laurence Juber and Steve Holley were excellent players and entirely professional, but *Back to the Egg* had not won critical accolades, and there were some in Paul's circle who thought Juber and Holley lacked their predecessors' rock and roll rawness.

Now, eight years of running a band was beginning to wear on Paul. And his experience recording on his own over the summer left him longing for the freedom to just pop into the studio and get to work—no teaching parts to other players, no dealing with other musicians' egos or opinions.

"I didn't know how to make a group," Paul later confessed. "I assumed I must have known because I'd been in the Beatles. But I didn't make the Beatles, it made itself, it was a chemical affair. It wasn't like that with Wings."[1]

Steve had thought Paul was disengaging from Wings when he visited him in Scotland during the summer, and that feeling never quite left him. "My gut instinct would be that he had probably already had enough of it, to be honest. I don't know whether it was a conscious thing."[2]

There were now, in effect, two Pauls—Paul McCartney, the front man of Wings, and Paul McCartney, the solo artist who had just completed a double album's worth of new material and was about to release a single on his own. At the moment, it was time to focus on the former, to pull together a setlist and get the band ready to tour.

Once Paul switched into band mode, he threw himself into it fully: his work ethic was as powerful as ever, and he was not about to go onstage giving anything less than his best. You could almost *see* the shift: when he finished mixing his summer recordings at Abbey Road, he spent a day (October 21) assembling five reels of tape marked "Compilation for Rehearsals," with master copies of tracks he wanted the band to work up for the tour (although as the final setlist shows, they were not limited to these):

Reel 1: 'Let 'Em In' / 'My Love' / 'Mull of Kintyre' / 'Time to Hide' / 'Cook of the House' / 'Silly Love Songs'
Reel 2: 'Goodnight Tonight' / 'Magneto and Titanium Man' / 'Go Now' / 'Listen to What the Man Said' / 'Say You Don't Mind' / 'With a Little Luck' / 'The Fool on the Hill'
Reel 3: 'Maybe I'm Amazed' / 'Every Night' / 'Let It Be' / 'No Words' / 'Band on the Run' / 'Getting Closer' / 'Spin It On'
Reel 4: 'Again and Again' / 'Arrow Through Me' / 'Smile Away' / 'Wonderful Christmastime' / 'Yesterday' / 'Got to Get You into My Life' / 'Coming Up'
Reel 5: 'I Need Love (Waterfalls)' / 'I've Had Enough' / 'Love Awake'

Four days later on October 25, Paul was back in London to be honored by the *Guinness Book of Records* as "the most successful composer of all time," the rationale being that 43 of his songs had sold more than a million copies, and 60 of his Beatles and Wings recordings had attained Gold Record status. The *Guinness Book*'s twenty-sixth edition also listed him as the world's most successful recording artist, having sold 100 million albums and 100 million singles. On the theory that Paul already had plenty of Gold and Platinum discs, Guinness had a Rhodium Record made for the ceremony at Les Ambassadeur's Club in Mayfair.

The "most successful composer" label was immediately questioned by writers and critics who pointed out that Beethoven, Mozart and Strauss, for starters, had not done badly in their day or since, but Norris McWhirter, the *Guinness Book*'s editor, fended those off, saying, "This is to do only with recorded music, and it is purely a quantitive question rather than one of quality. The work of Beethoven and Strauss was non-copyright, so their sales have never been audited."[3]

Another observer who took umbrage at the hoopla surrounding the award was George Harrison, who telephoned Paul to give him a piece of his mind.

"I know certain things got up his nose," Paul related, "and I remember I had one vile phone call where we just bitched at each other, and he just laid into me. And I said, 'eh, eh, eh—stop this' I said, 'I'm not having it, George, I'm just not up for this. . . . You sound like a fuckin' critic, and I've had enough of that.' So we had a very hairy telephone conversation where he was telling me what was wrong with what I was doing, trying to get into the *Guinness Book of Records*. I said, 'I didn't try—they put me in!' You don't ask to get in there, they ring you up and say, 'We're putting you in.' I think he gained the wrong impression from a lot of press."[4]

With Paul's reference tapes on hand for consultation, rehearsals began in earnest, mostly at the Royal Hippodrome Theatre in Eastbourne, a 516-seat hall built in 1883, not far from the McCartneys' home in Peasmarsh. Some rehearsals were also held at Lower Gate Farm, although Paul's music space there proved tight for a five-piece band. Nevertheless, a video showing Wings rehearsing 'Eleanor Rigby,' 'Got to Get You into My Life,' 'With a Little Luck' and 'Coming Up' was shot there, to be sent to Japan as an informal promo.

Rehearsals at the Royal Hippodrome were not without complications. "They'd left the back door open, and they'd moved guitar amplifiers off of the stage and onto backstage," Laurence remembered. "People were complaining about the noise." But the problems were quickly sorted, and with some trial and error, a setlist was hammered together.

The set was, in effect, a concise musical biography of Paul. With the exception of 'Go Now,' Denny's Moody Blues–era showpiece, the only cover was Eddie Cochran's 'Twenty Flight Rock,' the song Paul played at the Woolton Church Fete on July 6, 1957, the day he met John Lennon, and which led to John inviting Paul to join the Quarrymen.

When Paul included a few Beatles songs on his setlist for Wings' 1975–76 world tour, it was a major concession after years of resistance. Now he would be opening his concerts with 'Got to Get You into My Life.' Three more songs—'The Fool on the Hill,' 'Let It Be' and 'Yesterday'—would turn up later in the set.

'Every Night,' 'Hot as Sun' and 'Maybe I'm Amazed,' all from *McCartney*, represented Paul's post-Beatles/pre-Wings career (although 'Hot as Sun,' written in 1959, was also a glimpse of Paul's pre-Beatles work). Not a single hit from Wings Mark I was included; in fact, the setlist contained only five pre-*Back to the Egg* songs—'Band on the Run' (which closed the set), 'I've Had Enough' 'Mull of Kintyre,' 'Cook of the House' (Linda's first solo vocal spot on a Wings' show), and 'No Words,' one of Denny's three vocal turns (with 'Go Now' and 'Again and Again and Again').

More than a third of the set was recent work, with five songs from *Back to the Egg* ('Getting Closer,' 'Again and Again and Again,' 'Old Siam, Sir,' 'Spin It On' and 'Arrow Through Me'), the non-LP single 'Goodnight Tonight,' and two of Paul's new solo tracks, 'Coming Up' and 'Wonderful Christmastime,' which would be released as Paul's—not Wings'—new single before the tour began.

As in the 1975–76 tour, there were a few short teases: Denny's 'Go Now' was often preceded by the opening line of 'Tiptoe Through the Tulips,' and Paul sometimes brought out snippets of 'Baby Face' or other vaudeville hits. But overall, this was a more restrained production than the previous tour, without dry ice fog, bubbles or film backdrops—just some polystyrene snowflakes for 'Wonderful Christmastime.'

During the rehearsals, the band also decided on the gear they would be taking. Paul would be playing a new Yamaha BB1200 bass, as well as the Rickenbacker he played on the world tour, with a Fender Bassman 135 amplifier (with three cabinets), as well as his Epiphone Casino electric guitar and a Vox AC-30 amp, and two acoustic guitars—his Martin D28 and an Ovation, tuned a step low for 'Yesterday.'

Denny would play an early-1950's vintage Gibson Les Paul Standard, the Ibanez 2670 double-neck guitar he used in 1975–76, an Ovation Ademas acoustic guitar and Mexican mariachi guitar. He also brought a Fender Precision Bass, a pedal board (with a phase shifter, wah-wah and envelope follower) and a Charlie amplifier.

Laurence's gear included a 1960 Gibson Les Paul Standard and a new acquisition, a Gibson SG, along with two MESA/Boogie amplifiers and Marshall speaker cabinets, a custom-built pedal board and a Roland rack that included a synthesizer and vocoder (for 'Goodnight Tonight').

The keyboard arsenal, which would be used mostly by Linda, but also by Paul and Denny, included a Bösendorfer concert grand, a Fender Rhodes electric piano, a Hammond B3 organ, a

WONDERFUL CHRISTMASTIME

WORDS AND MUSIC BY McCARTNEY

WONDERFUL CHRISTMASTIME

PAUL McCARTNEY

WINGS

Paul McCartney, 'Wonderful Christmastime' single trade ad

clavinet, a Mellotron (with a refurbished collection of instrument and sound effects loops), and five synthesizers—her time-honored Minimoog, an ARP Pro Soloist, a Yamaha CS-80, a Prophet-5, and a Roland Jupiter string synthesizer.[5]

Steve Holly brought a brand-new black Tama kit with single-headed concert toms, a 14-inch-by-6.5-inch Tama snare, both 20-inch and 24-inch bass drums (he mostly used the 20-inch), and a selection of vintage and new Paiste and Zildjian cymbals. He also brought a pair of electronic Syndrums, for use in 'Coming Up.'[6]

Behind the scenes in London, Harvey Goldsmith had the dual task of putting together the Wings tour and helping Paul fulfill his promise to Kurt Waldheim to do something to alleviate the plight of Southeast Asian refugees. Goldsmith had already been discussing with other managers the idea of a series of concerts to celebrate the end of the 1970s; the Waldheim-McCartney request, as well as a flood of news reports about the refugees, gave him a more altruistic theme.

The Wings tour, which would be announced on November 7 (with tickets going on sale on November 10), was set to open at the Royal Court Theatre, Liverpool, on November 25 and 26, followed by concerts at the Manchester Apollo (November 28, 29); the Gaumont Theatre, Southampton (December 1); Brighton Centre (December 2); six shows in London (at the Lewisham Odeon on December 3, the Rainbow Theatre on December 5 and the Empire Pool, Wembley, on December 7, 8, 9 and 10); Birmingham Odeon (December 12); Newcastle City Hall (December 14); Edinburgh Odeon (December 15); and the Apollo, Glasgow (December 16 and 17).

As soon as the tour was announced, fans in Liverpool began camping outside the Royal Court Theatre, and it quickly became clear that two shows at the 1,200-seat theater would not meet the demand. So on November 9, another show was added, moving the tour's start date back to November 24.

Even that—and a two tickets per customer limit—proved inadequate. Paul was reluctant to add another show but agreed to a last-minute full-dress rehearsal in the form of a 5 P.M. show at the Royal Court Theatre on November 23, for which free tickets would be given to students at Paul's old school, the Liverpool Institute High School for Boys, as well as the Liverpool Institute High School for Girls, and a local school for disabled children.

"It's my way of saying 'thank you' for some very happy years," Paul told the *Daily Express*. "Everyone seems to knock their school days, but for me they have great memories."[7]

Goldsmith topped off the Wings tour with four nights of Concerts for Kampuchea, to benefit the UNICEF-Kampuchean Refugee Fund, which helped feed children fleeing from Pol Pot's despotic regime in Cambodia. The shows would not be announced until early December, but the bill Goldsmith assembled included performances by Queen on December 26, followed by Ian Dury and the Blockheads, the reggae band Matumbi, and the Clash on December 27; the Pretenders, the Specials, and the Who on December 28; and Elvis Costello and the Attractions, Rockpile and Wings—plus a reconvened Rockestra for the grand finale—on December 29. All four shows would be filmed and recorded by EMI.

—

'Wonderful Christmastime' was released on November 16, and though only Paul is heard on the recording, all of Wings—plus a crowd of extras—gathered at the Fountain Inn in Ashurst, West Sussex, to shoot a promotional video, directed by Russell Mulcahy. The video builds on the song's message of bright holiday spirit, showing the crowd at the Fountain Inn mixing cheerfully at the bar, or around a bonfire outside, with Paul and Wings alternately miming a performance of the song and making merry. Footage from the Royal Hippodrome rehearsals was woven in as well.

For the critics, the single was a slow-moving target.

I'm not surprised that this is a solo single—the other members of Wings were undoubtedly too proud to associate themselves with such a sloppy, poorly-executed song. 'Rudolph the Red-Nosed Reggae' on the flip is even worse.[8]

Chris Bohn, Melody Maker

Paul McCartney dons his Santa Claus drag, pulls out his pocket calculator and knocks off a grotesquely twee piece of festive nose-scrapings utilizing a tune of his own creation so twee and repellently banal that it makes 'Mull of Kintyre' sound like John Coltrane's 'Naima' by comparison. God knows McCartney has hit some musical troughs in his time but this hideous offering shuts down even 'Mary Had a Little Lamb' as our Macca's worst recording to date.[9]

Nick Kent, NME

The Great Christmas Crap Pumping Machine warms up this week, as Paulie leaps smugly aboard his rocket powered sleigh, sack in greasy mit. He's in the enviable situation of not having to try anymore and this is a tarnished tinsel song sounding as if it was composed in two minutes after a heavy Sunday lunch. Paulie's in little boy lost, granny stunning form, and there's lot of lines about choirs of children singing. It's awful. Not just awful, it's AWFUL.[10]

Robin Smith, Record Mirror

At Columbia Records, eyes squinted angrily in the direction of Walter Yetnikoff as the single failed to appear on *Billboard's* Hot 100 and charted poorly elsewhere—peaking at No. 94 in *Record World*, on December 29, and at No. 83 in *Cash Box*, on January 12, 1980. The single fared better in Britain, entering the singles chart at No. 61 on December 1 and remaining on the chart for eight weeks. But the Christmas number-one that Paul craved eluded him: the single peaked at No. 6 on January 5.

As the tour neared, there were two more details to be arranged. Wings' 1975–76 brass section—Steve Howard, Howie Casey, Thaddeus Richard and Tony Dorsey—agreed to return. They would be perched on a platform behind and above Steve's drums, between banks of speakers. Besides playing 'Got to Get You Into My Life,' 'No Words,' 'The Fool on the Hill,' 'Let It Be,' 'Hot as Sun,' 'Arrow Through Me,' 'Go Now,' 'Coming Up' and 'Band on the Run,' the quartet would open each concert with a short Renaissance fanfare and would undertake utility chores like shaking bells during 'Wonderful Christmastime.'

"He brought us in at the last minute," Tony Dorsey recalls. "I got a call from Alan Crowder, and he said, 'We need you to come on over for a couple of weeks, and after that we're going to Tokyo.' So I said, 'Okay, count me in!' But we didn't do a whole lot of rehearsing for that tour."[11]

Paul also wanted an opening act. Steve suggested Earl Okin, a singer-songwriter he had met recently. It was a peculiar choice: Okin had made some recordings for Parlophone—including a 1967 single, 'Yellow Petals' and 'I Can't Face the Animals'—when he was still a student. He went on to become a teacher and was now working as deputy headmaster at a school in London. But he also performed in folk clubs and toured with the likes of Ralph McTell and Fairport Convention.

"Steve saw me at the Cambridge Folk Festival, handling a big crowd of 25,000 people without any worries," Okin explained, "so later that year, when they were trying to find someone to open for Wings that would be different from the usual young rock band and wouldn't require the whole stage to be reset, he recommended me, and apparently Paul said, 'Well, it's the first time anybody's been enthusiastic about anybody, let's try him.' I got a call from Steve—it would have been a Tuesday, and he said, 'We're going on tour on Friday—this Friday—would you like to be on the tour with us?' So I resigned my post as assistant headmaster immediately, and the next evening I turned up at MPL" to discuss contracts.[12]

Goldsmith also hired Richard Ames, a British freelance tour manager who had recently overseen a Kate Bush tour and was managing an American tour with Sniff 'n' the Tears when Goldsmith lured him back to Britain to run the Wings tour. And he engaged TFA-Electrosound Ltd. to do the sound and lighting.

“From a UK touring setup point of view,” Ames explained, “it was all fairly simple and straightforward. This would have been pre-sleeper-bus touring, which meant that all the crew stayed in hotels every night. It wasn’t a 100 percent adrenaline full-on sort of touring operation. It was gentleman’s touring, so to speak.”[13]

As on the previous British tours, Wings traveled to the gigs by bus, arriving at each city in time to check into their hotels and make it to a 4 P.M. soundcheck the day of the show.

“The soundchecks were a laugh,” Earl Okin recalls, “because Paul just wanted to play ’50s rock and roll. And most of the time I think he played drums. We all found an instrument to play—I usually played piano because that’s my main instrument. I don’t think anybody sang, they just sort of played rock and roll.”[14]

The band arrived in Liverpool late in the day on November 20 for a few final days of rehearsal before the warm-up show. The McCartneys had a depressing stay at Rembrandt: the house had been broken into and largely cleaned out: a piano, two televisions, a stereo system, beds, carpets, and dining room and lounge furniture had been taken, the loss valued at £25,000 ($52,200); the police had arrested and charged a suspect.[15]

Howie Casey remembers Paul being nervous before the first show. “We were going down to the stage at the Royal Court Theatre,” the saxophonist said, “and Paul was at the door leading to the stage, looking out. And he turned to me and said, ‘I don’t know—I’m just wondering how it’s going to go down.’ He was nervous. I said, ‘*Come on*, Paul.’”[16] A moment later, he was singing ‘Got to Get You Into My Life’ before what one reporter described as a “sea of school uniforms and school scarves,” to chants of “We love Paul” and “We want Wings!”[17]

The warm-up show proved a good test of the setlist, which reflected Paul’s longstanding concern with a show’s ebb and flow, as well as his desire to surprise his audiences, particularly those who had seen Wings’ shows on past tours. ‘Got to Get You Into My Life’ was the perfect opener, in that sense: no one expected him to open with a Beatles tune, and the Beatles had never performed the song live. ‘Getting Closer,’ the mostly acoustic ‘Every Night,’ ‘Again and Again and Again,’ and another rocker, ‘I’ve Had Enough,’ followed before Paul had a vocal break, ceding the spotlight first to Denny for ‘No Words,’ then to Linda for ‘Cook of the House.’ It was back to rocking for ‘Old Siam, Sir,’ the live version’s opening octave leaps sounding like a sped-up version of Jimi Hendrix’s ‘Purple Haze.’

A piano set followed, with ‘Maybe I’m Amazed,’ ‘The Fool on the Hill’ and ‘Let It Be,’ after which Paul picked up his Epiphone Casino to play ‘Hot as Sun,’ as out-of-the-blue a selection as he could have found. Another pair of rockers, ‘Spin It On’ and ‘Twenty Flight Rock,’ preceded Denny’s turn at the piano for ‘Go Now’ and a block of recent work—‘Arrow Through Me,’ ‘Wonderful Christmastime,’ the not yet released ‘Coming Up,’ and ‘Goodnight Tonight’—ended the main part of the show, leaving ‘Yesterday,’ ‘Mull of Kintyre’ (for which a bagpiper was on hand to stand on the horn section’s platform and provide the song’s signature sound, with support from the bagpipe loops on Linda's Mellotron) and 'Band on the Run' (with space in the arrangement for an audience sing-along) as encores.

Before the show, Paul met with Bertram L. Parker, who had been his geography teacher when he was a student at the Institute and was now headmaster. Paul dedicated 'Mull of Kintyre' to "Blip," as Parker was known to the students, both in Paul's day and now.

Because the Friday afternoon concert was for students only, the Saturday evening show was treated as the tour opener, and it was followed by a post-concert press conference and a private party. As McCartney's first British concert in three years, it drew most of the music papers and several dailies from around the country.

For Steve Holley, the magic of performing with McCartney in Liverpool was impossible to resist. "I would think, 'How does this compare to what it must have been like to walk on stage with the Beatles?' I mean, that's really what you come back to all the time. You can't help it. I defy anybody that ever worked with Paul not to consider that."[18]

But the show proved a challenge for Earl Okin.

"They tried to boo me off the stage," Okin admitted. "It wasn't the whole audience, it was a small group of five to ten people sitting right in front of the sound desk, and they were shouting 'fuck off!' as the curtain came up, before I'd even done anything. I remember Paul saying to me, 'You've got some bottle—I'd have been off after ten minutes!'"

Okin's manager was convinced that the rowdy group was planted, either by another manager who wanted Okin replaced with their own clients, or even by MPL as a test to see how Okin handled a tough crowd. "The next night, it was the same venue," Okin added, "and it was lovely—I had to sign autographs."[19]

Peter Trollope of the *Liverpool Echo* quickly zeroed in on the newest Wings, reporting that "drummer Steve Holly and guitarist Laurence Juber give the group a better balanced sound than I've heard before. Holly is a steady drummer. There's nothing flash in his technique, but he adds the subtle touches. Laurence Juber is a revelation. He has never been in a group but sits like a hand in a glove with Wings. His playing is crisp and clear, and he provides some strong solos throughout." Trollope had kind words for Linda, too, noting that she "is now an integral part of the group, her keyboard work providing the foundation for the others to build on."[20]

Writers for the national music papers, however, were less committed to the "hometown hero returns" angle, and more invested, generally, in making Paul pay for 'Mull of Kintyre' and 'Wonderful Christmastime.'

McCartney, Mick Middles wrote in *Sounds*, "saw the giant rock 'n' roll lie and decided to prove to the world that he is but a nice little bloke who writes catchy pop tunes for quiet people." Wings, he added, is "a band who churn out endless chunks of bland plastic with about as much feeling, as much sincerity as a television quizmaster." He conceded that 'Maybe I'm

Amazed,' 'Let It Be' and 'Yesterday' "verged on the magnificent," but found the rest clinical and devoid of feeling.

"I could go on," he concluded, "but I'm sure you have no desire to read about the chantalong version of the dreaded 'Mull of Kintyre' or, even worse, the atmospheric falling of snowflakes during the embarrassing dirge entitled 'Wonderful Christmastime,' or the fact that they didn't play anything from the passable *Venus and Mars*. A mild evening of featherweight entertainment for deaf devotees."[21]

Penny Kiley, in *Melody Maker*, drew liberally from the run-on sentence school of scene painting to describe the show. "So there's Paul McCartney," she wrote, "singing his new Christmas single, there's fake snow falling from the roof, and Laurence Juber, the guitarist, is standing in the middle of the stage, covered in the stuff and wearing a half-witted grin, the brass section are playing bells, and suddenly rows of fairy lights are revealed forming the shapes of Christmas trees, and no one else could have got away with it."

She seemed momentarily willing to give in to the McCartney charm, writing that after the opening Beatles tune "the audience go politely mad and even your cynical reporter can't believe she's so near to the man her sister wanted to marry when she was eight years old." But lest a reader suspect that she was taken in, she reports that the band "closed with 'Band on the Run' and reminded me of when I used to like Wings."[22]

The most nuanced and thoughtfully reasoned take was Paul Du Noyer's review in a publication that had only recently been Paul's nemesis, *NME*.

"Only one stone's throw away from the '80s and we're still asking a man to walk in the shadow of what he was, or was imagined to be, in what's nearly the decade before last," Du Noyer wrote. "For ten years McCartney's seen his new work held up to an artificial light, viewed and valued, low or high, on every kind of terms except its own. . . . Between blinkered criticism and blind-eyed worship there's an underpopulated territory without much in the way of signposts. No wonder McCartney, the most response-conscious of artists, zig-zags so erratically, displays inconsistency and consumed identity. As much as he's drawn towards the open arms, he's still distracted by those turned backs."

Du Noyer tackled his own expectations head-on. Writing that at first the show "just didn't sound like megastar super-stadium stuff somehow," he quickly realized that it was not supposed to, and began wishing that Wings would play *only* small venues, "where McCartney can feed off the immediacy of the crowd and match every home-town heckler's wisecrack quip for quip."

"Wings aren't about complacency," he argued, "or about taking anything for granted or milking the easy applause. Instead they project as a solid, grass-roots English band of the old school, playing for fun—who just happen to be blessed with one of the better voices and a lot of the better songs which money could buy. . . . It might be impossible to like everything Wings do, and maybe at somewhere like Wembley I'd have liked it a lot less. But tonight was warm and informal—no BIG deal, just a little bit of magic."[23]

After the concert, Wings repaired to the Royal Court Theater's lounge for a press conference, attended by only half a dozen journalists. Paul appeared relaxed and in good humor, and began with a question of his own. "Tell me, Steve," he asked Holley, "what's it like being with a superstar like Denny?"[24] Steve and Laurence were introduced, and Paul was asked whether they would be contributing songs to the next album, giving Paul a chance to push the notion of Wings as a democracy, but keeping it light.

"Depends what they come up with, really," Paul replied. "Anyone with anything good is on, and hopefully, as much as they like. If they come up with the whole album . . . I won't let them do it!" About Wings recording methods, he said, "We just kind of book a studio and normally, like, I've got a few songs, Denny's got a couple and we just run through 'em all and see which ones we feel like playing that day." Linda added, "I've got this one in my pocket, Paul," to which he responded, "And Linda's got a few which I always reject."

Wings' appearance at the Royal Court Theatre raised the matter of performing in small venues, an idea Paul had been pushing for some time. Explaining that he chose the Royal Court because it was in danger of closing and he wanted to add his support—"'cos I used to come here as a kid and watch the plays"—he also noted that as much as he liked the intimacy of small theaters, there were downsides.

"It's like a double-edged sword because the trouble is you get letters from people saying, 'I queued all night and still didn't get a ticket,' so that makes it tempting to play a bigger place. But I must say, I do enjoy this kind of theater because you can actually feel the audience, and get a good sound, too. . . . But these tours don't make money unless you play somewhere like Wembley and it's silly to go out and do a job and not get paid for it."[25]

The remaining shows in Liverpool were less problem-free. Taxi drivers called a three-hour strike on Saturday to protest police harassment. "They blockaded the streets of Liverpool," Richard Ames remembers. "But they made an exception for Paul, and let him in and out."[26] And the final night, November 26, fans rushed the stage at the end of the concert, trampling several people in the front rows, but causing no grievous injuries.

Wings had November 27 off, but Paul took the band on a publicity-garnering trip down memory lane by way of a ferry across the Mersey. The ferry was the *Royal Iris*. "I played here on this very boat with the Beatles," he told the *Liverpool Echo*, referring to a floating gig the group played on July 6, 1962. "We only played here the once; I don't think we were invited back."[27]

That night, the band appeared on the BBC1's *Nationwide* program, in a piece about the tour with clips from the Eastbourne rehearsals and one of the Liverpool shows.

The tour wound its way through Manchester, Southampton and Brighton before the first of

Wings over Liverpool, November 27, 1979

Paul and Linda in Liverpool, November 27, 1979

the London concerts at the Lewisham Odeon, and everything was running smoothly—except that Paul and the band were increasingly annoyed by a low-level but audible buzz that began to plague the band's sound after the Liverpool shows. At soundcheck after soundcheck, technicians from Electrosound tried to get to the root of it, with no luck. But the buzz grew particularly acute in Brighton.

"The sound people were blaming the lights," Richard Ames related, "and the lighting people were saying that the lights don't buzz. 'Okay, but they might well *create* buzzes.' So there was this terrible circle of finger-pointing, without anyone coming to a conclusion. So the only option we had, which I organized, was a separate generator stuck outside each venue to isolate the PA."[28]

The generator helped, but no one was able to explain why, since when the problem was finally traced, the culprit turned out to be Laurence's custom-built pedal board. John Hammel, Wings' guitar technician, had vouched for it, and his expertise was such that no one wanted to challenge him.

But there were repercussions. Before the final Wembley show, on December 10, four Electrosound technicians replaced parts of the rig, and while they were able to eliminate the buzz on stage left by adding grounding connectors to Linda's Minimoog and ARP, the buzz on stage right, remained. The next morning, Electrosound's T. Marshall Bissett sent a memo to Harvey Goldsmith detailing their testing and hinting that the problem must come from the guitar equipment, including "two [MESA] Boogie amplifiers, well-known for their sensitivity to interference," or with Wings' equipment "some of which has been made for this tour." Bissett added that Electrosound "cannot accept the cost of the generator after Wembley, since that would be to concede that we were exclusively at fault in producing the buzz."[29]

"McCartney was amazingly calm about the whole thing," Ames recalls. "I never saw the man shout at anyone. He put up with it. But at the end of the UK tour, MPL told Harvey, 'We don't want to use [Electrosound] anymore.'"

By then, Electrosound had sent an identical sound and lighting rig to Japan by ship for the tour that was scheduled for January. It was too late to cancel it, but Paul had Ames get in touch with Robin Magruder at Showco, the company that had overseen the technical side of the 1975–76 world tour. Showco quickly assembled a new rig and had it flown to Tokyo. MPL had to foot the sizable shipping bill for both sound systems.

To some who attended Wings' Wembley concerts in 1976, this year's show seemed strangely tame. "Three years ago," Pauline McCloud observed in her *Daily Mirror* review of the December 7 show, "you almost had to stand on your seat to catch a glimpse of them. On Friday, the 8,000-strong audience sat politely in their seats erupting into total enthusiasm only at the end of the gig before the group allowed themselves to be drawn back on stage for the obligatory encore.

"Paul McCartney still maintains the same boyish charm. He manages to sing 'Fool on the Hill' and 'Let It Be' with the raw warmth that makes the hairs stand up on your neck. But does he really have to resort to fake snow and a Father Christmas descending from the cavernous heights of Wembley to grab some applause?"[30]

The press outside London was often more supportive. In Birmingham, for example, Jonathan Daumler-Ford of the *Birmingham Post* offered a concise assessment of the new lineup, which he found to be at its strongest in songs that featured "Juber and Denny Laine combining effectively on guitars for driving rock numbers that belie McCartney's silly love-song image." About the front man, he wrote, "I cannot think of another entertainer quite so comfortable on stage as McCartney. He was the genial host throughout and his casual repartee and personable manner put the finishing touches to a professional performance."[31]

In Newcastle, Barbara Day rhapsodized about McCartney's "boyish good looks and unfailing melodies" and reported that "the enthusiastic throng lapped up his every joke and gesture." She thought Linda's vocal on 'Cook of the House' was flat, but declared that "this was a classy show and proved McCartney is still at the top of the pop music tree, almost two decades after the Beatles began."[32]

As Okin remembered it, the Newcastle crowd's enthusiasm extended beyond Wings' front man—his observations helping to explain Denny's insistence on getting back on the road.

"There was an attractive blonde waitress," said Okin, "and Denny took a fancy to her. He spent the whole evening chatting her up and then disappeared with her. The next morning there was no Denny. Paul, I remember, was on the bus with his son sitting on his arm, and the conversation went, 'Where's Denny?' And the tour manager said, 'We don't know.' And Paul said, 'Well, has he scored?' And he went, 'Well, yeah.' Paul said, 'Oh well, that's fine, he'll come along when he comes along.'"

The bus left without Denny, leaving Okin to drive the guitarist to Scotland.

"Denny was just a wreck when he arrived. The place was snowbound—that was a very bad winter—and if you'd have laid Denny down in the snow, I'm not sure you would have been able to see where he was because his face was white. Anyway, he slept his way up to Edinburgh in the back of the car."[33]

The experience of playing before an audience helped tighten the band's sound in a way that was noticeable to the musicians. "From my perspective," Laurence recalled, "especially as we went further north, things got better and better."[34] Paul apparently agreed, and he hired the RAK Mobile to record the final four shows in Newcastle, Edinburgh and Glasgow.

Like Liverpool's Royal Court Theatre, the Apollo in Glasgow appealed to Paul's preservationist instincts. In April 1978, he read that George Green Ltd., which owned the Apollo, was preparing to sell the theater to the Mecca Organization, which planned to turn it into a bingo hall. Paul and the rest of Wings signed a petition to keep the Apollo as a music venue and privately committed to perform there.

"Glasgow is noted for the enthusiasm of its pop music audiences," Andrew Collier wrote in the *Glasgow Herald* after the December 16 show. "But the Wings concert produced an audience so frantically excited that it made other rock shows in the city seem positively sedate." Collier himself was less impressed. "This hugely popular band's performance was very clinical and average indeed," he wrote. "This was clearly a concert for the devoted faithful rather than casual observers."[35]

Paul had a surprise in store for the closing night audience, on December 17. Instead of a lone bagpiper standing on the horn riser for 'Mull of Kintyre,' Paul invited 14 members of the Campbeltown Pipe Band to join Wings for the multimillion-selling hit. He changed the staging, as well.

"That second night in Glasgow," Laurence reminisced, "the Campbeltown Pipe Band marched through the audience during 'Mull of Kintyre.' It was an amazing moment."[36]

For the concerts in Scotland, Wings and the entire production crew stayed at Dalhousie Castle, which was built between the thirteenth and fifteenth centuries and had been converted into a luxury hotel. The British musicians on the tour were taken with the castle's opulence. "The walls were about six feet thick," Earl Okin remembered, "and everyone's room was a different shape, with a four-poster bed."

For Tony Dorsey, though, it had all the qualities of a cinematic haunted castle. "It scared me to death, man," Tony said. "I'm standing in one of these rooms, and it's like an old horror movie. The wind is blowing, and the shadows are going *bump-bump-bump*. I couldn't sleep."[37]

Tony made the mistake of letting some of the others in on his impression of the place, and late on the final night, some of the entourage decided to play a prank at his expense.

"Tony Dorsey was very superstitious," Earl Okin said, "and my manager [John Jones] and Paul's bodyguard [Billy Francis] were naughty people. So in the middle of the storm, Paul's bodyguard, who was a very strong man, lowered my manager out the window by his feet. So now he's hanging outside in the middle of the storm, and below us was the window of Tony's room. So, my manager starts howling and rattling chains, and Tony got dressed and left."[38]

Dorsey never knew who was behind the prank—or even that it was a prank.

"I could imagine all kinds of ghosts and things going 'round in there," he said. "I got up at 5 o'clock that morning, got me a cab to the airport."[39]

With the tour ended and Christmas looming, Paul and Linda invited the band and some of the support staff to a Christmas lunch at Lympne Castle on December 20. It would have been a vegetarian meal, because after nearly eight years of flirting with the notion, Paul and Linda both had finally committed to giving up meat.

"All of us are vegetarians now," Linda proclaimed in a *Daily Express* interview published on the final day of the tour. "We don't eat meat or fish. Not only does that mean we don't eat cute little animals, but to my mind it's much healthier. I never thought the children would take to it and I certainly didn't force it on them, but they all enjoy my home cooking. I make vegetable stews, vegetarian sausages, thick pea soup: we're not macro-biotic and sparse, we eat well."[40]

Linda emphasized the family's vegetarian status in an interview on Capital Radio as well, telling Maggie Norden that the family would spend Christmas in London, and the family's holiday dinner would be veggie, although she had not yet settled on the menu. "It will be good whatever it is," she said. "But we'll let the turkeys live this Christmas in our house."[41]

There were also changes afoot at MPL. By the end of December, Brian Brolly's successor had been chosen, and the news was picked up in the press. The new managing director would be Stephen Shrimpton, formerly managing director of EMI Australia.

In the days leading up to the Kampuchea shows, Paul assembled a new Rockestra, inviting as many of the original players as could make it (Hank Marvin and David Gilmour were unavailable this time) and adding several others, including musicians from several of the bands on the Kampuchea bill, including guitarist James Honeyman-Scott from the Pretenders and Rockpile's two guitarists, Dave Edmunds and Bill Bremner. Robert Plant took part as well, joining his Led Zeppelin colleagues John Bonham and John Paul Jones, who played on the original session (leaving only Jimmy Page unaccounted for).

Otherwise, the band included Wings and its horn section, Tony Ashton and Gary Brooker on keyboards, Pete Townshend on guitar, Bruce Thomas and Ronnie Lane on bass, and Tony Carr, Morris Pert and Speedy Acquaye on drums and percussion.

One band in the Kampuchea lineup not represented in Rockestra was the Clash, and the lack of interest in a Clash-Wings collaboration may have been mutual; the band's latest single, 'London Calling,' included the line "phony Beatlemania has bitten the dust."

But in fact, phony Beatlemania was alive and well: on December 28, the day before the Wings/Rockestra performance, the *Daily Mirror* quoted an unidentified spokesman for Paul as saying that "George and Ringo have been asked to go tomorrow, and they said they will. We don't know about John. We haven't had a definite answer."[42]

Without John, it would have been closer to a reunion of Eric Clapton's wedding jam than a true Beatles get-together, but talk of even a partial Beatles reunion led Paul to counter his spokesman's claim.

"In the end," he said in a backstage interview with Shelli Sonstein of WPLJ-FM in New York, "there was so much talk about it all I just decided not to ask them anyway, just not to embarrass them. I think it's good enough this way. The main thing about any Beatles reunion is that, over the ten years that we've been split as a group, the four of us have never—when we've talked together, which we've done off and on—none of us has ever said, 'Hey, let's reunite.' It would need to be something much more positive even than that, and we haven't even had that. Everyone's attitude is, 'Well, that was it, it was the Beatles, it was great, we enjoyed it, but let sleeping dogs lie.'"[43]

Chris Thomas was enlisted to record the four evenings, and he brought in both the RAK mobile and Island mobile units, giving himself 48 tracks to work with. "Of course they [RAK and Island] were rivals," Thomas noted, "but I actually got them to do it in sync, so every single microphone went to a separate track. The whole idea was that every band could then take their performance and mix it to their satisfaction. But what happened was, I mixed the people I had worked with—Paul, and the Pretenders—and they had Bill Price at AIR Studios mix all the other people."[44]

The performances were filmed under the direction of Keith McMillan.

Wings played the set they had performed around Britain, minus 'Wonderful Christmastime,' and with 'Let It Be' moved to the Rockestra segment. After Wings finished with 'Band on the Run,' the curtain closed and the Scottish comedian Billy Connolly came out to say, "We've got a wee surprise for you here," and to introduce Rockestra by reading the list of participants (except for Plant, who joined the ensemble at the last minute and vanished after the first number).

Dressed in sparkling silver coats, with some players wearing matching top hats, the mammoth ensemble launched into a raucous performance of one of Paul's Little Richard favorites, 'Lucille,' followed by 'Let It Be.'

"Thank you, Peter," Paul said to Townshend before cueing the start of the 'Rockestra Theme.' He then turned to the audience and said, "Only lousy sod who wouldn't wear the silver suit. 'Cos he's a poof." Laurence walked up and crowned Townshend with a silver top hat, which Townshend wore for a few seconds before flinging it into the audience.

"Kampuchea was awkward," was how Steve Holley remembered the evening. "It was long. We were there from sort of nine o'clock in the morning, couldn't leave the building 'cos of security, and there weren't enough dressing rooms for everybody. So, a lot of the time it was just hanging in the stairwells and talking to people, and you couldn't really catch a break. So, that was long and arduous and wasn't a tremendous experience, really."[45]

Laurence agreed. "We didn't have quite the same energy as we had in Glasgow," he said. "The Kampuchea concert was a very long concert, and you'd already had full sets from Elvis Costello and Rockpile before Wings even got on stage. But of course, that's the one that was videoed."[46]

Soon after the dust settled on the Concerts for Kampuchea, Costello asked Paul to produce his next record. Paul said that he was flattered, but citing his already heavy workload, he had to decline.

Paul gave the band a brief New Year's break, but in early January, Wings were back in East Sussex to rehearse for their Japanese tour. Harvey Goldsmith had arranged the tour with Seijiro Udo, the founder of Udo Artists, Inc., one of Japan's oldest and most important promoters. Goldsmith had dispatched Ames to Tokyo immediately after Christmas to oversee last-minute details, including the arrival of the Electrosound and Showco sound and lighting rigs.

The tour would begin and end at the Nippon Budokan Hall in Tokyo, where the Beatles' performances in the summer of 1966 sparked protests by traditionalists who considered it sacrilege to hold rock concerts in the martial arts hall. Paul was scheduled to open the tour there on January 21, with concerts the next three days. Concerts at Aichi-Kien in Nagoya would follow on January 25 and 26, then on to Festival Hall in Osaka on January 28, with three final Budokan shows, January 31 through February 2.

The Tokyo Broadcasting Company and Yomiuri Shimbun, a newspaper group, signed on as sponsors, and soon after the itinerary was announced, 100,000 tickets—$1.8 million (£810,000) worth—were sold.

With the band reassembled in East Sussex, Paul tinkered with the setlist, adding and deleting songs and reconsidering the running order. 'Got to Get You Into My Life' remained the opener, but 'Jet' replaced 'Getting Closer,' which was dropped. Both 'Again and Again and Again' and 'Every Night' were retained, but their order was switched, and 'Every Night' was followed by 'Another Day,' a favorite in Japan. 'I've Had Enough,' 'No Words,' 'Cook of the House' and 'Old Siam, Sir' followed, and 'Spin It On' and 'Twenty Flight Rock' were moved up the setlist to follow them.

This was where Paul moved to the piano during the British tour, and he considered extending the piano set with 'The Long and Winding Road' and 'Lady Madonna,' both of which were rehearsed. But he opted instead to preface 'Maybe I'm Amazed,' 'The Fool on the Hill' and 'Let It Be' with 'Let 'Em In.' After 'Let It Be,' Paul turned over the piano to Denny for 'Go Now,' followed by another new addition, 'Silly Love Songs.' 'Wonderful Christmastime' was jettisoned, and the concert proper would end with 'Coming Up,' 'Goodnight Tonight' and another crowd-pleasing addition, 'Live and Let Die,' complete with lasers and pyro. For the encores, he replaced 'Mull of Kintyre' with 'Blackbird,' followed by 'Yesterday,' 'Band on the Run,' and a newly added closing rocker, 'Hi, Hi, Hi.'

"We were really primed to go to Japan," Lawrence said. "But we didn't rehearse for that long, because we were doing basically the same set, with a few new tunes."[47]

Before the McCartneys left London, there was business to be seen to, including a meeting with Tony Dorsey. As the leader of the horn section, Tony had been elected by the others to make the case to Paul for a higher pay. For the American and British tours, the horns were paid a weekly salary of £400 ($707 in 1976; $890 in 1979); for the US tour, they also received a $10,000 bonus (£5,600 in 1976).

"We knew other horn sections that toured with bands, and they were getting a lot more than we were,"[48] Howie Casey complained. Tony's meeting was a success: he got the band per-concert fees of $1,000 (£450) for the Japanese tour.

Tony raised a second issue, as well. The horns had a vague idea how well *Wings Over America* had sold and were feeling aggrieved at not receiving performance royalties. Tony proposed a 1 percent royalty, to be split between the four players. Paul demurred but agreed to pay the horns another $10,000 (£4,500), along with a friendly observation: "You're lucky to be working with me."[49]

Paul and Linda also met with Chris Thomas, who would be joining them in Tokyo. At one point, the discussion turned to the matter of having a supply of marijuana in Japan.

"I remember, I walked from AIR Studios to Soho Square," said Thomas, "and I said to Linda, 'Don't under any circumstances'—because she always used to talk about putting grass in James's nappy and smuggling it in. I said, 'You cannot do that. It's a different world. They'll lock you up there and they'll throw away the key. This is serious, you cannot do it this time.'"[50]

The McCartneys flew to New York on Monday, January 14, and checked into the Stanhope. Laurence Juber flew over on the same flight—"I had a girlfriend who was going to be in New York at the time," he explained. Juber also took the opportunity to prowl the music shops on West 48th Street, where he found a 1957 Gibson Les Paul Goldtop, a magnificent instrument that would be a superb addition to the set of guitars he was bringing to Japan.

While they were in town, Paul phoned the Dakota. According to Fred Seaman, John's assistant, Paul said that Linda had scored "some really dynamic weed," and they wanted to visit the Lennons at the Dakota. He mentioned, as well, that he and Linda would be staying at the Presidential Suite at the Okura Hotel in Tokyo—the suite John and Yoko preferred during their Tokyo visits—a point that, Seaman claims, appeared to vex John.[51]

Relations between Paul and Yoko had also never been worse. In a bid to scupper future house visits, Yoko had taken to screening telephone calls, and though John and Paul had spoken over Christmas when an ocean separated the pair, the second they set foot on American soil, Paul's attempts to speak with John were blocked. Only in town for a couple of days, the McCartneys did not see the Lennons that trip.

Laurence joined the McCartneys on the flight to Tokyo. The rest of Wings, along with Howie Casey, Chris Thomas and support staff from MPL, including Alan Crowder, flew from London, and the American contingent of the horn section flew from Atlanta. Everyone planned to meet in Tokyo the afternoon of January 16.

"Denny and I flew in from London," Steve related. "We'd already cleared Customs, and we were sitting on the coach waiting [for the others] to go to the hotel. Then Alan Crowder came onto the bus and said, 'Guys, we've got a bit of a problem here with luggage, go on to the hotel and we'll meet up with you later.' So we did. We were exhausted from the long flight, so I actually took a nap."[52]

The horn players, by then, were in Howie Casey's room celebrating the raise that Tony had negotiated. "I got in earlier than Tony, Thaddeus and Steve," Howie recalled, "but once they got in, an hour or so later, they came up to my room. I had bought some cigars in the duty-free, and some drinks, and I started to hand out the cigars—'Here you go, boys!'—because Tony had spoken to Paul and we got the money up to a realistic amount."

Back at Narita International Airport, the McCartneys and Juber had landed. Paul had been unable to sleep during the 14-hour flight, but he waved, joked and posed cheerfully for the crowd of photographers who greeted him as he walked off the plane. Also there to meet him were Billy Francis, his bodyguard, Mike Walley, MPL's travel agent, Seijiro Udo, the Japanese promoter, and Tatsuji Nagashima, the promoter who brought the Beatles to Japan 14 years earlier.

"Once we got off the flight," said Laurence, "we got sent to a holding area because they had to validate Paul's visa, which had been a whole big thing. He had to sign an affidavit saying he didn't smoke dope anymore. [MPL] had to jump through hoops to get the work permit to allow him to tour. So we had been held up for 90 minutes, or a couple of hours, waiting for all the bureaucracy to do its thing.

"And then we were just going through Customs. Linda and the kids had gone through, Paul was next to me, on my right, and I was the last one. I had the Les Paul I had bought in New York—I hand carried that—and I'm getting ready to open it for the guy to look at. They're on [Paul's] last suitcase, and the guy's kind of patting a jacket that's on top. And then he kind of looked quizzical and reached underneath and pulled out a bag of grass—at which point he must have pressed a button or something, because all these guys in suits came out of nowhere and escorted us to the back.

"Paul turned white—I think it was one of those 'Oh, God!' moments. They took him into a room and put me in another room. Linda was just basically panicking. I'm there with my Les Paul, and these guys came in with a screwdriver and pointed to the guitar. I had to take off the truss rod cover and the plastic plates on the back to show that there was nothing stashed away. And that was the last we saw of Paul."[53]

In the room Paul had been taken to, blue-uniformed inspectors wearing white gloves gave the rest of the family's luggage a thorough going-over. More marijuana was found in a suit jacket, a makeup bag and a coat,[54] each find photographed in the location where it was discovered. All told, the inspectors found about 220 grams—nearly eight ounces—of marijuana. The penalty for bringing grass into the country, Paul would soon learn, was seven years' imprisonment and a ¥500,000 (£925, $2,100) fine.

Paul was read the Japanese equivalent of Miranda rights and then questioned about whether the marijuana was his. His answers formed the basis of a statement, which he signed before he was taken out of the room, past Linda, whom he told he would probably be spending a night in jail, but not to worry. She snapped a photo as he was led away.

He was then taken to the Ministry of Health and Welfare, where another crowd of reporters and photographers was waiting as the now-handcuffed former Beatle was taken in for further questioning. A visit from the British consul was not heartening: another British subject was then in his third month of detention for bringing marijuana into Japan, and there was not a great deal the consulate could do. For now, all the consul could tell Paul was that he was being held without bail.

"People assume I was arrogant," Paul later reflected. "I wasn't. I was just being dumb. I'd got some good grass in America, if you wanna know the truth, and I was loath to flush it down the toilet. And I was silly enough to think I might get past. It was daft."[55]

Handcuffed again, Paul was led to the car that would take him to the Tokyo Metropolitan Police Detention Center, passing crowds of distraught Japanese fans lined up in the street hoping for a glimpse. Upon his arrival, he was assigned an institutional identity—he was now Prisoner 22—and was read the rules governing behavior in the jail. After surrendering his jewelry and other personal effects, he was shown to his cell, a nine-by-twelve room with a wooden floor, fluorescent ceiling lights, a bedroll, a seatless toilet and a sink.

At the Okura Hotel, Chris Thomas and Denny Laine shared an elevator up to the floor where they both had rooms, but by the time Chris unlocked his door, his telephone was ringing. It was Denny.

"Switch on the telly," Denny told him.

"What?"

"Switch on the telly."

"What channel?" Chris asked.

"It doesn't matter."

When Thomas turned on the television, he saw Paul surrounded by a group of dour-looking Japanese officials, a white towel over his wrists, hiding handcuffs. He didn't need a translation to know what had happened.

Howie, Thaddeus, Steve and Tony were enjoying their cigars and whisky when Alan Crowder knocked on their door. "I offered Alan a drink, and he said, 'No, no, no.' That wasn't like Alan—he always liked a drink. He said, 'Paul's in jail.' I said, 'Come on, Alan, you're taking the mickey.' He said, 'No, I'm serious. Paul's in jail.'"

"I didn't want to believe it, man," Tony Dorsey said. "I didn't want to hear that. Because I tried to tell Paul, 'Look, man, don't take any drugs over there.'"[56]

Steve Holley had just slipped into his nap when his phone rang. Answering groggily, he heard Linda at the other end of the line telling him that Paul had been arrested.

"I thought she was just having a practical joke," Steve said. "I said, 'Nice one, Linda, okay.' But I threw my clothes on, got in the elevator and went downstairs, and when the elevator doors opened, I was met with about 50 photographers, snapping away—*snap*, *snap*, *snap*, *snap*. I looked

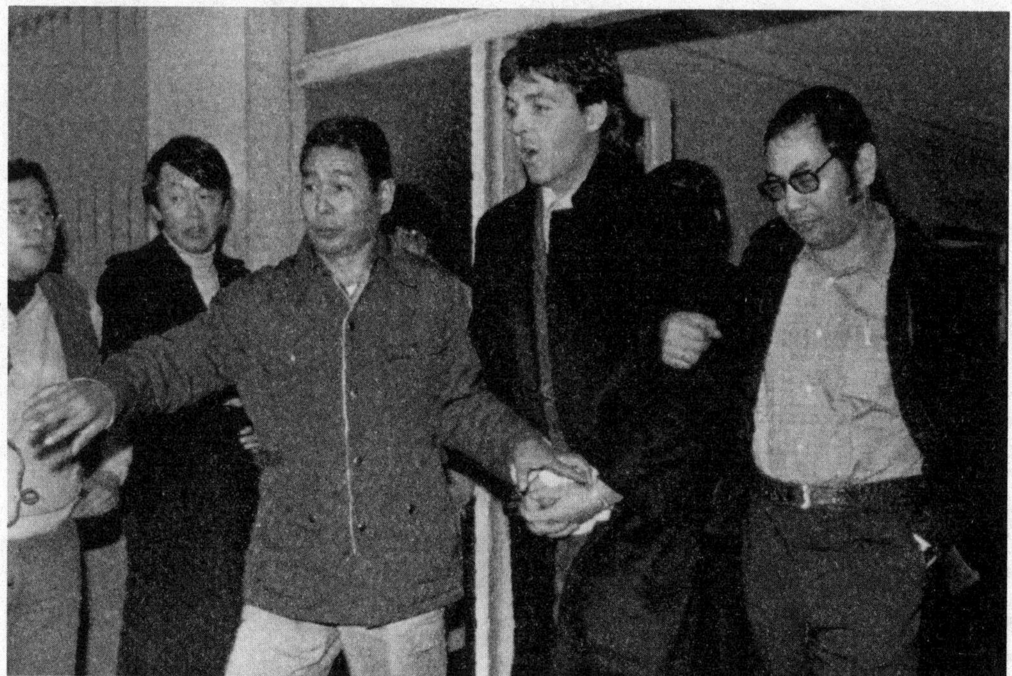

Paul is busted for cannabis possession in Japan, January 16, 1980

into the restaurant and saw a bunch of our crew with extremely long faces, sitting at the bar, and that's when I realized what had occurred.

"That," Steve said after a pause, "was a very bad day."

Some of the band adopted a positive attitude. "We were kind of hopeful that it would blow over," Laurence said, "because what would typically happen is, if a reggae band would come in with some weed, they'd just take it away from them and let them do the tour. But because some people in the Justice Department had got their noses out of joint because they had allowed for Paul's work permit, they wanted to make an example of him, I guess."[57]

By evening, the tour was canceled, and music by Paul and Wings, which had been saturating the airwaves, was effectively banned.

"When we all met up and got together—I think it must have been at the bar downstairs," Chris Thomas said, "people were saying, 'You know Tokyo, where can we go?' So I arranged for all of us to go to this club called Byblos, which was quite well known in those days. On the way there, there were posters for the gigs on literally every tree and lamppost. And when we came back from Byblos, there wasn't one to be seen."

In his cell, Paul was unable to sleep, even after the sleepless 14-hour flight and the enervating events of the day. His instinct to defy those who told him "you can't do that" had been strong since childhood, but over the past decade the phrase "you can't tell us what to do" had turned into a game for the McCartneys. Despite multiple brushes with the law between 1972 and 1976, their desire to push boundaries for kicks remained undiminished. And they had been lucky: fame often wrapped the couple in a protective blanket that guarded them from consequences that normal people feared.

In New York, photographer Bob Gruen asked John Lennon what Paul could have been thinking, flying to Japan with marijuana in his suitcase. "Well, as a Beatle," John told him, "he just never expected that anybody would ever open his bag. It just never happened."[58]

When Paul visited Hawaii in 1975, his decision to ignore local advice about bodysurfing in choppy waters nearly cost him his life. Now the same overconfidence landed him *"in a cage."*

"I can remember the first couple of nights," he later said, "'cos you see, my thing was rape. That was my big fear. I didn't know what was going to happen. 'Hello, this is your friendly jailor, I'd like a favor please.' *'NO!* Not even for a bowl of rice!' So, you know, I slept with my back to the wall, in the green suit I'd arrived in.

"It was hell."[59]

. . . to be continued.

ACKNOWLEDGMENTS

The pages of this volume were not populated with colorful tales and more information than any broadsheet reviewer could possibly digest (yes, we do enjoy an EMI matrix number or two), without the input of a legion of helpers.

Special thanks to Geoff Britton, whose interviews and diaries allowed us to better understand his tenure as Wings' second drummer and paint a vibrant and accurate portrait of his all-too-short time as McCartney's rhythm man. Landmark moments—like the precise day when Paul wrote 'Sally G,' and the specific time and the place Paul and Professor Longhair first crossed paths—are presented here thanks to Geoff's foresight not only to document his day-to-day life but also to hold on to his precious diaries even when some of the memories they contain are hard to revisit. A million thanks, Poker Man and your Magpie.

Distinctive praise also to recording engineers Peter Henderson, Alan O'Duffy and Tim Summerhayes, whose work diaries and session logs proved invaluable to the documenting of the *Venus and Mars*, *Wings at the Speed of Sound*, *London Town* and RAK mobile sessions.

For their generous interview time and openness to extended (and often extensive) correspondence we would like to thank Colin Allen, Richard Ames, Tom Anderson, Peter Asher, Gordon Bennett, Mike Bohen, Allen Branton, Peter Brown, Howie Casey, Marcy Cates, Margie Cates, Drummond Challis, Barry Chattington, John Christie, Tony Clark, Jeff Cummins, Warren Cunningham, Joseph Dera, Tony Dorsey, Genetic Drugs, Dan Ealey, Joe English, Nicholas Ferguson, Danny Fields, Paul Gambaccini, Dixie Gamble, David Gilmour, Graham Gouldman, Robert Grace, Bob Gruen, Steve Holley, Laurence Juber, Judd Lander, John Lang Brown, Nancy Lee Andrews, Sir Michael Lindsay-Hogg, David Litchfield, Bob Loveday, Morris Lyda, Hank Marvin, Angie McCartney, Mike McCartney, Jimmy McGeachy, Suzy Melville, Jim Miller, Zoot Money, Steve Morley, Leo Nocentelli, Humphrey Ocean, Earl Okin, May Pang, Ian Peacock, George Porter Jr., Aubrey Powell, Willy Russell, Tom Scott, Denny Seiwell, Sidney Smith, Roy Snyder, Ray Stevens, Eric Stewart, Brent Stoker, Sir Tom Stoppard, Peter Tattersall, Bruce Thomas, Chris Thomas, Steven Thomas, Rob Townsend, Fiachra Trench, Sam Trust, Eric Wishart and Walter Yetnikoff.

For allowing us access to documents, newspapers, magazine, photographs, and additional transcripts of interviews from their personal archives, we would like to extend special thanks to John Lennon expert Chip Madinger, Paul McCartney collector Benoît Dumetz, and world-renowned Beatles expert and author Mark Lewisohn.

Among the community of music experts and Beatles academics we spoke with, we would also like to doff our hats to Michael Ayre, Werner Burkhardt, Richard Buskin, Chris Charlesworth, Mark Cox, Peter Cross, Matthew Demakos, Edward Eikelenboom, Peter Gaveglia, Derek Graham, Sara Grant, Carol Lapidos, Mark Lapidos, Richard Lawrence, Eoghan Lyng, Abbey Maynard, Garry McGee, Sean Macreavy, Carl Magnus Palm, Luca Perasi, Paul Salley, Sara Schmidt, Alexis Schwarz, Bamiyan Shiff, Chloe Simmons, Jesse Tedesci, Peter Wadsworth, Paul Wane, Kenneth Womack, Chuck Yarborough, and finally Tom O'Dell and Elio Espana of Prism Films, whose interviews with Denny Laine feature in both this volume and our first book.

Very special thanks go out to the staff at the Boston University Libraries' Howard Gotlieb Archival Research Center, Northwestern University Libraries Charles Deering McCormick Library, the British Library in Boston Spa, Scotland's Land Information Service, HM Land Registry, and Registers of Scotland.

Thanks, as well, to Carrie Thornton, our effervescent editor; to Matthew Elblonk, our legendary literary agent; to Kate Lapin, our discerning copyeditor; and the amazing staff at Dey Street: Liate Stehlik, publisher; Benjamin Steinberg, deputy publisher; Leah Carlson-Stanisic, interior designer; Jessica Rozler, production editor; Owen Corrigan, art director; Allison Carney and Heidi Richter, directors of marketing and publicity; Kyran Cassidy, legal counsel; and Drew Henry, intrepid assistant editor.

And to all our family, friends and colleagues—some of whom (often colorfully) revealed their surprise when *Volume 1* was published in 2022—thank you for all the pub snug music tête-à-têtes, Macca-infused family gatherings, Beatles-skewed watercooler moments, and other eyeroll-inducing moments during the making of "the second one."

Several participants in the story, most of whom we interviewed for this book and for *Volume 1*, died while this volume was being prepared. We would like to offer our condolences to the families and friends of Wings co-founder Denny Laine, arranger and trombonist Tony Dorsey, recording engineers Tom Anderson, Brian Humphries and Tim Geelan, film director David Litchfield, drummer Gerry Conway, singer Holly McCracken, concert promoter John Morris, radio and television broadcaster Annie Nightingale, television presenter Sir Michael Parkinson, drummer Alan White, and Columbia Records executive Walter Yetnikoff. The pages of our volumes are all the richer for their contributions.

BIBLIOGRAPHY

Andrews, Eamonn: *For Ever and Ever, Eamonn: The Public and Private Life of Eamonn Andrews* (Grafton Books, London, 1989).

Becker, Frawley: *And the Stars Spoke Back* (Scarecrow Press, Lanham, MD, 2004).

Beerling, Johnny: *Radio 1—The Inside Story* (Trafford Publishing, Manchester, 2008).

Benitez, Vincent P.: *The Words and Music of Paul McCartney* (Praeger, Santa Barbara, 2010).

Benson, Harry: *Paul* (Taschen, Köln, 2022).

Blaney, John: *Lennon and McCartney Together Alone* (Outline Press, London, 2007).

Brown, Peter with Gaines, Steven: *All You Need Is Love: The End of the Beatles* (Monoray, London, 2024).

Caillat, Ken, and Steve Stiefel: *Making Rumours* (Turner Publishing Company, NJ, 2012).

Cassidy, David: *Could It Be Forever? My Story* (DBC, New York, 2007).

Coleman, Ray: *The Carpenters: The Untold Story* (HarperCollins, London, 1994).

Doyle, Tom: *Man on the Run* (Ballantine Books, London, 2014).

Du Noyer, Paul: *Conversations with McCartney* (Hodder & Stoughton, London, 2015).

Francis, Michael, with Paul Elliott: *Star Man the Right Hand Man of Rock 'N' Roll* (Simon & Schuster, New York, 2003).

Gambaccini, Paul: *Paul McCartney: In His Own Words* (Omnibus Press, New York, 1976).

Geller, Debbie, and Anthony Wall, editor: *The Brian Epstein Story* (Faber and Faber, London, 2000).

Gelly, Dave: *The Facts About a Pop Group* (Whizzard Publications Ltd., London, 1976).

Giuliano, Geoffrey: *Blackbird: The Life and Times of Paul McCartney* (Dutton, New York, 1991).

Giuliano, Geoffrey: *In Conversation with Ruth & Angie McCartney—Volume 3* (Icon Audio Arts, 2018).

Giuliano, Geoffrey: *In Conversation with Ruth & Angie McCartney—Volume 4* (Icon Audio Arts, 2018).

Giuliano, Geoffrey: *In Conversation with Ruth & Angie McCartney—Volume 6* (Icon Audio Arts, 2018).

Grundy, Stuart, with John Tobler: *The Record Producers* (BBC Books, London, 1982).

Helvin, Marie: *The Autobiography* (Orion, London, 2007).

Jones, Kenney: *Let the Good Times Roll* (Blink Publishing, London, 2018).

Juber, Laurence, with Marshall Terrill: *Guitar With Wings—A Photographic Memoir* (Dalton Watson Books, Deerfield, IL, 2014).

Killen, Buddy, with Tom Carter: *By the Seat of My Pants* (Simon & Schuster, New York, 1993).

Klein, Eddie: *McCartney II Archive Edition* (MPL/Hear Music/Concord, 2011).

Korinth, Axel: *Rock Show—Die (Ex-) Beatles in Deutschland 1971–1980* (Books on Demand, Germany, 2011).

Lawson, Twiggy: *Twiggy* (Granada Publishing Limited, St. Albans, 1975).

Lawson, Twiggy: *Twiggy in Black and White* (Simon & Schuster, London, 1997).

Lewisohn, Mark: *All These Years—Tune In (Special Edition)* (Little Brown, London, 2013).

Litchfield, David, and Schmitz, Caroline: *Bailey and I Volume 1* (Self-published, London, 2023).

Madinger, Chip, with Scott Raile: *Lennonology: Strange Days Indeed* (Open Your Books, Chesterfield, MO, 2015).

Madinger, Chip, with Mark Easter: *Eight Arms to Hold You—The Solo Beatles Compendium* (Open Your Books, Chesterfield, MO, 2018 edition).

Martin, George: *Making Music* (Frederick Muller Ltd., London, 1983).

McCartney, Linda: *Linda's Pictures* (Ballantine Books, New York, 1976).

McCartney, Mike: *The Macs—Mike McCartney's Family Album* (Delilah Communications Ltd., London, 1981).

McCartney, Paul, with Mark Lewisohn, editor: *Wingspan* (Bulfinch Press, London, 2002).

McCartney, Paul, with Paul Muldoon, editor): *The Lyrics 1956 to the Present* (Liverlight Publishing Corporation, New York, 2021).

McGee, Garry: *Band on the Run* (Taylor Trade Publishing, New York, 2003).

Miles, Barry: *Paul McCartney: Many Years from Now* (Henry Holt and Company, New York, 1997).

Miles, Barry: *Venus and Mars Archive Edition* (MPL Communications, London, 2014).

Miles, Barry: *Wings at the Speed of Sound* archive edition (MPL Communications, London, 2014).

Newman Del: *A Touch from God* (Apex, Clacton on Sea, London, 2010).

Norman, Philip: *Paul McCartney—The Life* (Little, Brown & Company, New York, 2016).

Ocean, Humphrey: *The Ocean View—Paintings and Drawings of Wings American Tour April to June 1976* (MPL Communications, Ltd., London, 1982).

Pang, May: *Instamatic Karma* (St. Martin's Press, New York, 2008).

Pang, May, with Henry Edwards: *Loving John* (Warner Books, New York, 1983).

Peckham, George: *George Peckham—Porky's Prime Cuts* (George Peckham/Apcor Books, Netherlands, 2018).

Perasi, Luca: *Paul McCartney: Music Is Ideas. The Stories Behind the Songs (Vol. 1) 1970–1989* (L.I.L.Y. Publishing, Italy, 2023).

Powell, Aubrey, Thorgerson, Storm, and Christopherson, Peter, ed.: *"Hands Across the Water"—Wings Tour USA* (Paper Tiger, London, 1978).

Sackett, Susan: *Inside Trek: My Secret Life with Star Trek Creator Gene Roddenberry* (Hawk Publishing, America, 2013).

Salley, Paul: *Little Wing: The Jimmy McCulloch Story* (Lotown Publishing, St. Louis, 2021).

Scheff, David with G. Barry Golson, editor: *All We Are Saying: The Last Major Interview with John Lennon and Yoko Ono* (St. Martin's Griffin, New York, 1981).

Seaman, Fred: *The Last Days of John Lennon—A Personal Memoir by Fred Seaman* (Birch Lane Press, New York, 1991).

Sounes, Howard: *Fab: An Intimate Life of Paul McCartney* (HarperCollins, New York, 2011).

Spizer, Bruce: *The Beatles Solo on Apple Records* (498 Productions, New Orleans, 2005).

Stardust, Alvin: *Tales from the Saddle* (Stanley Paul & Co. Ltd., London, 1984).

Taylor, Derek: *Fifty Years Adrift* (Genesis Publications, Guildford, 1984).

Welch, Chris: *Paul McCartney: The Definitive Biography* (Proteus, London, 1984).

Wenner, Jann: *Lennon Remembers* (Straight Arrow Books, San Francisco, 1971).

Womack, Kenneth: *Living the Beatles Legend: The Untold Story of Mal Evans* (Dey Street, New York, 2023).

PHOTO CREDITS

page ii: Denis O'Regan/Getty Images
page iv: James Andanson/Sygma via Getty Images
pages vi–vii: Ipol/Globe Photos, Inc.
page 49: Suzanne Vlamis-AP-Shutterstock
page 52: Globe Photos, Inc.
page 54: Fairchild Archive-Penske Media-Shutterstock
page 78: Anonymous-AP-Shutterstock
page 95: Margie and Marcy Cates
page 151: Geoffrey Britton
page 158: Ian Dickson-Shutterstock
page 166: Bob Gruen
page 200: Globe Photos, Inc.
page 202: Chris Harris/pt/Globe Photos, Inc.
page 230 (bottom): Associated Newspapers-Shutterstock
page 274: Associated Newspapers-Shutterstock
page 300: Derek Graham
page 376 (top): Gs-AP-Shutterstock
page 376 (bottom): Michael Marks/Globe Photos, Inc.
page 394 (top): Globe Photos, Inc.
page 394 (bottom): Allan S. Adler-ipol-Globe Photos, Inc.
page 414: Judith Kridler/Globe Photos, Inc.
page 416: Barb Fenwick
page 419: Allan S. Adler-Globe Photos, Inc.
page 437: Anonymous-AP-Shutterstock
page 459: Globe Photos, Inc.
page 486 (top): Tom Anderson
page 486 (bottom): Tom Anderson
page 491 (top): Tom Anderson
page 491 (bottom): Tom Anderson
page 527: Monty Fresco-Daily Mail-Shutterstock
page 533: ITV-Shutterstock
page 536: Jim Miller
page 537: Jim Miller
page 556: Jim Miller
page 557: Jim Miller
page 572: Anonymous-AP-Shutterstock
page 578: Globe Photos, Inc.
page 587: Globe Photos, Inc.
page 609: Ipol/Globe Photos, Inc.
page 648: Adrian Sinclair
page 658: Richard Young-Shutterstock
page 662: Ipol/Globe Photos, Inc.
page 663: David Thorpe/Ipol/Globe Photos, Inc.
page 664: Ipol/Globe Photos, Inc.
page 665: Ipol/Globe Photos, Inc.
page 670: Genetic Drugs
page 672: Genetic Drugs
page 692: Monty Fresco-Daily Mail-Shutterstock
page 704 (top): Picture Power/ipol/Globe Photos
page 704 (bottom): Picture Power/pol/Globe Photos
page 714: AP-Shutterstock

SELECTED DISCOGRAPHY

Albums

MIKE MCGEAR, *MCGEAR*

UK: Warner Bros. Records K 56051, September 27, 1974
USA: Warner Bros. Records BS 2825, September 27, 1974
Reissued: Deluxe remastered and expanded box set, Esoteric Recordings, ECLEC 32655
Original tracks: Sea Breezes / What Do We Really Know? / Norton / Leave It / Have You Got Problems / The Casket / Rainbow Lady / Simply Love You / Givin' Grease a Ride / The Man Who Found God on the Moon
Additional music tracks with reissue: Sweet Baby / Dance the Do / Sea Breezes (Without Orchestra) / Leave It (Extended Version) / Dance the Do (Rough First Mix) / What Do We Really Know? (Monitor Mix) / Paddy Pipes #1 / Do Nothing All Day / A to Z / Girls on the Avenue / Paddy Pipes #2 / All the Whales in the Ocean / Blowin' in the Bay / Keep Cool—Version 1 (Road Safety Ad) / Keep Cool—Version 2 (Road Safety Ad) / I Juz Want What You Got—Money! / Paddy Pipes #3 / Viv Stanshall Sings / Let's Turn the Radio On / Dance the Do (Radio Ad #1) / Dance the Do (Radio Ad #2)

WINGS, *VENUS AND MARS*

UK: Apple PCTC254, June 6, 1975
USA: Apple SMAS 11419, May 30, 1975
Reissued: Paul McCartney Archive Collection, Hear Music, HRM-35652-00, 2014
Original tracks: Venus and Mars / Rock Show / Love in Song / You Gave Me the Answer / Magneto and Titanium Man / Letting Go / Venus and Mars (Reprise) / Spirits of Ancient Egypt / Medicine Jar / Call Me Back Again / Listen to What the Man Said / Treat Her Gently—Lonely Old People / Crossroads Theme
Additional music tracks with reissue: Junior's Farm / Sally G / Walking in the Park with Eloise / Bridge Over the River Suite / My Carnival / Going to New Orleans (My Carnival) / Hey Diddle (Ernie Winfrey Mix) / Let's Love / Soily (From *One Hand Clapping*) / Baby Face (From *One Hand Clapping*) / Lunch Box/Odd Sox / 4th of July / Rock Show (Old Version) / Letting Go (Single Edit)

WINGS, *WINGS AT THE SPEED OF SOUND*

UK: Capitol PAS10010, April 2, 1976
USA: Capitol SW 11525, March 25, 1976
Reissued: Paul McCartney Archive Collection, Hear Music, HRM-35673-00, 2014
Original tracks: Let 'Em In / The Note You Never Wrote / She's My Baby / Beware My Love / Wino Junko / Silly Love Songs / Cook of the House / Time to Hide / Must Do Something About It / San Ferry Anne / Warm and Beautiful
Additional music tracks with reissue: Silly Love Songs (Demo) / She's My Baby (Demo) / Message to Joe / Beware My Love (John Bonham Version) / Must Do Something About It (Paul's Version) / Let 'Em In (Demo) / Warm and Beautiful (Instrumental Demo)

WINGS, *WINGS OVER AMERICA*

UK: Parlophone PAS720, December 24, 1976
USA: Capitol SW 11593, December 10, 1976
Reissued: Paul McCartney Archive Collection, Hear Music, HRM-34313-00, 2013
Original tracks: Venus and Mars / Rock Show / Jet / Let Me Roll It / Spirits of Ancient Egypt / Medicine Jar / Maybe I'm Amazed / Call Me Back Again / Lady Madonna / The Long and Winding Road / Live and Let Die / Picasso's Last Words (Drink to Me) / Richard Cory / Bluebird / I've Just Seen a Face / Blackbird / Yesterday / You Gave Me the Answer / Magneto and Titanium Man / Go Now / My Love / Listen to What the Man Said / Let 'Em In / Time to Hide / Silly Love Songs / Beware My Love / Letting Go / Band on the Run / Hi, Hi, Hi / Soily
Additional music tracks with reissue: (Live at the Cow Palace) Let Me Roll It / Maybe I'm Amazed / Lady Madonna / Live and Let Die / Picasso's Last Words (Drink to Me) / Bluebird / Blackbird / Yesterday

DENNY LAINE, *HOLLY DAYS*

UK: EMI EMA781, May 13, 1977
USA: Capitol Records ST11588, May 13, 1977
Original tracks: Heartbeat / Moondreams / Rave On / I'm Gonna Love You Too / Fool's Paradise / Lonesome Tears / It's So Easy / Listen to Me (Medley) / Look at Me / Take Your Time / I'm Looking for Someone to Love

WINGS, *LONDON TOWN*

UK: Parlophone PAS10012, March 31, 1978
USA: Capitol SW11777, March 31, 1978
Reissued: The Paul McCartney Collection, Parlophone, 0777 7 89265 2 8, 1993
Original tracks: London Town / Café on the Left Bank / I'm Carrying / Backward Traveller / Cuff Link / Children Children / Girlfriend / I've Had Enough / With a Little Luck / Famous Groupies / Deliver Your Children / Name and Address / Don't Let It Bring You Down / Morse Moose and the Grey Goose
Additional music tracks with reissue: Girls' School / Mull of Kintyre

WINGS, *WINGS GREATEST*

UK: Parlophone PCT256, December 1, 1978
US: Capitol SOO-11905, December 1, 1978
Original tracks: Another Day / Silly Love Songs / Live and Let Die / Junior's Farm / With a Little Luck / Band on the Run / Uncle Albert / Admiral Halsey / Hi, Hi, Hi / Let 'Em In / My Love / Jet / Mull of Kintyre

WINGS, *BACK TO THE EGG*

UK: Parlophone PCTC257, June 8, 1979
USA: Columbia FC 36057, June 8, 1979
Reissued: The Paul McCartney Collection, Parlophone, 0777 7 89136 2 7, 1993
Original tracks: Reception / Getting Closer / We're Open Tonight / Spin It On / Again and Again and Again / Old Siam, Sir / Arrow Through Me / Rockestra Theme / To You / After the Ball / Million Miles / Winter Rose / Love Awake / The Broadcast / So Glad to See You Here / Baby's Request
Additional music tracks with reissue: Daytime Nighttime Suffering / Wonderful Christmastime / Rudolph the Red-Nosed Reggae

WINGS, *ONE HAND CLAPPING*

International CD: MPL/Capitol/Universal 602465081640, June 14, 2024
International LP: MPL/Capitol/Universal 602465081596, June 14, 2024
Exclusive LP and 7-inch single from paulmccartney.com: 602465081633, June 14, 2024
One Hand Clapping / Jet / Soily / C Moon/Little Woman Love / Maybe I'm Amazed / My Love / Bluebird / Let's Love / All of You / I'll Give You a Ring / Band on the Run / Live and Let Die / Nineteen Hundred and Eighty Five / Baby Face / Let Me Roll It / Blue Moon of Kentucky / Power Cut / Love My Baby / Let It Be / The Long and Winding Road / Lady Madonna / Junior's Farm / Sally G / Tomorrow / Go Now / Wild Life / Hi, Hi, Hi
Additional music included with the paulmccartney.com LP, and from streaming and downloading platforms:
Blackpool / Blackbird / Country Dreamer / Twenty Flight Rock / Peggy Sue / I'm Gonna Love You Too

Singles

PAUL MCCARTNEY AND WINGS, 'JUNIOR'S FARM' B/W 'SALLY G'

UK: Apple R 5999, October 25, 1974
USA: Apple 1875, October 25, 1974

PAUL MCCARTNEY AND WINGS, 'SALLY G' B/W 'JUNIOR'S FARM'

USA: Apple 1875, January 17, 1975

WINGS, 'LISTEN TO WHAT THE MAN SAID' B/W 'LOVE IN SONG'

UK: Capitol R6006, May 16, 1975
USA: Capitol 4091, May 16, 1975

WINGS, 'LETTING GO' B/W 'YOU GAVE ME THE ANSWER'

UK: Capitol R6008, October 3, 1975
USA: Capitol 4145, September 19, 1975

WINGS, 'VENUS AND MARS/ROCK SHOW' B/W 'MAGNETO AND TITANIUM MAN'

UK: Parlophone R6010, October 25, 1975
USA: Capitol 4145, September 19, 1975

WINGS, 'SILLY LOVE SONGS' B/W 'COOK OF THE HOUSE'

UK: Parlophone R6006, April 30, 1976
USA: Capitol 4256, April 2, 1976

WINGS, 'LET 'EM IN' B/W 'BEWARE MY LOVE'

UK: Parlophone R6015, July 23, 1976
USA: Capitol 4293, June 18, 1976

WINGS, 'MAYBE I'M AMAZED (LIVE)' B/W 'SOILY (LIVE)'

UK: Parlophone R6017, February 4, 1977
USA: Capitol 4385, January 28, 1977

WINGS, 'MULL OF KINTYRE' B/W 'GIRLS' SCHOOL'

UK: Parlophone R6018, November 11, 1977
USA: Capitol 4504, November 11, 1977

WINGS, 'WITH A LITTLE LUCK' B/W 'BACKWARDS TRAVELLER/CUFF LINK'

UK: Parlophone R6019, March 24, 1978
USA: Capitol 4559, March 17, 1978

WINGS, 'I'VE HAD ENOUGH' B/W 'DELIVER YOUR CHILDREN'

UK: Parlophone R6020, June 16, 1978
USA: Capitol, 4594, June 16, 1978

WINGS, 'LONDON TOWN' B/W 'I'M CARRYING'

UK: Parlophone R6021, August 25, 1978
USA: Capitol 8908, August 21, 1978

WINGS, 'GOODNIGHT TONIGHT' B/W 'DAYTIME NIGHTTIME SUFFERING'

UK: Parlophone 6023, March 23, 1979
USA: Columbia 310939, March 23, 1979

WINGS, 'OLD SIAM, SIR' B/W 'SPIN IT ON'

UK: MPL R6026, June 1, 1979

WINGS, 'GETTING CLOSER' B/W 'SPIN IT ON'

USA: Columbia 3-11020, June 4, 1979

WINGS, 'ARROW THROUGH ME' B/W 'BABY'S REQUEST'

USA: Columbia 1-11070, August 10, 1979

WINGS, 'GETTING CLOSER' B/W 'BABY'S REQUEST'

UK: Parlophone R6027, August 17, 1979

PAUL MCCARTNEY, 'WONDERFUL CHRISTMASTIME' B/W 'RUDOLPH THE RED-NOSED REGGAE'

UK: Parlophone R6029, November 16, 1979
USA: Columbia 1-11612, November 16, 1979

Note: *All release dates are based on chart information rather than dates printed in the news columns of period music papers, which were often estimated dates for when buyers might expect to pick up 45s and LPs in record stores. Even trade ads often carried misleading release dates.*

SELECTED VIDEOGRAPHY

PROMO FILMS

Most promotional films listed here are available on the MPL box set The McCartney Years (MPL/Warner Music Group, 2007), or on Paul McCartney's archive series deluxe edition sets, and many are widely available through McCartney's official YouTube channel (in some cases, offered in 4K or HD). Those that remain unissued circulate widely on YouTube and bootleg DVDs.

PAUL MCCARTNEY & WINGS, 'BAND ON THE RUN' (ANIMATED)

Filming date: 1974
Director: Michael Coulson

PAUL MCCARTNEY & WINGS, 'JET' (ANIMATED)

Filming date: 1974
Director: Jim Quick

PAUL MCCARTNEY & WINGS, 'MAMUNIA' (ANIMATED)

Filming date: 1974
Director: Jim Quick

PAUL MCCARTNEY & WINGS, 'JUNIOR'S FARM' (*TOP OF THE POPS*)

Filming date: November 20, 1974
Directors: Johnny Pearson and Bruce Milliard
Producer: Robin Nash

WINGS, 'LETTING GO'

Filming date: September 1975
Director: Barry Chattington
Producer: Paul McCartney

WINGS, 'SILLY LOVE SONGS'

Filming date: November 1975 to May 1976
Director: Gordon Bennett
Producer: Paul McCartney

WINGS, 'MAYBE I'M AMAZED' (LIVE)

Filming date: May–June 1976
Director: Gordon Bennett
Producer: Paul McCartney

WINGS, 'MULL OF KINTYRE' #1

Filming date: October 13, 1977
Director: Sir Michael Lindsay-Hogg
Producer: Paul McCartney

WINGS, 'MULL OF KINTYRE' #2

Filming date: December 2, 1977
Producer/Director: Paul McCartney

WINGS, 'MULL OF KINTYRE' #3

Filming date: December 9, 1977
Director: Nicholas Ferguson
Producer: Paul McCartney

WINGS, 'LONDON TOWN'

Filming date: March 21, 1978
Director: Sir Michael Lindsay-Hogg
Producer: Paul McCartney

WINGS, 'WITH A LITTLE LUCK'

Filming date: March 21, 1978
Director: Sir Michael Lindsay-Hogg
Producer: Paul McCartney

WINGS, 'I'VE HAD ENOUGH'

Filming date: April 1978
Director: Keith McMillan
Producer: Paul McCartney

LINDA MCCARTNEY, 'ORIENTAL NIGHTFISH' (ANIMATED)

Filming date: 1977–78
Director: Ian Emes
Producers: Paul and Linda McCartney

WINGS, 'GOODNIGHT TONIGHT'

Filming date: April 3, 1979
Director: Keith McMillan
Producer: Paul McCartney

WINGS, 'OLD SIAM, SIR'

Filming date: June 1, 1979
Director: Keith McMillan
Producer: Paul McCartney

WINGS, 'BABY'S REQUEST'

Filming date: June 14, 1979
Director: Keith McMillan
Producer: Paul McCartney

WINGS, 'GETTING CLOSER'

Filming date: June 19, 1979
Director: Keith McMillan
Producer: Paul McCartney

PAUL MCCARTNEY, 'WONDERFUL CHRISTMASTIME'

Filming date: November 16, 1979
Director: Russell Mulcahy
Producer: Paul McCartney

Television Specials

PAUL MCCARTNEY & WINGS, *ONE HAND CLAPPING* (MPL, 1974)

Filming date: August and October 1974
Transmission date: Released as part of the *McCartney* Archive reissue, never broadcast
Director: David Litchfield
Producer: Paul McCartney

PAUL MCCARTNEY, *ROCKESTRA SPECIAL* (MPL, 1979)

Filming date: October 3–4, 1978
Transmission date: *Unreleased*
Director: Barry Chattington
Producer: Paul McCartney

PAUL MCCARTNEY, *WINGS OVER THE WORLD* (MPL, 1979)

Filming date: 1970–1976 (various)
Transmission date: March 16, 1979
Director: Various (compiled from footage shot by multiple directors)
Producer: Paul McCartney

WINGS, *BACK TO THE EGG TELEVISION SPECIAL* (MPL, 1979)

Filming date: June 1979
Transmission date: November 1979 (US), June 10, 1981 (UK)
Director: Keith McMillan
Producer: Paul McCartney

CONCERT TOURS

British Tour (September 1975)

September 9: Gaumont Theatre, Southampton, England
September 10: Bristol Hippodrome, Bristol, England
September 11: Capitol Theatre, Cardiff, Wales
September 12: Free Trade Hall, Manchester, England
September 13: Birmingham Hippodrome, Birmingham, England
September 15: Liverpool Empire Theatre, Liverpool, England
September 16: Newcastle City Hall, Newcastle, England
September 17: Hammersmith Odeon, Hammersmith, England
September 18: Hammersmith Odeon, Hammersmith, England
September 20: Usher Hall, Edinburgh, Scotland
September 21: The Apollo, Glasgow, Scotland
September 22: Capitol Theatre, Aberdeen, Scotland
September 23: Caird Hall, Dundee, Scotland

Australian Tour (November 1975)

November 1: Perth Entertainment Centre, Perth, Australia
November 4: Apollo Stadium, Adelaide, Australia
November 5: Apollo Stadium, Adelaide, Australia
November 7: Hordern Pavilion, Sydney, Australia
November 8: Hordern Pavilion, Sydney, Australia
November 10: Brisbane Festival Hall, Brisbane, Australia
November 11: Brisbane Festival Hall, Brisbane, Australia
November 13: Sidney Myer Music Bowl, Melbourne, Australia
November 14: Sidney Myer Music Bowl, Melbourne, Australia

Wings Over Europe Part 1 (March 1976)

March 20: Falkoner Teatret, Copenhagen, Denmark
March 21: Falkoner Teatret, Copenhagen, Denmark
March 23: Deutschlandhalle, West Berlin, West Germany
March 25: Sportpaleis, Rotterdam, Netherlands
March 26: Pavillon de Paris, Paris, France

Wings Over America (May–June 1976)

May 3: Tarrant County Convention Center, Fort Worth, USA
May 4: The Summit, Houston, USA
May 7: Detroit Olympia, Detroit, USA
May 8: Detroit Olympia, Detroit, USA
May 9: Maple Leaf Gardens, Toronto, Canada
May 10: Richfield Coliseum, Richfield, USA
May 12: The Spectrum, Philadelphia, USA
May 14: The Spectrum, Philadelphia, USA
May 15: Capital Center, Landover, USA
May 16: Capital Center, Landover, USA
May 18: Omni Coliseum, Atlanta, USA
May 19: Omni Coliseum, Atlanta, USA
May 21: Nassau Veterans Memorial Coliseum, Uniondale, USA
May 22: Boston Garden, Boston, USA
May 24: Madison Square Garden, New York, USA
May 25: Madison Square Garden, New York, USA
May 27: Riverfront Coliseum, Cincinnati, USA
May 29: Kemper Arena, Kansas City, USA
May 31: Chicago Stadium, Chicago, USA
June 1: Chicago Stadium, Chicago, USA
June 2: Chicago Stadium, Chicago, USA
June 4: St. Paul Civic Center, Saint Paul, USA
June 7: McNichols Sports Arena, Denver, USA
June 10: Kingdome, Seattle, USA
June 13: Cow Palace, Daly City, USA
June 14: Cow Palace, Daly City, USA
June 16: San Diego Sports Arena, San Diego, USA
June 18: Tucson Community Center, Tucson, USA
June 21: The Forum, Los Angeles, USA
June 22: The Forum, Los Angeles, USA
June 23: The Forum, Los Angeles, USA

Wings Over Europe Part 2 (September–October 1976)

September 19: Wiener Stadthalle, Vienna, Austria
September 21: Dom Sportova, Zagreb, Yugoslavia
September 25: Piazza San Marco, Venice, Italy
September 27: Olympiahalle, Munich, West Germany
October 19: Empire Pool, London, England
October 20: Empire Pool, London, England
October 21: Empire Pool, London, England

UK Tour (November–December 1979)

November 23: Royal Court Theatre, Liverpool, England
November 24: Royal Court Theatre, Liverpool, England
November 25: Royal Court Theatre, Liverpool, England
November 26: Royal Court Theatre, Liverpool, England
November 28: Manchester Apollo, Manchester, England
November 29: Manchester Apollo, Manchester, England
December 1: Gaumont Theatre, Southampton, England
December 2: Brighton Centre, Brighton, England
December 3: Lewisham Odeon, London, England
December 5: The Rainbow Theatre, London, England
December 7: Wembley Arena, London, England
December 8: Wembley Arena, London, England
December 9: Wembley Arena, London, England
December 10: Wembley Arena, London, England
December 12: Birmingham Odeon, Birmingham, England
December 14: Newcastle City Hall, Newcastle Upon Tyne, England
December 15: Edinburgh Odeon, Edinburgh, Scotland
December 16: The Apollo, Glasgow, Scotland
December 17: The Apollo, Glasgow, Scotland

The Concerts for Kampuchea (December 1979)

December 29: Hammersmith Odeon, London, England

NOTES

CHAPTER 1

1 Fong-Torres, Ben: "Beatles Talk: Let George Do It," *Rolling Stone*, April 11, 1974, p. 13.

2 Fielding, John: Filmed interview with John Lennon for *Weekend World*, first transmitted April 8, 1973.

3 Tyler, Andrew: "Please, Your Majesty, Can Our John Have a Free Pardon?," *NME*, January 19, 1974, p. 9.

4 Uncredited: "Beatles Hint at a Reunion," *NME*, January 19, 1974, p. 2.

5 Pang, May, with Henry Edwards: *Loving John* (Warner Books, New York, 1983), p. 173.

6 Salewicz, Chris: "Paul McCartney—An Innocent Man," *Q*, October 1986.

7 Goodman, Joan: Unedited *Playboy* interview transcripts, May 3, 1984, part 3, pp. 31–32. Courtesy of Charles Deering McCormick Library of Special Collections, Northwestern University Libraries.

8 Wigg, David: Radio interview with John Lennon for *Scene and Heard*, BBC Radio 1, recorded October 15, 1971.

9 Pang, May, Author interview [Kozinn], March 10, 2008.

10 Von Faber, Karin: "Paul McCartney: Goodbye, Kicks; So Long, Birds," *New York News Magazine*, April 7, 1974, pp. 24–26.

11 Uncredited: "McCartney Interview," *Hustler*, July 1974, p. 84.

12 Pete (Surname not given): "Pete Meets Mike McGear," *Jackie*, August 31, 1974, p. 18.

13 McCartney (McGear), Michael: Author interview (Kozinn), May 19, 2019.

14 McCartney (McGear), Michael: Author interview (Kozinn), May 19, 2019.

15 Stewart, Eric: *Things I Do for Love* (Self-published, London, 2017), p. 82.

16 Tattersall, Peter: Author interview (Sinclair), March 14, 2019.

17 Parade, James: "The Producers, Take 1: All in a Little Name," *Record Mirror*, September 22, 1979, p. 11.

18 Giuliano, Geoffrey: *In Conversation with Ruth & Angie McCartney, Volume 6* (Icon Audio Arts, 2018), Audiobook only.

19 Giuliano, Geoffrey: *In Conversation with Ruth & Angie McCartney, Volume 4* (Icon Audio Arts, 2018), Audiobook only.

20 Flattery, Paul: "Paul's Brother: 'I'm Adequate,'" *Rolling Stone*, August 29, 1974, p. 26.

21 McCartney (McGear), Michael: Author interview (Kozinn), May 19, 2019.

22 Robinson, Lisa: "The *Hit Parader* Interview: Paul and Linda McCartney," *Hit Parader*, May 1975, p. 37.

23 Katz, Robin: "Same Face—Different Name," *Sounds*, October 19, 1974, p. 31.

24 Tattersall, Peter: Author interview (Sinclair), March 14, 2019.

25 Gouldman, Graham: Author interview (Sinclair), March 15, 2019.

26 Fong-Torres, Ben: "Al Coury Owns Number One," *Rolling Stone*, October 5, 1978.

27 Coury, Al: *The Story of Band on the Run*, EMI/Capitol DPRO 7087 6 13558 2 6, from the 1999 reissue of *Band on the Run*.

28 Goodman, Arty: "For the Record," *Cash Box*, February 2, 1974, p. 20.

29 McCartney, Paul: Author interview (Kozinn), October 19, 1990.

30 McCartney (McGear), Michael: Author interview (Kozinn), May 19, 2019.

31 Brown, Mick: "The Gizmo: More Than a Gadget?" *Rolling Stone*, December 29, 1977.

32 Henderson, Stan: "Gizmono My Guitar," *NME*, July 20, 1974, p. 39.

33 Lyng, Eoghan: Unedited interview with Lol Creme, June 2022.

34 McCartney (McGear), Michael: Author interview (Kozinn), May 19, 2019.

35 McCartney (McGear), Michael: Author interview (Kozinn), May 19, 2019.

36 Poole, Chris: "What They Say About Stevie," *Record Mirror*, May 11, 1974, p. 15.

37 Trust, Sam: Author interview (Sinclair), April 13, 2022.

38 Trust, Sam: Author interview (Sinclair), April 13, 2022.

39 Lewisohn, Mark: *All These Years—Tune In (Special Edition)*, (Little Brown, London, 2013), pp. 1397–1398.

40 Welch, Chris: "Paul McCartney Interview," *Melody Maker*, December 1, 1973.

41 Geller, Debbie, with Anthony Wall, editor: *The Brian Epstein Story* (Faber and Faber, London, 2000), p. 138.

42 Recording Academy, Grammy Awards website, https://www.grammy.com/awards/16th-annual-grammy-awards.

43 Johnson, Derek, editor: "Wings Over Stockport," *NME*, February 9, 1974, p. 2.

44 Uncredited: "Paul McCartney & Wings, 'Jet,'" *Record World*, February 2, 1974, p. 1.

45 Horide, Rosemary: "Paul Makes the New Jet Set," *Disc*, February 16, 1974, p. 24.

46 Welch, Chris: "Paul McCartney & Wings—'Jet,'" *Melody Maker*, February 16, 1974, p. 14.

47 Shaar Murray, Charles: "Paul McCartney & Wings—'Jet'/'Let Me Roll It,'" *NME*, February 16, 1974, p. 16.

48 Jones, Peter: "Pick of the Week," *Record Mirror*, February 23, 1974, p. 16.

49 McCartney (McGear), Michael: Author interview (Kozinn), May 19, 2019.

50 Bentley, Cara: "The Bible Verse Read on the Moon as Buzz Aldrin Took Communion," *Christian News*, July 19, 2019.

51 Reproductions of manuscript pages for several songs are included in the *McGear* CD/DVD reissue, Esoteric/Cherry Red, 2019.

52 Thomas, Deborah: "A Dance You Can All Do Together," *Daily Mirror*, July 1, 1975, p. 7.

53 Coleman, Ray: *The Carpenters: The Untold Story* (HarperCollins, London, 1994), pp. 164–166.

54 McCartney (McGear), Michael: Author interview (Kozinn), May 19, 2019.

55 Uncredited: "Raver's Hot Licks," *Melody Maker*, February 22, 1975, p. 10.

56 Nicky and Sue: "Stockport in the Studio," Wings Official Fun Club newsletter, Summer (No. 1), 1974, p. 2.

57 Tattersall, Peter: Author interview (Sinclair), March 14, 2019.

58 Von Faber, Karin: "Paul McCartney: Goodbye, Kicks; So Long, Birds," *New York News Magazine*, April 7, 1974, pp. 24–26.

59 Salley, Paul: Interview with Gerry Conway, shared on Facebook, April 11, 2011.

60 Laine, Denny: Promotional interview with Rogers and Cowan, New York, July 1977.

61 Pike, Jeffrey: "Jimmy McCulloch," *Guitar*, January 1975, pp. 20–21.

62 Horide, Rosemary: "Wings in Full Flight," *Disc*, November 2, 1974, p. 13.

63 Webb, Julie: "Wings New Line-up Shock Sensation!," *NME*, December 7, 1974, pp. 12–13.

64 Pike, Jeffrey: "Jimmy McCulloch," *Guitar*, January 1975, pp. 20–21.

65 McCartney, Paul, interviewed on *The Today Show*, NBC-TV, March 8, 1974, broadcast on March 12 and 13, 1974.

CHAPTER 2

1 Erskine, Pete: "Henry Goes On with the Brain Drain," *Sounds*, March 9, 1974, p. 22.

2 Brandstein, Eve, Richard Kaufman, and Stuart Samuels, directors: *The Lost Weekend: A Love Story*, 2022.

3 Pang, May: Author interview (Kozinn), March 10, 2008.

4 Brandstein, Eve, Richard Kaufman, and Stuart Samuels, directors: *The Lost Weekend: A Love Story*, 2022.

5 Uncredited: "Teazers—Lennon Repents?" *NME*, March 30, 1974, p. 51.

6 Goodden, Joe: Interview with May Pang for *Beatles Bible* online, January 2011.

7 Salewicz, Chris: Audio interview with Paul McCartney for *Q Magazine*, September 1986.

8 Miles, Barry: *Many Years from Now* (Henry Holt and Company, New York, 1997), p. 558.

9 Haber, Joyce: "High Hopes for a One-Day Wonder," *Los Angeles Times*, March 28, 1974, p. 16.

10 Goodden, Joe: Interview with May Pang for *Beatles Bible* online, January 2011.

11 Pang, May, with Henry Edwards: *Loving John* (Warner Books, New York, 1983), p. 208.

12 Davis, Ivor: "John and Paul, Today All Their Troubles Seem So Far Away," *Daily Express*, April 8, 1974, p. 4.

13 Lewisohn, Mark: "The Paul McCartney Interview," *Club Sandwich*, Winter 1994, p. 7.

14 Miles, Barry: *Many Years from Now* (Henry Holt and Company, New York, 1997), p. 558.

15 Ibid.

16 Salewicz, Chris: Audio interview with Paul McCartney for *Q Magazine*, September 1986.

17 Brandstein, Eve, Richard Kaufman, and Stuart Samuels, directors: *The Lost Weekend: A Love Story*, 2022.

18 Pang, May, with Henry Edwards: *Loving John* (Warner Books, New York, 1983), p. 211.

19 Graham, Jenny: "Linda McCartney Says," *Animals Magazine*, Fall 1979, p. 26.

20 Fong-Torres, Ben: "Al Coury Owns Number One," *Rolling Stone*, October 5, 1978.

21 Miles, Barry: *Venus and Mars* Archive Edition (MPL Communications, London, 2014), p. 116.

22 Goodman, Arty: "For the Record," *Cash Box*, April 20, 1974, p. 16.

23 Budge, David: "N.Y.—Captain Beefheart—Plenty of Magic Left," *Cash Box*, May 4, 1974, p. 24.

24 Uncredited, "McCartney June Tour," *Sounds*, April 20, 1974, p. 22.

25 Becker, Frawley: *And the Stars Spoke Back* (Scarecrow Press, Lanham, MD, 2004), p. 224.

26 Hilburn, Robert: "McCartney on Beatles Breakup—Let It Be," *Los Angeles Times*, April 21, 1974, pp. 1, 52.

27 Coleman, Ray: "Lennon—a Night in the Life," *Melody Maker*, September 14, 1974, pp. 14–15.

28 Evans, Malcolm: *Living the Beatles Legend*, Malcolm Frederick Evans Archives, pp. 240–41. Also, Womack,

Kenneth: *Living the Beatles Legend—The Untold Story of Mal Evans* (Dey Street, New York, 2023), p. 448.

29 Hilburn, Robert: "McCartney on Beatles Breakup—Let It Be," *Los Angeles Times*, April 21, 1974, pp. 1, 52.

30 Uncredited reader question (possibly from Andrew Fitzharris): "Star-Probe," *Disc*, April 20, 1974, p. 17.

31 Lewisohn, Mark: "The Paul McCartney Interview," *Club Sandwich*, Winter 1994, p. 4.

32 Brown, Geoff: "McCartney: Life After Death," *Melody Maker*, November 30, 1974, p. 63.

33 Spizer, Bruce: *The Beatles Solo on Apple Records* (498 Productions, New Orleans, 2005), p. 199.

34 Brolly, Brian: Letter to Mo Ostin, with copies to Lee and John Eastman and Ron Kass, dated March 8, 1974.

35 McGear, Mike: Letter to Mo Ostin, dated April 3, 1974.

36 Regehr, Bob: Memo to Mo Ostin, dated April 10, 1974.

37 Ostin, Mo: Memo to Paul McCartney, via Brian Brolly, undated (April 1974).

38 Fielding, Sarah: "How Paul and Linda Got and Took Their Band on the Run," *Petticoat*, February 15, 1975, p. 6.

39 Gelly, Dave: *The Facts About a Pop Group* (Whizzard Publications Ltd., London, 1976), p. 43.

40 Peebles, Andy: Radio interview with Paul McCartney, BBC Radio 1, May 26, 1980.

41 Philips, Steven: Article for *With a Little Help from My Friends* Fanzine, 1978.

42 Britton, Geoff: Author interview (Sinclair), August 27, 2019.

43 Ibid.

44 Ibid.

45 Ibid.

46 Fielding, Sarah: "How Paul and Linda Got and Took Their Band on the Run," *Petticoat*, February 15, 1975, p. 6.

47 Brown, Geoff: "Wings," *Melody Maker*, November 30, 1974, p. 28.

48 Uncredited: *Wings Fun Club Newsletter* No. 3, December 1974.

49 Nevard, Nina: Warner Bros. Records interoffice memo to a large distribution list, August 6, 1974.

50 As noted in Paul's interview with Timothy White for "Not So Silly Love Songs," *Billboard*, March 17, 2001, p. 94.

51 Epand, Len: "The Generation Bridge," *Zoo World*, July 14, 1974, pp. 13–14.

52 Ibid.

53 Santiago, Iván: "The Peggy Lee Bio-Discography," https://peggyleediscography.com/p/LeeAtlantic.php.

54 Robinson, Lisa: "The *Hit Parader* Interview: Paul and Linda McCartney," *Hit Parader*, May 1975, p. 38.

55 Guyte, Jill: "Mrs. Misunderstood McCartney," *Woman's Own*, June 1, 1974, pp. 14–16.

56 Howell, Georgina: "Musician: Paul McCartney," *Vogue*, June 1974.

57 Uncredited: "Beatles' Reunion (Episode 50) Denied," *NME*, May 11, 1974, p. 2.

58 Charlesworth, Chris: "American News," *Melody Maker*, May 18, 1974, p. 30.

59 Russell, Willy: Author interview (Sinclair), May 14, 2020.

60 Doherty, Harry: "Stardom: She Owes It All to the Beatles," *Disc*, December 7, 1974, p. 32.

61 Neustatter, Angela: "Angela Neustatter Interviews Willy Russell," *Guardian*, August 14, 1974.

62 Russell, Willy: Author interview (Sinclair), May 14, 2020.

63 Lewisohn, Mark: "Fan Club Questions," *Club Sandwich* 78, Spring 1996.

64 Giuliano, Geoffrey: *In Conversation with Ruth & Angie McCartney—Volume 3* (Icon Audio Arts, 2018), Audiobook only.

65 Bailey, Jerry: "Paul McCartney Plans Social Life While Here," *The Tennessean*, May 24, 1974, p. 10.

66 Horide, Rosemary: "The Music & Wings," *Disc*, December 14, 1974, p. 12.

67 McCartney, Angie: Author interview by email (Sinclair), January 5, 2020.

68 Haber, Joyce: "One-Man Smash for Sammy Cahn" (entertainment news column), *Los Angeles Times*, June 12, 1974, p. 16.

CHAPTER 3

1 Bailey, Jerry, with Eve Zibart: "McCartney in Nashville for 3 Rs," *The Tennessean*, June 7, 1974, p. 1.

2 Uncredited: "Beatle Paul, Family Visiting Nashville," Associated Press report via *The Jackson Sun*, June 7, 1974, p. 5.

3 Knoedelseder, William K., Jr.: "CBS Records Goes Country: The Sale of Nashville Publisher Tree International for $40 Million Means the Japanese Now Own 'Heartbreak Hotel,'" *Los Angeles Times*, January 4, 1989.

4 Beck, Ken: "The Summer of McCartney, Part 1," *The Wilson Post*, July 29, 2009.

5 Uncredited: "Inside Paul McCartney's Secret Nashville Sessions," *Country Music Magazine*, January 2018, pp. 18–21.

6 Swingley, Pat: "The Woman at Paul's Side," *The Tennessean*, July 21, 1974, p. 70.

7 Miles, Barry: *Venus and Mars Archive Edition* (MPL Communications, London, 2014), p. 12.

8 Gamble, Dixie: Author interview (Sinclair), May 31, 2020.

9 Uncredited: Audio interview with Ernie Winfrey, SiriusXM, 2018.

10 Gamble, Dixie: Author interview (Sinclair), May 31, 2020.

11 Britton, Geoff: Author interview (Sinclair), March 27, 2020.

12 Ibid.

13 Christie, John: email exchange with author (Kozinn), October 1, 2019.

14 Cumming, Fox: "With a Little Help from His Friends," *Disc*, July 13, 1974, p. 10.

15 Britton, Geoff: Author interview (Sinclair), March 27, 2020.

16 Ibid.

17 Black, Johnny: Audio interview with Paul McCartney for *Mojo*, March 6, 2003.

18 Uncredited: "Inside Paul McCartney's Secret Nashville Sessions," *Country Music Magazine*, January 2018, pp. 18–21.

19 Britton, Geoff: Author interview (Sinclair), August 27, 2019.

20 Killen, Buddy, with Tom Carter: *By the Seat of My Pants* (Simon & Schuster, New York, 1993), pp. 216–217.

21 Ibid.

22 Rodgers, Nile: Audio interview with Paul McCartney for *Deep Hidden Meaning*, January 8, 2021.

23 Uncredited: "Inside Paul McCartney's Secret Nashville Sessions," *Country Music Magazine*, January 2018, pp. 18–21.

24 Horide, Rosemary: "The Basic Mr. McCulloch," *Disc*, June 21, 1975, p. 24.

25 Bohan, Mike: Press Conference, Nashville, Tennessee, July 17, 1974.

26 Zevallos, Hank: "Exclusive Interview with Paul McCartney," *Screen Stars*, September 1974, p. 38.

27 Bartlett, Stefan: "McCartney and Me," *Sunday Mercury*, January 24, 1988, p. 24.

28 Killen, Buddy, with Tom Carter: *By the Seat of My Pants* (Simon & Schuster, New York, 1993), p. 221.

29 Britton, Geoff: Diary entry, from Author interview (Sinclair), March 27, 2020.

30 Horne, Nicky: Audio interview with Paul McCartney for *Your Mother Won't Like This* on Capital Radio, September 17, 1975.

31 Allen, Colin: Email exchange with author (Sinclair), September 13, 2019.

32 Gambaccini, Paul: *Paul McCartney: In His Own Words* (Omnibus Press, New York, 1976), pp. 53–54.

33 Prism Films: Filmed interview with Denny Laine, published in multiple parts on YouTube, June 9, 2012. Taken from Part 11.

34 Chambers, Joe: Video interview with Ernie Winfrey for the Musician's Hall of Fame, April 2007.

35 Gamble, Dixie: Author interview (Sinclair), May 31, 2020.

36 Brown, Geoff: "Wings," *Melody Maker*, November 30, 1974, p. 29.

37 Uncredited: "Inside Paul McCartney's Secret Nashville Sessions," *Country Music Magazine*, January 2018, pp. 18–21.

38 Cates, Marcy: Email exchange with author (Sinclair), February 4, 2020.

39 Peel, John: "Paul McCartney & Wings 'Band on the Run' (EMI/Apple)," *Sounds*, July 13, 1974, p. 31.

40 Edmonds, Ben: "Paul McCartney & Wings: 'Band on the Run' (Apple)," *NME*, July 13, 1974, p. 15.

41 Battle, Bob: "Paul McCartney in Nashville," *Country Song Roundup*, November 1976, p. 11.

42 Britton, Geoff: Author interview (Sinclair), March 27, 2020.

43 Cates, Marcy: Email exchange with author (Sinclair), February 4, 2020.

44 Cates, Margie: Email exchange with author (Sinclair), February 12, 2020.

45 Dorsey, Tony: Author interview (Kozinn), October 8, 2019.

46 Johnson, James: "Right, Now Let's Number That Best McCartney," *NME*, August 17, 1974, pp. 7–8.

47 Courtney, Richard: Audio interview for the *From Me to You* show on Hippy Radio, March 12, 2014.

48 Chambers, Joe: Video interview with Ernie Winfrey for the Musicians Hall of Fame, April 2007.

49 Goodman, Joan: "Playboy Interview: Paul and Linda McCartney," *Playboy*, December 1984, p. 92.

50 Flippo, Chet: "King Picker," *Rolling Stone*, February 12, 1976.

51 Earle, Charles: "Chet Atkins," *In Review*, July 1998.

52 Miles, Barry: *Venus and Mars Archive Edition* (MPL Communications, London, 2014), p. 116.

53 Courtney, Richard: Audio interview for the *From Me to You* show on Hippy Radio, March 12, 2014.

54 Chambers, Joe: Video interview with Ernie Winfrey for the Musicians Hall of Fame, April 2007.

55 Courtney, Richard: Audio interview for the *From Me to You* show on Hippy Radio, March 12, 2014.

56 Gamble, Dixie: Author interview (Sinclair), May 31, 2020.

57 Peacock, Steve: "Paul McCartney & Wings—Yesterday & Today," *Street Life*, April 3–16, 1976, pp. 26–27.

58 Britton, Geoff: Author interview (Sinclair), March 27, 2020.

59 Ealey, Dan: Author interview (Sinclair), July 7, 2019.

60 Uncredited: "Pop Goes Old Man McCartney," *Daily Mirror*, August 13, 1974, p. 7.

61 Leigh, Spencer: "Paul McCartney & Wings," *Record Collector*, February 1993, p. 18.

62 Stoker, Brent: Author interview (Sinclair), September 28, 2019.

63 Killen, Buddy, with Tom Carter: *By the Seat of My Pants* (Simon & Schuster, New York, 1993), pp. 218–219.

64 Chambers, Joe: Video interview with Ernie Winfrey for the Musicians Hall of Fame, April 2007.

65 Britton, Geoff: Author interviews (Sinclair), August 27, 2019, and March 27, 2020.

66 Johnson, James: "Right, Now Let's Number That Best McCartney," *NME*, August 17, 1974, pp. 7–8.

67 Bohan, Mike: Press Conference, Nashville, Tennessee, July 17, 1974.

68 Brown, Geoff: "McCartney: Life After Death," *Melody Maker*, November 30, 1974, p. 63.

69 Uncredited: "Inside Paul McCartney's Secret Nashville Sessions," *Country Music Magazine*, January 2018, pp. 18–21.

CHAPTER 4

1 Uncredited: "Monogamy and Music: Life Around the Hearth for Paul and Linda," *People*, April 21, 1975, p. 24.

2 Madinger, Chip, and Scott Raile: *Lennonology, Vol. 1 Strange Days Indeed* (Open Your Books, Chesterfield, MO, 2015), p. 408.

3 Pang, May, with Henry Edwards: *Loving John* (Warner Books, New York, 1983), p. 222.

4 Coleman, Ray: "Lennon—a Night in the Life," *Melody Maker*, September 14, 1974, pp. 14–15.

5 Pang, May, with Henry Edwards: *Loving John* (Warner Books, New York, 1983), p. 238.

6 Gallo, Armando: "Wife, Player, Mother, Lover . . . Linda," *Sounds*, October 5, 1974, p. 8.

7 Fest for Beatles Fans (Beatlefest's name since 2002) website, https://www.thefest.com/history/.

8 McCartney, Linda: "Letter from Linda," *Mirabelle*, August 24, 1974.

9 Robinson, Lisa: "The *Hit Parader* Interview: Paul and Linda McCartney," *Hit Parader*, May 1975, p. 37.

10 Brown, Geoff: "McCartney: Life After Death," *Melody Maker*, November 30, 1974, p. 63.

11 Johnson, James: "Right, Now Let's Number That Best McCartney," *NME*, August 17, 1974, pp. 7–8.

12 Scott, Roger: Audio interview with Paul and Wings for Capital Radio, broadcast on June 14, 1979.

13 Miles, Barry: *Venus and Mars Archive Edition* (MPL Communications, London, 2014), p. 113.

14 Gambaccini, Paul: Audio interview with Paul McCartney for *An Evening with Paul McCartney*, BBC Radio 1, broadcast on April 1, 1979.

15 Scott, Roger: Audio interview with Paul McCartney and Denny Laine for Capital Radio, November 11, 1978.

16 Johnson, Derek: "Band on the Run Wings Upheaval," *NME*, August 10, 1974, p. 3.

17 Johnson, James: "Right, Now Let's Number That Best McCartney," *NME*, August 17, 1974, pp. 7–8.

18 Litchfield, David: Author interview (Sinclair), July 27, 2019.

19 Welch, Chris: *Paul McCartney: The Definitive Biography* (Proteus, London, 1984), p. 88.

20 Britton, Geoff: Author interview (Sinclair), March 27, 2020.

21 Moore, Carroll: "Waiting in the Wings," *Beat Instrumental*, December 1974, p. 59.

22 Litchfield, David: Author interview (Sinclair), July 27, 2019.

23 Ibid.

24 Ibid.

25 Gallo, Armando: "Wife, Player, Mother, Lover . . . Linda," *Sounds*, October 5, 1974, p. 8.

26 Newman Del: *A Touch from God* (Apex, Clacton on Sea, London, 2010), p. 36.

27 Conversation related by David Litchfield, Author interview (Sinclair), July 27, 2019.

28 Litchfield, David: Author interview (Sinclair), July 27, 2019.

29 Ibid.

30 Ibid.

31 Brown, Geoff: "McCartney: Life After Death," *Melody Maker*, November 30, 1974, p. 9.

32 Andrews, Nancy: Author interview (Sinclair), August 9, 2021.

33 Kaye, Lenny: "Paul Plays Ball," *Disc*, October 12, 1974, p. 22.

34 Gallagher, Dorothy: "Paul McCartney: Growing Up, Up and Away from the Beatles," *Redbook*, September 1974, p. 122.

35 Brown, Geoff: "McCartney: Life After Death," *Melody Maker*, November 30, 1974, pp. 8–9.

36 Ingham, Jonh, with Laurence Marks: "Wings: The Band That's Alright Tonight," *Circus*, September 1975, p. 31.

37 Lewisohn, Mark: The Paul McCartney Interview, *Club Sandwich*, No. 72, Winter, 1994, p. 9.

38 Hickey, William: "Aside Lines," *Daily Telegraph*, September 24 and 28, p. 9 in both cases.

39 Gallo, Armando: "Wife, Player, Mother, Lover . . . Linda," *Sounds*, October 5, 1974, p. 8.

40 Horide, Rosemary: "McCartney—School, My Kids, and Me," *Disc*, December 7, 1974, pp. 6–7.

41 Britton, Geoff: Author interview (Sinclair), August 27, 2019.

42 Horide, Rosemary: "McCartney: School, My Kids, and Me," *Disc*, December 7, 1974, pp. 6–7.

43 O'Duffy, Alan: Author interview (Sinclair) September 21, 2019.

44 Litchfield, David: Author interview (Sinclair), July 27, 2019.

45 Carr, Roy: "The Country Hams: 'Walking in the Park With Eloise' (EMI)," *NME*, October 26, 1974, p. 17.

46 Byrom, Sue: "The Country Hams: Walking in the Park With Eloise (EMI 2220)," *Record Mirror*, November 9, 1974, p. 35.

47 Horide, Rosemary: "McCartney: School, My Kids, and Me," *Disc*, December 7, 1974, p. 6.

CHAPTER 5

1 Hilburn, Robert: "Hard Day's Rite for Harrison," *Los Angeles Times*, October 25, 1974, p. 21.

2 Freeman, Alan: Audio interview with Alan Freeman for *Rock Around the World*, October 14, 1974.

3 Robinson, Lisa: "Being Born in Liverpool Does Carry With It . . . err . . . Certain Responsibilities," *NME*, December 11, 1976, pp. 22–23.

4 Robinson, Lisa: "The *Hit Parader* Interview: Paul and Linda McCartney," *Hit Parader*, May 1975, p. 36.

5 Horide, Rosemary: "The Music & Wings," *Disc*, December 14, 1974, p. 12.

6 Carr, Roy: "Wings: 'Junior's Farm'/'Sally G' (EMI)," *NME*, October 26, 1974, p. 17.

7 Jones, Allan: "Wings: 'Junior's Farm' (EMI)," *Melody Maker*, November 2, 1974, p. 17.

8 Byrom, Sue: "Wings: 'Junior's Farm' (EMI)," *Record Mirror*, November 2, 1974, p. 35.

9 Peel, John: "Good on Yer, Paul Baby," *Sounds*, November 2, 1974, p. 32.

10 Francis, Michael, with Paul Elliott: *Star Man: The Right Hand Man of Rock 'N' Roll* (Simon & Schuster, New York, 2003), p. 72.

11 Gambaccini, Paul: *Paul McCartney: In His Own Words* (Quick Fox, New York, 1983), p. 49.

12 Murray, Charles Shaar: "The Raps of Wacky Macca," *NME*, July 26, 1975, pp. 20–33.

13 Litchfield, David: Audio interview for *One Hand Clapping* documentary film, August 1974.

14 Britton, Geoff: Author interview (Sinclair), April 2, 2022.

15 Litchfield, David: Author interview (Sinclair), July 27, 2019.

16 Pike, Jeffrey: "Jimmy McCulloch," *Guitar*, January 1975, p. 20.

17 Edelson, Howie: "Winging It with Denny Laine," *Beatlefan*, July-October 2006.

18 Britton, Geoff: Author interview (Sinclair), August 27, 2019.

19 Ibid.

20 Andrews, Eamonn: *For Ever and Ever, Eamonn: The Public and Private Life of Eamonn Andrews* (Grafton Books, London, 1989), pp. 19–22.

21 Gambaccini, Paul: Audio interview with Paul McCartney for BBC Radio 1 *Rock Week*, broadcast on May 24, 1975.

22 Andrews, James: "Firebird in Jim's Wings," *Sounds*, May 31, 1975, p. 31.

23 Uncredited: "Geoff Britton," *Wings Official Fun Club*, No. 3, 1974, p. 10.

24 Britton, Geoff: Author interview (Sinclair), August 27, 2019.

25 Miles, Barry: *Venus and Mars Archive Edition* (MPL Communications, London, 2014), p. 116.

26 Litchfield, David: Author interview (Sinclair), July 27, 2019.

27 Pike, Jeffrey: "Jimmy McCulloch," *Guitar*, January 1975, p. 20.

28 Peebles, Andy: Audio interview with Paul McCartney for BBC Radio 1, May 26, 1980.

29 Ingham, Jonh, with Laurence Marks: *"Wings: The Band That's Alright Tonight,"* *Circus*, September 1975, p. 30.

30 McCartney, Paul: Author interview (Kozinn), May 11, 2007.

31 Britton, Geoff: Author interview (Sinclair), April 2, 2022.

32 Welch, Chris: *Paul McCartney: The Definitive Biography* (Proteus, London, 1984), p. 88.

33 Fielding, Sarah: "How Paul and Linda Got Wings and Took Their Band on the Run," *TV Times*, December 1974, p. 6.

34 Fielding, Sarah: "How Paul and Linda Got Wings and Took Their Band on the Run," *TV Times*, December 1974, p. 6.

35 Mills, Nancy: "John, Paul, George, Ringo . . . and Linda," *The Guardian*, December 18, 1974, p. 9.

36 Peacock, Steve: "Paul McCartney & Wings: Yesterday & Today," *Street Life*, April 3–16, 1976, p. 27.

37 Gambaccini, Paul: *Paul McCartney: In His Own Words* (Quick Fox, New York, 1983), pp. 39–40.

38 Russell, Willy: Author interview (Sinclair), May 14, 2020.

39 Robinson, Lisa: "Lennon on Sgt. Pepper Way," *NME*, October 26, 1974, p. 12.

40 Brown, Peter: Author interview (Kozinn), May 1, 2020.

41 Key, Ivor: "Beatlemania Is Back—with Added Guitar," *Daily Express*, November 14, 1974, p. 13.

42 Robinson, Lisa: "Lennon on Sgt. Pepper Way," *NME*, October 26, 1974, p. 12.

43 Horide, Rosemary: "Rock 'N' Roll Exile—Part 2," *Disc*, June 7, 1975, p. 11.

44 Thomas, Steve: Author interview (Sinclair), April 3, 2020.

45 Ibid.

46 Mills, Nancy: "Hey Linda, If Music Be the Food of Love, Play On . . . ," *Honey*, June 1975, p. 5.

47 Horide, Rosemary: "School, My Kids, and Me," *Disc*, December 7, 1974, p. 6.

48 Fielding, Sarah: "How Paul and Linda Got Wings and Took Their Band on the Run," *TV Times*, December 1974, p. 6.

49 Brown, Geoff: "McCartney: Life After Death," *Melody Maker*, November 30, 1974, pp. 8–9.

50 Ingham, Jonh, with Laurence Marks: "Wings: The Band That's Alright Tonight," *Circus*, September 1975, p. 31.

51 Pike, Jeffrey: "Jimmy McCulloch," *Guitar*, January 1975, p. 20.

52 Moore, Carroll: "Waiting in the Wings," *Beat Instrumental*, December 1974, p. 57.

53 Goodman, Joan: Audio interview with Paul McCartney, May 1983. Interview courtesy of Charles Deering McCormick Library of Special Collections, Northwestern University Libraries.

54 Block, Adam: "The Makka Material," *McCartney: Beatle on Wings*, Countrywide Publications K.49569, 1976, p. 63.

55 Tax information taken from *Melody Maker*, October 11, 1975, p. 18.

56 Gambaccini, Paul: "Dawn of the Age of Venus and Mars: McCartneys, Wings Take to the Stars," *Rolling Stone*, July 17, 1975, p. 12.

57 Book information taken from Paul Gambaccini: Audio interview with Paul McCartney for BBC Radio 1 *Rock Week*, broadcast on May 24, 1975.

58 Welch, Chris: "McCartney: Abbey Road Revisited," *Melody Maker*, May 31, 1975, p. 3.

59 Welch, Chris: "Just an Ordinary Superstar," *Melody Maker*, October 4, 1975, p. 56.

60 Welch, Chris: "McCartney—Abbey Road Revisited," *Melody Maker*, May 31, 1975, p. 3.

61 Ibid.

62 Mackie, Rob: "Pope Loony Wants to Noogaloo," *Sounds*, April 12, 1975, p. 12.

63 Goodman, Joan: Unedited *Playboy* interview transcripts, May 3, 1984, Part 2, p. 25. Courtesy of Charles Deering McCormick Library of Special Collections, Northwestern University Libraries.

64 Pang, May: *Instamatic Karma* (St. Martin's Press, New York, 2008), p. 98.

65 Salewicz, Chris: Unedited audio interview with Paul McCartney for *Q Magazine*, September 1986.

66 Charlesworth, Chris: "Rock On!," *Melody Maker,* March 8, 1975, p. 32.

67 Miles, Barry: *Venus and Mars* Archive Edition (MPL Communications, London, 2014), p. 109.

68 Pang, May: Author interview (Kozinn), March 10, 2008.

69 Fong-Torres, Ben: "Yesterday, Today and Paul," *Rolling Stone,* June 17, 1976, p. 22.

70 Robinson, Lisa: "Being Born in Liverpool Does Carry With It . . . err . . . Certain Responsibilities," *NME,* December 11, 1976, pp. 22–23.

71 Hennessey, Mike: "Sgt Pepper Show May Still Tour U.S.," *Billboard,* January 25, 1975, p. 3.

72 Block, Adam: "The Makka Material," *McCartney: Beatle on Wings,* Countrywide Publications K.49569, 1976, p. 57.

73 Welch, Chris: "Just an Ordinary Superstar," *Melody Maker,* October 4, 1975, p. 56.

74 Riley, Marc: Audio interview with David Bowie for BBC Radio 6 Music, 2004.

75 McCartney, Paul: Author interview (Kozinn), May 11, 2007.

76 Film treatment courtesy of the Isaac Asimov Collection, Howard Gotlieb Archival Research Center, Boston University. Treatment undated but most likely written in late 1974.

77 Ibid.

78 Pang, May: Author interview (Kozinn), March 10, 2008.

CHAPTER 6

1 Uncredited: "Paul McCartney: Getting Better All the Time, The Complete Interview—Live and Uncut!," *Reader's Digest*, 2001.

2 Information taken from legal documents, *McCartney v. Lennon, Harrison, Starkey, Apple Corps and Maclen Music Ltd* (J84-647) Part 3_212.

3 Carr, Roy: "They didn't have to be so nice," *NME*, May 17, 1975, p. 27.

4 Hamill, Pete: "Long Night's Journey into Day: A Conversation with John Lennon," *Rolling Stone*, June 5, 1975, p. 48.

5 Associated Press: "McCartney Due in N.O. for Album," *The Shreveport Times*, January 9, 1975, p. 11C.

6 Taylor, Derek: *Fifty Years Adrift* (Genesis Publications, Guildford, 1984), letter reproduced on p. 463.

7 Goodman, Joan: "Playboy Interview: Paul and Linda McCartney," *Playboy*, December 1984, p. 84.

8 Goodman, Joan: Unedited *Playboy* interview transcripts, May 3, 1984, Part 3, pp. 2–3. Courtesy of Charles Deering McCormick Library of Special Collections, Northwestern University Libraries.

9 Pang, May: *Instamatic Karma* (St. Martin's Press, New York, 2008), p. 137.

10 O'Duffy, Alan: Author interview (Sinclair), September 21, 2019.

11 Ibid.

12 Wirt, John: "Paul McCartney Recalls 1975 Mardi Gras, 'My Carnival' on 'Venus and Mars' Re-release," *The Advocate*, March 5, 2015 (based on historic reports from January 1975).

13 Welch, Chris: "Abbey Road Revisited," *Melody Maker*, May 31, 1975, p. 3.

14 White, Timothy: "When Toussaint Goes Marching In," *Crawdaddy*, May 1975, p. 48.

15 Conversation related by White, Timothy: "When Toussaint Goes Marching In," *Crawdaddy*, May 1975, p. 50.

16 Grace, Roberta: Author interview (Sinclair), May 20, 2021.

17 O'Duffy, Alan: Author interview (Sinclair), September 21, 2019.

18 Britton, Geoff: Author interview (Sinclair), April 17, 2020.

19 O'Duffy, Alan: Author interview (Sinclair), September 21, 2019.

20 Dorsey, Tony: Author interview (Kozinn), October 8, 2019.

21 Grace, Roberta: Author interview (Sinclair), May 20, 2021.

22 Block, Adam: "The Makka Material," *McCartney: Beatle on Wings*, K.49569, 1976, pp. 63–64.

23 O'Duffy, Alan: Author interview (Sinclair), September 21, 2019.

24 Dorsey, Tony: Author interview (Kozinn), October 8, 2019.

25 Britton, Geoff: Author interview (Sinclair), August 27, 2019.

26 Ingham, Jonh with Laurence Marks: "Wings: The Band That's Alright Tonight," *Circus*, September 1975, p. 33.

27 O'Duffy, Alan: Author interview (Sinclair), September 21, 2019.

28 Dorsey, Tony: Author interview (Kozinn), October 8, 2019.

29 Britton, Geoff: Author interview (Sinclair), April 17, 2020.

30 Welch, Chris: *Paul McCartney—The Definitive Biography* (Proteus, London, 1984), pp. 89–93.

31 Uncredited: "Britten Quits to Work on Film," *Disc*, March 8, 1975, p. 3. Uncredited: "Wings Man Quits," *NME*, March 8, 1975, p. 2.

32 Britton, Geoff: Author interview (Sinclair), August 27, 2019.

33 Gelly, Dave: *The Facts About a Pop Group* (Whizzard Publications Ltd., London, 1976).

34 Prince, Tony: Audio interview with Linda McCartney for Radio Luxembourg, March 1976.

35 Ingham, Jonh, with Laurence Marks: "Wings: The Band That's Alright Tonight," *Circus*, September 1975, p. 30.

36 SF: "Interview with Joe English," *Modern Drummer*, Winter 1985.

37 English, Joe: Author interview (Sinclair), July 9, 2024.

38 Uncredited: "Meeting Joe English," *Wings Official Fun Club*, No. 1, 1976, p. 7.

39 SF: "Interview with Joe English," *Modern Drummer*, Winter 1985.

40 Peacock, Steve: "Down the Laine," *Sounds*, August 2, 1975, p. 7.

41 Dorsey, Tony: Author interview (Kozinn), October 17, 2019.

42 Gambaccini, Paul: Audio interview with Paul McCartney for BBC Radio 1 *Rock Week*, broadcast on May 5, 1975.

43 Gambaccini, Paul: Audio interview with Paul McCartney for BBC Radio 1 *Rock Week*, broadcast on May 24, 1975.

44 Dorsey, Tony: Author interview (Kozinn), October 17, 2019.

45 Miles, Barry: *Venus and Mars* Archive Edition (MPL Communications, London, 2014), p. 47.

46 O'Duffy, Alan: Author interview (Sinclair), September 21, 2019.

47 O'Duffy, Alan: Author interview (Sinclair), September 21, 2019.

48 Read, Lorna: "Arranging What the Man Says," *Beat Instrumental*, November 1975, p. 6.

49 English, Joe: Author interview (Sinclair), July 9, 2024.

50 Block, Adam: "The Makka Material," *McCartney: Beatle on Wings*, K.49569, 1976, pp. 63–64.

51 Peacock, Steve: "Down the Laine," *Sounds*, August 2, 1975, p. 7.

52 Grace, Roberta: Author interview (Sinclair), May 20, 2021.

53 Uncredited: "Wings Take Off With New Member," *Beat Instrumental*, July 1975.

54 Horne, Nicky: Audio interview with Paul McCartney for *Your Mother Won't Like This* on Capital Radio, September 17, 1975.

55 Andrews, James: "Firebird in Jim's Wings," *Sounds*, May 31, 1975, p. 31.

56 O'Duffy, Alan: Author interview (Sinclair), September 21, 2019.

57 Fox-Cumming, Ray: "The Unknown Quantity," *Record Mirror & Disc*, October 4, 1975, p. 13.

58 McCartney, Paul: Via Paul McCartney's website newsletter, *You Gave Me the Answer: Professor Longhair Special*, February 28, 2019.

59 Murray, Charles Shaar: "The Raps of Wacky Macca," *NME*, July 26, 1975, pp. 20–33.

60 Gambaccini, Paul: Audio interview with Paul McCartney for BBC Radio 1 *Rock Week*, broadcast on May 24, 1975.

61 Ibid.

62 Read, Lorna: "Arranging What the Man Says," *Beat Instrumental*, November 1975, p. 4.

63 Dorsey, Tony: Author interview (Kozinn), October 17, 2019.

64 Uncredited: "Teazers," *NME*, February 15, 1975, p. 48.

65 Charlesworth, Chris: "Rock On!" *Melody Maker*, March 8, 1975, p. 32.

66 Horide, Rosemary: "Rock 'N' Roll Exile—Part 2," *Disc*, June 7, 1975, p. 11.

CHAPTER 7

1 Claw, D. J.: "Paul McCartney: Making Music at the Mardi Gras," *Blytheville Courier News*, March 10, 1975, p. 11.

2 Block, Adam: "The Makka Material," *McCartney: Beatle on Wings*, Countrywide Publications, K.49569, 1976, p. 64.

3 O'Duffy, Alan: Author interview (Sinclair), September 21, 2019.

4 Smith, Sidney: Author interview (Sinclair), February 11, 2021.

5 Ibid.

6 Horide, Rosemary: "The Lovely Linda," *Disc*, June 7, 1975, p. 7.

7 Nocentelli, Leo: Author interview (Sinclair), August 22, 2019.

8 Ingham, Jonh, with Laurence Marks: "Wings: The Band That's Alright Tonight," *Circus*, September 1975, p. 34.

9 Associated Press: "Ex-Beatles Emerges on Riverboat," via *The Shreveport Times*, February 14, 1975, p. 8A.

10 McConnell, Andy: "The McCartneys in New Orleans (Again)," *Sounds*, March 1, 1975, p. 10.

11 Dialogue taken from *Venus and Mars* archive edition DVD. Extra dialogue from Claw, D. J.: "Paul McCartney: Making Music at the Mardi Gras," *Blytheville Courier News*, March 10, 1975, p. 11.

12 Uncredited: "Band on the Bayou: The McCartneys' Cruise Through New Orleans," *Rolling Stone*, March 27, 1975, p. 11.

13 Smith, Sidney: Author interview (Sinclair), February 11, 2021.

14 Ibid.

15 Welch, Chris: "Abbey Road Revisited," *Melody Maker*, May 31, 1975, p. 3.

16 Kirsch, Bob: "A Day in the Life of . . . Bruce Wendell," *Billboard*, March 15, 1975, p. 35.

17 Welch, Chris: "Abbey Road Revisited," *Melody Maker*, May 31, 1975, p. 3.

18 Irwin, Colin: "McCartney's Country Romp," *Melody Maker*, February 15, 1975, p. 14.

19 Thirkettle, Lynne: "Disc: The Single Minded," *Disc*, February 8, 1975, p. 8.

20 Byrom, Sue: "Singles," *Record Mirror*, February 8, 1975, p. 21.

21 Shaar Murray, Charles: "Platters," *NME*, February 8, 1975, p. 19.

22 Smith, Sidney: Author interview (Sinclair), February 11, 2021.

23 O'Duffy, Alan: Author interview (Sinclair), September 21, 2019.
24 Gambaccini, Paul: Audio interview with Paul McCartney for BBC Radio 1 *Rock Week*, broadcast on May 24, 1975.
25 Gambaccini, Paul: Audio interview with Paul McCartney for BBC Radio 1 *Rock Week*, broadcast on May 5, 1975.
26 Mason, Dave: Author question answered during Facebook Q&A, February 5, 2021.
27 O'Duffy, Alan: Author interview (Sinclair), September 21, 2019.

CHAPTER 8

1 Ibid.
2 Bonici, Ray: Audio interview with Paul McCartney for *SFX Magazine*, April 17, 1982.
3 Uncredited: "Beatle's Wife on Drugs Charge," *Daily Express*, March 4, 1975, p. 1.
4 Brown, Peter: Unpublished interview with Mark Lewisohn, October 3, 2016.
5 Uncredited: "Beatle Wife Held on US Drug Charge," *Daily Mail*, March 4, 1975, p. 16.
6 Murray, Charles Shaar: "The Raps of Wacky Macca," *NME*, July 26, 1975, pp. 20–33.
7 Sabol, Blair: "Linda—Who Does She Think She Is? Mrs. Paul McCartney?," *Village Voice*, April 14, 1975, p. 6.
8 Ibid.
9 Gambaccini, Paul: Audio interview with Paul McCartney for BBC Radio 1 *Rock Week*, broadcast on May 5, 1975.
10 Scott, Tom: Author interview by email (Sinclair), September 21, 2019.
11 Gambaccini, Paul: Audio interview with Paul McCartney for BBC Radio 1 *Rock Week*, broadcast on May 5, 1975.
12 Scott, Tom: Author interview by email (Sinclair), September 21, 2019.
13 Caillat, Ken, and Steve Stiefel: *Making Rumours* (Turner Publishing Company, NJ, 2012), p. 239.
14 Irwin, Colin: "Cruising with Macca," *Melody Maker*, April 1, 1978, pp. 26–27.
15 Powell, Aubrey: Author interview (Sinclair), May 15, 2020.
16 Ibid.
17 Info taken from the *Los Angeles Times*, March 11, 1975, p. 2. Extra info taken from the *New York Times*, April 9, 1975. Quote taken from Uncredited: "Linda 'Not Guilty,'" *Daily Mail*, March 11, 1975, p. 4.
18 Caillat, Ken, and Steve Stiefel: *Making Rumours* (Turner Publishing Company, New Jersey, 2012), pp. 11–12.
19 O'Duffy, Alan: Author interview (Sinclair), September 21, 2019.
20 Dorsey, Tony: Author interview (Kozinn), October 8, 2019.
21 O'Duffy, Alan: Author interview (Sinclair), September 21, 2019.
22 O'Duffy, Alan: Author interview (Sinclair), September 21, 2019.
23 Melly, George: *Venus and Mars* album press kit, issued on May 31, 1975.
24 English, Joe: Author interview (Sinclair), July 9, 2024.
25 Powell, Aubrey: Author interview (Sinclair), May 15, 2020.
26 Ibid.
27 Goodman, Joan: Unedited *Playboy* interview transcripts, April 27, 1984, Part 1, pp. 90–91. Courtesy of Charles Deering McCormick Library of Special Collections, Northwestern University Libraries.
28 O'Duffy, Alan: Author interview (Sinclair), September 21, 2019.
29 Powell, Aubrey: Author interview (Sinclair), May 15, 2020.
30 McCartney, Paul: *You Gave Me the Answer*: Professor Longhair Special, paulmccartney.com, February 28, 2019.
31 Ibid.
32 Nocentelli, Leo: Author interview (Sinclair), August 22, 2019.
33 Sabol, Blair: "Linda—Who Does She Think She Is? Mrs. Paul McCartney?," *Village Voice*, April 14, 1975, p. 7.
34 O'Duffy, Alan: Author interview (Sinclair), September 21, 2019.
35 Ibid.
36 Benson, Harry: *Paul* (Taschen, Köln, 2022), p. 10.
37 Jones, Kenney: *Let the Good Times Roll* (Blink Publishing, London, 2018), pp. 212–213.

CHAPTER 9

1 Horide, Rosemary: "The Lovely Linda," *Disc*, June 7, 1975, p. 7.
2 Horide, Rosemary: "School, My Kids, and Me," *Disc*, December 7, 1974, pp. 1, 6–7.
3 English, Joe: Author interview (Sinclair), July 9, 2024.
4 Kaye, Roger: "From Wings to Gospel Rock," *Star Telegraph*, May 10, 1981, pp. 1F–10F.
5 Miles, Barry: *Wings at the Speed of Sound* archive edition (MPL Communications, London, 2014), p. 22.
6 Uncredited: "Drugs and Me, by Beatle Paul," *Daily Mirror*, April 3, 1975, p. 7.
7 Goodman, Joan: Audio interview with Linda McCartney, Tape 179B-A+B, May 2–6, 1983. Interview courtesy of Charles Deering McCormick Library of Special Collections, Northwestern University Libraries.
8 Uncredited: "Ex-Beatle Paul Helps Children," *Liverpool Echo*, April 18, 1975, p. 7.
9 Harris, Bob: Video interview with John Lennon for the BBC's *Old Grey Whistle Test*, broadcast on April 18, 1975.
10 Bonici, Ray: Audio interview with Paul McCartney for *SFX Magazine*, April 17, 1982.
11 Uncredited: "Capitol 3rd Qtr Sales Off 31.5%," *Cash Box*, May 17, 1975, p. 9.

12 Trust, Sam: Author interview (Sinclair), April 13, 2022.
13 Unsigned: "From the Music Capitals of the World," *Billboard*, June 28, 1975, p. 69.
14 Capitol Records press release issued on May 15, 1975.
15 Memo from Tony Brainsby to Brian Brolly, April 22, 1975.
16 Gambaccini, Paul: *London Town Special*, audio interview with Paul McCartney and Denny Laine for BBC Radio 1, March 31, 1978.
17 Allen, Colin: Email exchange with author (Sinclair), September 13, 2019.
18 McGear, Mike: Interview from the liner notes for the deluxe reissue of the *McGear* album, Esoteric Recordings, 2019, p. 27.
19 Money, Zoot: Author interview (Sinclair), September 29, 2019.
20 Gambaccini, Paul: "Dawn of the Age of Venus and Mars: McCartneys, Wings Take to the Stars," *Rolling Stone*, July 17, 1975, p. 12.
21 Clark, Tony: Author interview (Sinclair), February 16, 2017.
22 Peckham, George: *George Peckham—Porky's Prime Cuts* (George Peckham/Apcor Books, Netherlands, 2018), p. 120.
23 Gambaccini, Paul: "Dawn of the Age of Venus and Mars: McCartneys, Wings Take to the Stars," *Rolling Stone*, July 17, 1975, p. 9.
24 Gambaccini, Paul: "Dawn of the Age of Venus and Mars: McCartneys, Wings Take to the Stars," *Rolling Stone*, July 17, 1975, p. 12.
25 Ibid.
26 Litchfield, David: Author interview (Sinclair), July 27, 2019.
27 Loveday, Bob: Author interview (Sinclair), July 8, 2024.
28 Litchfield, David: Author interview (Sinclair), July 27, 2019.
29 Norden, Maggie: Audio interview with Paul and Linda McCartney for the *Hullabaloo* show, Capital Radio, broadcast on December 23, 1979.
30 Goodman, Joan: Unedited *Playboy* interview transcripts, May 3, 1984, Part 3, p. 16. Courtesy of Charles Deering McCormick Library of Special Collections, Northwestern University Libraries.
31 Goodman, Joan: Unedited *Playboy* interview transcripts, May 3, 1984, Part 2, pp. 31–32. Courtesy of Charles Deering McCormick Library of Special Collections, Northwestern University Libraries.
32 Uncredited: "Wings (Capitol 4091) Listen to What the Man Said," *Cash Box*, May 31, 1975, p. 24.
33 Peel, John: "Listen to . . . Another Winner," *Sounds*, May 17, 1975, p. 46.
34 Goddard, Lon: "Singles—Wings," *Disc*, May 24, 1975, p. 8.
35 Irwin, Colin: "Listen to What the Man Said (EMI)," *Melody Maker*, May 24, 1975, p. 16.
36 Fox-Cumming, Ray: "Spreading Summery Wings," *Record Mirror*, May 24, 1975, p. 25.
37 Philips, Kate: "Philosophical Dumb Crambo of the Week," *NME*, May 24, 1975, p. 15.
38 Percival, Eamonn: "Listening to What the Man Said," *Record Mirror*, May 31, 1975, p. 10.
39 Horide, Rosemary: "The Basic Mr. McCulloch," *Disc*, June 21, 1975, p. 24.
40 Welch, Chris: "Abbey Road Revisited," *Melody Maker*, May 31, 1975, p. 3.
41 Murray, Charles Shaar: "Paul Rolls It Home," *NME*, January 19, 1974, p. 12.
42 Murray, Charles Shaar: "The Raps of Wacky Macca," *NME*, July 26, 1975, p. 20.
43 Ibid.
44 Brown, Geoff: "McCartney: Life After Death," *Melody Maker*, November 30, 1974, pp. 8–9.
45 Ingham, Jonh with Laurence Marks: "Wings: The Band That's Alright Tonight," *Circus*, September 1975, p. 34.
46 Welch, Chris: "Wings: Shooting Stars!" *Melody Maker*, May 31, 1975, p. 22.
47 Flood, Mike: "Wings: Band on a Stroll," *Sounds*, May 31, 1975, p. 19.
48 Fox-Cumming, Ray: "Wings Fly to New Heights," *Record Mirror*, May 31, 1975, p. 27.
49 Horide, Rosemary: "Wonderful Wings," *Disc*, May 31, 1975, p. 20.
50 Nelson, Paul: "Venus & Mars: Wings' Non-stellar Flight," *Rolling Stone*, July 31, 1975, p. 52.
51 Nightingale, Ann: Audio interview with Linda McCartney for *Rock Around the World*, BBC Radio 1, December 1976.
52 Pearce, Garth: "The McCartney Memoirs," *Daily Express*, February 10, 1977, p. 7.
53 Ibid.
54 Santosuosso, Ernie: "'Giving Audiences What They Want'—McCartney," *Boston Globe*, May 24, 1976, p. 15.
55 Pearce, Garth: "The McCartney Memoirs," *Daily Express*, February 10, 1977, p. 7.
56 NAMM: Video interview with Rusty Brutsche of Showco, November 19, 2015.
57 Wiseman, Rich: "He Writes the Words for John," *Press and Sun Bulletin*, May 30, 1976, p. 13D.
58 Lyda, Morris: Author interview (Sinclair), October 7, 2021.
59 Ibid.
60 Peacock, Ian: Author interview (Sinclair), September 18, 2021.
61 Gambaccini, Paul: Audio interview with Paul McCartney for *The Birth of a Band* on BBC Radio 1, September 1975.
62 Wright, Michael: "The Gibson Interview—Denny Laine," *Gibson* [online], July 7, 2010.
63 Gambaccini, Paul: Audio interview with Paul McCartney for *The Birth of a Band* on BBC Radio 1, September 1975.
64 Read, Lorna: "Arranging What the Man Says," *Beat Instrumental*, November 1975, p. 5.
65 Welch, Chris: "And in the evening she's the singer in the band," *Melody Maker*, September 27, 1975, p. 8.

66 Trench, Fiachra: Author interview (Sinclair), October 31, 2019.
67 Goodman, Arty: "Wings: At the Speed of a Familiar Sound," unknown publication, May 20, 1976.
68 Murray, Charles Shaar: "The Raps of Wacky Macca," *NME*, July 26, 1975, pp. 20–33.
69 Pearce, Garth: "The McCartney Memoirs," *Daily Express*, February 9, 1977, p. 17.
70 McCartney, Ruth: "My Stepbrother Was a Beatle," *19 Magazine*, March 1983, pp. 56–57.
71 Welch, Chris: "Just an Ordinary Superstar," *Melody Maker*, October 4, 1975, p. 21.

CHAPTER 10

1 Brainsby, Tony: Letter to Paul McCartney, dated August 15, 1975.
2 Rudis, Al: "A Pilgrimage to See Saint Paul," *Sounds*, June 26, 1976, p. 23.
3 Peacock, Steve: "Paul McCartney & Wings—Yesterday & Today," *Street Life*, April 3–16, 1976, p. 27.
4 Connolly, Ray: "Connolly on McCartney," *Evening Standard*, December 2, 1972, p. 13.
5 Byrom, Sue: "Wings: Letting Go (EMI R 6008)," *Record Mirror & Disc*, September 13, 1975, p. 31.
6 MacDonald, Ian: "Platters," *NME*, September 13, 1975, p. 13.
7 Charlesworth, Chris, "Wings: Letting Go," *Melody Maker*, September 13, 1975, p. 19.
8 Pritchard, Terry: Memorandum to regional promoters, "Wings Over Britain," dated August 21, 1975.
9 Hughes, Wendy: "Long-Playing Success for McCartney at 33 1/3," *Sunday Times*, September 14, 1975.
10 Crowder, Alan J.: Memorandum—General Notes on Band Requirements on Tour, undated (September 1975).
11 McCartney, Paul, and Mark Lewisohn, editor: *Wingspan* (Bulfinch Press, London, 2002), Chapter 7.
12 Miles, Barry: *Wings at the Speed of Sound* archive edition (MPL Communications, London, 2014), p. 71.
13 Welch, Chris: "And in the evening she's the singer in the band," *Melody Maker*, September 27, 1975, p. 8.
14 Peacock, Ian: Author interview (Sinclair), September 18, 2021.
15 Lyda, Morris: Author interview (Sinclair), October 7, 2021.
16 Pearce, Garth: "The McCartney Memoirs," *Daily Express*, February 10, 1977, p. 7.
17 Harvey, Peter: "The Confident Front-Man," *Record Mirror & Disc*, October 11, 1975, p. 10.
18 Casey, Howie: Author interview (Sinclair), October 19, 2019.
19 Norden, Maggie: Audio interview with Paul McCartney for Capital Radio, September 18, 1975.
20 Fox-Cumming, Ray: "Wings at Home . . . in Southampton," *Record Mirror & Disc*, September 20, 1975, p. 10.
21 Mills, Bart: "It's Time Paul Came in from the Wings!" *Daily Mail*, September 11, 1975, p. 22.
22 Welch, Chris: "Fly Away, Paul," *Melody Maker*, September 20, 1975, pp. 8 and 50.
23 Welch, Chris: "Just an Ordinary Superstar," *Melody Maker*, October 4, 1975, p. 21.
24 Welch, Chris: "Fly Away, Paul," *Melody Maker*, September 20, 1975, pp. 8 and 50.
25 Spencer, Neil: "Just a Little Light Rocca from Macca," *NME*, September 20, 1975, pp. 5–6.
26 Welch, Chris: "Fly Away, Paul," *Melody Maker*, September 20, 1975, p. 50.
27 Ibid.
28 Hughes, Wendy: "Long-Playing Success for McCartney at 33 1/3," *Sunday Times*, September 14, 1975.
29 Welch, Chris: "Fly Away, Paul," *Melody Maker*, September 20, 1975, p. 9.
30 Northam, Randall: "Wings at the Birmingham Hippodrome," *Birmingham Post*, September 15, 1975, p. 2.
31 Charone, Barbara: "Have Guts Will Travel," *Sounds*, September 20, 1975, pp. 7–8.
32 Trollope, Peter: "Paul Comes Home in Triumph," *Liverpool Echo*, September 16, 1975, p. 3.
33 Uncredited: "England's Wings: Beating the Post-Beatle Stigma," *Rolling Stone*, November 6, 1975, p. 10.
34 Thompson, Steve: "Paul Tells Noisy Fans to Take It Easy," *Liverpool Daily Post*, September 16, 1975.
35 Uncredited: "England's Wings: Beating the Post-Beatle Stigma," *Rolling Stone*, November 6, 1975, p. 10.
36 Chattington, Barry: Author interview (Sinclair), December 15, 2018.
37 Trollope, Peter: "Paul Comes Home in Triumph," *Liverpool Echo*, September 16, 1975, p. 3.
38 Trollope, Peter: "Wings Has the Fans Flying in Ecstasy," *Liverpool Echo*, September 16, 1975.
39 Lyda, Morris: Author interview (Sinclair), October 7, 2021.
40 Giuliano, Geoffrey: *Geoffrey Giuliano in Conversation with Ruth and Angela McCartney, Volume 6* (Icon Audio Arts, Santa Monica, 2018).
41 Ibid.
42 Crawley, Philip: "Rock at Its Best," *Newcastle Journal*, September 19, 1975, p. 8.
43 Uncredited: "Tape Is Silent as in Wings," *Newcastle Evening Chronicle*, September 18, 1975, p. 13.
44 Uncredited: "Now McCartney Takes Wings Down East," *Thanet Times*, October 7, 1975, p. 14.
45 Charlesworth, Chris: "No—They Were Great!" *Melody Maker*, September 27, 1975, p. 38.
46 McCartney, Paul: Video interview for *Wings in the Netherlands*, Veronica TV, recorded on March 24–25, 1976.
47 Coleman, Ray: "Wings: Music for Yesterday—or Today?" *Melody Maker*, September 27, 1975, p. 38.
48 Uncredited: "England's Wings: Beating the Post-Beatle Stigma," *Rolling Stone*, November 6, 1975, p. 10.

49 Ibid.
50 Readers' Poll results, *Melody Maker*, September 20, 1975, pp. 36–37.
51 Dunn, Norman: "Top Gear as Supergroup Runs On," *Aberdeen Evening Express*, September 25, 1975, p. 11.
52 H.M.: "Vintage Music from Wings," *Aberdeen Evening Express*, September 23, 1975, p. 21.
53 Peacock, Ian: Author interview (Sinclair), September 18, 2021.
54 Dunn, Norman: "Top Gear as Supergroup Runs On," *Aberdeen Evening Express*, September 25, 1975, p. 11.
55 Uncredited: Audio interview with Paul McCartney for *London Town Special* on KRTH-101, broadcast on March 25, 1978.
56 The interview and review are quoted in Strachan, Graeme: "Paul McCartney Brought Out the Dundee Cake for Wife Linda at Caird Hall Gig in 1975," *Dundee Evening Telegraph* (Online), September 23, 2020.

CHAPTER 11

1 Miles, Barry: *Wings at the Speed of Sound* archive edition (MPL Communications, London, 2014), pp. 24–25.
2 Rockwell, John: "McCartney, Trying Wings in Three Shows, Talks of Yesterday," *New York Times*, May 21, 1976.
3 Uncredited: "Bottle SOS Starts Hunt," *Daily Mirror*, August 21, 1975, p. 3.
4 Beaton, Graeme: "Why Paul Keeps Flapping his Wings," *The Mirror* (Sydney), October 21, 1975.
5 Harvey, Peter: "The Confident Front-Man," *Record Mirror & Disc*, October 11, 1975, p. 10.
6 Miles, Barry: *Wings at the Speed of Sound* archive edition (MPL Communications, London, 2014), p. 66.
7 Peacock, Steve: Press kit for *Wings at the Speed of Sound*, issued to the press around March 25, 1976.
8 Miles, Barry: *Wings at the Speed of Sound* archive edition (MPL Communications, London, 2014), pp. 24–25.
9 Clark, Tony: Author interview (Sinclair), March 23, 2017.
10 Kaye, Roger: "From Wings to Gospel Rock," *Star Telegraph*, May 10, 1981, pp. 1F, 10F.
11 Welch, Chris: "TV Act I Couldn't Watch," *The Sun* (Sydney), October 20, 1975, p. 22.
12 Welch, Chris: "Linda—Jealous Fans Hated Me," *The Sun*, October 21, 1975, p. 30.
13 Uncredited: "Wings: 'Venus and Mars' 'Rock Show,'" *Billboard*, November 1, 1975, p. 72.
14 Uncredited: "Wings (Capitol P4175) 'Venus and Mars' 'Rock Show,'" *Cash Box*, November 1, 1975, p. 22.
15 Uncredited: "Wings, 'Venus and Mars' Rock Show,'" *Record World*, November 1, 1975, p. 1.
16 Goldman, Vivien: "Singles," *Sounds*, December 6, 1975, p. 28.
17 Byrom, Sue: "Singles—Another from *Venus*," *Record Mirror & Disc*, December 6, 1975, p. 29.
18 Uncredited: "Jet Waits for Pop Star," *The Times*, October 28, 1975, p. 4.
19 Uncredited: "Teenagers Hurt in Wild Crush—Beatles' Welcoming Crowd Jams Streets," *The Age*, June 15, 1964.
20 Uncredited: "No Mania for Ex-Beatle Paul," *The Age*, October 29, 1975, p. 3.
21 Spooner, Peter: "Rush for Tickets—It Was Like Beatlemania," *Sydney Morning Herald*, October 19, 1975, p. 8.
22 Scott, Phil: "Fake Tickets Alert for Wings Concerts," *Sydney Morning Herald*, November 2, 1975, p. 47.
23 Bennett, Gordon: Author interview (Sinclair), May 30, 2021.
24 Ibid.
25 Uncredited: "The Bodyguard in Paul's Life," *The West Australian*, November 5, 1975.
26 Gambaccini, Paul: Audio interview with Paul McCartney and Denny Laine, *London Town Special*, BBC Radio 1, March 31, 1978.
27 Kelton, Greg: "Rock Star Can Play It Cool," *Australian Advertiser*, November 5, 1975.
28 Stewart, Brandon: "Dog Breath," *Hamersley News*, November 20, 1975, p. 13.
29 Argo, Peter: "Paul Puts an End to All the Beatle Reunion Reports," *The West Australian*, November 3, 1975.
30 Ibid.
31 Kelton, Greg: "Rock Star Can Play It Cool," *Australian Advertiser*, November 5, 1975.
32 Horne, Nicky: Audio interview with Paul McCartney for *Your Mother Wouldn't Like It*, Capital Radio, March 26, 1976.
33 Hamilton, John: "Paul's Gig," *The Herald*, November 15, 1975.
34 Casey, Howie: Author interview (Sinclair), October 19, 2019.
35 Du Noyer, Paul: *Conversations with McCartney* (Hodder & Stoughton, London, 2015), p. 120.
36 From an unpublished fan memoir.
37 Bennett, Gordon: Author interview (Sinclair), May 30, 2021.
38 Welch, Chris: "Pressure Cooking," *Melody Maker*, March 27, 1976, p. 13.
39 McCartney, Paul: Audio interview at Tullamarine Airport, November 12, 1975.
40 Video recording of Wings' message to Japanese fans, recorded November 13, 1975.
41 Welch, Chris: "Pressure Cooking," *Melody Maker*, March 27, 1976, p. 13.
42 Lyda, Morris: Author interview (Sinclair), October 7, 2021.
43 Patterson, Bryan: "Paul Flies High on Dazzling Set of Wings," *The Age*, November 14, 1975, p. 2.
44 Hamilton, John: "Paul's Gig," *The Herald*, November 15, 1975.
45 Scott, Phil: "McCartney Plans to Tour Again," *The Sydney Morning Herald*, November 23, 1975, p. 121.
46 Creamer, Beverly: "The Click of Success," *Honolulu Star Bulletin*, December 3, 1975, p. G1.

47 Fallowell, Duncan: "Paul McCartney Today," *Chicago Tribune*, October 14, 1984, p. 6.

48 Creamer, Beverly: "The Click of Success," *Honolulu Star Bulletin*, December 3, 1975, p. G1.

49 Scott, Roger: Audio interview with Paul McCartney and Denny Laine, Capital Radio, November 11, 1978.

50 Gambaccini, Paul: Audio interview with Paul McCartney, *An Evening with Paul McCartney*, BBC Radio 1, broadcast on April 1, 1979.

51 The details of the time the McCartneys spent with Bailey and Helvin are drawn principally from Marie Helvin: *The Autobiography* (Orion, London, 2007), Kindle Edition; and Tom Horton: "Star Tracks," *The Honolulu Advertiser*, December 2, 1975, p. A3.

52 Helvin, Marie: *The Autobiography* (Orion, London, 2007), Kindle Edition.

53 Hamilton, John: "Paul's Gig," *The Herald*, November 15, 1975.

54 McCartney, Paul: Letter to Mal Evans, 1975, Malcolm Frederick Evans Archives.

55 Gruen, Bob: *Lennon: The New York Years* (Stewart, Tabori & Chang, New York, 2005), p. 112.

56 Evans, Malcolm: *Living the Beatles' Legend*, p. 205–206, Malcolm Frederick Evans Archives. Also, Kenneth Womack: *Living the Beatles Legend: The Untold Story of Mal Evans* (Dey Street, New York, 2023), p. 491.

57 Evans, Mal: Quoted in Sandford, Christopher: *McCartney* (Caroll & Graf, New York, 2006), p. 241.

58 Madinger, Chip, with Scott Raile: *Lennonology: Strange Days Indeed* (Open Your Books, Chesterfield, MO, 2015), p. 464.

59 Davies, Hunter: "The McCartneys Try Their Wings on the 'Long and Winding Road,'" *Sunday Times*, May 1, 1976.

60 Peacock, Steve: "Paul McCartney & Wings—Yesterday & Today," *Street Life*, April 3–16, 1976, p. 26.

61 Miles, Barry: *Wings at the Speed of Sound* archive edition (MPL Communications, London, 2014), p. 53.

62 Peacock, Steve: "Paul McCartney & Wings—Yesterday & Today," *Street Life*, April 3–16, 1976, p. 26.

63 A facsimile of the list is included in *Wings at the Speed of Sound* archive edition (MPL Communications, London, 2014).

CHAPTER 12

1 Horne, Nicky: Audio interview with Paul McCartney for Capital Radio, broadcast on March 26, 1976.

2 Henderson, Peter: Author interview (Sinclair), January 5, 2020.

3 Ibid.

4 English, Joe: Author interview (Sinclair), July 9, 2024.

5 SF: "Interview with Joe English," *Modern Drummer*, Winter 1985.

6 Details of the shooting were drawn from Snyder, Patrick, and Ziebarth, Dolores, "'6th Beatle' Mal Evans Killed in Los Angeles," *Rolling Stone*, February 12, 1976, p. 10; reports from the Associated Press, "Former Beatle Associate Shot During Fracas," *The Fresno Bee*, January 7, 1976, p. B5; and United Press International, "Beatles' Manager Is Killed," *The Napa Valley Register*, January 6, 1976, p. 2.

7 United Press International: "Beatles' Manager Is Killed," *The Napa Valley Register*, January 6, 1976, p. 2.

8 Peacock, Steve: Press kit for *Wings at the Speed of Sound*, issued to the press around March 25, 1976.

9 McCartney, Paul: Liner notes for *Working Classical*, 1999.

10 Henderson, Peter: Author interview (Sinclair), January 5, 2020.

11 Du Noyer, Paul: *Conversations with McCartney* (Hodder & Stoughton, London, 2015), pp. 119–120.

12 Iles, Jan: "Jim's Flight of Fancy," *Record Mirror & Disc*, August 14, 1976, p. 7.

13 Uncredited: "Jimmy in the Wings," *Bristol Evening Post*, March 26, 1976.

14 Herman, Gary: "Wings Over America—How Paul McCartney Pilots Them," *Circus*, June 17, 1976, p. 40.

15 Allen, Colin: Email exchange with author (Sinclair), September 13, 2019.

16 Goodman, Joan: Unedited *Playboy* interview transcripts, May 3, 1984, part 3, p. 16. Courtesy of Charles Deering McCormick Library of Special Collections, Northwestern University Libraries.

17 Miles, Barry: *Wings at the Speed of Sound* Archive Edition (MPL Communications, London, 2014), pp. 64–65.

18 Henderson, Peter: Author interview (Sinclair), January 5, 2020.

19 Uncredited: "Meeting Joe English," *Wings Official Fun Club*, No. 1, 1976, p. 7.

20 Ibid.

21 Edelson, Howie: "Winging It With Denny Laine," *Beatlefan*, July-October 2006.

22 Morris, Mark: Audio interview with Joe English for World of Faith Fellowship, January 17, 2019.

23 Allen, Colin: Email exchange with author (Sinclair), September 13, 2019.

24 Ibid.

25 Morris, Mark: Audio interview with Dayle English for World of Faith Fellowship, June 27, 2018.

26 Peacock, Steve: Press kit for *Wings at the Speed of Sound*, issued to the press around March 25, 1976.

27 Miles, Barry: *Wings at the Speed of Sound* Archive Edition (MPL Communications, London, 2014), pp. 64–65.

28 Ibid.

29 Henderson, Peter: Author interview (Sinclair), January 5, 2020.

30 Herman, Gary: "Wings Over America: How Paul McCartney Pilots Them," *Circus*, June 17, 1976, p. 41.

31 Charone, Barbara: "The World Doesn't Need Another Silly Love Song But Here I Go Again," *Sounds*, April 3, 1976, p. 29.

32 Mulhern, Tom: "Paul McCartney," *Guitar*, July 1990, p. 28.

33 Henderson, Peter: Author interview (Sinclair), January 5, 2020.
34 Edelson, Howie: "Winging It with Denny Laine," *Beatlefan*, July-October 2006.
35 Henderson, Peter: Author interview (Sinclair), January 5, 2020.
36 Ibid.
37 Snyder, Patrick: "Beatles Show: The Great White Shuck?" *Rolling Stone*, February 26, 1976.
38 Peacock, Steve: "Paul McCartney & Wings: Yesterday & Today," *Street Life*, April 3–16, 1976, p. 28.
39 Goodman, Joan: Unedited *Playboy* interview transcripts, May 3, 1984, part 2, p. 16. Courtesy of Charles Deering McCormick Library of Special Collections, Northwestern University Libraries.
40 McCartney, Paul: "Message to Joe," included as a bonus track on *Wings at the Speed of Sound* Archive Edition (MPL Communications / Concord Music Group, 2014).
41 McLeod, Pauline with Mark Dowdney: "Yeah! Yeah! Yeah!" *Daily Mirror*, January 23, 1976, p. 3.
42 Herman, Gary: "Wings Over America: How Paul McCartney Pilots Them," *Circus*, June 17, 1976, p. 40.
43 Blaney, John: *Lennon and McCartney Together Alone* (Outline Press, London, 2007), p. 114.
44 Henderson, Peter: Author interview (Sinclair), January 5, 2020.
45 Uncredited: "Hello Beatles!" *Daily Mirror*, January 28, 1976, p. 3.
46 Trench, Fiachra: Author interview (Sinclair), October 31, 2019.
47 McCartney, Paul: Quote via Sticking Out of My Back Pocket: "Warm and Beautiful," from paulmccartney.com, posted May 6, 2016.
48 Goodman, Joan: Unedited *Playboy* interview transcripts, May 3, 1984, part 2, pp. 5–6. Courtesy of Charles Deering McCormick Library of Special Collections, Northwestern University Libraries.
49 McCartney, Paul: Liner notes for *Working Classical*, 1999.
50 Horne, Nicky: Audio interview with Paul McCartney for *Your Mother Wouldn't Like It* show on Capital Radio, March 26, 1976.
51 Henderson, Peter: Author interview (Sinclair), January 5, 2020.
52 Horne, Nicky: Audio interview with Paul McCartney for *Your Mother Wouldn't Like It* show on Capital Radio, March 26, 1976.
53 Ibid.
54 Miles, Barry: *Wings at the Speed of Sound* Archive Edition (MPL Communications, London, 2014), pp. 64–65.
55 Trench, Fiachra: Author interview (Sinclair), October 31, 2019.
56 Peacock, Steve: Press kit for *Wings at the Speed of Sound*, issued to the press around March 25, 1976.
57 Welch, Chris: "Pressure Cooking," *Melody Maker*, March 27, 1976, p. 13.
58 English, Joe: Author interview (Sinclair), July 9, 2024.
59 Henderson, Peter: Author interview (Sinclair), January 5, 2020.
60 Welch, Chris: "Pressure Cooking," *Melody Maker*, March 27, 1976, p. 13.
61 Casey, Howie: Author interview (Sinclair), October 19, 2019.
62 Dorsey, Tony: Author interview (Kozinn), October 17, 2019.
63 Casey, Howie: Author interview (Sinclair), October 19, 2019.
64 Sinclair, Keith J.: "Steve Howard Interview," *ELO Beatles Forever* (Online), April 13, 2013.
65 Ibid.
66 Welch, Chris: "Pressure Cooking," *Melody Maker*, March 27, 1976, p. 13.
67 Henderson, Peter: Author interview (Sinclair), January 5, 2020.
68 Davies, Hunter: "The McCartneys Try Their Wings on the 'Long and Winding Road,'" *Sunday Times*, May 1, 1976.
69 Henderson, Peter: Author interview (Sinclair), January 5, 2020.
70 Herman, Gary: "Wings Over America: How Paul McCartney Pilots Them," *Circus*, June 17, 1976, p. 40.

CHAPTER 13

1 Powell, Aubrey: Author Interview (Sinclair), May 15, 2020.
2 Ocean, Humphrey: Author interview (Sinclair), May 11, 2020.
3 Dorsey, Tony: Author interview (Kozinn), October 17, 2019.
4 Bennett, Gordon: Author interview (Sinclair), May 30, 2020.
5 Callan, Paul: "Yeah! They ARE Coming Back," *Daily Mirror*, March 8, 1976, p. 13.
6 Peacock, Steve: "Paul McCartney & Wings—Yesterday & Today," *Street Life*, April 3–16, p. 27.
7 Giuliano, Geoffrey: *Geoffrey Giuliano in Conversation with Ruth and Angela McCartney, Volume 6* (Icon Audio Arts, Santa Monica, 2018).
8 Ibid.
9 Uncredited: "Jimmy in the Wings," *Bristol Evening Post*, March 26, 1976.
10 Herman, Gary: "Wings Over America: How Paul McCartney Pilots Them," *Circus*, June 17, 1976, p. 40.
11 Peacock, Steve: "Paul McCartney & Wings: Yesterday & Today," *Street Life*, April 3–16, pp. 26–27.
12 Ibid.
13 Chattington, Barry: Author interview (Sinclair), December 15, 2018.
14 Giuliano, Geoffrey: *Geoffrey Giuliano in Conversation with Ruth and Angela McCartney, Volume 6* (Icon Audio Arts, Santa Monica, 2018).
15 McCartney, Mike: *The Macs: Mike McCartney's Family Album* (Delilah Communications Ltd., London, 1981), pages unnumbered.

16 Goodman, Joan: "Playboy Interview: Paul and Linda McCartney," *Playboy*, December 1984, p. 82.

17 Giuliano, Geoffrey: *Geoffrey Giuliano in Conversation with Ruth and Angela McCartney, Volume 6* (Icon Audio Arts, Santa Monica, 2018).

18 Goodman, Joan: *Playboy* interview transcripts, April 27, 1984, Part 1, pp. 26–27. Courtesy of Charles Deering McCormick Library of Special Collections, Northwestern University Libraries.

19 Laine, Denny: "The Real McCartney," *The Sun*, February 2, 1984, p. 9.

20 Uncredited: Video interview for Danish Broadcasting Corporation DR1, recorded March 20, 1976.

21 Uncredited: Audio interview with Wings for Danish Radio, recorded March 21, 1976.

22 MPL Press Release, March 22, 1976.

23 Branton, Allen: Author interview (Sinclair), July 5, 2021.

24 Korinth, Axel: *Rock Show: Die (Ex-) Beatles in Deutschland 1971–1980* (Books on Demand, Germany, 2011), p. 61.

25 Video footage of Wings at Schipol Airport, Amsterdam, Veronica Television, March 24, 1976.

26 Buchan, Alasdair: "A Wild Young Genius of Rock," *Daily Mirror*, October 1, 1979, p. 23.

27 Video interview with Wings for the television feature *Wings in the Netherlands*, recorded on March 25, 1976, Veronica Television.

28 Welch, Chris: "Pressure Cooking," *Melody Maker*, March 27, 1976, p. 13.

29 Rockwell, John: "The Pop Life—3 British Groups Cut New Rock Discs," *New York Times*, April 22, 1976.

30 Tiven, Jon: "*At the Speed of Sound:* Wings," *Audio*, July 1976.

31 Holden, Stephen: "*Wings at the Speed of Sound*," *Rolling Stone*, May 20, 1976.

32 Charone, Barbara: "*Wings at the Speed of Sound* (Parlophone)," *Sounds*, March 27, 1976.

33 Welch, Chris: "Wings: *Wings at the Speed of Sound* (Capitol)," *Melody Maker*, March 27, 1976.

34 Horne, Nicky: Audio interview with Paul McCartney, recorded in Paris, March 26, 1976, *Your Mother Wouldn't Like It*, Capital Radio, London.

35 Cassidy, David: *Could It Be Forever? My Story* (DBC, New York, 2007), Kindle Edition.

36 Watts, Michael: "Paul McCartney: The Yellow Perils of Paulie," *Melody Maker*, January 26, 1980.

37 Uncredited: "Jimmy's Broken Wing," *Record Mirror & Disc*, April 10, 1976, p. 36.

38 Giuliano, Geoffrey: "Life on the McCartney Farm Cultivates Murderous Intent," *Vancouver Sun*, November 27, 1991, p. C6.

39 Callan, Paul: "When the Writing on the Wall Is Kids' Play," *Daily Mirror*, April 27, 1976, p. 13. Further information from an uncredited article in the *Daily Mail*, April 12, 1976.

CHAPTER 14

1 Carr, Roy: "The Trial of James Paul McCartney," *NME*, April 29, 1978, pp. 33–35.

2 Uncredited: "McCartney Honcho 'Rolling' at 36," *People*, July 1976.

3 McCartney, Paul: *The McCartney Years* DVD commentary for "Silly Love Songs," MPL, issued November 12, 2007.

4 Ibid.

5 Pearce, Garth: "The McCartney Memoirs," *Daily Express*, February 10, 1977, p. 7.

6 Dorsey, Tony: Author interview (Kozinn), October 8, 2019.

7 Beaumont, Mark: "A Fab Time," *Uncut*, August 2021, pp. 52–53.

8 Uncredited: "Wings—'Silly Love Songs' (Capitol P4256)," *Cash Box*, April 14, 1976, p. 15.

9 Coon, Caroline: "New Singles," *Melody Maker*, May 15, 1976, p. 3.

10 Farren, Mick: "Platters," *NME*, May 15, 1976, p. 18.

11 Ingham, Jonh: "Singles," *Sounds*, May 15, 1976, p. 44.

12 Byrom, Sue: "Singles," *Record Mirror & Disc*, May 8, 1976, p. 22.

13 Sex Pistols information from *NME*, March 27, 1976, p. 55. Patti Smith information from *Record Mirror & Disc*, April 24, 1976, p. 3. Ramones information from Danny Fields: "How the Ramones Invented Punk Over Two London Gigs," *Square Mile* (online), May 25, 2018.

14 Both sides of the manuscript are shown in McCartney and Muldoon (ed.): *The Lyrics 1956 to the Present*, pp. 56–57.

15 Prince, Tony: "Paul and Linda at It Again!" *Daily Mirror*, April 22, 1978.

16 Uncredited: Audio interview with Paul McCartney for *London Town Special* on KRTH-101, broadcast on March 25, 1978.

17 Fong-Torres, Ben: "Yesterday, Today and Paul," *Rolling Stone*, June 17, 1976, p. 38.

18 (Surname unknown), Stuart: Fan questionnaire mailed to John Lennon in 1976 (precise date unknown). First made available online via Lists of Note.

19 Michaels, Lorne: Offer to the Beatles, *NBC's Saturday Night*, April 24, 1976, available in *Saturday Night Live: The Complete First Season*, Universal, 2006.

20 Scheff, David: "The Playboy Interview: John Lennon," *Playboy*, January 1981.

21 Cocks, Jay: "McCartney Comes Back," *Time*, May 31, 1976, p. 43.

22 Crowley, John: "Wings Across America," *Record Mirror & Disc*, May 15, 1976, p. 7.

23 Stardust, Alvin: *Tales from the Saddle* (Stanley Paul & Co. Ltd., London, 1984), p. 13.

24 Uncredited: "Paul McCartney and Wings," *Teen Talk*, November 1976, p. 55.

25 Ibid.

26 Rockwell, John: "U.S. Tour of McCartney and Wings Is

Off to Triumphant Start in Fort Worth," *New York Times*, May 5, 1976.

27 Maimis, Tony: "Macca Back in the USA," *Sounds*, May 15, 1976, p. 51.

28 Orth, Maureen: "Paul Soars," *Newsweek*, May 4, 1976.

29 Edelson, Howie: "Winging It with Denny Laine," *Beatlefan*, July-October 2006.

30 Adamson, Dale: "Ex-Beatle McCartney Still Dazzles in Wings," *Houston Chronicle*, May 5, 1976.

31 Fields, Danny: Author interview (Kozinn), December 7, 2019.

32 Audience recording of the Olympia Stadium concert, Detroit, MI, May 7, 1976.

33 Ocean, Humphrey: *The Ocean View: Paintings and Drawings of Wings American Tour April to June 1976* (MPL Communications, Ltd., London, 1982), p. 11.

34 Lyda, Morris: Author interview (Sinclair), October 7, 2021.

35 Fong-Torres, Ben: "Yesterday, Today & Paul," *Rolling Stone*, June 17, 1976, p. 19.

36 McLeod, Pauline: "On the Wings of a Storm!" *Daily Mirror*, May 13, 1976, p. 11.

37 Uncredited: "Beatles Plan Reunion," *Daily Mirror*, May 4, 1976, p. 2.

38 Uncredited: "McCartney Tour May Bring Reunion," Associated Press via *Fort Worth Star Telegram*," April 28, 1976, p. 14a.

39 Lawson, Michael: "Beatles' Reunion Untrue But McCartney Wins Praise," *Edmonton Journal*, May 10, 1976, p. 11.

40 Goddard, Peter: "McCartney Backstage Full of Enthusiasm," *Toronto Star*, May 10, 1976.

41 Audience recording of the Richfield Coliseum concert, Cleveland, OH, May 10, 1976.

42 Bennett, Gordon: Author interview (Sinclair), May 30, 2021.

43 Some of Bennett's footage is included in *Wings Over the World* (MPL, 1979).

44 Ocean, Humphrey: Author interview (Sinclair), May 11, 2020.

45 Ocean, Humphrey: *The Ocean View: Paintings and Drawings of Wings American Tour April to June 1976* (MPL Communications, Ltd., London, 1982), p. 12.

46 Von Sternberg, Bob: "More Than Just Memories," *Akron Beacon Journal*, May 11, 1976, p. D-9.

47 The poem is quoted, with slight inaccuracies, in Jack Hafferkamp: "McCartney & Company, Flying High," *Chicago Daily News*, May 11, 1976.

48 Dorsey, Tony: Author interview (Kozinn), October 17, 2019.

49 Casey, Howie: Author interview (Sinclair), October 19, 2019.

50 Audience recording of the second Spectrum concert, Philadelphia, PA, May 14, 1976.

51 Lloyd, Jack: "McCartney Soars on Wings, Brings Back the Old Thrill," *The Philadelphia Enquirer*, May 13, 1976, p. 4-C.

52 Andrews, Nancy: Author interview (Sinclair), August 9, 2021.

53 Robinson, Lisa: "Hey It's a One-a Da Bodles . . . as Ringo's Pals Call Him," *NME*, October 16, 1976, p. 15.

54 Ibid.

55 Basham, Tom: "McCartney and Wings Take Off at Enthusiastic Largo Concert," *Baltimore Sun*, May 17, 1976, p. B1.

56 Rohter, Larry: "Exciting Show by Wings," *Washington Post*, May 18, 1976.

57 Smith, Jeanette: "McCartney Still a Superstar," *Washington Post*, May 18, 1976.

58 Ocean, Humphrey: Author interview (Sinclair), May 11, 2020.

59 Ocean, Humphrey: *The Ocean View: Paintings and Drawings of Wings American Tour April to June 1976* (MPL Communications, Ltd., London, 1982), p. 12.

60 Ocean, Humphrey: Author interview (Sinclair), May 11, 2020.

61 Ibid.

62 SF: "Interview with Joe English," *Modern Drummer*, Winter 1985.

63 Kaye, Roger: "From Wings to Gospel Rock," *Star Telegraph*, May 10, 1981, pp. 1F, 10F.

64 Casey, Howie: Author interview (Sinclair), October 19, 2019.

65 Goodman, Arty: "Wings: At the Speed of a Familiar Sound," unknown publication, May 20, 1976.

66 Willwerth, James: "McCartney Comes Back," *Time*, May 31, 1976.

67 Roman, Joe: "Wings Over Atlanta," *Atlanta Gazette*," May 19, 1976.

68 Jerome, Jim: "Daddy McCartney," *People*, June 7, 1976.

69 Ibid.

70 Rockwell, John: "McCartney, Trying Wings in Three Shows, Talks of Yesterday," *New York Times*, May 21, 1976.

71 Mieses, Stan: "The Cat Got Your Tongue, Paul?" *New York Daily News*, May 30, 1976, section 3, p. 1.

72 Robins, Wayne: "The Magic McCartney," *Newsday*, May 22, 1976.

73 Santosuosso, Ernie: "Sold-out Garden Awaits McCartney & Wings," *Boston Globe*, May 21, 1976, p. 17.

74 Fountas, Nick: "Wings Soar into Boston Garden," *Lowell Sun*, May 24, 1976.

75 Goodman, Joan: Unedited *Playboy* interview transcripts, May 3, 1984, part 3. Courtesy of Charles Deering McCormick Library of Special Collections, Northwestern University Libraries.

76 Dorsey, Tony: Author interview (Kozinn), October 17, 2019.

77 Casey, Howie: Author interview (Sinclair), October 19, 2019.

78 Dorsey, Tony: Author interview (Kozinn) October 17, 2019.

79 Powell, Aubrey: Author interview (Sinclair), May 15, 2020.

80 McCartney, Paul, with Mark Lewisohn, editor: *Wingspan* (Bulfinch Press, London, 2002).

81 Gilchrist, Roderick: "The Long and Winding Road Back to the Top for a Beatle Who Started Again," *Daily Mail*, May 26, 1976, p. 3.

82 Pearce, Garth: "The McCartney Memoirs," *Daily Express*, February 10, 1977, p. 7.

83 Fong-Torres, Ben: "Wings Tour Ends: Up, Up and Away," *Rolling Stone*, July 29, 1976, p. 9.

84 Palmer, Robert: "McCartney's Wings Brings National Tour to Garden," *New York Times*, May 25, 1976.

85 Campbell, Mary: "Paul Doubts Chances for Reunion," Associated Press by way of the *Springfield Leader and Press*, May 29, 1976, p. 10.

86 Steele, Allison: Audio interview with Paul and Linda McCartney at Madison Square Garden, May 24, 1976.

87 Casey, Howie: Author interview (Sinclair), October 19, 2019.

CHAPTER 15

1 Gambaccini, Paul: "Paul Won't Rest His Wings," *Rolling Stone*, December 15, 1976.

2 Coleman, Ray: "Starr Trek," *Melody Maker*, October 2, 1976, p. 17.

3 Gambaccini, Paul: "Ringo Remembers . . . ," *Rolling Stone*, November 4, 1976, p. 33.

4 Ibid.

5 Brennan, Peter: "$150 Beatles Blitz All Set to Blast U.S. Again," *San Antonio Express*, May 9, 1976, p. 7.

6 St. John, Michael: "Tragedy and Triumph of an Ex-Beatle," *Super Rock*, June 1977, p. 94.

7 Branton, Allen: Author interview (Sinclair), July 5, 2021.

8 Audience recording of the Riverfront Coliseum show, Cincinnati, OH, May 27, 1976.

9 Radel, Cliff: "McCartney Masterful on Coliseum Stage," *Cincinnati Enquirer*, May 29, 1976, pp. B-12.

10 Tatum, Bil: "'He' and Wings Heading for Top," *The Springfield Leader and Press*, June 5, 1976, pp. 2, 8.

11 Backstage audio interviews with Wings, Kemper Arena, Kansas City, MO, May 29, 1976.

12 Van Matre, Lynn: "Wings Moving On: We Shall Return, McCartney Vows," *Chicago Tribune*, June 3, 1976, pp. T1-T2.

13 Harris, George W.: "Denny Seiwell: On Sir Paul's Wings," *Jazz Weekly* (online), April 1, 2019.

14 Van Matre, Lynn: "Wings Moving On: We Shall Return, McCartney Vows," *Chicago Tribune*, June 3, 1976, pp. T1-T2.

15 Ibid.

16 Morley, Peter "Rocky": Facebook comment made on April 20, 2022.

17 King, Bill: "Inside Wings—An Interview with Joe English," *Beatlefan*, December 19, 1978.

18 Evans, Jim: "Blowin' in the Wings," *Record Mirror*, April 16, 1977, pp. 18.

19 Leonard, Roy: Backstage interviews at Chicago Stadium for the *Roy Leonard Show*, WLS, Chicago, IL, May 31, 1976.

20 Meyer, Bruce: "McCartney, 'Wings' Having Fun," United Press International, via *Press Democrat*, June 6, 1976, p. 10S.

21 Audience recording of the St. Paul Civic Center show, Saint Paul, MN, June 4, 1976.

22 Bream, Jon: "Paul McCartney: He Seeks Wings' Emergence from Beatles' Chrysalis," *Minneapolis Star*, June 8, 1976, p. 5C.

23 Beck, Marilyn: "Hotel Demands Deposit for Damage from Paul McCartney and His Group," *Democrat and Chronicle*, May 28, 1976, p. 3C.

24 Grein, Paul: "Promoters' Role Becomes Larger with Acts, Labels," *Billboard*, November 18, 1978, p. 39.

25 Audience recording of the McNichols Sports Arena show, Denver, CO, June 7, 1976.

26 Hilburn, Robert: "After the Flaps, McCartney's Wings Airborne," *Los Angeles Times*, June 20, 1976, p. 76.

27 Cunningham, Warren: Author interview (Sinclair) by email, July 6, 2021.

28 Uncredited: "McCartney Honcho 'Rolling' at 36," *People*, July 1976.

29 Peacock, Ian: Author interview (Sinclair), September 18, 2021.

30 English, Joe: Author interview (Sinclair), July 9, 2024.

31 Ibid.

32 MacDonald, Patrick: "McCartney in Dome Exciting Success," *Seattle Times*, June 11, 1976.

33 Iles, Jan: "Jim's Flight of Fancy," *Record Mirror & Disc*, August 14, 1976, p. 7.

34 Dorsey, Tony: Author interview (Kozinn), October 17, 2019.

35 Tremlett, George: "The Other McCartney," *The Sunday Telegraph Magazine*, August 14, 1977, p. 28.

36 Audience recording of the Kingdome show, Seattle, WA, June 10, 1976.

37 MacDonald, Patrick: "McCartney in Dome Exciting Success," *Seattle Times*, June 11, 1976.

38 Giuliano, Geoffrey: *Blackbird: The Life and Times of Paul McCartney* (Dutton, New York, 1991), pp. 207–8.

39 Audience recording of the second Cow Palace show, June 14, 1976.

40 Guthrie, Jim: "Wings Covers America," *Times Advocate*, June 27, 1976, p. 2–3.

41 Powell, Aubrey: Author interview (Sinclair), May 15, 2020.

42 Andrews, Nancy: Author interview (Sinclair), August 9, 2021.

43 Coleman, Ray: "Starr Trek," *Melody Maker*, October 2, 1976, p. 17.

44 Uncredited: "Thrills," *NME*, July 10, 1976, p. 21.

45 Uncredited: "Wings—, Let 'Em In' (MPL/ATV—EMI) (McCartney)," *Cash Box*, July 3, 1976, p. 24.

46 Uncredited: "Wings, 'Let 'Em In,'" *Record World*, July 3, 1976, p. 1.

47 Hancock, David: "Wings: 'Let 'Em In' (MPL E6015)," *Record Mirror & Disc*, July 31, 1976, p. 10.

48 Dadomo, Giovanni: "Wings: 'Let 'Em In' (MPL)," *Sounds*, July 31, 1976, p. 16.

49 Weinraub, Judith: "Linda McCartney's Camera Solo," *New York Times*, December 12, 1976.

50 Fleischman, Larry: "Wings' Concert 'Tremendous,'" *Tucson Daily Citizen*, June 19, 1976, p. 3.

51 Fong-Torres, Ben: "Wings Tour Ends: Up, Up and Away," *Rolling Stone*, July 29, 1976, p. 9.

52 Sackett, Susan: *Inside Trek: My Secret Life with Star Trek Creator Gene Roddenberry* (Hawk Publishing Group, 2002), Kindle Edition.

53 Sackett, Susan: Author interview (Sinclair) by email, April 28, 2020.

54 Hilburn, Robert: "Paul, Ringo Wing It in Mini-Reunion," *Los Angeles Times*, June 23, 1976, p. 1.

55 Hilburn, Robert: "Afterthoughts on Wings Tour," *Los Angeles Times*, June 26, 1976, p. 10–18R.

56 Eikelenboom, Edward (editor): "Wings Over America," *Maccazine*, vol. 45, issue 2, pp. 155–7.

57 Audience recording of the third Forum show, Los Angeles, June 23, 1976.

58 Branton, Allen: Author interview (Sinclair), July 5, 2021.

59 Uncredited, "The Raver," *Melody Maker*, July 3, 1976, p. 8.

60 White, Stuart: "The Only One Who Found Happiness," *News of the World*, November 6, 1977.

61 Fong-Torres, Ben: "Wings Tour Ends: Up, Up and Away," *Rolling Stone*, July 29, 1976, p. 9.

62 Goodman, Joan: Unedited *Playboy* interview transcripts, April 27, 1984, Part 1. Courtesy of Charles Deering McCormick Library of Special Collections, Northwestern University Libraries.

CHAPTER 16

1 Young, Sally: "Paul and Linda McCartney," *Woman's Weekly*, January 1977.

2 Ashford, Paul: "War & Peace," *International Musician*, September 1983, p. 42.

3 Muldoon, Paul: Audio interview with Paul McCartney for *McCartney: A Life in Lyrics* podcast, first broadcast in October 2023.

4 Slater, Jim: Video interview with Paul and Linda McCartney for the BBC show *Tonight*, broadcast on September 27, 1976.

5 Charlesworth, Chris: "Lennon Gets His Ticket to Ride," *Melody Maker*, August 7, 1976, p. 8.

6 Uncredited: "Beatles Return Hopes," *Liverpool Echo*, July 2, 1976, p. 1.

7 Uncredited: "Beatles Are Asked to Play for the Queen," *Daily Mail*, July 3, 1976, p. 11.

8 Campbell, Nicky: Audio interview with Paul McCartney, *The Nicky Campbell Show*, BBC Radio 1, November 19, 1991.

9 Baird, Pat: "McCartney to Buy E. H. Morris Music," *Record World*, July 10, 1976, p. 26.

10 Lichtman, Irv: "We Polish Old Silver—Eastman," *Billboard*, July 7, 1979, p. 12.

11 Goodman, Joan: "Playboy Interview: Paul and Linda McCartney," *Playboy*, December 1984, pp. 100, 102.

12 Brainsby, Tony: "Interview with Denny Laine," edited for clarity and concision. Press kit for *Holly Days* on May 6, 1977.

13 Nightingale, Annie: "Water Wings," *Record Mirror*, October 23, 1976, p. 12.

14 Gambaccini, Paul: "Water Wings," *Sounds*, August 20, 1977, p. 18.

15 Stevens, Ray: Author interview (Sinclair) by email, April 4, 2023.

16 Edelson, Howie: "Winging It with Denny Laine," *Beatlefan*, July-October 2006.

17 Nightingale, Anne: "In Tune: Paul and His New Songwriter . . . ," *Daily Express*, April 19, 1977, p. 20.

18 Gambaccini, Paul: Audio interview with Paul McCartney and Denny Laine, *London Town Special*, BBC Radio 1, March 31, 1978.

19 Horne, Nicky: Audio interview with Paul McCartney and Denny Laine, Capital Radio, March 22, 1978.

20 Gambaccini, Paul: Audio interview with Paul McCartney and Denny Laine, *London Town Special*, BBC Radio 1, March 31, 1978.

21 Uncredited: Rogers and Cowan (publicity firm) interview with Denny Laine for the *Holly Days* album, New York, May 1977.

22 Uncredited: "Beatlemania Strikes Again," *Melody Maker*, July 24, 1976, p. 5.

23 Carr, Roy: "Denny Laine . . . It's So Easy—Listen to Me / I'm Looking for Someone to Love (EMI)," *NME*, September 18, 1976, p. 21.

24 Coon, Caroline: "Denny Laine: 'It's So Easy / Listen to Me—Medley' (EMI)," *Melody Maker*, September 18, 1976, p. 42.

25 Uncredited: "Denny Laine (Capitol) P-4340) It's So Easy/Listen to Me," *Cash Box*, October 16, 1976, p. 18.

26 Gambaccini, Paul: "Paul Won't Rest His Wings," *Rolling Stone*, December 15, 1976.

27 Brown, David: "Not Fade Away . . . ," *Record Mirror & Disc*, September 11, 1976, p. 10–11.

28 Robinson, Lisa: "Being Born in Liverpool Does Carry With It . . . err . . . Certain Responsibilities," *NME*, December 11, 1976, pp. 22–23.

29 MacDonald, Fiona: "Scrambled Eggs Gave Paul His Greatest Hit-maker," *Australasian Post*, December 6, 1976, p. 20.

30 Rockwell, John: "The Pop Life," *New York Times*, September 17, 1976.

31 Bernstein, Sid: Full-page advertisement in the *New York Times*, September 19, 1976, p. 16D

32 Slater, Jim: Interview with Paul and Linda McCartney, *Tonight*, BBC, broadcast on September 27, 1976.

33 Lyda, Morris: Author interview (Sinclair), October 7, 2021.

34 Audience recording of the Zagreb concert, September 21, 1976.

35 Peacock, Ian: Author interview (Sinclair), September 18, 2021.

36 Nightingale, Annie: "Water Wings," *Record Mirror*, October 23, 1976, p. 12.

37 Pearce, Garth: "The McCartney Memoirs," *Daily Express*, February 10, 1977, p. 7.

38 Slater, Jim: Interview with Paul and Linda McCartney, *Tonight*, BBC, broadcast on September 27, 1976.

39 McLeod, Pauline: "Wings Give the Sinking City a Lift," *Daily Mirror*, September 27, 1976, p. 22.

40 Audience recording of the Venice concert, September 25, 1976.

41 Brown, Geoff: "Venetian Blinder," *Melody Maker*, October 2, 1976, pp. 56, 63.

42 Pearce, Garth: "Sinking Venice Rises to New Heights on Paul McCartney's Wings of Song," *Daily Express*, September 27, 1976, p. 13.

43 Horide, Rosemary: "Venice Preserved!," *Beat Instrumental*, December 1976, p. 7.

44 McCartney, Paul: Audio recording of the post-concert press conference, Venice, September 25, 1976.

45 Korinth, Axel: *Rock Show: Die (Ex-) Beatles in Deutschland 1971–1980* (Books on Demand, Germany, 2011), pp. 84–85.

46 Warfield, Dan: "Wings on the Road," *Stars and Stripes*, October 8, 1976, p. 15.

47 Uncredited: "Pistols Sign EMI Deal," *Sounds*, October 16, 1976, p. 2.

48 Gambaccini, Paul: "Paul Won't Rest His Wings," *Rolling Stone*, December 15, 1976.

49 Uncredited: Teazers, *NME*, October 30, 1976, p. 41.

50 Edelson, Howie: "Winging It with Denny Laine," *Beatlefan*, July–October 2006.

51 King, Bill: "Inside Wings—An Interview with Joe English," *Beatlefan*, December 19, 1978.

52 Nightingale, Annie: "Water Wings," *Record Mirror*, October 23, 1976, p. 12.

53 Descriptive material in this section drawn from Barry Chattington and BBC film footage, and Jonh Ingham, "Wings: She's a Good Cook, Eamonn," *Sounds*, October 30, 1976, pp. 22, 23, 30.

54 Ingham, Jonh: "Wings: She's a Good Cook, Eamonn," *Sounds*, October 30, 1976, pp. 22, 23, 30.

55 Denselow, Robin: "Wembley—Wings," *The Guardian*, October 20, 1976, p. 10.

56 Welch, Chris: "Jet-Lagged Wings," *Melody Maker*, October 30, 1976, p. 22.

57 Hill, Derrick: "My Life with Paul," *Liverpool Echo*, November 16, 1976, p. 6.

58 Ingham, Jonh: "Wings: She's a Good Cook, Eamonn," *Sounds*, October 30, 1976, pp. 22, 23, 30.

CHAPTER 17

1 Uncredited: "Peace Group Warns Critics," *Belfast Telegraph*, October 28, 1976, p. 8.

2 Brown, David: "Jimmy's New Branch Line," *Record Mirror & Disc*, November 20, 1976, p. 12.

3 Lyda, Morris: Author interview (Sinclair), November 7, 2021.

4 Goodman, Joan: Unedited *Playboy* interview transcripts, Linda McCartney interview, May 2–6, 1984, pp. 48–49. Courtesy of Charles Deering McCormick Library of Special Collections, Northwestern University Libraries.

5 O'Neill, Terry: "Linda: More Than a Rocker," *Melody Maker*, December 4, 1976, p. 26.

6 Uncredited: "Wings, Denver, Frampton in Major Movie Roles," *Melody Maker*, November 27, 1976, p. 5.

7 Cummins, Jeff: Author interview (Sinclair), March 19, 2020.

8 Ibid.

9 Powell, Aubrey: Author interview (Sinclair), May 15, 2020.

10 Ibid.

11 Griffin, Phil: Audio interview with Paul McCartney for Piccadilly Radio, November 1977.

12 Doherty, Harry: "Wings Need Clipping," *Melody Maker*, December 18, 1976, p. 16.

13 Fielder, Hugh: "Wings: Alive and Kicking," *Sounds*, December 18, 1976, p. 21.

14 Stewart, Tony: "Wings—A Complete Action Replay," *NME*, December 18, 1976, p. 26.

15 Tucker, Ken: "*Wings Over America*," Wings, Capitol SWCO-11593, *Rolling Stone*, February 10, 1977.

16 Winn, Paul B.: Letter to Denny Laine listing fees paid between 1973 and 1978, October 24, 1978.

17 Melville, Suzy: Author interview (Sinclair), May 7, 2020.

18 Emberton, Julie: "You'd Forgotten About Yoko, Hadn't You?" *NME*, January 22, 1977, p. 10

19 Uncredited: "Beatles Pay £3 Million," *Daily Mail*, January 11, 1977, p. 2.

20 Uncredited: "The Best of '76," *Sounds*, December 25, 1976, p. 14.

21 Uncredited: "Jaws," *Sounds*, February 12, 1977, p. 9.

22 Polti, Steve: "The Forgotten Story of How Muhammad Ali and a Jersey Guy Tried to Reunite the Beatles," *NJ.com*, June 9, 2016.

23 Gibbs, Garth: "Spell Out the Danger, Says Paul," *Daily Mirror*, January 18, 1977, p. 11.

24 Norden, Maggie: Audio interview with Paul McCartney for Capital Radio, October 1976.

25 Nightingale, Anne: "Singles of the Week," *Daily Express*, February 8, 1977, p. 24.

26 Coon, Caroline: "Singles," *Melody Maker*, February 19, 1977, p. 20.

27 Makowski, Pete: "Wings: 'Maybe I'm Amazed' (EMI/Capitol)," *Sounds*, February 19, 1977, p. 20.

28 Carr, Roy: "Wings: Maybe I'm Amazed / Soily (EMI)," *NME*, February 19, 1977, p. 22.

29 Uncredited: "Wings—Maybe I'm Amazed (3:45)," *Billboard*, February 12, 1977, p. 70.

30 Uncredited: "Wings—Maybe I'm Amazed (3:43)," *Cash Box*, February 12, 1977, p. 22.

31 Russell, Rosalind: "Wings: 'Maybe I'm Amazed' (Parlophone R6017)," *Record Mirror*, February 19, 1977, p. 10.

32 Simons, Judith: "Wings Are Spreading," *Daily Express*, February 8, 1977, p.3.

33 Pearce, Garth: "The McCartney Memoirs Part 1," *Daily Express*, February 9, 1977, pp. 16, 17.

34 Pearce, Garth: "The McCartney Memoirs Part 2," *Daily Express*, February 10, 1977, p. 7.

35 Pearce, Garth: "The McCartney Memoirs Part 3," *Daily Express*, February 11, 1977, p. 6.

36 Uncredited: Audio interview with Paul McCartney for *London Town Special* on KRTH-101, broadcast on March 25, 1978.

37 Gambaccini, Paul: *London Town Special*, audio interview with Paul McCartney and Denny Laine for BBC Radio 1, March 31, 1978.

38 Prince, Tony: "Paul and Linda At It Again!" *Daily Mirror*, April 22, 1978.

39 Douglas, Peter: "Wings Hit Virgins," *Beat Instrumental*, August 1977, p. 13.

40 Gambaccini, Paul: *London Town Special*, audio interview with Paul McCartney and Denny Laine for BBC Radio 1, March 31, 1978.

41 Horne, Nicky: Audio interview with Paul McCartney and Denny Laine for Capital Radio, March 22, 1978.

42 Lubin, Tom: "10 Years Later—George Martin Revisited," *Recording Engineer Producer*, February 1979, p. 36.

43 Horne, Nicky: Audio interview with Paul McCartney and Denny Laine for Capital Radio, March 22, 1978.

44 Uncredited: "Tour Threat to 'John, Paul, George, Ringo . . . and Bert . . .'" *Liverpool Echo*, April 28, 1977, p. 4.

45 McCartney, Paul: *Oobu Joobu* radio series, Week 3, Westwood 1, broadcast the weekend of June 10, 1995.

CHAPTER 18

1 Doherty, Harry: "Rock: It's All Over Now . . . ," *Melody Maker*, March 12, 1977, p. 17.

2 Clarke, Steve: "V-Signs at Queen's Pad Fails," *NME*, March 1977, p. 11.

3 Prophet, Sheila: "Mad Dogs and Englishmen," *Record Mirror*, March 12, 1977, p. 6.

4 McLean, Ralph: Audio interview with Geoff Emerick for Radio Ulster, broadcast on October 11, 2018.

5 Sally, Paul: Unedited interview with Geoff Emerick for his book *Little Wing*, provided by author, date unknown.

6 Meldrum, Ian: Video interview with Paul McCartney for ABC's *Countdown*, filmed on March 22, 1977.

7 Sally, Paul: Unedited interview with Geoff Emerick for his book *Little Wing*, provided by author, date unknown.

8 Uncredited: "Beatles' Live LP in the Works," *Rolling Stone*, April 7, 1977.

9 Scott, Roger: Audio interview with Paul McCartney and Denny Laine for Capital Radio, November 11, 1978.

10 Gambaccini, Paul: "McCartney and Wings at Sea," *Rolling Stone*, October 6, 1977, p. 12.

11 Gambaccini, Paul: "McCartney and Wings at Sea," *Rolling Stone*, October 6, 1977, p. 12.

12 Uncredited, "Allen Klein Indicted for Tax Evasion," *Record World*, April 16, 1977, p. 8.

13 Kaye, Roger: "From Wings to Gospel Rock," *Star Telegraph*, May 10, 1981, pp. 1F, 10F.

14 Morris, Mark: Audio interview with Dayle English for World of Faith Fellowship, June 27, 2018.

15 White, Randy: "Wife of 'Wings' Drummer Talks About Ex-Beatle," *Florida News-Press*, May 25, 1977, p. D1.)

16 Kaye, Roger: "From Wings to Gospel Rock," *Star Telegraph*, May 10, 1981, pp. 1F, 10F.

17 Evans, Jim: "Blowin' in the Wings," *Record Mirror*, April 16, 1977, p. 18.

18 Brown, David: "Denny Laine: 'Moondreams' (EMI2588)," *Record Mirror*, April 10, 1977, p. 10.

19 Edmands, Bob: "Denny Laine: Moondreams (EMI)," *NME*, April 30, 1977, p. 23.

20 Lewis, Al: "Denny Laine: 'Moondreams' (EMI)," *Sounds*, April 30, 1977, p. 24.

21 Madinger, Chip, and Mark Easter: *Eight Arms to Hold You—The Solo Beatles Compendium* (Open Your Books, Chesterfield, MO, 2018 edition), p. 230.

22 Uncredited: "MPL: Expanding Indie," *Record World*, April 16, 1977, pp. 8, 44.

23 Sheff, David: *All We Are Saying: The Last Major Interview with John Lennon & Yoko Ono* (Pan Books, London, 2020), p. 98.

24 Brown, David: "Percy 'Thrills' Thrillington: 'Uncle Albert/Admiral Halsey' (Regal Zonophone EMI2594)," *Record Mirror*, April 30, 1977, p. 10.

25 Humphries, Patrick: "Percy Thrillington—*Thrillington* (Regal Zonophone/EMI)," *NME*, May 21, 1977, p. 45.

26 Silverton, Pete: "Percy Thrillington—Thrillington (EMI EMC 3175)," *Sounds*, May 15, 1977, p. 41.

27 Douglas, Peter: "Wings Hit Virgins," *Beat Instrumental*, August 1977, p. 13.

28 Anderson, Tom: Author interview (Sinclair), March 9, 2016.

29 Vigars, Mark: "Wings Over the Caribbean," *Club Sandwich*, June/July 1977, p. 3.

30 Cummings, Howard: "Geoff Emerick," *Recording Engineer Producer*, December 1978, p. 47.

31 Crowder, Alan: "Extracts from Alan Crowder's Diary," *Club Sandwich*, June/July 1977, p. 2.

32 Gambaccini, Paul: "Water Wings," *Sounds*, August 20, 1977, p. 19.

33 Simons, Judith: "For the Record, Wings Call This Work!," *Daily Express*, August 15, 1977, p. 21.

34 Grundy, Stuart: Audio interview with Paul McCartney

for *Rock On*, BBC Radio 1, broadcast on November 12, 1977.

35 Crowder, Alan: "Extracts from Alan Crowder's Diary," *Club Sandwich*, June/July 1977, p. 2.

36 Many of the details of the band's non-recording activity in this chapter are from Trevor Jones's diary (unpublished).

37 Horne, Nicky: Audio interview with Paul McCartney and Denny Laine for Capital Radio, broadcast on March 22, 1978.

38 Anderson, Tom: Author interview (Sinclair), March 9, 2016.

39 Vigars, Mark: "Wings Over the Caribbean," *Club Sandwich*, June/July 1977, p. 3.

40 Prince, Tony: "Paul and Linda at It Again!" *Daily Mirror*, April 22, 1978.

41 Anderson, Tom: Author interview (Sinclair), March 9, 2016.

42 Yarborough, Chuck: "Recording the Grateful Dead, Paul McCartney and More: A Cleveland Recording Engineer's Story," *The Plain Dealer*, January 29, 2016. Taken from Yarborough's unedited transcript.

43 Uncredited: Audio interview with Paul McCartney for *London Town Special* on KRTH-101, broadcast on March 25, 1978.

44 Irwin, Colin: "Cruising with Macca," *Melody Maker*, April 1, 1978, p. 26–27.

45 Horne, Nicky: Audio interview with Paul McCartney and Denny Laine for Capital Radio, broadcast on March 22, 1978.

46 Crowder, Alan: "Extracts from Alan Crowder's Diary," *Club Sandwich*, June/July 1977, p. 2.

47 Welch, Chris: "Goodbye to Yesterday," *Melody Maker*, November 19, 1977, p. 8.

48 Gambaccini, Paul: "Water Wings," *Sounds*, August 20, 1977, p. 19.

49 English, Joe: Author interview (Sinclair), July 11, 2024.

50 Peebles, Andy: Audio interview with Paul McCartney for BBC Radio 1, broadcast on May 26, 1980.

51 McKay, Andy: "Tug of War," *Club Sandwich*, No. 26, 1982.

52 Ibid.

53 Wishart, Eric: "Will Wings Stay Together?" *Lennox Herald Dumbarton*, August 1977, p. 9.

54 Angus, Janet: "Geoff Emerick—Producer/Engineer," *Home Studio Recording*, July 1985, p. 43.

55 Wenner, Jann: *Lennon Remembers* (Straight Arrow Books, San Francisco, 1971), p. 84.

56 Uncredited: Audio interview with Paul McCartney for *London Town Special* on KRTH-101, broadcast on March 25, 1978.

57 Horne, Nicky: Audio interview with Paul McCartney and Denny Laine for Capital Radio, broadcast on March 22, 1978.

58 Gambaccini, Paul: *London Town Special*, audio interview with Paul McCartney and Denny Laine for BBC Radio 1, March 31, 1978.

59 Gambaccini, Paul: *London Town Special*, audio interview with Paul McCartney and Denny Laine for BBC Radio 1, March 31, 1978.

60 Horne, Nicky: Audio interview with Paul McCartney and Denny Laine for Capital Radio, broadcast on March 22, 1978.

61 Anderson, Tom: Author interview (Sinclair), March 9, 2016.

62 Yarborough, Chuck: "Recording the Grateful Dead, Paul McCartney and More: A Cleveland Recording Engineer's Story," *The Plain Dealer*, January 29, 2016. Taken from Yarborough's unedited transcript.

63 McCartney, Paul: "Paul Recalls '77," *Club Sandwich*, December 1977/January 1978, p. 21.

64 Anderson, Tom: Author interview (Sinclair), March 9, 2016.

65 Gambaccini, Paul: "Water Wings," *Sounds*, August 20, 1977, p. 19.

66 Gambaccini, Paul: "McCartney and Wings at Sea," *Rolling Stone*, October 6, 1977, p. 19.

67 Gambaccini, Paul: "Water Wings," *Sounds*, August 20, 1977, p. 19.

68 Gambaccini, Paul: "McCartney and Wings at Sea," *Rolling Stone*, October 6, 1977, p. 19.

69 Ibid.

70 Uncredited: "Flutter of Tiny Wings for Linda," *Daily Mirror*, June 3, 1977, p. 13.

CHAPTER 19

1 Evans, Jim: "Denny Laine: 'Holly Days' (EMI EMA 781)," *Record Mirror*, April 23, 1977, p. 14.

2 Uncredited: "Holly Days—Denny Laine—Capitol ST-11588," *Cash Box*, May 28, 1977, p. 20.

3 Farren, Mick: "Denny Laine—*Holly Days* (EMI)," *NME*, May 21, 1977, p. 44.

4 Marsh, Dave: "Denny Laine Decks the Hollys," *Rolling Stone*, June 16, 1977.

5 Parsons, Tony: "Suzy and the Red Stripes: Seaside Woman (Epic)," *NME*, July 30, 1977, p. 23.

6 Uncredited: "Suzy & The Red Stripes—Seaside Woman," *Billboard*, June 25, 1977, p. 34.

7 Uncredited: "Suzy and the Red Stripes (Epic/MPL 50403)—Seaside Woman," *Cash Box*, June 4, 1977, p. 22.

8 Uncredited: "Suzy and the Redstripes, 'Seaside Woman,'" *Record World*, June 11, 1977, p. 1.

9 Prophet, Sheila: "A Whole New Paul Game," *Record Mirror*, May 21, 1977, p. 38.

10 Jahr, Cliff: "Beatlemania Is a Scrapbook of Soggy Standards," *Rolling Stone*, July 14, 1977, p. 30.

11 Trust, Sam: Author interview (Sinclair), April 13, 2022.

12 Uncredited: "The Faces Are Familiar," *Daily News*, July 9, 1977, p. 7.

13 Bonici, Ray: "Paul McCartney Wings It Alone," *Music Express*, April 5, 1982.

14 Gilchrist, Roderick: "His America," *Daily Mail*, December 13, 1977, p. 2.

15 Michaels, Ken, Kit O'Toole, Kenneth Womack, and Tom Hunyady: Audio interview with Chris Thomas for *Talk More Talk* podcast, first broadcast on November 18, 2018.

16 Rodriguez, Robert: Audio interview with Chris Thomas for the *Something About the Beatles* podcast, first broadcast on December 25, 2018.

17 Ibid.

18 Michaels, Ken, Kit O'Toole, Kenneth Womack, and Tom Hunyady: Audio interview with Chris Thomas for *Talk More Talk* podcast, first broadcast on November 18, 2018.

19 Ibid.

20 Thomas, Chris: Unpublished interview with Mark Lewisohn, 2018.

21 King, Bill: "Inside Wings—An Interview with Joe English," *Beatlefan*, December 19, 1978.

22 Greig, Stuart: "Punk Star Rotten Razored," *Daily Mirror*, June 21, 1977, p. 1.

23 Rodriguez, Robert: Audio interview with Chris Thomas for the *Something About the Beatles* podcast, first broadcast on December 25, 2018.

24 Estridge, Bonnie: "All You Need Is Love and a Beatle Called Paul," *Woman*, April 30, 1977, pp. 28–30.

25 Hoffman, Ken: "Joe Talks Plain English on Spreading His New Wings," *Fort Lauderdale News*, September 7, 1978, p. 16C.

26 Douglas, Peter: "Wings Hit Virgins," *Beat Instrumental*, August 1977, p. 13.

27 Hodgkinson, Will: "The Thing With FEATHERS," Mojo, March 2024, p. 75.

28 Cowing, Emma: "How Macca Killed Off Punk Rock with the Bagpipes," *Daily Mail*, November 11, 2017, p. 37.

29 Edelson, Howie: "Winging It with Denny Laine," *Beatlefan*, July–October 2006.

30 Bartlett, Stefan: "McCartney and Me," *Sunday Mercury*, January 24, 1988, p. 24.

31 Edelson, Howie: "Winging It with Denny Laine," *Beatlefan*, July-October 2006.

32 Gambaccini, Paul: Audio interview with Paul McCartney for *An Evening with Paul McCartney*, BBC Radio 1, broadcast on April 1, 1979.

33 Scott, Roger: Audio interview with Paul McCartney and Denny Laine for Capital Radio, November 11, 1978.

34 Thomas, Steven: Author interview (Sinclair), April 3, 2020.

35 Yetnikoff, Walter: Email exchange with author (Kozinn), May 4, 2021.

36 Scott, Roger: Audio interview with Paul McCartney and Denny Laine for Capital Radio, November 11, 1978.

37 Summerhayes, Tim: Author interview (Sinclair) by email, February 7, 2020.

38 Sally, Paul: Unedited interview with Geoff Emerick for his book *Little Wing* provided by author, date unknown.

39 Summerhayes, Tim: Author interview (Sinclair) by email, February 7, 2020.

40 The account of Jimmy's redecoration of the farmhouse kitchen and the aftermath draws on information conveyed by a member of Paul's technical crew to a fan shortly after the incident, an account that corroborated some (though not all) of the details given by Jo Jo Laine in interviews over the years.

41 Edelson, Howie: "Winging It with Denny Laine," *Beatlefan*, July–October 2006.

42 English, Joe: Author interview (Sinclair), July 11, 2024.

43 Bonici, Ray: "Thoughts of Chairman Mac," *Record Mirror*, November 26, 1977, p. 8.

44 Hughes, Jillian: "Paul McCartney Living with His Legend," *Juke*, December 2, 1978, p. 11.

45 Scott, Roger: Audio interview with Paul McCartney and Denny Laine for Capital Radio, November 11, 1978.

46 Lang Brown, John: Author interview (Sinclair), March 1, 2020.

47 Uncredited: "The Emma Interview," *Emma*, July 1, 1978, p. 32.

48 Angus, Janet: "Geoff Emerick–Producer/Engineer," *Home Studio Recording*, July 1985, p. 43.

49 McGeachy, Jimmy: Author interview (Sinclair), April 15, 2021.

50 Scott, Roger: Audio interview with Paul McCartney and Denny Laine for Capital Radio, November 11, 1978.

51 McGeachy, Jimmy: Author interview (Sinclair), April 15, 2021.

52 Morris, Mark: Audio interview with Dayle English for World of Faith Fellowship, June 27, 2018.

53 Wishart, Eric: "Will Wings Stay Together?" *Lennox Herald Dumbarton*, August 1977, p. 9.

54 Crawley, Phillip: "Facing Up to the Changing Times," *Newcastle Journal*, September 9, 1977, p. 8.

55 Ibid.

56 Russell, Willy: Author interview (Sinclair), May 14, 2020.

57 Letter from Paul McCartney to the editor of the *Sunday Times*, undated and unpublished.

58 Simons, Judith: "McCartney and Son," *Daily Express*, September 14, 1977, p. 3.

59 Garbarini, Vic: "Paul McCartney: Lifting the Veil on the Beatles," *Musician*, August 1980.

CHAPTER 20

1 Bonici, Ray: "Thoughts of Chairman Mac," *Record Mirror*, November 26, 1977, p. 8.

2 Uncredited: Audio interview with Paul McCartney for Capital Radio, November 1977.

3 Giuliano, Geoffrey: Interview with Denny Laine for *Blackbird: The Life and Times of Paul McCartney* (Penguin Reprint Edition, New York, 1992).

4 Juber, Laurence: Author interview (Sinclair), March 10, 2020.

5 Bragg, Melvyn: *The South Bank Show: Final Cut* (Hodder & Stoughton, London, Kindle Edition), pp. 7–9.

6 Bairnson, Ian: Official Website, discography: https://www.ianbairnson.com/discography/mull/mull.htm.

7 McCartney, Paul: Interviewed for *The South Bank Show*, October 4, 1977, broadcast on January 14, 1978.

8 Malone, Mary: "Culture's Very Own Vulture," *Daily Mirror*, May 13, 1978, p. 13.

9 Hoffman, Ken: "Joe Talks Plain English on Spreading His New Wings," *Fort Lauderdale News*, September 7, 1978, p. 16C.

10 English, Joe: Author interview (Sinclair), July 11, 2024.

11 Kaye, Roger: "From Wings to Gospel Rock," *Star Telegraph*, May 10, 1981, pp. 1F, 10F.

12 Morris, Mark: Audio interview with Joe English for World of Faith Fellowship, January 17, 2019.

13 Hoffman, Ken: "Joe Talks Plain English on Spreading His New Wings," *Fort Lauderdale News*, September 7, 1978, p. 16C.

14 Hughes, Jillian: "Paul McCartney Living with His Legend," *Juke*, December 2, 1978, p. 11.

15 Edelson, Howie: "Winging It with Denny Laine," *Beatlefan*, July-October 2006.

16 McCartney, Paul: Audio interview for *The Beatles—Now and Then—The Last Beatles Song (Short Film)*, published on YouTube on November 1, 2023.

17 Griffin, Phil: Audio interview with Paul McCartney for Piccadilly Radio, November 1977.

18 Grundy, Stuart: Audio interview with Paul McCartney for *Rock On*, BBC Radio 1, November 12, 1977.

19 Lindsay-Hogg, Michael: Author interview (Sinclair), May 24, 2020.

20 Miller, Jim: Author interview (Sinclair), March 13, 2022.

21 Lindsay-Hogg, Michael: Author interview (Sinclair), May 24, 2020.

22 Miller, Jim: "The Day 'the Movies' Came to Kintyre," *Campbeltown Courier*, October 21, 1977, p. 5.

23 Watt, Michael: "Lennon Speaks," *Melody Maker*, October 15, 1977, p. 1.

24 Jackson, Peter: Audio interview with Sean Ono Lennon for *The Beatles—Now and Then—The Last Beatles Song (Short Film)*, issued on YouTube on November 2, 2023.

25 Hope, David: "Critics Anger Beatle Father," *The Liverpool Echo*, November 10, 1977, p. 1.

26 Gambaccini, Paul: *London Town Special*, audio interview with Paul McCartney and Denny Laine for BBC Radio 1, March 31, 1978.

27 Prince, Tony: "Paul and Linda at It Again!" *Daily Mirror*, April 22, 1978.

28 Ibid.

29 Sally, Paul: Unedited interview with Geoff Emerick for his book *Little Wing* provided by author, date unknown.

30 Gambaccini, Paul: *London Town Special*, audio interview with Paul McCartney and Denny Laine for BBC Radio 1, March 31, 1978.

31 Prince, Tony: "Paul and Linda At It Again!" *Daily Mirror*, April 22, 1978.

32 Horne, Nicky: Audio interview with Paul McCartney and Denny Laine for Capital Radio, March 22, 1978.

33 Welch, Chris: "Goodbye to Yesterday," *Melody Maker*, November 19, 1977, p. 8–9.

34 Ibid.

35 Bonici, Ray: "Thoughts of Chairman Mac," *Record Mirror*, November 26, 1977, p. 8.

36 Welch, Chris: "Goodbye to Yesterday," *Melody Maker*, November 19, 1977, pp. 8–9.

37 Bonici, Ray: "Thoughts of Chairman Mac," *Record Mirror*, November 26, 1977, p. 8.

38 Welch, Chris: "Jet-Lagged Wings," *Melody Maker*, October 30, 1976, p. 22.

39 Welch, Chris: "Goodbye to Yesterday," *Melody Maker*, November 19, 1977, pp. 8–9.

40 Horne, Nicky: Audio interview with Paul McCartney and Denny Laine for Capital Radio, March 22, 1978.

41 White, Stuart: "The Only One Who Found Happiness," *News of the World*, November 6, 1977.

42 Uncredited news column, *NME*, December 3, 1977, p. 71.

43 Beerling, Johnny: *Radio 1—The Inside Story* (Trafford Publishing, Manchester, 2008), p. 107.

44 Murray, Charles Shaar: "Wings: Mull of Kintyre (Capitol)," *NME*, November 19, 1977, p. 25.

45 Prophet, Sheila: "Wings: 'Mull of Kintyre' / 'Girls' School' (EMI R6018)," *Record Mirror*, November 19, 1977, p. 8.

46 Birch, Ian: "Alfresco Macca—Soft Centers," *Melody Maker*, November 19, 1977, p. 20.

47 Suck, Jane: "Wings—'Mull of Kintyre' / 'Girls' School' (EMI)," *Sounds*, November 26, 1977, p. 20.

48 Uncredited: "Wings—Girls' School (3:19) / Mull of Kintyre (3:31)," *Billboard*, November 19, 1977, p. 8.

49 Peebles, Andy: Audio interview with Paul McCartney for BBC Radio 1, May 26, 1980.

50 Sackett, Susan: *Inside Trek: My Secret Life with Star Trek Creator Gene Roddenberry* (Hawk Publishing, America, 2013), Kindle Edition.

51 Gelly, Dave: "Wings Work," issued in the press kit for *London Town* on March 31, 1978.

52 Gambaccini, Paul: *London Town Special*, audio interview with Paul McCartney and Denny Laine for BBC Radio 1, March 31, 1978.

53 Lee, Iain: Audio interview with Denny Laine for *Late Night Alternative* on talkRADIO, broadcast on June 15, 2018.

54 Gelly, Dave: "Wings Work," issued in the press kit for *London Town* on March 31, 1978.

55 Ibid.

56 Ferguson, Nicholas: Author interview (Sinclair), March 9, 2022.

57 Miller, Jim: "A Credit to the Town . . . " *Campbeltown Courier*, December 16, 1977, p. 1.

58 McGeachy, Jimmy: Author interview (Sinclair), April 15, 2021.

59 Miller, Jim: "A Credit to the Town . . . " *Campbeltown Courier*, December 16, 1977, p. 1.

60 Uncredited: Britain's Most Watched TV: The 1970s, British Film Institute website, updated June 28, 2005.

61 Lee, Iain: Audio interview with Denny Laine for *Late Night Alternative* on talkRADIO, broadcast on June 15, 2018.

62 Uncredited: "Wings with Yarwood," *Record Mirror*, December 17, p. 5.

63 Frost, Deborah: "Once There Was a Way to Get Back Homeward," *Record*, September 1984, p. 27.

64 Coburn, Bob: Audio interview with Paul McCartney for *Rockline*, October 24, 1984.

65 Griffin, Phil: Audio interview with Paul McCartney for Piccadilly Radio, November 1977.

66 Lawson, Twiggy: *Twiggy in Black and White* (Simon & Schuster, London, 1997), p. 209–11.

67 Griffin, Phil: Audio interview with Paul McCartney for Piccadilly Radio, November 1977.

CHAPTER 21

1 Uncredited: "Ken Maliphant: Management by Involvement," *Billboard*, January 28, 1978, p. 65.

2 Benson, Ross: "Melvyn and McCartney," *Daily Express*, January 7, 1978, p. 11.

3 Cowing, Emma: "How Macca Killed Off Punk Rock with the Bagpipes," *Daily Mail*, November 11, 2017, p. 37.

4 Doyle, Tom: *Man on the Run* (Ballantine Books, London, 2014), p. 204.

5 Gambaccini, Paul: *London Town Special*, audio interview with Paul McCartney and Denny Laine for BBC Radio 1, March 31, 1978.

6 Powell, Aubrey: Author interview (Sinclair), May 15, 2020.

7 Scott, Roger: Audio interview with Paul and Wings for Capital Radio, broadcast on June 14, 1979.

8 Uncredited: Audio interview with Denny Laine, Mersey Beatle '88, Eighth Annual Beatle Convention, Adelphi Hotel, Liverpool, August 29, 1988.

9 White, Timothy: "Not So Silly Love Songs," *Billboard*, March 17, 2001, p. 97.

10 Juber, Laurence: Author interview (Sinclair), March 10, 2020.

11 Juber, Laurence, with Marshall Terrill: *Guitar with Wings—A Photographic Memoir* (Dalton Watson Books, Deerfield, IL, 2014), p. 27.

12 Gambaccini, Paul: Audio interview with Paul McCartney for *An Evening with Paul McCartney*, BBC Radio 1, broadcast on April 1, 1979.

13 Holley, Steve: Author interview (Kozinn), November 9, 2023.

14 Holley, Steve: Author interview (Kozinn), July 1, 2020.

15 Holley, Steve: Author interview (Kozinn), November 9, 2023.

16 Holley, Steve: Author interview (Kozinn), July 1, 2020.

17 Ibid.

18 Lindsay-Hogg, Michael: Author interview (Sinclair), May 24, 2020.

19 Ibid.

20 Hall, Philip: "Wings: 'With a Little Love," *Record Mirror*, March 25, 1978, p. 10.

21 Goldman, Vivien: "Wings: 'With a Little Luck,'" *Sounds*, March 25, 1978, p. 58.

22 Birch, Ian: "Wings: 'With a Little Luck,'" *Melody Maker*, April 1, 1978, p. 16.

23 Rambali, Paul: "Wings: 'With a Little Luck,'" *NME*, April 8, 1978, p. 29.

24 Uncredited: "Wings—With a Little Luck (3:13)," *Billboard*, April 1, 1978, p. 87.

25 Carr, Roy: "The Trial of James Paul McCartney," *NME*, April 29, 1978, pp. 33–35.

26 Trollope, Peter: "McCartney Goes to Town," *Liverpool Echo*, April 8, 1978, p. 8.

27 Cain, Barry: "Sob Story," *Record Mirror*, March 25, 1978, pp. 16–17.

28 Irwin, Colin: "Cruising with Macca," *Melody Maker*, April 1, 1978, pp. 26–27.

29 Cain, Barry: "Juicy Lucy," *Record Mirror*, April 8, 1978, p. 3.

30 Irwin, Colin: "Cruising with Macca," *Melody Maker*, April 1, 1978, pp. 26–27.

31 Ibid.

32 Horne, Nicky: Audio interview with Paul McCartney and Denny Laine, Capital Radio, March 22, 1978.

33 Gambaccini, Paul: Audio interview with Paul McCartney for *An Evening with Paul McCartney*, BBC Radio 1, broadcast on April 1, 1979.

34 White, Cliff: "Macca, Longhair, and the LP Controversy," *NME*, April 15, 1978, pp. 18–19.

35 Maslin, Janet: "Paul and Carly—Family Affairs," *Rolling Stone*, June 15, 1978, p. 89.

36 Rockwell, John: "The Pop Life," *New York Times*, April 21, 1978.

37 Hilburn, Robert: "McCartney's on Target—After Eight Years," *Los Angeles Times*, April 9, 1978, pp. 1–2.

38 Edmands, Bob: "Can One Man on a White Horse Save the Western World?" *NME*, April 8, 1978, p. 36.

39 McAllilster, Donna: "Wingszzzzzzzzzzzzzz," *Sounds*, April 1, 1978, p. 35.

40 Simons, Judith: "Tickets to Write," *Daily Express*, April 8, 1978, p. 10.

41 Lindsay-Hogg, Michael: Author interview (Sinclair), May 24, 2020.

42 Uncredited: "Wings Making Ready to Fly," *NME*, April 8, 1978, p. 4.

43 Juber, Laurence: Author interview (Sinclair), March 10, 2020.

44 Ibid.

CHAPTER 22

1 Ibid.

2 Ibid.

3 Trench, Fiachra: Author interview (Sinclair), October 31, 2019.

4 Gambaccini, Paul: Audio interview with Paul McCartney, *An Evening with Paul McCartney*, BBC Radio 1, broadcast on April 1, 1979.

5 Traiman, Steve: "Keefco Bows in LA as Offshoot of British Outfit," *Billboard*, July 8, 1978, p. 22.

6 Juber, Laurence: Author interview (Sinclair), March 10, 2020.

7 Jackson, Lorne: "The Wild Ideas of Birmingham Filmmaker Ian Emes," *Birmingham Post*, August 6, 2010.

8 Pike, Kelly: "Wings: 'I've Had Enough,'" *Record Mirror*, June 24, 1978, p. 10.

9 Brazier, Chris: "Wings: 'I've Had Enough,'" *Melody Maker*, June 24, 1978, p. 22.

10 Lewis, Alan: "Wings: I've Had Enough," *Sounds*, June 24, 1978, p. 24.

11 Gambaccini, Paul: Audio interview with Paul McCartney, *An Evening with Paul McCartney*, BBC Radio 1, broadcast on April 1, 1979.

12 Oliver, Sally: "Why Our Marriage Is Still Going Strong," *Daily Mirror*, June 27, 1978, pp. 16–17.

13 Wigg, David: "Wings Fly the Flag!," *Daily Express*, June 17, 1978, p. 3.

14 Uncredited: "Wings Are Full Strength Again," *NME*, June 24, 1978, p. 4.

15 Juber, Laurence: Author interview (Sinclair), March 10, 2020.

16 Holley, Steve: Author interview (Kozinn), July 1, 2020.

17 John Eastman interview in Brown, Peter, with Steven Gaines: *All You Need Is Love--The End of the Beatles* (Monoray, London, 2024), p. 260.

18 Conversation relayed by Paul McCartney in Brown, Peter, with Steven Gaines: *All You Need Is Love—The End of the Beatles* (Monoray, London, 2024), pp. 30–31.

19 Rodriguez, Robert: Audio interview with Mike "Tree" Meideros for *Something About the Beatles* podcast, first broadcast on March 10, 2024.

20 Kelly, Ryan: "Wings: Business as Usual," *Smash Hits*, December 13–26, 1979, p. 31.

21 Uncredited: "Paul McCartney–Songwriter," *International Musician*, December 1979, p. 36.

22 Holley, Steve: Author interview (Kozinn), July 1, 2020.

23 Scott, Roger: Audio interview with Paul and Wings for Capital Radio, broadcast on June 14, 1979.

24 Holley, Steve: Author interview (Kozinn), July 1, 2020.

25 Garbarini, Vic: "Lifting the Veil on the Beatles," *Musician*, August 1980, p. 46.

26 Kopp, Bill: "Spin It On—Denny Laine on Wings' *Back to the Egg* at 40," *Rock & Roll Globe* [online], July 1, 2019.

27 Juber, Laurence: Author interview (Sinclair), March 10, 2020.

28 Juber, Laurence: Audio interview with Ken Michaels, *Every Little Thing* radio show, April 23, 2014.

29 Holley, Steve: Author interview (Kozinn), July 1, 2020.

30 Ibid.

31 Ibid.

32 Juber, Laurence: Author interview (Sinclair), March 10, 2020.

33 Holley, Steve: Author interview (Kozinn), July 1, 2020.

34 Kozinn, Allan, Ken Michaels, and Steve Marinucci: Audio interview with Laurence Juber, *Things We Said Today* podcast, posted May 30, 2015.

35 Juber, Laurence: Author interview (Sinclair), March 10, 2020.

36 Juber, Laurence with Marshall Terrill: *Guitar with Wings—A Photographic Memoir* (Dalton Watson, Deerfield, IL, 2014), p. 63.

37 Holley, Steve: Author interview (Sinclair and Kozinn) at the Fest for Beatles Fans, February 12, 2024.

38 Ibid.

39 McLeod, Pauline: "Paul Takes Two Under His Wings," *Daily Mirror*, July 17, 1978, p. 21.

40 Russell, Willy: Author interview (Sinclair), May 14, 2020.

41 The title page and character list are reproduced in Juber, Laurence, with Marshall Terrill: *Guitar with Wings—A Photographic Memoir* (Dalton Watson, Deerfield, IL, 2014), p. 78.

42 Williams, Mark: Audio interview with Paul McCartney for *Melody Maker* and *Back to the Egg* press kit, June 5, 1979.

43 Juber, Laurence: Author interview (Sinclair), March 10, 2020.

44 Michaels, Ken, Kit O'Toole, Kenneth Womack, and Tom Hunyady: Audio interview with Chris Thomas, *Talk More Talk* podcast, first broadcast on November 18, 2018.

45 Juber, Laurence, with Marshall Terrill: *Guitar with Wings—A Photographic Memoir* (Dalton Watson, Deerfield, IL, 2014), p. 78.

46 Juber, Laurence, with Marshall Terrill: *Guitar with Wings—A Photographic Memoir* (Dalton Watson, Deerfield, IL, 2014), p. 78.

47 Williams, Mark: Audio interview with Paul McCartney for *Melody Maker* and *Back to the Egg* press kit, June 5, 1979.

48 Gambaccini, Paul: Audio interview with Paul McCartney, *An Evening with Paul McCartney*, BBC Radio 1, broadcast on April 1, 1979.

49 Holley, Steve: Author interview (Kozinn), July 1, 2020.

50 Juber, Laurence: Author interview (Sinclair), March 10, 2020.

51 Holley, Steve: Author interview (Kozinn), July 1, 2020.

52 Peebles, Andy: Audio interview with Paul McCartney, BBC Radio 1, May 26, 1980.

53 Williams, Mark: Audio interview with Paul McCartney for *Melody Maker* and *Back to the Egg* press kit, June 5, 1979.

54 Smith, Robin: "Growing Two More Wings," *Record Mirror*, August 12, 1978, p. 12.

55 Birch, Ian: "Wings: 'London Town,'" *Melody Maker*, August 19, 1978, p. 19.

56 Brigg, Bev: "Wings: 'London Town,'" *Record Mirror*, August 26, 1978, p. 8.

57 Baker, Danny: "Singles," *NME*, August 26, 1978, p. 21.
58 Uncredited: "Wings—'London Town,'" *Billboard*, August 26, 1978, p. 104.
59 Gambaccini, Paul: Audio interview with Paul McCartney, *An Evening with Paul McCartney*, BBC Radio 1, broadcast on April 1, 1979.

CHAPTER 23

1 Gilchrist, Roderick: "McCartney Tells of 'That Day Linda Nearly Left Me,'" *Daily Mail*, June 12, 1980, p. 13.
2 O'Brien, Catherine: "Linda's Most Fragile Legacy," *The Daily Telegraph*, February 4, 1999, p. 21.
3 Bonici, Ray: "Don't Say Goodnight, Say Good Grief!," *Record Mirror*, May 5, 1979, p. 11.
4 Trollope, Peter: "Paul's Been Cooking Up Something Special," *Liverpool Echo*, June 23, 1979, p. 8.
5 Prentice, Thomson: "Moon the Loon's Last Party—by Annette," *Daily Mail*, September 9, 1978, p. 11.
6 Williams, Mark: Audio interview with Paul McCartney for *Melody Maker* and *Back to the Egg* press kit, June 5, 1979.
7 Scott, Roger: Audio interview with Paul McCartney and Wings, Capital Radio, June 14, 1979.
8 Williams, Mark: Audio interview with Paul McCartney for *Melody Maker* and *Back to the Egg* press kit, June 5, 1979.
9 Juber, Laurence: Author interview (Sinclair), March 10, 2020.
10 Williams, Mark: Audio interview with Paul McCartney for *Melody Maker* and *Back to the Egg* press kit, June 5, 1979.
11 Guion, David: "After the Ball, by Charles K. Harris," *Musicology for Everyone* website, posted April 27, 2011.
12 Juber, Laurence, with Marshall Terrill: *Guitar with Wings—A Photographic Memoir* (Dalton Watson, Deerfield, IL, 2014), p. 110.
13 Juber, Laurence, with Marshall Terrill: *Guitar with Wings—A Photographic Memoir* (Dalton Watson, Deerfield, IL, 2014), p. 110.
14 Juber, Laurence: Author interview (Sinclair), March 10, 2020.
15 Ibid.
16 McCartney, Paul (Paul Muldoon, ed.): *The Lyrics 1956 to the Present* (Liveright Publishing Corporation, New York, 2021), pp. 197–198.
17 Williams, Mark: Audio interview with Paul McCartney for *Melody Maker* and *Back to the Egg* press kit, June 5, 1979.
18 Ibid.
19 Holley, Steve: Author interview (Kozinn), July 1, 2020.
20 Ibid.
21 Uncredited: "ATV Growling at Beatles Song Pirates," *Billboard*, September 16, 1978, p. 20.
22 Chattington, Barry: Author interview (Sinclair), December 15, 2018.
23 Scott, Roger: Audio interview with Paul and Wings for Capital Radio, broadcast on June 14, 1979.
24 Ibid.
25 Thomas, Chris: Unpublished audio interview with Mark Lewisohn, 2018.
26 Michaels, Ken, Kit O'Toole, Kenneth Womack, and Tom Hunyady: Audio interview with Chris Thomas, *Talk More Talk* podcast, November 18, 2018.
27 Ibid.
28 Juber, Laurence: Author interview (Sinclair), March 10, 2020.
29 Williams, Mark: Audio interview with Paul McCartney for *Melody Maker* and *Back to the Egg* press kit, June 5, 1979.
30 Marvin, Hank: Author interview by email (Sinclair), February 21, 2020.
31 Thomas, Chris: Unpublished audio interview with Mark Lewisohn, 2018.
32 Holley, Steve: Author interview (Kozinn), July 1, 2020.
33 Powell, Aubrey: Author interview (Sinclair), May 15, 2020.
34 Juber, Laurence: Author interview (Sinclair), March 10, 2020.
35 Holley, Steve: Author interview (Kozinn), July 1, 2020.
36 Juber, Laurence: Author interview (Sinclair), March 10, 2020.
37 Leigh, Spencer: "Paul McCartney & Wings," *Record Collector*, February 1993, p. 23.
38 Juber, Laurence with Marshall Terrill: *Guitar with Wings—A Photographic Memoir* (Dalton Watson, Deerfield, IL, 2014), p. 150.
39 Williams, Mark: Audio interview with Paul McCartney for *Melody Maker* and *Back to the Egg* press kit, June 5, 1979.
40 Juber, Laurence with Marshall Terrill: *Guitar with Wings—A Photographic Memoir* (Dalton Watson, Deerfield, IL, 2014), p. 150.
41 Thomas, Steven: Author interview (Sinclair), April 3, 2020.
42 McLeod, Pauline: "Laine Longs for the Road," *Daily Mirror*, January 2, 1979, p. 23.
43 McLeod, Pauline: "A Rocker in the Hot Seat," *Daily Mirror*, January 15, 1979, p. 17.
44 Smith, Monty: "Wings—Wings Greatest," *NME*, January 13, 1979, p. 28.
45 Lazell, Barry: "Wings—Wings Greatest," *Sounds*, January 27, 1979, p. 22.
46 Uncredited: "Cuddly New Year, Kids!" *Sunday Mirror*, December 31, 1978, p. 4.

CHAPTER 24

1 McLeod, Pauline: "Laine Longs for the Road," *Daily Mirror*, January 2, 1979, p. 23.
2 Juber, Laurence: Author interview (Sinclair), March 10, 2020.

3 Holley, Steve: Author interview (Kozinn), July 1, 2020.
4 Connolly, Ray: "The Winged Wonder," *Newcastle Evening Chronicle*, April 21, 1979, p. 3.
5 White, Timothy: "Not So Silly Love Songs," *Billboard*, March 17, 2001, p. 95
6 Juber, Laurence, with Marshall Terrill: *Guitar with Wings—A Photographic Memoir* (Dalton Watson, Deerfield, IL, 2014), p. 154.
7 Juber, Laurence: Author interview (Sinclair), March 10, 2020.
8 Holley, Steve: Author interview (Kozinn), July 1, 2020.
9 Peebles, Andy: Audio interview with Paul McCartney for BBC Radio 1, May 26, 1980.
10 Holley, Steve: Author interview (Kozinn), July 1, 2020.
11 Juber, Laurence, with Marshall Terrill: *Guitar with Wings—A Photographic Memoir* (Dalton Watson, Deerfield, IL, 2014), p. 161.
12 Gambaccini, Paul: "A Conversation with Paul McCartney," *Rolling Stone*, July 12, 1979, pp. 39–46.
13 Segell, Michael: "Paul McCartney Signs with Columbia Records," *Rolling Stone*, March 22, 1979.
14 Harrington, Richard: "The Battle Over Record Royalties," *Washington Post*, October 26, 1980.
15 Yetnikoff, Walter: Author email interview (Kozinn), April 8, 2021.
16 Holley, Steve: Author interview (Kozinn), July 1, 2020.
17 Michaels, Ken, Kit O'Toole, Kenneth Womack, and Tom Hunyady: Audio interview with Chris Thomas, *Talk More Talk* podcast, November 18, 2018.
18 Thomas, Chris: Unreleased audio interview with Mark Lewisohn, 2018.
19 Peebles, Andy: Audio interview with Paul McCartney for BBC Radio 1, May 26, 1980.
20 Williams, Peter: "My Bust-Up with Paul McCartney," *Sunday People*, March 4, 1979, p. 30.
21 Niles, Richard: Podcast interview with Kate Robbins for *Radio Richard*, posted on YouTube, January 24, 2022.
22 Williams, Richard: Audio interview with Paul McCartney for the *Times*, December 28, 1981.
23 Watts, Michael: "George Harrison: Is There Life After Enlightenment?" *Melody Maker*, March 10, 1979, pp. 23–24.
24 Brown, Mick: "A Conversation with George Harrison," *Rolling Stone*, April 19, 1979, pp. 71–75.
25 Watts, Michael: "George Harrison: Is There Life After Enlightenment?" *Melody Maker*, March 10, 1979, pp. 23–24.
26 Thomas, Chris: Unpublished interview with Mark Lewisohn, 2018.
27 Birch, Ian: "Wings: Goodnight Tonight (EMI/Parlophone 12Y R6023)," *Melody Maker*, April 7, 1979, p. 31.
28 Hepworth, David: "Wings: 'Goodnight Tonight' (Parlophone)," *Sounds*, March 24, 1979, p. 26.
29 Nightingale, Anne: "Anne's Top Singles," *Daily Express*, March 29, 1979, p. 28.
30 Edmands, Bob: "Wings: Goodnight Tonight (Parlophone)," *NME*, March 24, 1979, p. 26.
31 Pike, Kelly: "Wings—Goodnight Tonight," *Record Mirror*, March 24, 1979, p. 11.
32 Gambaccini, Paul: "A Conversation with Paul McCartney," *Rolling Stone*, July 12, 1979, pp. 39–46.
33 Thomas, Chris: Unpublished interview with Mark Lewisohn, 2018.
34 Juber, Laurence, with Marshall Terrill: *Guitar with Wings—A Photographic Memoir* (Dalton Watson, Deerfield, IL, 2014), p. 161.
35 Gambaccini, Paul: "A Conversation with Paul McCartney," *Rolling Stone*, July 12, 1979, pp. 39–46.
36 Bonici, Ray: "Don't Say Goodnight, Say Good Grief!" *Record Mirror*, May 5, 1979, p. 11.
37 Scott, Roger: Audio interview with Paul and Wings, Capital Radio, broadcast on June 14, 1979.
38 Sheretta, Steven B.: "Ex-Beatle McCartney, Wife Buy 151-Acre Layout Near Monument," *Arizona Daily Star*, June 15, 1979, p. 1.
39 Sippel, John: "Apple Sues Capitol for $16 Mil," *Billboard*, June 9, 1979, p. 4.
40 Bushell, Garry: "Clobberin' Time (Slight Refrain)," *Sounds*, June 9, 1979, p. 22.
41 Goldman, Vivien: "Big Name (White) Section," *Melody Maker*, June 9, 1979, p. 32.
42 Parade, James, with Monique: "Wings: 'Old Siam, Sir' (EMI)," *Record Mirror*, June 16, 1979, p. 10.
43 Morley, Paul: "Wings: Old Siam, Sir (MPL)," *NME*, June 16, 1979, p. 21.
44 Uncredited: "Wings—Getting Closer," *Billboard*, June 16, 1979, p. 87.
45 Martin, George: *Making Music* (Frederick Muller Ltd., London, 1983), p. 62.
46 Holley, Steve: Author interview (Kozinn), July 1, 2020.

CHAPTER 25

1 Uncredited: Video interview with Keith McMillan for *RPM-2 Rock 2*, broadcast on BBC2, October 24, 1980.
2 Mitchell, Tony: "Wings *Back to the Egg* (MPL PCTC 257)," *Sounds*, June 9, 1979, p. 34.
3 Coleman, Ray: "Wings Chicken Out," *Melody Maker*, June 9, 1979, p. 36.
4 Gurr, Ronnie: "Bad Egg?" *Record Mirror*, June 9, 1979, p. 19.
5 White, Timothy: "Clipping Paul McCartney's Wings," *Rolling Stone*, August 23, 1979.
6 Rockwell, John: "The Pop Life," *New York Times*, June 29, 1979.
7 Du Noyer, Paul: "Macca Unscrambles," *NME*, June 9, 1979, pp. 40–41.
8 Uncredited: Video interview with Keith McMillan for *RPM-2 Rock 2*, broadcast on BBC2, October 24, 1980.
9 Williams, Mark: "Wings: Taking Off at Last?" *Melody Maker*, June 16, 1979, pp. 16–17.

10 Ibid.
11 Zibart, Eve: "From Penny Lane to Easy Street," *Washington Post*, June 18, 1979.
12 Juber, Laurence: Author interview (Sinclair), March 10, 2020.
13 Holley, Steve: Author interview (Kozinn), July 1, 2020.
14 Juber, Laurence: Author interview (Sinclair), March 10, 2020.
15 Uncredited: "Paul Goes on the Run . . . As Film Star," *Daily Mail*, June 30, 1979, p. 13.
16 Zibart, Eve: "From Penny Lane to Easy Street," *Washington Post*, June 18, 1979.
17 Klein, Eddie: "Recording" *McCartney II* Deluxe Edition book (MPL/Hear Music/Concord, 2011), pp. 34–35.
18 Garbarini, Vic: "Lifting the Veil on the Beatles," *Musician*, August 1980, p. 46.
19 Ibid.
20 Peebles, Andy: Audio interview with Paul McCartney for *McCartney on McCartney*, BBC Radio 1, May 26, 1980.
21 Gambaccini, Paul: "Paul McCartney Talking About *McCartney II*," Press kit for *McCartney II*, MPL, May 1980, p. 6.
22 Gambaccini, Paul: "Paul McCartney Talking About *McCartney II*," Press kit for *McCartney II*, MPL, May 1980, p. 7.
23 Gambaccini, Paul: "Paul McCartney Talking About *McCartney II*," Press kit for *McCartney II*, MPL, May 1980, p. 6.
24 DuNoyer, Paul: "McCartney on *McCartney II*," *McCartney II* Deluxe Edition book (MPL/Hear Music/Concord, 2011), pp. 16–17.
25 White, Timothy: "Farewell to the First Solo Era," *Musician*, February 1988, pp. 54–55.
26 Gambaccini, Paul: "Paul McCartney Talking About *McCartney II*," Press kit for *McCartney II*, MPL, May 1980, pp. 7–8.
27 Ibid.
28 Norden, Maggie: Audio interview with Paul and Linda McCartney, *Hullabaloo*, Capital Radio, broadcast on December 23, 1979.
29 Ibid.
30 Holley, Steve: Author interview (Kozinn), July 1, 2020.
31 Ibid.
32 Gambaccini, Paul: "Paul McCartney Talking About *McCartney II*," Press kit for *McCartney II*, MPL, May 1980, pp. 9–10.
33 Garbarini, Vic: "Lifting the Veil on the Beatles," *Musician*, August 1980, p. 46.
34 DuNoyer, Paul: "McCartney on *McCartney II*," *McCartney II* Deluxe Edition book (MPL/Hear Music/Concord, 2011), p. 19.
35 Gambaccini, Paul: "Paul McCartney Talking About *McCartney II*," Press kit for *McCartney II*, MPL, May 1980, p. 6.
36 White, Timothy: "Farewell to the First Solo Era," *Musician*, February 1988, pp. 54–55.
37 Ibid.
38 Norden, Maggie: Audio interview with Paul and Linda McCartney, *Hullabaloo*, Capital Radio, broadcast on December 23, 1979.
39 Thomas, Chris: Unpublished interview with Mark Lewisohn, 2018.
40 Pike, Kelly: "Suzy and the Red Stripes: Seaside Woman (A&M)," *Record Mirror*, August 11, 1979, p. 9.
41 Uncredited: "Wings—Arrow Through Me," *Billboard*, August 25, 1979, p. 75.
42 Tebbutt, Simon: "Wings: 'Baby's Request' (EMI)," *Record Mirror*, August 25, 1979, p. 8.
43 Birch, Ian: "Everything Else of the Week," *Melody Maker*, August 25, 1979, p. 24.
44 Bell, Max: "Wings: 'Getting Closer' (EMI)," *NME*, August 25, 1979, p. 23.
45 Sayer, Stan: "My Buddy and Me by Holly's Widow," *Daily Mirror*, September 10, 1979, p. 23.
46 Lichtman, Irv: "We Polish Old Silver," *Billboard*, July 7, 1979, p. 12.
47 Gambaccini, Paul: "British Rockers Unite in Concerts for Kampuchea," *Rolling Stone*, February 21, 1980, pp. 17–18.
48 Finn, Philip: "Hands Off," *Daily Express*, September 27, 1979, p. 1.
49 Uncredited: "Dick Clark Is Sued by Apple," *Billboard*, November 17, 1979, p. 71.
50 Gambaccini, Paul: "British Rockers Unite in Concerts for Kampuchea," *Rolling Stone*, February 21, 1980, pp. 17–18.
51 Holley, Steve: Author interview (Kozinn), July 1, 2020.
52 Uncredited: "Riddle of Pop Star's Drug Death," *Daily Mirror*, November 1, 1979, p. 5.
53 Uncredited: "Pop Man Is Found Dead," *Daily Mail*, September 28, 1979, p. 3.
54 Flanagan, Bill: "Boy You're Gonna Carry That Weight," *Musician*, May 1990, p. 42.
55 Thomas, Chris: Unpublished interview with Mark Lewisohn, 2018.

CHAPTER 26

1 Goodman, Joan: Unedited *Playboy* interview transcripts, May 3, 1984, part 3. Courtesy of Charles Deering McCormick Library of Special Collections, Northwestern University Libraries.
2 Holley, Steve: Author interview (Kozinn), July 1, 2020.
3 Foster, Howard: "Roll Over Beethoven," *Daily Mail*, October 25, 1979, p. 25.
4 Goodman, Joan: Unedited *Playboy* interview transcripts, April 27, 1984, part 1. Courtesy of Charles Deering McCormick Library of Special Collections, Northwestern University Libraries.
5 Juber, Laurence: "Laurence's Guitar Corner," *Club Sandwich*, No. 17, early 1980, p. 6. and MPL paperwork from the tour.

6 Holley, Steve: Email exchange with author (Kozinn), January 4, 2024, and MPL paperwork from the tour.
7 Pearce, Garth: "Image of Yesterday," *Daily Express*, November 22, 1979, p. 21.
8 Bohn, Chris: "Paul McCartney: 'Wonderful Christmastime' (EMI R6029)," *Melody Maker*, November 24, 1979, p. 28.
9 Kent, Nick: "Paul McCartney: 'Wonderful Christmastime' (Parlophone)," *NME*, November 24, 1979, p. 37.
10 Smith, Robin: "Oh No! Not Xmas Again," *Record Mirror*, December 1, 1979, p. 6.
11 Dorsey, Tony: Author interview (Kozinn), October 17, 2019.
12 Okin, Earl: Author interview (Sinclair), January 24, 2021.
13 Ames, Richard: Author interview (Sinclair), March 29, 2020.
14 Ibid.
15 Uncredited: "McCartney Burglary Charge," *Liverpool Echo*, November 7, 1979, p. 11.
16 Casey, Howie: Author interview (Sinclair), October 19, 2019.
17 Pearce, Garth: "Image of Yesterday," *Daily Express*, November 22, 1979, p. 21.
18 Holley, Steve: Author interview (Kozinn), July 1, 2020.
19 Okin, Earl: Author interview (Sinclair), January 24, 2021.
20 Trollope, Peter: "New Model, Rarin' to Go," *Liverpool Echo*, November 26, 1979, p. 7.
21 Middles, Mick: "Featherweight Champions," *Sounds*, December 8, 1979, p. 53.
22 Kiley, Penny: "Wings Over Scouse," *Melody Maker*, December 1, 1979, p. 35.
23 Du Noyer, Paul: "Wacca, Music in Another Gallery and the Criminal," *NME*, December 8, 1979, pp. 48–50.
24 Kiley, Penny: "Fab Macca: The Truth," *Melody Maker*, December 1, 1979, p. 10.
25 Nicholls, Mike: "The Homecoming," *Record Mirror*, December 8, 1979, p. 25.
26 Ames, Richard: Author interview (Sinclair), March 29, 2020.
27 Uncredited: "Paul Sails Down a River of Memories," *Liverpool Echo*, November 28, 1979, p. 7.
28 Ames, Richard: Author interview (Sinclair), March 29, 2020.
29 Bissett, Marshall T.: Letter to Harvey Goldsmith, December 11, 1979.
30 McLeod, Pauline: "Gliding to Earth," *Daily Mirror*, December 10, 1979, p. 23.
31 Daumler-Ford, Jonathan: "Wings at the Odeon Theatre, New Street," *Birmingham Post*, December 13, 1979, p. 18.
32 Day, Barbara: "It Was a Privilege and a Pleasure to See Paul," *Newcastle Evening Chronicle*, December 15, 1979, p. 3.
33 Okin, Earl: Author interview (Sinclair), January 24, 2021.
34 Juber, Laurence: Author interview (Sinclair), March 10, 2020.
35 Collier, Andrew: "McCartney Pleases the Faithful," *Glasgow Herald*, December 17, 1979, p. 5.
36 Juber, Laurence: Author interview (Sinclair), March 10, 2020.
37 Dorsey, Tony: Author interview (Kozinn), October 17, 2019.
38 Okin, Earl: Author interview (Sinclair), January 24, 2021.
39 Dorsey, Tony: Author interview (Kozinn), October 17, 2019.
40 Estridge, Bonnie: "Linda's Long Playing Love Song," *Daily Express*, December 17, 1979, p. 15.
41 Norden, Maggie: Audio interview with Paul and Linda McCartney, *Hullabaloo*, Capital Radio, December 23, 1979.
42 McLeod, Pauline: "Can This Be the Beatle Reunion?" *Daily Mirror*, December 28, 1979, p. 3.
43 Sonstein, Shelli: Audio interview with Paul McCartney, WPLJ-PM, broadcast on December 29, 1979.
44 Thomas, Chris: Unpublished audio interview with Mark Lewisohn, 2018.
45 Holley, Steve: Author interview (Kozinn), July 1, 2020.
46 Juber, Laurence: Author interview (Sinclair), March 10, 2020.
47 Ibid.
48 Casey, Howie: Author interview (Sinclair), October 19, 2019.
49 Ibid.
50 Thomas, Chris: Unpublished audio interview with Mark Lewisohn, 2018.
51 Seaman, Fred: *The Last Days of John Lennon—A Personal Memoir by Fred Seaman* (Birch Lane Press, New York, 1991), pp. 90–91.
52 Holley, Steve: Author interview (Kozinn), July 1, 2020.
53 Juber, Laurence: Author interview (Sinclair), March 10, 2020.
54 Kirk, Donald: "McCartney Jailed in Japan," *Boston Globe*, January 17, 1980.
55 Frost, Deborah: "Once There Was a Way to Get Back Homeward," *Record*, September 1984, p. 27.
56 Dorsey, Tony: Author interview (Kozinn), October 17, 2019.
57 Juber, Laurence: Author interview (Sinclair), March 10, 2020.
58 Cooper, Alice: Audio interview with Bob Gruen, *Nights with Alice Cooper*, January 15, 2021.
59 Goodman, Joan: Unedited *Playboy* interview transcripts, May 3, 1984, part 3, p. 30. Courtesy of Charles Deering McCormick Library of Special Collections, Northwestern University Libraries.

DEYST.

Page 721 constitutes an extension of the copyright page.

HarperCollins books may be purchased for educational, business, or sales promotional use. For information, please email the Special Markets Department at SPsales@harpercollins.com.

FIRST EDITION

DESIGNED BY LEAH CARLSON-STANISIC

Endpaper design by Jennifer Chung

Endpaper background texture © Octavio/stock.adobe.com

Library of Congress Cataloging-in-Publication Data has been applied for.

ISBN 978-0-06-300075-9

24 25 26 27 28 LBC 5 4 3 2 1

ıs liking for schoolboy pranks.

UNDAY, APRIL 3
ercy Thrillington trusts that all is friends were not offended by is April Fool's day little japes, o which he had no choice but to ccumb on account of his liking or school-boy pranks.

ONDAY, APRIL 4
ercy Thrillington has announced at this week is Health And Happness Week. The Thrillington pernal routine will be vigorous and ll commence each morning with enty alternating single handed sh-ups. Please read on tomorrow r further details.

UESDAY, APRIL 5
ercy Thrillington implores all aders to adapt their daily bath utine, in the cause of Health d Happiness Week. Five minutes day of "bath-bumping" works wonrs. Your participation is inted.

EDNESDAY, APRIL 6
has come to the attention of rcy Thrillington that the genal physical condition of the jority of London's residents is ite deplorable. He intends setng a personal example by taking morning jog through Hyde Park. l other interested parties are ked to gather at the Bayswater untain at 1.30.

URSDAY, APRIL 7
ving travelled extensively Percy rillington wishes to comment at the early morning faces of mmuting Londoners are amongst e most unhappy he has seen anyere in the world. In the cause Health and Happiness Week would l readers please smile warmly at eir immediate neighbours. Thank u.

ESDAY, APRIL 12
rcy Thrillington wishes to state at Health & Happiness Week has oven a big success & wishes to ank everyone for their kind parcipation. All readers are earstly implored to continue their od efforts today by not wasting eir free time.

rcy Thrillington will be in ris today to advise his dear iend from the world of fashion the design & musical presentaon of her new collection.

DNESDAY, APRIL 13
cy Thrillington is extremely ttered that rumours suggest

WEDNESDAY, APRIL 13
Percy Thrillington is extremely flattered that rumours suggest that he is to be invited to advise on Modern Music at the Paris Conservatoire, while he is visited that city.

THURSDAY, APRIL 14
Percy Thrillington would like to thank Oliver & Richard for all their help & endeavours.

Percy Thrillington has been persuaded to prolong his stay in Paris as he finds the springtime atmosphere most conducive to musical creativity.

FRIDAY, APRIL 15
Percy Thrillington returns by air from Paris today, thoroughly invigorated and inspired, in full preparation for next week's announcement of his masterpiece

MONDAY, APRIL 18
Percy Thrillington regrets that he is forced to postpone this evening's planned soiree where his closest friends were to hear a preview of "Thrillington," his first long playing record.

TUESDAY, APRIL 19
Percy Thrillington with an armful of "Thrillington" LP records, has gone to Amsterdam to visit friends and to astonish the Dutch with his musical prowess.

WEDNESDAY, APRIL 20
Percy Thrillington was delighted that Mrs. Bedworthy was able to purchase a copy of his new album at her local music purveyor.

THURSDAY, APRIL 21
Percy Thrillington thoroughly recommends that his album "Thrillington" is used for therapeutic and relaxing purposes, particularly following arduous activities.

FRIDAY, APRIL 22
Percy Thrillington has returned to Newbury and is preparing to stay with friends for the Badminton Horse Trials. He feels that a copy of his new album "Thrillington" would make an ideal gift for his hostess.

SUNDAY, APRIL 24
Percy Thrillington thoroughly recommends that his album "Thrillington" is used for therapeutic and relaxing purposes, particularly following arduous activities.

MONDAY, APRIL 25

ton" is used for therapeutic a relaxing purposes, particular following arduous activities.

MONDAY, APRIL 25
Percy Thrillington will today b attending the Berkley Dress Sho as he is assured that "Admira Halsey," a single taken from th "Thrillington" LP will be feature extensively.

TUESDAY, APRIL 26
Percy Thrillington, delighted b the ecstatic reception afforde to his single 'Admiral Halsey' a the Berkeley Dress Show, oblige to young beauties by placing hi moniker on the record sleeve clutched to their breasts.

WEDNESDAY, APRIL 27
Percy Thrillington will be attending a few days at Newmarket fo the racing, and has taken copie of his single, Admiral Halsey, fo the enjoyment of his many friend within the racing fraternity.

Percy Thrillington wishes to in form all his friends that he wil be taking an extended holiday in South America following th rigours of launching his first al bum Thrillington and the single Admiral Halsey. In his absence al enquiries should be directed t Miss Penelope Telfer-Smollett.

THURSDAY, APRIL 28
Percy Thrillington, pleased with his fortunes on the racecourse, was fortunate to meet an influential gentleman who assured him that Admiral Halsey could be included in the Trooping the Colour Ceremony in the near future.

FRIDAY, APRIL 29
Percy Thrillington wishes to inform all his friends that he will be taking an extended holiday in South America following the rigours of launching his first album 'Thrillington' and the single 'Admiral Halsey.' In his absence all enquiries should be directed to Miss Penelope Telfer-Smallett.

MONDAY, FEBRUARY 14
Percy Thrillington sends his warmest love and thanks to Miss Penelope Telfer-Smallett, Miss Debbie Dixon-Smythe, The Princess Francesca Visconte and Mrs. Ethel Bedworthy on this glorious St. Valentine's Day 1977.

WEDNESDAY, FEBRUARY 23
Percy Thrillington wishes to announce that today he has given up

ONDAY, FEBRUARY 14
ercy Thrillington sends his warmest love and thanks to Miss Peelope Telfer-Smallett, Miss ebbie Dixon-Smythe, The Princess rancesca Visconte and Mrs. Ethel edworthy on this glorious St. alentine's Day 1977.

VEDNESDAY, FEBRUARY 23
ercy Thrillington wishes to announce that today he has given up smoking, and craves support from ll his friends.

HURSDAY, FEBRUARY 24
ercy Thrillington is basking in he sun in Mustique, and sends ays of sunshine to his friends in og-bound London.

FRIDAY, FEBRUARY 25
ercy Thrillington wishes to advise his friends that he will be incommunicado for two days.

SUNDAY, FEBRUARY 27
Percy Thrillington wishes to announce that he has given up smoking, and craves support from all his friends.

MONDAY, FEBRUARY 28
Percy Thrillington wishes to advise all concerned that he will be represented at the Christie Sale of Chinese Ceramics by Miss Penelope Telfer-Smallett.

TUESDAY, MARCH 1
Percy Thrillington regrets that he will be unable to join Lady Metroland's party at the ROH performance of the Taming of the Shrew.

THURSDAY, MARCH 3
Percy Thrillington sends his congratulations to Mr. Sebastian McKindoe on the announcement of his engagement to Miss Sarah Wyatt.

FRIDAY, MARCH 4
Percy Thrillington will be attending the Torquay Relaxation Center for three days as from Saturday, March 5

MONDAY, MARCH 7
Percy Thrillington would like to send thanks to his friends for helping him acquire his latest Hispano Suiza.

TUESDAY, MARCH 8
Percy Thrillington wishes to thank Sir Jeremy Matthews-Ffitch and his party for a simply riveting evening at the opera.

WEDNESDAY, MARCH 9
Percy Thrillington looks forward

ning at the opera.

WEDNESDAY, MARCH 9
Percy Thrillington looks forward to meeting old school chums at the Canada Club Dinner.

THURSDAY, MARCH 10
Percy Thrillington wishes to advise that his gelding will not now be running at Sandown due to stable sickness.

FRIDAY, MARCH 11
Percy Thrillington regrets he will be unable to attend the Newbury Hunt this weekend due to prior commitments.

SUNDAY, MARCH 13
Percy Thrillington would like to send thanks to his friends for helping him acquire his latest Hispano Suiza.

TUESDAY, MARCH 15
Percy Thrillington has postponed all business engagements in order to spend time with a dear friend in Geneva.

WEDNESDAY, MARCH 16
Percy Thrillington wishes to advise friends that he is feeling thoroughly invigorated by the crisp & brisk skiing conditions in Gstaad.

THURSDAY, MARCH 17
Friends are mortified to hear Percy Thrillington has broken his arm skiing and wish him a speedy recovery.

FRIDAY, MARCH 18
Percy Thrillington is deeply irritated by the curtailment of his apres-ski enjoyment and is currently returning overland by private ambulance.

SUNDAY, MARCH 20
The princess Francesca Visconte is mortified to hear that Percy Thrillington has broken his arm skiing and wishes him a speedy recovery.

MONDAY, MARCH 21
Percy Thrillington is now en route to Paris despite the extreme inconvenience caused by a broken arm and suspected cracked rib.

TUESDAY, MARCH 22
Eccentricity is not one of my stronger attributes, dear ladies in Classified, but however, many thanks for your support, and to Mr. Stephen Clackson my sincere

TUESDAY, MARCH 22
Eccentricity is not one of m stronger attributes, dear ladie in Classified, but however, man thanks for your support, and t Mr. Stephen Clackson my sincer
thanks for preserving my much valued privacy. Regard, Percy Thrillington.

WEDNESDAY, MARCH 23
Percy Thrillington is returnin from Paris today with all hast to see his specialist in Harle St. to assess the damage incurre by the unfortunate incident i Gstaad.

THURSDAY, MARCH 24
Percy Thrillington wishes to ar nounce that, comforted by his spe cialist's verdict regarding hi condition he has departed, al smiles, for Yorkshire.

FRIDAY, MARCH 25
Percy Thrillington has been study ing form & is confident that h has picked a winner for this week end's activities at Doncaster.

SUNDAY, MARCH 27
Percy Thrillington will be er joying a day of retreat at hi Mayfair residence, following hi recent frenetic and frustratir experiences.

MONDAY, MARCH 28
Percy Thrillington is delighte with the efforts of those cor cerned at the YELLOWPLUSH GALLEI to humour his aesthetic needs.

TUESDAY, MARCH 29
Percy Thrillington despite exces sive demands on both social ar business time, hopes to lend hi support to today's DAFFODIL BALL

WEDNESDAY, MARCH 30
Percy Thrillington will be attenc ing tonight's production of Do Giovanni and awaits with eager ar ticipation a stimulating perfor mance from Miss Hayashi.

THURSDAY, MARCH 31
Percy Thrillington will be spenc ing the morning with his taile discussing plans for his spri wardrobe, and taking luncheon a his club in Pall Mall.

FRIDAY, APRIL 1
Percy Thrillington trusts that a his friends will not be offend by today's little japes, to whi he had to succumb, on account his liking for schoolboy pranks.

SUNDAY, APRIL 3